CONSUMER BEHAVIOUR

A European Perspective

Seventh Edition

Michael R. Solomon
Søren Askegaard
Margaret K. Hogg
Gary J. Bamossy

Pearson

Harlow, England • London • New York • Boston • San Francisco • Toronto • Sydney • Dubai • Singapore • Hong Kong
Tokyo • Seoul • Taipei • New Delhi • Cape Town • São Paulo • Mexico City • Madrid • Amsterdam • Munich • Paris • Milan

PEARSON EDUCATION LIMITED
KAO Two KAO Park
Harlow CM17 9SR
United Kingdom
Tel: +44 (0)1279 623623
Web: www.pearson.com/uk

7th European adaptation edition published by PEARSON EDUCATION LTD, Copyright © 2019.

First published by Prentice Hall Europe 1999 (print)
Second edition published 2002 (print)
Third edition published 2006 (print)
Fourth edition published 2010 (print)
Fifth edition published 2014 (print and electronic)
Sixth edition published 2016 (print and electronic)
Seventh edition published 2019 (print and electronic)

© Prentice Hall (print)
© Pearson Education Limited 2002, 2006, 2010 (print)
© Pearson Education Limited 2014, 2016, 2019 (print and electronic)

ISBN: 978-1-292-24542-3 (print)
       978-1-292-24546-1 (PDF)
       978-1-292-24543-0 (ePub)

British Library Cataloguing-in-Publication Data
A catalogue record for the print edition is available from the British Library

Library of Congress Cataloging-in-Publication Data
Names: Solomon, Michael R., author. | Askegaard, Søren, author. | Hogg,
    Margaret K., author.
Title: Consumer behaviour: a European perspective / Michael R. Solomon,
    Søren Askegaard, Margaret K. Hogg, Gary J. Bomossy.
Other titles: Consumer behavior
Description: Seventh Edition. | New York : Pearson, [2019] | Revised edition
    of Consumer behaviour, [2016] | Includes bibliographical references and
    indexes.
Identifiers: LCCN 2018061780| ISBN 9781292245423 (print) | ISBN 9781292245461
    (pdf) | ISBN 9781292245430 (epub)
Subjects: LCSH: Consumer behavior—Europe.
Classification: LCC HF5415.33.E85 S65 2019 | DDC 658.8/342—dc23 LC record available at https://lccn.loc.gov/2018061780

10 9 8 7 6 5 4 3 2 1
23 22 21 20 19

Front cover image: © elenabs / iStock / Getty Images Plus

Print edition typeset in 8.5/12 SST by Pearson CSC
Printed in Slovakia by Neografia

NOTE THAT ANY PAGE CROSS REFERENCES REFER TO THE PRINT EDITION

Brief contents

Contents

Companion Website

For open-access **student resources** specifically written
to complement this textbook and support your learning,
please visit **www.pearsoned.co.uk/solomon**

Lecturer Resources

For password-protected online resources tailored to support
the use of this textbook in teaching, please visit
www.pearsoned.co.uk/solomon

List of case studies

Case study number	Case study title/author(s)	Topic(s)/context
	Part D	
D.1	Influencer marketing: monetising online audiences through customer reviews Ben Koeck and David Marshall, University of Edinburgh Business School, UK	Blogging, influencer marketing; digital word of mouth – *online world*
D.2	What is generational marketing? And how does consumption contribute to strengthen links between generations? Elodie Gentina, IESEG Schooof Management, Paris and Lille	Cross-cultural study of sharing practices across generations between mothers and daughters (France and Japan)
D.3	Consumption ambivalence in family sharing: the case of intergenerational support in economically challenging times Katerina Karanika, Exeter University, UK	Family, self (especially family-level of the extended self and multiple selves); downward mobility (Greece)
	Part E	
E.1	Keep the faith: mediating Catholicism and consumption Leighanne Higgins, Lancaster University Management School, UK	Religion and consumption (Scotland)
E.2	'Miss u loads': online consumer memorialisation practices Darach Turley, Dublin City University, Ireland, and Stephanie O'Donohoe, University of Edinburgh, UK	Death and dying; self-concept; storytelling in the online virtual world – *online world*
E.3	Routes to heritage: acculturation among second-generation British Indian women Anuja Pradhan and Hayley Cocker, Lancaster University, UK	Myths, acculturation and second-generation British Asian citizens (UK)

Consumer behaviour as I see it...	Author	Topic
Giving and getting access...	Professor Giana Eckhardt Royal Holloway, University of London	We hear a lot about the current sharing economy, but a lot of what is called 'sharing' is actually better understood as access-based consumption. This commentary explores this concept.
Children and their favourite stores	Professor Stefania Borghini Bocconi University, Milan	Children are an important target market (as consumers in their own right; as influencers; and as future consumers). This commentary examines patterns of children's behaviour in retail settings.
Touching technology...	Associate Professor Rhonda Hadi Saïd School of Business, Oxford University	Technology is increasingly a multisensorial experience. This commentary explores the effects of what is called haptic feedback – the vibrating or similar sensation that technology uses to communicate with us.
What makes a real man?	Professor Jacob Östberg Stockholm University	Gender is one of the most important dimensions of consumer behaviour. In this commentary, the notion of masculinity and how it forms and is formed by consumption is discussed.
Luxury goods and luxury consumers: is status-enhancing consumption compatible with the notion of sustainability?	Professor Benjamin G. Voyer ESCP Europe (London) and LSE, London	Are luxury goods compatible with consumer values around sustainability? This commentary describes findings from a study which showed that consumers associated luxury brands with words related to unsustainability (e.g. pollution, greed). A follow-up focus group found that consumers felt that luxury was conceptually the opposite of sustainability.
Learning via word of mouth in offline (WOM) and online (eWOM) settings	Professor Peeter Verlegh Vrije Universiteit, Amsterdam, Netherlands	This commentary reports research which has examined brand loyalty in the context of influencing consumer behaviour via online word of mouth (eWOM) and offline word of mouth (WOM) respectively.
Compensatory materialism	L.J. Shrum HEC Paris	Most people have mixed feelings about materialism. This commentary approaches it slightly differently, as a way of compensating for a harmed self-image or self-esteem.

Consumer behaviour as I see it...	Author	Topic
Consumer behaviour in a data-rich world	Professor Vincent-Wayne Mitchell The University of Sydney Business School	Explores the advantages and disadvantages for consumers in the 21st century confronted with a data-rich world. Interconnectivity means access to more information for consumers, but also allows for the capturing of a lot more data about consumers by companies.
Selfies: how consumers are shaping new photography practices	Professor Stefania Farace Eastern Connecticut State University	What exactly do consumers engage with when they look at pictures online? In an experiment participants were shown a variety of images and asked to rate them. The researchers identified three recurring techniques (used by those taking photos) to encourage readers' engagement with a visual.
Gender, gender identity and consumer behaviour	Professor Pauline Maclaran Royal Holloway, University of London	Just as marketers can legitimate certain gender identities, so too they can also reinforce traditional gender norms that stereotype or marginalize certain groups. This commentary discusses challenges to societal gender norms (a form of resignification) that disrupt the continual repetition of the status quo with relation to gender and consumer diversity.
Coping with poverty	Kathy Hamilton University of Strathclyde	Poverty is a serious issue – also in consumer research. This commentary addresses how consumers apply various (more or less successful) coping strategies to try to alleviate the effects of poverty.
The dark side of the gift	Stephen Brown University of Ulster	Ever received an unwelcome gift? Or given one? Sure, come on! This introspection reflects on the dire consequences of not mastering the subtleties of gift-giving correctly.
Cultural change as glocalisation	Professor Dannie Kjeldgaard University of Southern Denmark	Through the example of youth culture, this commentary addresses how social change processes often come in the shape of glocalisation: local ways of adopting and relating to global trends.

Preface

We wrote this book because we're fascinated by the field of consumer behaviour. We hope that, as consumers and future managers, you find this study to be fascinating as well. Whether you're a student, manager or professor, we're sure you can relate to the trials and tribulations associated with last-minute shopping, preparing for a big night out, agonising over a purchase decision, fantasising about a week's skiing in the Swiss Alps, enjoying a holiday on a Greek island or commemorating a landmark event, such as graduating from university, getting a driver's licence or (dreaming about) winning the lottery.

Buying, having and being

Our understanding of this field goes beyond looking at the act of *buying* only, and extends to both *having* and *being* as well. Consumer behaviour is about much more than just buying things; it also embraces the study of how having (or not having) things affects our lives, and how our possessions influence the way we feel about ourselves and about each other – our state of being. In addition to understanding why people buy things, we also try to appreciate how products, services and consumption activities contribute to the broader social world we experience.

A European perspective on consumers and marketing strategy

An important objective for this new, seventh edition has been to ensure its continuing relevance to European audiences while retaining the accessibility and contemporary approach established over the last 12 editions of Michael Solomon's U.S. *Consumer Behaviour.* The significant level of European material in this latest edition includes extra references to European research, illustrative examples and cases from a European consumer context, as well as a number of European advertisements so that the reader can visualise different elements in the marketing applications of consumer behaviour theory.

The internationalisation of market structures makes it increasingly necessary for business people to acquire a clear understanding of cultural differences and similarities among consumers from various countries. One of the challenges of writing this book has been to develop materials which illustrate *local* as well as *pan-European* and *global* aspects of consumer behaviour. In this spirit, we have kept a number of American and other non-European examples to illustrate various similarities and differences on the global consumer scene. To illustrate the potential of consumer research to inform marketing strategy, the text contains numerous examples of specific applications of consumer behaviour concepts by marketing practitioners.

Digital consumer behaviour

As more of us go online every day, there's no doubt the world is changing – and consumer behaviour is constantly evolving in response to the Web and social media (e.g. Facebook, Instagram, Twitter). The seventh edition continues to highlight the new world of the digital consumer.

One of the most exciting aspects of the new digital world is that consumers can interact directly with other people who live either just down the street or half way across the world.

As a result, we are having to radically redefine the meaning of community. It's no longer enough to acknowledge that consumers like to talk to each other about products. Now we share opinions and get the up-to-date information about new films, music, cars, clothes . . . in electronic communities that might include a young parent from Aalborg or Aachen, a senior citizen from Odense or Les Moutiers, or a teenager from Amsterdam or Edinburgh. And many of us meet up in computer-mediated environments (CMEs) such as Facebook or Twitter. We have tried to thread material and examples about these new emerging consumer playgrounds throughout the text. These new ways of interacting in the marketplace create bountiful opportunities for marketing managers and consumers alike.

However, is the digital world always a rosy place? Unfortunately, just as in the 'real world', so inevitably the digital world comes with its own warnings (e.g. trolling). That said, it is difficult to imagine going back to a world without the Web, and it is changing the field of consumer behaviour all the time – so watch this space.

About the authors

Michael R. Solomon, PhD, is Professor of Marketing in the Haub School of Business at Saint Joseph's University in Philadelphia. Before joining the Saint Joseph's faculty in the fall of 2006, he was the Human Sciences Professor of Consumer Behavior at Auburn University. Before moving to Auburn in 1995, he was chair of the Department of Marketing in the School of Business at Rutgers University, New Brunswick, New Jersey. Professor Solomon began his academic career in the Graduate School of Business Administration at New York University (NYU), where he also served as Associate Director of NYU's Institute of Retail Management. He earned his BA.

degrees in psychology and sociology *magna cum laude* at Brandeis University and a PhD in social psychology at the University of North Carolina at Chapel Hill. In 1996 he was awarded the Fulbright/FLAD Chair in Market Globalization by the US Fulbright Commission and the Government of Portugal, and he served as Distinguished Lecturer in Marketing at the Technical University of Lisbon. He held an appointment as Professor of Consumer Behaviour at the University of Manchester (United Kingdom) from 2007 to 2013.

Professor Solomon's primary research interests include: consumer behaviour and lifestyle issues; branding strategy; the symbolic aspects of products; the psychology of fashion, decoration and image; services marketing; marketing in virtual worlds; and the development of visually oriented online research methodologies. He has published numerous articles on these and related topics in academic journals, and he has delivered invited lectures on these subjects in Europe, Australia, Asia, and Latin America. His research has been funded by the American Academy of Advertising, the American Marketing Association, the U.S. Department of Agriculture, the International Council of Shopping Centers, and the U.S. Department of Commerce. He currently sits on the editorial or advisory boards of *The Journal of Consumer Behaviour, Journal of Marketing Theory and Practice, Critical Studies in Fashion and Beauty* and *Journal for Advancement of Marketing Education,* and he served an elected six-year term on the Board of Governors of the Academy of Marketing Science. Professor Solomon has been recognised as one of the 15 most widely cited scholars in the academic behavioural sciences/ fashion literature, and as one of the 10 most productive scholars in the field of advertising and marketing communications.

Professor Solomon is a frequent contributor to mass media. His feature articles have appeared in such magazines as *Psychology Today, Gentleman's Quarterly,* and *Savvy.* He has been quoted in numerous national magazines and newspapers, including *Advertising Age, Adweek, Allure, Elle, Glamour, Mademoiselle, Mirabella, Newsweek,* the *New York Times, Self, Time, USA Today,* and the *Wall Street Journal.* He frequently appears on television and speaks on radio to comment on consumer behaviour issues, including appearances on *The Today Show, Good Morning America, Inside Edition, Newsweek on the Air,* the *Entrepreneur Sales and Marketing Show,* CNBC, Channel One, the *Wall Street Journal* Radio Network, the WOR Radio Network and National Public Radio. He acts as consultant to numerous companies on consumer behaviour and marketing strategy issues and often speaks to business groups throughout the United States and overseas. In addition to this text, Professor Solomon is co-author of the widely used textbook *Marketing: Real People, Real Choices.* He has three children, Amanda, Zachary and Alexandra, a son-in-law, Orly and three granddaughters, Rose, Evey and Arya. He lives in Philadelphia with his wife Gail and their 'other child' – a pug named Kelbie Rae.

Søren Askegaard is Professor of Consumption Studies at the University of Southern Denmark. He entered the atmosphere the same year as Yuri Gagarin left it. Søren has a post-graduate Diploma in Communication Studies from the Sorbonne University, Paris and PhD in Business Studies from Odense University, 1993.

Professor Askegaard's research interests generally are in the field of consumer culture theory and commercial symbolism. He is interested in debunking what is known as 'common sense', and he likes to act as a 'Martian' in his own society (as well as other societies), in order to catch a glimpse of all the funny, little – and not so little – things we do (and consume!), while thinking that it is 'perfectly normal'.

Professor Askegaard has given invited lectures at universities in Europe, Africa, Asia, North America and Latin America. He has served on a dozen programme committees for scientific conferences and is, among other things, co-organiser of the 2012 Consumer Culture Theory conference at Oxford University. He has been a visiting professor at universities in France, Sweden, Turkey and the USA.

Søren Askegaard served as associate editor for *The Journal of Consumer Research* 2008–14 and is currently a member of its editorial review board. He also serves on the editorial boards for four other journals. His research has been published in numerous international journals and anthologies. For his research accomplishment he has received four research awards, including the Danish Marketing Association's Research Award. In 2008, he received the Danish Academy for Business Research Award for making his and his colleagues' research beneficial to the business community in Denmark. He also serves as the honorary consul of France in Odense, Denmark.

His research has been widely quoted by the mass media in Denmark, where he is a frequent commentator on consumer and market issues. His research has also been featured in the Swedish media and on BBC Radio 4.

Margaret K. Hogg holds the Chair of Consumer Behaviour and Marketing in the Department of Marketing at Lancaster University Management School (LUMS). She read for an MA (Hons) in Politics and Modern History at Edinburgh University; postgraduate studies in History at the Vrije Universiteit, Amsterdam; an MA in Business Analysis at Lancaster University; and a PhD in Consumer Behaviour and Retailing at Manchester Business School. She worked for six years in marketing with 'K Shoes' in Kendal and she spent eight years at Manchester School of Management (MSM), UMIST before moving to LUMS in May 2004.

Professor Hogg's main areas of research interests are around the issues of identity, self and consumption within consumer behaviour. Her work has appeared in refereed journals including the *Journal of Advertising, Journal of Business Research, Journal of Marketing Management, European Journal of Marketing, International Journal of Advertising, Journal of Services Marketing, Journal of Consumer Policy, Marketing Management Journal, Advances in Consumer Research* and *Consumption, Markets and Culture*. She edited six volumes of papers on consumer behaviour in the Sage Major Works series (2005 and 2006) and has co-authored numerous book chapters. Professor Hogg regularly presents papers at international conferences including US, European and Asia-Pacific meetings of the Association for Consumer Research (ACR), and Consumer Culture Theory. She has given numerous seminar papers as an invited speaker (e.g. in Australia, New

Zealand and Europe). She is a regular reviewer for the UK Economic and Social Research Council (ESRC) and for the Social Sciences and Humanities Research Council of Canada; she was an Associate Editor (Buyer Behaviour) for *Journal of Business Research* for five years and she reviews regularly for the *Journal of Consumer Research, European Journal of Marketing, Journal of Marketing Management* and *Marketing Theory.* She has been on the conference programme committees for US and European meetings of the Association for Consumer Research (ACR).

Professor Hogg has taught extensively on consumer behaviour and research methods at undergraduate and postgraduate level and supervised and examined a wide range of PhD students.

Gary J. Bamossy, PhD, is Clinical Professor of Marketing at the McDonough School of Business, Georgetown University, in Washington DC. From 1985 to 1999 he was on the Faculty of Business and Economics at the Vrije Universiteit, Amsterdam, as *Hoogleraar, Marktkunde* (Professor of Marketing), and Director of Business Research for the VU's participation at the Tinbergen Research Institute. Prior to his appointment at Georgetown, he was Director of the Global Business Program and a member of the marketing faculty at the University of Utah (1999–2005).

Professor Bamossy's primary research interests are on the global diffusion of material culture, sustainable consumption, and trademark infringement. He has published numerous articles on these and related topics in academic journals and as chapters in research books. He has given invited lectures on materialism and sustainable consumption issues at universities, companies and government agencies in North America, Europe and Asia, and his work has been funded by the Dutch Science Foundation (KNAW), the Marketing Science Institute, the Davidson Institute (University of Michigan) and the Anglo-Dutch Scholar Forum. For the past several years, Dr Bamossy has served as an Invited Member by The Bank of Sweden, to nominate a candidate for the Nobel Memorial Prize in Economic Sciences.

Authors' acknowledgements

Søren Askegaard would like to thank Cristiano Smaniotto and Christian Dam for their excellent support in finding new material for a variety of chapters. He would also like to thank Caroline for her patience.

Margaret Hogg would like to say a very sincere 'thank you' to her family, Daniel, Robert, Julietta, Becca, Zoe and Elijah and to her late husband, Richard, for their generous, unstinting and loving support since she started this project.

Gary Bamossy would like to thank Anne Marie Parlevliet in Amsterdam for her excellent desk research on developments in the Netherlands and the EU, and Jerome West, for source work and critical discussions on the EU. Both of you have made my revision efforts enjoyable. A special thanks to Janeen, Joost, Lieke and Jason – whose world views and consumption practices continue to amaze, amuse, inspire and enlighten me.

Sandra Awanis thanks Professor Diana Haytko and Dr Charles Cui for their help in constructing the title and refining the ideas behind Case study A.1.

Publisher's acknowledgements

Text

5 The Financial Times Limited: Thompson, Christopher (2012), 'Valentine's boost for online dating sites', *Financial Times* (10 February 2012). **10 Crain Communications Inc:** Mucus to maxi pads: Marketing's dirtiest jobs by Jack Neff. Published on February 16, 2009. **12 Oxford University Press:** Adapted from Laurel A. Hudson and Julie L. Ozanne, 'Alternative ways of seeking knowledge in consumer research', *Journal of Consumer Research* 14(4) (1988): 508–21. **16 Emerald Publishing Limited:** Lilly Ye, Mousumi Bose and Lou Pelton, 'Dispelling the myth of Chinese consumers: A new generation of brand-conscious individualists', *Journal of Consumer Marketing* 29(3) (2012): 190–201. **16 Taylor & Francis Group:** Aliakbar Jafari and Christina Goulding, 'Globalization, reflexivity, and the project of the self: A virtual intercultural learning process', *Consumption, Markets and Culture,* 16(1) (2013): 84. **18 The MIT Press:** Erazim Kohák, 'Ashes, ashes… Central Europe after forty years', *Daedalus* 121 (Spring 1992): 197–215, at 219, quoted in Belk, 'Romanian Consumer Desires and Feelings of Deservingness', op. cit. **22 John Wiley & Sons:** Louise Hassan, Deirdre Shaw, Edward Shiu, Gianfranco Walsh and Sara Parry, 'Uncertainty in ethical consumer choice: A conceptual model, *Journal of Consumer Behaviour* 12 (2013): 182–93. **23 Sage Publications:** Adapted from Bente Halkier et al., 'Trusting, complex, quality conscious or unprotected? Constructing the food consumer in different European national contexts', *Journal of Consumer Culture* 7(3) (2007): 379–402. **26 Giana Eckhardt:** Giana Eckhardt. **37 American Psychological Association:** James Russell and Geraldine Pratt, 'A description of the affective quality attributed to environment', *Journal of Personality and Social Psychology* 38(2) (1980): 311–22. **38 Haymarket Media Group Ltd:** Laura Mazur, 'Web marketers must now adapt to the occasion', op. cit. **38 Oxford University Press:** Ritesh Saini and Ashwani Monga, 'How I decide depends on what I spend: Use of heuristics is greater for time than for money', *Journal of Consumer Research* 34 (April 2008): 921. **41 The New York Times Company:** Henry Fountain, quoted in 'The Ultimate Body Language: How You Line Up for Mickey', *New York Times* (18 September 2005). **42 Oxford University Press:** For a scale that was devised to assess these dimensions of the shopping experience, see Barry J. Babin, William R. Darden and Mitch Griffin, 'Work and/or fun: Measuring hedonic and utilitarian shopping value', *Journal of Consumer Research* 20 (March 1994): 644–56. **44 Financial Times:** Jonathan Eley 'Grocery watchdog hails improvement as Aldi holds top spot', *Financial Times* (25 June 2018), https://www.ft.com/content/6b00fff8-787f-11e8-8e67-1e1a0846c475 (accessed June 28 2018). **44 MGN Limited:** Zoe Chamberlain 'Aldi insider reveals 12 reasons why prices are so cheap - and it's fascinating', *The Mirror* (18 June 2018), https://www.mirror.co.uk/money/aldi-insider-reveals-12-reasons-12732619 (accessed 28 June 2018). **45 Guardian News and Media Limited:** Zoe Wood 'Tesco trials "shop and go" app in till-free store', *The Guardian* (28 June 2018), https://www.theguardian.com/business/2018/jun/28/tesco-shop-and-go-app-till-free-store (accessed June 29 2018). **46 Harvard Business Review:** Joseph C. Nunes and Xavier Dreze, 'Your loyalty program is betraying you', *Harvard Business Review* (April 2006): 124–131,. **46 Forrester Research, Inc:** Samantha Merlivat, Luca S. Paderni, Ryan Skinner, and Kasia Madej 'UK's Multichannel Consumers Demand Customer Life-Cycle Marketing: Discover The Touchpoints UK Consumers Turn To For Discovery, Exploration. Purchase Inquiries and Engagement', Forrester Report (7 April 2015). **47 European Union:** Eurostat, Date of extraction: 12 March 2018 © European Union. **48 European Union:** http://ec.europa.eu/eurostat/statistics-explained/index.php/E-commerce_statistics_for_individuals (accessed 14 March 2018). **49 Guardian News and Media Limited:** Zoe Wood and Nick Fletcher, 'Era ends as House of Fraser to axe 31 stores and 6,000 jobs', *The Guardian* (22 June 2018), https://www.theguardian.com/business/2018/jun/22/house-of-fraser-to-close-31-stores-with-6000-job-losses-as-cva-approved (accessed June 28). **50 Guardian News and Media Limited:** Zoe Wood, 'Asos app allows shoppers to snap up fashion', *The Guardian,* (15 July 2017), https://www.theguardian.com/business/2017/jul/15/asos-app-allows-shoppers-to-snap-up-fashion (accessed 14 March 2018). **51 Oxford University Press:** Avni M. Shah, Noah Eisenkraft, James R. Bettman and Tanya L. Chartrand, 'Paper or Plastic?: How We Pay Influences Post-Transaction Connection', *Journal of Consumer Research* 42(5) (2016): 688–708. **51**

Publisher's acknowledgements

Guardian News and Media Limited: Larry Elliott, 'I don't use contactless': The woman whose name is on British banknotes', *The Guardian* (21 February 2018), https://www.theguardian.com/money/2018/feb/21/i-dont-use-contactless-the-woman-whose-name-is-on-british-banknotes (accessed 14 March 2018). **54**
Professor Stefania Borghini: Professor Stefania Borghini, Bocconi University, Milan. **56 Guardian News and Media Limited:** Kira Cochrane, 'Why pop-ups pop up everywhere?', *The Guardian* (12 October 2010), http://www.guardian.co.uk/lifeandstyle/2010/oct/12/pop-up-temporary-shops-restaurants (accessed 13 March 2018). **56 Association for Consumer Research:** Stefania Borghini, John F. Sherry, Annamma Joy, 'Ordinary Spaces and Sense of Place' in Alan Bradshaw, Chris Hackley and Pauline Maclaran (eds), *European Association for Consumer Research Conference* 2010 RHUL: 33. **57 Elsevier:** Philip Kotler, 'Atmospherics as a marketing tool', *Journal of Retailing* (Winter 1973–74): 10 **59 Advertising Age:** Chairman-CEO A.G. Laffley, quoted in Jack Neff, 'P&G boosts design's role in marketing', *Advertising Age* (9 February 2004): 52. **61 Journal of Marketing:** Adapted from Jacob Jacoby, Carol K. Berning and Thomas F. Dietvorst, 'What about disposition?' *Journal of Marketing* 41 (April 1977): 23. **61 Guardian News and Media Limited:** Helen Pidd and Zoe Wood, 'How Oxfam became the rising star of UK's online fashion industry', *The Guardian* (14 January 2018), https://www.theguardian.com/business/2018/jan/14/how-oxfam-became-the-rising-star-of-uks-online-fashion-industry (accessed 14 March 2018). **61 UK Statistics Authority:** Katie Fisher 'UK Statistics on Waste' DEFRA (22 February 2018), https://assets.publishing.service.gov.uk/government/uploads/system/uploads/attachment_data/file/683051/UK_Statisticson_Waste_statistical_notice_Feb_2018_FINAL.pdf (accessed 29 June 2018). **63 European Association for Consumer Research:** Katherine White, Rhiannon MacDonnell and Darren Dahl, 'It's the Mindset that Matters: The Role of Construal Level and Message Framing in Influencing Consumer Conservation Behaviors' in Alan Brad-shaw, Chris Hackley and Pauline Maclaran (eds), *European Association for Consumer Research Conference* 2010 RHUL: 15. **63 Association for Consumer Research:** Jan Brace-Govan and Elizabeth Parsons, 'Reduce, Re-use, Recycle Practice Theory' in Alan Bradshaw, Chris Hackley and Pauline Maclaran (eds), *European Association for Consumer Research Conference* 2010 RHUL: 7. **63 Association for Consumer Research:** Barbara Philllips and Trina Sego 'The Role of Identity in Disposal: Lessons from Mothers' Disposal of Children's Products' in Alan Bradshaw, Chris Hackley and Pauline Maclaran (eds), *European Association for Consumer Research Conference*

2010 RHUL: 67. **63 Oxford University Press:** Remi Trudel, Jennifer J. Argo and Matthew D. Meng. 'The recycled self: Consumers' disposal decisions of identity-linked products', *Journal of Consumer Research* 43(2) (2016): 246–264. **63 University of Chicago Press:** Grant E. Donnelly, Cait Lamberton, Rebecca Walker Reczek and Michael I. Norton, 'Social recycling transforms unwanted goods into happiness', *Journal of the Association for Consumer Research* 2(1) (January 2017): 48–63. **64 Guardian News and Media Limited:** Jess Cartner-Morley, 'In search of the real deal', The Guardian (2 July 2008), http://www.guardian.co.uk/technology/2008/jul/02/ebay.consumeraffairs (accessed 13 March 2018). **64 Oxford University Press:** John F. Sherry Jr, 'A socio-cultural analysis of a Mid-western American flea market', *Journal of Consumer Research* 17 (June 1990): 13–30. **64 Guardian News and Media Limited:** John Sutherland, 'The price of nostalgia', *Guardian G2* (28 March 2005): 5 (http://www.guardian.co.uk/g2/story/0,,1446610,00.html) (accessed 13 March 2018). **64 The New York Times Company:** Quoted in Jenna Wortham, 'Neighborly borrowing, over the online fence', *New York Times* (28 August 2010), http://www.nytimes.com/2010/08/29/business/29ping.html?_r=1&scp=1&sq=collaborative%20consumption&st=cse (accessed 13 March 2018); https://www.crunchbase.com/organization/snapgoods-com (accessed 13 March 2018); www.neighborgoods.com (accessed 13 March 2018). **66 Boston Globe Media Partners, LLC:** Quoted in Stephanie Stoughton, 'Unemployed Americans turn to e-Bay to make money', *The Boston Globe* (16 October 2001). **67 Association for Consumer Research:** Zeynep Arsel and Susan Dobscha, 'Local Acts, Global Impacts? Examining the Pro-Social, Non-Reciprocal Nature of Freecyclers' in Alan Bradshaw, Chris Hackley and Pauline Maclaran (eds), *European Association for Consumer Research Conference* 2010 RHUL: 11–12. **72 Guardian News and Media Limited:** Zoe Wood 'Shop before you drop off. Bedtime retail rises', *The Guardian* (10 October 2015): 3; 'Online shopping sees 30% rise between midnight and 6am', http://www.theguardian.com/money/2014/oct/10/internet-online-shopping-30-per-cent-rise-midnight-6am-john-lewis (accessed 13 March 2018). **78 SANDRA AWANIS:** Sandra Awanis, Lancaster University Management School, UK. **78 Youth Policy Labs:** Youth Policy (2013), 'Adult Responsibilities, Right of Minors: Youth Rights – More than a Timely Slogan?', http://www.youthpolicy.org/blog/youth-policy-young-people/youth-rights-timely-slogan/ **81 KIRA STRANDBY:** Kira Strandby Campus Vejle, Denmark. **86 American Psychological Association:** Jerome S. Bruner, 'On perceptual readiness', *Psychological Review* 64 (March 1957): 123–52. **89 NEWSWEEK LLC:** Adam Bryant,

'Plastic surgery at AmEx', *Newsweek* (4 October 1999): 55. **89 Pantone LLC:** NY Fashion Week Spring (2018), https://www.pantone.com/fashion-color-trend-report-new-york-spring-2018 (accessed 3 August 2018). **90 Inter brand:** Dale Buss, 'Audio branding: BMW uses new sound signature to help redefine the brand,' *Brand Channel* (20 March 2013), http://www.brandchannel.com/home/post/2013/03/20/BMW-Sound-Signature-032013.aspx (accessed 23 February 2015). **95 RHONDA HADI:** Associate Professor Rhonda Hadi Saïd School of Business, Oxford University. **100 Emerald Publishing Limited:** Baxter, S., J. Ilicic, and A. Kulczynski, 'You see Froot, you think fruit: examining the effectiveness of pseudohomophone priming,' *European Journal of Marketing* 51 (5-6) (2017): 885-902. **102 Oxford University Press (journals only):** McCracken G., 'Culture and consumption: A theoretical account of the structure and movement of the cultural meaning of consumer goods', *Journal of Consumer Research* 13(1) (1986): 72, Copyright © 1986, Oxford University Press by permission of Oxford University Press. **105 Emerald Publishing Limited:** Teresa J. Domzal and Jerome B. Kernan, 'Reading advertising: The what and how of product meaning', *Journal of Consumer Marketing* 9 (Summer 1992): 48-64, at 49. **108 SAGE Publications:** Alladi Venkatesh, 'Ethnoconsumerism: A New Paradigm to Study Cultural and Cross-Cultural Consumer Behavior', in J.A. Costa and G. Bamossy (eds), *Marketing in a Multicultural World* (Thousand Oaks, CA: Sage, 1995). **110 American Marketing Association:** Stephen Brown, Robert V. Kozinets and John F. Sherry Jr, 'Teaching old brands new tricks: Retro branding and the revival of brand meaning', *Journal of Marketing* 67 (July 2003): 19-33. **117 Carolyn Strong:** Carolyn Strong, Cardiff business School strongc@cardiff.ac.uk. **123 American Psychological Association:** Mark Snyder and Steve Gangestad, 'On the nature of self-monitoring: Matters of assessment, matters of validity', *Journal of Personality & Social Psychology* 51 (1986): 125-39. **125 Jacob Ostberg:** Jacob Ostberg, Stockholm University. **126 CPA Highlights:** Quoted in Floyd Rudmin, 'Property crime victimization impact on self, on attachment, and on territorial dominance', *CPA Highlights, Victims of Crime Supplement* 9(2) (1987): 4-7. **126 Association for Consumer Research:** Quoted in Shay Sayre and David Horne, 'I Shop, Therefore I Am: The Role of Possessions for Self Definition', in Shay Sayre and David Horne (eds), *Earth, Wind, and Fire and Water: Perspectives on Natural Disaster* (Pasadena, CA: Open Door Publishers, 1996): 353-70. **129 Frontiers Media S.A:** Andrew D. Wilson and Sabrina Golonka, 'Embodied cognition is not what you think it is', *Frontiers in Psychology* (12 February 2013). **130 De Gruyter company:** Quoted in Susan Fournier,

'Breaking up is hard to do: The ups and downs of divorcing brands', *GfK Marketing Intelligence Review* 6(1) (May 2014), http://www.degruyter.com/view/j/gfkmir.2014.6.issue-1/gfkmir-2014-0005/gfkmir-2014-0005.xml (accessed 21 March 2015). **133 Elsevier:** Joan Meyers-Levy and Barbara Loken, Barbara (2015), 'Revisiting gender differences: What we know and what lies ahead', *Journal of Consumer Psychology* 25(1): 129-149. **137 Condé Nast:** Serena Williams' New Nike Ad Is the Definition of Empowering by Krystin Arneson (11 March 2018). **137 Inter brand:** Quoted in Barry Silverstein, 'Ever the Publicity Hound, Branson Readies to be an Airline Hostess', *BrandChannel* (18 November 2010). **138 The New York Times Company:** Stuart Elliott, 'Banana Republic Ads With Real-Life Unions Include a Gay Couple', *New York Times* (20 February 2014). **142 John Keats:** Woman! When I Behold Thee Flippant, Vain By John Keats. **143 Unilever Archives:** With kind permission from Unilever. **145 Organisation for Economic Co-operation and Development:** Created from data appearing in http://www.dailymail.co.uk/health/article-5070921/UK-HIGHEST-obesity-rate-Western-Europe.html. **147 Child and Teen Consumption:** Hounaida El Jurdi, Nacima Ourahmoune and Søren Askegaard, 'Beauty and the Social Imaginary: A Social Historical Analysis of the Lebanese Techno-Cosmetized Beauty Market', competitive paper presented at the 11th CCT conference, Lille July 2016. **147 Telegraph Media Group Limited:** https://www.telegraph.co.uk/news/2018/04/18/south-koreas-cosmetic-surgery-industry-faces-backlash-cultural/ (accessed August 11 2018). **148 Oxford University Press:** Rebecca Scott, Julien Cayla, and Bernard Cova (2017) 'Selling pain to the saturated self', *Journal of Consumer Research* 44(1): 22-43. **149 Dow Jones & Company, Inc:** Quoted in Wendy Bounds, 'Body-piercing gets under America's skin', *Wall Street Journal* (4 April 1994): B1(2), B4. **161 Guardian News and Media Limited:** Nell Frizzell, 'Vegans, vegetarians and now... reducetarians', *The Observer* (25 June 2017), https://www.theguardian.com/lifeandstyle/2017/jun/25/vegans-vegetarians-and-now-reducetarians (accessed March 7 2018). **168 Guardian News and Media Limited:** Rebecca Smithers, 'Tofu turkey with all the trimmings? Britain carves out a meat-free Christmas', *The Guardian* (2 December 2017), https://www.theguardian.com/lifeandstyle/2017/dec/02/christmas-vegan-vegetarian-cooking-flexitarian-diet-rebecca-smithers (accessed 12 March 2018). **172 Oxford University Press:** Judith Lynne Zaichkowsky, 'Measuring the involvement construct in marketing', *Journal of Consumer Research* 12 (December 1985): 341-52. **173 Elsevier:** Charles C. Cui, Mona Mrad and Margaret K.

Hogg, 'Brand addiction: Exploring the concept and its definition through an experiential lens', *Journal of Business Research* 87 (June 2018): 118–127, https://doi.org/10.1016/j.jbusres.2018.02.028. **174 Merriam-Webster, Incorporated:** www.merriam-webster.com/dictionary/worldwideweb. **175 Guardian News and Media Limited:** Sarah Butler 'Cheers? No thanks! Low- and no-alcohol lifestyle booms', *The Guardian* (26 January 2018), https://www.theguardian.com/society/2018/jan/26/cheers-no-thanks-low--and-no-alcohol-lifestyle-booms (accessed 29 June 2018). **180 Taylor & Francis Group:** Douglas and Isherwood, *The World of Goods,* quoted on 72–73. **182 Cambridge University Press:** William D. Wells and Douglas J. Tigert, 'Activities, interests, and opinions', *Journal of Advertising Research* 11 (August 1971): 27. **184 Strategic Business Insights:** http://www.strategicbusinessinsights.com/vals/international/ (accessed 15 April 2015). **184 Strategic Business Insights:** See VALS website for detailed descriptions of each of these six core groups of UK consumers: http://www.strategicbusinessinsights.com/vals/international/uk.shtml (accessed 7 March 2018). **185 Guardian News and Media Limited:** Julia Carrie Wong '"It might work too well": The dark art of political advertising online', *The Guardian* (March 22 2018), https://www.theguardian.com/technology/2018/mar/19/facebook-political-ads-social-media-history-online-democracy (accessed 29 June 2018). **189 Guardian News and Media Limited:** Simon Usborne 'Just do it: The experience economy and how we turned our backs on "stuff"', *The Guardian* (13 May 2017), https://www.theguardian.com/business/2017/may/13/just-do-it-the-experience-economy-and-how-we-turned-our-backs-on-stuff (accessed 29 June 2018). **190 Benjamin Voyer:** Benjamin Voyer. **190 Guardian News and Media Limited:** Edward Helmore 'So how do you make snakeskin handbags environmentally friendly?', *The Observer* (24 May 2015): 33, http://www.theguardian.com/fashion/2015/may/24/fashion-environment-sustainability (accessed 8 March 2018). **193 Taylor & Francis Group:** Richard W. Pollay, 'Measuring the cultural values manifest in advertising', *Current Issues and Research in Advertising* 6(1) (1983): 71–92. Copyright © 1983 Routledge. **195 Elsevier:** N.A. Nielsen, T. Bech-Larsen and K.G. Grunert, 'Consumer purchase motives and product perceptions: A laddering study on vegetable oil in three countries', *Food Quality and Preference* 9(6) (1998): 455–66. **196 UK Statistics Authority:** Katie Fisher, 'UK Statistics on Waste', DEFRA (22 February 2018), https://assets.publishing.service.gov.uk/government/uploads/system/uploads/attachment_data/file/683051/UK_Statisticson_Waste_statistical_notice_Feb_2018_FINAL.pdf accessed June 29

2018. **197 Guardian News and Media Limited:** Daniel Boffey, 'EU declares war on plastic waste', *The Guardian* (16 January 2018), https://www.theguardian.com/environment/2018/jan/16/eu-declares-war-on-plastic-waste-2030 (accessed 12 March 2018). **197 Guardian News and Media Limited:** Editorial, 'Water: Go Against the Flow', *The Guardian* (20 August 2008): 30, http://www.guardian.co.uk/commentisfree/2008/aug/20/water.food (accessed 8 March 2018). **197 Guardian News and Media Limited:** Editorial, 'Water: Go Against the Flow', *The Guardian* (20 August 2008): 30, http://www.guardian.co.uk/commentisfree/2008/aug/20/water.food (accessed 8 March 2018). **197 Guardian News and Media Limited:** Felicity Lawrence, 'Revealed: the massive scale of UK's water consumption', *The Guardian* (20 August 2008): 1, http://www.guardian.co.uk/environment/2008/aug/20/water.food1 (accessed 8 March 2018). **208 Eman Gadalla:** Eman Gadalla, Lancaster University Management School, UK, and Kathy Keeling, Alliance Manchester Business School, UK. **210 Ben Kerrane:** Ben Kerrane, Lancaster University Management School, UK, and Shona Bettany, Liverpool John Moores University, UK. **210 John Blake Publishing:** Russell, G. (2011), Arise Sir David Beckham: Footballer, Celebrity, Legend – the Biography of Britain's Best Loved Sporting Icon. London: John Blake Publishing Ltd. **210 SAGE Publications:** Gentry, J. and Harrison, R. (2010), 'Is advertising a barrier to male movement toward gender change?', *Marketing Theory* 10(1): 74–96. **214 Gabriele Morello:** Gabriele Morello, GMA-Gabriele Morello and Associates, Palermo, Italy. **218 Taylor & Francis Group:** Yaveroglu Donthu and Naveen Donthu, 'Advertising Repetition and Placement Issues in On-Line Environments', *Journal of Advertising* 37 (Summer 2008): 31–43. **224 The New York Times Company:** Quoted in 'Look-alikes mimic familiar packages', *New York Times* (9 August 1986): D1. **225 The New York Times Company:** Quoted in Rebecca R. Ruiz, 'Luxury Cars Imprint Their Brands on Goods From Cologne to Clothing', *New York Times* (February 2015). **227 The New York Times Company:** Quoted in John Grossmann, 'Using Smartphones and Apps to Enhance Loyalty Programs', *New York Times* (28 January 2015). **228 Peeter Verlegh:** Professor Peeter Verlegh, Vrije Universiteit Amsterdam, The Netherlands. **229 Guardian News and Media Limited:** Dean Burnett, 'What happens in your brain when you make a memory?', *The Guardian* (September 16 2015), https://www.theguardian.com/education/2015/sep/16/what-happens-in-your-brain-when-you-make-a-memory (accessed July 2 2018). **230 Guardian News and Media Limited:** Daniel Glaser, 'Head space: why our adolescent memories are so clear', The Guardian (22 October 2017), https://www.

theguardian.com/lifeandstyle/2017/oct/22/head-space-why-our-adolescent-memories-are-so-clear (accessed July 2 2018). **235 The New York Times Company:** Quoted in Jenna Wortham, 'A Growing App Lets You See It, Then You Don't', *New York Times* (8 February 2013). **236 Interbrand:** Mark J. Miller, 'Carnival Hopes to Jog Passengers' Positive Memories in New Cruise Campaign', *BrandChannel* (19 September 2013). **237 Guardian News and Media Limited:** Mark Cousins, 'How our visual memories are made', *The Guardian* (17 October 2015), https://www.theguardian.com/lifeandstyle/2017/oct/15/how-our-visual-memories-are-made (accessed 2 July 2018). **241 Guardian News and Media Limited:** Nicola Davis, 'Humans produce new brain cells throughout their lives say researchers', *The Guardian* (5 April 2018), https://www.theguardian.com/science/2018/apr/05/humans-produce-new-brain-cells-throughout-their-lives-say-researchers (accessed 2 July 2018). **251 John Wiley & Sons:** Torben Hansen, 'The role of trust in financial customer-seller relationships before and after the financial crisis', *Journal of Consumer Behaviour* 13 (2014): 442–52. **253 Taylor & Francis Group:** Athanasios Krystalis, Klaus G. Grunert, Marcia D. de Barcellos, Toula Perrea and Wim Verbeke, 'Consumer Attitudes towards Sustainability Aspects of Food Production: Insights from Three Continents', *Journal of Marketing Management* 28(3–4) (March 2012): 334–372. **254 PepsiCo:** Tagline of Pepsi. **254 The University of Chicago Press:** Priyali Rajagopal and Nicole Votolato Montgomery, 'I Imagine, I Experience, I Like: The False Experience Effect', *Journal of Consumer Research* 38 (October 2011): 578–594. **269 SAGE Publications:** Martin Fishbein, 'An investigation of the relationships between beliefs about an object and the attitude toward that object', *Human Relations* 16 (1983): 233–40. **271 Oxford University Press:** Olson, J. G., B. McFerran, A. C. Morales, and D. W. Dahl. 2016, 'Wealth and Welfare: Divergent Moral Reactions to Ethical Consumer Choices', *Journal of Consumer Research* 42(6): 879–96. **273 Taylor & Francis Group:** Caroline Moraes, Marylyn Carrigan and Isabelle Szmigin, 'The coherence of inconsistencies: Attitude-behaviour gaps and new consumption communities', *Journal of Marketing Management,* 28(1–2) (2012): 103–28. **276 Dow Jones & Company, Inc:** Choi Hae Won, 'Bill Gates, style icon? Oh yes – in Korea, where geek is chic', *Wall Street Journal* (4 January 2001): A1. **278 Dow Jones & Company, Inc:** Allessandra Galloni, 'Lee's cheeky ads are central to new European campaign', *Wall Street Journal Online* (15 March 2002). **279 Clio Awards:** https://www.adsoftheworld.com/media/integrated/7eleven_chlamydia_goes_viral (28 accessed July 2018). **282 Gary J Bamossy:** From Consumer Behavior, 2nd edn (1989), by John C. Mowen, Macmillan

Publishing Company. **291 Future Publishing Limited Quay House:** Kashfia Kabir 'What is OLED? The tech, the benefits, the best OLED TVs and OLED phones' (17 January 2018), https://www.whathifi.com/advice/what-oled-tech-benefits-best-oled-tvs-and-oled-phones (accessed 5 March 2018). **292 Kelkoo:** http://www.kelkoo.co.uk/c-100311823-televisions.html. **294 The New York Times Company:** Quoted in Matt Richtel, 'That devil on your shoulder likes to sleep in', *New York Times* (1 November 2014), http://www.nytimes.com/2014/11/02/business/that-devil-on-your-shoulder-likes-to-sleep in.html?module=Search&mabReward=relbias%3As%2C%7B%221%22%3A%22RI%3A6%22%7D (accessed 8 March 2018). **297 Oxford University Press:** Ying Zhang, Ayelet Fishback and Ravi Dhar, 'When thinking beats doing: The role of optimistic expectations in goal-based choice', *Journal of Consumer Research* 34 (December 2007): 567. **299 Oxford University Press:** Peter H. Bloch, Daniel L. Sherrell and Nancy M. Ridgway, 'Consumer search: An extended framework', *Journal of Consumer Research* 13(1) (1986): 120. Copyright © 1986, Oxford University Press by permission of Oxford University Press. **302 SAGE Publications:** Tracy W. Tuten and Michael R. Solomon, *Social Media Marketing,* 2nd edition, London: SAGE, 2016. **304 Guardian News and Media Limited:** Jamie Grierson and Ben Quinn, 'Google loses landmark "right to be forgotten" case', *The Guardian* (14 April 2018), https://www.theguardian.com/technology/2018/apr/13/google-loses-right-to-be-forgotten-case (accessed 30 June 2018). **305 Vincent-Wwyne Mitchell:** Professor Vincent-Wayne Mitchell The University of Sydney Business School. **306 Elsevier:** Meyrav Shoham, Sarit Moldovan and Yael Steinhart, 'Positively useless: Irrelevant negative information enhances positive impressions', *Journal of Consumer Psychology* 27(2) (2017): 147–159.. **310 Oxford University Press:** Stuart Rose, quoted in *Corporate Reputation Magazine,* Oxford University (Michaelmas 2014) 11: 5. **311 Journal of Marketing Research:** C. Whan Park, 'The effect of individual and situation-related factors on consumer selection of judgmental models', *Journal of Marketing Research* 13 (May 1976): 144–51. **311 Springer Nature:** Amna Kirmani and Peter Wright, 'Procedural learning, consumer decision making and marketing communication', *Marketing Letters* 4(1) (1993): 39–48. **313 Guardian News and Media Limited:** Rupert Neate, 'Ad men use brain scanners to probe our emotional response', *The Guardian* (14 January 2012), http://www.guardian.co.uk/media/2012/jan/14/neuroscience-advertising-scanners?INTCMP=SRCH (accessed 8 March 2018). **316 European Union:** *The Consumer Markets Scoreboard: Monitoring Consumer Outcomes in the Single Market,* COM (2008) 31, European Communities,

Luxembourg, 2008: 17. **319 Oxford University Press:** Ritesh Saini and Ashwani Monga, 'How I decide depends on what I spend', op. cit.: 915. **320 Association for Consumer Research:** Adapted from Calvin P. Duncan, 'Consumer Market Beliefs: A Review of the Literature and an Agenda for Future Research', in Marvin E. Goldberg, Gerald Gorn and Richard W. Pollay (eds), *Advances in Consumer Research* 17 (Provo, UT: Association for Consumer Research, 1990(17)): 729–35. **321 European Association for Consumer Research:** Raffaella Paciolla and Li-Wei Mai, 'The Impact of Italianate on Consumers' Brand Perceptions of Luxury Brands', in Alan Bradshaw, Chris Hackley and Pauline Maclaran (eds), *European Association for Consumer Research Conference* 2010 RHUL: 61. **322 Journal of Consumer Research:** Kelly, L. Haws, Rebecca Walker Reczek and Kevin L. Sample, 'Healthy Diets Make Empty Wallets: The Healthy = Expensive Intuition', *Journal of Consumer Research* 43(6) (2017): 992–1007. **324 Oxford University Press:** Scott I. Rick, Cynthia E. Cryder and George Loewenstein, 'Tightwads and Spendthrifts', *Journal of Consumer Research* 34 (April 2008): 767. **328 European Union:** https://ec.europa.eu/consumers/consumers_safety/safety_products/rapex/alerts/repository/content/pages/rapex/reports/docs/rapex_annual_report_2016_en.pdf. **329 European Union:** https://ec.europa.eu/consumers/consumers_safety/safety_products/rapex/alerts/repository/content/pages/rapex/reports/docs/rapid_alert_system_factsheet-2016.pdf. **336 Joonas Rokka:** Joonas Rokka, Emlyon Business School, France, and Nacima Ourahmoune, Kedge Business School, France. **338 Effi Raftopoulou:** Effi Raftopoulou, Salford University, UK. **341 Sheila Malone:** Sheila Malone, Lancaster University, UK. **341 The Economist Newspaper Limited:** Unger, B. (2014), 'Exclusively for everybody', *The Economist* (13 December 2014), http://www.economist.com/news/special-report/21635761-modern-luxury-industry-rests-paradoxbut-thriving-nonetheless-says-brooke?zid=319&ah=17af09b0281b01505c226b1e574f5cc1. **347 R.J.W. Hogg:** R.J.W. Hogg, London. **348 The New York Times Company:** Andrew Adam Newman, 'Campaign redefines running as a social activity', *New York Times* (8 July 2013), http://www.nytimes.com/2013/07/09/business/media/campaign-redefines-running-as-a-social-activity.html?_r=3&adxnnl=1&adxnnlx=1375297677-/ALie05m6JiubQ4oXE4qig (accessed 11 March 2018); also for more details on New Balance's Runnovation campaign. **348 Harcourt Brace Jovanovich:** Kenneth J. Gergen and Mary Gergen, *Social Psychology* (New York: Harcourt Brace Jovanovich, 1981): 312. **349 The New York Times Company:** Tamar Charry, 'Unconventional spokesmen talk up U.S. robotics' fast modems in a new TV campaign,' *New York Times* (6 February 1997), http://www.nytimes.com/1997/02/06/business/unconventional-spokesmen-talk-up-us-robotics-fast-modems-in-a-new-tv-campaign.html?scp=44&sq=Tamar+Charry&st=nyt (accessed 11 March 2018). **349 Oxford University Press:** C. Whan Park and V. Parker Lessig, 'Students and housewives: Differences in susceptibility to reference group influence', *Journal of Consumer Research* 4 (September 1977): 102–10. **350 Oxford University Press:** Adapted from William O. Bearden and Michael J. Etzel, 'Reference group influence on product and brand purchase decisions', *Journal of Consumer Research* 9(2) (1982): 185. Copyright © 1982, Oxford University Press by permission of Oxford University Press. **352 Guardian News and Media Limited:** Cited in Zoe Wood, 'Tweet and Tell: turning Twitter into complaints megaphone', *The Guardian* (6 January 2018), https://www.theguardian.com/money/2018/jan/05/tweet-and-tell-turning-twitter-into-complaints-megaphone. **353 Oxford University Press:** Katherine White and Darren W. Dahl, 'Are all out-groups created equal? Consumer identity and dissociative influence', *Journal of Consumer Research* 34 (December 2007): 525. **354 John Wiley & Sons:** Maria G. Piacentini, Andreas Chatzidakis and Emma N. Banister (2012), 'Making Sense of Drinking: The Role of Techniques of Neutralisation and Counter-Neutralisation in Negotiating Alcohol Consumption', *Sociology of Health and Illness* 34(6) forthcoming. **355 Forbes Media LLC:** Melanie Wells, Smooth Operator', *Forbes* (13 May 2002): 167–68. **356 Oxford University Press:** Ping Dong and Chen-Bo Zhong, 'Witnessing moral violations increases conformity in consumption', *Journal of Consumer Research* 44(4) (2017): 778–793. **361 American Marketing Association:** Reprinted with permission from *Journal of Marketing,* published by the American Marketing Association, Schau, Hope Jensen, Albert M. Muñiz, and Eric J. Arnould, September 2009, 73(5): 30–51. **361 McLibel Support Campaign:** http://www.mcspotlight.org/index.shtml. **362 Annual Reviews:** Penelope Eckert and Sally McConnell-Ginet, 'Think practically and look locally: Language and gender as community-based practice', *Annual Review of Anthropology* (1992): 461–90, at 464, cited in Emma Moore, 'Approaches to Identity: Lesson from Sociolinguistics', Seminar paper, Customer Research Academy, Manchester School of Management, UMIST, UK (22 April 2004): 2. **362 Periodicals Service Company:** Quoted in Barbara B. Stern and Stephen J. Gould, 'The consumer as financial opinion leader', *Journal of Retail Banking* 10 (Summer 1988): 43–52. **363 Oxford University Press:** Evan Weingarten and Jonah Berger, 'Fired Up for the Future: How Time Shapes Sharing',

Journal of Consumer Research 44(2) (2017): 432–447. **364 The New York Times Company:** Cathy Horyn, 'A store made for right now: You shop until it's dropped', *NYTOnline* (17 February 2004). **368 American Marketing Association:** Steven A. Baumgarten, 'The innovative communicator in the diffusion process', *Journal of Marketing Research* 12 (February 1975): 12–18. **369 SAGE Publications:** Adapted from Lawrence Feick and Linda Price, 'The market maven: A diffuser of marketplace information', *Journal of Marketing* 51 (January 1987): 83–7. **371 Association for Consumer Research:** John Deighton, Jacob Goldenberg and Andrew T. Stephen, 'Introduction to the Special Issue of The Consumer in a Connected World', *Journal of the Association for Consumer Research* April 2(2) (2017): 137–139. **372 Guardian News and Media Limited:** Mark Sweney, 'Home entertainment spending overtakes print sales for the first time', *The Guardian* (1 March 2018), https://www.theguardian.com/media/2018/mar/01/home-entertainment-spending-overtakes-print-sales-for-first-time. **373 Merriam-Webster, Incorporated:** The Merriam-Webster Dictionary. **373 John Wiley & Sons:** Barry Wellman, 'Physical place and cyberplace: The rise of personalized networking', *International Journal of Urban & Regional Research* 24(2) (2001): 227–52. **375 Guardian News and Media Limited:** Mark Sweney, '"Parents killed it": Why young users are ditching Facebook', *The Guardian* (16 February 2018), https://www.theguardian.com/technology/2018/feb/16/parents-killed-it-facebook-losing-teenage-users (accessed 5 March 2018). **377 Lifewire:** Daniel Nations, 'Is Web 3.0 really a thing?', *Lifewire* (24 March 2018), https://www.lifewire.com/what-is-web-3-0-3486623 (accessed 1 July 2018). **378 Pearson Education Ltd:** Donna Hoffman, 'Consumer Behavior as I See IT', *Consumer Behavior,* 10th edn, Michael R. Solomon (2012) Pearson. **378 American Marketing Association:** Ezgi Akpinar and Jonah Berger, 'Valuable Virality', *Journal of Marketing Research* 54(2) (2017): 318–330. **378 Guardian News and Media Limited:** Karen Kay, 'Millennial "influencers" who are the new stars of web advertising', *The Guardian* (28 May 2017), https://www.theguardian.com/fashion/2017/may/27/millenial-influencers-new-stars-web-advertising-marketing-luxury-brands (accessed February 27 2018). **378 Oxford University Press:** Quoted in Edward F. McQuarrie, Jessica Miller and Barbara J. Phillips, 'The Megaphone Effect: Taste and Audience in Fashion Blogging', *Journal of Consumer Research* 40(1) (2013): 136–58. **379 Guardian News and Media Limited:** Hannah Ellis-Petersen 'Makeup, advice, anxiety – how Zoella rose to be queen of the video bloggers', *The Guardian* (6 December 2014): 17, http://www.theguardian.com/technology/2014/dec/05/ zoella-sugg-internet-queen-fastest-selling-novel-youtube (accessed 11 March 2018). **379 Guardian News and Media Limited:** Dalmeet Singh Chawla, 'The young vloggers and their fans who are changing the face of youth culture', *The Observer* (28 September 2014): 20, http://www.theguardian.com/technology/2014/sep/28/vloggers-changing-future-advertising (accessed 11 March 2018). **379 Guardian News and Media Limited:** Cited in: Press Association, Growing social media backlash among young people, survey shows *The Guardian* (5 October 2017), https://www.theguardian.com/media/2017/oct/05/growing-social-media-backlash-among-young-people-survey-shows (accessed 11 March 2018). **380 Stefania Farace:** Professor Stefania Farace Eastern Connecticut State University. **386 Guardian News and Media Limited:** https://www.theguardian.com/technology/2017/jun/06/internet-of-things-smart-home-smart-city. **394 United Nations:** Livia Sz. Oláh, 'Changing families in the European Union: Trends and policy implications', Analytical paper, prepared for the United Nations Expert Group Meeting, 'Family policy development: achievements and challenges', New York, (14-15 May 2015): 1, http://www.un.org/esa/socdev/family/docs/egm15/Olahpaper.pdf. **395 European Union:** Eurostat (demo_pjangroup) and (proj_13npms) © European Union. http://ec.europa.eu/eurostat/statistics explained/index.php/File:Population_structure_by_major_age_groups,_EU-28,_2016-80_(%25_of_total_population).png (accessed 28 March 2018). **397 European Union:** 'Families with children in the EU', Source Eurostat: http://ec.europa.eu/eurostat/web/products-eurostat-news/-/EDN-20170531-1?ticket=ST-15846581-83zehqBMbtePwdVmwClyFA1zPMq7lkSzsEFq mvFaCovWqaYatypdp5VXddzx566DSXbgJuzlwzozmJYzy kBjfyKW-PHsIUMVSXYC6iO06UxAkYy-iaKcx2Twkzq8jEm3 SlqvQHdzsybqjxGjREyciHapJIIW. **398 Guardian News and Media Limited:** Tracy McVeigh, 'Why men still won't get their hands dirty at home', *The Guardian* (12 March 2017), https://www.theguardian.com/lifeandstyle/2017/mar/12/housework-men-assert-masculinity (accessed 3 April 2018). See also Tanja van der Lippe Judith Treas and Lukas Norbutas, 'Unemployment and the division of housework in Europe', *Work, Employment and Society* (1–20 March 2017), http://journals.sagepub.com/doi/full/10.1177/0950017017690495 accessed 3 April 2018. **399 Telegraph Media Group Limited:** Richard Alleyne, 'Facebook increasingly implicated in divorce,' *The Telegraph* (UK) (21 January 2011), http://www.telegraph.co.uk/technology/facebook/8274601/Facebook-increasingly-implicated-in-divorce.html (accessed 2 April 2018). **399 European Union:** http://ec.europa.eu/

eurostat/cache/infographs/womenmen/bloc-1b. html?lang=en (accessed 2 April 2018). **401 Oxford University Press:** Daniel Seymour and Greg Lessne, 'Spousal conflict arousal: Scale development', *Journal of Consumer Research* 11 (December 1984): 810–21. **404 Pearson Education Ltd:** Scott Ward, 'Consumer Socialization', in Harold H. Kassarjian and Thomas S. Robertson (eds), *Perspectives in Consumer Behavior* (Glenville, IL: Scott, Foresman, 1980): 380. **407 Guardian News and Media Limited:** Sarah Boseley, 'Amsterdam's solution to the obesity crisis: no fruit juice and enough sleep', *The Guardian* (14 April 2017), https://www. theguardian.com/society/2017/apr/14/amsterdam-solution-obesity-crisis-no-fruit-juice-enough-sleep (accessed 2 April 2018). **407 Pauline Maclaran:** Professor Pauline Maclaran Royal Holloway University of London. **413 Guardian News and Media Limited:** Patrick Collinson, 'UK millennials second worst-hit financially in developed world, says study', *The Guardian* (19 February 2018), https://www.theguardian.com/money/2018/ feb/19/uk-millennials-second-worst-hit-financially-in-developed-world-says-study (accessed 3 April 2018). **413 Guardian News and Media Limited:** Sally Weale, 'Boomerang offspring damage parents' wellbeing, study finds', *The Guardian* (7 March 2018), **413 Elsevier:** Marco Tosi and Emily Grundy, 'Returns home by children and changes in parents' well-being in Europe', *Social Science and Medicine* 200 (2018): 104, https://ac.els-cdn.com/ S0277953618300169/1-s2.0-S0277953618300169-main. pdf?_tid=6654de52-f182-49f9-af97-ee476fe980d4&acdn at=1522756067_806a4966745a73964dbcb2f49b1383ba (accessed 3 April 2018). **413 European Union:** Eurostat (online data codes: demo_pjangroup and proj_15npms) http://ec.europa.eu/eurostat/statistics-explained/ index.php/File:Population_pyramids,_EU-28,_2016_ and_2080_(%25_of_the_total_population).png (accessed 28 March 2018). **414 Guardian News and Media Limited:** Sally Weale, 'Boomerang children can be good for family relationships – study', *The Guardian* (June 29 2018), https://www.theguardian.com/education/2018/ jun/29/boomerang-children-can-be-good-for-family-relationships-study (accessed 1 July 2018). **416 European Union:** Eurostat (online data codes: demo_pjanind and proj_15ndbims), http://ec.europa.eu/eurostat/statistics-explained/index.php/File:Projected_old-age_ dependency_ratio,_EU-28,_2016-80_(%25).png (accessed 28 March 2018). **430 European Union:** Eurostat, http:// ec.europa.eu/eurostat/statistics-explained/index.php/ File:The_unadjusted_gender_pay_gap,_2013_%281% 29_-_difference_between_average_gross_hourly_ earnings_of_male_and_female_employees_as_%25_of_ male_gross_earnings.png. © European Union, 1995–2016. **431 An Hodgson:** Euromonitor International from national statistics. **432 GfK:** GfK, http://www.gfk. com/documents/press-releases/2014/20141022_pr_gfk-purchasing-power-europe_fin.pdf. © GfK GeoMarketing, study GfK Purchasing Power Europe 2012/2013. **433 Henley Business School:** 'Frontiers: Planning or consumer change in Europe 96/97', 2 (London: The Henley Centre, 1996). **436 Guardian News and Media Limited:** Golden chicken: you might as well light a cigarette with a burning tenner https://www. theguardian.com/lifeandstyle/2018/may/30/golden-chicken-you-might-as-well-be-lighting-a-fag-with-a-burning-tenner. **436 Goodyear Publishing Company:** Jonathan H. Turner, *Sociology: Studying the Human System,* 2nd edn (Santa Monica, CA: Goodyear, 1981). **438 Organisation for Economic Co-operation and Development:** OECD report 2017: https://www.oecd. org/els/soc/cope-divide-europe-2017-background-report.pdf. **439 Goodyear Publishing Company:** Jonathan H. Turner, *Sociology: Studying the Human System,* 2nd edn (Santa Monica, CA: Goodyear, 1981). **442 Organisation for Economic Co-operation and Development:** Homi Kharas, 'The Emerging Middle Class in Developing Countries', OECD Development Centre, Working Paper no. 285 (OECD 2010). © OECD 2010. **443 The New York Times Company:** Heather Timmons, 'Vogue's fashion photos spark debate in India', *New York Times* (31 August 2008), www.nytimes. com/2008/09/01/business/worldbusiness/01vogue. html?_r1&refbusi (accessed 1 September 2008). **444 The New York Times Company:** Heather Timmons, 'Vogue's fashion photos spark debate in India', *New York Times* (31 August 2008), www.nytimes.com/2008/09/01/ business/worldbusiness/01vogue.html?_r1&refbusi (accessed 1 September 2008). **445 Business Daily News Desk:** Doors, the new status symbol in Kenyan homes https://www.businessdailyafrica.com/lifestyle/design/ Doors-new-status-symbol-Kenyan-homes/4258320-4305908-l5mfix/index.html. **445 Simon & Schuster:** Durkheim (1958), quoted in Roger Brown, Social Psychology (New York: The Free Press, 1965). **446 Sociology and Social Research:** Edward O. Laumann and James S. House, 'Living room styles and social attributes: The patterning of material artifacts in a modern urban community', *Sociology and Social Research* 54 (April 1970): 321–42. **448 Association for Consumer Research:** Quoted in Richard Elliott, 'How do the unemployed maintain their identity in a culture of consumption?', in Hansen (ed.), *European Advances in Consumer Research* 2: 1–4, at 3. **448 SAGE Publications:** Adapted from Jeffrey F. Durgee, 'How Consumer Sub-Cultures Code Reality: A Look at Some Code Types', in Richard J. Lutz (ed.), *Advances in Consumer Research* 13 (Provo, UT: Association for Consumer Research, 1986

(13):332). **449 Kathy Hamilton:** Kathy Hamilton. **453 Hachette Book Group:** John Brooks, Showing off in America (Boston: Little, Brown, 1981): 13. **454 Emerald Publishing Limited:** Kira Strandby and Søren Askegaard, 'Weddings as Waste', *Research in Consumer Behavior* 15 (2013): 145–165. **454 Penguin Random House:** Thorstein Veblen, *The Theory of the Leisure Class* (1899; reprint, New York: New American Library, 1953): 45. **455 VNU eMedia, Inc:** Quoted in Miller, 'Baubles are back', op. cit.; Elaine Underwood, 'Luxury's tide turns', *Brandweek* (7 March 1994): 18–22. **457 SAGE Journals:** Adapted from B. Moingeon, 'La sociologie de P. Bourdieu et son apport au marketing', *Recherches et Applications en Marketing,* 8(2) (1993): 123. **459 Nike, Inc:** Nike slogan. **467 Benjamin Koeck and David Marshall:** Benjamin Koeck and David Marshall, University of Edinburgh Business School, UK. **470 ELODIE GENTINA:** Elodie Gentina, IESEG, Paris, France. **473 Katerina Karanika:** Katerina Karanika Exeter University, UK. **480 Damien Mcloughlin :** Damien Mcloughlin University College, Dublin, Ireland. **483 Macmillan Publishers:** Søren Askegaard, Dannie Kjeldgaard and Eric J. Arnould, 'Reflexive culture's consequences', in C. Nakata (ed.), Beyond Hofstede; Culture frameworks for global marketing and management (Chicago: Palgrave Macmillan, 2009): 101–24. **485 Copenhagen Business School Press:** Laurie Meamber and Alladi Venkatesh, 'Ethnoconsumerist Methodology for Cultural and Cross-Cultural Consumer Research', in R. Elliott and S. Beckmann (eds), Interpretive Consumer Research, Copenhagen: Copenhagen Business School Press, 2000: 87–108. **489 Rudyard Kipling:** The Ballad of East and West Poem by Rudyard Kipling. **493 Oxford University Press:** Dennis W. Rook, 'The ritual dimension of consumer behavior', *Journal of Consumer Research* 12(3) (1985): 251–64. The Journal of Consumer Research Copyright © 1985, Oxford University Press by permission of Oxford University Press. **496 Temple University Press:** Diane Barthel, *Putting on Appearances: Gender and Attractiveness* (Philadelphia: Temple University Press, 1988). **496 Oxford University Press:** Adapted from Julie A. Ruth, Cele C. Otnes and Frederic F. Brunel, 'Gift receipt and the reformulation of interpersonal relationships', *Journal of Consumer Research,* 25(4) (1999): 385–402, Table 1: 389. **499 Stephen Brown:** Stephen Brown, University of Ulster. **500 John Wiley & Sons:** Antje Cockrill and Mark M.H. Goode, 'DVD pirating intentions: Angels, devils, chancers and receivers', *Journal of Consumer Behaviour,* 11 (2012): 1–10. **506 Oxford University Press:** Robert V. Kozinets, John F. Sherry Jr, Diana Storm, Adam Duhachek, Krittinee Nuttavuthisit and Benet DeBerry-Spence, 'Ludic agency and retail spectacle', *Journal of Consumer Research* 31 (December 2004): 658–72. **507 John Wiley &**

Sons: Beverly Gordon, 'The souvenir: Messenger of the extra-ordinary', *Journal of Popular Culture* 20(3) (1986): 135–46. **510 Virginia Polytechnic Institute and State University:** Quoted in Ruth Ann Smith, 'Collecting as Consumption: A Grounded Theory of Collecting Behavior', unpublished manuscript, Virginia Polytechnic Institute and State University, 1994: 14. **511 Association for Consumer Research:** Jan Slater, 'Collecting the Real Thing: A Case Study Exploration of Brand Loyalty Enhancement Among Coca-Cola Brand Collectors', in Hoch and Meyer (eds), *Advances in Consumer Research* 27: 202–8. **511 Guardian News and Media Limited:** '"Christianity as default is gone": The rise of a non-Christian Europe'. **512 Ogilvy UK:** Ogilvy and Mather. **513 The Halal Journal:** Jonathan Bilal, A.J. Wilson, 'Muslim youth culture: A new wave of hip hop grunge', *The Halal Journal,* World Halal Forum 2012 Special Edition 32–38, www.halaljournal.com: 34. **513 Emerald Publishing Limited:** Jonathan Bilal, A.J. Wilson and J. Liu, 'The challenges of Islamic branding: Navigating emotions and halal', Figure 4 Classification of Islamic Brands (p. 34), *Journal of Islamic Marketing* 2(1): 28–42. **514 Bloomsbury Publishing:** 'Generation M: Young Muslims Changing the World' by Shelina Janmohamed, pub IB Taurus **515 Crain Communications Inc:** Claudia Penteado, 'Brazilian ad irks Church', *Advertising Age* (23 March 2000): 11. **543 John Wiley & Sons, Inc:** Deniz Atik and Cansu Yildirim, 'Motivations behind acquiring tattoos and feelings of regret: Highlights from an Eastern Mediterranean context', *Journal of Consumer Behaviour,* 13 (2014): 212–23. **544 Elle:** Ad appeared in Elle (September 1994). **544 Rolling Stone, LLC:** Jancee Dunn, 'How hip-hop style bum-rushed the mall', *Rolling Stone* (18 March 1999): 54–9. **544 The Wall Street Journal:** Quoted in Teri Agins, 'The rare art of "gilt by association": How Armani got stars to be billboards', *The Wall Street Journal Interactive Edition* (14 September 1999). **546 Elsevier:** Source: Adapted from Michael R. Solomon, 'Building Up and Breaking Down: The Impact of Cultural Sorting on Symbolic Consumption', in J. Sheth and E.C. Hirschman (eds), *Research in Consumer Behavior* (Greenwich, CT: JAI Press, 1988): 325–51. **549 SAGE Publishing:** Jennifer Smith Maguire, 'Provenance and the liminality of production and consumption: The case of wine promoters', *Marketing Theory* 10(3) (2010); 269–82. **554 Sheffield Publishing Company:** Arthur A. Berger, *Signs in Contemporary Culture: An Introduction to Semiotics* (New York: Longman, 1984): 86. Copyright © 1984. Reissued 1989 by Sheffield Publishing Company, Salem, WI. Reprinted with permission of the publisher. **556 Montgomery Advertiser:** Nicolas Marmie, 'Casablanca Gets a Rick's', *Montgomery Advertiser* (9 May 2004): 3AA. **557 Dannie Kjeldgaard:** Professor

Dannie Kjeldgaard, University of Southern Denmark. **557 Taylor & Francis Group:** Søren Askegaard, 'Experience economy in the making: Hedonism, play and coolhunting in automotive song lyrics', *Consumption, Markets and Culture,* 13(4) (2010): 351–371. **558 Guardian News and Media Limited:** https://www.theguardian.com/media/2018/jan/20/forget-product-placement-advertisers-buy-storylines-tv-blackish (accessed 22 August 2018). **559 The Washington post:** https://www.washingtonpost.com/news/wonk/wp/2015/06/12/jurassic-world-shows-just-how-weird-product-placement-has-become/?noredirect=on&utm_term=.3dbe4a6fbe99 (accessed 22 August 2018). **559 The Wall Street Journal:** Geoffrey A. Fowler, 'New star on Chinese TV: Product placements', *Wall Street Journal Online Edition* (2 June 2004): B1. **562 Beverage Marketing Corporation:** Beverage Marketing Corporation. http://www.bottledwater.org/public/2011%20BMC%20Bottled%20Water%20Stats_2.pdf\#overlay-context=economics/industry-statistics. **564 Emerald Publishing Limited:** Gordon R. Foxall and Seema Bhate, 'Cognitive style and personal involvement as explicators of innovative purchasing of health food brands', *European Journal of Marketing* 27(2) (1993): 5–16.. Used with permission. **567 Harvard Business Publishing:** W. Chan Kim and Renée Mauborgne, 'Value innovation: The strategic logic of high growth', *Harvard Business Review* (January–February 1997): 103–12. **568 Leighanne Higgins:** Leighanne Higgins, Lancaster University Management School, UK. **570 Darach Turley:** Darach Turley, Dublin City University, Ireland, and Stephanie O'donohoe, University of Edinburgh, UK. **572 Taylor & Francis Group:** Fajer Saleh al-Mutawa, Richard Elliott and Peter Nuttall, 'Foreign brands in local cultures: A socio-cultural perspective of postmodern brandscapes', *Journal of Consumer Behaviour,* 14 (2015): 137–44. **573 Odense University:** Anne F. Jensen and Søren Askegaard, 'In Pursuit of Ugliness. Searching for a Fashion Concept in the Era After Good Taste', *Working Paper in Marketing,* no. 17 (Odense: Odense University, 1998). **573 Anuja Pradhan and Hayley Cocker:** Anuja Pradhan and Hayley Cocker, Lancaster University, UK. **575 Macmillan Publisher:** Based on Susan Kaiser, *The Social Psychology of Clothing* (New York: Macmillan, 1985). **576 Macmillan Publisher:** Susan Kaiser, *The Social Psychology of Clothing* (New York: Macmillan, 1985). **576 Oxford University Press:** Quoted in Stephen Brown and Anthony Patterson, '"You're a Wizard, Harry!" Consumer responses to the Harry Potter phenomenon', *Advances in Consumer Research* 33 (2006): 155–60. **578 Oxford University Press:** Adapted from Lisa Peñaloza, 'Atravesando fronteras /border crossings: A critical ethnographic exploration of the consumer acculturation of Mexican immigrants', *Journal of Consumer Research,* 21(1) (1994): 32–54. Copyright © 1994, Oxford University Press by permission of Oxford University Press. **580 Oxford University Press:** Tuba Ustuner and Douglas B. Holt, 'Dominated consumer acculturation: The social construction of poor migrant women's consumer identity projects in a Turkish squatter', *Journal of Consumer Research* 34 (June 2007): 41. **580 Taylor & Francis Group:** Marius K. Luedicke (2011) 'Consumer acculturation theory: (crossing) conceptual boundaries', *Consumption Markets & Culture,* 14(3): 223. **580 Oxford University Press:** Source: Tuba Ustuner and Douglas B. Holt 'Dominated Consumer Acculturation: The Social Construction of Migrant Women's Consumer Identity Projects in a Turkish Squatter', *Journal of Consumer Research,* 34 (June 2007) Figure 2: 53. The Journal of Consumer Research by American Association for public opinion research. Reproduced with permission of University of Chicago Press. **581 Oxford University Press:** Marius K. Luedicke (2015) 'Indigenes' Responses to Immigrants' Consumer Acculturation: A Relational Configuration Analysis', *Journal of Consumer Research* 42(1) (1 June): 109–129. **581 Taylor and Francis Group:** Source: Luedicke (2011), 'Consumer acculturation theory: (crossing) conceptual boundaries', *Consumption Markets & Culture,* 14(3): 239, Figure 2.

Photographs

xix Michael R Solomon: Michael R Solomon. **xx Soren Askegaard:** Soren Askegaard. **xx Margaret K Hogg:** Margaret K Hogg. **xxi Gary J Bamossy:** Gary J Bamossy. **1, 2, 33, Getty Images:** 97/E+/Getty Images. **17 Getty Images:** Bloomberg/Getty Images. **22 Professor Robert Kozinets:** Courtesy of Professor Robert Kozinets. **26 Giana Eckhardt:** Giana Eckhardt. **35 Mary Boone Gallery:** Copyright Barbara Kruger, Courtesy: Mary Boone Gallery, New York. **40 H.J. Heinz Company Limited (UK):** Courtesy of H.J. Heinz Company Limited. **47 Shutterstock:** javi_indy/Shutterstock. **53 Alamy Stock Photo :** Gerard Ferry/Alamy Stock Photo. **54 Stefania Borghini:** Professor Stefania Borghini Bocconi University, Milan. **55 Getty Images:** Oli Scarff/Getty Images. **62 Guardian News and Media Ltd / Christopher Thomond:** Christopher Thomond/Guardian News & Media Ltd 2015. **65 Getty Images:** LIU JIN/Getty Images. **65 Alamy:** ZUMA Press, Inc./Alamy Stock Photo. **66 Alamy Stock Photo :** Alan Wilson/Alamy Stock Photo. **83, 84, 117, 160 Getty Images:** Emilija Manevska/Moment/Getty Images. **87 Shutterstock:** Patrick Foto/

Shutterstock. **89 Shutterstock:** vectorfusionart/ Shutterstock. **91 Alamy:** Rufus Stone/Alamy Stock Photo. **92 Shutterstock:** ra2studio/Shutterstock. **93 Sunkist Growers, Inc:** Sunkist Growers, Inc. **94 Shutterstock:** Suriyachan/Shutterstock. **95 Rhonda Hadi:** Associate Professor Rhonda Hadi Saïd School of Business, Oxford University. **101 Demner, Merlicek & Bergmann Werbegesellschaft mbH:** Demner, Merlicek & Bergmann Werbegesellschaft mbH. **107 Shutterstock:** Chrisdorney/Shutterstock. **110 Soren Askegaard:** Soren Askegaard. **110 Unilever Archives:** With kind permission from Unilever. **121 Alamy Stock Photo :** Simon leigh/ Alamy Stock Photo. **125 Michael R Solomon:** Michael R Solomon. **131 Getty Images:** Tony Latham/Corbis/Getty Images. **133 Gender-Neutral icon:** Gender-Neutral icon. **135 Alamy Stock Photo :** Chris Hellier/Alamy Stock Photo. **139 Alamy Stock Photo :** Nano Calvo/Alamy Stock Photo. **139 Shutterstock:** Tracey Nearmy/EPA/ Shutterstock. **141 Getty Images:** Vittorio Zunino Celotto /Getty Images. **143 Unilever Archives:** With kind permission from Unilever. **146 The Body Shop:** The Body Shop. **149 Getty Images:** Jamie Garbutt/Taxi/ Getty Images. **164 Shutterstock:** mubus7/Shutterstock. **167 Alamy Stock Photo :** Contraband Collection/Alamy Stock Photo. **178 Alamy:** Eric Audras/ONOKY - Photononstop/Alamy Stock Photo. **179 Alamy Stock Photo :** Fotograferen.net/Alamy Stock Photo. **187 Alamy Stock Photo :** Thiago Santos/Alamy Stock Photo. **188 Alamy Stock Photo :** CrowdSpark/Alamy Stock Photo. **190 BENJAMIN G. VOYER:** Professor Benjamin G. Voyer ESCP Europe (London) and LSE, London. **192 Shutterstock:** Ipatov/Shutterstock. **213, 214, 250, 291 Getty Images:** Noel Hendrickson/DigitalVision/Getty Images. **219 Alamy Stock Photo :** Ashley Cooper/Alamy Stock Photo. **224 123RF:** mitdesign/123RF. **225 Shutterstock:** David McHugh/Shutterstock. **228 Peeter Verlegh:** Professor Peeter Verlegh Vrije Universiteit, Amsterdam, The Netherlands. **232 Alamy Stock Photo :** Jeff Morgan 09/Alamy Stock Photo. **240 Alamy Stock Photo:** Clynt Garnham Business/Alamy Stock Photo. **242 Alamy Stock Photo:** Daniel Dempster Photography/ Alamy Stock Photo. **256 Gary J Bamossy:** Gary J Bamossy. **257 Alamy:** Mauritius images GmbH/Alamy Stock Photo. **259 L.J. Shrum:** L.J. Shrum, HEC Paris. **274 Shutterstock:** Shutterstock. **275 Getty Images:** David McNew/Getty Images. **277 Alamy:** Jeffrey Blackler/ Alamy Stock Photo. **277 Shutterstock:** Jonathan Hordle/ Shutterstock. **280 Brandhouse:** Brandhouse. **280 Alamy:** Steve Skjold/Alamy Stock Photo. **281 Getty Images:** Ullstein bild/Getty Images. **296 Shutterstock:** Songquan Deng/Shutterstock. **296 Shutterstock:** Bikeworldtravel/Shutterstock. **301 Alamy Stock Photo:** f8 archive/Alamy Stock Photo. **303 Alamy:** Newscast Online Limited/Alamy Stock Photo. **323 Shutterstock:** Gorodenkoff/Shutterstock. **336 Getty Images:** Francois Nascimbeni/Stringer/Getty Images. **345, 346, 392, 427 Getty Images:** Eva-Katalin/E+/Getty Images. **347 Shutterstock :** p2play/Shutterstock. **352 Shutterstock:** Paolo Paradiso/Shutterstock. **354 Alamy:** MARTIN DALTON/Alamy Stock Photo. **358 Unilever Archives:** With kind permission from Unilever. **364 Shutterstock :** IBL/Shutterstock **364 Shutterstock:** sirtravelalot/ Shutterstock. **367 The Image Works:** © Susan Goldman/ The Image Works. **374 Threadless.com:** Threadless.com. **381 Shutterstock:** Rex/Shutterstock. **393 Shutterstock:** Monkey Business Images/Shutterstock. **398 Shutterstock:** Luc Ubaghs/Shutterstock. **405 123RF:** Paha_l/123RF. **406 Alamy Stock Photo :** Christopher Stewart/Alamy Stock Photo. **407 Pauline Maclaran:** Professor Pauline Maclaran, Royal Holloway,University of London. **412 Shutterstock:** Sirtravelalot/Shutterstock. **417 Shutterstock:** Entertainment Press/Shutterstock. **449 Kathy Hamilton:** Kathy Hamilton, University of Strathclyde. **452 Magic Car Pics/Shutterstock:** Magic Car Pics/Shutterstock. **479, 480, 522 Getty Images:** Emma Falasco/EyeEm/Getty Images. **481 Getty Images:** Oli Scarff/Getty Images. **491 Caroline Penhoat:** Caroline Penhoat. **494 Alamy:** RubberBall/Alamy Stock Photo. **496 Getty Images:** Eva-Katalin/E+/Getty Images. **498 Getty Images:** Gen Nishino/Getty Images. **500 Getty Images:** Drazen/E+/Gettty Images. **502 Kira Strandby:** Kira Strandby. **503 Getty Images:** Heritage Images/ Hulton Archive/Getty Imahes. **505 Alamy Stock Photo :** Stephen Barnes/Northern Ireland News/Alamy Stock Photo. **509 Getty Images:** ullstein bild/Contributor/ Getty Images. **529 Shutterstock:** Eugenio Marongiu/ Shutterstock. **531 Shutterstock:** Alfredo Dagli Orti/ Shutterstock. **534 Shutterstock:** Thomas Frey/EPA/ Shutterstock. **534 Shutterstock:** Thomas Frey/EPA/ Shutterstock. **535 Dannie Kjeldgaard:** Professor Dannie Kjeldgaard, University of Southern Denmark. **547 Maidenform, Inc:** Copyright © 1994 by Maidenform, Inc. Used with permission. **550 Alamy:** keith morris/Alamy Stock Photo. **552 Alamy:** Agencja Fotograficzna Caro/ Alamy Stock Photo.

Part A
Consumers in the marketplace

This introductory part comprises two chapters. The first chapter gives an overview of the field of consumer behaviour. It examines how the field of marketing is influenced by the actions of consumers, and also how we as consumers are influenced by marketers. It also surveys consumer behaviour as a discipline of enquiry, and describes some of the different approaches that researchers use in order better to understand what makes consumers behave as they do. Next, it addresses contemporary consumer culture and, more particularly, its globalisation tendencies. The second chapter offers a broad overview of the consumer in the marketplace, through its investigation of the modern ritual of the shopping process. It also looks at various contemporary retail environments and the roles they play in consumers' social lives.

Chapter 1
Consumer behaviour and consumer society

Chapter objectives

When you finish reading this chapter you will understand why:

1.1 We use products to help us define our identities in different settings.

1.2 Consumer behaviour is a process involving many actors.

1.3 Many different types of specialists study consumer behaviour.

1.4 There are basically two differing perspectives (called paradigms) regarding how and what we should understand about consumer behaviour.

1.5 The society we live in today can be described as a consumer society.

1.6 Globalisation is important when trying to understand the consumer society.

1.7 Consumption is not just a private but also a political issue. The ethics of consumption is becoming more and more significant.

1.8 We are witnessing the appearance of new forms of collective consumption formats.

LIANE is working at her computer. It is early autumn and the beginning of a new term at her Higher Professional Nursing School in Amsterdam. Time for getting new books and study materials. As a full-time student in her final year of a full-time practical internship with exams, she is not surprised to find that several of the required books are unavailable at the campus bookshop.

She goes online to check if she can get her books from one of the internet bookshops. She uses her favorite portal www.athenaeum.nl/studieboeken, which she thinks might be able to deliver the books faster than its international competitors, but Athenaeum doesn't have all of the books in stock that she needs, and she really feels that she should get all them from the same store. On an impulse, Liane visits a website that sells used books and provides search facilities for a number of online booksellers. She searches for a couple of the titles she needs, but the search function on this site does not seem to be working properly. For a moment, she considers putting some of her used books up for sale on this site, then decides not to let herself be distracted and moves on to the UK version of Amazon. She has heard from friends that prices are a little steeper here (relative to the other internet book-shops), but she knows this site well by now. Besides, the books she wants are in stock and can be delivered in about a week, maybe less. Considering that the chances of the books she needs appearing in the campus bookshop on time seem pretty slim, Liane decides to go ahead and buy them online.

While filling out the Amazon order form, she thinks about what else she needs to get done. She and her friend are looking for an interesting topic for a course project and she wants to look at ideas for a relevant European project, so she clicks on CESSDA's website (https://www.cessda.eu/) for some inspiration. Also, she wants to visit a few of her favourite sites for news, music and travel. 'A little information update before meeting my friends this afternoon for coffee', she thinks to herself. She clicks back to the Amazon tab in her browser, hits 'OK' on her textbook order confirmation and is glad to have that out of the way. She navigates her way back to the CESSDA website and starts her search. All the while that she's getting the textbooks ordered, she is also thinking to herself that she should take a look at her personal performance data, which is logged on her activity tracker, Polar Loop. She finished a great workout and run at the gym the day before . . . now might be a good time to post the results of that impressive effort on her Facebook page! Suddenly Liane remembers that there were a couple of study plans to print out from the university website – and a few emails to answer. She checks her email account and is a little surprised to see that she has received so much mail today – it seems like everybody has just realised that summer is over and wants to get started on new projects. It makes her feel joyful, even invigorated . . .

DIANA STORM, UNIVERSITY OF SOUTHERN DENMARK

Introduction

This text is about **consumer behaviour**, written from a European perspective. But what does that mean exactly? Obviously, to write about a 'European' consumer or a 'European's consumer behaviour' is problematic. For that matter, one might even ask 'What and where is Europe'? For it is a concept as well as a continent, and the borders of both oscillate wildly. The most common present-day usage of the term 'Europe' seems to be shorthand for (and synonymous with) the European Union. The external borders of this supranational project are movable, having consistently shifted outward until Brexit made it evident that the project can also shrink. And a number of obviously 'European' countries have never been members.

Some of the general theory about the psychological or sociological influences on consumer behaviour may be common to all Western cultures. However, some theories may be culturally specific. Certain groups of consumers do show similar kinds of behaviour across national borders, and research on consumers in Europe suggests that we even use our understanding of the consumption environment to make sense of the foreign cultures we are visiting.[1] So, the ways in which people live their consumption life vary greatly from one European country to another, and sometimes even within different regions of the same country. As a student of consumer behaviour, you might also want to ask yourself: 'In which consumption situations do I seem to have a great deal in common with fellow students from other European countries? And in what ways do I seem to more closely resemble my compatriots? In what ways do subcultures in my country exert a strong influence on my consumption patterns, and how international are these subcultures?'

This book is about consumer behaviour theory in general, and we will illustrate our points with examples from various European markets as well as from other countries. Each chapter features 'Multicultural dimensions' boxes, which spotlight international aspects of consumer behaviour. From both a global and a pan-European perspective, these issues will be explored in depth.

Consumer behaviour: people in the marketplace

We use products to help us define our identities in different settings.

You can probably relate to at least some general aspects of Liane's behaviour. This book is about people like Liane. It concerns the products and services they buy and use, and the ways these fit into their lives. This introductory chapter briefly describes some important aspects of the field of consumer behaviour, including the topics studied, who studies them and some of the ways these issues are approached by consumer researchers.

But first, let's return to Liane. The sketch that started the chapter allows us to highlight some aspects of consumer behaviour that will be covered in the rest of the book:

- As a consumer, Liane can be described and compared to other individuals in a number of ways. For some purposes, marketers might find it useful to categorise Liane in terms of her age, gender, income or occupation. These are some examples of descriptive characteristics of a population, or **demographics**. In other cases, marketers would rather know something about Liane's interests in fashion, sports, fitness, music, or the way she spends her leisure time. This sort of information often comes under the category of **psychographics**, which refers to aspects of a person's lifestyle and **personality**. Knowledge of consumer characteristics plays an extremely important role in many marketing applications, such as defining the market for a product or deciding on the appropriate techniques to employ when targeting a certain group of consumers.

- Liane's purchase (and boycotting) decisions are heavily influenced by the opinions and behaviours of her friends. A lot of product information, as well as recommendations to use or avoid particular brands, is picked up in conversations among real people, rather than by way of television commercials, magazines or advertising messages. The bonds among Liane's group of friends are in part cemented by the products they all use, or specifically avoid. The growth of the Web has created thousands of online **consumption communities**, where members share opinions and recommendations about anything from healthy foods to iPhone apps. Liane forms bonds with fellow group members because they use the same products. There is also pressure on each group member to buy things that will meet with the group's approval, and often a price to pay in the form of group rejection or embarrassment when one does not conform to others' conceptions of what is good or bad, 'in' or 'out'.[2]

- As a member of a large society, people share certain cultural values or strongly held beliefs about the way the world should function. Other values are shared by members of subcultures, or smaller groups within the culture, such as ethnic groups, teens, people from certain parts of the country, even hipsters who listen to Arcade Fire, wear Band of Outsiders clothing and eat vegan tacos. The people who matter to Liane – her reference group – value the idea that women should be innovative, style-conscious, independent and up-front. While many marketers focus on either very young targets or the thirty-somethings, some are recognising that rapidly growing segment of older (50+) people.

- When browsing through the websites, Liane was exposed to many competing 'brands'. Many offerings did not grab her attention at all; others were noticed but rejected because they did not fit the 'image' with which she identified or to which she aspired. The use of market segmentation strategies means targeting a brand to specific groups of consumers rather than to everybody – even if that means that other consumers will not be interested or may choose to avoid that brand.

- Brands often have clearly defined images or 'personalities' created by product advertising, packaging, branding and other marketing strategies that focus on positioning a product a certain way, or by certain groups of consumers adopting the product. Leisure activities, in particular, are very much lifestyle statements: they say a lot about what a person is interested in, as well as something about the type of person they would like to be. People often choose a product offering, a service or a place, or subscribe to a particular idea, because they like its image, or because they feel its 'personality' somehow corresponds to their own. Moreover, a consumer may believe that by buying and using the product, its desirable qualities will somehow magically 'rub off'.

- When a product succeeds in satisfying a consumer's specific needs or desires, a Amazon did for Liane, it may be rewarded with many years of brand or store loyalty – a bond between product or outlet and consumer that may be very difficult for competitors to break. Often a change in one's life situation or self-concept is required to weaken this bond and thus create opportunities for competitors.

- Consumers' evaluations of products are affected by their appearance, taste, texture or smell. We may be influenced by the shape and colour of a package, as well as by more subtle factors such as the symbolism used in a brand name, in an advertisement, or even in the choice of a cover model for a magazine. These judgements are affected by – and often reflect – how a society feels that people should define themselves at that point in time. Liane's choice of a new hairstyle, for example, says something about the type of image women like her want to project. If asked, Liane might not be able to say exactly why she considered some websites and rejected others. Many product meanings are hidden below the surface of the packaging, the design and advertising, and this book will discuss some of the methods used by marketers and social scientists to discover or apply these meanings.

- Amazon.co.uk has a combined American and international image that appeals to Liane. A product's image is often influenced by its country of origin, which helps to determine its 'brand personality'. In addition, our opinions and desires are increasingly shaped by input from around the world, thanks to rapid advancements in communications and transportation systems (witness the internet!). In today's global culture, consumers often prize products and services that 'transport' them to different locations and allow them to experience the diversity of other cultures. While the global/European recession had an impact on many consumer behaviours,[3] young/single European consumers seem to be making use of the internet for another form of 'shopping' – with online dating websites reporting revenues of over half a billion euros! In the UK, the Office for National Statistics has added online dating as a category in its basket for measuring goods and services as a cost of living. As the financial analyst for online dating puts it: 'People don't cut back on hooking up, but meeting people online is cheaper – you get to sift through potential suitors'.[4]

The field of consumer behaviour covers a lot of ground: it is the study of the processes involved when individuals or groups select, purchase, use or dispose of products, services, ideas or experiences to satisfy needs and desires. Consumers take many forms, ranging from a six-year-old child pleading with her mother for wine gums to an executive in a large corporation deciding on an extremely expensive computer system. The items that are consumed can include anything from tinned beans to a massage, democracy, reggae music and even other people (the images of rock stars, for example). Needs and desires to be satisfied range from hunger and thirst to love, status or spiritual fulfilment. There is a growing interest in consumer behaviour, not only in the field of marketing but from the social sciences in general. This follows a growing awareness of the increasing importance of consumption in our daily lives, in our organisation of daily activities, in our identity formation, in politics and economic development and in the flows of global culture, where consumer culture seems to spread, albeit in new forms, from North America and Europe to other parts of the world. This spread of consumer culture via marketing is not always well-received by social critics and consumers (as we shall see in subsequent chapters).[5] Indeed, consumption can be regarded as playing such an important role in our social, psychological, economic, political and cultural lives that today it has become (for better and for worse) the 'vanguard of history'.[6]

Consumers are actors on the marketplace stage

Consumer identities are not forged mainly from within ourselves. The perspective of **role theory**, which this text emphasises, takes the view that much of consumer behaviour resembles actions in a play,[7] where each consumer has lines, props and costumes that are necessary for a good performance. Since people act out many different roles, they may modify their consumption decisions according to the particular 'play' they are in at the time. The criteria that they use to evaluate products and services in one of their roles may be quite different from those used in another role.

Another way of thinking about consumer roles is to consider the various 'plays' that the consumer may engage in. One classical role here is the consumer as a 'chooser' – somebody who, as we have seen with Liane, can choose between different alternatives and explores various criteria for making this choice. But the consumer can have many things at stake other than just 'making the right choice'. We are all involved in a communication system through our consumption activities, whereby we communicate our roles and statuses. We are also sometimes searching to construct our identity, our 'real selves', through various consumption activities. Or the main purpose of our consumption might be an exploration of a few of the many possibilities the market has to offer us, maybe in search of a 'real kick of pleasure'. On the more negative side, we might feel victimised by fraudulent or harmful offerings, and we may decide to take action against such risks from the marketplace by becoming active in consumer movements. Or we may react against the authority of the producers by co-opting their products and turning them into something else, as when military boots all of a sudden became 'normal' footwear for pacifist women. We may decide to take action as 'political consumers' and boycott products from companies or countries whose behaviour does not meet our ethical or environmental standards. Hence, as consumers we can be choosers, communicators, identity-seekers, pleasure-seekers, victims, rebels and activists – sometimes simultaneously.[8]

Consumer behaviour is a process

Consumer behaviour is a process involving many actors.

In its early stages of development, the field was often referred to as *buyer behaviour*, reflecting an emphasis on the interaction between consumers and producers at the time of purchase. Marketers now recognise, however, that consumer behaviour is an ongoing *process* – not merely what happens at the moment a consumer hands over money or a credit card and in turn receives some good or service.

The **exchange**, in which two or more organisations or people give and receive something of value, is an integral part of marketing.[9] While exchange remains an important part of consumer behaviour, the expanded view emphasises the entire consumption process, which includes the issues that influence the consumer before, during and after a purchase. Figure 1.1 illustrates some of the issues that are addressed during each stage of the consumption process.

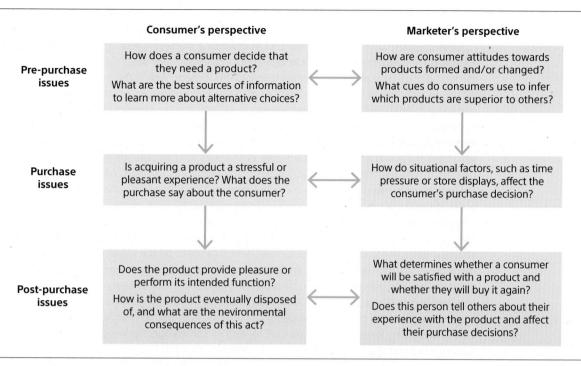

Consumer's perspective

Marketer's perspective

Pre-purchase issues

How does a consumer decide that they need a product?

What are the best sources of information to learn more about alternative choices?

⟷

How are consumer attitudes towards products formed and/or changed?

What cues do consumers use to infer which products are superior to others?

Purchase issues

Is acquiring a product a stressful or pleasant experience? What does the purchase say about the consumer?

⟷

How do situational factors, such as time pressure or store displays, affect the consumer's purchase decision?

Post-purchase issues

Does the product provide pleasure or perform its intended function?

How is the product eventually disposed of, and what are the nevironmental consequences of this act?

⟷

What determines whether a consumer will be satisfied with a product and whether they will buy it again?

Does this person tell others about their experience with the product and affect their purchase decisions?

Figure 1.1 Some issues that arise during stages in the consumption process

Consumer behaviour involves many different actors

A consumer is generally thought of as a person who identifies a need or desire, makes a purchase and then disposes of the product during the three stages of the consumption process. In many cases, however, different people may be involved in the process. The *purchaser* and *user* of a product may not be the same person, as when a parent chooses clothes for a teenager (and makes selections that can result in 'fashion suicide' from the teenager's point of view). In other cases, another person may act as an *influencer*, providing recommendations for (or against) certain products without actually buying or using them. For example, a friend, rather than a parent, accompanying a teenager on a shopping trip may pick out the clothes that they decide to purchase.

Finally, consumers may be organisations or groups in which one person may make the decisions involved in purchasing products that will be used by many, as when a purchasing agent orders the company's office supplies. In other organisational situations, purchase decisions may be made by a large group of people – for example, company accountants, designers, engineers, sales personnel and others – all of whom will have a say in the various stages of the consumption process. One important organisation is the family, where different family members play pivotal roles in decision-making regarding products and services used by all (see Chapter 10).

Consumer research and marketing strategy

Why should managers, advertisers and other marketing professionals bother to learn about consumer behaviour? Very simply, *understanding consumer behaviour is good business*. The basic marketing concept states that firms exist to satisfy needs. Marketers can only satisfy these needs to the extent that they understand the people or organisations who will use the products and services they are trying to sell. *Voilà!* That's why we study consumer behaviour.

Consumer response is the ultimate test of whether a marketing strategy will succeed. Thus, a marketer should incorporate knowledge about consumers into every facet of a successful marketing plan. Data about consumers help organisations to define the market and identify threats to and opportunities for a brand. And, in the wild and wacky world of marketing, nothing is forever: this knowledge also helps to ensure that the product continues to appeal to its core market. However, as we have already indicated, from a critical perspective not all is necessarily well in the 'land of happy consumers'. It is obvious, not least from the recent scandals concerning abuse of social media-based data, that knowledge about consumers can be used for the benefit of the organisations rather than for consumers. Although many marketing people would like to consider the marketplace a 'free site', where only exchanges are made that are considered free choices and beneficial for both parties, this is obviously a very naïve way of thinking. There is, therefore, a debate among people studying consumer behaviour as to whether these studies only have a purpose to serve the aforementioned strategic goals of commercial organisations (which tends to be the classical point of view), or a more critical and somewhat nuanced perspective that considers consumers as biologists consider fish, and not as fishermen consider fish![10] Indeed, as it has been underlined, even considering people as 'consumers' is already situating them in a market-society context where the impression might be given that being consumers is our primary mode of being. These critical reflections serve to remind us that, as with all knowledge, the knowledge of consumer behaviour can be used for good and bad, benevolent and dubious purposes.[11]

Market segmentation: to whom are we marketing?

Whether within or across national boundaries, effective **market segmentation** delineates segments whose members are similar to one another in one or more characteristics and different from members of other segments. Depending on its goals and resources, a company may choose to focus on just one segment or several, or it may ignore differences among segments by pursuing a mass-market strategy. In many cases, it makes a lot of sense to target a number of market segments. The likelihood is that no one will fit any given segment description exactly, and the issue is whether or not consumers differ from the profile in ways that will affect the chances of their adopting the products being offered.

Many segmentation variables form the basis for slicing up a larger market, and a great deal of this text is devoted to exploring the ways marketers describe and characterise different segments. The segmentation variables listed in Table 1.1 are grouped into four categories, which also indicate where in the text these categories are considered in more depth. Demographics are statistics that measure observable aspects of a population, such as birth rate, age distribution or income. The national statistical agencies of European countries and pan-European agencies such as Eurostat[12] are major sources of demographic data on families, but many private firms gather additional data on specific population groups. The changes and trends revealed in demographic studies are of great interest to marketers, because the data can be used to locate and predict the size of markets for many products, ranging from mortgages to baby food to health care for senior consumers. However, a word of caution is needed here: the last couple of decades have witnessed the growth of new consumer segments that are less dependent on demographics and more likely to borrow behavioural patterns and fashions across what were formerly more significant borders or barriers. It is now not so uncommon to see men and women, or grandmothers and granddaughters, having similar tastes. Hence, useful as demographic variables might be, marketers should beware of using them as the sole predictors of consumer tastes. We'll also consider other important characteristics that are not so easy to measure, which are both psychological and sociological in character, as indicated in Table 1.1.

Table 1.1 Variables for market segmentation

Category	Variables	Location of discussion
Demographics	Age	Chapter 10
	Gender	Chapter 4
	Social class, occupation, income	Chapter 11
	Ethnic group, religion	Chapters 12, 13
	Stage in life	Chapter 10
	Purchaser *vs* user	Chapter 9
Geographic	Region	Chapters 12, 13
	Country differences	All chapters
Psychographic	Self-concept, personality	Chapter 4
	Lifestyle	Chapters 5, 12, 13
Behavioural	Brand loyalty, extent of usage	Chapter 7
	Usage situation	Chapter 8
	Benefits desired	Chapter 5

Marketing opportunity
New segments

Marketers have come up with so many ways to segment consumers – from the overweight to overachievers – that you might think they had run out of segments. Hardly. Changes in lifestyle and other characteristics of the population are constantly creating new opportunities. The following is one such example of a new segment:

LBGT communities are targeted by many organisations these days. The city of Brussels, for example, has made a point of targeting this segment with a campaign focusing on the many events – cultural, musical, sportive and others – that allegedly make Brussels the 'capital' of LGBT tourism.[13] If Brussels does not seem tempting for the next 'gaycation', there are also various sea cruises specifically targeted to this segment, as well as many other commercial resources available.[14]

Consumer behaviour as a field of study

Many different types of specialist study consumer behaviour.

Although people have been consumers for a very long time, it is only recently that consumption *per se* has been the focus of formal study. In fact, while many business schools now require that marketing students take a consumer behaviour course, most universities and business schools did not even offer such a course until the 1970s. Much of the impetus for the attention now being given to consumer behaviour was the realisation by many business people that the consumer really *is* the boss.

Interdisciplinary influences on the study of consumer behaviour

Where do we find consumer researchers? Just about anywhere we find consumers. Consumer researchers work for manufacturers, retailers, marketing research firms, governments and non-profit organisations, and, of course, colleges and universities. Professional groups, such as the Association for Consumer Research, have been formed since the mid-1970s, and European academics and practitioners are major contributors to the growing literature on consumer behaviour.

You'll find researchers doing sophisticated experiments in laboratories that involve advanced neural imaging machinery, or simply interviewing shoppers in malls. They may conduct focus groups or run large-scale polling operations. And researchers work on many types of topic, from everyday household products and high-tech installations to professional services, museum exhibits and public policy issues such as the effect of advertising on children. Indeed, no consumer issue is too sacred: some intrepid investigators bravely explore 'delicate' categories such as incontinence products and birth-control devices. The marketing director for Trojan condoms notes that, 'Unlike laundry, where you can actually sit and watch people do their laundry, we can't sit and watch them use our product'. For this reason, Trojan relies on clinical psychologists, psychiatrists and cultural anthropologists to understand how men relate to condoms.[15]

Researchers approach consumer issues from different perspectives. You might remember a fable about blind men and an elephant. The gist of the story is that each man touched a different part of the animal and, as a result, the descriptions each gave of the elephant were quite different. This analogy applies to consumer research as well. A similar consumer phenomenon can be studied in different ways and at different levels depending on the training and interests of the researchers studying it.

Figure 1.2 covers some of the disciplines in the field and the level at which each discipline approaches research issues. These disciplines can be loosely characterised in terms of their focus on micro *vs* macro consumer behaviour topics. The fields closer to the top of the pyramid concentrate on the individual consumer (micro issues), while those towards the base are more interested in the aggregate activities that occur among larger groups of people, such as consumption patterns shared by members of a culture or subculture (macro issues).

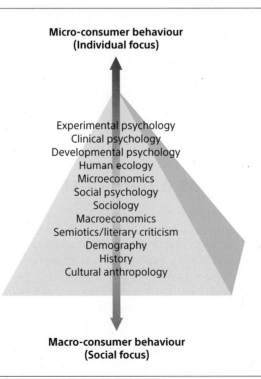

Figure 1.2 The pyramid of consumer behaviour

The issue of strategic focus

Many people regard the field of consumer behaviour as an applied social science. Accordingly, the value of the knowledge generated has traditionally been measured in terms of its ability to improve the effectiveness of marketing practice. Recently, though, some researchers have argued that consumer behaviour should not have a strategic focus at all; the field should not be a 'handmaiden to business'. It should instead focus on understanding consumption for its own sake, rather than because the knowledge can be applied by marketers.[16] This view is probably not held by most consumer researchers, but it has encouraged many to expand the scope of their work beyond the field's traditional focus on the purchase of consumer goods. And it has certainly led to some fierce debates among people working in the field! In fact, it can also be argued that business gets better research from non-strategic research projects because they are unbiased by strategic goals. Take a relatively simple and common consumer object, such as a women's magazine, found in every culture in a variety of versions. How much is there to say about the 'simple' act of buying such a magazine? Well, quite a lot. Table 1.2 lists some potential issues relevant for the marketing of or advertising in women's magazines, which can be researched based on the variety of disciplines influencing consumer research.

Table 1.2 Interdisciplinary research issues in consumer behaviour

Disciplinary focus	Magazine usage sample research issues
Experimental Psychology: product role in perception, learning and memory processes	How specific aspects of magazines, such as their design or layout, are recognised and interpreted; which parts of a magazine are most likely to be read
Clinical Psychology: product role in psychological adjustment	How magazines affect readers' body images (e.g. do thin models make the average woman feel overweight?)
Microeconomics/Human Ecology: product role in allocation of individual or family resources	Factors influencing the amount of money spent on magazines in a household
Social Psychology: product role in the behaviours of individuals as members of social groups	Ways that ads in a magazine affect readers' attitudes towards the products depicted; how peer pressure influences a person's readership decisions
Sociology: product role in social institutions and groups through a social group relationship	Pattern by which magazine preferences spread and role of magazines in the shaping of social behavior and social roles
Macroeconomics: product role in consumers' relations with the marketplace	Effects of the price of fashion magazines and expense of items advertised during periods of high unemployment
Semiotics/Literary Criticism: product role in the verbal and visual communication of meaning	Ways in which underlying messages communicated by models and ads in a magazine are interpreted
Demography: product role in the measurable characteristics of a population	Effects of age, income and marital status of a magazine's readers
History: product role in societal changes over time	Ways in which our culture's depictions of 'femininity' in magazines have changed over time
Cultural Anthropology: product role in a society's beliefs and practices	Ways in which fashions and models in a magazine affect readers' definitions of masculine *vs* feminine behaviour (e.g. the role of working women, sexual taboos)

This more critical view of consumer research has led to the recognition that not all consumer behaviour and/or marketing activity is necessarily beneficial to individuals or to society. As a result, current consumer research is likely to include attention to the 'dark side' of consumer behaviour, such as addiction, prostitution, homelessness, shoplifting or environmental waste. This activity builds upon the earlier work of researchers who, as we have seen, have studied consumer issues related to public policy, ethics and consumerism.

The issue of two perspectives on consumer research

1.4

There are basically two differing perspectives (called paradigms) regarding how and what we should understand about consumer behaviour.

One general way to classify consumer research is in terms of the fundamental assumptions the researchers make about what they are studying and how to study it. This set of beliefs is known as a **paradigm**. Like other fields of study, consumer behaviour is dominated by a paradigm, but some believe it is in the middle of a *paradigm shift*, which occurs when a competing paradigm challenges the dominant set of assumptions.

The basic set of assumptions underlying the current dominant paradigm is called **positivism**. This perspective has significantly influenced Western art and science since the late sixteenth century. It emphasises that human reason is supreme and that there is a single, objective truth that can be discovered by science. Positivism encourages us to stress the function of objects, to celebrate technology and to regard the world as a rational, ordered place with a clearly defined past, present and future. Some feel that positivism puts too much emphasis on material well-being, and that its logical outlook is dominated by an ideology that stresses the homogeneous views of a predominantly Western and male culture.

The newer paradigm of **interpretivism** questions these assumptions. Proponents of this perspective argue that our society places too much emphasis on science and technology, and that this ordered, rational view of consumers denies the complexity of the social and cultural world in which we live. Interpretivists stress the importance of symbolic, subjective experience, and the idea that meaning is in the mind – that is, we each construct our own meanings based on our unique and shared cultural experiences, so that there are no single right or wrong references. To the value we place on products, because they help us to create order in our lives, is added an appreciation of consumption as a set of diverse experiences. The major differences between these two perspectives are summarised in Table 1.3.

In addition to the cross-cultural differences in consumer behaviour discussed earlier, it is also clear that research styles differ significantly between Europe and North America and also

Table 1.3 Positivist *vs* interpretivist approaches to consumer behaviour

Assumptions	Positivist approach	Interpretivist approach
Nature of reality	Objective, tangible	Socially constructed
	Single	Multiple
Goal	Prediction	Understanding
Knowledge generated	Time-free	Time-bound
	Context-independent	Context-dependent
View of causality	Existence of real causes	Multiple, simultaneous shaping events
Research relationship	Separation between researcher and subject	Interactive, co-operative, with researcher being part of phenomenon under study

Source: Adapted from Laurel A. Hudson and Julie L. Ozanne, 'Alternative ways of seeking knowledge in consumer research', *Journal of Consumer Research* 14(4) (1988): 508–21. Copyright © 1988, Oxford University Press by permission of Oxford University Press.

within European countries. For example, studies have shown that European researchers tend to consider the cultural dimension far more than their American counterparts.[17] A recent and more 'bridging' perspective on approaches to the study of consumer research argues that the study of particular consumption contexts are not an end in themselves, but rather that studying human behaviour in a consumption context is useful for generating new constructs and theoretical insights. This approach, known as **consumer culture theory (CCT)**, embraces a variety of methodological approaches and recognises that managers can make use of multiple methods to better understand trends in the marketplace, such as the complexities of lifestyle, multicultural marketing and how consumers use media as part of their lives.[18]

Consumer research is still moving on. From its original emphasis on buying behaviour and the factors influencing the decision-making process, the field gradually widened to become a study of consumer behaviour in a more general sense, also taking into consideration what happened before and after the purchase. After the introduction of the interpretivist approach, a broader research perspective has included many new and non-psychological facets in the increasingly complex portraits of consumers. And it can be argued that the field increasingly looks beyond the single individual and their social background and environment to describe and analyse the complex relationships that have led us to start characterising our present society as a **consumer society**.[19] The facts of living in a consumer society and being surrounded by consumer culture permeate this text, but will be dealt with in more detail in Chapters 2, 12 and 13.

Consumer culture

1.5

The society we live in today can be described as a consumer society.

In contemporary modern society, it is hard to think of many kinds of social behaviour that do not involve consumption in one form or another. Consumption activities provide both meaning and structure to the way we live. A lot of our everyday imaginations are informed by **consumer culture** – our imaginations about health, perfect family life or the dream wedding take shape using consumer culture as negative or positive frames of reference.[20]

Many people use the notion of the consumer society in order to describe the current type of social organisation in the economically developed world. This is not only because we live in a world full of things, which we obviously do, but also because the most decisive step in the construction of consumer society is the new role of consumption activities. We used to define ourselves primarily through our role in the production process, i.e. our work. Increasingly, however, how we consume is more decisive for our personal and social identities than what we do for a living. The plethora of goods and their varieties in range and styles allows consumption choices to become clear (or sometimes purposefully ambiguous) statements about our personalities, values, aspirations, sympathies and antipathies, and our way of handling social relations. Furthermore, in times of economic crisis, consumers are time and again called upon to play their crucial part in keeping the economies running. The standard economic logic is that if consumers stop buying, producers will have to stop producing. It is in many ways as simple as that – and is one of the big challenges for a sustainable society. Consumption is, therefore, a matter to be taken seriously – on a personal, social and economic level.[21]

Modern consumer society is thus characterised by consumption-based identities, but related features of a consumer society include many of the other topics discussed in this book: shopping as a leisure activity combined with the variety of shopping possibilities, including shopping centres (the new 'temples of consumption'); easier access to credit; the growing attention to brand images and the communicative aspects of product and packaging, as well as the pervasiveness of promotion; the increasing political organisation of consumers in groups with a variety of purposes; and the sheer impossibility of trying not to be a consumer and still participating in ordinary social life.[22] 'Things' do matter.[23]

Popular culture

When it is said that contemporary culture is a consumer culture, we do not just refer to the central role of consumption in all of our daily activities.[24] We also underline the basic relationship between market forces, consumption processes and the basic characteristics of what we normally understand by 'a culture'. As we shall see, whether we talk about high culture (such as the fine arts, etc.) or **popular culture**, our contemporary culture is basically something 'to be consumed'. Whether we talk about our ways of travelling around, our styles of dress, our music, our cultural and sports events, tourism, fashion, or the care for our physical and mental selves, our ways of socialising are all deeply commercialised consumer markets.[25] We consume 'spaces' and 'places', both in our cities when we are enjoying their commercial and/or cultural areas and offerings, and when away on holiday. We are constantly consuming different styles and fashions, not only in clothing but also in food, home appliances, garden and interior design, music and so on. Marketing sometimes seems to exert a self-fulfilling prophecy on popular culture: as commercial influences on popular culture increase, marketer-created symbols make their way into our daily lives to a greater degree. Historical analyses of plays, best-selling novels and the lyrics of hit songs, for example, clearly show large increases over time in the use of brand names.[26]

Popular culture – the music, films, sports, books and other forms of entertainment consumed by the mass market – is both a product of and an inspiration for marketers. Our lives are also affected in more fundamental ways, ranging from how we acknowledge social events such as marriages, deaths or holidays to how we view societal issues such as global warming, gambling and addiction. The FIFA World Cup, Christmas shopping, tourism, newspaper recycling, cigarette smoking and Barbie dolls are all examples of products and activities that touch many of us in our lives. Marketing's role in the creation and communication of popular culture is especially emphasised in this text. Its cultural influence is hard to ignore, although many people fail to appreciate the extent to which their view of the world is influenced by the marketing system.

Consider the product characters that marketers use to create a personality for their products and brands. To speak of a **brand personality** is an example of the degree of anthropomorphism in marketing. From the Michelin Man to Ronald McDonald, popular culture is peopled with fictional heroes. A recent issue of an academic journal is consecrated to the study of such anthropomorphic figures and their impact on consumers and marketing.[27] In fact, it is likely that more consumers will recognise characters such as these than can identify former (or present!) prime ministers, captains of industry or artists. These characters may not exist, but many of us feel that we 'know' them, and they certainly are effective *spokes-characters* for the products and brands they promote.

Global consumer culture

1.6

Globalisation is important when trying to understand the consumer society.

Consumer culture is becoming increasingly globalised, and brands have become signs of a global ideology of cultural (and commercial) value and power.[28] In fact, the tempting imagery of contemporary consumer culture and marketing, the prime vehicles that bring this imagery about, may be considered some of the most important drivers of **globalisation**. The process of globalisation has attracted a tremendous amount of interest in the last couple of decades. But learning about the relationship between the global and the local in the practices of other cultures is more than just interesting – it is an essential task for any vww company that wishes to expand its horizons and become part of the international or global marketplace in the new millennium.

Global consumer culture represents an etic perspective, which focuses on commonalities across cultures. An etic approach assumes that there are common, general categories and measurements, which are valid for all cultures under consideration. One such etic study identified four major clusters of consumer styles when it looked at data from the US, the UK,

France and Germany: *price-sensitive consumers, variety seekers, brand-loyal consumers* and *information seekers*.[29] On the other hand, many marketers choose to study and analyse a culture using an emic perspective, which attempts to explain a culture based on the cultural categories and experiences of the insiders. We will take a closer look at this perspective in the discussion of ethnoconsumerism (see Chapter 13), but for now it will be sufficient to remember that, in spite of the fact that technology, media and cultural exchange processes are bringing us closer to each other in many ways, cultural differences continue to prevail. For example, cultures vary sharply in the degree to which references to sex and nudity (and other controversial issues) are permitted. One study analysed responses to advertising for 'controversial products', including potentially offensive ads related to sexual behaviour such as ads for condoms, female contraceptives, underwear and (prevention of) sexually transmitted diseases. It was found that results for what was deemed controversial differed highly between the UK and New Zealand on the one hand, and Turkey and Malaysia on the other. While negative reactions to sexual references differed, racist imagery was ranked among the most offensive in all samples. Good that we can agree on something like that![30]

A global consumer?

It is often asserted that global marketing works well with affluent people who are 'global citizens' and who are exposed to ideas from around the world through their travels, business contacts and media experiences, and as a result share common tastes.[31] One sector that comes across as inherently 'global' is the market for luxury goods, with its highly standardised and aesthetised marketing campaigns and its cosmopolitan target market. Still, one study distinguished between a European type of luxury brands, based more on history, rarity and craftsmanship and an American type of luxury brands based on storytelling, marketing imagery and marketing finesse.[32] The differing business cultures, we can assume, also cover differences in the cultural meaning of luxury products across the Atlantic Ocean. Furthermore, differences in the perception and valorisation of the concept of 'performance' (an important notion in many contemporary marketing campaigns) has led to different responses to the same advertisement in countries such as the US, Germany, France, Spain and Thailand.[33]

Another 'global segment' that is often referred to is young people, whose tastes in music and fashion are strongly influenced by international pop culture broadcasting many of the same images and sounds to multiple countries.[34] On the other hand, one study of the global youth culture concluded that although similar existential conditions were found, including the search for an identity and the feeling of being a member of a global youth consumer culture, the way these similar existential conditions are lived out in reality varies a lot from context to context.[35]

Coca-colonisation: exporting Western lifestyles

The West (and especially the US) is a *net exporter* of popular culture. Western symbols in the form of images, words and products have diffused throughout the world. This influence is eagerly sought by many consumers, who have learned to equate Western lifestyles in general (and the English language in particular) with modernisation and sophistication. As a result, people around the world are being exposed to a blizzard of Western products that are attempting to become part of local lifestyles.

The allure of Western consumer culture has spread as people in other societies slowly but surely fall under the spell of the global presence of consumer brands and practices, of far-reaching advertising campaigns, contact with tourists and the desire to form attachments with other parts of the world. Not least, the internet is becoming a global source of information about consumer culture, and facilitates a virtual intercultural learning process. In the process, however, the meanings of consumer objects and practices are transformed and adapted to local tastes. As one project demonstrates, the local youth culture in Iran is not just emulating the Western models of a consumer culture, but is reflexively constructing its own local version of a modern consumer culture through its confrontation with similarities and differences in visible lifestyles ('what people have'). This observation leads to an interpretation of what the 'other culture' may be like and a reflexive response to these interpretations in terms of finding out how oneself (and one's own culture) is different from and similar to the foreign culture, and finally a reflection on how one would like to respond to this difference in terms of individual and cultural change (see Figure 1.3).[36]

Consequently, the West is no longer the sole model for expanding consumer cultures. In the BRICS countries (Brazil, Russia, India, China and South Africa), but also in MINT countries (Mexico, Indonesia, Nigeria and Turkey)[37] and other places (Korea, Malaysia . . .), enormous new middle classes are producing consumer societies that, to some degree, not only emulate what is known from the West but also establish their own particular variant of consumer culture. One of the most evident contemporary showcases for studying the impact of a rapid introduction of consumer culture is in China. In the 1970s, the Chinese strove to attain what they called the 'three bigs': bikes, sewing machines and wristwatches. This wish list was later modified to become the 'new big six', adding refrigerators, washing machines and televisions. The list was then expanded with *colour* televisions, cameras and video recorders.[38] Today, in spite of huge urban–rural variations, Chinese middle classes constitute a power consumer market – 'a new generation of brand-conscious individualists'.[39]

The lure of Western consumption styles and the brands that carry these messages have been some of the most effective tools in spreading Western-style consumer culture across the globe. But these tools are now used in order to maintain a particular cultural identity. Branding strategies are used by increasingly strong Asian managers in order to construct a universe of 'Asianness' that can be used to maintain local brand value in the booming Asian markets. The Asia portrayed in these campaigns is not the traditional one of peasants working in rice fields but a modern, booming and busting, self-confident, transnational (not *a priori* tied to a specific country) Asian world.

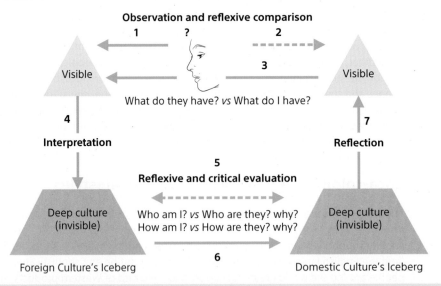

- The numbers indicate the seven stages of the reflexive process of virtual intercultural learning.
- The dashed arrows indicate reflexivity. Arrow 2 shows the reflexive comparision of the visible parts of the cultures and arrow 5 demonstrates reflexive evaluation of the invisible parts of the cultures.

Figure 1.3 The ongoing reflexive process of intercultural learning

Allakbar Jafari and Christina Goulding, 'Globlization, reflexivity, and the project of the self: a virtual intercultural learning process', *Consumption, Markets and Culture*, 16(1) (2013): 84.

Advertisement for Chow Tai Fook, indicating the existence of a vibrant Chinese luxury brand scene. The ad combines signs of Chinese culture with classical Western signs of a luxury brand.
Bloomberg/Getty Images

The result is a branding style that reinforces pride and self-confidence in the Asian region.[40] Consequently, there is a growth in Chinese luxury brands. Do names such as Chow Tai Fook, Lao Feng Xiang or Chow Sang Sang ring a bell? Well, in China they do – these are all prominent luxury jewellery brands in China, that recently broke the top 25 in a global ranking of luxury brands. Move over, France, Italy, Switzerland. . . the Chinese are coming.[41]

Multicultural dimensions

Until 1989, there was an imposed public dress code in the Himalayan kingdom of Bhutan. This dress code has relaxed somewhat since then, and while the traditional clothing of Bhutanese people is still dominant, there is an emerging 'Bhutanese streetwear' scene blending the traditional with the modern. Blogs on Bhutanese streetwear have existed since 2010. Even the fashion company Balenciaga has taken inspiration from the traditional Bhutanese clothing and used it in its designs.[42]

Marketing pitfall

However, 'cultural appropriation', such as the 'borrowing' discussed in the case of Bhutan, is becoming increasingly criticised. When the fashion house Dior launched a blouse directly emulating local styles from a Romanian craft tradition in the region of Bihor, without accrediting or much less paying the original creators for the inspiration, a counter-campaign 'Bihor vs Dior' was launched. This campaign – spread by YouTube – both exhibited the 'theft' and ridiculed the fashion industry in several ways, and is a centrepiece in the argument that consumers should buy 'the real thing' and through their consumption help keep this particular crafting tradition alive in Romania.[43] This case clearly demonstrates the current politicisation of consumption and consumption's ethical dimensions (something we shall return to later in the chapter).

Emerging consumer cultures in transitional economies

After the collapse of communism, Eastern Europeans emerged from a long winter of deprivation of consumer goods into a springtime of abundance. The picture is not all rosy, however, since attaining consumer goods is not easy for many in **transitional economies**, where the economic system is still 'neither fish nor fowl', and governments ranging from Vietnam to Romania struggle with the difficult adaptation from a controlled, centralised economy to a free market system.[44] These problems stem from such factors as the unequal distribution of income among citizens, as well as striking rural–urban differences in expectations and values, as is the case in, for example, Turkey, which we already established as a market of rapid growth. One study investigated how poor villagers migrating to a larger Turkish city coped with becoming acculturated to consumer society. The study basically concluded that these consumers-to-be would select one of three coping strategies. They would either shut out the whole modern consumer lifestyle altogether, trying to perpetuate village life in the poor shantytown outside the city, or collectively embrace the dreams proposed by consumer society by adopting ritualised consumption practices to the best of their humble means. A final strategy consists of giving up on both projects, which leads to shattered identities for the consumers involved, being able neither to maintain the traditional identity nor to adopt a consumer identity.[45] Such a transitional process can have heartbreaking consequences. In Turkey, one researcher met a rural consumer – a mother who deprived her child of nutritious milk from the family's cow and instead sold it in order to be able to buy sweets for her child because 'what is good for city kids is also good for my child'.[46]

Some of the consequences of the transition to a market economy thus include a loss of confidence and pride in the local culture, as well as alienation, frustration and an increase in stress as leisure time is sacrificed to work ever harder to buy consumer goods. The yearning for the trappings of Western material culture is perhaps most evident in parts of Eastern Europe, where citizens who threw off the shackles of communism now have direct access to coveted consumer goods from the US and Europe – if they can afford them. One analyst observed, '. . . as former subjects of the Soviet empire dream it, the American dream has very little to do with liberty and justice for all and a great deal to do with soap operas and the Sears Catalogue'.[47] A recent huge analysis of the acceptance of brands and advertisements in social media among 57,000 consumers in 60 countries demonstrated a profound difference: whereas 57 per cent of consumers in the Western countries dislike commercial content in **social media**, this figure is much lower in emerging market economies such as China, India, Mexico or Vietnam.[48]

Glocalisation

Based on these discussions, we are now able to reflect a little more on the character of the globalisation process. The conclusion we can safely draw is that globalisation is always inevitably a **glocalisation**, since all global phenomena exist and become meaningful in a local context. Even completely similar McDonald's restaurants, just to take one obvious example, have different meanings and play different roles for consumers when placed in Chicago, Bordeaux, Moscow or Middlesbrough. Yoga is popular in many parts of the world, now also in India! Yes, you read correctly. Not least due to its popularity in the West and modernised lifestyles including stressful work lives and fitness values, Indians are rediscovering the virtues of yoga. Given the popularity of yoga in the West in the last century, today it is indeed difficult to say whether yoga is more Indian or more Western.[49] In France, renowned for its sophisticated food culture, one of the regular top three national dishes in terms of popularity is couscous, a dish migrated to France from North Africa, but today immensely popular throughout the French population.[50] Likewise, an introspective account of a Thai consumer researcher's experience of a paradoxical glocal consumer identity, reflecting both differences within the Thai culture's upper and lower classes as well as her experiences of being an expatriate during her studies in the UK, witness the extent to which many of us (maybe, in particular, migrants) are today glocalised.[51]

Globalisation may even engender an increased focus on the local.[52] An anthropological study of developments in the British food culture revealed four different types of food consumption that are all consequences of globalisation.[53] The first is the *global food* culture, represented mainly by the ubiquitous fast food of burgers and pizzas and convenience products such as instant coffee that are found everywhere and belong nowhere in particular. Secondly, *expatriate food* refers to the search for authentic meals and products from other cultures – 'Indian', 'Mexican', 'Thai', etc. Thirdly, *nostalgia food* represents a search for local authenticity – in Britain, for example, Stilton cheese and sticky toffee puddings – from the local cultural heritage that is under pressure from globalisation. Finally, *creolisation* of food involves blending various traditions into new ones, such as Chinese dishes omitting ingredients considered unappetising in Western culture, spiced-down Indonesian food in the Netherlands, or Indianised versions of sandwiches. Similar processes are found in all European cultures.

It is interesting to note that all four are related to globalisation trends, but only global food leads to a tendency to standardise consumption patterns. We may consider these tendencies as relevant for all types of consumption, not just for consumption of food. So, whether we look at retailing, interior decoration, tourism or musical tastes, we may find at least these four tendencies, taking the notion of globalisation beyond the interpretation of it as homogenisation. Glocalisation also includes the increasing awareness of other styles and tastes, and the search for 'exotic authenticity', as well as the incorporation of this 'exoticism' into local habits and consumption styles. And finally, the exposure to all this 'otherness' often makes consumers more aware of their own cultural roots, and the tastes and consumption styles that they would define as 'our own'. All these offers of old and new, strange and familiar, authentic and creolised tend to coexist in the marketplace.[54] Therefore, it is not so strange that some authors discuss globalisation more in terms of fragmentation than in terms of homogenisation.[55]

The politics of consumption

Public policy and consumerism

1.7

Consumption is not just a private but also a political issue.

The ethics of consumption are becoming more and more significant. Public concern for the welfare of consumers has been an issue since at least the beginning of the twentieth century. This is normally referred to as **consumer policy**. The general purpose of such consumer policy measures and legislation is to protect consumers against the worst and most fraudulent abuses of marketing techniques. Partly as a result of consumers' efforts, many national and international agencies have been established to oversee consumer-related activities. Consumers themselves continue to have a lively interest in consumer-related issues, ranging from environmental concerns such as pollution caused by oil spills or toxic waste, the use of additives and genetically manipulated material in food, to excessive violence and sex on television. In a globalised world, corporations increasingly are held responsible for the entire production chain behind their products.

Whether intentionally or not, some marketers do violate their bond of trust with consumers. In some cases, these actions are illegal – as when a manufacturer deliberately mislabels the contents of a package, or 'just' of dubious morality – as when a retailer adopts a 'bait-and-switch' selling strategy, whereby consumers are lured into the store with promises of inexpensive products with the sole intention of getting them to switch to higher-priced goods. A similar problematic issue concerning the luring of consumers is the case of misleading claims, for instance on food product labels.[56] For example, what about a label such as '100 per cent fat-free strawberry jam'?

Marketing pitfall
Women for s@le!

The charge against abuse of marketing techniques has taken on new dimensions with the rise of the internet. Would you like to buy a Latvian girl for escort service? Or a Russian bride by mail order? The trade in women from Eastern Europe, Asia or Latin America has reached new heights with the easier contact made possible by the internet. Obvious problems are created by the difficulty of distinguishing between serious marriage bureaux or au pair agencies on the one side, and organised traders of women for various kinds of prostitution services on the other. According to human rights organisations, many women who believe that they are going to marry the prince of their dreams end up as 'sexual services workers', sometimes under slavery-like conditions. Do a search for 'mail-order brides' on Reddit (which positions itself as 'the front page of the internet') and follow some of those discussion threads.[57]

Dark sides of consumer culture

There is a growing concern that not all is well in consumer society, and the globalisation of consumer culture makes these problems even clearer because we can, so to speak, 'study the problems as they aggravate'. Many critics have attacked consumer society for a variety of reasons: that it erodes cultural differences; that it creates superficial and inauthentic forms of social interaction; and that it inspires competition and individualism rather than solidarity and community. While many of these assertions may or may not bear close scrutiny,[58] consumer society in general does represent some serious challenges for our future development, not least in terms of the pressure on the environment, so it may not be so strange that current times are characterised by a hefty public and scientific debate about the ethics and moralities of consumption.[59]

The central role of consumption in today's society has therefore led to an increasing interest in the social and political consequences of consumer society. The aggravating environmental crisis, the linkages between overconsumption and climate change, the unsustainability of many consumption practices and a feeling that a consumer orientation has turned politics into marketing and branding – all these factors contribute to the feeling that consumer society is not a care- and risk-free lifestyle. There have been several investigations of various types of **anti-consumption** practices and movements.[60] Some critics have coined the term 'affluenza'[61] to account for the negative sides of a society over-focused on its consumption. The successful animated movie from Pixar, *Wall-E*, is based on a grim projection of a future world as a victim of affluenza. On the other hand, as pointed out by a very influential consumer researcher, it might be wiser to analyse the pros and cons of consumer society in more detail concerning the variety of ways in which consumers can also make a positive difference, rather than making such sweeping 'consumption is bad' conclusions as indicated by the affluenza term.[62]

It has been suggested that we live in a **risk society**, where our ways of manufacturing goods are increasingly producing just as many, and even more, 'bads' or risks[63] – risks that the consumer will have to take into account in their decision-making. Lots of these risks are linked to our consumption processes, whether they concern something we eat or drink, chemicals in the paint and surface coating of various construction materials or the content of phtalates (plasticisers) in toys and so on. The sense of risks is compounded by recurring food scandals such as the addition of melanine in Chinese milk products, which has severely lowered consumer confidence in many foods 'made in China',[64] or the many scandals surrounding meat (for example the BSE scandal), or fake classifications of wine or olive oil.

One example of a product type where such risks have made consumers sceptical about the benefits suggested to them by the industry is that of genetically manipulated organisms (GMO). One fear, expressed by consumers in a study of acceptance or rejection of GMO foods in Sweden and Denmark, was of too great a concentration of power in a few giant corporations dominating both research and industry.[65] Similar results were found for several European countries in a cross-national study. Testing consumer attitudes and purchase intentions regarding GMO foods, it was concluded that an overall rejection of the technology, as such, was found in Denmark, Germany, the UK and Italy.[66] In connection with this study, various types of information material were also tested, some more informative, some more emotional, in order to estimate the potential of informational campaigns in changing negative attitudes. But whatever data were given to the consumers, it only made their attitude more negative – something that points to the deep-seated nature of this scepticism among European consumers. Instead, the demand for organic produce has increased tremendously in several European countries over the last few years. Although the economic crisis may have led to a temporary setback in this demand in, for example, the UK in the years between 2008 and 2013, European organic producers are still trying to catch up with the growing demand for organic produce experienced across European markets.[67] Other ways of eating sustainably, for example observing seasonality, avoiding excessive packaging and buying local produce, are also on the increase in a number of European countries, as testified by a study in Denmark, Finland, Norway and Sweden.[68]

The ethical consumer

The discussion above points to an increasing awareness of the political and moral consequences of consumption choices among many consumers. Consumers are not just individuals responsible solely for the private outcomes of their choices, they are also social citizens with social responsibilities.[69] How consumers feel these responsibilities and act upon them depends largely on how they perceive the robustness of nature in the face of so many consumers who intervene and use resources,[70] but also on their beliefs regarding technology and its role for society.[71] This social and moral consciousness means that what started out predominantly as a 'green' consumer is gradually being followed by, or perhaps is turning into, a 'political' or 'ethical' consumer (as they're increasingly known).[72,73] The **ethical consumers** use their buying pattern as a weapon against companies they don't like, and in support of the companies that reflect values similar to their own. This consumer type selects products according to the company's ethical behaviour, which includes respect for human rights, animal protection, environmental friendliness and support for various benevolent causes.

Large numbers of consumers are trying to reduce their reliance on possessions by downshifting. This means learning to get by with less, avoiding the use of credit cards and, in extreme cases, living totally 'off the grid' without using commercial services. Other evidence of the disenchantment among some people with a culture dominated by materialist values and

Participants at the anti-corporate Burning Man Festival find novel ways to express their individuality.
Courtesy of Professor Robert Kozinets

big corporations shows up in events that promote uniqueness and anti-corporate statements. Some of the more prominent examples are the 'Occupy' and 'We are the 99%' movements, but also the annual Burning Man project. This is a week-long annual anti-market event, where thousands of people gather at Black Rock Desert in Nevada to express themselves and proclaim their emancipation from corporate America. The highlight of the festival involves the burning of a huge figure of a man made out of wood that symbolises the freedom from market domination. Ironically, some critics point out that even this high-profile anti-market event is being commercialised as it becomes more popular each year.[74]

For ethical consumers, one big challenge is the uncertainty that consumers who would like to shop consciously may face. One study isolated four dimensions that contribute to this uncertainty: (1) complexity, i.e. the involvement of several factors such as fair trade, organic produce, animal welfare and so on; (2) ambiguity, i.e. uncertainty about what an ethical claim actually means; (3) conflict, i.e. trade-off between supporting trade with poor countries *vs* local produce; and (4) credibility, i.e. the trustworthiness of information provided by labels or claims.[75] For example, there has been a tremendous increase in the use of environmental labelling programmes throughout the world, and that is of course good. The problem is that many of these labels are not very transparent, so it is difficult for the consumer to actually know what kind of environmental responsibility is behind the label, and cases of 'greenwashing' may undermine the confidence in all labels, even the more serious ones.[76]

Although consumer boycott of, for example, South African produce during the apartheid regime has been known for some time, the term 'the political consumer' was first coined in Denmark in the 1990s following consumer protests against the dumping of a drilling platform in the North Sea and against France for its nuclear testing in the Pacific.[77] Today, political or ethical consumers are found in all countries, but significant differences are also found. One EU-based study concluded that Norwegian food consumers could generally be framed as trusting, Danish as complex, Italian as quality conscious and Portuguese as unprotected. Some results from that study are reproduced in Table 1.4.

Table 1.4 Political consumption activities among food consumers in four European countries (percentage of population) (all result: p = < 0.0001)

	Norway N = 1000	Denmark N = 1005	Italy N = 2006	Portugal N = 1000
During the last 12 months, I have been involved in the following activities:				
Refused to buy food types or brands to express opinion about a political or social issue	21%	35%	24%	25%
Bought particular food to support their sale	31%	38%	21%	14%
Participated in organised consumer boycott	3%	4%	13%	6%

Source: Adapted from Bente Halkier et al., 'Trusting, complex, quality conscious or unprotected? Constructing the food consumer in different European national contexts', *Journal of Consumer Culture*, 7(3), 2007: 379–402.

The ethical consumer is supported by such agencies as the Vancouver-based Adbusters,[78] which engages in twisting campaigns from major companies that, for some reason, have come under their spotlight for immoral or harmful behaviour. For example, they made a spoof on the well-known Coca-Cola polar bear campaign by depicting a family of bears on a tiny ice floe, with the sign 'Enjoy Climate Change' written in that well-known type from the Coca-Cola logo, thereby protesting against the company's use of ozone-harming gases in its vending machines.[79] This kind of 'peaceful' rebelliousness against what is seen as control over our minds and imagination by major companies is called 'culture jamming'.[80] Vigilante marketing is also emerging, where new ads and ideas for campaigns appear without either client or agency involvement. These are often generated by freelancers, fans or agencies looking for work.[81]

The global brands are generally the target of such consumer activism. One study examined consumers' experiences of the global coffee shop chain Starbucks.[82] The authors concluded that although Starbucks has created a lot of followers in and outside the US who see Starbucks as the quintessential cool café environment, it has also produced significant consumer resistance among consumers who perceive Starbucks as inauthentic and no better in terms of the café culture than McDonald's is for the global food culture. As such, they must fight a negative shadow of their own brand image, a so-called *doppelgänger* brand-image.[83]

However, not all organisations are on the defensive. Companies such as The Body Shop are founded on the idea of natural and non-animal-tested products and a maximum of environmental concern. But their concerns are becoming directed towards a broader array of social values. They took up the debate over beauty ideals by introducing 'Ruby', a Barbie-lookalike doll but one with considerably rounder forms, in order to fight the tyranny of thinness and the impossible body ideal of the supermodels that is also endorsed by Barbie's shape (see Chapter 4). The reaction was predictable: Mattel Inc., the producers of Barbie, took out an injunction against The Body Shop because Ruby's face was too like the original Barbie's.

Consumer boycotts

As we have seen, we live in a period where many consumers are becoming increasingly aware that their consumption pattern is part of a global political and economic system, to the extent that they become ethical consumers. Sometimes a negative experience can trigger an organised and devastating response, as when a consumer group organises a *boycott* of a company's products. These efforts can include protests against everything from investing in a politically undesirable country (as when Carlsberg and Heineken both withdrew their investments from Myanmar following protests against their support of a repressive regime), to efforts to discourage consumption of products from certain companies or countries (as during the boycott of French wines and other products during the nuclear testing in the Pacific in 1996 – an action that was implemented especially strongly in the Netherlands and in the Scandinavian countries). Four factors are found to predict boycott participation:

1 The desire to make a difference.

2 The scope for self-enhancement.

3 Counterarguments that inhibit boycotting.

4 The cost to the boycotter of constrained consumption.[84]

Boycotts are not always effective – studies show that normally only a limited percentage of a country's consumers participate in them. However, those who do are disproportionately vocal and well educated, so they are a group that companies especially do not want to alienate. One increasingly popular solution used by marketers is to set up a joint task force with the boycotting organisation, to try to iron out the problem. In the US, following yet another school shooting in early 2018, various companies (airlines, rental car agencies, hotel chains) followed consumer petitions and, following the dialogue, ended their relationships (membership advantages, screening of TV channel) with the NRA (National Rifle Association). Companies such as Apple, however, refrained from reacting to the call for consumer boycotting by referring to the importance of freedom of speech.[85] What do you think?

Multicultural dimensions

People are beginning to realise the power of consumer boycotts outside the Western world. In Morocco, what was initially a protest organised on Facebook, against what was considered unfair and unjustified price levels on dairy products, petrol and mineral water, has turned into a major protest action against the country's elite. The boycott against three of Morocco's companies evolved into a larger manifestation of discontent with the poverty, corruption and lack of interest of the ruling elite in 'ordinary people's life situations' as a sort of consumer-based 'Arab Spring', and has resulted in major falls in share value. While the protest boycotts are thus effective (and far more difficult to crack down on than demonstrations and unrest in the streets), there is of course the downside – that the boycott first and foremost harms local companies and hence workers, inducing workers from the targeted companies to organise counter-demonstrations. It is guessed that the protest will lead to lower prices, but most importantly the boycott is interpreted as a sign of a strengthened civil society in Morocco that may act again against other exploitative actions from the political and economic elite.[86]

Transformative consumer research (TCR)

Some consumer researchers are themselves organising not only to study, but also to rectify what they see as pressing social problems in the marketplace. This perspective is called **transformative consumer research (TCR)**. It promotes research projects that include the goal of helping people or encouraging social change. Scientists who subscribe to this perspective view consumers as collaborators who work with them to realise this change, rather than as a 'phenomenon' upon which to conduct research. As a consequence, they often use participatory action research methods – that is, research methods where the researcher actively works with a population in order to bring about the desired social change.[87]

Adherents of TCR typically work with at-risk populations, such as children, the disadvantaged and the disabled, or other types of stigmatised or underprivileged consumer groups. In that respect, it is linked to social marketing processes. Researchers typically take a critical stance towards the various ways in which marketplace offerings that 'look all right' may be detrimental to consumer well-being, For example, consumers use products that claim a 'high fibre content' or other types of so-called functional foods as quick solutions to improve their diet, but ultimately fail – first because the health benefits of these products may be dubious and secondly because there are no 'miracle foods' that provide short cuts to a healthy diet.[88] Other issues addressed by TCR researchers include the ways families confront various types of risk (economic, social, emotional),[89] how we can conceive of the tricky relationship between marketing and development in poorer parts of the world[90] or how poverty plays a role in the lives of consumers. In the case of poverty, one team of researchers has suggested that four dimensions characterise the way it is represented in society:

- social exclusion (based on individual incapacity rather than social factors);
- vulnerability (mainly defined from an economic perspective);
- pleasure (that poor people waste their money on excessive consumption of things they don't need); and
- contentment (something the poor should not be able to obtain).

The researchers argue that these representations easily lead us to apply a 'them and us' logic when considering poor populations, but they also show how an alternative more transformative view might be helpful in providing a better understanding of what it is like to be poor.[91]

One of the problems with TCR is that it may be linked to social marketing – that is, marketing for good social causes rather than for profit. But marketing, with its simplifying tendencies and persuasive techniques, may in and by itself be seen as a dubious practice, regardless of the cause, and as such it may not be embraced by consumers.[92] Another issue, which is particularly evident in the numerous TCR projects on health and nutrition, is that TCR researchers run the risk of imposing their own moral judgements on the types of consumption they study, which may be counter-productive to consumer well-being. To take one example, one may ask whether the many projects aimed at encouraging people to eat healthier food in order to prevent obesity do not, in fact, contribute to an overall anxiety about excess weight among people (especially girls) who may perceive themselves as too fat but who have no medical conditions whatsoever.[93]

Marketing pitfall

The name Rana Plaza, a building in Dhaka, capital of Bangladesh, will for a long time to come be connected with scandalous production conditions in the clothing industry. On 24 April 2013, Rana Plaza (which contained five factories producing garments for a large number of world-renowned fashion brands) collapsed, killing more than 1,000 workers and injuring an even larger number. At the time of writing, the owner of the building, as well as 40 other people, face severe punishment in the court in Dhaka.[94]

But what about the companies that placed their orders with this cheap production site with such inadequate safety standards? According to one consumer activist site, even if some of the brands that bought clothes from Rana Plaza have contributed to a fund that will pay compensation to the families of the victims, this fund is still waiting for the full compensation amount to be paid by all implicated companies.[95] What about the clothes you are wearing? Do you know where and how they were produced?

New forms of consumption: sharing stuff

1.8

We are witnessing the appearance of new forms of collective consumption formats.

Most of us have experienced situations where, for example, 'pay and-display' tickets for parking spaces are handed over from consumer to consumer, as the original buyer did not make use of the full parking time.[96] This practice of sharing what one has already bought but cannot use, or cannot use fully or all the time, is spreading rapidly both globally and to different types of consumption. We're witnessing the rise of the **sharing economy**,[97] where consumers want to share, lend each other[98] or rent to each other what they already possess. Thus, the concept of the sharing economy actually comprises far more than simply sharing. Furthermore, the notion of sharing fails to acknowledge the element of reciprocity that is always part of social communities formed around circulation of goods and services, which is why some researchers have suggested the alternative term of 'mutuality' to account for this new type of economy.[99] When one adds the rise of new consumer-to-consumer internet-based short-term renting services, the sharing economy is more appropriately called **access-based consumption**,[100] since what consumers are really doing is securing temporary access to resources rather than buying them for ownership.

Need to use a car? Go to Zipcar and rent one by the hour. Need to send something somewhere? Go to Nimber and get it shipped with someone going there anyway. Need accommodation in a different city, maybe even in a different country? Go to Airbnb and search for a friendly host located where you want to go. The access-based economy is revolutionising industries including taxis (Uber and Lyft), hospitality (Airbnb), music (Spotify), even errand running (TaskRabbit) and an increasing number of other consumption domains.

What is fuelling this revolution? Primarily, technology that dramatically lowers transaction costs, so that it's much easier to share assets and track them across large numbers of people.[101] Online payment systems make it easy to exchange money. Social networks create communities and build trust among strangers who can access each other's histories. Sellers can make money from assets they don't use very much – think about how many hours a typical owner actually uses an electric drill compared to how much it costs to buy one. Many of us only use our cars a few hours per week, but we still pay a monthly loan, maintenance, insurance and so on.

Consumer behaviour as I see it . . .
Giving and getting access . . .

Professor Giana Eckhardt
University of London, Royal Holloway

Did you use Airbnb rather than a hotel the last time you travelled? Or did you use Uber to get home rather than take a taxi? Or decide to rely on Zipcar instead of bringing your car to campus? If the answer is yes, you are a part of the Sharing Economy, heralded by sources ranging from *Fortune* magazine to President Obama as a major growth sector. The sharing economy represents a major shift in lifestyle for consumers: consumers no longer want to own, but prefer to access goods and services. That way, they do not have the obligations and burdens of ownership, such as finding a space to park their car or having to deal with the upkeep of their bicycle, when a bike-sharing service is more convenient. But what is sharing? Sharing is a form of social exchange that takes place among people known to each other, without any profit. Sharing is an established practice, and dominates particular aspects of our life, such as within the family. By sharing and collectively consuming the household space of the home, family members establish a communal identity, for example.

My colleague Fleura Bardhi and I are interested in whether the form of exchange happening in the 'sharing economy' is really sharing. We have found that when sharing is market-mediated – when a company is an intermediary between consumers who don't know each other – it is no longer sharing at all. Rather, consumers are paying to access someone else's goods or services for a particular period of time. It is an economic exchange, and we have labelled this 'access-based consumption'.

Our research on Zipcar, the world's leading car-sharing company, illustrates some of the characteristics of access-based consumption. Consumers don't feel any psychological sense of ownership over the cars, nor do they feel a sense of reciprocal obligations that arise when sharing with one another. They experience Zipcar in the anonymous way one experiences a hotel; they know others have used the cars, but have no desire to interact with them. They don't view other 'Zipsters' as co-sharers of the cars, but rather are mistrustful of them, and rely on the company to police the sharing system so that it's equitable for everyone. Finally, consumers do not want to be a part of a community, either with other Zipsters or with the company itself. Thus, our research challenges the romanticized view of the sharing economy as being collaborative and altruistically motivated.

It is important to highlight the benefits that access provides in contrast to the disadvantages of ownership and sharing. These consist of convenient and cost-effective access to valued resources, flexibility, and freedom from the financial, social, and emotional obligations embedded in ownership and sharing. There is still a lot to learn about sharing, access and ownership, though, and we are currently researching how these concepts may vary across generations, across cultures, and across social classes.

Question

Uber, the sharing economy alternative to taxis, that allows consumers to call the car via an app and choose a driver based on past user's ratings, positions itself squarely around its pricing, reliability, and convenience. This is encapsulated in its tagline, 'Better, faster and cheaper than a taxi'. In comparison, Lyft, which offers an almost identical service, positions itself as friendly ('We're your friend with a car'), and as a community ('Greet your driver with a fistbump'). Which positioning is more likely to be successful? Why? Use other examples from the sharing economy to support your answer.

Giana Eckhardt

However, it's not just convenience that explains the rise of the sharing economy. We can also point to changes in attitudes towards ownership, especially among younger consumers. A global survey that interviewed more than 10,000 respondents reported that one-third of millennials already use a sharing service, or expect to join one soon. Many people believe that overconsumption is putting our planet at risk, and half of the respondents say they could happily live without most of the items they own. This is consistent with discussions about the weak relationship researchers find between owning more 'stuff' and happiness.[102] A major study of Zipcar users did not reveal ethical and environmental concerns as the most important drivers of access-based consumption but highlighted economic advantages and daily conveniences as most important,[103] whereas other researchers studying, for example, access-based consumption in nursery and baby equipment did find concern about sustainability to be important.[104]

Chapter summary

Now that you have finished reading this chapter you should understand why:

1.1 **We use products to help us define our identities in different settings.** Consumption, private or collective, is part and parcel of most of the activities we engage in on a daily basis. If it is shallow to say that we are what we have (even though there is a truth to it), we might like 'we are what we do' better. But in a market and consumer culture such as ours, most activities are related to some form of consumption.

1.2 **Consumer behaviour is a process involving many actors.** Consumer behaviour is the study of the processes involved when individuals or groups select, purchase, use or dispose of products, services, ideas or experiences to satisfy needs and desires. A consumer may purchase, use and dispose of a product, but different people may perform these functions. In addition, we can think of consumers as role players who need different products to help them play their various parts.

1.3 Many different types of specialist study consumer behaviour. The field of consumer behaviour is interdisciplinary; it is composed of researchers from many different fields who share an interest in how people interact with the marketplace. We can categorise these disciplines by the degree to which their focus is micro (the individual consumer) or macro (the consumer as a member of groups or of the larger society).

1.4 There are basically two differing perspectives (called paradigms) regarding how and what we should understand about consumer behaviour. The positivist perspective emphasises the objectivity of science, and the consumer as a rational decision-maker. The interpretivist (or CCT) perspective, in contrast, stresses the subjective meaning of the consumer's individual experience and its insertion in a cultural context.

1.5 The society we live in today can be described as a consumer society. As was underlined in this chapter, most of the things we do involve some form of market consumption. Most of the resources we have access to are (for better or worse) mediated through the market, either directly with us as purchasers or indirectly with us as users. The consumer role is becoming increasingly important in many social relationships (again for better or worse).

1.6 Globalisation is important when trying to understand the consumer society. Consumer society and its characteristics are spreading on a global scale, and often go hand in hand with processes of development and modernisation. Globalisation does not necessarily mean that we are becoming one big homogenous mass; on the contrary – the process of *glocalisation* may contribute to produce new cultural differences.

1.7 Consumption is not just a private but also a political issue. The ethics of consumption are becoming more and more significant. Being a consumer is not a value-free position. Our choices as consumers relate in powerful ways to the rest of our lives and marketing activities exert an enormous impact on individuals. Consumer behaviour is relevant to our understanding of both public policy issues and the dynamics of popular culture. Global problems such as sustainability, climate change and inequality are deeply inscribed in consumer culture and its processes. Both consumers and organisations are discovering that ethical issues are at the core of the production and consumption processes.

1.8 We are witnessing the appearance of new forms of collective consumption formats. The internet has made consumer-to-consumer communications and offerings far easier, and we have therefore witnessed new formats of consumption emerging, based on either sharing or mutual usage, or on private marketisation of resources – so-called 'access-based consumption'.

Key terms

Access-based consumption (p. 26)
Anti-consumption (p. 20)
Brand personality (p. 14)
Consumer behaviour (p. 3)
Consumer culture (p. 13)
Consumer culture theory (CCT) (p. 13)
Consumer policy (p. 19)
Consumer society (p. 13)
Consumption communities (p. 4)
Demographics (p. 4)
Ethical consumers (p. 21)
Exchange (p. 6)
Global consumer culture (p. 14)
Globalisation (p. 14)
Glocalisation (p. 19)

Interpretivism (p. 12)
Market segmentation (p. 8)
Paradigm (p. 12)
Personality (p. 4)
Popular culture (p. 14)
Positivism (p. 12)
Psychographics (p. 4)
Risk society (p. 21)
Role theory (p. 6)
Sharing economy (p. 25)
Social media (p. 18)
Transformative Consumer Research (TCR) (p. 24)
Transitional economies (p. 18)

Consumer behaviour challenge

1 This chapter states that people play different roles and that their consumption behaviours may differ depending on the particular role they are playing. State whether you agree or disagree with this perspective, giving examples from your own life.

2 Some researchers believe that the field of consumer behaviour should be a pure, rather than an applied, science. That is, research issues should be framed in terms of their scientific interest rather than their applicability to immediate marketing problems. Do you agree?

3 In recent years there has been a large debate about the influence that internet shopping will have on our consumer lives. Try listing the changes that you personally have made in your buying and consumption patterns due to e-commerce. Compare these changes with changes experienced by other people from various social groups, e.g. somebody from your parents' generation, an IT geek or somebody with a lower educational background.

4 Name some products or services that are widely used by your social group. State whether you agree or disagree with the notion that these products help to form bonds within the group, and support your argument with examples from your list of products used by the group.

5 Some people believe that the sale of data on customers' social media habits, likes, buying habits and so on constitutes an invasion of privacy and should be banned. The recent scandal around Facebook and Cambridge Analytica only accentuates this. Comment on this issue from both a consumer's and a marketer's point of view.

6 List the three stages in the consumption process. Describe the issues that you considered in each of these stages when you made a recent important purchase.

7 State the differences between the positivist and interpretivist approaches to consumer research. For each type of inquiry, give examples of product dimensions that would be more usefully explored using that type of research over the other.

8 What aspects of consumer behaviour are likely to be of interest to a financial planner? To a university administrator? To a graphic arts designer? To a social worker in a government agency? To a nursing instructor?

9 Select a product and brand that you use frequently and list what you consider to be the brand's determinant attributes. Without revealing your list, ask a friend who is approximately the same age but of the opposite sex to make a similar list for the same product (the brand may be different). Compare and contrast the identified attributes and report your findings.

10 Collect ads for five different brands of the same product. Report on the segmentation variables, target markets and emphasised product attributes in each ad.

For additional material see the companion website at **www.pearsoned.co.uk/solomon**

Notes

1. Andrea Davies, James Fitchett and Avi Shankar, 'An Ethno-Consumerist Enquiry into International Consumer Behaviour', in Darach Turley and Stephen Brown (eds), *European Advances in Consumer Research: All Changed, Changed Utterly?*, 6th edn (Valdosta, GA: Association for Consumer Research, 2003): 102–7. See also: Frank Jacobs, 'Where is Europe?', *New York Times* (2012), http://opinionator.blogs.nytimes.com/2012/01/09/where-is-europe/ (accessed 23 August 2018).

2. See, for example, http://unhappyhipsters.com/ (accessed 23 August 2018) or http://www.parool.nl/parool/nl/34261/PS/article/detail/3976488/2015/04/24/9-hipsterfenomenen-waar-Amsterdam-wel-klaar-mee-is.dhtml (accessed 23 August 2018).

3. 'Recession: shifting consumer responses', *Euromonitor International* (March 2012), http://blog.euromonitor.com/survey-results/ (accessed 23 August 2018).

4. Christopher Thompson, 'Valentine's boost for online dating sites', *Financial Times* (10 February 2012); see also http://www.telegraph.co.uk/women/sex/online-dating/3356126/The-20-most-useful-dating-websites.html (accessed 23 August 2018).

5. Mike Featherstone (ed.), *Global Culture: Nationalization, and Modernity* (London: Sage, 1990). For a critical review of the effects and reception of (American-style) marketing, see Johnny K. Johansson, *In Your Face: How American Marketing Excess Fuels Anti-Americanism* (Upper Saddle River, NJ: Financial Times Prentice Hall, 2004).

6. Daniel Miller, 'Consumption as the Vanguard of History', in D. Miller (ed.), *Acknowledging Consumption* (London: Routledge, 1995): 1–57.

7. Erving Goffman, *The Presentation of Self in Everyday Life* (Garden City, NY: Doubleday, 1959); George H. Mead, *Mind, Self, and Society* (Chicago: University of Chicago Press, 1934); Michael R. Solomon, 'The role of products as social stimuli: A symbolic interactionism perspective', *Journal of Consumer Research* 10 (December 1983): 319–29.

8. Yiannis Gabriel and Tim Lang, *The Unmanageable Consumer* (London: Sage, 1995).

9. Frank Bradley, *Marketing Management: Providing, Communicating and Delivering Value* (London: Prentice-Hall, 1995).

10. See Matthias Bode and Søren Askegaard, 'Marketing and Consumer Research: An Uneasy Relationship', in Margit Keller, Bente Halkier, Terhi-Anna Wilska and Monica Truninger (eds) *The Routledge Handbook of Consumption* (London: Routledge, 2017): 61–71.

11. See, for example, the debate in James Fitchett, Georgios Patsiaouras and Andrea Davies, 'Myth and ideology in consumer culture theory', *Marketing Theory*, 14(4) (2104): 495–506 and Søren Askegaard, 'Consumer culture theory: Neoliberalism's "useful idiots"?', *Marketing Theory*, 14(4) (2014): 507–11.

12. https://ec.europa.eu/eurostat (accessed 30 August 2018).

13. https://www.vrt.be/vrtnws/en/2015/04/10/brussels_is_a_boominggaycapital-1-2300306/ (accessed 27 July 2018).

14. https://travelsofadam.com/2017/06/gay-travel-resources/, (accessed July 27 2018).

15. Jack Neff, 'Mucus to maxi pads: Marketing's dirtiest jobs, frank talk about diapers and condoms lifts taboos and helps make a difference in consumers' lives, say those in the trenches', *Advertising Age* (17 February 2009), www.adage.com (accessed 23 August 2018).

16. Morris B. Holbrook, 'The Consumer Researcher Visits Radio City: Dancing in the Dark', in E.C. Hirschman and M.B. Holbrook (eds), *Advances in Consumer Research* 12th edn (Provo, UT: Association for Consumer Research, 1985): 28–31.

17. Jean-Claude Usunier, 'Integrating the Cultural Dimension into International Marketing', Proceedings of the Second Conference on the Cultural Dimension of International Marketing (Odense: Odense University, 1995): 1–23.

18. Eric J. Arnould and Craig J. Thompson, 'Consumer culture theory (CCT): Twenty years of research', *Journal of Consumer Research* 31 (March 2005): 868–82.

19. Per Østergaard and Christian Jantzen, 'Shifting Perspectives in Consumer Research: From Buyer Behaviour to Consumption Studies' in S.C. Beckmann and R. Elliott (eds), *Interpretive Consumer Research* (Copenhagen: Copenhagen Business School Press, 2000): 9–23.

20. Rebecca Jenkins, Elizabeth Nixon and Mike Molesworth, '"Just normal and homely": The presence, absence and othering of consumer culture in everyday imagining', *Journal of Consumer Culture*, 11(2) (2011): 261–81.

21. Don Slater, 'The moral seriousness of consumption', *Journal of Consumer Culture*, 10(2) (2010): 280–4.

22. Celia Lury, *Consumer Culture* (New Brunswick, NJ: Rutgers University Press, 1996). Another excellent book on the rise of consumer culture is Don Slater, *Consumer Culture and Modernity* (Cambridge: Polity Press, 1997).

23. Daniel Miller, 'Why Some Things Matter', in D. Miller (ed.), *Material Cultures: Why Some Things Matter* (London: UCL Books, 1998): 3–21. See also Daniel Miller, *Stuff* (Cambridge: Polity Press, 2009).

24. Eric J. Arnould and Craig J. Thompson, 'Consumer culture theory (CCT): Twenty years of research', *Journal of Consumer Research*, 31(4) (March 2005): 868–82.

25. Steven Miles, *Consumerism – As a Way of Life* (London: Sage, 1998).

26. T. Bettina Cornwell and Bruce Keillor, 'Contemporary Literature and the Embedded Consumer Culture: The Case of Updike's Rabbit', in Roger J. Kruez and Mary Sue MacNealy (eds), *Empirical Approaches to Literature and Aesthetics: Advances in Discourse Processes* (Norwood, NJ: Ablex Publishing Corporation, 1996): 559–72; Monroe Friedman, 'The changing language of a consumer society: Brand name usage in popular American novels in the postwar era', *Journal of Consumer Research* 11 (March 1985): 927–37; Monroe Friedman, 'Commercial influences in the lyrics of popular American music of the postwar era', *Journal of Consumer Affairs* 20 (Winter 1986): 193.

27. *Journal of Marketing Management*, 29(1) (2013), special issue on anthropomorphic marketing.

28. Søren Askegaard, 'Brands as a Global Ideoscape', in J. Schroeder and M. Salzer-Mörling (eds), *Brand Culture* (London: Routledge, 2006): 91–102.

29. Martin McCarty, Martin I. Horn, Mary Kate Szenasy and Jocelyn Feintuch, 'An exploratory study of consumer style: Country differences and international segments', *Journal of Consumer Behaviour* 6(1) (2007): 48.

30. David Waller, Kim-Shyan Fam and B. Zafer Erdigan, 'Advertising of controversial products: A cross-cultural study', *Journal of Consumer Marketing*, 22(1) (2005): 6–13.

31. See, for example, Craig Thompson and Siok Kuan Tambyah, 'Trying to be cosmopolitan', *Journal of Consumer Research*, 26(3) (1999): 214–41.

32. Jean-Noël Kapferer, 'The Two Business Cultures of Luxury Brands', in J. Schroeder and M. Salzer-Mörling (eds), *Brand Culture* (London: Routledge, 2006): 67–76.

33. Sandra Diehl, Ralf Terlutter and Barbara Mueller, 'The Influence of Culture on Responses to the Globe Dimension of Performance Orientation in Advertising Messages – Results from the US, Germany, France, Spain, and Thailand', in A.Y. Lee and D. Soman (eds), *Advances in Consumer Research*, 35 (Duluth, MN: Association for Consumer Research, 2008): 269–75.

34. See also Ulf Hannerz, 'Cosmopolitans and Locals in World Culture', in Mike Featherstone (ed.), *Global Culture* (London: Sage, 1990): 237–52.

35. Dannie Kjeldgaard and Søren Askegaard, 'The glocalization of youth culture: The global youth segment as structures of common difference', *Journal of Consumer Research*, 33(2) (2006): 231–47.

36. Aliakbar Jafari and Christina Goulding, 'Globalization, reflexivity, and the project of the self: A virtual intercultural learning process', *Consumption, Markets and Culture*, 16(1) (2013): 65–90.

37. 'After the BRICS are the MINTs, but can you make any money from them?' *Forbes International* (1 June 2014), http://www.forbes.com/sites/chriswright/2014/01/06/

after-the-brics-the-mints-catchy-acronym-but-can-you-make-any-money-from-it/ (accessed 23 August 2018).

38. David K. Tse, Russell W. Belk and Nan Zhou, 'Becoming a consumer society: A longitudinal and cross-cultural content analysis of print ads from Hong Kong, the People's Republic of China, and Taiwan', *Journal of Consumer Research* 15 (March 1989): 457–72; see also Annamma Joy, 'Marketing in modern China: An evolutionary perspective', *CJAS* (June 1990): 55–67, for a review of changes in Chinese marketing practices since the economic reforms of 1978.

39. Lilly Ye, Mousumi Bose and Lou Pelton, 'Dispelling the myth of Chinese consumers: A new generation of brand-conscious individualists', *Journal of Consumer Marketing*, 29(3) (2012): 190–201.

40. Julien Cayla and Giana Eckhardt, 'Asian brands and the shaping of a transnational imagined community', *Journal of Consumer Research*, 35(2) (2008): 216–30.

41. https://jingdaily.com/6-chinese-brands-global-powers-of-luxury-goods/ (accessed 30 August 2018).

42. 'Mountain catwalk: Bhutan street fashion', https://www.bbc.com/news/world-asia-30631923 (accessed 23 August 2018).

43. https://www.calvertjournal.com/news/show/10465/bihor-not-dior-watch-the-new-campaign-reclaiming-romanian-folk-style (accessed 23 August 2018).

44. Material in this section adapted from Güliz Ger and Russell W. Belk, 'I'd like to buy the world a Coke: Consumptionscapes of the "less affluent world"', *Journal of Consumer Policy*, 19(3) (1996): 271–304; Russell W. Belk, 'Romanian Consumer Desires and Feelings of Deservingness', in Lavinia Stan (ed.), *Romania in Transition* (Hanover, NH: Dartmouth Press, 1997): 191–208; see also Güliz Ger, 'Human development and humane consumption: Well-being beyond the good life', *Journal of Public Policy and Marketing*, 16(1) (1997): 110–25.

45. Tuba Üstüner and Douglas B. Holt, 'Dominated consumer acculturation: The social construction of poor migrant women's consumer identity projects in a Turkish squatter', *Journal of Consumer Research*, 34(1) (2007): 41–56.

46. Güliz Ger, 'The positive and negative effects of marketing on socioeconomic development: The Turkish case', *Journal of Consumer Policy*, 15 (1992): 229–54.

47. Erazim Kohák, 'Ashes, ashes. . . Central Europe after forty years', *Daedalus*, 121 (Spring 1992): 197–215, at 219, quoted in Belk, 'Romanian Consumer Desires and Feelings of Deservingness', op. cit.

48. *Markedsføring* (10 November 2011).

49. Søren Askegaard and Giana Eckhardt, 'Glocal yoga: Re-appropriation in the Indian consumption scope', *Marketing Theory*, 12(1) (2012): 43–58.

50. Amina Béji-Bécheur, Nacima Ourahmoune and Nil Özça˘glar-Toulouse, 'The polysemic meaning of couscous consumption in France', *Journal of Consumer Behaviour*, 13 (2014): 196–203.

51. Rungpaka Amy Tiwaskul and Chris Hackley, 'Postmodern paradoxes in Thai–Asian consumer identity', *Journal of Business Research*, 65(4) (2012): 490–6.

52. Søren Askegaard and Dannie Kjeldgaard, 'Here, there and everywhere: Place branding and gastronomic glocalization in a macromarketing perspective', *Journal of Macromarketing*, 27(2) (2007): 138–47.

53. Allison James, 'Cooking the Books: Global or Local Identities in Contemporary British Food Cultures?' in David Howes (ed.), *Cross-Cultural Consumption* (London: Routledge, 1996): 77–92.

54. Søren Askegaard, Dannie Kjeldgaard and Eric Arnould, 'Reflexive Culture's Consequences', in C. Nakata (ed.), *Beyond Hofstede: Culture Frameworks for Global Marketing and Management* (Chicago: Palgrave Macmillan, 2009): 101–22.

55. A. Fuat Firat, 'Globalization of fragmentation – a framework for understanding contemporary global markets', *Journal of International Marketing*, 5(2) (1997): 77–86. See also T. Bettina Cornwell and Judy Drennan, 'Cross-cultural consumer/consumption research: Dealing with issues emerging from globalization and fragmentation', *Journal of Macromarketing*, 24(2) (2004): 108–21.

56. R. Pearce, 'Social responsibility in the marketplace: assymetric information in food labelling', *Business Ethics: A European Review*, 8(1) (1999): 26–36.

57. Teddy Wayne, 'The mail-order-bride trade is flourishing', *Business Week* (6 January 2011); *Information* (2–3 September 2000): 11; Victor Malarek, *The Natashas: The New Global Sex Trade Book* (Viking Canada, 2003). See also: 'New crackdown on sex trafficking', *BBC News* (3 October 2007), http://news.bbc.co.uk/2/hi/uk_news/7024646.stm (accessed 23 August 2018).

58. Daniel Miller, 'Consumption as the Vanguard of History', in D. Miller (ed.), *Acknowledging Consumption* (London: Routledge, 1995): 1–57; see also Cornelia Dröge, Roger Calantone, Madhu Agrawal and Robert Mackay, 'The consumption culture and its critiques: A framework for analysis', *Journal of Macromarketing* (Fall 1993): 32–45.

59. Panel discussion: 'Critical and Moral Stances in Consumer Studies', *Journal of Consumer Culture*, 10(2) (2010): 274–91.

60. See, for example, *Consumption, Markets and Culture*, 13(3) (2010), special issue on anti-consumption.

61. John de Graaf, David Waun and Thomas Naylor, *Affluenza: The All-Consuming Epidemic* (San Francisco: Berrett-Koehler Publishers, 2001).

62. Craig Thompson, 'A carnivalesque approach to the politics of consumption (or) grotesque realism and the analysis of the excretory economy', *ANNALS of the American Academy of Political and Social Science*, 611 (2007): 112–25. See also the already-cited panel discussion (op cit.).

63. Ulrich Beck, *Risk Society* (London: Sage Publications, 1992).

64. http://blogs.wsj.com/chinajournal/2008/10/01/seeking-sources-of-information-on-melamine-tainted-food/20090118 (accessed 23 August 2018).

65. Karin Ekström and Søren Askegaard, 'Daily consumption in risk society: The case of genetically modified foods', in S. Hoch and R. Meyer (eds), *Advances in Consumer Research* 27 (Provo, UT: Association for Consumer Research, 2000): 237–43.

66. Lone Bredahl, 'Determinants of Consumer Attitudes and Purchase Intentions with Regard to Genetically Modified Foods – Results from a Cross-National Survey', MAPP Working Paper no. 69 (Aarhus: The Aarhus School of Business, 2000).

67. http://www.foodnavigator.com/Policy/EU-organic-supply-demand-gap-uncertainty (accessed 23 August 2018).

68. Mari Niva, Johanna M$_k$el, Nina Kahma and Unni Kjærnæs, 'Eating sustainably? Practices and background factors of ecological food consumption in four Nordic countries', *Journal of Consumer Policy*, 37 (2014): 465–84.

69. Liisa Uusitalo, 'Consumers as Citizens – Three Approaches to Collective Consumer Problems', in K.G. Grunert and J. Thøgersen (eds), *Consumers, Policy and the Environment* (New York: Springer, 2005): 127–50. See also Yannis Gabriel

and Tim Lang, *The Unmanageable Consumer*, 2nd edn (London: Sage, 2006).

70. Suzanne Beckmann, 'In the Eye of the Beholder: Danish Consumer-Citizens and Sustainability', in K.G. Grunert and J. Thøgersen (eds), *Consumers, Policy and the Environment*, op. cit.: 265–99.

71. On consumers and their ideologised narratives about technology, see Robert V. Kozinets, 'Technology/ideology: How ideological fields influence consumers' technology narratives', *Journal of Consumer Research*, 34(6) (2008): 865–81.

72. Bente Halkier, 'Consequences of the politicization of consumption: The example of environmentally friendly consumption practices', *Journal of Environmental Policy and Planning* 1 (1999): 25–41.

73. Oliver M. Freestone and Peter McGoldrick, 'Motivations of the ethical consumer', *Journal of Business Research*, 79 (2008): 445–467. See also *Journal of Marketing Management*, 28(3–4) (March 2012).

74. Robert V. Kozinets, 'Can consumers escape the market? Emancipatory illuminations from burning man', *Journal of Consumer Research* 29 (June 2002): 20–38; see also Douglas B. Holt, 'Why do brands cause trouble? A dialectical theory of consumer culture and branding', *Journal of Consumer Research* 29 (June 2002): 70–90.

75. Louise Hassan, Deirdre Shaw, Edward Shiu, Gianfranco Walsh and Sara Parry, 'Uncertainty in ethical consumer choice: a conceptual model, *Journal of Consumer Behaviour*, 12 (2013): 182–93.

76. Guillaume Gruère, 'An analysis of the growth in environmental labelling and information schemes, *Journal of Consumer Policy*, 38(1) (2015): 1–18.

77. Richard Jones, 'Challenges to the notion of publics in public relations: Implications of the risk society for the discipline', *Public Relations Review*, 28(1) (2002): 49–62.

78. http://www.adbusters.org/ (accessed 23 August 2018).

79. www.cokespotlight.org (accessed 23 August 2018); see also www.adbusters.org (accessed 30 August 2018).

80. Kalle Lasn, 'Culture Jamming', in J.B. Schor and D.B. Holt (eds), *The Consumer Society Reader* (New York: The New Press, 2000): 414–32.

81. Nat Ives, 'Advertising: Unauthorized campaigns used by unauthorized creators become a trend', *New York Times* (23 December 2004).

82. Craig J. Thompson and Zeynep Arsel, 'The Starbucks brandscape and consumers' (anticorporate) experiences of glocalization', *Journal of Consumer Research* 31 (December 2004): 631–42.

83. Craig J. Thompson, Aric Rindfleisch and Zeynep Arsel, 'Emotional branding and the strategic value of the doppelganger brand image', *Journal of Marketing*, 70(1) (2006): 50–64.

84. Jill Gabrielle Klein, N. Craig Smith and Andrew John, 'Why we boycott: Consumer motivation for boycott participation', *Journal of Marketing*, 68 (July 2004): 92–109.

85. See, for example, https://www.cbsnews.com/news/companies-cutting-ties-with-nra-after-florida-school-shooting/ or https://9to5mac.com/2018/02/28/march1nraboy-cott-nra-boycott/ (both accessed 30 August 2018).

86. 'Det tavse oprør', *Weekendavisen* (20–26 July 2018): 10.

87. Julie L. Ozanne and Bige Saatcioglu, 'Participatory action research', *Journal of Consumer Research* 35 (October 2008): 423–39.

88. Lara Spiteri-Cornish, 'It's good for me: It has added fibre', *Journal of Consumer Behaviour*, 11 (2012): 292–302.

89. Simone Pettigrew, Laurel Anderson, Wendy Boland, Valérie-Inès de la Ville, Ilaisaane Fifita, Marie-Helène Fosse-Gomez, Marie Kindt, Laura Luukkanen, Ingrid Martin, Licie K. Ozanne, Dante Pirouz, Andrea Prothero and Tony Stovall, 'The experience of risk in families: Conceptualisations and implications for transformative research', *Journal of Marketing Management*, 30(17–18) (2014): 1,772–99.

90. Mark Tadajewski, Jessica Chelekis, Benet DeBerry-Spence, Bernardo Figueiredo, Olga Kravets, Krittinee Nuttavuthisit, Lisa Peñaloza and Johanna Moisander, 'The discourses of marketing and development: Towards critical transformative marketing research', *Journal of Marketing Management*, 30(17–18) (2014): 1,728–71.

91. Kathy Hamilton, Maria Piacentini, Emma Banister, Andres Barrios, Christopher Blocker, Catherine Coleman, Ahmet Ekici, Hélène Gorge, Martina Hutton, Françoise Passerard and Bige Saatcioğlu, 'Poverty in consumer culture: towards a transformative social representation', *Journal of Marketing Management*, 30(17–18) (2014): 1,833–57.

92. Teresa Pereira Heath and Andreas Chatzidakis, 'The transformative potential of marketing from the consumers' point of view', *Journal of Consumer Behaviour*, 11 (2012): 283–91.

93. Søren Askegaard, Nailya Ordabayeva, Pierre Chandon, Tracy Cheung, Zuzana Chytkova, Yann Cornil, Canan Corus, Julie Edell, Daniele Mathras, Astrid Junghans, Dorthe Brogård Kristensen, Ilona Mikkonen, Elisabeth Miller, Nada Sayarh and Carolina Werle, 'Moralities in food and health research', *Journal of Marketing Management*, 30(17–18) (2014): 1,800–32.

94. http://www.theguardian.com/world/2015/jun/01/rana-plaza-collapse-dozens-charged-with-murder-bangladesh (accessed 23 August 2018).

95. http://www.cleanclothes.org/ranaplaza (accessed 23 August 2018).

96. Gregorio Fuschillo and Bernard Cova, 'Subverting the market to help other consumer: The 'la repasse' phenomenon', *Journal of Consumer Behaviour*, 14(4) (2015).

97. Russell W. Belk, 'Sharing', *Journal of Consumer Research*, 36(5) (2010): 715–34.

98. Rebecca Jenkins, Mike Molesworth and Richard Scullion, 'The messy social lives of objects: Inter-personal borrowing and the ambiguity of possession and ownership', *Journal of Consumer Behaviour*, 13 (2014): 131–9.

99. Eric Arnould and Alexander Rose, 'Mutuality: Critique and substitute for Belk's "sharing"', *Marketing Theory*, 15 (2015).

100. Fleura Bardhi and Giana Eckhardt, 'Access-based consumption: The case of car sharing', *Journal of Consumer Research*, 39(4) (2012): 881–98.

101. John Harvey, Andrew Smith and David Golightly, 'Giving and sharing in the computer-mediated economy', *Journal of Consumer Behaviour*, 13 (2014).

102. See Marsha L. Richins, 'When wanting is better than having: Materialism, transformation expectations, and product-evoked emotions in the purchase process', *Journal of Consumer Research*, 40(1) (2013): 1–18.

103. Bardhi and Eckhardt (2012), op cit.

104. Maurizio Catulli, Julian Lindley, Nick Reed, Andrew Green, Hajra Hyseni and Sushma Kiri, 'What is mine is not yours: Further insight on what access-based consumption says about consumers', *Research in Consumer Behavior*, 15 (2013): 185–208.

Chapter 2
Shopping, buying and disposing

Chapter objectives

When you finish reading this chapter you will understand why:

2.1 Many factors at the time of purchase dramatically influence the consumer's decision-making process.

2.2 The information a store or website provides strongly influences a purchase decision, in addition to what a shopper already knows or believes about a product.

2.3 A salesperson is often the crucial connection to a purchase.

2.4 Getting rid of products when consumers no longer need or want them is a major concern both to marketers and to public policymakers.

GRACE'S Samsung smartphone was coming to the end of its life. She had three choices. She could buy a Samsung replacement (e.g. a Samsung Galaxy S9 or S9+); she could switch to an iPhone; or she could wait for the announcements about the new product ranges in September and choose a new smartphone when the new launches took place. She had a number of concerns, in addition to the cost. How confident could she be, if she bought an iPhone, that she would be able to operate it? Most especially, how easy would it be to set up the all-important links to her existing email account as she wanted to be able to check her emails easily? What was meant by all the different mobile operating systems she had read about: Apple's iOS and Android with the Samsung (had she got that right?). She was nervous about making everything work if she switched phones – would all the technology be compatible? She'd heard that 'everything is simple', but she'd learnt that was not always true. What should she do? She did a little bit of Web surfing for her homework, visiting a comparison site (e.g. kelkoo.co.uk). Then she went along to some of the providers with outlets on the high street (e.g. EE and Apple). To be honest, she was rather overwhelmed, although all the assistants were very helpful and friendly (not pushy at all, rather to her surprise). She decided to try and pick the brains of some of her friends, those who already had iPhones or the latest Samsung phone and also those who had changed their brand. In the end, after listening to everyone's stories, she decided she would stick with what she was most familiar with (i.e. Samsung). OK, she had made a decision. She would definitely upgrade to one of the latest Samsung smartphones – but which one? That would depend on the help and advice she got from the high-street store, once she had done some more homework on the Samsung website and identified the model she really fancied. She could, of course, always purchase via the EE website, but she thought it might be safer and better to make the purchase in-store, so that she could always go back and ask questions if she was having problems with understanding how to use all the various new functions – all the stores offered lessons these days, so that helped alleviate some of her anxiety that she would make a purchase and then be completely defeated by the complexity of the phone she had chosen.

MARGARET K. HOGG

Introduction

2.1

Many factors at the time of purchase dramatically influence the consumer's decision-making process.

In this chapter we seek to understand the consumer within the marketplace. Grace's experience illustrates some of the concepts to be discussed here as we examine factors that influence buying, shopping and disposing within the consumption cycle. Grace's story highlights the importance of the purchase context (online versus offline), as well as her fears about the post-purchase experience as we see how she faces a range of dilemmas when making consumption choices (more on consumer decision-making in Chapter 8, with the difficulties faced by Elijah when choosing among different televisions).

We begin the chapter by examining a number of important antecedent states that affect our consumer behaviour across all stages of the consumption cycle, including situational factors (e.g. social and physical surroundings), temporal factors and mood and shopping motivations. Our previous consumer experiences influence firstly our views about how best to collect information about the products we are interested in (note that Grace searched online and also in the high street), and secondly our decisions about where to purchase (e.g. online sites, high-street stores or a combination via click and collect). The importance of the retail environment means that marketing managers invest a lot of effort in the experiences that their customers have, either instore or online (e.g. store image, atmospherics, service levels, navigability of the website), so we spend some time in this chapter looking at 'servicescapes' (retailing as theatre), where the consumer has many of his/her experiences of the marketplace. Towards the end of the chapter we discuss disposing of products, and the increasingly important role played by consumer value systems about sustainability in influencing consumers' decisions on recycling.

Consumers' choices

Making a purchase is often not a simple, routine matter of going to a shop and choosing something. As illustrated in Figure 2.1, a consumer's choices are affected by many contextual factors, such as mood, time pressure and the particular situation or context for which the product is needed. In some situations, such as the purchase of a car or a home, the salesperson or the reference group (which we will discuss in Chapter 9) play a pivotal role in

Antecedent states	Purchase environment	Product disposal

• Moods and emotions
• Situational factors
• Temporal factors
• Shopping orientation
	• Shopping experience
	• Social and physical surroundings
	• Trends in the purchase environment
	• E-commerce: clicks and bricks
	  – Online retailing and mobile e-commerce
	• Servicescapes
	  – Store image
	  – Atmospherics
	• Instore decision-making
	  – Spontaneous shopping
	  – Point-of-purchase stimuli
	  – Place-based media
	• Sales interactions/sales person(s)
		• Disposal options
		• Lateral cycling

Figure 2.1 Issues related to purchase and post-purchase activities

the final choice. And people are using the Web to arm themselves with product and price information before they even enter a store.[1] Note Grace's initial search online using comparison sites, and then checking the product range on the Samsung website in the opening vignette; and similarly, Elijah's preliminary search for information about televisions via the

Barbara Kruger, 'I shop therefore I am'.
Copyright Barbara Kruger, Courtesy: Mary Boone Gallery, New York.

internet (see the opening vignette of Chapter 8). This all puts added pressure on retailers to deliver the value customers expect.

The store environment also exerts a major influence: shopping is like a stage performance, with the customer involved as either a member of the audience or as an active participant. The quality of the performance is affected by the other *cast members* (salespeople or other shoppers), as well as by the *setting* of the play (the image of a particular store and the 'feeling' it imparts) and *props* (store fittings and promotional material, which are used in an attempt to influence the shopper's decisions). However, certainly in the context of UK retailing, some stores are really being challenged in the face of rising rents, rising local council taxes and changing consumer buying habits towards online shopping. The most recent UK example of this is the House of Fraser department store chain (which has been in business for 169 years), which is rationalising its high-street offering by closing 31 stores at a cost of 6,000 jobs, all to be achieved by early 2019 (see longer discussion below about House of Fraser).

In addition, consumer activity also occurs *after* a product has been purchased and brought home. After using a product, the consumer must decide whether or not they are satisfied with it (see in Chapter 8, where we consider the role of both expectations and satisfaction in the post-purchase process). This final evaluative stage is especially important to marketers, who realise that the key to success is not necessarily just about selling a product once, but rather about forging a relationship with the consumer so that they will continue to buy in the future. Finally, we also consider how consumers go about disposing of or recycling products (e.g. second-hand goods) and how secondary markets (e.g. eBay; second-hand car dealers) often play a pivotal role in product acquisition.

Antecedent states

2.2

The information a store or website provides strongly influences a purchase decision, in addition to what a shopper already knows or believes about a product.

Antecedent states include a consumer's mood or physiological condition at the time of purchase, which can have a major impact on what is bought.[2] One reason for this is that behaviour is directed towards certain goal states (see Chapter 5). In addition, situational factors, usage contexts, time pressures and shopping orientations can also influence what is bought. The consumer's particular social identity, or the role that is being played at a given time (and thus their *situational self-image*), will also potentially be influential.[3]

Mood and emotions

A consumer's mood will have an impact on purchase decisions. Our moods can change radically during the day, so at different times we might be more or less interested in what a marketer offers. For example, stress can reduce a consumer's information-processing and problem-solving abilities.[4] Social media platforms are looking at ways to adapt quickly to situational changes. Theoretically, a user who posts near the end of his workday that 'It's Miller time' could immediately be served a promotion from MillerCoors or another beer company.[5]

Two dimensions determine whether a shopper will react positively or negatively to a store environment: *pleasure* and *arousal*. A person can enjoy or not enjoy a situation, and they can feel stimulated or not. As Figure 2.2 indicates, different combinations of pleasure and arousal levels result in a variety of emotional states. For example, an arousing situation can be either distressing or exciting, depending on whether the context is positive or negative (e.g. a street riot *vs* a street festival). Maintaining an upbeat mood in a pleasant context is one factor behind the success of theme parks such as Disneyland, which try to provide consistent doses of carefully calculated stimulation to patrons.[6]

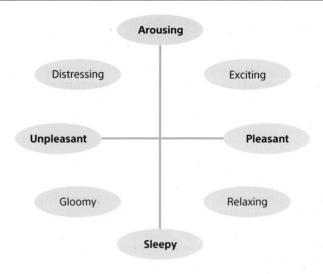

Figure 2.2 Dimensions of emotional states

Source: James Russell and Geraldine Pratt, 'A description of the affective quality attributed to environment', *Journal of Personality and Social Psychology* 38(2) (1980): 311–22.

A specific mood is some combination of pleasure and arousal. For example, the state of happiness is high in pleasantness and moderate in arousal, while elation would be high in both dimensions.[7] In general, a mood state (either positive or negative) biases judgements of products and services in that direction. Put simply, consumers like things better when they are in a good mood.

Moods can be affected by store design, the weather or other factors specific to the consumer. In addition, music and television programming can affect mood; this has important consequences for commercials.[8] When consumers hear happy music or watch happy programmes, they have more positive reactions to commercials and products, especially when the marketing appeals are aimed at arousing emotional reactions.[9] When we're in a good mood, we process ads with less elaboration. We pay less attention to the specifics of the message and we rely more on heuristics (see Chapter 8).[10] Another study has examined the impact of different types of music (and also colour) on consumers' enjoyment of food and wine.[11]

Our emotional reactions to marketing cues are so powerful that some high-tech companies study mood in very small doses (in 1/30-of-a-second increments) as they analyse people's facial reactions when they see ads or new products. They measure happiness as they look for differences between, for example, a *true smile* (which includes a relaxation of the upper eyelid) and a *social smile* (which occurs only around the mouth).[12]

Situational factors

A **consumption situation** includes a buyer, a seller and a product or service – but also many other factors, such as the reason we want to make a purchase and how the physical environment makes us feel. Situational effects can be behavioural (such as entertaining friends) or perceptual (e.g. feeling pressed for time).[13] Common sense tells us that people tailor their purchases to specific occasions, or that the way we feel at a specific time affects what we feel like buying or doing. In addition to the functional relationships between products and usage situation, another reason to take environmental circumstances into account is that the role a person plays at any time is partly determined by their *situational self-image:* 'Who am I right now?' (see also Chapter 4).[14] Someone trying to impress his girlfriend by playing the role of 'man about town' may spend more lavishly, ordering champagne rather than beer and buying flowers – purchases he would never consider when he is with his male friends in a pub and playing the role of 'one of the boys'. As this example demonstrates, knowledge of what consumers are doing at the time a product is consumed may improve predictions of product and brand choice.[15]

Situational segmentation

By systematically identifying important usage situations, market segmentation strategies can be developed to position products that will meet the specific needs arising from these situations. Many product categories are amenable to this form of segmentation.[16]

Situations can be used to fine-tune a segmentation strategy. A study of 2,500 online customers[17] identified 'occasion-based segmentation'. Using variables such as length of session, time spent on each page of the website and the user's familiarity with the site, seven different occasions were identified, which could be classified into two groups. The first group, 'Loitering, Information Please and Surfing', spent between 33 and 70 minutes online, and was more likely to purchase. The second group, 'Quickies, Just the Facts, Single Mission and Do It Again', remained online for much shorter periods. 'It's only by decoding the type of occasion – such as gathering product information – that marketers can fully harness the web's interactive powers by aiming messages and offers at the right place at the right time.'[18]

Marketing opportunity
Little and often: shoppers are abandoning the weekly shop

'We're moving into cities, working longer hours and living in smaller households – and it's making the weekly traipse round the out-of-town supermarket redundant. Why spend your Saturday food shopping when you can pick up a quick dinner for two on the way home from work? Today's shoppers top up as and when they need – a habit which supermarkets are capitalizing on, as growth in inner-city stores outpaces out-of-town superstores. At Sainsbury's, local stores now outnumber regular superstores. With the weekly routine vanishing, shoppers are seeking responsive, flexible ways to keep their shopping list updated and their cupboards full.'[19]

Temporal factors

Time is one of consumers' most precious and limited resources. Recent research indicates that there are significant time–money differences when consumers use heuristics ('rules-of-thumb for problem solving learnt by experiment or trial and error', Merriam-Webster http://www.merriam-webster.com/dictionary/heuristic) for decision-making: i.e. 'decisions related to time rather than money foster an enhanced use of heuristics', which suggests that although time and money seem to be economically equivalent, they are, in fact, psychologically different (see Chapter 8).[20] Our perspectives on time can affect many stages of decision-making and consumption, such as needs that are stimulated, the amount of information search we undertake and so on. Common sense tells us that more careful information search and deliberation occurs when we have the luxury of taking our time. In online marketing, **open rates** (the percentage of people who open an email message from a marketer) vary throughout the day. The peak time for high open rates is midday on weekdays (presumably when all those people at work take a lunch break).[21]

Economic time

Time is an economic variable; it is a resource that must be divided among activities.[22] Consumers try to maximise satisfaction by allocating time to the appropriate combination of tasks. Of course, people's allocation decisions differ. An individual's priorities determine their **time style**.[23] Time style incorporates dimensions such as economic time, past orientation, future orientation, time submissiveness and time anxiety.[24] Research identified four dimensions of time: social, temporal, planning and polychromic orientation. The *social dimension* refers to individuals' categorisation of time as either 'time for me' or 'time with/for others'. The *temporal orientation* depicts the relative significance individuals attach to past, present or future. The *planning orientation* dimension alludes to different time management styles varying on a continuum from analytic to spontaneous. And lastly, *polychromic orientation* denotes doing-one-thing-at-a-time versus multitasking time styles. These multiple dimensions of time style push and pull individuals in different directions, which ultimately leads to psychological conflicts. From these dimensions, five emergent symbolic metaphors of time were proposed,[25] which reflected different perspectives on time and the process by which the perspective was created:

Time is a pressure cooker: Women who personify this metaphor are usually analytic in their planning, other oriented, and monochronic in their time styles. They treat shopping in a methodical manner and they often feel under pressure and in conflict.

Time is a map: Women who exemplify this metaphor are usually analytic planners, have a future temporal orientation and a polychronic time style. They often engage in extensive information search and comparison shopping.

Time is a mirror: Women who come under this metaphor are also analytic planners and have a polychromic orientation. However, they have a past temporal orientation. Due to their risk averseness in time use, these women are usually loyal to products and services they know and trust.

Time is a river: Women whose time styles can be described through this metaphor are usually spontaneous in their planning orientation and have a present focus. They go on unplanned, short and frequent shopping trips undertaken on impulse.

Time is a feast: These women are analytic planners who have a present temporal orientation. They view time as something to be consumed in the pursuit of sensory pleasure and gratification and, hence, they are motivated by hedonic and variety-seeking desires in their consumption behaviour.[26]

Many consumers believe they are more pressed for time than ever before, a feeling called **time poverty**. This feeling may, however, be due more to perception than to fact. People may simply have more options for spending their time and feel pressured by the weight of it all. This sense of *time poverty* has made consumers very responsive to marketing innovations that allow them to save time. New online business concepts based on improved delivery are popping up all over the Web. Delivery of videos, groceries, or dry cleaning to customers' doors are just a few of the time-saving online possibilities.[27] In Hong Kong, rush-hour commuters no longer need to stand and queue to buy Underground tickets. Instead, a scanner automatically reads an Octopus card and automatically deducts the fare from their account. The card doesn't even require contact to be read, so people can just pass their entire bag over the scanner and race to catch their trains. A similar system was introduced in Greater London in July 2003 (Oyster card); and in Sydney, November 2014 (Opal card).[28]

Convenience, variety and new packaging are themes in this Heinz soup ad, which is addressed to the time-pressed consumer (illustrating time poverty as a theme within food ads, as well as the application of new technology to product packaging and preparation, e.g. these microwaveable and portable soups for lunch at the office).

Courtesy of H.J. Heinz Company Limited.

Psychological time

The fluidity of time is important for marketers to understand, because we are more likely to be in a consuming mood at certain times rather than others. We can identify time categories in terms of when people are likely to be receptive to marketing messages:[29]

- *Flow time:* In a flow state we become so absorbed in an activity we notice nothing else. Not a good time to be hitting people with ads.
- *Occasion time:* Special moments when something monumental occurs, such as a birth or an important job interview. Ads clearly relevant to the situation will be given our undivided attention.
- *Deadline time:* When we are working against the clock. This is the worst time to catch someone's attention.
- *Leisure time:* During down time, we are more likely to notice ads and perhaps try new things.
- *Time to kill:* Waiting for something to happen, such as catching a plane or sitting in a waiting room. This is bonus time, where we feel we have the luxury to focus on extraneous things. As a result, we are more receptive to commercial messages, even for products we do not normally use.

Waiting time

The psychological dimension of time – how we actually experience it – is an important factor in **queuing theory**, the mathematical study of waiting lines. As we all know, our experience when we wait has a big effect on our evaluations of what we get at the end of the wait. Although we assume that something must be pretty good if we have to wait for it, the negative feelings that long waits arouse can quickly turn people off.[30] In a survey, NCR Corp found queuing at retail outlets was one of the most frustrating consumer experiences, followed by registering at clinics or hospitals, checking in at airports and ordering at fast-food restaurants. On average, consumers estimate that they spend more than two days per year waiting in a queue for service, and half believe they waste between 30 minutes and two hours each week in queues.[31] Marketers use various devices to minimise psychological waiting time. These techniques range from altering customers' perceptions of the length of a queue to providing distractions that divert attention from waiting.[32] Queuing theory must take cultural differences into account, because these affect how we behave while we are waiting. A Disney executive claims that Europeans exhibit different behaviours depending on their nationality. He notes that at the Disneyland Resort Paris, British visitors are orderly but the French and Italians 'never saw a line they couldn't be in front of'.[33]

Social time

Social time has been proposed as an important but overlooked time dimension in consumer behaviour.[34] Social time refers to the time in relation to social processes and rhythms and schedules in society. It takes into account how determined our lives are by interrelated temporal phenomena, such as working hours, opening hours, eating hours and other institutionalised schedules. To most Western consumers, time is something that is neatly compartmentalised: we wake up in the morning, go to school or work, come home, eat, go out, go to bed, then do it all over again. This perspective is called linear separable time (or Christian time): events proceed in an orderly sequence and different times are well defined: 'There's a time and a place for everything'. In this worldwide 'modernised' conception of time, there is a clear sense of past, present and future, and the present is preferred to the past, whereas the future is generally rated better than the present.[35]

Some products and services are believed to be appropriate for certain times and not for others. Some products crossing cultural borders are also crossing over from consumption at one time of day to another time of day. In its home country of Italy, the cappuccino is known as a breakfast coffee. Now it has become popular all over Europe, and in these new markets it is drunk at all times of the day whenever a plain cup of coffee would traditionally have been appropriate. So, the cappuccino has moved from a 'breakfast time' category to a more general 'coffee time' category.[36,37,38]

Marketing opportunity
Online shopping sees 30 per cent rise between midnight and 6am. . .

'Retail giant John Lewis says Britons don't care what time it is when they can grab a bargain. Britons are so addicted to shopping that many are glued to their smartphones when most of their neighbours are asleep – buying games consoles, Lego and pillows. A study of tens of thousands of purchases made at John Lewis. . . provides a barometer of changing trends and tastes. The most revealing finding is perhaps the 30 per cent increase in online shopping between the hours of midnight and 6am. Brisk trade in the wee hours reflects "the degree to which customers are always on", said John Lewis former managing director Andy Street. Some late-night bestsellers are predictable: nocturnal gamers press the button to buy new consoles, while sleep-deprived parents splash out on toys and equipment to keep their children entertained. Lego figurines and nursery paraphernalia are among the top sellers around 4am. "Shopping has become much more spread over the day because the internet means it is no longer fixed to when things are open", said Neil Saunders, retail analyst at Conlumino. "But what has also changed is the rise of the tablet. They are much more portable, so you are able to take them to bed in a way you would never have dreamed of doing with a laptop."'[39]

Source: © The Guardian

Shopping orientation

Consumers can also be segmented in terms of their **shopping orientation**, or general attitudes about shopping. These orientations may vary depending on the particular product categories and store types considered. Many people feel insecure about shopping for a car, but they may love to browse in bookshops. A shopper's motivation influences the type of shopping environment that will be attractive or annoying; for example, a person who wants to locate and buy something quickly may find loud music, bright colours or complex layouts distracting, whereas someone who is there to browse may enjoy the sensory stimulation.[40] Our feelings about shopping are also influenced by the culture in which we live. Several shopping types have been identified, although the following list does not cover the whole range of possibilities: the economic shopper; the personalised shopper; the ethical shopper; the apathetic shopper; and the recreational shopper.[41] One type of shopper is missing from this list: *the hate-to-shop shopper.* They are emerging from research on a variety of examples of the aversive side of shopping, including the hassle of finding a parking space, shopping with a girl- or boyfriend with completely different shopping motivations, dealing with the fact that just when you've made a purchase you find something better or less expensive, or coping with intruding 'Can-I-help-you?' sales assistants.[42]

Purchase environment

The shopping experience

Some people shop often, even though they do not necessarily intend to buy anything at all, whereas others have to be dragged to the shopping centre. Shopping is a way to acquire needed products and services, but social motives for shopping are also important. Retailers need to understand the variety of shopping motivations because these all affect how consumers evaluate different aspects of their retail experience, such as atmospherics, promotion and marketing communications.[43] One scholar has suggested that shopping activities have a lot to do with love and caring for significant others, to the extent that shopping can be seen as a person's (often the mother's) personal sacrifice of time and devotion for the well-being of the family.[44]

Other scholars distinguish between shopping as an activity performed for utilitarian (functional or tangible) or hedonic (pleasurable or intangible) reasons.[45] These different motives are illustrated by scale items used by researchers to assess people's underlying reasons for shopping. One item that measures hedonic value is: 'During the trip, I felt the excitement of the hunt'. When that type of sentiment is compared to a functionally related statement such as: 'I accomplished just what I wanted to on this shopping trip', the contrast between these two dimensions is clear.[46] European research identified the following hedonic shopping motives:[47]

- *Anticipated utility:* Desire for innovative products, expectations of benefits or hedonistic states that will be provided by the product to be acquired.
- *Role enactment:* Taking on the culturally prescribed roles regarding the conduct of shopping activity, such as careful product and price comparisons, possibly discussed with other shoppers.
- *Choice optimisation:* Desire to find absolutely the best buy.
- *Negotiation:* To seek economic advantages and sports-like pleasure through bargaining interactions with sellers in a 'bazaar atmosphere'.
- *Affiliation:* Shopping centres are a natural place to affiliate. The shopping arcade has become a central meeting place for teenagers. It also represents a controlled, secure environment for other groups, such as the elderly.

- *Power and authority:* Entering a power game with the sales personnel and maybe feeling superior to the personnel.
- *Stimulation:* Searching for new and interesting things offered in the marketplace – shopping just for fun.

But note research that examines 'the effects of various marketing promotions on consumers' purchases of hedonic *(that are typically motivated by the desire for fun and sensual pleasure, and often are frivolous or luxurious)* versus utilitarian (*that are typically motivated by basic needs and often are practical or necessary)* products. . . Where the authors propose that non-quantity based promotions such as price discounts, rebates, coupons and loyalty rewards have a stronger positive effect on hedonic purchases than on utilitarian purchases, based on the notion that it is more difficult to justify hedonic consumption rather than utilitarian consumption, and that promotions provide a guilt-reducing justification for the acquisition of hedonic items. On the other hand, quantity-based promotions (buy three, get 30 per cent off) that require purchasing *additional units* of the hedonic product are not effective in justifying their purchase. It finds that quantity promotions are not as effective as price discounts for hedonic products, compared to utilitarian products. . . [because] . . . once consumers decide to purchase a luxury or hedonic product, they do not need a purchase justification, and a price promotion may simply weaken the product's perceived luxuriousness and status signal.'[48]

Social and physical surroundings

A consumer's physical and social environment can make a big difference in affecting their motives for product purchase. Important cues include the number and type of other consumers, as well as dimensions of the physical environment. Decor, smells (the use of scents in the retail environment can increase the pleasure and hedonic values derived from shopping)[49] and even temperature can significantly influence consumption.

In addition to physical cues, many of a consumer's purchase decisions are significantly affected by the groups or social settings in which these occur (as we shall see in Chapter 9). In some cases, the presence or absence of **co-consumers**, the other patrons in a setting, can be a determinant attribute (see the discussion in Chapter 8) and function as a product attribute, as when an exclusive resort or boutique promises to provide privacy to privileged customers. At other times, the presence of others can have positive value. A sparsely attended football match or an empty bar, in contrast, can be depressing sights.

The presence of large numbers of people in a consumer environment increases arousal levels, so a consumer's subjective experience of a setting tends to be more intense. This polarisation can be both positive and negative. While the experience of other people creates a state of arousal, the consumer's actual experience depends on their *interpretation of* and *reaction to* this arousal. Crowding may result in avoidance (leaving the store earlier), aggressiveness (rushing others), opportunism (using the extra time to find bargains) or self-blame (for coming into the store at the wrong hour).[50] It is important, therefore, to distinguish between *density* and *crowding.* Density refers to the actual number of people occupying a space, while the psychological state of crowding exists only if a negative affective state occurs as a result of this density.[51] For example, 100 students packed into a classroom designed for 75 may result in an unpleasant situation for all concerned, but the same number of people jammed together at a party occupying a room of the same size might just make for a great party.

In addition, the *type* of consumers who patronise a store or service can serve as a store attribute; and the *type* of consumers who use a product can influence evaluations. We may infer something about a store by examining its customers. For this reason, some restaurants require men to wear a jacket for dinner, and bouncers at some 'hot' nightspots hand-pick patrons from the queue based on whether they have the right 'look' for the club. Royal Ascot tightened up the dress code for its race meetings, banning the wearing of fascinators[52] from the Royal Enclosure, and announcing that all women's hats have to be 4 inches (10 cm) in diameter at the base, and banning strapless dresses; for men, waistcoats and ties are compulsory and the wearing of cravats is banned.[53]

Marketing opportunity
Grocery watchdog hails improvement as Aldi holds top spot

'Britain's supermarkets are treating their suppliers better, according to the UK's Grocery Code Adjudicator, as its fifth annual survey showed fewer of them are flagging serious problems with major retailers. Discounter Aldi came top of the GCA's annual survey of more than a thousand suppliers for a fifth consecutive year, with Tesco in second place and Waitrose in third. "The cornerstone of our success in the UK has been the long-term partnerships forged with suppliers", said Julie Ashfield, managing director of buying at Aldi. "We have engaged in honest dialogue with suppliers to give them clarity and stability in their dealing with us", she added. Industry observers said the German company tends to negotiate longer-term supply agreements with relatively few unplanned promotions, giving suppliers greater certainty over terms. Christine Tacon, the adjudicator, said: "My 2018 survey tells a very positive story and it is no coincidence that the four most-improved retailers this year have each faced increased scrutiny and heightened levels of GCA engagement through investigations and case studies." Tesco, the most improved retailer, was in 2016 found to have delayed payments to suppliers in order to flatter its own financial performance, while the Co-operative Group – Ms Tacon's former employer – was placed under investigation in March over delisting products and changes to quality control procedures. Sainsbury's slipped from second to fourth in the rankings, while Asda, the company it plans to take over, was third from bottom. In comments before a select committee last week, Sainsbury's chief executive Mike Coupe said that the objective would be "to bring standards of both businesses up to the best". Sainsbury's pays 97 per cent of its suppliers on time, but Asda generally has shorter payment terms. "If it is possible we will equalise those things", he added.'[54]

Aldi and Lidl have both become increasingly popular grocery outlets on the UK high street since the 2008 recession saw a major change in UK grocery shopping habits, which included a move away from Tesco and Sainsbury's. Some of Aldi's secrets for success in keeping prices low are described below.

Marketing opportunity
Aldi insider reveals 12 reasons why prices are so cheap – and it's fascinating

'Discounter Aldi has been crowned Britain's best supermarket[55] at a prestigious awards ceremony. The grocer, famed for its cut-price wines and cheap fruit and veg, fought off stiff competition from the likes of Lidl and the "big four" – to be crowned the nation's number one. . . Today, it attracts millions of shoppers each week. But have you ever wondered how Aldi is able to keep its prices so low?

1 Smaller choice = bigger discounts

"Most of our stores will have a maximum of 2,000 carefully curated products depending on the time of year", said communications director Mary Dunn. "At other supermarkets, you can expect to find 40,000 products."

2 Super-fast checkout tills

"The supermarket is famed for its incredibly efficient checkouts . . . There are multiple barcodes wrapped around every product sold in Aldi, which equates to faster checkout times."

3 Staff muck in with all jobs on the shop floor

"Many supermarkets have around 100 employees but we only have 30 to 40 in each store", said

Mary. . . "So a member of staff might be filling up carrier bags at the till, then jump on the till when people are waiting, close it when they're not and start cleaning. . . Everyone mucks in and does everything."

4 Shelf-ready packaging

All of its products arrive in shelf-ready packaging. . . which means it can be taken directly from the lorry onto the shelf. "It takes 30 seconds to change a pallet, which will include 198 products. This means we don't need 100 members of staff on the shop floor."

5 No loyalty cards or BOGOFs

It doesn't really offer typical discounts. "There are no loyalty cards or 'buy-one-get-one-free' deals at Aldi. Instead, Aldi offers 'Special Buys' on anything from electricals and clothes to gel nails and toys every Thursday and Sunday."

6 Super-organised lorries

Just like the packaging, everything is ordered on the lorry to go into certain sections of the store – again to save time.

7 Limited warehouse space

Most items can be found on the shop floor.

8 No mega-stores

"You'll not find an Aldi mega store – it goes against the Aldi business plan, which is to stock a limited number of products and have a smaller number of employees to keep the costs down for customers."

9 95 per cent own-label brands

Most of the products on offer are part of its own-brand range. Unlike other supermarkets, most of what is sold at Aldi is its own stock.

10 No clearance section

Ever wondered why there's not a clearance section full of items close to their best-before date in Aldi? "Wastage is limited – that's one of our KPIs (key performance indicators)", said Mary.

11 No grocery home deliveries

Aldi stores are DIY only. Aldi is one of the few supermarkets that doesn't offer home delivery on its groceries. . . "No-one does home delivery in a cost-efficient way", said Mary.

12 No staff discounts

"There are no staff discounts as this would impact on the price for customers", said Mary. "We offer the market-leading rates for pay and benefits."[56]

And yet, just to illustrate how dynamic and challenging the retail space is, particularly in the UK food sector, Tesco is already seeking innovations to restore its market-leading place. 'Tesco is trialling new "shop-and-go" technology that allows customers to scan and pay for their groceries on their smartphone and then walk out of the store without visiting a till. . . Tesco has installed the app, Scan Pay Go, on the mobiles of 100 staff who are able to use it to scan barcodes and then pay for their shopping. Traditional bricks-and-mortar retailers are investing in new technology as they try to keep pace with online rival Amazon, which opened an automated convenience store in the US earlier this year. The Co-op has already introduced pay-in-the aisle technology, while Sainsbury's tested a similar app in 2017.'[57]

Trends in the purchase environment

We see bumper stickers and T-shirts everywhere with the slogans 'Shop 'til you drop', 'When the going gets tough, the tough go shopping' and 'Born to shop'. Like it or not, shopping is a major activity for many consumers. However, the competition for shoppers among retailers is getting tougher. Retailers must now offer something extra to lure shoppers, whether that something is excitement or, increasingly, just plain bargains.[58]

In order to be able to compete in the European single market, many retail chains have undergone an internationalisation process. The ten biggest companies controlled 30 per cent of the turnover in daily goods in Europe in the mid to late 1990s, and the concentration was growing fast at the end of the 1990s. In 2016 the German-owned Schwarz emerged as the top European food retailer, with Tesco (UK) in second place (although its sales figures included fuel sales) and Carrefour (France) in third place.[59]

Store loyalty

Faced with a turbulent retailing environment, including economic recession, retailers highly value store-loyal consumers. Consumers now have an abundance of choices regarding where to shop, including electronic alternatives, which have proved particularly attractive in the economic downturn. People tend not to be as store-loyal as they once were.[60] Research suggests that loyalty programmes, properly designed and targeted, can serve five goals: 'keep customers from defecting; win greater share of wallet; prompt customers to make additional purchases; yield insights into customer behaviour; and help turn a profit'.[61] 'Levers of loyalty' were identified as: first, the divisibility of rewards (i.e. redeemable points divided into attractive-size clusters, such as two lots of 5,000 points rather than one set of 10,000 points); second, a sense of momentum for the members in the nature of rewards (more hedonic than utilitarian in emphasis); third, expansion of relationship (by encouraging the customer to buy more *different* products rather than simply more of the same product); and fourth, combined-currency flexibility (i.e. spending the alternative currencies represented by points such as air miles in smaller amounts in combination with cash purchase of an air ticket is more attractive than spending a lot of air miles in one go).[62] However, the same researchers warn of the dangers of designing schemes that reward the disloyal, reward volume over profit, give too much away in terms of profit margin and promise more than can be delivered.[63] A study of customer relationships in the Swedish superstore Gekås Ullared[64] identified the importance for customer relationships of both product features (e.g. price, assortment, availability) and also service (e.g. attitude of staff), along with aspects of the physical environment.[65] As marketing executives from Forrester argue: 'Consumers have come to rely on a plethora of channels, devices and touchpoints to guide them through their purchase decisions. This path to purchase has broken free from the linear conception of the traditional marketing funnel and is becoming increasingly difficult to anticipate. By following consumers in each phase of Forrester's customer life cycle – discover, explore, buy, use, ask, and engage – marketers can better understand what specific motivations, objectives, and preferences at each touchpoint will take consumers closer to their purchase decisions.'[66]

E-commerce: clicks *vs* bricks

As more and more websites pop up to sell everything from fridge magnets to cars, marketers continue to debate how this **cyberspace** marketplace in the online world will affect how they conduct business.[67] Will e-commerce replace traditional retailing, or learn to work in concert with it? Consumers worldwide spend about $1.5 trillion per year on e-commerce sites.[68] Analysts predict that soon about a quarter of these transactions will occur on a mobile device. Already, about three-quarters of the world's population has access to a mobile phone and users download about 30 billion apps in a year.[69] We're even more likely to use devices such as tablets when we're in the mood to shop. Their bigger screens make it easier to browse items, and are often even more efficient than computers because shoppers can zoom in or drag items to their carts with their fingers.[70] That helps to explain why, in recent years, people have purchased even more merchandise from tablets than they have from phones (or from the newer so-called **phablets**, which are a hybrid of a phone and a tablet). Tablets are diffused throughout the household as parents use tablets to keep their children entertained. 'One-in-three children aged between five and fifteen years old. . . have their own device. . . and 11% of three- to four-year-olds have one of their own.'[71]

In the year 2000, only 9 per cent of consumers wanted to buy food online (and a mere 1 per cent had actually tried it), and even the highest-scoring purchase product types such as travel and ticket purchases did not exceed 30 per cent at that point.[72] However, the last couple of decades has seen e-commerce take off globally, so that the e-market is increasingly important but with some marked variations across EU countries, as illustrated in Figure 2.3.

There will be over 18 million iPad users in the UK by 2019, up from 9.5 million in 2012, illustrating the growth potential for mobile marketing.

javi_indy/Shutterstock

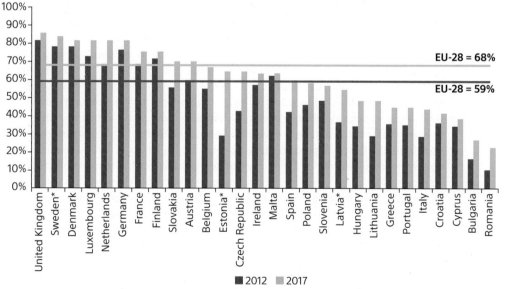

EU-28 = 68%

EU-28 = 59%

■ 2012   ■ 2017

(*) Estonia, Latvia and Sweden data for 2012 is not comparable to 2017 due to a change in the survey methodology.

Figure 2.3 EU individuals having ordered/bought goods or services over the internet (as at December 2017)

Source: Eurostat, Date of extraction: 12 March 2018 © European Union, Eurostat Tables, Graphs and Maps interface, http://ec.europa.eu/eurostat/statistics-explained/images/3/3e/Internet_users_who_bought_or_ordered_goods_or_services_for_private_use_in_the_previous_12_months%2C_2012_and_2017_%28%25_of_internet_users%29.png (accessed 27 July 2018)

Marketing opportunity

E-commerce statistics for individuals: 68 per cent of internet users in the EU shopped online in 2017

'Almost 7 out of 10 internet users in the 12 months prior to the [2017] survey (hereafter referred as "internet users") made online purchases in the same period. Overall, the share of e-shoppers in internet users is growing, with the highest proportions being found in the 16–24 and 25–54 age groups (71% each). The proportion of e-shoppers varied considerably across the EU, ranging from 23% of internet users in Romania to 86% in the UK. The most popular type of goods and services purchased online in the EU was clothes and sports goods (64% of e-buyers), followed by travel and holiday accommodation (53%). E-shoppers aged 16–24 were the top age group when it came to clothes and sports goods purchases (71%), those aged 25–54 in buying household goods (50%) and the older age group (55–74) in online purchases of travel and holiday accommodation (57%). In terms of frequency, the highest proportion of e-shoppers made purchases in the three months prior to the survey once or twice (35%) and the same proportion did so three to five times. In terms of amount spent, the highest proportion of e-buyers (40%) bought goods or services for a total of €100–499. . . Gender, age, level of education and employment situation all affect e-commerce activity. For men, the share of online shoppers among internet users was slightly higher than for women (69 and 66%, respectively), while people aged 25–34 are more active e-shoppers (77% of internet users) than other age groups. The proportion of internet users with a higher level of education shopping online (more than eight in 10) is 35 percentage points greater than that of internet users with lower education. Employees and the self-employed (73% of internet users) and students (70%) shop online far more than retired/inactive or unemployed people (54 and 52% respectively).'[73]

Research has shown an important distinction between online and offline shopping for food in terms of consumer responses. 'Consumers' shopping baskets contain relatively fewer vices (attractive but unhealthy products) when they shop in an online, versus offline, environment because of the difference in products' presentation in the two contexts. During online shopping, products are presented symbolically (i.e. using pictures), whereas an offline, bricks-and-mortar store presents products physically. The physical presentation (*vs.* symbolic) increases the vividness of products, whereas the symbolic product presentation in online stores induces sensory distance, making it harder for consumers to imagine the gratification they will get from consuming the product. Because consumers anticipate less gratification from symbolic, less vivid product presentations, they purchase relatively fewer vices in an online shopping environment than in an offline grocery store. In terms of practical implications for consumers, the findings suggest that simply changing the shopping channel used to buy groceries might aid them to decrease their purchases of unhealthy food products. For retailers, by raising consumers' awareness of online shopping, minimizing order lead times and overcoming risk perceptions, retailers might persuade and stimulate consumers to frequent their online stores, while nudging them to adopt healthier purchase patterns.'[74]

Marketers continue to debate how the online world affects their business in the face of the increasing number of websites. In particular, many lose sleep as they wonder whether e-commerce will replace traditional retailing, work in concert with it, or perhaps even fade away. Still, the rising availability of comparison shopping phone apps does threaten the existence of many retailers as consumers engage in what they call 'showrooming'. This means that a shopper visits a store such as Best Buy to explore options for big-ticket items like TVs or appliances, and then he or she finds a cheaper price for the specific model online.

For marketers, therefore, the growth of online commerce is a sword that cuts both ways: on the one hand, they can reach customers around the world even if they are physically located 100 miles from nowhere. On the other hand, their competition now comes not only from the shop across the street, but from thousands of websites spanning the globe. A second problem is that offering products directly to consumers has the potential to cut out the middleman – the loyal store-based retailers who carry the firm's products and who sell them at a marked-up price.[75] The 'clicks *vs* bricks' dilemma continues to rage in the marketing world, with some significant victims – for example, the UK's House of Fraser department store group.

Marketing pitfall
Era ends as House of Fraser to axe 31 stores and 6,000 jobs

'The closures [of 31 out of 59 stores] are a fresh blow to the UK's high streets, which are shedding stores and jobs at a faster rate than during the recession in 2009. Property experts calculate that 1m sq metres of store space has been dumped by retailers this year, which is more than in 2016 when the 160-store BHS chain went into administration.[76]

This trend is writ even larger in the US, with analysts predicting another record-breaking year of store closures as the collapsed Toys R Us chain and struggling Sears group beat a retreat. This is on top of a dire 2017, when a staggering 9.75m sq metres of retail space was closed in America as struggling main street veterans,[77] such as Macy's,[78] found themselves on the ropes.

When House of Fraser announced the plan this month [June 2018][79] its chair, Frank Slevin, gave a stark assessment of the 169-year old department store chain's predicament: "Our legacy store estate has created an unsustainable cost base which, without restructuring, presents an existential threat to the business."

The shadow cast by the digital high street is getting ever bigger. Last year one in every five pounds Britons spent on shopping was online, with the biggest shifts in clothing and footwear. Analysts at Retail Economics consultancy firm predict 50% of clothing and household goods will be bought online within a decade, double the current level.

The group of stores being closed by House of Fraser includes outlets in major cities such as London, Birmingham, Edinburgh and Cardiff, but others are dotted around the country in places such as Darlington, Shrewsbury and Carlisle. These once-grand stores are left over from a golden age when every major regional town and city could support its own independent department store. . .

"This is legacy space from a time when you were able to successfully trade a three- or four-storey shop in a medium-sized town", said Dan Simms, co-head of retail agency at Colliers International.

"With department stores you have to shovel a lot of money in to get money out. . . stores at the top end like Selfridges and Harvey Nichols are managing to do this."

"The department store is not necessarily a doomed format, it has just become stale", said Richard Lim, the chief executive of Retail Economics.

"They are incredibly expensive to operate and scale is a hindrance when you are trying to turn a business around. House of Fraser has got a mountain of debt so it doesn't have the money to innovate and refresh its stores."'[80]

Source: © 2018 Guardian News and Media Limited or its affiliated companies. All rights reserved.

One marketing opportunity, increasingly employed by European retailers, is click and collect – a multichannel strategy that allows companies to maximise the potential of both their online and offline retail offerings. Customers use the companies' websites to search for, order and pay for items (thus the 'click'), and then go to the retail branch in the local shopping mall or high street to collect the item (this saves a lot of the hassle that consumers have experienced in waiting around for the delivery of goods).

Table 2.1 Pros and cons of e-commerce

Benefits of e-commerce	Limitations of e-commerce
For the consumer	**For the consumer**
Shop 24 hours a day	Lack of security
Less travelling	Fraud
Can receive relevant information in seconds from any location	Can't touch items
More choice of products	Exact colours may not reproduce on computer monitors
More products available to less-developed countries	Expensive to order and then return
Greater price information	Potential breakdown of human relationships
Lower prices so that less affluent can purchase	
Participate in virtual auctions	
Fast delivery	
Electronic communities	
For the marketer	**For the marketer**
The world is the marketplace	Lack of security
Decreases costs of doing business	Must maintain site to reap benefits
Very specialised businesses can be successful	Fierce price competition
Real-time pricing	Conflicts with conventional retailers
	Legal issues not resolved

Source: Adapted from Michael R. Solomon and Elnora W. Stuart, *Welcome to Marketing.Com: The Brave New World of E-Commerce* (Englewood Cliffs, NJ: Prentice Hall, 2001).

Servicescapes: retailing as theatre

Shopping can no longer be regarded as a simple act of purchasing.[101] A retail culture has arisen,[102] where the act of shopping has taken on new entertainment and/or experiential dimensions as retailers compete for customers' attention, not to mention their loyalty. The act of shopping ties into a number of central existential aspects of human life, such as sexuality.[103] Furthermore, the customer may be regarded not as a passive recipient of the offerings of the purchase environment, but rather as an active co-creator of this very environment and the meanings attached to it,[104] in a situation analogous to the focus among 'market mavens' (see Chapter 9) on flexibility in the area of product supply and tailor-made marketing mixes for the individual consumer.[105] One of the most obvious trends in the retailing sector in Europe was the construction of shopping centres, often modelled on American prototypes, which often bring with them a whole new combination of leisure activities, shopping and social encounters in safe environments.[106]

Shopping centres have tried to gain the loyalty of shoppers by appealing to their social motives as well as providing access to desired goods. It is now typical to find such features as children's rides and climbing walls in a suburban shopping centre. The importance of creating a positive, vibrant and interesting image has led innovative marketers to blur the line between shopping and the theatre. Shopping centres and individual stores have to create environments that stimulate people and allow them to shop and be entertained at the same time.[107]

Hard Rock Café: one of the oldest and most well-established themed consumer environments.
Gerard Ferry/Alamy Stock Photo

However, new trends in shopping suggest a movement of consumers away from these out-of-town shopping experiences as online shopping continues to change patterns of consumer behaviour and retail patronage.

The first department stores in Europe can be seen as marking the introduction of a modern consumer culture, nourished by dreams of abundance.[108] In Dublin, the Powerscourt Townhouse Centre has succeeded in merging a variety of styles and features, including a grand piano on a stage in the central hall, to make a sort of new version of a Victorian marketplace atmosphere. Unlike the Mall of America, it does not appear as a carefully planned environment, but rather a happy blend of many consumption opportunities including an Italian restaurant, a modern hairstylist and an antique shop, all in a stylish classical setting.[109]

The quest to entertain means that many stores are going all-out to create imaginative environments that transport shoppers to fantasy worlds or provide other kinds of stimulation. This strategy is called **retail theming**. Innovative merchants today use four basic kinds of theming techniques:

1 *Landscape themes* rely upon associations with images of nature, earth, animals and the physical body.

2 *Marketscape themes* build upon associations with man-made places. An example is the Venetian Hotel in Las Vegas that lavishly recreates parts of the Italian city.

3 *Cyberspace themes* are built around images of information and communications technology. eBay's retail interface instils a sense of community among its vendors and traders.

4 *Mindscape themes* draw upon abstract ideas and concepts, introspection and fantasy, and often possess spiritual overtones. At the Seibu store in Tokyo, shoppers enter as neophytes at the first level. As they progress through the physical levels of the store each is themed to connote increasing levels of consciousness until they emerge at the summit as completed shoppers.[110]

Consumer behaviour as I see it . . .

Children and their favourite stores

Professor Stefania Borghini (Bocconi University, Milan)

'Marketing managers and retailers consider children important market targets. According to McNeal,[111] children combine three markets into one. They are a primary market that spends its own savings and allowances, they are powerful influencers on parental spending and, finally, they embody a future market of potential adults. In recent years, managers, researchers and policy makers have increasingly focused on children because of their significant impact on family decision-making and shopping experiences.

We have to take several factors into account in order to fully understand children's behaviour in retail settings. Research has tended to be scarce because of the ethical limitations on collecting data from this group of young consumers and, therefore, any information that becomes available is usually considered to be really significant. I briefly outline below some of the crucial empirical evidence that has been collected more recently about children's behavioural patterns in retail settings.

Favourite store for a child aged 8

Generally speaking, we know that the pre-purchase affective state can be salient.[112] We can also say that both children's affective state and their behaviour have a strong impact on the purchasing decisions made by the parent-child dyad in stores. Both the child's developmental stage and the type of store can also impact a child's interaction with commercial settings, as well as children's ability to develop constructive bonds with a retail site or shopping centre. We can see that stores are typical places where young children exert their "pester power". Parents therefore sometimes avoid shopping for food with their children because they find it a stressful and exhausting experience.[113] Parents have a preference for commercial settings where children can move around freely.[114]

Shopping particularly appeals to teenagers – especially girls – who spend the most time in shopping districts with their friends and peers and mothers, thoroughly enjoying themselves. For instance, girls aged 12–19 believe that shopping centres or malls offer multiple forms of benefits, including comfort, safety, accessibility, a pleasant atmosphere and a good retail mix.[115] Groups of female friends, or mothers and daughters, create memories, gender and family identities by shopping together and sharing joint purchasing experiences.[116]

A recent study carried out in Italy on children's perceptions of store design[117] reported that kids have quite sophisticated ideas about store layout and merchandising. Interviewed about their ideal stores, 200 boys and girls aged 8–11 years revealed very nuanced opinions about the potential influence of store design. A semiotic analysis of layouts confirmed that they are highly aware of the variety of commercial settings, and the related functional and architectural elements. Boys and girls envision and desire safe colourful places without adults where they can be the main actors, both sellers and buyers, addressing their personal interests. In such places they dream, learn and nurture their curiosity – in other words, they express themselves. This child's picture visualizes a place organized into different display areas for toys, chocolate, the internet, videos and also an area for reading and relaxing.'

Questions

Can you identify retail spaces that can be considered child-friendly? Which are, according to you, the features and design elements that make them suitable for this specific target audience? Please relate them to specific benefits (physical and psychological) for children and their families.

Stefania Borghini

A vintage pop-up market in Brick Lane, East London

Photograph by Oli Scarff/Getty Images.

Cutting-edge retailers are figuring out that they need to convert a store into a **being space** that resembles a commercial living room, where we can go to relax, be entertained, hang out with friends, escape the everyday or even learn. When you think of being spaces, Starbucks will probably come to mind. The coffee chain's stated goal is to become our 'third place', where we spend the bulk of our time in addition to home and work. Starbucks led the way when it fitted out its stores with comfy chairs and Wi-Fi. But there are many other marketers who are meeting our needs for exciting commercial spaces – no matter what those needs are.

Pop-up stores are appearing in many forms around the world. Typically, these are makeshift installations that do business only for a few days or weeks, and then disappear.

Spectacular consumption environments represent another example of servicescapes, where the emphasis is on *play,* and the co-creation of the experience by the producer and the consumer. Research within a themed retail environment, the ESPN Zone Chicago, examined the agency of the consumer in this type of environment and how the use of technology affected consumers' sense of reality. Consumers seemed to exercise creative control over the spectacular environment by using technology and their bodies to produce parts of the spectacle, and to create and alter space, suggesting a dialectical relationship between producers and consumers.[118] However, an alternative view of retail spaces from other research suggests that consumers also have bonds with what the researchers term 'ordinary places, i.e. small, informally branded or unthemed stores or restaurants' and these can often constitute consumers' favourite commercial spaces.[119]

Store image

With so many stores competing for customers, how do consumers select one over another? Like products, we can think of stores as having 'personalities'. Some stores have very clearly defined images (either good or bad). Others tend to blend into the crowd. They may not have anything distinctive about them and may be overlooked for that reason. This personality, or **store image**, is composed of many different factors. The design and general image of the store is central to the perception of the goods displayed there, whether we are talking about fashion,[120] food products[121] or any other type of good. Store features, coupled with such consumer characteristics as shopping orientation, help to predict which shopping outlets people will prefer.[122] Some of the important dimensions of a store's profile are location, merchandise suitability and the knowledge and congeniality of the sales staff.[123]

These features typically work together to create an overall impression. When shoppers think about stores, they may not say, 'Well, that place is fairly good in terms of convenience, the salespeople are acceptable and services are good'. They are more likely to say, 'That place gives me the creeps', or 'I always enjoy shopping there'. Consumers evaluate stores in terms of both their specific attributes *and* a global evaluation, or the **store gestalt** (see Chapter 3).[124] This overall feeling may have more to do with such intangibles as interior design and the types of people one finds in the store than with aspects such as returns policies or credit availability. As a result, some stores are likely to be consistently in consumers' evoked sets (see Chapter 8), whereas others will never be considered.[125]

Atmospherics

Retailers want you to come in – and stay. Careful store design increases the amount of space the shopper covers, and stimulating displays keep them in the aisles longer. This 'kerb appeal' translates directly to the bottom line. For example, researchers tracked grocery shoppers' movements by plotting the position of their mobile phones as they moved about a store; they found that when people lingered just 1 per cent longer, sales rose by 1.3 per cent.

Of course, grocers know a lot of tricks after years of observing shoppers. For example, they call the area just inside a supermarket's entrance the 'decompression zone'. People tend to slow down and take stock of their surroundings when they enter the store, so store designers use this space to promote bargains rather than to sell. Once they get a serious start, the first thing shoppers encounter is the produce section. Fruits and vegetables can easily be damaged, so it would be more logical to buy these items at the end of a shopping trip. But fresh, wholesome food makes people feel good (and righteous) so they're less guilty when they throw the crisps and biscuits into the shopping trolley later.[126]

Because a store's image is now recognised as a very important aspect of the retailing mix, store designers pay a lot of attention to **atmospherics**, or the 'conscious designing of space and its various dimensions to evoke certain effects in buyers'.[127] These dimensions include colours, scents and sounds. For any store or any shopping centre, one may think of this process as a careful *orchestration* of the various elements, each playing its part to form a whole.[128] A store's atmosphere, in turn, affects what we buy. In one study, researchers who asked shoppers how much pleasure they were feeling five minutes after they entered a store predicted the amount of time and money they spent there.[129] To boost the entertainment value of shopping (and to lure online shoppers back to bricks-and-mortar stores), some retailers now offer **activity stores** that let consumers participate in the production of the products or services they buy there.

Many elements of store design can be cleverly controlled to attract customers and produce desired effects on consumers. Light colours impart a feeling of spaciousness and serenity, and signs in bright colours create excitement. One study found that brighter in-store lighting influenced people to examine and handle more merchandise.[130]

In addition to visual stimuli, all sorts of cues can influence behaviours.[131] For example, music can affect eating habits. A study found that diners who listened to loud, fast music ate more food. In contrast, those who listened to Mozart or Brahms ate less and more slowly. The researchers concluded that diners who choose soothing music at mealtimes can increase weight loss by at least five pounds a month![132] Classical music can have a positive effect on consumers' evaluation of store atmosphere.[133]

In-store decision-making

Despite all their efforts to 'pre-sell' consumers through advertising, marketers are increasingly recognising the significant degree to which many purchases are strongly influenced by the store environment. Women tell researchers, for example, that store displays are one of the major information sources they use to decide what clothing to buy.[134] A Danish survey indicated that nine out of ten customers did not plan the purchase of at least one-third of the goods they acquired.[135] The proportion of unplanned purchases is even higher for other product categories such as food – it is estimated that about two out of every three supermarket purchases are decided in the aisles. And people with lists are just as likely to make spontaneous purchases as those without them.[136] Research evidence indicates that consumers have **mental budgets** for grocery trips that are typically composed of both an itemised portion and *in-store slack*. This means they typically decide beforehand on an amount they plan to spend, but then they have an additional amount in mind (slack) they are willing to spend on unplanned purchases – if they come across any they really want to have.[137] Here are some 'tricks of the trade':

- Sell sweets at eye level, midway along aisles, where shoppers' attention lingers longest.
- Use the ends of aisles to generate big revenues – endcap displays account for 45 per cent of soft-drink sales.
- Use free-standing displays toward the rear of the supermarket and on the left-hand side of aisles. Shoppers tend to move through a store in a counterclockwise direction and they are more likely to choose items from shelves to their left.
- Sprinkle the same product throughout the store, rather than grouping it in one spot, to boost sales through repetitive exposure.

- Group ingredients for a meal in one spot.
- Post health-related information on kiosks and shelf tags to link groceries to good health in shoppers' minds – even though only 23 per cent of them say they always look for nutritional information on labels.[138]

New media and technology in the retail scene

Mobile shopping apps on smartphones provide imaginative new ways for retailers to guide shoppers through the experience, as they do everything from locating merchandise to identifying the nearest restroom in a shopping centre, or looking for bargains. Some help you remember where you parked your car; others actually provide reward points when you visit certain stores. The apps also promise to provide a solution to the major hassles that drive consumers away from bricks-and-mortar stores, especially long check-out times and incompetent sales assistants. Some research indicates that when shoppers use in-store mobile technology their behaviour changes. Shoppers buy more unplanned items and also concentrate less on the information they find in the store. Ironically, if they talk on their phones while they shop they are less likely to buy items they planned to purchase and actually spend less because they are distracted.[139]

Other technology that has already arrived or is on the horizon includes: [140]

- **Augmented reality (AR)** superimposes a layer of digital information over a physical environment. AR apps such as Blippar allow the shopper to access additional information from product packages. For example, a woman who buys a Maybelline cosmetic product could hold her phone over the box to bring up a model who shares tips about how to apply makeup.
- **Virtual reality (VR)** is a computer-simulated interface that creates the impression that the user is physically present. In contrast to AR, VR substitutes a completely different sensory experience for the user. The UK-based Tesco grocery chain launched a virtual supermarket in Germany that allows shoppers to navigate a store in a 360-degree virtual environment, and the Marriott hotel chains offers a '4D Teleporter' that transports guests to exotic locales (at least virtually). The experience includes sensory inputs such as the sun on your face, wind in your hair, ground rumbling and sea spray hitting your skin.

Marketers are scrambling to engineer purchasing environments in order to increase the likelihood that they will be in contact with consumers at the exact time they make a decision.

Spontaneous shopping

When a shopper is prompted to buy something in a shop, one of two different processes may be at work:

- **unplanned buying** may occur when a person is unfamiliar with a store's layout or perhaps when under some time pressure; or, a person may be reminded to buy something by seeing it on a store shelf. About one-third of unplanned buying has been attributed to the recognition of new needs while within the store.[141]
- **impulse buying,** in contrast, occurs when the person experiences a sudden urge that they cannot resist.

For this reason, so-called impulse items such as sweets and chewing gum are conveniently placed near the checkout. Similarly, many supermarkets have installed wider aisles to encourage browsing, and the widest tend to contain products with the highest margin.

Low mark-up items that are purchased regularly tend to be stacked high in narrower aisles, to allow shopping trolleys to speed through.[142]

One particular type of occasion where a lot of impulse buying goes on is in the seasonal sales, which appeal especially to younger and price-conscious shoppers according to one British study.[143] In general, shoppers can be categorised in terms of how much advance planning they do. *Planners* tend to know what products and specific brands they will buy beforehand, *partial planners* know they need certain products but do not decide on specific brands until they are in the store, and *impulse purchasers* do no advance planning whatsoever.[144]

Point-of-purchase stimuli

Because so much decision-making apparently occurs while the shopper is in the purchasing environment, retailers are beginning to pay more attention to the amount of information in their stores, as well as to the way it is presented. It has been estimated that impulse purchases increase by 10 per cent when appropriate displays are used. Consumers' images of good-value-for-money purchases are in many cases induced not by careful price examinations but by powerful and striking in-store information.[145] That explains why US companies spend about $19 billion each year on **point-of-purchase (POP) stimuli**.[146] A POP can be an elaborate product display or demonstration, a coupon-dispensing machine, or someone giving out free samples of a new perfume in the cosmetics aisles. Research indicates that European consumers respond more positively to spray samplers than to vials and plugs in the promotion campaign for a fragrance.[147] Winning over consumers in the store with packaging and displays is regarded as 'the first moment of truth'.[148]

Much of the growth in point-of-purchase activity has been in new electronic technologies.[149] Videotronic, a German hardware producer, has specialised in compact in-store video displays, of which the latest feature is a touch-screen selection with various pieces of information that eventually provoke scent to be produced.[150] Some shopping trolleys have a small screen that displays advertising, which is keyed to the specific areas of the store through which the trolley is wheeled.[151] New interactive possibilities seem to enhance the effectiveness of POP information systems,[152] although the effect of in-store advertising and other POP continues to be difficult to assess. In-store *displays* are another commonly used device to attract attention in the store environment. While most displays consist of simple racks that dispense the product and/or related coupons, some highlight the value of regarding retailing as theatre by supplying the 'audience' with elaborate performances and scenery.

The salesperson: a lead role in the play

2.3

A salesperson is often the crucial connection to a purchase.

One of the most important in-store factors is the salesperson, who attempts to influence the buying behaviour of the customer.[153] This influence can be understood in terms of **exchange theory**, which stresses that every interaction involves an exchange of value; each participant gives something to the other and hopes to receive something in return.[154]

What 'value' does the customer look for in a sales interaction? There are a variety of resources a salesperson might offer. For example, they might offer expertise about the product to make the shopper's choice easier. Alternatively, the customer may be reassured because the salesperson is an admired or likeable person whose tastes are similar and who is seen as someone who can be trusted.[155] A long stream of research attests to the impact of a salesperson's appearance on sales effectiveness. In sales, as in much of life, attractive people appear to hold the upper hand.[156] In addition, it's not unusual for service personnel and customers to form fairly warm personal relationships; these have been termed *commercial* friendships (think of all those patient bartenders who double as therapists for many people). Researchers have found that commercial friendships are similar to other friendships in that they can involve affection, intimacy, social support, loyalty and reciprocal gift-giving. They also work to support marketing objectives such as satisfaction, loyalty and positive word of mouth.[157]

A buyer/seller situation is like many other dyadic (two-person group) encounters: it is a relationship where some agreement must be reached about the roles of each participant, when a process of *identity negotiation* occurs.[158] For example, if the salesperson immediately establishes him/herself as an expert, they are likely to have more influence over the customer through the course of the relationship. Some of the factors that help to determine a salesperson's role (and relative effectiveness) are their age, appearance, educational level and motivation to sell.[159] Another variable is similarity between the seller and the buyer. In fact, even **incidental similarity**, such as a shared birthday or growing up in the same place, can be enough to boost the odds of a sale.[160]

In addition, more effective salespeople usually know their customers' traits and preferences better than ineffective salespeople, since this knowledge allows them to adapt their approach to meet the needs of the specific customer.[161] The ability to be adaptable is especially vital when customers and salespeople differ in terms of their *interaction styles*.[162] Consumers, for example, vary in the degree of assertiveness they bring to interactions. At one extreme, non-assertive people believe that complaining is not socially acceptable and they may be intimidated in sales situations. Assertive people are more likely to stand up for themselves in a firm but non-threatening way. Aggressives may resort to rudeness and threats if they do not get their way.[163]

Product disposal

2.4

Getting rid of products when consumers no longer need or want them is a major concern both to marketers and to public policymakers.

Because we form strong attachments to some products, it can be painful to dispose of things. Our possessions anchor our identities; our past lives on in our things.[164] Although some of us have more problems than others in discarding things, we all have to get rid of our 'stuff' at some point, either because it has served its purpose or perhaps because it no longer fits with our view of ourselves. How do our changing consumer values around sustainability and environmentalism affect our consumer behaviour when disposing of products? In many cases we acquire a new product even though the old one still functions (e.g. our cars or our mobile phones). Reasons to replace an item include a desire for new features, a change in the individual's environment (e.g. moving to a house with a smaller kitchen so there is a need to change the large fridge for a more compact one), or a change in the person's role or self-image.[165]

Disposal options: recycling

When a consumer decides that a product is no longer of use, several choices are available. The person can (1) keep the item, (2) temporarily dispose of it, or (3) permanently dispose of it. Figure 2.4 provides an overview of consumers' disposal options. Compared with the original scheme, we have added the opportunity of 'to be recycled' in the lower left corner. This is interesting because it bears witness to the fact that thinking about recycling as a 'natural' thing to do is a rather more recent occurrence. The issue of **product disposal** is doubly vital because of its enormous public policy implications.

The following are some UK recycling statistics:

- The UK recycling rate for Waste from Households (WfH; including IBA metal) was 45.2 per cent in 2016, increasing from 44.6 per cent in 2015. There is an EU target for the UK to recycle at least 50 per cent of household waste by 2020.

- The recycling rate for WfH increased in all UK countries in 2016. The recycling rate for England was 44.9 per cent, compared with 43.0 per cent in Northern Ireland, 42.8 per cent in Scotland and 57.3 per cent in Wales.

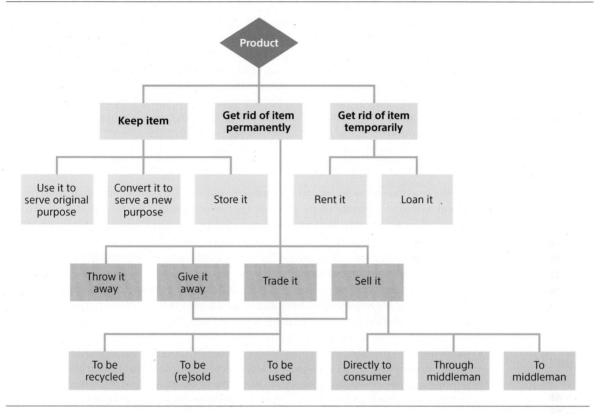

Figure 2.4 Consumers' disposal options

Source: Adapted from Jacob Jacoby, Carol K. Berning and Thomas F. Dietvorst, 'What about disposition?', *Journal of Marketing* 41(April) (1977): 23.

- UK biodegradable municipal waste (BMW) sent to landfill in 2016 was similar to that in 2015, remaining at approximately 7.7 million tonnes, or 22 per cent of the 1995 baseline value. The UK is therefore still on track to meet the EU target to restrict landfilled BMW to 35 per cent of the 1995 baseline by 2020.

- In 2016, 71.4 per cent of UK packaging waste was either recycled or recovered, compared to 64.7 per cent in 2015. This exceeds the EU target to recycle or recover at least 60 per cent of packaging waste.[166]

Marketing opportunity
Recycling of 'preloved' clothes: How Oxfam became the rising star of the UK's online fashion industry

'It's one of fashion's best-kept secrets, a website where you can buy luxury brands such as Burberry, Prada and Miu Miu, as well as the best of the high street, for a steal. Sales were up 33% at Christmas [2017] as shoppers bagged vintage and designer clothes for the party season but the company is not listed on the stock exchange like the web giant Asos and there is no chance of it ever being taken over. And

if you look closely, some of the clothes might seem familiar.

In fact they might actually be your clothes – because Oxfam has emerged as an unlikely rising star of the UK's fast-growing online fashion scene as it casts an increasingly canny eye over the branded cast-offs and vintage styles dumped in bin bags on its shops' doorsteps every day. "It is a big secret but when

→

people hear about our website they are really intrigued", says Oxfam trading director Andrew Horton, who wants to double the size of the web operation to reach 10% of retail sales over the next three years.[167]

. . . There are more than 125,000 one-off products listed on the Oxfam website, a vast catalogue that includes books as well as music and clothing. At Christmas the most searched-for brands on the website included Barbour, Gucci, Whistles and Boden. At

the moment, a trawl of Oxfam's designer boutique turns up a silk Hermès scarf, with a £190 price tag, and a Burberry trench coat for £110.

. . . The site's fashion credentials were boosted by Oxfam's first catwalk show at London Fashion Week in 2017, where models paraded the cream of its "preloved" clothes. The charity is repeating the exercise this year with stylist Bay Garnett currently assembling the collection.'[168]

We live in a throwaway society, which creates problems for the environment and also results in a great deal of unfortunate waste. Analysts say that one-third of the food produced globally is never consumed! To make matters worse, most food waste winds up in landfills where it decomposes and emits methane, a potent greenhouse gas.[169] There has been a recent initiative in France to persuade supermarkets not to throw away or destroy food, but rather donate it to charities for animal feed.[170]

One study reported that we never use as much as 12 per cent of the grocery products we buy; consumers buy nearly two-thirds of these **abandoned products** for a specific purpose such as a particular recipe and then change their plans. Because we don't use these items immediately, they slowly get pushed to the back of the cupboard and forgotten.[171] The consumers most likely to save things are older people and those who live alone.[172] A recent study examined whether messages framed around loss were more or less effective than messages framed around gain in influencing consumer behaviour towards recycling. The researchers found that 'loss frames were more efficacious paired with lower-level, concrete mindsets, whereas gain frames were more

France to force big supermarkets to give unsold food to charities. Legislation barring stores from spoiling and throwing away food is aimed at tackling epidemic of waste alongside food poverty

Source: Christopher Thomond/Guardian News & Media Ltd 2015.

effective paired with higher-level, abstract mindsets. . . [so that] a pairing of messages that activate more concrete (abstract) mindsets leads to enhancing processing efficiency, increased efficacy and, as a result, more positive recycling outcomes'.[173]

However, rather than assuming that disposal represents the terminal point for goods, rather disposal might 'be regarded as a new point in the valuing of objects and, by implication, also a new point in the relationship of people to goods'.[174] Training consumers to recycle has become a priority in many countries. Japan recycles about 40 per cent of its rubbish, and this relatively high rate of compliance is partly due to the social value the Japanese place on recycling.[175] Companies continue to search for ways to use resources more efficiently, often at the prompting of activist consumer groups. For example, McDonald's restaurants have bowed to pressure by eliminating the use of styrofoam packages, and its outlets in Europe experimented with edible breakfast plates made of maize.[176]

One study examined the relevant goals consumers have when they recycle. It used a means–end chain analysis (see Chapter 8) to identify how consumers link specific instrumental goals to more abstract terminal values. Researchers identified the most important lower-order goals to be 'avoid filling up landfills', 'reduce waste', 're-use materials' and 'save the environment'. They linked these to the terminal values of 'promote health/avoid sickness', 'achieve life-sustaining ends' and 'provide for future generations'.

Another study reported that the perceived effort involved in recycling was the best predictor of whether people would go to the trouble. This pragmatic dimension outweighed general attitudes towards recycling and the environment in predicting intention to recycle.[177] When researchers apply these techniques to study recycling and other product disposal behaviours, it will be easier for social marketers to design advertising copy and other messages that tap into the underlying values that will motivate people to increase environmentally responsible behaviour.[178] Of course, one way to ease the pain is to reward consumers for recycling. Gap tried this when it teamed up with Cotton Incorporated to collect old denim, which will be turned into insulation and donated to communities to help them build new houses. The sweetener in the deal: those who donated got a 30 per cent discount on new jeans purchases and a 40 per cent discount to those who buy the trousers on Gap's Facebook page.[179] In the UK, the major retailer M&S undertook a similar campaign in conjunction with the charity Oxfam, offering £5 store vouchers to customers who brought in their old M&S clothing and donated it to Oxfam.[180] The H&M store chain sponsors a garment recycling programme whereby customers can bring any garment from any brand in any condition into an H&M store. For every bag of clothes donated, H&M gives customers a 15 per cent discount on the next item they buy.[181]

Recent research examined the relationship between disposal and identity, using a study of mothers' disposal of their children's products to show how consumer behaviour 'is used to build, maintain and signal both individual and social identity' and to illustrate 'how complexities, conflicts and coping strategies are an inherent part of disposal as an identity marker'.[182] Other recent work has explored 'whether the presence (vs absence) of an identity link between the self and a product will influence consumers' disposal decisions (recycle vs. trash) of a product when they decide that they no longer want it. . . [and the authors showed] that consumers' identity links with products persist even when the products are no longer useful, and this connection profoundly influences disposal decisions. . . a consumer's decision to recycle an identity-linked product arises because the act of throwing such a product into the trash poses an identity threat. . . [therefore] we can increase overall recycle yield and decrease waste through design changes and marketing promotions by creating an identity link or making an existing identity link salient'.[183] There is also evidence that **social recycling** – 'disposing of used goods by allowing other consumers to acquire them at no cost. . . [has the potential] to transform unused physical resources into increased consumer happiness' and thus opening the way to 'maximise the ecological, interpersonal, and community utility of partially depleted resources'.[184]

Disposal options: lateral cycling (junk *vs* 'junque')

Interesting consumer processes occur during **lateral cycling**, where already-purchased objects are sold to others or exchanged for yet other things. Many purchases are made second-hand, rather than new. The reuse of other people's things is especially important in our throwaway society because, as one researcher put it, 'there is no longer an "away" to throw things to'.[185]

Flea markets, garage sales, classified advertisements, bartering for services, hand-me-downs, car-boot sales, charity shops and the black market all represent important alternative marketing systems that operate alongside the formal marketplace. In the US alone, there are more than 3,500 flea markets. Economic estimates of this **underground economy** range from 3 to 30 per cent of the gross national product of the US and up to 70 per cent of the gross domestic product of other countries. The new trend of **recommerce** (a play on the term *e-commerce*) shows that many consumers want to squeeze more value out of their possessions by selling or trading them.[186] This focus has given birth to the **swishing** movement, where people organise parties to exchange clothing or other personal possessions with others.[187]

Trade publications offer reams of practical advice to consumers who want to bypass formal retailers and swap merchandise. Interest in antiques, period accessories and specialised magazines catering for this niche is increasing, e.g. Lassco (London Architectural Salvage and Supply Company) is a reclamation business. '**Reclaimers** are not, strictly speaking, antique dealers, and very definitely not junk merchants. . . they are not in the business of plundering the past, they are in the business of rescuing large lumps of history from the wrecking ball. . . reclaiming is. . . part of the current craze for 'collectables' (architectural salvage is big on eBay)'.[188] Other growth areas include student markets for used computers and textbooks, as well as ski swaps, at which consumers exchange millions of dollars-worth of used ski equipment. A new generation of second-hand store owners is developing markets for everything from used office equipment to cast-off kitchen sinks. Many are non-profit ventures started with government funding.

The internet has revolutionised the lateral cycling process, as millions of people flock to eBay to buy and sell their 'treasures'. This phenomenally successful online auction site started as a trading post for Beanie Babies and other collectibles. Now two-thirds of the site's sales are for practical goods. eBay expects to sell $2 billion-worth of used cars and $1 billion-worth of computers a year. Coming next are event tickets, food, industrial equipment and property.[189] However, eBay hit a slight hiccup with the award by a French court against the company of €38.6 million in damages to 'LVMH, the luxury giant behind Louis Vuitton and Christian Dior, for negligence in allowing the sale of fake bags and clothes, and of perfume that it was not licensed to sell. The ruling comes hot on the heels of a judgement by another French court that ordered eBay to pay €20,000 to Hermès for allowing the sale of fake bags. . . As part of its case, LVMH presented evidence to the court that of the 300,000 products purporting to be Louis Vuitton or Christian Dior sold on the site in the second quarter of 2006, 90 per cent were fakes'.[190] In the case of LVMH's subsequent appeal, the court reduced the sum to €5.7 million but affirmed that eBay had been in the wrong. In 2012 a French appeal court ruled that a lower court did not have jurisdiction over eBay's US website but upheld the ruling as applied to its French and British sites'.[191]

Again, social media platforms offer new ways to recycle. Numerous **sharing sites** such as SnapGoods base their business models around allowing people to share, exchange and rent goods in a local setting. In fact, some research indicates that people who participate in these sites also benefit because they feel they are part of a community. One study found that when people post messages on Twitter (also part of a community), this releases oxytocin – a neurotransmitter that evokes feelings of contentment and is thought to help induce a sense of positive social bonding. The researcher observed that this interaction 'reduces stress hormones, even through the web. You're feeling a real physiological relationship to that person, even if they are online'.[192]

An eBay sign is seen at an office building in San Jose, California (28 May 2014). In terms of recycling, eBay expects to sell $2 billion worth of used cars and $1 billion worth of used computers a year.

Source: ZUMA Press, Inc/Alamy Images

Luxury items are often found for sale on eBay. eBay was successfully sued by LVMH (the corporation behind such luxury brands as Louis Vuitton and Christian Dior) for negligence in allowing the sale of fake bags and clothes.

LIU JIN/AFP/Getty Images

An economic slowdown was good news for auction sites such as eBay, because that is the kind of business that prospers when other businesses aren't doing well. As one analyst explained, 'The interesting thing about eBay is that it may benefit because some people may choose not to buy something new, like a computer or consumer electronics'. Hobbies and crafts also are selling strongly, which may be due to the number of people staying at home rather than travelling.

Despite its success, there's sometimes a bittersweet quality to eBay. Some of the sellers are listing computers, fancy cars, jewellery and other luxury items because they desperately need the money. As one vendor explained when he described the classic convertible he wanted to sell, 'I am out of money and need to pay my rent, so my toys have to be sold'. The site witnessed a particularly strong surge in these kinds of messages following 9/11, when many people were laid off in the wake of a sluggish economy. In the words of an accountant who lost his job, 'Things were bad before, and then they got really bad after the bombings. Everything completely dried up'. Noting that he used to sell merchandise on eBay as a hobby but is now forced to sell some of his own possessions, including his BMW and his wife's jewellery, he commented, 'If it weren't for eBay, I'm not sure what I'd be doing. We definitely would not be able to pay the bills'.[193]

Lateral cycling is literally a lifestyle for some people with an anti-consumerist bent who call themselves **freegans** (this label is a play on *vegans,* who shun all animal products). Freegans are modern-day scavengers who live off discards as a political statement against corporations and consumerism. They forage through supermarket waste bins and eat the slightly bruised produce or just-expired canned goods that we routinely throw out, and negotiate gifts of surplus food from sympathetic stores and restaurants. Freegans dress in cast-off clothes and furnish their homes with items they find on the street. They get the word on locations where people throw out a lot of stuff (end-of-semester student accommodation clear-outs are a prime target) and they check out postings at freecycle.org, where users post unwanted items and at so-called *freemeets* (flea markets where no one exchanges money).[194] **Freecycling** is the practice of giving away useful but unwanted goods to keep them out of landfills and maybe to help someone less fortunate in the process. Free recycling – which already existed in a number of forms offline (for

Flea markets are an important form of lateral cycling
Alan Wilson / Alamy Stock Photo

example, jumble sales and donations to charity shops and church institutions such as the Salvation Army) – has emerged online with the establishment of www.freecycle.org by a consumer in Tucson, Arizona, keen to give away a queen-size bed and some packaged peanuts. What started as an email circular to friends turned into a website for the exchange of unwanted items. 'Free, legal and appropriate for all ages': these are the only constraints on what is offered via the site. At freecycle.org, roughly three million people from more than 70 countries exchange unwanted items.[195] One study has examined how participation in freecycling served 'to increase community cohesion and personal and social sustainability goals'.[196]

If our possessions do indeed come to be a part of us, how do we bring ourselves to part with these precious items? Some researchers recently examined the ways consumers practice **divestment rituals**, where they take steps to gradually distance themselves from things they treasure so that they can sell them or give them away (more on rituals in Chapter 12). As they observed people getting items ready to be sold at garage sales, the researchers identified these rituals:

- *Iconic transfer ritual:* taking pictures and videos of objects before selling them.
- *Transition-place ritual:* putting items in an out-of-the way location such as a garage or attic before disposing of them.
- *Ritual cleansing:* washing, ironing, and/or meticulously wrapping the item.[197]

Chapter summary

Now that you have finished reading this chapter, you should understand why:

2.1 Many factors at the time of purchase dramatically influence the consumer's decision-making process. Many factors affect a purchase. These include the consumer's antecedent state (e.g. his or her mood, time pressure, or disposition towards shopping). Our moods are influenced by the degree of pleasure and arousal a store environment creates. Time is an important resource that often determines how much effort and search will go into a decision.

The usage context of a product is a segmentation variable; consumers look for different product attributes depending on the use to which they intend to put their purchase. The presence or absence of other people (co-consumers) – and the types of people they are – can also affect a consumer's decisions.

The shopping experience is a pivotal part of the purchase decision. In many cases, retailing is like theatre: the consumer's evaluation of stores and products may depend on the type of 'performance' he witnesses. The actors (e.g. salespeople), the setting (the store environment) and the props (e.g. store displays) influence this evaluation. Like a brand personality, a number of factors, such as perceived convenience, sophistication and expertise of salespeople, determine store image. With increasing competition from non-store alternatives, creating a positive shopping experience has never been more important.

Online shopping is growing in importance, and this new way to acquire products has both good (e.g. convenience) and bad (e.g. security) aspects.

2.2 The information a store or website provides strongly influences a purchase decision, in addition to what a shopper already knows or believes about a product. Because we don't make many purchase decisions until we're actually in the store, point-of-purchase (POP) stimuli are very important sales tools. These include product samples, elaborate package displays and in-store promotional materials such as 'shelf talkers'. POP stimuli are particularly useful in promoting impulse buying, which happens when a consumer yields to a sudden urge for a product. Increasingly, mobile shopping apps are also playing a key role.

2.3 A salesperson is often the crucial connection to a purchase. The consumer's encounter with a salesperson is a complex process and an important touchpoint. The outcome can be affected by such factors as the salesperson's similarity to the customer and his or her perceived credibility.

2.4 Getting rid of products when consumers no longer need or want them is a major concern to both marketers and to public policymakers. Product disposal is an increasingly important problem because of concerns about the environment, sustainability and waste. Recycling is one option that will become more crucial as consumers' environmental awareness grows. Lateral cycling occurs when we buy, sell or barter second-hand objects.

Key terms

Abandoned products (p. 62)
Activity stores (p. 57)
Atmospherics (p. 57)
Augmented reality (AR) (p. 58)
Being space (p. 56)
Bitcoin (p. 51)
Co-consumers (p. 43)
Consumption situation (p. 37)
Cryptocurrency (p. 51)
Cyberspace (p. 46)
Digital wallet (p. 51)
Divestment rituals (p. 67)
Exchange theory (p. 59)
Freecycling (p. 66)
Freegans (p. 66)
Impulse buying (p. 58)
Incidental similarity (p. 60)
Lateral cycling (p. 64)
Mental budgets (p. 57)
Mobile shopping apps (p. 58)
NFC (Near Field Communications) (p. 51)
Open rates (p. 39)

Phablets (p. 46)
Point-of-purchase stimuli (POP) (p. 59)
Pop-up stores (p. 56)
Pretailer (p. 50)
Product disposal (p. 60)
Queuing theory (p. 40)
Reclaimers (p. 64)
Recommerce (p. 64)
Retail theming (p. 53)
Sharing sites (p. 64)
Shopping orientation (p. 42)
Social recycling (p. 63)
Store gestalt (p. 56)
Store image (p. 56)
Swishing (p. 64)
Time poverty (p. 39)
Time style (p. 39)
Underground economy (p. 64)
Unplanned buying (p. 58)
Virtual reality (VR) (p. 58)
Visual search (p. 50)

Consumer behaviour challenge

1 Discuss some of the motivations for shopping described in the chapter. How might a retailer adjust their strategy to accommodate these motivations? What is the difference between unplanned buying and impulse buying?

2 Do you think shopping motives might be different between online and offline shopping? If so, why? What are the pros and cons of e-commerce?

3 What factors help determine store image? What are the two dimensions that determine whether we will react positively or negatively to a purchase environment?

4 Describe the difference between density and crowding. Why is this difference relevant in purchase environments?

5 The store environment is heating up as more and more companies put their promotional resources into point-of-purchase efforts. Shoppers are now confronted by videos at the checkout, computer monitors attached to their shopping trolleys and so on. Place-based media expose us to ads in non-shopping environments. Do you feel that these innovations are unacceptably intrusive? At what point might shoppers rebel and demand some peace while shopping? Do you see any market potential in the future for stores that 'counter-market' by promising a 'hands-off' shopping environment?

6 Find a spectacular consumption environment and examine how consumers' play is encouraged and constrained by producers. How is technology used by producers and consumers in this environment to create and alter the sense of reality and space in this spectacular environment? If you don't have a spectacular consumption environment near you, consider these questions (and the associated research findings) about the co-creation of meaning between producers and consumers within the context of the online world, such as computer games.

7 Is e-commerce going to replace the high-street retailer?

8 Discuss the changing trends across online and high-street shopping (e.g. click and collect) and identify the factors within consumer behaviour that have influenced the development of these trends (e.g. time scarcity). What new trends can you identify as online and offline consumer behaviour becomes increasingly integrated? Or will online and offline purchasing remain separate activities for different types of shoppers?

9 Are pop-up stores simply a fad, or a retailing concept that is here to stay?

10 Discuss the concept of 'time style'. Based on your own experiences, how might consumers be segmented in terms of their time styles?

11 What is time poverty, and how might it influence our purchase decisions?

12 Recent research (among American married and single women without children) has shown that there are major differences in individuals' attitudes and behaviours in relation to shopping across five metaphors of time: pressure cooker, map, mirror, river and feast. Consider how these temporal metaphors might vary across households (e.g. married with children), age (e.g. empty-nest households) and culture.

13 Conduct naturalistic observation at a local mall or shopping centre. Sit in a central location and observe the activities of mall staff and customers. Keep a log of the non-retailing activity you observe (special performances, exhibits, socialising, etc.). Does this activity enhance or detract from business conducted at the mall or shopping centre? As shopping centres become more like high-tech game rooms, how valid is the criticism that shopping areas are only encouraging more loitering by teenage boys, who do not spend a lot in stores and simply scare away other customers?

14 Select three competing clothing stores in your area and conduct a store image study for each one. Ask a group of consumers to rate each store on a set of attributes and plot these ratings on the same graph. Based on your findings, are there any areas of competitive advantage or disadvantage you could bring to the attention of store management? (This technique is described in Chapter 7.)

15 Discuss and critique the view that 'shoppers who blend store, mail-order catalogues and websites spend more'.[198]

16 New interactive tools are being introduced that allow surfers on sites such as landsend.com to view apparel product selections on virtual models in full, 360-degree rotational view. In some cases, the viewer can modify the bodies, face, skin-colouring and hairstyles of these models. In others, the consumer can project their own likeness into the space by scanning a photo into a 'makeover' programme.[199] Visit landsend.com or another site that offers a personalised model. Surf around. Try on some clothes. How was your experience? How helpful was this model? When you shop for clothes online, would you rather see how they look on a body with dimensions the same as yours, or on a different body? What advice can you give website designers who are

$\rightarrow$

trying to personalise these shopping environments by creating lifelike models to guide you through the site?

17 Choy and Loker[200] explored and classified internet sites supporting the wedding industry and the purchase of a wedding gown in their study of mass customisation. They identified four major categories: marketing, browsing, advice and customising. Choose another industry (e.g. mother and baby, travel, leisure, pets, music) and classify the websites according to their characteristics and strategies. What categories can you identify?

18 The mall or shopping centre of the future will most likely be less about purchasing products than about exploring them in a physical setting. This means that retail environments will have to

become places to build brand images, rather than just places to sell products. What are some strategies stores can use to enhance the emotional/sensory experiences they give to shoppers?

19 The movement away from a 'disposable consumer society' towards one that emphasises creative recycling creates many opportunities for marketers. Can you identify some?

20 What is the 'underground economy' and why is it important to marketers?

21 Interview people who are selling items at a flea market or garage sale. Ask them to identify some items to which they had a strong attachment. Then, see if you can prompt them to describe one or more divestment rituals they went through as they prepared to offer these items for sale.

For additional material see the companion website at **www.pearsoned.co.uk/solomon**

See Case studies A.1 and A.2 at the end of Part A:

Case study A.1: 'Help me! I can't pay!' Credit card targeting, young consumers and protectionist policy', Sandra Awanis (Lancaster University Management School, UK)

Case study A.2: Online shopping in Uganda: the exclusion of a rising middle class from the market, Kira Strandby (Campus Vejle, Denmark)

Notes

1. Brian T. Ratchford, Debabrata Talukdar and Myung-Soo Lee, 'The impact of the internet on consumers' use of information sources for automobiles: A re-inquiry', *Journal of Consumer Research* 34 (June 2007): 111–19.

2. Laurette Dube and Bernd H. Schmitt, 'The Processing of Emotional and Cognitive Aspects of Product Usage in Satisfaction Judgments', in Rebecca H. Holman and Michael R. Solomon (eds), *Advances in Consumer Research* 18 (Provo, UT: Association for Consumer Research, 1991): 52–6; Lalita A. Manrai and Meryl P. Gardner, 'The Influence of Affect on Attributions for Product Failure', in ibid.: 249–54.

3. Peter J. Burke and Stephen L. Franzoi, 'Studying situations and identities using experimental sampling methodology', *American Sociological Review* 53 (August 1988): 559–68.

4. Kevin G. Celuch and Linda S. Showers, 'It's Time To Stress *Stress*: The Stress-Purchase/Consumption Relationship', in Holman and Solomon (eds), *Advances in Consumer Research* 18: 284–9, op cit.; Lawrence R. Lepisto, J. Kathleen Stuenkel and Linda K. Anglin, 'Stress: An Ignored Situational Influence', in ibid.: 296–302.

5. Christopher Heine, 'Will Facebook ads soon reflect "what's on your mind?",' *ClickZ* (March 23 2011), http://www.clickz.com/clickz/news/2036901/facebook-ads-soon-reflect-whats-mind (accessed 25 July 2018).

6. See Eben Shapiro, 'Need a little fantasy? A bevy of new companies can help', *New York Times* (10 March 1991): F4.

7. John D. Mayer and Yvonne N. Gaschke, 'The experience and meta-experience of mood', *Journal of Personality and Social Psychology* 55 (July 1988): 102–11. See also: Michael J. Barone, Paul Miniard and Jean B. Romeo, 'The influence of positive mood on brand extension evaluations', *Journal of Consumer Research* 26 (March 2000): 386–400; Eduardo B. Andrade, 'Behavioral consequences of affect: Combining evaluative and regulatory mechanisms', *Journal of Consumer Research* 32 (December 2005): 355–62; Georgios A. Bakamitsos, 'A cue alone or a probe to think? The dual role of affect in product evaluations', *Journal of Consumer Research* 33 (December 2006): 403–12; Harper A. Roehm Jr and Michelle L. Roehm, 'Revisiting the effect of positive mood on variety seeking', *Journal of Consumer Research* 32 (September 2005): 330–36; Cheng Qiu and Catherine W.M. Yeung, 'Mood and comparative judgment: Does mood influence everything and finally nothing?', *Journal of Consumer Research* 34 (February 2008): 657–69; Alexander Fedorikhin and Vanessa M. Patrick, 'Positive mood and resistance to temptation: The interfering influence of elevated arousal', *Journal of Consumer Research* 37 (December 2010): 698–711; Cassie Mogilner, Jennifer Aaker and Sepandar D. Kamvar, 'How happiness affects choice', *Journal of Consumer Research* 39 (August 2012) published electronically; Fabrizio Di Muro and Kyle B. Murray, 'An arousal regulation explanation of mood effects on consumer choice',

Journal of Consumer Research 39 (October 2012): 574–84, https://doi.org/10.1086/664040 (accessed 25 July 2018).

8. Gordon C. Bruner, 'Music, mood, and marketing', *Journal of Marketing* 54 (October 1990): 94–104; Basil G. Englis, 'Music television and its influences on consumers, consumer culture, and the transmission of consumption messages', in Holman and Solomon (eds), *Advances in Consumer Research* 18: 111–14, op cit.; see also Steve Oakes, 'Examining the Relationships Between Background Musical Tempo and Perceived Duration Using Different Versions of a Radio Ad', in B. Dubois, T. Lowrey, L.J. Shrum and M. Vanhuele (eds), *European Advances in Consumer Research* 4 (Provo, UT: Association of Consumer Research, 1999): 40–4.

9. Marvin E. Goldberg and Gerald J. Gorn, 'Happy and sad TV programs: How they affect reactions to commercials', *Journal of Consumer Research* 14 (December 1987): 387–403; Gorn, Goldberg and Basu, 'Mood, awareness, and product evaluation': op. cit., 237–56; Curren and Harich, 'Consumers' mood states', op cit.

10. Rajeev Batra and Douglas M. Stayman, 'The role of mood in advertising effectiveness', *Journal of Consumer Research* 17 (September 1990): 203; John P. Murry, Jr, and Peter A. Dacin, 'Cognitive moderators of negative-emotion effects: Implications for understanding media context', *Journal of Consumer Research* 22 (March 1996): 439–47; see also Curren and Harich, 'Consumers' Mood States' op. cit.; Gorn, Goldberg, and Basu, 'Mood, awareness, and product evaluation' op. cit.

11. Neil Tweedie, 'Melody on the menu: How a sprinkle of Mozart might give your meal zing' *The Observer* 5 April (2015): 8–9, http://www.theguardian.com/science/2015/apr/05/music-enhance-enjoyment-wine-food (accessed 25 July 2018).

12. Jeffrey Zaslow, 'Happiness Inc', *Wall Street Journal* (18 March 2006): P1.

13. Pradeep Kakkar and Richard J. Lutz, 'Situational Influence on Consumer Behavior: A Review', in Harold H. Kassarjian and Thomas S. Robertson (eds), *Perspectives in Consumer Behavior,* 3rd edn (Glenview, IL: Scott, Foresman, 1981): 204–14.

14. Carolyn Turner Schenk and Rebecca H. Holman, 'A Sociological Approach to Brand Choice: The Concept of Situational Self-Image', in Jerry C. Olson (ed.), *Advances in Consumer Research* 7 (Ann Arbor, MI: Association for Consumer Research, 1980): 610–14.

15. Russell W. Belk, 'An exploratory assessment of situational effects in buyer behavior', *Journal of Marketing Research* 11 (May 1974): 156–63; U.N. Umesh and Joseph A. Cote, 'Influence of situational variables on brand-choice models', *Journal of Business Research* 16(2) (1988): 91–9; see also J. Wesley Hutchinson and Joseph W. Alba, 'Ignoring irrelevant information: Situational determinants of consumer learning', *Journal of Consumer Research* 18 (December 1991): 325–45.

16. Peter R. Dickson, 'Person–situation: Segmentation's missing link', *Journal of Marketing* 46 (Fall 1982): 56–64.

17. Booz-Allen Hamilton's Digital Consumer Project and Nielsen/NetRatings reported in Laura Mazur, 'Web marketers must now adapt to the occasion', *Marketing* (29 May 2003): 16.

18. Laura Mazur, 'Web marketers must now adapt to the occasion', op cit.

19. Canvas8 'Behaviours impacting on shopping' January 2015, www.canvas8.com [M.K.Hogg's private correspondence, granted access to this company's members-only lifestyles website 30 May 2015].

20. Ritesh Saini and Ashwani Monga, 'How I decide depends on what I spend: Use of heuristics is greater for time than for money', *Journal of Consumer Research* 34 (April 2008): 921.

21. Tanya Irwin, 'ReachMail: Email marketers should focus on mid-day', *Marketing Daily* (17 March 2011).

22. Carol Felker Kaufman, Paul M. Lane and Jay D. Lindquist, 'Exploring more than 24 hours a day: A preliminary investigation of polychronic time use', *Journal of Consumer Research* 18 (December 1991): 392–401.

23. Laurence P. Feldman and Jacob Hornik, 'The use of time: An integrated conceptual model', *Journal of Consumer Research* 7 (March 1981): 407–19; see also Michelle M. Bergadaa, 'The role of time in the action of the consumer', *Journal of Consumer Research* 17 (December 1990): 289–302; see also Niklas Woermann and Joonas Rokka, 'Timeflow: How consumption practices shape consumers' temporal experiences', *Journal of Consumer Research* 41(6) (April 2015): 1,486–508.

24. Jea-Claude Usunier and Pierre Valette-Florence, 'Individual time orientation: A psychometric scale', *Time and Society* 3(2) (1994): 219–41.

25. June Cotte, S. Ratneshwar and David Glen Mick, 'The times of their lives: Phenomenological and metaphorical characteristics of consumer timestyles', *Journal of Consumer Research* 31 (September 2004): 333–45.

26. Ibid.

27. Jared Sandberg, 'NoChores.com', *Newsweek* (30 August 1999): 30(2).

28. 'Plugged in: Hong Kong embraces the Octopus Card', *The New York Times on the Web* (8 June 2002).

29. David Lewis and Darren Bridger, *The Soul of the New Consumer: Authenticity – What We Buy and Why in the New Economy* (London: Nicholas Brealey Publishing, 2000).

30. Dhruv Grewal, Julie Baker, Michael Levy and Glenn B. Voss, 'The effects of wait expectations and store atmosphere evaluations on patronage intentions in service-intensive retail store', *Journal of Retailing* 79 (2003): 259–68; see also Shirley Taylor, 'Waiting for service: The relationship between delays and evaluations of service', *Journal of Marketing* 58 (April 1994): 56–69.

31. 'We're hating the waiting; 43 per cent prefer self-service', *Marketing Daily* (23 January 2007).

32. David H. Maister, 'The Psychology of Waiting Lines', in John A. Czepiel, Michael R. Solomon and Carol F. Surprenant (eds), *The Service Encounter: Managing Employee/Customer Interaction in Service Businesses* (Lexington, MA: Lexington Books, 1985): 113–24.

33. Henry Fountain, quoted in 'The ultimate body language: How you line up for Mickey', *New York Times* (18 September 2005).

34. Sigmund Grønmo, 'Concepts of Time: Some Implications for Consumer Research', in Thomas K. Srull (ed.), *Advances in Consumer Research* 16 (Provo, UT: Association for Consumer Research 1989): 339–45.

35. Gabriele Morello and P. van der Reis, 'Attitudes towards time in different cultures: African time and European time', *Proceedings of the Third Symposium on Cross-Cultural Consumer and Business Studies* (Honolulu: University of Hawaii, 1990); Gabriele Morello, 'Our attitudes towards time', *Forum* 96/2 (European Forum for Management Development, 1996): 48–51.

36. Søren Askegaard and Tage Koed Madsen, 'The local and the global: Traits of homogeneity and heterogeneity in European food cultures', *International Business Review* 7(6) (1998): 549–68; for a thorough discussion of food culture, see Claude Fischler, *L'Homnivore* (Paris: Odile Jacob, 1990).

37. 'Online shopping sees 30% rise between midnight and 6am, study says', http://www.theguardian.com/money/2014/oct/10/internet-online-shopping-30-per-cent-rise-midnight-6am-john-lewis (accessed 25 July 2018).

38. 'Online shopping sees 30% rise between midnight and 6am, study says', http://www.theguardian.com/money/2014/oct/10/internet-online-shopping-30-per-cent-rise-midnight-6am-john-lewis (accessed 25 July 2018).

39. Zoe Wood 'Shop before you drop off. Bedtime retail rises' *The Guardian* (10 October 2015): 3; 'Online shopping sees 30% rise between midnight and 6am, study says' http://www.theguardian.com/money/2014/oct/10/internet-online-shopping-30-per-cent-rise-midnight-6am-john-lewis (accessed 25 July 2018).

40. V.D. Kaltcheva and B.A. Weitz, 'When should a retailer create an exciting store environment?', *Journal of Marketing* 70(1) (Jan 2006): 107–18 (https://www.jstor.org/stable/30162076 (accessed 16 August 2018).

41. Gregory P. Stone, 'City shoppers and urban identification: Observations on the social psychology of city life', *American Journal of Sociology* 60 (1954): 36–45; Danny Bellenger and Pradeep K. Korgaonkar, 'Profiling the re-creational shopper', *Journal of Retailing* 56(3) (1980): 77–92.

42. Stephen Brown and Rhona Reid, 'Shoppers on the Verge of a Nervous Breakdown', in S. Brown and D. Turley (eds), *Consumer Research: Postcards from the Edge* (London: Routledge, 1997): 79–149.

43. Mark J. Arnold and Kristy E. Reynolds, 'Hedonic shopping motivations', *Journal of Retailing* 79 (2003): 90–1.

44. Daniel Miller, *A Theory of Shopping* (Cambridge: Polity Press, 1998).

45. For a scale that was devised to assess these dimensions of the shopping experience, see Barry J. Babin, William R. Darden and Mitch Griffin, 'Work and/or fun: Measuring hedonic and utilitarian shopping value', *Journal of Consumer Research* 20 (March 1994): 644–56.

46. Ibid.

47. Adapted from Andrea Groeppel-Klein, Eva Thelen and Christoph Antretter, 'The Impact of Shopping Motives on Store Assessment', in B. Dubois, T.M. Lowrey, L.J. Shrum and M. Vanhuele (eds), *European Advances in Consumer Research* 4: 63–72.

48. Ran Kivetz and Yuhuang Zheng, 'The effects of promotions on hedonic versus utilitarian purchases', *Journal of Consumer Psychology* 27(1) (2017): 59–68, http://dx.doi.org/10.1016/j.jcps.2016.05.005 (accessed 25 July 2018).

49. Anja Stöhr, 'Air-Design: Exploring the Role of Scents in Retail Environments', in B. Englis and A. Olofsson (eds), *European Advances in Consumer Research* 3 (Provo, UT: Association for Consumer Research, 1998): 126–32.

50. Delphine Dion, 'A Theoretical and Empirical Study of Retail Crowding', in Dubois, Lowrey, Shrum and Vanhuele (eds), *European Advances in Consumer Research* 4: 51–7.

51. Daniel Stokols, 'On the distinction between density and crowding: Some implications for future research', *Psychological Review* 79 (1972): 275–7.

52. Fascinators are worn on the head, but are smaller than hats and are seen as a way to wear some decoration on the head but without squashing the hair (as can happen with a hat). Fascinators are usually themed around feathers and netting, see http://www.prettycool.co.uk/fascinators--hats-79-c.asp (accessed 25 July 2018) for some illustrations.

53. http://www.guardian.co.uk/sport/2012/jan/18/royal-ascot-fascinators-hats-dresscode?INTCMP=SRCH (accessed 25 July 2018); http://www.guardian.co.uk/lifeandstyle/gallery/2012/jan/18/royal-ascot-dress-rules?INTCMP=SRCH (accessed 13 March 2018), article and picture illustrations of updated dress code for Royal Ascot for summer 2012 (e.g. no fascinators to be worn as hats).

54. Jonathan Eley, 'Grocery watchdog hails improvement as Aldi holds top spot', *Financial Times*, 25 June 2018 https://www.ft.com/content/6b00fff8-787f-11e8-8e67-1e1a0846c475 (accessed 25 July 2018).

55. https://www.mirror.co.uk/money/britains-favourite-grocer-revealed-12699049 (accessed 12 December 2018).

56. Zoe Chamberlain, '12 Aldi secrets revealed – insider spills the beans on why prices are so cheap', *The Mirror* (18 June 2018), https://www.mirror.co.uk/money/aldi-insider-reveals-12-reasons-12732619 (accessed 25 July 2018).

57. Zoe Wood, 'Tesco trials "shop and go" app in till-free store', *The Guardian* (28 June 2018), https://www.theguardian.com/business/2018/jun/28/tesco-shop-and-go-app-till-free-store (accessed 25 July 2018).

58. Nina Gruen, 'The retail battleground: Solutions for today's shifting marketplace', *Journal of Property Management* (July–August 1989): 14.

59. Veraart Research, http://www.retail-index.com/HOMESEARCH/FoodRetailers/tabid/3496/Default.aspx (accessed 25 July 2018).

60. Arieh Goldman, 'The shopping style explanation for store loyalty', *Journal of Retailing* 53 (Winter 1977–8): 33–46, 94; Robert B. Settle and Pamela L. Alreck, 'Hyperchoice shapes the marketplace', *Marketing Communications* (May 1988): 15.

61. Joseph C. Nunes and Xavier Dreze, 'Your loyalty program is betraying you', *Harvard Business Review* (April 2006): 124–131.

62. Joseph C. Nunes and Xavier Dreze, 'Your loyalty program is betraying you', *Harvard Business Review* (April 2006): 128–9.

63. Nunes and Dreze, 'Your loyalty program is betraying you', op cit.: 129–131.

64. http://www.halland.se/en/forest-lakes/278397/ (accessed 25 July 2018).

65. Daniel Hjelmgren, 'Creating positive experiences' in Alan Bradshaw, Chris Hackley and Pauline Maclaran (eds), *European Association for Consumer Research Conference* 2010, RHUL: 7.

66. Samantha Merlivat, Luca S. Paderni, Ryan Skinner, and Kasia Madej, 'UK's Multichannel Consumers Demand Customer Life-Cycle Marketing: Discover The Touchpoints UK Consumers Turn To For Discovery, Exploration. Purchase Inquiries and Engagement', Forrester Report (7 April 2015).

67. Some material in this section was adapted from Michael R. Solomon and Elnora W. Stuart, *Welcome to Marketing.com: The Brave New World of E-Commerce* (Upper Saddle River, NJ: Prentice Hall, 2001).

68. 'Global B2C ecommerce sales to hit $1.5 trillion this year,' emarketer.com (3 February 2014).

69. Alex Fitzpatrick, '75% of world has access to mobile phones,' *Mashable* (17 July 2012).

70. Claire Cain Miller, 'Do people actually shop on phones? The answer is decidedly yes,' *New York Times* (9 January 2013).

71. UK Ofcom figures reported in Mark Sweney 'From the toddler to the middle-aged TV binger – they're all taking to tablets', *The Guardian* (28 May 2015): 17.

72. Mikael Lundström, 'E-handel inget för svensson', *Info* 8 (2000): 52–4.

73. http://ec.europa.eu/eurostat/statistics-explained/index.php/E-commerce_statistics_for_individuals (accessed 25 July 2018).

74. Elke Huyghe, Julie Verstraeten, Maggie Geuens and Anneleen Van Kerchkhove, 'Clicks as a healthy alternative to bricks: How online grocery shopping reduces vice purchases', *Journal of Marketing Research* 54(1) (2017): 61–74.

75. Rebecca K. Ratner, Barbara E. Kahn and Daniel Kahneman, 'Choosing less-preferred experiences for the sake of variety', *Journal of Consumer Research* 26 (June 1999): 1–15.

76. https://www.theguardian.com/business/bhs (accessed 16 August 2018).

77. https://www.theguardian.com/business/2018/jan/13/us-retail-sector-job-losses-hitting-women-hardest-data (accessed 16 August 2018).

78. http://fortune.com/2017/01/04/macys-holiday-season-closings (accessed 16 August 2018).

79. https://www.theguardian.com/business/2018/jun/07/house-of-fraser-to-close-more-than-half-of-its-british-stores (accessed 16 August 2018).

80. Zoe Wood and Nick Fletcher, 'Era ends as House of Fraser to axe 31 stores and 6,000 jobs', *The Guardian* (22 June 2018), https://www.theguardian.com/business/2018/jun/22/house-of-fraser-to-close-31-stores-with-6000-job-losses-as-cva-approved (accessed 25 July 2018).

81. https://www.theguardian.com/business/2016/dec/10/future-shopping-mannequins-drones-shop-leave-without-paying-amazon-go (accessed 16 August 2018).

82. https://www.theguardian.com/business/johnlewis (accessed 16 August 2018).

83. Zoe Wood, 'Asos app allows shoppers to snap up fashion', *The Guardian* (15 July 2017), https://www.theguardian.com/business/2017/jul/15/asos-app-allows-shoppers-to-snap-up-fashion (accessed 25 July 2018).

84. A study of how online grocery shoppers negotiated three different store layouts, freeform, grid and racetrack, indicated that they found the freeform layout most useful for finding shopping list products within the store, and also by far the most entertaining to use. They also found the grid layout much easier to use than the other layouts. 'The grid layout is a rectangular arrangement of displays and long aisles that generally run parallel to one another. The freeform layout is a free-flowing and asymmetric arrangement of displays and aisles, employing a variety of different sizes, shapes and styles of display. In the racetrack/boutique layout, the sales floor is organized into individual, semi-separate areas, each built around a particular shopping theme', Adam P. Vrechopolous, Robert M. O'Keefe, Georgios I. Doukidis and George J. Siomkos, 'Virtual store layout: An experimental comparison in the context of grocery retail', *Journal of Retailing* 80 (2004): 13–22.

85. Jennifer Gilbert, 'Customer service crucial to online buyers', *Advertising Age* (13 September 1999): 52.

86. Bernard, 'Five bleeding-edge mobile marketing trends in 2017', op cit. Note that these AdAge (Advertising Age) statistics were cited in Rob Steffens, '30 mobile marketing statistics you need to know', *Bluleadz,* (March 2018) https://www.bluleadz.com/blog/30-mobile-marketing-statistics-you-need-to-know-infographic (accessed 25 July 2018).

87. Alisa Gould-Simon, 'How fashion retailers are redefining e-commerce with social media', *Mashable.com* (7 March 2011); http://modaoperandi.com/ (accessed 25 July 2018); https://www.net-a-porter.com/gb/en/ (accessed 25 July 2018).

88. For questionnaire items for researching consumers' online experiences see also: Mary Wolfinbarger and Mary C. Gilly, 'eTailQ: Dimensionalizing, measuring and predicting etail quality', *Journal of Retailing* 79 (2003): Table 4.

89. Datamonitor predicted that by the end of 2003 almost 60 million European consumers would bank online; Laura Mazur, 'Web marketers must now adapt to the occasion', *Marketing* (29 May 2003).

90. Bob Tedeschi, 'More e-commerce sites aim to add "sticky" content', *NYT Online* (9 August 2004).

91. Avni M. Shah, Noah Eisenkraft, James R. Bettman and Tanya L. Chartrand, 'Paper or plastic?: How we pay influences post-transaction connection', *Journal of Consumer Research,* 42(5) (2016): 688–708.

92. Kate Lyons, Rupert Jones and Patrick Collinson, 'Revealed: Cash eclipsed as Britain turns to digital payments', *The Guardian* (19 February 2018), https://www.theguardian.com/money/2018/feb/19/peak-cash-over-uk-rise-of-debit-cards-unbanked-contactless-payments (accessed 25 July 2018).

93. Larry Elliott, 'I don't use contactless': The woman whose name is on British banknotes', *The Guardian* (21 February 2018), https://www.theguardian.com/money/2018/feb/21/i-dont-use-contactless-the-woman-whose-name-is-on-british-banknotes (accessed 25 July 2018).

94. Vindu Goel, 'Coming soon to social media: Click to buy now', *New York Times* (17 July 2014).

95. Alex Washburn, 'Digital wallets: End of the beginning or beginning of the end?,' *Wired* (February 2015), http://www.wired.com/2015/02/digital-wallets-end-of-the-beginning-or-beginning-of-the-end/ (accessed 25 July 2018); Jacob Davidson, 'No, big companies aren't really accepting Bitcoin', *Money* (9 January 2015).

96. Alka Varma Citrin, Donald E. Stern, Eric R. Spangenberg and Michael J. Clark, 'Consumer need for tactile input: An internet retailing challenge', *Journal of Business Research* 56 (2003): 915–22. See also Joann Peck and Terry L. Childers, 'Individual differences in haptic information processing: The need for touch scale', *Journal of Consumer Research* 30 (December 2003): 430–42, whose scale includes both instrumental and autotelic factors that differentiate between need for touch as part of the pre-purchase decision-making process, and the need for touch as an end in itself. The importance of touch (particularly as an end in itself) points to this as a potential barrier to the use of e-commerce by some consumers across all product groups.

97. *Markedsføring* (17 February 2000): 20.

98. Kortney Stringer, 'Shoppers who blend store, catalog, web spend more', *The Wall Street Journal Online* (3 September 2004): A7.

99. Marc Gobé, *Emotional Branding: The New Paradigm for Connecting Brands to People* (New York: Allworth Press, 2001): xxv.

100. Ibid.
101. An excellent collection of articles on this topic is found in Pasi Falk and Colin Campbell (eds), *The Shopping Experience* (London: SAGE, 1997).
102. C. Gardner and J. Sheppard, *Consuming Passion: The Rise of Retail Culture* (London: Unwin Hyman, 1989).
103. Stephen Brown, 'Sex 'n' Shopping', Working Paper 9501 (University of Stirling: Institute for Retail Studies, 1995); see also Stephen Brown, 'Consumption Behaviour in the Sex 'n' Shopping Novels of Judith Krantz: A Post-structuralist Perspective', in Kim P. Corfman and John G. Lynch, Jr (eds), *Advances in Consumer Research* 23 (Provo, UT: Association for Consumer Research, 1996): 43–8.
104. Véronique Aubert-Gamet, 'Twisting servicescapes: Diversion of the physical environment in a re-appropriation process', *International Journal of Service Industry Management* 8(1) (1997): 26–41.
105. Stephen Brown, *Postmodern Marketing* (London: Routledge, 1995), discussion on pp. 50 ff.; Lars Thøger Christensen and Søren Askegaard, 'Flexibility in the marketing organization: The ultimate consumer orientation or Ford revisited?', *Marketing Today and for the 21st Century,* Proceedings of the XIV EMAC Conference (ed.), Michelle Bergadaà (Cergy-Pontoise: ESSEC, 1995): 1,507–14.
106. Turo-Kimmo Lehtonen and Pasi Mäenpää, 'Shopping in the East Centre Mall', in Falk and Campbell (eds), *The Shopping Experience:* 136–65.
107. Sallie Hook, 'All the retail world's a stage: Consumers conditioned to entertainment in shopping environment', *Marketing News* 21 (31 July 1987): 16.
108. Cecilia Fredriksson, 'The Making of a Swedish Department Store Culture', in Falk and Campbell (eds.), *The Shopping Experience:* 111–35.
109. Pauline Maclaran and Lorna Stevens, 'Romancing the Utopian Marketplace', in S. Brown, A.M. Doherty and B. Clarke (eds), *Romancing the Market* (London: Routledge, 1998): 172–86.
110. Millie Creighton, 'The Seed of Creative Lifestyle Shopping: Wrapping Consumerism in Japanese Store Layouts', in John F. Sherry Jr (ed.), *Servicescapes: The Concept of Place in Contemporary Markets* (Lincolnwood, IL: NTC Business Books, 1998): 199–228.
111. J.U. McNeal, *Kids as Customers: A Handbook of Marketing to Children* (New York: Lexington Books, 1992).
112. J. Nadeau and M. Bradley, 'Observing the influence of affective states on parent–child interactions and in-store purchase decisions', *Journal of Consumer Behavior* 11 (2012): 105–14.
113. A. Pettersson, U. Olsson and C. Fjellström, 'Family life in grocery stores – a study of interaction between adults and children', *International Journal of Consumer Studies* 28 (2004): 317–28.
114. C. Ebster, U. Wagner and D. Neumueller, 'Children's influence on in-store purchases', *Journal of Retailing and Consumer Services* 16(2) (2009): 145–54.
115. D.L. Haytko and J. Baker, 'It's all at the mall: Exploring adolescent girls' experiences', *Journal of Retailing* 80(1) (2004): 67–83.
116. S. Borghini, N. Diamond, R.V. Kozinets, M.A. McGrath, A. Muniz Jr and J.F. Sherry Jr, 'Why are themed brandstores so powerful? Retail brand ideology at American Girl Place', *Journal of Retailing* 85(3) (2009): 363–75; E. Gentina, I. Decoopman and A. Ruvio, 'Social comparison motivation of mothers with their adolescent daughters and its effects on the mother's consumption behaviour' *Journal of Retailing and Consumer Services* 20(1) (2013): 94–101.
117. S. Borghini, C. Mauri, 'Young shoppers in the marketplace. How children envision their ideal stores', *Working Paper,* (2015) Bocconi University.
118. Researchers identified two ludic (play-related) elements that help us understand the role of *play* in consumption environments: firstly, *Liminoid Real Estate:* This refers to the creation of new worlds through consumer play, which consumers interpret as different realities. This notion of transcendent surrender provides a link between play and religion, ritual, sacrifice and the sacred; and secondly *The Obverse Panapticon:* This refers to physical structures that are designed in a way that appeals to exhibitionistic desires of consumers by enabling them to be observed by others'; Robert V. Kozinets, John F. Sherry, Diana Storm, Adam Duhachek, Krittinee Nuttavuthisit and Benet DeBerry-Spence, 'Ludic agency and retail spectacle', *Journal of Consumer Research* 31 (December 2004): 658–72.
119. Stefania Borghini, John F. Sherry, Annamma Joy, 'Ordinary Spaces and Sense of Place' in Alan Bradshaw, Chris Hackley and Pauline Maclaran (eds), *European Association for Consumer Research Conference* 2010 RHUL: 33.
120. Patrick Hetzel and Veronique Aubert, 'Sales Area Design and Fashion Phenomena: A Semiotic Approach', in van Raaij and Bamossy (eds), *European Advances in Consumer Research* 1: 522–33.
121. Søren Askegaard and Güliz Ger, 'Product-Country Images as Stereotypes: A Comparative Analysis of the Image of Danish Food Products in Germany and Turkey', *MAPP Working Paper* 45 (Aarhus: The Aarhus School of Business, 1997).
122. Susan Spiggle and Murphy A. Sewall, 'A choice sets model of retail selection', *Journal of Marketing* 51 (April 1987): 97–111; William R. Darden and Barry J. Babin, 'The role of emotions in expanding the concept of retail personality', *Stores* 76 (April 1994) 4: RR7–RR8.
123. Most measures of store image are quite similar to other attitude measures, as discussed in Chapter 4. For an excellent bibliography of store image studies, see Mary R. Zimmer and Linda L. Golden, 'Impressions of retail stores: A content analysis of consumer images,' *Journal of Retailing* 64 (Fall 1988): 65–93.
124. Ibid.
125. Spiggle and Sewall, 'A choice sets model of retail selection', op. cit.
126. 'The science of shopping: The way the brain buys,' *The Economist* (18 December 2008).
127. Philip Kotler, 'Atmospherics as a marketing tool,' *Journal of Retailing* (Winter 1973–74): 10; Anna Mattila and Jochen Wirtz, 'Congruency of scent and music as a driver of in-store evaluations and behavior', *Journal of Retailing* 77 (Summer 2001): 273–89; J. Duncan Herrington, 'An Integrative Path Model of the Effects of Retail Environments on Shopper Behavior', in Robert L. King (ed.), *Marketing: Toward the Twenty-First Century* (Richmond, VA: Southern Marketing Association, 1991): 58–62; see also Ann E. Schlosser, 'Applying the functional theory of attitudes to understanding the influence of store atmosphere on store inferences', *Journal of Consumer Psychology* 7(4) (1998): 345–69.
128. Fabian Csaba and Søren Askegaard, 'Malls and the Orchestration of the Shopping Experience in a Historical

Perspective', in Arnould and Scott (eds), *Advances in Consumer Research* 26: 34–40.

129. Robert J. Donovan, John R. Rossiter, Gilian Marcoolyn and Andrew Nesdale, 'Store atmosphere and purchasing behavior', *Journal of Retailing* 70(3) (1994): 283–94.

130. Charles S. Areni and David Kim, 'The influence of in-store lighting on consumers' examination of merchandise in a wine store', *International Journal of Research in Marketing* 11(2) (March 1994): 117–25.

131. Jean-Charles Chebat, Claire Gelinas Chebat and Dominique Vaillant, 'Environmental background music and in-store selling', *Journal of Business Research* 54 (2001): 115–23; Judy I. Alpert and Mark I. Alpert, 'Music influences on mood and purchase intentions', *Psychology and Marketing* 7 (Summer 1990): 109–34.

132. Brad Edmondson, 'Pass the meat loaf', *American Demographics* (January 1989): 19.

133. Dhruv Grewal, Julie Baker, Michael Levy and Glenn B. Voss, 'The effects of wait expectations and store atmosphere evaluations on patronage intentions in service-intensive retail store', *Journal of Retailing* 79 (2003): 259–68.

134. 'Through the looking glass', *Lifestyle Monitor* 16 (Fall/Winter 2002).

135. 'Butikken er en slagmark', *Berlingske Tidende* (15 July 1996): 3.

136. Jennifer Lach, 'Meet you in aisle three', *American Demographics* (April 1999): 41.

137. Karen M. Stilley, J. Jeffrey Inman, and Kirk L. Wakefield, 'Planning to make unplanned purchases? The role of in-store slack in budget deviation', *Journal of Consumer Research* 37(2) (2010): 264–78.

138. Michael Moss, 'Nudged to the produce aisle by a look in the mirror', *New York Times* (27 August 2013), http://www.nytimes.com/2013/08/28/dining/wooing-us-down-the-produce-aisle.html?_r=0 (accessed 25 July 2018).

139. Michael Sciandra and Jeff Inman, 'Smart Phones, Bad Decisions? The Impact of In-store Mobile Technology Use on Consumer Decisions', in Simona Botti and Aparna Labroo (eds), *NA – Advances in Consumer Research* 41 (Duluth, MN: Association for Consumer Research, 2013).

140. Cooper Smith, 'How beacons – small, low-cost gadgets – will influence billions in US retail sales', *Tech Insider* (9 February 2015), http://www.businessinsider.com/beacons-impact-billions-in-reail-sales-2015-2 (accessed 25 July 2018); Zach Sokol, 'A Virtual Reality Tesco Is Opening Shop In Berlin,' *The Creators Project* (18 March 2014), http://thecreatorsproject.vice.com/blog/tescos-using-virtual-reality-goggles-to-possibly-allow-people-to-buy-groceries-from-bed (accessed 25 July 2018); Jordan Crook, 'With $45 million in funding, augmented reality platform Blippar is rethinking search', *Techcrunch* (6 March 2015), http://techcrunch.com/2015/03/06/with-45-million-in-funding-augmented-reality-platform-blippar-is-rethinking-search/#.h5cyu1:Ehw2 (accessed 25 July 2018).

141. Easwar S. Iyer, 'Unplanned purchasing: Knowledge of shopping environment and time pressure', *Journal of Retailing* 65 (Spring 1989): 40–57; C. Whan Park, Easwar S. Iyer and Daniel C. Smith, 'The effects of situational factors on in-store grocery shopping', *Journal of Consumer Research* 15 (March 1989): 422–33.

142. Michael Wahl, 'Eye POPping persuasion', *Marketing Insights* (June 1989): 130.

143. Peter McGoldrick, Erica J. Betts and Kathleen A. Keeling, 'Antecedents of Spontaneous Buying Behaviour During Temporary Markdowns', in Arnould and Scott (eds), *Advances in Consumer Research* 26: 26–33.

144. Cathy J. Cobb and Wayne D. Hoyer, 'Planned versus impulse purchase behavior', *Journal of Retailing* 62 (Winter 1986): 384–409; Easwar S. Iyer and Sucheta S. Ahlawat, 'Deviations from a Shopping Plan: When and Why Do Consumers Not Buy as Planned?' in Melanie Wallendorf and Paul Anderson (eds), *Advances in Consumer Research* 14 (Provo, UT: Association for Consumer Research, 1987): 246–9.

145. Andrea Groeppel-Klein, 'The Influence of the Dominance Perceived at the Point-of-Sale on the Price-Assessment', in Englis and Olofsson (eds), *European Advances in Consumer Research* 3: 304–11.

146. Emily Steel, 'Luring shoppers to stores', *Wall Street Journal* (26 August 2010), http://online.wsj.com/article/SB10001424 05274870454090457545184198006 3132.html (accessed 25 July 2018).

147. Dennis Desrochers, 'European consumers respond to spray samplers', *Global Cosmetic Industry* 171(16) (June 2003): 28.

148. Chairman-CEO A.G. Laffley, quoted in Jack Neff, 'P&G boosts design's role in marketing', *Advertising Age* (9 February 2004): 52.

149. William Keenan, Jr, 'Point-of-purchase: From clutter to technoclutter', *Sales and Marketing Management* 141 (April 1989): 96.

150. *Markedsføring* 13 (1999): 24.

151. Cyndee Miller, 'Videocart spruces up for new tests', *Marketing News* (19 February 1990): 19; William E. Sheeline, 'User-friendly shopping carts', *Fortune* (5 December 1988): 9.

152. Bernard Swoboda, 'Multimedia Customer Information Systems at the Point of Sale: Selected Results of an Impact Analysis', in Englis and Olofsson (eds), *European Advances in Consumer Research* 3: 239–46.

153. See Robert B. Cialdini, *Influence: Science and Practice,* 2nd edn (Glenview, IL: Scott, Foresman, 1988).

154. Richard P. Bagozzi, 'Marketing as exchange', *Journal of Marketing* 39 (October 1975): 32–9; Peter M. Blau, *Exchange and Power in Social Life* (New York: Wiley, 1964); Marjorie Caballero and Alan J. Resnik, 'The attraction paradigm in dyadic exchange', *Psychology and Marketing* 3(1) (1986): 17–34; George C. Homans, 'Social behavior as exchange', *American Journal of Sociology* 63 (1958): 597–606; Paul H. Schurr and Julie L. Ozanne, 'Influences on exchange processes: Buyers' preconceptions of a seller's trustworthiness and bargaining toughness', *Journal of Consumer Research* 11 (March 1985): 939–53; Arch G. Woodside and J.W. Davenport, 'The effect of salesman similarity and expertise on consumer purchasing behavior', *Journal of Marketing Research* 8 (1974): 433–6.

155. Paul Busch and David T. Wilson, 'An experimental analysis of a salesman's expert and referent bases of social power in the buyer–seller dyad', *Journal of Marketing Research* 13 (February 1976): 3–11; John E. Swan, Fred Trawick Jr, David R. Rink and Jenny J. Roberts, 'Measuring dimensions of purchaser trust of industrial salespeople', *Journal of Personal Selling and Sales Management* 8 (May 1988): 1.

156. For a study in this area, see Peter H. Reingen and Jerome B. Kernan, 'Social perception and interpersonal influence: Some consequences of the physical attractiveness stereotype in a personal selling setting', *Journal of Consumer Psychology* 2 (1993): 25–38.

157. Linda L. Price and Eric J. Arnould, 'Commercial friendships: Service provider–client relationships in context', *Journal of Marketing* 63 (October 1999): 38–56.

158. Mary Jo Bitner, Bernard H. Booms and Mary Stansfield Tetreault, 'The service encounter: Diagnosing favorable and unfavorable incidents', *Journal of Marketing* 54 (January 1990): 7–84; Robert C. Prus, *Making Sales* (Newbury Park, CA: Sage, 1989); Arch G. Woodside and James L. Taylor, 'Identity Negotiations in Buyer–Seller Interactions', in Elizabeth C. Hirschman and Morris B. Holbrook (eds), *Advances in Consumer Research* 12 (Provo, UT: Association for Consumer Research, 1985): 443–9.

159. Barry J. Babin, James S. Boles and William R. Darden, 'Salesperson stereotypes, consumer emotions, and their impact on information processing', *Journal of the Academy of Marketing Science* 23(2) (1995): 94–105; Gilbert A. Churchill Jr, Neil M. Ford, Steven W. Hartley and Orville C. Walker Jr, 'The determinants of salesperson performance: A meta-analysis', *Journal of Marketing Research* 22 (May 1985): 103–18.

160. Jiang Lan, Joandrea Hoegg, Darren W. Dahl and Amitava Chattopadhyay, 'The persuasive role of incidental similarity on attitudes and purchase intentions in a sales context', *Journal of Consumer Research* 36(5) (2010): 778–91.

161. Siew Meng Leong, Paul S. Busch and Deborah Roedder John, 'Knowledge bases and salesperson effectiveness: A script-theoretic analysis', *Journal of Marketing Research* 26 (May 1989): 164; Harish Sujan, Mita Sujan and James R. Bettman, 'Knowledge structure differences between more effective and less effective salespeople', *Journal of Marketing Research* 25 (February 1988): 81–6; Robert Saxe and Barton Weitz, 'The SOCCO scale: A measure of the customer orientation of salespeople', *Journal of Marketing Research* 19 (August 1982): 343–51; David M. Szymanski, 'Determinants of selling effectiveness: The importance of declarative knowledge to the personal selling concept', *Journal of Marketing* 52 (January 1988): 64–77; Barton A. Weitz, 'Effectiveness in sales interactions: A contingency framework', *Journal of Marketing* 45 (Winter 1981): 85–103.

162. Jagdish M. Sheth, 'Buyer–Seller Interaction: A Conceptual Framework,' in Beverlee B. Anderson (ed.), *Advances in Consumer Research* 3 (Cincinnati, OH: Association for Consumer Research, 1976): 382–6; Kaylene C. Williams and Rosann L. Spiro, 'Communication style in the salesperson–customer dyad', *Journal of Marketing Research* 22 (November 1985): 434–42.

163. Marsha L. Richins, 'An analysis of consumer interaction styles in the marketplace', *Journal of Consumer Research* 10 (June 1983): 73–82.

164. Russell W. Belk, 'The Role of Possessions in Constructing and Maintaining a Sense of Past', in Marvin E. Goldberg, Gerald Gorn and Richard W. Pollay (eds), *Advances in Consumer Research* 17 (Provo, UT: Association for Consumer Research, 1989): 669–76.

165. Jacob Jacoby, Carol K. Berning and Thomas F. Dietvorst, 'What about Disposition?' *Journal of Marketing* 41 (April 1977): 22–8.

166. Katie Fisher, 'UK Statistics on Waste', DEFRA (22 February 2018), https://assets.publishing.service.gov.uk/government/uploads/system/uploads/attachment_data/file/683051/UK_Statisticson_Waste_statistical_notice_Feb_2018_FINAL.pdf (accessed 25 July 2018).

167. https://www.oxfam.org.uk/shop/designer-boutique-women?intcmp=home-coll-designer-boutique (accessed 25 July 2018).

168. Helen Pidd and Zoe Wood, 'How Oxfam became the rising star of UK's online fashion industry', *The Guardian* (14 January 2018), https://www.theguardian.com/business/2018/jan/14/how-oxfam-became-the-rising-star-of-uks-online-fashion-industry (accessed 25 July 2018).

169. Ron Nixon, 'Food waste is becoming serious economic and environmental issue, report says,' *New York Times* (25 February 2015), http://www.nytimes.com/2015/02/26/us/food-waste-is-becoming-serious-economic-and-environmental-issue-report-says.html?_r=1 (accessed 25 July 2018).

170. Angelique Chrisafis, 'France to force big supermarkets to give unsold food to charities, *The Guardian* (23 May 2015): 3, http://www.theguardian.com/world/2015/may/22/france-to-force-big-supermarkets-to-give-away-unsold-food-to-charity (accessed 25 July 2018).

171. Brian Wansink, S. Adam Brasel and Steven Amjad, 'The mystery of the cabinet castaway: Why we buy products we never use', *Journal of Family & Consumer Sciences* 92(1) (2000): 104–7.

172. Jennifer Lach, 'Welcome to the Hoard Fest', *American Demographics* (April 2000): 8–9.

173. Katherine White, Rhiannon MacDonnell and Darren Dahl, 'It's the Mindset that Matters: The Role of Construal Level and Message Framing in Influencing Consumer Conservation Behaviors' in Alan Bradshaw, Chris Hackley and Pauline Maclaran (eds), *European Association for Consumer Research Conference* 2010 RHUL: 15.

174. Jan Brace-Govan and Elizabeth Parsons, 'Reduce, Re-use, Recycle Practice Theory' in Alan Bradshaw, Chris Hackley and Pauline Maclaran (eds), *European Association for Consumer Research Conference* 2010 RHUL: 7.

175. Mike Tharp, 'Tchaikovsky and toilet paper', *U.S. News and World Report* (December 1987): 62; B. Van Voorst, 'The recycling bottleneck', *Time* (14 September 1992): 52–4; Richard P. Bagozzi and Pratibha A. Dabholkar, 'Consumer recycling goals and their effect on decisions to recycle: A means–end chain analysis', *Psychology and Marketing* 11 (July/August 1994): 313–40.

176. 'Finally, something at McDonald's you can actually eat', *UTNE Reader* (May/June 1997): 12.

177. Debra J. Dahab, James W. Gentry and Wanru Su, 'New Ways to Reach Non-Recyclers: An Extension of the Model of Reasoned Action to Recycling Behaviors', in Frank R. Kardes and Mita Sujan (eds), *Advances in Consumer Research* 22 (Provo, UT: Association for Consumer Research): 251–256; for other research, cf. Catlin, R. Jesse and Yitong Wang, 'Recycling gone bad: When the option to recycle increases resource consumption, *Journal of Consumer Psychology* 23(1) (2013): 122–7; R. Trudel and J.J. Argo, 'The effect of product size and form distortion on consumer recycling behavior', *Journal of Consumer Research* 40(4) (2013): 632–43.

178. Richard P. Bagozzi and Pratibha A. Dabholkar, 'Consumer recycling goals and their effect on decisions to recycle', *Psychology & Marketing* 11(4) (1994): 313–40; see also L.J. Shrum, Tina M. Lowrey and John A. McCarty, 'Recycling as a marketing problem: A framework for strategy development', *Psychology & Marketing* 11 (July–August 1994):

393–416; Dahab, Gentry and Su, 'New Ways to Reach Non-Recyclers'.

179. 'Gap asks consumers to recycle their jeans', *RetailingToday. com* (5 October 2010).

180. http://www.look.co.uk/fashion/get-a-%C2%A35-ms-voucher-when-you-donate-to-oxfam (accessed 25 July 2018).

181. Alicia Ciccone, 'H&M launches garment recycling program across all markets', *Brandchannel* (21 February 2013).

182. Barbara Phillips and Trina Sego 'The Role of Identity in Disposal: Lessons from Mothers' Disposal of Children's Products' in Alan Bradshaw, Chris Hackley and Pauline Maclaran (eds), *European Association for Consumer Research Conference* 2010 RHUL: 67.

183. Remi Trudel, Jennifer J. Argo and Matthew D. Meng, 'The recycled self: Consumers' disposal decisions of identity-linked products', *Journal of Consumer Research* 43(2) (2016): 246–64.

184. Grant E. Donnelly, Cait Lamberton, Rebecca Walker Reczek and Michael I. Norton, 'Social recycling transforms unwanted goods into happiness', *Journal of the Association for Consumer Research* 2(1) (January 2017): 48–63.

185. John F. Sherry Jr, 'A socio-cultural analysis of a Mid-western American flea market', *Journal of Consumer Research* 17 (June 1990): 13–30.

186. 'Recommerce,' Trendwatching.com, October 2011, http://www.trendwatching.com/trends/recommerce/ (accessed 25 July 2018).

187. http://www.swishing.com/ (accessed 25 July 2018).

188. John Sutherland, 'The price of nostalgia', *Guardian G2* (28 March 2005): 5, (http://www.guardian.co.uk/g2/story/0,,1446610,00.html) (accessed 25 July 2018).

189. Saul Hansell, 'Meg Whitman and eBay, net survivors', *The New York Times on the Web* (5 May 2002).

190. Jess Cartner-Morley, 'In search of the real deal', *The Guardian* (2 July 2008), http://www.guardian.co.uk/technology/2008/jul/02/ebay.consumeraffairs (accessed 25 July 2018).

191. Martine Geller, 'LVMH and eBay settle litigation over fake goods', Reuters (17 July 2014), http://www.reuters.com/article/2014/07/17/us-lvmh-ebay-settlement-idUSKBN-0FM15G20140717 (accessed 25 July 2018).

192. Quoted in Jenna Wortham, 'Neighborly borrowing, over the online fence', *New York Times* (28 August 2010), http://www.nytimes.com/2010/08/29/business/29ping.html?_r=1&scp=1&sq=collaborative%20consumption&st=cse (accessed 25 July 2018); https://www.crunchbase.com/organization/snapgoods-com (accessed 25 July 2018); www.neighborgoods.com (accessed 25 July 2018).

193. Quoted in Stephanie Stoughton, 'Unemployed Americans turn to e-Bay to make money', *The Boston Globe* (16 October 2001).

194. https://freegan.info/ (accessed 25 July 2018); Steven Kurutz, 'Not buying it', *New York Times* (21 June 2007).

195. Rob Walker, 'Unconsumption', *New York Times Magazine* (7 January 2007): 19; Tina Kelley, 'Socks? With Holes? I'll Take It', *New York Times on the Web* (16 March 2004).

196. Zeynep Arsel and Susan Dobscha, 'Local Acts, Global Impacts? Examining the Pro-Social, Non-Reciprocal Nature of Freecyclers' in Alan Bradshaw, Chris Hackley and Pauline Maclaran (eds), *European Association for Consumer Research Conference* 2010 RHUL: 11–12.

197. John L. Lastovicka and Karen V. Fernandez, 'Three paths to disposition: The movement of meaningful possessions to strangers', *Journal of Consumer Research* 31 (March 2005): 813–23.

198. See Kortnery Stringer, 'Shoppers who blend store, catalog, web spend more', *The Wall Street Journal Online* (3 September 2004): A7 for a detailed discussion of these issues.

199. William Echison, 'Designers climb onto the virtual catwalk', *Business Week* (11 October 1999): 164.

200. Rita Choy and Suzanne Loker, 'Mass customization of wedding gowns: Design involvement on the internet', *Clothing and Textiles Research Journal* 22(1&2) (2004): 79–87.

Case study A.1

'Help me, I can't pay!': Credit card targeting, young consumers and protectionist policy

Sandra Awanis, Lancaster University Management School, UK

> What kind of twisted message do we send when we tell youth they are judged mature, responsible adults when they commit murder, but silly, brainless kids when they want to vote? . . . Double standards load the responsibilities of adults onto the shoulders of young people while only granting them the rights of minors.[1]

Power imbalance continues to prevail in the credit card industry, particularly with regard to the marketing that is directed towards the youth market. Extant literature has long highlighted credit card marketers' predatory approaches to targeting young consumers, as well as this cohort's vulnerability to indebtedness and to experiencing the negative outcomes of credit card use.[2] As such, it comes as no surprise that national governments began to implement policies to protect young people from accumulating extensive credit card debt. A noteworthy trend is the increase in the minimum age of credit card ownership from 17 or 18 to 21, which systematically restricts consumers under the age of 21 from accessing the credit card market and its offerings. Age-based restrictions on credit card ownership are currently being implemented by the United States (CARD Act 2009, Section 226.51), Brunei (Banking Order 2006, Section 66) and Indonesia (APMK 2012, Paragraph 16A). This case study examines the justifications behind such exclusionary regulation.

Credit card targeting practices

The rational purpose of credit cards is to allow for an inter-temporal allocation of income. They enable consumers to borrow future income to use in the present time, allowing people to balance their lifetime utility. However, credit card marketing is more often described as predatory rather than informative, and may be potentially harmful, particularly for inexperienced users. A major criticism of the credit card marketing that targets young people is the promotion of positive, aspirational images of credit card use that obscures the negative consequences of debt – for example, 'There are some things money can't buy. For everything else, there's MasterCard'. Moreover, credit card marketing is often accompanied by a lack of transparency in credit pricing structures. For example, consumers often do not realise that any spending on a credit card with a 0 per cent balance transfer deal will be charged at a much higher interest rate than their normal rate when the promotional period ends.

Credit cards aimed at younger consumers, particularly students, pose greater risks of misuse and indebtedness, as these product offerings tend not to take the usual criteria into account. For example, the marketing of student credit cards typically includes initiatives that: (1) encourage credit cards to be used frequently, for example to purchase groceries and other basic necessities; (2) suspend the traditional criteria for the issuing of a credit card (such as minimum income and prior credit history); (3) fail to provide information about the consequences of making only minimum payments (such as whether interest will be charged on the interest accrued from previous months); (4) offer premiums, discounts and promotions to encourage the student to sign up for a credit card; and (5) offer credit limits that are beyond the young person's income or ability to pay.

Young people as a target market segment

Young credit card users have a greater average lifetime earning potential than other age groups and a greater likelihood of developing long-term brand loyalty towards their first credit card.[3] Furthermore, young people tend to use their credit cards to withdraw cash without considering the consequences, and then pay significant interest and/or penalty charges. Research by Equifax in 2009 indicates that 30 per cent of UK students are unaware of their overall level of credit card spending, while 19 per cent only make the minimum payment on their balance. Meanwhile, a study conducted by FICO in 2014 shows that the percentage of UK student credit card balance had increased by 40 per cent from the previous year.

Young consumers also tend to display biological and psychological traits that can lead to risky credit card behaviour, including shopping impulsiveness,[4] lack of self-control[5] and an unrealistic overestimation of future income.[6] These traits increase their likelihood of

78

experiencing the negative outcomes of credit card use. Further, Generation Y consumers also face rising unemployment and the lack of financial education in school curricula.[7] Overall, these reports point to a general perception that young people are vulnerable to credit card misuse and suffer the resulting negative outcomes of credit card indebtedness.

Public policy responses and critiques

The age restriction on credit card ownership is aimed at protecting the young from developing problematic credit card habits. At first glance, such restrictions do seem to lead to a rapid decrease in credit card debt. For example, the Brunei Darussalam National Bank claimed that credit card debt decreased by more than 30 per cent the first year after the age limit was raised from 18 to 21.[8] However, sceptics argue that this may have been due to a simple reduction in the total number of credit card users. The policy does not prevent young people from developing bad habits when they reach the age at which they are allowed to take out a credit card. Furthermore, exclusionary policies assume that individuals under 21 years of age are unfit to use credit cards responsibly, creating a barrier for young people who intend to use credit cards to manage their finances or to build a credit rating from an early age. Access to credit represents an essential means of obtaining goods or services that society regards as an individual's right.[9] Hence, excluding young people from the possibility of obtaining a credit card can be seen as simply denying them their basic right to build a credit record from a young age and to start crafting a credit history.

The regulation also poses a threat to the credit card industry's already weakening market presence. The elimination of a lucrative target market segment leaves credit card issuers with inferior marketing strategies. For example, Standard Chartered Bank in Brunei Darussalam reported a 20 per cent drop in operating income following the increase in the minimum age requirement.[10] Similarly, an independent study by Deloitte predicted that the overall rate of lost business for the credit card industry as a result of the US CARD Act would range from 18 per cent to 38 per cent, depending on the financial institutions' reliance on credit card revenues.[11]

Industry representatives also predict that further policy restrictions will lead to increased operating costs that are likely to be passed on to consumers, such as through a withdrawal of promotional credit card rates.[12] Importantly, consumer research indicates that credit card overuse is a cultural and lifestyle issue that is not exclusive to the young consumer.[13] These competing

arguments thus raise a question about the efficacy of age-restrictive credit card policies in helping young consumers to achieve sustained financial well-being. Moreover, it may be too simplistic to generalise all young people as equally vulnerable to credit card misuse and indebtedness, as not all young consumers are in a position of such vulnerability.

Questions

1 To what extent are young consumers considered a vulnerable consumer group in the credit card industry? State arguments for and against.

2 What are the potential causes of young people's credit card misuse and indebtedness?

3 What alternative policies can governments employ to reduce problematic indebtedness among young people?

4 In the light of the above case study, how should credit card issuers treat their younger consumers?

Sources

[1]Youth Policy, 'Adult Responsibilities, Right of Minors: Youth Rights – More than a Timely Slogan?', (2013), http://www.youthpolicy.org/blog/youth-policy-young-people/youth-rights-timely-slogan/ (accessed 3 September 2018).

[2]M.J. Mason, J.F. Tanner, M. Piacentini, D. Freeman, T. Anastasia, W. Batat, W. Boland, M. Canbulut, J. Drenten, A. Hamby, P. Rangan and Z. Yang, 'Advancing a participatory approach for youth risk behavior: foundations, distinctions, and research directions', *Journal of Business Research* 66(8) (2012): 1,235–41; J.J. Xiao, C. Tang, J. Serido and S. Shim, 'Antecedents and consequences of risky credit behavior among college students: application and extension of the theory of planned behavior', *Journal of Public Policy & Marketing* 30(2) (2011): 239–45.

[3]J. Warwick and P.M. Mansfield, 'Credit card consumers: college students' knowledge and attitude', *Journal of Consumer Marketing* 17(7) (2000): 617–26.

[4]S. Pirog and J.A. Roberts, 'Personality and credit card misuse among college students: the mediating role of impulsiveness', *Journal of Marketing Theory and Practice* 15(1) (2007): 65–77.

[5]M.B. Pinto, P.M. Mansfield and D.H. Parente, 'Relationship of credit attitude and debt to self-esteem and locus of control in college-age consumers', *Psychological reports* 94(3) (2004): 1,405–18.

[6]J.M. Norvilitis, M.M. Merwin, T.M. Osberg, P.V. Roehling, P. Young and M.M. Kamas, 'Personality factors, money attitudes, financial knowledge, and credit-card debt in college students', *Journal of Applied Social Psychology* 36(6) (2006): 1,395–413.

[7]I. Szmigin and D. O'Loughlin, 'Students and the consumer credit market: towards a social policy agenda', *Social Policy & Administration* 44(5) (2010): 598–619.

[8]B.S. Begawan, 'Baiduri Bank says card debts down 30% since 2010', *Brunei Times* (22 October 2011).

[9]S. Finlay, *Consumer Credit Fundamentals,* 2nd edn (New York: Palgrave Macmillan, 2009).

[10]Oxford Business Group, 'The Report: Brunei Darussalam 2011', (2011), https://books.google.co.uk/books?id= x-MBjG1LahsC&printsec= frontcover&source=;gbs_ge_ summary_r&cad=;0#v=;onepage&q&f=false (accessed 3 September 2018).

[11]D. Cox and L. Breslaw, 'Credit crisis advisory: US credit card accountability, responsibility and disclosure', *Centre for Banking Solutions* 9 (July 2009): 1–6.

[12]P. Rodford, 'The US Credit Card Accountability, Responsibility and Disclosure (CARD) Act – Handle With Care', The UK Cards Association (2009).

[13]M.J. Bernthal, D. Crockett and R.L. Rose, 'Credit cards as life-style facilitators', *Journal of Consumer Research* 32(1) (2005): 130–45; L. Peñaloza and M. Barnhart, 'Living U.S. capitalism: the normalization of credit/debt', *Journal of Consumer Research* 38(4) (2011): 743–62.

Case study A.2

Online shopping in Uganda: the exclusion of a rising middle class from the market

Kira Strandby, Campus Vejle, Denmark

Introduction

The internet represents a plethora of shopping opportunities. It seems that anything can ship anywhere within hours in a somewhat hyper-globalised online shopping centre. Amazon Prime fills up consumers' pantries with foods from around the world. Consumers buy cheap electronics on Taobao, luxury fashion on Net-a-porter.com and sell off anything they don't need after all on eBay. For companies, this means near endless competition. For consumers, it means lower prices, increased choice and, in some cases, even empowerment.[1]

This might be true for many Western consumers, but many Ugandan consumers, as with others in developing contexts, are having a hard time seeing these opportunities unfold. In their experience, once they make their way to the online shops, money in hand, the doors lock right in front of them. African consumers can experience exclusion based on their IP addresses,[2] with some companies not even allowing consumers from certain countries access to their websites, let alone to purchase any goods. Others are excluded using more subtle methods, such as increased shipping rates for low-income countries. For example, Amazon only offers standard shipping to a few select countries in Africa, while consumers from most African countries are forced to pay the expedited or even priority courier rates, depending on their location.

From a marketer's point of view, this makes little or no sense. Many African countries are experiencing economic growth, which creates new markets and consumers. However, reaching them has proven a challenge. While the main challenges for Western e-commerce businesses are lack of technology acceptance,[3] trust,[4] and perceived financial risk,[5] there are additional challenges to consider in sub-Saharan Africa,[6] such as lack of access to formalised banking systems and delivery systems. The three stories below are actual examples of Ugandan consumers' experiences with online shopping.

David

'Electronics, I love them. There are very many cheap electronics on the internet, but, I can't buy them, sometimes I just wish I could even sometimes stubbornly I am forced to press buy, but I can't buy it.'

David is a young entrepreneurial guy, living in Kampala. During the day he works as a driver for an expatriate worker, but by night he develops websites and works as a graphic designer. Business is going great, except for one thing. He has no credit card. Whenever he needs to buy domains or pay hosting fees, he has to rely on his boss's willingness to help him and lend him his VISA card. He knows that this solution is unsustainable, as his boss won't be stationed in Uganda forever. However, when he applied for a card of his own at his bank, he was rejected. His bank, like every other bank in Uganda, asked for a deposit of $600 in order to issue a debit card – an insurmountable amount when your monthly salary rarely surpasses $100. The lack of a credit card also prevents him from buying apps for his phone, and from purchasing electronics online at a much lower price than they are available in Kampala. As the opening quote shows, he is frustrated to a point where he clicks 'buy' anyway, knowing that he has no way of going through with the transaction. He has money to spend, but no way of spending it.

Lauryn

'I had bad experiences with let's say Amazon, the thing gets here and then it's even more expensive to try to send it back, than if I was buying it. I'd rather order from a local shop here, because then they can take the responsibility, the warranty and all that stuff.'

Lauryn, a successful career woman and mother of four, has little patience with online shopping. From her perspective, it is slow and inconvenient, offering few merits other than the somewhat larger selection of goods. Thus, she prefers to pay a premium price for convenience. She finds the items she likes online and places an order with a local shop, which then orders the items and lets her return them if she doesn't want them after all. Sometimes she will use personal shoppers who come to her office with a selection of desired items, such as 'red shoes' or 'black dresses'. She's in the position of having experienced few financial limitations, which makes some of the perceived benefits of internet shopping irrelevant in her particular case.

James

'I also want to buy clothes, but the bad thing about the internet, you can also buy something that is not authentic. So, what I usually do, when my cousins go out [of the country], I tell them to bring, things back with them to come with them I send money through Western Union to them to buy things. They receive your money, they buy the product and they come back with it in six months, when they come to visit us. That's mostly it. And of course, with family members, they can always choose what is best for you. Unlike those other people who don't know who you are, and all they want to do is to make money. That's mostly about that. I use them to bring me whatever I want from out there.'

James, a 21-year-old university student, has all but given up on online shopping. As seen in the quote above, he experiences a significant degree of risk with e-commerce, afraid to receive counterfeit goods or of being conned in some way or another. Instead he relies on his family to do his international shopping for him, which is rather common as many Ugandans have migrated to the US, Europe and the Middle East. He had tried to buy a computer online, but was rejected on account of his location, with the vendor deeming the transaction too risky to be profitable. He has, however, been quite successful in spending his money online in another context, that of online betting. While payment methods in online stores rarely include mobile money options,[7] betting companies are more than happy to accept any kind of payment.

Questions

1 Reflect upon the experiences of the three consumers above. How do they compare to your own experience of online shopping?

2 Imagine that you are a market researcher in a global consulting firm. One of your clients wants to enter the Ugandan market through online distribution channels, but they are unsure of what to do. What would your advice be? Compose a strategy brief summarising your thoughts.

3 Sub-Saharan consumers experience exclusion from online markets. What could be a possible explanation for this? Should discrimination be illegal or is it entirely up to the online vendor?

4 Imagine that you are a consumer advocate. Write a brief describing why inclusion into the global markets is important to Ugandan consumers.

Sources

[1]G. D. Pires, J. Stanton and P. Rita, 'The Internet, Consumer Empowerment and Marketing Strategies', *European Journal of Marketing* 40(9/10) (2006): 936–49; J. Alba, J. Lynch, B. Weitz, C. Janiszewski, R. Lutz, A. Sawyer and S. Wood, 'Interactive Home Shopping: Consumer, Retailer, and Manufacturer Incentives to Participate in Electronic Marketplaces', *Journal of Marketing* 61(3) (1997): 38–53; M. Wolfinbarger and M.C. Gilly, 'Shopping online for freedom, control, and fun', *California Management Review* 43(2) (2001): 34–55.

[2]J. Burrell, *Invisible Users: Youth in the Internet Cafés of Urban Ghana* (Cambridge, MA: MIT Press, 2012).

[3]F. Davis, 'Perceived Usefulness, Perceived Ease of Use, and User Acceptance of Information Technology', *MIS Quarterly* 13(3) (1989): 319–40; C. Dennis, B. Merrilees, C. Jayawardhena and L.T. Wright, 'E-consumer Behaviour', *European Journal of Marketing* 43(9/10) (2009): 1,121–39; T.P. Monsuwe, B.G.C. Dellaert and K. de Ruyter, 'What drives consumers to shop online? A literature review', *International Journal of Service Industry Management* 15(1) (2004): 102–21.

[4]D. Gefen, E. Karahanna and D.W. Straub, 'Trust and TAM in online shopping: an integrated model', *MIS Quarterly* 27(1) (2003): 51–90.

[5]G. Pires, J. Stanton and A. Eckford, 'Influences on the perceived risk of purchasing online', *Journal of Consumer Behaviour* 4 (2004): 118–31; Z. Chen and A.J. Dubinsky, 'A Conceptual Model of Perceived Customer Value in E-Commerce: A Preliminary Investigation', *Psychology & Marketing* 20(4) (2003): 323–47; E. Chang and Y. Tseng, 'Research note: E-store image, perceived value and perceived risk', *Journal of Business Research* 66 (2013): 864–70.

[6]B. DeBerry-Spence and E.A. Elliot, 'African micro-entrepreneurship: The reality of everyday challenges', *Journal of Business Research* 65(12) (2012): 1,665–73.

[7]Mobile Money is the most common payment system in sub-Saharan Africa. It allows the user to use their cellphone as a bank account, with the same possibilities of transferring money and paying bills.

Further reading

E. Penz, 'Paradoxical Effects of the Internet from a Consumer Perspective', *Critical Perspectives on International Business* 3(4) (2007): 364–80.

Part B
How consumers see the world and themselves

The second part of this text deals with the questions of 'Who am I?' and 'How do I see the world?'. Building on the initial themes set out in the first part, these chapters examine how consumers' perceptions affect their understanding of the marketplace and how they elicit meanings from the offerings of consumer culture, how they use consumption in constructing their sense of self, and how motivations, values and lifestyles affect their consumption.

Chapter 3
Perception and meaning

Chapter objectives

When you finish reading this chapter you will understand why:

3.1 Perception is a three-stage process that translates perceptual stimuli into meaning.

3.2 All our sensory systems are addressed through marketing.

3.3 The concept of a perceptual selection is important for marketing communication.

3.4 We elicit meaning through the process of interpretation and the use of cultural categories in order to make sense of the world around us.

3.5 The universe of meanings pertaining to commercial products or services is what we usually call the 'brand'.

3.6 The field of semiotics helps us to understand how marketers use symbols to create meaning.

3.7 Contemporary culture can be understood as postmodern.

THE EUROPEAN VACATION has been wonderful, and this stop in Lisbon is no exception. Still, after two weeks of eating his way through some of the Continent's finest pastry shops and restaurants, Gary's getting a bit of a craving for his family's favourite snack – a good old American box of Oreos and an ice-cold carton of milk. Unbeknownst to his wife, Janeen, he had stashed away some cookies 'just in case' – this was the time to break them out.

Now, all he needs is the milk. On an impulse, Gary decides to surprise Janeen with a mid-afternoon treat. He sneaks out of the hotel room while she's napping and finds the nearest *grosa*. When he heads to the small refrigerated section, though, he's puzzled – no milk here. Undaunted, Gary asks the clerk, '*Leite, por favor?*' The clerk quickly smiles and points to a rack in the middle of the store piled with little white square boxes. No, that can't be right – Gary resolves to work on his Portuguese. He repeats the question, and again he gets the same answer.

Finally, he investigates and sure enough he sees the boxes with labels saying they contain something called ultra heat-treated (UHT) milk. Nasty! Who in the world would drink milk out of a little box that's been sitting on a warm shelf for who knows how long? Gary dejectedly returns to the hotel, his snack-time fantasies crumbling like so many stale cookies.

Gary Bamossy

Introduction

We live in a world overflowing with sensations. Wherever we turn, we are bombarded by a symphony of colours, sounds and odours. Some of the 'notes' in this symphony occur naturally, such as the barking of a dog, the shadows of the evening sky or the heady smell of a rose bush. Others come from people: the person sitting next to you might have dyed-blonde hair, bright-pink jeans and be wearing enough perfume to make your eyes water.

Marketers certainly contribute to this commotion. Consumers are never far from advertisements, product packages, radio and television commercials and advertising hoardings that clamour for their attention. Whether it is the (culturally learned) bias of being suspicious of unrefrigerated UHT milk, purchasing fresh fish from a vending machine in Spain,[1] or listening to a car blast out teeth-rattling Major Lazer and MØ cuts from booming car speakers, each of us copes with the bombardment of sensations in the marketplace as we pay attention to some stimuli and tune out others. When we do make a decision to purchase, we are responding not only to these influences but to our interpretations of them.

This chapter focuses on the process of perception, in which sensations are absorbed by the consumer and used to interpret the surrounding world. After discussing the stages of this process, the chapter examines how the five senses (sight, smell, sound, touch and taste) affect consumers. The chapter emphasises that the way in which a marketing stimulus is presented plays a role in determining whether the consumer will make sense of it, or even notice it at all. Finally, we discuss the process of interpretation, in which the stimuli that are noticed by the consumer are organised and assigned meaning. In the end, the most important thing is not only *that* you perceive but *what* you perceive – or, in other words, the meanings that you elicit and how you make sense of the world around you.

The perceptual process

Perception is a three-stage process that translates perceptual stimuli into meaning.

As you sit in a lecture hall, you may find your attention shifting. One minute you are concentrating on the lecture, and the next you catch yourself day-dreaming about the weekend ahead before you realise that you are missing some important points and tune back into the lecture.

People undergo stages of information processing, in which stimuli are inputted and stored. However, we do not process passively whatever information happens to be present. Only a very small number of the stimuli in our environment are ever noticed. Of these, an even smaller number are attended to. And the stimuli that do enter our consciousness are not processed objectively. The meaning of a stimulus is interpreted by the individual, who is influenced by their unique biases, needs and experiences. These three stages of **exposure**, **attention** and **interpretation** make up the process of perception. The stages involved in selecting and interpreting stimuli are illustrated in Figure 3.1, which provides an overview of the perceptual process.

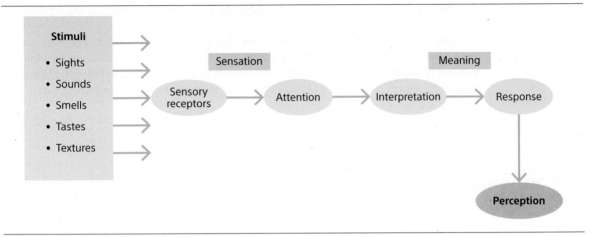

Figure 3.1 An overview of the perceptual process

From sensation to perception

Sensation refers to the immediate response of our sensory receptors (e.g. eyes, ears, nose, mouth, fingers) to such basic stimuli as light, colour and sound. **Perception** is the process by which these stimuli are selected, organised and interpreted. We process raw data (sensation); however, the study of perception focuses on what we add to or take away from these sensations as we assign meaning to them.

The subjective nature of perception is demonstrated by this 'Ugly Truth/Your beauty Up in Smoke' ad. Whether from smoking, or from other 'long-term' damaging behaviours to their appearance such as going to tanning salons, young people tend to discount or outright reject messages of 'This could be you if you continue to do this'. Such interpretations or assumptions stem from **schemas**, or organised collections of beliefs and feelings. That is, we tend to group the objects we see as having similar characteristics, and the schema to which an object is assigned is a crucial determinant of how we choose to evaluate this object at a later time. I'm youthful, beautiful, cool-looking now. . . these warnings don't apply to me, so I pay little or no attention to them.

The perceptual process can be illustrated by the purchase of a new aftershave. Men have learned to equate aftershave with romantic appeal, so we search for cues that (we believe) will increase our attractiveness. We make our selection by considering such factors as the image associated with each alternative and the design of the bottle, as well as the actual scent.

A perceptual process can be broken down into the following stages:[2]

1 *Primitive categorisation,* in which the basic characteristics of a stimulus are isolated: our male consumer feels he needs to bolster his image, so he chooses aftershave.

2 *Cue check,* in which the characteristics are analysed in preparation for the selection of a schema: everyone has his own unique, more-or-less developed schemas or categories for different types of aftershave, such as 'down-to-earth macho', 'mysterious' or 'fancy French'. We use certain cues, such as the colour of the bottle, to decide in which schema a particular cologne fits.

3 *Confirmation check,* in which the schema is selected; the consumer may decide that a brand falls into his 'mysterious' schema.

4 *Confirmation completion,* in which a decision is made as to what the stimulus is: the consumer decides he has made the right choice, and then reinforces this decision by considering the colour of the bottle and the interesting name of the aftershave.

The subjective nature of perception is demonstrated by this anti-smoking ad.
Patrick Foto/Shutterstock

Such considerations illustrate the importance of the perceptual process for product positioning. In many cases, consumers use a few basic dimensions to categorise competing products or services, and then evaluate each alternative in terms of its relative standing on these dimensions.

This tendency has led to the use of a very useful positioning tool – a **perceptual map**. By identifying the important dimensions and then asking consumers to place competitors within this space, marketers can answer some crucial strategic questions, such as which product alternatives are seen by consumers as similar or dissimilar, and what opportunities exist for new products that possess attributes not represented by current brands. Figure 3.2 offers a

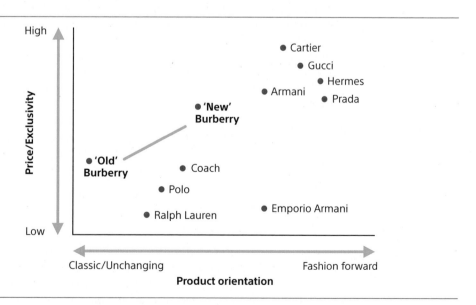

Figure 3.2 Perceptual map of the Burberry brand, relative to competitors

perceptual map of the iconic Burberry brand, showing its 'old' position from the 1980s and 1990s, and the shift in perceptions of the brand in more recent years.

Sensory systems

3.2

All our sensory systems are addressed through marketing.

When guests at Omni luxury hotels visit the hotel chain's website to reserve a room, they hear the sound of soft chimes playing. The signature scent of lemongrass and green tea hits them as they enter the lobby. In their rooms, they will find eucalyptus bath salts and Sensation Bars – minibars stocked with items such as mojito-flavoured jelly beans and miniature Zen gardens.

Welcome to the new era of **sensory marketing**, where companies pay extra attention to the impact of sensations on our product experiences. From hotels to carmakers to brewers, they recognise that our senses help us to decide which products appeal to us – and which ones stand out from a host of similar offerings in the marketplace. In this section, we'll take a closer look at how some smart marketers use our sensory systems to create a competitive advantage.

Sensory inputs evoke historical imagery, in which events that actually occurred are recalled. Fantasy imagery results when an entirely new, imaginary experience is the response to sensory data. These responses are an important part of **hedonic consumption**, or the multisensory, fantasy and emotional aspects of consumers' interactions with products.[3] These sensations we experience are context effects that subtly influence how we think about products we encounter. Here are some examples from consumer research:

- Respondents evaluated products more harshly when they stood on a tile floor rather than a carpeted floor.[4]
- Fans of romance movies rate them more highly when they watch them in a cold room (researchers say this is because they compensate for the low physical temperature with the psychological warmth the movie provides).[5]
- When a product is scented, consumers are more likely to remember other attributes about it after they encounter it.[6]
- A highly intensive sensory experience is not only preferable to most consumers in and by itself, but it also restores a better self-worth.[7]

Although we usually trust our sensory receptors to give us an accurate account of the external environment, new technology is making the linkage between our senses and reality more questionable. Computer-simulated environments, or **virtual reality**, allow surgeons to 'cut into' a person without drawing blood or an architect to see a building design from different perspectives. This technology, which creates a three-dimensional perceptual environment that the viewer experiences as being virtually real, is already being adapted to everyday pursuits, such as virtual reality games.

Enterprising business people will no doubt continue to find new ways to adapt this technology for consumers' entertainment – the recent developments in 'virtual catalogues' now allow a person to browse through a shop without leaving their armchair (still no progress on delivering smells to your Web browser, but it will come!). In this section, we will take a brief look at some of the processes involved in the business applications of sensory stimuli.

Vision

Sure, Apple's products usually work pretty well – but that's not why many people buy them. Sleek styling and simple, compact features telegraph an aura of modernity, sophistication and just plain 'cool'. Marketers rely heavily on visual elements in advertising, store design and packaging. They communicate meanings on the *visual channel* through a product's colour, size and styling.

Virtual reality, together with Artificial Intelligence, are some of the potentially most influential technologies when it comes to consumer behaviour.

vectorfusionart/ Shutterstock

Colours may even influence our emotions more directly. Evidence suggests that some colours (particularly red) create feelings of arousal and stimulate appetite, and others (such as blue) create more relaxed feelings – American Express launched its Blue card after its research found that people describe the colour as 'providing a sense of limitlessness and peace'.[8] Advertisements of products presented against a backdrop of blue are better liked than when shown against a red background, and cross-cultural research indicates a consistent preference for blue, whether people live in Canada or Hong Kong.[9] People even link moral judgements to colours; in a study, respondents evaluated undesirable consumer behaviours less negatively when described on a red (*vs* green) background while they evaluated desirable consumer behaviours more positively when described on a green (*vs* red) background.[10]

Some reactions to colour come from learned associations. In Western countries, black is the colour of mourning, whereas in some Eastern countries, notably Japan, white plays this role. In addition, we associate the colour black with power. Other reactions are a result of biological and cultural differences. Women are drawn towards brighter tones and they are more sensitive to subtle shadings and patterns. Some scientists attribute this to biology; females see colour better than males do, and men are 16 times more likely to be colour blind. It has also been established that the use of gender-stereotyped colours (pink and blue) activates gender-stereotypical associations for brands, such as 'warmth' or 'competence'. (Wait a minute, who said that competence – or warmth, for that matter – is gender specific? Well, remember that we talk stereotypes here.)[11]

Of course, fashion trends strongly influence our colour preferences, so it's no surprise that we tend to encounter a 'hot' colour in clothing and home designs in one season that is replaced by something else in the next season (as when the *fashionistas* proclaim: 'Brown is the new black!'). These styles do not happen by accident; most people don't know (but now *you* do) that a handful of firms produce *colour forecasts* that manufacturers and retailers buy so they can be sure they stock up on the next hot hue. For example, Pantone, Inc. (one of the colour arbiters), listed these colours among its favourites for Spring 2018 fashions:[12]

- Cherry tomato: "a tempestuous orangey red that exudes heat and energy [. . .] this courageous, never to be ignored, shade is viscerally alive".

- Little Boy Blue: "no longer for little boys only. Suggestive of expansiveness and continuity, this azure blue shade reassures us with its promise of a new day".

- Pink Lavender: Pink Lavender is a soft and romantic violet rose that charms with its soothing sense of quiescence.

In a given year, certain colours appear to be 'hot' and show up over and over again in clothing, home furnishings, cars and so on. But favourite colours disappear as fast as they come, to be replaced by another set of 'hot' colours the next year or season. Table 3.1 summarises how experts link specific colours to marketing contexts.

Smell

Odours can stir emotions or create a calming feeling. They can invoke memories or relieve stress. One study found that consumers who viewed ads for either flowers or chocolate and who were also exposed to flowery or chocolatey odours spent more time processing the product information and were more likely to try different alternatives within each product category.[13] Many consumers control the odours in their environments and this growing interest has spawned a lot of new products since Glade marketed the first air freshener to suburban families in 1956. Today, younger people are at the forefront of 'scented air' as they take advantage of plug-ins, fragrance fans, diffusers and potpourri. Almost anything is fair game to be scented today; even the country of Lithuania has created a perfume (appropriately called 'Lithuania') it uses in hotels and embassies to convey the country's image. And finally, Burger King in Japan sells a 'flame-grilled' fragrance to customers who want to smell like a Whopper![14]

Consumers' love of fragrances has contributed to a very large industry. Because this market is extremely competitive (30–40 new scents are introduced each year) and expensive (it costs an average of £30 million to introduce a new fragrance), manufacturers are scrambling to find new ways to expand the use of scents and odours in our daily lives. One trend, supported by the marketing efforts of, among others, Calvin Klein, is perfumes positioned as unisex. In addition to the perfume market, home-fragrance products (consisting primarily of potpourri, room sprays and atomisers, drawer liners, sachets and scented candles) represent an important market.

Sound

BMW recently began to use an audio watermark at the end of TV and radio ads around the world. 'The company wants to establish what the brand sounds like', so all of its messages end with a melody '. . . underscored by two distinctive bass tones that form the sound logo's

Table 3.1 Marketing applications of colours

Colour	Associations	Marketing applications
Yellow	Optimistic and youthful	Used to grab window shoppers' attention
Red	Energy	Often seen in clearance sales
Blue	Trust and security	Banks
Green	Wealth	Used to create relaxation in stores
Orange	Aggressive	Call to action: subscribe, buy or sell
Black	Powerful and sleek	Luxury products
Purple	Soothing	Beauty or anti-ageing products

Source: Adapted from Leo Widrich, 'Why Is Facebook Blue? The Science Behind Colors in Marketing', *Fast Company* (6 May 2013), http://www.fastcompany.com/3009317/why-is-facebook-blue-the-science-behind-colours-in-marketing?partner=newsletter (accessed 23 August 2018).

Marketing opportunity

Companies are highly interested in the use of fragrances. Already some years ago, the coffee shop chain Dunkin' Donuts used coffee-scenting in Seoul's public transportation system in order to increase coffee sales.[15] And world-renowned whisky producers Johnnie Walker made attempts to produce clothing with a hint of whisky-scent permanently imbued into the tweed.[16] Airlines such as Singapore Airlines, ANA and Turkish Airlines have applied scenting strategically, both in terms of scented towels but also light scenting of the cabin air for increased traveller pleasure. According to one agent assisting airline companies with strategic uses of odours, 'white tea and fig' is the most popular scent.[17]

melodic and rhythmic basis'. BMW claims this sound signature represents 'sheer driving pleasure'.[18]

Music and other sounds affect people's feelings and behaviours. Some marketers who come up with brand names pay attention to sound symbolism – the process by which the way a word sounds influences our assumptions about what it describes and attributes such as size. For example, consumers are more likely to recognise brand names that begin with a hard consonant such as a K (Kellogg's) or P (Pepsi). Consumers associate brand names with the stopping consonants 'k' and 't' with masculinity, whereas fricative (using air streams to form) consonants such as 'f' and 's' in brand names are associated with femininity.[19] We also tend to associate certain vowel and consonant sounds (or *phonemes*) with perceptions of large and small size. Mental rehearsal of prices containing numbers with small phonemes results in overestimation of price discounts, whereas mental rehearsal of prices containing numbers with large phonemes results in underestimation.[20] One study even found that the sound symbolism in a stock's ticker symbol helped to predict the company's performance during its first year of trading.[21] Two areas of research that have widespread applications in consumer contexts are the effects of background music on mood and the influence of speaking rate on attitude change and message comprehension. *Muzak* is heard by millions of people every day. This so-called 'functional music' is played in stores, shopping centres and offices either to relax or stimulate consumers. There is general agreement that muzak contributes to the well-being and buying activities of customers, but no scientific proof exists. Researchers have also been interested in the interaction between sensory stimuli – for example, in the perceived congruency between the appearance and the sound of the voice of brand spokespersons.[22]

The classic, contoured Coca-Cola bottle also attests to the power of touch. The bottle was designed approximately 90 years ago to satisfy the request of a US bottler for a soft-drink container that people could identify even in the dark.

© Rufus Stone/Alamy

Touch

Hint to retailers: follow Apple's lead and encourage customers to handle your products in the store! One recent study demonstrated the potential power of touch; the researchers found that participants who simply touched an item (an inexpensive coffee mug) for 30 seconds or less created a greater level of attachment to the product; this connection in turn boosted what they were willing to pay for it.[23] Britain's Asda grocery chain removed the wrapping from several brands of toilet tissue in its stores so that shoppers could feel and compare textures. The result, the retailer says, was soaring sales for its own in-store brand, resulting in a 50 per cent increase in shelf space for the line.[24]

Tactile cues have symbolic meaning. People associate the textures of fabrics and other products with underlying product qualities. The perceived richness or quality of the material in clothing, bedding or upholstery is linked to its 'feel' – whether it is rough or smooth, soft or stiff. A smooth fabric such as silk is equated with luxury, while denim is considered practical and durable. The vibration of a mobile phone against the owner's body signals a personal telephone call coming in, as well as some degree of respect about not disturbing others in the area. Some of these tactile/quality associations are summarised in Table 3.2. Fabrics that are composed of rare materials or that require a high degree of processing to achieve their smoothness or fineness tend to be more expensive and thus are seen as being classier. Similarly, lighter, more delicate textures are assumed to be feminine. Roughness is often positively valued for men, while smoothness is sought by women.

We have a tendency to want to touch objects, although typing or using a mouse are skills we have to learn. The proliferation of touchscreens on computers, ATM machines, digital

Technological change has made touching and feeling an increasingly important part of our interaction with technology (see Rhonda Hadi's 'Consumer behaviour as I see it . . .' later in the chapter.

ra2studio/Shutterstock

Table 3.2 Tactile oppositions to fabrics

Perception	Male	Female	
High-class	Wool	Silk	Fine
Low-class	Denim	Cotton	↕
	Heavy	Light	Coarse

cameras, GPS devices and e-readers is an outgrowth of a philosophy of computer design known as *natural user interface*. This approach incorporates habitual human movements that we don't have to learn. Sony decided to offer touchscreens on its e-readers after its engineers repeatedly observed people in focus groups automatically swipe the screen of its older, non-touch models. Touchscreens also appear on exercise machines, in hospitals and at airport check-in terminals.

Taste

Our taste receptors contribute to our experience of many products. Sensory analysis is used to account for the human perception of sensory product qualities. One study used sensory analysis to assess butter biscuits: the crispness, buttery-taste, rate of melt, density, 'molar packing' (the amount of biscuit that sticks to the teeth) and the 'notes' of the biscuit, such as sweetness, saltiness or bitterness.[25]

Food companies go to great lengths to ensure that their products taste as they should. Philips' highly successful Senseo coffee machine produces a creamy head of foam on the top of a cup of home-brewed coffee.[26] Companies may use a group of 'sensory panellists' as tasters – these consumers are recruited because they have superior sensory abilities, and are then given six months' training. Or they rely on lay people, i.e. ordinary consumers. In a blind

This ad metaphorically illustrates the natural quality and taste sensation of a lemon as a substitute for salt.

Sunkist Growers, Inc.

taste test, panellists rate the products of a company and its competitors on a number of dimensions. The results of such studies are important to discover both different consumer preferences and, thus, different consumer segments, and the positioning of a company or a brand in terms of the most important sensory qualities of the product.[27]

Perceptual selection

3.3

The concept of a perceptual selection is important for marketing communication.

Given that we encounter so many stimuli every single day and every single moment, it is obvious that marketers are interested in the processes by which we select what we pay attention to. However, as we shall see, sometimes it is equally important that we do not perceive any differences.

Sensory thresholds

If you have ever blown a dog whistle and watched pets respond to a sound you cannot hear, you will know that there are some stimuli that people simply are not capable of perceiving. And, of course, some people are better able to pick up sensory information than others. The science that focuses on how the physical environment is integrated into our personal, subjective world is known as **psychophysics**. By understanding some of the physical laws that govern what we are capable of responding to, this knowledge can be translated into marketing strategies.

The absolute threshold

When we define the lowest intensity of a stimulus that can be registered on a sensory channel, we speak of a threshold for that receptor. The **absolute threshold** refers to the minimum amount of stimulation that can be detected on a sensory channel. The sound emitted by a dog whistle is too high to be detected by human ears, so this stimulus is beyond our auditory absolute threshold. The absolute threshold is an important consideration in designing marketing stimuli. A billboard along the motorway might have the most entertaining story ever written, but this genius is wasted if the print is too small for passing motorists to read it.

The differential threshold

The **differential threshold** refers to the ability of a sensory system to detect changes or differences between two stimuli. A commercial that is intentionally produced in black and white might be noticed on a colour television because the intensity of colour differs from the programme that preceded it. The same commercial being watched on a black-and-white television would not be seen as different and might be ignored altogether.

The issue of when and if a change will be noticed is relevant to many marketing situations. Sometimes a marketer may want to ensure that a change is noticed, such as when merchandise is offered at a discount. In other situations, the fact that a change has been made is downplayed, as in the case of price increases or when the size of a product, such as a chocolate bar, is decreased.

A consumer's ability to detect a difference between two stimuli is relative. A whispered conversation that might be unintelligible on a noisy street can suddenly become public and embarrassing knowledge in a quiet library. It is the relative difference between the decibel level of the conversation and its surroundings, rather than the loudness of the conversation itself, that determines whether the stimulus will register.

The Pepsi logo over time.
Suriyachan/Shutterstock

The minimum change in a stimulus that can be detected is also known as the **JND**, which stands for 'just-noticeable difference'. In the nineteenth century, a German psychophysicist, Ernst Weber, found that the amount of change that is necessary to be noticed is related to the original intensity of the stimulus. The stronger the initial stimulus, the greater the change must be for it to be noticed. This relationship is known as **Weber's Law**. Many companies choose to update their packages periodically, making small changes that will not necessarily be noticed at the time. When a product icon is updated, the manufacturer does not want people to lose their identification with a familiar symbol.

Weber's Law, ironically, is a challenge to green marketers who try to reduce the sizes of packages when they produce concentrated (and more earth-friendly) versions of their products. Makers of laundry detergent brands have to convince their customers to pay the same price for about half the detergent. Also, because of pressure from powerful retailers such as Wal-Mart that want to fit more bottles on their shelves, the size of detergent bottles is shrinking significantly. Procter & Gamble, Unilever and Henkel all maintain that their new concentrated versions will allow people to wash the same number of loads with half the detergent. One perceptual trick they're using to try to convince consumers of this is the re-design of the bottle cap: both P&G and Church & Dwight use a cap with a broader base and shorter sides to persuade consumers that they need a smaller amount.[28]

Consumer behaviour as I see it . . .
Touching technology . . .

Associate Professor Rhonda Hadi, Saïd School of Business, Oxford University

Consumer engagement with technology is growing increasingly tactile in nature. Touchscreens have become the dominant mobile interface, wearable computing is strapping connectivity firmly onto our skin, and the Internet-of-Things is embedding digital capability into our tangible world. While these trends have cumulatively added multisensory richness to digital experiences, little research has explored how such shifts might influence consumer interactions with technology. Research in social psychology and marketing has long demonstrated the fundamental role touch plays in shaping consumer outcomes, but these considerations become more complex and the consequences more profound when the objects we touch are embedded with greater capabilities (e.g., allowing us to consume media, shop, and even monitor our own health).

Take, for example, the fact that an increasing proportion of everyday communication is mediated by technological devices consumers hold in their hands (e.g., mobile phones) or wear (e.g., smartwatches). These devices allow for the delivery of haptic feedback: applied forces, vibrations, or motions to the skin. Indeed, social etiquette often compels us to place devices on 'vibrate' mode and, accordingly, vibrotactile alerts often accompany the receipt of messages, call notifications, and other communications content (vibrotactile stimulation is so omnipresent that many people even report feeling 'phantom vibrations' – vibrating sensations that do not actually exist). Interestingly, my co-authors and I have found that these sensations might do more than just notify consumers. In our research, we find that users perceive messages accompanied by vibrotactile notifications to feel more personal than the same messages without vibrotactile notifications. We believe this is because sensations that typically require proximity (e.g., touch) activate a greater sense of psychological closeness than sensations that do not typically require proximity (e.g., hearing or sight).

$\rightarrow$

Marketers and product managers have also begun to explore how digital interactions might be enhanced through touch. For example, one major challenge marketers face when reaching consumers through mobile and wearable technology is the small screen size, which limits the scope for visual communication (in terms of both written text and graphical imagery). Perhaps in an effort to assuage this limitation, some brands have begun to experiment with haptic feedback in their mobile advertisements. For example, in mobile ads for Stoli vodka, users feel their phone vibrate when a woman shakes a cocktail. Meanwhile, wearable gadget designers are equally keen to exploit the power of touch: the Lumo sensor buzzes if you begin to slouch and the FitBit wristband vibrates when you hit your fitness goal.

As consumers rely on devices more and more, and as haptic technology becomes more sophisticated and nuanced (e.g., notifications from some new smartwatches are meant to feel as though someone is tapping your wrist), we believe touch will play an increasingly important role in shaping consumer judgments and behaviors.

Question

How might haptic feedback be used to enhance other digital interactions? Can you think of some contexts or scenarios where this might be the case?

Rhonda Hadi

Augmented reality

Perceptual selection processes become even more interesting as we enter the new age of **augmented reality**. This term refers to media that combine a physical layer with a digital layer to create a combined experience. If you've ever watched a 3D movie with those clunky glasses, you've experienced one form of augmented reality. Or, if you've seen those ads changing to new and different ads on the walls surrounding the football pitch, you've also encountered AR in a simple form.

More likely, though, in the next few years you'll live AR through your smartphone. New apps such as Google Goggles (for Android phones) and Layar (for Android and Apple devices) impose a layer of words and pictures onto whatever you see in your phone's viewer.

Augmented reality apps open new worlds of information (and marketing communications). Do you want to know the bio-sketch of the singer you see on a CD cover? Who painted that cool mural in your local bar? How much did that house you were looking at sell for last month? Just point your smartphone at each and the information will be superimposed on your screen.[29]

Web-based AR

These techniques use your PC and webcam to offer an enhanced experience, often via a marker, image or through motion capture. For example, the Fashionista dressing-room app you'll find in the online fashion boutique Tobi lets you 'virtually' try on clothing items using your webcam and a marker on a printed piece of paper.

Kiosk-based AR

This is similar to Web-based AR, but you can often find more powerful applications that use 3D or facial tracking. At a toy store, shoppers can hold up a boxed Lego set to an in-store kiosk, and the kiosk will show an image of them holding the put-together Lego creation. At several shopping malls in the US, Chevrolet showcases its key brands in kiosks that let shoppers use a virtual 'professional air sprayer' and their fingers to paint the car, then move on to choose the rims, tyres, decorative stripes and other elements. When visitors finish building their cars, they are handed a 6 × 9-inch card with an augmented reality marker on the back. The person holds the card up to a camera mounted on a 65-inch TV screen that reads the marker and creates a computer-generated 3D model of a Camaro. By moving the card, the person can 'drive' the car as they hear the engine roar.[30]

Mobile AR

These applications use the viewfinder on a mobile phone to access enhanced digital information. The iButterfly app that the Dentsu advertising agency created in Japan lets you track and find digital butterflies using your iPhone GPS and camera. Hold your iPhone camera up at designated spots and when you look at your surroundings through the camera, you'll see animated butterflies flapping by. Each iButterfly contains coupons for nearby businesses.[31] eBay's fashion app 'See It On' allows the user to virtually try on sunglasses in real time. The app uses facial recognition to identify the user and apply virtual sunglasses to their video image. The user is able to adjust the fit, choose different styles, frames, lenses and colours to find their perfect look. Within the app they can then browse through eBay to find the perfect pair at the perfect price.[32]

Attention

Attention is the degree to which consumers focus on stimuli within their range of exposure. Although we live in an 'information society', we can have too much of a good thing. Consumers are often in a state of **sensory overload**, where they are exposed to far more information than they can process. In our society, much of this bombardment comes from commercial sources, and the competition for our attention is steadily increasing. The average adult is exposed to about 3,500 pieces of advertising information every single day – up from about 560 per day 30 years ago. Because consumers are exposed to so many advertising stimuli, marketers are becoming increasingly creative in their attempts to gain attention for their products. Some successful advertisers, such as Apple, Nike, Gap and Dyson, have created a visual identity with their television ads, and then deliver more detailed product information in other places, such as websites and newspaper stories in which third-party experts provide independent reviews.[33]

Multitasking and attention

Getting the attention of young people in particular is a challenge – as your professor probably knows! As of 2010, more than half of teens reported that they engage in **multitasking**, where they process information from more than one medium at a time as they attend to their cell phones, TVs, instant messages and so on – and that's just during the time when they are doing homework![34] One study observed 400 people for a day and found that 96 per cent of them were multitasking about a third of the time they used media.[35] Marketing researchers struggle to understand this new condition as they figure out how to reach people who do many things at once.

What impact does all this multitasking have on consumers' ability to absorb, retain and understand information? One possible consequence: these bursts of stimulation provoke the body to secrete dopamine, which is addictive. When we go without these squirts, we feel bored. Some scientists warn that our cravings for increased stimulation distract us from more prolonged thought processes and reduce our ability to concentrate. Studies find that heavy multitaskers have more trouble focusing, and they experience more stress. One study found that people interrupted by email reported significantly more stress than those who were allowed to focus on a task. The good news is that the brains of internet users become more efficient at finding information, while some video-game players develop better eyesight. One team of researchers found that players of fast-paced video games can track the movement of a third-more objects on a screen than non-players. They say the games can improve reaction and the ability to pick out details amid clutter. For better or worse, technology seems to be rewiring our brains to try to pay attention to more stimuli. Today, we consume three times as much information each day as people did in 1960. We constantly shift attention: computer users at work change windows or check email or other programs nearly 37 times an hour and computer users in general visit an average of 40 websites a day.[36]

Because the brain's capacity to process information is limited, consumers are very selective about what they pay attention to. The process of **perceptual selection** means that people attend to only a small portion of the stimuli to which they are exposed. Consumers practise a form of 'psychic economy' as they pick and choose among stimuli to avoid being overwhelmed. How do we choose? Both personal and stimulus factors help to decide.

Personal selection factors

Experience, which is the result of acquiring and processing stimulation over time, is one factor that determines how much exposure to a particular stimulus a person accepts. Remember Gary's reaction to UHT milk in Portugal? Gary's perceptual filters based on his past experiences and beliefs about milk influenced what he decided to process. . . with some effort, he may have come to understand that UHT milk is perfectly good to drink!

Consumers are more likely to be aware of stimuli that relate to their current needs – a behaviour known as **perceptual vigilance**. A consumer who rarely notices car ads will become very much aware of them when she or he is in the market for a new car. A newspaper ad for a fast-food restaurant that would otherwise go unnoticed becomes significant when one sneaks a glance at the paper in the middle of a five o'clock class. And, individual variations in perceptual processing may account for some differences. Indeed, one study reported that women are better than men in terms of their ability to identify visually incongruent products that are promoted among competing products. Females discriminate relational information among competing advertisements and use this information to identify incongruent products that would otherwise go unidentified.[37]

The flip side of perceptual vigilance is **perceptual defence**. This means that people see what they want to see – and don't see what they don't want to see. If a stimulus is threatening to us in some way, we may not process it – or we may distort its meaning so that it's more acceptable. For example, a heavy smoker may block out images of cancer-scarred lungs because these vivid reminders hit a bit too close to home.

Still another factor is **adaptation** – the degree to which consumers continue to notice a stimulus over time. The process of adaptation occurs when consumers no longer pay attention to a stimulus because it is so familiar. A consumer can 'habituate' and require increasingly stronger 'doses' of a stimulus to notice it. For example, a commuter en route to work might read a billboard message when it is first installed, but after a few days it simply becomes part of the passing scenery.

Stimulus selection factors

In addition to the receiver's mind-set, characteristics of the stimulus itself play an important role in determining what we notice and what we ignore. Marketers need to understand these factors so that they can create messages and packages that will have a better chance of cutting through the clutter. For example, when researchers measured what ads consumers look at using infra-red eye-tracking equipment, they found that visually complex ads are more likely to capture attention.[38]

In general, we are more likely to notice stimuli that differ from others around them (remember Weber's Law). A message creates contrast in several ways:

- *Size*: the size of the stimulus itself, in contrast to the competition, helps to determine if it will command attention. Readership of a magazine ad increases in proportion to the size of the ad.[39]

- *Colour*: as we've seen, colour is a powerful way to draw attention to a product or to give it a distinct identity. When Black & Decker developed a line of tools it called DeWalt to target the residential construction industry, the company coloured the new line yellow instead of black; this made them stand out against other 'dull' tools.[40] It has also been demonstrated how the use of saturated colours increases the perceived size of the product among consumers.[41]

- *Position*: not surprisingly, we stand a better chance of noticing stimuli that are in places we're more likely to look. That's why the competition is so heated among suppliers to have their products displayed in stores at eye level. In magazines, ads that are placed towards the front of the issue, preferably on the right-hand side, also win out in the race for readers' attention. (Hint: The next time you read a magazine, notice which pages you're more likely to spend time looking at.)[42] When you are doing your 'Google search', how far down the screen do you typically go in reviewing results? Do you often scroll to the second page of results?

- *Novelty*: stimuli that appear in unexpected ways or places tend to grab our attention. One solution is to put ads in unconventional places, where there will be less competition for attention. These places include the backs of shopping carts, walls of tunnels, floors of sports stadiums and, yes, even public restrooms.[43] An outdoor advertising agency in London constructs huge ads in deserts and farm fields adjacent to airports, so that passengers who look out of the window can't help but pay attention. It prints the digital ads on pieces of PVC mesh that sit on frames a few inches above the ground.[44] Other entrepreneurs equip billboards with tiny cameras that use software to determine if a person is standing in front of an outdoor ad. Then the program analyses the viewer's facial features (such as cheekbone height and the distance between the nose and the chin) to judge their gender and age. Once the software categorises the passerby, it selects an advertisement tailored to this profile – a Spanish teenager, for example, sees a different message to the one shown to the middle-aged Asian woman who walks behind him.[45]

Interpretation: deciding what things mean

Interpretation refers to the meanings we assign to sensory stimuli. Just as people differ in terms of the stimuli that they perceive, the meanings we assign to these stimuli vary as well. Many of these meanings depend upon our socialisation within a society: Even sensory perception is culturally specific. A team of anthropologists created a 'kit' of stimuli to compare what people around the world perceive; this included colour chips, scratch-and-sniff cards, sounds recorded at different frequencies and so on. When they exposed the same stimuli to people in over 20 different cultures, the results were dramatic. For example, prior research on mostly English-speaking people indicated that the typical person is not very good at identifying the smell of everyday things such as coffee, peanut butter and chocolate – they usually identify about half of them correctly. However, people living on the Malay Peninsula were more accurate.

Some of these responses are driven by language differences. Researchers found that English and Dutch speakers used different metaphors from Farsi and Turkish people to describe pitch – the latter thought of sounds as being 'thin' or 'thick' rather than 'high' or 'low'. When Dutch speakers heard a tone while being shown a mismatched height bar (e.g. a high tone and a low bar) and were asked to sing the tone, they sang a lower tone, but this wasn't the case when they saw a thin or thick bar. In contrast, when Farsi speakers heard a tone and were shown a bar of mismatched thickness, they misremembered the tone – but not when they were shown a bar mismatched for height.[46] As we'll see in Part E of this text, culture matters – a lot.

Stimulus organisation

People do not perceive a single stimulus in isolation. Our brains tend to relate incoming sensations to imagery of other events or sensations already in our memory, based on some fundamental organisational principles. As pointed out by some researchers, 'you see froot, you think fruit',[47] as also illustrated by the ad for kitchen assembly pictured here. A number of perceptual principles describe how stimuli are perceived and organised.

The gestalt

These principles are based on work in **gestalt psychology**, a school of thought maintaining that people derive meaning from the totality of a set of stimuli, rather than from any individual stimulus. The German word *gestalt* roughly translates as 'whole', 'pattern' or 'configuration', and this perspective is best summarised by the saying, 'the whole is greater than the sum of its parts'. A piecemeal perspective that analyses each component of the stimulus separately will be unable to capture the total effect. The gestalt perspective provides several principles relating to the way stimuli are organised. Three of these principles, or perceptual tendencies, are illustrated in Figure 3.3.

The gestalt **principle of closure** implies that consumers tend to perceive an incomplete picture as complete. That is, we tend to fill in the blanks based on our prior experience. This principle explains why most of us have no trouble reading a neon sign even if one or two of its letters are burned out, or filling in the blanks in an incomplete message. The principle of closure is also at work when we hear only part of a jingle or theme. Utilisation of the principle of closure in marketing strategies encourages audience participation, which increases the chance that people will attend to the message.

The **principle of similarity** tells us that consumers tend to group together objects that share similar physical characteristics. That is, they group like items into sets to form an integrated whole. This principle is used by companies who have extended product lines but wish to keep certain features similar, such as the shape of a bottle, so that it is easy for the consumer to recognise that they are, in fact, buying a shampoo of brand X.

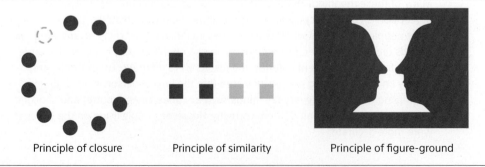

Principle of closure   Principle of similarity   Principle of figure-ground

Figure 3.3 Principles of stimulus organisation derived from gestalt psychology

We recognise patterns of stimuli, such as familiar words. In this Austrian ad consumers will tend to see the word 'kitchen', even though the letters are scrambled.

Source: Client: XXXLutz; Head of Marketing: Mag. Thomas Saliger; Agency: Demner, Merlicek & Bergmann; Account Supervisor: Andrea Kliment; Account Manager: Albin Lenzer; Creative Directors: Rosa Haider, Tolga Buyukdoganay; Art Directors: Tolga Buyukdoganay, Rene Pichler; Copywriter: Alistair Thompson.

Another important gestalt concept is the **figure–ground principle**, in which one part of a stimulus (the figure) will dominate while other parts recede into the background. This concept is easy to understand if one thinks of a photograph with a clear and sharply focused object (the figure) in the centre. The figure is dominant, and the eye goes straight to it. The parts of the configuration that will be perceived as figure or ground can vary depending on the individual consumer, as well as other factors. Similarly, in marketing messages that use the figure–ground principle, a stimulus can be made the focal point of the message or merely the context that surrounds the focus.

When we try to make sense of a marketing stimulus, whether a distinctive package, an elaborately staged television commercial or perhaps a model on the cover of a magazine, we do so by interpretation of its meaning in the light of associations we have with these images. For this reason, much of the meaning we take away is influenced by what we make of the symbolism we perceive. After all, on the surface, many marketing images have virtually no literal connection to actual products. What does a cowboy have to do with a bit of tobacco rolled into a paper tube? How can a celebrity such as former football star Gary Lineker enhance the image of a potato crisp? (Apparently many people think he can't!) [48]

The meaning of things

3.4

We elicit meaning through the process of interpretation and the use of cultural categories in order to make sense of the world around us.

For better or worse, we live in a world that is significantly influenced by marketers. We are surrounded by marketing stimuli in the form of advertisements, shops and products competing for our attention and our cash. Much of what we learn about the world is filtered by marketers, whether through conspicuous consumption depicted in glamorous magazine advertising or via the roles played by family figures in TV commercials. Ads show us how we ought to act with regard to recycling, alcohol consumption and the types of house or car we aspire to. In many ways we are heavily influenced by and depend upon marketers, since we rely on them to sell us products that are safe and perform as promised, to tell us the truth about what they are selling and to price and distribute these products fairly.

The meaning of consumption

One of the fundamental premises of consumer behaviour is that people often buy products not for what they *do,* but for what they *mean.*[49] This principle does not imply that a product's primary function is unimportant, but rather that the roles products play and the meaning that they have in our lives go well beyond the tasks they perform. The deeper meanings of a product may help it to stand out from other, similar goods and services – all things being equal, a person will choose the brand that has an image (or even a personality!) consistent with their underlying ideas. While this text takes multiple perspectives on how consumers view products in their lives, one of the recurring themes throughout is that consumer goods are an important medium in European (and other contemporary consumer) societies, that goods and services are loaded with both public and private meanings and that we, as consumers, are constantly drawing meanings out of our possessions and using them to construct our domestic and public worlds.

Research has demonstrated that the cultural symbolism of product meanings influences physiological processes such as taste. When we think we adhere to the values represented by a food or drink product or a brand, we also think that it tastes better.[50] So, such cultural symbols are very powerful and product meanings are, to some extent, self-fulfilling. Athletes swear by their favourite brand of sportswear and may lose self-confidence and perform poorly if they cannot wear it, although objectively speaking they cannot run faster or jump higher if they are wearing Nikes rather than Reeboks. These arch rivals are marketed in terms of their image – meanings that have been carefully crafted with the help of legions of rock stars, athletes, slickly produced commercials – and many millions of dollars. So, when you buy a Nike 'Swoosh' you may be doing more than choosing footwear – you may also be making a lifestyle statement about the type of person you are, or want to be. For a relatively simple item made of leather and laces, that's quite a feat!

As Figure 3.4 shows, meaning transfer is accomplished largely by such marketing vehicles as the advertising and fashion industries, which associate products with symbolic qualities. These goods, in turn, impart their meanings to consumers through different forms of ritual and are used to create and sustain consumer identities. We will take a much closer look at how these rituals work (see Chapter 12), and at the fashion system (see Chapter 13). In this chapter, the model serves the more general purpose of underlining the importance of meaning for understanding contemporary consumption.

One can make the objection to the model in Figure 3.4 that there is a feedback arrow missing between the individual consumer and the cultural values and symbols. Cultural values and symbols obviously only exist in so far as people enact and use them. Therefore, it is also important to remind ourselves that the advertising and fashion industries, even though they are highly influential, are not dictatorial in establishing product meanings. We all lend a helping hand. In a sense, in a consumer society we are all 'lifestyle experts' to some degree, and many of us are trying to assert our uniqueness by mixing and matching styles and

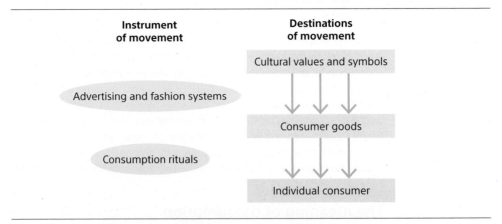

Figure 3.4 The movement of meaning

Source: Adapted from Grant McCracken, 'Culture and consumption: A theoretical account of the structure and movement of the cultural meaning of consumer goods', **Journal of Consumer Research** 13(1) (1986): 72. Copyright © 1986, Oxford University Press by permission of Oxford University Press.

products that we can find in the marketplace. In a very existential sense, we can say that we are what we consume – an issue we will discuss in more detail in the sections on consumption and the self (see Chapter 4).

Cultural categories

Meanings that are imparted to products reflect underlying **cultural categories,** which correspond to the basic ways we characterise the world.[51] Our culture makes distinctions between different times of the day, such as leisure and work hours, as well as other differences such as genders, occasions, groups of people and so on. The fashion system provides us with products that signify these categories. For example, the clothing industry gives us clothing to denote certain times (evening wear, resort wear), it differentiates between leisure clothes and work clothes and it promotes masculine, feminine or unisex styles.[52] Goods, then, are 'signs of the times' in which we live. The 'rocket designs' of the 1950s reflected the belief in the technological progress of that era. Political figures (and their relatives) and what they represent are also potential style icons. One of the first examples indicating the rise of consumer society was Jackie Kennedy. A European and more contemporary example is provided by royal families throughout Europe, whose female members, such as the princesses Diana or Kate in Great Britain, Mary in Denmark or Victoria in Sweden, become style icons for each cultural period. A dress Princess Catherine (Kate) was wearing during a public appearance subsequently sold out in eight minutes![53] Even royal toddlers are figures of emulation.[54] What is important to retain, then, is that meanings of consumer goods and their designs are not universal but relative to given social and historical contexts, or, to put it simply, are bound to particular times and particular places.

What do we do, when we consume? Product meanings in use

If consumption is not just about solving practical problems but is also about the personal and cultural meanings ascribed to consumption practices, then it raises the important question of the cultural purposes of consumption. For example, we do not eat just because we are hungry, since most eating behaviours are linked to a myriad of cultural meanings and rituals. We will take a closer look at this later in the text (see Chapter 13), but for now consider a more general explanation of consumption practices. In a fine proposal of a theory to answer this question, one consumer researcher has developed a classification scheme in an attempt to explore the different ways that products and experiences can provide meaning to people.[55] This consumption typology was derived from a two-year analysis of supporters of a baseball team in the US, but it is easily transferable to both a European context and to other types of consumption as well. But focusing on an event such as a baseball match – or, to make it more familiar to Europeans, a football match – is a useful reminder that when we refer to consumption, we are talking about intangible experiences, ideas and services (the thrill of a goal or the antics of a team mascot) in addition to tangible objects (such as the food and drink consumed at the stadium). This analysis identified four distinct types of consumption activities:

1 *Consuming as experience* – when the consumption is a personal, emotional or aesthetic goal in itself – the feeling of having been there. This would include activities such as the pleasure derived from learning how to interpret the offside rule, or appreciating the athletic ability of a favourite player.

2 *Consuming as integration* – using and manipulating consumption objects to express aspects of the self. For example, some fans express their solidarity with their team by identifying with the mascot and adopting some of its characteristic traits. Attending matches in person rather than watching them on TV allows the fan to integrate their experience more completely with their self.

3 *Consuming as classification* – the activities that consumers engage in to communicate their association with objects, both to self and to others. For example, spectators might dress up in the team's colours and buy souvenirs to demonstrate to others that they are diehard fans. Unfortunately, the more hard core fans express their contempt for opponents' supporters violently. There is a profound 'us' and 'them' dichotomy present here.

4 *Consuming as play* – consumers use objects to participate in a mutual experience and merge their identities with that of a group. For example, happy fans might scream in unison and engage in an orgy of jumping and hugging when their team scores a goal – this is a different dimension of shared experience compared with watching the game at home.

It is important to realise that these categories are not mutually exclusive, and that consumption activities may have traits of several or all of these aspects. On the other hand, one aspect may dominate in the understanding of one particular consumption situation.

Even though this typology takes its point of departure in the consumption of baseball, it has also proven useful in a European setting – for example, for analysing pet ownership as consumption.[56] In fact, a short exercise of imagining driving a car makes it easy to see how it can be applied to other types of consumption as well. You can drive/consume your car for the experience of it – just you and your car and the feeling of the oneness of the driver and the machine, or you can drive it as an extended self – a confirmation of your personality (maybe it is a hybrid model that serves to underline your environmental consciousness). You can drive your car based on the playful togetherness and the freedom of movement it gives to you and your friends. And finally, it is hard to think of a car that does not in some sense classify its driver, be it a cheerfully painted Citroën 2CV, a sporty convertible Mini or a black Mercedes Benz 500 SE.[57]

A branded world

3.5

The universe of meanings pertaining to commercial products or services is what we usually call the 'brand'.

One of the most important ways in which meaning is created in consumer society is through the **brand.** Although defining exactly what is a 'brand' is a complex task,[58] the point of departure is that it refers to those strategic processes whereby managers try to create and sustain meanings attached to products, services, organisations, etc. The problem arises when we add that the brand is not limited by these strategically intended meanings, but possibly first and foremost comes to life in the minds of consumers. Hence, what the brand means in the marketplace is ultimately decided by the consumer, not by the brand manager. In the twenty-first century, there has been a tremendous growth in the interest in brands, whether product or corporate, and their increasing importance as vehicles of meaning for people/consumers. Few people will raise an eyebrow at the suggestion that a university, a school, a kindergarten, a politician, a sports club or even a type of sports can be thought of in terms of being a brand. In fact, today, it is not unheard of to think about oneself as a brand that must compete in the marketplace for friends, partners, jobs, success, etc.[59]

As we have already seen (in Chapter 1), one of the hallmarks of marketing strategies at the beginning of the twenty-first century is an emphasis on building relationships with customers. The nature of these relationships can vary, and these bonds help us to understand some of the possible meanings products have for us. Here are some of the types of relationship a person may have with a brand:[60]

- Self-concept attachment: the product helps to establish the user's identity.
- Nostalgic attachment: the product serves as a link with a past self.
- Interdependence: the product is a part of the user's daily routine.
- Love: the product elicits bonds of warmth, passion or other strong emotion.

Brand identities are thus potentially very closely intertwined with consumer identities,[61] and brands can elicit deep emotional engagement from consumers.[62] These days, the idea of intertwining the self with brands through tattoos of brand logos or brand symbolism on the body doesn't seem strange to a lot of consumers, or to the advertising industry.[63] Even brands we do not like can be very important to us, because we often define ourselves in opposition to what we do not like.[64]

The role of semiotics for understanding brand and product meaning

3.6

The field of semiotics helps us to understand how marketers use symbols to create meaning.

For assistance in understanding how consumers interpret the meanings of symbols, some marketers are turning to a field of study known as **semiotics**, which examines how meanings are constructed in social sign systems.[65] Semiotics is important to the understanding of consumer behaviour, since it is a tool that helps us understand how meanings work in a social setting. Semiotics is a vast field, and it is beyond the scope of this text to provide more than a glimpse.[66]

But, simply put, products have learned meanings, and we rely on advertising (and other forms of social communication) to work out what those meanings are. As one set of researchers put it, 'advertising serves as a kind of culture/consumption dictionary; its entries are products, and their definitions are cultural meanings'.[67]

According to the semiotician Charles Sanders Peirce, every message has three basic components: an object, a sign and an interpretant. A marketing message such as a Marlboro ad can be read on different levels. On the lowest level of reading, the **object** would be the product that is the focus of the message (Marlboro cigarettes). The **sign** is the sensory imagery that represents the intended meanings of the object (the contents of the ad – in this case, the cowboy). The **interpretant** refers to the fact that someone has to interpret the relationship between the sign and the object. But it is not the interpreter, it is rather the meaning derived (for example, this man smokes these cigarettes). The funny way of expressing this can be seen as Peirce's way of indicating that meaning has to be 'meaning for someone' – that the meaning is not 'given' or 'out there'. If we continue the example, this particular man is not just any man. He is a cowboy – and not just any cowboy. The interpretant 'man (cowboy) smoking these cigarettes' in itself becomes a sign, especially since we have already seen many examples of these ads from this company. So, on the second, connotative level, this sign refers to the fictive personality of 'the Marlboro Man', and its interpretant consists of all the connotations attached to the Marlboro Man – for example his being a 'rugged, individualistic American'. On the third level, called the ideological level, the interpretant of the 'rugged, individualistic American' becomes a sign for what is stereotypically American. So, its object is 'America', and the interpretant is all the ideas and characteristics that we might consider as typically and quintessentially 'American'. This semiotic relationship is shown in Figure 3.5. By way of such a chain of meanings, the Marlboro ad both borrows from and contributes to reinforcing a fundamental 'myth of America'.

From the semiotic perspective of Peirce, signs are related to objects in one of three ways. They can resemble objects, be connected to them with some kind of causal or other relation, or be conventionally tied to them.[68]

An **icon** is a sign that resembles the product in some way (e.g. Apple Computers uses the image of an apple to represent itself). An **index** is a sign that is connected to a product because they are causally related (e.g. the pine tree on certain cleaning products conveys the conveys the meaning that it will cause the fresh, natural scent of pine). A **symbol** is a sign that is related to a product through purely conventional associations (e.g. the Mercedes star, which provides associations with German industrial quality and ingenuity). In other words, when someone asks us whether we would like to buy a product, we think not only about whether the product is similar in appearance to other products that we know

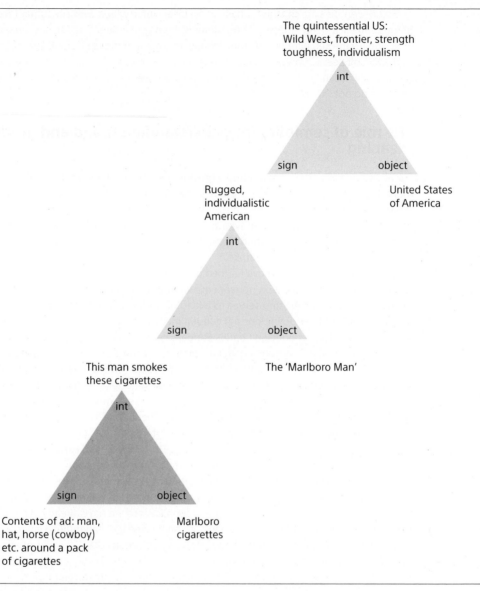

The quintessential US:
Wild West, frontier, strength
toughness, individualism

int

sign   object

Rugged,   United States
individualistic   of America
American

int

sign   object

This man smokes   The 'Marlboro Man'
these cigarettes

int

sign   object

Contents of ad: man,   Marlboro
hat, horse (cowboy)   cigarettes
etc. around a pack
of cigarettes

Figure 3.5 Relationship of components in semiotic analysis of meaning

(iconicity), but also how the product is perceived as physically related (produced by or producing some effect) to other things (indexicality) and what the product generally means to us and to others (symbolism).[69]

The use of symbols provides a powerful means for marketers to convey product attributes to consumers. For example, expensive cars, designer fashions and diamond jewellery – all widely recognised symbols of success – frequently appear in ads to associate products with affluence or sophistication. The rhetoric of advertising is an additional field of analysis that has been useful for the discussion of how advertising communicates its messages.[70] Semiotic analysis of ads has been connected to product and brand life cycles in order to establish some guidelines about when to use the most complex advertising forms.[71]

One aspect of the semiotics of consumption, which used to be relatively neglected compared to the semiotics of advertising, is the semiotics of goods as such. In recent years,

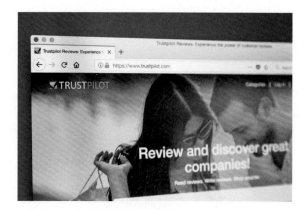

Peer-to-peer (and can this be trusted?) online evaluations have, for better and for worse, become a power factor in the market place
Chrisdorney/Shutterstock

instead of studying messages about commodities there has been an increased number of studies of commodities as messages.[72] The semiotics of consumer goods, then, focuses on the ability of goods to communicate either by themselves or in connection with other goods. A related field of study is symbolic consumption,[73] which focuses not so much on the products as a sign per se, but rather on the meanings attached to the act of consuming the product. Here, in many cases, the good becomes an indexical sign for some attributes that characterise the consumer, such as trendiness, wealth, femininity or others that place the consumer in some subcultural context.

Other uses of semiotics include industrial design[74] and design of distribution outlets. For example, in a semiotic study of the meanings and expectations consumers would attach to a new hypermarket, the researchers generated four different value profiles among potential customers. These profiles were linked to preferences for different designs of the hypermarket and its interior, thus helping the planners to conceive a type of hypermarket that was pleasing to most consumers.[75]

Semiotics plays a central role in much of the recent challenging consumer behaviour theory. The fact that consumers have become increasingly aware of how they communicate through their consumption as well as what they communicate has led to the designation of the present world as a 'semiotic world'.[76] Furthermore, it has been argued that we feel more confident in creating our own messages rather than just following what is proposed by marketing or fashion statements. This tendency to eclecticism means that we are increasingly likely to match things, such as articles of clothing, furniture or even lifestyles, that traditionally have not been perceived as fitting together. It does not follow that social meanings completely dissolve, but it does make attention to Peirce's observation of the importance of the 'interpretant' – that *meanings* are meanings for *someone* in a specific *context* – even more important. Consider, for example, the trustworthiness of product or service endorsements on social media. Which factors must we take into account in order to assess their trustworthiness?

A postmodern consumer culture?

3.7

Contemporary culture can be understood as postmodern.

Consumer society, then, is a society where social life is organised less around our identities as producers or workers in the production system, and more according to our roles as consumers in the consumption system. This expresses a relatively new idea. Until recently, many researchers treated culture as a sort of variable that would explain differences in what they saw as the central dimension in society: economic behaviour. However, in our post-industrial society it has become increasingly evident that the principles of economy are themselves

I. Pre-modern

No distinction between Culture and Economy. One implies the other

II. Modern

Culture and Economy are separate

Economy is accorded a superior status because of its relevance to the creation of 'productive' value

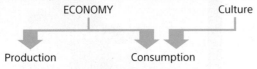

III. Postmodern-postindustrial

New perspectives on the relationship between Culture and Economy

Culture subsumes Economy

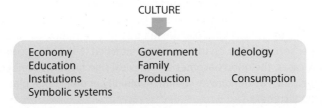

Figure 3.6 Relationship between culture and economy

Source: Alladi Venkatesh, 'Ethnoconsumerism: A New Paradigm to Study Cultural and Cross-Cultural Consumer Behavior', in J.A. Costa and G. Bamossy (eds), *Marketing in a Multicultural World* (Thousand Oaks, CA: Sage, 1995).

expressions of a specific kind of culture. Figure 3.6 provides an overview of this evolving approach to the relationship between culture and economy, indicating the all-encompassing influence that culture has on consumers.

Postmodernism

Figure 3.6 makes a reference to **postmodernism.** Many of the themes that we address in this text – such as the dominance of the brand (over whatever reality lies behind it), the possibility of engineering reality in the experience economy or the blurring of the fashion picture – are linked to major social changes. One proposed summary term for this change is postmodernism – one of the most widely discussed and disputed terms in consumer research in the past two decades.[77]

Postmodernists argue that we live in a period where the modern order, with its shared beliefs in certain central values of modernism and industrialism, is breaking up. Examples of these values include the fundamental belief in a progressing society, characterised by the benefits of economic growth and industrial production, and the infallibility of science. In opposition to currently held views, postmodernism questions the search for universal truths and values, and the existence of objective knowledge.[78] Thus, a keyword is 'pluralism', indicating the co-existence of various truths, styles and fashions. Consumers (and producers) are relatively free to combine elements from different styles and domains to create their own personal expression. This pluralism, it is argued, has significant consequences for how we regard theories of marketing and consumer behaviour. Most importantly, pluralism does not mean that anything goes in terms of method or theory, but it does mean that no single theory or method can pretend to be universal in its accounting for consumer behaviour or marketing practices.[79]

There have been several attempts to sum up features of postmodernism and their implications for contemporary market conditions.[80] Together with pluralism, one European researcher has suggested that postmodernism can be described by six key features:[81]

1 *Fragmentation*: the splitting-up of what used to be simpler and more mass-oriented, exemplified by the ever-growing product ranges and brand extensions in more and more specialised variations. The advertising media have also become fragmented, with increasingly specialised TV channels, magazines, radio stations and websites for placing one's advertising.

2 *De-differentiation*: postmodernists are interested in the blurring of distinctions between hierarchies such as 'high and low culture', 'advertising and programming' or 'politics and show business'. Examples would be the use of artistic works in advertising and the celebration of advertising as artistic works. Companies such as Coca-Cola, Nike and Guinness have their own museums. The blurring of gender categories also refers to this aspect of postmodernism.

Marketing opportunity

One of the new millennium's most significant break-throughs in terms of new types of products is the success of reality TV. From *Big Brother* onwards, following 'real people' in 'real situations', with real conflicts, affairs and feelings of whatever kind, has become a favourite pastime for a lot of people. Such programmes are good examples of what is called 'hyperreality', since they represent a kind of condensed form of an idea of which elements constitute ordinary people's 'reality'. One particular variation of reality TV is the sitcom that features real actors or comedians in the roles as 'themselves'. The story unfolds in a constructed universe (often constituted by a lot of other celebrities performing as 'themselves'), where we get a glimpse of the main characters' 'ordinary lives' and all their oddities. Examples include *Curb Your Enthusiasm* from the US and *Klovn* from Denmark. The success of reality TV may be based on a paradoxical relationship between consumers and this kind of 'hyperreality': we simultaneously accept that we are spectators of 'constructed realities', but central to this construction is a longing for authenticity and realism.[82]

3 *Hyperreality*: refers to the spreading of simulations and the 'making real of what was just a fantasy'. Disneyland (and other theme parks) are quintessentially hyperreal. Marketers are among the prime creators of hyperreality.[83] But consumers contribute too! Film director Quentin Tarantino lets some of his main characters in *Pulp Fiction* smoke a fictitious 'Red Apple' cigarette brand, which later appears on an advertising billboard in *Kill Bill*. Merchandise for this fictitious brand has subsequently been made real by certain consumers – presumably devoted Tarantino fans captured by the coolness of Red Apple smokers Butch Coolidge (Bruce Willis) and Mia Wallace (Uma Thurman) – through the production of T-shirts and ashtrays featuring the otherwise fictitious Red Apple brand![84]

Marketing pitfall

Sometimes companies may fall victim to their own hyperreality. It is the dream of many producers to create a strong brand with a solid position in cultural life. But as they do so, their brand images are incorporated into the general cultural sign system, and the company loses control over the signs attached to the brand name. For example, the name 'Barbie' today is far more than a brand name – it has almost become a name for a personality type. In 1997, when Danish pop group Aqua enjoyed a global success with the song 'Barbie Girl' (which contained lyrics alluding to the personal life of this hyperreal personality, such as 'you can dress my hair, undress me everywhere'), Mattel Inc. was not amused. It sued the pop group for abuse of the Barbie name and for destroying the pure and positive image of Barbie's world created through a long range of expensive campaigns. The case was dismissed by the US Supreme Court with reference to the lyrics being a parody. Ironically, in 2009 Mattel launched a series of campaigns where they made use of the song, albeit with altered 'no hanky-panky' lyrics.[85] But the important thing in this context is that it is yet another example of the blurring of marketing and popular culture, and the question is: can you patent culture?[86]

4 *Chronology*: this refers to the consumer's nostalgic search for the authentic, and a preoccupation with the past.[87] A postmodern way of looking at the same phenomenon is 'retro branding', conceptualised as 'the revival or re-launch of a brand from a prior historical period that differs from nostalgic brands by the element of updating'.[88] Retro brands are of relevance here as well because 'these revived brands invoke brand heritage, which triggers personal and communal nostalgia'.[89]

5 *Pastiche and parody*: **pastiche** refers to an imitation where the original is celebrated rather than scorned, in which case we talk about a parody. One book on postmodern marketing, *The Marketing Code,* is basically a pastiche of the novel *The Da Vinci Code* (complete with murders, suspense and a sectarian society that acts as a keeper of the ultimate secret) to discuss various marketing techniques, promoting the view that marketing is an art form rather than a science.[90] Such playful and ironic mixing of existing categories and styles is typical of pastiche. A good example of parody is the 'Festivus' festival – a sort of anti-commercial alternative to Christmas first popularised through its appearance in the sitcom *Seinfeld,* but which has since spread in certain consumer communities as a marker of anti-materialism and fatigue with the commercialisation of the Christmas holiday and its shopping frenzy.[91]

The seventeenth-century Danish landmark of the 'round tower' of Copenhagen has been recreated (in a slightly smaller version) in the simulated Danish environment of Solvang, California, founded as a 'little Denmark' by Danish immigrants in the nineteenth century, but gradually becoming more of a hyperreal theme park under the influence of marketing in the post-war period. The tower in Solvang houses a local pizza restaurant: Tower Pizza, of course!

Photo: Søren Askegaard.

Self-parody is one postmodern approach to communication.

Unilever

6   *Anti-foundationalism*: this last feature of postmodern marketing efforts refers not to parody but to an outright 'anti-campaign campaign'. For example, some campaigns are encouraging the receiver of the message not to take notice of the message, since somebody is trying to seduce and take advantage of them.

Of all these features of postmodernity, possibly **hyperreality** – referring to the 'becoming real' of what is initially simulation or 'hype'[92] – is the one that is most often used when we study marketing and consumer behaviour. It can be argued that modern (or postmodern!) marketing is inherently hyperreal, since the goal is to create some kind of enhanced reality around a product or a service. Semiotically speaking, advertisers create new relationships between objects and interpretants by inventing new connections between products and benefits, such as equating Marlboro cigarettes with the American frontier spirit.[93] To a large extent, over time the relationship between the symbol and reality is increasingly difficult to discern, and the 'artificial' associations between advertisement symbols, product symbols and the real world may take on a life of their own. We see this a lot in recent times when fans create products that correspond to 'realities' that never actually existed. These include Pinterest boards for food mentioned in the steamy novel *Fifty Shades of Gray* and *The Unofficial Mad Men Cookbook*, *The Unofficial Harry Potter Cookbook*, *The Unofficial Narnia Cookbook*, *A Feast of Ice and Fire* (*Game of Thrones*) and *Abbey Cooks Entertain* (*Downton Abbey*).[94]

Postmodernism has also been attached to such themes as the ability of readers to see through the hype of advertising.[95] This may suggest that we are becoming more skilled consumers and readers/interpreters of advertising, recognising ads as hyperreal persuasion or seduction attempts that do not intend to reflect our own daily experiences. Younger consumers, especially, may be prone to detect and enjoy the self-referencing or intertextuality of advertising.[96] Here, the self-consciousness of the brand as a brand and the ambivalence that follows from it is seen as the entertaining aspect of contemporary marketing.[97]

Chapter summary

Now that you have finished reading this chapter you should understand why:

3.1 Perception is a three-stage process that translates perceptual stimuli into meaning. Perception is the process by which physical sensations, such as sights, sounds and smells, are selected, organised and interpreted. The eventual interpretation of a stimulus allows it to be assigned meaning. A perceptual map is a widely used marketing tool that evaluates the relative standing of competing brands along relevant dimensions.

3.2 All our sensory systems are addressed through marketing. Marketing stimuli have important sensory qualities. We rely on colours, odours, sounds, tastes and even the 'feel' of products when we evaluate them.

3.3 The concept of a perceptual selection is important for marketing communication. Not all sensations successfully make their way through the perceptual process. Many stimuli compete for our attention, and we don't notice or accurately interpret the majority of them. People have different thresholds of perception. Some of the factors that determine which stimuli (above the threshold level) do get perceived include the amount of exposure to the stimulus, how much attention it generates and how it is interpreted. In an increasingly crowded stimulus environment, advertising clutter occurs when too many marketing-related messages compete for attention.

3.4 We elicit meaning through the process of interpretation and the use of cultural categories in order to make sense of the world around us. We interpret the stimuli to which we pay attention according to learned patterns and expectations. We don't attend to a stimulus in isolation. We classify and organise it according to principles of perceptual organization; a gestalt, or overall pattern, guides these principles. Specific grouping principles include closure, similarity and figure–ground relationships. The final step in the process of perception is interpretation. Symbols help us make sense of the world by providing us with an interpretation of a stimulus that others often share. The degree to which the symbolism is consistent with our previous experience affects the meaning we assign to related objects.

3.5 The universe of meanings pertaining to commercial products or services is what we usually call the 'brand'. Brands have become the most important symbolic vehicles in the marketplace. Consumption, branding and marketing have become some of the prime reflectors of current cultural values, norms and social roles. Economy and cultures of consumption are closely intertwined.

3.6 The field of semiotics helps us to understand how marketers use symbols to create meaning. A semiotic analysis involves the correspondence between social stimuli and the meaning of signs. The intended meaning may be literal (e.g. an icon, such as a street sign with a picture of children playing), or it may be indexical if it relies on shared characteristics (e.g. the red in a stop sign means danger). Meaning also can be conveyed by a symbol in which an image is given meaning by convention or by agreement of members of a society (e.g. stop signs are hexagonal, whereas yield signs are triangular).

3.7 Contemporary culture can be understood as postmodern. Postmodernism involves processes of social change in an era where the 'grand truths' of modernism, such as scientific knowledge or the progressiveness of economic growth, are no longer taken for granted. Postmodernism includes social processes such as fragmentation, de-differentiation, hyperreality, chronology, pastiche and anti-foundationalism.

Key terms

Absolute threshold (p. 94)	Pastiche (p. 110)
Adaptation (p. 98)	Perception (p. 86)
Attention (p. 85)	Perceptual defence (p. 98)
Augmented reality (p. 96)	Perceptual map (p. 87)
Brand (p. 104)	Perceptual selection (p. 98)
Cultural categories (p. 103)	Perceptual vigilance (p. 98)
Differential threshold (p. 94)	Postmodernism (p. 108)
Exposure (p. 85)	Principle of closure (p. 100)
Figure–ground principle (p. 101)	Principle of similarity (p. 100)
Gestalt psychology (p. 100)	Psychophysics (p. 94)
Hedonic consumption (p. 88)	Schemas (p. 86)
Hyperreality (p. 111)	Semiotics (p. 105)
Icon (p. 105)	Sensation (p. 86)
Index (p. 105)	Sensory marketing (p. 88)
Interpretant (p. 105)	Sensory overload (p. 97)
Interpretation (p. 85)	Sign (p. 105)
JND (p. 95)	Symbol (p. 105)
Multitasking (p. 97)	Virtual reality (p. 88)
Object (p. 105)	Weber's Law (p. 95)

Consumer behaviour challenge

1 Many studies have shown that our sensory detection abilities decline as we grow older. Discuss the implications of the absolute threshold for marketers attempting to appeal to the elderly.

2 Interview three to five male and three to five female friends regarding their perceptions of both men's and women's fragrances. Construct a perceptual map for each set of products. Based on your map of perfumes, do you see any areas that are not adequately served by current offerings? What (if any) gender differences did you obtain regarding both the relevant dimensions used by raters and the placement of specific brands along these dimensions?

3 Assume that you are a consultant for a marketer who wants to design a package for a new premium chocolate bar targeted to an affluent market. What recommendations would you provide in terms of such package elements as colour, symbolism and graphic design? Give the reasons for your suggestions.

4 Do you believe that marketers have the right to use any or all public spaces to deliver product messages? Where would you draw the line in terms of places and products that should be restricted?

5 Find one ad that is rich in symbolism and perform a semiotic analysis of it. Identify each type of sign used in the ad and the product qualities being communicated by each. Comment on the effectiveness of the signs that are used to communicate the intended message.

6 Using magazines archived in the library, track the packaging of a specific brand over time. Find an example of gradual changes in package design that may have been below the JND.

7 Collect a set of current ads for one type of product (e.g. personal computers, perfumes, laundry detergents or athletic shoes) from magazines, and analyse the colours employed. Describe the images conveyed by different colours and try to identify any consistency across brands in terms of the colours used in product packaging or other aspects of the ads.

8 Look through a current magazine and select one ad that captures your attention over the others. Give the reasons why.

9 Consider the characteristics of postmodernism – which phenomena from your own daily life could you describe as being examples of fragmentation, hyperreality, etc.?

For additional material see the companion website at **www.pearsoned.co.uk/solomon**

Notes

1. 'Fish vending machine in Munuia, Spain', http://guiagastronomika.diariovasco.com/noticias/maquina-dispensadora-pescado-201202231644.php (accessed 26 August 2018).
2. Jerome S. Bruner, 'On perceptual readiness', *Psychological Review* 64 (March 1957): 123–52.
3. Elizabeth C. Hirschman and Morris B. Holbrook, 'Hedonic consumption: Emerging concepts, methods, and propositions', *Journal of Marketing* 46 (Summer 1982): 92–101.
4. Joan Myers-Levy, Rui (Juliet) Zhu, and Lan Jiang, 'Context effects from bodily sensations: Examining bodily sensations induced by flooring and the moderating role of product viewing distance,' *Journal of Consumer Research* 37 (June 2010): 1–14.
5. Jiewen Hong and Yacheng Sun, 'Warm it up with love: The effect of physical coldness on liking of romance movies,' *Journal of Consumer Research* 39(2) (August 2012): 293–306.
6. Aradhna Krishna, May O. Lwin, and Maureen Morrin, 'Product scent and memory,' *Journal of Consumer Research* 37 (June 2010): 57–67.
7. R.K.Batra and T. Ghoshal, 'Fill up your senses: A theory of self-worth restoration through high-intensity sensory consumption', *Journal of Consumer Research* 44(4) (2017): 916–38.
8. Adam Bryant, 'Plastic surgery at AmEx', *Newsweek* (4 October 1999): 55.
9. Amitava Chattopadhyay, Gerald J. Gorn and Peter R. Darke, 'Roses Are Red and Violets Are Blue – Everywhere? Cultural Universals and Differences in Colour Preference Among Consumers and Marketing Managers' (unpublished manuscript, University of British Columbia, Fall 1999); Joseph Bellizzi and Robert E. Hite, 'Environmental colour, consumer feelings, and purchase likelihood', *Psychology & Marketing* 9 (1992): 347–63; Ayn E. Crowley, 'The two-dimensional impact of colour on shopping', *Marketing Letters* 4 (January 1993); Gerald J. Gorn, Amitava Chattopadhyay and Tracey Yi, 'Effects of Colour as an Executional Cue in an Ad: It's in the Shade' (unpublished manuscript, University of British Columbia, 1994).

10. Tine De Bock, Mario Pandelaere and Patrick Van Kenhove, 'When colours backfire: The impact of colour cues on moral judgment', *Journal of Consumer Psychology* 23(3) (2013): 341–8.

11. A.C. Hess and V. Melnyk, 'Pink or blue? The impact of gender cues on brand perceptions', *European Journal of Marketing* 50(9/10) (2016): 1,550–74.

12. Excerpted from https://www.pantone.com/fashion-color-trend-report-new-york-spring-2018 (accessed 26 August 2018).

13. Deborah J. Mitchell, Barbara E. Kahn and Susan C. Knasko, 'There's something in the air: Effects of congruent or incongruent ambient odor on consumer decision-making', *Journal of Consumer Research* 22 (September 1995): 229–38; for a review of olfactory cues in store environments, see also Eric R. Spangenberg, Ayn E. Crowley and Pamela W. Henderson, 'Improving the store environment: Do olfactory cues affect evaluations and behaviours?', *Journal of Marketing* 60 (April 1996): 67–80.

14. The Associated Press, 'Burger King to offer fragrance, Eau De Whopper', *New York Times* (20 March 2015), http://www.nytimes.com/2015/03/21/business/burger-king-to-offer-fragrance-eau-de-whopper.html?_r=0 (accessed 26 August 2018).

15. https://www.cnbc.com/id/48676703 (accessed 26 August 2018).

16. https://www.bbc.com/news/uk-scotland-highlands-islands-30292083 (accessed 26 August 2018).

17. https://edition.cnn.com/travel/article/airplane-cabin-fragrances/index.html (accessed 26 August 2018).

18. Dale Buss, 'Audio branding: BMW uses new sound signature to help redefine the brand', *Brand Channel* (20 March 2013), http://www.brandchannel.com/home/post/2013/03/20/BMW-Sound-Signature-032013.aspx (accessed 26 August 2018); Sheila Shayon, 'World Cup Winner: Coca-Cola for sonic branding', *BrandChannel* (12 July 2010), http://www.brandchannel.com/home/post/2010/07/12/Coca-Cola-World-Cup-Wavin-Flag.aspx (accessed 26 August 2018).

19. A. Guevremont and B. Grohmann, 'Consonants in brand names influence brand gender perceptions', *European Journal of Marketing* 49 (1/2) (2015): 101–22.

20. Bruce G. Vanden Bergh, Janay Collins, Myrna Schultz, and Keith Adler, 'Sound advice on brand names', *Journalism Quarterly* 61(4) (1984): 835–40; Eric Yorkston and Geeta Menon, 'A sound idea: Phonetic effects of brand names on consumer judgments', *Journal of Consumer Research* 31 (June 2004): 43–51; Keith S. Coulter and Robin A. Coulter, 'Small sounds, big deals: Phonetic symbolism effects in pricing', *Journal of Consumer Research* 37(2) (2010): 315–28.

21. L.J. Shrum, Sarah Roche and Tina M. Lowrey, 'What's in a Name: Sound Symbolism of Stock Ticker Symbols Predict Stock Performance', in (eds) June Cotte and Stacy Wood, *NA – Advances in Consumer Research* 42 (Duluth, MN: Association for Consumer Research, 2014): 654–5.

22. J. Ilicic, S. Baxter and A. Kulczynski, 'Names versus faces: Examining spokesperson-based congruency effects in advertising', *European Journal of Marketing* 49 (1/2) (2015): 62–81.

23. 'You can look – but don't touch', *Science Daily* (20 January 2009), www.sciencedaily.com (accessed 26 August 2018); Joann Peck and Suzanne B. Shu (2009), 'The effect of mere touch on perceived ownership', *Journal of Consumer Research* 36 (3): 434–47.

24. Sarah Ellison and Erin White, '"Sensory" marketers say the way to reach shoppers is the nose', *Advertising Age* (24 November 2000): 1–3.

25. Anne C. Bech, Erling Engelund, Hans Jørn Juhl, Kai Kristensen and Carsten Stig Poulsen, 'QFood. Optimal Design of Food Products', *MAPP Working Paper* 19 (Aarhus: The Aarhus School of Business, 1994); Hans Jørn Juhl, 'A Sensory Analysis of Butter Cookies – An Application of Generalized Procrustes Analysis', *MAPP Working Paper* 20 (Aarhus: The Aarhus School of Business, 1994).

26. Richard Tomkins, 'Products that aim for your heart', *Financial Times* (28 April 2005).

27. Andreas Scharf, 'Positionierung neuer bzw. modifizierter Nahrungsund Genußmittel durch integrierte Markt und Sensorikforschung', *Marketing ZFP* 1 (1st quarter 1995): 5–17.

28. Ellen Byron, 'Selling detergent bottles' big shrink suds makers' challenge: Convince consumers less isn't really less', *Wall Street Journal* (21 May 2007), www.wsj.com (accessed 26 August 2018).

29. Bob Teheschi, 'Seeing the world around you through your phone', *New York Times* (28 July 2010), http://www.nytimes.com/2010/07/29/technology/personaltech/29smart.html?emc=tnt&tntemail0=y (accessed 26 August 2018).

30. Patricia Odell, 'Chevy puts a new spin on an old model', *PROMO* (10 January 2011), https://www.chiefmarketer.com/chevy-puts-a-new-spin-on-an-old-model/ (accessed 26 August 2018).

31. Matthew Szymczyk, 'Digital marketing guide: Augmented reality', *Advertising Age* (27 February 2011), http://adage.com/article/special-report-digital-marketing-guide/digital-marketing-guide-augmented-reality/149109/ (accessed 26 August 2018).

32. 'Total immersion and eBay bring virtual "See It On" feature to eBay's Fashion App', *Business Wire* (1 February 2011), http://www.businesswire.com/news/home/20110201006053/en/Total-Immersion-eBay-Bring-Virtual-%E2%80%98See-On%E2%80%99 (accessed 26 August 2018).

33. Gary Silverman, 'Image is everything in attention wars', *Financial Times* (17 January 2005).

34. Joseph Burris, 'Plugged-in generation multi-tasking big time', *Baltimore Sun* (17 February 2010), http://articles.baltimoresun.com/2010-02-17/features/bal-md.pa.kids-17feb17_1_cell-phones-multi-tasking-parental-controls (accessed 26 August 2018).

35. Sharon Waxman, 'At an Industry media lab, close views of multitasking', *New York Times* (15 May 2006).

36. Matt Richtel, 'Attached to technology and paying a price', *New York Times* (6 June 2010), http://www.nytimes.com/2010/06/07/technology/07brain.html?pagewanted=1 (accessed 26 August 2018).

37. T.J. Noseworthy, J. Cotte and S.H. Lee, 'The effects of ad context and gender on the identification of visually incongruent products', *Journal of Consumer Research* 38(2) (2011): 358–75.

38. Rik Pieters, Michel Wedel and Rajeev Batra, 'The stopping power of advertising: Measures and effects of visual complexity', *Journal of Marketing*, 74 (September 2010): 48–60.

39. Roger Barton, *Advertising Media* (New York: McGraw-Hill, 1964).

40. Suzanne Oliver, 'New personality', *Forbes* (15 August 1994): 114.

41. H. Hagtvedt and S.A. Brasel, 'Color saturation increases perceived product size', *Journal of Consumer Research* 44 (2) (2017): 396–413.

42. Adam Finn, 'Print ad recognition readership scores: An information processing perspective', *Journal of Marketing Research* 25 (May 1988): 168–77.

43. Michael R. Solomon and Basil G. Englis, 'Reality engineering: Blurring the boundaries between marketing and popular culture', *Journal of Current Issues and Research in Advertising* 16(2) (Fall 1994): 1–18; Michael McCarthy, 'Ads are here, there, everywhere: Agencies seek creative ways to expand product placement', *USA Today* (19 June 2001): 1B.

44. Linda Stern, 'Bigger than at Times Square' (24 March 2008), www.newsweek.com (accessed 26 August 2018).

45. Stephanie Clifford, 'Billboards that look back', *New York Times* (31 May 2008).

46. T.M. Luhrmann, 'Can't place that smell? You must be American: How culture shapes our senses', *New York Times* (5 September 2014), http://www.nyTimes.com/2014/09/07/opinion/sunday/how-culture-shapes-our-senses.html?ref=international (accessed 26 August 2018).

47. S. Baxter, J. Ilicic and A. Kulczynski, 'You see Froot, you think fruit: Examining the effectiveness of pseudohomophone priming', *European Journal of Marketing* 51 (5/6) (2017): 885–902.

48. See http://news.bbc.co.uk/2/hi/talking_point/3270473.stm (accessed 26 August 2018) for a discussion on whether celebrities should endorse 'junk food'.

49. Sidney J. Levy, 'Symbols for sale', *Harvard Business Review* 37 (July–August 1959): 117–24.

50. Michael W. Allen, Richa Gupta and Arnaud Monnier, 'The interactive effect of cultural symbols and human values on taste evaluation', *Journal of Consumer Research* 35 (August 2008): 294–308.

51. Grant McCracken, 'Culture and consumption: A theoretical account of the structure and movement of the cultural meaning of consumer goods', *Journal of Consumer Research* 13 (June 1986): 71–84.

52. One example of such a cultural category is the definition of being 'a real woman'. For a cultural analysis of female identity and consumption of lingerie, see Christian Jantzen, Per Østergaard and Carla Sucena Vieira, 'Becoming a woman to the backbone. Lingerie consumption and the experience of female identity', *Journal of Consumer Culture* 6(2) (2006): 177–202.

53. 'Prince William stands dangerously close to the edge of a 328-foot cliff', *Vanity Fair* (17 April 2014), http://www.vanityfair.com/style/2014/04/prince-william-australia-edge-of-cliff?mbid=social_facebook (accessed 26 August 2018).

54. 'What is Prince George wearing in Christmas pictures? (£111 worth of toddler tailoring)', *The Daily Telegraph* (14 December 2014), http://www.telegraph.co.uk/news/uknews/prince-george/11292665/What-is-Prince-George-wearing-in-Christmas-pictures-111-worth-of-toddler-tailoring.html (accessed 26 August 2018).

55. Douglas B. Holt, 'How consumers consume: A typology of consumption practices', *Journal of Consumer Research* 22(1) (June 1995): 1–16.

56. Fiona Cheetham and Morven G. McEachern, 'Extending Holt's typology to encompass subject–subject relations in consumption: Lessons from pet ownership', *Consumption, Markets and Culture* 16(1) (2008): 91–115.

57. See Paul Hewer, Douglas Brownlie, Steven Treanor, Pauline Ferguson and Susan Hamilton, 'Peeps, Beemers and Scooby-doos; Exploring Community Value amongst Scottish Car Cruisers', in A.Y. Lee and D. Soman (eds), *Advances in Consumer Research,* 35 (Duluth, MN: Association for Consumer Research, 2008): 429–38.

58. Stephen Brown, 'Ambi-Brand Culture', in J. Schroeder and M. Salzer-Mörling (eds), *Brand Culture* (London: Routledge, 2006): 50–66.

59. Michael Solomon, Greg Marshall and Elnora Stuart, *Marketing: Real People, Real Choices* (Upper Saddle River, NJ: Prentice Hall, 2006).

60. Susan Fournier, 'Consumers and their brands: Developing relationship theory in consumer research', *Journal of Consumer Research* 24 (March 1998): 343–73.

61. Fabian F. Csaba and Anders Bengtsson, 'Rethinking Identity in Brand Management' in J. Schroeder and M. Salzer-Mörling (eds), *Brand Culture* (London: Routledge, 2006): 118–35.

62. Elisabeth A. Pichler and Andrea Hemetsberger, 'Driven by Devotion – How Consumers Interact with their Objects of Devotion', in A.Y. Lee and D. Soman (eds), *Advances in Consumer Research* 35 (Duluth, MN: Association for Consumer Research, 2008): 439–43.

63. Sofie Møller Bjerrisgaard, Dannie Kjeldgaard and Anders Bengtsson, 'Consumer-brand assemblages in advertising: An analysis of skin, identity and tattoos in ads', *Consumption, Markets and Culture* 16(3) (2013): 223–39.

64. Margaret Hogg and Emma Banister, 'Dislikes, distastes and the undesired self: Conceptualising and exploring the role of the undesired end state in consumer experience', *Journal of Marketing Management* 17(1–2) (2001): 73–104; Emma Banister and Margaret Hogg, 'Negative symbolic consumption and consumers' drive for self-esteem: The case of the fashion industry', *European Journal of Marketing* 38(7) (2004): 850–68.

65. See David Mick, 'Consumer research and semiotics: Exploring the morphology of signs, symbols, and significance', *Journal of Consumer Research* 13 (September 1986): 196–213.

66. For a general introduction, we can recommend Daniel Chandler, *Semiotics: The Basics* (London: Routledge, 2017). For a discussion of the use of semiotics in marketing and consumer behaviour, see Laura R. Oswald, *Marketing Semiotics* (Oxford: Oxford University Press, 2012).

67. Teresa J. Domzal and Jerome B. Kernan, 'Reading advertising: The what and how of product meaning', *Journal of Consumer Marketing* 9 (Summer 1992): 48–64, at 49.

68. Winfried Nöth, *Handbook of Semiotics* (London: Sage, 1994); David Mick, 'Consumer research and semiotics', op. cit.; Charles Sanders Peirce, in Charles Hartshorne, Paul Weiss and Arthur W. Burks (eds), *Collected Papers* (Cambridge, MA: Harvard University Press, 1931–58).

69. Professor Kent Grayson, Northwestern University, personal communication.

70. Jacques Durand, 'Rhetorical Figures in the Advertising Image', in Jean Umiker-Sebeok (ed.), *Marketing and Semiotics: New Directions in the Study of Signs for Sale* (Berlin: Mouton de Gruyter, 1987): 295–318.

71. C. Alsted and H.H. Larsen, 'Toward a semiotic typology of advertising forms', in H.H. Larsen, D.G. Mick and C. Alsted (eds), *Marketing and Semiotics: Selected Papers from the Copenhagen Symposium,* (Copenhagen: Handelshøjskolens Forlag, 1991): 75–103.

72. Winfried Nöth, 'The language of commodities: Groundwork for a semiotics of consumer goods', *International Journal of Research in Marketing* 4 (1988): 173–86.
73. See the early introduction of the field: Elizabeth C. Hirschman and Morris B. Holbrook (eds), *Symbolic Consumer Behaviour* (Ann Arbor, MI: Association for Consumer Research, 1981).
74. Odile Solomon, 'Semiotics and marketing: New directions in industrial design applications', *International Journal of Research in Marketing* 4 (1988): 201–15.
75. J.M. Floch, 'The contribution of structural semiotics to the design of a hypermarket', *International Journal of Research in Marketing* 4(3) (1988): 233–52.
76. James Ogilvy, 'This postmodern business', *Marketing and Research Today* (February 1990): 4–22.
77. Two special issues of *International Journal of Research in Marketing* 10(3) (1993) and 11(4) (1994), both edited by A. Fuat Firat, John F. Sherry Jr and Alladi Venkatesh, have been decisive for the introduction of themes of postmodernism in marketing and consumer research.
78. Craig J. Thompson, 'Modern truth and postmodern incredulity: A hermeneutic deconstruction of the metanarrative of "scientific truth" in marketing research', *International Journal of Research in Marketing* 10(3) (1993): 325–38.
79. Christina Goulding, 'Issues in representing the postmodern consumer', *Qualitative Market Research: An International Journal* 6(3) (2003): 152–9.
80. See, for example, A. Fuat Firat and Alladi Venkatesh, 'Postmodernity: The age of marketing', *International Journal of Research in Marketing* 10(3) (1993): 227–49; James Ogilvy, 'This postmodern business', *Marketing and Research Today* (February 1990): 4–22; W. Fred van Raaij, 'Postmodern consumption', *Journal of Economic Psychology* 14 (1993): 541–63.
81. Stephen Brown, *Postmodern Marketing* (London: Routledge, 1995): 106 ff.
82. Anita Biressi and Heather Nunn, *Reality TV: Realism and Revelation* (New York: Columbia University Press, 2013).
83. Fuat Firat and Venkatesh, 'Postmodernity: The age of marketing', op. cit.
84. Laurent Muzellec, 'Ceci n'est pas une brand. Postmodernism and Brand Management', paper presented at the 36th EMAC Conference (Reykjavik 2007).
85. Stuart Elliott, 'Years later, Mattel embraces "Barbie Girl"', *New York Times* (26 August 2009) http://mediadecoder.blogs.nytimes.com/2009/08/26/years-later-mattel-embraces-barbie-girl/?pagemode=print (accessed 26 August 2018).
86. Eric Arnould and Søren Askegaard, 'HyperCulture: The Next Stage in the Globalization of Consumption', paper presented at the 1997 Annual Association for Consumer Research Conference in Denver, Colorado (16–19 October).
87. Aurélie Kessous and Elyette Roux, 'A semiotic analysis of nostalgia as a connection to the past', *Qualitative Market Research: An International Journal* 11(2) (2008): 192–212.
88. Stephen Brown, Robert V. Kozinets and John F. Sherry Jr, 'Teaching old brands new tricks: Retro branding and the revival of brand meaning', *Journal of Marketing* 67 (July 2003): 19–33.
89. Ibid.
90. Stephen Brown, *The Marketing Code* (London: Cyan Books, 2006).
91. Ilona Mikkonen and Domen Bajde, 'Happy Festivus! Parody as playful consumer resistance', *Consumption Markets & Culture* 16(4) (2013): 311–37.
92. Fuat Firat and Venkatesh, 'Postmodernity: The age of marketing', *International Journal of Research in Marketing* 10(3) (1993): 227–49.
93. Jean Baudrillard, *Simulations* (New York: Semiotext(e), 1983).
94. Hellen Lundell, 'Fictional food: Consumers taking the lead on food fabrication', *Heartbeat* (18 June 2013), https://www.hartman-group.com/hartbeat/477/fictional-food-consumers-taking-the-lead-on-food-fabrication (accessed 30 August 2018).
95. Richard Elliott, Susan Eccles and Michelle Hodgson, 'Recoding gender representations: Women, cleaning products, and advertising's "New Man"', *International Journal of Research in Marketing* 10(3) (1993): 311–24.
96. Stephanie O'Donohoe, 'Raiding the postmodern pantry: Advertising intertextuality and the young adult audience', *European Journal of Marketing* 31(3/4) (1997): 234–53.
97. Stephanie O'Donohoe, 'Living with ambivalence: Attitudes towards advertising in postmodern times', *Marketing Theory* 1(1) (2001): 91–108.

Chapter 4
The self

Chapter objectives

When you finish reading this chapter you will understand why:

4.1 The self-concept is a complex and composite one.

4.2 Products and other types of consumption often play a key role in defining the self-concept.

4.3 The digital self is becoming increasingly important for our self-image.

4.4 Gender and gender roles contribute in determining the products we buy to fulfil these roles.

4.5 Body image is a key factor for our self-image in contemporary consumer culture.

4.6 Culture dictates certain types of beauty, including body decoration or mutilation.

MATTHEW, a marketing director, is a happily married man, and his two children aged six and eight provide immense joy in his life. However, at 42 he feels younger than his years, and somewhat anxious about his totally family-oriented life – he has a nice house, a magnificent garden and takes regular family holidays in sunny Dubai. But he has begun to feel the loss of his previous, extravagant, carefree life, one in which he perceived himself to be a well-dressed, admired individual of good taste and discernment who always turned heads when he entered the room. He has a slight nagging worry that 'Matthew the family man' is dominating his personality and has totally taken over his life's spirit. It's a life he very much loves and one that has his complete commitment, but one which he also views as very 'sensible and earnest'.

Some months into the development of these feelings, Matthew is contacted by his company's personnel department about replacing his company car. Three years earlier he had selected a sensible Audi 80 with the needs of the family in mind. In the meantime, he had bought his wife a BMW X5, which is always used for family travel. He has a widely envied budget allocated to car purchase, due to his long-term commitment and excellent contribution to company performance. As a result, he can select almost any car he desires. He drives past a Bentley garage on the way home every day but thought the price tag of £185k on the one in the window was a little excessive. After extensive thought and research he decides on a Porsche Panamera GTS.

The Porsche Panamera, a unique four-seater, four-door model, is a well-designed and admired car for drivers of good taste and discernment, created for the sporty, confident, powerful individual. The current media campaign portrays a successful mid-forties man being admired at the traffic lights, in the office car park and occasionally the local school collecting his children. While driving home Matthew plays his favourite music at full volume, exceeds the legal speed limit when he believes it is 'safe' to do so and generally feels more like the much-revered Matthew who graduated over 20 years ago. Catching a glimpse of himself in the rear view mirror he decides he really doesn't look his age. . .

Carolyn Strong, Cardiff Business School

Introduction

4.1

The self-concept is a complex and composite one.

Matthew is not alone in feeling that his self-image and possessions affect his 'value' as a person. Consumers' insecurities about their appearance are rampant: one survey concluded that 44 per cent of British women and 31 per cent of British men are generally dissatisfied with their bodies[1] – and if we narrow the issue to being unhappy with one aspect of the appearance, these numbers may rise to percentages in the 70s (for men) and 80s (for women).[2] Even among married couples, the sense of presenting one's self is guarded. When it comes to being naked in front of one's partner, one-third of women are too shy to take their clothes off in front of their husband. In the same study, 80 per cent of women reported having real difficulty in showering or changing clothes in front of other women in the gym.[3] Reflecting this discontent, various types of fitness and other 'body improvement practices' are growing – in Europe (2018) by just under 4 per cent.[4] New cosmetics for men and new clinical 'beauty procedures' have grown rapidly in Europe in the past few years, and the men's personal care market is projected to reach almost €150 billion by 2022![5] But as we have already seen, 'self' and consumption are not just about body, beauty and personal care. Many products, from cars to aftershave, are bought because the person is trying to highlight or hide some aspect of the self. In this chapter, we will focus on how consumers' feelings about themselves shape their consumption habits, particularly as they strive to fulfil their society's expectations about how a male or female should look and act.

Does the self exist?

Most of us can't boast of coming close to Katy Perry's almost 110 million followers on Twitter, but many of us do have hundreds of followers, in addition to legions of Facebook friends.[6] The explosion of these and other social networking services enables everyone to focus on him- or herself and share mundane or scintillating details about their lives with anyone who's interested (*why* they are interested is another story!).

Today it seems natural to think of ourselves as a potential celeb waiting for our 15 minutes of fame (as the pop icon Andy Warhol once predicted). However, the idea that each single human life is unique rather than a part of a group only developed in late medieval times (between the eleventh and fifteenth centuries). Furthermore, the emphasis on the unique nature of the self is much greater in Western societies.[7] Many Eastern cultures stress the importance of a *collective self,* where a person derives his or her identity in large measure from a social group. Both Eastern and Western cultures believe the self divides into an inner, private self and an outer, public self. But where they differ is in terms of which part they see as the 'real you' – the West tends to subscribe to an independent understanding of the self, which emphasises the inherent separateness of each individual.

Non-Western cultures, in contrast, tend to focus on an interdependent self where we define our identities largely by our relationships with others.[8] For example, a Confucian perspective stresses the importance of 'face' – others' perceptions of the self and maintaining one's desired status in their eyes. One dimension of face is *mien-tzu* – the reputation one achieves through success and ostentation. Some Asian cultures developed explicit rules about the specific garments and even colours that certain social classes and occupations were allowed to display. These traditions live on today in Japanese style manuals that provide very detailed instructions for dressing and how to address people of differing status.[9]

That orientation is a bit at odds with such Western conventions as 'casual Friday', which encourages employees to express their unique selves (at least short of muscle shirts and flip-flops). However casual we may think we are, it does not prevent us from 'just checking'. In the UK, a study of image consciousness showed that women in Liverpool check their appearance up to 71 times a day, while men check their appearance up to 66 times daily.[10]

The self can be understood from many different theoretical vantage points. A psychoanalytical or Freudian perspective regards the self as a system of competing forces riddled with conflict, while behaviourists tend to regard the self as a collection of conditioned responses (see Chapter 7). From a cognitive orientation, the self is an information-processing system, an organising force that serves as a nucleus around which new information is processed.[11]

Self-concept

The **self-concept** refers to the beliefs a person holds about their attributes, and how they evaluate these qualities. While one's overall self-concept may be positive, there are certainly parts of the self that are evaluated more positively than others. For example, Matthew felt better about his professional identity than he did about his pending 'middle-age' identity.

Components of the self-concept

The self-concept is a very complex structure. It is composed of many attributes, some of which are given greater emphasis when the overall self is being evaluated. Attributes of self-concept can be described along such dimensions as their content (for example, facial attractiveness *vs* mental aptitude), positivity or negativity (i.e. self-esteem), intensity, stability over time and accuracy (that is, the degree to which one's self-assessment corresponds to reality).[12] As we will see later in the chapter, consumers' self-assessments can be quite distorted, especially with regard to their physical appearance. In addition, our own estimates of how much we change over time vary as well: a study that included both young and old people asked over 19,000 respondents about their preferences in the past (foods, vacations, hobbies and bands) and also to predict how their tastes will change in the future. Regardless of age, people acknowledged that their prior choices had changed quite a bit over time, but they still tended to predict that they would not change as they got older.[13]

Self-esteem

Self-esteem refers to the positivity of a person's self-concept. People with low self-esteem do not expect that they will perform very well, and they will try to avoid embarrassment, failure or rejection. In developing a new line of snack cakes, for example, the company Sara Lee found that consumers low in self-esteem preferred portion-controlled snack items because they felt they lacked self-control.[14] In contrast, people with high self-esteem expect to be successful, will take more risks and are more willing to be the centre of attention.[15] Self-esteem is often related to acceptance by others. As you probably remember, teenagers who are members of high-status groups have higher self-esteem than their excluded classmates.[16] Alberto-Culver uses a self-esteem appeal to promote a new product that reflects our changing society: 'Soft & Beautiful Just for Me Texture Softener' – an alternative to hair pressing or relaxing. It is targeted at Caucasian mothers who don't know how to care for the hair of their multiracial children who have 'hair texture' issues. The self-esteem portion of the campaign, dubbed 'Love Yourself. Love Your Hair', includes a website (texturesoftener.com) that offers 'conversation starters' to help parents find ways to talk to their daughters about self-image.[17]

Marketing communications can influence a consumer's level of self-esteem. Exposure to ads can trigger a process of *social comparison,* where the person tries to evaluate their self by comparing it to the people depicted in these artificial images. This form of comparison appears to be a basic human motive, and many marketers have tapped into this need by supplying idealised images of happy, attractive people who just happen to be using their products. We even feel better about our self-image when we own and display products that are thought to be of high aesthetic value![18]

The social comparison process was illustrated in a study that showed that female college students tend to compare their physical appearance with advertising models. Furthermore, study participants who were exposed to beautiful women in advertisements afterwards expressed lowered satisfaction with their own appearance, as compared to controls.[19] Another study demonstrated that young women's perceptions of their own body shapes and sizes can be altered after being exposed to as little as 30 minutes of television programming.[20] Finally, in what would seem to be a counter-intuitive finding, one study showed that while female subjects felt badly about themselves after viewing ads with thin female models, they also evaluated the brands being paired with the thin models more highly. Further, the subjects who saw ads depicting normal-weight models did not feel bad about themselves, but they did rate the brands lower.[21]

Self-esteem advertising attempts to change product attitudes by stimulating positive feelings about the self.[22] One strategy is to challenge the consumer's self-esteem and then show a linkage to a product that will provide a remedy. Sometimes compliments are derived by comparing the person to others. It can also increase consumer self-esteem to be exposed to celebrity endorsers that for some reason or another have a relatively negative public image, in particular if your self-esteem is already low.[23] One UK advertising campaign run in London's Underground system and sponsored by Protein World managed to have its self-esteem advertising backfire by showing an impossibly in-shape model in a bikini on the beach, asking 'Are you Beach Body Ready?'. Following the mass of complaints received by Transport for London, Protein World and the Advertising Standards Agency, the posters were removed from all Tube stations. Many of the posters were vandalised, and both consumers and Unilever took to social media to respond to the ad. Speaking of their 'Campaign for Real Beauty', the Dove spokesperson said: 'that over the decade between 2004 and 2015, the percentage of women finding that the media set unrealistic standards for beauty fell from 75 to 66 %. As is underlined in this statement, the "Campaign for Real Beauty" seems to have had an effect since the degree of diversity is increasing but there is still a long way to go before the request for a more diversified portrayal of the female body in the media can be said to have been satisfied'.[24]

Real and ideal selves

Self-esteem is influenced by a process where the consumer compares their actual standing on some attribute to some ideal. A consumer might ask, 'Am I as attractive as I would like to be?', 'Do I make as much money as I should?' and so on. The **ideal self** is a person's conception of how they would like to be, while the **actual self** refers to our more realistic appraisal of the qualities we have or lack.

The much debated 'beach body ready' campaign, accused of producing eating disorders and a distorted beauty ideal.
Source: Reproduced with kind permission of Unilever PLC and group companies.
Simon leigh/Alamy Stock Photo

We choose some products because we think they are consistent with our actual self, whereas we buy others to help us to reach more of an ideal standard. And we often engage in a process of **impression management**, where we work hard to 'manage' what others think of us by strategically choosing clothing and other cues that will put us in a good light.[25] The phenomenon of impression management is, for example, crucial to understanding the phenomenon of selfies.[26] One study investigated how consumers use brands in selfie contexts and concluded that while the exposure is, of course, potentially beneficial for the brands, consumers' use of the brands – since not controlled by any brand manager – also represented a challenge for the firms.[27]

The ideal self is partly moulded by elements of the consumer's culture, such as heroes or people depicted in advertising who serve as models of achievement or appearance.[28] Products may be purchased because they are believed to be instrumental in helping us achieve these goals. Some products are chosen because they are perceived to be consistent with the consumer's actual self, while others are used to help reach the standard set by the ideal self. In a recent study looking at the willingness of young healthy adults to take (legal) drugs to enhance their social, emotional and cognitive traits, people were far more reluctant to take drugs that promised to enhance traits that they considered fundamental to their self-identity (social comfort), and more likely to take drugs that were viewed as being less central to their self-identity, such as performance-enhancing drugs for memory. Advertising messages that promoted 'enabling' rather than 'enhancing' were more favourably received as well. Apparently, boosting one's ability to concentrate is more easily accepted than boosting one's mood![29]

Fantasy: bridging the gap between the selves

While most people experience a discrepancy between their real and ideal selves, for some consumers this gap is larger than for others. These people are especially good targets for marketing communications that employ *fantasy* appeals.[30] A fantasy or daydream is a self-induced shift in consciousness, which is sometimes a way of compensating for a lack of external stimulation or of escaping from problems in the real world.[31] Many products and services are successful because they appeal to consumers' tendency to fantasise. An ad may transport us to an unfamiliar, exciting situation; things we purchase may permit us to 'try on' interesting or provocative roles. And, with today's technology, such as the **virtual makeovers** that several websites offer, consumers can experiment with different looks before they actually take the plunge in the real world. *Vogue*'s 'Makeup Simulation' application (now available in Japan) allows women to see how brands such as Clinique would look on their (simulated) faces. Johnson & Johnson's ROC Skincare offers its 'Skin Correxion Tool' to simulate the effects of anti-ageing products.[32]

Multiple selves

In a way, each of us is really a number of different people – your mother probably would not recognise the 'you' that emerges while you're on holiday with a group of friends! We have as many selves as we do different social roles. Depending on the situation, we act differently, use different products and services and we even vary in terms of how much we like ourselves. A person may require a different set of products to play a desired role: she may choose a sedate, understated perfume when she is being her professional self, but splash on something more provocative on Saturday night as she becomes her *femme fatale* self. The dramaturgical perspective on consumer behaviour views people much like actors who play different roles. We each play many roles, and each has its own script, props and costumes.[33]

The self can be thought of as having different components, or *role identities,* and only some of these are active at any given time. Some identities (e.g. husband, boss, student) are more central to the self than others, but others (e.g. stamp collector, dancer or advocate for greater equality in the workplace) may be dominant in specific situations.[34] Indeed, some roles may conflict with one another – for example, one study of Iranian young people living in the UK described what the authors termed the **torn self**, where respondents struggle with retaining an authentic culture while still enjoying Western freedom (and dealing with assumptions of others who believe they might be terrorists).[35] A not-dissimilar 'unmanageable multiplicity' of moral anxiety and tension is found among consumers who try to shop and consume in an ethically correct way.[36] Strategically, this means a marketer may want to ensure the appropriate role identity is active when products are proposed to fulfill a particular role – for example, when fortified drink and energy bar companies hand out free product samples to runners at a marathon.

If each person potentially has many social selves, how does each develop? How do we decide which self to 'activate' at any point in time? The sociological tradition of **symbolic interactionism** stresses that relationships with other people play a large part in forming the self.[37] According to this perspective, we exist in a symbolic environment. We assign meaning to any situation or object when we interpret the symbols in this environment. As members of society, individuals learn to agree on shared meanings. Thus, we 'know' that a red light means stop, the 'golden arches' mean fast food and 'blondes have more fun'. That knowledge is important in understanding consumer behaviour because it implies that our possessions play a key role as we evaluate ourselves and decide 'who we are'.[38]

The looking-glass self

Bloomingdales (an upscale American department store that would be thought of as 'high street' in London) and some other clothing stores are testing interactive dressing rooms: when you choose a garment, the mirror superimposes it on your reflection so that you can see how it would look on your body without having to go to the trouble of trying it on.[39] Exciting stuff – but in a way this fancy technology simply simulates the 'primping' process many shoppers undergo when they prance in front of a mirror and try to imagine how a garment will look on them – and whether others will approve or not.

Sociologists call the process of imagining others' reactions as 'taking the role of the other', or the **looking-glass self**.[40] According to this view, our desire to define ourselves operates as a sort of psychological sonar: we take readings of our own identity when we 'bounce' signals off others and try to project their impression of us. Like the distorted mirrors in a funhouse, our appraisal of who we are varies depending on whose perspective we consider and how accurately we predict their evaluations of us. In symbolic interactionist terms, we *negotiate* these meanings over time. Essentially, we continually ask ourselves the question, 'Who am I in this situation?'. Those around us greatly influence how we answer this query because we also ask, 'Who do other people think I am?'. We tend to pattern our behaviour on the perceived expectations of others, as a form of self-fulfilling prophecy. When we act the way we assume others expect us to act, we often confirm these perceptions.

A confident career man may sit morosely at a nightclub, imagining that others see him as a dowdy, unattractive man with little sex appeal (regardless of whether these perceptions are true). These 'signals' influence the man's actual behaviour. If he doesn't believe he's attractive, he may choose frumpy, unflattering clothing that actually does make him less attractive. However, the next morning at work his self-confidence at the office may cause him to assume that others hold his 'executive self' in even higher regard than they actually do (we all know people like that)!

Self-consciousness

Have you ever walked into a class in the middle of a lecture? If you were convinced that all eyes were on you as you awkwardly searched for a seat, you can understand the feeling of self-consciousness. In contrast, sometimes we behave with shockingly little self-consciousness. For example, we may do things in a stadium, at a riot, or at a party that we would never do if we were highly conscious of our behaviour (and we add insult to injury when we post these escapades on our Facebook page!).[41] Of course, certain cues in the environment – such as walking in front of a mirror – are likely to promote self-consciousness. That feeling may, in turn, influence behaviour. For example, one pair of researchers is looking at whether grocery shoppers who push a cart with an attached mirror will buy more healthy foods because their heightened self-consciousness makes them more weight conscious.[42]

Some people seem to be more sensitive in general to the image they communicate to others. However, we all know people who act as if they're oblivious to the impression they are making. A heightened concern about the nature of one's public 'image' also results in more concern about the social appropriateness of products and consumption activities. Consumers who score high on a scale of public self-consciousness express more interest in clothing and use more cosmetics than others who score lower.[43] In one study, highly self-conscious subjects expressed greater willingness to buy personal products, such as a douche or a gas-prevention remedy, that are somewhat embarrassing to buy but may avoid awkward public incidents later.[44]

Similarly, high self-monitors are more attuned to how they present themselves in their social environments, and their estimates of how others will perceive their product choices influence what they choose to buy.[45] A scale to measure self-monitoring asks consumers how much they agree with statements such as 'I guess I put on a show to impress or entertain others', or 'I would probably make a good actor'. Perhaps not surprisingly, publicly visible types such as college football players and fashion models tend to score higher on these dimensions.[46]

Self-consciousness on steroids – perhaps that's what we're experiencing in what historians, looking back, might call 'The Era of the Selfie'. We have already mentioned that the **selfie,** or a picture a smartphone user takes of him- or herself on a smartphone (whether or not it's attached to a 'selfie stick'), is a common form of communication, especially for millennials. It is becoming an increasingly central topic for consumer researchers also.[47] While the selfie is, positively speaking, a new resource for playful self-expression as well as one way of challenging social norms about the representation of, for example, women,[48] it also has a downside. It carries with it new problems in terms of the urge to always be 'on' – to optimise the impression management process – and produces an anxiety about relative performance in the universe of selfie coolness.[49]

What explains the infatuation many of us seem to have with photographing ourselves? One simple reason: because we can. Obviously, the widespread adoption of smartphones makes it easy to do. But there may be other reasons as well. One explanation hinges on the concept of the empty self. This perspective points to the decline of shared points of reference over the last

50 years as we have witnessed a decline in family, community and traditions. As a result, people have shifted inward and a focus on the self is an unconscious way to compensate for what we have lost. Indeed, when we look at young people (more on this in Chapter 13), we do observe a decline in marriage rates and a low amount of trust people place in government, corporations and organised religion. The increasing focus on self-reliance in turn creates a culture of narcissism, where we are obsessed with what we do and feel the need to constantly record it (updating our relationship status on Facebook, posting selfies and photos of our meals on Instagram, etc.).[50] Perhaps that's an overly bleak assessment, but it does help to explain why the average millennial checks his or her smartphone 43 times per day, and why 83 per cent of millennials report that they sleep with their smartphones next to them every night.[51] Here's the irony: research shows that while people believe taking pictures during an event enhances their enjoyment, the opposite is true. There is a tendency to become preoccupied with documenting the moment – the more pictures people take, the less they say they enjoy the actual experience.[52]

The tangled web

Job applicants who post selfies (that must have been a pretty wild party. . .) may come to regret their actions as potential employers start to check out their pages before they look at the would-be candidates' résumés. Some people even turn to services such as Reputation.com, which scour the internet to remove embarrassing postings before the boss (or Mum) sees them.[53] Cell phones have spawned yet another way for teens to share intimate details about themselves online. The phenomenon of sexting, where kids post nude or semi-nude photos of themselves online, is growing. In one recent survey of a sample of college students, more than half of respondents admitted to sexting as minors – and most were unaware that these acts have potential legal consequences.[54] Your online photos may be a lot more public than you think – and marketers find ways to use them, too. Digital marketing companies scan photo-sharing sites such as Instagram, Flickr and Pinterest when they work for major advertisers. They use software to scan the photos to identify whether a person is holding a brand with a logo (such as a Coke can) and what the person is doing in the picture. This information is used to send targeted messages to consumers and to provide feedback to clients about how people use their brands. For example, Kraft Foods pays a company to find out what people drink when they eat macaroni and cheese.[55]

Products that shape the self: you are what you consume

4.2

Products and other types of consumption often play a key role in defining the self-concept.

The selfie phenomenon reminds us how the reflected self helps to shape self-concept, which implies that people see themselves as they imagine others see them. Since what others see includes a person's clothing, jewellery, furniture, car and so on, it stands to reason that these products also help to determine the perceived self. A consumer's products place them in a social role, which helps to answer the question, 'Who am I *now*?'.

People use an individual's consumption behaviours to help them make judgements about that person's social identity. In addition to considering a person's clothes, grooming habits and such like, we make inferences about personality based on a person's choice of leisure activities (squash *vs* football), food preferences (vegetarians *vs* 'steak and chips' people), cars or home decorating choices. People who are shown pictures of someone's sitting room, for example, are able to make surprisingly accurate guesses about their personality.[56] In the same way that a consumer's use of products influences others' perceptions, the same products can help to determine their *own* self-concept and social identity.[57]

A consumer exhibits *attachment* to an object to the extent that it is used by that person to maintain their self-concept.[58] Objects can act as a sort of security blanket by reinforcing our identities, especially in unfamiliar situations. For example, students who decorate their room or house with personal items are less likely to drop out. This coping process may protect the self from being diluted in an unfamiliar environment.[59]

The use of consumption information to define the self is especially important when an identity is yet to be adequately formed – something that occurs when a consumer plays a new or unfamiliar role. **Symbolic self-completion theory** predicts that people who have an incomplete self-definition tend to complete this identity by acquiring and displaying symbols associated with it.[60] Adolescent boys may use 'macho' products such as cars and cigarettes to bolster their developing masculinity: these items act as a 'social crutch' to be leaned on during a period of uncertainty about identity. Logically, then, it was found that consumers who have fewer role-identity resources are more likely to present this role-identity outwardly compared to (typically elder) consumers who have more role-identity resources (possessions, heirlooms) but are less likely to feel the need to sport them publicly.[61]

Consumer behaviour as I see it . . .

What makes a real man?

Professor Jacob Östberg
Stockholm University

What is a real man? What kind of appearances and behaviors are you allowed to engage in and still be judged by your surroundings as a real man? What does the process look like whereby the criteria for making such judgments are constantly negotiated and renegotiated? These are the kinds of issues I have been looking at in my research over the years.

Basic semiotic theory tells us that meaning is difference. In that sense the category man is only meaningful in relation to other categories such as women, boys, and elders. While voices are increasingly heard to move away from a binary view of gender towards more fluidity, for most people a man is still largely defined in opposition to a woman, as the main counterpart in the key binary opposition. So much of our organisation of society is built upon this binary opposition that it is hard to circumvent, even for those actively trying.

In a paper I wrote a couple of years ago I decided to address the elephant in the room, that someone is typically viewed as a man because that person (supposedly) has a penis.[62] While this might indeed sound neatly binary, almost like the zeros and ones of a computer, in reality the designator of 'having'

and 'not having' turned out to be more complicated. Upon analyzing advertising and popular culture it became clear that there are plenty of normative accounts of a particular size of this bodily feature, despite a lack of explicit representations in mainstream cultural outlets. These messages are so ubiquitous that men are bombarded with the archaic imperative: thou shalt sport a banana in thy pocket. All in all, men are caught in a discursive crossfire where they are potentially made to feel anxious about their anxiousness and embarrassed about their embarrassedness.

From these more archaic conundrums of masculinity, we have recently engaged in a series of projects looking at masculinity in flux, responding to potentially shifting expectations of how a real man should be. When we transit into new roles in life – e.g., from child to adult, from single to in a relationship, from unemployed to employed, or as in this case from being just any man to being a father – we typically look for templates of how we should sufficiently conform to the new role that we are about to enter.

In a recent project we charted global reactions to Swedish photographer Johan Bävman's photo exhibition, Swedish Dads.[63] This exhibition shows images of stay-at-home fathers in their natural settings. The exhibition has toured Swedish embassies around the world and has garnered lots of international media attention. When Bävman was about to go on parental leave himself, he realised that he did not know what kind of man he was supposed to be. There was a paucity of depictions of men taking the main responsibility for children. He could not look at his own father, depictions in the media typically show men using babies and small children as props in their own identity game, and depictions in advertising, finally, typically show incompetent dads being rescued by various market offerings in order to manage 'babysitting' their own children.

In order to fill this void of realistic images of stay-at-home fathers, Bävman started taking photos of men in his surroundings. In the research we trace how these images were spread around the world and what reactions they got. There were two types of reactions: those celebrating the Swedish dads and the political system that enabled them to take on board this progressive fatherhood role, and those

condemning the Swedish dads for betraying true manhood. There were even those suggesting that this horrible social experiment would be the end of the Swedish population, as no sexual attraction could possibly occur when men behaved like Mister Mom and the women, supposedly, like men, figuratively wearing the pants in the family. Without sexual attraction, no sex, and without sex, no kids, and without kids, no future for the Swedish population.

I find studying various ways in which templates of being a 'real man' gets constructed at the intersection of marketing, popular culture and consumers' lived lives both interesting and important. Not least since men typically try to handle the insecurities thereby instilled in them by resorting to marketplace solutions, and we see how companies tread a thin line between reinforcing the insecurities and providing remedies.

Questions

What are the social consequences of not conforming to the behaviours and appearances connected to a particular gender? What are some character traits that you associate with being a real man? How do these character traits overlap with what are typically depicted as problematic aspects of masculinity?

Jacob Östberg

Loss of self

The contribution of possessions to self-identity is perhaps most apparent when these treasured objects are lost or stolen. One of the first acts performed by institutions that want to repress individuality and encourage group identity, such as prisons or convents, is to confiscate personal possessions.[64] Victims of burglaries and natural disasters commonly report feelings of alienation, depression or of being 'violated'. One consumer's comment after being robbed is typical: 'It's the next worse thing to being bereaved; it's like being raped'.[65] Burglary victims exhibit a diminished sense of community, reduced sense of privacy and take less pride in their house's appearance than do their neighbours.[66] On a less dramatic note, another study demonstrates how everyday products that are more closely linked to one's identity are more likely to be recycled rather than trashed.[67]

The dramatic impact of product loss is highlighted by studying post-disaster conditions, when consumers may literally lose almost everything but the clothes on their backs following a fire, hurricane, flood or earthquake. Some people are reluctant to undergo the process of recreating their identity by acquiring all new possessions. Interviews with disaster victims reveal that some are reluctant to invest the self in new possessions and so become more detached about what they buy. This comment from a woman in her fifties is representative of this attitude: 'I had so much love tied up in my things. I can't go through that kind of loss again. What I'm buying now won't be as important to me'.[68]

Self/product congruence

Because many consumption activities relate to self-definition, it is not surprising to learn that consumers demonstrate consistency between their values and the things they buy.[69] **Self-image congruence models** suggest that we choose products when their attributes match some aspect of the self.[70] These models assume a process of *cognitive matching* between product attributes and the consumer's self-image.[71] Over time we tend to form relationships with products that resemble the bonds we create with other people – these include love, unrequited love (we yearn for it but can't have it), respect and perhaps even fear or hate ('why is my computer out to get me?').[72] Researchers even report that after a 'break-up' with a brand, people tend to develop strong negative feelings and will go to great lengths to discredit it, including bad-mouthing and even vandalism. As the saying (sort of) goes, 'Hell hath no fury like a (wo)man scorned'.[73]

While results are somewhat mixed, the ideal self appears to be more relevant as a comparison standard for highly expressive social products such as perfume. In contrast, the actual self is more relevant for everyday functional products. These standards are also likely to vary by usage situation. For example, a consumer might want a functional, reliable car to commute to work every day, but a flashier model with more 'zing' when going out on a date in the evening. Sadly, there are examples of people using products in which the goal of enhancing the ideal self ends up conflicting with and damaging the actual self. The body-building craze that swept through the world resulted in an increasing number of young men using anabolic steroids for body-building. This steroid use may 'bulk up' the physique (and provide a faster attainment of the ideal self), but it also causes male infertility, high blood pressure and an increase in the risk of heart attacks.[74]

Marketing pitfall

The pursuit of a healthy, fit body cannot be a problem, can it? Well, psychiatric doctors and mental health workers are increasingly worried about the consequences of excessive fitness and exercise practice. Rather than the consumer gaining control over his or her body, in the cases of 'obsessive fitness orientation', it is the body and its alleged 'needs' that overtakes control. As a consequence, the consumer hit by this type of obsession increasingly sacrifices other aspects of his or her social life to spending all the time possible in the fitness centre.[75] This trend may be further encouraged through the process of 'fitspiration' – the promotion of ever-more optimised and fit bodies on social media.[76]

An exploration of the conflicts Muslim women who choose to wear headscarves experience illustrates how even a simple piece of cloth reflects a person's aesthetic, political and moral dimensions.[77] The Turkish women in the study expressed the tension they felt in their ongoing struggle to reconcile ambiguous religious principles that simultaneously call for modesty and beauty. Society sends Muslim women contradictory messages in modern-day Turkey. Although the Koran denounces waste, many of the companies that produce religious headscarves introduce new designs each season and, as styles and tastes change, women are encouraged to purchase more scarves than are necessary. Moreover, the authors point out that a wearer communicates her fashion sense by the fabrics she selects and by the way she drapes and ties her scarf. In addition, veiling sends contradictory images about the proper sex roles of men and women. On the one hand, women who cover their heads by choice feel a sense of empowerment. On the other, the notion that Islamic law exhorts women to cover themselves lest they threaten men's self-restraint and honour is a persistent sign that men exert control over women's bodies and restrict their freedom.

Marketing opportunity

While many environments in the Muslim world do not encourage female participation in sports, this is far from true everywhere. And, as a consequence of globalisation, women in the Muslim world are increasingly enthusiastic about the pleasures of sports. However, they may also be keen on observing the modesty required by their cultural environments. As a compromise solution, Nike has designed a uniform for observant women in Somalia who want to play sports without abandoning the traditional hijab (a robe that wraps around the head and loosely drapes over the entire body). The company streamlined the garment so that volleyball players could move but still keep their bodies covered.[78] Since then, Nike has engaged in intensive market research and product testing in terms of use and appearance of various prototypes and finally announced the global 'pro-Hijab' in 2017.[79]

While these findings make some intuitive sense, we cannot blithely assume that consumers will always buy products whose characteristics match their own. It is not clear that consumers really see aspects of themselves in down-to-earth, functional products that do not have very complex or human-like images. It is one thing to consider a brand personality for an expressive, image-oriented product such as perfume and quite another to impute human characteristics to a toaster.

One study found that 'polarising' products (i.e., products that produce highly divergent reactions from others in terms of whether they like or dislike them) carry more self-expression potential than bland products.[80] Of course, this raises the issue of how different and socially marginalised one wants to appear – it is not a problem to provoke and stand out, but most of us want to remain accepted at the same time, at least among our peers. Another problem is the old 'chicken-and-egg' question: do people buy products because the products are seen as similar to the self, or do they *assume* that these products must be similar because they have bought them? The similarity between a person's self-image and the images of products purchased does tend to increase with ownership, so this explanation cannot be ruled out.

The extended self

As noted earlier, many of the props and settings consumers use to define their social roles in a sense become a part of their selves. Those external objects that we consider a part of us comprise the **extended self**. In some cultures, people literally incorporate objects into the self – they lick new possessions, take the names of conquered enemies (or in some cases eat them) or bury the dead with their possessions.[81] Others don't go that far, but many people do cherish possessions as if they were a part of them. Many material objects, ranging from personal possessions and pets to national monuments or landmarks, help to form a consumer's identity. Just about everyone can name a valued possession that has a lot of the self 'wrapped up' in it, whether it is a treasured photograph, a trophy, an old shirt, a car or a cat. Indeed, it is often possible to construct a pretty accurate 'biography' of someone just by cataloguing the items on display in their bedroom or office.

In an important study on the self and possessions, four levels of the extended self were described. These range from very personal objects to places and things that allow people to feel like they are rooted in their larger social environments:[82]

- *Individual level*: consumers include many of their personal possessions in self-definition. These products can include jewellery, cars, clothing and so on. The saying 'You are what you wear' reflects the belief that one's things are a part of what one is.

- *Family level*: this part of the extended self includes a consumer's residence and its furnishings. The house can be thought of as a symbolic body for the family and often is a central aspect of identity.
- *Community level*: it is common for consumers to describe themselves in terms of the neighbourhood or town from which they come. For farming families or residents with close ties to a community, this sense of belonging is particularly important.
- *Group level*: our attachments to certain social groups can be considered a part of self. A consumer may feel that landmarks, monuments or sports teams are a part of the extended self.

Embodied cognition

To what extent do the products we buy influence the way we define ourselves? Social scientists who study relationships between thoughts and behaviours increasingly talk about the theory of **embodied cognition** A simple way to explain this perspective is that 'states of the body modify states of the mind'.[83] In other words, our behaviours and observations of what we do and buy shape our thoughts rather than vice versa. One of the most powerful examples is the idea that our body language actually changes how we see ourselves – in one of the most widely viewed TED talk ever, a social psychologist discusses how **power posing** (standing in a confident way even if you don't feel confident) affects brain activity – again, the self-fulfilling prophecy at work.[84]

The embodied cognition approach is consistent with consumer behaviour research that demonstrates how changes in self-concept can arise from usage of brands that convey different meanings. Indeed, one pair of researchers used the term **enclothed cognition** in their work, which showed how the symbolic meaning of clothing changes how people behave. In one study they asked respondents to wear a lab coat, which people associate with attentiveness and precise work. Indeed, they found that subjects who wore the lab coat displayed enhanced performance on tasks that required them to pay close attention. But they also introduced a twist: when respondents were told the garment was, in fact, a painter's coat rather than a doctor's lab coat, the effects went away. In other words, the respondents interpreted the symbolic meaning of the clothing and then altered their behaviour accordingly.[85]

The digital self

4.3

The digital self is becoming increasingly important for our self-image.

We've already talked about impression management, but our wired world takes this process to a new level.[86] Today we have access to 'post-production' tools to engineer our identities. These free or inexpensive applications allow virtually anyone to dramatically modify his or her **digital self** at will, as we strategically 'modify' the profile photos we post on Facebook or the descriptions we share on online dating sites. In addition, many of us create additional identities in the form of avatars in virtual worlds in MMOGs (massive multiplayer online games) such as *World of Warcraft*. Americans alone spend about $1.6 billion per year buying virtual goods just for their avatars. Our physical bodies continue to merge with our digital environments – we're moving from 'you are what you wear' to 'you are what you post'. We also take pieces of these digital identities back with us to the physical world. Respondents in one study placed more value on digital items that reflect their physical identities, such as digital photos and written communications.[87] However, as we have already seen, digital selves are not just about freedom to 'be whomever you want', they also pose a problem – not least because various sides of our digital self may come back and haunt us in a dramatic fashion long after we thought we had deleted and gotten rid of these 'former selves'.[88]

The tangled web

'I can leave Facebook whenever I want!' Actually, for many people it's not so easy. Researchers looked at Facebook posts, blogs, discussion groups and online magazines to find 'break-up stories' that would help them to understand what people go through when they decide to end their relationship with this social network. Many people talked about the things they're missing – friends' birthdays, the chance to play online games and the ability to use various online services. Their descriptions were laced with strong emotions ranging from sadness to the kind of relief an addict might feel if he or she succeeds in breaking out of a bad habit. Here are a few excerpts from the study:[89]

- 'Deleting my Facebook account was a four-day affair. It took me that long to disentangle myself from the service and to let others know how else they could find me. "Disentangling" entailed deleting my photos, "unliking" everything and dis-connecting all of the third-party services that used Facebook Connect to log me in.'
- 'I found a tiny link at the bottom of the security settings page for "how to deactivate Facebook".

After clicking the link, a page popped up with photos of me and my friends. "Jake will miss you", one caption read. "Jules will miss you", "Aaron will miss you". All of my friends were smiling at me and telling me please don't go.'
- 'I reactivated my Facebook account. Rejecting it felt, well, extreme. You can't get away from it. It's everything. It's everywhere. We can't reject it entirely. But I am approaching it this time with new wariness. . . '
- '(. . .) my decision to jettison Facebook has drawn me closer to those that matter and allowed peripheral acquaintances to fade away naturally. I can no longer just toss a meaningless "Happy Birthday, ugly!" on my friends' Facebook walls, but instead must call them to express such sentiments.'
- 'I have toyed with the idea of logging back in, but prying Facebook's sticky tentacles out of my life has inexorably improved my life, and I urge you to give it a shot, if only for a week.'

Wearable computing

Get ready for the invasion of **wearable computing**. Whether devices we wear on our wrist (such as the Apple Watch), on our face (Google Glass), or woven into our clothing, increasingly our digital interactions will become attached to our bodies – and perhaps even inserted into our bodies as companies offer ways to implant computer chips into our wrists. There are obvious privacy concerns as these products pick up steam, but advocates argue they offer numerous benefits as well. These attachable computers will be cheaper, provide greater accuracy because sensors are closer to our bodies and be more convenient because we won't have to carry around additional hardware.[90] Already, numerous wearables with big health implications are available or under development:[91]

- sensing for sleep disorders by tracking breath, heart rate and motion;
- detecting the possible onset of Alzheimer's by monitoring a person's gait via a GPS embedded in his or her shoes;
- tracking ingestion of medication via sensors that are activated by stomach fluid;
- measuring blood sugar via a contact lens with a chip that can track activity in a patient's tears;
- assessing the impact of blows to a football player's head via sensors inserted in his helmet.

Both in Australia and in Sweden there have been larger-scale experiments with such wearable computing for performing such things as opening doors, paying in stores and other

Wearable computing is still at the experimental stage – but many foresee much more widespread use in the future.

Source: Tony Latham/Corbis

Tony Latham/Corbis/Getty Images

daily tasks.[92] The question is still – what are the real uses (and the real dangers!) of such built-in technology?

Virtual makeovers

New virtual makeover technologies make it even easier for each of us to involve the digital self as we choose products to adorn our physical selves. These platforms allow the shopper to superimpose images on their faces or bodies so that they can quickly and easily see how products would alter appearance – without taking the risk of actually buying the item first. L'Oréal Paris offers a Makeup Genius app that turns the front-facing iPhone and iPad camera into a make-up mirror so that the customer can virtually try on hundreds of cosmetics products. The shopper can change facial expressions and lighting conditions; the virtual make-up stays on her face. The online glasses merchant Warby Parker allows consumers to upload a picture of themselves and try on frames virtually. Other apps such as Perfect365 and Facetune let you touch up your photo so that you can remove a pimple, a wrinkle, or even a few pounds before you post it on Instagram or Facebook for others to admire.[93]

Gender roles

4.4

Gender and gender roles contribute in determining the products we buy to fulfil these roles.

Gender identity is a very important component of a consumer's self-concept. People often conform to their culture's expectations about how those of their gender should act, dress, speak and so on. Of course, these guidelines change over time, and they can differ radically across societies. Some societies are highly dichotomised, with little tolerance for deviation from gender norms. In other societies this is not the case, and greater freedom in behaviour, including behaviour stemming from sexual orientation, is allowed. In certain societies, lip-service is paid to gender equality but inequalities are just under the surface; in others, there is greater sharing of power, of resources and of decision-making. To the extent that our culture is everything that we learn, then virtually all aspects of the consumption process must be affected by culture. It is not always clear to what extent gender differences are innate rather than culturally shaped – but they are certainly evident in many consumption decisions.[94]

Consider the gender differences market researchers have observed when comparing the food preferences of men and women. Women eat more fruit, men are more likely to eat meat. As one food writer put it, 'Boy food doesn't grow. It is hunted or killed'. Indeed, consumers do tend to view meat as a masculine product. In one case, a company that sells soy patties found that men viewed the food as feminine, so its solution was to add artificial grill marks on the patties to make them look like cuts of meat.[95]

Men are more likely to eat Frosted Flakes or Corn Flakes, while women prefer multigrain cereals. Men are more likely than women to consume soft drinks, while women account for the bulk of sales of bottled water. The sexes also differ sharply in the quantities of food they eat: when researchers at Hershey's discovered that women eat smaller amounts of sweets, the company created a white-chocolate confection called Hugs, one of the most successful food launches of all time. However, a man in a Burger King Whopper ad ditches his date at a fancy restaurant, complaining that he is 'too hungry to settle for chick food'. Pumped up on Whoppers, a swelling mob of men shake their fists, punch one another, toss a van off a bridge and sing, 'I will eat this meat until my innie turns into an outie', and 'I am hungry. I am incorrigible. I am man'.[96]

Gender differences in socialisation

A society's assumptions about the proper roles of men and women are communicated in terms of the ideal behaviours that are stressed for each sex (in advertising, among other places).[97] It is likely, for instance, that many women eat smaller quantities because they have been 'trained' to be more delicate and dainty. In many societies, males are controlled by **agentic goals**, which stress self-assertion and mastery. Females, on the other hand, are taught to value **communal goals**, such as affiliation and the fostering of harmonious relations.[98] For example, in an American context it has been argued that an association between 'feminine caring' as a social stereotype and 'caring for the environment' leads to men being generally less prone to engage in environmental issues and sustainable consumption in order to preserve their 'manhood'.[99]

Every society creates a set of expectations regarding the behaviours appropriate for men and women, and finds ways to communicate these expectations. This training begins very young: even children's stories about birthdays reinforce sex roles. A recent analysis showed that while stereotypical depictions have decreased over time, female characters in children's books are still far more likely to take on nurturant roles, such as baking and gift-giving. The adult who prepares the birthday celebration is almost always the mother – often no adult male is present at all. On the other hand, the male figure in these stories is often cast in the role of a miraculous provider of gifts.[100] Not surprisingly, we observe the same gender difference in social media: women are just more enthusiastic about connecting with others. Although there are more men online on the global internet, women spend about 8 per cent more time online, averaging 25 hours per month on the Web. Women around the world spend 20 per cent more time on retail sites overall than men. In a typical month, about 76 per cent of all women globally interact with a social networking site, as compared to only 70 per cent of men. And, women spend significantly more time on social networking sites than men, with women averaging 5.5 hours per month compared to 4 hours for men.[101]

Macho marketers?

Marketing historically has been defined largely by men, so it still tends to be dominated by male values. Competition rather than cooperation is stressed, and the language of warfare and domination is often used. Strategists often use distinctly masculine concepts: 'market penetration' or 'competitive thrusts', for example. Marketing articles in academic journals also emphasise agentic rather than communal goals. The most pervasive theme is power and control over others. Other themes include instrumentality (manipulating people for the good of an organisation) and competition.[102] This bias may diminish in years to come, as more marketing researchers begin to stress such factors as emotions and aesthetics in purchase decisions, and as increasing numbers of women graduate in marketing. But for the time being it seems a slow process. Marketers tend to reinforce cultural expectations regarding the 'correct' way for boys and girls, men and women, to look and act. A comprehensive review of current research literature reported five basic conclusions about gender differences:[103]

1 Males are more self-oriented, while females are more other-oriented.
2 Females are more cautious responders.
3 Females are more responsive to negative data.
4 Males process data more selectively and females more comprehensively.
5 Females are more sensitive to differentiating conditions and factors.

Gender *vs* sexual identity

Sex-role identity is a state of mind as well as body. A person's biological gender (i.e. male or female) does not totally determine whether they will exhibit **sex-typed traits**, or characteristics that are stereotypically associated with one sex or the other. A consumer's subjective feelings about their sexuality are crucial as well.[104] Indeed, Facebook in the UK now offers its users a choice of 50 options for gender identity, ranging from *agender* to *twospirit,* while the Oxford English Dictionary now includes the gender-neutral honorific 'Mx' to represent transgender people that do not want to be represented by gender.[105] At the same time, new evidence is emerging about the effects of biology on consumer behaviour. *Neuroendocrinological science* focuses on the potential role of hormonal influences on preferences for different kinds of products or people.[106] Much of this work is based on evolutionary logic that underscores how people are 'wired' from birth to seek out mates who are most likely to produce optimal offspring that will be more likely to survive in a competitive environment. However, it has been argued that such a reduction of all cultural traits to direct evolutionary advantages is (of course) a too-simple understanding

We can expect to see gender-neutral icons like this one popping up on public restrooms and other locations as the third-gender movement gains momentum.

Source: Gender Neutral Icon, https://yle.fi/uutiset/osasto/news/finnish_ngo_debuts_new_symbol_for_gender-neutral_bathrooms/9696361

of culture, but also of biology and of Darwin's thesis of evolutionary selection.[107] For example, a couple of controversial evolutionary studies found that ovulating women are more likely to prefer variety in product choice; the authors report that this variety-seeking relates to a desire to be exposed to new men during this time.[108] We predict that the discussion of biology versus culture will become even more prevalent in the years to come. We can hope it will evade the most idiotic simplifications and excesses.

Unlike 'maleness' and 'femaleness', 'masculinity' and 'femininity' are *not* biological characteristics. A behaviour that is considered masculine in one culture may not be viewed as such in another. For example, the norm in northern Europe, and in Scandinavia in particular, is that men are stoical, while cultures in southern Europe and in Latin America allow men to show their emotions. Each society determines what 'real' men and women should and should not do.

Sex-typed products

Many products also are *sex-typed:* they take on masculine or feminine attributes, and consumers often associate them with one sex or another.[109] The sex-typing of products is often created or perpetuated by marketers (e.g. princess telephones, boys' and girls' toys and babies' colour-coded nappies). Even brand names appear to be sex-typed: those containing alphanumerics (e.g. Formula 409, 10W40, Clorox 2) are assumed to be technical and hence masculine.[110] Our gender also seems to influence the instrumentality of the products we buy. Studies have shown that men tend to buy instrumental and leisure items impulsively, projecting independence and activity, while women tend to buy symbolic and self-expressive goods concerned with appearance and emotional aspects of self. Similarly, one study found masculinity to be linked to functional products whereas femininity was linked to hedonic products.[111] Other research has shown, for example, that men take a more self-oriented approach to buying clothing – stressing its use as an expressive symbol of personality and functional benefits, while women have 'other-oriented' concerns – choosing to use clothes as a symbol of their social and personal interrelatedness with others.[112]

Androgyny

The British department store Selfridges is known for unusual promotions and events (this is the store where actress Lindsay Lohan ripped off her clothes and ran through the aisles, much to the delight of the London tabloids).[113] The store went brand-free for two years, to give customers a break, and gender-free in its Agender Project, which featured unisex fashion lines and put mannequins in storage to 'show the collections in a non-gender-specific way'. One possible motivation for the experiment: the store found that more female shoppers were buying menswear for themselves and wanted to encourage men to be adventurous about crossing to the other side of the aisle as well.[114] Come on, guys, rock those skirts. . .

Masculinity and femininity are not opposite ends of the same dimension. **Androgyny** refers to the possession of both masculine and feminine traits.[115] Researchers make a distinction between *sex-typed people,* who are stereotypically masculine or feminine, and *androgynous people,* whose mixture of characteristics allows them to function well in a variety of social situations.[116]

Differences in sex-role orientation can influence responses to marketing stimuli, at least under some circumstances.[117] For example, research evidence indicates that females are more likely to undergo elaborate processing of message content, so they tend to be more sensitive to specific pieces of information when forming a judgement, while males are more influenced by overall themes.[118] In addition, women with a relatively strong masculine component in their

This Turkish ad uses a particular Japanese male stereotype, the Sumo wrestler, to allude to the strength of a glue brand.

Chris Hellier/Alamy Stock Photo

sex-role identity prefer ad portrayals that include non-traditional women.[119] Some research indicates that sex-typed people are more sensitive to the sex-role depictions of characters in advertising, although women appear to be more sensitive to gender-role relationships than men. A study demonstrated that sex-role assumptions travel into cyberspace as well. The researchers asked each volunteer to interact with another respondent via a chat room. They showed subjects an avatar to represent the other person, with images ranging from an 'obviously female' blonde, to one with no clear gender, to a strong-jawed male. The subjects rated their partners as less 'credible' when they saw an androgynous avatar than when they saw one with sex-typed facial characteristics.[120]

Sex-typed people in general are more concerned with ensuring that their behaviour is consistent with their culture's definition of gender appropriateness.

Female gender roles

Gender roles for women are changing rapidly. Social changes, such as the dramatic increase in the proportion of women in waged work, have led to an upheaval in the way women are regarded by men, the way they regard themselves and in the products they choose to buy. Modern women now play a greater role in decisions regarding traditionally male purchases. For example, more than 60 per cent of new car buyers under the age of 50 are female, and women even buy almost half of all condoms sold.[121]

Segmenting women

In the 1949 movie *Adam's Rib,* Katharine Hepburn played a stylish and competent lawyer. This was one of the first films to show that a woman can have a successful career and still be

Marketing pitfall

In an earlier era, wealthy women avoided the sun at all costs lest people get the impression that they had to work for a living outdoors. Today the situation is reversed as people equate a tanned complexion with health, physical activity and an abundance of leisure time. Indoor tanning at salons with names like Eternal Summer and Tan City are very popular among many American young people, despite evidence that links this practice to skin cancer. An analysis found that tanning beds account for as many as 400,000 cases of skin cancer in the United States each year, including 6,000 cases of melanoma, which is the deadliest form of the disease. The rate of melanoma among women under 40 has risen significantly in recent years. Public health officials report that a third of Caucasian teenage girls say they have engaged in indoor tanning. And, about half of the top-rated colleges in the US offer tanning beds either on campus or in off-campus housing.[122] Is skin cancer too high a price to pay to attain an ideal of beauty?

This does not mean, however, that we should conclude that 'the browner the better'. Global reality is actually rather the reverse. An ad on Malaysian television showed an attractive college student who can't get a second glance from a boy at the next desk. 'She's pretty', he says to himself, 'but. . . '. Then she applies Pond's Skin Lightening Moisturizer by Unilever plc, and she reappears looking several shades paler. Now the boy wonders, 'Why didn't I notice her before?'. In many Asian cultures, people also historically equate light skin with wealth and status, and they associate dark skin with the labouring class that toils in the fields. This stereotype persists today: in a survey, 74 per cent of men in Malaysia, 68 per cent in Hong Kong and 55 per cent in Taiwan said they were more attracted to women with fair complexions. About a third of the female respondents in each country said they used skin-whitening products. Olay has a product it calls 'White Radiance', and L'Oréal sells a 'White Perfect' line.[123]

happily married. Today, the evolution of a new managerial class of women has forced marketers to change their traditional assumptions about women as they target this growing market. For example, Suzuki is going out of its way to appeal to the growing number of women in India who are achieving financial independence and buying their own cars. Its Zen Estilo (*Estilo* means 'style' in Spanish) model comes in eight colours, including 'purple fusion', 'virgin blue' and 'sparkling olive'.[124] Ironically, it seems that in some cases marketers have overcompensated for their former emphasis on women as housewives. Many attempts to target the vast market of females employed outside the home tend to depict all these women in glamorous, executive positions. This portrayal ignores the fact that the majority of women do not hold such jobs, and that many work because they have to, rather than for self-fulfillment. This diversity means that not all women should be expected to respond to marketing campaigns that stress professional achievement or the glamour of working life.

Although women continue to be depicted in traditional roles, this situation is changing as advertisers scramble to catch up with reality. For example, the highly successful Dove Real Beauty campaign has significantly changed women's perceptions of what is 'beautiful', particularly with respect to the notion of beauty and natural ageing. The campaign shows women in various roles, and at varying ages, and the notion of 'beauty' is central to the discussions.[125] Women are now as likely as men to be central characters in television commercials. But, as one study indicated, while women increasingly embrace a view on menstruation as 'natural', they also incorporate the dominant marketing discourse that it is something to 'protect yourself against'.[126] Gender roles, as much as we discuss and challenge them (or maybe exactly because we do that) remain full of paradoxes.

Some ads now feature *role reversal,* where women occupy traditional men's roles. In other cases, women are portrayed in romantic situations, but they tend to be more sexually dominant. Ironically, current advertising is more free to emphasise traditional female traits now that sexual equality is becoming more of an accepted fact. This freedom is demonstrated in a

Marketing opportunity
#MeToo Marketing?

A 'Me-too' campaign used to be a pejorative expression, referring to campaigns that were just emulating successful competitors without any originality. Maybe no longer so. In the future, we may look back on 2017 and say 'this was the year'. This was the year when numerous organisations, private as well as public, started to 'walk the talk'. For years most people have agreed that discrimination against and power-based exploitation of women is not acceptable. Yet, as the #MeToo campaign has demonstrated, there may have been more 'talk' than 'walk' about this issue in far too many contexts. Following the ubiquitous public debates about gender and power relations, the world of advertising is changing as well. In the sometimes not-so-ethically correct world of marketing, even the smarmiest players in the corporate world seem to be changing.[127]

Much of this chapter deals with the many ways in which everyone, but in particular women, can feel bad about themselves (and the remedies that marketers propose to help alleviate the problem). But the times they are (maybe) a-changing. The 2018 Nike campaign, featuring tennis star Serena Williams, underlines that 'there's no wrong way to be a woman'.[128]

German poster for a women's magazine. The caption reads, 'Today's women can sometimes show weakness, because they are strong'.

Male sex roles

While the traditional concept of the ideal male as a tough, aggressive, muscular man who enjoys 'manly' sports and activities is not dead, society's definition of the male role is evolving. As with female roles, this evolution is a slow process. When global entrepreneur and CEO of Virgin Airlines Richard Branson lost a racing bet to the owner of AirAsia, his 'sentence' was to dress as a female flight attendant for the winner's airline. The winner gloated, '. . . I'm looking forward to him sucking up to me as a stewardess!'.[129] Starting in the late 1990s, men were allowed to be more compassionate and to have close friendships with other men. In contrast to the depiction of macho men who do not show feelings, some marketers were promoting men's 'sensitive' side. An emphasis on male bonding was the centre-piece of many ad campaigns, especially for beers.[130] Just as for women, however, the true story is more complicated than that. Indeed, scholars of **masculinism** study the male image and the complex cultural meanings of masculinity.[131] Like women, men receive mixed messages about how they are supposed to behave and feel. One of the biggest marketing buzzwords in the first decade of the 21st century was the **metrosexual** – a straight, urban male who is keenly interested in fashion, home design, gourmet cooking and personal care. Next came the *hipster,* also an urban male but this time defined more by an opposition to being stylish (which of course becomes a style in itself) and sporting a beard (since metrosexuals and men in general did not in the early 2000s). Is hipster even a thing to talk about in 2018?[132] And what's next?

Some analysts argue that men are threatened because they do not necessarily recognise themselves in the powerful male stereotypes against which feminists protest.[133] One study examined how American men pursue masculine identities through their everyday consumption. The researchers suggest that men are trying to make sense out of three different models of masculinity that they call *breadwinner, rebel* and *man-of-action hero,* as they figure out just who they are supposed to be. On the one hand, the breadwinner model draws from the American myth of success and celebrates respectability, civic virtues, pursuit of material success and organised achievement. The rebel model, on the other hand, emphasises rebellion, independence, adventure and potency. The man-of-action hero is a synthesis that draws from the better of the other two models.[134] In a different cultural context, namely

Sweden, consumer researchers have also studied how men negotiate and 'feminise' their masculinity through engagement in home cooking and establishing more equal gender roles in terms of household responsibilities.[135]

One consequence of the continual evolution of sex roles is that men are concerned as never before with their appearance. Men spend $7.7 billion on grooming products globally each year. A wave of male cleansers, moisturisers, sunscreens, depilatories and body sprays is washing up on US shores, largely from European marketers. L'Oréal Paris reports that men's skincare products are now its fastest-growing sector. In Europe, 24 per cent of men younger than the age of 30 use skincare products – and 80 per cent of young Korean men do. Men are a bit more store-loyal than women when shopping for beauty cosmetics (for bricks-and-mortar stores), and a bit more likely to make use of the internet once they have found a brand that works for them.[136]

Beefcake: the depiction of men in advertising

Men as well as women are often depicted in a negative fashion in advertising. They frequently come across as helpless or bumbling.

Just as advertisers are criticised for depicting women as sex objects, so the same accusations can be made about how males are portrayed – a practice correspondingly known as 'beefcake'.[137]

Lesbian, gay, bisexual and transgender (LGBT) consumers

Gay and lesbian consumers are being more actively targeted by marketers, and companies are acknowledging this societal shift towards more and more acceptance.[138] With over a dozen European countries recognising same-sex marriage, it's not surprising to see more and more marketing communications that routinely include gay couples. A recent Banana Republic campaign features pairs of models who also are couples in real life. One of these is two men, both interior designers. The chief creative officer of the agency that created the campaign observed that the goal is 'to reflect our world and how we live in a true, genuine way'.[139] Even the Oreo cookie brand took a public stand when, in support of Gay Pride Month, the company posted a photo on its Facebook page of an Oreo with six different colours of cream – one for each colour of the rainbow – a symbol gay rights supporters use to show diversity. The Facebook post drew many thousands of comments. Some called for a product boycott, but most like this one were more supportive: 'I didn't think it was possible for me to love Oreos more than I already did!'[140]

The percentage of the population that is gay and lesbian is difficult to determine, and efforts to measure this group have been controversial.[141] However, the respected research company Yankelovich Partners Inc., which has tracked consumer values and attitudes since 1971 in its annual Monitor survey, now includes a question about sexual identity in its survey. This study was virtually the first to use a sample that reflects the population as a whole, instead of polling only smaller or biased groups (such as readers of gay publications), whose responses may not be representative of all consumers. About 6 per cent of respondents identified themselves as gay/homosexual/lesbian. As of 2018, there has been tremendous growth in marketing and public relations firms that specialise in consulting with and for companies of all sizes regarding the LGBT market, globally.

As civil rights gains are made by gay activists, the social climate is becoming more favourable for firms targeting this market segment.[142] In one of the first academic studies in this field, the conclusion was that gays and lesbians did not qualify as a market segment because they did not satisfy the traditional criteria of being identifiable, accessible and of

**The significance of and
support for the LGBTQ market
is growing.**

Nano Calvo/Alamy Stock Photo

sufficient size.[143] Subsequent studies have argued that the segmentation criteria rely on
outdated assumptions regarding the nature of consumers, marketing activities and the ways in
which media are used in the contemporary marketplace. Here, the argument is that
identifiability is an unreliable construct for socially subordinated groups, and really is not the
issue anyway. How marketers segment (by race, ethnicity, gender or, in this case, sexuality) is
not as important as whether the group itself expresses consumption patterns in identifiable
ways. Similarly, the accessibility criterion continues with the assumption of active marketers
who contact passive consumers. This criterion also needs to take into account the dramatic
changes in media over the past two decades, in particular the use of speciality media by
marketers to access special-interest segments. As many as 65 per cent of gay and lesbian
internet users go online more than once a day and over 70 per cent make purchases online.[144]
Finally, sufficient size assumes separate campaigns are necessary to reach each segment – an
assumption that ignores consumers' ability and willingness to explore multiple media.[145] More
importantly, the LGBT community is becoming better organised, particularly in terms of having
its 'consumer voice' heard. Global companies are all now aware of and working for high ratings
from the LGBT segment.[146]

Body image

4.5

Body image is a key factor for our self-image in contemporary consumer culture.

For many women, trying on jeans is a painful exercise. Levi Strauss recently launched an online fitting service called the Curve ID system to make the process a little more comfortable. The digital offering is available in 20 languages and 50 countries; it is based on 60,000 women's figures worldwide and its goal is to provide a more customised experience to ease the frustration many women feel as they search for the perfect pair of jeans.[147] A person's physical appearance is a large part of their self-concept. **Body image** refers to a consumer's subjective evaluation of their physical self. As was the case with the overall self-concept, this image is not necessarily accurate. A man may think of himself as being more muscular than he really is, or a woman may think she is fatter than is the case. In fact, it is not uncommon to find marketing strategies that exploit consumers' tendencies to distort their body images by preying upon insecurities about appearance, thereby creating a gap between the real and the ideal physical self and, consequently, the desire to purchase products and services to narrow that gap. Whether these perceptions are accurate is almost a moot point, because our body insecurities weigh us down whether they're justified or not. A Dove campaign in China asks, 'If I only have an A-cup breast, will you still love me?'. This advertising preys on insecurities in that country about meeting the proper man and getting married. Many Chinese women worry about being labelled a 'leftover woman' or a 'spinster' – terms for women who reach the age of 26 and are still single.[148]

Body cathexis

A person's feelings about their body can be described in terms of **body cathexis**. Cathexis refers to the emotional significance of some object or idea to a person, and some parts of the body are more central to self-concept than others. One study of young adults' feelings about their bodies found that these respondents were most satisfied with their hair and eyes and had least positive feelings about their waists. These feelings were related to consumption of grooming products. Consumers who were more satisfied with their bodies were more frequent users of such 'preening' products as hair conditioner, hairdryers, aftershave, artificial tanning products, toothpaste and pumice soap.[149] In a large-scale study of older women in six European countries, the results showed that women would like to 'grow old beautifully', and that they were prepared to follow diets, exercise and use cosmetics to reach this goal. Wrinkles were the biggest concern, and Greek and Italian women were by far the most concerned about how to combat ageing, with northern European women expressing more agreement with the statement that ageing was natural and inevitable.[150]

Ideals of beauty

A person's satisfaction with the physical image they present to others is affected by how closely that image corresponds to the image valued by their culture. In fact, infants as young as two months show a preference for attractive faces.[151] An ideal of beauty is a particular model, or exemplar, of appearance. Ideals of beauty for both men and women may include physical features (big breasts or small, bulging muscles – or not), as well as clothing styles, cosmetics, hairstyles, skin tone (pale *vs* tan) and body type (petite, athletic, voluptuous, etc.).

Is beauty universal?

It's no secret that despite the popular saying 'You can't judge a book by its cover', people can and do. Fairly or not, we assume that more attractive people are smarter, more interesting and more competent – researchers have long since called this the '*what is beautiful is good*' stereotype.[152] Indeed, recent research evidence indicates there is a lot of truth (or rather self-fulfilling prophesy) to this assumption – beautiful people are generally happier than average- or below-average-looking people and economists calculate that about half of that boost stems from the fact that they make more money![153] By the way, this bias affects both men and women – men with above-average looks earn about 5 per cent more than those of average appearance, and those who are below-average in appearance make an average of 9 per cent less than the norm.

Research indicates that preferences for some physical features over others are 'wired in' genetically, and that these reactions tend to be the same among people around the world. Specifically, people appear to favour features associated with good health and youth, attributes linked to reproductive ability and strength, and symmetrical faces. But as anthropologists have demonstrated, there are widely differing culturally instituted norms about what counts as 'beautiful'. One Western female anthropologist was pitied by her female informants in Niger because she was so skinny (although the Niger women did not seem to feel the same kind of shame as Western women if they did not live up to their plump ideal).[154] Indeed, it has been estimated that about 80 per cent of known societies have idealised plumper women.[155] However, the current globalisation of a particular Western ideal represents a challenge for such alternative ways of thinking. Looking at the global phenomenon of beauty contests, one anthropologist has introduced the notion of *Global Structures of Common Difference* to indicate that while technically, for example, the Miss World competition is a celebration of different beauties from all over the world, it is actually a particular type of beauty that is celebrated. Power is not distributed equally![156] Nigeria is a neighbouring country to Niger and thus another place with a preference for plumper women. After having performed poorly for years, Nigeria sent a tall, slim (and locally not-so-adored) contestant to the 2001 Miss World finals. . . and she won. Such events are, of course, contributing to changes in beauty ideals in West Africa.[157]

As suggested by this Emporio Armani ad, luxury brands may be promoting uniform(ising) global standards of beauty.
Photo by Vittorio Zunino Celotto/Getty Images

Schoolgirls learn about the (ir)reality of the Barbie-based body ideal.
Tracey Nearmy/EPA/Shutterstock

Consequently, advertising and other forms of mass media play a highly significant role in determining which forms of beauty are considered desirable at any point in time. An ideal of beauty functions as a sort of cultural yardstick. Consumers compare themselves to some standard (often advocated by the fashion media) and are dissatisfied with their appearance to the extent that it does not match up to it. These mass-media portrayals have been criticised not only on social grounds, but on issues of health as well. In a study of New Zealand print advertisements over the period 1958–88, the findings confirmed that advertising models became thinner and less curvaceous over the 30-year period, resulting in contemporary models being approximately 8.5kg lighter than they would be if they had the same body shape as models of the late 1950s. To achieve the currently fashionable body shape, a young woman of average height would have to weigh approximately 42kg, which is far below the recommended level for good health.[158] Clearly, what constitutes 'beauty' for women involves a number of complex relationships – a study in the Netherlands found that Dutch women consider friendliness, self-confidence, happiness and humour to be the most important pillars of female beauty, while only 2 per cent found 'pretty' to be a description of female beauty. A majority of the over 3,200 women in the study felt that the media's depiction of the 'ideal' female beauty was unrealistic. Most of the women in the study complained slightly of their weight and the shape of their body.[159]

Ideals of beauty over time

While beauty may be only skin deep, throughout history and across cultures women, in particular, have worked very hard to attain it. They have starved themselves, painfully bound their feet, inserted plates into their lips, spent countless hours under hairdryers, in front of mirrors and beneath ultraviolet lights, and have undergone breast reduction or enlargement operations to alter their appearance and meet their society's expectations of what a beautiful woman should look like.

Periods of history tend to be characterised by a specific 'look' or ideal of beauty. American history can be described in terms of a succession of dominant ideals. For example, in sharp contrast to today's emphasis on health and vigour, in the early 1800s it was fashionable to appear delicate to the point of looking ill. The poet John Keats described the ideal woman of that time as 'a milk white lamb that bleats for man's protection'. Other looks have included the voluptuous, lusty woman (as epitomised by Lillian Russell in the late 19th century), the athletic Gibson Girl of the 1890s, the small, boyish flapper of the 1920s (as exemplified by Clara Bow), the voluptuous Marilyn Monroe in the 1950s, the skinny supermodels of the millennium and the current tendency towards 'strong' and 'fit' models.[160] The actress Marilyn Monroe died in

1962, but she represents a cultural ideal of beauty that persists to this day. The global cosmetic company M.A.C. introduced a line of cosmetics named after her and Macy's launched a Marilyn clothing line.[161] However, if the icon lives, the body ideal may not – Marilyn would probably be judged too chubby to represent an ideal model anno 2018.

Throughout much of the nineteenth century, the desirable waistline for American women was 18 inches – a circumference that required the use of corsets pulled so tight that they routinely caused headaches, fainting fits and possibly even the uterine and spinal disorders common among women of the time. While modern women are not quite as 'strait-laced', many still endure such indignities as high heels, body waxing, eye-lifts and liposuction. These practices, in addition to the millions spent on cosmetics, clothing, health clubs and fashion magazines, remind us that – rightly or wrongly – the desire to conform to current standards of beauty is alive and well.

Is the ideal getting real?

Fed up because you don't get mistaken for a svelte supermodel on the street? Dove's well-known Campaign for Real Beauty featuring women with imperfect bodies in their underwear may help. One ad reads, 'Let's face it, firming the thighs of a size 8 supermodel wouldn't have been much of a challenge'. Unilever initiated the campaign after its research showed that many women didn't believe its products worked because the women shown using them were so unrealistic.[162] When the company asked 3,200 women around the world to describe their own looks, most summed themselves up as 'average' or 'natural'. Only 2 per cent called themselves 'beautiful'.

Marketers of the Dove brand sensed an opportunity, and they set out to reassure women about their insecurities by showing them as they are – wrinkles, freckles, pregnant bellies and all. Taglines ask 'Oversized or Outstanding?' and 'Wrinkled or Wonderful?'. The brand also continues to publish regular reports on female well-being (or lack thereof), insecurity induced

☐ fat?
☐ fit?

Does true beauty only squeeze into size 8?

campaignforrealbeauty.co.uk 🕊 | Dove

The Dove campaign emphasises that our ideals about beauty, and what is beautiful, vary over time, place and age.

Unilever

by self-doubt and depreciation of one's own body and so on. In 2016, the third of such reports concluded that 'additionally, 7 in 10 girls with low body-esteem say they won't be assertive in their opinion or stick to their decision if they aren't happy with the way they look, while 9 out of 10 (87 per cent) of women will stop themselves from eating or will otherwise put their health at risk'.[163]

However, Unilever's experience with Chinese women reminds us, again, that appearance norms are strongly rooted in culture. Dove's Campaign for Real Beauty flopped in China when Unilever's research showed that many Chinese women *do* believe they can attain the kind of air-brushed beauty they see in advertising. As a result, the company scrapped the campaign there and instead launched a Chinese version of *Ugly Betty* – a successful American sitcom, which was in turn adapted from a Colombian telenovela. The show, *Ugly Wudi,* focuses on fictional ad agency employee Lin Wudi, who strives to unveil her own beauty – aided by the numerous Dove products that appear in the show. As you might expect, it helps that the actress who played Wudi has perfect skin and actually is quite attractive once you strip away the oversized glasses and the fake braces.[164]

We can also distinguish among ideals of beauty for men in terms of facial features, musculature and facial hair – who could confuse Johnny Depp with Mr Bean? In fact, one national survey that asked both men and women to comment on male aspects of appearance found that the dominant standard of beauty for men is a strongly masculine, muscled body – though women tend to prefer men with less muscle mass than men themselves strive to attain.[165] Advertisers appear to have the males' ideal in mind – a study of men appearing in advertisements found that most ads sport the strong and muscular physique of the male stereotype.[166]

Working on the body

Because many consumers are motivated to match up to an ideal appearance, they often go to great lengths to change aspects of their physical selves. From cosmetics to plastic surgery, tanning salons to diet drinks, a multitude of products and services are directed towards altering or maintaining aspects of the physical self in order to present a desirable appearance. It is difficult to overstate the importance of the physical self-concept (and the desire by consumers to improve their appearance) to many marketing activities.

Sizeism

As reflected in the expression 'you can never be too thin or too rich', many Western societies have an obsession with weight. Even primary school children perceive obesity as worse than being disabled.[167] The pressure to be slim is continually reinforced, both by advertising and by peers. Americans, in particular, are preoccupied by what they weigh. They are continually bombarded by images of thin, happy people. However, larger consumers are fighting back against these stereotypes. As it has been proclaimed more and more often, 'big is beautiful'[168] A recent study focused on **fatshionistas** – plus-sized consumers who want more options from mainstream fashion marketers. A blog post that the study's researchers found sums up the alienation many of these women feel:

> For many of us who were fat as children and teens, clothes shopping was nothing short of tortuous. Even if our parents were supportive, the selection of 'husky' or 'half-sizes' for kids was the absolute pits. When that sort of experience is reinforced as a child, we often take it into adulthood. . . We simply have been socialized not to expect better than to be treated as fashion afterthoughts.

Researchers have investigated the triggers that mobilise women to try to change the market in order to make it friendlier to shoppers who don't conform to a pencil-thin ideal of beauty. They found that, indeed, these consumers can agitate for change, especially when they create a common community of like-minded people (the 'Fat Acceptance Movement') who can rally behind others who have successfully challenged the status quo. So, there is upheaval and resistance in the fashion market, since consumers now can form communities with other like-minded and like-bodied consumers through social media.[169]

How realistic are appearance standards? In Europe, the public discourse on appearance and body weight is becoming more active and visible, particularly with respect to the weight of European children. One study reports that one in three children in the EU aged 6–9 is overweight.[170] The EU has launched a 'platform' on diet, physical activity and health as a public policy approach to the issue of weight. Obesity is especially acute in Mediterranean countries, underscoring concerns that people in the southern region are turning away from the traditional diet of fish, fruits and vegetables to fast food, high in fat and refined carbohydrates.[171] Still, many consumers focus on attaining an unrealistic ideal weight, sometimes by relying on height and weight charts that show what one should weigh. These expectations are communicated in subtle ways. Even fashion dolls, such as the ubiquitous Barbie, reinforce the ideal of thinness. The dimensions of these dolls, when extrapolated to average female body sizes, are unnaturally long and thin.[172] In spite of Americans' obsession about weight, as a country the US continues to have a greater percentage of obesity in the general population relative to all European countries, as shown in Figure 4.1. Within Europe, female and male consumers from Hungary, the UK, Finland and Germany lead the EU in measures of obesity.[173]

Body image distortions

While many people perceive a strong link between self-esteem and appearance, some consumers unfortunately exaggerate this connection even more, and make great sacrifices to attain what they consider to be a desirable body image. Women tend to be taught to a greater degree than men that the quality of their bodies reflects their self-worth, so it is not surprising that most major distortions of body image occur among females.

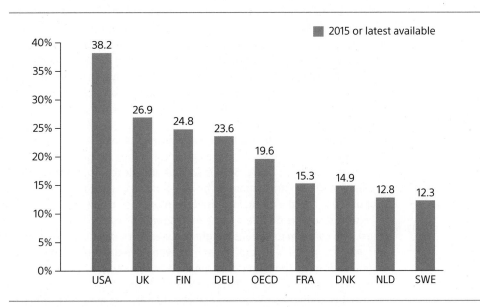

Figure 4.1 Obese population comparison

Source: OECD (2017), OECD Health Statistics 2017, www.oecd.org/health/health-data.htm

There are 3 billion women who don't look like supermodels and only 8 who do.

THE BODY SHOP
KNOW YOUR MIND LOVE YOUR BODY

The Body Shop taps into the growing sentiment against unrealistic ideals of beauty.

Reproduced with the kind permission of The Body Shop.

Men do not tend to differ in ratings of their current figure, their ideal figure and the figure they think is most attractive to women. In contrast, women rate both the figure they think is most attractive to men and their ideal figure as much thinner than their actual figure.[174] In one survey, two-thirds of college women admitted resorting to unhealthy behaviour to control weight. Advertising messages that convey an image of slimness help to reinforce these activities by arousing insecurities about weight.[175]

A distorted body image has been linked to the rise in eating disorders, which are particularly prevalent among young women. People with anorexia regard themselves as fat, and starve themselves in the quest for thinness. This condition may be accompanied by bulimia, which involves two stages. First, binge-eating (usually in private), where more than 5,000 calories may be consumed at one time. The binge is then followed by induced vomiting, abuse of laxatives, fasting and/or overly strenuous exercise – a 'purging' process that reasserts the woman's sense of control.

Most eating disorders are found among white teenage girls and students. Victims often have brothers or fathers who are hypercritical of their weight. In addition, binge eating may be encouraged by one's peers. Groups such as athletic teams and social clubs at school may develop positive norms regarding binge eating. In one study of a female social club, members' popularity within the group increased the more they binged.[176]

Eating disorders do affect some men as well. They are common among male athletes who must also conform to various weight requirements, such as jockeys, boxers and male models.[177] In general, though, most men who have distorted body images consider themselves to be too light rather than too heavy: society has taught them that they must be muscular to be masculine. Men are more likely than women to express their insecurities about their bodies by becoming addicted to exercise. In fact, striking similarities have been found between male compulsive runners and female anorexics. These include a commitment to diet and exercise as a central part of one's identity and a susceptibility to body image distortions.[178]

Cosmetic surgery

The website for the International Society of Aesthetic Plastic Surgery (http://www.isaps.org) lists hundreds of clinics available for plastic surgery,[179] and several other websites point out to Western Europeans that the options for highly skilled, safe and very affordable cosmetic surgery can be found in Eastern European countries such as Poland and the Czech Republic. There is no longer much (if any) psychological stigma associated with having this type of operation: it is commonplace and accepted among many segments of consumers.[180]

Many women turn to surgery either to reduce weight or to increase sexual desirability. Liposuction, where fat is removed with a vacuum-like device, has become the most widespread cosmetic surgery since its introduction in the 1970s.[181] Some women believe that larger breasts will increase their allure and undergo breast augmentation procedures. Although some of these procedures have generated controversy due to possible negative side effects, it is unclear whether potential medical problems will deter large numbers of women from choosing surgical options to enhance their (perceived) femininity. The importance of breast size to self-concept resulted in an interesting and successful marketing strategy undertaken by an underwear company. While conducting focus groups on bras, an analyst noted that small-chested women typically reacted with hostility when discussing the subject. They would unconsciously cover their chests with their arms as they spoke and felt that their needs were ignored by the fashion industry. To meet this overlooked need, the company introduced a line of A-cup bras called 'A-OK' and depicted wearers in a positive light. A new market segment was born. Other companies are going in the opposite direction by promoting bras that create the illusion of a larger cleavage. In Europe and the US, both Gossard and Playtex are aggressively marketing specially designed bras offering 'cleavage enhancement', which use a combination of wires and internal pads to create the desired effect. Recently, the market for women's bras has had to contend with at least one natural development: unaugmented breasts (no surgery) are getting bigger by themselves, as a result of using the pill and changes in diet. The average cup size in Britain has grown from 34B to 36C over the past 30 years. While female consumers dominate the cosmetic surgery market, one should not conclude that it is an exclusively female consumption domain. In fact, men now account for 13 per cent of cosmetic surgery patients.[182]

Marketing pitfall
Cosmetic surgery gone amok?

Cosmetic surgery has gone from being for the very few – typically, famous movie stars keen to preserve their youthful appearance a bit longer – to becoming a mass consumption phenomenon.[183] Some countries such as Lebanon have become international hubs for plastic surgery, drawing visitors for a 'holiday under the knife'.[184] In South Korea, it is not unusual to get a plastic surgery operation as a graduation gift.[185] However, slowly this 'tyranny of beauty' is mobilising an increasing number of protesters – according to a local source, the protests represent a logical local consequence of the global #MeToo campaign, drawing increased attention to 'cultural violence against women'.[186] Another problematic aspect of the unholy alliance between the ideal of beauty and cosmetic surgery is the emergent phenomenon of *Snapchat Dysmorphia*.[187] Snapchat filters that are smoothing our skin, giving us fuller lips and bigger eyes are increasingly used as templates for cosmetic surgery. Our self-image is suffering from not being able to live up to the beautified versions of it on the pictures on social media. Consequently, we try to live up to the ideal image of ourselves, that we have ourselves created – a chase for perfection that ultimately only harms our self-esteem, and our wallets. Snapchat Dysmorphia de facto makes us hyperreal versions of ourselves (see Chapter 3).

Body decoration and mutilation

The body is adorned or altered in some way in every culture. Decorating the self serves a number of purposes.[188]

- *To separate group members from non-members.* The Chinook Indians of North America used to press the head of a newborn baby between two boards for a year, permanently altering its shape. In Western societies, teenagers go out of their way to adopt distinctive hair and clothing styles that will distinguish them from adults.

- *To place the individual in the social organisation.* Many cultures engage in rites of passage at puberty, when a boy symbolically becomes a man. Young men in Ghana paint their bodies with white stripes to resemble skeletons to symbolise the death of their child status. In Western culture, this rite may involve some form of mild self-mutilation or engaging in dangerous activities.

- *To place the person in a gender category.* The Tchikrin Indians of South America insert a string of beads in a boy's lip to enlarge it. Western women wear lipstick to enhance femininity. At the turn of the century, small lips were fashionable because they represented women's submissive role at that time.[189] Today big, red lips are provocative and indicate an aggressive sexuality. Some women, including a number of famous actresses and models, have collagen injections or lip inserts to create large, pouting lips (known in the modelling industry as 'liver lips').[190]

- *To enhance sex-role identification.* Wearing high heels, which podiatrists agree are a prime cause of knee and hip problems, backaches and fatigue, can be compared with the traditional Oriental practice of foot-binding to enhance femininity.

- *To indicate desired social conduct.* The Suya of South America wear ear ornaments to emphasise the importance placed in their culture on listening and obedience. In Western societies gay men may wear an earring to signal how they expect to be identified.

- *To indicate high status or rank.* The Hidates Indians of North America wear feather ornaments that indicate how many people they have killed. In our society, some people wear glasses with clear lenses, even though they do not have eye problems, to increase their perceived intellectual or fashion status.

- *To provide a sense of security.* Consumers often wear lucky charms, amulets, rabbits' feet and so on to protect them from the 'evil eye'. Some modern women wear a 'mugger whistle' around their necks for a similar reason.

One study focused on the phenomenon of Tough Mudders, one of the fastest growing athletic events. Participants must endure a 10–12 mile run where they undergo tests of their physical and mental capacities. The challenges and pains include fundamental human fears such as electricity, being submerged in water, heights, etc. Tough Mudder consumers reported the significance for their self-images in completing the self-inflicted pains, but in addition pointed to the scars, marks and wounds left by the race as memories helping to create 'the story of a fulfilled life'.[191]

Tattoos

Tattoos – both temporary and permanent – are a popular form of body adornment.[192] This body art can be used to communicate aspects of the self to onlookers and may serve some of the same functions that other kinds of body painting do in primitive cultures. In fact, much of the recent literature and discourse on tattoos centres on the theme of users as 'Modern Primitives'.[193] Tattoos (from the Tahitian *ta-tu*) have deep roots in folk art. Until recently, the

Body decoration can be permanent, or temporary, in order to distinguish oneself, shock others, signify group membership, or express a particular mood or message.

Jamie Garbutt/Taxi/Getty Images

images were crude and were primarily either death symbols (e.g. a skull), animals (especially panthers, eagles and snakes), pin-up women or military designs. More current influences include science fiction themes, Japanese symbolism and tribal designs.

A tattoo may be viewed as a fairly risk-free (?) way of expressing an adventurous side of the self. Tattoos have a long history of association with people who are social outcasts. For example, the faces and arms of criminals in sixth-century Japan were tattooed as a way of identifying them, as were Massachusetts prison inmates in the nineteenth century. These emblems are often used by marginal groups, such as bikers or Japanese *yakuze* (gang members), to express group identity and solidarity. In Europe today, the growth of tattoos on individuals of all ages and social classes can be seen both as a form of communication, and a growth in commodification. European consumers are more and more often using their own skin as part of their expression of consumer culture.[194]

Body piercing

Decorating the body with various kinds of metallic inserts has evolved from a practice associated with some fringe groups to become a popular fashion statement. Piercings can range from a hoop protruding from a navel to scalp implants, where metal posts are inserted in the skull (do not try this at home!). Publications such as *Piercing Fans International Quarterly* are seeing their circulations soar, and websites featuring piercings and piercing products are attracting numerous followers. This popularity is not pleasing to hard-core piercing fans, who view the practice as a sensual, consciousness-raising ritual and are concerned that now people just do it because it is 'trendy'. As one customer waiting for a piercing remarked, 'If your piercing doesn't mean anything, then it's just like buying a pair of platform shoes'.[195]

Chapter summary

Now that you have finished reading this chapter you should understand why:

4.1 **The self-concept is a complex and composite one.** Rather than a simple understanding of one's self as a fairly homogenous concept in the style of 'I am who I am', it is more fruitful to think of the self as something that is highly composite. The symbolic interactionist perspective of the self implies that each of us actually has many selves, depending on the specific roles and interactions we engage in. Furthermore, we have both actual and ideal selves that are influencing our behaviour. Finally, since our self-image is deeply dependent on how others see us, we engage in impression management.

4.2 **Products and other types of consumption often play a key role in defining the self-concept.** Consumers' self-concepts are reflections of their attitudes towards themselves. Whether these attitudes are positive or negative, they will help to guide many purchase decisions; we can use products to bolster self-esteem or to 'reward' the self. Products therefore often play a pivotal role in defining the self-concept. We choose many products because we think that they are similar to our personalities. However, we also play different roles, and we require a different set of products as props to play each role. We view many things other than the body as part of who we are. People use valued objects, cars, homes and even attachments to sports teams or national monuments to define the self, when they incorporate these into the extended self.

4.3 **The digital self is becoming increasingly important for our self-image.** Our self-image is largely a reflection of how others see us, the various forms in which we represent ourselves on social media platforms play an increasingly pivotal role in our self-construction. It can even go so far that we try to reshape our physical selves to better resemble the image we present online.

4.4 **Gender and gender roles contribute in determining the products we buy to fulfil these roles.** Society's expectations of masculinity and femininity help to determine the products we buy to be consistent with these expectations. A person's sex-role identity is a major component of self-definition. Conceptions about masculinity and femininity, largely shaped by society, guide the acquisition of 'sex-typed' products and service. Advertising and other media play an important role because they socialise consumers to be male and female. Although traditional women's roles have often been perpetuated in advertising depictions, this situation is changing somewhat. The media do not always portray men accurately either.

4.5 **Body image is a key factor for our self-image in contemporary consumer culture.** The way we think about our bodies (and the way our culture tells us we should think) is a key component of self-esteem. A person's conception of his or her body also provides feedback to their self-image. A culture communicates specific ideals of beauty, and consumers go to great lengths to attain these. Our desire to live up to cultural expectations of appearance can be harmful. Sometimes these activities are carried to an extreme, as people try too hard to live up to cultural ideals. One common manifestation is eating disorders – diseases in which women, in particular, become obsessed with thinness.

4.6 **Culture dictates certain types of beauty, including body decoration or mutilation.** Every culture dictates certain types of body decoration or mutilation. Body decoration or mutilation may serve such functions as separating group members from non-members, marking the individual's status or rank within a social organisation or within a gender category (e.g. homosexual), or even providing a sense of security or good luck. Many consumer activities involve manipulating the body, whether through dieting, cosmetic surgery, piercing or tattooing.

Key terms

Actual self (p. 120)
Agentic goals (p. 132)
Androgyny (p. 134)
Body cathexis (p. 140)
Body image (p. 140)
Communal goals (p. 132)
Digital self (p. 129)
Embodied cognition (p. 129)
Enclothed cognition (p. 129)
Extended self (p. 128)
Fatshionistas (p. 144)
Ideal self (p. 120)
Impression management (p. 121)

Looking-glass self (p. 122)
Masculinism (p. 137)
Metrosexual (p. 137)
Power posing (p. 129)
Self-concept (p. 119)
Self-image congruence models (p. 127)
Sex-typed traits (p. 133)
Symbolic interactionism (p. 122)
Symbolic self-completion theory (p. 125)
Torn self (p. 122)
Virtual makeovers (p. 121)
Wearable computing (p. 130)

Consumer behaviour challenge

1 How might the creation of a self-conscious state be related to consumers who are trying on clothing in changing rooms? Does the act of preening in front of a mirror change the dynamics by which people evaluate their product choices? Why?

2 Is it ethical for marketers to encourage infatuation with the self?

3 List three dimensions by which the self-concept can be described.

4 Compare and contrast the real *vs* the ideal self. List three products for which each type of self is likely to be used as a reference point when a purchase is considered.

5 Watch a series of ads featuring men and women on television. Try to imagine the characters with reversed roles (the male parts played by women, and vice versa). Can you see any differences in assumptions about sex-typed behaviour?

6 To date, the bulk of advertising targeted at gay consumers has been placed in exclusively gay media. If it was your decision, would you consider using mainstream media to reach the gay market, who constitute a significant proportion of the general population? Or, bearing in mind that members of some targeted segments have serious objections to this practice, especially when the product (e.g. alcohol, cigarettes) may be viewed as harmful in some way, do you think gays should be singled out at all by marketers?

7 Do you agree that marketing strategies tend to have a male-oriented bias? If so, what are some possible consequences for specific marketing activities?

8 Construct a 'consumption biography' of a friend or family member. Make a list of and/or photograph their favourite possessions, and see if you or others can describe this person's personality just from the information provided by this catalogue.

9 Some consumer advocates have protested at the use of super-thin models in advertising, claiming that these women encourage others to starve themselves in order to attain the 'waif' look. Other critics respond that the media's power to shape behaviour has been overestimated, and that it is insulting to people to assume that they are unable to separate fantasy from reality. What do you think?

For additional material see the companion website at **www.pearsoned.co.uk/solomon**

Notes

1. https://yougov.co.uk/news/2015/07/21/over-third-brits-unhappy-their-bodies-celebrity-cu/ (accessed 28 August 2018).

2. Daniel Goleman, 'When ugliness is only in patient's eye, body image can reflect mental disorder', *New York Times* (2 October 1991): C13. See also: Duncan Robertson, 'Too shy to strip in front of a man' (28 March 2007), www.dailymail.co.uk/news/article-445068/Too-shy-strip-man.html (accessed 28 August 2018).

3. Duncan Robertson, 'Too shy to strip in front of a man', *Daily Mail* (28 March 2007), based on a survey of 3,500 women for SHUC, a bathroom equipment company, www.dailymail.co.uk/news/article-445068/Too-shy-strip-man.html (accessed 28 August 2018).

4. https://www2.deloitte.com/content/dam/Deloitte/de/Documents/consumer-business/European%20Health%20and%20Fitness%20Report_2018_extract.pdf (accessed 28 August 2018).

5. https://www.prnewswire.com/news-releases/mens-personal-care-market-to-reach-166-billion-globally-by-2022-allied-market-research-597595471.html (accessed 28 August 2018).

6. https://www.statista.com/statistics/273172/twitter-accounts-with-the-most-followers-worldwide/ (accessed 28 August 2018).

7. Harry C. Triandis, 'The self and social behavior in differing cultural contexts', *Psychological Review* 96(3) (1989): 506–20; H. Markus and S. Kitayama, 'Culture and the self: Implications for cognition, emotion, and motivation', *Psychological Review* 98 (1991): 224–53.

8. P. Wong, and M.K. Hogg, 'Exploring cultural differences in the extended self' in A. Ruvio and R. Belk (eds), *Identity and Consumption* (London: Routledge, 2013); P. Wong, M.K. Hogg and M. Vanharanta, 'Consumption narratives of extended possessions and the extended self', *Journal of Marketing Management* (2013); Markus and Kitayama, 'Culture and the Self', op. cit.

9. Nancy Wong and Aaron Ahuvia, 'A Cross-Cultural Approach to Materialism and the Self', in Dominique Bouchet (ed.), *Cultural Dimensions of International Marketing* (Denmark: Odense University, 1995): 68–89.

10. http://www.dailymail.co.uk/news/article-491741/British-women-look-mirror-71-times-day-survey-reveals.html (accessed 28 August 2018).

11. Anthony G. Greenwald and Mahzarin R. Banaji, 'The self as a memory system: Powerful, but ordinary', *Journal of Personality and Social Psychology* 57(1) (1989): 41–54; Hazel Markus, 'Self schemata and processing information about the self', *Journal of Personality and Social Psychology* 35 (1977): 63–78.

12. Morris Rosenberg, *Conceiving the Self* (New York: Basic Books, 1979); M. Joseph Sirgy, 'Self-concept in consumer behavior: A critical review', *Journal of Consumer Research* 9 (December 1982): 287–300.

13. John Tierney, 'Why You Won't Be the Person You Expect to Be?', *New York Times* (3 January 2013), http://www.nytimes.com/2013/01/04/science/study-in-science-shows-end-of-history-illusion.html?_r=0 (accessed 28 August 2018).

14. Emily Yoffe, 'You are what you buy', *Newsweek* (4 June 1990): 59. See also 'Therapy hope for eating disorders' (2008), http://news.bbc.co.uk/2/hi/health/7779468.stm (accessed 28 August 2018) and http://www.eatingdisorderexpert.co.uk/ (accessed 28 August 2018).

15. Roy F. Baumeister, Dianne M. Tice and Debra G. Hutton, 'Self-presentational motivations and personality differences in self-esteem', *Journal of Personality* 57 (September 1989): 547–75; Ronald J. Faber, 'Are Self-Esteem Appeals Appealing?', in Leonard N. Reid (ed.), *Proceedings of the 1992 Conference of the American Academy of Advertising* (1992): 230–5.

16. B. Bradford Brown and Mary Jane Lohr, 'Peer-group affiliation and adolescent self-esteem: An integration of ego identity and symbolic-interaction theories', *Journal of Personality and Social Psychology* 52(1) (1987): 47–55.

17. Christine Bittar, 'Alberto-Culver Ties Hair Relaxer to Self-Esteem', *MarketingDaily* (15 February 2007), https://www.mediapost.com/publications/article/55577/alberto-culver-ties-hair-relaxer-to-self-esteem.html (accessed 28 August 2018).

18. Claudia Townsend and Sanjay Sood, 'Self-Affirmation Through the Choice of Highly Aesthetic Products', *Journal of Consumer Research* 39(3) (2012): 415–28.

19. Marsha L. Richins, 'Social comparison and the idealized images of advertising', *Journal of Consumer Research* 18 (June 1991): 71–83; Mary C. Martin and Patricia F. Kennedy, 'Advertising and social comparison: Consequences for female pre-adolescents and adolescents', *Psychology and Marketing* 10(6) (November/December 1993): 513–30.

20. Philip N. Myers Jr and Frank A. Biocca, 'The elastic body image: The effect of television advertising and programming on body image distortions in young women', *Journal of Communication* 42 (Summer 1992): 108–33.

21. Jeremy Kees, Karen Becker-Olsen and Milos Mitric, 'The Use of Thin Models in Advertising: The Moderating Effect of Self-Monitoring on Females' Body Esteem and Food Choices', in John Kozup, Charles R. Taylor and Ronald Paul Hill (eds), *Marketing and Public Policy Proceedings* (Philadelphia, PA: American Marketing Association, 2008).

22. Jeffrey F. Durgee, 'Self-esteem advertising', *Journal of Advertising* 14(4) (1986): 21.

23. M. Sääksjärvi, K. Hellén, and G. Balabanis, 'Sometimes a celebrity holding a negative public image is the best product endorser', *European Journal of Marketing,* 50(3/4) (2016): 421–41.

24. Oliver Wheaton, '"Yes. We are beach body ready": New advert pokes fun at Protein World poster', (2015) http://metro.co.uk/2015/04/30/yes-we-are-beach-body-ready-dove-pokes-fun-at-world-protein-poster-with-new-advert-5175375/ (accessed 28 August 2018).

25. For the seminal treatment of this process, see Erving Goffman, *The Presentation of Self in Everyday Life* (New York: Doubleday, 1959).

26. K. Pounders, C.M. Kowalczyk and K. Stowers. 'Insight into the motivation of selfie postings: impression management and self-esteem', *European Journal of Marketing* 50(9/10) (2016).: 1,879–92.

27. J. Rokka and R. Canniford, 'Heterotopian selfies: How social media destabilizes brand assemblages', *European Journal of Marketing* 50(9/10) (2016): 1,789–813.

28. Sigmund Freud, *New Introductory Lectures in Psycho-analysis* (New York: Norton, 1965).

29. Jason Riis, Joseph P. Simmons and Geoffrey P. Goodwin (2008) 'Preferences for enhancement pharmaceuticals: The reluctance to enhance fundamental traits', *Journal of Consumer Research* 35 (October 2008): 495–508.

30. Harrison G. Gough, Mario Fioravanti and Renato Lazzari, 'Some implications of self versus ideal-self congruence on the revised adjective check list', *Journal of Personality and Social Psychology* 44(6) (1983): 1,214–20.

31. Steven Jay Lynn and Judith W. Rhue, 'Daydream believers', *Psychology Today* (September 1985): 14.

32. Parham Aarabi, 'How brands are using facial recognition to transform marketing', *VB News (*13 April 2013), http://venturebeat.com/2013/04/13/marketing-facial-recognition/ (accessed 28 August 2018).

33. Erving Goffman, *The Presentation of Self in Everyday Life* (Garden City, NY: Doubleday, 1959); Michael R. Solomon, 'The role of products as social stimuli: A symbolic interactionism perspective', *Journal of Consumer Research* 10 (December 1983): 319–29.

34. Yinlong Zhang and L.J. Shrum (2009) 'The influence of self-construal on impulsive consumption', *Journal of Consumer Research* 35(5) (February 2009): 838–50.

35. Aliakbar Jafari and Christina Goulding, '"We are not terrorists!" UK-based Iranians, consumption practices and the "torn self"', *Consumption Markets and Culture,* 11 (June 2008): 73–91.

36. M.J. Carrington, B. Neville and R. Canniford, 'Unmanageable multiplicity: Consumer transformation towards moral self-coherence', *European Journal of Marketing* 49 (7/8) (2015): 1,300–25.

37. George H. Mead, *Mind, Self and Society* (Chicago: University of Chicago Press, 1934).

38. Debra A. Laverie, Robert E. Kleine and Susan Schultz Kleine, 'Reexamination and extension of Kleine, Kleine, and Kernan's Social Identity Model of Mundane Consumption: The mediating role of the appraisal process', *Journal of Consumer Research* 28 (March 2002): 659–69.

39. Jennifer Elias, 'Can this company finally get the retail fashion world online?', *Fast Company* (24 June 2014), http://www.fastcolabs.com/3026831/can-this-company-finally-get-the-retail-fashion-world-online (accessed 28 August 2018).

40. Charles H. Cooley, *Human Nature and the Social Order* (New York: Scribner's, 1902).

41. J.G. Hull and A.S. Levy, 'The organizational functions of the self: An alternative to the Duval and Wicklund Model of Self-Awareness', *Journal of Personality & Social Psychology* 37 (1979): 756–68; Jay G. Hull, Ronald R. Van Treuren, Susan J. Ashford, Pamela Propsom and Bruce W. Andrus, 'Self-consciousness and the processing of self-relevant information', *Journal of Personality & Social Psychology* 54(3) (1988): 452–65.

42. Michael Moss, 'Nudged to the produce aisle by a look in the mirror', *New York Times* (27 August 2013), http://www.nytimes.com/2013/08/28/dining/wooing-us-down-the-produce-aisle.html?_r=0 (accessed 28 August 2018).

43. Arnold W. Buss, *Self-Consciousness and Social Anxiety* (San Francisco: Freeman, 1980); Lynn Carol Miller and Cathryn Leigh Cox, 'Public self-consciousness and makeup use', *Personality & Social Psychology Bulletin* 8(4) (1982): 748–51; Michael R. Solomon and John Schopler, 'Self-consciousness and clothing', *Personality & Social Psychology Bulletin* 8(3) (1982): 508–14.

44. Loraine Lau-Gesk and Aimee Drolet, 'The publicly self-conscious consumer: Prepare to be embarrassed', *Journal of Consumer Psychology* 18 (April 2008): 127–36.

45. Morris B. Holbrook, Michael R. Solomon and Stephen Bell, 'A re-examination of self-monitoring and judgments of furniture designs', *Home Economics Research Journal* 19 (September 1990): 6–16; Mark Snyder, 'Self-Monitoring Processes', in Leonard Berkowitz (ed.), *Advances in Experimental Social Psychology* (New York: Academic Press, 1979): 85–128.

46. Mark Snyder and Steve Gangestad, 'On the nature of self-monitoring: Matters of assessment, matters of validity', *Journal of Personality & Social Psychology* 51 (1986): 125–39; Timothy R. Graeff, 'Image congruence effects on product evaluations: The role of self-monitoring and public/private consumption', *Psychology & Marketing* 13 (August 1996): 481–99; Richard G. Netemeyer, Scot Burton and Donald R. Lichtenstein, 'Trait aspects of vanity: Measurement and relevance to consumer behavior', *Journal of Consumer Research* 21 (March 1995): 612–26.

47. R. Kedzior, D.E. Allen and J. Schroeder, 'The selfie phenomenon – consumer identities in the social media marketplace', *European Journal of Marketing* 50(9/10) (2016): 1,767–72; see also W.M. Lim, 'Understanding the selfie phenomenon: current insights and future research directions', *European Journal of Marketing* 50(9/10) (2016): 1,773–88.

48. D.C. Murray, 'Notes to self: the visual culture of selfies in the age of social media', *Consumption Markets & Culture* 18(6) (2015): 490–516.

49. R. Kedzior and D.E. Allen, 'From liberation to control: Understanding the selfie experience', *European Journal of Marketing* 50(9/10) (2016): 1,893–902.

50. Philip Cushman, 'Why the self is empty: Toward a historically situated psychology', *American Psychologist* 45 (1990): 599–611.

51. Peter Noel Murray, 'Are selfies and smartphones the new comfort food? How millennials satisfy the "empty self"', *Psychology Today* (2 October 2014), https://www.psychologytoday.com/blog/inside-the-consumer-mind/201410/are-selfies-and-smartphones-the-new-comfort-food (accessed 28 August 2018).

52. Gia Nardini, Robyn A. LeBoeuf and Richard J. Lutz, 'When a Picture is Worth Less Than a Thousand Words', *Association for Consumer Research 2013 North American Conference,* Chicago (USA) (4 October 2013).

53. http://www.reputation.com/ (accessed 28 August 2018).

54. Heidi Strohmaier, Megan Murphy and David DeMatteo, 'Youth sexting: Prevalence rates, driving motivations, and the deterrent effect of legal consequences', *Sexuality Research and Social Policy* 11(3) (September 2014): 245–55,

http://link.springer.com/article/10.1007/s13178-014-0162-9 (accessed 28 August 2018).

55. Douglas Macmillan and Elizabeth Dwoskin, 'Smile! Marketing firms are mining your selfies', *Wall Street Journal* (October 9, 2014), http://www.wsj.com/articles/smile-marketing-firms-are-mining-your-selfies-1412882222?KEYWORDS=selfies (accessed 28 August 2018).

56. Jack L. Nasar, 'Symbolic meanings of house styles', *Environment and Behavior* 21 (May 1989): 235–57; E.K. Sadalla, B. Verschure and J. Burroughs, 'Identity symbolism in housing', *Environment and Behavior* 19 (1987): 599–687.

57. Douglas B. Holt and Craig J. Thompson, 'Man-of-action heroes: The pursuit of heroic masculinity in everyday consumption', *Journal of Consumer Research* 31 (September 2004): 425–40; Michael R. Solomon, 'The role of products as social stimuli: A symbolic interactionism perspective', *Journal of Consumer Research* 10 (December 1983): 319–28; Robert E. Kleine III, Susan Schultz-Kleine and Jerome B. Kernan, 'Mundane consumption and the self: A social-identity perspective', *Journal of Consumer Psychology* 2(3) (1993): 209–35; Newell D. Wright, C.B. Claiborne and M. Joseph Sirgy, 'The Effects of Product Symbolism on Consumer Self-Concept', in John F. Sherry Jr and Brian Sternthal (eds), *Advances in Consumer Research* 19 (Provo, UT: Association for Consumer Research, 1992): 311–18; Susan Fournier, 'A Person-Based Relationship Framework for Strategic Brand Management', PhD dissertation, University of Florida, 1994.

58. A. Dwayne Ball and Lori H. Tasaki, 'The role and measurement of attachment in consumer behavior', *Journal of Consumer Psychology* 1(2) (1992): 155–72.

59. William B. Hansen and Irwin Altman, 'Decorating personal places: A descriptive analysis', *Environment and Behavior* 8 (December 1976): 491–504.

60. R.A. Wicklund and P.M. Gollwitzer, *Symbolic Self-Completion* (Hillsdale, NJ: Lawrence Erlbaum, 1982).

61. R. E. Kleine, S.S. Kleine and D.R. Ewing, 'Differences in symbolic self-completion and self-retention across role-identity cultivation stages', *European Journal of Marketing* 51 (11/12) (2017): 1,876–95.

62. Jacob Ostberg, 'Thou shalt sport a banana in thy pocket: Gendered body size ideals in advertising and popular culture', *Marketing Theory* 10(1) (2010): 45–73.

63. Susanna Molander, Astrid Kleppe Ingeborg and Jacob Ostberg, 'Hero shots: Involved fathers conquering new discursive territory in consumer culture', accepted for forthcoming publication in *Consumption, Markets and Culture* (2018).

64. Erving Goffman, *Asylums* (New York: Doubleday, 1961).

65. Quoted in Floyd Rudmin, 'Property crime victimization impact on self, on attachment, and on territorial dominance', *CPA Highlights, Victims of Crime Supplement* 9(2) (1987): 4–7.

66. Barbara B. Brown, 'House and Block as Territory', paper presented at the Conference of the Association for Consumer Research, San Francisco, 1982.

67. R. Trudel, J.J. Argo and M.D. Meng, 'The recycled self: Consumers' disposal decisions of identity-linked products', *Journal of Consumer Research* 43(2) (2016): 246–64.

68. Quoted in Shay Sayre and David Horne, 'I Shop, Therefore I Am: The Role of Possessions for Self-Definition', in Shay Sayre and David Horne (eds), *Earth, Wind, and Fire and Water: Perspectives on Natural Disaster* (Pasadena, CA: Open Door Publishers, 1996): 353–70. Recently in Germany, the 'loss of self' was taken to the ultimate extreme when a 43-year-old German from Berlin answered an advert on the internet looking for someone to offer to be killed and eaten. With his consent, he was killed, cut into pieces, frozen and placed in the freezer next to the takeaway pizza. See 'Cannibal to face murder charge at retrial', *Guardian* (23 April 2005), http://www.guardian.co.uk/international/story/0,,1468373,00.html (accessed 28 August 2018).

69. Deborah A. Prentice, 'Psychological correspondence of possessions, attitudes, and values', *Journal of Personality and Social Psychology* 53(6) (1987): 993–1,002.

70. Jennifer L. Aaker, 'The malleable self: The role of self-expression in persuasion', *Journal of Marketing Research* 36 (February 1999): 45–57; Sak Onkvisit and John Shaw, 'Self-concept and image congruence: Some research and managerial implications', *Journal of Consumer Marketing* 4 (Winter 1987): 13–24. For a related treatment of congruence between advertising appeals and self-concept, see George M. Zinkhan and Jae W. Hong, 'Self-Concept and Advertising Effectiveness: A Conceptual Model of Congruency, Conspicuousness, and Response Mode', in Rebecca H. Holman and Michael R. Solomon (eds), *Advances in Consumer Research* 18 (Provo, UT: Association for Consumer Research, 1991): 348–54.

71. C.B. Claiborne and M. Joseph Sirgy, 'Self-Image Congruence as a Model of Consumer Attitude Formation and Behavior: A Conceptual Review and Guide for Further Research', paper presented at the Academy of Marketing Science Conference, New Orleans, 1990.

72. Susan Fournier and Julie L. Yao, 'Reviving brand loyalty: A reconceptualization within the framework of consumer-brand relationships', *International Journal of Research in Marketing* 14(5) (December 1997): 451–72; Caryl E. Rusbult, 'A longitudinal test of the investment model: The development (and deterioration) of satisfaction and commitment in heterosexual involvements', *Journal of Personality and Social Psychology* 45(1) (1983): 101–17.

73. Allison R. Johnson, Maggie Matear and Matthew Thomson, 'A coal in the heart: Self-relevance as a post-exit predictor of consumer anti-brand actions', *Journal of Consumer Research* 38(1) (June 2011): 108–25.

74. Liz Hunt, 'Rise in infertility linked to craze for body building', *The Independent* (12 July 1995): 12; MaryGrace Taylor, '7 horrifying consequences of taking steroids', *Men's Health* (16 February 2018), https://www.menshealth.com/health/g18199455/7-horrifying-consequences-of-taking-steroids/ (accessed 30 August 2018). See also 'Learn more about use and abuse of anabolic steroids' (10 September 2016), http://menshealth.about.com/cs/fitness/a/anab_steroids.htm (accessed 28 August 2018).

75. https://www.telegraph.co.uk/health-fitness/body/i-was-addicted-to-exercise-heres-how-to-spot-the-signs/ (accessed 28 August 2018).

76. C.C. Simpson and S. E. Mazzeo, 'Skinny is not enough: A content analysis of fitspiration on Pinterest', *Health Communication* 32(5) (2017): 560–7.

77. Özlem Sandikci and Güliz Ger, 'Aesthetics, Ethics and Politics of the Turkish Headscarf', in Susanne Küchler and Daniel

Miller (eds), *Clothing as Material Culture* (Oxford: Berg, 2005): Chapter 4.

78. Marc Lacey, 'Where showing skin doesn't sell, a new style is a hit', *New York Times* (20 March 2006).

79. https://news.nike.com/news/nike-pro-hijab (accessed 28 August 2018).

80. B. Rozenkrants, S.C. Wheeler and B. Shiv, 'Self-expression cues in product rating distributions: When people prefer polarizing products', *Journal of Consumer Research* 44(4) (2017): 759–77.

81. Ernest Beaglehole, *Property: A Study in Social Psychology* (New York: Macmillan, 1932).

82. Russell W. Belk, 'Possessions and the extended self', *Journal of Consumer Research* 15 (September 1988): 139–68.

83. Andrew D. Wilson and Sabrina Golonka, 'Embodied cognition is not what you think it is', *Frontiers in Psychology* (12 February 2013), http://journal.frontiersin.org/article/10.3389/fpsyg.2013.00058/full (accessed 28 August 2018).

84. Amy Cuddy, 'Your Body Language May Shape Who You Are', TED talk filmed June 2012, http://www.ted.com/talks/amy_cuddy_your_body_language_shapes_who_you_are?language=en (accessed 28 August 2018).

85. Adam Hajo and Adam D. Galinsky, 'Enclothed cognition', *Journal of Experimental Social Psychology* 48(4) (July 2012): 918–25.

86. Adapted from Jagdish N. Sheth and Michael R. Solomon, 'Extending the extended self in a digital world', *Journal of Marketing Theory and Practice* 22(2) 2014: 123–32; see also Russell W. Belk, 'Extended self in a digital world', *Journal of Consumer Research* 40(3) (2013): 477–500.

87. Nick Yee, Jeremy N. Bailenson, Mark Urbanek, Francis Chang and Dan Merget, 'The Unbearable Likeness of Being Digital: The persistence of nonverbal social norms in online virtual environments', *Cyberpsychology & Behavior* 10(1) (2007): 116–21.

88. F. Kerrigan and A. Hart, 'Theorising digital personhood: A dramaturgical approach', *Journal of Marketing Management* 32(17/18) (2016): 1,701–21.

89. Quoted in Susan Fournier, 'Breaking up is hard to do: The ups and downs of divorcing brands', *GfK Marketing Intelligence Review* 6(1) (May 2014), http://www.degruyter.com/view/j/gfkmir.2014.6.issue-1/gfkmir-2014-0005/gfkmir-2014-0005.xml (accessed 28 August 2018).

90. Nick Bilton, 'Wearable technology that feels like skin', *New York Times* (8 October 2014), http://www.nytimes.com/2014/10/09/fashion/wearable-technology-that-feels-like-skin.html?smid=nytcore-iphone-share&smprod=nytcore-iphone&_r=0 (accessed 28 August 2018).

91. Adapted from a presentation by Prof. Thanigavelan Jambulingam, Saint Joseph's University (22 January 2015).

92. https://www.theguardian.com/technology/2017/nov/01/under-the-skin-how-insertable-microchips-could-unlock-the-future (accessed 28 August 2018).

93. Hilary Stout, 'Mirror, Mirror in the App: What's the Fairest Shade and Shadow of Them All?', *New York Times* (14 May 2014), http://www.nytimes.com/2014/05/15/business/mirror-mirror-in-the-app-whats-the-fairest-shade-of-all.html?_r=0 (accessed 28 August 2018).

94. Janeen Arnold Costa, 'Introduction', in J.A. Costa (ed.), *Gender Issues and Consumer Behavior* (Thousand Oaks, CA: Sage, 1994).

95. Paul Rozin, Julia M Hormes. Myles S. Faith and Brian Wansink, 'Is meat male?: A quantitative multimethod framework to establish metaphoric relationships', *Journal of Consumer Research* 39(3) (2012): 629–43.

96. Rozin, Hormes, Faith and Wansink, 'Is meat male? A quantitative multimethod framework to establish metaphoric relationships', op cit. See also Nina M. Lentini, 'McDonald's tests "Angus Third Pounder" in California', *MarketingDaily* (27 March 2007).

97. For an up-to-date overview of gender and consumer behaviour research that has a strong global perspective, see Cele C. Otnes and Linda Tuncay Zayer (eds), *Gender, Culture and Consumer Behavior* (London: Routledge, 2012).

98. Joan Meyers-Levy, 'The influence of sex roles on judgment', *Journal of Consumer Research* 14 (March 1988): 522–30.

99. A.R. Brough, J.E.B. Wilkie, J.J. Ma, M.S. Isaac and D. Gal, 'Is eco-friendly unmanly? The green-feminine stereotype and its effect on sustainable consumption', *Journal of Consumer Research* 43(4) (2016): 567–82.

100. Kimberly J. Dodson and Russell W. Belk, 'Gender in Children's Birthday Stories' in Janeen Costa (ed.), *Gender, Marketing, and Consumer Behavior* (Salt Lake City, UT: Association for Consumer Research, 1996): 96–108.

101. Gavin O'Malley, 'Study: Men Are from Hulu, Women Are from Facebook', Online Media Daily (28 July 2010).

102. Elizabeth C. Hirschman, 'A Feminist Critique of Marketing Theory: Toward Agentic-Communal Balance', working paper, School of Business, Rutgers University, New Brunswick, NJ, 1990.

103. Joan Meyers-Levy and Barbara Loken, 'Revisiting gender differences: What we know and what lies ahead', Journal of Consumer Psychology 25(1) (2015): 129–49.

104. Eileen Fischer and Stephen J. Arnold, 'Sex, gender identity, gender role attitudes, and consumer behavior', Psychology and Marketing 11(2) (March/April 1994): 163–82.

105. Matthew Sparks, 'Facebook sex changes: Which of 50 genders are you?' (2014), http://www.telegraph.co.uk/technology/facebook/10637968/Facebook-sex-changes-which-one-of-50-genders-are-you.html (accessed 28 August 2018); see also: Barbara Herman, 'Mr., Ms., or Mx? Oxford English Dictionary Adopts Gender-Neutral Honorific', (2015), http://www.ibtimes.com/mr-mrs-or-mx-oxford-english-dictionary-adopts-gender-neutral-honorific-1907977 (accessed 28 August 2018).

106. Julie King, 'What Biology Can Tell Us About Consumers', Canada One (1 March 2011); see also https://www.sciencedirect.com/topics/neuroscience/neuroendocrinology (accessed 30 August 2018).

107. Raymond Tallis, Aping Mankind (London: Routledge, 2016).

108. Kristina M. Durante, Vladas Griskevicius, Sarah E. Hill, Carin Perilloux and Norman P. Li, 'Ovulation, female competition, and product choice: Hormonal influences on consumer behavior', Journal of Consumer Research 37(6) (April 2011): 921–34; Kristina M. Durante and Ashley Rae Arsena, 'Playing the field: The effect of fertility on women's desire for variety', Journal of Consumer Research 41(6) (2015): 1,372–91.

109. Kathleen Debevec and Easwar Iyer, 'Sex Roles and Consumer Perceptions of Promotions, Products, and Self: What Do We Know and Where Should We Be Headed', in Richard J. Lutz (ed.), Advances in Consumer Research 13 (Provo, UT: Association for Consumer Research, 1986): 210–14; Joseph A. Bellizzi and Laura Milner, 'Gender positioning of a traditionally male-dominant product', Journal of Advertising Research (June/July 1991): 72–9.

110. Janeen Arnold Costa and Teresa M. Pavia, 'Alpha-numeric brand names and gender stereotypes', Research in Consumer Behavior 6 (1993): 85–112.

111. B. Schnurr, 'What's best for whom? The effect of product gender depends on positioning', European Journal of Marketing 52(1/2) (2018): 367–91.

112. Helga Dittmar, Jane Beattie and Susanne Friese, 'Gender identity and material symbols: Objects and decision considerations in impulse purchases', Journal of Economic Psychology 16 (1995): 491–511; Jason Cox and Helga Dittmar, 'The functions of clothes and clothing (dis)satisfaction: A gender analysis among British students', Journal of Consumer Policy 18 (1995): 237–65.

113. Lucy Vine, 'Lindsay Lohan gets naked and streaks in London's Selfridges laughing hysterically', Mirror (23 June 2014), http://www.mirror.co.uk/3am/celebrity-news/lindsay-lohan-gets-naked-streaks-3746464 (accessed 28 August 2018).

114. Quoted in Mark J. Miller, 'Selfridges Will Go Gender-Free in Latest Retail Experiment', Brandchannel (29 January 2015), http://www.brandchannel.com/home/post/2015/01/29/150129-Selfridges-Gender-Free.aspx?utm_campaign=150129-Selfridges-Agender&utm_source=newsletter&utm_medium=email (accessed 28 August 2018).

115. Sandra L. Bem, 'The measurement of psychological androgyny', Journal of Consulting and Clinical Psychology 42 (1974): 155–62; Deborah E.S. Frable, 'Sex typing and gender ideology: Two facets of the individual's gender psychology that go together', Journal of Personality and Social Psychology 56(1) (1989): 95–108.

116. S.L. Bem, 'The measurement of psychological androgyny', Journal of Consulting and Clinical Psychology 42(2) (1974): 155.

117. See D. Bruce Carter and Gary D. Levy, 'Cognitive aspects of early sex-role development: The influence of gender schemas on preschoolers' memories and preferences for sex-typed toys and activities', Child Development 59 (1988): 782–92; Bernd H. Schmitt, France Le Clerc and Laurette Dube-Rioux, 'Sex typing and consumer behavior: A test of gender schema theory', Journal of Consumer Research 15 (June 1988): 122–7.

118. Carol Gilligan, In a Different Voice: Psychological Theory and Women's Development (Cambridge, MA: Harvard University Press, 1982); Joan Meyers-Levy and Durairaj Maheswaran, 'Exploring differences in males' and females' processing strategies', Journal of Consumer Research 18 (June 1991): 63–70.

119. Lynn J. Jaffe and Paul D. Berger, 'Impact on purchase intent of sex-role identity and product positioning', Psychology and Marketing (Fall 1988): 259–71; Lynn J. Jaffe, 'The unique predictive ability of sex-role identity in explaining women's response to advertising', Psychology and Marketing 11(5) (September/October 1994): 467–82.

120. Kristine L. Nowak and Christian Rauth, 'The influence of the avatar on online perceptions of anthropomorphism, androgyny, credibility, homophily, and attraction', Journal of Computer-Mediated Communication 11(1) (2006): 153–78.

121. Sexual Health, U.K., Mintel, July 2011; see also Julie Candler, 'Woman car buyer – don't call her a niche anymore', Advertising Age (21 January 1991): S-8; see also Robin Widgery and Jack McGaugh, 'Vehicle message appeals and the new generation woman', Journal of Advertising Research (September/October 1993): 36–42; Blayne Cutler, 'Condom mania', American Demographics (June 1989): 17.

122. Sherry L. Pagoto, Stephenie C. Lemon, Jessica L. Oleski, Jonathan M. Scully, Gin-Fei Olendzki, Martinus M. Evans, Wenjun Li, L. Carter Florence, Brittany Kirkland and Joel J. Hillhouse, 'Availability of Tanning Beds on US College Campuses', JAMA Dermatol 151(1) (2015): 59–63, http://archderm.jamanetwork.com/article.aspx?articleid=1919438 (accessed 28 August 2018); Sabrina Tavernise, 'Warning: That tan could be hazardous: Indoor tanning poses cancer risks, teenagers learn', New York Times (10 January 2015), http://www.nytimes.com/2015/01/11/health/indoor-tanning-poses-cancer-risks-teenagers-learn.html?_r=1 (accessed 28 August 2018).

123. Andrew Adam Newman, 'Celebrating Black Beauty and advocating diversity', New York Times (18 April 2013), http://www.nytimes.com/2013/04/19/business/media/celebrating-black-beauty-and-advocating-diversity.html (accessed 28 August 2018); Thomas Fuller, 'A vision of pale beauty carries risks for Asia's women', International Herald Tribune Online (14 May 2006).

124. Eric Bellman, 'Suzuki's stylish compacts captivate India's women', Wall Street Journal (11 May 2007): B1.

125. http://campaignforrealbeauty.co.uk (accessed 28 August 2018).

126. T.D. Malefyt and M. McCabe, 'Women's bodies, menstruation and marketing "protection": Interpreting a paradox of gendered discourses in consumer practices and advertising campaigns', Consumption Markets & Culture 19(6) (2016): 555–75.

127. https://www.wired.com/story/metoo-is-changing-even-the-smarmiest-advertisers/ (accessed 28 August 2018).

128. https://www.glamour.com/story/serena-williams-nike-ad (accessed 28 August 2018).

129. Quoted in Barry Silverstein, 'Ever the Publicity Hound, Branson Readies to be an Airline Hostess', BrandChannel (18 November 2010), http://www.brandchannel.com/home/post/2010/11/18/Richard-Branson-Loses-Bet.aspx (accessed 28 August 2018).

130. Gordon Sumner, 'Tribal rites of the American male', Marketing Insights (Summer 1989): 13.

131. Barbara B. Stern, 'Masculinism(s) and the Male Image: What Does It Mean to Be a Man?' in Tom Reichert and Jacqueline Lambiase (eds), Sex in Advertising: Multi-disciplinary Perspectives on the Erotic Appeal (Mahwah, NJ: Erlbaum, 2003).

132. Ellinor Block, 'Hipster Style – Is It even a Thing in 2018?', https://www.whowhatwear.co.uk/hipster-style (accessed 28 August 2018).

133. Diego Rinallo, 'Metro/Fashion/Tribes of men: Negotiating the boundaries of men's legitimate consumption', in B. Cova, R. Kozinets and A. Shankar (eds), Consumer Tribes: Theory, Practice, and Prospects (Oxford, UK: Elsevier/Butterworth-Heinemann, 2007).

134. Douglas B. Holt and Craig J. Thompson, 'Man-of-action heroes: The pursuit of heroic masculinity in everyday consumption', Journal of Consumer Research 31 (September): 425–40.

135. M. Klasson and S. Ulver, 'Masculinising domesticity: an investigation of men's domestic foodwork', Journal of Marketing Management 31(15/16) (2015): 1,652–75.

136. 'Beauty Retailing: U.K.', Mintel (January 2012); see also Vivian Manning-Schaffel, 'Metrosexuals: A Well-Groomed Market?', www.brandchannel.com (accessed 28 August 2018).

137. Maples, 'Beefcake marketing', op. cit.

138. D.A. Black, S.G. Sanders and L.J. Taylor, 'The economics of lesbian and gay families', Journal of Economic Perspectives 21(2) (2007): 53–70; Riccardo A. Davis, 'Marketers game for gay events', Advertising Age (30 May 1994): S-1(2); Cyndee Miller, 'Top marketers take bolder approach in targeting gays', Marketing News (4 July 1994): 1(2); see also Douglas L. Fugate, 'Evaluating the US male homosexual and lesbian population as a viable target market segment', Journal of Consumer Marketing 10(4) (1993): 46–57; Laura M. Milner, 'Marketing to Gays and Lesbians: A Review', unpublished manuscript, the University of Alaska, 1990.

139. Stuart Elliott, 'Banana Republic ads with real-life unions include a gay couple', New York Times (20 February 2014), http://www.nytimes.com/2014/02/21/business/media/banana-republic-ads-with-real-life-unions-includes-a-gay-couple.html?_r=1 (accessed 28 August 2018).

140. https://www.adweek.com/creativity/oreo-surprises-26-million-facebook-fans-gay-pride-post-141440/ (accessed 30 August 2018).

141. Projections of the incidence of homosexuality in the general population are often influenced by assumptions of the researchers, as well as the methodology they employ (e.g. self-report, behavioural measures, fantasy measures). For a discussion of these factors, see Edward O. Laumann, John H. Gagnon, Robert T. Michael and Stuart Michaels, The Social Organization of Homosexuality (Chicago: University of Chicago Press, 1994).

142. Lisa Peñaloza, 'We're here, we're queer, and we're going shopping! A critical perspective on the accommodation of gays and lesbians in the U.S. marketplace', Journal of Homosexuality 31(1/2) (1966): 9–41.

143. Fugate, 'Evaluating the U.S. male homosexual and lesbian population as a viable target market segment'; see also Laumann, Gagnon, Michael and Michaels, The Social Organization of Homosexuality, op cit.

144. Laura Koss-Feder, 'Out and about', Marketing News (25 May 1998): 1(2); Rachel X. Weissman, 'Gay market power', American Demographics 21(6) (June 1999): 32–3.

145. Peñaloza, 'We're here, we're queer, and we're going shopping!', op. cit.

146. https://www.glassdoor.com/blog/companies-lgbtq-equality/ (accessed 30 August 2018); see also https://www.ranker.com/list/gay-friendly-companies/coreybarger (accessed 30 August 2018).

147. Sheila Shayon, 'Levi's for Women: Shape, Not Size, Matters', BrandChannel (17 September 2010), http://www.brandchannel.com/home/post/2010/09/17/Levis-Women-Curve-ID-Digital.aspx (accessed 28 August 2018); http://us.levi.com/shop/index.jsp?categoryId=3146849&AB=CMS_Home_CurveID_081010 (accessed 28 August 2018).

148. Abe Sauer, 'How Unilever is Translating the Dove Real Beauty Campaign for China', BrandChannel (15 July 2013), http://www.brandchannel.com/home/post/2013/07/15/Dove-Real-Beauty-China-Campaign-071513.aspx (accessed 28 August 2018).

149. Dennis W. Rook, 'Body Cathexis and Market Segmentation', in Michael R. Solomon (ed.), The Psychology of Fashion (Lexington, MA: Lexington Books, 1985): 233–41.

150. 'Nederlandse vrouw krijt lachend rimpels', De Telegraaf (26 April 1997): TA5.

151. Jane E. Brody, 'Notions of beauty transcend culture, new study suggests', New York Times (21 March 1994): A14.

152. Karen K. Dion, 'What Is Beautiful Is Good', Journal of Personality and Social Psychology 24 (December 1972): 285–90.

153. Sharon Jayson, 'Study: Beautiful People Cash in on Their Looks', USA Today (31 March 2011), http://www.usatoday.com/money/perfi/basics/2011-03-30-beauty30_ST_N.htm (accessed 28 August 2018).

154. Rebecca Popenoe, 'Ideal', in D. Kulick and A. Menley (eds.), Fat: The Anthropology of an Obsession, (New York: Penguin, 2004): 9–28.

155. P.J. Brown, 'Culture and the evolution of obesity', Human Nature 2(1) (1991): 31–57.

156. R. Wilk, 'Learning to be local in Belize: global systems of common difference', in D. Miller (ed.), Worlds Apart: Modernity Through the Prism of the Local (London: Polity, 1995): 110–33.

157. Popenoe (2004), op.cit.

158. Michael Fay and Christopher Price, 'Female body-shape in print advertisements and the increase in anorexia nervosa', European Journal of Marketing 28 (1994): 12.

159. 'Vrouwen hebben complexe relatie met schoonheid' ('Women have a complex relationship with beauty') De Telegraaf (31 January 2005).

160. M. Tiggemann and M. Zaccardo, 'Strong is the new skinny: A content analysis of fitspiration images on Instagram', Journal of Health Psychology 23(8) (2018): 1,003–11.

161. Mark J. Miller, 'Macy's Introduces Marilyn Monroe Collection to a Racier Generation', BrandChannel (6 March 2013), http://www.brandchannel.com/home/post/2013/03/06/Macys-Marilyn-Monroe-030613.aspx (accessed 28 August 2018).

162. Erin White, 'Dove "Firms" with Zaftig Models: Unilever Brand Launches European Ads Employing Non-Supermodel Bodies', Wall Street Journal (21 April 2004): B3.

163. https://www.prnewswire.com/news-releases/new-dove-research-finds-beauty-pressures-up-and-women-and-girls-calling-for-change-583743391.html (accessed 30 August 2018).

164. Geoffrey A. Fowler, 'Unilever Gives "Ugly Betty" A Product-Plug Makeover in China', Wall Street Journal (29 December 2008).

165. Jill Neimark, 'The beefcaking of America', Psychology Today (November/December 1994): 32(11).

166. Richard H. Kolbe and Paul J. Albanese, 'Man to man: A content analysis of sole-male images in male-audience magazines', Journal of Advertising 25(4) (Winter 1996): 1–20.

167. 'Girls at 7 think thin, study finds', New York Times (11 February 1988): B9.

168. See for example E. Rothblum and S. Solovay, eds. (2009), The Fat Studies Reader, New York University Press.

169. A.A. Harju and A. Huovinen, 'Fashionably voluptuous: normative femininity and resistant performative tactics in fashion blogs', Journal of Marketing Management 31(15/16) (2015): 1,602–25.

170. https://www.theguardian.com/society/2016/may/31/one-in-three-children-aged-six-to-nine-in-europe-overweight-or-obese-study (accessed 30 August 2018).

171. Dirk Smeesters, Thomas Mussweiler and Naomi Mandel, 'The Effects of Thin and Heavy Media Images on Overweight and Underweight Consumers: Social Comparison Processes and Behavioral Implications', Journal of Consumer Research 36 (April 2010): 930–49; Brent McFerran, Darren W. Dahl, Gavan J. Fitzsimons and Andrea C. Morales, 'I'll have What She's Having: Effects of Social Influence and Body Type on the Food Choices of Others', Journal of Consumer Research 36 (April 2010): 915–29; David Dubois, Derek D. Rucker and Adam D. Galinsky, 'Super-Size Me: Product Size as a Signal of Status', Journal of Consumer Research 38 (April 2012): 1,047–62; see also Beth Carney, 'In Europe, the fat is in the fire', Business Week (8 February 2005).

172. Elaine L. Pedersen and Nancy L. Markee, 'Fashion dolls: Communicators of ideals of beauty and fashion', paper presented at the International Conference on Marketing Meaning, Indianapolis, 1989; Dalma Heyn, 'Body hate', Ms. (August 1989): 34; Mary C. Martin and James W. Gentry, 'Assessing the internalization of physical attractiveness norms', Proceedings of the American Marketing Association Summer Educators' Conference (Summer 1994): 59–65.

173. http://www.oecd.org/health/obesity-update.htm (accessed 30 August 2018).

174. Debra A. Zellner, Debra F. Harner and Robbie I. Adler, 'Effects of eating abnormalities and gender on perceptions of desirable body shape', Journal of Abnormal Psychology 98 (February 1989): 93–6.

175. Robin T. Peterson, 'Bulimia and anorexia in an advertising context', Journal of Business Ethics 6 (1987): 495–504.

176. Christian S. Crandall, 'Social contagion of binge eating', Journal of Personality and Social Psychology 55 (1988): 588–98.

177. Judy Folkenberg, 'Bulimia: Not for women only', Psychology Today (March 1984): 10.

178. Eleanor Grant, 'The exercise fix: What happens when fitness fanatics just can't say no?', Psychology Today 22 (February 1988): 24.

179. http://www.isaps.org/news/isaps-global-statistics (accessed 30 August 2018).

180. Annette C. Hamburger and Holly Hall, 'Beauty quest', Psychology Today (May 1988): 28.

181. E. Bellini, M.P. Grieco and E. Raposio, 'A journey through liposuction and liposculture', Annals of Medicine and Surgery 24 (2017): 53–60.

182. https://www.plasticsurgery.org/documents/News/Statistics/2017/plastic-surgery-statistics-full-report-2017.pdf (accessed 30 August 2018).

183. Søren Askegaard, Martine Cardel Gertsen and Roy Langer, 'The body consumed: Reflexivity and cosmetic surgery', Psychology and Marketing 19(10) (2002): 793–812.

184. Hounaida El Jurdi, Nacima Ourahmoune and Søren Askegaard, 'Beauty and the Social Imaginary: A Social Historical Analysis of the Lebanese Techno-Cosmetized Beauty Market', competitive paper presented at the 11th CCT conference, Lille, July 2016.

185. https://www.theatlantic.com/international/archive/2013/06/south-korean-high-schoolers-get-plastic-surgery-for-graduation/277255/ (accessed 28 August 2018).

186. https://www.telegraph.co.uk/news/2018/04/18/south-koreas-cosmetic-surgery-industry-faces-backlash-cultural/ (accessed 28 August 2018).

187. https://www.bbc.co.uk/bbcthree/article/9ca4f7c6-d2c3-4e25-862c-03aed9ec1082 (accessed 28 August 2018); see also https://www.huffingtonpost.com/entry/snapchat-dysmorphia_us_5a8d8168e4b0273053a680f6?guccounter=1 (accessed 28 August 2018).

188. Ruth P. Rubinstein, 'Color, Circumcision, Tattoos, and Scars', in Solomon (ed.), The Psychology of Fashion: 243–54; Peter H. Bloch and Marsha L. Richins, 'You look "mahvelous": The pursuit of beauty and marketing concept', Psychology and Marketing 9 (January 1992): 3–16.

189. Sondra Farganis, 'Lip service: The evolution of pouting, pursing, and painting lips red', Health (November 1988): 48–51.

190. Michael Gross, 'Those lips, those eyebrows: New face of 1989 (new look of fashion models)', New York Times Magazine (13 February 1989): 24.

191. Rebecca Scott, Julien Cayla and Bernard Cova, 'Selling pain to the saturated self', Journal of Consumer Research 44 (1) (2017): 22–43.

192. Dannie Kjeldgaard and Anders Bengtsson, 'Consuming the Fashion Tattoo', in Geeta Menon and Akshay R. Rao (eds), Advances in Consumer Research 32 (Duluth, MN: Association for Consumer Research, 2005): 172–7.

193. Mike Featherstone (ed.), Body Modification (Thousand Oaks, CA: Sage, 2000); Anne M. Velliquette and Jeff B. Murray, 'The New Tattoo Subculture', in Susan Ferguson (ed.), Mapping the Social Landscape: Readings in Sociology (Mountain View, CA: Mayfield, 1999): 56–68; Anne M. Velliquette, Jeff B. Murray and Elizabeth H. Creyer, 'The Tattoo Renaissance: An Ethnographic Account of Symbolic Consumer Behavior', in Joseph W. Alba and J. Wesley Hutchinson (eds), Advances in Consumer Research 25 (Provo, UT: Association for Consumer Research, 1998): 461–7; Anne M. Velliquette, 'Modern Primitives: The Role of Product Symbolism in Lifestyle Cultures and Identity', dissertation, University of Arkansas Press, 2000; Margo DeMello, Bodies of Inscription: A Cultural History of the Modern Tattoo Community (Durham, NC: Duke University Press, 2000); Anne Veliquette and Gary Bamossy, 'Modern Primitives: The Role of the Body and Product Symbolism in Lifestyle Cultures and Identity', in Andrea Groppel-Klein and Franz-Rudolf Esch (eds), European Advances in Consumer Research 5 (Valdosta, GA: Association for Consumer Research, 2001): 21–2.

194. Jonathan Schroeder, 'Branding the Body: Skin and Consumer Communication', in Darach Turley and Stephen Brown (eds), European Advances in Consumer Research: All Changed, Changed Utterly? 6 (Valdosta, GA: Association for Consumer Research, 2003): 23; Maurice Patterson and Richard Elliott, 'Harsh Beauty: The Alternative Aesthetic of Tattooed Women', in Turley and Brown (eds), European Advances in Consumer Research 6: 23; Dannie Kjeldgaard and Anders Bengtsson, 'Acts, Images, and Meaning of Tattooing', in Turley and Brown (eds), European Advances in Consumer Research 6: 24; Jonathan Schroeder and Janet Borgerson, 'Skin Signs: The Epidermal Schema in Contemporary Marketing Communications', in Turley and Brown (eds), European Advances in Consumer Research 6: 26; Roy Langer, 'SKINTWO: (Un)covering the Skin in Fetish Carnivals', in Turley and Brown (eds), European Advances in Consumer Research 6: 27.

195. Quoted in Wendy Bounds, 'Body-piercing gets under America's skin', Wall Street Journal (4 April 1994): B1(2), B4.

Chapter 5
Motivation, lifestyles and values

Chapter objectives

When you finish reading this chapter you will understand why:

5.1 It is important for marketers to recognise that products can satisfy a range of consumer needs.

5.2 Consumers experience different kinds of motivational conflicts that can impact their purchase decisions.

5.3 The way we evaluate and choose a product depends on our degree of involvement with the product, the marketing message and/or the purchase situation.

5.4 A lifestyle defines a pattern of consumption that reflects a person's choices of how to spend his or her time and money, and these choices are essential to defining consumer identity.

5.5 It can often be more useful to identify *patterns* of consumption than knowing about *individual* purchases when organisations craft a lifestyle marketing strategy.

5.6 Psychographics go beyond simple demographics to help marketers understand and reach different consumer segments.

5.7 Underlying values often drive consumer motivations. Products thus take on meaning because a person thinks they will help him or her to achieve some goal that is linked to a value, such as individuality or freedom. A set of core values characterises each culture, to which most of its members adhere.

ANDREW and his German girlfriend, Alexandra, have just found a table for lunch at a restaurant in Kolonaki (Athens) that Andrew found recommended on TripAdvisor.[1] It had been Andrew's turn to choose where to eat as Alexandra had suggested the Cretan restaurant where they had had dinner the previous night. Andrew studies the menu hard. He is reflecting on what a man will do for love. Alexandra is keen that they both eat healthily. She's not yet managed to persuade him to follow her conversion to vegetarianism. However, she's slowly but surely persuading him to give up burgers and pizzas for healthier, preferably organic, fare. At least while they are on holiday he can hide from tofu and the other vegan delights that confront him as the menu choices at their favourite local café when he visits her in St. Andrews.

Alexandra is still prepared to eat dairy products, so she is not a vegan. She argues that eating this way not only cuts out unwanted fat, but is also good for the environment. Just Andrew's luck to fall head-over-heels for a green, organic-food-eating environmentalist who is into issues of sustainability. As Andrew gamely tries to decide between the stuffed artichokes with red pepper vinaigrette and the grilled, marinated croquettes, he wonders if he might be able to choose the *soutzoukakia smyrneika* (meatballs cooked with cumin, cinnamon and garlic in a tomato sauce) – after all, they are on holiday and in Greece!

Margaret K. Hogg

Introduction

As a lacto-ovo-vegetarian (rather than a lacto-vegetarian or a vegan),[2] Alexandra is certainly not alone in believing that eating organic foods are good for the body, the soul and the planet.[3] The forces that drive people to buy and use products are generally straightforward, as when a person chooses what to have for lunch. As hard-core vegans demonstrate, however, even the consumption of basic food products may also be related to wide-ranging beliefs regarding what is appropriate or desirable. Among the more general population there are strong beliefs about genetically modified foods, which have proved difficult to alter via information campaigns.[4] There has been a lively debate in Europe about genetically modified foods compared with the US, although genetic modification for medical purposes has not met with such widespread hostility in Europe. Consumers see 'functional foods as placed midway on the combined "naturalness–healthiness continuum" from organically processed to genetically modified'[5] but tend to remain unconvinced that genetically modified foods can offer any significant health benefits.[6]

Concerns about adult, and more especially childhood, obesity, for instance, mean that diet has become a burning issue for many European governments.[7] It is obvious our menu choices have deep-seated consequences. In some cases, our emotional responses create a deep commitment to the product. Sometimes people are not even fully aware of the forces that drive them towards some products and away from others. Often a person's *values* – their priorities and beliefs about the world – influence these choices, as in Alexandra's case. Choices are not always straightforward. Often there are trade-offs to be made (as in Andrew's case).

Marketing opportunity
Vegans, vegetarians and now. . . reducetarians

'According to the Vegan Society,[8] there were three-and-a-half times as many vegans in 2016 [in the UK] as 10 years earlier. The NHS states that more than 1.2 million people in the UK are vegetarian. *And a YouGov survey found that 25% of people in Britain have cut back how much meat they eat* [emphases added]. . . Brian Kateman, the co-founder of the Reducetarian movement,[9] a group committed simply to eating less meat. . . is a self-described pragmatist. He grew up eating steaks and buffalo wings, but as a student decided to go vegetarian. . . . "I'm a utilitarian", he says. "I'm more interested in outcomes than processes. The reason people eat less meat isn't for some badge, some public status, it's because it has a meaningful impact on the world. . . It's about moderation for everyday omnivores". According to the reducetarians, to eat less meat is an accomplishment; but to eat meat occasionally isn't a failure.'[10]

The motivation process: why ask why?

5.1

It is important for marketers to recognise that products can satisfy a range of consumer needs.

To understand motivation is to understand *why* consumers do what they do. Why do some people choose to bungee jump off a bridge (which is close to being an important rite of passage for young Europeans on their gap year visiting New Zealand), while others choose to do gardening for their relaxation,[11] while still others spend their leisure time on social media? Whether to quell the pangs of hunger, as in the case of Andrew and Alexandra, to kill boredom, or to attain some deep spiritual experience, we do everything for a reason – even if we can't always articulate what that reason is. Marketing students are taught that the goal of marketing is to satisfy consumers' needs. However, this insight is of little value unless we can discover *what* those needs are and *why* they exist.

Motivation refers to the processes that cause people to behave as they do. From a *psychological perspective,* motivation occurs when a **need** is aroused that the consumer wishes to satisfy. Once a need has been activated, a state of tension exists that drives the consumer to attempt to reduce or eliminate the need. This need may be *utilitarian* (a desire to achieve some functional or practical benefit, as when Alexandra eats green vegetables for nutritional reasons), or it may be *hedonic* (an experiential need, involving emotional responses or fantasies, as when Andrew thinks longingly about Greek cuisine). The distinction between the two is, however, a matter of degree. The desired end-state is the consumer's **goal**. Marketers try to create products and services that will provide the desired benefits and permit the consumer to reduce this tension.

Does a person even need to be aware of their motivation in order to achieve a goal? The evidence suggests that motives can lurk beneath the surface, and cues in the environment can activate a goal even when we don't know it. The effects of **incidental brand exposure** are now being explored; here are some initial thoughts:

- People who were exposed to a sign in a room of the brand name 'Apple' enhanced their motivation to be different and unique compared to others who saw a sign with the IBM brand name.[12]
- College students who used a 'cute' ice cream scoop to help themselves to ice cream took a larger amount than those who used a plain scoop; the idea was that the whimsical object drove them to be more self-indulgent, even though they weren't aware of this effect.[13]

Whether the need is utilitarian or hedonic, a discrepancy exists between the consumer's present state and some ideal state. This gulf creates a state of tension. The magnitude of this tension determines the urgency the consumer feels to reduce the tension. This degree of arousal is called a 'drive'. A basic need can be satisfied in any number of ways, and the specific path a person chooses is influenced both by their unique set of experiences and by the values instilled by cultural, religious, ethnic or national background. In Alexandra's case, her German upbringing meant that lunch was her mother's home-cooked food, and this would normally have been her main meal of the day. Supper was usually a cold spread of breads, cheeses and cold meats, with soup in the winter or salad in the summer (a meal known as *abendbrot* in German). However, patterns of family eating are changing now in Germany.[14]

These personal and cultural factors combine to create a **want**, which is one manifestation of a need. For example, hunger is a basic need that must be satisfied by all; the lack of food creates a tension state that can be reduced by the intake of such products as paella, bouillabaisse, pasta, cheeses, smoked herring, chocolate biscuits or bean sprouts. The specific route to drive reduction is culturally and individually determined. Once the goal is attained, tension is reduced and the motivation recedes (for the time being). Motivation can be described in terms of its *strength,* or the pull it exerts on the consumer, and its *direction,* or the particular way the consumer attempts to reduce motivational tension.

Motivational strength

The degree to which a person is willing to expend energy to reach one goal as opposed to another reflects their underlying motivation to attain that goal. Many theories have been advanced to explain why people behave the way they do. Most share the basic idea that people have some finite amount of energy that must be directed towards certain goals. A conceptual distinction has been made between goal setting and goal striving.[15] Bagozzi and Dhokalia's modelling of goals has been extended by examining consumers' willingness to *persistently* strive to achieve goals. In a study of assisted reproductive technologies, researchers identified the important interplay between culture and cognition in affecting consumers' persistence in achieving goals – in this case, the highly emotional goal of parenthood.[16]

Biological *vs* learned needs

Early work on motivation ascribed behaviour to *instinct,* the innate patterns of behaviour that are universal in a species. This view is now largely discredited. The existence of an instinct is difficult to prove or disprove. The instinct is inferred from the behaviour it is supposed to explain (this type of circular explanation is called a *tautology*).[17] It is like saying that a consumer buys products that are status symbols because they are motivated to attain status, which is hardly a satisfactory explanation.

Drive theory

Drive theory focuses on biological needs that produce unpleasant states of arousal (e.g. your stomach grumbles during the first lecture of the day – you missed breakfast). We are motivated to reduce the tension caused by this arousal. Tension reduction has been proposed as a basic mechanism governing human behaviour.

In a marketing context, tension refers to the unpleasant state that exists if a person's consumption needs are not fulfilled. A person may be grumpy or unable to concentrate very well if they haven't eaten. Someone may be dejected or angry if they cannot afford that new car they want. This state activates goal-oriented behaviour, which attempts to reduce or eliminate this unpleasant state and return to a balanced one, called **homeostasis**. Some researchers believe that this need to reduce arousal is a basic mechanism that governs

This gym advertises no contract required (so no long-term expensive commitment to obtain membership) and also the ease of online registration to appeal to potential customers keen to pursue healthy activities.

mubus7/Shutterstock

much of our behaviour. Indeed, there is research evidence for the effectiveness of so-called **retail therapy**; apparently the act of shopping restores a sense of personal control over one's environment and as a result can alleviate feelings of sadness.[18]

Those behaviours that are successful in reducing the drive by satisfying the underlying need are strengthened and tend to be repeated. (This *reinforcement* aspect of the learning process will be discussed in Chapter 6.) Your motivation to leave your lecture early to buy a snack would be greater if you hadn't eaten in the previous 24 hours than if you had eaten breakfast only two hours earlier. If you did sneak out and experienced indigestion after, say, wolfing down a packet of crisps, you would be less likely to repeat this behaviour the next time you wanted a snack. One's degree of motivation, then, depends on the distance between one's present state and the goal.

Drive theory, however, runs into difficulties when it tries to explain some facets of human behaviour that run counter to its predictions. People often do things that *increase* a drive state rather than decrease it. For example, people may delay gratification. If you know you are going out for a five-course dinner, you might decide to forgo a snack earlier in the day even though you are hungry at that time. And the most rewarding thing may often be the tension of the drive state itself, rather than its satisfaction.

Expectancy theory

Most explanations of motivation currently focus on cognitive rather than biological factors in order to understand what drives behaviour. **Expectancy theory** suggests that behaviour is largely pulled by expectations of achieving desirable outcomes – *positive incentives* – rather than being pushed from within. We choose one product over another because we expect this choice to have more positive consequences for us. Thus, the term **drive** is used here more loosely to refer to both physical and cognitive, i.e. learned, processes.

Motivational direction

Motives have direction as well as strength. They are goal oriented in that they drive us to satisfy a specific need. Most goals can be reached by a number of routes, and the objective of a company is to convince consumers that the alternative it offers provides the best chance to attain that goal. For example, a consumer who decides that they need a pair of jeans to help them reach their goal of being accepted by others can choose among Levi's, Wranglers, Diesel, Calvin Klein, Pepe, Gap, Hugo Boss, Stone Island and many other alternatives, each of which promises to deliver certain functional as well as symbolic benefits.

Needs *vs* wants

The specific way a need is satisfied depends on the individual's unique history, learning experiences and their cultural environment. A need reflects a basic goal, such as keeping yourself nourished or protected from the elements. The particular form of consumption used to satisfy a need is termed a want. A want is a specific manifestation of a need and represents the pathway for achieving the objective, which in turn depends a lot upon our unique personalities, cultural upbringing and our observations about how others we know satisfy the same need. Therefore, personal and cultural factors come into play at this point. For example, two classmates may feel their stomachs rumbling during a lunchtime lecture. If neither person has eaten since the night before, the strength of their respective needs (hunger) would be about the same. However, the way each person goes about satisfying this need might be quite different. The first person may be a vegetarian like Alexandra, who fantasises about large bowls of salad, whereas the second person like Andrew might be equally aroused by the prospect of a large plateful of Greek meatballs in tomato sauce. However, in some cases we don't even know we have a 'want' until we can no longer have it.

We can be motivated to satisfy either utilitarian or hedonic needs. When we focus on a *utilitarian need,* we emphasise the objective, tangible attributes of products, such as miles per gallon in a car, the amount of fat, calories and protein in a cheeseburger or the durability of a pair of blue jeans. *Hedonic needs* are subjective and experiential; here we might look to a product to meet our needs for excitement, self-confidence or fantasy – perhaps to escape the mundane or routine aspects of life.[19] Many items satisfy our hedonic needs. Luxury brands, in particular, thrive when they offer the promise of pleasure to the user. Of course, consumers can be motivated to purchase a product because it provides *both* types of benefits. For example, a mink coat might be bought because it feels soft against the skin, because it keeps one warm through the long cold winters of northern Europe and because it has a luxurious image. But, again, the distinction tends to hide more than it reveals, because functionality can bring great pleasure to people and is an important value in the modern world.[20] Indeed, recent research on novel consumption experiences indicates that even when we choose to do unusual things (like eating bacon ice cream or staying in a freezing ice hotel), we may do so because we have what the authors term a **productivity orientation**. This refers to a continual striving to use time constructively: trying new things is a way to check them off our checklist of experiences we want to achieve before moving on to others.[21]

Motivational conflicts

5.2

Consumers experience different kinds of motivational conflicts that can impact their purchase decisions.

A goal has *valence,* which means that it can be positive or negative. A positively valued goal is one towards which consumers direct their behaviour; they are motivated to *approach* the goal and will seek out products that will help them to reach it. However, not all behaviour is motivated by the desire to approach a goal. As we will see in the discussion of negative reinforcement (Chapter 6), consumers may instead be motivated to *avoid* a negative outcome.[22] They will structure their purchases or consumption activities to reduce the chances of attaining this end result. For example, many consumers work hard to avoid rejection, a negative goal. They will stay away from products that they associate with social disapproval. Products such as deodorants and mouthwash frequently rely on consumers' negative motivation by depicting the onerous social consequences of underarm odour or bad breath.

Because a purchase decision can involve more than one source of motivation, consumers often find themselves in situations where different motives, both positive and negative, conflict with one another.[23] Because marketers are attempting to satisfy consumers' needs, they can also be helpful by providing possible solutions to these dilemmas. As shown in Figure 5.1, three general types of conflicts can occur: approach–approach; approach–avoidance; and avoidance–avoidance.

Approach–approach conflict

In an **approach–approach conflict**, a person must choose between two desirable alternatives. As a student, Alexandra might be torn between going home for the holidays or going on a skiing trip with friends. Or, she might have to choose between two pairs of fashionable boots.

The **theory of cognitive dissonance** is based on the premise that people have a need for order and consistency in their lives and that a state of tension is created when beliefs or behaviours conflict with one another. The conflict that arises when choosing between two alternatives may be resolved through a process of *cognitive dissonance reduction,* where people are motivated to reduce this inconsistency (or dissonance) and thus eliminate an unpleasant tension.[24]

Post-decision dissonance occurs when there is a psychological inconsistency between two or more beliefs or behaviours. It often occurs when a consumer must make a choice between two

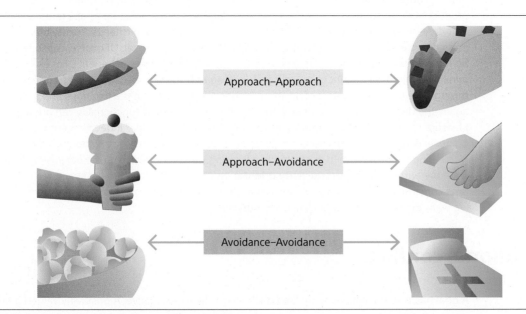

Figure 5.1 Three types of motivational conflict

products, where both alternatives usually possess both good and bad qualities. By choosing one product and not the other, the person gets the bad qualities of the chosen product and loses out on the good qualities of the one not chosen.

This loss creates an unpleasant, dissonant state that the person is motivated to reduce. People tend to convince themselves, after the fact, that the choice they made was the right one by finding additional reasons to support the alternative they chose, or perhaps by 'discovering' flaws with the option they did not choose (sometimes we call this 'rationalisation'). A marketer can resolve an approach–approach conflict by bundling several benefits together. For example, many low-calorie products claim that they have 'all the taste' *and* 'half the calories' (e.g. Müller Light Yoghurts), while being 'deliciously thick and creamy tasting and still fat free', thus allowing the consumer to avoid having to choose between better taste and fewer calories.

Approach–avoidance conflict

Many of the products and services we desire have negative consequences attached to them as well. We may feel guilty or ostentatious when buying a status-laden product such as a fur coat, or we might feel like a glutton when contemplating a box of chocolates. When we desire a goal but wish to avoid it at the same time, an **approach–avoidance conflict** exists. Some solutions to these conflicts include the proliferation of fake furs, which eliminate guilt about harming animals to make a fashion statement; and the success of low-calorie and diet foods, such as those produced by WeightWatchers, that promise good food without the calories (https://www.weight watchers.com/uk/). Some marketers counter consumer resistance to

This ad points to the negative consequences of drug addiction for those tempted to start.

Contraband Collection/ Alamy Stock Photo

over-consumption and spending by promising more (benefits) from less, whereas other marketers try to overcome guilt by convincing consumers that they deserve luxuries. Sometimes consumers go outside the conventional marketplace to satisfy their needs, wants and desires – for instance, drag-racing in Moscow where young Russian car fanatics fulfil their drive for thrill-seeking outside the law.[25]

Avoidance–avoidance conflict

Sometimes consumers find themselves 'caught between a rock and a hard place'. They may face a choice between two undesirable alternatives, for instance the option of either investing more money into an old car with more repairs or buying a new one. Marketers frequently address an **avoidance–avoidance conflict** with messages that stress the unforeseen benefits of choosing one option (e.g. by emphasising special credit plans to ease the pain of new car payments).

Marketing opportunity
The popular 'flexitarian' trend continues to sweep the UK

'As the popular "flexitarian" trend continues to sweep the UK, major retailers such as Tesco and Marks & Spencer are hoping that even occasional carnivores might consider swapping their traditional turkey for an exotic vegan or vegetarian centrepiece. Flexitarianism has been one of the most striking food trends of 2017, with one in three people trying to reduce their meat intake. According to the Vegan Society, more than half of UK adults are now adopting "vegan buying behaviour", while the number of full-time vegans in the UK has grown four-fold in the past 10 years. . . [At Tesco] Derek Sarno has overseen the supermarket's biggest ever vegan and vegetarian Christmas offering this year [December 2017], which has doubled the number of festive centrepieces compared with last year, including, for the first time, two vegan dinners – turmeric-spiced cauliflower wellington and, for those who cannot let go of their nut roast, a pecan and peanut roast with maple-roasted carrot and parsnip. . . Marks & Spencer is showcasing more meat-free Christmas dinner main courses than meat-based ones, after its vegetarian range sold out in record time last year [2016]. . . and its butternut and sweet potato rosti became its bestselling vegetarian product ever. . . [At the online retailer Ocado] vegan cheeseboards include a Christmas platter from the Greek manufacturer Violife that is made up of three vegan cheese blocks – blu, cranberry after-dinner and mature. It is selling out fast in Ocado and Sainsbury's, and will be followed by a vegan feta next year [2018]. Finally, for those who fancy a tipple, the vegan version of Baileys Irish Cream, called Baileys Almande and made with almond milk, was recently launched in the US and can now be snapped up in the UK through Whole Foods Markets and thegoodnessproject.co.uk.'[26]

How can we classify consumer needs?

Another approach to classifying needs and wants (apart from utilitarian versus hedonic, as discussed above) is to consider two basic types of need. People are born with a need for certain elements necessary to maintain life, such as food, water, air and shelter. These are called *biogenic needs.* People have many other needs, however, that are not innate. We acquire *psychogenic needs* as we become members of a specific culture. These include the need for status, power, affiliation and so on. Psychogenic needs reflect the priorities of a culture, and their effect on behaviour will vary in different environments. For example, an Italian consumer may be driven to devote a good portion of their income to products that permit them to display their individuality, whereas their Scandinavian counterpart may work equally hard to ensure that they do not stand out too much from their group.

This distinction is revealing because it shows how difficult it is to distinguish needs from wants. How can we tell what part of the motivation is a psychogenic need and what part is a want? Both are profoundly formed by culture, so the distinction is problematic at best. As for the biogenic needs, we know from anthropology that satisfaction of these needs leads to some of the most symbolically rich and culturally based activities of humankind. The ways we want to eat, dress, drink and provide shelter are far more interesting to marketers than our need to do so. Hence, the idea of satisfaction of biogenic needs is more or less a given thing for marketing and consumer research because it is, on the most basic level, nothing more than a simple prerequisite for us to be here. Beyond that level, and of much greater interest (and challenge) to marketers, is a concept embedded in culture, such as wants.[27]

Some classifications of consumer needs

Much research has been done on classifying human needs. On the one hand, some psycho-logists have tried to define a universal inventory of needs that could be traced systematically to explain virtually all behaviour. One such effort, developed by Henry Murray, delineates a set of 20 psychogenic needs that (sometimes in combination) result in specific behaviours. These needs include such dimensions as *autonomy* (being independent), *defendance* (defending the self against criticism) and even *play* (engaging in pleasurable activities).[28]

Murray's needs structure serves as the basis for a number of widely used personality tests, such as the Thematic Apperception Technique (TAT) and the Edwards' Personal Preference Schedule (EPPS). In the TAT, test subjects are shown four to six ambiguous pictures and are asked to write answers to four questions about the pictures. These questions are: (1) What is happening? (2) What has led up to this situation? (3) What is being thought? (4) What will happen? Each answer is then analysed for references to certain needs and scored whenever that need is mentioned. The theory behind the test is that people will freely project their own subconscious needs onto the stimulus. By getting their responses to the picture, you are really getting at the person's true needs for achievement or affiliation, or whatever other need may be dominant. Murray believed that everyone has the same basic set of needs, but that individuals differ in their priority ranking of these needs.[29]

Other motivational approaches have focused on specific needs and their ramifications for behaviour. For example, individuals with a high *need for achievement* strongly value personal accomplishment.[30] They place a premium on products and services that signify success because these consumption items provide feedback about the realisation of their goals. These consumers are good prospects for products that provide evidence of their achievement. One study of working women found that those who were high in achievement motivation were more likely to choose clothing they considered business-like, and less likely to be interested in clothing that accentuated their femininity.[31] Some other important needs that are relevant to consumer behaviour include the following:

- *Need for affiliation* (to be in the company of other people):[32] this need is relevant to products and services that are 'consumed' in groups and alleviate loneliness, such as team sports, bars and shopping centres.
- *Need for power* (to control one's environment):[33] many products and services allow consumers to feel that they have mastery over their surroundings, ranging from cars with 'souped up' engines and loud sound systems that impose the driver's musical tastes on others, to luxury resorts that promise to respond to every whim of their pampered guests.

- *Need for uniqueness* (to assert one's individual identity):[34] products can satisfy this need by pledging to accentuate a consumer's distinctive qualities. For example, Cachet perfume claims to be 'as individual as you are'.

Maslow's hierarchy of needs

Psychologist Abraham Maslow originally developed his influential **hierarchy of needs** to understand personal growth and how people attain spiritual '**peak experiences**'. Marketers later adapted his work to understand consumer motivations.[35] Maslow proposed a hierarchy of biogenic and psychogenic needs that specifies certain levels of motives. This *hierarchical* structure implies that the order of development is fixed – that is, we must attain a certain level before we activate a need for the next, higher one. Marketers embraced this perspective because it (indirectly) specifies certain types of product benefits people might look for, depending on their stage of mental or spiritual development or on their economic situation.[36] However, as we shall see, it contains many problems, and we devote space to it here because it is a 'standard' in marketing knowledge rather than because we are entirely convinced of its theoretical and practical value.

Maslow's levels are summarised in Figure 5.2. At each level, different priorities exist in terms of the product benefits a consumer is looking for. Ideally, an individual progresses up the hierarchy until their dominant motivation is a focus on 'ultimate' goals, such as justice and beauty. Unfortunately, this state is difficult to achieve (at least on a regular basis); most of us have to be satisfied with occasional glimpses, or *peak experiences.* One study of men aged 49 to 60 found respondents engaged in three types of activities to attain self-fulfilment: (1) sport and physical activity; (2) community and charity; and (3) building and renovating.

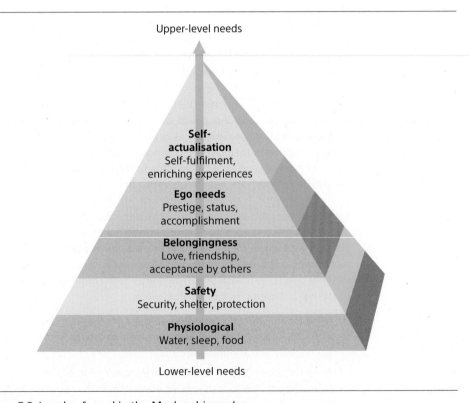

Figure 5.2 Levels of need in the Maslow hierarchy

Regardless of whether these activities related to their professional work, these so-called *magnetic points* gradually took the place of those that were not as fulfilling.[37]

The implication of Maslow's hierarchy is that one must first satisfy basic needs before progressing up the ladder (i.e. a starving man is not interested in status symbols, friendship or self-fulfilment).[38] This suggests that consumers value different product attributes depending upon what is currently available to them.

The application of this hierarchy by marketers has been somewhat simplistic, especially as the same product or activity can satisfy a number of different needs. One example would be gardening, which has been found to satisfy needs at every level of the hierarchy:[39]

- *Physiological*: 'I like to work in the soil'.
- *Safety*: 'I feel safe in the garden'.
- *Social*: 'I can share my produce with others'.
- *Esteem*: 'I can create something of beauty'.
- *Self-actualisation*: 'My garden gives me a sense of peace'.

Another problem with taking Maslow's hierarchy too literally is that it is culture-bound. The assumptions of the hierarchy may be restricted to a highly rational, materialistic and individualistic Western culture. People in other cultures may question the order of the levels as specified. A religious person who has taken a vow of celibacy, for example, would not necessarily agree that physiological needs must be satisfied before self-fulfilment can occur. Neither do all people in Western cultures seem to live according to Maslow's hierarchy. In fact, spiritual survival might be seen as a stronger motivator than physical survival, as can be seen from patriots or freedom fighters giving their lives for the idea of nation, or religious fanatics for their beliefs.[40]

Similarly, many Asian cultures value the welfare of the group (belongingness needs) more highly than the needs of the individual (esteem needs). The point is that Maslow's hierarchy, while widely applied in marketing, is only helpful to marketers in so far as it reminds us that consumers may have different need priorities in different consumption situations and at different stages in their lives – not because it exactly specifies a consumer's progression up the ladder of needs. It also does not take account of the cultural formation of needs.

Satisfying needs via social media

Our online behaviours can also satisfy needs at different levels of Maslow's hierarchy, especially when we participate in social networks such as Facebook. **Web**-based companies can build loyalty if they keep these needs in mind when they design their offerings:

- We satisfy physiological needs when we use the Web to research topics such as nutrition or medical questions.
- The Web enables users to pool information and satisfy safety needs when they call attention to bad practices, flawed products, or even dangerous predators.
- Profile pages on Facebook and MySpace let users define themselves as individuals.
- Online communities, blogs and social networks provide recognition and achievement to those who cultivate a reputation for being especially helpful or expert in some subject.
- Users can seek help from others and connect with people who have similar tastes and interests.
- Access to invitation-only communities provides status.
- Spiritually based online communities can provide guidance to troubled people.[41]

Consumer involvement

The way we evaluate and choose a product depends on our degree of involvement with the product, the marketing message and/or the purchase situation.

Do consumers form strong relationships with products and services? People can become pretty attached to products. As we have seen, a consumer's motivation to attain a goal increases their desire to expend the effort necessary to acquire the products or services they believe will be instrumental in satisfying that goal. However, not everyone is motivated to the same extent – one person might be convinced they can't live without the latest Apple iPhone, while another is perfectly happy with their three year-old Samsung. Involvement can help us understand *why* different consumers may approach the same choice situation from very different perspectives.

Involvement is defined as 'a person's perceived relevance of the object based on their inherent needs, values, and interests'.[42] The word *object* is used in the generic sense and refers to a product (or a brand), an advertisement or a purchase situation. Consumers can find involvement in all these *objects.* Figure 5.3 shows that because involvement is a motivational construct, different antecedents can trigger it. These factors can be something about the person, something about the object, or something about the situation.

Any or all of these factors can combine to determine the consumer's motivation to process product-related information at a given point in time. When consumers are intent on doing what they can to satisfy a need, they will be motivated to pay attention and process any information felt to be relevant to achieving their goals. On the other hand, a person may not bother to pay any attention to the same information if it is not seen as relevant to satisfying some need. Alexandra, for instance, who prides herself on her knowledge of the environment and green issues, may read everything she can find about the subject, while another person may skip over this information without giving it a second thought.

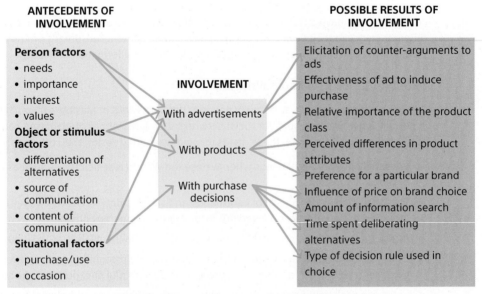

INVOLVEMENT = f (Person, Situation, Object)

The level of involvement may be influenced by one or more of these factors.
Interactions among persons, situation, and object factors are likely to occur.

Figure 5.3 Conceptualising components of involvement

Involvement can therefore be viewed as the motivation to process information.[43] To the degree that there is a perceived linkage between a consumer's needs, goals or values and product knowledge, the consumer will be motivated to pay attention to product information. When relevant knowledge is activated in memory, a motivational state is created that drives behaviour (e.g. shopping). As felt involvement with a product increases, the consumer devotes more attention to ads related to the product, exerts more cognitive effort to understand these ads and focuses more attention on the product-related information in them.[44] However, this kind of 'rational' involvement may be the exception rather than the rule.[45]

Figure 5.4 summarises the relationship between involvement and our three types of decision-making (see also Chapter 8 on decision-making). Not surprisingly, we tend to find higher levels of involvement in product categories that demand a big investment of money (such as houses) or self-esteem (for example, clothing) and lower levels for mundane categories such as household cleaners.[46] Still, bear in mind that virtually anything can qualify as highly involving to some people.

Cult products such as those made by Apple or Harley-Davidson, or football clubs such as Manchester United, Paris Saint-Germain, Bayern Munich, Juventus, A.C. Milan, Real Madrid or Barcelona, command fierce consumer loyalty, devotion and maybe even worship by consumers.[47] A large majority of consumers agree that they are willing to pay more for a brand when they feel a personal connection to the company.[48] And sometimes their feelings can come close to **brand addiction**, defined as 'a consumer's psychological state that involves mental and behavioral preoccupation with a particular brand, driven by uncontrollable urges to possess the brand's products, and involving positive affectivity and gratification'.[49]

Levels of involvement

We can think of a person's degree of involvement as a continuum, ranging from absolute lack of interest in a marketing stimulus at one end to obsession at the other. The type of information processing that will occur thus depends on the consumer's level of involvement. It can range from *simple processing,* where only the basic features of a message are considered, all the way to *elaboration,* where the incoming information is linked to one's pre-existing knowledge system.[50]

Inertia

Consumption at the low end of the involvement continuum is characterised by **inertia**, where decisions are made out of habit because the consumer lacks the motivation to consider alternatives (see also how inertia and brand loyalty fit into habitual decision-making, in Chapter 8). At the high end of involvement, we can expect to find the type of passionate

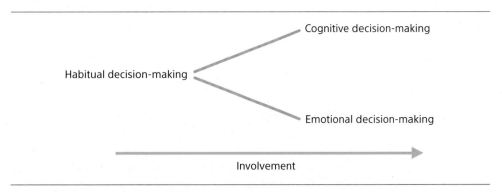

Figure 5.4 Involvement and decision-making

intensity reserved for people and objects that carry great meaning for the individual. For the most part, a consumer's involvement level with products falls somewhere in the middle, and the marketing strategist must determine the relative level of importance to understand how much elaboration of product information will occur.

When consumers are truly involved with a product, an ad or a website, they enter what has been called a **flow state**. This state is the Holy Grail of Web designers, who want to create sites that are so entrancing that the surfer loses all track of time as they become engrossed in the site's contents. The Web is 'a part of the internet accessed through a graphical user interface and containing documents often connected by hyperlinks' (www.merriam-webster.com/dictionary/worldwideweb). Flow is an optimal experience characterised by:

- a sense of playfulness
- a feeling of being in control
- concentration and highly focused attention
- mental enjoyment of the activity for its own sake
- a distorted sense of time
- a match between the challenge at hand and one's skills.[51]

Types of involvement

As previously defined, involvement can take many forms. It can be cognitive, as when a 'web-head' is motivated to learn all they can about the latest spec of a new multimedia PC, or emotional, as when the thought of a new Armani suit gives a clothes horse goose pimples.[52] Further, the very act of buying the Armani suit may be very involving for people who are passionately devoted to shopping. To complicate matters further, advertisements, such as those produced for Nike or Adidas, may themselves be involving for some reason (for example, because they make us laugh, cry, or inspire us to work harder). It seems that involvement is a fuzzy concept, because it overlaps with other things and means different things to different people. Indeed, the consensus is that there are actually several broad types of involvement related to the product, the message or the perceiver.[53]

Product involvement

Product involvement is related to a consumer's level of interest in a particular product. Many sales promotions are designed to increase this type of involvement. Perhaps the most powerful way to enhance product involvement is to invite consumers to play a role in designing or personalising what they buy. **Mass customisation** is the personalisation of products and services for individual customers at a mass-production price.[54] Improved manufacturing techniques in many industries are allowing companies to produce made-to-order products for many customers at a time. This design revolution recognises the changing role of digital technologies in consumers' lives, where the emphasis is as much on the form as on the function of these IT products.[55]

Marketing opportunity

When we have the opportunity to personalise a product, our involvement increases because the item reflects our unique preferences. But how about when we build the product ourselves? Researchers term this the **IKEA Effect** – self-made (or at least self-assembled) products including furniture, Lego and even origami enhance the value we attach to them because our own labour is involved.[56]

When a consumer is highly involved with a specific product, this means he or she exhibits **brand loyalty**: repeat purchasing behaviour that reflects a conscious decision to continue buying the same brand.[57] Note that this definition states that the consumer not only buys the brand on a regular basis, but that he or she also has a strong positive attitude toward it rather than simply buying it out of habit. In fact, we often find that a brand-loyal consumer has more than simply a positive attitude; frequently she or he is passionate about the product. 'True-blue' users react more vehemently when a company alters, redesigns or eliminates a favourite brand. One simple test to find out if you're brand loyal: if the store is temporarily out of your favourite brand, will you buy a different product or wait until you can get your first choice?

Although everyone wants to cultivate brand-loyal customers, there is a wrinkle that sometimes confounds even the most effective marketers. We often engage in *brand switching*, even if our current brand satisfies our needs. When researchers for British brewer Bass Export studied the American beer market, they discovered that many drinkers have a repertoire of two to six favourite brands rather than one clear favourite.[58] However, drinking trends are changing, with a growth in low- and no-alcohol lifestyles – especially among the younger generation of consumers (aged 16 to 24), a quarter of whom report not drinking.[59]

Marketing opportunity
Cheers? No thanks! Low- and no-alcohol lifestyle booms

'About 5 million people will drink their first beer or glass of wine in a month next week as "dry January" comes to an end. But for an increasing number of people it will be an entirely dry year, because low- and no-alcohol is now a fast-growing lifestyle choice. Sales of beer and cider with less than 1.2% alcohol grew by nearly 30% last year compared with 2015, while demand for low- and no-alcohol wine was up 8%, according to analysis firm Kantar Worldpanel. The trend is creating a new market for major drinks companies, craft brewers and retailers.

While non-boozers were once limited to the grim choice of a decidedly uncool Kaliber, a juice or a lime soda, there are now dozens of options on the market. Budweiser launched its alcohol-free beer in the UK in November, Heineken unveiled a no-alcohol version of its beer last year, while Tesco introduced a choice of five wines with less than 0.5% alcohol before Christmas. Next month discounter Aldi is joining the trend, putting two low-alcohol wines on its shelves.

Tesco's. . . wine expert Alexandra Runciman, says: "Consumption of alcohol in the UK is down by 18% over the last decade and we're seeing more customers looking for a quality wine-drinking experience without the alcohol." Drinking rates among British adults are at their lowest since 2005. A recent Office for National Statistics survey found the proportion who drank alcohol at least once a week declined from 64.2% to 56.9% last year. Almost 100,000 people officially signed up to the "dry January" challenge this year – about 40% up on 2017 – while millions more joined in unofficially. The trend is particularly prevalent among young people: more than a quarter of 16- to 24-year-olds do not drink.

The UK's bestselling low-alcohol beer is Becks Blue, but . . . British craft brewers, such as Big Drop and Nirvana, which both produce beers with less than 0.5% alcohol, are helping drive the trend because they focus on flavour. "We do a lot of beer tastings and people say 'goodness me it tastes like beer'. They are extremely surprised how good it can be. They used to boil the beer to remove the alcohol and it wasn't good. But people have come up with modern ways of removing the alcohol that keeps the flavour", says Stuart Elkington, founder of specialist online store Dry Drinker.

Andy Crossan, consumer insight director at Kantar Worldpanel, says the big drinks firms and brands are having to adapt as young people spearhead change. "With 20 million adults in Great Britain happy to consider low- and non-alcoholic drinks, and with a number of recent high-profile launches in the zero-alcohol market, we expect this part of the alcohol industry to continue to thrive", he says. And there are signs that the 'no and low' trend is moving beyond beer and wine. Diageo, which makes Smirnoff and Johnnie Walker, last year bought a stake in Seedlip, a start-up company producing an alcohol-free spirit designed to be drunk instead of gin in cocktails. It was the drink conglomerate's first investment in a non-alcoholic drinks company in its 258-year history.'[60]

Sometimes, it seems we simply like to try new things – we crave variety as a form of stimulation or to reduce boredom. **Variety-seeking**, the desire to choose new alternatives over more familiar ones, even influences us to switch from our favourite products to ones we like less. This can occur even before we become *satiated,* or tired, of our favourite. Research supports the idea that we are willing to trade enjoyment for variety because the unpredictability *itself* is rewarding.[61]

We're especially likely to look for variety when we are in a good mood, or when there isn't a lot of other stuff going on.[62] So, even though we have favourites, we still like to sample other possibilities. However, when the decision situation is ambiguous, or when there is little information about competing brands, we tend to opt for the safe choice.

Message involvement

Message-response involvement (also known as *advertising involvement*), refers to the consumer's interest in processing marketing communications.[63] Note Jay-Z's celebrated campaign to promote his autobiographical *Decoded* book, for instance. The agency Droga5 created a national scavenger hunt when it hid all 320 pages of the book (mostly blown-up versions) in outdoor spots in 13 cities that somehow related to the text on each page (e.g. on cheeseburger wrappers in New York). Coldplay took a leaf out of Droga5's book to promote its album *Ghost Stories.* The band hid lyric sheets inside ghost stories in libraries around the world and gave out clues on Twitter.[64] This represents an emerging way to engage consumers: In **alternate reality games (ARGs)**, thousands of people participate in a fictional story or competition to solve a mystery. As these novel scavenger hunts illustrate, media vehicles possess different qualities that influence our motivation to pay attention to what they tell us, known as message involvement. Print is a *high-involvement medium* (whether it appears on a 'dead tree' or in an e-book). The reader actively processes the information and (if desired) he or she is able to pause and reflect on it before turning the page.[65] In contrast, television is a *low-involvement medium* because it requires a passive viewer who exerts relatively little control (remote-control 'zapping' notwithstanding) over content. In fact, some messages (including really-well-made advertisements) are so involving that they trigger a stage of **narrative transportation**, where people become immersed in the storyline (much like the flow state we described earlier). One study showed that people who are feeling lucky engage in this process when they look at an advertisement for a lottery; once immersed, it is hard to distract them from the message.[66] (See Chapter 7 for a discussion of the role of message characteristics in changing attitudes.)

Strategies to increase message involvement

Although consumers differ in their levels of involvement with respect to a product message, marketers do not have to simply sit back and hope for the best. By being aware of some basic factors that increase or decrease attention, they can take steps to increase the likelihood that product information will get through. A marketer can boost a person's motivation to process relevant information via one or more of the following techniques:[67]

- *Use novel stimuli,* such as unusual cinematography, sudden silences or unexpected movements, in commercials.[68]
- *Use prominent stimuli,* such as loud music and fast action, to capture attention in commercials. In print formats, larger ads increase attention. Also, viewers look longer at coloured pictures than at black-and-white ones.
- *Include celebrity endorsers* to generate higher interest in commercials. As we'll see in Chapter 7, people process more information when it comes from someone they admire.

- *Provide value* that customers appreciate.[69]
- *Invent new media platforms* to grab attention. An Australian firm created hand stamps that nightclubs used to identify paying customers; the stamps included logos or ad messages so party-goers' hands became an advertising platform.[70]
- *Encourage viewers to think about actually using the product.* If a person can imagine this product, he or she is more likely to want to obtain the real thing.[71]
- *Create* **spectacles** where the message is itself a form of entertainment.[72]
- *Let customers make the messages* – **consumer-generated content**, where freelancers and fans film their own commercials for favourite products, is another important marketing trend. The explosion in consumer-generated media means that this reliance on word of mouth, over other forms of referral, looks set to increase.[73] 'Social media advertising is big business.'[74] This important trend helps to define the so-called era of Web 2.0; the rebirth of the internet as a social, interactive medium from its original roots as a form of one-way transmission from producers to consumers. This practice creates a high degree of *message–response involvement* (also called *advertising involvement*), which refers to the consumer's interest in processing marketing communications.[75]

The quest to heighten message involvement is fuelling the rapid growth of **interactive mobile marketing**, where consumers participate in real-time promotional campaigns via their smartphones, usually by text-messaging entries to on-air TV contests. These strategies are very popular in the UK, for example, where revenue from phone and text-messaging services for TV programmes brings in almost half-a-billion dollars (over 680 million euros) a year. In the past, viewers have sent over 500,000 text-message votes within two days during the reality show *Big Brother*.[76]

Situational involvement

Situational involvement refers to differences that may occur when buying the same object for different contexts. Here the person may perceive a great deal of social risk or none at all. For example, when you want to impress someone you may try to buy a brand or a product with a certain image that you think reflects good taste. When you have to buy a gift for someone in an obligatory situation, such as a wedding gift for a cousin you do not really like, you may not care what image the gift portrays. Or you may actually pick something cheap that reflects your desire to distance yourself from that cousin. Again, some smart retailers are realising the value of increasing purchase situation involvement by appealing to hedonic shoppers who are looking to be entertained or otherwise engaged, in addition to just 'buying stuff'.[77] (See also the creation of themed retailing venues and other strategies in Chapter 2.)

Many of us experience heightened purchase situation involvement when we log on to our favourite social media sites. Some of the most successful new applications involve some form of **social game**: a multi-player, competitive, goal-oriented activity with defined rules of engagement and online connectivity among a community of players.

Brands can utilise social games for marketing in several ways. When the Microsoft search engine Bing ran an ad that offered players the chance to earn *FarmVille* cash for becoming a fan of Bing on Facebook, the brand won 425,000 new fans in the first day.[78] One specific tactic we will see more of in the booming world of social games is **transactional advertising**, which rewards players if they respond to a request.[79] The offers can be for *virtual goods* (which players can use in the game or offer as gifts to friends), *currency* (used to advance in the game) or *codes* (used to unlock prizes and limited-access player experiences).

Television is considered a low-involvement medium because it requires a passive viewer who exerts relatively little control. This is in contrast to other types of alternative reality games (as discussed above) which involve more viewer interactions in order to generate greater degrees of message involvement.

Eric Audras/ONOKY - Photononstop/Alamy Stock Photo

Lifestyles, consumer identity and consumption choices

5.4

A lifestyle defines a pattern of consumption that reflects a person's choices of how to spend his or her time and money, and these choices are essential to defining consumer identity.

Consumers choose products, services and activities that help them define a unique *lifestyle.* This section first explores how marketers approach the issue of lifestyle and how they use information about these consumption choices to tailor products and communications to individual lifestyle segments, and second how marketers use **psychographics** to obtain a more nuanced picture of consumer behaviour.

Are you an **e-sports** fan?[80] Millions of people watch e-sports on television.[81] Consumers who choose to spend hours watching their heroes play videogames are making a choice – how to spend their time? how to spend their money? Each of us makes similar choices every day and often two quite similar people in terms of basic categories such as gender, age, income and place of residence still prefer to spend their time and money in markedly different ways. We often see this strong variation among students at the same university, even though many of them come from similar backgrounds. A typical university student may dress much like his friends, hang out in the same places and like the same foods, yet still indulge a passion for marathon running, stamp collecting or jazz. According to *The Urban Dictionary,* some of the undergraduates or postgraduates at your university may fall into one of these categories: metro, hasher or emo.[82]

Lifestyle: who we are, what we do

In traditional societies, class, caste, village or family largely dictate a person's consumption options. In a modern consumer society, however, people are freer to select the products, services and activities that define themselves and, in turn, create a social identity they communicate to others. Our choice of goods and services makes a statement about who we are and about the types of people with whom we wish to identify – and even some whom we wish to avoid. **Lifestyle** refers to a pattern of consumption that reflects a person's choices about how they spend time and money, but in many instances it also refers to the attitudes and values attached to these behavioural patterns. Many of the factors discussed in this book, such as a person's self-concept, reference group and social class, are used as 'raw ingredients' to fashion a unique lifestyle. In an economic sense, your lifestyle represents the way you elect to allocate income, both in terms of relative allocations to different products and services and to specific alternatives within these categories.[83] Other somewhat similar distinctions describe consumers in terms of their broad patterns of consumption, such as people who devote a high proportion of their total expenditure to food, or advanced technology or to such information-intensive goods as entertainment and education. Often, these allocations create a new kind of status system based less on income than on accessibility to information about goods and how these goods function as social markers.[84]

Lifestyles may be considered as group identities. Marketers use demographic and economic approaches in tracking changes in broad societal priorities, but these approaches do not begin to embrace the symbolic nuances that separate lifestyle groups. Lifestyle is more than the allocation of discretionary income. It is a statement about who one is in society and who one is not. Group identities, whether of hobbyists, athletes, amateur footballers (e.g. Bobby's friends in Chapter 9) or drug users, take their form based on acts of expressive symbolism. The self-definitions of group members are derived from the common symbol system to which the group is dedicated. Such self-definitions have been described by a number of terms, including *lifestyle, public taste, consumer group, symbolic community* and *status culture*.[85] Many people in similar social and economic circumstances may follow the same general consumption pattern. Still, each person provides a unique 'twist' to this pattern, which allows them to inject some individuality into a chosen lifestyle.

Lifestyles don't last for ever, and are not set in stone. Unlike deep-seated values, people's tastes and preferences evolve over time, so that consumption patterns that were viewed favourably at one point in time may be laughed at or sneered at a few years later. If you don't believe that, simply think back to what you, your friends and your family were wearing, doing and eating five or ten years ago: where *did* you find those clothes? Why was prawn cocktail or Black Forest gateau so popular at dinner parties in the 1980s? Because people's attitudes regarding physical fitness, social activism, sex roles for men and women, the importance of home life and family and many other things do change, it is vital for marketers to monitor the social landscape continually to try to anticipate where these changes will lead. An example of this is given above, in the discussion of how low- or no-alcohol consumption is a new lifestyle choice being adopted by an increasing number of UK consumers (especially 16–24 year-olds).[86]

A study of clubbing (or 'raves') illustrates how a social activity is co-created by producers and consumers. These experiences started in the UK as spontaneous gatherings in empty warehouses. Although these events are banned in many places, the consumer researchers showed how the promoters and the clubbers cooperate with local authorities to make possible this 'contained illegality'. For example, by regulating the drugs (particularly Ecstasy) that are consumed and instituting safeguards to prevent violence.
Fotograferen.net/Alamy Stock Photo

Lifestyle marketing

The lifestyle concept is one of the most widely used in modern marketing activities. It provides a way to understand consumers' everyday needs and wants, and a mechanism to allow a product or service to be positioned in terms of how it will allow a person to pursue a desired lifestyle. A **lifestyle marketing perspective** recognises that people sort themselves into groups on the basis of the things they like to do, how they like to spend their leisure time and how they choose to spend their disposable income.[87] These choices, in turn, create opportunities for market segmentation strategies that recognise the potency of a consumer's chosen lifestyle in determining both the types of products purchased and the specific brands more likely to appeal to a designated lifestyle segment. The growing number of niche magazines and websites that cater to specialist interests reflects the spectrum of choices available to us in today's society. The downside of this is obvious to the newspaper industry: several major papers have already had to shut down their print editions because people consume most of their information online; and many surviving newspapers have put up paywalls to allow them to charge readers for accessing their online editions. In the UK, *The Guardian* remains a rare exception to this trend within the British newspaper industry.

5.5

It can often be more useful to identify *patterns* of consumption than know about *individual* purchases when organisations craft a lifestyle marketing strategy.

A goal of lifestyle marketing is to allow consumers to pursue their chosen ways to enjoy their lives and express their social identities. For this reason, a key aspect of this strategy is to focus on people who use products in desirable social settings. The desire to associate a product with a specific social situation is a long-standing one for advertisers, whether they include the product in a round of golf, a family barbecue or a night at a glamorous club surrounded by the hip-hop elite.[88] Thus, people, products, and settings combine to express a *consumption style,* as Figure 5.5 illustrates.

Product complementarity and co-branding strategies

We get a clearer picture of how people use products to define lifestyles when we see how they make choices in a variety of product categories. A lifestyle marketing perspective implies that we must look at *patterns of behaviour* to understand consumers. As one study noted, 'All goods carry meaning, but none by itself. . . The meaning is in the relations between all the goods, just as music is in the relations marked out by the sounds and not in any one note'.[89] Indeed,

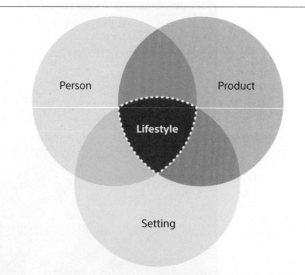

Figure 5.5 Consumption styles

many products and services do seem to 'go together', usually because the same types of people tend to select them. In many cases, products do not seem to 'make sense' if companion products don't accompany them, or are incongruous in the presence of other products that have a very different personality (e.g. a Chippendale chair in a high-tech office or Lucky Strike cigarettes with a solid-gold lighter).

An important part of lifestyle marketing, therefore, is to identify the set of products and services that consumers associate with a specific lifestyle. In fact, research evidence suggests that even a relatively unattractive product becomes more appealing when consumers link it with other products that they do like.[90] The meshing of objects from many different categories to express a single lifestyle idea is at the heart of many consumption decisions, including coordinating an outfit for a big day (shoes, garments, fragrance, etc.), decorating a room (tables, carpet, wallpaper, etc.), and designing a restaurant (menu, ambiance, waitperson uniforms, etc.). Many people today evaluate products not just in terms of function, but also in terms of how well their design coordinates with other objects and furnishings.

Marketers who understand these cross-category relationships may pursue **co-branding strategies**, where they team up with other companies to promote two or more items. Some marketers even match up their spokes characters in ads – for instance, the Pillsbury Doughboy appeared in a commercial with the Sprint Guy to sell mobile phones.[91] **Product complementarity** occurs when the symbolic meanings of different products relate to one another.[92] Consumers use these sets of products we call a **consumption constellation** to define, communicate and perform social roles.[93] For example, we identified the American 'yuppie' of the 1980s by such products as a Rolex watch, a BMW car, a Gucci briefcase, a squash racket, fresh pesto, white wine and Brie cheese. We identify Ralph Lauren's classic lifestyle brand as built around American taste that evokes images of country homes and sheepdogs.[94] Researchers find that even children are adept at creating consumption constellations, and as they get older they tend to include more brands in these cognitive structures.[95]

Psychographics

5.6

Psychographics go beyond simple demographics to help marketers understand and reach different consumer segments.

Marketers often find it useful to develop products that appeal to different lifestyle groups – simply knowing a person's income does not necessarily predict which type of car he or she might drive. Consumers can share the same demographic characteristics and still be very different people. For this reason, marketers need a way to 'breathe life' into demographic data to identify, understand and target consumer segments that will share a set of preferences for their products and services. (See Chapter 4 for the important differences in consumers' self-concepts and personalities that play a big role in determining product choices.) When marketers combine personality variables with a knowledge of lifestyle preferences, they have a powerful lens that they can focus on consumer segments. This tool is known as **psychographics,** which involves the 'use of psychological, sociological and anthropological factors. . . to determine how the market is segmented by the propensity of groups within the market – and their reasons – to make a particular decision about a product, person, ideology, or otherwise hold an attitude or use a medium'.[96]

Psychographic research was first developed in the 1960s and 1970s to address the short-comings of two other types of consumer research: motivational research and quantitative survey research. **Motivational research**, which involves intensive personal interviews and projective tests, yields a lot of information about individual consumers. The information gathered, however, is often idiosyncratic and not deemed necessarily to be very useful or reliable.[97] At the other extreme, *quantitative survey research,* or large-scale demographic surveys, yields only a little information about a lot of people. As some researchers observed, 'The marketing manager who wanted to know why people ate the competitor's corn flakes was told "32 per cent of the respondents said *taste,* 21 per cent said *flavour,* 15 per cent said *texture,* 10 per cent said *price,* and 22 per cent said *don't know* or *no answer*".[98] Marketers often find it useful to develop products that appeal to different lifestyle subcultures. When marketers combine personality variables with knowledge of lifestyle preferences, they have a powerful lens that they can focus on consumer segments.

In many applications, the term 'psychographics' is used interchangeably with 'lifestyle' to denote the separation of consumers into categories based on differences in choices of consumption activities and product usage. While there are many psychographic variables that can be used to segment consumers, they all share the underlying principle of going beyond surface characteristics to understand consumers' motivations for purchasing and using products. Demographics allow us to describe *who* buys, but psychographics helps us understand *why* they buy.

How do we perform a psychographic analysis?

Some early attempts at lifestyle segmentation 'borrowed' standard psychological scales (often used to measure pathology or personality disturbances) and tried to relate scores on these tests to product usage. As might be expected, such efforts were largely disappointing. These tests were never intended to be related to everyday consumption activities and yielded little in the way of explanation for purchase behaviours. The technique is more effective when the variables included are more closely related to actual consumer behaviours. If you want to understand purchases of household cleaning products, you are better off asking people about their attitudes towards household cleanliness than testing for personality disorders.

Psychographic studies can take several different forms:

- *A lifestyle profile* looks for items that differentiate between users and non-users of a product.
- *A product-specific profile* identifies a target group and then profiles these consumers on product-relevant dimensions.
- *A general lifestyle segmentation* places a large sample of respondents into homogeneous groups based on the similarities in their overall preferences.
- *A product-specific segmentation* tailors questions to a product category. For example, if a researcher wants to conduct research for a stomach medicine, they might rephrase the item, 'I worry too much' as, 'I get stomach problems if I worry too much'. This allows them to more finely discriminate among users of competing brands.[99]

AIOs

Most contemporary psychographic research attempts to group consumers according to some combination of three categories of variables – activities, interests and opinions – which are known as **AIOs**. Using data from large samples, marketers create profiles of customers who resemble each other in terms of their activities and patterns of product usage.[100] The dimensions used to assess lifestyle are: **Activities** (Work, Hobbies, Social events, Holiday, Entertainment, Club membership, Community, Shopping, Sports); **Interests** (Family, Home, Job, Community, Recreation, Fashion, Food, Media, Achievements); **Opinions** (Themselves, Social issues, Politics, Business, Economics, Education, Products, Future, Culture); and Demographics (Age, Education, Income, Occupation, Family size, Dwelling, Geography, City size, Stage in life cycle).[101]

To group consumers into common AIO categories, researchers give respondents a long list of statements and respondents are asked to indicate how much they agree with each one. Lifestyle is thus teased out by discovering how people spend their time, what they find interesting and important and how they view themselves and the world around them, as well as demographic information.

Typically, the first step in conducting a psychographic analysis is to determine which lifestyle segments are producing the bulk of customers for a particular product. According to a very general rule of thumb that marketers call the **80/20 rule**, only 20 per cent of a product's users account for 80 per cent of the volume of product a company sells. Researchers attempt to determine who uses the brand and try to isolate heavy, moderate and light users. They also look for patterns of usage and attitudes towards the product. In some cases, just a few lifestyle segments account for the majority of brand users.[102] Marketers primarily target these heavy users, even though they may constitute a relatively small number of total users.

After marketers identify and understand their heavy users, they consider more specifically how these customers relate to the brand. Heavy users may have quite different reasons for using the product; they can be further subdivided in terms of the *benefits* they derive from using the product or service. For instance, marketers at the beginning of the walking-shoe craze assumed that purchasers were basically burned-out joggers. Subsequent psychographic research showed that there were actually several different groups of 'walkers', ranging from those who walk to get to work to those who walk for fun. This realisation resulted in shoes aimed at different segments.

How do we use psychographic data?

Marketers use the data from psychographic surveys in a variety of ways:

- *To define the target market.* This information allows the marketer to go beyond simple demographic or product usage descriptions (such as 'middle-aged men' or 'frequent users').

- *To create a new view of the market.* Sometimes marketers create their strategies with a 'typical' customer in mind. This stereotype may not be correct because the actual customer may not match these assumptions. For example, marketers of a facial cream for women were surprised to find their key market of heavy users was composed of older, widowed women, rather than the younger, more sociable women to whom they were pitching their appeals.

- *To position the product.* Psychographic information can allow the marketer to emphasise features of the product that fit in with a person's lifestyle. A company that wants to target people whose lifestyle profiles show a high need to be around other people might focus on its product's ability to help meet this social need.

- *To better communicate product attributes.* Psychographic information can offer very useful input to advertising creatives who must communicate something about the product. The artist or writer obtains a much richer mental image of the target consumer than they can obtain through simply looking at dry statistics, and this insight improves their ability to 'talk' to that consumer.

- *To develop product strategy.* Understanding how a product fits, or does not fit, into consumers' lifestyles allows the marketer to identify new product opportunities, chart (social) media strategies and create environments most consistent and harmonious with these consumption patterns. For example, inexpensive airline tickets have become very popular in Germany, with intra-country fares often lower than the price of a train ticket. The increase in flights has sparked environmental worries among 'the greens', even though the greens are one of the market segments most likely to book the low-fare airline tickets. Research has shown that conflicting values (in this case, low fares *vs* air pollution and the carbon footprint) can be addressed in promotions by better understanding the motives that cause the tensions.[103]

- *To market social and political issues.* Psychographic segmentation can be an important tool in political campaigns, and policy-makers can also employ the technique to find similarities among types of consumers who engage in destructive behaviours, such as drug users, excessive gamblers or binge drinkers.

Psychographic segmentation typologies

Marketers are constantly on the lookout for new insights that will allow them to identify and reach groups of consumers that are united by a common lifestyle. To meet this need, many research companies and advertising agencies have developed their own **lifestyle segmentation typologies**, which divide people into segments. Respondents answer a battery of questions that allow the researchers to cluster them into a set of distinct lifestyle groups. The questions usually include a mixture of AIOs, plus other items relating to their perceptions of specific brands, favourite celebrities, (social) media preferences and so on. These systems are usually sold to companies wanting to learn more about their customers and potential customers.

At least at a superficial level, many of these typologies are fairly similar to one another, in that a typical typology breaks up the population into roughly five–ten segments. Unfortunately, it is often difficult to compare or evaluate different typologies, since the methods and data used to devise these systems are frequently *proprietary* – this means that the information is developed and owned by the company, and the company feels that it would not be desirable to release this information to outsiders.

Such psychographic segmentation typologies and their associated lifestyle analyses have been widely used in Europe and the US.[104] The best-known lifestyle segmentation system is the **Values and Lifestyles System (VALS2™)** that SRI International developed, initially for the US and Canada and later for international markets. The VALS2™ system is adapted for specific countries in order to take account of 'cultural differences in the relationship between attitudes and behaviors as they exist'.[105] A battery of items (a mixture of psychological attitudes – empirically proven to link with consumerism – and key demographics) is used, for instance, to classify UK adults into six core groups, each with distinctive characteristics: activators, traditionalists, achievers, seekers, pragmatics and constraineds.[106] 'Measures of primary motivations – *Tradition, Achievement,* and *Self-Expression* – and high/low resources and innovation define the segments'.[107] Their typology arranges groups vertically by their resources (including such factors as income, education, energy levels and eagerness to buy) and horizontally by self-orientation.

The value of lifestyle segmentation typologies

Generally, lifestyle analyses of consumers are exciting because they seek to provide an approximately complete sociological view of the market and its segments and trends, but their general character is their biggest weakness, since the underlying assumption – that these general segments have relatively homogeneous patterns of consumer behaviour – is far from proven.[108] Add to this the generally weak theoretical foundation and the problems of reliability and validity linked to the large-scale questionnaires and to the operationalisation of complex social processes in simple variables, and it is understandable why some marketers see lifestyles more as a way of 'thinking the market' and as an input to creative strategies, than as descriptions of segments defined by their consumer behaviour.[109]

Behavioural targeting

The latest and hottest extension of lifestyle marketing is **behavioural targeting**, which refers to presenting people with advertisements based on their internet use. In other words, with today's technology it has become fairly easy for marketers to tailor the ads you see to websites you have visited. Some critics feel this is a mixed blessing because it implies that big companies are tracking where we go and keeping this information.

Tangled web

'It might work too well': the dark art of political advertising online: European elections

Digital campaigns have evolved from banner ads 20 years ago . . . Has the rise of micro-targeting become a threat to democracy?

The UK has seen a rapid shift to digital campaigning following the Conservative party's embrace of Facebook in the 2015 general election. The Tories outspent Labour by a factor of 10 on Facebook advertisements, a decision that many political observers saw as decisive. In a country that bans political ads on television, Facebook enabled the Conservatives to reach 80.65% of users in targeted constituencies with its promoted posts and video ads, according to marketing materials created by Facebook. The Vote Leave campaign in the 2016 Brexit referendum went on to spend almost its entire budget on Facebook advertising, an investment that resulted in about 1bn targeted digital ads being served to voters over the course of a 10-week campaign. Though it is impossible to parse the exact impact of Facebook advertisements amid all the other factors that shape an electoral result (including organic Facebook content), the platform is increasingly cited as a factor in the growing electoral might of far-right groups in Europe.

The radical right-wing Alternative for Germany (AfD) party reportedly worked with a US campaign consultancy and Facebook itself to target German voters susceptible to its anti-immigrant message during the 2017 election in which AfD surged in popularity to become the third-largest party in parliament.

Campaigning in Italy's recent election, which saw the rise of anti-establishment parties, including the populist Five Star Movement and the far-right League, largely took place on social media. Facebook advertisements and targeting information gathered by Italian transparency group Openpolis found that the neo-fascist Brothers of Italy party ran a Facebook ad targeting Italian adults who are interested in the paramilitary police force, the *carabinieri*. After the polls closed in Italy, the League's Matteo Salvini shared some words of gratitude with the press: "Thank God for the internet. Thank God for social media. Thank God for Facebook."

Mark Zuckerberg says Facebook has taken steps to achieve "an even higher standard of transparency". Starting this summer, the platform has promised that every political ad will be linked back to the page that paid for it. The pages themselves will display every ad that they're running, as well as demographic information about the audience that they are reaching, a measure that Mark Zuckerberg claimed would "bring Facebook to an even higher standard of transparency" than the law requires for television or other media. A version of these reforms is already live in Canada, where users can see all the ads being run by a political candidate in a designated tab on their page.

But there is good reason to be sceptical. Since 2014, Facebook has had a transparency tool for all ads served on the platform. . . So far so good, but a new study by computer scientists found that Facebook's ad explanations were "often incomplete and sometimes misleading" in a way that "may allow malicious advertisers to easily obfuscate ad explanations that are discriminatory or that target privacy-sensitive attributes".

Alan Mislove, a professor of computer science at Northeastern University and one of the study's co-authors, said that he gave Facebook credit for having the feature at all, noting that it is one of the only examples of a company offering any kind of explanation of how an algorithm actually works. But the findings do not paint a particularly pretty picture of Facebook's ability to self-regulate. "They've built this incredibly powerful platform that allows very narrow targeting, a very powerful tool that anyone on the internet can use, so that scares me", Mislove said. "And up until very recently, there was very little accountability."[110]

There are important privacy issues still to be resolved but, interestingly, many consumers seem more than happy to trade-off some of their personal information in exchange for information they consider more useful to them.[111] Microsoft, for instance, combines personal data from the users of its free Hotmail email service – the biggest in the world – with information it gains from monitoring their searches. When you sign up for Hotmail, the service asks you for personal information including your age, occupation and address (though you are not required to answer). If you use Microsoft's search engine Bing,[112] the company keeps a record of the words you search for and the results you click on. Microsoft's behavioural targeting system will allow its advertising clients to send different ads to each person surfing the Web.[113]

MySpace[114] uses personal details users put on their profile pages and blogs to sell highly targeted advertising in ten broad categories including finance, autos, fashion and music. Facebook plans to use sophisticated software to decide how receptive a user will be to an ad based not only on their personal information but that of their friends – even if they haven't explicitly expressed interest in that topic.[115] However, behavioural lifestyle marketing brings threats as well as opportunities for consumers, as represented by **cybercrime** – criminal behaviour online, such as theft of money or theft of identity.

Values

Underlying values often drive consumer motivations. Products thus take on meaning because a person thinks they will help him or her to achieve some goal that is linked to a value, such as individuality or freedom. A set of core values characterises each culture, to which most of its members adhere.

Generally speaking, a **value** can be defined as a belief about some desirable end-state that transcends specific situations and guides selection of behaviour.[116] Thus, values are general and different from attitudes in that they do not apply to specific situations only. A person's set of values plays a very important role in their consumption activities, since many products and services are purchased because (it is believed) they will help us to attain a value-related goal. Two people can believe in and exhibit the same behaviours (for example, vegetarianism) but their underlying **belief systems** may be quite different (animal activism *vs* health concerns). The extent to which people share a belief system is a function of individual, social and cultural forces. Advocates of a belief system often seek out others with similar beliefs, so that social networks overlap and, as a result, believers tend to be exposed to information that supports their beliefs (e.g. environmentalists rarely socialise with factory farmers).[117]

Core values

Every culture has a set of **core values** that it imparts to its members.[118] For example, people in one culture might feel that being a unique individual is preferable to subordinating one's identity to the group, while another group may emphasise the virtues of group membership. In many cases, values are universal. Who does not desire health, wisdom or world peace? But on the other hand, values can vary across cultures and do change over time. Concerns about the consequences of what is often called a 'value crisis' have been voiced in European societies. For instance, one may wonder what happened to the traditional Scandinavian modesty – in both Denmark and Sweden people are now showing more willingness to share their private lives with thousands of others in either talk shows or docu-soaps of the *Big Brother* variety.

Or, take the core value of cleanliness: everyone wants to be clean, but some societies are more fastidious than others and won't accept products and services that they think cut corners. Italian women on average spend 21 hours a week on household chores other than cooking – compared with only four hours for Americans, according to Procter & Gamble's research. The Italian women wash kitchen and bathroom floors at least four times a week,

Cleanliness is a core value in many cultures
Thiago Santos/Alamy Stock Photo

Americans only once. Italian women typically iron nearly all their wash, even socks and sheets, and they buy more cleaning supplies than women elsewhere do.

So, they should be ideal customers for cleaning products, right? That's what Unilever thought when it launched its all-purpose Cif spray cleaner there, but it flopped. Similarly, P&G's best-selling Swiffer wet mop bombed big time. Both companies underestimated this market's desire for products that are tough cleaners, not time-savers. Only about 30 per cent of Italian households have dishwashers, because many women don't trust machines to get dishes as clean as they can get them by hand, manufacturers say. Many of those who do use machines tend to thoroughly rinse the dishes before they load them into the dishwasher. Young Italian women increasingly work outside the home, but they still spend nearly as much time as their mothers did on housework.

When Unilever did research to determine why Italians didn't take to Cif, they found that these women weren't convinced that a mere spray would do the job on tough kitchen grease or that one product would adequately clean different surfaces (it turns out that 72 per cent of Italians own more than eight different cleaning products). The company reformulated the product and reintroduced it with different varieties instead of as an all-in-one. It also made the bottles 50 per cent bigger, because Italians clean so frequently, and changed its advertising to emphasise the products' cleaning strength rather than convenience. P&G also reintroduced its Swiffer, this time adding beeswax and a Swiffer duster, which is now a bestseller. It sold five million boxes in the first eight months – twice the company's forecasts.[119]

Value systems

Every culture is characterised by its members' endorsement of a **value system**. These end-states may not be equally endorsed by everyone and, in some cases, values may even seem to contradict one another (e.g. Westerners in general appear to value both conformity and individuality, and seek to find some accommodation between the two). Nonetheless, it is usually possible to identify a general set of *core values* that uniquely define a culture.

In many cases, values are universal. What sets cultures apart is the *relative importance,* or ranking, of these universal values. This set of rankings constitutes a culture's value system.[120] For example, one study found that North Americans have more favourable attitudes towards advertising messages that focus on self-reliance, self-improvement and the achievement of personal goals, as opposed to themes stressing family integrity, collective goals and the feeling of harmony with others. Korean consumers exhibited the reverse pattern.[121]

Nonetheless, it is usually possible to identify a general set of core values that uniquely define a culture. Core values such as freedom, youthfulness, achievement, materialism and activity characterise American culture. Of course, these values evolve over time. For example, some analysts argue that our focus on acquiring physical objects is shifting a bit towards the consumption of experiences instead. This movement is consistent with research that shows that experiential purchases provide greater happiness and satisfaction because they allow us to connect with others and form a bigger part of our social identities. Indeed, one study demonstrated that highly materialistic consumers actually experience pleasure before a purchase because they believe it will transform their lives, but they then experience negative emotions after they buy the item when they realise this is not the case.[122] We find that many consumers value sustainability, and reward companies that are environmentally friendly.

Many promotions and advertisements appeal to people's values to persuade them to change or modify their behaviours. In 2017, a giant whale made entirely of plastic was seen near Tower Bridge in London to raise awareness of ocean pollution. This was part of Sky's Ocean Rescue campaign. The whale was covered with 250 kg worth of plastic, which is the same amount that pollutes the ocean every second. The plastic whale toured UK beaches and seas, visiting Newquay, Cardiff and Birmingham, as well as other locations.

CrowdSpark/Alamy Stock Photo

Marketing opportunity
Just do it: the experience economy and how we turned our backs on 'stuff'

'New figures show we are continuing to spend less money on buying things, and more on doing things – and telling the world about it online afterwards, of course. From theatres to pubs to shops, businesses are scrambling to adapt to this shift. The latest figures come from Barclaycard, which processes about half of all Britain's credit and debit card transactions. Figures for April show a 20% increase in spending in pubs compared with the same month last year. Spending in restaurants went up 16%, while theatres and cinemas enjoyed a 13% rise. Meanwhile, department stores suffered a 1% drop, vehicle sales were down 11% and spending on household appliances fell by 2.5%.

Barclaycard says the trend began to emerge about a year ago. And retailers are feeling it. In March, Simon Wolfson, chief executive of Next, blamed the clothing chain's first fall in profits for eight years on the move from buying things to doing things.[123] More startlingly, IKEA, the world's biggest furniture retailer, told a *Guardian* conference last year that consumption of many goods had reached a limit. "If we look on a global basis, in the west we have probably hit peak stuff",[124] said Steve Howard, the company's head of sustainability. . . .

And as we consume less, we are doing more. "If you think about the 20th century, the big dominant value system was materialism, the belief that if we had more stuff we'd be happier", says James Wallman, a trend forecaster and the author of *Stuffocation: Living More with Less*,[125] in which he charts the move from possessions to experience. "The big change to what I call experientialism is more about finding happiness and status in experiences instead."

The happiness bit perhaps stands to reason, but studies suggest the anticipation of an experience has a crucial, additional value. . . We are also less likely to compare experiential purchases than we are products, in a way that means we are all happy with what we buy, regardless of what we can afford. "So, if you have a Nissan and your neighbour has a Porsche, there's no doubt who has the better car, and if you ask the Nissan driver to swap, they will", Wallman says. "But if you ask people who went on holiday to the Seychelles or South Wales, it's clear who had the fancier holiday, but surveys show the person who went to Wales won't swap because they had an equally good time."[126]

How do we find out what a culture values? We term the process of learning the beliefs and behaviours endorsed by one's own culture **enculturation**. In contrast, we call the process of learning the value system and behaviours of another culture (often a priority for those who wish to understand consumers and markets in foreign countries) **acculturation**.[127] (See Chapter 13 for a detailed discussion of acculturation.) Core values must be understood in the local context – that is, the meaning of the values changes when the cultural context shifts. This is a serious challenge to the idea that it is possible to compare value systems by studying the rankings of universal sets of values across countries:

- A **custom** is a norm that controls basic behaviours, such as division of labour in a household or how we practise particular ceremonies.
- A **more** ('mor-ay') is a custom with a strong moral overtone. It often involves a *taboo,* or forbidden behaviour, such as incest or cannibalism. Violation of a more often meets with strong sanctions.
- **Conventions** are norms that regulate how we conduct our everyday lives. These rules often deal with the subtleties of consumer behaviour, including the 'correct' way to furnish one's house, wear one's clothes or host a dinner party.

All three types of **crescive** (or unspoken) **norms** may jointly define a culturally appropriate behaviour. For example, a more may tell us what kind of food it's OK to eat. These norms vary across cultures, so a meal of dog is taboo in the United States, Hindus shun steak and Muslims avoid pork products. A custom dictates the appropriate hour at which we should serve a meal. Conventions tell us how to eat the meal, including such details as the utensils we use, table etiquette and even the appropriate apparel to wear at dinnertime. We often take these conventions for granted. We just assume that they are the 'right' things to do (again, until we travel abroad). Much of what we know about these norms we learn *vicariously* as we observe the behaviours of actors in television commercials, sitcoms, print ads and other media. That reminds us why the marketing system is such an important element of culture.

And as part of the debate around the issues raised by Professor Benjamin Voyer, also look at Edward Helmore's news item where he argues that 'care for the planet is becoming more than a whim for a global fashion giant that wants to make sustainability pay [with the question] so how do you make snakeskin handbags environmentally friendly?'.[128]

Consumer behaviour as I see it. . .

Luxury goods and luxury consumers: is status-enhancing consumption compatible with the notion of sustainability?

Professor Benjamin G. Voyer
ESCP Europe (London) and LSE, London

'What do you typically associate with luxury and luxury goods? High-quality, well-crafted products – or perhaps simply a waste of money? The display of refined tastes – or merely an attempt to show off? Luxury goods constitute a unique product and service category in marketing and are interesting for one simple reason: they often challenge everything we know about traditional products and services. The buying behaviour of luxury consumers – and the meaning of luxury possessions – has been the focus of much research. Luxury consumption has been linked to wealth, social class, and economic power. Research suggests that consumers use luxury goods to enhance their status, especially when buying brands with prominent designer logos.

Recently, researchers have started to look at conspicuous consumption from a different angle, examining whether or not status-enhancing consumption was compatible with the notion of sustainability. Throughout history, luxury goods have been associated with unsustainability or unhealthiness – Plato, for instance, suggested that societies in which people were consuming luxury goods were 'unhealthy'; 'healthy' societies, on the other hand, were those in which people would limit themselves to necessities. Overall, luxury consumption has often been seen as a social and moral transgression, denoting values of hedonism, expense and affluence.

In this context, could it be that consumers actually find sustainable luxury goods less desirable than non-sustainable ones? We pursued this question in a series of studies (conducted with colleague Daisy Beckham) and looked at whether luxury was seen as compatible with sustainability. In the first study, we found that consumers were more likely to associate luxury brands with words related to unsustainability (e.g. pollution, smoke, greed, fumes) *vs* words related to sustainability (e.g. conservation, green, trees, ecology).

In another study, we looked at the effect of a 'sustainability label' on consumers' perceptions of luxury goods. We asked participants to rate a series of six luxury handbags, three of them being randomly described as sustainable. We found that luxury bags receiving the label 'sustainable edition' were rated, on average, as being less luxurious than bags without such a label. The only consumers who responded favourably to a sustainability label were those who valued sustainability as an important decision criterion when buying a handbag. A follow-up focus group revealed that participants perceived luxury as being conceptually opposed to the idea of sustainability, and that for some, sustainable luxury products would not carry the same status-enhancing effects as regular luxury products.

What is the bottom line on all this? Given that many consumers use luxury goods to communicate about social status, which is typically associated with breaking norms and rules, it seems that a sustainability label is paradoxically detrimental to the marketing of luxury goods. This is something that can be counterintuitive for luxury brands, which often communicate product features that are thought to enhance the perception of quality and prestige of their products (e.g. 'Made in France' labels).'

Questions

Given the growing importance of sustainability in marketing and buying behaviour, what can luxury companies do to promote sustainable goods? Is the promotion of sustainable luxury goods doomed to fail?

Benjamin Voyer

How do values link to consumer behaviour?

Despite their importance, values have not been as widely applied to direct examinations of consumer behaviour as might be expected. One reason is that broad-based concepts such as freedom, security or inner harmony are more likely to affect general purchasing patterns rather than differentiate between brands within a product category. For this reason, some researchers have found it convenient to make distinctions among broad-based *cultural values* such as security or happiness, *consumption-specific values* such as convenient shopping or prompt service and *product-specific values* such as ease of use or durability, which affect the relative importance that people place on possessions in different cultures.[129] One way we can clearly see the impact of shifting cultural values on consumption is to look at the increasing emphasis placed on the importance of health and wellbeing.

A study of product-specific values looked in depth at Australians who engage in extreme sports such as surfing, snowboarding and skateboarding. The researchers identified four dominant values that drove brand choice: freedom, belongingness, excellence and connection. For example, one female surfer they studied embraced the value of belongingness. She expressed this value by wearing popular brands of surfing apparel even when these major brands had lost their local roots by going mainstream. In contrast, another surfer in the study valued connection; he expressed this by selecting only locally made brands and going out of his way to support local surfing events.[130]

While some aspects of brand image such as sophistication tend to be common across cultures, others are more likely to be relevant in specific places. The characteristic of peacefulness is valued to a larger extent in Japan, while the same holds true for passion in Spain and ruggedness in the US.[131] Because values drive much of consumer behaviour (at least in a very general sense), we might say that virtually all consumer research ultimately is related to the identification and measurement of values. This process can take many forms, ranging from qualitative research techniques such as ethnography to quantitative techniques such as laboratory experiments and large-scale surveys. This section will describe some specific attempts by researchers to measure cultural values and apply this knowledge to marketing strategy.

A number of companies track changes in values through large-scale surveys. For instance, one Young and Rubicam study tracked the new segment of single, professional career women without any ambitions of having a family. They are among the highest-consuming segments and are characterised by central values such as freedom and independence.[132]

Such ideas are reflected in a relatively recent theory of consumer value. According to this theory, value for a consumer is the consumer's evaluation of a consumer object in terms of which general benefit the consumer might get from consuming it.[133] As such, the value at stake in consumption is tied much more to the consumption experience than to general existential

Research has identified four dominant values that drive brand choice among extreme sports' enthusiasts: freedom, belongingness, excellence and connection. (Research by Pascale Quester, Michael Beverland and Francis Farrelly (2006), 'Brand-personal values fit and brand meanings: Exploring the role individual values play in ongoing brand loyalty in extreme sports subcultures', Advances in Consumer Research 33(1)).

Ipatov/Shutterstock

values of the person. Thus, it is suggested that the consumer experience may generate eight distinct types of consumer value:

1 *Efficiency:* referring to all products aimed at providing various kinds of convenience for the consumer.

2 *Excellence:* addressing situations where the experience of quality is the prime motivation.

3 *Status:* when the consumer pursues success and engages in impression management and conspicuous consumption.

4 *(Self-)esteem:* situations where the satisfaction of possessing something is in focus, as is the case with materialism.

5 *Play:* the value of having fun in consuming.

6 *Aesthetics:* searching for beauty in one's consumption, e.g. designer products, fashion or art.

7 *Ethics:* referring to motivations behind consumption, e.g. morally or politically correct consumption choices.

8 *Spirituality:* experiencing magical transformations or sacredness in the consumption, as felt by devoted collectors.[134]

The Rokeach Value Survey

The psychologist Milton Rokeach identified a set of **terminal values**,[135] or desired end-states, that apply (in various degrees) to many different cultures. The *Rokeach Value Survey,* a scale used to measure these values, also includes a set of **instrumental values**,[136] which are composed of actions needed to achieve these terminal values (Table 5.1).[137]

Some evidence indicates that differences on these global values do translate into product-specific preferences and differences in media usage. Nonetheless, marketing researchers have not widely used the Rokeach Value Survey.[138] One reason is that our society is evolving into smaller and smaller sets of *consumption micro-cultures* within a larger culture, each with its own set of core values.

Table 5.1 Terminal and instrumental values

Instrumental values	Terminal values
Ambitious	A comfortable life
Broadminded	An exciting life
Capable	A sense of accomplishment
Cheerful	A world of peace
Clean	A world of beauty
Courageous	Equality
Forgiving	Family security
Helpful	Freedom
Honest	Happiness
Imaginative	Inner harmony
Independent	Mature love
Intellectual	National security
Logical	Pleasure
Loving	Salvation
Obedient	Self-respect
Polite	Social recognition
Responsible	True friendship
Self-controlled	Wisdom

Source: Richard W. Pollay, 'Measuring the Cultural Values Manifest in Advertising', *Current Issues and Research in Advertising* 6(1) (1983): 71–92. Copyright © 1983 Routledge.

The list of values (lov)

The **List of Values** identifies nine consumer values that can be related to differences in consumption behaviours, and thus has more direct marketing applications. It includes the following values: sense of belonging, fun and enjoyment in life, excitement, warm relationships with others, self-fulfilment, being well respected, a sense of accomplishment, self-respect and security. The nine consumer segments identified by LOV include consumers who place priorities on such values as a sense of belonging, excitement, warm relationships with others and security.[139] A comparative study of French and German consumers, which used this instrument, found that the values of sense of belonging and self-respect were far more popular in Germany, whereas the values of fun and enjoyment in life, self-fulfillment and self-accomplishment were chosen as the most important values in France significantly more often.[140]

However, the cross-cultural validity of such value instruments is, at best, difficult to establish since the meaning of values may differ significantly in different cultural contexts.[141] For example, the LOV did not do very well in a test of its cross-cultural validity.[142]

Schwartz Value Survey

This very elaborate set of values, containing 56 different values organised in ten so-called motivational domains, has been demonstrated to be among the more cross-culturally valid set of instruments.[143] The structuring of values in interrelated motivational domains provides a

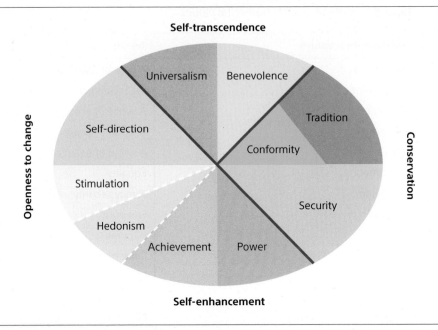

Figure 5.6 The motivational domains of the Schwartz value survey

theoretical framework for this approach to values, which many researchers find more satisfactory compared to other value inventories. More specifically, it has been demonstrated to distinguish between cultures[144] and types of media consumption behaviour[145] better than the traditional dichotomy of **individualism** and collectivism. The values are located in a space demarcated by the poles of 'openness to change' *vs* 'conservation', and 'self-transcendence' *vs* 'self-enhancement'. These dimensions seem relatively universal for a lot of syndicated lifestyle and value surveys. A mapping of the motivational domains can be seen in Figure 5.6.

The means–end chain model

Another research approach that incorporates values is termed a **means–end chain model**. This approach assumes that people link very specific product attributes (indirectly) to terminal values: we choose among alternative means to attain some end-state that we value (such as freedom or safety). Thus, we value products to the extent that they provide the means to some end we desire. Through a technique called **laddering**, researchers can uncover consumers' associations between specific attributes and these general consequences. Using this approach, consumers are helped to climb up the 'ladder' of abstraction that connects functional product attributes with desired end-states.[146] Based upon consumer feedback, researchers create *hierarchical value maps* that show how specific product attributes get linked to end-states (see Figure 5.7).

To understand how laddering works, consider somebody who expresses a liking for a light beer. Probing might reveal that this attribute is linked to the consequence of not getting drunk. A consequence of not getting drunk is that they will be able to enjoy more interesting conversations, which in turn means that they will be more sociable. Finally, better sociability results in better friendship – a terminal value for this person.[147]

Figure 5.7 shows three different hierarchical value maps, or sets of ladders, from a study of consumers' perceptions and motivations with regard to cooking oils. The three ladders demonstrate some important differences between the three markets. Health is the central

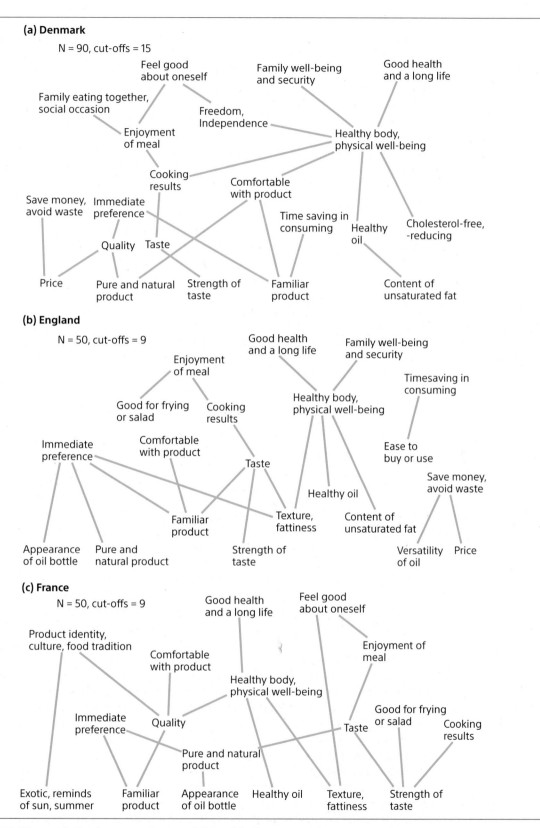

Figure 5.7 Hierarchical value maps for vegetable oil in three countries

Source: N.A. Nielsen, T. Bech-Larsen and K.G. Grunert, 'Consumer purchase motives and product perceptions: a laddering study on vegetable oil in three countries', *Food Quality and Preference* 9(6) (1998): 455–66.

concept most often referred to for the Danes and is linked to several personal values. The British also focus on health but the links to personal values are fewer and less differentiated, indicating a lower product involvement. Saving money and avoiding waste are more important to the British than to the other samples. The French focus a lot on previous knowledge of the product, indicating more routine with buying oils. Theirs is also the only culture that links oil (especially olive oil) with cultural identity and fundamental food culture.[148] These ladders illustrate the central importance of cultural and contextual differences for consumers' motivation structures.

Laddering is not without problems, however, since the laddering technique might generate invalid answers if the respondent is pushed up the ladder by too strong an emphasis on the sequence in the means–end chain. Consumers should be allowed to jump back and forth, to make loops and forks and take blind alleys, which requires more skill on the part of the interviewer but is also a more accurate representation of the respondents' thought processes.[149] Furthermore, it has been argued that in researching the demand for status goods, using laddering techniques can be problematic since motivations for conspicuous consumption are difficult for consumers to express or reveal.[150]

Syndicated surveys

A number of companies who track changes in values through large-scale surveys sell the results of these studies to marketers, who often also pay a fee to receive regular updates on changes and trends. This approach originated in the mid-1960s. It is often useful to go beyond simple demographics like a person's age to understand the values and preferences a group of people might have in common. These services include VALS by Strategic Business Insight (as discussed earlier in the chapter).

Sustainability: a new core value?

Are European consumers finally going green? In a US 2007 survey, 8 out of 10 US consumers said they believed it is important to buy green brands and products from green companies, and that they will pay more to do so. The US consumer's focus on personal health is merging with a growing interest in global health. Some analysts call this new value **conscientious consumerism**.[151] One study has suggested that 'the translation of concern over sustainability to sustainable consumption practices is based on the promotion of self-efficacy, through the reduction of ambivalent feelings by enforcing knowledge-based trust between institutions and individuals'.[152] In the UK, recycling of household waste increased from 44.6 per cent (in 2015) to 45.2 per cent (in 2016). 'The recycling rate for England was 44.9%, compared with 43.0% in Northern Ireland, 42.8% in Scotland and 57.3% in Wales. . . In 2016, 71.4% of UK packaging waste was either recycled or recovered compared to 64.7% in 2015.'[153]

Consumers who practice **LOHAS** – an acronym for 'lifestyles of health and sustainability' (others refer to this segment as *cultural creatives*) – worry about the environment, want products to be produced in a sustainable way and spend money to advance what they see as their personal development and potential. These consumers represent a great market for products such as organic foods, energy-efficient appliances and hybrid cars, as well as alternative medicine, yoga tapes and eco-tourism.

Marketers and retailers are responding, in turn, with thousands of new eco-friendly products and programmes. Kellogg's, for instance, has introduced organic and vegan cereals with new plant-based 'no added sugar'.[154] We are seeing a significant increase in products with better-for-you positioning, but new products that take an ethical stance are also driving this trend, whether the claim links to fair trade, sustainability or ecological friendliness. Whereas in the past it was sufficient for companies to offer recyclable products, this new movement is creating a whole new vocabulary as consumers begin to demand food, fragrances and other items that are made with no *GMOs* (genetically modified ingredients), are hormone-free, involve no animal clones or animal testing, are locally grown and cage-free, to name a few.[155]

Not content to wait for companies to change their practices, ordinary consumers are taking action. Many are joining organisations such as Slow Food to agitate for lifestyle changes. One such movement, called 'Local First', stresses the value of buying locally made products. This group (some members call themselves 'locavores') values small community businesses, but it is also reacting to the waste it sees occurring as people import things they need from long distances.[156]

Still other consumers are rebelling against the huge market for bottled water, with some brands coming from as far away as Fiji. These imports create pollution because of the tanker ships that have to move them halfway around the world and the waste from millions of discarded plastic bottles.[157] The environmental effect of an object seemingly as innocent as a plastic water bottle points to the concern that many now have about the size of their **carbon footprint**. This measures in units of carbon dioxide the impact that human activities have on the environment in terms of the amount of greenhouse gases they produce.[158]

Marketing opportunity (or threat?)
Plastic bottles and the EU

'A million plastic bottles are bought around the world every minute and despite the rise in recycling culture over the past few decades, just 7% of those collected last year were turned into new bottles. Most end up in landfill or in the ocean and by 2050 plastic waste is estimated to outweigh all the fish in the sea.[159]

'The EU is waging war against plastic waste as part of an urgent plan to clean up Europe's act and ensure that every piece of packaging on the continent is reusable or recyclable by 2030. . . Following China's decision to ban imports of foreign recyclable material, Brussels [has] launched a plastics strategy designed to change minds in Europe, potentially tax damaging behaviour, and modernise plastics production and collection by investing €350m (£310m) in research. . . . the vice-president of the commission, Frans Timmermans, said Brussels' priority was to clamp down on "single-use plastics that take five seconds to produce, you use it for five minutes and it takes 500 years to break down again". In the EU's sights, Timmermans said, were throw-away items such as drinking straws, "lively coloured" bottles that do not degrade, coffee cups, lids and stirrers, cutlery and takeaway packaging. . . "If we don't do anything about this, 50 years down the road we will have more plastic than fish in the oceans."'[160]

Another emerging environmental issue for the developed world is the **virtual water footprint**, which represents how much water is required to produce a product: 'when virtual water is taken into account, consumers in developed nations are leaving a large water footprint not just in their own countries but across the globe too'.[161] In the case of the UK, for instance, under 40 per cent of the country's total footprint is met from its own resources; more than 60 per cent is met by the rest of the world. 'A can of fizzy drink might contain 0.35 litres of water, for instance, yet it also requires about 200 litres to grow and process the sugar that goes into it.'[162] This means that the average Briton consumes about 4,645 litres of water a day once these hidden factors are included. World Water Forum experts are 'increasingly talking of fresh water as "the new oil"'.[163]

Greenwashing

Consumers sometimes just don't believe the green claims that companies make about their brands. According to one report, more than 95 per cent of consumer products marketed as 'green', including all toys surveyed, make misleading or inaccurate claims. Another survey found that the number of products claiming to be green has increased by 73 per cent since 2009 – but of the products investigated, almost a third had fake labels, and 70 made green claims without offering any proof to back them up.[164]

All of this hype results in so-called **greenwashing**[165] and causes consumers not to believe the claims marketers make and, in some cases, consumers actually avoid brands that promise they are green. One survey reported that 71 per cent of respondents say they will stop buying a product if they feel they've been misled about its environmental impact, and 37 per cent are so angry about greenwashing that they believe this justifies a complete boycott of everything the company makes.[166]

The 'why' of consumption

As we have seen in this chapter, there are many reasons why we want to engage in consumption activities. One of the main lessons is that the 'why?' question cannot stand alone, but must be asked with reference to a number of other questions such as 'who?' (indicating personal, group and cultural differences), 'when?' and 'where?' (indicating situational and contextual differences), 'how?' (pointing to the reflexive and emotional processes involved) and finally 'what' kind of consumption items and consumer behaviour are we talking about?

Chapter summary

Now that you have finished reading this chapter you should understand why:

5.1 **It's important for marketers to recognise that products can satisfy a range of consumer needs.** Marketers try to satisfy consumer needs, but the reasons people purchase any product can vary widely. The identification of consumer motives is an important step to ensuring that a product will satisfy appropriate needs. Traditional approaches to consumer behaviour focus on the abilities of products to satisfy rational needs (utilitarian motives), but hedonic motives (e.g. the need for exploration or for fun) also play a key role in many purchase decisions. As Maslow's hierarchy of needs demonstrates, the same product can satisfy different needs, depending on the consumer's state at the time. In addition to this objective situation (e.g. have basic physiological needs already been satisfied?), we must also consider the consumer's degree of involvement with the product.

5.2 **Consumers experience different kinds of motivational conflicts that can impact their purchase decisions.** Motivation refers to the processes that lead people to behave as they do. It occurs when a need is aroused that the consumer wishes to satisfy. A goal has *valence,* which means that it can be positive or negative. We direct our behaviour towards goals we value positively; we are motivated to *approach* the goal and to seek out products that will help us to reach it. However, we may also be motivated to *avoid* a negative outcome rather than achieve a positive outcome.

5.3 **The way we evaluate and choose a product depends on our degree of involvement with the product, the marketing message and/or the purchase situation.** Product involvement can range from very low, where purchase decisions are made via inertia, to very high, where consumers form very strong bonds with what they buy. In addition to considering the degree to which consumers are involved with a product, marketing strategists also need to assess consumers' extent of involvement with marketing messages and with the purchase situation.

5.4 **A lifestyle defines a pattern of consumption that reflects a person's choices of how to spend his or her time and money, and these choices are essential to define consumer identity.** A consumer's *lifestyle* refers to the ways she chooses to spend time and money and how her consumption choices reflect these values and tastes. Lifestyle research is useful for tracking societal consumption preferences and also for positioning specific products and services to different segments. Marketers segment based on lifestyle differences; they often group consumers in terms of their AIOs (activities, interests and opinions).

5.5 **It can often be more useful to identify *patterns* of consumption than to know about *individual* purchases when organisations craft a lifestyle marketing strategy.** We associate interrelated sets of products and activities with social roles to form *consumption constellations.* People often purchase a product or service because they associate it with a constellation that, in turn, they link to a lifestyle they find desirable.

5.6 **Psychographics go beyond simple demographics to help marketers understand and reach different consumer segments.** *Psychographic* techniques classify consumers in terms of psychological, subjective variables in addition to observable characteristics (demographics). Marketers have developed systems to identify consumer 'types' and to differentiate them in terms of their brand or product preferences, media usage, leisure-time activities and attitudes toward broad issues such as politics and religion.

5.7 **Underlying values often drive consumer motivations. Products thus take on meaning because a person thinks they will help him or her to achieve some goal that is linked to a value, such as individuality or freedom. All cultures form a value system that sets them apart from other cultures. Each culture is characterised by a set of core values to which many of its members adhere**. Some researchers have developed lists to account for such value systems and used them in cross-cultural comparisons. One approach to the study of values is the means–end chain, which tries to link product attributes to consumer values via the consequences that usage of the product will have for the consumer.

Key terms

80/20 rule (p. 183)
Acculturation (p. 189)
Activities (p. 182)
AIOs (p. 182)
Alternate reality games (ARGs) (p. 176)
Approach–approach conflict (p. 166)
Approach–avoidance conflict (p. 167)
Avoidance–avoidance conflict (p. 168)
Behavioural targeting (p. 184)
Belief systems (p. 186)
Brand addiction (p. 173)
Brand loyalty (p. 175)
Carbon footprint (p. 197)
Co-branding strategies (p. 181)
Conscientious consumerism (p. 196)
Consumer-generated content (CGC) (p. 177)

Consumption constellation (p. 181)
Conventions (p. 189)
Core values (p. 186)
Crescive norms (p. 189)
Cult products (p. 173)
Custom (p. 189)
Cybercrime (p. 186)
Drive (p. 164)
Drive theory (p. 163)
Enculturation (p. 189)
E-sports (p. 178)
Expectancy theory (p. 164)
Flow state (p. 174)
Goal (p. 162)
Greenwashing (p. 198)
Hierarchy of needs (p. 170)
Homeostasis (p. 163)

Incidental brand exposure (p. 162)
Individualism (p. 194)
Inertia (p. 173)
Instrumental values (p. 192)
Interactive mobile marketing (p. 177)
Interests (p. 182)
Involvement (p. 172)
Laddering (p. 194)
Lifestyle (p. 178)
Lifestyle marketing perspective (p. 180)
Lifestyle segmentation typologies (p. 184)
List of Values (LOV) (p. 193)
LOHAS (p. 196)
Mass customisation (p. 174)
Means–end chain model (p. 194)
More (p. 189)
Motivation (p. 162)
Motivational research (p. 181)
Narrative transportation (p. 176)
Need (p. 162)
Opinions (p. 182)

Peak experiences (p. 170)
Product complementarity (p. 181)
Product involvement (p. 174)
Productivity orientation (p. 165)
Psychographics (p. 178)
Retail therapy (p. 164)
Situational involvement (p. 177)
Social game (p. 177)
Spectacles (p. 177)
Terminal values (p. 192)
Theory of cognitive dissonance (p. 166)
Transactional advertising (p. 177)
Value (p. 186)
Values and Lifestyles System (VALS2™) (p. 184)
Variety-seeking (p. 176)
Value system (p. 187)
Virtual water footprint (p. 197)
Want (p. 163)
Web (p. 171)

Consumer behaviour challenge

1 What is motivation, and how is motivation relevant to consumer behaviour? What is the difference between a need and a want?

2 Describe three types of motivational conflicts, citing an example of each from current marketing campaigns.

3 What is cognitive dissonance? Why is it important for marketers to understand how this works?

4 Devise separate promotional strategies for an article of clothing, each of which stresses one of the levels of Maslow's hierarchy of needs.

5 What is consumer involvement? Give examples of the three types of consumer involvement. How do these types of involvement relate to motivation?

6 'High involvement is just a fancy term for expensive.' Do you agree?

7 Describe how a man's level of involvement with his car would affect how he is influenced by different marketing stimuli. How might you design a strategy for a line of car batteries for a segment of low-involvement consumers, and how would this strategy differ from your attempts to reach a segment of men who are very involved in working on their cars?

8 Collect a sample of ads that appeal to consumers' values. What value is being communicated in each ad, and how is this done? Is this an effective approach to designing a marketing communication?

9 'University students' concerns about ethics, sustainability, the environment, carbon footprints, genetically modified foods and vegetarianism are just passing fads; a way to look cool.' Do you agree?

10 Describe at least two alternative techniques that marketing researchers have used to measure values. What might be the cultural issues to be considered when applying these techniques?

11 Core values evolve over time. What do you think are the three-to-five core values that best describe your country today? Can you see differences between present-day core values and those of your parents' and grandparents' generations? What might be the implications for marketing managers?

12 Compare and contrast the concepts of lifestyle and social class. How does lifestyle differ from income?

13 In what situations is demographic information likely to be more useful than psychographic data, and vice versa?

14 Define psychographics, and describe three ways that marketers might use it.

15 What are three specific kinds of AIOs?

16 Behavioural targeting techniques give marketers access to a wide range of information about a consumer by telling them what websites they visit. Do you believe this 'knowledge power' presents any ethical problems with regard to consumers' privacy? Should governments regulate access to such information? Should consumers have the right to limit access to these data?

17 What is the basic philosophy behind a lifestyle marketing strategy?

18 Discuss some concrete situations in which international similarities in lifestyles may be more relevant than national cultural differences for market segmentation and for the understanding of consumer behaviour.

19 Compile a set of recent ads that attempt to link consumption of a product with a specific lifestyle. How is this goal usually accomplished?

20 There are, of course, people of most lifestyle types in all European countries, but their numbers vary. Try to determine which lifestyles are the most common in some European countries that you know.

21 Extreme sports. Chat rooms. Vegetarianism. Can you predict what will be 'hot' in the near future? Identify a lifestyle trend that is just surfacing in your country. Describe this trend in detail and justify your prediction. What specific styles and/or products are part of this trend?

For additional material see the companion website at **www.pearsoned.co.uk/solomon**

See Case studies B.1 and B.2 at the end of Part B:

Case study B.1: 'Virtual consumption: are consumers truly enjoying their "Second Life"?', Eman Gadalla (Lancaster University Management School) and Kathy Keeling (Alliance Manchester Business School) UK

Case study B.2: 'Contemporary fatherhood and the use of technology: exploring the transition to first-time fatherhood', Ben Kerrane (Manchester Metropolitan University) and Shona Bettany (Liverpool John Moores University) UK

Notes

1. https://www.tripadvisor.co.uk/Restaurants-g189400-Athens_Attica.html (accessed 27 July 2018).

2. For detailed definitions of different types of vegetarianism see https://www.vegsoc.org/definition (accessed 27 July 2018).

3. See Susan Baker, Keith E. Thompson and Julia Engelken, 'Mapping the values driving organic food choice: Germany vs the UK', *European Journal of Marketing* 38 (2004): 995 ff. Their study showed that although there were similarities between German and UK consumers of organic products in terms of values related to health, well-being and enjoyment, there were differences in terms of product attributes linked to achieving these values. A major difference was that UK consumers did not necessarily link organic food with the environment.

4. Tino Bech-Larsen and Klaus G. Grunert, 'The Influence of Tasting Experience and Health Benefits on Nordic Consumers' Rejection of Genetically Modified Foods', in Andrea Groppel-Klein and Franz-Rudolf Esch (eds), *European Advances in Consumer Research* 5 (Valdosta, GA: Association for Consumer Research, 2001): 11–14.

5. Ibid.

6. Ibid.

7. Laura Smith, 'Childhood obesity fuelled by cartoons', *The Guardian* (24 February 2005): 5; https://www.theguardian.com/society/2005/feb/24/food.foodanddrink2 (accessed 27 July 2018).

8. https://www.vegansociety.com/ (last accessed 16 August 2018).

9. https://reducetarian.org/ (last accessed 16 August 2018).

10. Nell Frizzell, 'Vegans, vegetarians and now. . . reducetarians', *The Observer* (25 June 2017), https://www.theguardian.com/lifeandstyle/2017/jun/25/vegans-vegetarians-and-now-reducetarians (accessed 27 July 2018).

11. Paul Hewer, 'Consuming Gardens: Representations of Paradise, Nostalgia and Postmodernism', in Darach Turley and Stephen Brown (eds), *European Advances in Consumer Research* 6 (Valdosta, GA: Association for Consumer Research, 2003): 327–31.

12. Grainne Fitzsimons, Tanya L. Chartrand and Gavan J. Fitzsimons, 'Automatic Effects of Brand Exposure on Motivated

Behavior: How Apple Makes You "Think Different"', *Journal of Consumer Research* 35 (2008): 21–35.

13. Gergana Y. Nenkov and Maura L. Scott, 'So Cute I Could Eat It Up: Priming Effects of Cute Products on Indulgent Consumption', *Journal of Consumer Research,* (August 2014), https://www.jstor.org/stable/10.1086/676581 (accessed 16 August 2018).

14. https://germanfoods.org/german-food-facts/german-meals-and-manners/ (accessed 27 July 2018)

15. Richard Bagozzi and Utpal Dholakia, 'Goal setting and goal striving in consumer behavior', *Journal of Marketing* 63 (October 1999): 19–23.

16. Eileen Fischer, Cele C. Otnes and Linda Tuncay, 'Pursuing parenthood: integrating cultural and cognitive perspectives on persistent goal striving', *Journal of Consumer Research* 34 (December 2007): 425–40.

17. Robert A. Baron, *Psychology: The Essential Science* (Needham, MA: Allyn & Bacon, 1989).

18. Scott I. Rick, Beatriz Pereira and Katherine A. Burson, 'The Benefits of Retail Therapy: Making Purchase Decisions Reduces Residual Sadness', *Journal of Consumer Psychology,* 24(3) (2014): 373–80.

19. Russell W. Belk, Guliz Ger and Søren Askegaard, 'The Fire of Desire: A Multisited Inquiry into Consumer Passion', *Journal of Consumer Research* 30 (2003): 326–51; see also Yu Chen, 'Possession and Access: Consumer Desires and Value Perceptions Regarding Contemporary Art Collection and Exhibit Visits', *Journal of Consumer Research* 35 (April 2009): 925–40.

20. Søren Askegaard and A. Fuat Firat, 'Towards a Critique of Material Culture, Consumption, and Markets', in S. Pearce (ed.), *Experiencing Material Culture in the Western World* (London: Leicester University Press, 1997): 114–39.

21. Anat Keinan and Ran Kivetz, 'Productivity Orientation and the Consumption of Collectable Experiences', *Journal of Consumer Research* 37(6) (April 2011): 935.

22. See, for instance, the discussion in Emma N. Banister and Margaret K. Hogg, 'Negative symbolic consumption and consumers' drive for self-esteem: the case of the fashion industry', *European Journal of Marketing* 38(7) (2004): 850–68.

23. Thomas Kramer and Song-Oh Yoon, 'Approach–Avoidance motivation and the use of affect as information', *Journal of Consumer Psychology* 17(2) (2007): 128–38.

24. Leon Festinger, *A Theory of Cognitive Dissonance* (Stanford, CA: Stanford University Press, 1957).

25. Jeannie Whalen, 'Meet the leader of the pack: Moscow's drag-racing queen Katya Karenina organizes illicit matches under the nose of the city police force', *The Wall Street Journal* (9 December 2002), jeanne.whalen@wsj.com.

26. Rebecca Smithers, 'Tofu turkey with all the trimmings? Britain carves out a meat-free Christmas', *The Guardian,* 2 December 2017, https://www.theguardian.com/lifeandstyle/2017/dec/02/christmas-vegan-vegetarian-cooking-flexitarian-diet-rebecca-smithers (accessed 27 July 2018).

27. Jean Baudrillard, 'La genèse idéologique des besoins', *Cahiers internationaux de sociologie* 47 (1969): 45–68.

28. See Paul T. Costa and Robert R. McCrae, 'From catalog to classification: Murray's needs and the five-factor model', *Journal of Personality and Social Psychology* 55 (1988): 258–65; Calvin S. Hall and Gardner Lindzey, *Theories of Personality,* 2nd edn (New York: Wiley, 1970); James U. McNeal and Stephen W. McDaniel, 'An analysis of need-appeals in

television advertising', *Journal of the Academy of Marketing Science* 12 (Spring 1984): 176–90.

29. Michael R. Solomon, Judith L. Zaichkowsky and Rosemary Polegato, *Consumer Behaviour: Buying, Having, and Being,* Canadian edition (Scarborough, Ontario: Prentice Hall Canada, 1999).

30. See David C. McClelland, *Studies in Motivation* (New York: Appleton-Century-Crofts, 1955).

31. Mary Kay Ericksen and M. Joseph Sirgy, 'Achievement Motivation and Clothing Preferences of White-Collar Working Women', in Michael R. Solomon (ed.), *The Psychology of Fashion* (Lexington, MA: Lexington Books, 1985): 357–69.

32. See Stanley Schachter, *The Psychology of Affiliation* (Stanford, CA: Stanford University Press, 1959).

33. Eugene M. Fodor and Terry Smith, 'The power motive as an influence on group decision making', *Journal of Personality and Social Psychology* 42 (1982): 178–85.

34. C.R. Snyder and Howard L. Fromkin, *Uniqueness: The Human Pursuit of Difference* (New York: Plenum, 1980).

35. Abraham H. Maslow, *Motivation and Personality,* 2nd edn (New York: Harper & Row, 1970).

36. An integrative view of consumer goal structures and goal-determination processes proposes six discrete levels of goals wherein higher-level (versus lower-level) goals are more abstract, more inclusive and less mutable. In descending order of abstraction, these goal levels are life themes and values, life projects, current concerns, consumption intentions, benefits sought and feature preferences. See Cynthia Huffman, S. Ratneshwar and David Glen Mick, 'Consumer Goal Structures and Goal-Determination Processes: An Integrative Framework', in S. Ratneshwar, David Glen Mick and Cynthia Huffman (eds), *The Why of Consumption* (London: Routledge, 2000): 9–35.

37. Henry, Paul (2006), 'Magnetic points for lifestyle shaping: the contribution of self-fulfillment, aspirations and capabilities', *Qualitative Market Research* 9(2): 170.

38. See, however, Primo Levi, *If This Is A Man* (London: Abacus by Sphere Books, 1987) 161: his discussion of the importance of friendship for surviving extreme conditions of deprivation and his description of the loss of his concentration camp friend and companion Alberto.

39. Study conducted in the Horticulture Department at Kansas State University, cited in 'Survey tells why gardening's good', *Vancouver Sun* (12 April 1997): B12; see also Paul Hewer and Douglas Brownlie (2006), 'Constructing "Hortiporn": On the aesthetics of stylized exteriors', *Advances in Consumer Research* 33(1).

40. Richard Maddock, 'A Theoretical and Empirical Substructure of Consumer Motivation and Behaviour', in Flemming Hansen (ed.), *European Advances in Consumer Research* 2 (Provo, UT: Association for Consumer Research, 1995): 29–37.

41. Adapted in part from Jack Loechner, 'Emotional Business Bonding on Social Networks', *Research Brief,* Center for Media Research (27 December 2007).

42. Judith Lynne Zaichkowsky, 'Measuring the involvement construct in marketing', *Journal of Consumer Research* 12 (December 1985): 341–52.

43. Andrew Mitchell, 'Involvement: A Potentially Important Mediator of Consumer Behaviour', in William L. Wilkie (ed.), *Advances in Consumer Research* 6 (Provo, UT: Association for Consumer Research, 1979): 191–6.

44. Richard L. Celsi and Jerry C. Olson, 'The role of involvement in attention and comprehension processes', *Journal of Consumer Research* 15 (September 1988): 210–24.

45. Ton Otker, 'The highly involved consumer: A marketing myth?' *Marketing and Research Today* (February 1990): 30–6.

46. Barbara J. Phillips and Edward F. McQuarrie, 'Narrative and persuasion in fashion advertising', *Journal of Consumer Research* 37 (October 2010): 368–92; Ronald E. Goldsmith, Leisha R. Flynn and Ronald A. Clark, 'Materialistic, brand engaged, and status consuming consumers and clothing behaviors', *Journal of Fashion Marketing and Management* 16(1) (2012): 102–20.

47. Robert W. Pimentel and Kristy E. Reynolds, 'A model for consumer devotion: Affective commitment with proactive sustaining behaviors,' *Academy of Marketing Science Review*, 5 (2004).

48. Tanya Irwin, 'Breakout brands connect with customers', *Marketing Daily* (4 November 2012).

49. Charles C. Cui, Mona Mrad and Margaret K. Hogg, 'Brand addiction: Exploring the concept and its definition through an experiential lens', *Journal of Business Research* 87 (June 2018): 118–27, https://doi.org/10.1016/j.jbusres.2018.02.028 (accessed 27 July 2018)

50. Anthony G. Greenwald and Clark Leavitt, 'Audience involvement in advertising: four levels', *Journal of Consumer Research* 11 (June 1984): 581–92.

51. Mihaly Csikszentmihalyi, *Flow: The Psychology of Optimal Experience* (New York: HarperCollins, 1991); Donna L. Hoffman and Thomas P. Novak, 'Marketing in hypermedia computer-mediated environments: Conceptual foundations', *Journal of Marketing* 60 (July 1996): 50–68.

52. Judith Lynne Zaichkowsky, 'The Emotional Side of Product Involvement', in Paul Anderson and Melanie Wallendorf (eds), *Advances in Consumer Research* 14 (Provo, UT: Association for Consumer Research): 32–5.

53. For a discussion of interrelationship between situational and enduring involvement, see Marsha L. Richins, Peter H. Bloch and Edward F. McQuarrie, 'How enduring and situational involvement combine to create involvement responses', *Journal of Consumer Psychology* 1(2) (1992): 143–53. For more information on the involvement construct see 'Special issue on involvement', *Psychology and Marketing* 10(4) (July/August 1993).

54. Joseph B. Pine II and James H. Gilmore, *Markets of One – Creating Customer-Unique Value through Mass Customization* (Boston: Harvard Business School Press, 2000).

55. http://search.ft.com/ftArticle?queryText=personalization&y=4&aje=false&x=16&id=070913000705&ct=0 (accessed 26 April 2008); http://adfarm.mediaplex.com/ad/fm/54649?mpt=5640053&mpvc= (accessed 27 April 2008).

56. Michael I. Norton, Daniel Mochon and Dan Ariely, 'The IKEA Effect: When Labor Leads to Love', *Journal of Consumer Psychology* 22(3) (2012): 453–60.

57. Jacob Jacoby and Robert Chestnut, *Brand Loyalty: Measurement and Management* (New York: Wiley, 1978).

58. David F. Midgley, 'Patterns of Interpersonal Information Seeking for the Purchase of a Symbolic Product', *Journal of Marketing Research* 20 (February 1983): 74–83.

59. Sarah Butler, 'Cheers? No thanks! Low- and no-alcohol lifestyle booms', *The Guardian* (26 January 2018), https://www.theguardian.com/society/2018/jan/26/cheers-no-thanks-low--and-no-alcohol-lifestyle-booms (accessed 27 July 2018).

60. Ibid.

61. Cyndee Miller, 'Scotland to U.S.: "This Tennent's for You"', *Marketing News* (29 August 1994): 26.

62. Rebecca K. Ratner, Barbara E. Kahn and Daniel Kahneman, 'Choosing Less-Preferred Experiences for the Sake of Variety', *Journal of Consumer Research* 26 (June 1999): 1–15.

63. Rajeev Batra and Michael L. Ray, 'Operationalizing Involvement as Depth and Quality of Cognitive Responses', in Alice Tybout and Richard Bagozzi (eds), *Advances in Consumer Research* 10 (Ann Arbor, MI: Association for Consumer Research, 1983): 309–13.

64. Tim Nudd, 'Coldplay Hides Lyrics From New Album Inside Libraries in 9 Countries: Look for the Ghost Stories', *Adweek* (1 May 2014), http://www.adweek.com/adfreak/coldplay-hides-lyrics-new-album-inside-libraries-9-countries-157410 (accessed 27 July 2018)

65. Herbert E. Krugman, 'The Impact of Television Advertising: Learning Without Involvement,' *Public Opinion Quarterly* 29 (Fall 1965): 349–56.

66. Brent McFerran, Darren W. Dahl, Gerald J. Gorn and Heather Honea, 'Motivational Determinants of Transportation into Marketing Narratives', *Journal of Consumer Psychology* 20(3) (2010): 306–16.

67. David W. Stewart and David H. Furse, 'Analysis of the Impact of Executional Factors in Advertising Performance', *Journal of Advertising Research* 24 (1984): 23–6; Deborah J. MacInnis, Christine Moorman and Bernard J. Jaworski, 'Enhancing and Measuring Consumers' Motivation, Opportunity, and Ability to Process Brand Information from Ads', *Journal of Marketing* 55 (October 1991): 332–53.

68. Elaine Sciolino, 'Disproving Notions, Raising a Fury', *New York Times* (21 January 2003).

69. Louise Story, 'Times Sq. Ads Spread via Tourists' Cameras', *New York Times* (11 December 2006).

70. 'Ads That Stay with You,' *Newsweek* (19 November 2007), www.newsweek.com/Id/68904 (accessed 27 July 2018).

71. R.S.Elder and A. Krishna, The "visual depiction effect" in advertising: facilitating embodied mental simulation through product orientation', *Journal of Consumer Research* 38(6) (2012): 988 –1,003.

72. Stephanie Clifford, 'Axe body products puts its brand on the Hamptons club scene', *New York Times* (22 May 2009): B6; Alana Semuels, 'Honda finds a groovy new way to pitch products: The musical road', *Los Angeles Times* (13 October 2008); Eric Pfanner, 'A live promotion, at 14,000 feet', *New York Times* (6 June 2008); Les Luchter, 'Jameson Whiskey texts targets on N.Y. streets', *Marketing Daily* (8 August 2008); Doreen Carvajal, 'Dancers in the crowd bring back "Thriller"', *New York Times* (10 March 2008); Eric Pfanner, 'When consumers help, ads are free', *New York Times* (21 June 2009).

73. The Nielsen Company Press Release, 'Over 875 Million Consumers Have Shopped Online – the Number of Internet Shoppers Up 40 per cent in Two Years', http://www.earthtimes.org (accessed 16 August 2018).

74. http://www.adweek.com/socialtimes/social-ad-spend-stats-trends/503712 (accessed 27 July 2018).

75. Rajeev Batra and Michael L. Ray, 'Operationalizing Involvement as Depth and Quality of Cognitive Responses', in Alice Tybout and Richard Bagozzi, eds., *Advances in Consumer Research* 10 (Ann Arbor, MI: Association for Consumer Research, 1983): 309–13.

76. Li Yuan, 'Television's new joy of text shows with vote by messaging are on the rise as programmers try to make live TV matter', *Wall Street Journal* (20 July 2006): B1.

77. Mark J. Arnold and Kristy E. Reynolds, 'Hedonic shopping motivations', *Journal of Retailing* 79 (2003): 77–95.

78. Drew Elliott, 'Opportunities for Brands in Social Games', *Ogilvy PR Blog* (May 2010).

79. Andiara Petterle, 'Reaching Latinos through virtual goods', *Media Post* (10 June 2010).

80. Karyne Levy, 'Here's why Amazon just paid nearly $1 billion for a site where you watch people play video games', *Business Insider* (25 August 2014), http://www.businessinsider.com/heres-why-amazon-paid-almost-1-billion-for-twitch-2014-8#ixzz3VnhCim1P (accessed 27 July 2018).

81. Paul Mozur, 'For South Korea, e-sports is national pastime', *New York Times* (19 October 2014), http://www.nytimes.com/2014/10/20/technology/league-of-legends-south-korea-epicenter-esports.html (accessed 27 July 2018).

82. These definitions are adapted from entries in *The Urban Dictionary,* www.urbandictionary.com (accessed 27 July 2018).

83. Pierre Valette-Florence, *Les styles de vie* (Paris: Nathan, 1994); Benjamin Zablocki and Rosabeth Moss Kanter, 'The differentiation of life-styles', *Annual Review of Sociology* (1976): 269–97.

84. Mary T. Douglas and Baron C. Isherwood, *The World of Goods* (New York: Basic Books, 1979).

85. Richard A. Peterson, 'Revitalizing the culture concept', *Annual Review of Sociology* 5 (1979): 137–66.

86. Sarah Butler 'Cheers? No thanks! Low- and no-alcohol lifestyle booms', *The Guardian* (26 January 2018) https://www.theguardian.com/society/2018/jan/26/cheers-no-thanks-low--and-no-alcohol-lifestyle-booms (accessed 27 July 2018).

87. Søren Askegaard, 'Livsstilsundersøgelser: henimod et teoretisk fundament', doctoral dissertation, School of Business and Economics: Odense University, 1993.

88. William Leiss, Stephen Kline and Sut Jhally, *Social Communication in Advertising* (Toronto: Methuen, 1986).

89. Douglas and Isherwood, *The World of Goods,* 72–3.

90. Christopher K. Hsee and France Leclerc, 'Will Products Look More Attractive When Presented Separately or Together?' *Journal of Consumer Research* 25 (September 1998): 175–86.

91. Brian Steinberg, 'Whose Ad Is This Anyway? Agencies Use Brand Icons to Promote Other Products; Cheaper Than Zeta-Jones', *Wall Street Journal* (4 December 2003).

92. Michael R. Solomon, 'The Role of Products as Social Stimuli: A Symbolic Interactionism Perspective', *Journal of Consumer Research* 10 (December 1983): 319–29.

93. Michael R. Solomon and Henry Assael, 'The Forest or the Trees? A *Gestalt* Approach to Symbolic Consumption', in Jean Umiker-Sebeok, ed., *Marketing and Semiotics: New Directions in the Study of Signs for Sale* (Berlin: Mouton de Gruyter, 1988), 189–218; Michael R. Solomon, 'Mapping Product Constellations: A Social Categorization Approach to Symbolic Consumption', *Psychology & Marketing* 5(3) (1988): 233–58; see also Stephen C. Cosmas, 'Life Styles and Consumption Patterns', *Journal of Consumer Research* 8(4) (March 1982): 453–5; Russell W. Belk, 'Yuppies as Arbiters of the Emerging Consumption Style', in Richard J. Lutz, ed., *Advances in Consumer Research* 13 (Provo, UT: Association for Consumer Research, 1986): 514–19.

94. Quoted in 'Polo/Ralph Lauren Corporation History', *Funding Universe,* http://www.fundinguniverse.com/company-histories/polo-ralph-lauren-corporation-history/ (accessed 27 July 2018); Mark J. Miller, 'Ralph Lauren Ready to Open First Restaurant in New York City', *Brandchannel* (12 December 2014).

95. Lan Nguyen Chaplin and Tina M. Lowrey, 'The Development of Consumer-Based Consumption Constellations in Children', *Journal of Consumer Research,* 36(5) (2010): 757–77.

96. See Lewis Alpert and Ronald Gatty, 'Product Positioning by Behavioral Life Styles', *Journal of Marketing* 33 (April 1969): 65–9; Emanuel H. Demby, 'Psychographics Revisited: The Birth of a Technique', *Marketing News* (2 January 1989): 21; William D. Wells, 'Backward Segmentation', in Johan Arndt (ed.), *Insights into Consumer Behavior* (Boston: Allyn & Bacon, 1968): 85–100.

97. Bill Schlackman, 'An Historical Perspective', in S. Robson and A. Foster (eds), *Qualitative Research in Action* (London: Edward Arnold, 1989): 15–23.

98. William D. Wells and Douglas J. Tigert, 'Activities, interests, and opinions', *Journal of Advertising Research* 11 (August 1971): 27.

99. Piirto Heath, 'Psychographics: "Q'est-ce que c'est"?', *American Demographics* (November 1995).

100. Alfred S. Boote, 'Psychographics: mind over matter', *American Demographics* (April 1980): 26–9; William D. Wells, 'Psychographics: a critical review', *Journal of Marketing Research* 12 (May 1975): 196–213.

101. These lifestyle dimensions are based on William D. Wells and Douglas J. Tigert, 'Activities, interests and opinions', *Journal of Advertising Research* 11 (August 1971): 27–35.

102. Joseph T. Plummer, 'The concept and application of life style segmentation', *Journal of Marketing* 38 (January 1974): 33–7.

103. J.E. Burroughs and A. Rindfleisch, 'Materialism and well-being: a conflicting values perspective', *Journal of Consumer Research* 29(3): 348–70; Hugh Williamson, 'All the rage in Germany: cheap flights', *Financial Times* (26 March 2004).

104. For information about international lifestyle segmentation approaches in the US, e.g. the psychographic segmentation typology VALS2™ and its associated lifestyle analyses, go to http://www.strategicbusinessinsights.com/vals/ and www.strategicbusinessinsights.com/vals/presurvey.shtml (accessed 27 July 2018).

105. http://www.strategicbusinessinsights.com/vals/international/ (accessed 27 July 2018).

106. See VALS website for detailed descriptions of each of these six core groups of UK consumers: http://www.strategicbusinessinsights.com/vals/international/uk.shtml (accessed 27 July 2018).

107. Ibid.

108. Valette-Florence, *Les Styles de vie,* op. cit.

109. Askegaard, 'Livsstilsundersøgelser: henimod et teoretisk fundament', op. cit.

110. Julia Carrie Wong, '"It might work too well": the dark art of political advertising online', *The Guardian* (22 March 2018) https://www.theguardian.com/technology/2018/mar/19/facebook-political-ads-social-media-history-online-democracy (accessed 27 July 2018).

111. 'Consumers Willing to Trade Off Privacy for Electronic Personalization', sourced from www.mediapost.com (accessed 16 August 2018).

112. https://www.bing.com/ (accessed 27 July 2018).

113. Aaron O. Patrick, 'Microsoft ad push is all about you: "Behavioral Targeting" aims to use customer preferences to hone marketing pitches', *Wall Street Journal* (26 December 2006): B3; Brian Steinberg, 'Next up on Fox: Ads that can change pitch', *Wall Street Journal* (21 April 2005): B1; Bob Tedeschi, 'Every click you make, they'll be watching you', *New York Times Online* (3 April 2006); David Kesmodel, 'Marketers push online ads based on your surfing habits', *Wall Street Journal on the Web* (5 April 2005).

114. https://myspace.com/ (accessed 27 July 2018).

115. Associated Press, 'MySpace launches targeted ad program', *New York Times Online* (18 September 2007); Vauhini Vara, 'Facebook gets personal with ad targeting plan', *Wall Street Journal* (23 August 2007): B1.

116. Shalom H. Schwartz and Warren Bilsky, 'Toward a universal psychological structure of human values', *Journal of Personality and Social Psychology* 53 (1987): 550–62.

117. Ajay K. Sirsi, James C. Ward and Peter H. Reingen, 'Microcultural analysis of variation in sharing of causal reasoning about behavior', *Journal of Consumer Research* 22 (March 1996): 345–72.

118. Richard W. Pollay, 'Measuring the cultural values manifest in advertising', *Current Issues and Research in Advertising* (1983): 71–92.

119. Deborah Ball, 'Women in Italy like to clean but shun the quick and easy: Convenience doesn't sell when bathrooms average four scrubbings a week', *Wall Street Journal* (25 April 2006): A1.

120. Milton Rokeach, *The Nature of Human Values* (New York: Free Press, 1973).

121. Sang-Pil Han and Sharon Shavitt, 'Persuasion and culture: Advertising appeals in individualistic and collectivistic societies', *Journal of Experimental Social Psychology* 30 (1994): 326–50.

122. Thomas Gilovich, Amit Kumar, Amit and Lily Jampol, 'A wonderful life: Experiential consumption and the pursuit of happiness', *Journal of Consumer Psychology* 25(1) (2015): 152–65; Marsha L. Richins, 'When wanting is better than having: Materialism, transformation expectations, and product-evoked emotions in the purchase process', *Journal of Consumer Research* 40(1) (June 2013): 1–18.

123. https://www.theguardian.com/business/2017/mar/23/next-price-rises-profits-fall-pound-brexit (accessed 16 August 2018).

124. https://www.theguardian.com/business/2016/jan/18/weve-hit-peak-home-furnishings-says-ikea-boss-consumerism (accessed 16 August 2018).

125. https://www.theguardian.com/books/2015/jan/07/stuffocation-living-more-with-less-james-wallman-review (accessed 16 August 2018).

126. Simon Usborne, 'Just do it: The experience economy and how we turned our backs on "stuff"', *The Guardian* (13 May 2017), https://www.theguardian.com/business/2017/may/13/just-do-it-the-experience-economy-and-how-we-turned-our-backs-on-stuff (accessed 27 July 2018).

127. See, for instance, the discussion of acculturation issues and British South East Asian women in A.M. Lindridge, M.K. Hogg and M. Shah, 'Imagined multiple worlds: How South Asian women in Britain use family and friends to navigate the "border crossings" between household and societal contexts', *Consumption, Markets and Culture* 7(3) (September 2004): 211–38.

128. Edward Helmore, 'So how do you make snakeskin handbags environmentally friendly?', *The Observer* (24 May 2015): 33, http://www.theguardian.com/fashion/2015/may/24/fashion-environment-sustainability (accessed 27 July 2018).

129. Donald E. Vinson, Jerome E. Scott and Lawrence R. Lamont, 'The role of personal values in marketing and consumer behaviour', *Journal of Marketing* 41 (April 1977): 44–50; John Watson, Steven Lysonski, Tamara Gillan and Leslie Raymore, 'Cultural values and important possessions: A cross-cultural analysis', *Journal of Business Research* 55 (2002): 923–31.

130. Quester, Pascale, Michael Beverland and Francis Farrelly (2006), 'Brand-personal values fit and brand meanings: exploring the role individual values play in ongoing brand loyalty in extreme sports subcultures', *Advances in Consumer Research* 33(1).

131. Jennifer Aaker, Veronica Benet-Martinez and Jordi Garolera, 'Consumption symbols as carriers of culture: A study of Japanese and Spanish brand personality constructs', *Journal of Personality and Social Psychology* (2001).

132. *Markedsføring* (25 August 2000): 8; see also Amelia Hill and Anushka Asthana, 'She's young, gifted and ahead of you at the till', *Observer* (2 January 2005): 7, http://observer.guardian.co.uk/uk_news/story/0,6903,1382042,00.html (accessed 27 July 2018). This describes 10 million twenty-to-thirty somethings in UK 'who are the new darlings of the retailers and politicians want their vote'. They are key decision makers and spenders in homeware stores.

133. Morris B. Holbrook, *Consumer Value* (London: Routledge, 1999).

134. Ibid. This book contains a chapter by various consumer researchers on each of the value types.

135. A comfortable life; an exciting life; a sense of accomplishment; a world at peace; a world of beauty; equality; family security; freedom; happiness; inner harmony; mature love; national security; pleasure; salvation; self-respect; social recognition; true friendship; and wisdom.

136. Ambitious; broad-minded; capable; cheerful; clean; courageous; forgiving; helpful; honest; imaginative; independent; intellectual; logical; loving; obedient; polite; responsible; and self-controlled.

137. Milton Rokeach, *Understanding Human Values* (New York: The Free Press, 1979); see also J. Michael Munson and Edward McQuarrie, 'Shortening the Rokeach Value Survey for Use in Consumer Research', in Michael J. Houston (ed.), *Advances in Consumer Research* 15 (Provo, UT: Association for Consumer Research, 1988): 381–6.

138. B.W. Becker and P.E. Conner, 'Personal values of the heavy user of mass media', *Journal of Advertising Research* 21 (1981): 37–43; D.E. Vinson, J.E. Scott, L.M. Lamont, 'The role of personal values in marketing and consumer behavior', *Journal of Marketing* 41(2) (1977): 44–50.

139. Sharon E. Beatty, Lynn R. Kahle, Pamela Homer and Shekhar Misra, 'Alternative Measurement Approaches to Consumer Values: The List of Values and the Rokeach Value Survey', *Psychology & Marketing* 2 (1985): 181–200; Lynn R. Kahle and Patricia Kennedy, 'Using the List of Values (LOV) to Understand Consumers', *Journal of Consumer Marketing* 2 (Fall 1988): 49–56; Lynn Kahle, Basil Poulos and Ajay Sukhdial, 'Changes in Social Values in the United States During the Past Decade', *Journal of Advertising Research* 28 (February–March 1988): 35–41; see also Wagner A. Kamakura and Jose Alfonso Mazzon, 'Value Segmentation: A Model for the Measurement of Values and Value Systems', *Journal of*

Consumer Research 18 (September 1991): 28; Jagdish N. Sheth, Bruce I. Newman and Barbara L. Gross, *Consumption Values and Market Choices: Theory and Applications* (Cincinnati, OH: South-Western, 1991).

140. Pierre Valette-Florence, Suzanne C. Grunert, Klaus G. Grunert and Sharon Beatty, 'Une comparaison franco-allemande de l'adhésion aux valeurs personnelles', *Recherche et Applications en Marketing* 6(3) (1991): 5–20.

141. Klaus G. Grunert, Suzanne C. Grunert and Sharon Beatty, 'Cross-cultural research on consumer values', *Marketing and Research Today* 17 (1989): 30–9.

142. Suzanne C. Grunert, Klaus G. Grunert and Kai Kristensen, 'Une méthode d'estimation de la validité interculturelle des instruments de mesure: Le cas de la mesure des valeurs des consommateurs par la liste des valeurs LOV', *Recherche et Applications en Marketing* 8(4) (1993): 5–28. Beatty, Kahle, Homer and Misra, 'Alternative measurement approaches to consumer values': 181–200; Lynn R. Kahle and Patricia Kennedy, 'Using the List of Values (LOV) to understand consumers', *Journal of Consumer Marketing* 2 (Fall 1988): 49–56; Lynn Kahle, Basil Poulos and Ajay Sukhdial, 'Changes in social values in the United States during the past decade', *Journal of Advertising Research* 28 (February/March 1988): 35–41; see also Wagner A. Kamakura and Jose Alfonso Mazzon, 'Value segmentation: a model for the measurement of values and value systems', *Journal of Consumer Research* 18 (September 1991): 28; Jagdish N. Sheth, Bruce I. Newman and Barbara L. Gross, *Consumption Values and Market Choices: Theory and Applications* (Cincinnati: South-Western Publishing Co., 1991).

143. Shalom H. Schwartz and Warren Bilsky, 'Toward a theory of universal content and structure of values: extensions and cross-cultural replications', *Journal of Personality and Social Psychology* 58 (1990): 878–91; Shalom H. Schwartz, 'Universals in the Content and Structure of Values: Theoretical Advance and Empirical Test in 20 Countries', in M. Zanna (ed.), *Advances in Experimental Social Psychology* 25 (San Diego, CA: Academic Press, 1992): 1–65.

144. Shalom H. Schwartz, 'Beyond Individualism/Collectivism: New Cultural Dimensions of Values' in U. Kim et al. (eds), *Individualism and Collectivism* (Thousand Oaks, CA: Sage, 1994): 85–119.

145. Sarah Todd, Rob Lawson and Haydn Northover, 'Value Orientation and Media Consumption Behavior', in B. Englis and A. Olofsson (eds), *European Advances in Consumer Behaviour* 3 (Provo, UT: Association for Consumer Research): 328–32.

146. Thomas J. Reynolds and Jonathan Gutman, 'Laddering theory, method, analysis, and interpretation', *Journal of Advertising Research* (February/March 1988): 11–34; Beth Walker, Richard Celsi and Jerry Olson, 'Exploring the Structural Characteristics of Consumers' Knowledge', in Melanie Wallendorf and Paul Anderson (eds), *Advances in Consumer Research* 14 (Provo, UT: Association for Consumer Research, 1986): 17–21.

147. Andreas Hermann, 'Wertorientierte produktund werbegestaltung', *Marketing ZFP* 3 (3rd quarter 1996): 153–63.

148. N.A. Nielsen, T. Bech-Larsen and K.G. Grunert, 'Consumer purchase motives and product perceptions: A laddering study on vegetable oil in three countries', *Food Quality and Preference* 9(6) (1998): 455–66.

149. Klaus G. Grunert and Suzanne C. Grunert, 'Measuring subjective meaning structures by the laddering method: Theoretical considerations and methodological problems', *International Journal of Research in Marketing* 12(3) (1995): 209–25. This volume of *IJRM* is a special issue on means–end chains and the laddering technique.

150. Roger Mason, 'Measuring the Demand for Status Goods: An Evaluation of Means–End Chains and Laddering', in Hansen (ed.), *European Advances in Consumer Research* 2: 78–82.

151. Emily Burg, 'Whole foods is consumers' favorite green brand', *Marketing Daily*, mediapost.com (10 May 2007).

152. Cristina Cardigo and Paulo Rita, 'Fostering Sustainable Consumption Practices Through Consumer Empowerment' in Alan Bradshaw, Chris Hackley and Pauline Maclaran (eds), *European Association for Consumer Research Conference*, 2010, RHUL: 55.

153. Katie Fisher, 'UK Statistics on Waste', DEFRA (22 February 2018), https://assets.publishing.service.gov.uk/government/uploads/system/uploads/attachment_data/file/683051/UK_Statisticson_Waste_statistical_notice_Feb_2018_FINAL.pdf (accessed 16 August 2018).

154. https://www.kelloggs.co.uk/en_GB/who-we-are/press-release/kelloggs-goes-organic.html (accessed 27 July 2018).

155. Adrienne W. Fawcett, 'Conscientious consumerism drives record new product launches in 2006', *New York Times* (24 January 2007).

156. Mya Frazier, 'Farmstands vs Big Brands: With Consumers Interested in Locally Produced Goods, Marketers Scramble to Get in on a Movement Going Mainstream', adgage.com (5 June 2007).

157. Cecilia M. Vega, 'Mayor to cut off flow of city money for bottled water', http://sfgate.com/cgi-bin/article.cgi?f=/c/a/2007/06/22/BAGE8QJVIL1.DTL (accessed 27 July 2018).

158. Note that a carbon footprint comprises two parts, the direct/primary footprint and the indirect/secondary footprint: firstly, the primary footprint is a measure of our direct emissions of CO_2 from the burning of fossil fuels including domestic energy consumption and transportation (e.g. car and plane); and secondly the secondary footprint is a measure of the indirect CO_2 emissions from the whole life cycle of products we use – those associated with their manufacture and eventual breakdown.

159. Ekaterina Ochagavia and Josh Strauss, 'We need to talk about plastic bottles', *The Guardian* (29 June 2017), https://www.theguardian.com/environment/video/2017/jun/29/we-need-to-talk-about-plastic-bottles (accessed 27 July 2018).

160. Daniel Boffey, 'EU declares war on plastic waste', *The Guardian* (16 Jan 2018), https://www.theguardian.com/environment/2018/jan/16/eu-declares-war-on-plastic-waste-2030 (accessed 27 July 2018).

161. Editorial, 'Water: Go against the flow', *The Guardian* (20 August 2008): 30, http://www.guardian.co.uk/commentisfree/2008/aug/20/water.food (accessed 27 July 2018).

162. Ibid.

163. Felicity Lawrence, 'Revealed: The massive scale of UK's water consumption', *The Guardian* (20 August 2008): 1, http://www.guardian.co.uk/environment/2008/aug/20/water.food1 (accessed 27 July 2018).

164. Wendy Koch, '"Green" product claims are often misleading', *USA Today* (26 October 2010), http://content.usatoday.com/communities/greenhouse/post/2010/10/green-product-claims/1?csp=34money&utm_source=feedburner&utm_medium=feed&utm_campaign=Feed%3A$+$Usatodaycom-Money-TopStories$+$%28Money$+$-$+$Top$+$Stories%29 (accessed 27 July 2018).

165. See Gary Bamossy and Basil Englis video: 'In Green', http://vimeo.com/10409261, which gets into the 'burnout' of Green; see also Amy DuFault and Jennifer Kho, 'Sustainability: Is it a dirty word?', *The Guardian* (March 25 2015), https://www.theguardian.com/sustainable-business/2015/mar/25/sustainability-eco-green-natural-buzzwords-greenwashing (accessed 27 July 2018).

166. Mark Dolliver, 'Thumbs down on corporate green efforts', *Adweek* (31 August 2010); Sarah Mahoney, 'Americans hate faux green marketers', *Marketing Daily* (25 March 2011).

Case study B.1

Virtual consumption: are consumers truly enjoying their 'Second Life'?

Eman Gadalla, Lancaster University Management School, UK, and **Kathy Keeling**, Alliance Manchester Business School, UK

One of the distinctive features of virtual worlds (VWs) is the tangible representation of the user, that is, the avatar, which provides a focus for social interaction and helps engender identity, presence and social facilitation.[1] Avatars are the only means by which consumers in VWs present themselves to others and create a virtual identity (that is, how they would like to be regarded by themselves and by others). Although in real life it might be challenging, expensive or simply impossible to change one's physical attributes, avatars can be instantly redesigned online by means of graphic technology. Consumers can choose either to design an avatar that is identical or representative of themselves, or to create one that reflects their fantasies, imagination or the person they wish to be. Since each avatar is both part of the perceived environment and a representation of the user to others, VWs potentially offer a high level of mutual awareness[2] and produce feelings not only of presence, but also of co-presence.[3] Therefore, VWs provide interactive customer experiences to educate, entertain, display information and offer an appealing visual aesthetic encounter. Additionally, VWs such as *Second Life* have their own economies with convertible currencies (such as linden dollars), intellectual property and free market exchange. One of the most popular activities in VWs is virtual consumption (that is, consuming virtual products online).

Because of these unique characteristics, marketers and advertisers are interested in using VWs as sites for engaging consumers in deeper and more sustaining ways. To provide customers with an enjoyable virtual experience, it is important to understand how consumers perceive VWs and to identify their different motivations and values. Kelly, Thomas, Mark and Mary are *Second Life* users who met online in *Second Life* and became friends; they live in different countries around the world, and each of them has a different character and uses *Second Life* for a different reason. They meet regularly in *Second Life* to shop, play and attend events. In one of their meetings they decided to talk about why they use *Second Life* and to discuss whether or not they fully enjoy their virtual experience. In the following sections we will introduce each user and provide a summary of their different opinions regarding *Second Life* in general and virtual consumption activities in particular.

Kelly is a 33-year-old single woman who lives in the US; she is mainly interested in consuming the beauty of the virtual context. Kelly appreciates the time and effort taken to create and design virtual contexts such as Hyde Park, and she enjoys attractive store designs. Kelly explained that she uses *Second Life* to have fun, as well as to enjoy the aesthetics, environment and music. Since joining *Second Life*, Kelly has become interested only in high-quality stores, which highlights the importance she places on product quality. Despite the fact that these products can only be virtually consumed in *Second Life*, buying good-quality products has a significant effect on her virtual experience in general and her avatar appearance in particular. It is important to Kelly to stand out in *Second Life*. She likes her avatar to be unique and attractive; she does not want to do this with an extraordinary 'skin' for her avatar, such as a cat or a lion, but wants to be human in *Second Life* too, wearing fancy and stylish clothes, human skins and shapes. In her real life, she feels her appearance must be relatively sober and modest, appropriate for her job as a lawyer.

Kelly complains that *Second Life* store owners do not update their stock regularly and that it is very boring seeing the same merchandise over and over again. Kelly is always hunting for new high-quality stores in *Second Life*, which proves to be very difficult; she has, on occasion, spent many linden dollars on outfits only to put them on her avatar and discover that even with a fair amount of editing, the garments look unattractive. This is a waste of time and money. She feels that stores should prioritise the overall design concept; some stores are better at doing this than others.

Thomas is a 30-year-old married man with three young children who lives in the UK. His main *Second Life* purchasing interest is buying Gothic outfits for his avatar. His priority is to find affordable and reasonably priced virtual products; he does not want his virtual consumption to affect his real life because, although he is buying virtual products that are not delivered in real life, he is still paying real money. Even though linden dollars represent very small sums of real money, he considers that because of the attractive nature of *Second Life,* large amounts of money can be spent unintentionally, and this could impact his real-life budget. He must therefore stay within budget in *Second Life* as he has more pressing requirements on his wallet and other important spending priorities in real life. He complains about overpriced products, noting that it is not acceptable to sell an overpriced product even if it is of high quality. He appreciates the amount of work that can go into making a product, but maintains that the price should be realistic. If a product is well made it can demand a reasonably high price, but overpricing a product just to make money quickly is not acceptable – in Thomas's opinion, this is just greed. He tends to look for good designers whose clothes are cheaper in price but of the same quality as the most popular designers. He managed to find a good store that sells moderately priced outfits; within this store, the purchasing process is always fast and simple, with no delay. Thomas is very loyal to this store and would not switch to another one.

Mary is a married woman in her fifties who lives in France; she uses a beautiful fairy avatar. She notes that while in some stores the customer service is excellent, other stores provide appalling service or almost no service at all. One of her most memorable virtual experiences is when she went shopping for furniture for her virtual house. She went to one store where a very helpful salesperson showed her around, displaying the different products and options available. She enjoyed the guided tour and felt that she had received excellent customer service that was friendly and fun. She also bought a flag for another project and then noticed that it had a fault. She contacted the creator/store owner who quickly responded to her complaint and sent her a replacement. Mary was impressed by the excellent and fast response. She generally would like salespeople to be friendly and knowledgeable, otherwise she will spend her money elsewhere. In addition, she prefers talking to a live avatar, rather than a scripted bot; she uses *Second Life* mainly to communicate and interact with others and does not like to go into an empty place and feel like a trespasser. She explained the importance of customer service, stating that this makes her feel good about herself and more confident about her purchases. Simply put, make someone feel at home as well as answering their questions and concerns, and they will be regular and loyal customers.

Mark, who uses a female avatar, is a married man in his forties who lives in China. He noted that one distinguishing feature of *Second Life* that can attract customers is the use of demos (that is, product demonstrations that can allow the product to be evaluated). He explained that demos of skins, hair or clothing are important because there is a huge difference between how they look on a picture of a model and how they look on the customer. Mark was hoping to buy a large spaceship, which is sold in different *Second Life* stores. He went to a popular store that had a large demonstration area where the spaceships they sold could be viewed. Mark browsed the menu and viewed the different spaceships sold. The store had set it up so that the majority of functions were working, and this meant he could get a real feel for the product. Having this ability to view such large and expensive items in depth is a great advantage. Mark felt that this store was of high quality and he intends to continue visiting it for any future purchases.

Questions

1 How does the self-concept affect how consumers behave in virtual worlds? Reflect on the real-world and virtual identities of the four *Second Life* users: Kelly, Thomas, Mark and Mary.

2 Consumers can become very attached to their virtual life in general, and virtual products in particular. Discuss the different components of involvement in *Second Life* and identify different strategies to increase consumer involvement.

3 Virtual experience may generate different types of consumer values. Discuss how values are linked to consumer behaviour in virtual worlds.

4 What reasons can you find for why consumers would want to engage in virtual consumption activities? Reflect on the why of virtual consumption.

5 Create a *Second Life* account and spend time teleporting your avatar between islands, exploring different activities and enjoying freebies, then reflect on your own virtual experience.

6 Discuss the possibility and likely extent of future migration to 3D immersive environments. Think about the opportunities and the challenges of moving from the internet as we know it to the future internet, that is, 3D internet.

Sources

[1]M. Gerhard, D.J. Moore and D. Hobbs, 'Embodiment and co-presence in collaborative interfaces', *International Journal of Human Computer Studies* 61(4) (2004): 453–80.

[2]M. Slater and S. Wilbur, 'A framework for immersive virtual environments (FIVE): speculations on the role of presence in virtual environments', *Presence Teleoperators and Virtual Environments* 6(6) (1997): 603–16.

[3]M. Gerhard, D.J. Moore and D. Hobbs, 'Embodiment and co-presence in collaborative interfaces', *International Journal of Human Computer Studies* 61(4) (2004): 453–80.

Case study B.2

Contemporary fatherhood and the use of technology: exploring the transition to first-time fatherhood

Ben Kerrane, Manchester Metropolitan University, UK, and **Shona Bettany**, Liverpool John Moores University, UK

I'm a strong person, I'm a strong family man, I'm a strong husband and a strong father.[1]

When men become fathers for the first time they experience what has been termed a 'male identity crisis',[2] encountering various pressures (social, economic, historical) as they strive to meet 'the many conflicting and contradictory demands made of them due to their male sex role'.[3] What does it mean to be a father, and what does this role involve? Existing studies of fatherhood have explored the different epochs of fatherhood over recent decades,[4] charting the development of the father role from that of moral teacher, through breadwinner (with fathers having sole responsibility for the financial support of their family), towards more recent articulations of the nurturing/involved father role.

Contemporary men such as David Beckham often feel the need to 'have it all' in their role as fathers. On the one hand, they want to be able to provide financially for their children, and on the other, they also want to be involved in the provision of care for their children (for example, changing nappies, participating in childcare and helping with night-time feeds). Gone are the days, it would appear, when fathers concentrated only on the financial responsibility for their family. But are these days indeed past? Despite many opportunities opening-up to fathers (such as flexible working practices and shared parental leave schemes, which aim to encourage fathers to have greater involvement in contemporary family life), many adult men still feel defined 'as a man' by their ability to financially support their family.[5] The father-as-breadwinner discourse, bound up in notions of hegemonic masculinity and the pressure to conform to orthodox gender norms around 'being a man', still endures.[6]

Men also report feeling helpless during the transition to new fatherhood, especially so during their partner's pregnancy when they are uncertain about what their role involves. Pregnancy is a process that they cannot physically experience, unlike their female partner who is able to feel the baby kick and move around inside her. Because of this lack of (embodied) connection with their unborn child, many men turn to consumption as a virtual umbilical cord to help feel connected with their unborn child.[7]

In this case study, we explore the experiences of Paul, who has recently become a father for the first time. Using interview data both before and after the birth of his first child, we chart contradictions in Paul's expectations of fatherhood and the role he subsequently assumes. Before his son was born, Paul was adamant that he would 'have it all', and that he would play a very different role from that of his own father (who was, for example, out drinking at the local pub when Paul was born). Paul wanted to improve on his own father's example, and to be a more hands-on father. However, when the realities of new fatherhood emerged (the sleepless nights, diminished free time, tiredness), Paul could not wait to revert back to the breadwinner role of fatherhood (in which he would be responsible for putting food on the table, and little else). To help ease his conscience, however, and to go some way to participating in the care of his newborn child, Paul turned to consumption (particularly of high-technology items) to help take some of the baby work off him – much to his partner's dismay.

Paul's story

Paul was delighted to hear that he was going to become a father for the first time. When we spoke with him before the birth of his son, Max, he was determined that he was going to be the best father that he could be. For Paul, this involved playing a hands-on parenting role, and taking equal care of his newborn child alongside his wife. Paul reminisced a lot about the role that his own father had played in his upbringing, positioning it as a role that he himself wanted to steer clear of. Paul recalled that when he was little, his own father worked very long hours, which meant that he was often absent from the family home. This fatherhood role was a million miles away from the father Paul wanted to be: 'I don't want to be a deadbeat dad. I do want to provide, bring in money, but I also want to be there, making bottles, changing nappies. I do want to have it all, really. I want to be hands-on.'

Like other fathers we have spoken with, Paul felt very unsure as to what he should be doing during his wife's pregnancy. During this stage, he helped to get the baby's room prepared, building the flat-pack cot and assembling other pieces of nursery furniture. But he was struggling to come to terms with the potential demands of impending fatherhood, and in particular he began to question quite how his life would change on becoming a father for the first time.

Paul was a keen runner, for example, and he was adamant (in keeping with his need to 'have it all') that when the baby came he would still be able to carry on running. To help support this activity that he loved so much, Paul decided to buy a BabyJogger™ pushchair (a three-wheeled pushchair, purposely designed to enable parents to go urban running with their child): 'I've always been a runner. I've run for years, and I was certain the baby wouldn't stop me [running]. The pram is brilliant for that, the BabyJogger™ . . . 20-inch wheels, rear suspension, it's a good bit of kit, and you can go out in all weathers with it, spend time with the baby, carry on with your life as before.'

Paul's wife, Jenny, however, was not overly enamoured with this purchase, and questioned how safe her (at this point, unborn) child would be when strapped into this pushchair. But this did not daunt Paul, who also became highly involved in purchasing baby surveillance equipment, such as pressure pads that slipped under the baby's mattress and detected if the baby stopped breathing or moving around, and a state-of-the-art video camera that he positioned at the end of the cot and then hooked up to the TV downstairs, enabling him to view the cot from a distance via the TV. Paul, through these acts of consumption, felt that he was engaging with his unborn child, and that he was performing the anticipatory caring duties involved in being a father.

When Paul's son, Max, was born, Paul flooded his Facebook account with pictures of his new baby, and he proudly took Max to meet family and friends. The responsibilities of being a father weighed heavily on Paul's shoulders, however, and his paid work commitments took on a new significance for him. What if Jenny decided not to return to paid work? Could they afford to live on one wage alone? For Paul, this caused a lot of tension and stress – so much so that he decided to return to work earlier than expected, and he did not fully utilise his entitlement of two weeks' statutory paternity leave:

'I felt an enormous sense of responsibility after the baby was born. I was tired – Max didn't sleep much to start with, he still doesn't. Work became really important. If I wasn't fit for work because I was too tired, I didn't know what would happen. Would I lose my job?

So I became fixated on going to work. I practically ran out of the door to work because it was easier there, away from the baby. And I'd done my bit to help – the products were in place to help look after Max: the cameras, the surveillance kit, the pressure pad mattress and the like. I'd done my bit. I knew the baby was going to be safe when I wasn't there.'

What emerges through Paul's story are the many contradictions in his experience of becoming a father for the first time. His ideals of being a hands-on father, financially and emotionally supporting his child, were soon replaced with the enduring norm that many men experience as part of their fatherhood role (as enacted in the breadwinner discourse of fatherhood). Despite Paul's good intentions, he soon reverted back to gender role norms, and justified his escape to work through the very consumption objects that he had initially bought to help him care for his child.

Questions

1 What role do you think fathers play in contemporary family life?

2 What role do you think fathers *should* play in contemporary family life?

3 Can you identify any cultural expectations for fathers from different cultural groups?

4 What role did consumption play in the case to help Paul transition to the role of first-time father?

5 What potential tensions can you highlight or infer from the case between Paul and his wife, Jenny, about their respective expectations or constructions of the roles of new fathers and new mothers?

6 How has technology been positioned by Paul, and subsequently re-positioned within this case, to help support him in the conduct of his fathering duties?

Sources

[1]David Beckham, quoted in G. Russell, *Arise Sir David Beckham: Footballer, Celebrity, Legend – the Biography of Britain's Best Loved Sporting Icon* (London: John Blake Publishing Ltd, 2011).

[2]J.H. Pleck, 'American fathering in a historical perspective', in M.S. Kimmel (ed.), *Changing Men: New Directions in Research on Men and Masculinity* (Newbury Park, CA: Sage, 1987): 83–97.

[3]J. Gentry and R. Harrison, 'Is advertising a barrier to male movement toward gender change?', *Marketing Theory* 10(1) (2010): 74–96.

[4]M.E. Lamb, 'Introduction: The emergent American father', in M.E. Lamb (ed.), *The Father Role: A Cross-Cultural Perspective* (Hillside, NJ: Lawrence Erlbaum, 1987): 1–26; M.E. Lamb, 'The changing roles of fathers', in J.L. Shapiro, M.J. Diamond and M. Greenburg (eds), *Becoming a Father* (New York: Springer,

1995): 18–35; J.H. Pleck, 'American fathering in a historical per-spective', in M.S. Kimmel (ed.), *Changing Men: New Directions in Research on Men and Masculinity* (Newbury Park, CA: Sage, 1987): 83–97.

[5]K. Henwood and J. Procter, 'The "good father": Reading men's accounts of paternal involvement during the transition to first-time fatherhood', *British Journal of Social Psychology* 42(3) (2003): 337–55.

[6]S. Bettany, B. Kerrane and M.K. Hogg, 'The material-semiotics of fatherhood: the co-emergence of technology and contem-porary fatherhood', *Journal of Business Research* 67(7) (2014): 1,544–51.

[7]VOICE Group, 'The involved ostrich: mothers' perceptions of fathers' participation in the transition to parenthood', *Advances in Consumer Research* 36 (2009): 254–60.

Part C
Consumers as decision-makers

This part explores how individuals make choices and discusses many of the internal influences involved in the process of consumer decision-making. Chapter 6 considers how decisions are affected by what we have learned and what we have remembered. Chapter 7 provides an overview of how attitudes are formed and changed, and also discusses how influences such as advertising affect our consumer choices and our predisposition to make certain consumption decisions. Chapter 8 focuses on the basic sequence of steps we undertake when making a decision.

Chapter 6
Learning and memory

Chapter objectives

When you finish reading this chapter you will understand why:

6.1 It is important to understand how consumers learn about products and services.

6.2 Conditioning results in learning.

6.3 There is a difference between classical and instrumental conditioning, and both processes help consumers to learn about products.

6.4 Learned associations with brands generalise to other products, and this is important to marketers.

6.5 We learn about products by observing others' behaviour.

6.6 Our brains process information about brands to retain them in memory.

6.7 The other products we associate with an individual product influence how we will remember it.

6.8 Products help us to retrieve memories from our past.

6.9 Marketers measure our memories about products and ads.

MARIO ROSSI is a 60-year-old Italian insurance man, and still very active in his field. He is a pleasant, sociable and easy-going fellow, and has made a very good career for himself. Together with his wife and four children, he lives in a comfortable flat in the suburbs of Rome. Although Rome is full of historical sites to visit, Mario is a staunch nature lover, and he prefers to 'get back to nature' in his free time.

Mario's dog, Raphael, recognises the sound of his master's old Fiat drawing up outside as he arrives home late after work, and begins to get excited at the prospect of having his master back home. Mario's 'first love' was a Fiat 126, and in spite of his good income he keeps the old car running. Relaxing and sipping a glass of Chianti is just what he needs after a hard day's work. The pieces of furniture in his sitting room, and even his television set, are not the latest models, but he likes it that way – the old objects give him a sense of security. Slowly unwinding, he looks forward to spending the weekend with his family and friends at his house in the countryside. He grew up there, and is very attached to the old villa and everything in it.

He often imagines what it will be like when he retires, when he will be able to live there permanently, surrounded by his family. It will be like the good old days, when he was a boy and life was uncomplicated, less chaotic. He pictures them all sitting around the table enjoying a leisurely meal (with pasta, of course!) made from home-grown produce, and afterwards sitting together.

This peaceful fantasy is in stark contrast to the reality of last weekend. His two eldest sons had gone off to a football match. The youngest ones restlessly complained about the fact that there was still such a slow Wi-Fi internet connection in the house, and then went into another room to settle down in front of the television for what they called an afternoon's entertainment!

Gabriele Morello, GMA-Gabriele Morello and Associates, Palermo, Italy

Introduction

6.1

It is important to understand how consumers learn about products and services

Learning refers to a relatively permanent change in behaviour that comes with experience. This experience does not have to affect the learner directly: we can learn vicariously by observing events that affect others.[1] We also learn even when we are not trying to do so. Consumers, for example, recognise many brand names and can hum many product jingles, even for those product categories they themselves do not use. This casual, unintentional acquisition of knowledge is known as *incidental learning.* Like the concept of perception discussed in an earlier chapter, learning is an ongoing process. Our knowledge about the world is constantly being revised as we are exposed to new stimuli and receive feedback that allows us to modify behaviour in other, similar situations. The concept of learning covers a lot of ground, ranging from a consumer's simple association between a stimulus such as a product logo (such as Coca-Cola) and a response (e.g. 'refreshing soft drink'), to a complex series of cognitive activities (such as writing an essay on learning for a consumer behaviour exam). Psychologists who study learning advance several theories to explain the learning process. These theories range from those that focus on simple stimulus–response connections (*behavioural theories*) to perspectives that regard consumers as solvers of complex problems who learn abstract rules and concepts when they observe what others say and do (*cognitive theories*). It's important for marketers to understand these theories as well, because basic learning principles are at the heart of many consumer purchase decisions.

In this chapter we will explore how learned associations among feelings, events and products – and the memories they evoke – are an important aspect of consumer behaviour.

Behavioural learning theories

6.2

Conditioning results in learning

Behavioural learning theories assume that learning takes place as the result of responses to external events. Psychologists who subscribe to this viewpoint do not focus on internal thought processes. Instead, they approach the mind as a 'black box' and emphasise the observable aspects of behaviour, as depicted in Figure 6.1. The observable aspects consist of things that go into the box (the stimuli, or events perceived from the outside world) and things that come out of the box (the responses, or reactions, to these stimuli).

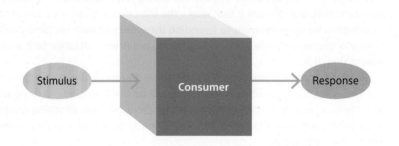

Figure 6.1 The consumer as a 'black box': a behaviourist perspective on learning

This view is represented by two major approaches to learning: classical conditioning and instrumental conditioning. People's experiences are shaped by the feedback they receive as they go through life. Similarly, consumers respond to brand names, scents, jingles and other marketing stimuli based on the learned connections they have formed over time. People also learn that actions they take result in rewards and punishments, and this feedback influences the way they respond in similar situations in the future. Consumers who are complimented on a product choice will be more likely to buy that brand again, while those who get food poisoning at a new restaurant will not be likely to patronise it in the future.

Marketing opportunity

Popcorn is the scent usually associated with a trip to the cinema. But in a European cinema, you might just smell bread, chocolate or whatever else an advertiser wants you to.

A company called Cinescent is giving marketers the chance to pump out the scent of their brands in German theatres, where it first tested the technology for Beiersdorf's Nivea. For the test, a specially made 60-second spot showed a typical sunny beach scene, with people lying around on deck chairs or sunbathing on towels while waves crashed and seagulls cried in the background. As people wondered what the ad was for, the scent of Nivea sun cream permeated the cinema, and a Nivea logo appeared on screen along with the words, 'Nivea. The scent of summer'. The results were significant: cinema exit polls showed a 515 per cent rise in recall for the Nivea ad compared with movie-goers who saw the spot without the scent. The same ad, when combined with only a subliminal whiff of scent, scored a 25 per cent lift. Cinescent works by pumping smells through the cinema's air-conditioning system to distribute a scent that covers other odours without being overpowering. Using this method, much finer fragrance molecules reach the audience, minimising the allergy

and irritation problems encountered by previous attempts, when smells were dispensed via boxes located among the audience. Now, '4D cinema' is on the horizon – entertainment presentation systems that combine a 3D film with physical effects that occur in the theatre in synchronisation with the film. Effects simulated in a 4D film may include rain, wind, strobe lights and vibration. Seats in 4D venues may vibrate or move a few inches during the presentations. Other common chair effects include air jets, water sprays and leg and back ticklers. Hall effects may include smoke, rain, lightning, air bubbles and smells (gunpowder? fresh coffee? burning rubber?).

Mike Hope-Milne, enterprise director at Pearl & Dean, which sells cinema advertising, is so impressed by the German results that he is bringing the technology to the UK. 'We are talking to a handful of clients, including sun cream, bread, coffee, perfume, air fresheners and chocolate manufacturers. It is most cost-effective when working with scent-based products that have the scent oils already to hand', he said.

One of the advertisers lined up is a car manufacturer that wants to promote its Cabriolet version by evoking the smell of fresh country air and newly cut grass. The argument is that scents provide a dynamic psychological and emotional trigger that can be invaluable to brands.

Mr Hope-Milne is also hoping to drum up new business with the technology, noting that three of the companies he's talking to have never advertised in cinemas before. 'It's encouraging people to reappraise the medium', he said. The Cinescent idea works best, he said, when advertising a product that appeals to a broad audience. 'Perfume is probably a bit of a risk and is better off using sampling'.[2]

Classical conditioning

6.3

There is a difference between classical and instrumental conditioning, and both processes help consumers to learn about products.

Classical conditioning occurs when a stimulus that elicits a response is paired with another stimulus that initially does not elicit a response on its own. Over time, this second stimulus causes a similar response because it is associated with the first stimulus. This phenomenon was first demonstrated in dogs by Ivan Pavlov, a Russian physiologist doing research on digestion in animals.

Pavlov induced classically conditioned learning by pairing a neutral stimulus (a bell) with a stimulus known to cause a salivation response in dogs (he squirted dried meat powder into their mouths). The powder was an unconditioned stimulus (UCS) because it was naturally capable of causing the response. Over time, the bell became a conditioned stimulus (CS): it did not initially cause salivation, but the dogs learned to associate the bell with the meat powder and began to salivate at the sound of the bell only. The drooling of these canine consumers over a sound, now linked to feeding time, was a conditioned response (CR), just as Mario's dog Raphael begins to get excited hearing his master's Fiat 126 coming close to home.

This basic form of classical conditioning primarily applies to responses controlled by the autonomic (e.g. salivation) and nervous (e.g. eye blink) systems. That is, it focuses on visual and olfactory cues that induce hunger, thirst or sexual arousal. When these cues are consistently paired with conditioned stimuli, such as brand names, consumers may learn to feel hungry, thirsty or aroused when later exposed to the brand cues.

Classical conditioning can have similar effects for more complex reactions, too. Even a credit card becomes a conditioned cue that triggers greater spending, especially since it is a stimulus that is present only in situations where consumers are spending money. People learn that they can make larger purchases when using credit cards, and they also have been found to leave larger tips than they do when using cash.[3] Conditioning effects are more likely to occur after the conditioned and unconditioned stimuli have been paired a number of times.[4] Repeated exposures increase the strength of stimulus–response associations and prevent the decay of these associations in memory.

Conditioning will not occur or will take longer if the CS is only occasionally presented with the UCS. One result of this lack of association may be **extinction**, which occurs when the effects of prior conditioning are reduced and finally disappear. This can occur, for example, when a product is over-exposed in the marketplace so that its original allure is lost. Some research indicates that the intervals between exposures may influence the effectiveness of this strategy as well as the type of medium the marketer uses; the most effective repetition strategy is a combination of spaced exposures that alternate in terms of media that are more and less involving, such as television advertising complemented by print media.[5]

6.4

Learned associations with brands generalise to other products, and this is important to marketers.

Stimulus generalisation refers to the tendency of stimuli similar to a CS to evoke similar, conditioned responses.[6] Pavlov noticed in subsequent studies that his dogs would sometimes salivate when they heard noises that only resembled a bell (e.g. keys jangling). People react to other, similar stimuli in much the same way that they responded to an original stimulus, and this generalisation is called a *halo effect*. A chemist shop's bottle of own-brand mouthwash deliberately packaged to resemble Listerine mouthwash may evoke

Net profit

How often should an advertiser repeat the ads it places on websites? The answer depends on whether the ad relates to the website's content, and whether or not competing ads are also present on the site. The study found support for the general idea that repetitive ad messages resulted in higher recall and interest in learning more about the advertised product (in this case, a laptop).

However, repeating the same ad was primarily effective when competitors also showed ads on the site. Otherwise, it was better to vary the ad messages for the laptop (presumably because people tuned out from the ad if it appeared repeatedly). These ads were also more effective when they appeared on a site where the content related to the advertised product.[7]

a similar response among consumers, who assume that this 'me-too' product shares other characteristics of the original. These 'look-alikes' tactics work, and companies have targeted well-known brands ranging from Unilever's Blue Band margarine and Calvé peanut butter, to Hermès scarves. Similar colours, shapes and designs are all stimuli that consumers organise and interpret and, up to a point, these tactics are perfectly legal.[8] When the quality of the me-too product turns out to be lower than that of the original brand, consumers may exhibit even more positive feelings towards the original. However, if they perceive the quality of the two competitors to be about equal, consumers may conclude that the price premium they pay for the original is not worth it.[9]

Stimulus discrimination occurs when a stimulus similar to a CS is not followed by a UCS. In these situations, reactions are weakened and will soon disappear. Part of the learning process involves making a response to some stimuli but not to other, similar stimuli. Manufacturers of well-established brands commonly urge consumers not to buy 'cheap imitations' because the results will not be what they expect.

Operant conditioning

Operant conditioning, also known as instrumental conditioning, occurs as the individual learns to perform behaviours that produce positive outcomes and to avoid those that yield negative outcomes. This learning process is most closely associated with the psychologist B.F. Skinner, who demonstrated the effects of instrumental conditioning by teaching animals to dance, pigeons to play ping-pong and so on, by systematically rewarding them for desired behaviours.[10]

While responses in classical conditioning are involuntary and fairly simple, those in instrumental conditioning are made deliberately to obtain a goal and may be more complex. The desired behaviour may be learned over a period of time, as intermediate actions are rewarded in a process called *shaping*. For example, the owner of a new shop may award prizes to shoppers just for coming in, hoping that over time they will continue to drop in and eventually buy something.

Also, classical conditioning involves the close pairing of two stimuli. Instrumental learning occurs as a result of a reward received following the desired behaviour and takes place over a period in which a variety of other behaviours are attempted and abandoned because they are not reinforced. A good way to remember the difference is to keep in mind that in instrumental learning the response is performed because it is instrumental to gaining a reward or avoiding a punishment. Consumers over time come to associate with people who reward them and to choose products that make them feel good or satisfy some need.

Operant conditioning (instrumental learning) occurs in one of three ways. When the environment provides **positive reinforcement** in the form of a reward, the response is strengthened, and appropriate behaviour is learned. For example, a woman who is

Positive reinforcement occurs after consumers try a new product and like it.
Ashley Cooper/Alamy Stock Photo

complimented after wearing Obsession perfume will learn that using this product has the desired effect, and she will be more likely to keep buying the product. **Negative reinforcement** also strengthens responses so that appropriate behaviour is learned. A perfume company, for example, might run an ad showing a woman sitting alone on a Saturday night because she did not use its fragrance. The message to be conveyed is that she could have avoided this negative outcome if only she had used the perfume. In contrast to situations where we learn to do certain things in order to avoid unpleasantness, **punishment** occurs when a response is followed by unpleasant events (such as being ridiculed by friends for wearing an offensive-smelling perfume). We learn not to repeat these behaviours.

When trying to understand the differences between these mechanisms, keep in mind that reactions from a person's environment to behaviour can be either positive or negative and that these outcomes or anticipated outcomes can be applied or removed. That is, under conditions of both positive reinforcement and punishment, the person receives a reaction after doing something. In contrast, negative reinforcement occurs when a negative outcome is avoided: the removal of something negative is pleasurable and hence is rewarding. Finally, when a positive outcome is no longer received, extinction is likely to occur, and the learned stimulus–response connection will not be maintained (as when a woman no longer receives compliments on her perfume). Thus, positive and negative reinforcement strengthen the future linkage between a response and an outcome because of the pleasant experience. This tie is weakened under conditions of both punishment and extinction because of the unpleasant experience. The relationships among these four conditions are easier to understand by referring to Figure 6.2.

An important factor in operant conditioning is the set of rules by which appropriate reinforcements are given for a behaviour. The issue of what is the most effective reinforcement schedule to use is important to marketers, because it relates to the amount of effort and resources they must devote to rewarding consumers in order to condition desired behaviours:

- *Fixed-interval reinforcement.* After a specified period has passed, the first response that is made brings the reward. Under such conditions, people tend to respond slowly immediately after being reinforced, but their responses speed up as the time for the next reinforcement approaches. For example, consumers may crowd into a store for the last day of its seasonal sale and not reappear again until the next one.

- *Variable-interval reinforcement.* The time that must pass before reinforcement is delivered varies around some average. Since the person does not know exactly when to expect the reinforcement, responses must be performed at a consistent rate. This logic is behind retailers' use of so-called secret shoppers – people who periodically test for service quality by posing as customers at unannounced times. Since store employees never know exactly when to expect a visit, high quality must be constantly maintained.

- *Fixed-ratio reinforcement.* Reinforcement occurs only after a fixed number of responses. This schedule motivates people to contnue performing the same behaviour over and over again. For example, a consumer might keep buying groceries at the same store in order to earn a gift after collecting a certain number of points on their store card.

- *Variable-ratio reinforcement.* The person is reinforced after a certain number of responses, but they do not know how many responses are required. People in such situations tend to respond at very high and steady rates, and this type of behaviour is very difficult to extinguish. This reinforcement schedule is responsible for consumers' attraction to slot machines. They learn that if they keep feeding money into the machine, they will eventually win something (if they don't go broke first).

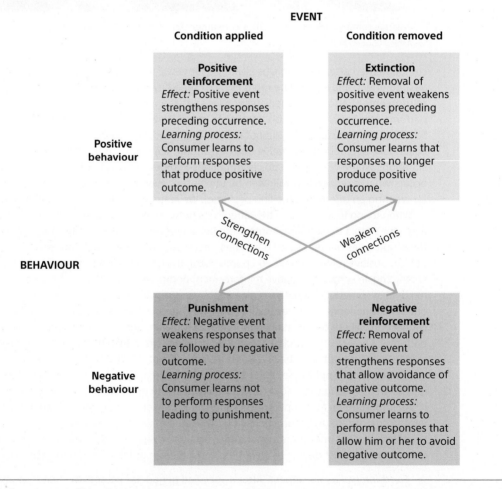

Figure 6.2 Four types of learning outcome

Cognitive learning theory

Cognitive learning occurs as a result of mental processes. In contrast to behavioural theories of learning, cognitive learning theory stresses the importance of internal mental processes. This perspective views people as problem-solvers who actively use information from the world around them to master their environment. Supporters of this viewpoint also stress the role of creativity and insight during the learning process.

The issue of consciousness

A lot of controversy surrounds the issue of whether or when people are aware of their learning processes. While behavioural learning theorists emphasise the routine, automatic nature of conditioning, proponents of cognitive learning argue that even these simple effects are based on cognitive factors: that is, expectations are created that a stimulus will be followed by a response (the formation of expectations requires mental activity). According to this school of thought, conditioning occurs because subjects develop conscious hypotheses and then act on them.

There is some evidence for the existence of non-conscious procedural knowledge. People apparently do process at least some information in an automatic, passive way, which is a condition that has been termed 'mindlessness'.[11] When we meet someone new or encounter a new product, for example, we have a tendency to respond to the stimulus in terms of existing categories, rather than taking the trouble to formulate different ones. Our reactions are activated by a trigger feature – some stimulus that cues us towards a particular pattern. For example, men in one study rated a car in an ad as superior on a variety of characteristics if a seductive woman (the trigger feature) was present in the ad, despite the fact that the men did not believe the woman's presence actually had an influence.[12] A study that reviewed the literature on knowledge (a meta-analysis) took the approach of looking at what consumers know, versus what they think they know. Results suggest that we are better at having objective knowledge about products (as opposed to services), and that we have a stronger sense of subjective knowledge (what we think we know) when the information comes to us from an expert in the product category.[13] Ultimately, our ability to retrieve information comes from our actual knowledge, as well as from what we think we know. Another study also suggests that our subjective knowledge about the 'fairness' of how the product was manufactured (ethical, humane working conditions) influences how we evaluate brands.[14]

Nonetheless, many modern theorists are beginning to regard some instances of conditioning as cognitive processes, especially where expectations are formed about the linkages between stimuli and responses. Indeed, studies using masking effects, in which it is difficult for subjects to learn CS/UCS associations, show substantial reductions in conditioning.[15] For example, an adolescent girl may observe that women on television and in real life seem to be rewarded with compliments and attention when they smell nice and wear alluring clothing. She works out that the probability of these rewards occurring is greater when she wears perfume, and deliberately wears a popular scent to obtain the pay-off of social acceptance.

Observational learning

6.5

We learn about products by observing others' behaviour.

Observational learning occurs when people watch the actions of others and note the reinforcements they receive for their behaviours. This type of learning is a complex process: people store these observations in memory as they accumulate knowledge, perhaps using this information at a later point to guide their own behaviours. This process of imitating the behaviour of others is called 'modelling'. For example, a woman shopping for a new kind of perfume may remember the reactions a friend received when wearing a certain brand several months earlier, and she will base her behaviour on her friend's actions. In order for

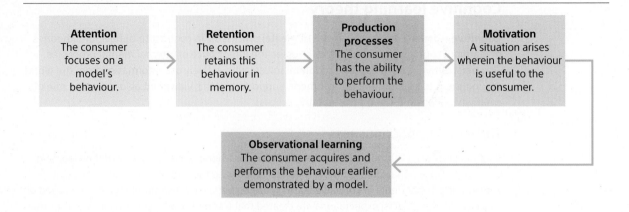

Figure 6.3 Components of observational learning

observational learning in the form of modelling to occur, four conditions must be met (see Figure 6.3):[16]

1 The consumer's attention must be directed to the appropriate model who, for reasons of attractiveness, competence, status or similarity, it is desirable to emulate.

2 The consumer must remember what is said or done by the model.

3 The consumer must convert this information into actions.

4 The consumer must be motivated to perform these actions.

Marketing applications of learning principles

6.6

Our brains process information about brands to retain them in memory.

Understanding how consumers learn is very important to marketers. After all, many strategic decisions are based on the assumption that consumers are continually accumulating information about products and that people can be 'taught' to prefer some alternatives over others. And once information (for instance, about products and brands) is learned, it is stored in memory (and hopefully retrieved). (The key interrelationship between memory and learning is discussed in greater detail later in this chapter under objective 6.8.)

Behavioural learning applications

Many marketing strategies focus on the establishment of associations between stimuli and responses. Behavioural learning principles apply to many consumer phenomena, ranging from the creation of a distinctive brand image to the perceived linkage between a product and an underlying need.

How marketers take advantage of classical conditioning principles

The transfer of meaning from an unconditioned stimulus to a conditioned stimulus explains why 'made-up' brand names such as Marlboro, Coca-Cola or IBM can exert such powerful effects on consumers. The association between the Marlboro Man and the cigarette is so strong that in some cases the company no longer even includes the brand name in its ad. When nonsense syllables (meaningless sets of letters) are paired with such evaluative words as beauty or success, the meaning is transferred to the nonsense syllables. This change in the symbolic significance of initially meaningless words shows that complex meanings can be conditioned. Other studies have shown that attitudes formed through classical conditioning are enduring.[17]

These conditioned associations are crucial to many marketing strategies that rely on the creation and perpetuation of positive **brand equity**, in which a brand has strong positive associations in a consumer's memory and commands a lot of loyalty as a result.[18] As we will see in the next chapter, a product with brand equity holds a tremendous advantage in the marketplace.

Repetition

One advertising researcher argues that more than three exposures are wasted. The first creates awareness of the product, the second demonstrates its relevance to the consumer and the third serves as a reminder of the product's benefits.[19] However, even this bare-bones approach implies that repetition is needed to ensure that the consumer is actually exposed to (and processes) the ad at least three times. Marketers attempting to condition an association must ensure that the consumers they have targeted will be exposed to the stimulus a sufficient number of times.

On the other hand, it is possible to have too much of a good thing. Consumers can become so used to hearing or seeing a marketing stimulus that they cease to pay attention to it (see Chapter 3). This problem, known as advertising wear-out, can be reduced by varying the way in which the basic message is presented.

6.7

The other products we associate with an individual product influence how we will remember it.

Conditioning product associations

Advertisements often pair a product with a positive stimulus to create a desirable association. Various aspects of a marketing message, such as music, humour or imagery, can affect conditioning. In one study, subjects who viewed a photograph of pens paired with either pleasant or unpleasant music were more likely later to select the pen that appeared with pleasant music.[20]

The order in which the conditioned stimulus and the unconditioned stimulus is presented can affect the likelihood that learning will occur. Generally speaking, the unconditioned stimulus should be presented prior to the conditioned stimulus. The technique of forward conditioning, such as showing a soft drink (the CS) and then playing a jingle (the UCS), is generally most effective.[21] Because sequential presentation is desirable for conditioning to occur, classical conditioning is not very effective in static situations, such as in magazine ads, where (in contrast to TV or radio) the marketer cannot control the order in which the CS and the UCS are perceived.

Just as product associations can be formed, so they can be extinguished. Because of the danger of extinction, a classical conditioning strategy may not be as effective for products that are frequently encountered, since there is no guarantee they will be accompanied by the CS. A bottle of Pepsi paired with the refreshing sound of a carbonated beverage being poured over ice may seem like a good example of conditioning. Unfortunately, the product would also be seen in many other contexts where this sound was absent, reducing the effectiveness of the conditioning.

By the same reasoning, a novel tune should be chosen over a popular one to pair with a product, since the popular song might also be heard in many situations in which the product is not present.[22] Music videos in particular may serve as effective UCSs because they often have an emotional impact on viewers and this effect may transfer to ads accompanying the video.[23]

Applications of stimulus generalisation

The iconic (and deceased) reggae singer Bob Marley's name and image appears on a vast range of products, including caps, lanyards, T-shirts, rolling papers, handbags and purses, belts and buckles, beach towels and knapsacks. His daughter Cedella launched High Tide swimwear to further extend the franchise, and his son Rohan created the Marley Coffee brand; each

Advertising often pairs a product with a positive stimulus (e.g. 'you deserve the best') or with positive features (e.g. the features of this razor identified here) or with positive outcomes (e.g. here the implicit 'you get a clean shave').

mitdesign/123RF

variety is named after a different Marley tune.[24] In one 20-month period, Procter & Gamble introduced almost 90 new products. Not a single product carried a new brand name. In fact, roughly 80 per cent of all new products are actually extensions of existing brands or product lines.[25] Strategies based on stimulus generalisation include the following:

- *Family branding,* in which a variety of products capitalise on the reputation of a company name. Companies such as Campbell's, Heinz, Philips and Sony rely on their positive corporate images to sell different product lines.

- *Product-line extensions,* in which related products are added to an established brand. Dole, which is associated with fruit, was able to introduce refrigerated juices and juice bars, while Sun Maid went from raisins to raisin bread. The gun manufacturer Smith & Wesson launched its own line of furniture and other home items. Starbucks Corp. and Jim Beam Brands teamed up to make Starbucks Coffee Liqueur. Condé Nast is opening bars and clubs linked to its *Vogue* and *GQ* magazines around the world.[26]

- *Licensing,* in which well-known names are 'rented' by others. This strategy is increasing in popularity as marketers try to link their products and services with well-established figures. Companies as diverse as McDonald's, Disney, Vogue and Harley-Davidson have authorised the use of their names on products.

- Marketers are increasingly capitalising on the public's enthusiasm for films[27] and popular TV programmes by developing numerous *product tie-ins.*

- *Lookalike packaging,* in which distinctive packaging designs create strong associations with a particular brand. This linkage is often exploited by makers of generic or private-label brands who wish to communicate a quality image by putting their products in very similar packages. As one chemist chain store executive commented, 'You want to tell the consumer that it's close to the national brand. You've got to make it look like, within the law, close to the national brand. They're at least attracted to the package'.[28]

Marketing opportunity

Luxury car makers are jumping into the licensing pool in droves. Bentley lends its name to colognes, furniture, skis, handbags and even a hotel suite at the St Regis hotel in New York that costs over $10,500 a night. The Ferrari prancing horse logo pops up on chess sets, Tod's loafers and Oakley sunglasses. Lamborghini, Maserati and Tesla now sell leather goods. Porsche (which, like Lamborghini and Bentley, now is owned by Volkswagen) has gone a step farther; it operates Porsche Design retail stores around the world. A spokeswoman observed, 'Luggage, bikes, desk pieces, couture clothing – it all provides a continuation of the Porsche driving experience'.[29]

Applications of stimulus discrimination

An emphasis on communicating a product's distinctive attributes vis-à-vis its competitors is an important aspect of positioning, in which consumers learn to differentiate a brand from its competitors (see Chapter 3). This is not always an easy task, especially in product categories where the brand names of many of the alternatives look and sound alike. For example, one survey showed that many consumers have a great deal of trouble distinguishing between products sold by the top computer manufacturers. With a blur of names like OmniPlex, OptiPlex, Premmia, Premium, ProLinea, ProLiant, etc., this confusion is not surprising.[30]

Companies with a well-established brand image try to encourage stimulus discrimination by promoting the unique attributes of their brands, such as the constant reminders for American Express Travellers Cheques: 'Ask for them by name . . . '. On the other hand, a brand name that is used so widely that it is no longer distinctive becomes part of the public domain and can be used by competitors, as has been the case for such products as aspirin, cellophane, yo-yos and escalators.

Many marketing strategies focus on the establishment of associations between stimuli and responses. In this ad Premier Inn promotes its first-class standard of service and accommodation, as well as the modest pricing of its rooms.
David McHugh/Shutterstock

How marketers take advantage of instrumental conditioning principles

Principles of instrumental conditioning are at work when a consumer is rewarded or punished for a purchase decision. Business people shape behaviour by gradually reinforcing consumers for taking appropriate actions. For example, a car dealer might encourage a reluctant buyer to try sitting in a showroom model, then suggest a test drive and so on.

Marketers have many ways of reinforcing consumers, ranging from a simple thank you after a purchase to substantial rebates and follow-up phone calls. For example, a life insurance company obtained a much higher rate of policy renewal among a group of new customers who received a thank you letter after each payment, compared to a control group that did not receive any reinforcement.[31]

A popular technique known as **frequency marketing** reinforces regular purchasers by giving them prizes with values that increase along with the amount purchased. This operant learning strategy was pioneered by the airline industry, which introduced 'frequent-flyer' programmes in the early 1980s to reward loyal customers. Well over 20 per cent of food stores now offer frequent-buyer promotions (e.g. the Marks and Spencer Sparks card). Manufacturers in the fast-moving consumer goods (FMCG) category also make use of this technique in food stores (e.g. Tesco Club Card). In some industries, these reinforcers take the form of clubs, including the Hilton Hotel Club. Club members usually earn bonus points to set against future purchases, and some get privileges such as magazines and free telephone numbers and sometimes even invitations to exclusive outings.

Gamification: The new frontier for learning applications

Many of us grew up playing games, and some of us never stopped. In some sense, all of life is a game, insofar as there are winners and losers and challenges we must solve to reach various objectives. Many organisations are going to the next level; they're borrowing from basic principles of gaming to motivate consumers and employees across a broad spectrum of activity.

The fast-growing strategy of gamification turns routine actions into experiences as it adds gaming elements to tasks that might otherwise be boring or routine. Millennials have grown up playing games; these activities structure their learning styles and influence the platforms to which they will gravitate.[32] Important elements of gaming include:

- a dynamic digital environment (whether in-store, on a laptop, or on a tablet or phone) that resembles a sophisticated videogame platform;
- multiple short- and long-term goals;
- rapid and frequent feedback;
- a reward for most or all efforts in the form of a badge or a virtual product;
- friendly competition in a low-risk environment;
- a manageable degree of uncertainty.

At its most basic, gamification is simply about providing rewards to customers to encourage them to buy even more. These mechanisms used to take the form of buy-10-get-one-free punch cards, but today a host of sophisticated phone apps dispense rewards to eager shoppers – sometimes with a twist when marketers tinker with the reinforcement schedule. Indeed, research shows that when a business 'preloads' a frequent buyer card with a few punches, this makes the reward look more attainable and motivates consumers to complete the rest. In a study on what the researchers term the **endowed progress effect**, a car wash gave one set of customers a buy-eight-get-one-free card, while a second set of customers got a 10-wash card that had been punched twice. Researchers reported that almost twice as many people in the second condition redeemed their cards, even though in both cases customers had to pay for eight car washes to get a free one. The connection to basic learning processes is clear. As one marketing professor explained, 'All organisms, in different ways, are drawn to goals. The closer we are to achieving our goals, the more motivated we are to keep doing something. As mice on a runway get closer to a food pellet, they run faster. . . as people get closer to having a completed card, the time between visits gets smaller.'[33]

Many domains of human activity (and business) share the common need to motivate and reward people to achieve ascending levels of mastery. These include:

- *Store and brand loyalty* – Foursquare gives people virtual badges when they check in at a local café or restaurant; some of them check in as often as they can to compete for the honour of being named 'mayor' of the location.

- *Social marketing* – more than 75 utilities have begun using a service from a company called Opower that awards badges to customers when they reduce their energy consumption; customers can compare their progress with their neighbours' progress and broadcast their achievements on Facebook.

- *Employee performance* – some restaurants use a service called Objective Logistics to rank the performances of waiters on a leader board, rewarding the good ones with plum shifts and more lucrative tables.[34]

How marketers take advantage of cognitive learning principles

Consumers' ability to learn vicariously by observing how the behaviour of others is reinforced makes the lives of marketers much easier. Because people do not have to be directly reinforced for their actions, marketers do not necessarily have to reward or punish them for purchase behaviours. Instead, they can show what happens to desirable models who use or do not use their products and know that consumers will often be motivated to imitate these actions at a later date. For example, a perfume commercial may depict a woman surrounded by a throng of admirers who are providing her with positive reinforcement for using the product. Needless to say, this learning process is more practical than providing the same personal attention to each woman who actually buys the perfume.

Consumers' evaluations of models go beyond simple stimulus–response connections. For example, a celebrity's image is often more than a simple reflexive response of good or bad: it is a complex combination of many attributes.[35] In general, the degree to which a model will be emulated depends upon their social attractiveness. Attractiveness can be based upon several components, including physical appearance, expertise or similarity to the evaluator.

These factors will be addressed further in our discussions of personal characteristics that make a communication's source more or less effective in changing consumers' attitudes (see Chapter 7). In addition, many applications of consumer problem-solving are related to ways in which information is represented in memory and recalled at a later date. This aspect of cognitive learning is the focus of Part C.

Consumer behaviour as I see it . . .

Learning via word of mouth in offline (WOM) and online (eWOM) settings[36]

Professor Peeter Verlegh, Vrije Universiteit, Amsterdam, Netherlands

'Consumers who want to learn more about a product or service have many different sources of information at their disposal. First of all, consumers may learn from their own experience, by trying or using a product. Second, they may rely on information provided by marketers, including for example advertising, packaging and company-owned websites. A third source is other consumers. In recent years, the information from other consumers – generally referred to as 'word of mouth' – has become more and more important. There may be several reasons for this, including a general distrust towards advertising, but the most important driver appears to be the greatly increased availability of this type of information: whereas the dissemination of word of mouth used to be limited to personal communications, it is now available in great quantities, in the form of online reviews, unboxing videos, blogs and product-related posts on Twitter, Facebook and other social media platforms.

I have been fascinated by word of mouth for quite some time, and have studied a variety of questions. More recently, I have started to look at differences between online and offline word of mouth. Together with Jiska Eelen and Peren Ozturan (also at the Vrije Universiteit, Amsterdam) I have conducted research that examines the relationship between brand loyalty and word of mouth in offline (face-to-face) and online settings. It is often assumed that loyal consumers are the ones who are more likely to talk about a brand, but there has not been a lot of research on this relationship, especially not in the context of fast-moving consumer goods like soft drinks or shampoo. In our research, we found that loyal (compared to non-loyal) customers are more likely to engage in face-to-face conversations about a brand. Loyalty does not necessarily influence the likelihood of engaging in online word of mouth (so-called eWOM). In the online world, it is much more important to motivate consumers to talk about your brand, for example by establishing a strong connection with a consumer's personal identity, or by simply telling them how much you appreciate and need their support. We were especially proud of this research, because it combined insights from a large-scale consumer survey with data gathered in follow-up experiments, and because it deals with a question that is relevant to marketers and provides them with specific recommendations.

Questions

Word of mouth is a potent influence on consumers: we tend to believe what other consumers tells us, much more than marketing messages. But what happens when marketers are trying to influence word of mouth, by stimulating it through (for example) rewards or contests? Are we still prepared to trust word of mouth from consumers if we know they have been rewarded, or otherwise stimulated to write or talk about their experiences? And how do we know whether an online review has been paid for, or even faked? Do we need regulations, or are consumers able to "sense" that a review is not authentic, perhaps by the language that the reviewers use? Plenty of questions for you to think about and discuss, and for me to study. . . '.[37]

The role of learning in memory

6.8

Products help us to retrieve memories from our past.

Memory involves a process of acquiring information and storing it over time so that it will be available when needed. Contemporary approaches to the study of memory employ an

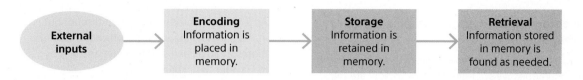

Figure 6.4 The memory process

information-processing approach. They assume that the mind is in some ways like a computer: data are input, processed and output for later use in revised form. In the **encoding** stage, information is entered in a way the system will recognise. In the **storage** stage, this knowledge is integrated with what is already in memory and 'warehoused' until needed. During **retrieval**, the person accesses the desired information.[38] The memory process is summarised in Figure 6.4.

Insights for marketing
What happens in your brain when you make a memory?

'We all have memories, as far as I can remember. But where do these memories come from and how do they get made? People often compare the brain to a computer, but the brain doesn't have USB slots that allow you to pick up new information by jamming a flash drive in your ear. That would be convenient, if a little painful. In truth, "memory" is not one single solid thing. It is a term covering lots of types of recollections that are surprisingly distinct, and used constantly in different combinations by a typical human.

Short-term memory – like writing your name with a sparkler

We've all heard about short-term and long-term memory. While people tend to use the phrase "short-term memory" to refer to our recall of things that happened recently – in the last hour or day – technically speaking, it's actually far more fleeting. Short-term memory typically lasts between 15 and 30 seconds: it's a bit like writing your name in the air with a sparkler. Any memory that can be recalled after that length of time is a long-term memory.

In computer terms, short-term memory is like the RAM – it holds the information we're currently working with or using for cognitive tasks (thinking). This can be new information delivered by our senses, for example, or old information retrieved from the long-term memory. Neuroscientists theorise that all this thinking is supported by patterns of neuron activity in the prefrontal cortex (that bit at the front of your brain).

Long-term memory – information becomes a physical 'thing'

Luckily, for memories we actually want to keep, there's also long-term memory. If short-term memory is the RAM of a computer, long-term memory is the hard drive, which keeps everything from your failed screenplays to Minesweeper scores. Unlike short-term memories, long-term memories have a physical presence in the brain, and aren't dependant purely on specific patterns of activity. Neurons make new physical connections and synapses with each other when a new long-term memory is formed. This connection endures whether it's being used or not.

Long-term memory can be split into explicit and implicit memory. Implicit memories include habits and skills that we can do automatically, such as rolling a cigarette, driving a car, forging your boss's signature on expense forms. Explicit memories are things we're consciously aware of and are intentionally trying to remember. There are two kinds of explicit memory: episodic and semantic. Episodic memory is memory for things and events that happened to you. Semantic memory is for more general knowledge. Knowing that Paris is the capital of France is a semantic memory; remembering being sick on your trip to Paris is an episodic memory.

Encoding – a terrifyingly complex tapestry in real time

When we actually want to learn something, it is long-term memories we are interested in. So how are they formed? The first step is to encode a piece of information – otherwise it quickly disappears, like breath on a mirror. Information is channelled to the hippocampus, the brain region crucial for the formation of new memories and one of the only places in the brain where brand new neurons are regularly generated. The hippocampus links all of the relevant information together and encodes it into a new memory by forming new synapses. It's basically like someone knitting a terrifyingly complex tapestry in real time.

But not all information is equal in the eyes of the hippocampus. "Important" things are encoded more readily and effectively than routine or incomprehensible things, like an uneventful daily commute, or the lyrics of a dance song in a language you don't recognise. The hippocampus will prioritise those that have been rehearsed repeatedly in the short-term memory, or those with a strong emotional component. The hippocampus is selective because it is very busy. Long-term memories have an actual physical presence in the brain. Neurons make new physical connections and synapses with each other when a new long-term memory is formed.

Finding a home for your memories

Coding a memory is all well and good, but it is useless if it has nowhere to go. Finding a storage place is the next step. Newer memories, once consolidated, appear to reside in the hippocampus for a while. But as more memories are formed, the neurons that represent a specific memory migrate further into the cortex. As a result, memories are stored throughout the brain. It's a bit like the internet, which is made of information spread all across the planet and accessed via countless connections.

Similar memories tend to clump together – spoken memories near the language centres, visual memories near the visual cortex – and there's a lot of redundancy too; you can have several memories for the same thing. Every time they are activated they are strengthened. Human memories aren't stored like books in a library; they're constantly being updated and tweaked.

Recalling memories you've forgotten you forgot

So how do you go about getting the bits you need out of this weird, ever-shifting library of information? It might seem as though lots of the so-called long-term memories have actually turned to dust because there are plenty of things you've forgotten: old addresses, passwords, deadlines for articles about the memory system that you promised to write. The problem here is not that it has disappeared, but rather that you can't recall it. It's a bit like losing a glove – you still own a glove, it's in your home somewhere, but you can't use it.

Recall is a very impressive but slightly mysterious process. When we want to access a memory from the dark recesses of our brain, signals from our frontal cortex link to that memory via uncertain means, and the memory is reconstructed from the information available. The more often you use the memory, the easier it is to find.'[39]

As suggested by Mario's memories and musings at the beginning of the chapter, many of our experiences are locked inside our heads, and we maintain those memories and recall those experience's if prompted, by the right cues. Consider 'the so-called reminiscence bump, based on many well-established studies about memory, [which] refers to the way we recall memories from adolescence and early adulthood more vividly as we grow older – compared to, say, remembering something from last week. So much of what we remember isn't to do with our mental state now, but about the state of our brain when the memory was first "processed". It could be down to the emotional intensity of our earlier years, or the lack of banal distraction that plagues so many adult lives, no one knows for sure. Either way, it seems it's not growing old that stops us remembering events from last year, it's just that they weren't experienced or laid down that strongly in the first place.'[40]

Marketers rely on consumers to retain information they have learned about products and services, trusting that it will later be applied in situations where purchase decisions must be made. During the consumer decision-making process, this internal memory is combined with external memory – which includes all the product details on packages in shopping lists, and through other marketing stimuli – to permit brand alternatives to be identified and evaluated.[41] Research supports the idea that marketers can distort a consumer's recall of a product experience. What we think we 'know' about products can be influenced by advertising messages to which we are exposed after using them. This *post-experience advertising* is more likely to alter actual memories when it is very similar to or activates memories about the actual experience. For example, advertising can make a remembered product experience more favourable than it actually was.[42]

Encoding information for later retrieval

The way information is encoded or mentally programmed helps to determine how it will be represented in memory. In general, incoming data that are associated with other information already in memory stand a better chance of being retained. For example, brand names that are linked to physical characteristics of a product category (such as Coffee-mate creamer or Sani-flush toilet bowl cleaner) or that are easy to visualise (e.g. Tide or Omo detergent) tend to be more easily retained in memory than more abstract brand names.[43] The grocery shopping list is a good example of a powerful external memory aid. When consumers use shopping lists, they buy approximately 80 per cent of the items on the list. The likelihood that a shopper will purchase a particular list item is higher if the person who wrote the list also participates in the shopping trip. This means that if marketers can induce a consumer to plan to purchase an item before she goes shopping, there is a high probability that she will buy it. One way to encourage this kind of advance planning is to provide peel-off stickers on packages so that, when the consumer notices the supply is low, she can simply peel off the label and place it directly on a shopping list.[44] Or, a retailer can support a phone app that generates a shopping list for the user (you already can choose from an abundance of apps that do this).[45]

Today, one of the biggest memory problems relates to our need to retain the numerous passwords we have to remember to function in our high-tech society. In fact, one in nine consumers keeps their passwords written down in electronic form – making the whole system so insecure that government regulators require online banks to add more layers of authentication. Both Google/Firefox and the Mac OS systems offer add-ons to manage your many passwords and take the strain off your memory.

Types of memory

A consumer may process a stimulus simply in terms of its sensory meaning, such as its colour or shape. When this occurs, the meaning may be activated when the person sees a picture of the stimulus. We may experience a sense of familiarity on seeing an ad for a new snack food we recently tasted, for example.

In many cases, though, meanings are encoded at a more abstract level. *Semantic meaning* refers to symbolic associations, such as the idea that rich people drink champagne or that fashionable men wear an earring.

Episodic memories are those that relate to events that are personally relevant, such as Mario's.[46] As a result, a person's motivation to retain these memories will be strong. Couples often have 'their song' that reminds them of their first date or wedding. The memories that might be triggered upon hearing this song would be quite different and unique for them.

Commercials sometimes attempt to activate episodic memories by focusing on experiences shared by many people. Recall of the past may have an effect on future behaviour. A university fundraising campaign can get higher donations by evoking pleasant memories. Some especially vivid associations are called *flashbulb* memories. These are usually related to some highly significant event. One method of conveying product information is through a *narrative* or a story. Much of the social information that an individual acquires is represented in memory this way. Therefore, utilising this method in product advertising can be an effective marketing

This ad for Audi requires the reader to invest a high level of effort to understand it.

Jeff Morgan 09/Alamy Stock Photo

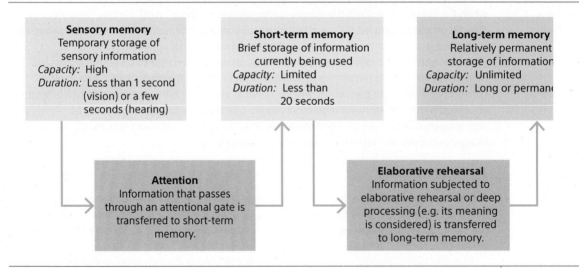

Figure 6.5 Relationships among memory systems

technique. Narratives persuade people to construct a mental representation of the information they are viewing. Pictures aid in this construction and allow for a more developed and detailed mental representation.[47]

Memory systems

According to the information-processing perspective, there are three distinct memory systems: sensory memory, short-term memory (STM) and long-term memory (LTM). Each plays a role in processing brand-related information. The interrelationships of these memory systems are summarised in Figure 6.5.

Sensory memory permits storage of the information we receive from our senses. This storage is very temporary: it lasts a couple of seconds at most. For example, a person might be walking past a bakery and get a brief, but enticing, whiff of bread baking inside. While this sensation would only last for a few seconds, it would be sufficient to allow the person to determine if they should investigate further. If the information is retained for further processing, it passes through an attentional gate and is transferred to short-term memory.

Short-term memory (STM) also stores information for a limited period of time, and its capacity is limited. Similar to a computer, this system can be regarded as working memory: it holds the information we are currently processing. Verbal input may be stored acoustically (in terms of how it sounds) or semantically (in terms of its meaning).

The information is stored by combining small pieces into larger ones in a process known as 'chunking'. A chunk is a configuration that is familiar to the person and can be manipulated as a unit. For example, a brand name can be a chunk that summarises a great deal of detailed information about the brand.

Initially, it was believed that STM was capable of processing five to nine chunks of information at a time, and for this reason phone numbers were designed to have seven digits.[48] It now appears that three to four chunks is the optimum size for efficient retrieval (seven-digit phone numbers can be remembered because the individual digits are chunked, so we may remember a three-digit exchange as one piece of information).[49]

Long-term memory (LTM) is the system that allows us to retain information for a long period of time. In order for information to enter into long-term memory from short-term memory, elaborative rehearsal is required. This process involves thinking about the meaning of a stimulus and relating it to other information already in memory. Marketers sometimes assist in the process by devising catchy slogans or jingles that consumers repeat on their own.

Storing information in memory

Relationships among the types of memory are a source of some controversy. The traditional perspective, known as multiple-store, assumes that STM and LTM are separate systems. More recent research has moved away from the distinction between the two types of memory, instead emphasising the interdependence of the systems. This work argues that, depending upon the nature of the processing task, different levels of processing occur that activate some aspects of memory rather than others. These approaches are called **activation models of memory**.[50] The more effort it takes to process information (so-called deep processing), the more likely it is that information will be placed in long-term memory.

Activation models propose that an incoming piece of information is stored in an associative network containing many bits of related information organised according to some set of relationships. The consumer has organised systems of concepts relating to brands, stores and so on.

Knowledge structures

These storage units, known as **knowledge structures**, can be thought of as complex spiders' webs filled with pieces of data. This information is placed into nodes, which are connected by associative links within these structures. Pieces of information that are seen as similar in some ways are chunked together under some more abstract category. New, incoming information is interpreted to be consistent with the structure already in place.[51] According to the hierarchical processing model, a message is processed in a bottom-up fashion: processing begins at a very basic level and is subject to increasingly complex processing operations that require greater cognitive capacity. If processing at one level fails to evoke the next level, processing of the ad is terminated and capacity is allocated to other tasks.[52]

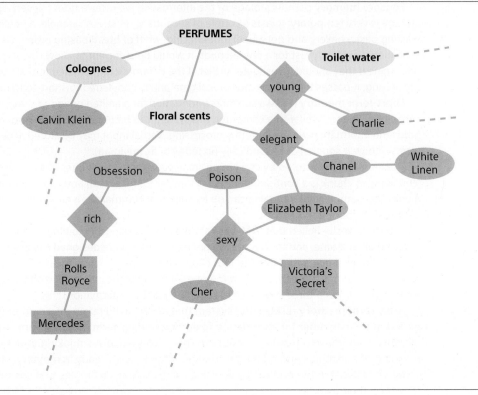

Figure 6.6 An associative network for perfumes

Links form between nodes as an associative network is developed. For example, a consumer might have a network for 'perfumes'. Each node represents a concept related to the category. This node can be an attribute, a specific brand, a celebrity identified with a perfume, or even a related product. A network for perfumes might include concepts including the names Chanel, Obsession and Charlie, as well as attributes such as 'sexy' and 'elegant'.

When asked to list perfumes, the consumer would recall only those brands contained in the appropriate category. This group constitutes that person's **evoked set**. The task of a new entrant that wants to position itself as a category member (e.g. a new luxury perfume) is to provide cues that facilitate its placement in the appropriate category. A sample network for perfumes is shown in Figure 6.6.

Spreading activation

A meaning can be activated indirectly: energy spreads across nodes at varying levels of abstraction. As one node is activated, other nodes associated with it also begin to be triggered. Meaning thus spreads across the network, bringing up concepts including competing brands and relevant attributes that are used to form attitudes towards the brand.

This process of spreading activation allows consumers to shift back and forth between levels of meaning. The way a piece of information is stored in memory depends upon the type of meaning assigned to it. This meaning type will, in turn, determine how and when the meaning is activated. For example, the memory trace for an ad could be stored in one or more of the following ways:

- *Brand-specific:* in terms of claims made for the brand.
- *Ad-specific:* in terms of the medium or content of the ad itself.
- *Brand identification:* in terms of the brand name.

- *Product category:* in terms of how the product works, where it should be used, or experiences with the product.
- *Evaluative reactions:* in terms of whether 'that looks like fun'.[53]

Levels of knowledge

Knowledge is coded at different levels of abstraction and complexity. Meaning concepts are individual nodes (e.g. elegant) and these may be combined into a larger unit, called a *proposition* (also known as a belief). A proposition links two nodes together to form a more complex meaning, which can serve as a single chunk of information. For example, a proposition might be that 'Chanel is a perfume for elegant women'.

Propositions are, in turn, integrated to produce a complex unit known as a **schema**. A schema is a cognitive framework that is developed through experience. Information that is consistent with an existing schema is encoded more readily.[54] The ability to move up and down between levels of abstraction greatly increases processing flexibility and efficiency. For this reason, young children, who do not yet have well-developed schemas, are not able to make efficient use of purchase information compared with older children.[55]

One type of schema that is relevant to consumer behaviour is a script – a sequence of procedures that is expected by an individual. For example, consumers learn service scripts that guide expectations and purchasing behaviour in business settings. Consumers learn to expect a certain sequence of events, and they may become uncomfortable if the service departs from the script. A service script for your visit to the dentist might include such events as: (1) driving to the dentist; (2) reading old magazines in the waiting room; (3) hearing your name called and sitting in the dentist's chair; (4) having the dentist probe your teeth; (5) having the dentist scale and polish your teeth; and so on. This desire to follow a script helps to explain why such service innovations as automatic bank machines and self-service petrol stations have met with initial resistance from some consumers, who have trouble adapting to a new sequence of events.[56]

The tangled web

Social networks such as Facebook have revolutionised how people store and share memories. However, at least some users are starting to feel that maybe these platforms do this a bit too well: they don't necessarily want others (especially employers, parents and other authority figures) to know about all of their 'awesome' experiences. As a result, a number of newer platforms, including Wickr, Vidburn and even Facebook's own Poke, allow photos or messages to be viewed for a few seconds before they vanish into cyberspace. The biggest hit is Snapchat, which posts and then destroys more than 60 million photos or messages every day – already a tenth of the activity that occurs on the much-bigger Facebook platform. One of Snapchat's founders explained the thinking behind the app: 'It became clear how awful social media is. There is real value in sharing moments that don't live forever.'[57]

Retrieving information for purchase decisions

Retrieval is the process whereby information is accessed from long-term memory. As evidenced by the popularity of the board game *Trivial Pursuit,* or the television programmes *Who Wants to Be a Millionaire?* or *Mastermind,* people have a vast quantity of information stored in their heads that is not necessarily available on demand. Although most of the information entered in long-term memory does not go away, it may be difficult or impossible to retrieve unless the appropriate cues are present.

Factors influencing retrieval

Individual cognitive or physiological factors are responsible for some of the differences we see in retrieval ability among people.[58] Some older adults consistently display inferior recall ability for current items, such as prescription drug instructions, although they may recall events that happened to them when they were younger with great clarity.[59] The recent popularity of puzzles, such as Sudoku, and centres that offer 'mental gymnastics' attest to emerging evidence that we can keep our retrieval abilities sharp by exercising our minds, just as we keep our other muscles toned by working out on a regular basis.

The tangled web

It hasn't been smooth sailing for the cruise industry lately, following several highly publicised incidents where things were not exactly ship-shape on board. One of the most embarrassing and high-profile accidents stranded several thousand guests on a Carnival ship in the Gulf of Mexico with no electricity or working toilets – but plenty of smartphones to record the dismal conditions. Carnival's potential cruisers are skittish, so the cruise line launched a $25 million PR offensive to lure people back on board. The campaign asked past customers to use social media to post images and videos of happy experiences that would contribute to Carnival's 'Moments that Matter' commercial. The ad's voice-over said, 'We never forget the moments that matter. We hang them on our walls. We share them with everyone. And hold onto them forever. Since the day we first set sail, millions of lasting moments have been made with us. What will yours be?' Sure enough, the campaign received more than 30,000 submissions – presumably from passengers who enjoyed both the midnight chocolate buffet and working plumbing.[60]

In one major study, only 23 per cent of the respondents could recall a new product introduced in the past year.[61] That's not an encouraging finding for marketers.

Other factors that influence retrieval are situational – they relate to the environment in which the message is delivered. Not surprisingly, recall is enhanced when we pay more attention to the message in the first place. Some evidence indicates that we can retrieve information about a *pioneering brand* (the first brand to enter a market) more easily from memory than we can for *follower brands,* because the first product's introduction is likely to be distinctive and, for the time being, no competitors divert our attention.[62] In addition, we are more likely to recall descriptive brand names than those that do not provide adequate cues as to what the product is.[63]

Not surprisingly, the way a marketer presents their message influences the likelihood we will be able to recall it later. The **spacing effect** describes the tendency for us to recall printed material more effectively when the advertiser repeats the target item periodically, rather than presenting it repeatedly in a short time period.[64] The viewing environment of a marketing message also affects recall. For example, General Electric found that its commercials fared better in television shows with continuous activity, such as stories or dramas, compared to variety shows or talk shows that are punctuated by a series of acts.[65] Finally, a large-scale analysis of TV commercials found that viewers recall commercials shown first in a series of ads better than those they see last.[66]

State-dependent retrieval

In a process termed 'state-dependent retrieval', people are better-able to access information if their internal state is the same at the time of recall as it was when the information was learned.

This phenomenon, called the *mood congruence effect,* underscores the desirability of matching a consumer's mood at the time of purchase when planning exposure to marketing communications. A consumer is more likely to recall an ad, for example, if their mood or level of arousal at the time of exposure is similar to that in the purchase environment. By recreating the cues that were present when the information was first presented, recall can be enhanced.[67]

Familiarity and recall

As a general rule, prior familiarity with an item enhances its recall. Indeed, this is one of the basic goals of marketers who are trying to create and maintain awareness of their products. The more experience a consumer has with a product, the better use that person is able to make of product information.[68] Finally, research suggests a **highlighting effect**, where the order in which consumers learn about brands determines the strength of association between these brands and their attributes. Consumers more strongly associate common attributes with early-learned brands and unique attributes with late-learned brands. More generally, we are more likely to recognise words, objects and faces we learn early in life than similar items we learn later. This applies to brands as well; managers who introduce new entries into a market with well-established brand names need to work harder to create learning and memory linkages by exposing consumers to information about them more frequently.[69]

However, there is a possible fly in the ointment: as noted earlier in the chapter, some evidence indicates that over-familiarity can result in inferior learning and/or recall. When consumers are highly familiar with a brand or an advertisement, they may attend to fewer attributes because they do not believe that any additional effort will yield a gain in knowledge.[70] For example, when consumers are exposed to the technique of radio replay, where the audio track from a television ad is replayed on the radio, they do very little critical, evaluative processing and instead mentally replay the video portion of the ad.[71]

Salience and recall

The salience of a brand refers to its prominence or level of activation in memory. Stimuli that stand out in contrast to their environment are more likely to command attention (see Chapter 3), which, in turn, increases the likelihood that they will be recalled. Almost any technique that increases the novelty of a stimulus also improves recall (a result known as the von Restorff effect).[72] This effect explains why unusual advertising or distinctive packaging tends to facilitate brand recall.[73]

Introducing a surprise element in an ad can be particularly effective (see Chapter 3). This strategy aids recall even if the stimulus is not relevant to the factual information being presented.[74] In addition, so-called mystery ads, where the brand is not identified until the end, are more effective at building associations in memory between the product category and that brand – especially in the case of novel brands.[75]

Pictorial *vs* verbal cues

There is some evidence for the superiority of visual memory over verbal memory, but this advantage is unclear because it is more difficult to measure recall of pictures.[76] However, the available data indicate that information presented in pictorial form is more likely to be recognised later.[77] Certainly, visual aspects of an ad are more likely to grab a consumer's attention. In fact, eye-movement studies indicate that about 90 per cent of viewers look at the dominant picture in an ad before they bother to view the copy.[78] One commentator argues: 'We have work lives and love lives, but we also have looking lives. If we're lucky enough to have eyesight, an inner photo album accrues throughout our lives. On its pages are the sunsets we've seen, the dead bodies, and many other defining images – these are the visual shocks and pleasures which help us understand and read emotion. . . There seem to be two different streams within our brain's rear visual cortex. The first, the ventral stream, assesses objects. It's the "what" function, and tells you, if you are on a tennis court, that this is a ball barrelling towards you. The second, the dorsal stream, assesses the position and movement of the ball, the "where" function.'[79]

While pictorial ads may enhance recall, they do not necessarily improve comprehension. One study found that television news items presented with illustrations (still pictures) as a backdrop result in improved recall for details of the news story, even though the understanding of the story's content does not improve.[80] Visual imagery can be especially effective when it includes verbal cues that relate to the consumer's existing knowledge.

Factors influencing forgetting

Marketers obviously hope that consumers will not forget their products. However, in a poll of more than 13,000 adults, more than half were unable to remember any specific ad they had seen, heard or read in the previous 30 days.[81] Forgetting is obviously a problem for marketers.

Early memory theorists assumed that memories fade due to the simple passage of time. In a process of decay, the structural changes in the brain produced by learning simply go away. But forgetting also occurs due to **interference**: as additional information is learned, it displaces the earlier information.

Stimulus–response associations will be forgotten if the consumers subsequently learn new responses to the same or similar stimuli in a process known as *retroactive interference*. Or prior learning can interfere with new learning, a process termed *proactive interference*. Since pieces of information are stored in memory as nodes that are connected to one another by links, a meaning concept that is connected by a larger number of links is more likely to be retrieved. But, as new responses are learned, a stimulus loses its effectiveness in retrieving the old response.[82]

These interference effects help to explain problems in remembering brand information. Consumers tend to organise attribute information by brand.[83] Additional attribute information regarding a brand or similar brands may limit the person's ability to recall old brand information. Recall may also be inhibited if the brand name is composed of frequently used words. These words cue competing associations and result in less retention of brand information.[84]

In one study, brand evaluations deteriorated more rapidly when ads for the brand appeared with messages for 12 other brands in the same category than when the ad was shown with ads for 12 dissimilar products.[85] By increasing the salience of a brand, the recall of other brands can be impaired.[86] On the other hand, calling a competitor by name can result in poorer recall for one's own brand.[87]

Finally, a phenomenon known as the *part-list cueing effect* allows marketers to utilise the interference process strategically. When only a portion of the items in a category are presented to consumers, the omitted items are not as easily recalled. For example, comparative advertising that mentions only a subset of competitors (preferably those that the marketer is not very worried about) may inhibit recall of the unmentioned brands with which the product does *not* compare favourably.[88]

Products as memory markers

Products and ads can themselves serve as powerful retrieval cues. Indeed, the three types of possessions most valued by consumers are furniture, visual art and photos. The most common explanation for this attachment is the ability of these things to summon memories of the past.[89] Products are particularly important as markers when our sense of the past is threatened, as when a consumer's current identity is challenged due to some change in role caused by divorce, moving, graduation and so on.[90] Products have mnemonic qualities that serve as a form of external memory by prompting consumers to retrieve episodic memories.

For example, family photography allows consumers to create their own retrieval cues, with the 11 billion amateur photos taken annually forming a kind of external memory bank for our culture.

Researchers are just beginning to probe the effects of autobiographical memories on buying behaviour. These memories appear to be one way that advertisements create emotional responses: ads that succeed in getting us to think about our own past also appear to get us to like these ads more – especially if the linkage between the nostalgia experience and the brand is strong.[91] Researchers argue that films we've seen a second (or third) time, and books that we've re-read, even after years since the first reading, add to a deeper sense of understanding and appreciation for the film or book.[92]

The marketing power of nostalgia

Marketers often resurrect popular characters and stories from days gone by; they hope that consumers' fond memories will motivate them to revisit the past. We had a 1950s revival in the 1970s, and consumers in the 1980s got a heavy dose of memories from the 1960s. Today, it seems that popular characters only need to be gone for a few years before someone tries to bring them back. **Nostalgia** describes a bittersweet emotion where we view the past with both sadness and longing.[93] References to 'the good old days' are increasingly common, as advertisers call up memories of youth – and hope these feelings will translate to what they are selling today. Researchers find that valued possessions can evoke thoughts about prior events on several dimensions, including sensory experiences, friends and loved ones and breaking away from parents or former partners.[94] That helps to explain the popularity of photo-sharing sites such as Flickr – this platform alone hosts over five billion pictures and offers a 'Share This' tool for use on Facebook and Twitter.[95]

Many European companies are making use of nostalgic appeals, some of which are based on the not-too-distant past. Berlin's Humboldt University and City Museum staged a fashion show of the 1960s, displaying clothes, appliances and posters from the communist era. The show, entitled *Ostalgie,* which is a play on words for 'East nostalgia' in the German language, gave a nostalgic view of a time when goods might have been shoddy but when there was no unemployment or homelessness. There is growing interest in the Trabant car (the joke used to be that you could double the value of a Trabant by filling it with sand), which has resulted in a new model, the Son of Trabant, built in the same factory where they used to build the original. Likewise, Western European multinationals are relaunching local brands of East European origin in response to a backlash against the incursion of foreign products. From cigarettes to yoghurt, multinationals are trying to lure consumers by combining yesteryear's product names with today's quality. Local brands such as Nestlé's Chokito or Unilever's Flora margarine are now among the companies' best-selling products in Eastern European markets. Much as Americans two decades ago tuned in to *The Wonder Years* for a glimpse of simpler times, Russians are waxing nostalgic for the late communist period with *The Eighties,* a coming-of-age comedy that pokes fun at banned Western music, cabbage soup and the need to boil laundry. *The Eighties,* which has also been sold to broadcasters in Ukraine, Latvia and Estonia, is one of a growing number of TV shows being made behind the old Iron Curtain and that are also aimed at export markets. As the purchasing power of Eastern Europeans grows, TV series producers, including Sony (SNE), Amsterdam-based Endemol and Time Warner's (TWX) HBO, are creating more original programming in Eastern Europe to give locals an alternative to their standard fare of imported cop shows and soaps.[96]

Considerable care goes into the production values of campaigns that are intended to evoke nostalgia. Mulino Bianco, the Italian producer of cakes, biscuits and cereals, carefully developed a campaign depicting the quiet aspects of rural life to increase sales of cakes, which are typically served only on special occasions. The campaign showed a white farmhouse on a green hill, next to a watermill. Parents, children and friends were shown in a slow, relaxed, informal atmosphere, far from the hectic urban commitments of work. The object was to evoke a relationship between 'the good old days' and cakes, and to present cakes as genuine food to be eaten every day during normal meals. In Italy, where the tension to escape from the hectic urban life is high, the campaign was quite successful. In France, where eating habits are different and the appeal to rural life is weaker, the same campaign was not successful.[97]

As you notice from the examples above, food can be a particularly nostalgic product category. A study looked at how favourite recipes stimulate memories of the past. When the researchers asked informants to list three of their favourite recipes and to talk about these choices, they found that people tended to link them with memories of past events such as childhood memories, family holidays, milestone events (such as dishes they only make on special holidays, like corned beef and cabbage on St Patrick's Day), heirlooms (recipes handed down across generations) and the passing of time (e.g. only eating blueberry cobbler in the summer).[98] Indeed, one of the most famous literary references is from the classic (3,000-page) novel *Remembrance of Things Past* by the French novelist Marcel Proust. The narrator dips a pastry (a *madeleine*) into his tea, and this action unleashes a flood of memories that drive the rest of the book.

Memory and aesthetic preferences

In addition to liking ads and products that remind us of our past, our prior experiences also help to determine what we like now. Some research indicates that people's tastes in such products as films and clothing are influenced by what was popular during certain critical periods of their youth. For example, liking for specific songs appears to be related to how old a person was when those songs were popular: on average, songs that were popular when an individual was 23 to 24 years old are the most likely to be favoured.[99] In addition, it seems that men form preferences for women's clothing styles that were in vogue when these men were in their early twenties.[100]

More generally, many marketers understand that life-long brand loyalties are formed at a fairly early age: they view the battle for the hearts (and wallets) of students and young adults as a long-term investment. (See Chapter 10, where these age-related preferences will be further addressed.)

The visual aspects of display are important, not just for attracting and keeping attention, but also for more subtle cues about the status of the product or retail outlet. For example, here the clean lines of the lettering and use of green link the product to nature and the countryside, as well as environmental and sustainability issues, which are all central to the Barbour branding.

Clynt Garnham Business/Alamy Stock Photo

Marketing opportunity
Humans produce new brain cells throughout their lives, say researchers

'Humans continue to produce new neurons in a part of their brain involved in learning, memory and emotion throughout adulthood, scientists have revealed, countering previous theories that production stopped after adolescence. . . Many new neurons are produced in the hippocampus in babies, but it has been a matter of hot debate whether this continues into adulthood – and if so, whether this rate drops with age, as seen in mice and non-human primates.

Although some research had found new neurons in the hippocampus of older humans, a recent study scotched the idea, claiming that new neurons in the hippocampus were at undetectable levels by our late teens.

Now another group of scientists have published research that pushes back, revealing the new neurons are produced in this brain region in human adults and do not drop off with age. . . "The exciting part is that the neurons are there throughout a lifetime", said Dr Maura Boldrini from Columbia University in New York and first author of the new study published in the journal *Cell Stem Cell*. "It seems that indeed humans are different from mice – where [neuron production] goes down with age really fast – and this could mean that we need these neurons for our complex learning abilities and cognitive behavioural responses to emotions", she said.

Boldrini and colleagues looked at the hippocampus in 28 men and women aged between 14 and 79, collected just hours after they had died. Importantly, Boldrini notes, all of the individuals were healthy before death, unlike in many previous studies. Using a number of techniques, the team examined the degree of new blood-vessel formation, the volume and the number of cells of different stages of maturity, in an area known as the dentate gyrus – the region of the hippocampus where new neurons are produced.'[101]

6.9

Marketers measure our memories about products and ads.

Measuring memory for advertising

Because advertisers pay so much money to place their messages in front of consumers, they are naturally concerned that people will actually remember these messages at a later point. It seems that they have good reason to be concerned. In one study, less than 40 per cent of television viewers made positive links between commercial messages and the corresponding products; only 65 per cent noticed the brand name in a commercial; and only 38 per cent recognised a connection to an important point.[102]

More worryingly, only 7 per cent of television viewers can recall the product or company featured in the most recent television commercial they watched. This figure represents less than half the recall rate recorded in 1965 and may be attributed to such factors as the increase of 30- and 15-second commercials, the highly fragmented media consumption of consumers in the twenty-first century and the practice of airing television commercials in clusters rather than in connection with single-sponsor programmes.[103] Small wonder that noticing a brand is becoming more difficult, especially among young consumers. A recent study of 'digital natives' (consumers in their twenties, who grew up with computers, smartphones and tablets) shows that, during non-working hours, they switch media venues up to 27 times an hour![104]

Recognition *vs* recall

One indicator of good advertising is, of course, the impression it makes on consumers. But how can this impact be defined and measured? Two basic measures of impact are recognition and recall. In the typical recognition test, subjects are shown ads one at a time and asked if they have seen them before. In contrast, free recall tests ask consumers to produce independently previously acquired information and then perform a recognition test on it.

Visual aspects of an ad can really grab a consumer's attention, especially when they are novel. This ad is particularly effective, not least because it really plays with the notion of trompe-l'oeil (i.e. using realistic imagery to create an illusion); and like many examples of trompe-l'oeil this ad uses the wall space of a building for its setting (which is typically how this art form has been reproduced in many European cities).

Daniel Dempster Photography/Alamy Stock Photo

Under some conditions, these two memory measures tend to yield the same results, especially when the researchers try to keep the viewers' interest in the ads constant.[105] Generally, though, recognition scores tend to be more reliable and do not decay over time in the way recall scores do.[106] Recognition scores are almost always better than recall scores because recognition is a simpler process and more retrieval cues are available to the consumer.

Both types of retrieval play important roles in purchase decisions. Recall tends to be more important in situations where consumers do not have product data at their disposal, and so they must rely upon memory to generate this information.[107] On the other hand, recognition is more likely to be an important factor in a store, where consumers are confronted with thousands of product options and information (i.e. where external memory is abundantly available) and where the task may simply be to recognise a familiar package. Unfortunately, package recognition and familiarity can have a negative consequence in that warning labels may be ignored, since their existence is taken for granted and not really noticed.[108]

The Starch Test

A widely used commercial measure of advertising recall for magazines is called the Starch Test, a syndicated service founded in 1932.[109] This service provides scores on a number of aspects of consumers' familiarity with an ad, including such categories as 'noted', 'associated' and 'read most'. It also scores the impact of the component parts of an overall ad, giving such information as 'seen' for major illustrations and 'read some' for a major block of copy.[110] Such factors as the size of the ad, whether it appears towards the front or the back of the magazine, if it is on the right or left page and the size of illustrations play an important role in affecting the amount of attention given to an ad, as determined by Starch scores.

Problems with memory measures

While the measurement of an ad's memorability is important, the ability of existing measures to assess these dimensions accurately has been criticised for several reasons.

Response biases

Results obtained from a measuring instrument are not necessarily due to what is being measured, but rather to something else about either the instrument or the respondent. This form of contamination is called a **response bias**. For example, people tend to give 'yes' responses to questions regardless of what is asked. In addition, consumers are often eager to be 'good subjects' by pleasing the experimenter. They will try to give the responses they think experimenters are looking for. In some studies, the claimed recognition of bogus ads (ads that have not been seen before) is almost as high as the recognition rate of real ads.[111]

Memory lapses

People are also prone to forgetting information unintentionally. Typical problems include omitting (the leaving out of facts), averaging (the tendency to 'normalise' things and not report extreme cases) and telescoping (the inaccurate recall of time).[112] These distortions call into question the accuracy of various product usage databases that rely upon consumers to recall their purchase and consumption of food and household items. In one study, for example, people were asked to describe what portion of various foods – small, medium or large – they ate in a normal meal; however, different definitions of 'medium' were used (e.g. 185ml *vs* 375ml). Regardless of the measurement specified, about the same number of people claimed they normally ate 'medium' portions.[113]

Memory for facts *vs* feelings

Although techniques are being developed to increase the accuracy of memory scores, these improvements do not address the more fundamental issue of whether recall is necessary for advertising to have an effect. In particular, some critics argue that these measures do not adequately tap the impact of 'feeling' ads, where the objective is to arouse strong emotions rather than to convey concrete product benefits. Many ad campaigns, including those for Hallmark cards, Chevrolet and Pepsi, use this approach.[114] An effective strategy relies on a long-term build-up of feeling, rather than on a one-shot attempt to convince consumers to buy the product.

Also, it is not clear that recall translates into preference. We may recall the benefits touted in an ad but not believe them. Or the ad may be memorable because it is so obnoxious, and the product becomes one we 'love to hate'. The bottom line is that while recall is important, especially for creating brand awareness, it is not necessarily sufficient to alter consumer preferences. To accomplish this, marketers need more sophisticated attitude-change strategies (see Chapter 7).

Chapter summary

Now that you have finished reading this chapter you should understand why:

6.1 **It's important to understand how consumers learn about products and services.** Learning is a change in behaviour that is caused by experience. Learning can occur through simple associations between a stimulus and a response, or via a complex series of cognitive activities.

6.2 **Conditioning results in learning.** Behavioural learning theories assume that learning occurs as a result of responses to external events. Classical conditioning occurs when a stimulus that naturally elicits a response (an unconditioned stimulus) is paired with another stimulus that does not initially elicit this response. Over time, the second stimulus (the conditioned stimulus) elicits the response even in the absence of the first.

6.3 **There is a difference between classical and instrumental conditioning.** Operant, or instrumental, conditioning occurs as the person learns to perform behaviours that produce positive outcomes and avoid those that result in negative outcomes. Whereas classical conditioning involves the pairing of two stimuli, instrumental learning occurs when reinforcement is the result of following a response to a stimulus. Reinforcement is positive if a reward follows a response. It is negative if the person avoids a negative outcome by not performing a response. Punishment occurs when an unpleasant event follows a response. Extinction of the behaviour will occur if reinforcement no longer occurs.

6.4 **Learned associations with brands generalise to other products, and this is important to marketers.** This response can also extend to other, similar stimuli in a process we call 'stimulus generalisation'. This process is the basis for such marketing strategies as licensing and family branding, where a consumer's positive associations with a product transfer to other contexts.

6.5 **We learn about products by observing others' behaviour.** Cognitive learning occurs as the result of mental processes. For example, observational learning occurs when the consumer performs a behaviour as a result of seeing someone else performing it and being rewarded for it.

6.6 **Our brains process information about brands to retain them in memory.** Memory is the storage of learned information. The way we encode information when we perceive it determines how we will store it in memory. The memory systems we call sensory memory, short-term memory and long-term memory each play a role in retaining and processing information from the outside world.

6.7 **The other products we associate with an individual product influence how we will remember it.** We don't store information in isolation; we incorporate it into knowledge structures where our brains associate it with other related data. The location of product information in associative networks, and the level of abstraction at which it is coded, help to determine when and how we will activate this information at a later date. Some factors that influence the likelihood of retrieval include the level of familiarity with an item, its salience (or prominence) in memory and whether the information was presented in pictorial or written form.

6.8 **Products help us to retrieve memories from our past.** Products also play a role as memory markers; consumers use them to retrieve memories about past experiences (autobiographical memories), and we often value them because they are able to do this. This function also encourages the use of nostalgia in marketing strategies.

6.9 **Marketers measure our memories about products and ads.** We can use either recognition or recall techniques to measure memory for product information. Consumers are more likely to recognise an advertisement if it is presented to them than they are to recall one without being given any cues. However, neither recognition nor recall automatically or reliably translates into product preferences or purchases.

Key terms

Activation models of memory (p. 233)
Behavioural learning theories (p. 215)
Brand equity (p. 223)
Classical conditioning (p. 217)
Cognitive learning (p. 221)
Encoding (p. 229)
Endowed progress effect (p. 227)
Evoked set (p. 234)
Extinction (p. 217)
Frequency marketing (p. 226)
Highlighting effect (p. 237)
Interference (p. 238)
Knowledge structures (p. 233)
Learning (p. 215)
Long-term memory (p. 233)
Memory (p. 228)

Negative reinforcement (p. 219)
Nostalgia (p. 239)
Observational learning (p. 221)
Operant conditioning (p. 218)
Positive reinforcement (p. 218)
Punishment (p. 219)
Response bias (p. 243)
Retrieval (p. 229)
Schema (p. 235)
Sensory memory (p. 233)
Short-term memory (p. 233)
Spacing effect (p. 236)
Stimulus discrimination (p. 218)
Stimulus generalisation (p. 217)
Storage (p. 229)

Consumer behaviour challenge

1 Identify three patterns of reinforcement and provide an example of how each is used in a marketing context.

2 Describe the functions of short-term and long-term memory. What is the apparent relationship between the two?

3 Devise a 'product jingle memory test'. Compile a list of brands that are or have been associated with memorable jingles, such as Opal Fruits or Heinz Baked Beans. Read this list to friends and see how many jingles are remembered. You may be surprised at the level of recall.

4 Identify some important characteristics for a product with a well-known brand name. Based on these attributes, generate a list of possible brand extension or licensing opportunities, as well as some others that would be unlikely to be accepted by consumers.

5 Collect some pictures of 'classic' products that have high nostalgia value. Show these pictures to consumers and allow them to make free associations. Analyse the types of memories that are evoked and think about how these associations might be employed in a product's promotional strategy.

For additional material see the companion website at **www.pearsoned.co.uk/solomon**

Notes

1. Robert A. Baron, *Psychology: The Essential Science* (Boston: Allyn & Bacon, 1989).

2. 'Coming Soon: 4DMovie Theatres with Smell-o-Vision', *Bloomberg News* (April 2015); see also Sarah Dowdey, 'Does What You Smell Determine What you Buy?', *How Stuff Works*, The Discovery Channel (2012), http://money.howstuffworks.com/scent-marketing.htm (accessed 28 July 2018); see also Emma Hall, 'What's that Smell in the Movie Theater? It's an Ad', *Adage* (24 July 2008), http://adage.com/article?article_id=129864 (accessed 27 July 2018).

3. Richard A. Feinberg, 'Credit cards as spending facilitating stimuli: a conditioning interpretation', *Journal of Consumer Research* 13 (December 1986): 348–56.

4. R.A. Rescorla, 'Pavlovian conditioning: it's not what you think it is', *American Psychologist* 43 (1988): 151–60; Elnora W. Stuart, Terence A. Shimp and Randall W. Engle, 'Classical conditioning of consumer attitudes: four experiments in an advertising context', *Journal of Consumer Research* 14 (December 1987): 334–9; Terence A. Shimp, Elnora W. Stuart and Randall W. Engle, 'A program of classical conditioning experiments testing variations in the conditioned stimulus and context', *Journal of Consumer Research* 18(1) (June 1991): 1–12.

5. C. Janiszewski, H. Noel and A.G. Sawyer, 'A Meta-analysis of the Spacing Effect in Verbal Learning: Implications for Research on Advertising Repetition and Consumer Memory', *Journal of Consumer Research* 30(1) (2003): 138–49.

6. Baron, *Psychology*, op. cit.

7. Yaveroglu Donthu and Naveen Donthu, 'Advertising Repetition and Placement Issues in On-Line Environments', *Journal of Advertising* 37 (Summer 2008): 31–43.

8. Caitlin Ingrassia, 'Counterfeiter, imitators: fine line, *The Wall Street Journal* (16 January 2004), http://online.wsj.com/article/0,,SB107421653820930400,00.html?mod=article-outset-box (accessed 27 July 2018); see also: 'AH moet twee verpakkingen aanpassingen' (video), *RTL Nieuws* (28 April 2005); see also: Ryan S. Elder and Krishna Aradhna, 'The "Visual Depiction Effect" in Advertising: Facilitating Embodied Mental Simulation through Product Orientation', *Journal of Consumer Research,* 38(6) (April 2012): 988–1,003.

9. Judith Lynne Zaichkowsky and Richard Neil Simpson, 'The Effect of Experience with a Brand Imitator on the Original Brand', *Marketing Letters* 7(1) (1996): 31–9.

10. For a comprehensive approach to consumer behaviour based on operant conditioning principles, see Gordon R. Foxall, 'Behavior analysis and consumer psychology', *Journal of Economic Psychology* 15 (March 1994): 5–91. Foxall also sets out some consumer behaviour based on a neo-behaviourist perspective. By identifying environmental determinants, he develops four classes of consumer behaviour: *accomplishment, pleasure, accumulation* and *maintenance*. For an extensive discussion on this approach, see the entire special issue of Gordon R. Foxall, 'Science and interpretation in consumer behavior: a radical behaviourist perspective', *European Journal of Marketing* 29(9) (1995): 3–99.

11. Ellen J. Langer, *The Psychology of Control* (Beverly Hills, CA: Sage, 1983); Klaus G. Grunert, 'Automatic and strategic processes in advertising effects', *Journal of Marketing* 60 (1996): 88–91.

12. Robert B. Cialdini, *Influence: Science and Practice,* 2nd edn (New York: William Morrow, 1984).

13. Jay P. Carlson, Leslie H. Vincent, David M. Hardesty and William O. Bearden (2009) 'Objective and subjective knowledge relationships: a quantitative analysis of consumer research findings', *Journal of Consumer Research* 35 (February 2009): 864–76.

14. Andrew D. Gershoff, Ran Kivetz and Anat Keinan, 'Consumer Response to Versioning: How Brands' Production Methods Affect Perceptions of Unfairness', *Journal of Consumer Research,* 39 (August 2012) 382–98; see also Chris Nuttall and Richard Waters, 'Apple responds to critical report on Foxconn', *Financial Times* (29 March 2012).

15. Chris T. Allen and Thomas J. Madden, 'A closer look at classical conditioning', *Journal of Consumer Research* 12 (December 1985): 301–15.

16. Albert Bandura, *Social Foundations of Thought and Action: A Social Cognitive View* (Englewood Cliffs, NJ: Prentice Hall, 1986); Baron, *Psychology*, op. cit.

17. Allen and Madden, 'A closer look at classical conditioning', op. cit.; Chester A. Insko and William F. Oakes, 'Awareness and the conditioning of attitudes', *Journal of Personality and Social Psychology* 4 (November 1966): 487–96; Carolyn K. Staats and Arthur W. Staats, 'Meaning established by classical conditioning', *Journal of Experimental Psychology* 54 (July 1957): 74–80; Randi Priluck Grossman and Brian D. Till, 'The persistence of classically conditioned brand attitudes', *Journal of Advertising* 21(1) (Spring 1998): 23–31.

18. Stijn M.J. van Osselaer and Joseph W. Alba, 'Consumer learning and brand equity', *Journal of Consumer Research* 27(1) (June 2000): 1–16; Kevin Lane Keller, 'Conceptualizing, measuring, and managing customer-based brand equity', *Journal of Marketing* 57 (January 1993): 1–22; Patrick Barwise, 'Brand equity: Snark or boojum?', *International Journal of Research in Marketing* 10 (1993): 93–104; W. Fred van Raaij and Wim Schoonderbeer, 'Meaning Structure of Brand Names and Extensions', in W. Fred van Raaij and Gary J. Bamossy (eds), *European Advances in Consumer Research* 1 (Provo, UT: Association for Consumer Research, 1993): 479–84; Gil McWilliam, 'The Effect of Brand Typology on Brand Extension Fit: Commercial and Academic Research Findings', in van Raaij and Bamossy (eds), *European Advances in Association for Consumer Research* 1: 485–91; Elyette Roux and Frederic Lorange, 'Brand Extension Research: A Review', in van Raaij and Bamossy (eds), *European Advances in Consumer Research* 1: 492–500; 'The art of perception', *Marketing* (28 November 1996): 25–9.

19. Herbert Krugman, 'Low recall and high recognition of advertising', *Journal of Advertising Research* (February/March 1986): 79–86.

20. Gerald J. Gorn, 'The effects of music in advertising on choice behavior: a classical conditioning approach', *Journal of Marketing* 46 (Winter 1982): 94–101.

21. Calvin Bierley, Frances K. McSweeney and Renee Vannieuwkerk, 'Classical conditioning of preferences for stimuli', *Journal of Consumer Research* 12 (December 1985): 316–23; James J. Kellaris and Anthony D. Cox, 'The effects of background music in advertising: a reassessment', *Journal of Consumer Research* 16 (June 1989): 113–18.

22. Frances K. McSweeney and Calvin Bierley, 'Recent developments in classical conditioning', *Journal of Consumer Research* 11 (September 1984): 619–31.

23. Basil G. Englis, 'The Reinforcement Properties of Music Videos: "I Want My. . . I Want My. . . I Want My. . . MTV"' (paper presented at the meeting of the Association for Consumer Research, New Orleans, 1989).

24. Mark J. Miller, 'Bob Marley Brand Expands from Music to Coffee to Swimwear', Brandchannel (21 February 2012).

25. Bernice Kanner, 'Growing pains – and gains: brand names branch out', *New York* (13 March 1989): 22.

26. Dale Buss, 'Condé Nast Extends Magazine Brands into Bar and Restaurant Scene', *Broad Channel* (12 April 2013).

27. Product placements in film and TV programmes are also a very common marketing approach to building learning and awareness, and to associate a product or service with a particular actor, or popular cultural event.

28. Quoted in 'Look-alikes mimic familiar packages', *New York Times* (9 August 1986): D1; 'Action fails to match spirit of lookalike law', *Marketing* (27 March 1997): 19.

29. Quoted in Rebecca R. Ruiz, 'Luxury Cars Imprint Their Brands on Goods From Cologne to Clothing', *New York Times* (February 2015).

30. Laurie Hays, 'Too many computer names confuse too many buyers', *Wall Street Journal* (29 June 1994): B1 (2 pp.).

31. Blaise J. Bergiel and Christine Trosclair, 'Instrumental learning: its application to customer satisfaction', *Journal of Consumer Marketing* 2 (Fall 1985): 23–8.

32. Several books have recently been published on this topic: G. Zichermann and C. Cunningham, *Gamification by Design: Implementing Game Mechanics in Web and Mobile Apps* (Sebastopol, CA: O'Reilly Media, 2011); J. McGonigal, *Reality Is Broken: Why Games Make Us Better and How They Can Change the World* (New York, NY: Vintage Books, 2011); and B. Reeves and J.L. Read, *Total Engagement: Using Games and Virtual Worlds to Change the Way People Work and Businesses Compete* (Boston, MA: Harvard Business Press, 2013).

33. Quoted in John Grossmann, 'Using Smartphones and Apps to Enhance Loyalty Programs', *New York Times* (28 January 2015); Joseph C. Nunes and Xavier Drèze, 'The Endowed Progress Effect: How Artificial Advancement Increases Effort', *Journal of Consumer Research* 32 (March 2006): 504–12.

34. Nick Wingfield, 'All the World's a Game, and Business Is a Player', *New York Times* (23 December 2012).

35. Terence A. Shimp, 'Neo-Pavlovian Conditioning and Its Implications for Consumer Theory and Research', in Thomas S. Robertson and Harold H. Kassarjian (eds), *Handbook of Consumer Behavior* (Englewood Cliffs, NJ: Prentice Hall, 1991).

36. See Chapter 9 for an extended discussion of word-of-mouth communication.

37. J. Eelen, P. Özturan and P.W.J. Verlegh, 'The differential impact of brand loyalty on traditional and online word of mouth: the moderating roles of self-brand connection and the desire to help the brand', *International Journal of Research in Marketing* 34(4): 872–91.

38. K.K. Desai and Wayne Hoyer, 'Descriptive characteristics of memory-based consideration sets: influence of usage occasion frequency and usage location familiarity', *Journal of Consumer Research* 27(3) (December 2000): 309–23; R.C. Atkinson and R.M. Shiffrin, 'Human Memory: A Proposed System and Its Control Processes', in K.W. Spence and J.T. Spence (eds), *The Psychology of Learning and Motivation: Advances in Research and Theory* (New York: Academic Press, 1968): 89–195.

39. Dean Burnett, 'What happens in your brain when you make a memory?', *The Guardian* (16 September 2015) https://www.theguardian.com/education/2015/sep/16/what-happens-in-your-brain-when-you-make-a-memory (accessed 28 July 2018).

40. Daniel Glaser, 'Head space: why our adolescent memories are so clear', *The Guardian* (October 22 2017), https://www.theguardian.com/lifeandstyle/2017/oct/22/head-space-why-our-adolescent-memories-are-so-clear (accessed 28 July 2018).

41. James R. Bettman, 'Memory factors in consumer choice: a review', *Journal of Marketing* (Spring 1979): 37–53. For a study that explored the relative impact of internal versus external memory on brand choice, see Joseph W. Alba, Howard Marmorstein and Amitava Chattopadhyay, 'Transitions in preference over time: the effects of memory on message persuasiveness', *Journal of Marketing Research* 29 (November 1992): 406–17. For other research on memory and advertising, see H. Shanker Krishnan and Dipankar Chakravarti,

'Varieties of Brand Memory Induced by Advertising: Determinants, Measures, and Relationships', in David A. Aaker and Alexander L. Biel (eds), *Brand Equity and Advertising: Advertising's Role in Building Strong Brands* (Hillsdale, NJ: Lawrence Erlbaum Associates, 1993): 213–31; Bernd H. Schmitt, Nader T. Tavassoli and Robert T. Millard, 'Memory for print ads: understanding relations among brand name, copy, and picture', *Journal of Consumer Psychology* 2(1) (1993): 55–81; Marian Friestad and Esther Thorson, 'Remembering ads: the effects of encoding strategies, retrieval cues, and emotional response', *Journal of Consumer Psychology* 2(1) (1993): 1–23; Surendra N. Singh, Sanjay Mishra, Neeli Bendapudi and Denise Linville, 'Enhancing memory of television commercials through message spacing', *Journal of Marketing Research* 31 (August 1994): 384–92.

42. Kathryn R. Braun, 'Postexperience advertising effects on consumer memory', *Journal of Consumer Research* 25 (March 1999): 319–34. See also: Gal Zauberman, Rebecca K. Ratner and B. Kyu Kim (2008), 'Memories as assets: strategic memory protection in choice over time', *Journal of Consumer Research* 35 (February 2009): 715–28.

43. Kim Robertson, 'Recall and recognition effects of brand name imagery', *Psychology and Marketing* 4 (Spring 1987): 3–15.

44. Lauren G. Block and Vicki G. Morwitz, 'Shopping Lists as an External Memory Aid for Grocery Shopping: Influences on List Writing and List Fulfillment', *Journal of Consumer Psychology* 8(4) (1999): 343–75.

45. Tanya Menoni, '11 Time-Saving Grocery List Apps for the iPhone', *About Tech,* http://ipod.about.com/od/bestiphoneapps/tp/6-Time-Saving-Iphone-Grocery-List-Apps.htm (accessed 28 July 2018).

46. Endel Tulving, 'Remembering and knowing the past', *American Scientist* 77 (July/August 1989): 361.

47. Andrew W. Perkins and Mark R. Forehand, 'Implicit Self Referencing: The Effect of Non-Volitional Self-Association on Brand and Product Attitude', *Journal of Consumer Research,* 39 (June 2012): 142–56; see also Rashmi Adaval and Robert S. Wyer Jr, 'The role of narratives in consumer information processing', *Journal of Consumer Psychology* 7(3) (1998): 207–46.

48. George A. Miller, 'The magical number seven, plus or minus two: some limits on our capacity for processing information', *Psychological Review* 63 (1956): 81–97.

49. James N. MacGregor, 'Short-term memory capacity: limitation or optimization?', *Psychological Review* 94 (1987): 107–8.

50. See Catherine A. Cole and Michael J. Houston, 'Encoding and media effects on consumer learning deficiencies in the elderly', *Journal of Marketing Research* 24 (February 1987): 55–64; A.M. Collins and E.F. Loftus, 'A spreading activation theory of semantic processing', *Psychological Review* 82 (1975): 407–28; Fergus I.M. Craik and Robert S. Lockhart, 'Levels of processing: a framework for memory research', *Journal of Verbal Learning and Verbal Behavior* 11 (1972): 671–84.

51. Walter A. Henry, 'The effect of information-processing ability on processing accuracy', *Journal of Consumer Research* 7 (June 1980): 42–8.

52. Anthony G. Greenwald and Clark Leavitt, 'Audience involvement in advertising: four levels', *Journal of Consumer Research* 11 (June 1984): 581–92; see also Anirban Mukhopadhyay, Jaideep Sengupta and Suresh Ramanathan,

'Recalling past temptations: an information processing perspective on the dynamics of self-control', *Journal of Consumer Research* 35 (December 2008): 586–99.

53. Kevin Lane Keller, 'Memory factors in advertising: the effect of advertising retrieval cues on brand evaluations', *Journal of Consumer Research* 14 (December 1987): 316–33. For a discussion of processing operations that occur during brand choice, see Gabriel Biehal and Dipankar Chakravarti, 'Consumers' use of memory and external information in choice: macro and micro perspectives', *Journal of Consumer Research* 12 (March 1986): 382–405.

54. Susan T. Fiske and Shelley E. Taylor, *Social Cognition* (Reading, MA: Addison-Wesley, 1984).

55. Deborah Roedder John and John C. Whitney Jr, 'The development of consumer knowledge in children: a cognitive structure approach', *Journal of Consumer Research* 12 (March 1986): 406–17.

56. Michael R. Solomon, Carol Surprenant, John A. Czepiel and Evelyn G. Gutman, 'A role theory perspective on dyadic interactions: the service encounter', *Journal of Marketing* 49 (Winter 1985): 99–111.

57. Quoted in Jenna Wortham, 'A Growing App Lets You See It, Then You Don't', *New York Times* (8 February 2013).

58. S. Danziger, S. Moran and V. Rafaely, 'The influence of ease of retrieval on judgment as a function of attention to subjective experience', *Journal of Consumer Psychology* 16(2) (2006): 191–5.

59. Roger W. Morrell, Denise C. Park and Leonard W. Poon, 'Quality of instructions on prescription drug labels: effects on memory and comprehension in young and old adults', *The Gerontologist* 29 (1989): 345–54.

60. Mark J. Miller, 'Carnival Hopes to Jog Passengers' Positive Memories in New Cruise Campaign', Brandchannel *(*19 September 2013).

61. Aaron Baar, 'New Product Messages Aren't Making Intended Impressions', *Marketing Daily* (6 March 2008).

62. Frank R. Kardes, Gurumurthy Kalyanaram, Murali Chandrashekaran and Ronald J. Dornoff, 'Brand retrieval, consideration set composition, consumer choice, and the pioneering advantage' (unpublished manuscript, University of Cincinnati: Ohio, 1992).

63. Judith Lynne Zaichkowsky and Padma Vipat, 'Inferences from Brand Names', paper presented at the European meeting of the Association for Consumer Research, Amsterdam (June 1992).

64. H. Noel, 'The spacing effect: enhancing memory for repeated marketing stimuli', *Journal of Consumer Psychology* 16(3) (2006): 306–20; for an alternative explanation, see S.L. Appleton-Knapp, R.A. Bjork and T.D. Wickens, 'Examining the spacing effect in advertising: encoding variability, retrieval processes, and their interaction', *Journal of Consumer Research* 32(2) (2005): 266–76.

65. Herbert E. Krugman, 'Low recall and high recognition of advertising', *Journal of Advertising Research* (February–March 1986): 79–86.

66. Rik G.M. Pieters and Tammo H.A. Bijmolt, 'Consumer memory for television advertising: a field study of duration, serial position, and competition effects', *Journal of Consumer Research* 23 (March 1997): 362–72.

67. Margaret G. Meloy, 'Mood-driven distortion of product information', *Journal of Consumer Research* 27(3) (December 2000): 345–59.

68. Eric J. Johnson and J. Edward Russo, 'Product familiarity and learning new information', *Journal of Consumer Research* 11 (June 1984): 542–50.

69. Marcus Cunha Jr and Juliano Laran, 'Asymmetries in the Sequential Learning of Brand Associations: Implications for the Early Entrant Advantage', *Journal of Consumer Research* 35(5) (2009): 788–99; Andrew W. Ellis, Selina J. Holmes and Richard L. Wright, 'Age of acquisition and the recognition of brand names: on the importance of being early', *Journal of Consumer Psychology* 20(1) (2010): 43–52.

70. Eric J. Johnson and J. Edward Russo, 'Product Familiarity and Learning New Information', in Kent Monroe (ed.), *Advances in Consumer Research* 8 (Ann Arbor, MI: Association for Consumer Research, 1981): 151–5; John G. Lynch and Thomas K. Srull, 'Memory and attentional factors in consumer choice: concepts and research methods', *Journal of Consumer Research* 9 (June 1982): 18–37.

71. Julie A. Edell and Kevin Lane Keller, 'The information processing of coordinated media campaigns', *Journal of Marketing Research* 26 (May 1989): 149–64.

72. Lynch and Srull, 'Memory and attentional factors in consumer choice', op. cit.

73. Joseph W. Alba and Amitava Chattopadhyay, 'Salience effects in brand recall', *Journal of Marketing Research* 23 (November 1986): 363–70; Elizabeth C. Hirschman and Michael R. Solomon, 'Utilitarian, Aesthetic, and Familiarity Responses to Verbal Versus Visual Advertisements', in Thomas C. Kinnear (ed.), *Advances in Consumer Research* 11 (Provo, UT: Association for Consumer Research, 1984): 426–31.

74. Susan E. Heckler and Terry L. Childers, 'The role of expectancy and relevancy in memory for verbal and visual information: what is incongruency?', *Journal of Consumer Research* 18 (March 1992): 475–92.

75. Russell H. Fazio, Paul M. Herr and Martha C. Powell, 'On the development and strength of category–brand associations in memory: the case of mystery ads', *Journal of Consumer Psychology* 1(1) (1992): 1–13.

76. Hirschman and Solomon, 'Utilitarian, aesthetic, and familiarity responses to verbal versus visual advertisements', op. cit.

77. Terry Childers and Michael Houston, 'Conditions for a picture-superiority effect on consumer memory', *Journal of Consumer Research* 11 (September 1984): 643–54; Terry Childers, Susan Heckler and Michael Houston, 'Memory for the visual and verbal components of print advertisements', *Psychology and Marketing* 3 (Fall 1986): 147–50.

78. Werner Krober-Riel, 'Effects of Emotional Pictorial Elements in Ads Analyzed by Means of Eye Movement Monitoring', in Kinnear (ed.), *Advances in Consumer Research* 11: 591–6.

79. Mark Cousins, 'How our visual memories are made', *The Guardian* (October 17 2015), https://www.theguardian.com/lifeandstyle/2017/oct/15/how-our-visual-memories-are-made (accessed 28 July 2018).

80. Hans-Bernd Brosius, 'Influence of presentation features and news context on learning from television news', *Journal of Broadcasting and Electronic Media* 33 (Winter 1989): 1–14.

81. Raymond R. Burke and Thomas K. Srull, 'Competitive interference and consumer memory for advertising', *Journal of Consumer Research* 15 (June 1988): 55–68.

82. Ibid.

83. Johnson and Russo, 'Product Familiarity and Learning New Information', op. cit.

84. Joan Meyers-Levy, 'The influence of brand names association set size and word frequency on brand memory', *Journal of Consumer Research* 16 (September 1989): 197–208.

85. Michael H. Baumgardner, Michael R. Leippe, David L. Ronis and Anthony G. Greenwald, 'In search of reliable persuasion effects: II. Associative interference and persistence of persuasion in a message-dense environment', *Journal of Personality and Social Psychology* 45 (September 1983): 524–37.

86. Alba and Chattopadhyay, 'Salience effects in brand recall', op. cit.

87. Margaret Henderson Blair, Allan R. Kuse, David H. Furse and David W. Stewart, 'Advertising in a new and competitive environment: persuading consumers to buy', *Business Horizons* 30 (November/December 1987): 20.

88. Lynch and Srull, 'Memory and attentional factors in consumer choice', op. cit.

89. Russell W. Belk, 'Possessions and the extended self', *Journal of Consumer Research* 15 (September 1988): 139–68.

90. Russell W. Belk, 'The Role of Possessions in Constructing and Maintaining a Sense of Past', in Marvin E. Goldberg, Gerald Gorn and Richard W. Pollay (eds), *Advances in Consumer Research* 16 (Provo, UT: Association for Consumer Research, 1990): 669–78.

91. Hans Baumgartner, Mita Sujan and James R. Bettman, 'Autobiographical memories, affect and consumer information processing', *Journal of Consumer Psychology* 1 (January 1992): 53–82; Mita Sujan, James R. Bettman and Hans Baumgartner, 'Influencing consumer judgments using autobiographical memories: a self-referencing perspective', *Journal of Marketing Research* 30 (November 1993): 422–36.

92. Christel Antonia Russell and Sidney J. Levy, 'The Temporal and Focal Dynamics of Volitional Reconsumption: A Phenomenological Investigation of Repeated Hedonic Experiences', *Journal of Consumer Research,* 39 (August 2012): 341–9.

93. Katherine E. Loveland, Dirk Smeesters and Naomi Mandel, 'Still Preoccupied with 1995: The Need to Belong and Preferences for Nostalgic Products', *Journal of Consumer Research,* 37 (October 2010): 393–408; Xinyue Zhou, Tim Wildschut, Constatine Sekikides Kan Shi and Cong Feng, 'Nostalgia: The Gift that Keeps on Giving', *Journal of Consumer Research* 39 (June 2012): 39–50; Fleura Bardhi, Giana M. Eckhardt and Eric J. Arnould, 'Liquid Relationship to Possessions', *Journal of Consumer Research* 39 (October 2012): 510–29; see also Susan L. Holak and William J. Havlena, 'Feelings, fantasies, and memories: an examination of the emotional components of nostalgia', *Journal of Business Research* 42 (1998): 217–26.

94. Morris B. Holbrook and Robert M. Schindler, 'Nostalgic Bonding: Exploring the Role of Nostalgia in the Consumption Experience', *Journal of Consumer Behavior* 3(2) (December 2003): 107–27.

95. Alexia Tsotsis, 'Flickr Dips Its Toes Into Social with Twitter and Facebook "Share This" Features' (30 March 2011), *TechCrunch,* http://techcrunch.com/2011/03/30/flickr-dips-its-toes-into-social-with-twitter-and-facebook-share-this-features/ (accessed 28 July 2018).

96. Kirsten Schweizer, 'Eastern Europeans tune in to Communist Nostalgia on TV', Bloomberg Business (7 March 2013), http://www.bloomberg.com/bw/articles/2013-03-07/eastern-europeans-tune-in-to-communist-nostalgia-on-tv (accessed 28 July 2018).

97. Gabriella Stern, 'VW hopes nostalgia will spur sales of retooled Beetle, fuel US comeback', *Wall Street Journal, Europe* (7 May 1997): 4; 'Ostalgie for the day when they'd never had it so good', *The Independent* (10 February 1997); Almar Latour, 'Shelf wars', *Central European Economic Review* 4 (Dow Jones, May 1997); G. Morello, *The Hidden Dimensions of Marketing* (Amsterdam: Vrije Universiteit, 1993): 13.

98. Stacy Menzel Baker, Holli C. Karrer and Ann Veeck, 'My Favorite Recipes: Recreating Emotions and Memories Through Cooking', *Advances in Consumer Research* 32(1) (2005): 304–5.

99. Morris B. Holbrook and Robert M. Schindler, 'Some exploratory findings on the development of musical tastes', *Journal of Consumer Research* 16 (June 1989): 119–24.

100. See Morris B. Holbrook, 'Nostalgia and consumption preferences: some emerging patterns of consumer tastes', *Journal of Consumer Research* 20 (September 1993): 245–56; Robert M. Schindler and Morris B. Holbrook, 'Critical periods in the development of men's and women's tastes in personal appearance', *Psychology and Marketing* 10(6) (November/December 1993): 549–64; Morris B. Holbrook and Robert M. Schindler, 'Age, sex, and attitude toward the past as predictors of consumers' aesthetic tastes for cultural products', *Journal of Marketing Research* 31 (August 1994): 412–22.

101. Nicola Davis, 'Humans produce new brain cells throughout their lives say researchers', *The Guardian* (April 5 2018), https://www.theguardian.com/science/2018/apr/05/humans-produce-new-brain-cells-throughout-their-lives-say-researchers (accessed 28 July 2018).

102. 'Only 38 per cent of T.V. audience links brands with ads', *Marketing News* (6 January 1984): 10.

103. 'Terminal television', *American Demographics* (January 1987): 15.

104. Brian Steinberg, 'Young Consumers Switch Media 27 Times an Hour', *Advertising Age* (9 April 2012), http://adage.com/article/news/study-young-consumers-switch-media-27-times-hour/234008/?utm_source=digital_email&utm_medium=newsletter&utm_campaign=adage (accessed 28 July 2018).

105. Richard P. Bagozzi and Alvin J. Silk, 'Recall, recognition, and the measurement of memory for print advertisements', *Marketing Science* (1983): 95–134.

106. Adam Finn, 'Print ad recognition readership scores: an information processing perspective', *Journal of Marketing Research* 25 (May 1988): 168–77.

107. Bettman, 'Memory factors in consumer choice', op. cit.

108. Mark A. deTurck and Gerald M. Goldhaber, 'Effectiveness of product warning labels: effects of consumers' information processing objectives', *Journal of Consumer Affairs* 23(1) (1989): 111–25.

109. Campaign, 'History of advertising: No 161: A Starch Test score sheet', https://www.campaignlive.co.uk/article/history-advertising-no-161-starch-test-score-sheet/1381938#ix1W84YFjdBE0w02.99; https://www.campaignlive.co.uk/article/history-advertising-no-161-starch-test-score-sheet/1381938 (accessed 28 July 2018).

110. Finn, 'Print ad recognition readership scores', op. cit.

111. Iris W. Hung and Anirban Mukhopadhyay, 'Lenses of the Heart: How Actors' and Observers' Perspectives Influence Emotional Experiences', *Journal of Consumer Research* 38 (April 2012): 1,103–15; see also Surendra N. Singh and Gilbert A. Churchill Jr, 'Response-bias-free recognition tests to measure advertising effects', *Journal of Advertising Research* 29 (June/July 1987): 23–36.

112. William A. Cook, 'Telescoping and memory's other tricks', *Journal of Advertising Research* 27 (February/March 1987): 5–8.

113. 'On a diet? Don't trust your memory', *Psychology Today* (October 1989): 12.

114. Hubert A. Zielske and Walter A. Henry, 'Remembering and forgetting television ads', *Journal of Advertising Research* 20 (April 1980): 7–13.

Chapter 7
Attitudes

Chapter objectives

When you finish reading this chapter you will understand why:

7.1 Attitudes have various functions for the consumer.

7.2 Attitudes are formed in several ways, and build on different types of hierarchies between affective, behavioural and cognitive elements.

7.3 Consistency is important in attitude formation.

7.4 Attitude models measure attitude by identifying specific components and combining them to measure and predict a consumer's attitude towards a product or a brand.

7.5 Attitudes, as important as they are, have never proven to be very closely linked to consumers' behaviour.

7.6 Marketers engage in persuasive argumentation in order to change or confirm our attitudes towards products or brands.

T'S A FRIDAY EVENING, and Leah, Lynn and Nicki are hanging out at Leah's flat in Manchester. While waiting for the late hours to arrive so they can go out, they are doing some channel surfing. Leah clicks to the sports channel and the three friends see there's a football game on, being televised from Russia. Portugal is playing against Spain. Leah has been a fan for as long as she can remember – perhaps as a result of having three older brothers and growing up in a house that had Manchester United souvenirs in every room. She loves the subtle intensity of the game, of any game – the traps, the moves, the way players make it look easy to move a ball around a huge field as if it were a small patch of grass. Furthermore, she's proud of Manchester United's rich history as a club and the huge fanbase it has all over the world. In spite of some less-than-satisfactory seasons recently, fans' attitudes haven't changed so much, although many miss Sir Alex Ferguson as the club manager.

Nicki's a glutton for thrills and chills – at least when it comes to the national team of England: she remembers how her father got her all fired up about England's strong team and its possibilities at the last European Championship, and then they lost to Iceland! This time, England sailed smoothly through the qualifiers so she has high hopes. But this game does not include the English team, and so she is somewhat less interested.

Lynn, on the other hand, doesn't know a corner kick from a penalty kick. For her, the most interesting part of the match is the footage being shown of the Portuguese player Christiano Ronaldo. She thinks he is the cutest thing – and even considered asking her boyfriend to get a haircut like Ronaldo's. Still, football doesn't really float her boat – but as long as she gets to hang out with her girlfriends she doesn't really care if they watch non-contact sports like football or contact sports like *I'm a Celebrity Get Me Out of Here!*

Søren Askegaard

The power of attitudes

All over Europe, football has a long and rich tradition, but as a sport it has been dominated by male patronage at the stadiums and male viewership on the television. However, female football is gaining momentum – not just in the US, where it has been big for some time, but also in countries in Europe, such as the Netherlands, Germany and the Scandinavian countries.

Not surprisingly, football clubs, sports-gear producers and other market agents generally welcome female consumers among their ranks. For example, Leah is just the kind of fan that sponsoring companies such as Nike, Gatorade and Adidas hope will turn more women into an ongoing source of football fanaticism. It is obvious that a variety of hero myths are necessary in order to mobilise such new fan groups. However, in the wake of players' stardom as male sex symbols rather than as footballers, from Beckham to Ronaldo and other contemporary players, certain people believe that too much focus is moving away from the sport and onto something that should be secondary. According to this attitude, it is one (acceptable) thing to use the hero myth to sell something related to the sport,[1] it is another to sell something completely unrelated to the sport.

Any which way, football is big business, but how it operates in the life of the single consumer is very much a question of attitude, as we have seen with Leah, Nicki and Lynn. As you'll see throughout this chapter, and this text in general, attitudes can vary significantly along gender lines, and from one culture to another. Attitudes obviously also vary over time. Since most of us are also consuming banking services and other financial products, we may be able to relate to the attitudinal statement, 'I have confidence in the financial sector'. How would that rate in an attitude measurement before or after the financial crisis? You probably guessed it![2] Effectively, part of the problem is exactly that the shift in attitudes vis-à-vis the financial sector was provoking much lower degrees of confidence, which in itself contributed to an aggravation of the crisis.

The term **attitude** is widely used in popular culture. You might be asked, 'What is your attitude towards abortion?' A parent might scold, 'Young man, I don't like your attitude'. Some bars even euphemistically refer to Happy Hour as 'an attitude adjustment period'. For our purposes, though, an attitude is a lasting, general evaluation of people (including oneself), objects, advertisements or issues.[3] Anything towards which one has an attitude is called an **attitude object (A$_o$)**.

This chapter will consider the contents of an attitude, how attitudes are formed, how they can be measured and review some of the surprisingly complex relationships between attitudes and behaviour. Both as a theoretical concept and as a tool to be used in the marketplace, the notion and dynamics of attitudes remain one of the most studied and applied of all behavioural constructs.[4] In the final part of the chapter, we will take a closer look at how attitudes can be changed – as this is certainly an issue of prime importance to marketers.

The function of attitudes

7.1

Attitudes have various functions for the consumer.

The **functional theory of attitudes** was initially developed by the American psychologist Daniel Katz to explain how attitudes facilitate social behaviour.[5] According to this pragmatic approach, attitudes exist because they serve a function for the person. That is, they are determined by a person's motives. Consumers who expect that they will need to deal with similar information at a future time will be more likely to start forming attitudes in anticipation of an event.[6]

Two people can each have the same attitude towards an object for very different reasons. As a result, it can be helpful for a marketer to know why an attitude is held before attempting to change it. The following are attitude functions, as identified by Katz:

- *Utilitarian function.* The utilitarian function is related to the basic principles of reward and punishment. We develop some of our attitudes towards products simply on the basis of whether these products provide pleasure or pain. If a person likes the taste of a cheeseburger, that person will develop a positive attitude towards cheeseburgers. Ads that stress straightforward product benefits (e.g. you should drink Coke Zero 'just for the taste of it' – and for the alleged consequences on your weight!) appeal to the utilitarian function.

- *Value-expressive function.* Attitudes that perform a value-expressive function express the consumer's central values or self-concept. A person forms a product attitude not because of its objective benefits, but because of what the product says about them as a person (e.g. 'What sort of woman reads *Elle?*'). Value-expressive attitudes are highly relevant to lifestyle analyses, where consumers cultivate a cluster of activities, interests and opinions to express a particular social identity.

- *Ego-defensive function.* Attitudes that are formed to protect the person, from either external threats or internal feelings, perform an ego-defensive function. An early marketing study indicated that housewives in the 1950s resisted the use of instant coffee because it threatened their conception of themselves as capable homemakers.[7] Notice how this attitude has certainly changed! Products that promise to help a man project a 'macho' image (e.g. Marlboro cigarettes) may be appealing to his insecurities about his masculinity. Another example of this function is deodorant campaigns that stress the dire, embarrassing consequences of underarm odour.

- *Knowledge function.* Some attitudes are formed as the result of a need for order, structure or meaning. This need is often present when a person is in an ambiguous situation or is confronted with a new product (e.g. 'Bayer wants you to know about pain relievers').

An attitude can serve more than one function, but in many cases a particular one will be dominant. By identifying the dominant function that a product serves for consumers (i.e. what benefits it provides), marketers can emphasise these benefits in their communications and packaging. Ads relevant to the function prompt more favourable thoughts about what is being marketed and can result in a heightened preference for both the ad and the product.

One American study determined that, for most people, coffee serves more of a utilitarian function than a value-expressive function. As a consequence, subjects responded more positively to copy for a fictitious brand of coffee that read, 'The delicious, hearty flavour and aroma of Sterling Blend coffee comes from a blend of the freshest coffee beans' (i.e. a utilitarian appeal) than they did to copy that read, 'The coffee you drink says something about the type of person you are. It can reveal your rare, discriminating taste' (i.e. the

Table 7.1 Comparison among types of citizens in terms of sustainability-related characteristics

	Indifferent ambivalent	Environmentally conscious	Animal well-being conscious	Small farming supporters	Food-safety conscious	Industrial production-oriented
EU	59.1%	17.1%	12.3%	11.5%	–	–
Brazil	71.6%	16.0%	–	12.4%	–	–
China	44.1%	–	–	–	31.5%	23.0%

Source: Adapted from Athanasios Krystalis, Klaus G. Grunert, Marcia D. de Barcellos, Toula Perrea and Wim Verbeke, 'Consumer Attitudes towards Sustainability Aspects of Food Production: Insights from Three Continents', *Journal of Marketing Management* 28(3/4) (March 2012): 334–72.

value-expressive function). In European countries with a strong 'coffee culture', such as Germany, the Benelux and Scandinavian countries, ads are more likely to stress the value-expressive function, in which the more social and ritualistic aspects of coffee consumption are expressed.[8] Attitudes, then, obviously vary with cultural context. A large-scale comparative study of attitudes towards sustainability principles in pork production resulted in a typology of consumers that showed some clear differences between the EU, Brazil and China (see Table 7.1). While the results for the EU and Brazil were fairly similar (although the level of ambivalence or indifference towards the sustainability issue is higher in Brazil than in Europe), the issue of animal welfare came out as significant in the EU sample, unlike Brazil, where it did not appear. In China, the segment of the indifferent showed a higher degree of indifference but, perhaps surprisingly, this segment was smaller than on the other two continents. China, having been plagued by a number of food production scandals, was shown to have segments that were far more concerned about food safety and industrial farming (as opposed to small-scale farming in EU and Brazil).[9] The same food-safety issue might also explain the fact that personal (rather than social) motives seem to dominate the small but emerging demand for organic produce in China.[10]

As we saw in the experiences of the three Manchester women watching a football game, the importance of an attitude object may differ quite a bit for different people. Understanding the centrality of an attitude to an individual and to others who share similar characteristics can be useful to marketers who are trying to devise strategies that will appeal to different customer segments. A study of football-game attendance illustrates that varying levels of commitment result in different fan 'profiles'.[11] The study identified three distinct clusters of fans:[12]

- One cluster consisted of the real diehard fans, like Leah, who were highly committed to their team and who displayed an enduring love of the game. To reach these fans, the researchers recommended that sports marketers should focus on providing them with greater sports knowledge and relate their attendance to their personal goals and values.

- A second cluster was like Nicki – their attitudes were based on the unique, self-expressive experience provided by the game. They enjoyed the stimulation of cheering for a team and the drama of the competition itself. These people are more likely to be 'brand switchers', fair-weather fans who shift allegiances when the home team no longer provides the thrills they need. This segment can be appealed to by publicising aspects of the visiting teams, such as advertising the appearance of stars who are likely to give the fans a game they will remember.

- A third cluster was like Lynn – they were looking, above all, for camaraderie. These consumers attended games primarily to take part in small-group activities, such as a pre- or post-game party that might accompany the event. Marketers could appeal to this cluster by providing improved peripheral benefits, such as making it easier for groups to meet at the stadium, improving parking and offering multiple-unit pricing.

How do we form attitudes?

7.2

Attitudes are formed in several ways, and build on different types of hierarchies between affective, behavioural and cognitive elements.

We all have lots of attitudes, and we do not usually question how we got them. No one is born with the conviction that, for example, Pepsi is better than Coke, or that heavy metal music liberates the soul. So where do these attitudes come from?

An attitude can form in several different ways, depending on the particular hierarchy of effects in operation. It can occur because of classical conditioning, in which an attitude object, such as the name 'Pepsi', is repeatedly paired with a catchy jingle ('You're in the Pepsi Generation . . . '). Or it can be formed through instrumental conditioning, in which consumption of the attitude object is reinforced (Pepsi quenches the thirst). Alternatively, the learning of an attitude can be the outcome of a very complex cognitive process. For example, a teenager may come to model the behaviour of friends and media endorsers such as Beyoncé, and drink Pepsi because they believe that this will allow them to fit in with the desirable lifestyle Pepsi commercials portray.

Is it possible to build positive attitudes to, and even recall of, experiences of something that does not exist? Indeed! Experiments have shown that advertisements, especially those with more vivid imagery, can even lead consumers to believe that they have had experiences with a product that does not, in fact, exist – a belief that, in turn, is likely to reinforce the attitude towards the product, a phenomenon known as the 'false experience effect'.[13] Such research demonstrates a certain unreliability of attitudes as expressed by consumers.

The ABC model of attitudes and hierarchies of effects

Most researchers agree that an attitude has three components: affect, behaviour and cognition. **Affect** refers to the way a consumer feels about an attitude object. *Behaviour* involves the person's intentions to do something with regard to an attitude object (but, as will be discussed later, an intention does not always result in an actual behaviour). **Cognition** refers to the beliefs a consumer has about an attitude object. These three components of an attitude can be remembered as the **ABC model of attitudes**.

This model emphasises the interrelationships between knowing, feeling and doing. Consumers' attitudes towards a product cannot be determined simply by identifying their beliefs about it. For example, a researcher may find that shoppers 'know' a particular digital camera has a 10X optical zoom lens, records in full HD and is Wi-Fi-enabled, but such findings do not indicate whether they feel these attributes are good, bad or irrelevant, or whether they would actually buy the camera.

While all three components of an attitude are important, their relative importance will vary depending upon a consumer's level of motivation with regard to the attitude object. Attitude researchers have developed the concept of a **hierarchy of effects** to explain the relative impact of the three components. Each hierarchy specifies that a fixed sequence of steps occurs en route to an attitude. Three different hierarchies are summarised in Figure 7.1.

The standard learning hierarchy

Think → Feel → Do: Leah's positive attitude towards football closely resembles the process by which most attitudes have been assumed to be constructed. A consumer approaches a product decision as a problem-solving process. First, they form beliefs about a product by accumulating knowledge (beliefs) regarding relevant attributes. Next, the consumer evaluates these beliefs and forms a feeling about the product (affect).[14] Over time, Leah assembled information about the sport, began to recognise the players and learned which teams were superior to others. Finally, based on this evaluation, the consumer engages in a relevant behaviour, such as buying the product or supporting a particular team by wearing its shirt. This careful choice process often results in the type of loyalty displayed by Leah: the consumer 'bonds' with the product over time and is not easily persuaded to experiment with other brands. The standard learning

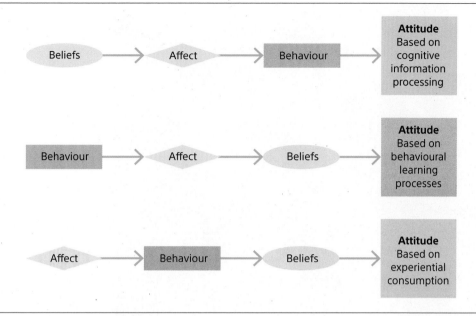

Figure 7.1 Three hierarchies of effects

hierarchy assumes that a consumer is highly involved in making a purchase decision.[15] The person is motivated to seek out a lot of information, carefully weighs alternatives and comes to a thoughtful decision. As we have seen (see Chapter 4), this process is likely to occur if the decision is important to the consumer or in some way central to the consumer's self-concept. If you understand the level of fan support for Manchester United, then you will appreciate just how central Leah's attitudes about football (or, in this case, Manchester United) are for her.

While the attitudes that Leah holds towards Manchester United may be well understood to be positive, it is not always an easy and straightforward task to assume that any related product purchases she makes will be consistent with her positive attitudes towards the team. Imagine that Leah is considering the purchase of some Nike football shoes for herself, and as part of gathering information about the shoes, she comes across an article on globalisation and Nike's use of outsourcing the labour for making football shoes to factories in low labour-cost countries such as Vietnam. Leah's attitudes towards globalisation, coupled with her own cognitive beliefs about the labour conditions in these factories, may in fact lead her to have a negative affect towards the Nike shoes. At the same time, Leah's attitude towards buying a well-made football shoe at a very competitive price might be quite positive! So possibly she is likely to still buy the shoes. In a different context, it has been shown that satisfaction with the brand's performance is more directly related to brand loyalty than corporate image.[16]

The low-involvement hierarchy

Do → Feel → Think: In contrast to Leah, Nicki's interest in the attitude object (football) is, at best, lukewarm. She is not particularly knowledgeable about the sport, and she may have an emotional response to an exciting game but not to a specific team (excluding the English national team). Nicki is typical of a consumer who forms an attitude via the *low-involvement hierarchy of effects*. In this sequence, the consumer does not initially have a strong preference for one brand over another, but instead acts on the basis of limited knowledge and then forms an evaluation only after the product has been purchased or used.[17] The attitude is likely to come about through behavioural learning, in which the consumer's choice is reinforced by good or bad experiences with the product after purchase. Nicki will probably be more likely to tune in to future England games if she can avoid disappointments such as the Iceland match.

While Leah may have very positive attitudes towards soccer, and for the soccer boot made by one of her favourite brands, Nike, she still needs to sort out her conflicting attitudes towards globalisation and the labour practices that Nike and other shoe manufacturers use.

Photo: Gary Bamossy

The possibility that consumers simply do not care enough about many decisions to assemble a set of product beliefs carefully and then evaluate them is important, because it implies that all of the concern about influencing beliefs and carefully communicating information about product attributes may be largely wasted. Consumers are not necessarily going to pay attention anyway; they are more likely to respond to simple stimulus–response connections when making purchase decisions. For example, a consumer choosing between paper towels might remember that 'Brand X absorbs more quickly than Brand Y', rather than bothering to compare systematically all of the brands on the shelf. Such automatically evoked attitudes are also called *implicit attitudes* and may have significant influences on purchase decisions.[18] A similar effect has been shown to exist when we compare consumers buying store brands and manufacturer brands respectively – store brand buyers directly associate it with a good cost efficiency, whereas manufacturer brand buyers automatically associate it with high quality.[19]

The notion of low involvement on the part of consumers is a bitter pill for some marketers to swallow. Who wants to admit that what they market is not very important or involving? A brand manager for, say, a brand of chewing gum or cat food may find it hard to believe that consumers do not put that much thought into purchasing their product because they themselves spend many of their waking (and perhaps sleeping) hours thinking about it.

For marketers, the ironic silver lining to this low-involvement cloud is that, under these conditions, consumers are not motivated to process a lot of complex brand-related information. Instead, they will be swayed by principles of behavioural learning, such as the simple responses caused by conditioned brand names, point-of-purchase displays and so on. This results in what we might call the *involvement paradox*: the less important the product is to consumers, the more important are many of the marketing stimuli (e.g. packages, jingles) that must be devised to sell it.

The experiential hierarchy

Feel → Do → Think: In recent years, researchers have begun to stress the significance of emotional response as a central aspect of an attitude. According to the experiential hierarchy of effects, consumers act on the basis of their emotional reactions (just as Lynn enjoys watching TV with her friends, regardless of what is on). Although the factors of beliefs and behaviour are recognised as playing a part, a consumer's overall evaluation of an attitude object is considered by many to be the core of an attitude.

This perspective highlights the idea that attitudes can be strongly influenced by intangible product attributes such as package design, and by consumers' reactions to accompanying stimuli such as advertising and even the brand name. As an example, consider one Swedish study that underlined the importance of book covers with sexually charged images in forming of the attitude towards the book.[20] Such emotional involvement and feelings of connectedness also play a role in relation to sales people. Another study concluded that an incidental similarity between a customer and a salesperson, such as a shared birthday or originating from the same town, can lead to a more positive attitude and a higher likelihood of purchase.[21] Numerous studies indicate that the mood a person is in when exposed to a marketing message influences how the ad is processed, the likelihood that the information presented will be remembered and how the person will feel about the advertised item and related products in the future.[22] Furthermore, feelings may not be uniform, as we saw with Leah, Manchester United and Nike shoes – they can be a mix of positive and negative. There are indications that people with Eastern cultural backgrounds are better at accepting mixed emotions in the formation of an attitude than Westerners, since they have a less dichotomising way of looking at life, and instead understand the balancing of contradictory principles, as seen in the principle of yin and yang.[23]

This campaign attemps to change people's attitudes towards throwing cigarette butts in the streets - you may reflect on the usage of hierachy (or hierarchies?) of effects.

Mauritius images GmbH/Alamy Stock Photo

One important debate about the experiential hierarchy concerns the independence of cognition and affect. On the one hand, the *cognitive–affective model* argues that an affective judgement is the last step in a series of cognitive processes. Earlier steps include the sensory registration of stimuli and the retrieval of meaningful information from memory to categorise these stimuli.[24] On the other hand, the *independence hypothesis* takes the position that affect and cognition involve two separate, partially independent systems; affective responses do not always require prior cognitions.[25] A song that has more than 100 million listens on Spotify may possess the same attributes as many other songs (dominant bass guitar, raspy vocals, persistent downbeat), but beliefs about these attributes cannot explain why one song becomes a classic while another sharing the same characteristics ends up in the bargain bin on iTunes! The independence hypothesis does not eliminate the role of cognition in experience. It simply balances this traditional, rational emphasis on calculated decision-making by paying more attention to the impact of aesthetic, subjective experience. This type of holistic processing has long been believed to be more salient when consumers are choosing well-known products and less so with innovations, when there is more risk involved. However, recent research has demonstrated that this is not the case.[26] One recent experimental study even concluded that consumers find that cookies taste worse if they come from a company that has donated to a political party the consumer dislikes. The moral dislike or the formation of a particular attitude translates into a worse taste.[27]

Marketers who are concerned with understanding consumers' attitudes have to contend with an even more complex issue: in decision-making situations, people form attitudes towards objects other than the product itself that can influence their ultimate selections. One additional factor to consider is attitudes towards the act of buying in general, or attitudes towards a particular shop.[28] Our evaluation of a product can be determined solely by our appraisal of how it is depicted in marketing communications – that is, we do not hesitate to form attitudes about products we have never even seen personally, much less used. Furthermore, attitudes may be very complex in their form. Think about your own attitudes towards, for example, something like 'materialism'. Most people have quite split attitudes, since they tend to think of materialism as a bad thing but at the same time have many positive attitudes towards (the prospect of) owning or having access to various material possessions.[29]

Materialism

It can be debated whether **materialism** is a value or an attitude. Here we consider it more as an attitude, since it has been demonstrated that only a few people value materialism *per se* and most consider it a means to some end. As such, it has the character of an attitude. Materialism refers to the importance people attach to worldly possessions. Westerners in general (and Americans in particular) are often stereotyped as being members of a highly materialistic society where people often gauge their worth and that of others in terms of how much they own. If you take a materialistic attitude, you are more likely to value possessions for their status and appearance-related meanings, whereas those who do not emphasise this attitude tend to prize products that connect them to other people or that provide them with pleasure in using them.[30] As a result, products valued by 'high materialists' are more likely to be publicly consumed and to be more expensive.[31] The priorities of materialism tend to emphasise the well-being of the individual versus the group, which may conflict with family or religious values. That conflict may help to explain why people with highly materialistic attitudes tend to be less happy.[32] A study comparing specific items that low versus high materialists value found that people low in materialism value cherished items such as a mother's wedding gown, picture albums, a rocking chair from childhood or a garden, whereas those who scored high preferred things such as jewellery, china or a holiday home.[33] Materialistic attitudes are also linked to the self-concept (see 'Consumer behaviour as I see it' by L.J. Shrum below). One study reported that consumers who are 'love-smitten' with their possessions tend to use these relationships to compensate for loneliness and a lack of affiliation with social networks.[34]

Cross-cultural differences in materialism have also been analysed. One study of 12 countries resulted in the following ranking in degree of materialism, from highest to lowest: Romania, US, New Zealand, Ukraine, Germany, Turkey, Israel, Thailand, India, UK, France and Sweden.[35] From these results, several conclusions can be drawn. First of all, materialism is not directly linked to affluence, as has often been proposed. On the contrary, some of the most materialistic cultures are the ones where most consumers (feel that they) lack a lot of things. But this is obviously not the only explanation, since the US, New Zealand and Germany score relatively high as well, and India scores low. Since neither wealth, 'Westernness', nor any other single variable can explain these differences, it must be concluded that materialism is a consequence of several factors, including such things as social stability, access to information, reference models and historical developments and cultural values.

This study was followed up by another based on qualitative in-depth interviews, adding more insight into consumers' different ways of coping with their own materialism, which was generally perceived as something negative. Basically, two ways of dealing with materialism were found – justifying oneself *vs* excusing oneself; either you condemn materialism and provide an explanation of why your personal materialism is a particularly good one, or you admit to being a 'bad' materialist but provide an excuse for being so.[36] We can conclude that whereas materialism is an important aspect of consumer culture, it is also a very complex concept that has both positive and negative aspects to it.[37] If materialism is used in a simple way, it typically will conceal more than it will reveal when it comes to understanding consumers and consumption.

Consumer behaviour as I see it . . .

Compensatory materialism

L.J. Shrum HEC Paris

The concept of materialism is one with which almost everyone is familiar. When I ask my students if they know what materialism is, they unanimously say 'Yes'. However, when I then ask them to define it, they become less certain, finding a precise articulation of materialism to be remarkably elusive. Nevertheless, there seems to be a generally shared belief that materialism is a bad thing, that it reflects a shallow character, that it pertains to a disproportionate focus on possessions, often at the expense of more communal virtues, and that it invariably leads to bad outcomes, such as financial problems and generally less happiness.

There is little dispute that these beliefs surely have some basis in fact. Indeed, most academic definitions of materialism revolve around the same viewpoints as those of the students: extrinsic motivation, focus on short-term, hedonistic urges, preferences for possessions over experiences, just to name a few. However, my colleagues and I have recently taken a different perspective, one that views materialism in terms of constructing and maintaining important aspects of the self-concept.[38] More specifically, people are motivated to maintain a positive self-concept, and at times aspects of their self-concept can be threatened. For example, some people may be very insecure about important aspects of their identity, such as belonging, power and control (efficacy), self-esteem and so on. In other cases, even people who are secure in their self-concepts may experience momentary threats to aspects of their self-concept (turned down for membership in an exclusive club, poor performance in an exam, fired from a job). In all of these cases, people are motivated to 'repair' the

→

damaged self-concept, and one way they may do so is through symbolic consumption that signals – either to themselves or others – mastery, success or competence in the threatened self-domain.

My colleagues and I tested this reasoning across a number of studies. For example, Jaehoon Lee and I demonstrated that when people feel threats to their self-esteem, they compensate through behaviours that are associated with being a good person, such as helping others and donating to charities. In contrast, when they feel threats to their feelings of power and control, they compensate with behaviours aimed at getting more attention and signalling status, such as expressing preferences for clothing with large logos.[39] In another series of studies, Nimish Rustagi and I showed that when people feel threats to their intelligence, their preference increases for products that are symbolic of intelligence (e.g., encyclopedia, subscription to intellectual magazines).[40]

Although these examples of materialistic consumption are relatively benign, one important question is whether they 'work', that is, are they successful in restoring the damaged self-concept? We find that often they are not. In general, we find that people are unaware of the link between the self-threats and their compensatory consumption. Thus, in instances in which the compensatory consumption is not successful, it may potentially result in an insidious effect in which people are constantly using consumption to repair a damaged self-concept that is never repaired. However, we also find that in some instances, symbolic consumption can successfully restore the damaged self-concept, suggesting that under some circumstances, materialism can have a positive effect.[41]

Questions

Can you think of examples in which you may have compensated for threats to your self-concept through symbolic consumption? Try to be specific about what aspect of your self-concept was threatened, and how a specific purchase or product preference symbolically relates to the self-threat.

What about people who have chronic deficits in their self-concept (e.g., chronically low self-esteem, feelings of powerlessness, etc.)? Do you think they also try to restore or boost their self-concept? What do you think are the long-term consequences of such compensatory consumption?

Affect

The **attitude towards the advertisement (A$_{ad}$)** is defined as a predisposition to respond in a favourable or unfavourable manner to a particular advertising stimulus during a particular exposure occasion. The feelings generated by advertising can have a direct impact on brand attitudes. Commercials can evoke a wide range of emotional responses, from disgust to happiness. Further, there is evidence that emotional responses will vary from one group

Marketing opportunity

Zumba began in the 1990s as a Colombian dance fitness programme, but it became an international sensation. Every week about 14 million people in more than 150 countries take classes that combine elements of dance moves adapted from various sources such as hip-hop, salsa, merengue, mambo, belly dancing and Bollywood, with some squats and lunges thrown in for good measure. The Zumba company started as an infomercial producer, but the regimen was popularised when the CEO's brother, an out-of-work advertising executive, had a revelation and convinced him to change focus. The brother recalls that he saw a movie billboard with some exuberant dancers: 'Immediately, I called my brother and said, "You're selling the wrong thing. You're selling fitness when you should be selling this emotion". I wanted to turn Zumba into a brand where people felt that kind of free and electrifying joy.' The two invented the tagline, 'Ditch the workout; join the party!' and the rest is history.[42]

of consumers to another. This points to the central role of affect in the formation of our attitudes and also to processes of persuasion, which will be discussed at the end of the chapter.

Even if we may not all be in good-enough shape to endure a Zumba work-out, many of our decisions are driven by our emotional responses to products. Social scientists refer to these raw reactions as *affect.* That explains why so many marketing activities and messages focus on altering our moods or linking their products to an *affective* response – although different types of emotional arousal may be more effective in some contexts than others.[43] Emotional experience, for example, has been shown to be very important in forming attitudes towards service brands such as coffee shops or fast-food outlets.[44] These connections make sense to anyone who has ever 'teared up' during a sappy TV commercial or written an angry letter after getting shabby treatment at a hotel. In today's world of social media, such emotional evaluations are becoming increasingly salient, whether the sentiments are positive or negative, for companies and brands.[45]

Types of affective responses

Affect describes the experience of emotionally laden states, but the nature of these experiences ranges from evaluations, to moods, to full-blown emotions. Evaluations are valenced (i.e. positive or negative) reactions to events and objects that are not accompanied by high levels of physiological arousal. For example, when a consumer evaluates a movie as being positive or negative, this usually involves some degree of affect accompanied by low levels of arousal (possible exceptions such as *Fifty Shades of Grey* notwithstanding!). **Moods** involve temporary positive or negative affective states accompanied by moderate levels of arousal. Moods tend to be diffuse and not necessarily linked to a particular event (e.g. you might have just 'woken up on the wrong side of the bed this morning'). **Emotions**, such as happiness, anger and fear, tend to be more intense and often relate to a specific triggering event, such as receiving an awesome gift.[46]

Marketing opportunity

It's very common for people to express their moods and also their emotional reactions to products online, meaning that these posts can be a treasure trove for marketers who want to learn more about how their offerings make people feel. A technique called **sentiment analysis** refers to a process (sometimes also called *opinion mining*) that scours the social media universe to collect and analyse the words people use when they describe a specific product or company. When people feel a particular way, they are likely to choose certain words that tend to relate to an emotion. From these words, the researcher creates a word-phrase dictionary (sometimes called a *library*) to code the data. A program scans the text to identify whether the words in the dictionary appear. Consider this example, based on Canon's PowerShot A540. A review on *Epinions*, a product review site, included this statement: 'The Canon PowerShot A540 had good aperture and excellent resolution'. A sentiment analysis would extract the entities of interest from the sentence, identifying the product as the Canon PowerShot A540 and the relevant dimensions as aperture and resolution. The sentiment would then be extracted for each dimension: the sentiment for aperture is *good* while that for resolution is *excellent*. Text-mining software would collect these reactions and combine them with others to paint a picture of how people are talking about the product. There are several sentiment analysis programs that do similar things – see the explanation on www.brandwatch.com.[47] However. . . see also the upcoming box of marketing pitfalls!

Marketers find many uses for affective states. They often try to link a product or service with a positive mood or emotion (just think of a sappy Hallmark greeting card). Of course, a variety of products from alcohol to chocolate are consumed at least partly for their ability to enhance moods. Numerous companies evaluate the emotional impact of their ads; some, such as Unilever and Coca-Cola, use sophisticated technology that interprets how viewers react to ads by analysing their facial expressions.[48]

A study shows that this emotional element is especially potent for decisions that involve outcomes the person will experience shortly, as opposed to those that involve a longer time frame.[49] Another study attests to the interplay between our emotions and how we access information in our minds that allows us to make smarter decisions. These researchers reported evidence for what they call an 'emotional oracle effect': people who trusted their feelings were able to predict future events better than those who did not. This occurred for a range of situations, including the presidential election, the winner of *American Idol,* movie box office success and the stock market. The most likely reason is that those with more confidence were better able to access information they had learned that could help them make an informed forecast.[50]

As we shall discuss a little later in this chapter, cognitive dissonance occurs when our various feelings, beliefs or behaviours don't line up – and we may be motivated to alter one or more of these to restore consistency. Mood congruency refers to the idea that our judgements tend to be shaped by our moods. For example, consumers judge the very same products more positively when they are in a positive (as opposed to negative) mood. This is why advertisers attempt to place their ads after humorous TV programming, or create uplifting ad messages that put viewers in a good mood. Similarly, retailers work hard to make shoppers happy by playing 'up-beat' background music and encouraging staff to be friendly. Then, of course, there's the traditional 'three-martini' business lunch. . .

Marketing pitfall

That Facebook is not just an innocent virtual meeting platform for friends should be clear to most people following the Cambridge Analytica scandal.[51] However, there have been less obvious incidents of abuse before. Facebook routinely has adjusted its users' news feeds – without their knowledge – to see what happens when they see different ad formats or numbers of ads. The company got into hot water a few years back when it admitted that it had manipulated the news feeds of over 600,000 randomly selected users to change the number of positive and negative posts they saw. The goal was to determine if these posts then influenced what users posted. Sure enough, moods are contagious: people who saw more positive posts responded by writing more positive posts. Similarly, seeing more negative content prompted the viewers to be more negative in their own posts. While Facebook argued that users give blanket consent to the company's research as a condition of using the service, many critics suggested the company had crossed an ethical boundary.[52]

The terms 'affect', 'mood' and 'emotion' are all deeply inscribed in a psychological approach to consumer behaviour, looking predominantly at the individual level. Recently, it has been argued that emotions might be looked at from a more cultural perspective as a collectively shared emotional disposition towards discourses and practices in consumer society, such as, for example, the avid emotions that may follow from positive versus negative attitudes towards vegetarianism. To distinguish this collective dimension of emotions from the more standard psychological types of emotions, the researcher chose to name this phenomenon 'sentiments'.[53]

Levels of commitment to an attitude

It is important to distinguish between types of attitudes, since not all are formed the same way.[54] A highly brand-loyal consumer such as Leah, the Manchester United fan, has an enduring, deeply held positive attitude towards an attitude object, and this involvement will be difficult to weaken. On the other hand, another consumer such as Nicki, who likes the drama and excitement more than other, possibly more subtle aspects of football, may have a mildly positive attitude towards a product but be quite willing to abandon it when something better comes along. This section will consider the differences between strongly and weakly held attitudes, and briefly review some of the major theoretical perspectives that have been developed to explain how attitudes form and relate to one another in the minds of consumers.

Consumers vary in their commitment to an attitude, and the degree of commitment is related to their level of involvement with the attitude object.[55] Consumers are more likely to consider brands that engender strong positive attitudes.[56] Let's look at three (increasing) levels of commitment:

- *Compliance*: at this lowest level of involvement, an attitude is formed because it helps in gaining rewards or avoiding punishments from others. This attitude is very superficial: it is likely to change when the person's behaviour is no longer monitored by others or when another option becomes available. A person may drink Pepsi because that is the brand the café sells and it is too much trouble to go elsewhere for a Coca-Cola.

- *Identification*: a process of identification occurs when attitudes are formed in order for the consumer to be similar to another person or group. Advertising that depicts the social consequences of choosing some products over others is relying on the tendency of consumers to imitate the behaviour of desirable models (see Chapter 9 on group influences).

- *Internalisation*: at a high level of involvement, deep-seated attitudes are internalised and become part of the person's value system. These attitudes are very difficult to change because they are so important to the individual. For example, many consumers had strong attitudes towards Coca-Cola and reacted very negatively when the company attempted to switch to the New Coke formula. This allegiance to Coke was obviously more than a minor preference for these people: the brand had become intertwined with their social identities, taking on patriotic and nostalgic properties.

Attitudes and consistency

7.3

Consistency is important in attitude formation.

The consistency principle

Have you ever heard someone say, 'Pepsi is my favourite soft drink. It tastes terrible', or 'I love my husband. He's the biggest idiot I've ever met'? If we disregard the use of irony, perhaps not very often, for the simple reason that these beliefs or evaluations are not consistent with one another. According to the **principle of cognitive consistency**, consumers value harmony among their thoughts, feelings and behaviours, and they are motivated to maintain uniformity among these elements. This desire means that, if necessary, consumers will change their thoughts, feelings or behaviours to make them consistent with their other experiences. The consistency principle is an important reminder that attitudes are not formed in a vacuum. A significant determinant of the way an attitude object will be evaluated is how it fits with other related attitudes we already hold.

Marketing pitfall
Attitudes to countries: Who do we love?

Is it more important to be spectacular and entertaining than actually good? For a number of years, the Chinese government has spent huge sums on trying to improve its image in the West. Understanding the salience of 'soft power' – the power of cultural attractiveness rather than the power of armies and weapons – the Chinese government has concentrated massive efforts on being more present on the global news scene, and in universities numerous China-sponsored 'Confucius Institutes' have sprung up, promoting Chinese language and culture among foreign students. These institutes have been accused of, if not actively promoting the party politics governing China, at least glossing over some of the negative human rights records of the regime. Unfortunately, if numbers presented in *The Economist* are to be believed, these efforts have so far been in vain. The general attitude to China is not more positive today than it was ten years ago except among young people, where there seems to be a somewhat more positive attitude – but they are the consumers of the future, so maybe the Chinese are just investing in long-term effects?[57] Try to consider your own attitude (or those of your friends) to China – a major cultural power or a major threat. . . or something more complex than that?

Cognitive dissonance theory revisited

We have discussed the role played by cognitive dissonance when consumers are trying to choose between two desired products (see Chapter 5). Cognitive dissonance theory has other important ramifications for attitudes, since people are often confronted with situations in which there is some conflict between their attitudes and behaviours.[58] The theory focuses on situations where two cognitive elements are inconsistent with one another. Dissonance can, for example, be related to mixed feelings about having a smoking habit, and reduction can occur by either eliminating, adding or changing elements. For example, the person could stop smoking (eliminating), or remember Great Aunt Sophia who smoked until the day she died at age 90 (adding). Changing can be illustrated by, for example, insisting that the social gains from smoking outweigh the health risks. Researchers found that consumers try to compensate for what they perceive as non-ethical behaviour by engaging in perceived ethical behaviour in other contexts.[59] To provide an even more concrete example, environmentally conscious consumers employ various rationales for explaining why they continue to fly even though they know it to be a highly unsustainable type of consumption.[60]

Dissonance theory can help to explain why evaluations of a product tend to increase after it has been purchased, i.e. post-purchase dissonance. The cognitive element 'I made a stupid decision' is dissonant with the element 'I am not a stupid person', so people tend to find even more reasons to like something after buying it. Gamblers have been shown to evaluate their chosen horses more highly and to be more confident of their success after placing a bet than before. Since the gambler is financially committed to their choice, they reduce dissonance by increasing the attractiveness of the chosen alternative relative to the unchosen ones.[61] Similar effects have been found for technological products, but it has also been found that such increased positivity is fragile.[62] One implication of this phenomenon is that consumers actively seek support for their purchase decisions, so marketers should supply them with additional reinforcement to build positive brand attitudes.

Balance theory

Balance theory is basically a variation of cognitive dissonance theory that considers relations among elements a person might perceive as belonging together.[63] This perspective involves relations (always from the perceiver's subjective point of view) among three elements, so the resulting attitude structures are called *triads*. Each triad contains: (1) a person and their perceptions of (2) an attitude object and (3) some other person or object. These perceptions can be positive or negative. More importantly, people *alter* these perceptions in order to make relations among them consistent. The theory specifies that people desire relations among elements in a triad to be harmonious, or balanced. If they are not, a state of tension will result until perceptions are changed and balance is restored.

To see how balance theory might work, consider the following scenario:

- Monica would like to go out with Anthony, who is in her consumer behaviour class. In balance theory terms, Monica has a positive sentiment relation with Anthony.

- One day, Anthony attends class wearing clothing that allows his fellow students to see his tattoo. Anthony has a positive unit relation with the tattoo. It belongs to him and is literally a part of him.

- Monica does not like tattooed men. She has a negative sentiment relation with tattoos.

According to balance theory, Monica faces an unbalanced triad, and she will experience pressure to restore balance by altering some aspect of the triad, as shown in Figure 7.2. She could, for example, decide that she does not like Anthony after all. Or her liking for Anthony could prompt a change in her attitude towards tattoos. Finally, she could choose to 'leave the field' by thinking no more about Anthony and his controversial tattoo. Note that while the theory does not specify which of these routes will be taken, it does predict that one or more of Monica's perceptions will have to change in order to achieve balance. While this distortion is an over-simplified representation of most attitude processes, it helps to explain a number of consumer behaviour phenomena. Consider, for example, how consumers tend to perceive the same dish – say, a pasta salad – as more healthy when it is classified as a salad than when it is classified as a pasta dish. Since consumers, and especially dieters, have established negative associations with the pasta category and positive with the salad category, these negative and positive associations rub off on a dish classified under one or the other, even if the dish is the same.[64] Similarly, consumers may have mixed attitudes about luxury consumption, considering it both an ostentatious display of wealth (negative) and a sign of style consciousness and good taste (positive). Hence, for the marketer, it may be worthwhile stressing the style consciousness rather than the conspicuous consumption element in promoting luxury goods.[65]

Balance theory reminds us that when perceptions are balanced, attitudes are likely to be stable. On the other hand, when inconsistencies are observed we are more likely to observe changes in attitudes. Balance theory also helps to explain why consumers like to be associated with positively valued objects. Forming a unit relation with a popular product (buying and wearing fashionable clothing or driving a high-performance car) may improve one's chances of being included as a positive sentiment relation in other people's triads.

This 'balancing act' is at the heart of celebrity endorsements, in which marketers hope that the star's popularity will transfer to the product, or when a non-profit organisation gets a celebrity to discourage harmful behaviours.[66] We will consider this strategy in more detail towards the end of the chapter. For now, it pays to remember that creating a unit relation between a product and a star can backfire if the public's opinion of the celebrity endorser shifts from positive to negative. This happened when Pepsi pulled an ad featuring Madonna after she released a controversial music video involving religion and sex. The strategy can also cause trouble if people question the star–product unit relation, as when Oxfam criticised movie star Scarlett Johansson for appearing in a (banned) Superbowl ad for Sodastream and she subsequently withdrew as an Oxfam ambassador. An Israeli company, Sodastream had a production plant on the West Bank (internationally acknowledged as being occupied territory), so consequently Scarlett Johansson and Oxfam could no longer be seen as a consistent unity.

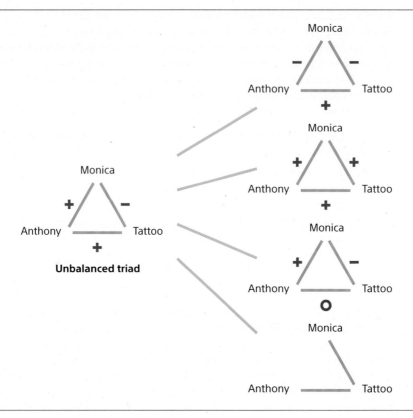

Figure 7.2 Alternative routes to restoring balance in a triad

Self-perception theory

Do attitudes necessarily change following behaviour because people are motivated to feel good about their decisions? **Self-perception theory** provides an alternative explanation of dissonance effects.[67] It assumes that people use observations of their own behaviour to determine what their attitudes are, just as we assume that we know the attitudes of others by watching what they do. The theory states that we maintain consistency by inferring that we must have a positive attitude towards an object if we have bought or consumed it (assuming that we freely made this choice). Thus, buying a product out of habit may result in a positive attitude towards it after the fact – namely, why would I buy it if I didn't like it? On the other hand, if consumers are somehow forced to form an opinion about a consumption option, that may lead to them altering their preferences – in other words, the formation of an attitude can lead a consumer to change habits.[68]

Self-perception theory helps to explain the effectiveness of a sales strategy called the **foot-in-the-door technique**, which is based on the observation that a consumer is more likely to comply with a request if they have first agreed to comply with a smaller request.[69] The name of this technique comes from the practice of door-to-door selling, when the salesperson was taught to plant their foot in a door so the prospect could not slam it shut. A good salesperson knows that they are more likely to get an order if the customer can be persuaded to open the door and talk. By agreeing to do so, the customer has established that they are willing to listen. Placing an order is consistent with this self-perception. This technique is especially useful for inducing consumers to answer surveys or to donate money to charity. When salespeople ask consumers to make a series of choices, these decisions are cognitively demanding and deplete the resources the person has available to monitor his behaviour. As a result, the target will opt for easier decisions down the road; in some cases, it may be easier just to comply with the request than to search for reasons why you shouldn't.[70]

Social judgement theory

Social judgement theory assumes that people assimilate new information about attitude objects in the light of what they already know or feel.[71] The initial attitude acts as a frame of reference, and new information is categorised in terms of this existing standard. Just as our decision that a box is heavy depends in part on other boxes we have lifted, so we develop a subjective standard when making judgements about attitude objects.

One important aspect of the theory is the notion that people differ in terms of the information they will find acceptable or unacceptable. They form **latitudes of acceptance and rejection** around an attitude standard. Ideas that fall within a latitude will be favourably received, while those falling outside this zone will not. There are plenty of examples of how latitudes of acceptance and rejection are influencing marketing practices and consumers' behaviour in Europe. Due to issues of health and obesity, there has been a move over the last decade or so towards banning sugary soft drinks from primary schools, and now also secondary schools, in Europe.[72] Nowadays, in more and more European countries, pubs, bars, restaurants and other public facilities have faced new legislation banning smoking in public rooms. The widespread acceptance of this legislation, also among smokers, reflects these changing attitudes towards smoking.

Messages that fall within the latitude of acceptance tend to be seen as more consistent with one's position than they actually are. This process is called an *assimilation effect*. On the other hand, messages falling in the latitude of rejection tend to be seen as even further from one's position than they actually are, resulting in a *contrast effect*.[73] The working of social judgement theory is the social psychological explanation why so many people today choose to live in 'information bubbles', where they only expose themselves to messages with which they already tend to agree.

Measuring attitudes

7.4

Attitude models measure attitude by identifying specific components and combining them to measure and predict a consumer's attitude towards a product or a brand.

A consumer's overall evaluation of a product sometimes accounts for the bulk of their attitude towards it. When market researchers want to assess attitudes, it can often be sufficient for them simply to ask the consumer, 'How do you feel about Heineken?' or 'How do you feel about Brexit?'.

However, as is obvious from the second question, attitudes can be a lot more complex than that. One problem is that a product or service may be composed of many attributes or qualities – some of which may be more important than others to particular people. Another problem is that a person's decision to act on their attitude is affected by other factors, such as whether it is felt that buying a product will meet with approval of friends or family (if Leah's closest friends are strongly opposed to using cheap labour for the making of Nike soccer boots, this may be a key reason for her not to buy Nike). For these reasons, attitude models have been developed that try to specify the different elements that might work together to influence people's evaluations of attitude objects.

Measuring attitude elements

Let us start at the simpler end. Suppose a supermarket chain wanted to measure shoppers' attitudes towards its retail outlets, the firm might administer one of the following types of attitude scales to consumers by mail, phone or in person.[74]

Single-item scales

One simple way to assess consumers' attitudes towards a store or product is to ask them for their general feelings about it. Such a global assessment does not provide much information about specific attributes, but it does give managers some sense of consumers' overall attitudes. This single-item approach often uses a Likert scale, which measures respondents' overall level of agreement with or feelings about an attitude statement:

How satisfied are you with your grocery store?

□ **Very satisfied**   □ **Somewhat satisfied**   □ **Satisfied**   □ **Not at all satisfied**

Multiple-item batteries

Attitude models go beyond such a simple measure, since they acknowledge that an overall attitude may often be composed of consumers' perceptions about multiple elements. For this reason, many attitude measures assess a set of beliefs about an issue and combine these reactions into an overall score. For example, the supermarket might ask customers to respond to a set of Likert scales and combine their responses into an overall measure of store satisfaction:

1Q My supermarket has a good selection of produce.

2Q My supermarket maintains sanitary conditions.

3Q I never have trouble finding exotic foods at my supermarket.

Measured on a scale like the following:

□ **Agree**   □ **Agree**   □ **Neither agree**   □ **Disagree**   □ **Disagree**

  strongly   somewhat   nor disagree   somewhat   strongly

The *semantic-differential scale* is useful for describing a person's set of beliefs about a company or brand, and it is also used to compare the images of competing brands. Respondents rate each attribute on a series of rating scales, where each end is anchored by adjectives or phrases, such as this one:

My supermarket is

Dirty 1–2–3–4–5–6–7 Clean

Semantic-differential scales can be used to construct a profile analysis of the competition, where the images of several stores or products can be compared visually by plotting the mean ratings for each object on several attributes of interest. This simple technique can help to pinpoint areas where the product or store diverges sharply from its competitors (in either a positive or a negative way).

Multi-attribute attitude models

Sometimes various attitudes need to be weighed against each other. For this reason, **multi-attribute attitude models** have been extremely popular among marketing researchers. This type of model assumes that a consumer's attitude (evaluation) of an attitude object (A_o) will depend on the beliefs they have about several or many attributes of the object. The use of a multi-attribute model implies that an attitude towards a product or brand can be predicted by identifying these specific beliefs and combining them to derive a measure of the consumer's overall attitude. We will describe how these work, using the example of a consumer evaluating a complex attitude object that should be very familiar: a university.

Basic multi-attribute models specify three elements:[75]

1 *Attributes* are characteristics of the A^o. Most models assume that the relevant characteristics can be identified; that is, the researcher can include those attributes that consumers take into consideration when evaluating the A°. For example, scholarly reputation is an attribute of a university.

2 *Beliefs* are cognitions about the specific A° (usually relative to others like it). A belief measure assesses the extent to which the consumer perceives that a brand possesses a particular attribute. For example, a student might have a belief that a particular university has a strong academic standing in consumer research.

3 *Importance weights* reflect the relative priority of an attribute to the consumer. Although an A° can be considered on a number of attributes, some will be more important than others (i.e. they will be given greater weight), and these weights are likely to differ across consumers. In the case of universities, for example, one student might stress the school's reputation for project-based learning, while another might assign greater weight to the social environment in which the university is located – for example, in terms of access to internships.

The Fishbein model

The most influential multi-attribute model is the Fishbein model, named after its primary developer.[76] The model measures three components of attitude:

1 *salient beliefs* people have about an A_o (those beliefs about the object that are considered during evaluation);

2 *object-attribute linkages,* or the probability that a particular object has an important attribute;

3 *evaluation* of each of the important attributes.

Note, however, that the model makes some assumptions that may not always be warranted. It assumes that we have been able to specify adequately all the relevant attributes that, for example, a student will use in evaluating their choice about which college to attend. The model also assumes that they will go through the process (formally or informally) of identifying a set of relevant attributes, weighing them and summing them. Although this particular decision is likely to be highly involving, it is still possible that their attitude will be formed by an overall affective response (a process known as *affect-referral*).

By combining these three elements, a consumer's overall attitude towards an object can be computed. (We will see later how this basic equation has been modified to increase its accuracy.) The basic formula is

$$A_{ijk} = \Sigma B_{ijk} I_{ik}$$

where i = attribute; j = brand; k = consumer; I = the importance weight given to attribute i by consumer k; B = consumer k's belief regarding the extent to which brand j possesses attribute i; and A = a particular consumer k's attitude score for brand j. The overall attitude score (A) is obtained by multiplying a consumer's rating of each attribute for all the brands considered by the importance rating for that attribute.

To see how this basic multi-attribute model might work, let's suppose we want to predict which phone a young girl, Sandra, is likely to buy. Sandra has now reduced her choice to three possibilities. Since she must now decide between these, we would first like to know which attributes Sandra will consider in forming an attitude towards each phone. We can then ask her to assign a rating regarding how well each phone performs on each attribute and also determine the relative importance of the attributes to her. An overall attitude score for each phone can then be computed by summing scores on each attribute (after weighing each by its relative importance). These hypothetical ratings are shown in Table 7.2. Based on this analysis, it seems that Sandra has the most favourable attitude towards the Samsung Galaxy.

Table 7.2 The basic multi-attribute model: Sandra's phone decision

Attribute (i)	Importance (I)	iPhone	Samsung Galaxy	Huawei P20
		Beliefs (b)		
Price	6	2	5	9
Brand reputation	5	10	8	5
Size	4	7	7	6
Camera	3	10	9	4
Memory	2	7	7	5
Customisation	1	3	7	10
Attitude score		137	146	135

Note: These hypothetical ratings are scored from 1 to 10, and higher numbers indicate 'better' standing on an attribute. For a negative attribute (e.g. price), higher scores indicate that the phone is believed to have 'less' of that attribute (i.e. to be cheaper).

Do attitudes predict behaviour?

7.5

Attitudes, as important as they are, have never proven to be very closely linked to consumers' behaviour.

Although multi-attribute models have been used by consumer researchers for many years, they have been plagued by a major problem: in many cases, knowledge of a person's attitude is not a very good predictor of behaviour. In a classic demonstration of 'Do as I say, not as I do', many studies have obtained a very low correlation between a person's reported attitude towards something and their actual behaviour towards it.

Consequently, for many years some researchers have been so discouraged that they have questioned whether attitudes are of any use at all in understanding behaviour.[77]

Theory of reasoned action

The original Fishbein model, which focused on measuring a consumer's attitude towards a product, has been extended in a number of ways to improve its predictive ability. The revised version is called the **theory of reasoned action**.[78] Some of the modifications to this model are considered here.

Intentions *vs* behaviour

As the old saying goes, 'The road to hell is paved with good intentions'. Many factors might interfere with actual behaviour, even if the consumer's intentions are sincere. You might save up with the intention of buying an iPod. In the interim, though, any number of things – having to spend your savings on unexpected expenses or finding that the desired model has been replaced by a new (and more expensive) one – could happen. It is not surprising, then, that in some instances past purchase behaviour has been found to be a better predictor of future behaviour than is a consumer's behavioural intention.[79] The theory of reasoned action aims to measure behavioural intentions, recognising that certain uncontrollable factors inhibit prediction of actual behaviour.

Social pressure

The theory acknowledges the power of other people in influencing behaviour. Most of our behaviour is not determined in isolation. Much as we sometimes may hate to admit it, what we think others would like us to do may be more relevant than our own individual preferences. In the case of Sandra's phone choice, note that she is very positive about purchasing a less expensive model. However, if she feels that this choice would be unpopular (perhaps her friends will think she is mad), she might ignore or downgrade this preference when making her final decision. A new element, the subjective norm (SN), was thus added to include the effects of what we believe other people think we should do. The value of SN is arrived at by including two other factors: (1) the intensity of a normative belief (NB) that others believe an action should be taken or not taken; and (2) the motivation to comply (MC) with that belief (i.e. the degree to which the consumer takes others' anticipated reactions into account when evaluating a course of action or a purchase). One study demonstrated how hotel guests were more likely to re-use towels if told that 'most guests in this hotel choose to re-use towels' than if told that doing so was 'good for the environment'. If told that most guests 'in this room' have chosen to re-use towels, the effect was even stronger. Social pressure also works even if you are never confronted with those exercising it.[80]

Multicultural dimensions

Under given cultural conditions, social pressure may even be at work in such a way that it promotes what is considered unethical consumer behaviour. It all depends on the cultural valorisation of different ethical principles. One recent experimental study concluded that when a distinction between resourceful consumers and consumers receiving government assistance is introduced, there is a difference in how the morality of making such choices is looked upon. Basically, when poor consumers made ethical choices, they were perceived as less moral compared to when income earners and, in particular, high-income consumers made the exact same choice. The fact that you 'have not earned your own money' makes spending it on ethical but more costly choices frowned upon.[81] This study was carried out in the US – would the effect of social pressure be the same in a European country? Why? Or Why not?

Attitude towards buying

Some models measure **attitude towards the act of buying (A_{act})**, rather than only the attitude towards the product itself. In other words, the focus is on the perceived consequences of a purchase. Knowing how someone feels about buying or using an object proves to be more valid than merely knowing the consumer's evaluation of the object itself.[82]

To understand this distinction, consider a problem that might arise when measuring attitudes towards condoms. Although a group of college students might have a positive attitude towards condom use, does this necessarily predict that they will buy and use them? A better prediction would be obtained by asking the students how likely they are to buy condoms. While a person might have a positive A_o towards condoms, their A_{act} might be negative due to the embarrassment or the inconvenience involved. Different shopping contexts, such as seasonal sales, are also met with different attitudes, since consumers weigh the benefits and costs of such sales differently. One factor to consider is whether such sales are actually sales or just a marketing trick. In order to improve the trustworthiness, and therefore the positive attitude, it has been suggested that shops produce a 'seasonal sales charter', promising good ethical conduct in their sales policies.[83]

Finally, in these days when more and more shopping takes place online, it is also useful to consider yet another attitude type: attitude towards the site (A_{site}). One study concluded, however, that affect (mood state based mainly on interactivity and aesthetics of the website) was more influential in producing purchase intentions than the attitude towards the website.[84]

Obstacles to predicting behaviour

Despite such improvements, attitude models continue to be lacking in their predictive power. One study added an emotional dimension to predicting the usage of electric cars, and concluded that the emotional component, together with the attitudes towards the car, were actually the strongest determinants of usage intentions.[85] We will look at emotions in terms of their persuasive function later in the chapter. Other obstacles to predicting behaviour are as follows:

1 Attitude models were developed to deal with actual behaviour (e.g. taking a slimming pill), not with the outcomes of behaviour (e.g. losing weight), which are assessed in some studies.

2 Some outcomes are beyond the consumer's control, such as when the purchase requires the co-operation of other people. For instance, someone might seek a mortgage, but this intention will be worthless if they cannot find a banker to give them one.

3 The basic assumption that behaviour is intentional may be invalid in a variety of cases, including those involving impulsive acts, sudden changes in one's situation, novelty-seeking or even simple repeat-buying. One study found that such unexpected events as having guests, changes in the weather or reading articles about the health qualities of certain foods exerted a significant effect on actual behaviours.[86]

4 Measures of attitude often do not really correspond to the behaviour they are supposed to predict, either in terms of the A_o or when the act will occur. One common problem is a difference in the level of abstraction employed. For example, knowing a person's attitude towards sports cars may not predict whether they will purchase a Mazda MX5. It is very important to match the level of specificity between the attitude and the behavioural intention.

5 A similar problem relates to the time-frame of the attitude measure. In general, the longer the time between the attitude measurement and the behaviour it is supposed to assess, the weaker the relationship will be. For example, predictability would improve markedly by asking consumers the likelihood of their buying a house in the next week as opposed to within the next five years.

6 Attitudes formed by direct, personal experience with an A_o are stronger and more predictive of behaviour than those formed indirectly, such as through advertising.[87] This underscores the importance of strategies that induce trial (e.g. by widespread product sampling to encourage the consumer to try the product at home, by taste tests, test drives, etc.), as well as those that maximise exposure to marketing communications.

7 Attitude research usually assumes that reasons for doing something and not doing something are logically inverse. However, a study comparing attitudes in favour of charitable giving versus attitudes against charitable giving concluded that the reasons were indeed different, but not just each other's opposite.[88]

Beyond attitudes?

Clearly, studies of attitudes have not been living up to what was expected in terms of predicting consumer behaviour. Therefore, researchers have been trying to approach the problem from a different angle, suggesting that attitudes and behaviour will almost always be inconsistent since they represent consumers' long-term and short-term interests respectively (which are not necessarily the same). They may also represent a difference between individual and collective interests and thus create a social dilemma – something that is evident in, for example, the consistent discrepancy between how many people say they would like to buy environmentally safe products and what they actually do buy.[89] Some researchers go even further along that path and reject the idea that formulating it as a gap is the right way to approach the issue. They argue that expecting such a consistency is an over-rationalising and simplified view of consumers' complex social lives, and suggest considering consumer behaviour in relation to 'green consumerism' as what they call 'coherent inconsistencies'.[90] A similar conclusion, but drawn from a psychoanalytic approach, also underlines how morality is not rooted in rational processes but rather in unconscious feelings of guilt.[91] Finally, from a critical perspective it is argued that addressing the discrepancy between ethical attitudes and ethical behaviour as a gap is not only a simplification of a complex issue, but actually serves the ideological purpose of prolonging the problem by responsibilising the individual consumer (and thereby taking responsibility away from capitalism), rather than promoting political action.[92]

Marketing pitfall

Animal welfare is an increasingly salient social issue for farmers, and animal rights activists have targeted a variety of production types all over Europe. Fur farming, for example, has been prohibited for more than a decade in countries such as Austria and the UK following massive consumer protests and activities. In order to try to avoid a similar fate, the fur industry in Denmark openly admitted to the problems of the business, but also underlined that while such problems exist, they are smaller in Denmark than elsewhere due to the high standards in the industry.[93] And opinions are very divided, as some have raised serious criticism over the logics applied by and the sometimes very dubious methods of the anti-fur campaigners.[94]

Multicultural dimensions

The theory of reasoned action has primarily been applied in the West. Certain assumptions inherent in the model may not necessarily apply to consumers from other cultures. Several of the following diminish the universality of the theory of reasoned action:

- The model was developed to predict the performance of any voluntary act. Across cultures, however, many consumer activities, ranging from taking exams and entering military service to receiving an inoculation or even choosing a marriage partner, are not necessarily voluntary.

- The relative impact of subjective norms may vary across cultures. For example, Asian cultures tend to value conformity and face-saving, so it is possible that subjective norms involving the anticipated reactions of others to the choice will have an even greater impact on behaviour for many Asian consumers.

- The model measures behavioural intentions and thus presupposes that consumers are actively anticipating and planning future behaviours. The intention concept assumes that consumers have a linear time sense, i.e. they think in terms of past, present and future. As will be discussed in a later chapter, this time perspective is not held by all cultures.

- A consumer who forms an intention is (implicitly) claiming that they are in control of their actions. Some cultures tend to be fatalistic and do not necessarily believe in the concept of free will. Indeed, one study comparing students from the US, Jordan and Thailand found evidence for cultural differences in assumptions about fatalism and control over the future.[95]

How do marketers change attitudes?

As consumers, we are constantly bombarded by messages inducing us to change our attitudes. These persuasion attempts can range from logical arguments to graphic pictures,

This ad uses humour (including a cultural reference to Monthy Python's classic sketch 'Ministry of Silly Walks') in order to persuade Belgian consumers that a trip to London is no big deal with the Eurostar train.

Shutterstock

Marketers engage in persuasive argumentation in order to change or confirm our attitudes towards products or brands.

and from intimidation by peers to exhortations by celebrity spokespeople. And communications flow both ways – the consumer may seek out information sources in order to learn more about these options, for instance by surfing the net. The increasing choice of ways to access marketing messages is changing the way we think about persuasion attempts. Our focus will be on some basic aspects of communication that specifically help to determine how and if attitudes will be created or modified. This objective relates to **persuasion**, which refers to an active attempt to change attitudes. Persuasion is, of course, the central goal of many marketing communications.

Consumers: ad readers or ad users?

In a traditional communications model, advertising is essentially viewed as the process of transferring information to the buyer before a sale. As such, there is a 'real' meaning of the ad based on the intentions of the sender of the message. This meaning can then be transferred to the consumer, if the message is clear enough and the medium is easy to get access to. In other words, if there is not too much 'noise' (as it was called!) on the line, the message should pass undistorted to the consumer. From this perspective, the power of creating the content of the message lies exclusively with the sender.[96]

Is this an accurate picture of the way we relate to marketing communications? In **reader-response theory**,[97] it is argued that it is better to conceive of the communication process as consisting of two communicators, both actively engaged in a process of making sense in and of some message. Instead of the 'machine-like' transmission of information, advertising must be understood as a particular type of communication, a particular genre, and it is understood and interpreted by consumers using particular strategies. Persuading consumers through advertising is not a technical but a cultural process.[98] In other words, when there is uncertainty about how consumers understand and interpret ads, this cannot be explained by 'noise' disturbing the 'real message', but must instead be understood based on consumers' own personal and cultural backgrounds.[99]

Proponents of **uses and gratification theory** add to this argument that consumers are an active, goal-directed audience who draw on mass media as a resource to satisfy needs. Instead of asking what media do *for* or *to* people, they ask what people do *with* the media.[100] Research with young people in the UK finds that they rely on advertising for many gratifications, including entertainment (some report that the 'adverts' are better than the programmes), escapism, play (some report singing along with jingles, others make posters out of magazine ads) and self-affirmation (ads can reinforce their own values or provide role models).[101]

Credibility and attractiveness

Regardless of whether a message is received by passive or, as it seems, more active consumers, common sense tells us that the same words uttered or written by different people can have very different effects. Research on *source effects* has been carried out for more than 50 years. By attributing the same message to different sources and measuring the degree of attitude change that occurs after listeners hear it, it is possible to determine which aspects of a communicator will induce attitude change.[102] Two particularly important source characteristics are *credibility* and *attractiveness*.[103]

Source credibility refers to a source's perceived expertise, objectivity or trustworthiness. This characteristic relates to consumers' beliefs that a communicator is competent and is willing to provide the necessary information to evaluate competing products adequately. A credible source can be particularly persuasive when the consumer has not yet learned much about a product or formed an opinion of it.[104] The decision to pay an expert or a celebrity to promote a product can be a very costly one, but researchers have concluded that, on average, the investment is worth it simply because the announcement of an endorsement contract is often used by market analysts to evaluate a firm's potential profitability, thereby affecting its expected return. On average, then, the impact of endorsements appears to be so positive that it offsets the cost of hiring the spokesperson.[105] The credibility is reinforced if the consumer/advertisement reader thinks that the source's qualifications are relevant to the product he or she endorses. On the other hand, teen idol Justin Bieber has promoted almost anything, including nail polish![106]

What's more, the early evidence indicates that celebrities exert the same impact on messages we receive from social media platforms. Brand endorsements streamed by celebrities directly to friends and followers on platforms such as Facebook and Twitter are generally more effective than conventional display ads placed on social media pages. For hints on how to use celebrities and social media strategically, check out sproutsocial.com.[107]

More generally, star power works because celebrities represent *cultural meanings* – they symbolise important categories such as status and social class (a 'sports-turned-into business icon' such as David Beckham[108]), or working-class celebrities (such as Cheryl (Tweedy)

Celebrity endorsement in advertising. Note that in 2011 TAG Heuer dropped the collaboration with Tiger Woods following the scandals concerning his private life; see the discussion on balance theory.

David McNew/Getty Images

and Katie Price[109]), gender (a 'manly man' like Mel Gibson, or a strong feminine character, such as Kate Winslet), age (the boyish Cristiano Ronaldo or the mature and serene George Clooney) and even personality types (the engaged humanitarian Leonardo di Caprio or the domestic glamour of Nigella).[110] Ideally, the advertiser decides what meanings the product should convey (that is, how it should be positioned in the marketplace), and then chooses a celebrity who has come to evoke that meaning. The product's meaning thus moves from the manufacturer to the consumer, using the star as a vehicle.[111] More recently, it has been suggested that this process does not just *happen* to the consumer but is something that we actively, creatively and purposefully *participate* in.[112]

These celebrities are not only credible due to their status. A good number of them are also credible simply because they are good looking. **Source attractiveness** refers to the source's perceived social value. This quality can emanate from the person's physical appearance, personality, social status, or their similarity to the receiver (we like to listen to people who are like us). For example, it has been found that high-power communicators resonate better with a high-power audience, communicating a message based on competence, whereas a low-power communicator is more persuasive to a low-power audience with a message based on warmth.[113] This kind of similarity effect is presumably also at the roots of the success of bloggers and YouTubers as product endorsers, since they are perceived by consumers as 'people just like ourselves'. In other words, well-adapted compelling sources have great value, and endorsement deals are constantly in the works.

Multicultural dimensions
Does this work for you?

Park Jin Sung combs through a rack of button-down shirts at a clothes shop in Seoul. After close examination, he picks out one in light blue that has a stiff, narrow collar and buttons spaced just right, so that the top two can be left open without exposing too much chest. 'Bill would wear this. The collar on this other one is too floppy. Definitely not Bill's style', Mr Park says. William H. Gates, Chairman of Microsoft Corp., may not be considered the epitome of chic in Europe, but in Seoul, Korea, he is a serious style icon. Young South Koreans believe that 'dressing for success' means copying Mr Gates's wardrobe, down to his round, tortoise-shell glasses, unpolished shoes and wrinkle-free trousers.[114] While Bill Gates doesn't even try to be an endorser of style in Korea, or elsewhere, some celebrities choose to maintain their credibility by endorsing products only in other countries. Many celebrities who do not do many American advertisements appear frequently in Japan. Mel Gibson endorses Asahi beer, Sly Stallone appears for Kirin beer, Sean Connery plugs Ito hams and the singer Sheena was featured in ads for Shochu liquor – dressed in a kimono and wig. Even the normally reclusive comedian and film director Woody Allen featured in a campaign for a large Tokyo department store.[115] Japander.com is a website where consumers can see Hollywood stars in Japanese commercials – for example, Nathalie Portman for Lux soap or Nicholas Cage promoting a video game (both in 2006).[116]

Types of message appeals

The *way* something is said can be as significant as *who* says it. A persuasive message can tug at the heartstrings or scare you, make you laugh, make you cry or leave you yearning to learn more, depending on the **appeal** used. In this section, we will briefly review the major alternatives available to communicators who wish to appeal to a message recipient.

The first alternative often considered is whether to use rational or emotional appeals; or, in other words, appeal to the head or to the heart? As with other types of appeals, there is no single given 'right' or 'wrong' answer to this question. The answer always depends upon the nature of the product, the type of relationship consumers have with it and the current competitive situation in the market. Conventional measures of advertising effectiveness

This ad for veganism clearly uses an emotional appeal.

Jeffrey Blackler/Alamy Stock Photo

Supermodel Claudia Schiffer used to 'seduce' investors to consider investing in Germany.

Jonathan Hordle/Shutterstock

are oriented towards cognitive responses, and 'feeling' ads may be penalised because the reactions are not as easy to articulate.[117] Moreover, while we do admit to the emotional impact of many a good advertising campaign, we are usually less willing to admit a persuasive effect. As market agents, we prefer to see ourselves as fairly rational decision-makers, although – as this text makes clear – that is far from the truth about consumers.

Echoing the widely held belief that 'sex sells', many marketing communications – for everything from perfumes to cars – feature heavy doses of erotic suggestions that range from subtle hints to blatant displays of flesh. Of course, the prevalence of sex appeals varies from country to country. American firms run ads abroad that would not go down well in the US. For example, a 'cheeky' ad campaign designed to boost the appeal of American-made Lee Jeans among Europeans features a series of bare buttocks. The messages are based on the concept that if bottoms could choose jeans, they would opt for Lee: 'Bottoms feel better in Lee Jeans'.[118]

Does sex work? Although the use of sex does appear to draw attention to an ad, it may actually be counter-productive to the marketer. Ironically, a provocative picture can be *too* effective; it attracts so much attention that it hinders processing and recall of the ad's other contents, such as the brand. Some researchers also suggest that strong use of sexual appeals are generally received negatively.[119] In one survey, an overwhelming 61 per cent of the respondents said that sexual imagery in a product's ad made them less likely to buy it.[120] However, as in all attitude measurements, it is important to remember that such statements are highly influenced by the moral picture that consumers like to present, not only to the researcher, but also to themselves. Perhaps not surprisingly, female nudity in print ads generates negative feelings and tension among female consumers, whereas men's reactions are more positive – although women with more liberal attitudes towards sex are more likely to be receptive.[121] Women also respond more positively to sexual themes when they occur in the context of a committed relationship rather than just gratuitous lust.[122] Furthermore, that moral picture is deeply dependent on the 'spirit of the times' and prevalent public discourse. For example, the use of (female) sexual imagery in commercial messages has come under new attack and scrutiny following 2017's globally impactful #MeToo campaigning.

Multicultural dimensions
Sexy ads. . . but with a hint of modesty

A few years ago, when supermodel Giselle Bundchen appeared in ads for H&M in Saudi Arabia and Dubai, the naked arms and upper part of her breast were covered through the addition of a photoshopped t-shirt and top, so that the model would show less naked skin. Such modifications are often made in order to comply with local standards of etiquette and not to alienate local consumers.[123]

Marketing opportunity
Sex, fame and humour – a combination only for the big and powerful?

Is the use of sexy and famous endorsers only for the big corporations? Cocio, a Danish producer of choc-olate milk and ice coffee thinks not, and has aligned itself with actress Eva Mendes in an attempt to further enhance its market shares nationally but especially internationally. A first execution using Eva Mendes was launched a couple of years ago, and now a new TV commercial should hopefully follow up on the success. Two young boys are hitchhiking on a rainy night, when Eva Mendes arrives in a classic Volkswagen Cocio van.

She stops and invites them to either 'squeeze up with her' or 'sit in the back'. One boy is obviously thrilled by the possibility of rubbing thighs with Eva Mendes, but his friend, discovering the chocolate milk cargo in the back, pulls him back there, exclaiming: 'How lucky can you be!'. Eva Mendes, through her skin colour, also metaphorically expresses the Cocio product (see the section on metaphors below).[124]

And what about humour? Does humour work? Overall, humorous advertisements do get attention. One study found that recognition scores for humorous alcohol ads were better than average. However, the verdict is mixed as to whether humour affects recall or product attitudes in a significant way.[125] One function it may play is to provide a source of *distraction*. A funny ad inhibits the consumer from *counter-arguing* (thinking of reasons why they don't agree with the message), thereby increasing the likelihood of message acceptance.[126]

Humour is more likely to be effective when the brand is clearly identified and the funny material does not 'swamp' the message. This danger is similar to that of beautiful models diverting attention from copy points. Furthermore, subtle humour is usually better, as it presents the product or brand as 'clever'. Finally, the humour can make fun of the brand (and its producers), something which makes them appear as 'more cool', but generally should not make fun of the potential consumer.

Marketing pitfall
When humour backfires

One of the reasons the use of humour is so widespread is that it is such a versatile tool.

Prior to the summer holidays of 2018, the global chain 7-Eleven was trying to use a humorous approach to promoting safe sex (and encouraging people to buy their condoms at 7-Eleven). Both a viral video and posters were made, drawing heavily on pictures and sounds of Norwegian national romanticism but adding that Norway is also one of the countries in Europe with the highest percentage of people suffering from Chlamydia, thus encouraging tourists to 'protect themselves from the locals'.[127] The campaign, featured on the American show *Last Week Tonight,* backfired on 7-Eleven when at least some Norwegians reacted with little amusement that such posters would be some of the first encounters with Norway for incoming tourists.[128] How do you respond to humorous ads from different countries in Europe? Do they all strike you as 'funny', and does the approach improve your attitude towards the advertiser?

Marketing opportunity
Most popular YouTube clip: Celebrities rule!

In May 2015, YouTube asked its users for a popular vote on the best commercial shown on YouTube during the last ten years. In order to get some structure on the competition, YouTube had pre-selected 20 ads among the ones with most views and likes. And the winner became the ad 'The Selfie Shoot' for Turkish Airlines, featuring football star Lionel Messi and basketball ace Kobe Bryant roaming the world for impressive selfies to send to each other.[129] The rise of YouTube has made exposure to the most popular ads grow exponentially, like it or not. . .

A fear appeal
from South
Africa

Courtesy of
brandhouse

WHO'S DRIVING YOU HOME TONIGHT? NEVER DRINK AND DRIVE — DRIVE DRY

Fear appeals highlight the negative consequences that can occur unless the consumer changes a behaviour or an attitude. The arousal of fear is a common tactic for social policy issues, such as encouraging consumers to change to a healthier lifestyle by stopping smoking, using contraception, taking more exercise, eating a more balanced diet, drinking without driving (by relying on a designated driver in order to reduce physical risk to themselves or others). It can also be applied to social risk issues by threatening one's success with the opposite sex, career and so on. One French study made a direct comparison of fear appeals, guilt appeals and shame appeals in terms of persuading consumers to refrain from excessive alcohol consumption; fear and shame were found to have the biggest persuasive impact.[130]

Does fear work? Fear appeals, it has been argued, are usually most effective when only a moderate amount of fear is induced and when a solution to the problem is presented.[131] If the threat is too great, the audience tends to deny that it exists as a way to rationalise the danger. This approach also works better when source credibility is high.[132] Fear also seems to be effective in driving consumers to make decisions rather than deferring decisions until later.[133] Finally, researchers have found that shock effects are considerably more accepted when it is for social causes, i.e. not-for-profit organisations, than when it is for a for-profit company.[134]

Some of the research on fear appeals may be confusing a threat (the literal content of a message, such as saying 'engage in safe sex or die' in the case of the AIDS campaign) with fear (an emotional response to the message). According to this argument, greater fear does

Humourous ads like this one grab our attention.

Steve Skjold/Alamy Stock Photo

This Moroccan ad uses a powerful metaphor to create fear appeal.

Ullstein bild/Getty Images

result in greater persuasion – but not all threats are equally effective because different people will respond differently to the same threat. Therefore, the strongest threats are not always the most persuasive because they may not have the desired impact on the perceiver. For example, raising the spectre of AIDS is about the strongest threat that can be delivered to sexually active young people – but this tactic is only effective if they believe they will get the disease. Because many young people (especially those who live in fairly affluent areas) do not believe that 'people like them' will be exposed to the AIDS virus, this strong threat may not actually result in a high level of fear.[135] The bottom line is that more precise measures of actual fear responses are needed before definitive conclusions can be drawn about the impact of fear appeals on consumption decisions.

Fear, humour or any other communicative strategy – most of them remind us that marketers today are story-tellers who supply visions of reality similar to those provided by authors, poets and artists. These communications take the form of stories often because the product benefits they describe are intangible and must be given tangible meaning by expressing them in a form that is concrete and visible. Advertisers (consciously or not) rely on various literary devices to communicate these meanings. To do this, they often use metaphors, which involves placing two dissimilar things in a close relationship by expressing one thing in terms of another. 'Love is a battlefield' is one example of a metaphor. 'Argument is war' is another.[136] Such usage of metaphors is both an expression and a development of some of those cultural values and symbols used by the advertising industry in connection with providing meaning to a product or brand (as we saw in McCracken's model of movement of meanings in Chapter 3).

The elaboration likelihood model

Some major features of the persuasion process, such as the qualities of the source and the appeals, have been discussed. Which aspect has more impact in persuading consumers to change their attitudes? Should marketers worry more about *what* is said, or *how* it is said and *who* says it?

The answer is, it depends. Variations in a consumer's level of involvement (as discussed in Chapter 5), result in the activation of very different cognitive processes when a message is received. Research indicates that this level of involvement will determine which aspects of a communication are processed. The situation appears to resemble a traveller who comes to a fork in the road: one or the other path is chosen, and this choice has a big impact on the factors that will make a difference in persuasion attempts.

The **elaboration likelihood model (ELM)** assumes that once a consumer receives a message they begin to process it.[137] Depending on the personal relevance of this information, one of two routes to persuasion will be followed. Under conditions of high involvement,

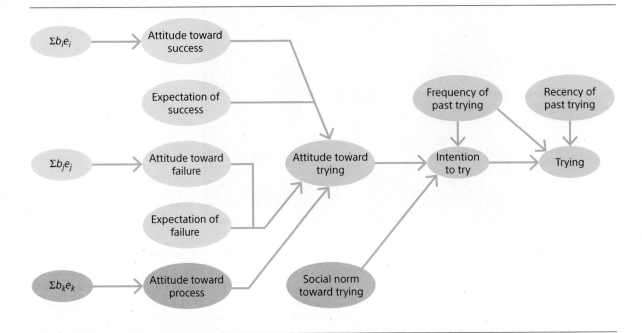

Figure 7.3 The elaboration likelihood model of persuasion

Source: John C. Mowen, *Consumer Behavior,* 2nd edn (Basingstoke, UK: Macmillan Publishing Company, 1989).

the consumer takes the *central route* to persuasion. Under conditions of low involvement, a *peripheral route* is taken instead. This model is shown in Figure 7.3.

The central route to persuasion

When a consumer finds the information in a persuasive message to be relevant or somehow interesting, they will carefully attend to the message content. The person is likely to actively think about the arguments presented and generate *cognitive responses* to these arguments. On hearing a radio message warning about drinking alcohol while pregnant, for example, an expectant mother might say to herself, 'She's right. I really should stop drinking alcohol now that I'm pregnant'. Or she might offer counter-arguments, such as, 'That's a load of nonsense. My mother had a cocktail every night when she was pregnant with me, and I turned out OK'. If a person generates counter-arguments in response to a message, it is less likely that they will yield to the message, whereas the generation of further supporting arguments by the consumer increases the probability of compliance.[138]

The central route to persuasion is likely to involve the traditional hierarchy of effects, as discussed earlier in the chapter. Beliefs are carefully formed and evaluated, and the resulting strong attitudes will be likely to guide behaviour. The implication is that message factors, such as the quality of arguments presented, will be important in determining attitude change. Prior knowledge about a topic results in more thoughts about the message but also increases the number of counter-arguments.[139]

The peripheral route to persuasion

In contrast, the peripheral route is taken when the person is not motivated to think deeply about the arguments presented. Instead, the consumer is likely to use other cues in deciding on the suitability of the message. These cues might include the product's package, the attractiveness of the source or the context in which the message is presented. Sources of information extraneous to the actual message content are called *peripheral cues* because they surround the actual message.

The peripheral route to persuasion highlights the paradox that in the case of low involvement (discussed in Chapter 6), when consumers do not care about a product, the stimuli associated with it increase in importance. The implication here is that low-involvement products may be purchased chiefly because the marketer has done a good job in designing a 'sexy' package, choosing a popular spokesperson, or perhaps just creating a pleasant shopping environment.

In a recent overview of research based on the ELM, it is concluded that the model has its limits and it might be useful to develop new versions of it. First of all, ELM does not really allow for a continuum of processing styles between the central and the peripheral route to persuasion, something which makes it quite simplistic. Secondly, the explosion of the media scene and the interactivity between different media types has complexified the simple message structure that ELM builds on.[140]

A competing theory of persuasion based on the notion of transportation has been suggested by some social psychologists. The idea of transportation is that instead of the cognitive evaluation that is seen as the root of persuasion in ELM, the decisive factor is the degree to which a consumer becomes immersed in the messages (or narratives as they are preferably called) and thereby lets him- or herself become 'transported' to (and hence persuaded to accept) a different point of view.[141] This approach to persuasion was used in a study of the *X Factor* reality show, where there were rich possibilities of studying completely immersed consumers/viewers of the show.[142] How about you? Do you also get 'transported'?

Chapter summary

7.1 **Attitudes have various functions for the consumer.** An attitude is a predisposition to evaluate an object (here we are most interested in products or brands), positively or negatively. A key to understanding attitude is therefore to understand the function that the attitude plays for the consumer (such as utilitarian or ego-defensive).

7.2 **Attitudes are formed in several ways, and build on different types of hierarchies between affective, behavioural and cognitive elements.** Attitude researchers traditionally assumed that attitudes were learned in a predetermined sequence, consisting first of the formation of beliefs (cognitions) regarding an attitude object, followed by an evaluation of that object (affect) and then some action (behaviour). However, depending on the consumer's level of involvement and the circumstances, attitudes can result from other hierarchies of effects.

7.3 **Consistency is important in attitude formation.** One organising principle of attitude formation is the importance of consistency among attitudinal components – that is, some parts of an attitude may be altered to conform with others. Such theoretical approaches to attitudes as cognitive dissonance theory, balance theory and congruity theory stress the vital role of consistency.

7.4 **Attitude models measure attitude by identifying specific components and combining them to measure and predict a consumer's attitude towards a product or a brand.** The complexity of attitudes is underscored by multi-attribute attitude models, in which sets of beliefs and evaluations are identified and combined to predict an overall attitude. Factors such as subjective norms and the specificity of attitude scales have been integrated into attitude measures to improve predictability.

7.5 **Attitudes, as important as they are, have never proven to be very closely linked to consumers' behaviour.** There are a number of possible explanations for why this is the case, including, for example, the discrepancy between the attitude to doing something and the attitude towards the outcome of such action. More generally, though, it is argued that attitudes are too simple for explaining and understanding the complex social context in which our consumer behaviour unfolds. In other words, we are much more walking fragments of social patterns of behaviour than we are people who constantly form attitudes and base our decisions on those attitudes.

7.6 **Marketers engage in persuasive argumentation in order to change or confirm our attitudes towards products or brands.** Persuasion refers to an attempt to change consumers' attitudes. Two important elements that characterise a message source are its attractiveness and credibility. Although celebrities are often used with the purpose of enhancing these characteristics, their credibility is not always as strong as marketers might hope. Some elements of a message that help to determine its effectiveness in terms of attitude change are whether an emotional or a rational appeal is employed and whether the message includes fear, humour or sexual references. The relative influence of the source versus the message depends on the receiver's level of involvement with the communication. The elaboration likelihood model specifies that a less-involved consumer will more likely be swayed by source effects, whereas a more-involved consumer will be more likely to attend to and process components of the actual message.

Social marketing refers to attempts to change consumers' attitudes and behaviours in ways that are beneficial to society as a whole.

Key terms

ABC model of attitudes (p. 254)
Affect (p. 254)
Appeal (p. 276)
Attitude (p. 251)
Attitude object (A_o) (p. 251)
Attitude towards the act of buying (A_{act}) (p. 271)
Attitude towards the advertisement (A_{ad}) (p. 260)
Balance theory (p. 264)
Cognition (p. 254)
Elaboration likelihood model (ELM) (p. 281)
Emotions (p. 261)
Foot-in-the-door technique (p. 266)
Functional theory of attitudes (p. 252)

Hierarchy of effects (p. 254)
Latitudes of acceptance and rejection (p. 267)
Materialism (p. 258)
Moods (p. 261)
Multi-attribute attitude models (p. 268)
Persuasion (p. 274)
Principle of cognitive consistency (p. 263)
Reader-response theory (p. 274)
Self-perception theory (p. 266)
Sentiment analysis (p. 261)
Social judgement theory (p. 267)
Source attractiveness (p. 276)
Source credibility (p. 275)
Theory of reasoned action (p. 270)

Consumer behaviour challenge

1 Consider the hierarchy of effects. Think of situations where you, as a consumer, have gone through the different hierarchies. Which hierarchies have applied to which situations?

2 Think of a behaviour exhibited by an individual that is inconsistent with their attitudes (e.g. attitudes towards cholesterol, drug use or even buying things to attain status or be noticed). Ask the person to elaborate on why they behave this way, and try to identify how the person has resolved any dissonant elements.

3 Using a series of semantic-differential scales, devise an attitude survey for a set of competing cars. Identify areas of competitive advantage or disadvantage for each model you incorporate.

4 Construct a multi-attribute attitude model for a set of local restaurants. Based on your findings, suggest how the restaurant managers can improve their establishments' image using the strategies described in the chapter.

5 A government agency wants to encourage the use of designated drivers by people who have been drinking. What advice could you give the organisation about constructing persuasive communications? Discuss some factors that might be important, including the structure of the communications, where they should appear and who should deliver them. Should fear appeals be used, and if so, how?

6 The Coca-Cola company pulled a UK internet promotion campaign after parents accused it of targeting children by using references to a notorious pornographic movie. As part of its efforts to reach young social media users for its Dr Pepper brand, the company took over consenting users' Facebook status boxes. Then, the company would

post mildly embarrassing questions such as 'Lost my special blankie. How will I go sleepies?', and 'What's wrong with peeing in the shower?'. But when a parent discovered that her 14-year-old daughter's profile had been updated with a message that directly referred to a hardcore porn film, the plan backfired and Coke had to pull the promotion.[143] What does it take to get the attention of jaded young people, who get exposed to all kinds of messages in cyberspace? What guidelines (if any) should marketers follow when they try to talk to young people on social media platforms?

7 Why would a marketer consider saying negative things about their product? When is this strategy feasible? Can you find examples of it?

8 Create a list of celebrities who match up with products in your country. What are the elements of the celebrities and products that make for a 'good match'? Why? Which celebrities have a global or European-wide appeal, and why?

9 A marketer must decide whether to incorporate rational or emotional appeals in a communication strategy. Describe conditions that are more favourable to one or the other in terms of changing consumers' attitudes.

For additional material see the companion website at **www.pearsoned.co.uk/solomon**

Notes

1. See, for example, Sven Bergvall and Mikolaj Dymek, 'Uncovering Sport Game Covers – The Consumption of Video Game Packages', in K. Ekström and H. Brembeck (eds), *European Advances in Consumer Research* 7 (Valdosta, GA: Association for Consumer Research, 2007): 310–16.
2. Torben Hansen, 'The role of trust in financial customer-seller relationships before and after the financial crisis', *Journal of Consumer Behaviour* 13 (2014): 442–52.
3. Robert A. Baron and Donn Byrne, *Social Psychology: Understanding Human Interaction,* 5th edn (Boston: Allyn & Bacon, 1987).
4. D. Albarracín, B.T. Johnson and M.P. Zanna (eds), *The Handbook of Attitudes* (Mahwah, NJ: Erlbaum, 2005); see also J.R. Priester, D. Nayakankuppan, M.A. Fleming and J. Godek, 'The A(2)SC(2) model: The influence of attitudes and attitude strength on consideration set choice', *Journal of Consumer Research* 30(4) (2004): 574–87 for a study on how the strength of attitudes influences and guides a consumer's consideration of brands.
5. Daniel Katz, 'The functional approach to the study of attitudes', *Public Opinion Quarterly* 24 (Summer 1960): 163–204;

Richard J. Lutz, 'Changing brand attitudes through modification of cognitive structure', *Journal of Consumer Research* 1 (March 1975): 49–59.
6. Russell H. Fazio, T.M. Lenn and E.A. Effrein, 'Spontaneous attitude formation', *Social Cognition* 2 (1984): 214–34.
7. Mason Haire, 'Projective techniques in marketing research', *Journal of Marketing* 14 (April 1950): 649–56.
8. Sharon Shavitt, 'The role of attitude objects in attitude functions', *Journal of Experimental Social Psychology* 26 (1990): 124–48; see also J.S. Johar and M. Joseph Sirgy, 'Value-expressive versus utilitarian advertising appeals: When and why to use which appeal', *Journal of Advertising* 20 (September 1991): 23–34.
9. Athanasios Krystalis, Klaus G. Grunert, Marcia D. de Barcellos, Toula Perrea and Wim Verbeke, 'Consumer attitudes towards sustainability aspects of food production: Insights from three continents', *Journal of Marketing Management* 28(3/4) (March 2012): 334–72.
10. John Thøgersen and Yanfeng Zhou, 'Chinese consumers' adoption of a "green" innovation: The case of organic food', *Journal of Marketing Management* 28(3/4) (March

2012): 313–33. See also PRNewswire, 'China Organic Food Market Outlook to 2020 – Rising Food Safety Concerns and Urban Population to Prosper Market Growth', (15 September 2016), https://www.prnewswire.com/news-releases/china-organic-food-market-outlook-to-2020---rising-food-safety-concerns-and-urban-population-to-prosper-market-growth-300329233.html (accessed 31 August 2018).

11. For the original work that focused on the issue of levels of attitudinal commitment, see H.C. Kelman, 'Compliance, identification, and internalization: Three processes of attitude change', *Journal of Conflict Resolution* 2 (1958): 51–60.

12. Lynn R. Kahle, Kenneth M. Kambara and Gregory M. Rose, 'A functional model of fan attendance motivations for college football', *Sports Marketing Quarterly* 5(4) (1996): 51–60.

13. Priyali Rajagopal and Nicole Votolato Montgomery, 'I imagine, I experience, I like: The false experience effect', *Journal of Consumer Research* 38 (October 2011): 578–94.

14. For a study that found evidence of simultaneous causation of beliefs and attitudes, see Gary M. Erickson, Johny K. Johansson and Paul Chao, 'Image variables in multi-attribute product evaluations: Country-of-origin effects', *Journal of Consumer Research* 11 (September 1984): 694–9.

15. Michael Ray, 'Marketing Communications and the Hierarchy-of-Effects', in P. Clarke (ed.), *New Models for Mass Communications* (Beverly Hills, CA: Sage, 1973): 147–76.

16. Jung Chae Suh and Youjae Yi, 'When brand attitudes affect the customer satisfaction–loyalty relation: The moderating role of product involvement', *Journal of Consumer Psychology* (2006)16(2): 145–55.

17. Herbert Krugman, 'The impact of television advertising: Learning without involvement', *Public Opinion Quarterly* 29 (Fall 1965): 349–56; Robert Lavidge and Gary Steiner, 'A model for predictive measurements of advertising effectiveness', *Journal of Marketing* 25 (October 1961): 59–62.

18. Melanie A. Dempsey and Andrew A. Mitchell, 'The influence of implicit attitudes on choice when consumers are confronted with conflicting attribute information', *Journal of Consumer Research* 37 (December 2010): 614–25.

19. Athanasios Krystallis, 'Motivation and cognitive structures of store versus manufacturer brand consumers', *Journal of Consumer Behaviour* 14(3) (2015).

20. Magnus Söderlund, 'Judging Fiction Books by the Cover: An Examination of the Effects of Sexually Charged Cover Images', in S. Borghini, M.A. McGrath and C.C. Otnes (eds), *European Advances in Consumer Research* 8 (Duluth, MN: Association for Consumer Research, 2008): 500–4.

21. Lan Jiang, Joandrea Hoegg, Darren W. Dahl and Amitava Chattopadhyay, 'The Persuasive Role of Incidental Similarity on Attitudes and Purchase Intentions in a Sales Context', *Journal of Consumer Research* 36 (February 2010): 778–91.

22. For some studies on this topic see Andrew B. Aylesworth and Scott B. MacKenzie, 'Context is key: The effect of program-induced mood on thoughts about the ad', *Journal of Advertising* 27(2) (Summer 1998): 15–17 (at 15); Angela Y. Lee and Brian Sternthal, 'The effects of positive mood on memory', *Journal of Consumer Research* 26 (September 1999): 115–28; Michael J. Barone, Paul W. Miniard and Jean B. Romeo, 'The influence of positive mood on brand extension evaluations', *Journal of Consumer Research* 26 (March 2000): 386–401. For a study that compared the effectiveness of emotional appeals across cultures, see Jennifer L. Aaker

and Patti Williams, 'Empathy versus pride: The influence of emotional appeals across cultures', *Journal of Consumer Research* 25 (December 1998): 241–61.

23. See, for example, Özlem H. Sanaktekin, 'Moderating Role of Valence Sequence in the Mixed Affective Approach', in S. Borghini, M.A. McGrath and C.C. Otnes (eds), *European Advances in Consumer Research* 8 (Duluth, MN: Association for Consumer Research, 2008): 150–54.

24. Punam Anand, Morris B. Holbrook and Debra Stephens, 'The formation of affective judgments: The cognitive–affective model versus the independence hypothesis', *Journal of Consumer Research* 15 (December 1988): 386–91; Richard S. Lazarus, 'Thoughts on the relations between emotion and cognition', *American Psychologist* 37(9) (1982): 1,019–24.

25. Robert B. Zajonc, 'Feeling and thinking: Preferences need no inferences', *American Psychologist* 35(2) (1980): 151–75.

26. Jesse King and Paul Slovic, 'The affect heuristic in early judgments of product innovations', *Journal of Consumer Behaviour* 13 (2014): 411–28.

27. A. Tal, Y. Gvili, M. Amar and B. Wansink, 'Can political cookies leave a bad taste in one's mouth? Political ideology influences taste', *European Journal of Marketing* 51 (11/12) (2017): 2,175–91.

28. Dirk Morschett, Bernhard Swoboda and Hanna Schramm-Klein, 'Shopping Orientations as Determinants of Attitude Towards Food Retailers and Perception of Store Attributes', in K. Ekström and H. Brembeck (eds), *European Advances in Consumer Research* 7 (Duluth, MN: Association for Consumer Research, 2006): 160–67.

29. Güliz Ger and Russell W. Belk, 'Accounting for materialism in four cultures', *Journal of Material Culture* 4(2) (1999): 183–204.

30. Marsha L. Richins, 'Special possessions and the expression of material values', *Journal of Consumer Research* 21 (December 1994): 522–33.

31. Ibid.

32. James E. Burroughs and Aric Rindfleisch, 'Materialism and well-being: A conflicting values perspective', *Journal of Consumer Research* 29 (December 2002): 348ff.

33. Marsha L. Richins, 'Special possessions and the expression of material values', *Journal of Consumer Research* 21 (December 1994): 522–33.

34. John L. Lastovicka and Nancy J. Sirianni, 'Truly, madly, deeply: Consumers in the throes of material possession love', *Journal of Consumer Research* 38 (August 2011): 323–42.

35. Güliz Ger and Russell Belk, 'Cross-cultural differences in materialism', *Journal of Economic Psychology* 17 (1996): 55–77.

36. Güliz Ger and Russell Belk, 'Accounting for materialism in four cultures', *Journal of Material Culture* 4(2) (1999): 183–204.

37. L.J. Shrum, Tina Lowrey, Mario Pandelaere, Ayalla Ruvio, Elodie Gentina, Pia Furchheim, Maud Herbert, Liselot Hudders, Inge Lens, Naomi mandel, Agnes Nairn, Adriana Samper, Isabella Soscia and Laurel Steinfeld, 'Materialism: the good, the bad and the ugly', *Journal of Marketing Management* 13(17/18) (2014): 1,858–81.

38. L.J. Shrum, Nancy Wong, Farrah Arif, Sunaina Chugani, Alexander Gunz, Tina M. Lowrey, Agnes Nairn, Mario Pandelaere, Spencer M. Ross, Ayalla Ruvio, Kristin Scott and Jill Sundie, 'Reconceptualizing materialism as identity goal pursuits: Functions, processes, and consequences', *Journal of Business Research* 66 (2013): 1,179–85.

39. Jaehoon Lee and L.J. Shrum, 'Conspicuous consumption versus charitable behavior in response to social exclusion: A differential needs explanation', *Journal of Consumer Research* 39 (2012): 530–44.

40. Nimish Rustagi and L.J. Shrum, 'Undermining the Restorative Potential of Compensatory Consumption: A Product's Explicit Identity Connection Impedes Self-Repair', in Ryan Hamilton and Cait Lamberton (eds), *Advances in Consumer Psychology* (Dallas, TX: Society for Consumer Psychology, 2018).

41. Rustagi and Shrum (2018), op. cit.

42. http://www.zumba.com/en-US (accessed 1 September 2018); quoted in Alexandra Bruell, 'How Zumba Built a Brand with a Cult Following in Just a Few Years,' *Ad Age/CMO Strategy* (20 August 2012), http://adage.com/article/cmo-interviews/zumba-built-a-cult-a-years/236737/ (accessed 1 September 2018).

43. Fabrizio Di Muro and Kyle B. Murray, 'An arousal regulation explanation of mood effects on consumer choice', *Journal of Consumer Research* 39(3) (October 2012): 574–84, http://www.jstor.org/stable/10.1086/664040 (accessed 1 September 2018); Cassie Mogilner, Jennifer Aaker and Sepandar D. Kamvar, 'How happiness affects choice', *Journal of Consumer Research* 39(2) (August 2012): 429–43, http://www.jstor.org/stable/10.1086/663774 (accessed 1 September 2018); for a study that looks at cross-cultural differences in expression of emotion, see Ana Valenzuela, Barbara Mellers and Judi Strebel, 'Pleasurable surprises: A cross-cultural study of consumer responses to unexpected incentives', *Journal of Consumer Research* 36(5) (2010): 792–805; see also Samuel K. Bonsu, Aron Darmody and Marie-Agnes Parmentier, 'Arrested emotions in reality television,' *Consumption Markets & Culture* 13(1) (2010): 91–107; parts of this section were adapted from Michael R. Solomon, Rebekah Russell-Bennett and Josephine Previte, *Consumer Behaviour: Buying, Having, Being,* 3rd edn (Frenchs Forest, NSW: Pearson Australia, 2012).

44. C.G. Ding and T.H. Tseng, 'On the relationships among brand experience, hedonic emotions, and brand equity', *European Journal of Marketing* 49(7/8) (2015): 994–1,015.

45. F.V. Ordenes, S. Ludwig, K. De Ruyter, D. Grewal and M. Wetzels. 'Unveiling what is written in the stars: Analyzing explicit, implicit, and discourse patterns of sentiment in social media', *Journal of Consumer Research* 43(6) (2017): 875–94.

46. Portions of this section are adapted from Michael R. Solomon, Katherine White and Darren W. Dahl, *Consumer Behaviour: Buying, Having, Being* 6th Canadian edn (Toronto: Pearson, 2014).

47. https://www.brandwatch.com/blog/understanding-sentiment-analysis/ (accessed 7 September); Tracy Tuten and Michael R. Solomon, *Social Media Marketing* 2nd edn (London: SAGE, 2016); Jennifer Van Grove, 'How a Sentiment Analysis Startup Profits by Checking Emotion in E-mail', *Mashable* (20 January 2011), [[check-powermath]]???http://mashable.com/2011/01/20/lymbix/?utm_source=feedburner&utm_medium=email&utm_campaign=Feed%3A+Mashable+%28Mashable%29 (accessed 1 September 2018).

48. Steve McClellan, 'Unilever, Coca-Cola Utilize Facial Analysis To Enhance Ad Tests', *Mediapost* (18 January 2013), http://www.mediapost.com/publications/article/191418/unilever-coca-cola-utilize-facial-analysis-to-enh.

49. Hannah H. Chang and Michel Tuan Pham, 'Affect as a decision-making system of the present', *Journal of Consumer Research* 40(1) (2013): 42–63.

50. Michel Tuan Pham, Leonard Lee and Andrew T. Stephen, 'Feeling the future: The emotional Oracle effect', *Journal of Consumer Research* 39(3) (October 2012): 461–77.

51. https://www.theguardian.com/news/series/cambridge-analytica-files (accessed 1 September 2018).

52. Vindu Goel, 'Facebook tinkers with users' emotions in news feed experiment, stirring outcry', *New York Times* (29 June 2014), http://www.nytimes.com/2014/06/30/technology/facebook-tinkers-with-users-emotions-in-news-feed-experiment-stirring-outcry.html (accessed 1 September 2018).

53. Ahir Gopaldas, 'Marketplace sentiments', *Journal of Consumer Research* 41(3) (2014): 995–1,014.

54. Kelman, 'Compliance, identification, and internalization', op. cit.: 51–60.

55. See Sharon E. Beatty and Lynn R. Kahle, 'Alternative hierarchies of the attitude–behaviour relationship: The impact of brand commitment and habit', *Journal of the Academy of Marketing Science* 16 (Summer 1988): 1–10.

56. J.R. Priester, D. Nayakankuppan, M.A. Fleming and J. Godek, 'The A(2)SC(2) model: The influence of attitudes and attitude strength on consideration set choice', *Journal of Consumer Research* 30(4) (2004): 574–87.

57. https://www.economist.com/china/2017/03/23/china-is-spending-billions-to-make-the-world-love-it (accessed 1 September 2018).

58. Leon Festinger, *A Theory of Cognitive Dissonance* (Stanford, CA: Stanford University Press, 1957).

59. Diana Gergory-Smit, Andrew Smith and Heidi Winklhofer, 'Emotions and dissonance in "ethical" consumption', *Journal of Marketing Management* 29(11/12) (2013): 1,201–23.

60. S. McDonald, C.J. Oates, M. Thyne, A.J. Timmis and C. Carlile, 'Flying in the face of environmental concern: Why green consumers continue to fly', *Journal of Marketing Management* 31(13/14) (2015): 1,503–28.

61. Robert E. Knox and James A. Inkster, 'Postdecision dissonance at post time', *Journal of Personality and Social Psychology* 8(4) (1968): 319–23.

62. Ab Litt and Zakary L. Tormala, 'Fragile enhancement of attitudes and intentions following difficult decisions', *Journal of Consumer Research* 37 (December 2010): 584–98.

63. Fritz Heider, *The Psychology of Interpersonal Relations* (New York: Wiley, 1958).

64. Caglar Irmak, Beth Vallen and Stephanie Rosen Robinson, 'The impact of product name on dieters' and nondieters' food evaluations and consumption', *Journal of Consumer Research* 38 (August 2011): 390–405.

65. C. Ki, K. Lee and Y.K. Kim, 'Pleasure and guilt: How do they interplay in luxury consumption?', *European Journal of Marketing* 51(4) (2017): 722–47.

66. Debra Z. Basil and Paul M. Herr, 'Attitudinal balance and cause-related marketing: An empirical application of balance theory', *Journal of Consumer Psychology* 16(4) (2006): 391–403.

67. Daryl J. Bem, 'Self-Perception Theory', in Leonard Berkowitz (ed.), *Advances in Experimental Social Psychology* (New York: Academic Press, 1972): 1–62.

68. Michail Kokkoris and Ulrich Kühnen, 'The need to have an opinion as a driver of consumer choice', *Journal of Consumer Behaviour* 14 (2015): 92–102.

69. Jonathan L. Freedman and Scott C. Fraser, 'Compliance without pressure: The foot-in-the-door technique', *Journal of Personality and Social Psychology* 4 (August 1966): 195–202; for further consideration of possible explanations for this effect, see William DeJong, 'An examination of self-perception mediation of the foot-in-the-door effect', *Journal of Personality and Social Psychology* 37 (December 1979): 221–31; Alice M. Tybout, Brian Sternthal and Bobby J. Calder, 'Information availability as a determinant of multiple-request effectiveness', *Journal of Marketing Research* 20 (August 1988): 280–90.

70. Bob Fennis, Loes Janssen and Kathleen D. Vohs, 'Acts of benevolence: A limited-resource account of compliance with charitable requests', *Journal of Consumer Research* (December 2009): 906–25.

71. Muzafer Sherif and Carl I. Hovland, *Social Judgment: Assimilation and Contrast Effects in Communication and Attitude Change* (New Haven, CT: Yale University Press, 1961); for a recent treatment see Yong-Soon Kang and Paul M. Herr, 'Beauty and the beholder: Toward an integrative model of communication source effects', *Journal of Consumer Research* 33 (June 2006): 123–30.

72. https://www.foodbev.com/news/european-soft-drinks-industry-commits-to-school-sugar-ban/ (accessed 7 September 2018).

73. Joan Meyers-Levy and Brian Sternthal, 'A two-factor explanation of assimilation and contrast effects', *Journal of Marketing Research* 30 (August 1993): 359–68.

74. A number of criteria beyond the scope of this book are important in evaluating methods of attitude measurement, including such issues as reliability, validity and sensitivity. For an excellent treatment of attitude-scaling techniques, see David S. Aaker and George S. Day, *Marketing Research*, 4th edn (New York: Wiley, 1990).

75. William L. Wilkie, *Consumer Behavior* (New York: Wiley, 1986).

76. Martin Fishbein, 'An investigation of the relationships between beliefs about an object and the attitude toward that object', *Human Relations* 16 (1983): 233–40.

77. Allan Wicker, 'Attitudes versus actions: The relationship of verbal and overt behavioral responses to attitude objects', *Journal of Social Issues* 25 (Autumn 1969): 65.

78. Icek Ajzen and Martin Fishbein, 'Attitude–behavior relations: A theoretical analysis and review of empirical research', *Psychological Bulletin* 84 (September 1977): 888–918.

79. Richard P. Bagozzi, Hans Baumgartner and Youjae Yi, 'Coupon Usage and the Theory of Reasoned Action', in Holman and Solomon (eds), *Advances in Consumer Research* 18: 24–7; Edward F. McQuarrie, 'An alternative to purchase intentions: The role of prior behavior in consumer expenditure on computers', *Journal of the Market Research Society* 30 (October 1988): 407–37; Arch G. Woodside and William O. Bearden, 'Longitudinal Analysis of Consumer Attitude, Intention, and Behavior Toward Beer Brand Choice', in William D. Perrault Jr (ed.), *Advances in Consumer Research* 4 (Ann Arbor, MI: Association for Consumer Research, 1977): 349–56.

80. Noah J. Goldstein, Robert B. Cialdini and Vladas Griskevicius, 'A room with a viewpoint: Using social norms to motivate environmental conservation in hotels', *Journal of Consumer Research* 35 (October 2008): 472–82.

81. J.G. Olson, B. McFerran, A.C. Morales and D.W. Dahl, 'Wealth and welfare: Divergent moral reactions to ethical consumer choices', *Journal of Consumer Research* 42(6) (2016): 879–96.

82. Michael J. Ryan and Edward H. Bonfield, 'The Fishbein Extended Model and consumer behavior', *Journal of Consumer Research* 2 (1975): 118–36.

83. Christine Gonzalez and Michaël Korchia, 'Attitudes Toward Seasonal Sales: An Exploratory Analysis of the Concept and its Antecedents', in K. Ekström and H. Brembeck (eds), *European Advances in Consumer Research* 7 (Duluth, MN: Association for Consumer Research, 2006): 485–94.

84. Anis Allagui and Jean-Francois Lemoine, 'Web Interface and Consumers' Buying Intention in e-Tailing: Results from an Online Experiment', in S. Borghini, M.A. McGrath and C.C. Otnes (eds), *European Advances in Consumer Research* 8 (Duluth, MN: Association for Consumer Research, 2008): 24–30.

85. Ingrid Moons and Patrick de Pelsmacker, 'Emotions as determinants of electric car usage intention', *Journal of Marketing Management* 28(2/3) (March 2012): 195–237.

86. Joseph A. Cote, James McCullough and Michael Reilly, 'Effects of unexpected situations on behavior–intention differences: A garbology analysis', *Journal of Consumer Research* 12 (September 1985): 188–94.

87. Russell H. Fazio, Martha C. Powell and Carol J. Williams, 'The role of attitude accessibility in the attitude-to-behavior process', *Journal of Consumer Research* 16 (December 1989): 280–8; Robert E. Smith and William R. Swinyard, 'Attitude–behavior consistency: The impact of product trial versus advertising', *Journal of Marketing Research* 20 (August 1983): 257–67.

88. A. Chatzidakis, S. Hibbert and H. Winklhofer, 'Are consumers' reasons for and against behaviour distinct?', *European Journal of Marketing* 50(1/2) (2016): 124–44.

89. Geertje Schuitema and Judith de Groot, 'Green consumerism: The influence of product attributes and values on purchasing intentions', *Journal of Consumer Behaviour* 14 (2015): 57–69.

90. Caroline Moraes, Marylyn Carrigan and Isabelle Szmigin, 'The coherence of inconsistencies: Attitude-behaviour gaps and new consumption communities', *Journal of Marketing Management* 28(1/2) (2012): 103–28.

91. A. Chatzidakis, 'Guilt and ethical choice in consumption: A psychoanalytic perspective', *Marketing Theory* 15(1) (2015): 79–93.

92. M.J. Carrington, D. Zwick and B. Neville, 'The ideology of the ethical consumption gap', *Marketing Theory* 16(1) (2016): 21–38.

93. Jesper Uggerhøj, CEO Kopenhagen Fur, 'Green Conscience' (2018), https://issuu.com/kopenhagenfur/docs/kopenhagen_fur_news_february_2018 (accessed 7 September 2018).

94. See, for example, https://www.truthaboutfur.com (accessed 7 September 2018).

95. Joseph A. Cote and Patriya S. Tansuhaj, 'Culture Bound Assumptions in Behavior Intention Models', in Thom Srull (ed.), *Advances in Consumer Research* 16 (Provo, UT: Association for Consumer Research, 1989): 105–9.

96. For a good introduction to various classical perspectives on human communication, see R. Aubrey Fischer, *Perspectives on Human Communication* (New York: Macmillan, 1978).

97. See, for example, Umberto Eco, *The Role of the Reader* (Bloomington: Indiana University Press, 1979).

98. See, for example, Linda M. Scott, 'The bridge from text to mind: Adapting reader-response theory to consumer research', *Journal of Consumer Research* 21 (December 1994): 461–80.

99. David G. Mick and Claus Buhl, 'A meaning-based model of advertisement experiences', *Journal of Consumer Research* 19 (December 1992): 317–38.

100. First proposed by Elihu Katz, 'Mass communication research and the study of popular culture: An editorial note on a possible future for this journal', *Studies in Public Communication* 2 (1959): 1–6; for a more recent discussion of this approach, see Stephanie O'Donohoe, 'Advertising uses and gratifications', *European Journal of Marketing* 28(8/9) (1994): 52–75.

101. Mark Ritson and Richard Elliott, 'The social uses of advertising: An ethnographic study of adolescent advertising audiences', *Journal of Consumer Research* 25(3) (December 1999): 260–78.

102. Carl I. Hovland and W. Weiss, 'The influence of source credibility on communication effectiveness', *Public Opinion Quarterly* 15 (1952): 635–50.

103. Herbert Kelman, 'Processes of opinion change', *Public Opinion Quarterly* 25 (Spring 1961): 57–78; Susan M. Petroshuis and Kenneth E. Crocker, 'An empirical analysis of spokesperson characteristics on advertisement and product evaluations', *Journal of the Academy of Marketing Science* 17 (Summer 1989): 217–26.

104. S. Ratneshwar and Shelly Chaiken, 'Comprehension's role in persuasion: The case of its moderating effect on the persuasive impact of source cues', *Journal of Consumer Research* 18 (June 1991): 52–62.

105. Jagdish Agrawal and Wagner A. Kamakura, 'The economic worth of celebrity endorsers: An event study analysis', *Journal of Marketing* 59 (July 1995): 56–62.

106. Robert Klara, 'Brands by Bieber', Brandweek (1 January 2011), http://www.adweek.com/news/advertising-branding/brands-bieber-126241 (accessed 1 September 2018).

107. https://sproutsocial.com/insights/how-to-work-with-influencers-on-social-media/ (accessed 7 September 2018); see also Rebekah Carter, 'Facebook vs Twitter: Which is best for your brand?' (11 April 2018), https://sproutsocial.com/insights/facebook-vs-twitter/ (accessed 7 September 2018).

108. Chris Hackley and Rungpaka Amy Hackley, 'Marketing and the cultural production of celebrity in the era of media convergence', *Journal of Marketing Management* 31(5/6) (2015): 461–77.

109. Hayley Cocker, Emma Banister and Maria Piacentini, 'Producing and consuming celebrity identity myths: unpacking the classed identities of Cheryl Cole and Katie Price', *Journal of Marketing Management* 31(5/6) (2015): 502–24.

110. Lorna Stevens, Benedetta Cappellini and Gilly Smith, 'Nigellissima: a study of glamour, performativity and embodiment', *Journal of Marketing Management* 31(5/6) (2015): 577–98.

111. Grant McCracken, 'Who is the celebrity endorser? Cultural foundations of the endorsement process', *Journal of Consumer Research* 16(3) (December 1989): 310–21.

112. Emma Banister and Hayley Cocker, 'A cultural exploration of consumers' interactions and relationships with celebrities', *Journal of Marketing Management* 30(1/2) (2014): 1–29.

113. D. Dubois, D.D. Rucker and A.D. Galinsky, 'Dynamics of communicator and audience power: The persuasiveness of competence versus warmth', *Journal of Consumer Research* 43(1) (2016): 68–85.

114. Choi Hae Won, 'Bill Gates, style icon? Oh yes – in Korea, where geek is chic', *Wall Street Journal* (4 January 2001): A1.

115. Marie Okabe, 'Fading yen for foreign stars in ads', *Singapore Straits Times* (1986).

116. www.japander.com (accessed 1 September 2018).

117. H. Zielske, 'Does day-after recall penalize "feeling" ads?', *Journal of Advertising Research* 22 (1982): 19–22.

118. Allessandra Galloni, 'Lee's cheeky ads are central to new European campaign', *Wall Street Journal Online* (15 March 2002).

119. Michael S. LaTour and Tony L. Henthorne, 'Ethical judgments of sexual appeals in print advertising', *Journal of Advertising* 23(3) (September 1994): 81–90.

120. Rebecca Gardyn, 'Where's the lovin'?', *American Demographics* (February 2001): 10.

121. Jaideep Sengupta and Darren W. Dahl, 'Gender-related reactions to gratuitous sex appeals', *Journal of Consumer Psychology* 18 (2008): 62–78.

122. Darren W. Dahl, Jaideep Sengupta and Kathleen Vohs, 'Sex in advertising: Gender differences and the role of relationship commitment', *Journal of Consumer Research* 36 (August 2009): 215–31.

123. http://www.marieclaire.co.uk/news/fashion/520111/gisele-censored-in-middle-east-s-h-m-campaign.html (accessed 1 September 2018).

124. Lars Winther, 'Cocio skal ud I verden', *Food & Culture* 2 (2011): 30.

125. Thomas J. Madden, 'Humor in Advertising: An Experimental Analysis' (working paper, no. 83–27, University of Massachusetts, 1984); Thomas J. Madden and Marc G. Weinberger, 'The effects of humor on attention in magazine advertising', *Journal of Advertising* 11(3) (1982): 8–14; Weinberger and Spotts, 'Humor in U.S. versus U.K. TV commercials'; see also Ashesh Mukherjee and Laurette Dubé, 'The Use of Humor in Threat-Related Advertising', unpublished manuscript, McGill University (June 2002).

126. David Gardner, 'The distraction hypothesis in marketing', *Journal of Advertising Research* 10 (1970): 25–30.

127. https://www.adsoftheworld.com/media/integrated/7eleven_chlamydia_goes_viral (accessed 1 September 2018).

128. https://www.nrk.no/kultur/norsk-nasjonalromantisk-kondomsjokk-pa-hbo-1.14099836 (accessed 1 September 2018).

129. *Markedsføring* (6 June 2015).

130. Imene Becheur, Hayan Dib, Dwight Merunka and Pierre Valette-Florence, 'Emotions of Fear, Guilt or Shame in Anti-Alcohol Messages: Measuring Direct Effects on Persuasion and the Moderating Role of Sensation Seeking', in S. Borghini, M.A. McGrath and C.C. Otnes (eds), *European Advances in Consumer Research* 8 (Duluth, MN: Association for Consumer Research, 2008): 99–108.

131. Michael L. Ray and William L. Wilkie, 'Fear: The potential of an appeal neglected by marketing', *Journal of Marketing* 34(1) (1970): 54–62.

132. Brian Sternthal and C. Samuel Craig, 'Fear appeals: Revisited and revised', *Journal of Consumer Research* 1 (December 1974): 22–34.

133. N.V. Coleman, P. Williams, A.C. Morales and A.E. White, 'Attention, attitudes, and action: When and why incidental

fear increases consumer choice', *Journal of Consumer Research* 44(2) (2017): 283–312.

134. Sara Parry, Rosalind Jones, Philip Stern and Matthew Robinson, 'Shockvertising': An exploratory investigation into attitudinal variations and emotional reactions to shock advertising', *Journal of Consumer Behaviour* 12 (2013): 112–21.

135. Prof. Herbert J. Rotfeld, Auburn University, personal communication (9 December 1997); Herbert J. Rotfeld, 'Fear appeals and persuasion: assumptions and errors in advertising research', *Current Issues and Research in Advertising* 11(1) (1988): 21–40; Michael S. LaTour and Herbert J. Rotfeld, 'There are threats and (maybe) fear-caused arousal: Theory and confusions of appeals to fear and fear arousal itself', *Journal of Advertising* 26(3) (Fall 1997): 45–59.

136. For a classical discussion of the importance of metaphors in our culture, see George Lakoff and Mark Johnson, *Metaphors We Live By* (Chicago, IL: University of Chicago Press, 1980).

137. Richard E. Petty, John T. Cacioppo and David Schumann, 'Central and peripheral routes to advertising effectiveness: The moderating role of involvement', *Journal of Consumer Research* 10(2) (1983): 135–46.

138. Jerry C. Olson, Daniel R. Toy and Philip A. Dover, 'Do cognitive responses mediate the effects of advertising content on cognitive structure?', *Journal of Consumer Research* 9(3) (1982): 245–62.

139. Julie A. Edell and Andrew A. Mitchell, 'An Information Processing Approach to Cognitive Responses', in S.C. Jain (ed.), *Research Frontiers in Marketing: Dialogues and Directions* (Chicago: American Marketing Association, 1978).

140. Philip Kitchen, Gayle Kerr, Don Schultz, Rod McColl and Heather Pals, 'The elaboration likelihood model: review, critique and research agenda', *European Journal of Marketing* 48(11/12) (2014): 2,033–50.

141. Melanie Green and Timothy Brock, 'The role of transportation in the persuasiveness of public narratives', *Journal of Personality and Social Psychology* 79(5) (2000): 701–21.

142. Brendan Richardson, 'It's a fix! The mediative influence of the X factor tribe on narrative transportation as persuasive process', *Journal of Consumer Behaviour* 12 (2013): 122–32.

143. Vikram Dodd, 'Coca-Cola forced to pull Facebook promotion after porn references', Guardian.co.uk (18 July 2010), http://www.guardian.co.uk/business/2010/jul/18/coca-cola-facebook-promotion-porn (accessed 1 September 2018).

Chapter 8
Decision-making

Chapter objectives

When you finish reading this chapter you will understand why:

8.1 The three categories of consumer decision-making are cognitive, habitual and affective.

8.2 A cognitive purchase decision is the outcome of a series of stages that results in the selection of one product over competing options.

8.3 The way information about a product choice is framed can prime a decision, even when the consumer is unaware of this influence.

8.4 We often rely on 'rules of thumb', heuristics or mental short cuts for habitual and routine decision-making.

ELIJAH is really frustrated with his TV. The final straw was when he found it really hard to follow the Six Nations Rugby matches. When he finally went next door – in total exasperation – to watch the rugby on Zoe's new 4K Ultra HD Blu-ray player, he realised what he had been missing out on. Budget or not, it was time to act, as he felt he was miles behind all his friends in getting the latest digital television technology.[1]

Where to start looking? The Web, naturally. Elijah does a quick search on YouTube for OLED TVs (Organic Light-Emitting Diode) – 'a type of display technology that makes it possible to reach dark black levels from ultra-thin screens while, at the same time, making TVs more efficient and eco-friendly'.[2] Elijah then checks out an independent online consumer guide – there's no point in slogging around the shops at this early stage. After narrowing down his options, he ventures out to look at the possible Smart TVs that he has identified. He knows he will get some good advice at the small specialist high-street retailer about the merits of particular brands, so he decides to start there; and then he can hunt around for the best buy by visiting a couple of comparison-shopping websites such as Kelkoo.

(http://www.kelkoo.co.uk/c-100311823-televisions.html) and PriceRunner. He reckons he'll probably find the most affordable models at one of the out-of-town 'big shed' retailers. At the local specialist retailer, Elijah asks some questions of the friendly shop assistant, and gets some useful advice and tips about what features to think about when making his purchase, and one or two recommendations about current good buys. Before leaving the shop, Elijah asks the salesperson to write down the model names and numbers (and prices) for him. Elijah then does some more searching online, this time visiting the manufacturers' and brand websites in order to compare the respective features of the different models more carefully. He reckons that he has now collected all the information he needs for making his decision.

Elijah starts to look at the new OLED TVs. He knows his friend Ehaan has a set by Prime Wave that he really likes, and his fellow hockey player, Lily, has warned him to stay away from the Kamashita. Although Elijah finds a Prime Wave model loaded with tons of features, he chooses the less-expensive Precision 2000X because it will fit neatly onto the wall of the open-plan living room/kitchen in his small terraced house, it had been highly recommended by the high-street specialist retailer, it comes within his budget and, most importantly, it has the feature of a sleep timer.

Margaret K. Hogg

Introduction

8.1

The three categories of consumer decision-making are cognitive, habitual and affective.

Every consumer decision we make is a response to a problem. In Elijah's case it is the perceived need for a new TV, partly because the screen on his existing TV is too small, and partly because he feels he has fallen behind with the trends. Elijah is probably right to feel that he has not kept up with the Joneses. Of course, the type and scope of problems that consumers face vary enormously. Our needs range from simple physiological priorities, such as quenching our thirst, to abstract intellectual quandaries like choosing a university degree course, or aesthetic problems such as what to wear at next summer's Glastonbury Festival.

Because some purchase decisions are more important than others, the amount of effort we put into each one differs. Sometimes the decision-making process is almost automatic; we seem to make snap judgements based on very little information. At other times the decision-making process is far more onerous. A person may literally spend days or weeks agonising over an important purchase such as a new home, a car, or even an iPhone versus an Android phone. We make some decisions very thoughtfully and rationally as we carefully weigh the pros and cons of different choices – while in other cases we let our emotions guide us to one choice over another as we react to a problem with great enthusiasm or even disgust. Still other actions actually contradict what those rational models predict. For example, **purchase momentum** occurs when our initial impulse purchases actually increase the likelihood that we will buy even more (instead of less as we satisfy our needs); it's like we get 'revved up' and plunge into a spending spree (we've all been there!).[3]

Hyperchoice

Ironically one of the biggest problems that many modern consumers face is not having *too few* choices but having *too many*. We describe this profusion of options as **consumer hyperchoice**, a condition where the large number of available options forces us to make repeated choices that may drain our psychological energy while, at the same time, decreasing our abilities to make smart decisions.[4] A German study has argued that, in the face of choice under conditions of high product variety, consumers might disengage and evade the choice process by choosing an avoidant option. In effect, the consumers become paralysed when faced with too much choice.[5] Although we tend to assume that more choice is always better, in fact this preference varies across the world. In some cultures, people prefer to have hard choices made for them. For example, one study compared American and French consumers who live in different medical cultures: the US norm is to emphasise patient autonomy, whereas in France it's more typical for a doctor to make important decisions on behalf of the patient. The researchers studied families that had to decide whether to take their gravely ill infants off life-support. Although the American parents claimed the right to make this almost impossible choice, they also had greater problems with their grief and coping processes than the French parents who left this decision to their doctors.[6]

Given the range of choices to be made, researchers now realise that decision-makers actually possess a *repertoire* of strategies. In a thought process we call **constructive processing**, we evaluate the effort we'll need to make a particular choice and then tailor the amount of cognitive 'effort' we expend to get the job done.[7] When the task requires a well-thought-out, rational approach, we'll invest the brainpower to do it. Otherwise, we look for short cuts or mental heuristics such as 'I'll do what I usually do', or perhaps we make 'gut' decisions based on our emotional reactions. In some cases, we may actually create a **mental budget** that helps us to estimate what we will consume over time so that we can regulate what we do in the present – for instance, the dieter using the 5:2 principle carefully regulates what they consume on their fasting days.[8] Research also hints that people differ in terms of their **cognitive processing style**. Some of us tend to have a *rational system of cognition* that processes information analytically and sequentially using rules of logic, whereas others rely on an *experiential system of cognition* that processes information more holistically and in parallel.[9]

Self-regulation

One way to think about consumer decision-making is in terms of three broad categories, as Figure 8.1 shows. We're going to consider each of these types of decision-making in turn, but bear in mind that they don't necessarily work independently of one another. These ideas really

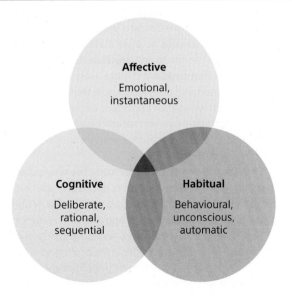

Figure 8.1 Three broad and interrelated types of consumer decision-making

relate to types of decision-making because they remind us that, depending on the situation and the importance of what we are dealing with, our choices can be dominated by 'hot' emotions, 'cold' information processing, or even 'lukewarm' snap decisions. Think, for example, about Emily, who has decided to embark on a weight-loss programme. A person's efforts to change or maintain her actions over time, whether these involve dieting, living on a budget, or training to run a marathon, involve planning that is a form of **self-regulation**. If we have a self-regulatory strategy, this means that we specify in advance how we want to respond in certain situations. These 'if-then plans' or **implementation intentions** may dictate how much weight we give to different kinds of information (emotional or cognitive), a timetable to carry out a decision, or even how we will deal with disruptive influences that might interfere with our plans (such as a bossy salesperson who tries to steer us to a different choice).[10]

Emily, for instance, may engage in cognitive decision-making as she carefully selects a diet and perhaps compiles a list of foods that are 'banned' from her kitchen. Secondly, she may have to recognise that she has a behavioural pattern of snacking on junk food in the mid-afternoon whether she's really hungry or not. Emily may have to 'argue' with herself as she weighs the long-term benefits of a successful diet against short-term temptations such as that inviting chocolate bar sitting on her desk. In some cases, this involves some creative tinkering with the facts – for example, consumers engage in **counteractive construal** when they exaggerate the negative aspects of behaviours that will interfere with the ultimate goal.[11] Emily may inflate the number of calories the snack contains as one way to resist its lure. But, as every dieter knows, we don't always win this argument.

In recent years, researchers and marketers have become more aware of the role they can play in changing consumer behaviour by helping people to regulate their own actions. This help may take the form of simple feedback, such as a phone app for dieters, or perhaps a wearable computing device that tells you how many steps you take in a day (and how many more you should take). These applications provide a **feedback loop** to help with self-regulation. The basic premise is simple: provide people with information about their actions in real time, and then give them a chance to change those actions so that you push them to improve. A common feedback loop we increasingly see while we are driving along comes from those 'dynamic speed displays' that use a radar sensor to flash 'Your Speed' when you pass one. This isn't new information; all you have to do is look at your own speedometer to know the same thing. Yet, on average, these displays result in a 10 per cent reduction in driving speed among motorists for several miles following exposure to the feedback loop.[12]

Now, the bad news: As any frustrated dieter knows, self-regulation doesn't necessarily work. Just because we devise a well-meaning strategy doesn't mean we'll follow it. Sometimes our best-laid intentions go awry literally because we're too tired to fight temptation. Research shows that our ability to self-regulate declines as the day goes on. The **Morning Morality Effect** shows that people are more likely to cheat, lie or even commit fraud in the afternoon than in the morning. Scientists know that the part of the brain they call the **executive control centre**, which we use for important decision-making, including moral judgements, can be worn down or distracted by even simple tasks such as memorising numbers.[13] As one researcher nicely put it, 'To the extent that you're cognitively tired, you're more likely to give in to the devil on your shoulder'.[14]

Other studies show that, ironically, the very act of planning itself can undermine our ability to attain goals. When a person is not happy with his or her progress towards a goal, such as weight loss, the act of thinking about what he or she needs to do to improve performance can cause emotional distress. This angst in turn results in less self-control.[15]

Finally, emotional responses also drive many of our choices, such as feelings of inferiority or low self-esteem, or of anger, guilt or disgust. In some situations, people consume products (especially food) as a reaction to prior life experiences such as the loss of a loved one or perhaps abuse as a child. Obviously these would be extreme cases, but they illustrate the role that emotion often plays — a dieter like Emily may feel elated when she weighs in at 3 lbs less than last week; however, if she fails to make progress she may become discouraged and actually sabotage herself with a binge on chocolate bars.[16]

Types of consumer decisions: extended, limited and habitual problem-solving

A different but also helpful way to characterise the decision-making process (which links to the more detailed discussion below of the steps in the cognitive decision-making process) is to consider the amount of effort that goes into the decision each time we must make it. Consumer researchers have found it convenient to think in terms of a continuum, which is anchored at one end by extended problem-solving and at the other extreme by habitual decision-making (see later in the chapter). Many decisions fall somewhere in the middle, and so we characterise these as limited problem-solving. This continuum is presented in Figure 8.2.

Extended problem-solving

Decisions involving **extended problem-solving** correspond most closely to the traditional cognitive decision-making perspective (see the next section on 'Cognitive decision-making'). As indicated in Table 8.1, we usually initiate this careful process when the decision we have to make relates to our self-concept (see Chapter 4), and we feel that the outcome may be risky in some way. In that case we try to collect as much information as possible, both from our memory (internal search) and from outside sources such as Google or YouTube (as Elijah did when looking for information about Smart TVs – external search). Based on the importance of the decision, we carefully evaluate each product alternative, often considering the attributes of one brand at a time and seeing how each brand's attributes shape up to some set of desired characteristics or outcomes that we hope to achieve through our choice (see the section on decision-making rules later in the chapter).

Limited problem-solving

Limited problem-solving is usually more straightforward and simple. In this case we are not nearly as motivated to search for information or to evaluate each alternative rigorously. Instead, we are likely to use simple *decision rules* to choose among alternatives. These cognitive short cuts (see below) enable consumers to fall back on general guidelines, instead of having to start from scratch every time we need to make a decision.

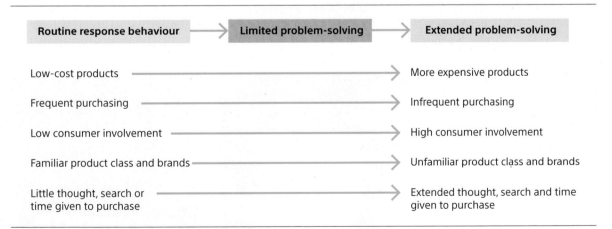

Figure 8.2 A continuum of buying decision behavior

Table 8.1 Characteristics of limited *vs* extended problem-solving

	Limited problem-solving	**Extended problem-solving**
Motivation	Low risk and involvement	High risk and involvement
Information search	Little search	Extensive search
	Information processed passively	Information processed actively
	In-store decision likely	Multiple sources consulted prior to store visits
Alternative evaluation	Weakly held beliefs	Strongly held beliefs
	Only most prominent criteria used	Many criteria used
	Alternatives perceived as basically similar	Significant differences perceived among alternatives
	Non-compensatory strategy used	Compensatory strategy used
Purchase	Limited shopping time; may prefer self-service	Many outlets visited if necessary
	Choice often influenced by store displays	Communication with store personnel often desirable

Cognitive decision-making

8.2

A cognitive purchase decision is the outcome of a series of stages that results in the selection of one product over competing options.

Now, let's go back and look more closely at the three different decision-making perspectives we described earlier (Figure 8.1), starting with the classic cognitive decision-making approach. Traditionally, consumer researchers approached decision-making from an **information-processing perspective**, i.e. a **rational perspective**. According to this view, people calmly and carefully integrate as much information as possible with what they already know about a product, painstakingly weigh the pluses and minuses of each alternative and arrive at a satisfactory decision. This kind of careful, deliberate thinking is especially relevant to activities such as financial planning that call for a lot of attention to detail, and many choices that impact a consumer's quality of life (unfortunately, most of us seem to be better at planning for the short term than thinking ahead to the future).[17]

When marketing managers believe that their customers do, in fact, undergo this kind of planning, they should carefully study the steps in decision-making to understand just how consumers weigh information, form beliefs about options and choose the criteria they will use to select one option over others. With these insights in mind, they can develop products and promotional strategies that supply the specific information people look for in the most effective formats.[18]

Two of the most powerful global brands.

Songquan Deng/Shutterstock.com
Bikeworldtravel/Shutterstock.com.

However, even the traditional view of decision-making recognises that we tend to be 'cognitive misers', who do what we can to simplify our choices if possible. The **economics of information** perspective assumes that we collect just as much data as we need to make an informed decision. We form expectations of the value of additional information and continue to search to the extent that the rewards of doing so (what economists call the *utility*) exceed the costs. This utilitarian assumption also implies that we collect the most valuable units of information first. We absorb additional pieces only to the extent that we think they will add to what we already know.[19] In other words, we'll put ourselves out to collect as much information as we can, so long as the process isn't too onerous or time-consuming.[20]

Steps in the cognitive decision-making process

Elijah's situation, which we described in the opening vignette, is similar to that encountered by many consumers at different points in their lives (even deciding not to make any decision is still a decision). Elijah did not suddenly wake up and crave a new Smart TV. He went through several steps between feeling the need (translated into a want) for a better-quality television picture for watching sport, and actually purchasing a new television.

These steps can be described as: (1) problem recognition; (2) **information search**; (3) evaluation of alternatives; (4) product choice; and (5) post-purchase evaluation. After the decision is made, the quality of that decision affects the final step in the process, when learning occurs based on how well the choice worked out (see Figure 8.3). This learning process influences the likelihood that the same choice will be made the next time the need for a similar decision occurs. There is also evidence that suggests that 'more optimistic expectations of future goal pursuit . . . have a greater impact on immediate choices'.[21]

STEP 1: Problem recognition

Problem recognition occurs when we experience a significant difference between our current state of affairs and some desired or ideal state. We realise that to get from here to there we need to solve a problem, which may be large or small, simple or complex. A person who unexpectedly runs out of petrol has a problem, as does the person who becomes dissatisfied with the image of their car, even though there may be nothing mechanically wrong with it. Although the quality of Elijah's TV had not changed, for example, his *standard of comparison* had altered, and he was confronted with a desire he did not have prior to watching his friend Zoe's 4K Ultra HD Blu-ray player.

Problem creation

Figure 8.4 shows that a problem can arise in one of two ways. As in the case of the person who runs out of petrol, the quality of the consumer's *actual state* can sometimes move downwards or decrease (*need recognition*). On the other hand, as in the case of the person who craves a high-performance car, the consumer's *ideal state* can move upward (*opportunity recognition*). Either way, a gulf occurs between the actual state and the ideal state.[22] In Elijah's case, a problem was perceived as a result of opportunity recognition – his ideal state in terms of the television reception and viewing quality that he wanted.

Marketers' role in problem creation

While problem recognition can and does occur naturally, this process is often spurred on by marketing efforts. In some cases, marketers attempt to create *primary demand*, where consumers are encouraged to use a product or service regardless of the brand they choose. Such needs are often encouraged in the early stages of a product's life cycle – as, for example, when mobile phones and then smartphones[23] were first introduced. *Secondary demand,*

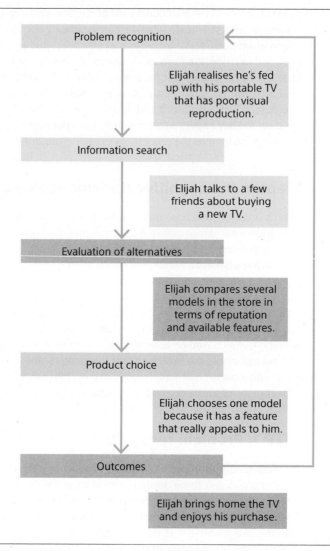

Figure 8.3 Steps in consumer decision-making

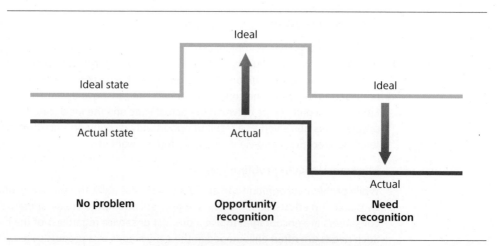

Figure 8.4 Problem recognition: shifts in actual or ideal states

where consumers are prompted to prefer a specific brand instead of others (e.g. Apple iPhones), can occur only if primary demand already exists. At this point, marketers must convince consumers that a problem can be best solved by choosing their brand over others in the same category.

STEP 2: Information search

Once a problem has been recognised, consumers need adequate information to resolve it. Information search is the process by which the consumer surveys their environment for appropriate data to make a reasonable decision. In this section we will review some of the factors this search involves.[24]

Types of information search

A consumer may recognise a need and then search the marketplace for specific information (a process called *pre-purchase search*). On the other hand, many consumers, especially veteran shoppers, enjoy browsing just for the fun of it, or because they like to stay up to date with what's happening in the marketplace. Those shopaholics are engaging in *ongoing search*.[25] Some differences between these two types of search are described in Table 8.2.

Internal vs external search

Information sources can be roughly broken down into two kinds: internal and external. Whether we are hard-core shoppers or not, each of us has some degree of knowledge already in memory about many products, either as a result of prior experiences or simply from living in a consumer culture. When confronted with a purchase decision, we may engage in *internal search* by scanning our own memory bank to assemble information about different product alternatives (see Chapter 5). Usually, though, even the most market-aware of us needs to supplement this knowledge with external search, by which we obtain the information from advertisements, social media, friends, or just plain people-watching.

How much do we search?

As a general rule, we search more when the purchase is important, when we have more of a need to learn more about the purchase, or when it's easy to obtain the relevant information.[26]

Table 8.2 A framework for consumer information search

	Pre-purchase search	**Ongoing search**
Determinants	Involvement in the purchase Market environment Situational factors	Involvement with the product Market environment Situational factors
Motives	Making better purchase decisions	Building a bank of information for future use Experiencing fun and pleasure
Outcomes	Increased product and market knowledge Better purchase decisions Increased satisfaction with the purchase outcome	Increased product and market knowledge, leading to – future buying efficiencies – personal influences Increased impulse buying Increased satisfaction from search and other outcomes

Source: Peter H. Bloch, Daniel L. Sherrell and Nancy M. Ridgway, 'Consumer search: an extended framework', *Journal of Consumer Research* 13(1) 1986: 120. Copyright © 1986, Oxford University Press by permission of Oxford University Press.

Consumers differ in the amount of search they tend to undertake, regardless of the product category in question. All things being equal, younger, better-educated people who enjoy the shopping/fact-finding process tend to conduct more information searches. Women are more inclined to search than men, as are those who place greater value on style and the image they present.[27]

Does knowing something about the product make it more or less likely that we will engage in search? The answer to this question isn't as obvious as it first appears. Product experts and novices use very different strategies when they make decisions. 'Newbies', who know little about a product, should be the most motivated to find out more about it. However, experts are more familiar with the product category, so they should be better able to understand the meaning of any new product information they might acquire.

So, who searches more? The answer is neither. Search tends to be greatest among those consumers who are *moderately knowledgeable* about the product. Typically, we find an inverted-U relationship between knowledge and external search effort, as Figure 8.5 shows. People with very limited expertise may not feel they are competent to search extensively. In fact, they may not even know where to start. Elijah, who did not spend a lot of time researching his purchase, is typical. He visited one store, did a couple of searches on the internet and looked only at brands with which he was already familiar. In addition, he focused on only a small number of product features.[28]

Because experts have a better sense of what information is relevant to the decision, they engage in *selective search*, which means their efforts are more focused and efficient. In contrast, novices are more likely to rely on the opinions of others and on 'non-functional' attributes, such as brand name and price, to distinguish among alternatives. Finally, novice consumers may process information in a 'top-down' rather than a 'bottom-up' manner – they focus less on details than on the big picture. For instance, they may be more impressed by the sheer amount of technical information an ad presents than by the actual significance of the claims it makes.[29]

Online search and decision-making

With the tremendous number of websites and apps available and the huge number of people who spend so much of their day online, how can people organise information and decide where to click? A **cybermediary** is often the answer. This term describes a website or app that helps to filter and organise online market information so that customers can identify and evaluate alternatives more efficiently. Many consumers regularly link to comparison-shopping sites, such as Bizrate.com or Pricerunner.co.uk, for example, which list many online

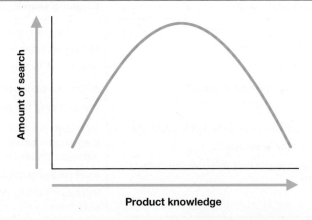

Figure 8.5 The relationship between amount of information search and product knowledge

retailers that sell a given item along with the price each site charges.[30] Elijah used Kelkoo and Pricerunner for his price comparison searches. *Directories* and *portals*, such as Yahoo!, are general services that tie together a large variety of different sites. *Forums, fan clubs* and *user groups* offer product-related discussions to help customers sift through options. **Intelligent agents** are sophisticated software programs that use *collaborative filtering* technologies to learn from past user behaviour in order to recommend new purchases.[31] When you let Amazon.com suggest a new book, the site uses an intelligent agent to propose novels based on what you and others like you have bought in the past.

What's the most common way for us to conduct information search today? 'Google it', of course! Although there are other **search engines** out there, such as Microsoft's Bing, Yahoo! or even YouTube, Google's version of the software that examines the Web for matches to terms such as 'home theatre system' or 'tattoo removal services' is so dominant – with 96 per cent of the world's mobile search market – that the name has become a verb. However, even a giant like Google can't rest on its laurels, because changes in how we search will probably reduce our reliance on search engines. Increasingly, consumers are bypassing Google as they go directly on their smartphones or tablets to apps such as Yelp to read and write product reviews.[32] Elijah also used the internet for informal information gathering, and then for price searching when looking for his new Smart TV, thus integrating the net into his search activities.

However, as anyone who's ever Googled knows, the Web delivers enormous amounts of product and retailer information in seconds. The biggest problem Web surfers face these days is to narrow down their choices, not to beef them up. In cyberspace, simplification is key. Still, the sad reality is that in many cases we simply don't search as much as we might. If we Google a term, most of us are only likely to look at the first few results at the top of the list.

Indeed, that's one reason why **search engine optimisation (SEO)** is so important today; this term refers to the procedures companies use to design the content of websites and posts to maximise the likelihood that their content will show up when someone searches for a relevant term. Their goal is to persuade people to access their content above all others'. Just like an expert fisherman chooses his spot and carefully selects the right bait to catch a fish, SEO experts create online content that will attract the attention of the *search algorithms*, or mathematical formula, that companies such as Google use to determine which entries will turn up in a search. The algorithm will hunt for certain keywords, and it also will consider who uses them. For example, if a lot of influential people share an entry, the formula will weight it more.

This ad shows how both the internet and smartphone apps can be used in decision-making, in this case in terms of managing financial decisions and money management using digital banking.

f8 archive/Alamy Stock Photo

Site creators try to ensure that they use the right keywords and that these show up in one or more elements of the post, including:

- *Meta tag:* code embedded in a Web page. Meta tags are visible to site visitors but only by viewing the source code for the page.
- *Title tag:* an HTML tag that defines the page's title. The title is displayed in the browser's title bar, in search engine results and in RSS feeds.
- *Heading tag:* an HTML tag that is used to section and describe content.
- *Title:* the headline or the main indicator of a page's content. While a traditional headline in a magazine article may be indirect, an optimised title needs to be more literal. Search algorithms are smart, but they don't get puns or jokes. For example, a print ad for an expensive Louis Vuitton handbag may read 'High Fashion Replicas Indistinguishable from the Real Thing'. An optimised title might read 'Shop Wise: 5 Tips for Ensuring that a Vuitton Bag is Real, Not Fake, Fashion', to ensure that the search would index on keywords such as *Vuitton, shop* and *bag.* Titles also should use a **hook** that increases the likelihood people will click on it. Social media pros refer to this careful crafting of a title that markets the content as 'link-baiting'.[33]

Can you imagine choosing a restaurant before you check it out online? Increasingly, many of us rely on online reviews to steer us towards and away from specific restaurants, hotels, films, clothes, music and just about everything else. A survey of 28,000 respondents in 56 countries reported that online user ratings are the second most-trusted source of brand information (after recommendations from family and friends).

Regardless of their accuracy, customer product reviews are a key driver of satisfaction and loyalty. Another advantage these reviews provide is that consumers learn about other, less popular options they may like as well – and at the same time products such as films and books that aren't 'blockbusters' are more likely to sell. At the online DVD rental company Netflix, for example, fellow subscribers recommend about two-thirds of the films that people order.[34] The huge growth in demand for user reviews in turn fuels new opinion-based sites, such as TripAdvisor for travel and Zomato for restaurants. People who take the time to post to these sites don't do it for money, but they do generate an income in the form of props for good recommendations. Analysts refer to this reward system as the **reputation economy**: many thousands of consumers devote significant time to editing Wikipedia entries, serving as brand advocates, or uploading clips to YouTube simply because they enjoy the process and want to boost their reputation as knowledgeable advisors.[35]

This aspect of online customer review is one important factor that's fuelling an important business model called the **long tail**.[36] The basic idea is that companies no longer need to rely solely on big hits (such as blockbuster movies or best-selling books) to find profits. Companies can also make money if they sell small amounts of items that only a few people want – *if* they sell enough different items. For example, Amazon.com maintains a stock of nearly four million books, compared to the 100,000 or so you'll find in a large retail store such as Waterstone's. Most of these stores will sell only a few thousand copies (if that), but the nearly four million books that Waterstone's *doesn't* carry make up a quarter of Amazon's revenues. Other examples of the long tail include successful microbreweries and TV networks that make money on reruns of old shows on channels such as ITV3 or Gold in the UK.

Researchers work hard to understand how consumers find information online, and in particular how they react to and integrate recommendations received from different kinds of online agents into their own product choices. An **electronic recommendation agent** is a software tool that tries to understand a human decision-maker's multi-attribute preferences for a product category as it asks the user to communicate his/her preferences. Based on those data, the software then recommends a list of alternatives sorted by the degree to which they fit these criteria. These agents do appear to influence consumers' decision-making, though some evidence indicates that they're more effective when they recommend a product based

Ask Jeeves, one of the popular search engines/shopping 'bots' available on the Web to simplify the consumer decision-making process via online searches.

Newscast Online Limited/Alamy Stock Photo

on utilitarian attributes (functionality such as nutritional value) rather than hedonic attributes (such as design or taste).[37] Although engineers continually improve the ability of electronic recommendation agents to suggest new things we might like, we still rely on other people to guide our search. About 80 per cent of online shoppers rely on customer reviews before they buy. We call the people who supply these reviews **brand advocates**. Yahoo! estimates that 40 per cent of people who spend time online are advocates and that they influence purchases two to one over non-advocates. Marketers who adjust their strategies to acknowledge this impact find it's worth their while.[38]

Do consumers always search rationally?

This assumption of rational search is not always supported. As we've seen, consumers don't necessarily engage in a rational search process where they carefully identify every alternative before choosing the one they prefer. The amount of external search that we do for most products is surprisingly small, even when we would benefit from having more information. For example, lower-income shoppers, who have more to lose by making a bad purchase, actually search *less* prior to buying than more affluent people do.[39] Like Elijah, some consumers typically visit only one or two stores and often don't seek out unbiased information sources prior to making a purchase decision, especially when there is little time to do so.[40] This pattern is especially prevalent for decisions regarding durable goods such as appliances or cars, even when these products represent significant investments. There is also some evidence that even having information available on the product packaging does not necessarily mean that consumers make use of it.

This tendency to avoid external search is less prevalent when consumers consider the purchase of symbolic items such as clothing. In those cases, not surprisingly, people tend to do a fair amount of external search, although most of it involves seeking the opinions of peers.[41] Although the stakes may be lower financially, people may see these self-expressive decisions as having dire social consequences if they make the wrong choice. The level of perceived risk, a concept to be discussed next, is high.

Perceived risk

As a rule, purchase decisions that involve extensive search also entail some kind of **perceived risk**, or the belief that the product has potentially negative consequences from using or not using the product or service. Perceived risk may be present if the product is expensive or is complex and difficult to understand, or if the brand is unfamiliar. Mood effects on consumers'

	Buyers most sensitive to risk	Purchases most subject to risk
Monetary risk	Risk capital consists of money and property. Those with relatively little income and wealth are most vulnerable.	High-price items that require substantial expenditures are most subject to this form of risk.
Functional risk	Risk capital consists of alternate means of performing the function or meeting the need. Practical consumers are most sensitive.	Products or services whose purchase and use requires the buyer's exclusive commitment and precludes redundancy are most sensitive.
Physical risk	Risk capital consists of physical vigour, health and vitality. Those who are elderly, frail, or in ill health are most vulnerable.	Mechanical or electrical goods (such as vehicles or flammables), drugs and medical treatment, and food and beverages are most sensitive.
Social risk	Risk capital consists of self-esteem and self-confidence. Those who are insecure and uncertain are most sensitive.	Socially visible or symbolic goods, such as clothes, jewellery, cars, homes, or sports equipment are most subject to it.
Psycho-logical risk	Risk capital consists of affiliations and status. Those lacking self-respect or attractiveness to peers are most sensitive.	Expensive personal luxuries that may engender guilt; durables; and services whose use demands self-discipline or sacrifice are most sensitive.

Figure 8.6 Five types of perceived risk

attitudes and perceptions about risk are stronger when brands are unfamiliar.[42] Perceived risk can also be a factor when a product choice is visible to others and we run the risk of embarrassment if we make the wrong choice.[43]

Figure 8.6 lists five kinds of risk – including objective (e.g. physical danger) and subjective factors (e.g. social embarrassment) – as well as the products that tend to be affected by each type. As this figure notes, perceived risk is less of a problem for consumers who have greater 'risk capital' because they have less to lose by making a poor choice. For example, a highly self-confident person might worry less about the social risk inherent in a product, whereas a more vulnerable, insecure consumer might be reluctant to take a chance with a product or brand that might not be seen as cool and thus not be accepted by peers. Within the EU, complaints about the physical risks associated with consumer products are particularly related to the categories of toys, clothing, textiles and fashion items, electrical appliances, motor vehicles, lighting equipment and childcare articles and children's equipment.[44] A study of Italian consumers suggested that the issue of food safety was the major determining influence in the motivation of regular consumers of organic foods, whereas occasional organic food consumers were influenced by ethical issues.[45]

Professor Mitchell highlights the risk to privacy in the current data-rich age; and this is an ongoing hot topic. In 2014 the European Court of Justice (ECJ) ruled that 'irrelevant' and outdated data should be erased on request. Since then, Google has received requests to

Consumer Behaviour as I See it . . .

Consumer behaviour in a data-rich world

Professor Vincent-Wayne Mitchell
The University of Sydney Business School

'A general conclusion we can draw about consumer behaviour in the 21st century is that "life's more complicated". For example, some say 90% of the world's data has been created in the past two years, and that consumers are estimated to make around 35,000 decisions each day. Therefore, more consumers are facing more decisions with more data than ever before. This has implications for two main stakeholders who have to deal with this, namely: consumers themselves, and companies.

For consumers, choice and information overload will become greater problems at every stage of the consumer decision-making process. As we live more complicated lives, there are more opportunities for marketers to identify and promote to us, "need" opportunities or "problems" for which they have a product. As more people spend more time online, they can be exposed to problem identification, search and purchase within seconds rather than hours, days or weeks as it used to be. Thus, decision-making cycles are radically reduced. Yet, thanks to the internet, search for solutions and information about them has become bewildering and, in some categories, overwhelming. This means that the evaluation of choices is more complicated. When faced with more choices and more data about those choices, but shorter decision-making cycles, extended decision-making in a faster-paced world is likely to diminish, being replaced by simpler heuristic-based decision-making. These heuristics, such as purchasing on cheapest price, most well-known product, or top-rated reviews on TripAdvisor, simplify the decision. However, this type of low-involvement decision-making is more prone to cognitive biases such as confirmation bias, anchoring, bandwagon effects, and recency bias. Other examples include the problems of; salience, i.e., taking into account only easily recognized features; and the clustering illusion, which is seeing patterns in random events which don't really exist. As the brain is a pattern-recognizing machine, this is a natural consequence of having so much information. Thus, we might expect consumers to make more 'sub-optimal' decisions in the future.

For companies such as retailers, Google, Facebook and credit card providers, who are able to track our decision-making processes, this means companies are beginning to know us better than we know ourselves. Knowing what consumers have bought is one of the greatest predictors of what we will buy in the future, so it's extremely valuable information to companies. However, companies are aware of and can exploit the cognitive biases we are prone to in data-rich environments. For example, in the search and evaluation phases, the number of brands consumers can consider expands rather than narrows as customers are able to access more information. This means new brands are better able to influence and interrupt the decision-making process by entering the consideration set than before. Also, because of the highly-targeted message ability of platforms such as Facebook, brands can feed us information that confirms our existing biased views on products, thus exacerbating confirmation bias. Finally, a major source of search information are other consumers' actions, preferences and opinions and these influence us. In this hyper-interconnected world, decisions about the adoption of new products are made more quickly because information about others' adoption is more readily available, which reduces risk and speeds up adoption. As a consequence, product life cycles become shorter as people move on more quickly to buy the latest thing. In contrast, anti-consumption messages, such as boycotts, also spread more quickly.

Interconnectivity and the abundance of others' data should facilitate consumer power in the 21st century marketplace as never before. However, the explosion of data about consumers, as companies find more ways to track consumers' search, evaluation, purchase and post-purchase behaviour, has pros and cons. It can have advantages for consumers in that they receive more targeted messages and product suggestions. However, it also poses a larger privacy risk for consumers than ever before. Some suggest that personal data are the new 'oil' and consumers need to be rightly wary of the by-product of mining, processing and exploiting for massive profit this valuable asset, which is privacy loss and consequent damage. Like a secret, once given away it's almost impossible to get back and control of it is lost forever, making life in this more complicated world, even more complicated.'

Question

Identify and evaluate the implications for consumers and companies of this data-rich world.

remove at least 2.4million links from search results. Search engine firms can reject applications if they believe the public interest in accessing the information outweighs a right to privacy. . . A Google spokesperson said: 'We work hard to comply with the right to be forgotten, but we take great care not to remove search results that are in the public interest and will defend the public's right to access lawful information'.[46] The right to be forgotten has been the subject of two court cases in the UK. In one the complainant was unsuccessful in getting his/her information removed from his/her profile; but in the second case the complainant successfully argued in court his/her case for the removal of information about spent convictions from his/her online profile.[47]

STEP 3: Evaluation of alternatives

Much of the effort we put into a purchase decision occurs at the stage in which a choice must be made from the available alternatives. This may not be easy; modern consumer society abounds with choices. In some cases, there may be literally hundreds of different brands (as in cigarettes) or different variations of the same brand (as in shades of lipstick), each clamouring for our attention.

Ask a friend to name all the brands of perfume she can think of. The odds are she will reel off three to five names rather quickly, then stop and think awhile before she comes up with a few more. She's probably very familiar with the first set of brands, and in fact she probably wears one or more of these. Her list may also contain one or two brands that she doesn't like; to the contrary, they come to mind because she thinks she doesn't like the way they smell or she might think that they are unsophisticated. Note also that there are many, many more brands on the market that she did not name at all.

If your friend goes to buy perfume, it is likely that she will consider buying some or most of the brands she listed initially. She might also entertain a few more possibilities if these come to her attention while she's at the fragrance counter (for example, if an employee approaches her with a scent sample as she walks down the shopping aisle).

Identifying alternatives

How do we decide which criteria are important, and how do we narrow-down product alternatives to an acceptable number and eventually choose one instead of the others? The answer varies depending upon the decision-making process we are using. Social media does not necessarily make things easier. A recent study established that 'irrelevant reviews that are negatively valenced signal to consumers that they can be confident that their information is complete, and that their positive impression is accurate, thus boosting positive evaluations. This effect is not intuitive, as consumers and sellers alike expect irrelevant information to undermine, rather than support related positive information'.[48] What this means for marketers is that it might be useful for sellers 'to accept and encourage a small number of irrelevant reviews with negative ratings, rather than trying to prevent consumers from seeing them.'[49]

A consumer engaged in extended problem-solving (as described above, Table 8.1) may carefully evaluate several brands, whereas someone making a habitual decision may not consider any alternatives to their normal brand. Furthermore, some evidence indicates that we do more extended processing in situations that arouse negative emotions due to conflicts among the available choices. This is most likely to occur when there are difficult trade-offs – for example, when a person must choose between the risks involved in undergoing a heart bypass operation versus the potential improvement in their life if the operation is successful.[50]

We call the alternatives a consumer knows about their **evoked set**; and the ones they actually consider their **consideration set** (because often we do not seriously consider every single brand in a category because of issues such as price, a prior negative experience and so on).[51] The evoked set comprises those products already in memory (the retrieval set), plus those prominent in the retail environment. For example, recall that Elijah did not know much about the technical aspects of Smart TVs, and he had only a few major brands in memory. Of these, two were acceptable possibilities and one was not. The alternatives that the consumer is aware of but would not consider buying are their *inept set*, while those not under consideration at all comprise the *inert set*. You can easily guess which set marketers want their brands to appear in. These categories are depicted in Figure 8.7.

Consumers often include a surprisingly small number of alternatives in their evoked set. One study combined results from several large-scale investigations of consumers' evoked sets. It found that people overall include a small number of products in these sets, although this amount varies by product category and across countries.[52]

For obvious reasons, a marketer who finds that their brand is not in their target market's evoked set has cause to worry. You don't often get a second chance to make a good first impression. A consumer is not likely to place a product in her evoked set after she has already considered it and rejected it. Indeed, we are more likely to add a new brand to the evoked set than one that we had previously considered but passed over, even after a marketer has provided additional positive information about the brand.[53,54] For marketers, consumers' unwillingness to give a rejected product a second chance underlines the importance of ensuring that it performs well from the time it is first introduced.

Product categorisation

Remember that when consumers process product information, they do not do so in a vacuum. Instead, they evaluate a product stimulus in terms of what they already know about a product

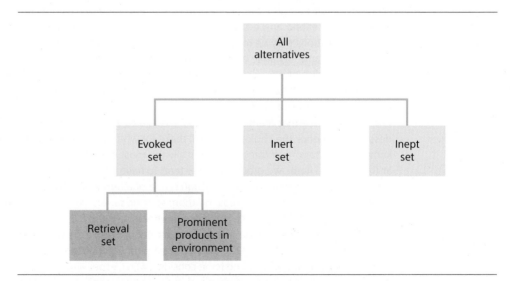

Figure 8.7 Identifying alternatives: getting in the game

or other similar products. A person evaluating a particular digital camera will most likely compare it with other digital cameras rather than with a 35mm camera or a smartphone. Since the category in which a product is placed determines the other products it will be compared with, *categorisation* is a crucial determinant of how a product is evaluated. These classifications derive from different product attributes, including appearance (e.g. we assume that chocolates in silver or gold wrappings are more upscale), price (we view items with price endings in .99 as cheaper than those that end in .00), or previously learned connections (if it has the name 'Porsche' on it, it must be expensive).[55] And, sometimes, companies like to play with these categories; they create new ones when they introduce **hybrid products** that feature characteristics from two distinct domains. Thus, we have the crossover utility vehicle (CUV), which mixes a passenger car and a sport utility vehicle (SUV).

A recent study that examined how consumers use calorie information demonstrates why the categories we use to define products are important. When people saw menus that listed the calorie count of individual items, they chose more dietetic items. However, when the lower-calorie items were grouped into a single 'low-calorie' category on the menu, diners actually selected them less frequently. The researchers explain that consumers have negative associations with low-calorie labels, so they're more likely to dismiss these options in the early stages of the decision process. As a result, individual items are less likely to make it into diners' consideration sets so, ironically, this menu information results in less healthier choices overall.[56]

The products in a consumer's evoked set are likely to share some similar features. This process can either help or hurt a product, depending on what people compare it with. When faced with a new product, consumers refer to their already existing knowledge in familiar product categories to form new knowledge.[57] We tend to place the new product into an existing category rather than create a whole new category.[58] Of course, that's one of the big hurdles a new form of technology has to clear: before people will buy a smartphone, tablet, MP3 player or GPS, they need to make sense of the category to which it belongs.

It is important to understand how consumers cognitively represent this information in a **knowledge structure** – a set of beliefs and the way we organise these beliefs in our minds.[59] (We discussed these knowledge structures in Chapter 6.)[60] Their make-up matters to marketers because they want to ensure that customers correctly group their products.

Levels of categorisation

Not only do people group things into categories, but these groupings occur at different levels of specificity. Typically, we represent a product in a cognitive structure at one of three levels. To understand this idea, consider how someone might respond to these questions about an ice cream: what other products share similar characteristics, and which would be considered as alternatives to eating an ice cream?

These questions may be more complex than they first appear. At one level, an ice cream is similar to an apple, because both could be eaten as a dessert. At another level, an ice cream is similar to a slice of pie, because both are eaten for dessert and both are fattening. At still another level, an ice cream is similar to an ice cream sundae – both are eaten for dessert, are made of ice cream and are fattening.

It is easy to see that the items a person associates with – say, the category 'fattening dessert' – influence the choices they will make for what to eat after dinner. The middle level, known as the *basic level category*, is typically the most useful in classifying products, because at this level the items we group together tend to have a lot in common with each other, but still permit us to consider a broad enough range of alternatives. The broader *superordinate category* is more abstract, whereas the more specific *subordinate category* often includes individual brands.[61] These three levels are depicted in Figure 8.8.

Of course, not all items fit equally well into a category. Apple pie is a better example of the subordinate category 'pie' than is rhubarb pie, even though both are types of pie. Apple pie is thus more *prototypical*, and would tend to be considered first, especially by category novices. In contrast, pie experts will tend to have knowledge about both typical and atypical category examples.[62]

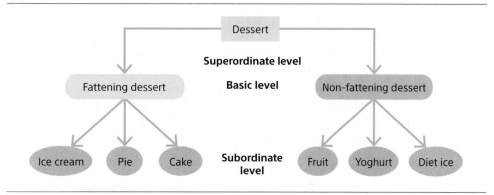

Figure 8.8 Levels of abstraction in categories of dessert

Strategic implications of product categorisation

The way we categorise products has many strategic implications. This process affects which products consumers will compare with our product and also the criteria they will use to decide if they like us or our competitors.

Position a product

The success of a *positioning strategy* often hinges on the marketer's ability to convince the consumer that their product should be considered within a given category. For example, the orange juice industry tried to reposition orange juice as a drink that could be enjoyed all day long ('It's not just for breakfast any more'). On the other hand, soft drinks companies are now attempting the opposite by portraying carbonated drinks as suitable for breakfast consumption. They are trying to make their way into consumers' 'breakfast drink' category, along with orange juice, grapefruit juice, tea and coffee. Of course, this strategy can backfire, as PepsiCo discovered when it introduced Pepsi AM and positioned it as a coffee substitute. The company did such a good job of categorising the drink as a morning beverage that customers wouldn't drink it at any other time, and the product failed.[63]

Identify competitors

At the abstract, superordinate level, many different product forms compete for membership. The category 'entertainment' might comprise both bowling and the ballet, but not many people would consider the substitution of one of these activities for the other. Products and services that, on the surface, are quite different, however, actually compete with each other at a broad level for consumers' discretionary cash. While bowling or ballet may not be a likely trade-off for many people, it is feasible, for example, that a symphony orchestra might try to lure away season ticket-holders to the ballet by positioning itself as an equivalent member of the category 'cultural event'.[64]

We are often faced with choices between non-comparable categories, where we cannot directly relate the attributes of one category to those in another category (the old problem of comparing apples and oranges). When we can create an overlapping category that encompasses both items (for instance, entertainment, value, usefulness) and then rate each alternative in terms of that superordinate category comparison, the process is easier.[65]

Create an exemplar product

As we saw with the case of apple pie versus rhubarb pie, if a product is a really good example of a category, it is more familiar to consumers and they will more easily recognise and recall it.[66] The characteristics of **category exemplars** tend to exert disproportionate influence on how people think of the category in general.[67] In a sense, brands that are strongly associated with a category 'call the shots' by defining the evaluative criteria that should be used to evaluate all category members.

However, being a bit less than prototypical is not necessarily a bad thing. Products that are moderately unusual within their product category may stimulate more information processing and positive evaluations, because they are neither so familiar that we will take them for granted nor so different that we will not consider them at all.[68] A brand that is strongly discrepant may occupy a unique niche position, whereas those that are moderately discrepant remain in a distinct position within the general category.[69]

Locate products in a store

Product categorisation can also affect consumers' expectations regarding the places where they can locate a desired product, either instore or on a retailer's website. If products do not clearly fit into categories (is a carpet furniture?), this may diminish our ability to find them, or work out what they are meant to do once we have found them.

Evaluative criteria

When Elijah was looking at different Smart TVs, he focused on one or two product features and completely ignored several others. He narrowed down his choices by only considering two specific brand names, and from the Prime Wave and Precision models he chose one that featured stereo capability. A survey carried out by different European manufacturers showed that they had identified a range of criteria used by consumers in Germany, the Netherlands and Czech Republic when choosing televisions. Purchase price, design and technology emerged as key considerations for consumer decision-making in this product category.[70]

Evaluative criteria are the dimensions we use to judge the merits of competing options. In comparing alternative products, Elijah could have chosen from among any number of criteria, ranging from very functional attributes ('does this TV have a remote control?') to experiential ones ('does this TV's sound reproduction make me imagine I'm in a concert hall?').

Another important point is that criteria on which products *differ* from one another carry more weight in the decision process than do those where the alternatives are *similar*. If all brands being considered rate equally well on one attribute (e.g. if all TVs come with remote control), consumers will have to find other reasons to choose one over another. **Determinant attributes** are the features we actually use to differentiate among our choices.

Reflecting consumers' renewed interest in ethical and sustainable marketing (see Chapter 5), it makes sense that a company's reputation for social responsibility is emerging as one of the most important determinant attributes when people choose among brands. Each year Harris Interactive and *The Wall Street Journal* conduct a survey and rank corporate reputations on 20 attributes in six categories: financial performance, social responsibility, workplace environment, quality of products and services, vision and leadership and emotional appeal.[71] A US survey (2015) by Harris Interactive placed Wegmans Food Markets first, followed by Amazon, Samsung, Costco and Johnson & Johnson. Apple is ranked 9th, Google 10th and Microsoft 15th.[72] In the light of the controversies surrounding the tax status and accounting practices of some multinationals in Europe, it seems unlikely that some of these companies would rank so highly in a European listing. The corporate world's overall reputation remains dismal in the light of other scandals, e.g. Parmalat, Madoff and Satyam.[73] 'There are those businesses that really espouse sustainability and those who talk the talk . . . There is a lot of greenwash, but a lot are doing the right thing, and a gap is appearing' argues Stuart Rose, former CEO and Board Chairman of Marks and Spencer in an interview with the Centre for Corporate Reputation at Oxford University (2014).[74]

Marketers can play a role in educating consumers about which criteria should be used as determinant attributes. For example, research indicated that many consumers view the use of natural ingredients as a determinant attribute. The result was promotion of toothpaste made from baking soda, which the company Church & Dwight already manufactured for its Arm & Hammer brand.[75] The decision about which attributes to use is the result of *procedural learning*, in which a person undergoes a series of cognitive steps before making a choice. These steps include identifying important attributes, remembering whether competing brands differ on those attributes and so on. In order for a marketer to recommend a new decision criterion effectively, their communication should convey three pieces of information:[76]

1 It should point out that there are significant differences among brands on the attribute.

2 It should supply the consumer with a decision-making rule, such as if (deciding among competing brands), then . . . (use the attribute as a criterion).

3 It should convey a rule that can be easily integrated with how the consumer has made this decision in the past. Otherwise, the recommendation is likely to be ignored because it requires too much mental work.

Decision rules we use when we care

We can see that we use different rules to choose among competing products depending on the decision's complexity and how important the choice is to us. Sometimes we carefully weigh alternatives but sometimes we just use a simple heuristic (see below). We can describe the processes we use when we are giving more thought to these decisions by dividing the types of rules we use into two categories: *compensatory* and *non-compensatory*. To aid the discussion of some of these rules, Table 8.3 summarises the attributes of the Smart TV sets Elijah considered. It is now possible to see how some of these rules result in different brand choices.

Non-compensatory decision rules

We use **non-compensatory decision rules** when we feel that a product with a low standing on one attribute cannot compensate for this flaw by doing better on another attribute. Simple non-compensatory decision rules are therefore short cuts to making choices. In other words, we simply eliminate all options that do not meet some basic standards. A consumer like Elijah who uses the decision rule, 'Only buy well-known brand names', would not consider a new brand, even if it were equal or superior to existing ones. When people are less familiar with a product category or are not very motivated to process complex information, they tend to use simple, non-compensatory rules, which are summarised below:[77]

When a person uses the **lexicographic rule**, they select the brand that is the best on the most important attribute selected. If they feel two or more brands are equally good on that

Table 8.3 Hypothetical alternatives for a Smart TV

	Brand ratings			
Attribute	Importance ranking	Kamashita	Prime Wave	Precision
Size of screen	1	Excellent	Excellent	Excellent
Stereo broadcast capability	2	Good	Poor	Excellent
Brand reputation	3	Poor	Excellent	Excellent
On-screen programming	4	Poor	Excellent	Poor
Cable-ready capability	5	Good	Good	Good
Sleep timer	6	Good	Poor	Excellent

attribute, the consumer then compares them on the second most-important attribute. This selection process goes on until the tie is broken. In Elijah's case, because both the Prime Wave and Precision models were tied on his most important attribute (screen size), he chose the Precision because of its rating on his second most-important attribute – its stereo capability.

Using the **elimination-by-aspects rule**, the buyer also evaluates brands on the most important attribute. In this case, though, they impose specific cut-offs. For example, if Elijah had been more interested in having a sleep timer on his Smart TV (if that had had a higher importance ranking), he might have stipulated that his choice 'must have an excellent sleep timer'. Because the Precision model had an excellent one and the Prime Wave did not, he would have stuck to his choice of the Precision.

Whereas the two former rules involve processing by attribute, the **conjunctive rule** entails processing by brand. As with the elimination-by-aspects procedure, the decision-maker establishes cut-offs for each brand. They choose a brand if it meets all of the cut-offs, while failure to meet any one cut-off means they will reject it. If none of the brands meets all of the cut-offs, they may delay the choice, change the decision rule, or modify the cut-offs they choose to apply.

If Elijah had stipulated that all attributes had to be rated 'good' or better, he would not have been able to choose any of the options. He might then have modified his decision rule, conceding that it was not possible to attain these high standards in the price range he was considering. In this case, Elijah might decide that he could live without on-screen programming, so he would again consider the Precision model.

Compensatory decision rules

Unlike non-compensatory decision rules, **compensatory decision rules** give a product a chance to make up for its shortcomings. Consumers who employ these rules tend to be more involved in the purchase and so they are willing to exert the effort to consider the entire picture in a more exacting way. The willingness to let good and bad product qualities balance each other out can result in quite different choices. For example, if Elijah had not been concerned about having good stereo reception, he might have chosen the Prime Wave model. But because this brand doesn't feature a good version of this highly ranked attribute, it doesn't stand a chance when he uses a non-compensatory rule.

Two basic types of compensatory rules have been identified. When using the *simple additive rule*, the consumer merely chooses the alternative that has the largest number of positive attributes. This choice is most likely to occur when their ability or motivation to process information is limited. One drawback to this approach for the consumer is that some of these attributes may not be very meaningful or important. An ad containing a long list of product benefits may be persuasive, despite the fact that many of the benefits included are actually standard within the product class and are not determinant attributes at all.

The *weighted additive rule* is a more complex version.[78] When using this rule, the consumer also takes into account the relative importance of positively rated attributes, essentially multiplying brand ratings by importance weights. If this process sounds familiar, it should. The calculation process strongly resembles the multi-attribute attitude model described earlier (see Chapter 6).

Researchers argue that the difficulties faced by consumers in making decisions derive not just from the evaluation and trading-off of different attributes (as described by the different decision rules above), but also derive from some degree of incompatibility between the *task* of choosing itself, and the valence of the alternatives within the decision set. When the consumer experiences conflict between the task of choosing and the valence of the alternatives then they face greater difficulties in making decisions, and take longer to make the decision. In the case of Elijah, for instance, if he had been faced with choices between Smart TVs that he had not liked, then this would have compounded the difficulty involved in the task itself, i.e. making a decision. When all of the alternatives are unattractive, then decision-making increases in difficulty. The conflict Elijah would have faced in making a decision, when confronted by alternatives that he did not like, would have been heightened because he was faced with making a choice that he did not wish to make; and he would have taken longer to make a decision.[79]

Neuromarketing: how your brain reacts to alternatives

Is there a 'buy button' in your brain? Some corporations are teaming up with neuroscientists to find out.[80] **Neuromarketing** uses *functional magnetic resonance imaging* (or *fMRI*) – a brain-scanning device that tracks blood flow as we perform mental tasks. Researchers have discovered that regions in the brain, such as the amygdala, the hippocampus and the hypothalamus, are dynamic switchboards that blend memory, emotions and biochemical triggers. These interconnected neurons shape the ways that fear, panic, exhilaration and social pressure influence our choices.

Scientists know that specific regions of the brain light up in these scans to show increased blood flow when a person recognises a face, hears a song, makes a decision, or senses deception. Now scientists are trying to harness this technology to measure consumers' reactions to film trailers, choices about cars, the appeal of a pretty face and loyalty to specific brands. British researchers recorded brain activity as shoppers toured a virtual store. They claim to have identified the neural region that becomes active when a shopper decides which product to pluck from a supermarket shelf. DaimlerChrysler took brain scans of men as they looked at photos of cars and confirmed that sports cars activated their reward centres. The company's scientists found that the most popular vehicles – the Porsche- and Ferrari-style sports cars – triggered activity in a section of the brain they call the *fusiform face area,* which governs facial recognition. A psychiatrist who ran the study commented, 'They were reminded of faces when they looked at the cars. The lights of the cars look a little like eyes.'[81]

Scientists have also identified types of consumers based on their responses to images of shoes, cars, chairs, wristwatches, sunglasses, handbags and water bottles. All of these objects set off a rush of activity in a part of the cortex that neuroscientists know links to a sense of identity and social image. At one extreme were people whose brains responded intensely to 'cool' products and celebrities with bursts of activity, but who didn't respond at all to 'uncool' images. They dubbed these participants 'cool fools', likely to be impulsive or compulsive shoppers. At the other extreme were people whose brains reacted only to the unstylish items, a pattern that fits well with people who tend to be anxious, apprehensive or neurotic.

Marketing opportunity
Neuro-marketing and neuroscience

Gemma Calvert, a former Oxford University neurologist who founded *Neurosense*, said that neuromarketing . . . is now so advanced that she is "able to predict how customers will behave" . . . "**Neuroscience** has completely changed our understanding of the brain. This information is not a flash-in-the-pan", she says. "We are trying to find out what aspects of the images [in adverts] are having effect on the reward system – and making them [the brand] more likeable." Her company's website lists clients including McDonald's, Unilever, Procter & Gamble and GlaxoSmithKline . . . She said the research has led to brands changing their logos, packaging and even theme tunes: "We are changing the way brands understand themselves so they can better understand their audiences". The techniques are also used in the development of new products: "There are lots of products that have been developed with knowledge about the brain and psychology that's been derived from this stuff", she said.'[82]

STEP 4: Product choice

Once we assemble and evaluate the relevant options in a category, we have to choose one.[83] Recall that the decision rules guiding choice can range from very simple and quick strategies to complicated processes requiring much attention and cognitive processing.[84] The choice can be influenced by integrating information from sources such as prior experience with the product or a similar one, information present at the time of purchase and beliefs about the brands that have been created by advertising.[85]

Decision-making does not get any easier, as we often find that there are more and more features to evaluate. We deal with 50-button remote controls, digital cameras with hundreds of mysterious features and book-length manuals, and cars with dashboard systems worthy of the space shuttle. Experts call this spiral of complexity **feature creep**, also known as **feature fatigue** or **feature bloat**.[86] As evidence that the proliferation of gizmos is counter-productive, Philips Electronics found that at least half of returned products have nothing wrong with them – consumers simply couldn't figure out how to use them! What's worse, on average the person spent only 20 minutes trying to figure out how to use the product before giving up.

Why don't companies avoid this problem? One reason is that when we look at a new product in a store we tend to think that the more features there are, the better. It is only once we get the product home and try to use it that we realise the virtues of simplicity. We tend to rely on indirect experience when choosing products, so that before using a product our preference tends to be for many features and capabilities. It is only after we have had direct experience of a product that we tend to prefer simpler products that we find easier to use.[87] In one study,[88] consumers selected from among three models of a digital device that varied in terms of how complex each was. More than 60 per cent chose the one with the most features. Then, the participants got the chance to choose from up to 25 features to customise their product – the average person chose 20 of these add-ons. But when they actually used the devices, it turns out that the large number of options only frustrated them – they ended up being much happier with the simpler product.[89]

Marketing pitfall
Brand switching

Consumers are often observed to engage in brand switching, even if their current brand satisfies their needs.[90] Sometimes it seems that people simply like to try new things – we crave variety as a form of stimulation or to reduce boredom. Variety seeking, the desire to choose new alternatives over more familiar ones, even influences us to switch from our favourite products to ones we like less. This can occur even before we become satiated, or tired of our favourite product.[91]

Variety seeking is a choice strategy that occurs as a result of pleasurable memories of ringing the changes.[92] Variety seeking is especially likely to occur when we are in a good mood, or when there is relatively little stimulation elsewhere in our environment.[93] In the case of foods and beverages, variety seeking can occur due to a phenomenon known as sensory-specific satiety. Put simply, this means the pleasantness of a recently consumed food item drops, while the pleasantness of uneaten foods remains unchanged.[94] So, even though we have favourites, we still like to sample other possibilities. Ironically, consumers may actually switch to less-preferred options for variety's sake even though they enjoy the more familiar option more. On the other hand, when the decision situation is ambiguous or when there is little information about competing brands, we tend to opt for the safe choice by selecting familiar brands and maintaining the status quo.

Brand familiarity influences confidence about a brand, which in turn affects purchase intention.[95] Still, the tendency of consumers to shift brand choices over time means that marketers can never relax in the belief that once they have won a customer, they are necessarily theirs forever.[96]

STEP 5: Post-purchase evaluation

The true test of our decision-making process is whether we are happy with the choice we made after we undertake all these decision-making stages. **Post-purchase evaluation** closes the loop; it occurs when we experience the product or service we selected and decide whether it meets (or maybe even exceeds) our expectations.

Our overall reactions to a product after we've bought it – what researchers call **consumer satisfaction/dissatisfaction (CS/D)** – obviously play a big role in our future behaviour. We evaluate the things we buy as we use them and integrate them into our daily consumption activities.[97] Our post-purchase product experiences are an important part of our satisfaction (or dissatisfaction) with a product or service, and these experiences and post-purchase evaluations play a big role in our future purchasing choices. Despite evidence that customer satisfaction is steadily declining in many industries, good marketers are constantly on the lookout for sources of dissatisfaction that they can improve on.[98] Customer satisfaction has a real impact on profitability.

What exactly do consumers look for in products? That's easy: they want quality and value.[99] However, these terms have slippery meanings that are hard for us always to pin down. We infer quality when we rely on cues as diverse as brand name, price, product warranties and even our estimate of how much money a company invests in its advertising.[100]

Marketing pitfall

Satisfaction or dissatisfaction is more than a reaction to how well a product or service performs. According to the **expectancy disconfirmation model**, we form beliefs about product performance based on our prior experience with the product or communications about the product that imply a certain level of quality.[101] When something performs the way we thought it would, we may not think much about it. If it fails to live up to expectations, this may create negative feelings. However, if performance happens to exceed our expectations, we're very happy.

This perspective underscores the importance of managing expectations. We often trace a customer's dissatisfaction to his or her erroneous expectations of the company's ability to deliver a product or service. No company is perfect. Figure 8.9 illustrates the alternative strategies a firm can choose in these situations. When confronted with unrealistic expectations about what it can do, the firm can either accommodate these demands by improving the range or quality of the products it offers, alter the expectations, or perhaps even choose to abandon the customer if it is not feasible to meet their needs.[102] Expectations are altered, for example, when waiters tell patrons in advance that the portion size they have ordered will not be very big, or when new car buyers are warned of strange smells they will experience when first driving their new vehicle. A firm can also under-promise, as when Xerox inflates the time it will take for a service rep to visit. When the rep arrives a day earlier, the customer is impressed. It's just not realistic to think that everything will always turn out perfectly.

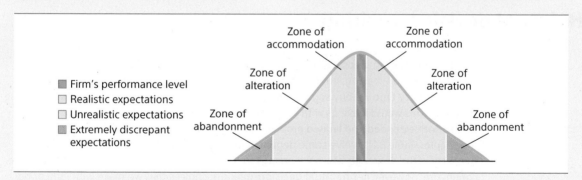

Figure 8.9 Customer expectation zones: managing quality expectations

Satisfaction levels are determined not only by the product purchased, but also by the expectations about the quality of alternatives that were *not* purchased. In other words, the higher the expectations about unselected alternatives, the lower the level of satisfaction with the chosen good.[103] A general conclusion that one should draw from such a discussion is that consumer goals may be multiple and the product or service offer so complex to evaluate that any measurement of satisfaction must be used with caution.[104] An Italian study argued that consumers' schematic knowledge about a product, or the hopes associated with the subsequent consumption of the product, determined consumers' satisfaction judgements depending on their motivation and level of involvement.[105]

Acting on dissatisfaction

If a person is not happy with a product or service, what can be done? Reasons for complaining include bad service, unsafe products, failure to respect consumer legislation and lack of transparency or availability of information.[106] Essentially, a consumer can take one or more possible courses of action:[107]

1 **Voice response:** the consumer can appeal directly to the retailer for redress (e.g. a refund).

2 **Private response:** express dissatisfaction about the store or product to friends and/or boycott the store. As will be discussed in Chapter 9, negative word of mouth (WOM) can be very damaging to a retailer's reputation.

3 **Third-party response:** the consumer can take legal action against the merchant, register a complaint with the Ombudsman, or perhaps write a letter to a newspaper.

A number of factors influence which route is taken, including different national systems for consumer protection, consumers' perception of the likelihood of success and consumers' different expectations of the outcome of a complaint. Within the EU, 'country-level analysis suggests that consumers living in northern Europe are more likely to launch a complaint than other Europeans. A socio-economic analysis of results indicates that citizens with higher education levels tend to be more assertive if they are not satisfied with their purchases and proceed to launch a complaint (21 per cent)'.[108] Action is more likely to be taken for expensive products, such as household durables, cars and clothing, than for inexpensive products.[109] Ironically, marketers should *encourage* consumers to complain to them: people are more likely to spread the word about unresolved negative experiences to their friends than they are to boast about positive occurrences.[110] Complaint management is not as good an alternative as high-quality service in the first place.[111] In addition, consumers who are satisfied with a store are more likely to complain; they take the time to complain because they feel connected to the store.

Habitual decision-making

The decision-making steps we've reviewed are all well and good within the context of cognitive decision-making, but common sense tells us we don't undergo this elaborate sequence every time we buy something.[112] If we did, we'd spend our entire lives making these decisions. This would leave us with very little time to enjoy the things we eventually decide to buy. Both extended and limited problem-solving modes (discussed at the beginning of the chapter, Table 8.1) involve some degree of information search and deliberation, though they vary in the degree to which we engage in these activities. At the other end of the choice continuum, however, lies **habitual decision-making**: choices that we make with little or no conscious effort. Many purchase decisions are so routine that we may not realise we have made them until we look in our shopping trolleys. We make these choices with minimal effort and without conscious control; researchers call this process *automaticity*.[113] We purchase some items with virtually no advance planning at all.[114] For a detailed update of research on the habit-driven consumer, see Drolet and Wood (2017).[115]

Habitual decision-making describes the choices we make with little or no conscious effort. In fact, the amount of external search we do for most products is surprisingly small.[116] Although decisions we make on the basis of little conscious thought may seem dangerous, or at best stupid, this process actually is quite efficient in many cases. The journalist Malcolm Gladwell hit the bestseller list with his book *Blink,* which demonstrated how snap judgements that occur in the blink of an eye can be surprisingly accurate.[117] When a person buys the same brand over and over, does this mean it's just a habit or is he or she truly loyal to that product? The answer is, it depends. In some cases, the explanation really is just **inertia** – that is, it involves less effort to throw a familiar package into the shopping trolley. **Brand loyalty** is a totally different story. This describes a pattern of repeat purchasing behaviour that involves a conscious decision to continue buying the same brand (these topics are also discussed in Chapter 5 in the context of 'involvement').

As you might imagine, though both inertia and brand loyalty yield the same result, the latter is harder to achieve – but also far more valuable because it represents a true commitment by the consumer. Here's one simple test that may help to tell the difference. If the consumer discovers that a store is out of his or her normal brand, will he or she just choose another one or defer the purchase in order to find this brand somewhere else? If the answer is 'my way or the highway', that marketer has a loyal customer.

The development of habitual, repetitive behaviour allows consumers to minimise the time and energy spent on mundane purchase decisions. On the other hand, habitual decision-making poses a problem when a marketer tries to introduce a new way of doing an old task. In this case, consumers must be convinced to 'unfreeze' their former habit and replace it with a new one – perhaps by using digital banking rather than the local branch of the bank, or using an ATM machine instead of a live bank teller, or switching to self-service petrol pumps instead of being served by an attendant. We discuss heuristics, or mental short cuts (and rules of thumb), in more detail later in the chapter. But before then, we stop for a moment to look at research on how our unconscious impacts our behaviour.

Behavioural economics: priming and nudging

The way information about a product choice is framed can prime a decision, even when the consumer is unaware of this influence.

There is growing interest, among both researchers and policy makers, in the power of the unconscious to influence our daily decisions.[118] In particular, many researchers focus on the role of priming: cues in the environment that make us more likely to react in a certain way, even though we're unaware of these influences. Consider this example. A study of the influence of computer company logos found that, when consumers were primed with either an Apple or an IBM logo briefly flashed on a screen, their behaviours changed even though they weren't even aware they had seen the logo. Creativity, non-conformity and innovation are traits many consumers associate with the Apple brand, while they link tradition, intelligence and responsibility with IBM.[119] Sure enough, those who saw the Apple logo subsequently provided more creative and innovative responses than those who saw the IBM logo.

Researchers continue to identify factors that bias our decisions – and many of these are factors that operate beneath the level of conscious awareness. In one study, respondents' attitudes toward an undesirable product – curried grasshoppers – improved when they were asked to approach it. This physical movement typically links to liking; even our own body movements or other physiological reactions can influence what goes on in our minds.[120] To help understand this process, try to force yourself to smile or frown and then carefully gauge your feelings – you may find that the old prescription to 'put on a happy face' to cheer yourself up may actually have some validity.[121]

Often, it's just a matter of **framing** – how we pose the question to people, or what exactly we ask them to do. For example, people hate losing things more than they like getting things; economists call this 'tendency loss aversion'. In one study, teachers who had the opportunity to improve student performance didn't make the grade in terms of improved test scores. However, those who got the extra money at the beginning of the year and were told they would lose it if their students did not show sufficient progress managed to raise their students' scores.

To see how framing works, consider the following scenario. You've won a free ticket to a sold-out football game. At the last minute, though, a sudden snowstorm makes it somewhat dangerous to get to the stadium. Would you still go? Now, assume the same game and snowstorm – except this time you paid a small fortune for the ticket. Would you head out in the storm in this case? This all relates to the **psychology of loss aversion (PLA)**, which means we emphasise our losses more than our gains. For example, for most people losing money is more *unpleasant* than gaining money is *pleasant*.

Researchers who work on **prospect theory** analyse how the value of a decision depends upon gains or losses; they identify principles of **mental accounting** that relate to the way we frame the question, as well as external issues that shouldn't influence our choices – but do anyway. In this case, researchers find that people are more likely to risk their personal safety in the storm if they *paid* for that football ticket described above, rather than if it's a freebie. Only the most die-hard fan would fail to recognise that this is an irrational choice, because the risk is the same regardless of whether you got a great deal on the ticket. Researchers call this decision-making bias the **sunk-cost fallacy**: if we've paid for something, we're more reluctant to waste it.

The notion that even subtle changes in a person's environment can strongly influence the choices he or she makes has emerged centre stage in the study of consumer behaviour in recent years. Unlike standard economic theory, which regards people as rational decision-makers, the rapidly growing field of **behavioural economics** focuses on the effects of psychological and social factors on the economic decisions we make – and many of these choices are anything but 'rational'. Indeed, it turns out that it's quite possible to modify the choices of individuals and groups merely by tinkering with the way we present information to them. This research holds enormous implications, especially for public policy issues, because the way organisations frame their messages can exert a big influence on the numbers of consumers who will stop smoking, eat healthy foods or save more money for retirement. There are important ethical issues as well, especially as studies continue to identify ways that organisations, including governments and companies, can subtly but powerfully influence what we 'freely' choose to do.[122]

Much of the emerging work in behavioural economics focuses on the role of **priming** – cues in the environment that make us more likely to react in a certain way, even though we're unaware of these influences. A *prime* is a stimulus that encourages people to focus on some specific aspect of their lives, such as their financial well-being or the environment:

- A group of undergraduates was primed to think about money; they saw phrases like 'she spends money liberally', or pictures that would make them think of money. Then this group and a control group that wasn't focused on money answered questions about moral choices they would make. Those students who had been primed to think of money consistently exhibited weaker ethics: they were more likely to say they would steal a ream of paper from the university's copying room and more likely to say they would lie for financial gain.[123]

- When people see pictures of 'cute' products, they are more likely to engage in indulgent behaviour such as eating larger portions of ice cream.[124]

- For a field study taking place in a wine store, researchers played either stereotypically French or German music on alternate days. On the days when French music was in the background people bought more French than German wine, and the reverse happened on German music days. Follow-up questionnaires indicated customers were not aware of the impact of the music on their choices.[125]

Much of the current work in behavioural economics demonstrates how a **nudge** – a deliberate change by an organisation that intends to modify behaviour – can result in dramatic effects.[126] A simple 'nudge' that changes how people act is to switch from asking consumers to 'opt-in' to a programme to asking them to 'opt-out' of a programme if they don't want to participate. In Europe, countries that ask drivers to indicate if they want to be an organ donor convince less than 20 per cent of drivers to do so. In contrast, those that require drivers to opt-out if they *don't* want to be donors get more than 95 per cent participation. This **default bias** – where we are more likely to comply with a requirement than to make the effort not to comply – can be applied to numerous choice situations. For example, people are more likely to save for retirement if their employers automatically deduct a set amount from their pay cheques than if they have to set up this process themselves. It is also how many software companies and social media platforms encourage users to adopt their products and privacy policies (e.g. when you must opt-out of Facebook's right to share your data with others).[127] As a footnote to this section, the struggle remains to win greater support for organ donation in the UK.[128]

8.4

We often rely on 'rules of thumb', heuristics or mental short cuts for habitual and routine decision-making.

Decision-making biases, heuristics and mental short cuts

The default bias we previously described illustrates that we often take the easy way out when we make decisions. Unlike the cognitive decision strategies we've already described , which we use when we want to arrive at the best result (a **maximising** solution), in fact we are often quite content to exert less mental effort and simply receive an adequate outcome (a **satisficing** solution). This 'good enough' perspective on decision-making is called **bounded rationality**, and is one way to reduce the costs (or resources) of the decision-making process. These two extremes (maximising versus satisficing) have huge implications for marketing and retailing strategy, because they imply very different approaches to customers. Indeed, the maximiser strongly resembles the high-involvement consumer we have discussed (see Chapter 5), who is going to go all out to obtain as much information as they can before they decide. In contrast, the satisficer resembles the low-involvement consumer, who will probably use some simple short cuts to just pick something decent and get on with their life.

Heuristics: mental short cuts

We've seen that many habitual decisions that we make are subject to mental accounting biases. In addition, we often fall back on other short cuts to simplify our choices. For example, Elijah relied on certain assumptions as substitutes for a prolonged information search. In particular, he assumed the advice from the salesperson was sound, so he did not bother to investigate any of the retailer's competitors. This assumption served as a short cut to more extended information processing.[129] We refer to these short cuts as **heuristics**. These 'mental rules of thumb' range from the very general ('higher-priced products are higher-quality products' or 'buy the same brand as I bought last time') to the very specific ('buy Tate and Lyle Silver Spoon, the brand of sugar my mother always bought for her baking'). We can see some of these short cuts in Elijah's decision-making. Elijah could have chosen a heuristic approach based either on compromise or anchoring. A compromise strategy might have involved following one of the options used by his friends in choosing a new Smart TV – Lily might have done an exhaustive Web-based search, Zoe might have visited every high-street and out-of-town stockist and Ehaan might have read all the independent consumer reports. Elijah's compromise would have been to have done some Web-searching, visit one high-street retailer and then make a purchase after visiting just one large out-of-town stockist.[130] Alternatively, Elijah could have pursued **anchoring** (Tversky and Kahneman, 1974),[131] i.e. 'the tendency to rely heavily, or anchor, on one piece of information in order to arrive at a decision'.[132] Research has 'demonstrated that decision-making is more heuristic in situations that involve spending time rather than money'.[133]

Sometimes these short cuts may not be in our best interests. A car buyer who personally knows one or two people who have had problems with a particular vehicle, for example, might assume that he would have similar trouble with it rather than taking the time to find out that it actually has an excellent repair record.[134] Table 8.4 lists a set of **market beliefs** that many of us share. Let's summarise a few of the most prevalent heuristics we commonly use:

Co-variation: relying on a product signal

One short cut we often use is to infer hidden dimensions of products from attributes we can observe. In these cases, the visible element acts as a **product signal** that communicates some underlying quality. This explains why someone trying to sell a used car takes great pains to be sure the car's exterior is clean and shiny. Potential buyers often judge the vehicle's mechanical condition by its appearance, even though this means they may drive away in a shiny, clean death trap.[135]

When we only have incomplete product information, we often base our judgements on our beliefs about **co-variation** – the associations we make between events that may or may not actually influence one another.[136] For example, a consumer may judge product quality by the length of time a manufacturer has been in business. Other signals or attributes consumers tend to believe co-exist with good or bad products include well-known brand names, country of origin, price and the retail outlets that carry the product.

Table 8.4 Common market beliefs

Brand	All brands are basically the same.
	Generic products are just name brands sold under a different label at a lower price.
	The best brands are the ones that are purchased the most.
	When in doubt, a national brand is always a safe bet.
Store	Specialised shops are good places to familiarise yourself with the best brands; but once you know what you want, it's cheaper to buy it at a discount outlet.
	A store's character is reflected in its window displays.
	Salespeople in specialised shops are more knowledgeable than other sales personnel.
	Larger stores offer better prices than small stores.
	Locally owned stores give the best service.
	A store that offers good value on one of its products probably offers good value on all of its items.
	Credit and return policies are most lenient at large department stores.
	Stores that have just opened usually charge attractive prices.
Prices/ discounts/ sales	Sales are typically run to get rid of slow-moving merchandise.
	Stores that are constantly having sales don't really save you money.
	Within a given store, higher prices generally indicate higher quality.
Advertising and sales promotions	'Hard-sell' advertising is associated with low-quality products.
	Items tied to 'giveaways' are not good value (even with the freebie).
	Coupons represent real savings for customers because they are not offered by the store.
	When you buy heavily advertised products, you are paying for the label, not for higher quality.
Product/ packaging	Largest-sized containers are almost always cheaper per unit than smaller sizes.
	New products are more expensive when they're first introduced; prices tend to settle down as time goes by.
	When you are not sure what you need in a product, it's a good idea to invest in the extra features, because you'll probably wish you had them later.
	In general, synthetic goods are lower in quality than goods made of natural materials.
	It's advisable to stay away from products when they are new to the market; it usually takes the manufacturer a little time to sort out the bugs.

Source: Adapted from Calvin P. Duncan, 'Consumer Market Beliefs: A Review of the Literature and an Agenda for Future Research', in Marvin E. Goldberg, Gerald Gorn and Richard W. Pollay (eds), *Advances in Consumer Research* 17 (Provo, UT: Association for Consumer Research, 1990): 729–35.

Country of origin as a product signal

Modern consumers choose among products made in many countries. European consumers may buy Portuguese, Italian or Brazilian shoes, Japanese cars, clothing imported from Taiwan or smartphones and microwave ovens produced in South Korea. A product's 'address' matters. Consumers' reactions to these imports are mixed. In some cases, people have come to assume that a product made overseas is of better quality (cameras, cars), whereas in other cases the knowledge that a product has been imported tends to lower perceptions of product quality (clothing apparel).[137] In general, people tend to rate their own country's products more favourably than foreign-sourced products, and products from industrialised countries are rated better than those from developing countries. **Ethnocentrism** is the tendency to prefer products or people of one's own culture to those of other countries. Ethnocentric consumers are likely to feel it is wrong to buy products made elsewhere, particularly because this may have a negative effect on the domestic economy. Marketing campaigns that stress the desirability of buying locally appeal to ethnocentric consumers. The Consumer Ethnocentric Scale (CETSCALE) for measuring this trait was originally developed in the US[138] and its applicability in other cultural contexts, such as Spain, has been examined.[139]

As briefly discussed when we were talking about persuasive communication (see Chapter 7), a product's **country of origin** in some cases is an important piece of information in the decision-making process.[140] A product's origin, then, is often used as a signal of quality. Certain items are strongly associated with specific countries, and products from those countries often attempt to benefit from these linkages. Sometimes, however, the country of origin can act as a negative signal. Reports of poor experiences with goods has undermined some national manufacturing reputations – for example, that of China.

Countries, in their turn, can be very protective of product names that potentially provide them with an important competitive advantage in winning customers. The EU has been trying to achieve a global trade agreement to protect some of its product names, such as Champagne and wines such as Beaujolais, Chianti and Madeira, cheeses such as Roquefort, Feta and Gorgonzola, as well as meat products such as Parma ham and Mortadella. This has been opposed in some non-EU countries, where these names are seen as generic.[141] Country of origin can function as a **stereotype** – a knowledge structure based on inferences across products. These stereotypes may be biased or inaccurate, but they do play a constructive role in simplifying complex choice situations.[142] A study of UK consumers' brand perceptions of Italian goods across a range of categories (e.g. luxury design, fashion, food and beverages) showed that 'brand image, brand trust and brand experience . . . [were all] highly important in influencing the relationship between consumers and Italian luxury brands'.[143]

Research evidence indicates that learning of a product's country of origin is not necessarily good or bad. Instead, it often has the effect of stimulating the consumer's interest in the product to a greater degree. The purchaser thinks more extensively about the product and evaluates it more carefully.[144] The origin of the product can act as a product attribute that combines with other attributes to influence evaluations.[145] In addition, the consumer's own expertise with the product category moderates the effects of this attribute. When other information is available, experts tend to ignore country-of-origin information, whereas novices continue to rely on it. However, when other information is unavailable or ambiguous, both experts and novices will rely on this attribute in helping to reach a decision.[146]

Market beliefs: is it better if I have to pay more for it?

We constantly make assumptions about companies, products and stores. These market beliefs then become the short cuts that guide our decisions – regardless of whether or not these beliefs are accurate.[147] Recall, for instance, that Elijah chose to shop either at an out-of-town 'big shed' retailer or online, because he *assumed* the prices would be more competitive there than at a specialised shop. A large number of market beliefs have been identified – some of these are listed in Table 8.4. How many of these do you share?

Do higher prices mean higher quality? The assumption of a *price–quality relationship* is one of the most pervasive market beliefs.[148] Novice consumers may, in fact, consider price as the *only* relevant product attribute. Experts also consider this information, although they tend to use price for its informational value, especially for products they know vary widely in quality (e.g. virgin wool). When this quality level is more standard or strictly regulated (e.g. Harris Tweed sports jackets), experts do not weigh price in their decisions. For the most part, this belief is justified – you do tend to get what you pay for. However, let the buyer beware: the price–quality relationship is not always justified.[149]

Marketing pitfall

Researchers recently found that 'Consumers may frequently rely on the "healthy = expensive" intuition to make inferences and judgments of food products in a variety of consumption situations, including in stores and in restaurants, due to a lack of motivation to process systematically in addition to a lack of opportunity or ability to do so. The findings show that consumers rely on this lay theory when specific information is either missing or lacking detail, or when consumers cannot rely on prior knowledge to interpret a health claim. Given this, consumers and public policy-makers need to be aware that marketers could use an understanding of the "healthy = expensive" intuition to charge more for healthy products or, worse, to successfully promote products through meaningless health-related claims (e.g., using the term "natural", which is a non-regulated product claim, unlike "organic") by coupling such claims with higher prices. Therefore, policy-makers must guard against unscrupulous uses of ambiguous health terms and higher prices.'[150]

Familiar brand names

Do we choose familiar brand names because of loyalty or habit? Branding is a marketing strategy that often functions as a heuristic. When you fall in love with a brand, it may be your favourite for a lifetime (e.g. fans of the iPhone). People form preferences for a favourite brand, and then they literally may never change their minds in the course of a lifetime. In a study of the market leaders in 30 product categories by the Boston Consulting Group, it was found that 27 of the brands that were number one in 1930 in the US still remain at the top now. These include such perennial American favourites as Ivory Soap, Campbell's Soup and Gold Medal Flour.[151] As this study demonstrates, in a sense some brands are well known because they are well known; we assume that if so many people choose a product, it must be good. Clearly, choosing a well-known brand name is a powerful heuristic. One study has applied cultural theory to understanding how brands become icons over time.[152]

Indeed, our tendency to prefer a number-one brand to the competition is so strong that it seems to mimic a pattern that scientists find in other domains, ranging from earthquakes to linguistics, known as **Zipf's Law**. In the 1930s, a linguist, George Kingsley Zipf, found that 'the' – the most-used English word – occurs about twice as often as 'of' (second place), which occurs about twice as often as 'and' (third) and so on. Since then, scientists have found similar relationships between the size and frequency of earthquakes and a variety of other natural and artificial phenomena.

A marketing researcher decided to apply Zipf's Law to consumer behaviour. His firm asked Australian consumers to identify the brands of toilet paper and instant coffee they use and to rank them in order of preference. As the model predicted, people spend roughly twice as much of their toilet-paper budget on the top choice than on the second-ranked brand, about twice as much on the number-two brand as on the third-ranked brand and about twice as much on the number-three brand as on the number-four brand. One ramification is that a brand that moves from number two to number one in a category will see a much greater jump in sales than will, say, a brand that moves from number four to number three. Brands that dominate their markets are as much as 50 per cent more profitable than their nearest competitors.[153]

Inertia

Many people tend to buy the same brand just about every time they go shopping. This consistent pattern is often due to inertia – we buy a brand out of habit merely because it requires less effort. If another product is introduced that is for some reason easier to buy (for instance, it is cheaper, or the original product is out of stock), we will not hesitate to change our minds. A competitor who is trying to change a buying pattern based on inertia often can do so rather easily, because the shopper won't hesitate to jump to the new brand if it offers the right incentive. When we have little to no underlying commitment to a particular brand, marketers find it easy to 'unfreeze' our habit when they use promotional tools such as point-of-purchase displays, extensive couponing or noticeable price reductions. Some analysts predict that we are going to observe this kind of fickle behaviour more and more as consumers flit from one brand to the next.

Brand loyalty: a 'friend', tried and tested

This kind of fickleness or promiscuity will not occur if true **brand loyalty** exists. In contrast to inertia, brand loyalty describes repeat purchasing behaviour that reflects a *conscious* decision to continue buying the same brand.[154] For brand loyalty to exist, a pattern of repeat purchase must be accompanied by an underlying positive attitude towards the brand, rather than simply buying the same brand out of habit. Brand loyalty may be initiated by customer preference based on objective reasons, but after the brand has existed for a long time and is heavily advertised it can also create an emotional attachment, either by being incorporated into the consumer's self-image or because it is associated with prior experiences.[155] Purchase decisions based on brand loyalty also become habitual over time, though in these cases the underlying commitment to the product is much firmer.

Compared to inertia (a situation in which the consumer passively accepts a brand), a brand-loyal consumer is actively (sometimes passionately) involved with their favourite. Because of the emotional bonds that can exist between brand-loyal consumers and products, 'true-blue' users react more vehemently when these products are altered, redesigned or withdrawn.[156] Recall, for example, when Coca-Cola replaced its tried-and-tested formula with 'New Coke' in the 1980s.

A few decades ago, marketers struggled with the problem of *brand parity,* which refers to consumers' beliefs that there are no significant differences among brands. For example, one survey at that time found that more than 70 per cent of consumers worldwide believed that all paper towels, all soaps and all crisps were alike.[157] Some analysts even proclaimed the death of brand names, predicting that private-label or generic products that offered the same value for less money would kill off the tried-and-tested products.

This image illustrates the impact of advances in neuroscience in helping us better understand consumer behaviour.

In the Modern Brain Study/Neurological Research Laboratory this man is wearing a brainwave scanning headset and sits in a chair with closed eyes. Monitors show the EEG reading and a graphical model of the brain.

Gorodenkoff/Shutterstock

However, the reports of this death appear to be premature – major brands are making a dramatic come-back. With too many alternatives (many of them unfamiliar names) to choose from, people seem to be looking for a few clear signals of quality. Following a period in the late 1980s and early 1990s when people had strong doubts about the ability of large companies to produce quality products, more recent surveys indicate that consumers are slowly beginning to trust major manufacturers again.[158] Brand names are very much alive.

Affective decision-making

We now turn to the third broad category of decision-making (Figure 8.1) to look at affective aspects of decision-making. Many of our decisions are driven by our emotional responses to products or services. Social scientists refer to these raw reactions as **affect**. That explains why so many marketing activities and messages focus on altering our moods or linking products to an 'affective' response, although different types of emotional arousal may be more effective in some contexts than in others.[159] These connections make sense – for instance, writing an angry letter after getting poor service at a hotel or from an airline. One study looked at 'the pain of paying', and argued that immediate emotions experienced at the point of choice could affect consumer behaviour. These researchers examined the emotion of 'pain of paying' and identified that the 'anticipatory pain of paying drives "tightwads" to spend less than they would ideally spend. "Spendthrifts", by contrast, experience too little pain of paying and typically spend more than they would ideally like to spend.'[160]

Marketing opportunity

One study shows that this emotional element is especially potent for decisions that involve outcomes the person will experience shortly, as opposed to those that involve a longer time frame.[161] Another study attests to the interplay between our emotions and how we access information in our minds that allows us to make smarter decisions. These researchers reported evidence for what they call an 'emotional oracle effect': people who trusted their feelings were able to predict future events better than those who did not. This occurred for a range of situations, including the US presidential election, the winner of *American Idol*, cinema box office successes and the stock market. The likely reason is that those with more confidence were better able to access information they had learned that could help them make an informed forecast.[162]

Positive affect

Our feelings also can serve as a source of information when we weigh-up the pros and cons of a decision. Put simply, the fact that the prospect of owning a specific brand will make a person feel good is a determinant attribute – even if the brand is similar on a functional level to other competing brands. That helps to explain why many of us will willingly pay a premium for a product that, on the surface, seems to do the same thing as a less expensive alternative – whether in the case of the hottest new Apple iPhone, or a Ralph Lauren shirt. A passionate commitment to one brand has famously been termed a 'lovemark' by the head of the Saatchi & Saatchi advertising agency. Consumer–brand relationships involve a range of feelings (e.g. love, obsession). A recent study has identified a range of feelings that characterise **brand addiction**, including acquisitiveness, anxiety-irritability, compulsive urges, dependence and gratification. Brand addiction has been defined as 'a consumer's psychological state that involves mental and behavioral preoccupation with a particular brand, driven by uncontrollable urges to possess the brand's products, and involving positive affectivity and gratification'.[163]

Negative affect

Many researchers believe that the primitive emotion of disgust evolved to protect us from contamination; we learned over the years to avoid putrid meat and other foul substances linked to pathogens. As a result, even the slight odour of something nasty elicits a universal reaction – the wrinkling of the nose, curling of the upper lips and protrusion of the tongue. Wrinkling the nose has been shown to prevent pathogens from entering through the nasal cavity and sticking out the tongue aids in the expulsion of tainted food and is a common precursor to vomiting. So, what does this have to do with marketing and persuasion? Well, disgust also exerts a powerful effect on our judgements. People who experience this emotion become harsher in their judgements of moral offences and offenders. In one experiment, people who sat in a foul-smelling room or at a desk cluttered with dirty food containers judged acts such as lying on a résumé or keeping a wallet found on the street as more immoral than individuals who were asked to make the same judgements in a clean environment. In another study, survey respondents who were randomly asked to complete the items while they stood in front of a hand sanitiser gave more conservative responses than those who stood in another part of the hallway.[164]

Advertisers used to avoid using negative imagery so that they wouldn't turn people off, but many now realise that it actually can be productive to elicit extreme feelings such as disgust in order to get their message across. A Febreze TV ad, for instance, shows blindfolded volunteers sitting in an ultra-filthy room – but fooled into thinking that they smell something pleasant, thanks to the household odour killer.[165] For a detailed discussion of the novel phenomena of embodied cognition and sensory marketing, see Krishna, Lee, Li and Schwarz (2017).[166]

Chapter summary

Now that you have finished reading this chapter you should understand why:

8.1 **The intertwined three categories of consumer decision-making are cognitive, habitual and affective.** Consumer decision-making is a central part of consumer behaviour, but the way we evaluate and choose products (and the amount of thought we put into these choices) varies widely, depending on such dimensions as the degree of novelty or risk related to the decision. We almost constantly need to make decisions about products. Some of these decisions are very important and entail great effort, whereas we make other decisions on a virtually automatic basis. Perspectives on decision-making range from a focus on habits that people develop over time to novel situations involving a great deal of risk in which consumers must carefully collect and analyse information before making a choice. The way we evaluate and choose a product depends on our degree of involvement with the product, the marketing message and/or the purchase situation. Product involvement can range from very low, where purchase decisions are made via inertia, to very high, where consumers form very strong bonds with what they buy.

8.2 **A cognitive purchase decision is the outcome of a series of stages that results in the selection of one product over competing options.** A typical decision involves several steps. The first is problem recognition, when we realise we must take some action. This recognition may occur because a current possession malfunctions or perhaps because we have a desire for something new. Once the consumer recognises a problem and sees it as sufficiently important to warrant some action, he or she begins the process of the second step, information search. This search may range from performing a simple memory scan to determine what he or she has done before to resolve the same problem, to carrying out extensive fieldwork during which he or she consults a variety of sources to amass as much information as possible. The Web has changed the way many of us search for information. Today, our problem is more likely to be weeding out excess detail rather than searching for more information. Comparative search sites and intelligent agents help to filter and guide the search process. We may rely on cybermediaries, such as Web portals, to sort through massive amounts of information as a way to simplify the decision-making process. In the evaluation of alternatives third stage, the options a person considers constitute his or her evoked set. Members of the evoked set usually share some characteristics; we categorise them similarly. The way the person mentally groups products influences which alternatives he/she will consider, and usually we associate some brands more strongly with these categories (i.e. they are more prototypical). When the consumer eventually must make a product choice from among alternatives (the fourth step), they use one of several decision rules. Non-compensatory rules eliminate alternatives that are deficient on any of the criteria they've chosen. Compensatory rules, which they are more likely to apply in high-involvement situations, allow them to consider each alternative's good and bad points more carefully to arrive at the overall best choice. Once the consumer makes a choice, she/he engages in the final stage, post-purchase evaluation, to determine whether it was a good choice; this assessment, in turn, influences the process the next time the problem occurs.

8.3 **The way information about a product choice is framed can prime a decision, even when the consumer is unaware of this influence.** Principles of mental accounting demonstrate that the way a problem is framed and whether it is put in terms of gains or losses influences what we decide. In addition, other cues in the environment – including very subtle ones of which we may not even be aware – may prime us to choose one option over another. A prime is a stimulus that encourages people to focus on some specific aspect of their lives. Much of the current work in behavioural economics demonstrates how a nudge – a deliberate change by an organisation that intends to modify behaviour – can result in dramatic effects.

8.4 **We often rely on 'rules of thumb', heuristics or mental short cuts for habitual and routine decision-making.** In many cases, people engage in surprisingly little research. Instead, they rely on various mental short cuts, such as brand names or price, or they may simply imitate others' choices. We may use heuristics, or mental rules of thumb, to simplify decision-making. In particular, we develop many market beliefs over time. One of the most common beliefs is that we can determine quality by looking at the price. Other heuristics rely on well-known brand names or a product's country of origin as signals of product quality. When we consistently purchase a brand over time, this pattern may be the result of true brand loyalty or simply inertia because it's the easiest thing to do.

Key terms

Affect (p. 324)
Anchoring (p. 319)
Behavioural economics (p. 318)
Bounded rationality (p. 319)
Brand addiction (p. 324)
Brand advocates (p. 303)
Brand loyalty (p. 317)
Category exemplars (p. 309)
Cognitive processing style (p. 293)
Compensatory decision rules (p. 312)

Conjunctive rule (p. 312)
Consideration set (p. 307)
Constructive processing (p. 293)
Consumer hyperchoice (p. 292)
Consumer satisfaction/dissatisfaction (CS/D) (p. 315)
Counteractive construal (p. 294)
Country of origin (p. 321)
Co-variation (p. 320)
Cybermediary (p. 300)

Consumer behaviour challenge

1 Identify the differences between the cognitive, habitual and affective perspectives on decision-making. Give an example of the type of purchase that each perspective would help to explain.

2 If people are not always rational decision-makers, is it worth the effort to study how purchasing decisions are made? What techniques might be employed to understand affectively based consumption choices and to translate this knowledge into marketing strategy?

3 What is prospect theory? Does it support the argument that we are rational decision-makers?

4 Give an example of the sunk-cost fallacy.

5 Define the three levels of product categorisation described in the chapter. Diagram these levels for a health club.

6 Describe the difference between a superordinate category, a basic-level category and a subordinate category. Can you provide an example of each category level? What is an example of an exemplar product?

7 Describe the relationship between a consumer's level of expertise and how much they are likely to search for information about a product.

→

8 List three types of perceived risk and give an example of each.

9 List three product attributes that can be used as quality signals and provide an example of each.

10 Explain the 'evoked set'. Why is it difficult to place a product in a consumer's evoked set after it has already been rejected? What strategies might a marketer use in an attempt to accomplish this goal?

11 How does a brand function as a heuristic?

12 Discuss two different non-compensatory decision rules and highlight the difference(s) between them. How might the use of one rule versus another result in a different product choice?

13 Form a group of three. Pick a product and develop a marketing plan based on each of the three approaches to consumer decision-making: cognitive, habitual and affective. What are the major differences in emphasis among the three perspectives? Which is the most likely type of problem-solving activity for the product you have selected? What characteristics of the product make this so?

14 Find a person who is about to make a major purchase. Ask that person to make a chronological list of all the information sources consulted prior to making a decision. How would you characterise the types of sources used (i.e. internal versus external, (social) media versus personal, etc.)? Which sources appeared to have the most impact on the person's decision?

15 Perform a survey of country-of-origin stereotypes. Compile a list of five countries and ask people what products they associate with each. What are their evaluations of the products and what are the likely attributes of these different products? The power of a country stereotype can also be demonstrated in another way. Prepare a brief description of a product, including a list of features, and ask people to rate it in terms of quality, likelihood of purchase and so on. Make several versions of the description, varying only the country from which it comes. Do ratings change as a function of the country of origin?

16 In the past few years, several products made in China have been recalled because they are dangerous or even fatal to use (see https://ec.europa.eu/consumers/consumers_safety/safety_products/rapex/alerts/repository/content/pages/rapex/reports/docs/rapex_annual_report_2016_en.pdf (accessed 29 July 2018) for an up-to-date list). If the Chinese government hired you as a consultant to help it repair some of the damage to the reputation of products made there, what actions would you recommend?

17 What is neuromarketing, and is it dangerous? Identify the advantages and disadvantages of neuromarketing from the perspective firstly of the consumer, secondly of the market researcher and thirdly of the marketing brand manager.

18 Ask a friend to 'talk through' the process they used to choose one brand rather than others during a recent purchase. Based on this description, can you identify the decision rule that they probably employed?

19 Technology has the potential to make our lives easier by reducing the amount of clutter we need to work through in order to access the information on the internet that really interests us. On the other hand, intelligent agents that make recommendations based only on what we and others like us have chosen in the past perhaps potentially limit us – they reduce the chance that we will stumble upon something (e.g. a book on a topic we've never heard of, or a music group that's different from the style we usually listen to). Will the proliferation of shopping bots make our lives too predictable by only giving us more of the same? If so, is this a problem?

20 Read Rust, Thompson and Hamilton's article in *Harvard Business Review* (February 2006: 98ff) on 'Defeating feature fatigue'.[167] Summarise their main arguments and examples into a paragraph. Working in groups of three, write a brief for a marketing manager: first, explain why consumers prefer capability to usability; second, identify the disadvantages for both consumers and managers of consumers' tendency to prefer capability to usability; and third, suggest strategies that managers might adopt to counter feature fatigue among consumers.

21 'Too many features can make a product overwhelming for consumers and difficult to use'.[168] Debate this statement in class, using the material on adoption and diffusion from Chapter 13 in this text. How might marketing managers overcome barriers to adoption of their technically sophisticated products?

22 Think of a product you recently shopped for online. Describe your search process. How did you become aware you wanted/needed the product? How did you evaluate alternatives? Did you end up buying online? Why, or why not? What factors would make it more or less likely that you would buy something online rather than in a traditional store?

23 How do a consumer's prior expectations about product quality influence their satisfaction with the product after they buy it? List three actions a consumer can take if they are dissatisfied with a purchase.

24 Consider the five types of perceived risk in Figure 8.6 within the context of making a decision to purchase a new diamond. Review the following websites and discuss the kinds of risk you would consider in buying a diamond on the Web: http://www.mouawad.com/ and www.bluenile.com.

25 Find examples of electronic recommendation agents on the Web. Evaluate these – are they helpful? What characteristics of the sites you locate are likely to make you buy products you wouldn't have bought on your own?

26 It is increasingly clear that many postings on blogs and product reviews on websites are fake, or are posted there to manipulate consumers' opinions. For example, a mini-scandal erupted in 2007 when the press learned that the CEO of Whole Foods had regularly been blasting competitor Wild Oats on blogs under a pseudonym.[169] How big a problem is this if consumers are increasingly looking to consumer-generated product reviews to guide their purchase decisions? What steps, if any, can marketers take to tackle this problem?

27 Visit the EC website about systems of consumer protection in the EC *inter alia*: https://ec.europa.eu/consumers/consumers_safety/safety_products/rapex/alerts/repository/content/pages/rapex/reports/docs/rapid_alert_system_factsheet-2016.pdf (accessed 29 July 2018). Debate in class the reasons why there is increasing concern about 'keeping consumers safe'; and how far is it the role of national governments or international institutions (like the EU) to undertake this? What about the traditional view of the consumer's responsibility, i.e. buyer beware or *caveat emptor*?

For additional material see the companion website at **www.pearsoned.co.uk/solomon**

See Case studies C.1, C.2 and C.3 at the end of Part C:

Case study C.1: 'When rapper buys a champagne house: Jay-Z and Ace of Spades', Joonas Rokka (EMLYON, France) and Nacima Ourahmoune (Kedge Business School, France)

Case study C.2: 'Changing attitudes towards alcohol consumption: emotion and information appeals', Effi Raftopoulou (Salford University, UK)

Case study C.3: 'Ethical luxury: some consumption dilemmas of ethics and sustainability', Sheila Malone (Lancaster University, UK)

Notes

1. http://www.hdtvtest.co.uk/ (accessed 29 July 2018).
2. Kashfia Kabir, 'What is OLED? The tech, the benefits, the best OLED TVs and OLED phones', (17 January 2018), https://www.whathifi.com/advice/what-oled-tech-benefits-best-oled-tvs-and-oled-phones (accessed 29 July 2018).
3. Ravi Dhar, Joel Huber and Uzma Khan, 'The Shopping Momentum Effect', paper presented at the Association for Consumer Research, Atlanta, GA, October 2002.
4. David Glen Mick, Susan M. Broniarczyk and Jonathan Haidt, 'Choose, choose, choose, choose, choose, choose, choose: emerging and prospective research on the deleterious effects of living in consumer hyperchoice', *Journal of Business Ethics* 52 (2004): 207–11; see also Barry Schwartz, *The Paradox of Choice: Why More Is Less* (New York: Ecco, 2005).
5. Frank Huber, Sören Köcher, Frederik Meyer and Johannes Vogel, 'The Paralyzed Customer: An Empirical Investigation of Antecedents and Consequences of Decision Paralysis' in Alan Bradshaw, Chris Hackley and Pauline Maclaran (eds), *European Association for Consumer Research Conference* 2010 RHUL: 82.
6. Simona Botti, Kristina Orfali and Sheena S. Iyengar, 'Tragic Choices: Autonomy and emotional responses to medical decisions', *Journal of Consumer Research* 36 (October 2009): 337–52; cf. also Hazel Rose Markus and Barry Schwartz, 'Does choice mean freedom and well being?' *Journal of Consumer Research* 37(2) (2010): 344–55.
7. James R. Bettman, 'The Decision Maker Who Came in from the Cold' (presidential address), in Leigh McAllister and

Michael Rothschild, eds., *Advances in Consumer Research* 20 (Provo, UT: Association for Consumer Research, 1993): 7–11; John W. Payne, James R. Bettman and Eric J. Johnson, 'Behavioral decision research: A constructive processing perspective', *Annual Review of Psychology* 4 (1992): 87–131.

8. Parthasarathy Krishnamurthy and Sonja Prokopec, 'Resisting that triple-chocolate cake: Mental budgets and self-control', *Journal of Consumer Research* 37 (June 2010): 68–79.

9. Thomas P. Novak and Donna L. Hoffman, 'The fit of thinking style and situation: New measures of situation-specific experiential and rational cognition', *Journal of Consumer Research* 36 (December 2009): 56–72.

10. Peter M. Gollwitzer and Paschal Sheeran, 'Self-regulation of consumer decision making and behavior: The role of implementation intentions', *Journal of Consumer Psychology* 19 (2009): 593–607.

11. Ying Zhang, Szu-chi Huang and Susan M. Broniarczyk, 'Counteractive construal in consumer goal pursuit', *Journal of Consumer Research* 37 (June 2010): 129–42.

12. Thomas Goetz, 'Harnessing the power of feedback loops', *Wired* (19 June 2011), http://www.wired.com/2011/06/ff_feedbackloop/all/1 (accessed 29 July 2018).

13. Maryan Kouchadki and Isaac H. Smith, 'The morning morality effect: The influence of time of day on unethical behavior', *Psychological Science* 25(1) (January 2014): 95–102.

14. Quoted in Matt Richtel, 'That devil on your shoulder likes to sleep in', *New York Times* (1 November 2014), http://www.nytimes.com/2014/11/02/business/that-devil-on-your-shoulder-likes-to-sleep-in.html?module=Search&mabReward=relbias%3As%2C%7B%221%22%3A%22RI%3A6%22%7D (accessed 29 July 2018).

15. Claudia Townsend and Wendy Liu, 'Is planning good for you? The differential impact of planning on self-Regulation', *Journal of Consumer Research* 39(4) (December 2012): 688–703.

16. Ibid.

17. John G. Lynch, Richard G. Netemeyer, Stephen A. Spiller and Alessandra Zammit, 'A generalizable scale of propensity to plan: The long and the short of planning for time and for money', *Journal of Consumer Research* 37 (June 2010): 108–28; Anick Bosmans, Rik Pieters and Hans Baumgartner, 'The get ready mind-set: How gearing up for later impacts effort allocation now', *Journal of Consumer Research* 37 (June 2010): 98–107.

18. John C. Mowen, 'Beyond consumer decision-making', *Journal of Consumer Marketing* 5(1) (1988): 15–25.

19. Itamar Simonson, Joel Huber and John Payne, 'The relationship between Prior Brand Knowledge and Information Acquisition Order', *Journal of Consumer Research* 14 (March 1988): 566–78.

20. John R. Hauser, Glenn L. Urban and Bruce D. Weinberg, 'How consumers allocate their time when searching for information', *Journal of Marketing Research* 30 (November 1993): 452–66; George J. Stigler, 'The economics of information', *Journal of Political Economy* 69 (June 1961): 213–25. For a set of studies focusing on online search costs, see John G. Lynch, Jr., and Dan Ariely, 'Wine online: Search costs and competition on price, quality, and Distribution', *Marketing Science* 19(1) (2000): 83–103.

21. Ying Zhang, Ayelet Fishback and Ravi Dhar, 'When thinking beats doing: The role of optimistic expectations in goal-based choice', *Journal of Consumer Research* 34 (December 2007): 567.

22. Gordon C. Bruner III and Richard J. Pomazal, 'Problem recognition: The crucial first stage of the consumer decision process', *Journal of Consumer Marketing* 5(1) (1988): 53–63.

23. http://www.knowyourmobile.com/nokia/nokia-3310/19848/history-mobile-phones-1973-2007-these-are-handsets-made-it-happen (accessed 29 July 2018); http://pocketnow.com/2014/07/28/the-evolution-of-the-smartphone (accessed 29 July 2018).

24. For a study that examined trade-offs in search behaviour among different channels, cf. Judi Strebel, Tulin Erdem and Joffre Swait, 'Consumer search in high technology markets: Exploring the use of traditional information channels', *Journal of Consumer Psychology* 14(1&2) (2004): 96–104.

25. Peter H. Bloch, Daniel L. Sherrell and Nancy M. Ridgway, 'Consumer search: An extended framework', *Journal of Consumer Research* 13 (June 1986): 119–26.

26. Richard Thaler, 'Mental accounting and consumer choice', *Marketing Science* 4 (3) (1985): 199–214.

27. Girish N. Punj and Richard Staelin, 'A model of consumer search behavior for new automobiles', *Journal of Consumer Research* 9 (March 1983): 366–80. For recent work on online search that decomposes search strategies in terms of type of good, cf. Peng Huang, Nicholas H. Lurie and Sabyasachi Mitra, 'Searching for experience on the web: An empirical examination of consumer behavior for search and experience goods', *Journal of Marketing* 73 (March 2009): 55–69.

28. Cathy J. Cobb and Wayne D. Hoyer, 'Direct observation of search behavior'; William L. Moore and Donald R. Lehmann, 'Individual differences in search behavior for a nondurable'; Girish N. Punj and Richard Staelin, 'A model of consumer search behavior for new automobiles'; Brian T. Ratchford, M. S. Lee and D. Toluca, 'The impact of the internet on information search for automobiles', *Journal of Marketing Research* 40(2) (2003): 193–209.

29. James R. Bettman and C. Whan Park, 'Effects of prior knowledge and experience and phase of the choice process on consumer decision processes: A protocol analysis', *Journal of Consumer Research* 7 (December 1980): 234–48.

30. Michael Porter, *Competitive Advantage* (New York: Free Press, 1985).

31. Jeffrey M. O'Brien, 'You're sooooooo predictable', *Fortune* (27 November 2006): 230.

32. Claire Cain Miller, 'Mobile apps drive rapid change in searches', *New York Times* (7 January 2013).

33. Tracy W. Tuten and Michael R. Solomon, *Social Media Marketing*, 2nd edition (London: SAGE, 2016).

34. 'Customer product reviews drive online satisfaction and conversion', *Marketing Daily* (24 January 2007).

35. Sangkil Moon, Paul K. Bergey and Dawn Iacobucci, 'Dynamic effects among movie ratings, Movie revenues, and viewer satisfaction', *Journal of Marketing* 74 (January 2010): 108–21; Anya Kamenetz, 'The perils and promise of the reputation economy', *Fast Company* (3 December 2008).

36. Chris Anderson, *The Long Tail: Why the Future of Business Is Selling Less of More* (New York: Hyperion, 2006).

37. Joseph Lajos, Amitava Chattopadhyay and Kishore Sengupta, 'When Electronic Recommendation Agents Backfire: Negative Effects on Choice Satisfaction, Attitudes, and Purchase Intentions', *INSEAD Working Paper Series* (2009).

38. Emily Burg, 'Leverage user-generated content to boost brands', *Marketing Daily* (13 March 2007).

39. Cathy J. Cobb and Wayne D. Hoyer, 'Direct observation of search behavior,' *Psychology & Marketing* 2 (Fall 1985): 161–79.

40. Sharon E. Beatty and Scott M. Smith, 'External search effort: An investigation across several product categories', *Journal of Consumer Research* 14 (June 1987): 83–95; William L. Moore and Donald R. Lehmann, 'Individual differences in search behavior for a nondurable', *Journal of Consumer Research* 7 (December 1980): 296–307.

41. David F. Midgley, 'Patterns of interpersonal information seeking for the purchase of a symbolic product', *Journal of Marketing Research* 20 (February 1983): 74–83.

42. Alexander Fedorikhin and Catherine A. Cole, 'Mood effects on attitudes, perceived risk and choice: moderators and mediators', *Journal of Consumer Psychology* 14(1&2) (2004): 2–12.

43. For a discussion of 'collective risk', where consumers experience a reduction in perceived risk by sharing their exposure with others who are also using the product or service, see an analysis of Hotline, an online file-sharing community in Markus Geisler, 'Collective Risk', working paper, Northwestern University (March 2003).

44. *Safe Rapid Alert System for dangerous products*, http://ec.europa.eu/consumers/consumers_safety/safety_products/rapex/reports/docs/rapex_infographic_final_en.pdf (accessed 29 July 2018).

45. Gianluigi Guido, M. Irene Prete and Giovanni Pino, 'Purchasing motivations of regular and occasional organic food consumers: The incidence of food safety and ethical concern' in Alan Bradshaw, Chris Hackley and Pauline Maclaran (eds), *European Association for Consumer Research Conference* 2010 RHUL: 17.

46. Jamie Grierson and Ben Quinn, 'Google loses landmark "right to be forgotten" case', *The Guardian* (14 April 2018), https://www.theguardian.com/technology/2018/apr/13/google-loses-right-to-be-forgotten-case (accessed 29 July 2018).

47. For a fuller discussion of these two UK court cases, see Jamie Grierson and Ben Quinn, ibid.

48. Meyrav Shoham, Sarit Moldovan and Yael Steinhart, 'Positively useless: Irrelevant negative information enhances positive impressions', *Journal of Consumer Psychology* 27(2) (2017): 147–59.

49. Ibid.

50. Mary Frances Luce, James R. Bettman and John W. Payne, 'Choice processing in emotionally difficult decisions', *Journal of Experimental Psychology: Learning, Memory, and Cognition* 23 (March 1997): 384–405; example provided by Prof. James Bettman, personal communication (17 December 1997).

51. Some research suggests that structural elements of the information available, such as the number and distribution of attribute levels, will influence how items in a consideration set are processed; cf. Nicholas H. Lurie, 'Decision making in information-rich environments: The role of information structure', *Journal of Consumer Research* 30 (March 2004): 473–86.

52. John R. Hauser and Birger Wernerfelt, 'An evaluation cost model of consideration sets', *Journal of Consumer Research* 16 (March 1990): 393–408.

53. Robert J. Sutton, 'Using empirical data to investigate the likelihood of brands being admitted or re-admitted into an established evoked set', *Journal of the Academy of Marketing Science* 15 (Fall 1987): 82.

54. Stephen A. Spiller, 'Opportunity cost consideration', *Journal of Consumer Research* 38(4) (2011): 595–610; Philp M. Fernbach, Christina Kan and John G. Lynch, 'Squeezed: coping with constraint through efficiency and prioritization', *Journal of Consumer Research* 41(5) (2015): 1,204–27.

55. Cf., for example, Kenneth C. Manning and David E. Sprott, 'Price endings, left-digit effects, and choice', *Journal of Consumer Research* 36(2) (2009): 328–35; Sandra J. Milberg, Francisca Sinn and Ronald C. Goodstein, 'Consumer reactions to brand extensions in a competitive context: Does fit still matter?', *Journal of Consumer Research* 37(3) (2010): 543–53; David Sleeth-Keppler and Christian S. Wheeler, 'A multidimensional association approach to sequential consumer judgments', *Journal of Consumer Psychology* 21(1) (2011): 14–23; Aner Sela, Jonah Berger and Wendy Liu, 'Variety, vice, and virtue: How assortment size influences option choice', *Journal of Consumer Research* 35(6) (2009): 941–51.

56. Jeffrey R. Parker and Donald R. Lehmann, 'How and when grouping low-calorie options reduces the benefits of providing dish-specific calorie information', *Journal of Consumer Research* 41(1) (2014): 213–35; cf. also Avni M. Shah, James R. Bettman, Peter A. Ubel, Punam Anand Keller and Julie A. Edell, 'Surcharges plus unhealthy labels reduce demand for unhealthy menu items', *Journal of Marketing Research* 51(6) (2014): 773–89.

57. Cyndee Miller, 'Hemp is latest buzzword', *Marketing News* (17 March 1997): 1.

58. Stuart Elliott, 'A Brand Tries to Invite Thought', *New York Times* (7 September 2007).

59. Alba and Hutchinson, 'Dimensions of consumer expertise' and Joel B. Cohen and Kunal Basu, 'Alternative models of categorization: toward a contingent processing framework', *Journal of Consumer Research* 13 (March 1987): 455–72.

60. Robert M. McMath, 'The perils of typecasting', *American Demographics* (February 1997): 60.

61. Eleanor Rosch, 'Principles of Categorization', in E. Rosch and B.B. Lloyd (eds), *Recognition and Categorization* (Hillsdale, N.J.: Erlbaum, 1978).

62. Michael R. Solomon, 'Mapping product constellations: A social categorization approach to symbolic consumption', *Psychology and Marketing* 5(3) (1988): 233–58.

63. McMath, 'The perils of typecasting', op. cit.

64. Elizabeth C. Hirschman and Michael R. Solomon, 'Competition and Cooperation Among Culture Production Systems', in Ronald F. Bush and Shelby D. Hunt (eds), *Marketing Theory: Philosophy of Science Perspectives* (Chicago: American Marketing Association, 1982): 269–72.

65. Michael D. Johnson, 'The differential processing of product category and noncomparable choice alternatives', *Journal of Consumer Research* 16 (December 1989): 300–9.

66. Mita Sujan, 'Consumer knowledge: Effects on evaluation strategies mediating consumer judgments', *Journal of Consumer Research* 12 (June 1985): 31–46.

67. Rosch, 'Principles of categorization', op. cit.

68. Joan Meyers-Levy and Alice M. Tybout, 'Schema congruity as a basis for product evaluation', *Journal of Consumer Research* 16 (June 1989): 39–55.

69. Mita Sujan and James R. Bettman, 'The effects of brand positioning strategies on consumers' brand and category perceptions: Some insights from schema research', *Journal of Marketing Research* 26 (November 1989): 454–67.

70. Lutz Stobbe, EuP Preparatory Studies, 'Televisions' (Lot 5) Final Report on Task 3 "Consumer Behaviour and Local Infrastructure" (TREN/D1/40 lot 5-2005), compiled by Deutsche

Umwelthilfe and Fraunhofer IZM (contractor, Fraunhofer Institute for Reliability and Microintegration, IZM: Berlin) (2 August 2007): 5.

71. James Surowiecki, 'Feature Presentation', *The New Yorker* (28 May 2007).

72. The 2015 Harris Poll Reputation Quotient® (RQ®): The Reputations of the 100 Most Visible Companies Among the U.S. General Public.

73. Sikka, Prem, 'Sleeping watchdogs', http://www.guardian.co.uk/commentisfree/2009/jan/14/corporatefraud (accessed 29 July 2018).

74. Stuart Rose, quoted in *Corporate Reputation Magazine*, Oxford University, 1 (Michaelmas 2014): p. 5.

75. Jack Trout, 'Marketing in tough times', *Boardroom Reports* 2 (October 1992): 8.

76. Amna Kirmani and Peter Wright, 'Procedural learning, consumer decision making and marketing communication', *Marketing Letters* 4(1) (1993): 39–48.

77. C. Whan Park, 'The effect of individual and situation-related factors on consumer selection of judgmental models', *Journal of Marketing Research* 13 (May 1976): 144–51.

78. Joseph W. Alba and Howard Marmorstein, 'The effects of frequency knowledge on consumer decision making', *Journal of Consumer Research* 14 (June 1987): 14–25.

79. Anish Nagpal and Parthasarathy Krishnamurthy, 'Attribute conflict in consumer decision making: the role of task compatibility', *Journal of Consumer Research* 34 (February 2008): 696–705.

80. Carmen Nobel, 'Neuromarketing: Tapping Into the "Pleasure center" of consumers', *Forbes* (1 February 2013); www.neurosciencemarketing.com/blog (accessed 29 July 2018); Martin Reimann, Oliver Schilke, Bernd Weber, Carolin Neuhaus and Judith L. Zaichkowsky, 'Functional magnetic resonance imaging in consumer research: A review and application', *Psychology & Marketing* 28(6) (2011): 608–37; sandra blakeslee, 'If you have a "buy button" in your brain, what pushes it?', *New York Times* (19 October 2004); Clive Thompson, 'There's a sucker born in every medial prefrontal cortex', *New York Times* (26 October 2003).

81. Ibid.

82. Rupert Neate, 'Ad men use brain scanners to probe our emotional response', *The Guardian* (14 January 2012), http://www.guardian.co.uk/media/2012/jan/14/neuroscience-advertising-scanners?INTCMP=SRCH (accessed 29 July 2018).

83. William P. Putsis Jr and Narasimhan Srinivasan, 'Buying or just browsing? The duration of purchase deliberation', *Journal of Marketing Research* 31 (August 1994): 393–402.

84. Robert E. Smith, 'Integrating information from advertising and trial: Processes and effects on consumer response to product information', *Journal of Marketing Research* 30 (May 1993): 204–19.

85. Ibid.

86. Roland T. Rust, Debora V. Thompson and Rebecca W. Hamilton, 'Defeating feature fatigue', *Harvard Business Review* 84 (February 2006): 100.

87. Rebecca W. Hamilton and Debora Viana Thompson, 'Is there a substitute for direct experience? Comparing consumers' preferences after direct and indirect product experiences', *Journal of Consumer Research* 34 (December 2007): 546–55.

88. Debora V. Thompson, Rebecca W. Hamilton and Roland T. Rust, 'Feature fatigue: When product capabilities become too much of a good thing', *Journal of Marketing Research* 42 (November 2005): 431–42; Roland T. Rust, Debora V.

Thompson and Rebecca W. Hamilton, 'Defeating feature fatigue', op. cit.: 98–107.

89. Smith, 'Integrating information from advertising and trial: processes and effects on consumer response to product information', op. cit.

90. Cyndee Miller, 'Scotland to U.S.: "This Tennent's for you"', *Marketing News* (29 August 1994): 26.

91. Jeff Galak, Joseph P. Redden and Justin Kruger (2009), 'Variety amnesia: Recalling past variety can accelerate recovery from satiation', *Journal of Consumer Research* 36(4) (2009): 575–84.

92. Rebecca K. Ratner, Barbara E. Kahn and Daniel Kahneman, 'Choosing less-preferred experiences for the sake of variety', *Journal of Consumer Research* 26 (June 1999): 1–15.

93. Satya Menon and Barbara E. Kahn, 'The impact of context on variety seeking in product choices', *Journal of Consumer Research* 22 (December 1995): 285–95; Barbara E. Kahn and Alice M. Isen, 'The influence of positive affect on variety seeking among safe, enjoyable products', *Journal of Consumer Research* 20 (September 1993): 257–70.

94. J. Jeffrey Inman, 'The Role of Sensory-Specific Satiety in Consumer Variety Seeking Among Flavors' (unpublished manuscript, A.C. Nielsen Center for Marketing Research, University of Wisconsin-Madison, July 1999).

95. Michael Laroche, Chankon Kim and Lianxi Zhou, 'Brand familiarity and confidence as determinants of purchase intention: An empirical test in a multiple brand context', *Journal of Business Research* 37 (1996): 115–20.

96. Barbara E. Kahn, 'Understanding Variety-Seeking Behavior From a Marketing Perspective' (unpublished manuscript, University of Pennsylvania, University Park, 1991); Leigh McAlister and Edgar A. Pessemier, 'Variety-seeking behavior: An interdisciplinary review', *Journal of Consumer Research* 9 (December 1982): 311–22; Fred M. Feinberg, Barbara E. Kahn and Leigh McAlister, 'Market share response when consumers seek variety', *Journal of Marketing Research* 29 (May 1992): 228–37; Kahn and Isen, 'The influence of positive affect on variety seeking among safe, enjoyable products', op. cit.

97. Rama Jayanti and Anita Jackson, 'Service Satisfaction: Investigation of Three Models', in Rebecca H. Holman and Michael R. Solomon, eds., *Advances in Consumer Research* 18 (Provo, UT: Association for Consumer Research, 1991): 603–10; David K. Tse, Franco M. Nicosia and Peter C. Wilton, 'Consumer satisfaction as a process', *Psychology & Marketing* 7 (Fall 1990): 177–93. For a recent treatment of satisfaction issues from a more interpretive perspective, see Susan Fournier and David Mick, 'Rediscovering satisfaction', *Journal of Marketing* 63 (October 1999): 5–23.

98. Constance L. Hayes, 'Service takes a holiday', *New York Times* (23 December 1998): C1.

99. Robert Jacobson and David A. Aaker, 'The strategic role of product quality', *Journal of Marketing* 51 (October 1987): 31–44. For a review of issues regarding the measurement of service quality, see J. Joseph Cronin, Jr. and Steven A. Taylor, 'Measuring service quality: A re-examination and extension', *Journal of Marketing* 56 (July 1992): 55–68.

100. Amna Kirmani and Peter Wright, 'Money talks: Perceived advertising expense and expected product quality', *Journal of Consumer Research* 16 (December 1989): 344–53; Donald R. Lichtenstein and Scot Burton, 'The relationship between perceived and objective price-quality', *Journal of Marketing Research* 26 (November 1989): 429–43; Akshay R. Rao and

Kent B. Monroe, 'The effect of price, brand name, and store name on buyers' perceptions of product quality: An integrative review', *Journal of Marketing Research* 26 (August 1989): 351–7; Shelby Hunt, 'Post–transactional communication and dissonance reduction', *Journal of Marketing* 34 (January 1970): 46–51; Daniel E. Innis and H. Rao Unnava, 'The Usefulness of Product Warranties for Reputable and new Brands', in Rebecca H. Holman and Michael R. Solomon, eds., *Advances in Consumer Research* 18 (Provo, UT: Association for Consumer Research, 1991): 317–22; Terence A. Shimp and William O. Bearden, 'Warranty and other extrinsic cue effects on consumers' risk perceptions', *Journal of Consumer Research* 9 (June 1982): 38–46.

101. Gilbert A. Churchill, Jr., and Carol F. Surprenant, 'An investigation into the determinants of customer satisfaction', *Journal of Marketing Research* 19 (November 1983): 491–504; John E. Swan and I. Frederick Trawick, 'Disconfirmation of expectations and satisfaction with a retail service', *Journal of Retailing* 57 (Fall 1981): 49–67; Peter C. Wilton and David K. Tse, 'Models of consumer satisfaction formation: An extension', *Journal of Marketing Research* 25 (May 1988): 204–12. For a discussion of what may occur when customers evaluate a new service for which comparison standards do not yet exist, see Ann L. McGill and Dawn Iacobucci, 'The Role of Post-Experience Comparison Standards in the Evaluation of Unfamiliar Services', in John F. Sherry, Jr. and Brian Sternthal, eds., *Advances in Consumer Research* 19 (Provo, UT: Association for Consumer Research, 1992): 570–8; William Boulding, Ajay Kalra, Richard Staelin and Valarie A. Zeithaml, 'A dynamic process model of service quality: From expectations to behavioral intentions', *Journal of Marketing Research* 30 (February 1993): 7–27.

102. Jagdish N. Sheth and Banwari Mittal, 'A framework for managing customer expectations', *Journal of Market Focused Management* 1 (1996): 137–58.

103. Andreas Herrmann, Frank Huber and Christine Braunstein, 'A Regret Theory Approach to Assessing Customer Satisfaction when Alternatives are Considered', in Dubois, Lowrey, Shrum and Vanhuele (eds), *European Advances in Consumer Research* 4: 82–8.

104. Kjell Grønhaug and Alladi Venkatesh, 'Products and services in the perspectives of consumer socialisation', *European Journal of Marketing* 21(10) (1987); Folke Ölander, 'Consumer Satisfaction – A Sceptic's View', in H.K. Hunt (ed.), *Conceptualization and Measurement of Consumer Satisfaction and Dissatisfaction* (Cambridge, MA: Marketing Science Institute, 1977): 453–88.

105. Alessandro M. Peluso and Gianluigi Guido, 'Testing antecedents and moderators in product evaluation: Towards a new model of consumer satisfaction' in Alan Bradshaw, Chris Hackley and Pauline Maclaran (eds), *European Association for Consumer Research Conference* 2010 RHUL: 15.

106. *The Consumer Markets Scoreboard: Monitoring Consumer Outcomes in the Single Market*, COM 31, European Communities, Luxembourg 2008: 17.

107. Mary C. Gilly and Betsy D. Gelb, 'Post-purchase consumer processes and the complaining consumer', *Journal of Consumer Research* 9 (December 1982): 323–8; Diane Halstead and Cornelia Droge, 'Consumer Attitudes Toward Complaining and the Prediction of Multiple Complaint Responses', in Holman and Solomon (eds), *Advances in Consumer Research* 18: 210–16; Jagdip Singh, 'Consumer complaint intentions and behavior: definitional and taxonomical issues', *Journal of Marketing* 52 (January 1988): 93–107.

108. *The Consumer Markets Scoreboard: Monitoring Consumer Outcomes in the Single Market,* COM 31, European Communities, Luxembourg, 2008: 17.

109. Alan Andreasen and Arthur Best, 'Consumers complain – does business respond?', *Harvard Business Review* 55 (July/August 1977): 93–101.

110. John A. Schibrowsky and Richard S. Lapidus, 'Gaining a competitive advantage by analysing aggregate complaints', *Journal of Consumer Marketing* 11(1) (1994): 15–26.

111. Veronica Liljander, 'Consumer Satisfaction with Complaint Handling Following a Dissatisfactory Experience with Car Repair', in Dubois, Lowrey, Shrum and Vanhuele (eds), *European Advances in Consumer Research* 4: 270–5.

112. Richard W. Olshavsky and Donald H. Granbois, 'Consumer decision-making – fact or fiction', *Journal of Consumer Research* 6 (September 1989): 93–100.

113. Joseph W. Alba and J. Wesley Hutchinson, 'Dimensions of consumer expertise', *Journal of Consumer Research* 13 (March 1988): 411–54.

114. Malcolm Gladwell, *Blink: The Power of Thinking Without Thinking* (New York: Little Brown & Company, 2005): 48–71.

115. Aimee Drolet and Wendy Wood, 'The habit-driven consumer: Introduction to the Special Issue', *Journal of the Association for Consumer Research* 2(3) (July 2017): 275–8 inter alia.

116. Geoffrey C. Kiel and Roger A. Layton, 'Dimensions of consumer information seeking behavior', *Journal of Marketing Research* 28 (May 1981): 233–9; see also Narasimhan Srinivasan and Brian T. Ratchford, 'An empirical test of a model of external search for automobiles', *Journal of Consumer Research* 18 (September 1991): 233–42; Alex Mindlin, 'Buyers Search Online, but Not by Brand', *New York Times* (13 March 2006); Cathy J. Cobb and Wayne D. Hoyer, 'Direct observation of search behavior', *Psychology & Marketing* 2 (Fall 1985): 161–79; Sharon E. Beatty and Scott M. Smith, 'External search effort: An investigation across several product categories', *Journal of Consumer Research* 14 (June 1987): 83–95; William L. Moore and Donald R. Lehmann, 'Individual differences in search behavior for a nondurable', *Journal of Consumer Research* 7 (December 1980): 296–307.

117. Gladwell, 2005, op. cit.

118. J. A. Bargh and T. L. Chartrand, 'The unbearable automaticity of being', *American Psychologist* 54(7) (1999): 462–79; J. A. Bargh and M. J. Ferguson, 'Beyond behaviourism: On the automaticity of higher mental processes', *Psychological Bulletin* 126(6) (2000): 925–45.

119. Gavan Fitzsimons, 'LB As I See It', in M. Solomon, *Consumer Behaviour*, 10th edn (Harlow, UK: Pearson, 2012).

120. Ibid.

121. Ibid.

122. Steven J. Levitt and Stephen G. Dubner, *Freakonomics: A Rogue Economist Explores the Hidden Side of Everything* (New York, NY: Harper Perennial, 2009); Dan Ariely, *Predictably Irrational: The Hidden Forces That Shape Our Decisions* (New York, NY: HarperCollins, 2008).

123. Eduardo Porter, 'How money affects morality', *New York Times* (3 January 2013), http://economix.blogs.nytimes.com/2013/06/13/how-money-affects-morality/ (accessed 29 July 2018).

124. Gergana Y. Nenkov and Maura L. Scott, 'So cute I could eat it up: Priming effects of cute products on indulgent consumption', *Journal of Consumer Research* 41(2) (August 2014): 326–41.

125. Adrian C. North, David J. Hargreaves and Jennifer McKendrick, 'The influence of in-store music on wine selections', *Journal of Applied Psychology* 84(2) (April 1999): 271–6.

126. Rob Girling, 'Design's next frontier: Nudging consumers into making better life choices', *Fast Company* (15 February 2012), http://www.fastcodesign.com/1669055/designs-next-frontier-nudging-consumers-into-making-better-life-choices?partner=homepage_newsletter (accessed 29 July 2018); for examples in the health and wellness area, cf. Zoe Chance, Margarita Gorlin and Ravi Dhar, 'Why choosing healthy foods is hard, and how to help: Presenting the 4Ps framework for behavior change', *Customer Needs and Solutions* 1(4) (2014): 253–62.

127. Richard H. Thaler and Cass R. Sunstein, *Nudge: Improving Decisions About Health, Wealth, and Happiness* (New York: Penguin Books, 2009); Rob Girling, 'Design's next frontier: nudging consumers Into making better life choices', *Fast Company* (29 February 2012), http://www.fastcodesign.com/1669055/designs-next-frontier-nudging-consumers-into-making-better-life-choices?partner=homepage_newsletter (accessed 29 July 2018); John A. Bargh and Tanya L. Chartrand, 'The unbearable automaticity of being', *American Psychologist* 54(7) (1999): 462–79; J.A. Bargh and M.J. Ferguson, 'Beyond behaviourism: On the automaticity of higher mental processes', *Psychological Bulletin* 126(6) (2000): 925–45.

128. Cole Moreton, 'Organ donation saves lives. Why don't more people sign up for it?', *The Guardian* (20 September 2017) https://www.theguardian.com/commentisfree/2017/sep/11/organ-donation-saves-lives-jemima-layzell-waiting-list (accessed 29 July 2018).

129. Robert A. Baron, *Psychology: The Essential Science* (Boston: Allyn & Bacon, 1989); Valerie S. Folkes, 'The availability heuristic and perceived risk', *Journal of Consumer Research* 15 (June 1989): 13–23; Daniel Kahneman and Amos Tversky, 'Prospect theory: An analysis of decision under risk', *Econometrica* 47 (1979): 263–91.

130. Example developed from Ritesh Saini and Ashwani Monga, 'How I decide depends on what I spend: Use of heuristics is greater for time than for money', *Journal of Consumer Research* 34 (April 2008): 914–22.

131. Amos Tversky and Daniel Kahneman, 'Judgment under uncertainty: Heuristics and biases', *Science* 27(185) (September 1974): 1,124–31.

132. Saini and Monga, 'How I decide depends on what I spend', op. cit.: 915.

133. Saini and Monga, 'How I Decide Depends on What I Spend', op. cit.: 920.

134. Wayne D. Hoyer, 'An Examination of consumer decision-making for a common repeat purchase product', *Journal of Consumer Research* 11 (December 1984): 822–9; Calvin P. Duncan, 'Consumer Market Beliefs: A review of the literature and an agenda for future research', in Marvin E. Goldberg, Gerald Gorn, and Richard W. Pollay, eds., *Advances in Consumer Research* 17 (Provo, UT: Association for Consumer Research, 1990): 729–35; Frank Alpert, 'Consumer market beliefs and their managerial implications: An empirical examination', *Journal of Consumer Marketing* 10(2) (1993): 56–70.

135. Beales *et al.*, 'Consumer search and public policy', op. cit.

136. Gary T. Ford and Ruth Ann Smith, 'Inferential beliefs in consumer evaluations: An assessment of alternative processing strategies', *Journal of Consumer Research* 14 (December 1987): 363–71; Deborah Roedder John, Carol A. Scott and James R. Bettman, 'Sampling data for covariation assessment: The effects of prior beliefs on search patterns', *Journal of Consumer Research* 13 (June 1986): 38–47; Gary L. Sullivan and Kenneth J. Berger, 'An investigation of the determinants of cue utilization', *Psychology and Marketing* 4 (Spring 1987): 63–74.

137. Durairaj Maheswaran, 'Country of origin as a stereotype: Effects of consumer expertise and attribute strength on product evaluations', *Journal of Consumer Research* 21 (September 1994): 354–65; Ingrid M. Martin and Sevgin Eroglu, 'Measuring a multi-dimensional construct: Country image', *Journal of Business Research* 28 (1993): 191–210; Richard Ettenson, Janet Wagner and Gary Gaeth, 'Evaluating the effect of country of origin and the "Made in the U.S.A." campaign: a conjoint approach', *Journal of Retailing* 64 (Spring 1988): 85–100; C. Min Han and Vern Terpstra, 'Country-of-origin effects for uni-national and bi-national products', *Journal of International Business* 19 (Summer 1988): 235–55; Michelle A. Morganosky and Michelle M. Lazarde, 'Foreign-made apparel: Influences on consumers' perceptions of brand and store quality', *International Journal of Advertising* 6 (Fall 1987): 339–48.

138. See Sung-Tai Hong and Dong Kyoon Kang, 'Country-of-origin influences on product evaluations: The impact of animosity and perceptions of industriousness brutality on judgments of typical and atypical products', *Journal of Consumer Psychology* 16(3) (2006): 232–9; Richard Jackson Harris, Bettina Garner-Earl, Sara J. Sprick and Collette Carroll, 'Effects of foreign product names and country-of-origin attributions on advertisement evaluations', *Psychology & Marketing* 11 (March–April 1994): 129–45; Terence A. Shimp, Saeed Samiee and Thomas J. Madden, 'Countries and their products: A cognitive structure perspective', *Journal of the Academy of Marketing Science* 21 (Fall 1993): 323–30; Durairaj Maheswaran, 'Country of origin as a stereotype: Effects of consumer expertise and attribute strength on product evaluations', *Journal of Consumer Research* 21 (September 1994): 354–65; Ingrid M. Martin and Sevgin Eroglu, 'Measuring a multi-dimensional construct: Country image', *Journal of Business Research* 28 (1993): 191–210; Richard Ettenson, Janet Wagner and Gary Gaeth, 'Evaluating the effect of country of origin and the "Made in the U.S.A." campaign: A conjoint approach', *Journal of Retailing* 64 (Spring 1988): 85–100; C. Min Han and Vern Terpstra, 'Country-of-origin effects for uni-national and bi-national products', *Journal of International Business* 19 (Summer 1988): 235–55; Michelle A. Morganosky and Michelle M. Lazarde, 'foreign-made apparel: Influences on consumers' perceptions of brand and store quality', *International Journal of Advertising* 6 (Fall 1987): 339–48.

139. Teodoro Luque-Martinez, Jose-Angel Ibanez-Zapata and Salvador del Barrio-Garcia, 'Consumer ethnocentrism measurement – an assessment of the reliability and validity of the CETSCALE in Spain', *European Journal of Marketing* 34(11&12) (2000): 1,353ff.

140. Richard Jackson Harris, Bettina Garner-Earl, Sara J. Sprick and Collette Carroll, 'Effects of foreign product names and country-of-origin attributions on advertisement evaluations', *Psychology and Marketing* 11 (March/April 1994): 129–45; Terence A. Shimp, Saeed Samiee and Thomas J. Madden, 'Countries and their products: A cognitive structure perspective', *Journal of the Academy of Marketing Science* 21 (Fall 1993): 323–30.

141. 'EU steps up global battle over Parma ham, Roquefort cheese', *NYT online* (28 August 2003).

142. Durairaj Maheswaran, 'Country of origin as a stereotype: Effects of consumer expertise and attribute strength on product evaluations', *Journal of Consumer Research* 21 (September 1994): 354–65.

143. Raffaella Paciolla and Li-Wei Mai, 'The Impact of Italianate on Consumers' Brand Perceptions of Luxury Brands', in Alan Bradshaw, Chris Hackley and Pauline Maclaran (eds), *European Association for Consumer Research Conference* 2010 RHUL: 61.

144. Sung-Tai Hong and Robert S. Wyer Jr, 'Effects of country-of-origin and product-attribute information on product evaluation: An Information processing perspective', *Journal of Consumer Research* 16 (September 1989): 175–87; Marjorie Wall, John Liefeld and Louise A. Heslop, 'Impact of country-of-origin cues on consumer judgments in multi-cue situations: A covariance analysis', *Journal of the Academy of Marketing Science* 19(2) (1991): 105–13.

145. Wai-Kwan Li and Robert S. Wyer Jr, 'The role of country of origin in product evaluations: Informational and standard-of-comparison effects', *Journal of Consumer Psychology* 3(2) (1994): 187–212.

146. Maheswaran, 'Country of origin as a stereotype', op. cit.

147. Calvin P. Duncan (1990), 'Consumer Market Beliefs: A Review of the Literature and an Agenda For Future Research', in Marvin E. Goldberg, Gerald Gorn, and Richard W. Pollay (eds), *NA – Advances in Consumer Research* 17 (Provo, UT : Association for Consumer Research): 729–36.

148. Chr. Hjorth-Andersen, 'Price as a risk indicator', *Journal of Consumer Policy* 10 (1987): 267–81.

149. David M. Gardner, 'Is there a generalized price–quality relationship?', *Journal of Marketing Research* 8 (May 1971): 241–3; Kent B. Monroe, 'Buyers' subjective perceptions of price', *Journal of Marketing Research* 10 (1973): 70–80.

150. Kelly, L. Haws, Rebecca Walker Reczek and Kevin L. Sample, 'Healthy diets make empty wallets: The healthy = expensive intuition', *Journal of Consumer Research* 43(6) (2017): 992–1,007.

151. Richard W. Stevenson, 'The brands with billion-dollar names', *New York Times* (28 October 1988): A1.

152. Douglas B. Holt, *How Brands Become Icons: The Principles of Cultural Branding* (Boston, MA: Harvard Business School Press, 2004).

153. Richard W. Stevenson, 'The brands with billion-dollar names', *New York Times* (28 October 1988): A1; Eric Pfanner, 'Zipf's Law, or the Considerable Value of Being Top Dog, as Applied to Branding', *New York Times* (21 May 2007); Ronald Alsop, 'Enduring brands hold their allure by sticking close to their roots', *Wall Street Journal*, centennial edn (1989): B4.

154. Jacob Jacoby and Robert Chestnut, *Brand Loyalty: Measurement and Management* (New York: Wiley, 1978).

155. Anne B. Fisher, 'Coke's brand loyalty lesson', *Fortune* (5 August 1985): 44.

156. Jacoby and Chestnut, *Brand Loyalty,* op. cit.

157. Ronald Alsop, 'Brand loyalty is rarely blind loyalty', *The Wall Street Journal* (19 October 1989): B1.

158. Betsy Morris, 'The brand's the thing', *Fortune* 72(8) (4 March 1996).

159. Fabrizio Di Muro and Kyle B. Murray, 'An arousal regulation Explanation of mood effects on consumer choice', *Journal of Consumer Research* 39(3) (October 2012): 574–84; Cassie Mogilner, Jennifer Aaker and Sepandar D. Kamvar, 'How happiness affects choice', *Journal of Consumer Research* 39(2) (August 2012): 429–43. For a study that looks at cross-cultural differences in expression of emotion, cf. Ana Valenzuela, Barbara Mellers and Judi Strebel, 'Pleasurable Surprises: A cross-cultural study of consumer responses to unexpected incentives', *Journal of Consumer Research* 36(5) (2010): 792–805; see also Samuel K. Bonsu, Aron Darmody and Marie-Agnes Parmentier, 'Arrested emotions in reality television', *Consumption Markets & Culture* 13(1) (2010): 91–107. Parts of this section were adapted from Michael R. Solomon, Rebekah Russell-Bennett and Josephine Previte, *Consumer Behaviour: Buying, Having, Being,* 3rd edn. (Frenchs Forest, NSW: Pearson Australia, 2012).

160. Scott I. Rick, Cynthia E. Cryder and George Loewenstein, 'Tightwads and spendthrifts', *Journal of Consumer Research* 34 (April 2008): 767.

161. Hannah H. Chang and Michel Tuan Pham, 'Affect as a decision-making system of the present', *Journal of Consumer Research* 40(1) (2013): 42–63.

162. Michel Tuan Pham, Leonard Lee and Andrew T. Stephen, 'Feeling the future: The emotional oracle effect', *Journal of Consumer Research* 39(3) (October 2012): 461–77.

163. Charles C. Cui, Mona Mrad and Margaret K. Hogg, 'Brand addiction: Exploring the concept and its definition through an experiential lens', *Journal of Business Research* 87(118) (June 2018): 127, https://doi.org/10.1016/j.jbusres.2018.02.028 (accessed 29 July 2018).

164. Peter Lieberman and David Pizarro, 'All politics is olfactory', *New York Times* (23 October 2010), http://www.nytimes.com/2010/10/24/opinion/24pizarro.html?_r=1&ref=-todayspaper (accessed 29 July 2018).

165. Andrea C. Morales, Eugenia C. Wu and Gavan J. Fitzsimons, 'How disgust enhances the effectiveness of fear appeals', *Journal of Marketing Research* 49(3) (2012): 383–93; Bruce Horowitz, 'Gross ads disgust consumers into action', *USA Today* (27 February 2012).

166. Aradhna Krishna, Spike W.S. Lee, Xiuping Li and Norbert Schwarz, 'Embodied cognition, sensory marketing, and the conceptualization of consumers' Judgment and decision processes: Introduction to the issue', *Journal of the Association for Consumer Research* 2(4) (October 2017): 377–81, inter alia.

167. Roland T. Rust, Debora V. Thompson and Rebecca W. Hamilton, 'Defeating feature fatigue', *Harvard Business Review* 84 (February 2006): 98.

168. Debora V. Thompson, Rebecca W. Hamilton and Roland T. Rust, 'Feature fatigue: When product capabilities become too much of a good thing', *Journal of Marketing Research* 42 (November 2005): 431–42.

169. David Kesmodel and John R. Wilke, 'Whole foods Is hot, wild oats a dud – so said "Rahodeb" then again, Yahoo poster was a whole foods staffer, the CEO to be precise', *Wall Street Journal* (12 July 2007): A1.

Case study C.1

When a rapper buys a champagne house: Jay-Z and Ace of Spades

Joonas Rokka, Emlyon Business School, France, and **Nacima Ourahmoune**, Kedge Business School, France

A traditional family champagne house

Armand de Brignac is a small traditional champagne brand that produces champagne according to classic winemaking practices, using a refined knowledge of the champagne terroir and grapes, and sold by the Cattier champagne house (est. 1763), which until recently had remained an independent family-owned business employing 20 people. The attention to detail, quality and excellence in the production of Armand de Brignac over the years has contributed to a reputation of the highest standard. Despite being fashionable and distinctive, however, the brand became dormant and was discontinued in the late 1940s. However, it was resurrected in 2006; that same year it attracted worldwide public attention, and in 2009 it went on to be named top finisher in an expert blind tasting of 100 champagne brands organised by *Fine Champagne* magazine.[1]

The brand is perhaps better known as 'Ace of Spades' because of the brand logo, familiar from playing cards. It is also easily identifiable through its distinctive opaque metallic bottles that stand out from other champagne brands. The eye-catching appearance of the iconic golden bottle is down to the vision of the André Courrèges fashion house, which evokes French haute couture and its reputation for opulence. Each bottle is also packaged in a beautiful black lacquered wooden box, bearing an engraved plaque in pewter (no paper is used), covered with a luxurious black velvet fabric (hand-produced) and stamped with the royal crest of the brand. The name Armand de Brignac evokes the aristocracy, although it is actually the invention of one of the family members and was inspired by a character in a novel.

The most impressive bottle is called the 'Midas', after the legendary king who turned everything he touched into gold. The bottle underlines the combination of royalty and golden opulence as important codes in the brand's narrative. In part, the emblematic Midas bottle was created in response to clients' wishes for bigger bottles suitable for sharing in nightclubs, even though the size of the bottle brought some technical challenges. As a consequence, the Cattier house later came up with the idea of producing the most expensive

Armand de Brignac Brut Gold
Francois Nascimbeni/Stringer/Getty Images

champagne in the world (selling at around $200,000 per bottle, compared to $300 for a regular bottle), underlining the increasingly conspicuous brand image of Armand de Brignac.

From traditional champagne brand to global pop culture phenomenon

Rather unexpectedly, the brand suddenly surged into the global spotlight as one of the hottest wine brands – at least in the eyes of a specific consumer group. The driver for this unprecedented success was none other than the famous rapper Jay-Z, who is married to fellow music superstar Beyoncé. He showed off a golden bottle of Ace of Spades in his hit music video *Show Me What You Got* in 2006.[2] Beyoncé's hit *Drunk in Love* (featuring Jay-Z) similarly echoed new-found love for Armand de Brignac, spreading the word to new audiences worldwide.[3]

This 'strategic act' was quite unlike the conventional celebration of luxury and status products that populate many hip-hop music videos. It was, in fact, an apparent response to comments made by Frederic Rouzaud, managing director of Louis Roederer, the maker of Cristal champagne, Jay-Z's former favourite brand. Jay-Z publicly announced that he would boycott all Louis Roederer products after Mr Rouzaud, unhappy that his champagne brand had become associated with hip-hop culture, famously said, 'Unfortunately, we can't forbid people from buying it'. This was enough for Jay-Z and his followers. They quickly needed a new brand to support, which turned out to be lucky for Armand de Brignac.

In November 2014 it was announced that Jay-Z had bought the Armand de Brignac brand.

Armand de Brignac – a luxury brand between two worlds

Champagne represents a complex world of contradictions between tradition and modernity, between references to aristocracy and simple craftsmanship, between religious symbolism and pure profit. It speaks of the deep dynamic of the French social class system, from the aristocracy to the bourgeois. Consuming and displaying champagne connotes certain tastes and social distinctions. Its link to a specific place, a given terroir, followed by its acquisition by an 'outsider' had a sudden destabilising impact on the normal course of business in the region.

More precisely, Armand de Brignac was caught between the tensions of two distinct and contradictory cultural worlds – hip-hop and the French elite. Such a cultural clash frequently leads to conflict, as evidenced by Louis Roederer's strong reaction to the emergence of 'non-legitimate' new customers from the hip-hop scene. The loud 'bling bling' and conspicuous displays of wealth and success of the rap stars was simply too much for the conservative side of traditional champagne lovers. Beneath these reactions lay the notion that an appreciation of champagne requires an appreciation of traditional culture and values that the hip-hop crowd supposedly did not possess. The case of Jay-Z championing a champagne brand thus illustrates the tensions between the old and new worlds, in which the role and meanings of luxury are challenged and contested. It also illustrates how consumption habits, even the most traditional and established, are constantly in flux in an increasingly connected world.

Finding a balance in the eyes of distinct customers

This case study offers two alternative brand strategies with regard to a heterogeneous client base. First, in the case of Louis Roederer, the brand attempted to reinforce its image among its more conservative customer base by dismissing undesired new clients. This strategy was undoubtedly effective for its positioning but clearly limited opportunities for serving a new and potentially profitable clientele. Cattier, on the other hand, was successful – and remains so, at least for the time being – in finding a more balanced position by serving two types of clientele at the same time. Cattier was able to maintain a high standard of production and a quality brand image while gradually adapting traditional codes of luxury to become more visible and conspicuous. At the same time, the brand was sure to benefit from the favourable winds, propelled by popular culture, that constantly work to re-appropriate and re-define the role of champagne consumption.

Questions

1 What makes the champagne brand Armand de Brignac so popular among hip-hop consumers, and what exactly does it communicate?

2 How does the popular image of Armand de Brignac champagne among hip-hop culture influence other consumer groups, and how will that eventually influence the success of the brand?

3 Is it possible for a single brand to serve the needs and tastes of a highly disparate consumer base effectively – for example, clients looking for refined and sophisticated culinary experiences as well as flamboyant hip-hop clients?

4 What factors influence the acceptance of a brand among such distinctive and different consumer groups?

5 What would you do if you were the management of the Armand de Brignac brand after the take-over by Jay-Z?

6 What would you do if you were the management of Louis Roederer after the crisis with Jay-Z?

Sources

[1]'The best champagnes of the year – a golden surprise!', *Fine Champagne* (18 September 2009), http://www.fine-magazines.com (accessed 3 September 2018).

[2]See https://www.youtube.com/watch?v=FS4U-HAHwps (accessed 3 September 2018).

[3]See https://www.youtube.com/watch?v=p1JPKLa-Ofc (accessed 3 September 2018).

Case study C.2

Changing attitudes towards alcohol consumption: emotional and information appeals

Effi Raftopoulou, Salford University, UK

The issue of alcohol misuse has become ever more significant in the past few decades. The European Union (EU) has a particular problem, since it is home to the world's heaviest drinkers and has the highest proportion of ill health and premature death due to alcohol.[1]

Alcohol misuse is a multi-faceted problem in terms of both its manifestations and its consequences. It includes frequent, long-term use of alcohol as well as short-term excessive use, both of which can result in health risks and wider social harm. In particular, heavy occasional drinking is common across Europe, with overall consumption being double the global average and 20 per cent of the population stating that they drink heavily on occasion.[2] Alcohol is also recognised as the third most-important factor in disease liability in Europe (after smoking and obesity).

The problem is even more prevalent in the UK. An indication of this is the fact that, although overall consumption of alcohol has fallen in the EU since 1990, it has increased in the UK by 3 per cent.[3] Alcohol is estimated to cost England around £21billion in healthcare, crime and lost productivity costs, while the number of deaths attributed to alcohol rose by 19 per cent between 2001 and 2012.[4] Issues associated with alcohol misuse include alcohol-related crime, antisocial behaviour and domestic abuse, personal injury and death. Death due to alcohol is linked both to fatal injury and to alcohol-specific conditions including chronic liver disease.

But what are the markers of alcohol misuse? The picture varies from country to country. In the UK, it is estimated that every year over 13 per cent of the population will binge-drink, while 3 per cent will show signs of alcohol dependence. At the same time, 2 per cent of people will be admitted to hospital with an alcohol-related condition, 1 per cent will be a victim of alcohol-related crime[5] and over 0.4 per cent of 11–15 year-olds will be drinking weekly.[6] In addition to this, an estimated 7.5 million people are unaware of the damage their drinking could be causing.[7] This poses a great challenge for governments in their efforts to minimise the impact of alcohol misuse in society.

The World Health Organisation (WHO) has introduced a strategy to support EU states in reducing alcohol-related harm. This strategy focuses on protecting young people, children and the unborn child; reducing injuries and deaths from alcohol-related road accidents; preventing alcohol-related harm among adults and reducing the negative impact on the workplace; and informing, educating and raising awareness about the impact of harmful and hazardous alcohol consumption, and about appropriate consumption patterns.[8]

In this bleak context, marketing plays a dual role. On the one hand, marketing campaigns promoting alcohol are seen to increase people's alcohol consumption, particularly the under-18s,[9] and, on the other hand, social marketing initiatives are seen to assist efforts by governments to reduce the impact of alcohol. The latter are considered to be a useful tool in a government's effort to provide information and to change attitudes and behaviours regarding alcohol consumption.

Three UK examples

In the UK there are numerous campaigns targeting alcohol misuse, reflecting the different dimensions of the problem. Drinkaware, for example, an independent charity supported by voluntary donations from the drinks industry and major UK supermarkets, runs a number of different campaigns. The 'Why Let Good Times Go Bad?' campaign focused on students' excessive alcohol consumption. One of its advertisements portrays, on the left-hand side of the picture, a young girl in her twenties having fun and dancing, and features the caption 'Dance floor', while the other half of the picture shows the same girl in a bad state in a toilet with a caption that reads 'Toilet floor'. The campaign focuses on appealing to the emotions and tries to associate excessive drinking with a feeling of embarrassment.[10]

A second campaign run by the UK Government as part of the 'Change for Life' campaign focuses almost exclusively on informational content. The aim of this campaign is to encourage healthy living and, in relation to alcohol, to inform people about the risks of drinking, to help them understand how much alcohol they consume and to introduce some strategies to help them drink less. It includes a number of interactive tools, such as a guide that explains alcohol units and a mobile phone app that tracks how much the user drinks and spends. One advertisement features anthropomorphic cartoon characters sitting on a sofa having a drink, while glasses of wine and beer are sneaking up on them from behind the sofa. The caption reads 'Don't let drink sneak up on you' and aims to alert people to the fact that even if they only have a drink or two in the evening to wind down, if this is a recurring habit it can still cause significant problems.[11]

Finally, THINK!, an organisation promoting road safety, runs campaigns aiming to prevent drink driving, and is famous for its hard-hitting messages. One of its more recent campaigns showed three men visiting a pub toilet. The camera showed them in front of a rectangular mirror washing their hands when, all of a sudden, the mirror breaks with a loud crash and a woman's injured head comes through. The image was designed to resemble a car's front windscreen during a collision with a person and aimed to shock the audience and make the implications of drink driving clear. Road safety campaigns have a long history of using emotional appeals to achieve their goals.[12]

Emotion or information?

Emotional appeals – aiming to arouse both positive and negative emotions – are prevalent in advertising. They are thought to have a significant influence on attitudes, and the strength of the emotion generated is usually thought to correlate with the effectiveness of the advertising campaign. Some researchers, however, question the effectiveness of emotional appeals and suggest that the audience does not always react in predicted ways.[13] For example, it is suggested that an advertisement that creates too much fear can often make the audience switch off and not engage with the message. It is also argued that negative emotions such as fear and anger can differentially affect a person's desire to look for information or the accessibility of information for that person.[14]

In addition, advertisers have also been accused of manipulation by playing on people's emotions.[15] The Code of Advertising Practice[16] also tries to prevent excessive use of emotion in advertising and recommends that fear, violent images and distress should not be used without good reason or disproportionately, and that advertisers should avoid causing distress or offence to members of the public.

Questions

1 The three advertisements discussed use different types of appeals: information, embarrassment and fear. Discuss the effectiveness of each different type of appeal.

2 The use of emotional appeals is often deemed necessary by organisations that are trying to change long-standing attitudes (for example in campaigns against smoking). Is the use of emotional appeals in such advertisements justified and if so, why (or if not, why not)?

3 Alcohol misuse is a very complicated problem that affects many different target audiences. Carry out an internet search for campaigns targeting alcohol misuse, then try to identify the relevant target audiences and the main objectives of the campaign. How do you evaluate the approach chosen by the organisation in question compared to those discussed in the case study?

Sources

[1]WHO (European website) (2015), http://www.euro.who.int/en/health-topics/disease-prevention/alcohol-use/data-and-statistics (accessed 3 September 2018).

[2]WHO (Regional Office for Europe), 'Status report on alcohol and health in 35 European countries' (2013), http://www.euro.who.int/__data/assets/pdf_file/0017/190430/Status-Report-on-Alcohol-and-Health-in-35-European-Countries.pdf (accessed 3 September 2018); WHO (European website) (2015), http://www.euro.who.int/en/health-topics/disease-prevention/alcohol-use/data-and-statistics (accessed 3 September 2018).

[3]WHO (Regional Office for Europe), 'Status report on alcohol and health in 35 European countries' (2013), http://www.euro.who.int/__data/assets/pdf_file/0017/190430/Status-Report-on-Alcohol-and-Health-in-35-European-Countries.pdf (accessed 3 September 2018).

[4]Alcohol Concern (2015), https://www.alcoholconcern.org.uk (accessed 3 September 2018).

[5]HM Government, 'The government's alcohol strategy 2012' (2012), https://www.gov.uk/government/uploads/system/uploads/attachment_data/file/224075/alcohol-strategy.pdf (accessed 3 September 2018).

[6]Ibid.

[7]Alcohol Concern (2015), https://www.alcoholconcern.org.uk (accessed 3 September 2018).

[8]WHO (Regional Office for Europe), 'Status report on alcohol and health in 35 European countries' (2013), http://www.euro.who.int/__data/assets/pdf_file/0017/190430/Status-Report-on-Alcohol-and-Health-in-35-European-Countries.pdf (accessed 3 September 2018).

[9]HM Government, 'The government's alcohol strategy 2012' (2012), https://www.gov.uk/government/uploads/system/

uploads/attachment_data/file/224075/alcohol-strategy.pdf (accessed 3 September 2018).

[10]G. Stone, 'Drinkaware ramps up campaign', The Drinks Business (2011), http://www.thedrinksbusiness.com/2011/08/drinkaware-ramps-up-campaign (accessed 3 September 2018).

[11]Change for Life (2015).

[12]THINK! (2015), http://think.direct.gov.uk/drink-driving.html (accessed 3 September 2018).

[13]M.C. Campbell, 'When attention-getting advertising tactics elicit consumer inferences of manipulative intent', *Journal of Consumer Psychology* 4(3) (1995): 225–54.

[14]R.L. Nabi, 'Do discrete emotions differentially influence information accessibility, information seeking, and policy preference?', *Communication Research* 30(2) (2003): 224–47.

[15]L. Brennan and W. Binney, 'Fear, guilt, and shame appeals in social marketing', *Journal of Business Research* 63(2) (2010): 140–6.

[16]Advertising Standards Authority (ASA) (2015), https://www.asa.org.uk/ (accessed 3 September 2018).

Case study C.3

Ethical luxury: some consumption dilemmas of ethics and sustainability

Sheila Malone, Lancaster University, UK

Luxury consumption is generally characterised by notions of opulence and indulgence. It is an industry that comes with high prices and conspicuous consumption practices. Luxury products are sought after for authentic and prestigious reasons. They open-up the world of the 'one-off' product never to be replicated again and are normally accessible only to a minority. Luxury goods are rarely thought of as sustainable or ethical due to their antithetical positioning and elitist characteristics. For instance, the luxury tourism market, based on the notion of exclusivity, may be defined as 'having the latest, the rarest and the best'.[1] This often means having access to areas that only high-end travellers can afford, resulting in 'increased credibility and status amongst their peers'. Such consumption practices are rarely, if ever, linked with the principles of sustainable development or a consumer's desire to fulfil their ethical beliefs and values in a luxurious manner. Currently, the global market for luxury goods is growing, reaching €253bn in 2015.[2] According to Dubois and Duquesne,[3] luxury goods are a status symbol offering emotional value rather than functional utility. As a result, 'luxury has been portrayed as a menace to martial spirit and moral fibre'.[4] It is this portrayal of the luxury goods industry that has traditionally separated the world of ethical practices and luxury consumption. Nonetheless, the relationship between ethics and luxury is growing closer, with industries such as jewellery, clothes, food and tourism striving to attain a greater ethical-luxury nexus. Despite such efforts, the link between ethics and luxury has brought with it many questions in terms of sustainability. Many luxury organisations are successfully integrating ethics into their business operations as this provides a competitive advantage and a sense of place based on craftsmanship. However, the question remains: how can ethics be actualised in luxury consumption practices? In general, ethical consumption is considered to be an act of compromise in the face of conflicting hedonic, social and environmental concerns.[5] It is associated with a waste hierarchy of reduce, reuse and recycle, and is evident in the growth of second-hand stores and swap shops,[6] and in the rise of the sharing economy as a way of promoting more traditional ways of living. This is particularly noteworthy as the future of luxury consumption hinges upon the millennial generation, who, according to *The Economist*,[7] 'want luxury goods to be made in ways that damage neither workers nor the environment'.

Bridging the fashion gap: the rise of ethical luxury

We often see media headlines highlighting the scandals of high-street fast-fashion production processes with the use of 'sweatshops' and cheap labour. On the one hand, the fast-fashion model encourages a throwaway culture as it typically has four fashion seasons per year. Retailers such as Zara can produce a new clothing line every two to six weeks, often replicating luxury fashion-house styles. The speed with which such products can reach the market is 'enabling the masses to get a taste of Michelin-starred quality on a McDonald's budget'.[8] Fast fashion allows mainstream consumers to realise their dreams of owning luxury products. However, the stark reality is evident in the environmental impact of the fast-fashion industry, as 350,000 tonnes (€180m worth) of clothing goes into landfill each year.[9] On the other hand, luxury fashion tends to be considered unsustainable due to its haute-couture nature; that is, the true cost of luxury is often evident in the demand for exclusive custom-fit clothing, which is often made from contested materials such as fur and leather. An interesting premise with regard to the ethicality of luxury products is that they tend to be made from superior quality materials and are developed using bespoke craftsmanship. It is the attention to detail involved in producing a luxury item that creates a high-quality piece that can be kept forever. The products are based on longevity – a one-off piece that lasts a lifetime – as opposed to an item to be consumed in the here and now.

The term 'eco-fashion' conjures up the hippie movement of the 1960s and '70s, based on environmental concerns, during which ecologically sensitive fashion often meant shapeless recycled clothing.[10] Winge goes one step further in distinguishing between eco-dress and eco-fashion.[11] Eco-dress is associated with the hippie movement, whereas eco-fashion currently represents luxurious and cultivated taste. The rise of 'ecolux fashion'[12] highlights the growing desire for luxurious fashion pieces that are sustainable. Such efforts are demonstrated in an annual luxury sustainable fashion show. In Europe, eco-fashion[13] has become more prominent; some of the producers are smaller companies making clothing and accessories from organic cotton sourced from suppliers using Fairtrade practices. A further stream of ethical luxury is evident in the growth of a sharing culture and the rise in collaborative consumption organisations, such as One Night Stand, Bag Borrow or Steal, LuxTNT and handbagsbydesigners. co.uk. These organisations are enabling customers to access luxury goods through hiring a designer product. The rise in the sharing economy is evident in the ethical luxury market, with second-hand luxury available from outlets such as stylesequel and InstantLuxe.

A report by the consumer organisation Ethical Consumer identified the top luxury fashion brands in terms of their ethical efforts.[14] Calvin Klein and Tommy Hilfiger shared the top position, with brands such as Armani, Missoni, Paul Smith and Valentino, among others, sharing second place. However, Ethical Consumer reports that 'a designer item can no longer be assumed to have been hand-made in Italy, but is far more likely to have been produced in China or another similarly low-cost country'. The influence of attitudes and personal values has a weaker effect on consumption behaviour in relation to luxury goods.[15] Therefore, the attitude–behaviour gap in relation to ethical behaviour is higher for luxury goods. In this case, the place for ethical considerations in the luxury market is challenging.

Ethical consumer behaviour: a case of ethical luxury

A report by the WWF highlighted that, in Western markets, environmental and social issues are no longer the sole concern of a minority.[16] It is clear that socially conscious people are a sizeable proportion of mainstream, brand-conscious consumers who want to purchase the quality they expect at a reasonable price, but with an emphasis on social and environmental performance. We are currently experiencing a global wave of environmental awareness among urban middle-class consumers, and the consequent changing attitudes towards brands. 'The wealthy are increasingly concerned about environmental issues'.[17] Based on 2,000 interviews with high-earning individuals, the report identified not only that such issues relate to shopping differently, but also that a shift in

mind-set is evident as some customers (such as voluntary simplifiers) begin to reduce their consumption practices. With a growing consumer segment focused on lifestyles of health and sustainability (LOHAS), and celebrities around the world showing support for more sustainable luxury items, it is clear that ethical issues associated with traditional luxury consumption are at a crossroads of change.

Defined by Cooper-Martin and Holbrook,[18] ethical consumer behaviour relates to the 'decision-making, purchases and other consumption experiences that are affected by the consumer's ethical concerns'. Given the abundant interpretations, various terms have been associated with ethical practices, such as 'socially conscious',[19] 'environmentally concerned',[20] 'socially responsible',[21] 'Fairtrade' and 'ethical consumers'.[22]

The rise in the number of ethical consumers with a desire for a luxury lifestyle is demonstrable in the upsurge in ethical luxury brands in the UK, such as La Jewellery Ltd, an upmarket bespoke ethical jeweller. It claims to sell 'accessible and affordable [jewellery] while still keeping it exclusive'. Likewise, Beautiful Soul London, an ethical luxury fashion house, states: 'The label is committed to a conscious approach to fabric sourcing and environmental impact and is committed to local, UK-based production. These collections are produced in the most exquisite fabrics, including British lace, British wool, sustainable, organic and Fairtrade fabrics giving customers an alternative, more ethical choice that does not compromise luxury'. Other companies, such as DePloy, Beyond Skin and Number 22 Eco-Luxury Boutique, and designers such as Katherine Hooker, are creating classic eco-lux pieces for celebrities such as Meryl Streep, Kate and Pippa Middleton, Zoe Saldana, Taylor Swift and Cat Deeley. As consumers are demanding more information about sourcing and manufacturing, Joy et al.[23] suggest that luxury fashion has the potential to overcome some of the ethical issues associated with the fast fashion industry: 'because of their long-standing concern for quality and craft, luxury brands could effectively counteract some of the problems endemic to fast fashion and provide leadership on issues relating to sustainability'.

Questions

1 How do models of consumer decision-making take into account the ethical concerns of consumers? Using traditional decision-making models, outline an ethical luxury consumer's decision-making process. How does a consumer's ethical decision-making process compare with those outlined in the discussion of consumer decision-making?

2 In the case of ethical luxury, research has shown that the wealthy are increasingly concerned about environmental issues.[24] What is the role of ethical consumer behaviour in luxury products and services? Is ethical consumer behaviour based on consumers' socio-economic status?

3 Can the luxury sector truly be ethical or is the ethical association a functional alibi to consume more high-end products without experiencing feelings of guilt?

Sources

[1]VisitBritain, 'Luxury tourism trends summary' (2010), http://www.visitbritain.org (accessed 3 September 2018).

[2]Bain & Company, 'Luxury goods worldwide market study' (2015), http://www.bain.com/publications/articles/luxury-goods-worldwide-market-study-spring-2014.aspx (accessed 3 September 2018).

[3]B. Dubois and P. Duquesne, 'The market for luxury goods: income versus culture', *European Journal of Marketing* 27(1) (1993): 35–44.

[4]B. Unger, 'Exclusively for everybody', *The Economist* (13 December 2014), http://www.economist.com/news/special-report/21635761-modern-luxury-industry-rests-paradoxbut-thriving-nonetheless-says-brooke?zid=;319&ah=;17af09b0281b-01505c226b1e574f5cc1 (accessed 3 September 2018).

[5]D.A. Fennell, *Tourism Ethics* (Clevedon: Channel View Publications, 2006).

[6]Keynote, 'Green & ethical consumer', Market Report (2013), https://www.keynote.co.uk/market-report/lifestyle/green-ethical-consumer (accessed 3 September 2018).

[7]B. Unger, 'Exclusively for everybody', *The Economist* (13 December 2014).

[8]F. Adu-Yeboah, 'Goodbye Primark: Michael Kors says fast fashion "will die out"', *International Business Times* (9 July 2014), http://www.ibtimes.co.uk/goodbye-primark-michael-kors-says-fast-fashion-will-die-out-1456013 (accessed 3 September 2018).

[9]WRAP, 'Working together for a world without waste. Evaluating the financial viability and resource implications for new business models in the clothing sector' (2013), http://www.wrap.org.uk/sites/files/wrap/Clothing%20REBM%20Final%20Report%2005%2002%2013_0.pdf (accessed 3 September 2018).

[10]L. Welters, 'The natural look: American style in the 1970s', *Fashion Theory* 12(4) (2008): 489–510.

[11]T.M. Winge, 'Green is the new black: celebrity chic and the "green" commodity fetish', *Fashion Theory* 12(4) (2008): 511–24.

[12]http://www.ecoluxelondon.org/

[13]http://www.ecofashionworld.com/

[14]Ethical Consumer, 'Style over substance: why ethics are not in fashion for designer labels' (2011), http://www.ethical-consumer.org/portals/0/downloads/luxury%20fashion.pdf (accessed 3 September 2018).

[15]I.A. Davies, Z. Lee and I. Ahonkhai, 'Do consumers care about ethical-luxury?', *Journal of Business Ethics* 106(1) (2012): 37–51.

[16]WWF, 'Let them eat cake: satisfying the new consumer appetite for responsible brands' (2005), http://www.wwf.org.uk (accessed 3 September 2018).

[17]Ledbury Research, 'Sustainable luxury' (2013).

[18]E. Cooper-Martin and M.B. Holbrook, 'Ethical consumption experiences and ethical space', *Advances in Consumer Research* 20 (1993): 113–18.

[19]W.T. Anderson Jr and W.H. Cunningham, 'The socially conscious consumer', *Journal of Marketing* 36(3) (1972): 23–31; F.E. Webster Jr, 'Determining the characteristics of the socially conscious consumer', *Journal of Consumer Research* 2(3) (1975): 188–96; G. Brooker, 'The self-actualizing socially conscious consumer', *Journal of Consumer Research* 3(2) (1976): 107–12.

[20]L.R. Tucker Jr., 'Identifying the environmentally responsible consumer: The role of internal–external control of reinforcements', *The Journal of Consumer Affairs* 14(2) (1980): 326–40; R.D. Straughan and J.A. Roberts, 'Environmental segmentation alternatives: A look at green consumer behavior in the new millennium', *Journal of Consumer Marketing* 16(6) (1999): 558–75.

[21]J.A. Roberts, 'Profiling levels of socially responsible consumer behavior: a cluster analytic approach and its implications for marketing', *Journal of Marketing Theory and Practice* 3(4) (1995): 97–117.

[22]M. Carrigan and A. Attalla, 'The myth of the ethical consumer – do ethics matter in purchase behaviour?', *Journal of Consumer Marketing* 18(7) (2001): 560–78; S. Malone, 'Ethical tourism: the role of emotion', in C. Weeden and K. Boluk (eds) *Managing Ethical Consumption in Tourism* (London: Routledge, 2014).

[23]A. Joy, J.F. Sherry, A. Venkatesh, J. Wang and R. Chan, 'Fast fashion, sustainability, and the ethical appeal of luxury brands', *Fashion Theory: The Journal of Dress, Body & Culture* 16(3) (2012): 273–96.

[24]Ledbury Research, 'Sustainable luxury' (2013).

Part D
European consumers and their social groups

The chapters in this part consider the range of social influences that help to determine who we are, as well as our consumer behaviour. Chapter 9 looks at the influences that groups and social media have on consumer behaviour, the role of brand communities as a social context and the particular influences that word of mouth and opinion leaders exert on our consumption deliberations. Chapter 10 provides a discussion of family structures in Europe. The chapter also points out the strong influence that age has on our behaviours as consumers, with an emphasis on the bonds we share with others who were born at roughly the same time. Chapter 11 focuses on factors that define our social class, and how membership of a social class exerts a strong influence on what we buy with the money we make.

Chapter 9
Groups and social media

Chapter objectives

When you finish reading this chapter you will understand why:

9.1 Other people and groups, especially those that possess social power, influence our decisions.

9.2 Word-of-mouth communication is the most important driver of product choice.

9.3 Opinion leaders' recommendations are more influential than others' when we decide what to buy.

9.4 Social media changes the way we learn about and select products.

BOBBY tries to play sport just about every day. The obsession that started with football has expanded to include cricket, tennis and squash (depending on the season). He will happily leave work early to play for his company team, especially the 11-a-side league on a Monday evening. The original work team that Bobby played for now includes some of his closest friends, but things have changed a lot since he started. A few players used to go for drinks after work but commitments mean most players now want to get straight home after the match, while younger players seem less keen on celebrating an important victory when they have an early start at work the next day. The other new innovation is that the captain selects the team by sending out a WhatsApp broadcast and the squad are all in one group where they can talk and share pictures together. There is also a player who acts as social media secretary, posting upcoming fixtures, results and stories on Facebook and Instagram.

Recently, Bobby decided he needed new football boots, and now he has some money to spend he thinks it would be good to upgrade to the next level. Bobby has noticed a clear divide between the older players, like himself, who want traditional black boots, and the garishly coloured pairs worn by the younger players.

His friend Pete pointed out that his Nike Mercurial Vapors had an excellent fit, acting like a sock round the ankle, but Bobby decided that the colours just did not suit him. He considered buying a pair of Puma Kings, but his team kit was from Puma and he did not like the material. He thought he might go for Adidas Copa Mundials. But then he surfed the Web for the best football boots for 2018 and found Pantofola D'Oro Lazzarini, an elegant black-leather Italian boot described as the 'best for the old-fashioned footballing fashionista'.[1] That made up his mind. Some people want to stand out in the crowd, to be individual and different, but football is a team game. . . and most of his friends were now wearing quite classic football boots. They must be showing their age.

R.J.W. Hogg, London

Introduction

Like Bobby, we all belong to many different types of groups, some formal and some informal, some from our personal worlds (e.g. fellow football players) and some from our professional worlds (e.g. work colleagues). Our behaviour is often heavily influenced by the groups to which we belong, and we often seek affirmation from our fellow group members via our consumption choices. This chapter focuses on how other people – whether fellow footballers and team mates, coworkers, friends and family or just casual acquaintances – influence our purchase decisions. It considers how our preferences are shaped by our positive group memberships, as well as by our dissociative reference groups, by our desire to please or be accepted by others, and even by the actions of famous people whom we've never met. Finally, it explores why some people are more influential than others in affecting consumers' product preferences, and how marketers go about finding those people and enlisting their support in the persuasion process.

Groups

Other people and groups, especially those that possess social power, influence our decisions.

Humans are social animals. We belong to groups, try to please others and look to others' behaviour for clues about what we should do in public settings. In fact, our desire to 'fit in' or to identify with desirable individuals or groups is the primary motivation for many of our consumption behaviours. We may go to great lengths to please the members of a group whose acceptance we covet,[2,3] and to avoid the group with which we do not wish to be

Adidas original in Adidas store at Ximending, in Taipei, Taiwan. Adidas is a global brand, and the multinational corporation (based in Germany) designs and manufactures shoes, clothing and accessories.

p2play/Shutterstock

associated.[4] **Social identity theory** argues that each of us has several 'selves' that relate to groups.[5] These linkages are so important that we think of ourselves not just as 'I', but also as 'we'. In addition, we favour others that we feel share the same identity – even if that identity is superficial and virtually meaningless. In numerous experiments that employ the **minimal group paradigm**, researchers show that even when they arbitrarily assign subjects to one group or another, people favour those who wind up in the same group.[6]

Bobby's football team is an important part of his identity, and this membership influences many of his buying decisions. Bobby doesn't model himself on just any footballer – only the people with whom he really identifies can exert that kind of influence. For example, Bobby primarily identifies with other sport enthusiasts, especially football players. The English Football League represents one of Bobby's most important reference groups, whereas the English Rugby Union represents one of his **dissociative groups**.

Marketing opportunity

We tend to think of running as something you do on your own, but today you're much more likely to run with a group. People train with friends and participate in charity runs together. Many of us are moving away from running alone at home; sales of home cardio equipment such as treadmills are way down. Instead people gravitate to competitions, obstacle courses, fitness classes or free family events such as Parkrun in the UK (http://www.parkrun.org.uk/). New Balance is picking up on this trend as the shoe manufacturer promotes its 'Runnovation' campaign in the US, which focuses on running as a social activity. One print ad carries the headline, 'Redefine girls' night out' as it shows a group of women running together. 'Some go out. Others go out and make excellent happen. The night is yours. This is Runnovation'.[7]

Social power

Why are groups so persuasive? The answer lies in the potential power they wield over us. **Social power** describes 'the capacity to alter the actions of others'.[8] To the degree to which you are able to make someone else do something, regardless of whether that person does it willingly, you have power over that person. The following classification of power bases helps us to distinguish among the reasons a person exerts power over another, the degree to which the influence is voluntary and whether this influence will continue to have an effect even when the source of the power isn't around:[9]

- **Referent power**. If a person admires the qualities of a person or a group, he tries to copy the referent's behaviours (e.g. choice of clothing, cars, leisure activities). Prominent people in all walks of life affect our consumption behaviours by virtue of product endorsements (e.g. Beyoncé for Ivy Park), distinctive fashion statements (e.g. Kendal Jenner's displays of high-end designer clothing) or championing causes (e.g. Angelina Jolie for the UNHCR). Referent power is important to many marketing strategies because consumers voluntarily modify what they do and buy in order to identify with a referent.

- **Information power**. A person possesses information power simply because they know something others would like to know. Editors of trade publications such as *Women's Wear Daily* often possess tremendous power because of their ability to compile and disseminate information that can make or break individual designers or companies. People with information power are able to influence consumer opinion by virtue of their (assumed) access to the knowledge that provides some kind of competitive advantage.

- **Legitimate power**. Sometimes we grant power by virtue of social agreements, such as the authority we give to police officers, soldiers and, yes, even professors. The legitimate power a uniform confers wields authority in consumer contexts, including teaching hospitals where medical students used to don white coats to enhance their standing with patients (although this practice has now largely been abandoned to try and prevent the spread of hospital infections).[10] Marketers 'borrow' this form of power to influence consumers. For example, an ad that shows a model who wears a white doctor's coat adds an aura of legitimacy or authority to the presentation of the product ('I'm not a doctor, but I play one on TV').

- **Expert power**. To attract the casual internet user, US Robotics Corporation signed up British physicist Stephen Hawking to endorse its modems. A company executive commented, 'We wanted to generate trust. So we found visionaries who use US Robotics technology, and we let them tell the consumer how it makes their lives more productive'. Hawking.[11] who had Lou Gehrig's disease and spoke via a synthesiser, said in one TV spot, 'My body may be stuck in this chair, but with the internet my mind can go to the end of the universe'.[12] Hawking's expert power derived from the knowledge he possessed about a content area. This helps to explain the weight many of us assign to professional critics' reviews of restaurants, books, movies and cars – even though, with the advent of blogs and open-source references such as Wikipedia, it's getting a lot harder to tell just who really is an expert.[13]

- **Reward power**. A person or group with the means to provide positive reinforcement (see Chapter 6) has reward power. The reward may be the tangible kind, as when an employee is given a pay rise. Or it can be more intangible, such as the approval the judges on *Strictly Come Dancing* or *The Voice* deliver to contestants.

- **Coercive power**. We exert coercive power when we influence someone because of social or physical intimidation. A threat is often effective in the short term, but it doesn't tend to stick because we revert to our original behaviour as soon as the bully leaves the scene. Fortunately, marketers rarely try to use this type of power (unless you count those annoying calls from telemarketers). However, we can see elements of this power base in the fear appeals we've talked about (see Chapter 7), as well as in intimidating salespeople who try to succeed with a 'hard sell'.

Reference groups

A **reference group** is 'an actual or imaginary individual or group conceived of having significant relevance upon an individual's evaluations, aspirations, or behaviour'.[14] Reference groups influence consumers in three ways: informational, utilitarian and value-expressive.[15] In this chapter we'll focus on how other people, whether fellow-bikers, co-workers, friends, family or simply casual acquaintances, influence our purchase decisions. We'll consider how our group memberships shape our preferences because we want others to accept us, or even because we mimic the actions of famous people we've never met. We'll also explore why some people, in particular, affect our product preferences and how marketers find those people and enlist their support to persuade consumers to jump on the bandwagon.

When are reference groups important?

Recent research on smoking cessation programmes powerfully illustrates the impact of reference groups. The study found that smokers tend to quit in groups: when one person quits, this creates a ripple effect that motivates others in their social network to give up cigarettes as well. The researchers followed thousands of smokers and non-smokers for more than 30 years, and also tracked their networks of relatives, co-workers and friends. They discovered that, over the years, the smokers tended to cluster together (on average in groups of three). As the overall US smoking rate declined dramatically during this period, the number of clusters in the sample decreased but the remaining clusters stayed the same size; this indicated that people quit in groups rather than as individuals. Not surprisingly, some social connections were more powerful than others. A spouse who quit had a bigger impact than did a friend, whereas friends had more influence than siblings. Co-workers had an influence only in small firms where everyone knew everyone else.[16]

Reference group influences don't work the same way for all types of products and consumption activities. For example, we're not as likely to take others' preferences into account when we choose products that are not very complex, that are low in perceived risk (see Chapter 8) or that we can 'try before we buy'.[17] In addition, knowing what others prefer may influence us at a general level (e.g. owning or not owning a computer, eating junk food versus healthy food), whereas at other times this knowledge guides the specific brands we desire within a product category (e.g. if we wear Levi's jeans versus Diesel jeans, or smoke Marlboro cigarettes rather than a national brand).

Two dimensions that influence the degree to which reference groups are important are whether we will consume the item publicly or privately and whether it is a luxury or a necessity. As a rule, reference group effects are more robust for purchases that are: (1) luxuries (e.g. yachts) rather than necessities, because products that we buy using discretionary income are subject to individual tastes and preferences, whereas necessities do not offer this range of choice; and (2) socially conspicuous or visible to others (e.g. living room furniture or clothing), because we do not tend to be swayed as much by the opinions of others if no one but ourselves will ever see what we buy.[18] The relative effects of reference group influences on some specific product classes are shown in Figure 9.1. Obviously this does not mean that a reference group cannot exert influence on the consumption of private necessities.

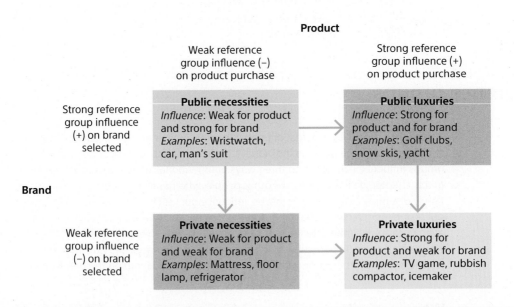

Figure 9.1 Relative effects of reference groups

Source: Adapted from William O. Bearden and Michael J. Etzel, 'Reference group influence on product and brand purchase decisions', *Journal of Consumer Research*, 9(2) (1982): 185. Copyright © 1982, Oxford University Press by permission of Oxford University Press.

Types of reference groups

Although two or more people are normally required to form a group, the term 'reference group' is often used a bit more loosely to describe any external influence that provides social cues.[19] The referent may be a cultural figure and have an impact on many people (e.g. Pope Francis or Michelle Obama), or a sportsman (e.g. Lionel Messi, Cristiano Ronaldo, Roger Federer or Andy Murray), or a person or group whose influence only operates in the consumer's immediate environment (e.g. Bobby's various football teams, 5-a-side and 11-a-side). Reference groups that affect consumption can include parents, fellow football enthusiasts and team members, classmates, other leisure activity enthusiasts, a political party or even sports clubs such as Manchester City and bands such as Little Mix, The Rolling Stones and Coldplay.

Some people influence us simply because we feel similar to them. Have you ever experienced a warm feeling when you pull up at a light next to someone who drives the exact same car as yours? One reason that we feel a bond with fellow brand users may be that many of us are a bit narcissistic; we feel an attraction to people and products that remind us of ourselves. That may explain why we feel a connection to others who happen to share our name. Research on the name-letter effect finds that, other things being equal, we like others who share our names or even initials better than those who don't.[20]

Some groups and individuals exert a greater influence than others and affect a broader range of consumption decisions. For example, our parents may play a pivotal role in forming our values towards many important issues, such as attitudes about marriage and the family or where to go to university. We call this **normative influence** – that is, the reference group helps to set and enforce fundamental standards of conduct. In contrast, a Harley-Davidson club or Manchester City fan club exerts comparative influence, whereby decisions about specific brands or activities are affected.[21]

Formal *vs* informal groups

A reference group can take the form of a large, formal organisation that has a recognised structure, regular meeting times and officers. Or it can be small and informal, such as a group of friends or students living in a university hall of residence. Marketers tend to have more control over the influencing of formal groups because they are more easily identifiable and accessible.

In general, small, informal groups exert a more powerful influence on individual consumers. These groups tend to be more involved in our day-to-day lives and to be more important to us, because they are high in normative influence. Larger, formal groups tend to be more product- or activity-specific and thus are high in comparative influence.

Membership *vs* aspirational reference groups

A membership reference group consists of people we actually know; whereas although we don't know those in an aspirational reference group, we can admire them anyway. The latter group is likely to consist of successful business people, athletes, performers, or whosoever appeals to us. Not surprisingly, many marketing efforts that specifically adopt a reference group appeal concentrate on highly visible, widely admired figures (such as well-known athletes or performers) and link these people to brands so that the products they use or endorse also take on this aspirational quality.[22] For instance, David Beckham endorses a number of different products including Armani.[23] One study of business students who aspired to the 'executive' role found a strong relationship between products they associated with their ideal selves (see Chapter 5) and those they assumed that real executives own.[24] Of course, it's worth noting that as social media usage increases, the

Both offline and online we seek out people similar to ourselves. This group of friends might be seen as part of an identificational membership reference group, drawn together by similar likes (e.g. sharing leisure activities; clothing; drinks) and dislikes.

Paolo Paradiso/Shutterstock

line between those we 'know' and those we 'friend' gets blurrier. Still, whether offline or online, we tend to seek out others who are similar. Indeed, one study even found that people on Twitter tend to follow others who share their mood: people who are happy tend to re-tweet or reply to others who are happy, while those who are sad or lonely tend to do the same with others who also post negative sentiments.[25] However, as Allyson Stewart-Allen (chief executive of the brand consultancy International Marketing Partners) points out: 'Social media is a minefield for brands. But they have to be on it because they are being talked about. They have to be part of the conversation'.[26] Twitter is 'now a customer-service megaphone, where a careless word or tweet can generate customer anger with the potential to inflict real damage on sales'.[27]

Identificational reference groups

Because we tend to compare ourselves with those who are similar to us, many promotional strategies include 'ordinary' people whose consumption activities provide informational social influence. How can we predict which people you know will become part of your **identificational membership reference group**? Several factors make it more likely:

- *Propinquity.* As physical distance between people decreases and opportunities for inter-action increase, relationships are more likely to form. We call this physical nearness **propinquity**. An early study on friendship patterns in a housing complex showed this factor's strong effects: residents were far more likely to be friends with the people next door than with those who lived only two doors away. Furthermore, people who lived next to a staircase had more friends than those at the ends of a corridor (presumably, they were more likely to 'bump into' people using the stairs).[28] Physical structure has a lot to do with who we get to know and how popular we are.

- *Mere exposure.* We come to like persons or things simply as a result of seeing them more often, which social scientists call the **mere exposure phenomenon**.[29] Greater frequency of contact, even if unintentional, may help to determine one's set of local referents. The same effect holds when evaluating works of art or even political candidates.[30] One study predicted 83 per cent of the winners of political primaries solely by the amount of media exposure given to candidates.[31]

- *Group cohesiveness.* **Cohesiveness** refers to the degree to which members of a group are attracted to each other and how much each person values their group membership. As the value of the group to the individual increases, so too does the likelihood that the group will influence their consumption decisions. Smaller groups tend to be more cohesive because in larger groups the contributions of each member are usually less important or noticeable. By the same token, groups often try to restrict membership to a select few, which increases the value of membership to those who are admitted. Exclusivity of membership is a benefit often promoted by credit-card companies, book clubs and so on, even though the actual membership base might be fairly large.

Positive *vs* negative reference groups

Reference groups may exert either a positive or a negative influence on consumption behaviours. In most cases, we model our behaviour to be consistent with what we think the group expects us to do. Sometimes, however, we also deliberately do the opposite if we want to distance ourselves from other people or groups who function as avoidance or dissociative groups. We may carefully study the dress or mannerisms of a disliked group and scrupulously avoid buying anything that might identify us with that group. Many consumers find it difficult to express what they want, whereas they can quite clearly express what they do not want. In fact, some researchers suggest that the phenomenon of distaste is far more decisive for our consumption choices but harder to study than tastes, since our choices are quite obvious compared to all the non-selected alternatives.[32] For example, rebellious adolescents often resent parental influence and may deliberately do the opposite of what their parents would like as a way of making a statement about their independence.[33]

The motivation to distance oneself from a negative reference group can be as or more powerful than the desire to please a positive group.[34] That is why advertisements occasionally show an undesirable person using a competitor's product to subtly make the point that you can avoid winding up like that kind of person by staying away from the products they buy. As a once-popular book reminded us, 'Real men don't eat quiche!'.[35] Today, others have adapted this avoidance group appeal to point out the ways we define ourselves by not consuming some products or services. Research suggests that 'dissociative reference groups have a greater impact on consumers' self-brand connections, product evaluations, and choices than do products associated with out-groups more generally'.[36]

When reference groups are important

Reference group influences are not equally powerful for all types of products and consumption activities, as we have seen above. However, we know that we can get away with more when we are in a group – for instance, in the purchase of services. With more people in a group, it becomes less likely that any one member will be singled out for attention. People in larger groups, or those in situations where they are unlikely to be identified, tend to focus less attention on themselves, so normal restraints on behaviour are reduced. You may have observed that people sometimes behave more wildly at fancy-dress parties, at hen or stag parties or partying on, for example, charter holidays, than they would normally do. This phenomenon is known as **de-individuation**. This is a process in which individual identities get submerged within a group.

Multicultural dimensions

University parties sometimes illustrate the dark side of de-individuation, when students are encouraged by their peers to consume almost superhuman volumes of alcohol in group settings. For most, social pressure to abandon all inhibitions is the culprit.[37] Binge drinking is also increasingly recognised as a problem in the UK,[38] and not only among university students. A UK study identified how students seek to 'neutralise potential feelings of guilt and stigmatisation regarding their alcohol consumption. . . Analysis highlights the importance of alcohol consumption in students' lifestyles, but also the potential identity conflicts experienced by all drinkers, regardless of the amount consumed. Heavy drinkers primarily employ neutralisation techniques as a means of rationalising the negative impacts of their actions, whereas abstainers and near-abstainers mainly use counter-neutralisation techniques as a means of reinforcing their commitment to lifestyles that run counter to mainstream student-life expectations. However, regardless of the amount of alcohol consumed, all participants employed neutralising and counter-neutralising arguments in some social situations.[39]

Social loafing has a similar effect. It happens when we do not devote as much effort to a task because our contribution is part of a larger group effort.[40] Waiting staff are painfully aware of social loafing: people who eat in groups tend to tip less per person than when they are eating alone.[41] For this reason, many restaurants automatically add on a fixed gratuity for groups of six or more.

Furthermore, the decisions we make as part of a group tend to differ from those that each of us might choose if we were on our own. The **risky shift effect** refers to the observation that, in many cases, group members show a greater willingness to consider riskier alternatives following group discussion than they would if each group member made his or her decision without talking about it with others.[42] Psychologists propose several explanations for this increased riskiness. One possibility is that something similar to social loafing occurs. As more people are involved in a decision, each individual is less accountable for the outcome, resulting in diffusion of responsibility.[43] The practice of placing blanks in at least one of the rifles used by a firing squad was one way of diffusing each soldier's responsibility for the death of a prisoner, because it was never certain who actually shot him. Another explanation is termed the 'value hypothesis', which states that our culture values risky behaviour, so when people make decisions in groups they conform to this expectation.[44]

Costumes hide our true identities and encourage de-individuation.

Martin Dalton/Alamy Images.

Research evidence for the risky shift is mixed. A more general finding is that group discussion tends to increase **decision polarisation**. Therefore, whichever direction the group members were leaning towards before discussion began – whether towards a risky choice or towards a more conservative choice – becomes even more extreme in that direction after discussion. Group discussions regarding product purchases tend to create a risky shift for low-risk items, but they yield more conservative group decisions for high-risk products.[45]

Group shopping

Even shopping behaviour changes when people do it in groups. For example, people who shop with at least one other person tend to make more unplanned purchases, buy more and cover more areas of a store than those who go alone.[46] These effects are due to both normative and informational social influence. Group members may buy something to gain the approval of the others, or the group may simply be exposed to more products and stores by pooling information within the group. For these reasons, retailers are well advised to encourage group shopping activities.

The famous 'Tupperware party' is a successful example of a **home shopping party** that capitalises on group pressure to boost sales.[47] A company representative makes a sales presentation to a group of people who have gathered in the home of a friend or acquaintance. The shopping party works because of **informational social influence**. Participants model the behaviour of others who provide them with information about how to use certain products, especially since the home party is likely to be attended by a relatively homogeneous group (e.g. neighbourhood friends). Normative social influence also operates because others can easily observe our actions. Pressures to conform may be particularly intense and may escalate as more and more group members begin to 'cave in' (this process is sometimes termed the *bandwagon effect*). In addition, these parties may activate de-individuation and/ or the risky shift. As consumers get caught up in the group, they may find themselves willing to try new products they would not normally consider. These same dynamics underlie the Botox party. The craze for Botox injections that paralyse facial nerves to reduce wrinkles (for up to six months) is fuelled by gatherings where dermatologists or plastic surgeons redefine the definition of 'house calls'. For patients, mixing cocktail hour with cosmetic injections takes some of the anxiety out of the procedure. Egged on by the others at the party, a doctor can dewrinkle many patients in an hour. An advertising executive who worked on the Botox marketing strategy explained that the **membership reference group** appeal is more effective than the traditional route that uses a celebrity spokesperson to tout the injections in advertising: 'We think it's more persuasive to think of your next-door-neighbour using it'.[48]

Conformity

In every age there are those who 'march to the beat of their own drum'. However, most people tend to follow society's expectations regarding how they should act and look (with a little improvisation here and there, of course). **Conformity** refers to a change in beliefs or actions as a reaction to real or imagined group pressure. In order for a society to function, its members develop **norms**, or informal rules that govern behaviour. If such a system of agreements and rules did not evolve, chaos would result. Imagine the confusion if a simple norm such as sitting down to attend class did not exist.

We conform in many small ways every day – even though we don't always realise it. Unspoken rules govern many aspects of consumption. In addition to norms regarding appropriate use of clothing and other personal items, we conform to rules that include gift-giving (we expect birthday presents from loved ones and get upset if they do not materialise), sex roles (men were often expected to pick up the bill on a first date, though this convention is changing) and personal hygiene (we are expected to shower or bathe regularly to avoid offending others).

The pressure to conform conflicts with another motivation that we've already discussed: the need to be unique. How can we reconcile these two goals? One study suggests that we try to have it both ways. We line up with a group on one dimension, such as choosing a popular brand, but we differentiate ourselves on another by choosing a unique attribute such as colour.[49] Another study identified another interaction and argued that 'conformity can buffer the negative psychological consequences of moral violations and. . . moral considerations can serve as an important basis for consumer choice. . . consumers' heightened conformist attitudes are reflected in their preferences for majority-endorsed products and brands. . . [and] exposure to moral violations increases consumers' subsequent conformity tendencies, which, in turn, increases their preference for majority-endorsed products'.[50]

Within limits, people approve of others who exhibit non-conforming behaviour. This may be because we assume someone who makes unconventional choices is more powerful or competent, so he or she can afford to go out on a limb. Researchers term this the **Red Sneakers Effect** (to describe a brave person who sports a pair of red sports shoes or trainers in a professional setting). Indeed, they find that non-conforming behaviours under some conditions do lead to more positive impressions – but these disappear if the observer is unsure *why* the brave soul is violating a norm, or if they decide the violator is not doing so intentionally (i.e. he or she is just clueless!).[51]

We also observe conformity in the online world; research supports the idea that consumers are more likely to show interest in a product if they see that it is already very popular. One study analysed how millions of Facebook users adopted apps to personalise their pages. Researchers tracked, on an hourly basis, the rate at which 2,700 apps were installed by 50 million Facebook users. They discovered that once an app had reached a rate of about 55 installations a day, its popularity started to soar. Facebook friends were notified when one of their online buddies adopted a new app, and they could also see a list of the most popular ones. Apparently, this popularity feedback was the key driver that determined whether still more users would download the software.[52]

Types of social influence

Just as the bases for social power can vary, so the process of social influence operates in several ways.[53] Sometimes a person is motivated to model the behaviour of others because this mimicry is believed to yield rewards such as social approval or money. At other times, the social influence process occurs simply because the person honestly does not know the correct way to respond and is using the behaviour of the other person or group as a cue to ensure that they are responding correctly.[54] **Normative social influence** occurs when a person conforms to meet the expectations of a person or group.

In contrast, **informational social influence** refers to conformity that occurs because the group's behaviour is taken as evidence of reality: if other people respond in a certain way in an ambiguous situation, we may mimic their behaviour because this appears to be the correct thing to do.[55]

Reasons for conformity

Conformity is not an automatic process, and many factors contribute to the likelihood that consumers will pattern their behaviour after others'.[56] Among the factors that affect the likelihood of conformity are the following:

- *Cultural pressures.* Different cultures encourage conformity to a greater or lesser degree. The American slogan 'Do your own thing' in the 1960s reflected a movement away from conformity and towards individualism. In contrast, Japanese society is characterised by the dominance of collective well-being and group loyalty over individuals' needs. Most European societies are situated somewhere between these two 'extreme' cultures. In an analysis of the reading of a soft drinks TV commercial, Danish consumers stressed the group solidarity that they saw in the ad, an aspect not mentioned at all by the American sample.[57] In another study, groups of passengers who arrived at an airport were asked to complete a survey. They were offered a handful of pens to use – for example, four orange and one green. People of European descent more often chose the one pen that stood out, while Asian people were more likely to choose the colour that was like the majority of others.[58]

- *Fear of deviance.* The individual may have reason to believe that the group will apply sanctions to punish non-conforming behaviours. It is not unusual to observe adolescents shunning a peer who is 'different' or a corporation or university passing over a person for promotion because they are not a 'team player'.

- *Commitment.* The more people are dedicated to a group and value their membership in it, the more motivated they are to do what the group wants. Rock groupies and followers of religious sects may do anything that is asked of them, and terrorists (or martyrs and freedom fighters, depending on the perspective) may be willing to die for the good of their cause. According to the **principle of least interest**, the person that is least committed to staying in a relationship has the most power, because that party doesn't care as much if the other person rejects them.[59]

- *Group unanimity, size and expertise.* As groups gain in power, compliance increases. It is often harder to resist the demands of a large number of people than just a few, and this difficulty is compounded when the group members are perceived to know what they are talking about.

- *Susceptibility to interpersonal influence.* This trait refers to an individual's need to have others think highly of them. This enhancement process is often accompanied by the acquisition of products the person believes will impress their audience and by the tendency to learn about products by observing how others use them.[60] Consumers who are low on this trait have been called role-relaxed – they tend to be older, affluent and to have high self-confidence. Based on research identifying role-relaxed consumers, Subaru created a communications strategy to reach these people. In one commercial, a man is heard saying, 'I want a car. . . Don't tell me about wood panelling, about winning the respect of my neighbours. They're my neighbours. They're not my heroes'.

- *Environmental cues.* One study reported that people are more likely to conform when they make decisions in a warm room. Apparently, the warmth caused participants to feel closer to other decision-makers and this feeling led them to assume the others' opinions were more valid. In one part of the study the researchers analysed betting behaviour at a racetrack over a three-year period. Sure enough, people were more likely to bet on the favourite horse on warmer days.[61]

Social comparison: 'How am I doing?'

Informational social influence implies that sometimes we look to the behaviour of others to provide a yardstick about reality. **Social comparison theory** asserts that this process occurs as a way of increasing the stability of one's self-evaluation, especially when physical evidence is unavailable.[62] Social comparison even applies to choices for which there are no objectively correct answers. Such stylistic decisions as tastes in music and art are assumed to be a matter of individual choice, yet people often assume that some choices are 'better' or more 'correct' than others.[63]

Although people often like to compare their judgements and actions with those of others, they tend to be selective about precisely who they will use as benchmarks. Similarity between the consumer and others used for social comparison boosts confidence that the information is accurate and relevant (though we may find it more threatening to be outperformed by someone similar to ourselves).[64] We tend to value the views of obviously dissimilar others only when we are reasonably certain of our own.[65]

Social comparison theory has been used to explore the effects of advertising images on women's self-perceptions of their physical attractiveness and their levels of self-esteem.[66] Many early studies showed that social comparison, when studied in terms of only self-evaluation, is likely to have a negative effect on self-esteem. However, the incorporation of the specific goal (self-evaluation, self-improvement or self-enhancement)[67] suggests that social comparison can have either positive or negative effects on self-feelings depending on the goal for social comparison.[68] One study suggests that the direction of spontaneous social comparison and social evaluation processes may be determined by fairly subtle cues. Whereas most advertising research suggests that comparisons with idealised models lead to contrast, this study found evidence that comparisons can also lead to assimilation of standards into the self-evaluation.[69]

In general, people tend to choose a co-oriented peer, or a person of equivalent standing, when performing social comparison. For example, a study of adult cosmetics users found that women were more likely to seek information about product choices from similar friends to reduce uncertainty and to trust the judgements of similar others.[70] The same effects have been found for evaluations of products as diverse as men's suits and coffee.[71]

Resistance to influence

Many people pride themselves on their independence, unique style or ability to resist the best efforts of salespeople and advertisers to buy products.[72] Indeed, individuality should be encouraged by the marketing system: innovation creates change and demand for new products and styles.

Anti-conformity *vs* independence

It is important to distinguish between independence and anti-conformity; in **anti-conformity**, defiance of the group is the actual object of behaviour.[73] Some people will go out of their way not to buy whatever happens to be in fashion. Indeed, they may spend a lot of time and effort to ensure that they will not be caught 'in style'. This behaviour is a bit of a paradox, because in order to be vigilant about not doing what is expected, one must always be aware of what is expected. In contrast, truly independent people are oblivious to what is expected; they 'march to the beat of their own drum'.

Reactance and the need for uniqueness

People have a deep-seated need to preserve freedom of choice. When they are threatened with a loss of this freedom, they try to overcome this loss. This negative emotional state

This advert for deodorant illustrates a message appeal based on conforming to the unspoken rule about personal hygiene in many societies.

With kind permission from Unilever

is termed **reactance**, and results when we are deprived of our freedom to choose.[74] This feeling can drive us to value forbidden things, even if they wouldn't be that interesting to us otherwise. For example, efforts to censor books, television shows or rock music because some people find the content objectionable may result in an increased desire for these products by the public.[75] Similarly, extremely overbearing promotions that tell consumers they must or should use a product may lose customers in the long run, even those who were already loyal to the advertised brand. Reactance is more likely to occur when the perceived threat to one's freedom increases as the threatened behaviour's importance to the consumer also increases.

If you have ever arrived at a party or wedding wearing the same outfit as someone else, you know how upsetting it can be – a reaction resulting from a search for uniqueness.[76] Consumers who have been led to believe they are not unique are more likely to try to compensate by increasing their creativity, or even to engage in unusual experiences. In fact, this is one explanation for the purchase of relatively obscure brands. People may try to establish a unique identity by deliberately not buying market leaders.

This desire to carve out a unique identity was the rationale behind Saab's shift from stressing engineering and safety in its marketing messages to appealing to people to 'find your own road'. According to a Saab executive, 'Research companies tell us we are moving into a period where people feel good about their choices because it fits their own self-concept rather than social conventions'.[77]

Brand communities and consumer tribes

Some marketing researchers are embracing a new perspective on reference groups as they identify groups built around a shared allegiance to a product or activity. A brand community is a group of consumers who share a set of social relationships based upon usage of or interest in a product.[78] Such **brand communities** can range from core members of 'social clubs' or organisations to 'felt' memberships of some imagined community. For example, drivers of the classic British-produced MG cars in the US consider each other somehow linked through their MG ownership, and they engage in various types of communal commitment and sharing of help and information, as they feel that they have a common cause in preserving this 'pristine brand'. Just the fact that they drive the same brand of cars makes the MG owners feel part of a special group of people set apart from the rest of society: a brand community.[79] Memberships of brand communities can also be very important in conveying a sense of authenticity and confirmation of one's identity as a member of some (youth) subculture oriented towards consumption of a particular style of fashion or type of music.[80] Finally, brand communities can be a valuable asset for a corporate organisation to make sure it is aligned with what its consumers see as its core value – as, for example, is the case with Liverpool FC and its international fan base and their maintenance of the 'you'll never walk alone' tradition.[81]

Brand communities do not have to be about expensive products such as computers or cars. A very active virtual brand community has formed around the hazelnut-based spread Nutella,[82] where consumers write or talk about themselves online, join in Nutella consumption situations and share their funniest or happiest 'Nutella moments'.[83] Some consumers form communities around brands, but some consumer communities form their own brands. Communities around websites such as www.outdoorseiten.net and www.skibuilders.com have engaged in developing equipment and branding based on what community members felt was lacking in the marketplace.[84]

Unlike other kinds of communities, these members typically do not live near each other – and they often meet only for brief periods at organised events called **brand-fests**, such as those sponsored by Jeep, Saturn or Harley-Davidson. These brand-fests help owners to 'bond' with fellow enthusiasts and strengthen their identification with the product, as well as with others they meet who share their passion. In virtually any category, you'll find passionate brand communities (in some cases devoted to brands that don't even exist anymore, such as the Apple Newton – a discontinued personal digital assistant).

Researchers find that people who participate in these events feel more positive about the products as a result and this enhances brand loyalty. They are more forgiving than others of product failures or lapses in service quality, and less likely to switch brands even if they learn that competing products are as good or better. Furthermore, these community members become emotionally involved in the company's welfare, and they often serve as brand missionaries by carrying its marketing message to others.[85]

There is also evidence that brand community members do more than help the product build buzz; their inputs actually create added value for themselves and other members as they develop better ways to use and customise products. For example, it's common for experienced users to coach 'newbies' in ways to maximise their enjoyment of the product so that more and more people benefit from a network of satisfied participants. In other cases, members benefit because their communities empower them to learn; for example, a study that looked at people who suffered from thyroid problems, and who indicated they were uninformed and ill-prepared to make decisions about their treatment, later exhibited more active involvement and informed decision-making after they participated in an online community with others who shared their health issues.[86] Figure 9.2 demonstrates this process of **collective value creation**.[87]

What do people, as consumers, get out of participating in a brand community? Based on an overview of brand community studies, it has been concluded that, beyond the mere production of a social identity (as an Apple user, a Star Trek fan or an MG driver), the following elements were highlighted:[88]

- *Social networking*: making sure that the community is inclusive and welcoming, keeping it together, making friends.

- *Community engagement*: making sure that the network is kept alive through active discussions, debates, differentiations.

- *Impression management*: promoting and justifying one's particular interest to others outside the community.

- *Brand use*: becoming better at what one is already interested in through learning from others inside the community.

The Tangled Web

The Web has spawned the rise of a new kind of avoidance group: anti-brand communities. These groups also coalesce around a celebrity, store or brand – but in this case they're united by their disdain for it. The site starbucked.com asked, 'Starbucked enough by corporate crap product and service?' and provided the locations of independent coffee houses.[89] The UK-based anti-McDonald's site www.McSpotlight. org claims, 'McDonald's spends over $2 billion a year broadcasting their glossy image to the world. This is a small space for alternatives to be heard'. At Hel*Mart. com you can find links to numerous groups that oppose the practices of the US corporate Wal-Mart.

One team of researchers that studies these communities observes that they tend to attract social idealists who advocate non-materialistic lifestyles. After they interviewed members of online communities who oppose these three companies, they concluded that these anti-brand communities provide a meeting place for those who share a moral stance, a support network to achieve common goals, a way to cope with workplace frustrations (many members actually work for the companies they bash!) and a hub for information, activities and related resources.[90]

The notion of a **consumer tribe** is similar to a brand community: it is a group of people who share a lifestyle and who can identify with each other through a shared allegiance to an activity or a product. Although these tribes are often unstable and short-lived, at least for a time members identify with others through shared emotions, moral beliefs, styles of life and, of course, the products they jointly consume as part of their tribal affiliation. Some companies,

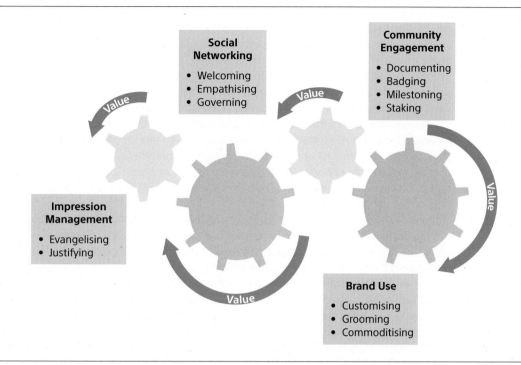

Figure 9.2 Collective value creation (Shau, Muniz and Arnould)

Source: Reprinted with permission from Hope Jensen Schau, Albert M. Muniz and Eric J. Arnould, *Journal of Marketing* 73(5) (September 2009): 30–51 (published by the American Marketing Association, Schau).

especially those that are more youth oriented, are using **tribal marketing** to link their product to the needs of a group as a whole. Many tribes devoted to activities such as skateboarding or football are youth oriented. However, there are also plenty of tribes with older members, such as car enthusiasts who gather to celebrate such products as the Citroën and Mini Cooper in Europe, and the Ford Mustang in the US.[91]

Other research has identified **communities of practice** as a potentially valuable way of understanding and interpreting group behaviour. Communities of practice are 'an aggregate of people who come together around mutual engagement in an endeavour'.[92] Developed from work in socio-linguistics, communities of practice are usually defined by three characteristics: 'mutual engagement; a joint enterprise; and a shared repertoire'.[93] A study of Bolton schoolgirls showed how consumption symbols (e.g. Rockport shoes) could be combined with other social symbols (e.g. language) in order to create meanings related to group identity.[94] 'We are surrounded by stylistic material, and as long as we can position ourselves in relation to the sources of that material, and attribute meaning to it, we can use it.'[95]

Word-of-mouth communication

Word-of-mouth communication is the most important driver of product choice.

Despite the abundance of formal means of communication (such as newspapers, magazines and television, as well as less formal channels in social media), much information about the world is conveyed by individuals on an informal basis.[96] **Word-of-mouth (WOM)** is product information that individuals transmit to other individuals. Despite the huge sums of money marketers pump into lavish ads, WOM is far more powerful: it influences up to 50 per cent of all consumer goods sales.[97] If you think carefully about the content of your own conversations in the course of a normal day, you will probably agree that much of what you discuss with friends, family members or co-workers is product related. Whether you compliment someone on her dress and ask her where she bought it, recommend a new restaurant to a friend or complain to your neighbour about the shoddy treatment you got at the bank, you are engaging in word-of-mouth communication (WOM). Recall, for example, that Bobby's choice of football boots was directly initiated by comments and suggestions from his friends and team mates. This kind of communication can be an efficient marketing tool. There is also evidence that such conversations particularly increase consumers' happiness in the context of experiential purchases.[98]

Information obtained from those we know or talk to directly tends to be thought of as more reliable and trustworthy than that received through more formal channels and, unlike advertising, it is often backed up by social pressure to conform to these recommendations.[99] Another factor in the importance of WOM is the decline in people's faith in institutions. As traditional endorsers are becoming increasingly problematical to use – celebrities because they can be unreliable, and classical authority figures because of the withering of their authority – and, indeed, as people are becoming more cynical about all sorts of commercial communications, consumers turn to sources that they feel are above commercial exploitation: friends and family.[100] The importance of personal, informal product communication to marketers is further underscored by one advertising executive, who stated, 'Today, 80 per cent of all buying decisions are influenced by someone's direct recommendations'.[101] In one survey, 69 per cent of interviewees said they relied on a personal referral at least once over the course of a year to help them choose a restaurant, 36 per cent reported they used referrals to decide on computer hardware and software and 22 per cent got help from friends and associates to decide where to travel.[102] Marketers have been aware of the power of WOM for many years, but recently they've been more aggressive about trying to promote and control it, instead of sitting back and hoping people will like their products enough to talk them up. Companies such as BzzAgent enlist thousands of 'agents' who try new products and spread the word about those they like.[103] Many sophisticated marketers today also precisely track WOM.

In the 1950s, communications theorists began to challenge the assumption that advertising primarily determines what we buy. As a rule, advertising is more effective when it reinforces our existing product preferences than when it tries to create new ones.[104] Studies in both industrial and consumer purchase settings underline the idea that, although information from impersonal sources is important for creating brand awareness, consumers rely on word of mouth in the later stages of evaluation and adoption.[105] Quite simply, the more positive information consumers get about a product from peers, the more likely they will be to adopt that product.[106] The influence of others' opinions is, at times, even more powerful than one's own perceptions.

WOM is especially powerful when the consumer is relatively unfamiliar with the product category. We would expect such a situation in the case of new products (e.g. medications to prevent hair loss), or those that are technologically complex (e.g. smart home assistants such as Amazon Alexa or Google Assistant).[107] One way to reduce uncertainty about the wisdom of a purchase is to talk about it. Talking gives the consumer an opportunity to generate supporting arguments for the purchase and to garner support for this decision from others.

Numerous professionals, such as doctors, accountants and lawyers, as well as service providers such as lawn-care companies and cleaning services, depend primarily on word of mouth to generate business. In many cases, consumers recommend a service provider to a friend or co-worker, and in other cases business people make recommendations to their customers.

Buzz building

Many marketers spend lavishly to create marketing messages that they hope will convince hordes of customers that they are the best. There's the rub – in many cases they may be trying too hard! We can think of this as the corporate paradox – the more involved a company appears to be in the dissemination of news about its products, the less credible it becomes.[108] Consumer word of mouth is typically the most convincing kind of message. **Buzz** is word of mouth that is viewed as authentic and generated by customers. In contrast, hype is dismissed as inauthentic – corporate propaganda planted by a company with an axe to grind. So, the challenge to marketers is to get the word out and about without it looking like they are trying too hard. The contemporary situation of convergence between different social and mass media creates even more possibilities but also pitfalls for operating in the hype/buzz zone, as witnessed by a discussion of celebrities and consumption in a UK marketing journal.[109]

Some marketers try to borrow the veneer of buzz by mounting 'stealth' campaigns that seem as if they are untouched by the corporate world. Buzz building has become the mantra for many companies that recognise the power of underground word of mouth.[110] Indeed, a small cottage industry has sprung up as some firms begin to specialise in the corporate promotion business by planting comments on websites that are made to look as if they originated from actual consumers. An example from the car industry includes Volkswagen's campaign for the Beetle in 2011, where a mixture of impressive billboards in urban environments and the opportunity for downloading apps that permitted playing with the billboard scenery in an augmented reality format created a lot of. . . buzz.[111] A recent study has identified the role of time, and its impact on sharing via word of mouth. The authors argue: 'that the effect of temporal location on word of mouth is driven by arousal, such that the same event is more arousing when it is happening in the future (vs. past); but whether arousal increases or decreases sharing depends on how the thing being discussed reflects on the sharer. People are more willing to talk about their experiences if they were to take place in the future as opposed to the past, however when the topic being discussed reflects badly on the sharer, arousal decreases sharing. Furthermore, it demonstrates that the strength of the social link between the sharer and the sharing target moderates the effect of temporal location and self-presentation on sharing behaviour. For weak ties, the relationship between arousal and sharing is reversed, such that events are not more likely to be talked about if they are in the future. . . the findings suggest that companies and organizations trying to increase word of mouth should encourage people to think about the future to boost buzz.'[112]

Guerrilla marketing

Streetwise strategies of **guerrilla marketing** started in the mid-1970s, when pioneering DJs promoted their parties through graffiti-style flyers. This type of grass-roots effort epitomises guerrilla marketing – promotional strategies that use unconventional locations and intensive word-of-mouth campaigns to push products. The term implies that the marketer 'ambushes' the unsuspecting recipient. These campaigns often recruit legions of real consumers who agree to engage in some kind of street theatre or other activity to convince others to use the product or service.

Big companies are buying into guerrilla marketing strategies in a big way. Coca-Cola did it for a Sprite promotion, Nike did it to build interest in a new shoe model.[113] Upmarket fashion companies are adopting this strategy, in order to offer shoppers a different retailing experience compared with conventional retail outlets. Comme des Garçons Guerrilla Store opened in New York in February 2004: '[I]n the first example of provisional retailing by an established fashion house, the store plans to close in a year even if it is making money. All 20 stores that the Tokyo-based company plans to open by next year, including one in Brooklyn in September [2004], will adopt the same guerrilla strategy, disappearing after a year'.[114]

Negative word of mouth

Word of mouth is a two-edged sword that can cut both ways for marketers. Informal discussions among consumers can make or break a product or store. Furthermore, consumers weigh **negative word-of-mouth** more heavily than they do positive comments. Especially

Low-angle view of young man dunking basketball into a hoop against a clear blue sky. This image is full of movement and impact , and you almost feel the force of his jump as he aims at the net, despite the fact that the image is actually static. The ad illustrates the marketing of athletic shoes, and how many styles first become popular in the inner city and then spread by word of mouth.

sirtravelalot/Shutterstock

'Ed Sheeran's album Divide was the biggest selling entertainment product of 2017 . . . [reflecting] the dramatic growth in the popularity of paid-for digital services.'

IBL/Shutterstock

when we're considering a new product or service, we're likely to pay more attention to negative information than positive information and tell others of our nasty experience.[115] Research shows that negative WOM reduces the credibility of a firm's advertising and influences consumers' attitudes toward a product as well as their intention to buy it.[116] And negative WOM is even easier to spread online. Many dissatisfied customers and disgruntled former employees have been 'inspired' to create websites just to share their tales of woe with others. For example, a website for people to complain about the Dunkin' Donuts chain became so popular the company bought it in order to control the bad press it was getting. It grew out of a complaint by the original owner because he could not get skimmed milk for his coffee.[117]

As we transmit information to one another, it tends to change. The resulting message usually does not resemble the original at all. The British psychologist Frederic Bartlett used the method of serial reproduction to examine how content mutates. A subject is asked to reproduce a stimulus, such as a drawing or a story. Another subject is given this reproduction and asked to copy that, and so on. Messages tend to change as the figures are constantly reproduced by different individuals. Bartlett found that distortions almost inevitably follow a pattern: they tend to change from ambiguous forms to more conventional ones as subjects try to make them consistent with pre-existing schemas. He called this process 'assimilation', and he noted that it often occurs as people engage in 'levelling' (when they omit details to simplify the structure) or 'sharpening' (when they exaggerate prominent details).

Opinion leadership

9.3

Opinion leaders' recommendations are more influential than others' when we decide what to buy.

Although consumers get information from personal sources, they tend not to ask just anyone for advice about purchases. If you decide to buy a new stereo, you will most likely seek advice from a friend who knows a lot about sound systems. This friend may own a sophisticated system, or they may subscribe to specialised magazines such as *Stereo Review* and spend free time browsing through electronics stores. On the other hand, you may have another friend who has a reputation for being stylish and who spends their free time reading fashion and lifestyle magazines and shopping at trendy boutiques. While you might not bring up your stereo problem with them, you may take them with you to shop for a dress for a special occasion, such as a wedding.

The nature of opinion leadership

Everyone knows someone who is knowledgeable about products and whose advice others take seriously. This individual is an opinion leader, a person who is frequently able to influence others' attitudes or behaviours.[118] Clearly, some people's recommendations carry more weight than others'. **Opinion leaders** are extremely valuable information sources because they possess the social power we discussed earlier in the chapter:

- They are technically competent, so they possess expert power.[119]
- They prescreen, evaluate and synthesise product information in an unbiased way, so they possess knowledge power.[120]
- They are socially active and highly interconnected in their communities.[121]
- They are likely to hold offices in community groups and clubs and to be active outside of the home. As a result, opinion leaders often wield legitimate power by virtue of their social standing.

- They tend to be similar to the consumer in terms of their values and beliefs, so they possess referent power. Note that although opinion leaders are set apart by their interest or expertise in a product category, they are more convincing to the extent that they are homophilous rather than heterophilous. **Homophily** refers to the degree to which a pair of individuals is similar in terms of education, social status and beliefs.[122] Effective opinion leaders tend to be slightly higher in terms of status and educational attainment than those they influence, but not so high as to be in a different social class.

- Opinion leaders are often among the first to buy new products, so they absorb much of the risk. This experience reduces uncertainty for the rest of us, who are not as courageous. Furthermore, whereas company-sponsored communications tend to focus exclusively on the positive aspects of a product, the hands-on experience of opinion leaders makes them more likely to impart both positive and negative information about product performance. Thus, they are more credible because they have no 'axe to grind'.

Whereas individual behavioural and psychological traits are the most important in identifying opinion leaders, there are some indications that opinion leadership does not function the same way in different cultures. For example, there are cultural differences in how much people rely on impersonal *vs* personal information. In a study of opinion leadership in 14 European countries plus the US and Canada, the countries most characterised by the use of impersonal information-seeking (from consumer magazines, etc.) were Denmark, Norway, Sweden and Finland, whereas the countries least characterised by impersonal information-seeking were Italy, Portugal and Spain.[123]

How influential is an opinion leader? The extent of an opinion leader's influence

When marketers and social scientists initially developed the concept of the opinion leader, they assumed that certain influential people in a community would exert an overall impact on group members' attitudes. Later work, however, began to question the assumption that there is such a thing as a generalised opinion leader – somebody whose recommendations we seek for all types of purchases. Very few people are capable of being expert in a number of fields. Sociologists distinguish between those who are monomorphic, or expert in a limited field, and those who are polymorphic, or expert in several fields.[124] Even opinion leaders who are polymorphic, however, tend to concentrate on one broad domain, such as electronics or fashion.

Research on opinion leadership generally indicates that although opinion leaders do exist for multiple product categories, expertise tends to overlap across similar categories.[125] A reexamination of the traditional perspective on opinion leadership reveals that the process isn't as clear-cut as some researchers thought. The original framework is called the **two-step flow model of influence**. It proposes that a small group of influencers disseminate information because they can modify the opinions of a large number of other people. When the authors ran extensive computer simulations of this process, they found that the influence was driven less by influentials and more by the interaction among those who are easily influenced; they communicate the information vigorously to one another and they also participate in a two-way dialogue with the opinion leader as part of an **influence network**. These conversations create **information cascades**, which occur when a piece of information triggers a sequence of **interactions** (much like an avalanche). They concluded that 'influentials are only modestly more important than average individuals'[126] and thus influentials are less central to the process of diffusion of innovations or early adoption than hitherto (Mark Sweney, 'Home entertainment spending overtakes print sales for the first time', The Guardian (1 March 2018), https://www.theguardian.com/media/2018/mar/01/home-entertainment-spending-overtakes-print-sales-for-first-time (accessed 2 March 2018).) assumed.[127]

Role-playing computer games involve thousands of players worldwide in interactive, online communities.
© Susan Goldman/The Image Works

The tangled Web

It's not unusual for us to observe *herding behaviour* among consumers as they blindly mimic what others in their group do. Information cascades can bias what people choose as they take their cues from what others select rather than choosing what they genuinely like. In a study that looked at how an individual's music preferences depend upon knowing what other people choose, test subjects listened to 72 songs by new bands. A control group made their own individual judgements about which songs to select, but in other groups the participants could see how many people downloaded particular songs. This feedback made a huge difference in what people chose. For example, if a song spiked early in the study and respondents could see a lot of people choosing it, many more people jumped on the bandwagon and downloaded it as well. And it turns out these cascades occurred regardless of whether or not people genuinely liked the songs. The same thing happened when the subjects were given false information about which songs a lot of other people were downloading.[128]

It's worth noting that consumer researchers and other social scientists continue to debate the dynamics of these networks. For example, the jury is still out about just how influential it is when different people tweet about a product. An online service called 'Klout' claimed to measure precisely just how influential each of us is.[129] Although many marketers today focus on identifying key influencers and motivating them to spread the word about a brand, another camp believes that it's more productive simply to get your message out to as many people as possible. They argue that it's very difficult to predict what will trigger a cascade, so it's better to hedge your bets by simply getting the word out as widely as possible.[130] The science of understanding online influence is racing to keep up with the mushrooming usage of these new platforms.

Types of opinion leaders *vs* other consumer types

Early conceptions of the opinion leader role assumed a static, one-way process: the opinion leader absorbs information from the mass media and in turn transmits data to opinion receivers. This view has turned out to be overly simplified; it confuses the functions of several different types of consumers. Furthermore, research has shown some evidence that the flow of influence is not one-way but two-way, so that opinion leaders are influenced by the responses of their followers.[131] This would reflect a more complex communication situation (as discussed in Chapter 7).

Opinion leaders may or may not be purchasers of the products they recommend. Early purchasers are known as innovators and like to take risks and try new things (see Chapter 13). Researchers call opinion leaders who are also early purchasers **innovative communicators**. One study identified a number of characteristics of male university students who were innovative communicators for fashion products. These men were among the first to buy new fashions, and their fashion opinions were incorporated by other students into their own clothing purchases. Other characteristics of these men included:[132]

- They were socially active.
- They were appearance-conscious and narcissistic (i.e. they were quite fond of themselves and self-centered).
- They were involved in rock culture.
- They were heavy magazine readers.
- They were likely to own more clothing, and a broader range of styles, than other students.

Opinion leaders also are likely to be **opinion seekers**. They are generally more involved in a product category and actively search for information. As a result, they are more likely to talk about products with others and to solicit others' opinions as well.[133] Contrary to the static view of opinion leadership, most product-related conversation does not take place in a 'lecture' format in which one person does all of the talking. A lot of product-related conversation is prompted by the situation and occurs in the context of a casual interaction rather than as formal instruction.[134] One study, which found that opinion seeking is especially high for food products, revealed that two-thirds of opinion seekers also view themselves as opinion leaders.[135] This updated view of interpersonal product communication is contrasted with the traditional view in Figure 9.3.

The market maven

A **market maven** is a person who likes to transmit marketplace information of all types. Market mavens are not necessarily interested in the products they recommend and may not necessarily be early purchasers of products; they are just interested in staying on top of what is happening in the marketplace. They come closer to the function of a generalised opinion

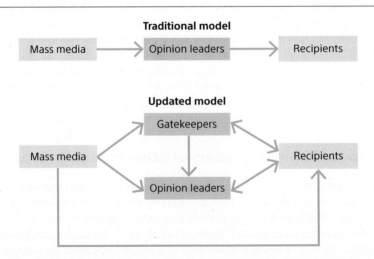

Figure 9.3 Updated opinion leadership model

leader because they tend to have a solid overall knowledge of how and where to procure products. They are also more confident in their ability to make smart purchase decisions. Researchers use scale items to identify market mavens (see Figure 9.4): respondents are asked to indicate how much they agree or disagree with the statements.[136]

The surrogate consumer

In addition to everyday consumers who are instrumental in influencing others' purchase decisions, a class of marketing intermediary called the **surrogate consumer** often influences what we buy. A surrogate consumer is a person whom we hire to provide input into our purchase decisions. Unlike the opinion leader or market maven, the surrogate is usually compensated for their advice (e.g. personal shoppers in major department flagship stores, or the M&S innovation to recruit fashion and design students as interns to provide instore styling advice to their customers).[137]

Interior designers, stockbrokers or professional shoppers can all be thought of as surrogate consumers. Whether or not they actually make the purchase on behalf of the consumer, surrogates' recommendations can be enormously influential. The consumer, in essence, relinquishes control over several or all decision-making functions, such as information search, the evaluation of alternatives, or the actual purchase. For example, a client may commission an interior designer to update their house, and a broker may be entrusted to make crucial buy/sell decisions on behalf of investors. The involvement of surrogates in a wide range of purchase decisions tends to be overlooked by many marketers, who may be mistargeting their communications to end-consumers instead of to the surrogates who are actually sifting through product information and deciding among product alternatives on behalf of their clients, and therefore making the final recommendations about purchase.[138]

How do we find opinion leaders?

Because most opinion leaders are everyday consumers rather than celebrities, they are hard to find. A celebrity or an influential industry executive is, by definition, easy to locate. That person has national or at least regional visibility or is listed in published directories. In contrast, opinion leaders tend to operate at the local level and may influence only a small group of consumers rather than an entire market segment. And yet, because opinion leaders

1. I like introducing new brands and products to my friends.

2. I like helping people by providing them with information about many kinds of products.

3. People ask me for information about products, places to shop, or sales.

4. If someone asked me where to get the best buy on several types of products, I could tell him or her where to shop.

5. My friends think of me as a good source of information when it comes to new products or sales.

6. Think about a person who has information about a variety of products and likes to share this information with others. This person knows about new products, sales, stores, and so on, but does not necessarily feel he or she is an expert on one particular product. How well would you say this description fits you?

Figure 9.4 Scale items used to identify market mavens

Source: Adapted from Lawrence Feick and Linda Price, 'The market maven: a diffuser of marketplace information', *Journal of Marketing* 51 (January 1987): 83–7.

are so central to consumer decision-making, marketers are very interested in identifying these influential people for a product category. In fact, many ads are intended to reach the influentials rather than the average consumer, especially if the ads contain a lot of technical information.

Professional opinion leaders

Perhaps the easiest way to find opinion leaders is to target people who are paid to give expert opinions. Professional opinion leaders are people such as doctors or scientists who obtain specialised information from technical journals and other practitioners. Marketers who are trying to gain consumer acceptance for their products sometimes find it easier to try to win over professional opinion leaders, who (they hope) will, in turn, recommend their products to clients. Of course, this approach may backfire if it is carried to an extreme and compromises the credibility of professional opinion leaders. In several countries, the medical industry has a dubious reputation of 'bribing' doctors with invitations to product presentations disguised as conferences, often held in glamorous places. An examination of registers of gifts and donations to doctors in the UK showed the scale of sponsorship by pharmaceutical companies of all-expenses-paid conference trips around the world ran into millions of pounds.[139]

Consumer opinion leaders

Consumer opinion leaders tend to operate at the local level and may influence five to ten consumers rather than an entire market segment. In some cases, companies have tried to identify influentials and involve them directly in their marketing efforts, hoping to create a 'ripple effect' as these consumers sing the company's praises to their friends.

Because of the difficulties involved in identifying specific opinion leaders in a large market, most attempts to do so instead focus on exploratory studies. Researchers aim to identify the profile of a representative opinion leader and then generalise these insights to the larger market. This knowledge helps marketers target their product-related information to appropriate settings and media.

Self-designation

The most commonly used technique to identify opinion leaders is simply to ask individual consumers whether they consider themselves to be opinion leaders. However, there are obvious problems with self-designation. Although respondents who report a greater degree of interest in a product category are more likely to be opinion leaders, the results of surveys intended to identify self-designated opinion leaders must be viewed with some skepticism. Some people have a tendency to inflate their own importance and influence, whereas others who really are influential might not admit to this quality or be conscious of it.[140] Just because we transmit advice about products does not mean other people take that advice. For someone to be considered a bona fide opinion leader, opinion seekers must actually heed their advice. An alternative is to select certain group members (key informants) who, in turn, are asked to identify opinion leaders. The success of this approach hinges on locating those who have accurate knowledge of the group and on minimising their response biases (the tendency to inflate one's own influence on the choices of others). Figure 9.5 shows one of the measurement scales researchers use for this kind of self-designation.

Sociometry

A Web-based service has been created that is based on the popular play *Six Degrees of Separation*. The basic premise of the plot is that everyone on the planet is separated by only six other people. A variation is the popular game called 'Six Degrees of Kevin Bacon', which challenges players to link the actor Kevin Bacon with other players in much the same way.[141]

Please rate yourself on the following scales relating to your interactions with friends and neighbours regarding_____.

1. In general, do you talk to your friends and neighbours about_____:

   very often   *never*
      5   4   3   2   1

2. When you talk to your friends and neighbours about_____ do you:

   give a great deal of information   *give very little information*
      5   4   3   2   1

3. During the past six months, how many people have you told about a new_____?

   told a number of people   *told no one*
      5   4   3   2   1

4. Compared with your circle of friends, how likely are you to be asked about new_____?

   very likely to be asked   *not at all likely to be asked*
      5   4   3   2   1

5. In discussion of new_____, which of the following happens most?

   you tell your friends about_____   *your friends tell you about_____*
      5   4   3   2   1

6. Overall in all of your discussions with friends and neighbours are you:

   often used as a source of advice   *not used as a source of advice*
      5   4   3   2   1

Figure 9.5 A revised and updated version of the opinion leadership scale

Source: Adapted from Terry L. Childers, 'Assessment of the psychometric properties of an opinion leadership scale', *Journal of Marketing Research* 23 (May 1986): 184–8; and Leisa Reinecke Flynn, Ronald E. Goldsmith and Jacqueline K. Eastman, 'The King and Summers opinion leadership scale: revision and refinement', *Journal of Business Research* 31 (1994): 55–64.

More conventional **sociometric methods** trace communication patterns among group members and allow researchers to systematically map out the interactions that take place among group members. By interviewing participants and asking them to whom they go for product information, researchers can identify those who tend to be sources of product-related information. In many cases, one or a few people emerge as the 'nodes' in a map – and, voila, we have found our opinion leaders. This method is the most precise, but it is very hard and expensive to implement because it involves very close study of interaction patterns in small groups. For this reason, sociometric techniques are best applied in a closed, self-contained social setting, such as in hospitals, prisons and army bases, where members are largely isolated from other social networks.

Sociometric techniques don't just look at who talks (or texts) to whom; they also consider the types of relationships among members of a social network. **Tie strength** refers to the nature of the bond between people. It can range from *strong primary* (one's spouse) to *weak secondary* (an acquaintance whom one rarely sees). Although strong ties are important, weak ties are as well because they perform a bridging function. This type of connection allows a consumer access between subgroups. For example, you might have a regular group of friends that is a primary reference group (strong ties). If you have an interest in tennis, one of these friends might introduce you to a group of people in her book group who play tennis. As a result, you gain access to their valuable expertise through this bridging function. This referral process demonstrates the strength of even weak ties.

We use sociometric analyses to better understand referral behaviour and to locate strengths and weaknesses in terms of how one's reputation flows through a community.[142] To understand how a network guides what we buy, researchers studied a group of women who lived together in a college. They found evidence that subgroups, or cliques, within the college were likely to share preferences for various products.[143] The main effects of the now-digitally connected world on social networks are probably 'visibility, speed and convenience'.[144]

Online opinion leaders

The internet makes opinion leaders even more powerful – it's like giving steroids to a football player (only legal). Instead of reaching only those within earshot, now an influential person can sway the opinions of thousands or even millions of people around the world. In online groups, sometimes opinion leaders are called **power users**. They have a strong communication network that gives them the ability to affect purchase decisions for a number of other consumers, directly and indirectly.[145]

The social media revolution

Social media changes the way we learn about and select products.

The odds are that you've interacted with social media today. If you've checked into your Facebook page, fired off a tweet, or read a restaurant review on TripAdvisor, you are part of the social media revolution that is changing how consumers interact with the marketplace and with one another. Sometimes people define social media in terms of hardware (such as Android smartphones) or software (e.g. Wikipedia), but really it's first and foremost an online community: the collective participation of members who together build and maintain a site.[146] Indeed, many of us become so enmeshed in our social networks that we feel the need to check them constantly to be sure we stay on top of what our (online) friends are up to 24/7 (oops, better stop reading this chapter and scan your Facebook or Twitter posts). Do you know anyone like that? Some refer to this compulsion as FOMO (**fear of missing out**). Certainly, there are advantages to always feeling connected, but perhaps the downside is a vague feeling of regret or inadequacy that lurks in the background in case we chose not to be somewhere – or, even worse, we weren't invited in the first place.[147] Whether we feel left out or not, it seems clear that our passion for social media exerts a big impact on our emotions and experiences during the course of a typical day. Indeed, one study even found that people on Twitter tend to follow others who share their mood: people who are happy tend to retweet or reply to others who are happy, while those who are sad or lonely tend to do the same with others who also post negative sentiments.[148]

The tangled Web
Home entertainment spending overtakes print sales for first time

Mark Sweney reports that: 'UK music, video and games sales are higher than those of magazines, books and newspapers last year. Ed Sheeran's album *Divide* was the biggest-selling entertainment product of 2017.

The soaring popularity of services such as Netflix, Amazon and Spotify has pushed the amount consumers spend on home entertainment products past the amount spent on books, magazines and newspapers for the first time. UK consumers spent a record £7.2bn last year [2017] on all forms of music, video and games, from CDs, DVDs and vinyl records to console software and subscriptions to music and TV streaming services. That surpassed the £7.1bn

spent by consumers on the "printed word" books, magazines and newspapers, according to a report from the Entertainment Retailers Association.

The report credits the "dramatic growth" in the popularity of paid-for digital services such as Netflix, Amazon, Apple, Deezer and Spotify as the key factor behind booming sales of entertainment. "It is an extraordinary testament to the appeal and resonance of digital entertainment services that they have helped home entertainment to hit this milestone", said Kim Bayley, the chief executive of the ERA.

Entertainment sales were fuelled by hits including Ed Sheeran's album *Divi*de, the video games *FIFA 18* and *Call of Duty: WWII* and the movies *Beauty and the Beast* and *Rogue One: A Star Wars Story.*

Spending on printed-word products peaked in 2007 at £8.3bn and has struggled since then to replace revenue lost from traditional physical formats with new digital income. Sales of consumer ebooks are at their lowest level since 2011, the year the ebook craze took off as Jeff Bezos's market-dominating Amazon Kindle took the UK by storm. . .

The ERA said the statistics showed the dramatic change in consumer habits as they shifted from buying physical products to digital consumption and formats. Five years ago, 80% of revenues were generated by "buy to own" formats such as DVDs and CDs. Now 56% of revenues come from digital sources including video streaming, electronic movie rental, subscriptions, online multiplayer games and in-app and mobile purchases.

Two physical products, however, have bucked the downward sales trend. The vinyl revival is still going strong with sales of LPs up nearly 35% last year [2017]. Sales of boxed software for games consoles, such as the Nintendo Switch, Xbox and PlayStation, have also made a comeback, rising by 5% to £750m – the first growth in a decade. . . .Overall consumer spending on home entertainment rose 8.8% last year [2017] – faster than other leisure sectors including: eating out, up 7.7%; alcoholic drinks, up 6%; overseas holidays, up 4.4%; and gambling, up 1%.'[149]

Social media and community

These new communications platforms can be varied, but social networking sites share some basic characteristics:

- *They improve as the number of users increase.* For example, Amazon's ability to recommend books to you based on what other people with similar interests buy gets better as it tracks more and more people who enter search queries.

- *Their currency is eyeballs.* Google makes money as it charges advertisers according to the number of people who see their ads after they type in a search term.

- *They are free and in perpetual change.* Wikipedia, the online encyclopedia, gets updated constantly by volunteer editors who 'correct' others' errors.

- *They categorise entries according to a* **folksonomy** *rather than a* taxonomy *(a pre-established labelling hierarchy).* Instead, sites rely on users to sort content. For example, people who upload their photos to Flickr tag them with the labels they think best describe the pictures.

In some ways, online communities are not much different from those we find in our physical environment. *The Merriam-Webster Dictionary* (online version, of course) defines **community** as 'a unified body of individuals, unified by interests, location, occupation, common history, or political and economic concerns'. In fact, one social scientist refers to an online community as a **cyberplace**, where 'people connect online with kindred spirits, engage in supportive and sociable relationships with them, and imbue their activity online with meaning, belonging, and identity'.[150]

Online social networks and brand communities

Let's take a closer look at the social fabric of social media. Each online platform, such as Facebook, Pinterest or Twitter, consists of a **social network** – a set of socially relevant nodes connected by one or more relations.[151] **Nodes** are members of the network (e.g. the 600-million-plus Facebook users). Ties stem from various affiliations, such as kinship, friendship and affective ties, shared experiences and shared hobbies and interests. When we think of community, we tend to think of people but, in principle, members of a network can be organisations, articles, countries, departments or any other definable unit. A good example is

At threadless.com, users vote on which T-shirt designs the company will print and sell.
© Threadless.com, 2009.

your university alumni association. The association is a community of networked individuals and organisations. Social networks are sometimes called **social graphs**, though this term may also refer to a diagram of the interconnections of units in a network.

Flows occur between nodes. Flows are exchanges of resources, information or influence among members of the network. On Facebook you share news, updates about your life, opinions on favourite books and films, photos, videos and notes. As you share content, you create flows from among those in your network. In social media, these flows of communication go in many directions at any point in time and often on multiple platforms – a condition we term **media multiplexity**. Flows are not simply two-way or three-way; they may go through an entire community, a list or group within a network, or several individuals independently. For marketers, flows are especially important because they are the actionable components of any social network system in terms of the sharing of information, delivery of promotional materials and sources of social influence.

Successful online communities possess several important characteristics:

- *Standards of behaviour.* Rules that specify what members can and can't do on the site. Some of these rules are spelled out explicitly (e.g. if you buy an item on eBay, you agree that you have entered into a legal contract to pay for it), but many of them are unspoken. A simple example is discouragement of the practice of **flaming**, when a POST CONTAINS ALL CAPITAL LETTERS TO EXPRESS ANGER.

- *Member contributions.* A healthy proportion of users need to contribute content. If not, the site will fail to offer fresh material and ultimately traffic will slow. Participation can be a challenge though. Remember the 80/20 rule? It applies to online consumption as well. The fact is that most members of an online community are **lurkers**: that's kind of a creepy term, but it just means they absorb content that others post rather than contributing their own. Researchers estimate that only 1 per cent of a typical community's users regularly participate, and another 9 per cent do so only intermittently. The remaining 90 per cent just observe what's on the site. Although they don't contribute content, they do offer value to advertisers that simply want to reach large numbers of people.

But what happens when we want to engage consumers more actively? How can a site convert lurkers into active users? The easier it is to participate, the more likely it is that the community can generate activity among a larger proportion of visitors. In part, this means ensuring that there are several ways to participate that vary in ease of use. Facebook is an example of an online community that has figured out how to offer several forms of participation. Members can post status updates (very easy), make comments, upload pictures, share notes and links, play social games, answer quizzes, decorate their profiles, upload videos and create events (a bit harder), among other forms of participation.

The tangled Web
Is Facebook losing the younger generation?

The longer-term viability of Facebook as a means of reaching younger consumers is starting to be questioned. Younger users are moving away from Facebook towards Snapchat, for instance. They sense that Facebook is being taken over by their parents' generation. In 2018 it is estimated that 'more than 3 million under-25s in the UK and US will quit Facebook or stop using it regularly. . . about 44% of Snapchat users are aged 18 to 24, while just 20% of Facebook's are now in that key age range'.[152] As Richard Broughton, an analyst at Ampere, commented: 'I don't know about calling peak at Facebook globally, but one of Facebook's biggest challenges is that it is saturating core markets, western markets, where it has really slowed down'.[153]

- *Degree of connectedness.* Powerful groups are cohesive; this means the members identify strongly with them and are highly motivated to stay connected. Online groups may be even more cohesive than physical groups, even though many of the members will never meet one another in person. For example, compared to the 'six degrees of separation' norm we discussed, researchers estimate that Facebook's members, on average, have only four degrees of separation from each other. While some users have designated only one friend and others have thousands, the median is about 100 friends. The researchers found that most pairs of Facebook users could be connected through four intermediate users, and this number shrank to three within a single country (even the US).[154] Because many of us devote so much time and energy to our online group relationships, connectedness also reflects our real-world relationships (it's quite common for people to learn that their partner has broken up with them only after they see a change in 'relationship status' on Facebook). One study that analysed 1.3 million Facebook users and about 8.6 billion links among them reported that couples who are in a relationship are more likely to stay together if they share a lot of mutual Facebook friends – and they're more likely to break up within a few months if this indicator dips sharply, because it implies their social lives aren't overlapping very much.[155]

- *Network effects.* The quality of the site improves as the number of users increase. For example, Amazon's ability to recommend books to you based on what other people with similar interests buy gets better as it tracks more and more people who enter search queries.

Social object theory suggests that social networks will be more powerful communities if there is a way to activate relationships among people and objects. In this perspective, an object is something of common interest and its primary function is to mediate the interactions between people. All relationships have social objects embedded in the relationship. In the online world, a site such as Facebook provides venues for several object formats, to ensure that relationships can thrive within the site's framework. One factor that drives Facebook's stunning success is that it offers so many objects for users to share, including events, family and friends, quizzes and so on. Other **social networking** sites (SNSs) provide a more specialised or focused set of objects. For example, consider how each of these SNSs incorporates objects as part of its mission: on Flickr, users participate because they want to share photos – these images are the objects that give meaning to the platform and motivate people to visit; and video is the social object around which YouTube centres.

Object sociality, the extent to which an object can be shared in social media, is clearly related to an audience's unique interests – by virtue of tying the site relationships to a specific object such as photos of people's dogs, or bookmarked websites that provide details about the history of alternative music. The audience becomes specialised, at least to a degree. Importantly, though, SNSs oriented around object sociality are likely to be passion-centric. That is, the people who join those communities not only share an interest in the object in question, but chances are also high that they are obsessed with it.

The power of online communities

All communities, whether they are online or in the physical world, share important characteristics: participants experience a feeling of membership, a sense of proximity to one another (even though in online groups other members' physical selves may be thousands of miles away) and in most cases some interest in the community's activities. Members may identify with one another due to a common mission (e.g. a Twitter campaign to donate money for oil-spill relief) or simply because they come from the same neighbourhood.

Communities help members meet their needs for affiliation, resource acquisition, entertainment and information. Above all else, communities are social. Whether online or offline, they thrive when the members participate, discuss, share and interact with others as well as recruit new members to the community. Members do vary in their degree of participation, but the more active the membership, the healthier the community.

Social media provides the fuel that fans the fires of online communities. In the Web 1.0 era, people visited a lot of websites to get content that interested them. But these really weren't communities, because the flow of information was all one way. In today's Web 2.0

environment, all that has changed as interactive platforms enable online communities to exhibit the following basic characteristics:[156]

- **Conversations**. Communities thrive on communication among members. These conversations are not based on talking or writing, but on a hybrid of the two. If you communicate with a friend via Facebook chat, you may feel that you actually 'talked' to her.

- **Presence**. Though online communities exist virtually rather than at a physical location, the better ones supply tangible characteristics that create the sensation of actually being in a place. This is particularly true for virtual-world communities that include three-dimensional depictions of physical spaces, but it also applies to visually simplistic online communities such as message-board groups. Presence is defined as the effect that people experience when they interact with a computer-mediated or computer-generated environment.[157] Social media sites can enhance a sense of presence by enabling interactions among visitors and making the environment look and feel real.[158]

- **Collective interest**. Just as your offline communities are based on family, religious beliefs, social activities, hobbies, goals, place of residence and so on, your online communities also need commonalities to create bonds among the members. These groups come together to allow people to share their passions, whether these are for indie bands, white wines or open-source apps.

- **Democracy**. The political model of most online communities is democratic: leaders emerge due to the reputation they earn among the general membership. In this context, democracy is a descriptive term that refers to rule by the people. The leaders are appointed or elected by the community based on their demonstrated ability to add value to the group. The huge growth in demand for user reviews in turn fuels new opinion-based sites, such as TripAdvisor for travel, hotels and restaurants. People who take the time to post to these sites don't do it for money, but they do generate an income in the form of props for good recommendations. Many thousands of consumers devote significant time to edit Wikipedia entries, serving as **brand advocates**, or uploading clips to YouTube simply because they enjoy the process and want to boost their reputation as knowledgeable advisors.[159]

However, a recent study has posed the question: Does 'liking' lead to 'loving?', and these researchers examined 'whether joining a brand's social network site (by "liking" their Facebook page) results in any changes in subsequent consumer behavior – either of the consumers who join, or of the friends of those who join. The results. . . show that the mere act of "liking" a brand on Facebook has no positive direct effect on consumer attitudes or purchases.'[160] Their conclusion was that, 'Despite the fact that marketers spend billions of dollars each year on social media to establish and maintain a presence on social networking sites, the results suggest that investing in increasing membership in the form of mere "likes" is not a fruitful approach for improving brand attitudes or increasing purchases.'[161]

But note: 'Web 3.0 is the next fundamental change, both in how websites are created and, more importantly, how people interact with them'.[162] And yet answering the question what will Web 3.0 look like is more difficult: 'The truth is that predicting the Web 3.0 future is a guessing game. A fundamental change in how we use the web could be based on an evolution of how we are using the web now, a breakthrough in web technology, or just a technological breakthrough in general. . . The ever-present Web 3.0 has to do with the increasing popularity of mobile internet devices and the merger of entertainment systems and the web. The merging of computers and mobile devices as a source for music, movies, and more puts the internet at the center of both our work and our play. Within a decade, internet access on our mobile devices (cell phones, smartphones, pocket PCs) has become as popular as text messaging. This will make the internet always present in our lives – at work, at home, on the road, out to dinner, the internet will be wherever we go.'[163]

How and why do consumers use social media?

In search of a deeper understanding of consumers' use of social media, and particularly of how social media can best-satisfy consumers' basic needs and lead to the most positive outcomes, Hoffman and Novak argued that 'the fundamental interactivity of social media allows for four higher-order goals: connect, create, consume, and control. These "4Cs" capabilities of social media undoubtedly explain in part why so many people spend so much of their time using social media and why social media are so popular.' In earlier research they had found that 'individuals who experience flow during their online navigational experiences are more likely to achieve positive outcomes compared to individuals who cannot attain these compelling online experiences'. Using this as a starting point, they studied how the 4Cs of connecting, creating, consuming and controlling social media experiences are used to organise consumers' social media goals '. . . Results suggested that connect goals ("social" goals) are associated with relatedness needs, an external locus of control, intrinsic motivation to connect with others, and positive evaluations of the social media groups to which consumers belong (private collective self-esteem). Consumers' pursuit of create goals is associated with autonomy, competence, and relatedness needs; an external locus of control; higher social media involvement; and contribution to sense of self (identity self-esteem). Consume goals ('non-social' goals) appear to be intrinsically motivated and negatively associated with autonomy and competence. Control goals satisfy autonomy and competence needs, and are associated with an external locus of causality and social media knowledge.' Hoffman and Novak concluded that 'different social media goals are supported by different needs and motivations'.[164]

Digital word of mouth

Viral marketing occurs when an organisation motivates visitors to forward online content to their friends; the message quickly spreads, much like a cold virus moves among residents of an office. It usually takes off when the online content is entertaining or just plain weird. One study examines **valuable virality**: 'Many brands now create content that they hope consumers will view and share with peers. While some campaigns indeed go "viral", their value to the brand is limited if they do not boost brand evaluation or increase purchase.'[165] There's no doubt many of us love to share the news with others: news about new styles, new music and especially new stuff that we've bought. Of course, we do this in the form of online reviews in forums such as TripAdvisor. However, the urge to share even creates new genres of communication, such as **haul videos**, which feature a proud fashionista describing clothing items she just bought, and **unboxing videos**, which illustrate in painstaking detail exactly how to remove electronics products from their boxes and assemble them for use.

The viral marketing explosion highlights the power of the **Megaphone Effect**: Web 2.0 makes a huge audience available to everyday consumers. 'In just a few years, the power of blogs and platforms such as Instagram has created a new marketing genre that has seen brands investing heavily in collaborations with the big names in the online space.'[166] Some fashion bloggers build an impressive following as they share their views about what's hot and what's not. For example, over 30,000 people read this post:

> Found the perfect grey socks while shopping at Uniqlo in Tokyo with my mom/favorite shopping partner (she's always down to stop randomly to eat and shares my love for finding wearable things in unlikely places). Vaguely sheer and just the right length. This sounds extremely trivial, and sort of is, but I've been looking for something like them forever now.[167]

The UK **vlogger** Zoella (or Zoe Sugg) has had over 300million views of her videos on beauty and life advice. Zoella is 'one of the new breed of online celebrities, an expanding group of video bloggers. . . who, thanks to their YouTube channels, have developed a worldwide following. . . one YouTube statistics website estimates she has potential earnings of over £300,000, with brands willing to pay up to £4,000 for a single mention or endorsement on a vlog'.[168] These vloggers are 'independent young video bloggers. . . who film their thoughts and observations for thousands of followers to enjoy online [and this] is already setting the future shape of marketing and advertising'.[169,170] However, a word of warning – recent studies on social media suggest that young people are turning away from social media, disillusioned by online abuse and fake news. Charlotte Robertson, co-founder of Digital Awareness UK said: 'We speak to thousands of students on a daily basis about safe internet use and it's encouraging to see that they are employing smart strategies such as **digital detoxing** to take control of their social media use'.[171] Marketers will need to stay alert to how best to reach this new generation of consumers as they potentially turn away from (or are turned off by) social media.

Online word of mouth is everywhere, and it differs from the way that people talk about products face to face. Figure 9.6 provides an overview of strategies marketers can follow to increase the likelihood that consumers will spread the word about their brands.

Researchers report that written communication about brands is more likely to include mentions of interesting or unusual brands, and the motivation to post about these items is driven to a greater extent by the desire for self-enhancement. When people share their opinions about products with their social networks, they may do so to satisfy one of several goals: to manage the impression they make on others; to regulate emotions by expressing affective reactions; to share and acquire information; to bond with others; and to persuade others to change their opinions.[172] Unlike a spontaneous conversation in the physical world, when consumers write about products they have more time to think strategically about what they're saying – and about how these judgments reflect on them.[173] Indeed, much of what we post is actually about ourselves; one study reported that 80 per cent of tweets people send focus on themselves rather than other topics.[174] However, evidence suggests that consumers need to be careful – particularly in online platforms – because consumers 'may perceive boastful sources as having more expertise and, therefore, be more persuaded by them'.[175]

A study that analysed Twitter data illustrates the care people take to portray themselves in a positive light – but to avoid acting like they're bragging when they tweet about products they've bought or experienced. When the researchers looked at posts regarding two luxury brands – Louis Vuitton and Mercedes – they found that people commonly mention these items 'in passing' as they comment on what they're doing or feeling at the moment, or even try to downplay the brand's positive characteristics to avoid looking too snobbish.[176]

Other researchers identified a somewhat similar phenomenon they call the Dispreferred Marker Effect: online posts that are really negative may make the writer look harsh and judgemental, so people sometimes soften them by couching them in *dispreferred markers*, including phrases such as, 'I'll be honest', 'God bless it',"] or 'I don't want to be mean, but. . . '. Sure enough, readers of these kinds of posts evaluated the writer more positively than they did posters who just laid out the bad news, warts and all.[177]

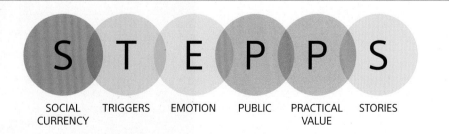

Figure 9.6 STEPPS

Source: Jonah Berger, 'Contagious: Why things catch on', Harvard Business Review Webinar (21 September 2016).

Digital opinion leaders

Quick, what's your Klout score? 'Klout' claimed to precisely measure just how influential each of us was in cyberspace. The site assessed more than 12 billion pieces of data every day to compute a score from 0 to 100 for anyone who was online. Several indicators went into this number, including the ratio of comments or retweets a person generated compared to the amount of content he or she posted, as well as the relative influence of the people who shared this content. Not surprisingly, celebrities including Justin Bieber and Zooey Deschanel boasted very high Klout scores, but plenty who are influential in other walks of life did too. And 'Klout for Business' allowed brands to identify consumers with high scores, so they could try to enlist them in spreading digital word of mouth about their brands.

Earlier in the chapter we saw that opinion leaders are people who are more influential than most when they recommend purchases to others. In online groups, opinion leaders sometimes are called power users. They have a strong communications network that gives them the ability to affect purchase decisions for a number of other consumers, directly and indirectly.[178]

Much like their offline counterparts, power users are active participants at work and in their communities. Their social networks are large and well developed. Others trust them and find them to be credible sources of information about one or more specific topics. They tend to have a natural sense of intellectual curiosity, which may lead them to new sources of information. And they post an awful lot of brand-related content. Forrester Research has dubbed these brand-specific mentions **influence impressions**. In advertising lingo, an *impression* refers to a view or an exposure to an advertising message. Forrester estimates that, each year, American consumers generate 256 billion influence impressions as people talk about their lives with each other, telling stories and experiences that invariably include brands.[179] These influence impressions are primarily delivered by – you guessed it – power users. Only 6.2 per cent of social media users are responsible for about 80 per cent of these brand mentions. Forrester calls these influencers **mass connectors**.

Zoella (or Zoe Sugg), UK vlogger on beauty and life advice.'
Source: Rex/Shutterstock

Consumer Behaviour As I See It . . .

Selfies: how consumers are shaping new photography practices

Professor Stefania Farace
Eastern Connecticut State University

'**Selfies** are literally everywhere. We share information, opinions, and personal stories with others by taking and posting photos of ourselves on social media sites. Why are some of our selfies more engaging than others?

My research (originally at Maastricht University, Netherlands) with Tom van Laer, Ko de Ruyter, and Martin Wetzels details experiments aimed at determining exactly what people engage with when they look at pictures online. Research participants were shown a range of images and told to rate them on aspects such as the narrative perspective, content and style. They were also asked to indicate how likely they would be to comment on the various pictures if they saw them on social media platforms.

We were able to isolate what elements people find the most and least engaging in selfies. This research revealed three recurring techniques that encourage consumer engagement. First, viewers really prefer you to take your picture (selfie), not someone else ('elsie'). The reason for this finding is that when we deal with selfies, viewers identify better with the story directly told by the main character compared to a story told by a third person. Producers of 'elsies' serve more as reporters of other represented participants' experiences than of their own, therefore making identification with the story character more difficult.

Second, it's essential to show yourself doing something meaningful: it's literally more engaging for viewers to see a picture of yourself doing something rather than merely posing for a portrait picture. We ran studies with actions toward (product) consumption but also with actions beyond product consumption (i.e. a hand wave) and found the same effect: having a selfie with someone doing something is better than a static selfie.

Third, unedited selfies attract less attention on social media than those that have been improved via the use of a filter or other stylistic alterations (i.e., lenses, emojis). Whether you tweak your photo to make it look more trendy, eccentric or professional, we found that post-snap improvements contribute to increase viewers' engagement with the selfie. It may be that in the online era, where our digital selves are not always true representations of our real selves, we are simply less keen on images that are faithful representations of reality.

Everyday consumers are shaping new photography practices on social media which open new and exciting opportunities for marketing practice and research. A big challenge for marketers will be to understand consumer photography and perhaps contribute to shape new photography practices. For example, Nixie, Intel's wearable drone, allows consumers to take selfies with a wristband that can launch itself off a consumer's arm. As a result, photos are taken without the consumer having to interrupt the action he/she is performing. These tools contribute to the massive growth of consumer photographs shared online. In the future, I will collect real consumer photographs and, through the use of visual and text mining techniques, analyze how selfies and text (e.g., written descriptions, captions, hashtags) in social media posts jointly affect consumer engagement.'

Questions

What are the pitfalls for businesses aiming to encourage consumers to take selfies with their brands to help social media consumption? Considering that consumers are looking for accurate information about products before they make a purchase (e.g., product reviews), if brands use tools to create images that are not a faithful representation of daily life, could online strategies backfire?

Net profit

As we saw earlier (in Chapter 2), consumption in online spaces such as websites, virtual worlds and video games is growing rapidly. Indeed, **digital virtual consumption (DVC)** may well be the next frontier of marketing. In 2011, Americans spent about $1.6 billion buying **virtual goods** for their avatars in **virtual worlds** such as *Second Life*, and **MMOGs (massively multi-player online games)** such as *World of Warcraft*.[180] The majority of virtual worlds are 3D and employ sophisticated computer graphics to produce photorealistic images. Furthermore, individuals who enter these worlds (or at least their avatars) can walk, fly, teleport, try on clothes, try out products, attend in-world events (educational classes, concerts, political speeches, etc.) and interact in real time (via textchat, IM and VoIP) with other avatars around the world. This unprecedented level of interactivity facilitates consumers' engagement and often creates the *flow state* we discussed above (and in Chapter 5). Some forward-thinking marketers understand that these platforms are the next stage that they can use to introduce their products into people's lives, whether real or virtual. Today, for example, people who play *The Sims* can import actual pieces of furniture from IKEA into their virtual homes. The use of this sort of platform to accelerate purchases for real homes is unexplored territory.

Chapter summary

Now that you have finished reading this chapter you should understand why:

9.1 Other people and groups, especially those that possess social power, influence our decisions. We belong to or admire many different groups, and a desire for them to accept us often drives our purchase decisions. Individuals or groups whose opinions or behaviour are particularly important to consumers are reference groups. Both formal and informal groups influence the individual's purchase decisions, although such factors as the conspicuousness of the product and the relevance of the reference group for a particular purchase determine how influential the reference group is.

- **Individuals have influence in a group to the extent that they possess social power.** Types of social power include information power, referent power, legitimate power, expert power, reward power and coercive power.

- **Brand communities unite consumers who share a common passion for a product.** Brand-fests, which companies organise to encourage this kind of community, can build brand loyalty and reinforce group membership.

- **We conform to the desires of others for two basic reasons:** (1) people who model their behaviour after others because they take others' behaviour as evidence of the correct way to act are conforming because of informational social influence; and (2) those who conform to satisfy the expectations of others or to be accepted by the group are affected by normative social influence. Group members often do things they would not do as individuals because their identities become merged with the group; they become deindividuated.

9.2 Word-of-mouth communication is the most important driver of product choice. Much of what we know about products we learn through word-of-mouth (WOM) communication rather than formal advertising. We tend to exchange product-related information in casual conversations. Although WOM often is helpful to make consumers aware of products, it can also hurt companies when damaging product rumours or negative WOM occurs.

9.3 Opinion leaders' recommendations are more influential than others' when we decide what to buy. Opinion leaders who are knowledgeable about a product and whose opinions are highly regarded tend to influence others' choices. Specific opinion leaders are somewhat hard to identify, but marketers who know their general characteristics can try to target them in their media and promotional strategies. Other influencers include market mavens, who have a general interest in marketplace activities, and surrogate consumers, who are compensated for their advice about purchases.

9.4 Social media changes the way we learn about and select products. Social media platforms significantly increase our access to others' opinions about products and services. Virtual consumption communities unite those who share a common passion for products that include apparel, cars, music, beer, political candidates, etc. Many social media users post content online that satisfies the motive for self-enhancement as well as the desire to share opinions and experiences about products and services. Consumers may engage with these brands via social games. Viral marketing techniques enlist individuals to spread online word of mouth about brands. Online opinion leaders play a pivotal role in disseminating influential recommendations and product information.

Key terms

Anti-conformity (p. 358)
Brand advocates (p. 377)
Brand communities (p. 359)
Brand-fests (p. 359)
Buzz (p. 362)
Coercive power (p. 349)
Cohesiveness (p. 353)
Collective interest (p. 377)
Collective value creation (p. 360)
Communities of practice (p. 361)
Community (p. 373)
Conformity (p. 355)
Consumer tribe (p. 360)
Conversations (p. 377)
Cyberplace (p. 373)
Decision polarisation (p. 355)
De-individuation (p. 353)
Democracy (p. 377)
Digital detoxing (p. 379)
Digital virtual consumption (DVC) (p. 382)
Dissociative groups (p. 348)
Expert power (p. 349)
Fear of Missing Out (FOMO) (p. 372)
Flaming (p. 375)
Folksonomy (p. 373)
Guerrilla marketing (p. 363)
Haul videos (p. 378)

Home shopping party (p. 355)
Homophily (p. 366)
Hype (p. 363)
Identificational membership reference group (p. 352)
Influence impressions (p. 380)
Influence network (p. 366)
Information cascades (p. 366)
Information power (p. 348)
Informational social influence (p. 355)
Innovative communicators (p. 368)
Interactions (p. 366)
Legitimate power (p. 349)
Lurkers (p. 375)
Market maven (p. 368)
Mass connectors (p. 380)
Media multiplexity (p. 375)
Megaphone Effect (p. 378)
Membership reference group (p. 355)
Mere exposure phenomenon (p. 352)
Minimal group paradigm (p. 348)
MMOGS (massively multi-player online games) (p. 382)
Negative word of mouth (p. 363)
Nodes (p. 373)
Normative influence (p. 351)
Normative social influence (p. 356)

Consumer behaviour challenge

1 Compare and contrast the five bases of power described in the text. Which are most likely to be relevant for marketing efforts?

2 Why is referent power an especially potent force for marketing appeals? What factors help to predict whether or not reference groups will be a powerful influence on a person's purchase decisions?

3 Identify the differences between a membership and an aspirational reference group. Give an example of each.

4 What is a brand community, and why is it of interest to marketers?

5 Evaluate the strategic soundness of the concept of guerrilla marketing. For what types of product category is this strategy most likely to be a success?

6 Discuss some factors that determine the amount of conformity likely to be observed among consumers.

7 Define de-individuation. Does de-individuation cause binge drinking? What can or should be done to discourage this type of behaviour?

8 What is the risky shift? How does this affect going shopping with friends? See if you can demonstrate risky shift. Get a group of friends together and ask each privately to rate the likelihood, on a scale from 1 to 7, that they would try a controversial new product (e.g. a credit card that works with a chip implanted in a person's wrist). Then ask the group to discuss the product and rate the idea again. If the average rating changes from the first rating, you have just observed a risky shift.

9 Under what conditions are we more likely to engage in social comparison with dissimilar others versus similar others? How might this dimension be used in the design of marketing appeals?

10 Discuss some reasons for the effectiveness of home shopping parties as a selling tool. What other products might be sold this way? Are home shopping parties, which put pressure on friends and neighbours to buy, ethical?

11 Discuss some factors that influence whether membership groups will have a significant influence on a person's behaviour.

12 Why is word-of-mouth communication often more persuasive than advertising? Which is more powerful, positive or negative word-of-mouth? Describe some ways in which marketers use the internet to encourage positive WOM.

13 What is viral marketing? Guerrilla marketing? Hype? Buzz? Give an example of each.

14 Is there such a thing as a generalised opinion leader? What is likely to determine if an opinion leader will be influential with regard to a specific product category? How can marketers use opinion leaders to help them promote their products or services?

15 The adoption of a certain brand of shoe or apparel by athletes can be a powerful influence on students and other fans. Should secondary school and university coaches be paid to determine what brand of athletic equipment their players will wear?

16 The power of unspoken social norms often becomes obvious only when these norms are violated. To witness this result first hand, try one of the following: stand facing the back wall in a lift; serve dessert before the main course; offer to pay cash for dinner at a friend's home; wear pyjamas to class; or tell someone not to have a nice day.

17 Identify a set of avoidance groups for your peers. Can you identify any consumption decisions that are made with these groups in mind?

18 Identify fashion opinion leaders at your university or business school. Do they fit the profile discussed in the chapter?

19 Although social networking is red-hot, could its days be numbered? Many people have concerns about privacy issues. Others feel that platforms such as Facebook are too overwhelming. What are your views? Will people start to tune-out of all of these networks?[181]

20 What are sociometric techniques? Conduct a sociometric analysis within your hall of residence or neighbourhood. For a product category such as music or cars, ask each individual to identify other individuals with whom they share information. Systematically trace all of these avenues of communication and identify opinion leaders by locating individuals who are repeatedly named as providing helpful information.

21 The strategy of viral marketing gets customers to sell a product to other customers on behalf of the company. That often means convincing your friends to climb on the bandwagon, and sometimes you get a small percentage return (or other reward) if they end up buying something.[182] Some might argue that means you are selling out your friends (or at least selling to your friends) in exchange for a marketing reward. Others might say you are just sharing the wealth with those you care about. Have you been involved in viral marketing by passing along names of your friends or sending them to a website such as hotmail.com? If so, what happened? How do you feel about this practice? Discuss the pros and cons of viral marketing.

22 Mobile social networking is the next frontier in technology, as companies race to adapt platforms such as Facebook to our mobile phones. Marketers are not far behind, especially because there are 3.3 billion mobile phone subscribers worldwide; that number is far greater than the number of internet users. Mobile social networks are appealing in part because companies can identify precisely where users are in the physical world. For example, the SpaceMe service from GyPSii displays a map that identifies your friends' locations as well as photos, videos and other information about them. A Dutch network called Bliin lets users update their location every 15 seconds.[183] This enhanced capability creates some fascinating marketing possibilities – but perhaps it also raises some ethical red flags? What do you see as the opportunities and the threats as we move into a world where our whereabouts are known to others? (Check also the long relevant section on mobile e-commerce in Chapter 2.)

23 Trace a referral pattern for a service provider such as a hair stylist by tracking how clients came to choose them. See if you can identify opinion leaders who are responsible for referring several clients to the businessperson. How might the service provider take advantage of this process to grow their business?

24 Work in pairs to read and synthesise the main arguments in the article Ezgi Akpinar and Jonah Berger, 'Valuable Virality', *Journal of Marketing Research,* 54(2) (2017): 318–30. Define 'valuable virality' and discuss the potential importance of the issues identified by the two authors for brand and marketing managers.

25 Read, summarise and critique the *Guardian* article by Adam Greenfield, 'Rise of the machines: who is the 'internet of things' good for?', *The Guardian* (6 June 2017), https://www.theguardian.com/technology/2017/jun/06/internet-of-things-smart-home-smart-city (accessed 31 July 2018).

For additional material see the companion website at www.pearsoned.co.uk/solomon

Notes

1. Source: https://www.t3.com/features/best-football-boots (accessed 31 July 2018).
2. Melanie Rickey, 'The 10 best shoes', *The Observer New Review* (31 May 2015): 6, http://www.theguardian.com/culture/2015/may/29/the-10-best-shoes (accessed 31 July 2018).
3. Joel B. Cohen and Ellen Golden, 'Informational social influence and product evaluation', *Journal of Applied Psychology* 56 (February 1972): 54–9; Robert E. Burnkrant and Alain Cousineau, 'Informational and normative social influence in buyer behavior', *Journal of Consumer Research* 2 (December 1975): 206–15; Peter H. Reingen, 'Test of a list procedure for inducing compliance with a request to donate money', *Journal of Applied Psychology* 67 (1982): 110–18.
4. Katherine White and Darren W. Dahl, 'To be or not to be? The influence of dissociative reference groups on consumer preferences', *Journal of Consumer Psychology* 16(4) (2006): 404–14; Katherine White and Darren W. Dahl, 'Are all out-groups created equal? Consumer identity and dissociative influence', *Journal of Consumer Research* 34 (December 2007): 525–36.
5. N.V. Coleman and P. Williams, 'Feeling like myself: emotion profiles and social identity', *Journal of Consumer Research* 20 (2013): 203–22; and A. Reed and M.R. Forehand, 'The ebb and flow of consumer identities: The role of memory, emotions and threats', *Current Opinion in Psychology* 10 (2016): 94–100 for more discussion of social identity theory in the context of consumption.
6. Henri Tajfel and John C. Turner, 'The Social Identity Theory of Intergroup Behaviour', in S. Worchel and W. G. Austin (eds.), *Psychology of Intergroup Relations* (Chicago, IL: Nelson-Hall, 1986): 7–24.
7. Andrew Adam Newman, 'Campaign redefines running as a social activity', *New York Times* (8 July 2013), http://www.nytimes.com/2013/07/09/business/media/campaign-redefines-running-as-a-social-activity.html?_r=3&adxnnl=1&adxnnlx=1375297677-/ALie05m6JiubQ4oXE4qig (accessed 31 July 2018); also, for more details on New Balance's Runnovation campaign, http://www.adweek.com/agencyspy/new-balance-wants-to-make-runnovation-into-a-thing-gives-it-an-anthem/51664 (accessed 31 July 2018).
8. Kenneth J. Gergen and Mary Gergen, *Social Psychology* (New York: Harcourt Brace Jovanovich, 1981): 312.
9. J.R.P. French, Jr. and B. Raven, 'The Bases of Social Power', in D. Cartwright (ed), *Studies in Social Power* (Ann Arbor, MI: Institute for Social Research, 1959): 150–67.
10. Michael R. Solomon, 'Packaging the Service Provider', *The Service Industries Journal* 5 (March 1985): 64–72.
11. Stephen Hawking, born 8 January 1942-died 14 March 2018.
12. Tamar Charry, 'Unconventional spokesmen talk up U.S. robotics' fast modems in a new TV campaign', *New York Times* (6 February 1997), http://www.nytimes.com/1997/02/06/business/unconventional-spokesmen-talk-up-us-robotics-fast-modems-in-a-new-tv-campaign.html?scp=44&sq=Tamar+Charry&st=nyt (accessed 31 July 2018).
13. Patricia M. West and Susan M. Broniarczyk, 'Integrating multiple opinions: The role of aspiration level on consumer response to critic consensus', *Journal of Consumer Research* 25 (June 1998): 38–51.
14. C. Whan Park and V. Parker Lessig, 'Students and house-wives: differences in susceptibility to reference group influence', *Journal of Consumer Research* 4(2) (September 1977): 102–10.
15. C. Whan Park and V. Parker Lessig, 'Students and housewives: Differences in susceptibility to reference group influence', *Journal of Consumer Research* 4(2) (September 1977): 102.
16. Gina Kolata, 'Study finds big social factor in quitting smoking', *New York Times* (22 May 2008).
17. Jeffrey D. Ford and Elwood A. Ellis, 'A re-examination of group influence on member brand preference', *Journal of Marketing Research* 17 (February 1980): 125–32; Thomas S. Robertson, *Innovative Behavior and Communication* (New York: Holt, Rinehart & Winston, 1980), ch. 8.
18. William O. Bearden and Michael J. Etzel, 'Reference group influence on product and brand purchase decisions', *Journal of Consumer Research* 9 (1982): 183–94.
19. Kenneth J. Gergen and Mary Gergen, *Social Psychology* (New York: Harcourt Brace Jovanovich, 1981).
20. Stephanie Rosenbloom, 'Names that match forge a bond on the internet', *New York Times* (10 April 2008), www.nytimes.com/2008/04/10/us/10names.html?ref=us (accessed 31 July 2018).
21. Harold H. Kelley, 'Two Functions of Reference Groups', in Harold Proshansky and Bernard Siedenberg (eds), *Basic Studies in Social Psychology* (New York: Holt, Rinehart & Winston, 1965): 210–14.
22. A. Benton Cocanougher and Grady D. Bruce, 'Socially distant reference groups and consumer aspirations', *Journal of Marketing Research* 8 (August 1971): 79–81.
23. Jason Gregory, 'David Beckham Bares His Body in the latest Armani Campaign', 11 June 2009.
24. A. Benton Cocanougher and Grady D. Bruce, 'Socially distant reference groups and consumer aspirations', *Journal of Marketing Research* 8 (August 1971): 79–81.
25. Nick Bilton, 'Twitter users congregate based on mood, study says', *New York Times* (16 March 2011).
26. Cited in Zoe Wood, 'Tweet and Tell: turning Twitter into complaints megaphone', *The Guardian* (6 January 2018), https://www.theguardian.com/money/2018/jan/05/tweet-and-tell-turning-twitter-into-complaints-megaphone (accessed 31 July 2018).
27. Ibid.
28. L. Festinger, S. Schachter and K. Back, *Social Pressures in Informal Groups: A Study of Human Factors in Housing* (New York: Harper, 1950).
29. R.B. Zajonc, H.M. Markus and W. Wilson, 'Exposure effects and associative learning', *Journal of Experimental Social Psychology* 10 (1974): 248–63.
30. D.J. Stang, 'Methodological factors in mere exposure research', *Psychological Bulletin* 81 (1974): 1,014–25; R.B. Zajonc, P. Shaver, C. Tavris and D. Van Kreveid, 'Exposure, satiation and stimulus discriminability', *Journal of Personality and Social Psychology* 21 (1972): 270–80.
31. J.E. Grush, K.L. McKeogh and R.F. Ahlering, 'Extrapolating laboratory exposure research to actual political elections', *Journal of Personality and Social Psychology* 36 (1978): 257–70.
32. Richard Wilk, 'A critique of desire: Distaste and dislike in consumer behavior', *Consumption, Culture and Markets* 1(2) (1997): 175–96; see also Pierre Bourdieu, *Distinction: A Social Critique of the Judgement of Taste* (London: Routledge,

1984); E.N. Banister and M.K. Hogg, 'Negative symbolic consumption and consumers' drive for self-esteem: The case of the fashion industry', *European Journal of Marketing* 7 (2004): 850–68; B.S. Turner and J. Edmunds, 'The distaste of taste: Bordieu, cultural capital and the Australian postwar elite', *Journal of Consumer Culture* 2(2) (2002): 219–40.

33. Jonah Berger and Lindsay Rand, 'Shifting signals to help health: Using identity signaling to reduce risky health behaviors', *Journal of Consumer Research* 35(3) (2008): 509–18.

34. Basil G. Englis and Michael R. Solomon, 'To be and not to be: reference group stereotyping and *The Clustering of America*', *Journal of Advertising* 24 (Spring 1995): 13–28; Michael R. Solomon and Basil G. Englis, 'I Am Not, Therefore I Am: The Role of Anti-Consumption in the Process of Self-Definition', Special Session at the Association for Consumer Research meetings, October 1996, Tucson, Arizona.

35. Bruce Feirstein, *Real Men Don't Eat Quiche* (New York: Pocket Books, 1982).

36. Katherine White and Darren W. Dahl, 'Are all out-groups created equal? Consumer identity and dissociative influence', *Journal of Consumer Research* 34 (December 2007): 525.

37. J. Craig Andrews and Richard G. Netemeyer, 'Alcohol Warning Label Effects: Socialization, Addiction, and Public Policy Issues', in Ronald P. Hill (ed.), *Marketing and Consumer Research in the Public Interest* (Thousand Oaks, CA: Sage, 1996): 153–75; 'National study finds increase in college binge drinking', *Alcoholism and Drug Abuse Weekly* (27 March 2000): 12–13; Emma Banister and Maria Piacentini, '"Binge Drinking: Do They Mean Us?" Living Life to the Full in Students' Own Words', in C. Pechmann and L. Price (eds), *Advances in Consumer Research* 33 (forthcoming).

38. Maria Piacentini and Emma N. Banister, 'Getting hammered? Students coping with alcohol', *Journal of Consumer Behaviour* 5(2) (Spring 2006).

39. Maria G. Piacentini, Andreas Chatzidakis and Emma N. Banister (2012), 'Making Sense of Drinking: The Role of Techniques of Neutralisation and Counter-Neutralisation in Negotiating Alcohol Consumption', *Sociology of Health and Illness* 34(6): 841–857.

40. B. Latane, K. Williams and S. Harkins, 'Many hands make light the work: The causes and consequences of social loafing', *Journal of Personality and Social Psychology* 37 (1979): 822–32.

41. S. Freeman, M. Walker, R. Borden and B. Latane, 'Diffusion of responsibility and restaurant tipping: Cheaper by the bunch', *Personality and Social Psychology Bulletin* 1 (1978): 584–7.

42. Nathan Kogan and Michael A. Wallach, *Risk Taking* (New York: Holt, Rinehart & Winston, 1964).

43. Nathan Kogan and Michael A. Wallach, 'Risky shift phenomenon in small decision-making groups: A test of the information exchange hypothesis', *Journal of Experimental Social Psychology* 3 (January 1967): 75–84; Kogan and Wallach, *Risk Taking, op cit.;* Arch G. Woodside and M. Wayne DeLozier, 'Effects of word-of-mouth advertising on consumer risk taking', *Journal of Advertising* (Fall 1976): 12–19.

44. Roger Brown, *Social Psychology* (New York: The Free Press, 1965).

45. David L. Johnson and I.R. Andrews, 'Risky shift phenomenon tested with consumer product stimuli', *Journal of Personality and Social Psychology* 20 (1971): 382–5; see also Vithala R. Rao and Joel H. Steckel, 'A polarization model for describing group preferences', *Journal of Consumer Research* 18 (June 1991): 108–18.

46. Donald H. Granbois, 'Improving the study of customer in-store behavior', *Journal of Marketing* 32 (October 1968): 28–32.

47. Len Strazewski, 'Tupperware locks in new strategy', *Advertising Age* (8 February 1988): 30.

48. Melanie Wells, 'Smooth operator', *Forbes* (13 May 2002): 167–8.

49. Cindy Chan, Jonah Berger and Leaf Van Boven, 'Identifiable but not identical: Combining social identity and uniqueness motives in choice', *Journal of Consumer Research* 39(3) (October 2012): 561–73.

50. Ping Dong and Chen-Bo Zhong, 'Witnessing moral violations increases conformity in consumption', *Journal of Consumer Research,* 44(4) (2017): 778–93.

51. Silvia Bellezza, Francesca Gino and Anat Keinan, 'the red sneakers effect: Inferring status and competence from signals of nonconformity', *Journal of Consumer Research* 41(1) 2014): 35–54.

52. Tanya Irwin, 'Study: Facebook users show "herding instinct"', *Marketing Daily* (12 October 2010).

53. See Robert B. Cialdini, *Influence: Science and Practice,* 2nd edn (New York: Scott, Foresman, 1988) for an excellent and entertaining treatment of this process.

54. For the seminal work on conformity and social influence, see Solomon E. Asch, 'Effects of Group Pressure Upon the Modification and Distortion of Judgments', in D. Cartwright and A. Zander (eds), *Group Dynamics* (New York: Harper & Row, 1953); Richard S. Crutchfield, 'Conformity and character', *American Psychologist* 10 (1955): 191–8; Muzafer Sherif, 'A study of some social factors in perception', *Archives of Psychology* 27 (1935): 187.

55. Robert E. Burnkrant and Alain Cousineau, 'Informational and normative social influence in buyer behavior', *Journal of Consumer Research* 2 (December 1975): 206–15.

56. For a study attempting to measure individual differences in proclivity to conformity, see William O. Bearden, Richard G. Netemeyer and Jesse E. Teel, 'Measurement of consumer susceptibility to interpersonal influence', *Journal of Consumer Research* 15 (March 1989): 473–81.

57. Douglas B. Holt, Søren Askegaard and Torsten Ringberg, '7 ups and Downs', unpublished manuscript, Penn State University.

58. T.M. Luhrmann, 'Wheat people vs. rice people: Why are some cultures more individualistic than others?', *New York Times* (3 December 2014), http://www.nytimes.com/2014/12/04/opinion/why-are-some-cultures-more-individualistic-than-others.html?ref=international (accessed 31 July 2018).

59. John W. Thibaut and Harold H. Kelley, *The Social Psychology of Groups* (New York: Wiley, 1959); W.W. Waller and R. Hill, *The Family: A Dynamic Interpretation* (New York: Dryden, 1951).

60. Bearden, Netemeyer and Teel, 'Measurement of consumer susceptibility to interpersonal influence'; Lynn R. Kahle, 'Observations: role-relaxed consumers: A trend of the nineties', *Journal of Advertising Research* (March/April 1995): 66–71; Lynn R. Kahle and Aviv Shoham, 'Observations: Role-relaxed consumers: empirical evidence', *Journal of Advertising Research* (May/June 1995): 59–62.

61. Xun Huang, Meng Zhang, Michael K. Hui and Robert S. Wyer Jr, 'Warmth and conformity: The effects of ambient temperature on product preferences and financial decisions', *Journal of Consumer Psychology,* 24(2) (2014): 241–50.

62. Leon Festinger, 'A theory of social comparison processes', *Human Relations* 7 (May 1954): 117–40.

63. Chester A. Insko, Sarah Drenan, Michael R. Solomon, Richard Smith and Terry J. Wade, 'Conformity as a function of the consistency of positive self-evaluation with being liked

and being right', *Journal of Experimental Social Psychology* 19 (1983): 341–58.

64. Abraham Tesser, Murray Millar and Janet Moore, 'Some affective consequences of social comparison and reflection processes: the pain and pleasure of being close', *Journal of Personality and Social Psychology* 54(1) (1988): 49–61.

65. L. Wheeler, K.G. Shaver, R.A. Jones, G.R. Goethals, J. Cooper, J.E. Robinson, C.L. Gruder and K.W. Butzine, 'Factors determining the choice of a comparison other', *Journal of Experimental Social Psychology* 5 (1969): 219–32.

66. M.L. Richins, 'Social comparison and the idealized images of advertising', *Journal of Consumer Research* 18 (June 1991): 71–83; M.C. Martin and P.F. Kennedy, 'Advertising and social comparison: consequences for female preadolescents and adolescents', *Psychology and Marketing* 10(6) (1993): 513–29; M.C. Martin and P.F. Kennedy, 'Social Comparison and the Beauty of Advertising Models: The Role of Motives in Comparison', in Chris T. Allen and Deborah Roedder John (eds), *Advances in Consumer Research* 21 (Provo, UT: Association for Consumer Research, 1994): 365–71; M.C. Martin and N.J. Gentry, 'Stuck in the model trap: the effects of beautiful models in ads on female pre-adolescents and adolescents', *Journal of Advertising* 26(2) (Summer 1997): 19–33.

67. See J.V. Wood, 'Theory and research concerning social comparisons of personal attributes', *Psychological Bulletin* 106 (September 1989): 231–48 for a detailed exposition of the evolving debates around the theory of social comparison.

68. Martin and Kennedy, 'Advertising and social comparison'; Martin and Kennedy, 'Social Comparison and the Beauty of Advertising Models'; Martin and Gentry, 'Stuck in the model trap'; Margaret K. Hogg, Margaret Bruce and Kerry Hough, 'Female images in advertising: the implications of social comparison for marketing', *International Journal of Advertising* 18(4) (1999): 445–73; Margaret K. Hogg and Aikaterini Fragou, 'Social comparison goals and the consumption of advertising: towards a more contingent view of young women's consumption of advertising', *Journal of Marketing Management* 19(7&8) (September 2003): 749–80.

69. Michael Hafner, 'How dissimilar others may still resemble the self: assimilation and contrast after social comparison', *Journal of Consumer Psychology* 14(1&2) (2004): 187–96.

70. George P. Moschis, 'Social comparison and informal group influence', *Journal of Marketing Research* 13 (August 1976): 237–44.

71. Robert E. Burnkrant and Alain Cousineau, 'Informational and normative social influence in buyer behavior', *Journal of Consumer Research* 2(3) (December 1975): 206–15 ; M. Venkatesan, 'Experimental study of consumer behavior conformity and independence', *Journal of Marketing Research* 3 (November 1966): 384–7.

72. Kenneth J. Gergen and Mary Gergen, *Social Psychology* (New York: Harcourt Brace Jovanovich, 1981).

73. L.J. Strickland, S. Messick and D.N. Jackson, 'Conformity, anticonformity and independence: their dimensionality and generality', *Journal of Personality and Social Psychology* 16 (1970): 494–507.

74. Jack W. Brehm, *A Theory of Psychological Reactance* (New York: Academic Press, 1966).

75. R.D. Ashmore, V. Ramchandra and R. Jones, 'Censorship as an Attitude Change Induction', paper presented at meeting of Eastern Psychological Association, New York, 1971; R.A. Wicklund and J. Brehm, *Perspectives on Cognitive Dissonance* (Hillsdale, NJ: Erlbaum, 1976).

76. C.R. Snyder and H.L. Fromkin, *Uniqueness: The Human Pursuit of Difference* (New York: Plenum Press, 1980).

77. Everett M. Rogers, *Diffusion of Innovations,* 3rd edn (New York: Free Press, 1983); cf. also Duncan J. Watts and Peter Sheridan Dodds, 'Influentials, networks, and public opinion formation', *Journal of Consumer Research* 34 (December 2007): 441–58; Morris B. Holbrook and Michela Addis, 'Taste versus the market: An extension of research on the consumption of popular culture', *Journal of Consumer Research* 34 (October 2007): 415–24.

78. Albert Muñiz and Thomas O'Guinn, 'Brand communities', *Journal of Consumer Research,* 27(4) (2001): 412–32.

79. Thomas W. Leigh, Cara Peters and Jeremy Shelton, 'The consumer quest for authenticity: The multiplicity of meanings within the MG subculture of consumption', *Journal of the Academy of Marketing Science* 34(4) (2006): 482–93.

80. Richard Elliott and Andrea Davies, 'Symbolic Brands and Authenticity of Identity Performance', in J. Schroeder and M. Salzer-Mörling, eds, *Brand Culture* (London: Routledge, 2006): 155–70.

81. Siwarit Pongsakornrungsilp and Jonathan E. Schroeder, 'Understanding value co-creation in a co-consuming brand community', *Marketing Theory* 11(3) (2011): 303–24.

82. https://www.nutella.com/en/uk (accessed 31 July 2018).

83. Bernard Cova and Stefano Pace, 'Brand community of convenience products: new forms of customer empowerment – the case "my Nutella The Community"', *European Journal of Marketing* 40(9&10) (2006): 1,087–105; see also www.nutellaville.it (accessed 31 July 2018).

84. Johann Füller, Marius Luedicke and Gregor Jawecki, 'How Brands Enchant: Insights from Observing Community Driven Brand Creation', in A.Y. Lee and D. Soman, eds, *Advances in Consumer Research* (Duluth, MN: Association for Consumer Research, 2008): 359–66.

85. James H. McAlexander, John W. Schouten and Harold F. Koenig, 'Building brand community', *Journal of Marketing* 66 (January 2002): 38–54; Albert Muniz and Thomas O'Guinn, 'Brand community', *Journal of Consumer Research* (March 2001): 412–32.

86. Rama K. Jayanti and Jagdip Singh, 'Framework for distributed consumer learning in online communities', *Journal of Consumer Research* 36(6) (2010): 1,058–81.

87. Hope Jensen Schau, Albert M. Muñiz and Eric J. Arnould, 'How brand community practices create value', *Journal of Marketing* 73 (September 2009): 30–51.

88. Ibid.

89. www.starbucked.com (accessed 26 April 2015); http://www.mcspotlight.org/index.shtml (accessed 31 July 2018); http://www.hel-mart.com/links.php (accessed 26 April 2015).

90. Candice R. Hollenbeck and George M. Zinkhan, 'Consumer activism on the internet: The role of anti-brand communities', *Advances in Consumer Research* 33(1) (2006): 479–85.

91. Veronique Cova and Bernard Cova, 'Tribal aspects of postmodern consumption research: The case of French in-line roller skaters', *Journal of Consumer Behavior* 1 (June 2001): 67–76.

92. Penelope Eckert and Sally McConnell-Ginet, 'Think practically and look locally: Language and gender as community-based practice', *Annual Review of Anthropology* (1992): 461–90, at 464, cited in Emma Moore, 'Approaches to Identity: Lesson from Sociolinguistics', Seminar paper, Customer Research Academy, Manchester School of Management, UMIST, UK (22 April 2004): 2.

93. Etienne Wenger, *Communities of Practice: Learning, Meaning and Identity* (Cambridge: Cambridge University Press, 1998), cited in Moore, 'Approaches to Identity', op. cit.

94. Emma Moore, 'Learning Style and Identity: A Socio-Linguistic Analysis of a Bolton High School', unpublished Ph.D. dissertation, University of Manchester (2003).

95. Penelope Eckert, 'Constructing Meaning in Socio-Linguistic Variation', paper presented at the Annual Meeting of the American Anthropological Association, New Orleans, USA (November 2002), cited in Moore 'Approaches to Identity', op. cit.: 3.

96. See for instance the *Daily Princetonian*'s editorial about Facebook.com as 'possibly the biggest word-of-mouth trend to hit campus since St Ives Medicated Apricot Scrub found its ways into the women's bathroom', cited by Peter Applebome, 'On campus, hanging out by logging on', *NYT Online* (1 December 2004); see also note 99.

97 Jacques Bughin, Jonathan Doogan and Ole Jørgen Vetvik, 'A New Way To Measure Word-Of-Mouth Marketing', *McKinsey Quarterly* (April 2010).

98. Wilson Bastos and Merrie Brucks, 'How and Why Conversational Value Leads to Happiness for Experiential and Material Purchases', *Journal of Consumer Research* 44(3) (2017): 598–612.

99. Johan Arndt, 'Role of product-related conversations in the diffusion of a new product', *Journal of Marketing Research* 4 (August 1967): 291–5.

100. '"Word-of-mouth" to become true measure of ads', *Marketing* (9 February 1995): 7.

101. Quoted in Barbara B. Stern and Stephen J. Gould, 'The consumer as financial opinion leader', *Journal of Retail Banking* 10 (Summer 1988): 43–52.

102. Douglas R. Pruden and Terry G. Vavra, 'Controlling the grapevine', *Marketing Management* (July–August 2004): 23–30.

103. www.bzzagent.com (accessed 31 July 2018).

104. Elihu Katz and Paul F. Lazarsfeld, *Personal Influence* (Glencoe, IL: Free Press, 1955).

105. John A. Martilla, 'Word-of-mouth communication in the industrial adoption process', *Journal of Marketing Research* 8 (March 1971): 173–8; see also Marsha L. Richins, 'Negative word-of-mouth by dissatisfied consumers: a pilot study', *Journal of Marketing* 47 (Winter 1983): 68–78.

106. Johan Arndt, 'Role of product-related conversations in the diffusion of a new product', op. cit.

107. See https://techcrunch.com/2017/10/08/comparing-alexa-google-assistant-cortana-and-siri-smart-speakers/ (accessed 31 July 2018).

108. This section is based upon a discussion in Michael R. Solomon, *Conquering Consumerspace: Marketing Strategies for a Branded World* (New York: AMACOM, 2003); see also David Lewis and Darren Bridger, *The Soul of the New Consumer: Authenticity – What We Buy and Why in the New Economy* (London: Nicholas Brealey Publishing, 2000).

109. *Journal of Marketing Management* 31(5&6) (2015). These two issues of this journal were devoted entirely to the themes of celebrity, convergence and transformation.

110. Jeff Neff, 'Pressure points at IPG', *Advertising Age* (December 2001): 4.

111. http://bengnyexperience.blogspot.com/2011/10/volkswagen-launches-new-beetle-with-ar.html (accessed 31 July 2018).

112. Evan Weingarten and Jonah Berger, 'Fired Up for the Future: How Time Shapes Sharing', *Journal of Consumer Research* 44(2) (2017): 432–47.

113. Constance L. Hays, 'Guerrilla marketing is going mainstream', *New York Times on the Web* (7 October 1999).

114. Cathy Horyn, 'A store made for right now: you shop until it's dropped', *NYTOnline* (17 February 2004).

115. Richard J. Lutz, 'Changing brand attitudes through modification of cognitive structure', *Journal of Consumer Research* 1 (March 1975): 49–59; for some suggested remedies to bad publicity, see Mitch Griffin, Barry J. Babin and Jill S. Attaway, 'An Empirical Investigation of the Impact of Negative Public Publicity on Consumer Attitudes and Intentions', in Rebecca H. Holman and Michael R. Solomon (eds), *Advances in Consumer Research* 18 (Provo, UT: Association for Consumer Research, 1991): 334–41; Alice M. Tybout, Bobby J. Calder and Brian Sternthal, 'Using information processing theory to design marketing strategies', *Journal of Marketing Research* 18 (1981): 73–9; see also Russell N. Laczniak, Thomas E. DeCarlo and Sridhar N. Ramaswami, 'Consumers' responses to negative word-of-mouth communication: An attribution theory perspective', *Journal of Consumer Psychology* 11(1) (2001): 57–74.

116. Robert E. Smith and Christine A. Vogt, 'The effects of integrating advertising and negative word-of-mouth communications on message processing and response', *Journal of Consumer Psychology* 4(2) (1995): 133–51; Paula Fitzgerald Bone, 'Word-of-mouth effects on short-term and long-term product judgments', *Journal of Business Research* 32 (1995): 213–23.

117. 'Dunkin' donuts buys out critical web site', *The New York Times on the Web* (27 August 1999); for a discussion of ways to assess negative WOM online, see David M. Boush and Lynn R. Kahle, 'Evaluating negative information in online consumer discussions: From qualitative analysis to signal detection', *Journal of Euro Marketing* 11(2) (2001): 89–105.

118. Everett M. Rogers, *Diffusion of Innovations,* 3rd edn (New York: Free Press, 1983); cf. also Duncan J. Watts and Peter Sheridan Dodds, 'Influentials, networks, and public opinion formation', *Journal of Consumer Research* 34 (December 2007): 441–58; Morris B. Holbrook and Michela Addis, 'Taste versus the market: An extension of research on the consumption of popular culture', *Journal of Consumer Research* 34 (October 2007): 415–24.

119. Dorothy Leonard-Barton, 'Experts as negative opinion leaders in the diffusion of a technological innovation', *Journal of Consumer Research* 11 (March 1985): 914–26; Rogers, *Diffusion of Innovations;* See also Jan Kratzer and Christopher Lettl, 'Distinctive roles of lead users and opinion leaders in the social networks of school-children', *Journal of Consumer Research* 36 December (2009): 646–59.

120. Herbert Menzel, 'Interpersonal and Unplanned Communications: Indispensable or Obsolete?', in Edward B. Roberts (ed.), *Biomedical Innovation* (Cambridge, MA: MIT Press, 1981): 155–63.

121. Meera P. Venkatraman, 'Opinion leaders, adopters, and communicative adopters: A role analysis', *Psychology & Marketing* 6 (Spring 1989): 51–68. Herbert Menzel, 'Interpersonal and Unplanned Com-munications: Indispensable or Obsolete?', in Edward B. Roberts (ed.), *Biomedical Innovation* (Cambridge, MA: MIT Press, 1981): 155–63.

122. Everett M. Rogers, *Diffusion of Innovations,* 3rd edn (New York: Free Press, 1983).

123. Niraj Dawar, Philip M. Parker and Lydia J. Price, 'A cross-cultural study of interpersonal information exchange', *Journal of International Business Studies* (3rd quarter 1996): 497–516.

124. Robert Merton, *Social Theory and Social Structure* (Glencoe, IL: Free Press, 1957).

125. King and Summers, 'Overlap of opinion leadership across consumer product categories', op. cit; see also Ronald E. Goldsmith, Jeanne R. Heitmeyer and Jon B. Freiden, 'Social values and fashion leadership', *Clothing and Textiles Research Journal* 10 (Fall 1991): 37–45; J.O. Summers, 'Identity of women's clothing fashion opinion leaders', *Journal of Marketing Research* 7 (1970): 178–85.

126. Ibid., 442.

127. Ibid., 441–58.

128. Cass R. Sunstein and Reid Hastie, 'Making Dumb Groups Smarter', *Harvard Business Review* (December 2014), https://hbr.org/2014/12/making-dumb-groups-smarter (accessed 31 July 2018); Matthew J. Salganik, Peter Sheridan Dodds and Duncan J. Watts, 'Experimental Study of Inequality and Unpredictability in an Artificial Cultural Market', *Science* 311 (10 February 2006): 854–6, http://www.princeton.edu/~mjs3/salganik_dodds_watts06_full.pdf (accessed 31 July 2018); Matthew J. Salganik and Duncan J. Watts, 'Leading the Herd Astray: An Experimental Study of Self-fulfilling Prophecies in an Artificial Cultural Market', *Social Psychology Quarterly* 71(4) (2008): 338–55, http://www.princeton.edu/~mjs3/salganik_watts08.pdf (accessed 31 July 2018).

129. http://klout.com/home (accessed February 26 2018).

130. Matthew Creamer, 'Your Followers Are No Measure of Your Influence', *Advertising Age* (3 January 2011), http://adage.com/article/special-report-influencers-2010/facebook-followers-measure-influence/147957/ (accessed 31 July 2018).

131. Gerrit Antonides and Gulden Asugman, 'The communication structure of consumer opinions', in Flemming Hansen (ed.), *European Advances in Consumer Research* 2 (Provo, UT: Association for Consumer Research, 1995): 132–7.

132. Steven A. Baumgarten, 'The innovative communicator in the diffusion process', *Journal of Marketing Research* 12 (February 1975): 12–18.

133. Laura J. Yale and Mary C. Gilly, 'Dyadic perceptions in personal source information search', *Journal of Business Research* 32 (1995): 225–37.

134. Russell W. Belk, 'Occurrence of Word-of-Mouth Buyer Behavior as a Function of Situation and Advertising Stimuli', in Fred C. Allvine (ed.), *Combined Proceedings of the American Marketing Association series* 33 (Chicago: American Marketing Association, 1971): 419–22.

135. Lawrence F. Feick, Linda L. Price and Robin A. Higie, 'People Who Use People: The Other Side of Opinion Leadership', in Richard J. Lutz (ed.), *Advances in Consumer Research* 13 (Provo, UT: Association for Consumer Research, 1986): 301–5.

136. For discussion of the market maven construct, see Lawrence F. Feick and Linda L. Price, 'The market maven', *Managing* (July 1985): 10; scale items adapted from Lawrence F. Feick and Linda L. Price, 'The market maven: a diffuser of marketplace information', *Journal of Marketing* 51 (January 1987): 83–7.

137. https://www.marksandspencer.com/s/women/fit-style-studio (accessed 31 July 2018).

138. Michael R. Solomon, 'The missing link: surrogate consumers in the marketing chain', *Journal of Marketing* 50 (October 1986): 208–18.

139. Sarah Boseley and Rob Evans, 'Drug giants accused over doctors' perks', *The Guardian* (23 August 2008): 1–2.

140. William R. Darden and Fred D. Reynolds, 'Predicting opinion leadership for men's apparel fashions', *Journal of Marketing Research* 1 (August 1972): 324–8. A modified version of the opinion leadership scale with improved reliability and validity can be found in Terry L. Childers, 'Assessment of the psychometric properties of an opinion leadership scale', *Journal of Marketing Research* 23 (May 1986): 184–8.

141. http://www.thekevinbacongame.com/ (accessed 11 March 2018).

142. Peter H. Reingen and Jerome B. Kernan, 'Analysis of referral networks in marketing: Methods and illustration', *Journal of Marketing Research* 23 (November 1986): 370–8.

143. Peter H. Reingen, Brian L. Foster, Jacqueline Johnson Brown and Stephen B. Seidman, 'Brand congruence in interpersonal relations: A social network analysis', *Journal of Consumer Research* 11 (December 1984): 771–83; see also James C. Ward and Peter H. Reingen, 'Sociocognitive analysis of group decision-making among consumers', *Journal of Consumer Research* 17 (December 1990): 245–62.

144. John Deighton, Jacob Goldenberg and Andrew T. Stephen, 'Introduction to the Special Issue of *The Consumer in a Connected World*', *Journal of the Association for Consumer Research* April 2(2) (2017): 137–9. See the complete Special Issue for range of articles on the topic area.

145. Ed Keller and Jon Berry, *The Influentials* (New York: Simon & Schuster, 2003).

146. The material in this section is adapted from Tracy Tuten and Michael R. Solomon, *Social Media Marketing* (Englewood Cliffs, NJ: Pearson, 2012).

147. Jenna Wortham, 'Feel like a wallflower? Maybe it's your Facebook wall', *New York Times* (9 April 2011), http://www.nytimes.com/2011/04/10/business/10ping.html?_r=0 (accessed 31 July 2018); Lizzie Crocker, 'Are twenty-somethings too afraid of missing out?', *The Daily Beast* (9 November 2012), http://www.thedailybeast.com/articles/2012/11/09/are-twentysomethings-too-afraid-of-missing-out.html (accessed 31 July 2018).

148. Nick Bilton, 'Twitter users congregate based on mood, study says', *New York Times* (16 March 2011), http://bits.blogs.nytimes.com/2011/03/16/twitter-users-congregate-based-on-mood-study-says/ (accessed 31 July 2018).

149. Mark Sweney, 'Home entertainment spending overtakes print sales for the first time', *The Guardian* (1 March 2018), https://www.theguardian.com/media/2018/mar/01/home-entertainment-spending-overtakes-print-sales-for-first-time (accessed 31 July 2018).

150. Barry Wellman, 'Physical place and cyberplace: The rise of personalized networking', *International Journal of Urban & Regional Research* 24(2) (2001): 227–52.

151. Alexandra Marin and Barry Wellman, 'Social Network Analysis: An Introduction', in *Handbook of Social Network Analysis* (London: SAGE, 2010).

152. Mark Sweney, '"Parents killed it": Why Facebook is losing its teenage users', *The Guardian* (16 February 2018), https://www.theguardian.com/technology/2018/feb/16/parents-killed-it-facebook-losing-teenage-users (accessed 31 July 2018).

153. Ibid.

154. 'Facebook Users Have Four Degrees of Separation from Each Other!', *IBN Live* (23 November 2011).

155. Steve Lohr, 'Researchers draw romantic insights from maps of Facebook networks', *New York Times* (28 October 2013), http://bits.blogs.nytimes.com/2013/10/28/spotting-romantic-relationships-on-facebook/ (accessed 31 July 2018).

156. John Coate, 'Cyberspace innkeeping: Building online community' (1998), http://www.cervisa.com/innkeeping (accessed 31 July 2018).

157. T.B. Sheridan, 'Further musings on the psychophysics of presence', *Presence: Teleoperators and Virtual Environments* 5 (1994): 241–6.

158. Matthew Lombard and Theresa Ditton, 'At the heart of it all: The concept of presence', *Journal of Computer Mediated Communication* 3(2) (1973).

159. Sangkil Moon, Paul K. Bergey and Dawn Iacobucci, 'Dynamic effects among movie ratings, movie revenues, and viewer satisfaction', *Journal of Marketing* 74 (January 2010): 108–21; https://www.yelp.com/search?find_desc=restaurants&find_loc=Manchester,+Greater+Manchester,+United+Kingdom (accessed 31 July 2018); Anya Kamenetz, 'The

perils and promise of the reputation economy', *Fast Company* (3 December 2008), www.fastcompany.com/magazine/131/on-the-internet-everyone-knows-youre-a-dog.html (accessed 31 July 2018).

160. Leslie K. John, Oliver Emrich, Sunil Gupta and Michael I. Norton, 'Does "liking" lead to loving? The impact of joining a brand's social network on marketing outcomes', *Journal of Marketing Research* (2017):144–55.

161. Ibid.

162. Daniel Nations, 'Is Web 3.0 really a thing?', *Lifewire* (March 24, 2018), https://www.lifewire.com/what-is-web-3-0-3486623 (accessed 31 July 2018).

163. Ibid.

164. Donna Hoffman, 'Consumer Behavior as I See IT', in Michael R. Solomon, *Consumer Behavior,* 10th edn, (Harlow, UK: Pearson, 2012); Donna L Hoffman and Thomas Novak 'Why do people use social media? Empirical findings and a new theoretical framework for social media goal pursuit', SSRN (17 January 2012), https://dx.doi.org/10.2139/ssrn.1989586

165. Ezgi Akpinar and Jonah Berger, 'Valuable virality', *Journal of Marketing Research* 54(2) (2017): 318–30.

166. Karen Kay, 'Millennial "influencers" who are the new stars of web advertising', *The Guardian* (28 May 2017), https://www.theguardian.com/fashion/2017/may/27/millenial-influencers-new-stars-web-advertising-marketing-luxury-brands (accessed 31 July 2018).

167. Quoted in Edward F. McQuarrie, Jessica Miller and Barbara J. Phillips, 'The Megaphone Effect: Taste and audience in fashion blogging', *Journal of Consumer Research* 40(1) (2013): 136–58.

168. Hannah Ellis-Petersen, 'Makeup, advice, anxiety – how Zoella rose to be queen of the video bloggers', *The Guardian* (6 December 2014): 17, http://www.theguardian.com/technology/2014/dec/05/zoella-sugg-internet-queen-fastest-selling-novel-youtube (accessed 31 July 2018).

169. Dalmeet Singh Chawla, 'The young vloggers and their fans who are changing the face of youth culture', *The Observer* (28 September 2014): 20, http://www.theguardian.com/technology/2014/sep/28/vloggers-changing-future-advertising (accessed 31 July 2018).

170. Hannah Ellis-Petersen 'Makeup, advice, anxiety', op. cit.

171. Cited in: Press Association, 'Growing social media backlash among young people, survey shows', *The Guardian* (5 October 2017), https://www.theguardian.com/media/2017/oct/05/growing-social-media-backlash-among-young-people-survey-shows (accessed 31 July 2018).

172. Jonah Berger, 'Word of mouth and interpersonal communication: A review and directions for future research', *Journal of Consumer Psychology* 24(4) (2014): 586–607; Eva Buechel and Jonah Berger, 'Facebook Therapy: Why People Share Self-Relevant Content Online', presented at the 2012 Association for Consumer Research conference, Vancouver: BC.

173. Jonah Berger and Raghuram Iyengar, 'Communication channels and word of mouth: How the medium shapes the message', *Journal of Consumer Research* 40(3) (2013):567–79; cf. also Andreas B Eisingerich, HaeEun Helen Chun, Yeyi Liu, He Jia and Simon J. Bell, 'Why recommend a brand face-to-face but not on Facebook? How word-of-mouth on online social sites differs from traditional word-of-mouth', *Journal of Consumer Psychology* 25(1) (2015): 120–8.

174. John Tierney, 'Good news beats bad on social networks', *New York Times* (18 March 2013), http://www.nytimes.com/2013/03/19/science/good-news-spreads-faster-on-twitter-and-facebook.html (accessed 31 July 2018).

175. Grant Packard, Andrew D. Gershoff and David B. Wooten, 'When boastful word of mouth helps vs. hurts social perceptions and persuasion', *Journal of Consumer Research* 43(1) (2016): 26–42.

176. Tejvir Sekhon, Barbara Bickart, Remi Trudel and Susan Fournier, 'Being a Likable Braggart: How Consumers Use Brand Mentions for Self-presentation on Social Media', in *Consumer Psychology in a Social Media World* (Armonk, NY: M.E. Sharpe), in press; cf. also Yinjong Zhang, Lawrence Feick and Vikas Mittal, 'How males and females differ in their likelihood of transmitting negative word of mouth', *Journal of Consumer Research* 40(6) (2014): 1097–108.

177. Ryan Hamilton, Kathleen D. Vohs and Ann L. McGill, 'We'll be honest, this won't be the best article you'll ever read: The use of dispreferred markers in word-of-mouth communication', *Journal of Consumer Research* 41(1) (June 2014): 197–212.

178. Ed Keller and Jon Berry, *The Influentials* (New York: Simon & Schuster, 2003).

179. 'Introducing peer influence analysis: 500 billion peer impressions each year', *Empowered* (20 April 2010).

180. Janice Denegri-Knot and Mike Molesworth, 'Concepts and practices of digital virtual consumption', *Consumption Markets & Culture* 13(2) (2010): 109–32; Natalie T. Wood and Michael R. Solomon, 'Adonis or Atrocious: Spokesavatars and Source Effects in Immersive Digital Environments', in Matthew S. Eastin, Terry Daugherty and Neal M. Burns (eds), *Handbook of Research on Digital Media and Advertising: User Generated Content Consumption* (Hershey, PA: IGI Global, 2011): 521–34.

181. Quoted in Suzanne Vranica, 'Ad houses will need to be more nimble, clients are demanding more and better use of consumer data, web', *The Wall Street Journal* (2 January 2008): B3.

182. Thomas E. Weber, 'Viral marketing: Web's newest ploy may make you an unpopular friend', *The Wall Street Journal Interactive Edition* (13 September 1999).

183. Victoria Shannon, 'Social networking moves to the cellphone', *New York Times* (6 March 2008), www.nytimes.com/2008/03/06/technology/06wireless.html?ex=1362459600&en=571b090085db559d&ei=5088&partner=rssnyt&emc=rss (accessed 31 July 2018).

Chapter 10
European families: types, structures, decision-making and age cohorts

Chapter objectives

When you finish reading this chapter you will understand why:

10.1 Marketers often need to understand consumers' behaviour, rather than a consumer's behaviour.

10.2 Our traditional notions about families are outdated; many important demographic dimensions of a population relate to family and household structure.

10.3 Members of a family unit play different roles and have different amounts of influence when the family makes purchase decisions.

10.4 Children learn over time what and how to consume.

10.5 We have many things in common with others because they are about the same age (age cohorts).

10.6 Teens are a critically important age segment for marketers.

10.7 Baby boomers continue to be the most powerful age segment economically in the EU.

10.8 Seniors continue to increase in size and spending power as a market segment, and marketers are making more and better efforts to understand this segment.

In the Netherlands, children get their first (main) set of Christmas gifts on 5 December, which is St Nicolas Eve (*Sinterklass*).[1] Children then get presents again on Christmas Eve. Christmas is celebrated over two days in the Netherlands (25 and 26 December). *Tweede Kerstdag* (second Christmas day) is usually spent visiting family. Although it was still three days before Christmas, Liane was intent on making a large cauldron of Dutch pea soup, while her partner Joost was in the process of chopping ingredients for several Indonesian dishes. They agreed that all these dishes taste best if they are cooked a few days before actually eating them.

Although pea soup isn't always a part of Christmas dinner in the Netherlands, it definitely has its place in the Dutch 'winter menu'. The best pea soup is thick in texture with peas, potatoes, celeriac root, onions, leek, carrots and generous chunks of ham. Hot pea soup and dark bread topped with thinly sliced bacon (*Snert met roggebrood en spek*) leaves everyone feeling warm and content. The only concession to 'store-bought' ingredients that Liane will make is to add a sliced *Unox rookworst* (sausage) on the day the soup is served. Joost, on the other hand, turns his nose up at the very idea of using anything from a package. While many Dutch rely on prepared Indonesian seasoning from Conimex, Joost considers himself a serious cook, and uses only traditional, freshly prepared dishes, which means lots of chopping, blending, mixing and marinating for days!

As in many other European countries, Christmas is a busy family time in the Netherlands. Everyone has social events to attend, some of which are personal and joyful, while others seem more 'obligatory'. For Joost and Liane, the Dutch tradition of celebrating two Christmas days is particularly helpful as they try to find time to visit everyone. Joost's parents divorced 18 years ago and his mother lives in the east of the Netherlands, while his father is two hours away in Amsterdam. In addition to Joost's parents, there is also Liane's family. Family, food and lots of train travel. . . all part of the Christmas season for Joost and Liane in the Netherlands.

Gary J. Bamossy and Margaret K. Hogg

Introduction

10.1

Marketers often need to understand consumers' behaviour, rather than a consumer's behaviour.

Joost and Liane's determination to celebrate Christmas with their families is fairly typical of the joint nature of many consumer decisions. The individual decision-making process we have already described in detail (see Chapter 8) is, in many cases, overly simplistic. This is because more than one person often participates in the problem-solving sequence, from initial problem recognition and information search to evaluation of alternatives and product choice. To further complicate matters, these decisions often include two or more people, or families, all with differing expectations, who may not have the same level of investment in the outcome, the same tastes and preferences, or the same consumption priorities.

A happy family enjoying the snow and skiing on holiday.

Shutterstock

Whether they are choosing a tin of tuna or buying a new multimedia entertainment system for the home, consumers commonly work together. This section of the chapter examines issues related to *collective decision-making,* where more than one person is involved in the purchasing process for products or services that may be used by multiple consumers. We focus specifically on one of the most important organisations of which many of us claim membership – the family unit. We will consider how members of a family negotiate among themselves, and how important changes in the modern family structure are affecting this process. The chapter concludes by discussing how we use age in consumer research as a predictor of behaviour, and the appeals that marketers make to diverse age subcultures.

The family

10.2

Our traditional notions about families are outdated; many important demographic dimensions of a population relate to family and household structure.

Constructing and deconstructing the family in Europe

While it might still be too early to draw definite conclusions, it is reasonable to speculate that historians will regard the period from the 1990s to 2018 as one of the most politically, socially and economically turbulent time-frames in modern history. Radical political and market changes throughout Western and Eastern Europe are reflections and outcomes of intense social change in European societies that have been under way since the 1950s. While the extent and pace of changes, and the national perceptions of social change, have differed from one country to another, it is clear that many of our social institutions have been altered over the past four decades, not least of which is the notion of 'family'. In January 2017, the population of the EU28 was estimated to be just over 511 million.[2] While the newest EU member countries have more similarities than differences with the 'former 15' EU members in terms of family structure, there are some important trends in age distributions, marriage patterns, employment, salary rates between men and women and ageing of the populations of our individual member states, which will have a major impact on consumption patterns of European families in the decades to come.[3]

A report summarised the different structures and policy provisions affecting family life and relationships within Europe as follows:

'*Scandinavia* (Denmark, Finland, Iceland, Norway and Sweden), the Social Democratic welfare regime type with mainly universal social provisions, promoting dual-earner families and gender equality;

Anglo-Saxon countries (United Kingdom and Ireland), the Liberal welfare regime type with usually means-tested policy support and market-based solutions regarding welfare provision;

Western Europe (Belgium, France, Luxembourg and the Netherlands), the Conservative welfare regime type that supports men's primacy in the labour market but also provides possibilities for women to combine paid work and family responsibilities;

German-speaking countries (Austria, Germany and Switzerland), also the Conservative welfare regime type but less supportive for women's labour force participation than countries in the "Western Europe" group;

Southern Europe (Greece, Cyprus, Italy, Malta, Portugal, Spain), the Mediterranean or Familistic welfare regime type with extremely limited policy provision for families and pronounced gender role differentiation (Saraceno, 2008; Lewis, 2006);

Central-Eastern Europe (Bulgaria, Croatia, Czech Republic, Estonia, Hungary, Latvia, Lithuania, Poland, Romania, Slovakia, Slovenia), the Transition Post-Socialist cluster with large variations in the range of state support for families and for women to facilitate the combination of paid work and family.'[4]

Before moving on to a discussion of the forces that have changed our notions of family, and what these changes mean in terms of consumer behaviour, we need to spend a moment tackling the thorny question, 'What is the family, and how do we gather data about it?'. There is a great deal of family diversity throughout Europe, and the conceptualisation of *family* is based on ideology, popular mythology and conventions that are firmly rooted in each country's historical, political, religious, economic and cultural traditions.[5] As May and Dawson argue in their overview: 'In terms of key [academic] works within the field of families and relationships, major influences include Morgan (1996) on family practices, Finch and Mason (1993) on negotiating family responsibilities, Weeks et al. (2001) on same-sex intimacies and Smart's (2007) recent work on personal life. Two of the articles, by Finch (2007) and Jamieson (1999), have also themselves become important points of reference in sociological debates.'[6]

Certainly, European governments have had a strong history of requiring regular and up-to-date socio-demographic information on the behaviour of families (birth rates, fertility rates, divorce rates), and about family forms (size, structure and organisation). This sort of information is an essential component in governments' policy-making processes. Yet, despite a long history of international collaboration and the growing need for reliable information about demographic trends in Europe, data on households and families in the EU are still far from comparable, particularly from a historical perspective.[7] In today's Europe, increasing migration rates, falling fertility rates and delaying marriage until later in life (or cohabitation instead of marriage) all influence the reporting and analyses of statistics used to paint a portrait of the European family (see Figure 10.1).

From both a statistical as well as a sociological perspective, 'family' is hard to nail down. However, one thing is certain – the concept of family will continue to exist and will manifest itself in varying forms over time and across countries throughout Europe. Figure 10.2 provides an overview of the many components that make up our notion of a European household.

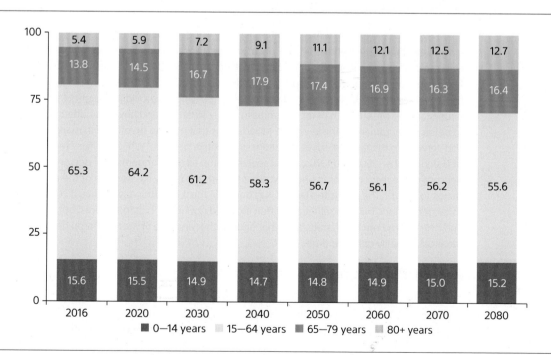

Figure 10.1 Population structure by major age groups, EU28, 2016–80 (% of total population), [Note: 2016 estimate provisional, 2020–80 projections]

Source: Eurostat (demo_pjangroup) and (proj_13npms) © European Union, http://ec.europa.eu/eurostat/statistics-explained/index.php/File:Population_structure_by_major_age_groups,_EU-28,_2016-80_(%25_of_total_population).png (accessed 28 March 2018).

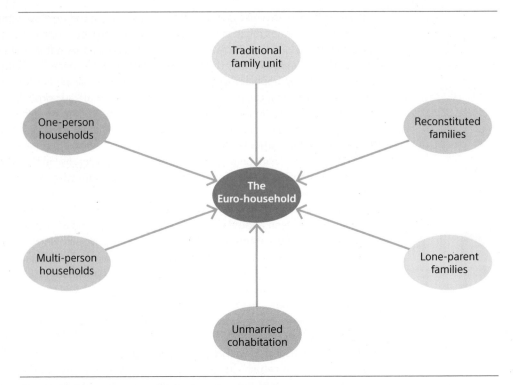

Figure 10.2 Components of the 'modern family'

Defining the modern family

Some experts have argued that as traditional family living arrangements have declined, people are placing even greater emphasis on the role of siblings, close friends and other relatives to provide companionship and social support.[8] Many marketers have focused on the renewed interest in family life brought about by the more flexible definitions of what constitutes a family. Research on the family has shown this social unit to be of key importance in providing insights for marketers in understanding the strength of relationships in family structure, and how this understanding leads to better development of the key value propositions that need to be offered in marketing goods and services to the family, such as vacations and mobile phones.[9] While families were indeed out of fashion in the 1960s and 1970s, being seen by some as an infringement of personal freedom, 90 per cent of the respondents in one survey confirmed that family life was one of the most important things to them.[10] The **extended family** was once the most common family unit. It consisted of three generations living together and often included not only the grandparents, but aunts, uncles and cousins. The **nuclear family**, a mother and a father and one or more children became the more usual family unit over time.

Just what is a household?

For statistical purposes, Eurostat has implemented the United Nation's definition of the family unit based on the 'conjugal family concept'. *The family* is defined in the narrow sense of a family nucleus as follows: 'The persons within a private or institutional household who are related as husband and wife or as parent and never-married child by blood or adoption'. Thus, a family nucleus comprises a married couple without children or a married couple with one or more never-married children of any age, or one parent with one or more never-married children of any age. The definition tries to take into account, whenever possible, couples who report that they are living in consensual unions, regardless of whether they are legally married.

Under the more recent European Community Household Panel, a **family household** is more broadly defined as a 'shared residence and common housekeeping arrangement'.

Statistics from 2016 showed that in the EU there were '220 million households, almost a third of which (65.6 million) had dependent children. . . A dependent child is [defined as] any child aged below 15, or any person aged between 15 and 24, who is socially and economically dependent on another household member (parent or adult). Among the EU Member States, the highest proportion of households with children was recorded in Ireland (41%), ahead of Cyprus and Poland (both 38%), Malta, Portugal and Slovakia (all 36%). In contrast, only about a fifth of households had children in Germany and Finland (22%), followed by Sweden (25%), Austria (26%) and Greece (27%). . . At EU level, almost half of all households with children (47%, or 31 million households) had only one child, while 40% (26 million) had two children and 13% (8.5 million) three children or more.'[11]

Marketers are interested in both of these units (families and households), not only for their similarities, but as a way of understanding differences. Changes in consumers' family structures, such as cohabitation, delayed marriage and delayed childbirth, the return of mothers to the workforce and the upheaval caused by divorce, often represent opportunities for marketers as normal purchasing patterns become unfrozen and people make new choices about products and brands.[12]

Age of the family

Since 1960 the EU has seen a trend of falling numbers of marriages and an increase in the number of divorces. Moreover, people are remarrying more often than they did before the 1960s, and men are more likely to form a new family than women. Couples marry youngest in Portugal and oldest in Denmark, and the greatest age difference between husbands and wives is to be found in Greece. Overall, consumers aged between 35 and 44 were responsible for the largest increase in the number of households, growing by almost 40 per cent since 1980. The 'crude marriage rate' (number of marriages per thousand of a country's population) had fallen from 7.9 in 1970, to 4.9 in 2007 – a reduction in marriage rates of 38 per cent.[13] A key segment to change in the coming 20 years will be the significant increase in adults living alone – a segment that will increase to over 62 million households by 2025.[14]

Family size

Worldwide, surveys show that many women today want smaller families. Ironically, while populations boom in some underdeveloped parts of the world, industrialised countries face future crises because there will be relatively fewer young people to support their elders. For population levels to remain constant, the fertility rate has to be 2.0 so that the two children can replace their parents. That's not happening in places such as Spain, Italy, Malta, Cyprus, Poland, Portugal and Greece, where the fertility rate is 1.4 or lower according to 2016 statistics from the EU.[15] As a benchmark, the US rate is 2.1.[16] A UK study predicts that one in five women born in the 1960s to 1980s will remain childless – a halving of the birth rate of their mother's generation.[17] The **fertility rate** is determined by the number of births per year per 1,000 women of childbearing age. For several decades now, fertility rates in the EU have remained clearly below population replacement levels of 2.1 – a trend that is reinforced by the enlargement of the EU to the EU28. In 2016 the estimated fertility rate for EU 28 was 1.60, with the UK on 1.79.[18] A variety of European studies on the dynamics that underlie family size show that size is dependent on such factors as educational level, the availability of birth control and religion. Not only is the EU's fertility rate below replacement rate, the median age of women giving birth for the first time rose to 29 years of age in 2015.[19]

Recent research has also shown that the division of labour within the household between partners (husband and wife, or however the relationship is defined) also matters in Europe. Consider the situation of women in Italy and the Netherlands. While there is a greater percentage of Dutch women than Italian women in the workforce, the fertility rate in the

Netherlands is higher (1.66 in the Netherlands, compared to 1.34 in Italy).[20] In both countries, people tend to have traditional views about gender roles, but Italian society is considerably more conservative in this regard, and this seems to be a decisive difference. Women who take on more than 75 per cent of the housework and child care are less likely to want to have another child than women whose husbands or partners share the load. Put differently, Dutch fathers change more nappies, pick up more kids after soccer practice and clean up the living room more often than Italian fathers; therefore, relative to the population, there are more Dutch babies than Italian babies being born. In Europe, many countries with greater gender equality have a greater social commitment to day care and other institutional support for working women, which gives those women the possibility of having second or third children.[21] A recent study undertaken by Dutch and Canadian researchers showed that: 'The total amount of housework differed between the [27 European countries plus Israel] countries studied, with Ukraine having the highest weekly hours of housework for both women (31.2 hours a week) and men (16.6). The lowest hours reported by women were in Denmark (12.4), while men in Portugal only managed to rouse themselves for 4.7 hours. The share of housework for women differs between countries: in Greece, for example, women did 82% of housework, compared with 61% in Sweden. . . The research found that women in the UK spend more than twice as much time doing housework as men: 15.7 hours a week compared with 6.3 hours. The gap closes if the woman is in work and her partner is unemployed, but only slightly.'[22]

Marketers keep a close eye on the population's birth rate to gauge how the pattern of births will affect demand for products in the future. Even when a married couple does live with children, the structure of family size is declining – the number of European households comprising one or two people is increasing, and the number of households with four or more people is falling.[23] The number of unmarried adults and one-person households is steadily rising (they now account for 26 per cent of European households, and are projected to be the fastest-growing segment through to the year 2025). Some marketers are beginning to address the fact that this group is under-represented in advertising.[24] Gold Blend coffee built a very popular TV ad campaign around a romance between two single neighbours, while Procter & Gamble introduced Folger's Singles 'single-serve' coffee bags for people who live alone and don't need a full pot.[25] On the other hand, many singles report that they avoid buying single-size food portions or eating alone in restaurants since both remind them of their unattached status – they prefer takeaway food.[26]

How realistic are these role models for your country and your generation?

Source: Luc Ubaghs/Shutterstock.

Single men and women constitute quite different markets. More than half of single men are under the age of 35, while among people over the age of 65 women account for 80 per cent of one-person households. Despite single males' greater incomes, single women dominate many markets because of their spending patterns. Single women are more likely than single men to own a home, and they spend more on housing-related items and furniture. Single men, in contrast, spend more overall in restaurants and on cars. However, these spending patterns are also significantly affected by age: middle-aged single women, for example, spend *more* than their male counterparts on cars.[27]

The tangled Web

Facebook has an impact on couples' relationships, perhaps because the platform makes it easier for people to rekindle old romances. In a recent survey of lawyers, two-thirds of divorce lawyers identified Facebook as the primary source of evidence in their cases. The large majority reports that evidence for infidelity also turns up on online photo albums, profile pages and tweets.[28] As one lawyer noted, the

'. . . huge popularity as well as the lure of sites such as Second Life. . . and Illicit Encounters are tempting couples to cheat on each other'. Apparently, many divorces occur when partners find 'flirty messages' on their spouse's Facebook wall. She also offered some timely advice to people in the middle of divorce proceedings: 'Avoid posting photos of your new lover until it's all over'.[29]

Non-traditional family structures

The European Community Household Panel regards any occupied housing unit as a household, regardless of the relationships between people living there. Thus, one person living alone, three room-mates or two lovers all constitute households. Less traditional households will rapidly increase if trends persist. One-parent households are increasing steadily throughout Europe (most common in the UK, Denmark and Belgium, least common in Greece); although these households are, in the majority of cases, headed by women, there is also an increasing trend for fathers to take on this role.[30] An EU report from 2016 identified that '7.7 % of women aged 25–49 lived alone with children, compared with 1.1 % of men of the same age. For singles without children in this age group, the share was 9.5 % for women and 16.1 % for men. Another group where there are large differences between women and men is for singles aged 65 and over: the share of elderly women living alone (40.1 %) was twice the share for men (19.7 %).'[31]

Members of a family unit play different roles and have different amounts of influence when the family makes purchase decisions.

Effects of family structure on consumption

A family's needs and expenditures are affected by factors such as the number of people (children and adults) in the family, their ages and whether one, two or more adults are employed outside of the home.

Two important factors determining how a couple spend time and money are: (1) whether they have children; and (2) whether the woman works. Couples with children generally have higher expenses, and not just for the 'basics' such as food and utilities bills. Studies in the UK estimate that the costs of keeping a teenager 'in the style to which they aspire' can run close to £66,000 per year, and that the costs of getting a child from birth to the age of 21 is approaching a staggering £230,000.[32] In addition, a recently married couple make very different expenditures compared with people with young children, who in turn are quite different from a couple with children in college, and so on. Families with working mothers must often make allowances for additional expenses such as nursery care (which can vary widely – e.g. the UK has some of the highest costs of child care in Europe[33]) and a working wardrobe for the woman.

The family life cycle

Recognising that family needs and expenditures change over time, the concept of the **family life cycle (FLC)** has been widely used by marketers. The FLC combines trends in income and family composition with the changes in demands placed upon this income. As we grow older, our preferences for products and activities tend to change. In many cases, our income levels tend to rise (at least until retirement), so that we can afford more as well. In addition, many purchases that must be made at an early age do not have to be repeated very often. For example, we tend to accumulate durable goods, such as furniture, and only replace them as necessary.

A life cycle approach to the study of the family assumes that pivotal events alter role relationships and trigger new stages of life that modify our priorities. These events include the birth of a first child, the departure of the last child from the house, the death of a spouse, retirement of the principal wage earner and divorce.[34] Movement through these life stages is accompanied by significant changes in expenditures on leisure, food, durables and services, even after the figures have been adjusted to reflect changes in income.[35]

This focus on longitudinal changes in priorities is particularly valuable in predicting demand for specific product categories over time. For example, the money spent on eating out and holidays by a couple with no children will probably be diverted for quite different purchases after the birth of a child. While a number of models have been proposed to describe family life cycle stages, their usefulness has been limited because in many cases they have failed to take into account such important social trends as the changing role of women, the acceleration of alternative lifestyles, childless and delayed-child marriages and single-parent households.

Four variables are necessary to describe these changes: age, marital status, the presence or absence of children in the home and their ages. In addition, our definition of 'marital status' (at least for analysis purposes) must be relaxed to include any couple living together who are in a long-term relationship. Thus, while room-mates might not be considered 'married', a man and a woman who have established a household would be, as would two homosexual men or lesbian women who have a similar understanding.

Life cycle effects on buying

As might be expected, consumers classified into different stages of a family life cycle show marked differences in consumption patterns. Young bachelors and newly-weds have the most 'modern' sex-role attitudes, are the most likely to exercise regularly, to go to pubs, concerts, the cinema and restaurants, and to go dancing; and they consume more alcohol. Families with young children are more likely to consume health foods such as fruit, juice and yoghurt, while those made up of single parents and older children buy more junk foods. The monetary value of homes, cars and other durables is lowest for bachelors and single parents, but increases as people go through the full nest and childless couple stages. Perhaps reflecting the bounty of wedding gifts, newly-weds are the most likely to own appliances such as toasters, ovens and electric coffee grinders. Baby-sitter and day-care usage is, of course, highest among single-parent and full nest households, while home maintenance services (e.g. lawn mowing) are most likely to be employed by older couples and bachelors. Recent studies have shown that families also place a significant emotional and financial attachment on possessions that they own when those possessions are part of the family's bonding and history. This goes well beyond our earlier notion of the importance of 'inheritance', and considers our sense of family well-being, continuity, history and the important role as 'caretaker' of the family's identity over generations.[36]

The growth of these additional categories creates many opportunities for enterprising marketers. For example, divorced people undergo a process of transition to a new social role. This change is often accompanied by the disposal of possessions linked to the former role and the need to acquire a set of possessions that help to express the person's new identity as they experiment with new lifestyles.[37]

The intimate corporation: family decision-making

The decision-making process within a household unit in some ways resembles a business conference. Certain matters are put up for discussion, different members may have different priorities and agendas and there may be power struggles to rival any tale of corporate intrigue. In just about every living situation, whether a conventional family, students sharing a house or apartment or some other non-traditional arrangement, group members seem to take on different roles – just as purchasing agents, engineers, account executives and others do within a company.

Household decisions

Two basic types of decisions are made by families.[38] In a **consensual purchase decision**, the group agrees on the desired purchase, differing only in terms of how it will be achieved. In these circumstances, the family will probably engage in problem-solving and consider alternatives until the means for satisfying the group's goal is found. For example, a household considering adding a dog to the family but concerned about who will take care of it might draw up a chart assigning individuals to specific duties.

Unfortunately, life is not always that easy. In an **accommodative purchase decision**, group members have different preferences or priorities and cannot agree on a purchase that will satisfy the minimum expectations of all involved. It is here that bargaining, coercion, compromise and the wielding of power are all likely to be used to achieve agreement on what to buy or who gets to use it. Family decisions are often characterised by an accommodative rather than a consensual decision. Conflict occurs when there is incomplete correspondence in family members' needs and preferences. While money is the most common source of conflict between marriage partners, television choices come a close second![39] Some specific factors determining the degree of family-decision conflict include the following:[40]

- *Interpersonal need* (a person's level of investment in the group). A child in a family situation may care more about what their family buys for the house than a college student who is living in student accommodation.

- *Product involvement and utility* (the degree to which the product in question will be used or will satisfy a need). A family member who is an avid coffee drinker will obviously be more interested in the purchase of a new coffee-maker to replace a malfunctioning one than a similar level of expenditure for some other item.

- *Responsibility* (for procurement, maintenance, payment and so on). People are more likely to have disagreements about a decision if it entails long-term consequences and commitments. For example, a family decision about getting a dog may involve conflict regarding who will be responsible for walking and feeding it.

- *Power* (or the degree to which one family member exerts influence over the others in making decisions). In traditional families, husbands tend to have more power than wives, who in turn have more than the oldest child and so on. In family decisions, conflict can arise when one person continually uses the power they have within the group to satisfy their priorities.

In general, decisions will involve conflict among family members to the extent that they are important or novel and/or if individuals have strong opinions about good and bad alternatives. The degree to which these factors generate conflict determines the type of decision the family will make.[41]

Sex roles and decision-making responsibilities

Traditionally, some buying decisions, termed **autocratic decisions**, were made by one spouse. Men, for instance, often had sole responsibility for selecting a car, while most decorating choices fell to women. Other decisions, such as holiday destinations, were made jointly; these are known as **syncratic decisions**. According to a study conducted by Roper Starch Worldwide, wives tend to have the most say when buying groceries, children's toys, clothes and medicines. Syncratic decisions are common for cars, holidays, homes, appliances, furniture, home electronics, interior design and long-distance phone services. As the couple's education increases, more decisions are likely to be made together.[42]

Identifying the decision-maker

The nature of consumer decision-making within a particular product category is an important issue for marketers, so that they know who to target and whether or not they need to reach both spouses to influence a decision. Researchers have paid special attention to which spouse plays the role of what has been called the **family financial officer (FFO)**, who keeps track of the family's bills and decides how any surplus funds will be spent. Among newly-weds, this role tends to be played jointly, and then over time one spouse or the other tends to take over these responsibilities.[43] Spouses usually exert significant influence on decision-making, even after one of them has died. An Irish study found that many widows claim to sense the continued presence of their dead husband, and to conduct 'conversations' with them about household matters.[44]

In traditional families (and especially those with low educational levels), women are primarily responsible for family financial management. While the man is usually the wage-earner, the woman in these traditional family structures typically decides how the money is spent.[45] Each spouse 'specialises' in certain activities.[46] The pattern is different among families where spouses adhere to more modern sex-role norms. These couples believe that there should be more shared participation in family maintenance activities. In these cases, husbands assume more responsibility for laundering, house cleaning, day-to-day shopping and so on, in addition to such traditionally 'male' tasks as home maintenance and waste removal.[47] Of course, cultural background is an important determinant of the dominance of the husband or wife. Husbands tend to be more dominant in decision-making among couples with a strong Mediterranean ethnic identification, for example.[48] Even in northern Europe, the pattern of traditional 'male' and 'female' roles is still fairly strong.

Four factors appear to determine the degree to which decisions will be made jointly or by one or other spouse:[49]

1 *Sex-role stereotypes.* Couples who believe in traditional sex-role stereotypes tend to make individual decisions for sex-typed products (i.e. those considered to be 'masculine' or 'feminine').

2 *Spousal resources.* The spouse who contributes more resources to the family has the greater influence.

3 *Experience.* Individual decisions are made more frequently when the couple has gained experience as a decision-making unit.

4 *Socio-economic status.* More joint decisions are made by middle-class families than in either higher- or lower-class families.

Despite recent changes in decision-making responsibilities, women are still primarily responsible for the continuation of the family's **kin network system**: they perform the rituals intended to maintain ties among family members, both immediate and extended. This function includes such activities as coordinating visits among relatives, phoning, emailing, texting and WhatsApping to family members, sending greetings cards, making social engagements and so on.[50] This organising role means that women often make important decisions about the family's leisure activities, and are more likely to decide with whom the family will socialise.

Heuristics in joint decision-making

The *synoptic ideal* calls for the husband and wife to take a common view and act as joint decision-makers. According to this ideal, they would very thoughtfully weigh alternatives, assign to one another well-defined roles and calmly make mutually beneficial consumer decisions. The couple would act rationally, analytically and use as much information as possible to maximise joint utility. In reality, however, spousal decision-making is often characterised by the use of influence or methods that are likely to reduce conflict. A couple 'reaches' rather than 'makes' a decision. This process has been described as 'muddling through'.[51]

One common technique for simplifying the decision-making process is the use of *heuristics* (see Chapter 8). Some decision-making patterns frequently observed when a couple makes decisions in buying a new house illustrate the use of heuristics:

- The couple's areas of common preference are based upon salient, objective dimensions rather than more subtle, hard-to-define cues. For example, a couple may easily agree on the number of bedrooms they need in the new home, but will have more difficulty achieving a common view of how the home should look.

- The couple agrees on a system of task specialisation, where each is responsible for certain duties or decision areas and does not interfere in the other's. For many couples, these assignments are likely to be influenced by their perceived sex roles. For example, the wife may seek out houses in advance that meet their requirements, while the husband will first determine whether the couple can obtain a mortgage.

- Concessions are based on the intensity of each spouse's preferences. One spouse will yield to the influence of the other in many cases simply because their level of preference for a certain attribute is not particularly intense, whereas in other situations they will be willing to exert effort to obtain a favourable decision.[52] In cases where intense preferences for different attributes exist, rather than attempt to influence each other spouses will 'trade off' a less-intense preference for a more strongly felt one. For example, a husband who is indifferent to kitchen design may yield on this to his wife but expect that, in turn, he will be allowed to design his own garage workshop. It is interesting to note that many men apparently want to be very involved in making certain decorating decisions and setting budgets – more than women want them to be. According to one survey, 70 per cent of male respondents felt the husband should be involved in decorating the family room, while only 51 per cent of wives wanted them to be.[53]

Children as decision-makers: consumers-in-training

10.4

Children learn over time what and how to consume.

Anyone who has had experience of supermarket shopping with one or more children knows that children often have a say in what their parents buy, especially for products such as breakfast cereal.[54] In addition, children are increasingly being recognised as a potential market for traditionally adult products (e.g. smartphones are just a very early example of this).

Parental yielding occurs when a parental decision-maker is influenced by a child's request and 'surrenders'. The likelihood of this occurring is partly dependent on the dynamics within a particular family – as we all know, parental styles range from permissive to strict, and they also vary in terms of the amount of responsibility children are given to make decisions.[55] The strategies children use to request purchases were documented in one study. While most children simply asked for things, other common tactics included saying they had seen it on television (or nowadays, probably as likely, on social media advertising), saying that a sibling or friend had it, or bargaining by offering to do chores. Other actions were less innocuous; they included directly placing the object in the trolley and continuous whining – often a 'persuasive' behaviour![56]

Consumer socialisation

Children do not spring from the womb with consumer skills already in memory. **Consumer socialisation** has been defined as the process 'by which young people acquire skills, knowledge, and attitudes relevant to their functioning in the marketplace'.[57] Where does this knowledge come from? Friends and teachers certainly participate in this process. For instance, children talk to one another about consumer products, and this tendency increases with age.[58] Especially for young children, though, the two primary socialisation sources are the family and media. Research has highlighted children's very varied experiences within the family, such that the family represents not a homogeneous but rather a heterogeneous consumption environment in which children grow up.[59]

Influence of parents

Parents' influences in consumer socialisation are both direct and indirect. They deliberately try to instil their own values about consumption in their children ('You're going to learn the value of the pound/euro'). Parents also determine the degree to which their children will be exposed to other information sources, such as television, salespeople and peers.[60] Grown-ups serve as significant models for observational learning (see Chapter 6). Children learn about consumption by watching their parents' behaviour and imitating it. This modelling is facilitated by marketers who package adult products in child-friendly versions.

The process of consumer socialisation begins with infants, who accompany their parents to shops where they are initially exposed to marketing stimuli. Within the first two years of life, children begin to make requests for desired objects. As children learn to walk, they also begin to make their own selections when they are out shopping. By the age of five, most children are making purchases with the help of parents and grandparents, and by eight most are making independent purchases and have become fully fledged consumers (Figure 10.3).[61]

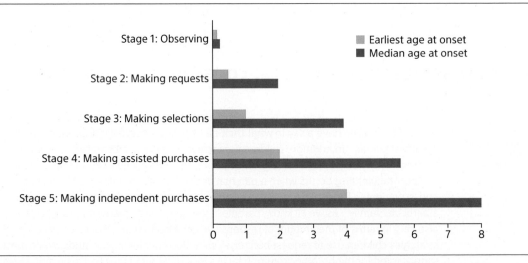

Figure 10.3 Five stages of consumer development by earliest age at onset and median age at onset

By eight years old children have become capable of making certain consumption choices and are independent consumers in parts of the marketplace. This picture captures perfectly a young consumer making choices and is an example of early decision-making by children.

Paha_l/123RF

Marketing pitfall

Three dimensions combine to produce different 'segments' of parental styles. Parents characterised by certain styles have been found to socialise their children differently.[62] 'Authoritarian parents', who are hostile, restrictive and emotionally uninvolved, do not have warm relationships with their children, are active in filtering the types of media to which their children are exposed and tend to have negative views about advertising. 'Neglecting parents' also do not have warm relationships, but they are more detached from their children and exercise little control over what their children do. In contrast, 'indulgent parents' communicate more with their children about consumption-related matters and are less restrictive. They believe that children should be allowed to learn about the marketplace without much interference. Along these lines, one study found that kids whose parents use products to shape behaviour are more likely to be materialistic as adults.[63]

Influence of television and social media

It is no secret that children watch television and use social media a lot. As a result, they are constantly bombarded with messages about consumption, both contained in commercials and in the TV programmes themselves. Television and social media teach people about a culture's values and myths. The more a child is exposed to television, whether the programme is a local 'soap' or Disney's blockbuster *Frozen,* the more they will accept the images depicted there as 'real'.[64] Without question, advertising starts to influence us at a very early age. As we've seen, many marketers push their products to kids to encourage them to build a lifelong habit. The National Institute of Health projects that a ban on fast-food advertising to children would cut the national obesity rate by as much as 18 per cent.[65] In two studies, British researchers compared the effects of television advertising on the eating habits of 152 children between the ages of 5 and 11. The children watched 10 ads followed by a cartoon. In one session, the children saw ads for toys before they watched a video. In another session, the researchers replaced the toy ads with food ads that commonly run during children's programmes. After both viewings, held two weeks apart, the children were allowed to snack as much as they wanted from a table of low-fat and high-fat snacks, including grapes, cheese-flavoured rice cakes, chocolate buttons and potato chips. The 5–7-year-old kids who saw the

This picture of a young woman from the Far East captures the impact of technology on children's consumer behaviour in today's global world. Children receive numerous marketing messages via social media.

Christopher Stewart/Alamy Stock Photo

food ads ate 14–17 per cent more calories than those who saw the toy ads. The results were even more dramatic among 9–11-year-olds. Those in the food ad condition ate between 84 and 134 per cent more calories than did those in the toy ad condition.[66] In the Netherlands, programmes have been developed to give children under the age of 12 'advertising lessons', in order to teach young children to develop a critical eye towards the messages and visuals in commercials.[67] A recent social-marketing campaign in Amsterdam has tackled the issue of obesity in children, trying to change both eating habits and patterns of (in)activity – with some success, as the city reported a drop of 12 per cent between 2012 and 2015 in the number of overweight and obese children.[68]

Social marketing challenge

'Some of the policies Amsterdam is using to crack obesity:

- a ban on bringing juice to schools and focus investment in more water fountains around the city;

- cooking classes to teach healthy varieties of ethnic dishes: pizzas with a broccoli base, kebabs with lean chicken instead of pork, honey and dates substituted for sugar;

- city refusal to sponsor any event joint-funded by a fast-food company;
- parents encouraged to put small children on bikes without pedals instead of wheeling them in buggies;
- focus on the first 1,000 days of a child's life, including counselling for pregnant women and mothers;
- families encouraged to eat dinner together;
- sports-centre membership and activities subsidised for low-income families.'[69]

Sex-role socialisation

Children pick up on the concept of gender identity at an earlier age than was previously believed – perhaps as young as the age of one or two. By the age of three, most children categorise driving a truck as masculine and cooking and cleaning as feminine.[70] Even cartoon characters who are portrayed as helpless are more likely to wear frilly or ruffled dresses.[71] Toy companies perpetuate these stereotypes by promoting gender-linked toys with commercials that reinforce sex-role expectations through their casting, emotional tone and copy.[72]

One function of child's play is to rehearse for adulthood. Children 'act out' different roles they might assume later in life and learn about the expectations others have of them. The toy industry provides the props children use to perform these roles.[73] Depending on which side of the debate you are on, these toys either reflect or teach children about what society expects of males versus females. While pre-school boys and girls do not exhibit many differences in toy preferences, after the age of five they part company: girls tend to stick with dolls, while boys gravitate towards 'action figures' and high-tech diversions. Industry critics charge that this is because the toy industry is dominated by males, while toy company executives counter that they are simply responding to children's natural preferences.[74] A campaign 'Let Toys be Toys'[75] has successfully persuaded about a dozen major UK retailers (including Marks and Spencer and Boots) to remove 'boys' and 'girls' signage from their toy departments.[76]

Consumer behaviour as I see it . . .

Gender, gender identity and consumer behaviour

Professor Pauline Maclaran
Royal Holloway University of London

'Gender is an important dynamic in consumer behaviour and I'm sure we have all found ourselves making purchases to reinforce our sense of gender identity. In this respect we are often helped by the many brands that have well-known gender connotations as, for example, Harley Davidson with masculinity or American Girl with femininity. Indeed, the term "the pink pound" is used to describe the thriving marketplace that has arisen around gay identities. But just as marketers can legitimate certain gender identities, so they can also reinforce traditional gender norms that stereotype or even marginalise some groups. In the past this has been a big problem, especially in relation to the representation of female consumers in advertising. Typically, images emphasized women as housewives, immersed in domestic duties or caring for their families when, of course, they were not being depicted as decorative sex objects! Men on the other hand were portrayed in more professional, commanding and confident roles.

Although such stereotypical imagery can still be found, most savvy marketers have long (1990s onwards) recognized the need to redress such images and keep up with the changing role of women in society, especially their spending power. Consequently nowadays, images of female empowerment abound in advertising, as well as more nuanced portrayals of different masculinities. Take, for example, the metrosexual who cares about fashion and how he looks, a type of masculinity that clearly defies traditional notions of what it means to be a man.

Despite these advances, it's fair to say that media forms in popular culture – and advertising is one of these – still have a long way to go to truly represent the gender diversity in our society. There is still an overriding emphasis on opposite sex relationships (male/female) rather than lesbian, gay, transgender or bi-sexual relationships. And in terms of representing the family, marketers still lag behind, with representations of the nuclear family (mother, father plus two kids) still dominant despite the fact that the family unit has changed radically in recent years with many permutations of divorced,

single parent or same sex couples with or without children. Recognising these changes can give marketers a competitive edge. For example, nursery chain Mamas & Papas challenged traditional family representations in an innovative campaign that depicted same sex couples and single parents.

Challenges like these to societal gender norms are a type of resignification of meaning because they disrupt the continual repetition of the status quo (i.e., the idea of the nuclear family and the naturalization of opposite sex desire). In a recent study I did with Cele Otnes we looked at how the TV series *Elementary* (based on Sherlock Holmes) defies expected gender norms, particularly with the casting of a female (Joan) Watson, played by Lucy Liu as well as a transgender Ms Hudson, Sherlock's famous housekeeper.[77] Over time such resignifications can influence societal gender norms and help to collapse binary divisions of masculinity and femininity. In turn, this paves the way for more inclusive representations of consumer diversity.

Question

Find an advertisement that you believe reinforces in some way gender norms. In what ways do you think that resignifications could be incorporated to challenge these norms?

Cognitive development

The ability of children to make mature, 'adult' consumer decisions obviously increases with age (not that grown-ups always make mature decisions). Children can be segmented by age in terms of their **stage of cognitive development**, or ability to comprehend concepts of increasing complexity. Some recent evidence indicates that young children are able to learn consumption-related information surprisingly well, depending on the format in which the information is presented (for instance, learning is enhanced if a video-taped vignette is presented to small children repeatedly).[78]

The foremost proponent of the idea that children pass through distinct stages of **cognitive development** was the Swiss psychologist Jean Piaget, who believed that each stage is characterised by a certain cognitive structure the child uses to handle information.[79] In one classic demonstration of cognitive development, Piaget poured the contents of a short, squat glass of lemonade into a taller, thinner glass. Five-year-olds, who still believed that the shape of the glass determined its contents, thought this glass held more liquid than the first glass. They are in what Piaget termed a *pre-operational stage of development.* In contrast, six-year-olds tended to be unsure, but seven-year-olds knew the amount of lemonade had not changed.

Many developmental specialists no longer believe that children necessarily pass through these fixed stages at the same time. An alternative approach regards children as differing in information-processing capability, or the ability to store and retrieve information from memory (see Chapter 6). The following three segments have been identified by this approach:[80]

- *Limited.* Below the age of six, children do not employ storage and retrieval strategies.
- *Cued.* Children between the ages of six and twelve employ these strategies, but only when prompted.
- *Strategic.* Children aged twelve and older spontaneously employ storage and retrieval strategies.

This sequence of development underscores the notion that children do not think like adults, and they cannot be expected to use information in the same way. It also reminds us that they do not necessarily form the same conclusions as adults when presented with product information. For example, children are not as likely to realise that something they see on television is not 'real', and as a result they are more vulnerable to persuasive messages. The remaining section of this chapter considers the role that age plays in our consumption, but from the perspective of how age groups (cohorts) influence our behaviours, and how consumers from different generations truly differ in their approaches to consumption.

Age and consumer identity

10.5

We have many things in common with others because they are about the same age (age cohorts).

The era in which a consumer grows up creates for that person a cultural bond with the millions of others born during the same time period. As we grow older, our needs and preferences change, often in unison with others who are close to our own age. For this reason, a consumer's age exerts a significant influence on their identity. All things being equal, we are more likely than not to have things in common with others of our own age. In the remaining section of this chapter, we explore some of the important characteristics of some key age groups and consider how marketing strategies must be modified to appeal to diverse age subcultures.

Age cohorts: 'my generation'

An **age cohort** consists of people of similar ages who have undergone similar experiences. They share many common memories about cultural heroes (e.g. Clint Eastwood *vs* Zac Efron, or Frank Sinatra *vs* Kurt Cobain *vs* Robert Pattinson), important historical or sporting events (e.g. the 1968 student demonstrations in Paris *vs* the fall of the Berlin Wall in 1989 *vs* the MeToo[81] movement in 2017 against harassment particularly in the workplace *vs* the Australian cricket ball tampering scandal, 2018[82]) and so on. Although there is no universally accepted way to divide people into age cohorts, each of us seems to have a pretty good idea of what we mean when we refer to 'my generation'. The age cohorts have been given various labels by market researchers, e.g. Baby boomers, Generation X, Generation Y and Millenials, which map approximately onto different age spans.[83]

Marketers often target products and services to one or more specific age cohorts. They recognise that the same offering will probably not appeal to people of different ages, nor will the language and images they use to reach them. In some cases, separate campaigns are developed to attract consumers of different ages. For example, travel agencies throughout Europe target youth markets during the months of May and June for low-cost summer holidays to Mallorca, and then target middle-aged, more affluent consumers for the same destination during September and October. What differs in the two campaigns are the media used, the images portrayed and the prices offered.

The appeal of nostalgia

Because consumers within an age group confront crucial life changes at roughly the same time, the values and symbolism used to appeal to them can evoke powerful feelings of nostalgia. Adults aged 30+ are particularly susceptible to this phenomenon.[84] However, young people as well as old are influenced by references to their past. In fact, research indicates that some people are more disposed to be nostalgic than others, regardless of age.

Product sales can be dramatically affected by linking a brand to vivid memories and experiences, especially for items that are associated with childhood or adolescence. Vespa scooters, Hornby electric trains and the coupon 'saving points' from Douwe Egberts coffee are all examples of products that have managed to span two or more generations of loyal consumers, giving the brand a strong equity position in competitive and crowded markets.

Many advertising campaigns have played on the collective memories of consumers by using older celebrities to endorse their products, such as campaigns by Hendrick's Gin and Baileys Original Irish Cream.[85] To assess just how pervasive nostalgia is, pay attention to television commercials and notice how often they are produced against a background of 'classic songs'. *Memories* magazine, which was founded to exploit the nostalgia boom, even offers advertisers a discount if they run old ads next to their current ones.

The teen market

10.6
Teens are a critically important age segment for marketers.

With a spending capacity of more than 61 billion euros per year, the European youth market of teens is a powerful demographic and an important culture to understand intimately for businesses looking to grow and maintain relevancy in the future. In 1956 the label 'teenage' first entered the (American) vocabulary, as Frankie Lymon and the Teenagers became the first pop group to identify themselves with this new subculture. The concept of teenager is a post-World War II cultural construction; throughout most of history a person simply made the transition from child to adult (often accompanied by some sort of ritual or ceremony, as we will see in a later chapter). As anyone who has been there knows, puberty and adolescence can be both the best of times and the worst of times. Many exciting changes happen as individuals leave the role of child and prepare to assume the role of adult. These changes create a lot of uncertainty about the self, and the need to belong and to find one's unique identity as a person becomes extremely important. At this age, choices of activities, friends and 'looks' are crucial to social acceptance. Teenagers actively search for cues from their peers and from advertising for the 'right' way to look and behave. Advertising geared to teenagers is typically action-oriented and depicts a group of 'in' teenagers using the product. Teenagers use products to express their identities, to explore the world and their new-found freedom in it, and also to rebel against the authority of their parents and other socialising agents. Marketers often do their best to assist in this process. The range of consumer products targeted at teenagers (and particularly younger ones) is greater than ever. Then again, so is teenagers' disposable income from part-time jobs and weekly pocket money.[86]

Teenagers in every culture grapple with fundamental developmental issues when they transition from childhood to adulthood. Throughout history, young people have coped with insecurity, parental authority and peer pressure (although each generation has trouble believing it's not the first!). According to Teenage Research Unlimited, the five most important social issues for teens are AIDS, race relations, child abuse, abortion and the environment. Today's teens often have to cope with additional family responsibilities as well, especially if they live in non-traditional families where they have significant responsibility for shopping, cooking and housework. It's hard work being a teen in the modern world. The Saatchi & Saatchi advertising agency identified four basic conflicts common to all teens:

1 *Autonomy vs belonging*. Teenagers need to acquire independence, so they try to break away from their families. On the other hand, they need to attach themselves to a support

structure, such as peers, to avoid being alone. A thriving internet subculture has developed to serve this purpose, as has text messaging via mobile phones.[87] The internet (worldwide Web) has become the preferred method of communication for many young people, since its anonymity makes it easier to talk to people of the opposite sex, or of different ethnic and racial groups.[88]

2 *Rebellion vs conformity.* Teenagers need to rebel against social standards of appearance and behaviour, yet they still need to fit in and be accepted by others. Cult products that cultivate a rebellious image are prized for this reason.

3 *Idealism vs pragmatism.* Teenagers tend to view adults as hypocrites, while they see themselves as being sincere. They have to struggle to reconcile their view of how the world should be with the realities they perceive around them.

4 *Narcissism vs intimacy.* Teenagers can be obsessed with their appearance and needs. On the other hand, they also feel the desire to connect with others on a meaningful level.[89]

Marketers have a difficult time 'defining' the values of today's European teens, perhaps because they are living in such socially dynamic and demanding times. A study among 500 young opinion leaders aged 14–20 across 16 European countries suggests that this age group's credo should be: 'Don't define us – we'll define ourselves'. Respondents were asked their opinions on a wide range of subjects, from new technology to family relationships, divorce, drugs, alcohol, politics, fashion, entertainment, sex and advertising. Some of the highlights of this study are:[90]

- Living life to the 'fullest' is mandatory; ambition drives them, as does the fear of failure. Young Eastern Europeans strongly believe that hard work will give them a higher standard of living and that education is their passport to this better life.

- They perceive the 'digitised' future as one that lacks warmth – something Europe's teenagers, a divorce-experienced generation, is actively seeking.

- Immersive and engaging technology that allows for '24-hour commerce' will lead to further stress for this generation, and a blurring of home/office means they will work longer and harder than any previous generation.

- This is a very visually literate generation, with a clear understanding of an advertising commercial's aims. Clichés will not be tolerated, and will lead to immediate rejection, particularly in the Nordic countries. Only Eastern European teens have yet to develop this level of 'advertising cynicism'.

- This generation is both brand-aware and brand-dismissive. It represents an opportunity, but not a homogeneous market. The successful marketer will be aware that, for these consumers, an aspirational quality is essential, that heritage is an advantage and that nothing is forever.

'Generation X' (or 'Baby Busters' or 'Slackers')

The cohort of consumers born between 1966 and 1976 consists of over 30 million Europeans and has been labelled 'Generation X', 'slackers' or 'busters'. They were profoundly affected by the economic downturn in the first part of the 1990s, and then again in the new/ongoing recession of 2012. So-called Generation X ('Gen-Xers') or baby busters include many people, both in and out of higher education, whose tastes and priorities are felt in fashion, popular culture, politics and marketing. While the percentage of Europeans in this age group is high in terms of completing upper secondary education (71 per cent), this group also had a large drop-out rate, with one in five Europeans between the ages of 18 and 24 leaving the education system without completing a qualification beyond lower secondary schooling.

This picture shows a mother and daughter sitting on sofa with other family members in the background. Is the daughter about to leave for university (and the parents are approaching the empty nest)? Or is the daughter back from university and about to return to the family home (boomerang children)?

Sirtravelalot/Shutterstock

Marketing to busters or marketing bust?

Although the income of this age cohort is below expectations, they still constitute a formidable market segment. Because many busters have been doing the family shopping for a long time, marketers are finding that they are far more sophisticated about evaluating advertising and products. They see advertising as a form of entertainment but are turned off by over-commercialisation.[91] They dislike advertising that either contains a lot of hype or takes itself too seriously. Gen-Xers are quite a diverse group – they don't all wear reversed baseball caps and work in temporary, low-paid, mindless jobs.

Baby boomers

Baby boomers continue to be the most powerful age segment economically in the EU.

The baby boomers cohort (born between 1946 and 1965, sometimes divided into two: 1946–54 and 1955–65) are the source of many fundamental cultural and economic changes. The reason: power in numbers. As the World War II ended, boomers' parents turned to new lives and began to establish families and careers at a record pace. Imagine a large python that has swallowed a mouse: the mouse moves down the length of the python, creating a moving bulge as it goes. So it is with baby boomers. In 2003 there were 76 million elderly people aged 65 and over in the (then) EU27 countries, compared with only 38 million in 1960. The ageing baby boomers, coupled with extended longevity and the overall lower fertility levels in the EU, means that the population will continue to grow older for the coming decades.[92]

The market impact of boomers

Figure 10.4 shows a series of age pyramids of the European population for all ages for the period from 2016 to 2080.[93] Over the next two or three decades, the high number of baby boomers will swell the number of elderly people. By 2080, the pyramid will take more the shape of a block, narrowing slightly in the middle of the pyramid (around the age 45–54 years) and then considerably near the base. This increase in the proportion of older citizens and decrease in the proportion of youth is often referred to as the 'greying and de-greening' of the European population – a structural trend that has major implications for the marketing of goods and services.

As teenagers in the 1960s and 1970s, this generation created a revolution in style, politics and consumer attitudes. As they have aged, their collective will has been behind cultural events as diverse as the Paris student demonstrations and the hippie movement in the 1960s,

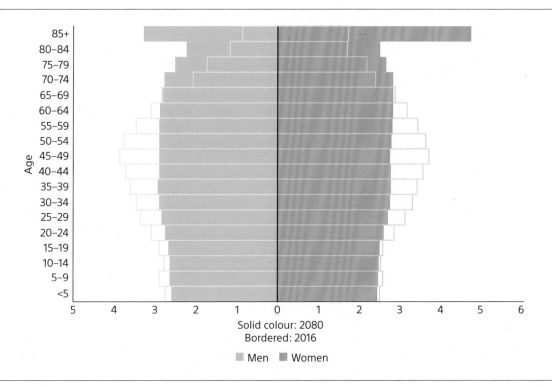

Figure 10.4 European Age Pyramids: Population pyramids, EU-28, 2016 and 2080 (% of the total population)

Source: Eurostat (online data codes: demo_pjangroup and proj_15npms), http://ec.europa.eu/eurostat/statistics-explained/index.php/
File:Population_pyramids,_EU-28,_2016_and_2080_(%25_of_the_total_population).png (accessed 1 August 2018).

and Thatcherism and yuppies in the 1980s. Now that they are older, they continue to influence popular culture in important ways, redefining 'chronological age' and what 'retirement' means.

This 'mouse in the python' is moving into its mid-fifties to early-seventies and is the age group that exerts an important impact on consumption patterns. Most of the growth in the market will be accounted for by people who are in – or starting to pass – their peak earning years. Boomers tend to have different emotional and psychological needs from those who came before them, and this is being played out again throughout European markets. Boomers are busy rethinking their role in 'retirement' (which is to say, new identities and new consumption activities). Boomers see themselves not so much in chronological age, but as simply entering into a new life stage that is full of new opportunities.[94]

However, many of these boomers are faced with a **boomerang generation** as their adult children return to live in the family home (often after completing their university education) because some millennials are unable to afford to live independently or gather the resources to get a start on the ladder of home ownership. 'Britain's millennial generation, born since 1981, have suffered a bigger reversal in financial fortunes than their counterparts in most other developed countries except Greece. . . the report by the Resolution Foundation[95] paints a gloomy picture for all young adults across the developed world – apart from the Nordic countries. It highlights how incomes are depressed, jobs scarce and home ownership is slumping for the millennial generation compared with the baby boomers that preceded them.'[96]

Another recent study found that 'couples who had enjoyed a new lease of life when their children flew the nest, with improved marital relationships and new hobbies, may regard their offspring's return as "a violation" of an exciting stage of their lives'.[97] The study authors argued that 'Returns to the parental home were associated with a decline in parents' QoL [quality of life] in Nordic countries where autonomy has a greater value and public support systems facilitate independence of younger and older family generations. By contrast, there was no association in Southern and Eastern European societies where people rely more on the family and shelter is an important form of support that parents provide to their adult children. . . we found that home returning had a less negative and non-significant association with parents' QoL in Southern Europe where an interplay between cultural systems and welfare institutions fosters family *interdependence.* However, we also found no associations in Western European societies where there is a higher heterogeneity in family attitudes and welfare state arrangements. Many other factors related to gender roles, care services and family cultures might explain these results. . .

We analysed transitions into unemployment and/or divorce/separation as possible confounding factors in the association between returns home and changes in parents' QoL. Parents' QoL decreased when a child became unemployed, and increased when a child started living with a partner. These findings are consistent with the concept of linked lives. . . However, these life course factors did not explain the decrease of parents' QoL associated with boomerang moves.'[98] However, a qualitative study painted a more optimistic picture, arguing that 'children coming home to live after university "enrich the whole family"'.[99]

Marketing opportunity
Boomerang children can be good for family relationships – study

'Boomerang children who return to live with their parents after university can be good for families, leading to closer, more supportive relationships and increased contact between the generations, a study has found. The findings contradict research published earlier this year [and discussed above] showing that returning adult children trigger a significant decline in their parents' quality of life and wellbeing. While no one is claiming that moving back into the family home after the freedom of university is free of tensions, the new study by the London School of Economics is more nuanced and finds there are "numerous advantages" for parents and children.

The young adults taking part in the study were "more positive than might have been expected" about moving back home – the stigma is reduced as so many of their peers are in the same position, and they acknowledged the benefits of their parents' financial and emotional support. Daughters were happier than sons, often slipping back easily into teenage patterns of behaviour, the study found. Parents on the whole were more ambivalent, expressing concern about the likely duration of the arrangement and how to manage it. But they acknowledged that things were different for graduates today, who leave university with huge debts and fewer opportunities.

The families featured in the study were middle-class and tended to view the achievement of adult independence for their children as a "family project". Parents accepted that their children required support as university students and then as graduates returning home, as they tried to find jobs paying enough to enable them to move out and get on the housing ladder.

But a key area of concern for the report's authors is that while middle-class children may benefit from the so-called boomerang trend, graduates from poorer backgrounds will not have access to the same financial support and will therefore be at greater disadvantage as they try to make their way in the world.

The parents in the study were aware of the implications for the "post-children" phase of their lives, but they recognised that their children needed a level of parental support that was not necessary when they themselves were entering adulthood. Their overwhelming response was: "I'm still your parent. I want to help." "However", the study says, "day-to-day tensions about the prospects of achieving different dimensions of independence, which in a few extreme cases came close to conflict, characterised the experience of a majority of parents and a little over half the graduates." Areas of disagreement included chores, money and social life. While parents were keen to help, they also wanted different relationships from those they had with their own parents, and continuing to support their adult children allowed them to remain close.

The study, 'Helicopter Parenting and Boomerang Children: How Parents Support and Relate to Their Student and Co-Resident Graduate Children', by Anne West and Jane Lewis, was based on interviews with 54 people – parents and graduate children who had lived with their parents for between three months and seven and a half years after returning from university.

While much of the focus of recent debate in this area has been about intergenerational inequality between baby-boomer parents and their less fortunate children, the study authors were also keen to highlight the dangers of intragenerational inequality.'[100]

The grey market

Seniors continue to increase in size and spending power as a market segment, and marketers are making more and better efforts to understand this segment.

The old widowed woman sits alone in her clean but sparsely furnished apartment, while the television blares out a soap opera. Each day, she slowly and painfully makes her way out of the apartment and goes to the corner shop to buy essentials – bread, milk and vegetables, always being careful to pick the least expensive offering. Most of the time she sits in her rocking chair, thinking sadly of her dead husband and the good times she used to have.

Is this the image you have of a typical elderly consumer? Until recently, many marketers did. As a result, they largely neglected the elderly in their feverish pursuit of the baby boomer market. But as our population ages and people are living longer and healthier lives, the game is rapidly changing as the boomers constitute an increasingly important part of the grey market. A lot of businesses are beginning to replace the old stereotype of the poor recluse. The newer, more accurate image is of an elderly person who is active, interested in what life has to offer and is an enthusiastic consumer with the means and willingness to buy many goods and services.

Grey power: shattering stereotypes

By 2020 the world will have 13 'super-aged' societies (where 20 per cent of the population is 65 or older). Most of these societies will be in Europe (Germany, Italy, the Netherlands, the UK, France, Sweden, Portugal, Slovenia and Croatia). This fastest-growing age segment can be explained by the ageing of 'boomers' and an increase in awareness of healthy lifestyles and nutrition, coupled with improved medical diagnoses and treatment. Over the past 50 years, the life expectancy of men and women has risen steadily by around 10 years for each sex. Throughout the EU, women live longer than men. Estimates are that the life expectancy of women and men may reach 84 and 78 years respectively by the year 2020.[101] Not only is this segment growing and living longer, but older adults have large amounts of discretionary income since, typically, they have paid off their mortgage and no longer have the expense of raising and educating children.

Most elderly people lead more active, multi-dimensional lives than we assume. Many engage in voluntary work, continue to work and/or are involved in daily care of a grandchild.

Seniors' economic clout

There is abundant evidence that the economic health of elderly consumers is good and getting better. Some of the important areas that stand to benefit from the surging **grey market** include holidays, cars, home improvements, cruises and tourism, cosmetic surgery and skin treatments, health, finance and legal matters and 'how-to' books for learning to cope with retirement.

It is crucial to remember that income alone does not capture the spending power of this group. As mentioned above, elderly consumers are no longer burdened with the financial obligations that drain the income of younger consumers. Elderly consumers are far more likely to own their home, have no mortgage or have a (low-cost or subsidised) rented house or apartment. Across Europe, approximately 50 per cent of pensioners' incomes still comes from state pensions, yet it is clear that older consumers are time-rich, and have a significant amount of discretionary income to spend. The relatively high living standards of future retirees (the baby boomers) and the stability of public finances (until the current economic climate, which has spurred such government policies as austerity in the UK) in different European states has led to an active discussion of pension reform plans throughout the EU. Nonetheless, pensions will continue to play an important role in the discretionary incomes of Europe's retired population. As a final note on the two major demographic trends in Europe, let's link together the 'greying' and the 'de-greening' populations. Figure 10.5 shows the dependency ratio of the number of people in the EU28 countries over the age of 65, relative to the number of people aged 15–64 (those who are theoretically still employed).[102] This will have significant implications for social security payments, and the offerings of goods and services.

Researchers have identified a set of key values that are relevant to older consumers. For marketing strategies to succeed, they should be related to one or more of these factors:[103]

- *Autonomy.* Mature consumers want to lead active lives and to be self-sufficient. Financial services and financial planning are increasing markets for the elderly segment, who have a strong need to remain independent. While companies are the largest purchasers of cars in the UK, the majority of private buyers are 'greys' – a further sign of their financial muscle and desire for autonomy.[104]

- *Connectedness.* Mature consumers value the bonds they have with friends and family. While the 'grey' do not relate well to their own age group (most elderly report feeling, on average, ten years younger than they are, and feel that 'other' elderly behave 'older' than they do), they do value information that communicates clear benefits to cohorts in their age group. Advertisements that avoid patronising stereotypes are well received.

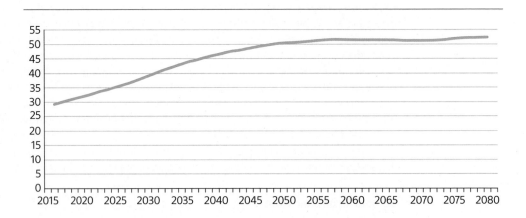

Figure 10.5 Projected old-age dependency ratio, EU-28, 2016–80 (%)

Source: Eurostat (online data codes: demo_pjanind and proj_15ndbims), http://ec.europa.eu/eurostat/statistics-explained/index.php/File:Projected_old-age_dependency_ratio,_EU-28,_2016-80_(%25).png (accessed 1 August 2018).

- *Altruism.* Mature consumers want to give something back to the world. Thrifty Car Rental found in a survey that over 40 per cent of older consumers would select a rental car company if it sponsored a programme that gives discounts to senior citizens' centres. Based on this research, the company launched its highly successful 'Give a Friend a Lift' programme.
- *Personal growth.* Mature consumers are very interested in trying new experiences and developing their potential. By installing user-friendly interactive touch-screen computer stations in European stores, the health retailer GNC has found that older consumers have become better-educated about health issues and are loyal to the brand.[105]

Perceived age: you're only as old as you feel

The 'grey' market does not consist of a uniform segment of vigorous, happy, ready-to-spend consumers – nor is it a group of senile, economically marginalised, immobile people. In fact, research confirms the popular wisdom that age is more a state of mind than of body. A person's mental outlook and activity level has a lot more to do with their longevity and quality of life than does *chronological age,* or the actual number of years lived. In addition to these psychological dimensions of age, there are also cultural influences on what constitutes ageing, and perceptions of what is 'elderly' across different European markets.[106]

A better yardstick to categorise the elderly is **perceived age**, or how old a person *feels.* Perceived age can be measured on several dimensions, including 'feel-age' (how old a person feels) and 'look-age' (how old a person looks).[107] The older consumers get, the younger they feel relative to actual age. For this reason, many marketers emphasise product benefits rather than age appropriateness in marketing campaigns, since many consumers will not relate

Saga Magazine in the UK (targeted at over-50s) is the best-selling monthly subscription magazine with over 25,000 subscribers
Source: ABC 255-544 January-June 2018
Entertainment Press/Shutterstock

to products targeted to their chronological age.[108] A study investigated what the authors call **consumer identity renaissance**; this refers to the redefinition process people undergo when they retire. The research identified two different types of identity renaissance: *revived* (revitalisation of previous identities) or *emergent* (pursuit of entirely new life projects). Even though many retirees cope with losses (of professional identity, spouses and so on), many of them focus on moving forward. They engage in a host of strategies to do this, including *affiliation,* where they reconnect with family members and friends (in many cases online), and *self-expression.* This latter strategy may involve revisiting an activity they never had time to adequately pursue when they were younger, learning new skills, or perhaps moving into an urban area to re-engage with cultural activities.[109]

Marketing pitfall

Some marketing efforts targeted at the elderly have backfired because they reminded people of their age or presented their age group in an unflattering way. One of the more infamous blunders was committed by Heinz. A company analyst found that many elderly people were buying baby food because of the small portions and easy chewing consistency, so Heinz introduced a line of 'Senior Foods' made especially for denture wearers. Needless to say, the product failed. Consumers did not want to admit that they required strained foods (even to the supermarket cashier). They preferred to purchase baby foods, which they could pretend they were buying for a grandchild.

In the Netherlands, a country where bicycles are an important mode of personal transportation, a specially designed 'elderly bicycle' was a resounding failure in spite of its competitive product benefits. While conventional marketing wisdom would suggest that a firm communicate its unique functional benefits to a target market, this wisdom backfired for the Dutch 'greys'. Positioning the bicycle as an easy-to-pedal 'senior bicycle' was met with a negative response, as the Dutch elderly who still ride a bicycle (a common sight in Holland) feel too young to be riding a 'senior' bike.[110]

Segmenting seniors

The senior subculture represents an extremely large market: the number of Europeans aged 62 and over exceeds the entire population of Canada.[111] Because this group is so large, it is helpful to think of the mature market as consisting of four sub-segments: an 'older' group (aged 55–64), an 'elderly' group (aged 65–74), an 'aged' group (aged 75–84) and finally a 'very old' group (85+).[112]

The senior market is well suited for segmentation. Older consumers are easy to identify by age and stage in the family life cycle. Most receive social security benefits, so they can be located without much effort, and many subscribe to one of the magazines targeted to the elderly. *Saga Magazine* in the UK has over 255,000 monthly readers. Selling holidays and insurance to the over-50s, the parent company also makes use of a database with over 4 million over-50s.

Several segmentation approaches begin with the premise that a major determinant of elderly marketplace behaviour is the way a person deals with being old.[113] *Social ageing theories* try to understand how society assigns people to different roles across the lifespan. For example, when someone retires they may reflect society's expectations for someone at this life stage – this is a major transition point when people exit from many relationships.[114] Some people become depressed, withdrawn and apathetic as they age, some are angry and resist the thought of ageing and some appear to accept the new challenges and opportunities this period of life has to offer.

In general, the elderly have been shown to respond positively to ads that provide an abundance of information. Unlike other age groups, these consumers are not usually amused, or persuaded, by imagery-oriented advertising. A more successful strategy involves the construction of advertising that depicts the aged as well-integrated, contributing members of society, with emphasis on them expanding their horizons rather than clinging precariously to life.

Effective ways of reaching this segment of older consumers include taking account of the following:[115]

'Rather than using age definitions, understanding senior citizens and developing promotional efforts on the basis of lifestyles, attitudes, interests, self-perceptions of age and aging, social roles, relative physical health, employment status and degree of social isolation has been . . . fruitful [for marketers and their promotional campaigns] . . . The great majority of senior citizens tend to be active, independent, learning, growing psychologically, socially and spiritually, productive and interested in a wide variety of products and services . . . As older consumers' interests, desires, behavior and purchasing patterns have become better understood, the senior market has become particularly attractive to certain industries. For example, the travel industry . . . Market researchers have discovered that older consumers also seek material possessions, particularly products and services that will keep them healthy and active . . . Because they are less peer-conscious, older consumers are less responsive to advertising appeals that emphasize status or what is fashionable. Special promotions that include discounts for senior citizens have proven effective in many instances . . . More important in building brand loyalty in the senior market are objectivity in advertising, attention to customer service, speed, convenience and a personal touch. Some have found older consumers particularly responsive to advertising containing testimonials . . . Increasingly, marketers are also tailoring their media plans to senior citizens. Older people read newspapers more often than their younger counterparts . . . As the 21st century began, most marketers and agencies were becoming aware that older consumers comprised a very diverse, greatly expanding, potentially highly profitable market. The[y] . . . were better-educated consumers than their predecessors and were more interested in cultural activities and an active lifestyle.'

Chapter summary

Now that you have finished reading this chapter you should understand why:

10.1 **Marketers often need to understand consumers' behavior, rather than a consumer's behaviour.** Collective decision-making occurs whenever two or more people are involved in evaluating, selecting or using a product or service.

10.2 **Our traditional notions about families are outdated; many important demographic dimensions of a population relate to family and household structure.** Some of the most important of these relate to family structure, e.g. the birth rate, the marriage rate and the divorce rate. In Europe, collecting reliable and comparable data regarding the family unit has not always been a straightforward process.

- **A household is an occupied housing unit.** The number and type of European households is changing in many ways – for example, through delays in getting married and having children and in the composition of family households, which increasingly are headed by a single parent. New perspectives on the family life cycle, which focus on how people's needs change as they move through different stages in their lives, are forcing marketers to consider more seriously such consumer segments as homosexuals, divorcees and childless couples when they develop targeting strategies.

10.3 Members of a family unit play different roles and have different amounts of influence when the family makes purchase decisions. Spouses, in particular, have different priorities and exert varying amounts of influence in terms of effort and power. Children are also increasingly influential during a widening range of purchase decisions.

10.4 Children learn over time what and how to consume. Some of this knowledge is instilled by parents and friends, but a lot of it comes from exposure to mass media and advertising. Since children are, in some cases, so easily persuaded, the ethical aspects of marketing to them are hotly debated among consumers, academics and marketing practitioners.

10.5 We have many things in common with others because they are about the same age (age cohorts). Consumers who grew up at the same time share many cultural memories, so they may respond to marketers' nostalgia appeals that remind them of these experiences.

10.6 Teens are a critically important age segment for marketers. Teenagers are making a transition from childhood to adulthood, and their self-concepts tend to be unstable. They are receptive to products that help them to be accepted and enable them to assert their independence. Because many teenagers receive allowances and/or earn pocket money, but have few financial obligations, they are a particularly important segment for many non-essential or expressive products, ranging from chewing gum to hair gel, to clothing fashions and music. Because of changes in family structure, many teenagers are taking more responsibility for their families' day-to-day shopping and routine purchase decisions.

- **'Generation X-ers', consumers born between 1966 and 1976, are a difficult group for marketers to 'get a clear picture of'.** They were affected by the economic downturn following the market crash in 2008. Their tastes and priorities are felt in fashion, popular culture, politics and marketing.

10.7 Baby boomers continue to be the most powerful age segment economically in the EU. As this group has aged, its interests have changed and marketing priorities have changed as well. The needs and desires of baby boomers have a strong influence on demands for housing, childcare, cars, clothing and so on. Only a small proportion of boomers fit into an affluent, materialistic category. However, many of their children's opportunities in the job and housing market have been severely affected (the boomerang generation – millennials).

10.8 Seniors continue to increase in size and spending power as a market segment, and marketers are making more and better efforts to understand this segment. Many marketers traditionally ignored the elderly because of the stereotype that they are inactive and spend too little. This stereotype is no longer accurate. Most of the elderly are healthy, vigorous and interested in new products and experiences – and they have the consumers' self-concepts and perceived ages, which tend to be more youthful than their chronological ages. Marketers should emphasise the concrete benefits of products, since this group tends to be sceptical of vague, image-related promotions. Personalised service is of particular importance to this segment.

Key terms

Accommodative purchase decision (p. 401)
Age cohort (p. 409)
Autocratic decisions (p. 402)
Boomerang generation (p. 413)
Cognitive development (p. 408)

Consensual purchase decision (p. 401)
Consumer identity renaissance (p. 418)
Consumer socialisation (p. 404)
Extended family (p. 396)
Family financial officer (FFO) (p. 402)

Consumer behaviour challenge

1 Review a number of popular media that are published in countries in southern Europe, as well as media targeted for northern European countries. How do the ads' depictions of *family* seem to differ by region? In what sorts of consumption situations do they seem largely similar? Why?

2 For each of the following five product categories – groceries, cars, holidays, furniture and appliances – describe the ways in which you believe a married couple's choices would be affected if they had children.

3 In identifying and targeting newly divorced couples, do you think marketers are exploiting these couples' situations? Are there instances where you think marketers may actually be helpful to them? Support your answers with examples.

4 Arrange to interview two married couples, one younger and one older. Prepare a response form listing five product categories – groceries, furniture, appliances, holidays and cars – and ask each spouse to indicate, without consulting the other, whether purchases in each category are made by joint or unilateral decisions and to indicate whether the unilateral decisions are made by the husband or the wife. Compare each couple's responses for agreement between husbands and wives relative to who makes the decisions, and compare both couples' overall responses for differences relative to the number of joint versus unilateral decisions. Report your findings and conclusions.

5 Collect ads for three different product categories in which the family is targeted. Find another set of ads for different brands of the same items in which the family is not featured. Prepare a report on the effectiveness of the approaches.

6 Observe the interactions between parents and children in the breakfast cereal section of a local supermarket. Prepare a report on the number of children who expressed preferences, how they expressed their preferences and how parents responded, including the number who purchased the child's choice.

7 Select a product category and, using the life cycle stages given in the text, list the variables that will affect a purchase decision for the product by consumers in each stage of the cycle.

8 Consider three important changes in modern European family structure. For each, find an example of a marketer who has attempted to be conscious of this change as reflected in product communications, retailing innovations or other aspects of the marketing mix. If possible, also try to find examples of marketers who have failed to keep up with these developments.

9 Why did baby boomers have such an important impact on consumer culture in the second half of the twentieth century?

10 How has the baby boomlet changed attitudes towards child-rearing practices and created demand for different products and services?

11 Is it practical to assume that people aged 55 and older constitute one large consumer market? What are some approaches to further segmenting this age subculture?

12 What are some important variables to keep in mind when tailoring marketing strategies to the elderly?

13 Find good and bad examples of advertising targeted at elderly consumers. To what degree does advertising stereotype the elderly? What elements of ads or other promotions appear to determine their effectiveness in reaching and persuading this group?

For additional material see the companion website at **www.pearsoned.co.uk/solomon**

Notes

1. https://www.whychristmas.com/cultures/holland.shtml (accessed 1 August 2018).

2. http://ec.europa.eu/eurostat/statistics-explained/index.php/Population_and_population_change_statistics (accessed 1 August 2018).

3. For an excellent summary of the key issues relating to families and family life in the EU, along with associated graphs extracted from Eurostat statistics, see Livia Sz. Oláh, 'Changing families in the European Union: Trends and policy implications, analytical paper prepared for the United Nations Expert Group Meeting, 'Family policy development: Achievements and challenges', New York (May 14-15 2015), http://www.un.org/esa/socdev/family/docs/egm15/Olahpaper.pdf (accessed 1 August 2018).

4. Livia Sz. Oláh, op. cit. Her references included J. Lewis, 'Gender and welfare in modern Europe: Past and present', Suppl 1 in *The Art of Survival: Gender and History in Europe, 1450-2000* (2006): 39–54; and C. Saraceno (ed.), *Families, Ageing and Social Policy: Intergenerational Solidarity in European Welfare States* (Cheltenham: UK, Edward Elgar, 2008).

5. For an excellent overview of the academic debates about studying and understanding family, families and family life, see the introduction to the e-Special Issue of *Sociology* (2018) on 'Families and Relationships' edited by Vanessa May and Matt Dawson, and the associated articles that they discuss (pages 1–10); and also their detailed bibliography, http://journals.sagepub.com/doi/abs/10.1177/0038038518760427 (accessed 1 August 2018).

6. Vanessa May and Matt Dawson, 'Introduction to e-Special Issue on Families and Relationships', *Sociology* (2018): 8; and their references: J. Finch, 'Displaying families', *Sociology* 41(1) (2007): 65–81; J. Finch and J. Mason, *Negotiating Family Responsibilities* (London: Routledge, 1993); L. Jamieson, 'Intimacy transformed? A critical look at the "pure relationship"', *Sociology* 33(3) (1999): 477–94; D. Morgan, *Family Connections: An Introduction to Family Studies* (Cambridge: Polity Press, 1996); C. Smart, *Personal Life: New Directions in Sociological Thinking* (Cambridge: Polity Press, 2007); J. Weeks, B. Heaphy and C. Donovan, *Same Sex Intimacies* (London: Routledge, 2001).

7. T. Eggerickx and F. Bégeot, 'Les recensements en Europe dans les années 1990. De la diversité des pratiques nationales à la comparabilité internationales des résulats', *Population* 41(2) (1993): 327–48. Standardisation efforts continue. See Eurostat website for variety of statistics and information about EU, 28 http://ec.europa.eu/eurostat/statistics-explained/index.php/Main_Page (accessed 1 August 2018); see also Eurostat website for 2017 edition of *The Life of Women and Men in Europe: A Statistical Portrait*, http://ec.europa.eu/eurostat/cache/infographs/womenmen/wide-menu.html?lang=en (accessed 1 August 2018); see as well 'People in the EU: Statistics on Household and Family Structures' for analysis based on 2017 data, http://ec.europa.eu/eurostat/statisticsexplained/index.php/People_in_the_EU_%E2%80%93_statistics_on_household_and_family_structures#Families (accessed 1 August 2018).

8. Robert Boutilier, 'Diversity in family structures', *American Demographics Marketing Tools* (1993): 4–6; W. Bradford Fay, 'Families in the 1990s: Universal values, uncommon experiences', *Marketing Research* 5(1) (Winter 1993): 47.

9. Amber M. Epp and Linda L. Price, 'Family identity: A framework of identity interplay in consumption practices', *Journal of Consumer Research* (June 2008): 50–70; see also David Cheal, 'The ritualization of family ties', *American Behavioral Scientist* 31 (July/August 1988): 632.

10. 'Women and men in the European Union: A statistical portrait' (Luxembourg: Office for Official Publications of the European Communities, 1996); 'Families come first', *Psychology Today* (September 1988): 11.

11. 'Families with children in the EU' Source Eurostat, http://ec.europa.eu/eurostat/web/products-eurostat-news/-/EDN-20170531-1?ticket=ST-15846581-83zehqBMbtePwdVmwClyFA1zPMq7lkSzsEFqmvFaCovWqaYatypdp5VXddzx566DSXbgJuzlwzozmJYzykBjfyKW-PHslUMVSXY-C6iO06UxAkYy-iaKcx2Twkzq8jEm3SIqvQHdzsybqjxGjREyciHapJllWTop of Form (accessed 1 August 2018).

12. Alan R. Andreasen, 'Life status changes and changes in consumer preferences and satisfaction', *Journal of Consumer Research* 11 (December 1984): 784–94; James H. McAlexander, John W. Schouten and Scott D. Roberts, 'Consumer behavior and divorce', *Research in Consumer Behavior* 6 (1993): 153–84.

13. Europe in Figures, *Eurostat Yearbook 2011,* p. 129. See also: 'Men and women in the European Union: A statistical portrait' (Luxembourg: Office for Official Publications of the European Communities, 1995); 'The big picture', *American Demographics* (March 1989): 22–7; Thomas G. Exter, 'Middle-aging households', *American Demographics* (July 1992): 63.

14. 'Trends in households in the European Union: 1995–2025', *Eurostat, Statistics in Focus,* Theme 3-24/2003 (Luxembourg: Office for Official Publications of the European Communities, 2004).

15. http://ec.europa.eu/eurostat/tgm/table.do?tab=table&init=1&language=en&pcode=tps00199&plugin=1 (accessed 1 August 2018).

16. Natalie Angier, 'The changing American family', *New York Times* (25 November 2013), http://www.nytimes.com/2013/11/26/health/families.html?_r=0 (accessed 1 August 2018); Erik Eckholm, '07 U.S. Births Break Baby Boom Record', *New York Times* (18 March 2009), www.nytimes.com/2009/03/19/health/19birth.html?_r=1 (accessed 1 August 2018).

17. 'The population of the EU on 1 January, 1995', *Statistics in Focus. Population and Social Conditions,* 8 (Luxembourg: Office for Official Publications of the European Communities, 1995); see also *The Life of Women and Men in Europe: A Statistical Portrait,* Eurostat statistical book, published in 2008 and based largely on 2006 data, http://ec.europa.eu/eurostat/documents/3217494/5698400/KS-80-07-135-EN.PDF/101b2bc8-03f8-4f49-b4e4-811fff81b174 (accessed 1 August 2018); Nicholas Timmins, 'One in five women to remain childless', *The Independent* (4 October 1995).

18. http://ec.europa.eu/eurostat/tgm/table.do?tab=table&init=1&language=en&pcode=tps00199&plugin=1 (accessed 1 August 2018).

19. http://ec.europa.eu/eurostat/cache/infographs/womenmen/bloc-1a.html?lang=en (accessed 1 August 2018).

20. http://ec.europa.eu/eurostat/tgm/table.do?tab=table&init=1&language=en&pcode=tps00199&plugin=1 (accessed 1 August 2018).

21. Russell Shorto (2008), 'No babies?', *New York Times* (29 June 2008), http://www.nytimes.com/2008/06/29/maga zine/29Birth-t.html?_r=2&oref=slogin&oref=slogin (accessed 1 August 2018).

22. Tracy McVeigh, 'Why men still won't get their hands dirty at home', *The Guardian* (12 March 2017), https://www. theguardian.com/lifeandstyle/2017/mar/12/house-work-men-assert-masculinity (accessed 1 August 2018); see also Tanja van der Lippe Judith Treas & Lukas Norbutas, 'Unemployment and the division of housework in Europe', *Work, Employment and Society* (March 2017): 1–20, http:// journals.sagepub.com/doi/full/10.1177/0950017017690495 (accessed 1 August 2018).

23. 'Men and women in the European Union: A statistical portrait', op. cit.: 72.

24. Peg Masterson, 'Agency notes rise of singles market', *Advertising Age* (9 August 1993): 17.

25. Christy Fisher, 'Census data may make ads more single minded', *Advertising Age* (20 July 1992): 2.

26. Calmetta Y. Coleman, 'The unseemly secrets of eating alone', *The Wall Street Journal* (6 July 1995): B1 (2).

27. Stephanie Shipp, 'How singles spend', *American Demographics* (April 1988): 22–7; Patricia Braus, 'Sex and the single spender', *American Demographics* (November 1993): 28–34.

28. Erik Sass, 'Facebook is now leading source of evidence in divorce cases', *Social Media & Marketing Daily* (10 March 2011).

29. Richard Alleyne, 'Facebook increasingly implicated in divorce', *The Telegraph* (UK) (21 January 2011), http://www. telegraph.co.uk/technology/facebook/8274601/Face-book-increasingly-implicated-in-divorce.html (accessed 1 August 2018).

30. 'Men and women in the European Union: A statistical portrait', op. cit.: 76.

31. http://ec.europa.eu/eurostat/cache/infographs/women men/bloc-1b.html?lang=en (accessed 1 August 2018).

32. John Bingham, 'Average cost of raising a child in UK £230,000', *The Daily Telegraph* (22 January 2015), http:// www.telegraph.co.uk/news/uknews/11360819/Average -cost-of-raising-a-child-in-UK-230000.html (accessed 1 August 2018).

33. 'Child care costs: How the UK compares with the world', datablog from *The Guardian,* https://www.theguardian.com/ news/datablog/2012/may/21/child-care-costs-compared-britain#data (accessed 1 August 2018); see also Livia Sz. Oláh, 'Changing families in the European Union: Trends and policy implications', United Nations Expert Group Meeting, 'Family policy development: Achievements and challenges', New York (14–15 May 2015): 39 for diagram of formal child care for each country of EU28, before and after 3 years of age, http://www.un.org/esa/socdev/family/docs/egm15/ Olahpaper.pdf (accessed 1 August 2018).

34. Mary C. Gilly and Ben M. Enis, 'Recycling the Family Life Cycle: A Proposal for Redefinition', in Andrew A. Mitchell (ed.), *Advances in Consumer Research* 9 (Ann Arbor, MI: Association for Consumer Research, 1982): 271–6.

35. Charles M. Schaninger and William D. Danko, 'A conceptual and empirical comparison of alternative household life cycle models', *Journal of Consumer Research* 19 (March 1993): 580–94; Robert E. Wilkes, 'Household life-cycle stages, transitions, and product expenditures', *Journal of Consumer Research* 22(1) (June 1995): 27–42.

36. Carolyn F. Curasi, Linda L. Price and Eric J. Arnould (2004), 'How individuals' cherished possessions become families'

inalienable wealth', *Journal of Consumer Research* 31 (December): 609–22; Tonya Williams Bradford (2009), 'Intergenerationally gifted asset disposition', *Journal Consumer Research* 36(1) (June): 93–111.

37. James H. McAlexander, John W. Schouten and Scott D. Roberts, 'Consumer Behavior and Divorce', in *Research in Consumer Behavior* (Greenwich, CT: JAI Press, 1992); Michael R. Solomon, 'The role of products as social stimuli: a symbolic interactionism perspective', *Journal of Consumer Research* 10 (December 1983): 319–29; Melissa Martin Young, 'Disposition of Possession During Role Transitions', in Rebecca H. Holman and Michael R. Solomon (eds), *Advances in Consumer Research* 18 (Provo, UT: Association for Consumer Research, 1991): 33–9.

38. Harry L. Davis, 'Decision making within the household', *Journal of Consumer Research* 2 (March 1972): 241–60; Michael B. Menasco and David J. Curry, 'Utility and choice: an empirical study of wife/husband decision making', *Journal of Consumer Research* 16 (June 1989): 87–97; for a review, see Conway Lackman and John M. Lanasa, 'Family decision-making theory: an overview and assessment', *Psychology and Marketing* 10(2) (March/April 1993): 81–94.

39. Shannon Dortch, 'Money and marital discord', *American Demographics* 11(3) (October 1994).

40. Daniel Seymour and Greg Lessne, 'Spousal conflict arousal: scale development', *Journal of Consumer Research* 11 (December 1984): 810–21.

41. For research on factors influencing how much influence adolescents exert in family decision-making, see Ellen Foxman, Patriya Tansuhaj and Karin M. Ekstrom, 'Family members' perceptions of adolescents' influence in family decision making', *Journal of Consumer Research* 15(4) (March 1989): 482–91; Sharon E. Beatty and Salil Talpade, 'Adolescent influence in family decision making: a replication with extension', *Journal of Consumer Research* 21(2) (September 1994): 332–41; also see K.M. Palan and R.E. Wilkes, 'Adolescent Parent Interaction in Family Decision Making', *Journal of Consumer Research.* 24 (September 1997): 159–69.

42. Diane Crispell, 'Dual-earner diversity', *American Demographics* (July 1995): 32–7.

43. Robert Boutilier, *Targeting Families: Marketing To and Through the New Family* (Ithaca, NY: American Demographics Books, 1993).

44. Darach Turley, 'Dialogue with the departed', in F. Hansen (ed.), *European Advances in Consumer Research* 2 (Provo, UT: Association for Consumer Research, 1995): 10–13.

45. Dennis L. Rosen and Donald H. Granbois, 'Determinants of role structure in family financial management', *Journal of Consumer Research* 10 (September 1983): 253–8.

46. Robert F. Bales, *Interaction Process Analysis: A Method for the Study of Small Groups* (Reading, MA: Addison-Wesley, 1950); for a cross-gender comparison of food shopping strategies, see Rosemary Polegato and Judith L. Zaichkowsky, 'Family food shopping: strategies used by husbands and wives', *The Journal of Consumer Affairs* 28 (1994): 2.

47. Alma S. Baron, 'Working parents: shifting traditional roles', *Business* 37 (January/March 1987): 36; William J. Qualls, 'Household decision behavior: the impact of husbands' and wives' sex role orientation', *Journal of Consumer Research* 14 (September 1987): 264–79; Charles M. Schaninger and W. Christian Buss, 'The relationship of sex role norms to household task allocation', *Psychology and Marketing* 2 (Summer 1985): 93–104.

48. Cynthia Webster, 'Effects of Hispanic ethnic identification on marital roles in the purchase decision process', *Journal of Consumer Research* 21(2) (September 1994): 319–31; for a study that examined the effects of family depictions in advertising among Hispanic consumers, see Gary D. Gregory and James M. Munch, 'Cultural values in international advertising: An examination of familial norms and roles in Mexico', *Psychology and Marketing* 14(2) (March 1997): 99–120.

49. Gary L. Sullivan and P.J. O'Connor, 'The family purchase decision process: A cross-cultural review and framework for research', *Southwest Journal of Business and Economics* (Fall 1988): 43; Marilyn Lavin, 'Husband-dominant, wife-dominant, joint', *Journal of Consumer Marketing* 10(3) (1993): 33–42; Nicholas Timmins, 'New man fails to survive into the nineties', *The Independent* (25 January 1996). See also Roger J. Baran, 'Patterns of Decision Making Influence for Selected Products and Services Among Husbands and Wives Living in the Czech Republic', in Hansen (ed.), *European Advances in Consumer Research* 2; Jan Pahl, 'His money, her money: Recent research on financial organization in marriage', *Journal of Economic Psychology* 16 (1995): 361–76; Carole B. Burgoyne, 'Financial organization and decision-making within Western "households"', *Journal of Economic Psychology* 16 (1995): 421–30; Erich Kirchler, 'Spouses' joint purchase decisions: Determinants of influence tactics for muddling through the process', *Journal of Economic Psychology* 14 (1993): 405–38.

50. Micaela DiLeonardo, 'The female world of cards and holidays: Women, families, and the work of kinship', *Signs* 12 (Spring 1942): 440–53.

51. C. Whan Park, 'Joint decisions in home purchasing: A muddling through process', *Journal of Consumer Research* 9 (September 1982): 151–62; see also William J. Qualls and Françoise Jaffe, 'Measuring Conflict in Household Decision Behavior: Read My Lips and Read My Mind', in John F. Sherry Jr and Brian Sternthal (eds), *Advances in Consumer Research* 19 (Provo, UT: Association for Consumer Research, 1992).

52. Kim P. Corfman and Donald R. Lehmann, 'Models of co-operative group decision-making and relative influence: An experimental investigation of family purchase decisions', *Journal of Consumer Research* 14 (June 1987).

53. Alison M. Torrillo, 'Dens are men's territory', *American Demographics* 11(2) (January 1995).

54. Charles Atkin, 'Observation of parent–child interaction in supermarket decision-making', *Journal of Marketing* 42 (October 1978).

55. Les Carlson, Ann Walsh, Russell N. Laczniak and Sanford Grossbart, 'Family communication patterns and marketplace motivations, attitudes, and behaviors of children and mothers', *Journal of Consumer Affairs* 28(1) (Summer 1994): 25–53; see also Roy L. Moore and George P. Moschis, 'The role of family communication in consumer learning', *Journal of Communication* 31 (Autumn 1981): 42–51.

56. Ben Kerrane, M.K. Hogg and Shona Bettany, 'Children's strategies in practice: Exploring the co-constructed nature of children's influence strategies in family consumption', *Journal of Marketing Management,* 28(7&8) (2012): 809–35; see also Leslie Isler, Edward T. Popper and Scott Ward, 'Children's purchase requests and parental responses: Results from a diary study', *Journal of Advertising Research* 27 (October/November 1987).

57. Scott Ward, 'Consumer Socialization', in Harold H. Kassarjian and Thomas S. Robertson (eds), *Perspectives in Consumer Behavior* (Glenville, IL: Scott, Foresman, 1980): 380.

58. Thomas Lipscomb, 'Indicators of materialism in children's free speech: Age and gender comparisons', *Journal of Consumer Marketing* (Fall 1988): 41–6.

59. B. Kerrane and M.K. Hogg, 'Shared or non-shared: Children's different consumer socialisation experiences within the family environment', *European Journal of Marketing,* 47(3&4) (2013): 506–24, http://dx.doi.org/10.1108/03090561311297436 (accessed 1 August 2018).

60. George P. Moschis, 'The role of family communication in consumer socialization of children and adolescents', *Journal of Consumer Research* 11 (March 1985): 898–913.

61. James U. McNeal and Chyon-Hwa Yeh, 'Born to shop', *American Demographics* (June 1993): 34–9.

62. Les Carlson, Sanford Grossbart and J. Kathleen Stuenkel, 'The role of parental socialization types on differential family communication patterns regarding consumption', *Journal of Consumer Psychology* 1(1) (1992): 31–52.

63. Marsha L. Richins and Lan Nguyen, 'Material parenting: How the use of goods in parenting fosters materialism in the next generation', *Journal of Consumer Research* 41 (2015): 6.

64. See Patricia M. Greenfield, Emily Yut, Mabel Chung, Deborah Land, Holly Kreider, Maurice Pantoja and Kris Horsley, 'The program-length commercial: A study of the effects of television/toy tie-ins on imaginative play', *Psychology and Marketing* 7 (Winter 1990): 237–56 for a study on the effects of commercial programming on creative play.

65. Emily Bryson York, 'NIH: Banning fast food ads will make kids less fat', *Advertising Age* (19 November 2008).

66. Andrew Martin, 'Kellogg to curb marketing of foods to children', *New York Times* (14 June 2007); Tara Parker-Pope, 'Watching food ads on TV may program kids to overeat', *Wall Street Journal* (10 July 2007): D1.

67. Roos van Tongerloo, 'Kind krijgt lesje reclame kijken', *De Telegraaf* (26 May 2015); see also http://www.mediarakkers.nl/ (accessed 1 August 2018).

68. Sarah Boseley, 'Amsterdam's solution to the obesity crisis: no fruit juice and enough sleep', *The Guardian* (14 April 2017), https://www.theguardian.com/society/2017/apr/14/amsterdam-solution-obesity-crisis-no-fruit-juice-enough-sleep (accessed 1 August 2018).

69. Sarah Boseley, op. cit.

70. Glenn Collins, 'New studies on "girl toys" and "boy toys"', *New York Times* (13 February 1984): D1.

71. Susan B. Kaiser, 'Clothing and the social organization of gender perception: A developmental approach', *Clothing and Textiles Research Journal* 7 (Winter 1989): 46–56.

72. D.W. Rajecki, Jill Ann Dame, Kelly Jo Creek, P.J. Barrickman, Catherine A. Reid and Drew C. Appleby, 'Gender casting in television toy advertisements: Distributions, message content analysis, and evaluations', *Journal of Consumer Psychology* 2(3) (1993): 307–27.

73. Lori Schwartz and William Markham, 'Sex stereotyping in children's toy advertisements', *Sex Roles* 12 (January 1985): 157–70.

74. Joseph Pereira, 'Oh boy! In toyland, you get more if you're male', *The Wall Street Journal* (23 September 1994): B1 (2); Joseph Pereira, 'Girls' favorite playthings: Dolls, dolls, and dolls', *The Wall Street Journal* (23 September 1994): B1 (2).

75. http://www.lettoysbetoys.org.uk/ (accessed 1 August 2018).

76. Kira Cochrane, 'The fightback against gendered toys', *The Guardian* (22 April 2014), https://www.theguardian.com/lifeandstyle/2014/apr/22/gendered-toys-stereotypes-boy-girl-segregation-equality (accessed 1 August 2018).

77. P. MacLaran and C. Otnes, 'Reinvigorating the Sherlock Myth: Elementary Gender-Bending, in J. Sherry and E. Fischer (eds), *Contemporary Consumer Culture Theory* (New York: Routledge, 2017): 152–72.

78. Laura A. Peracchio, 'How do young children learn to be consumers? A script-processing approach', *Journal of Consumer Research* 18 (March 1992): 4, 25–40; Laura A. Peracchio, 'Young children's processing of a televised narrative: is a picture really worth a thousand words?', *Journal of Consumer Research* 20(2) (September 1993): 281–93; see also M. Carole Macklin, 'The effects of an advertising retrieval cue on young children's memory and brand evaluations', *Psychology and Marketing* 11(3) (May/June 1994): 291–311.

79. Jean Piaget, 'The child and modern physics', *Scientific American* 196(3) (1957): 46–51; see also Kenneth D. Bahn, 'How and when do brand perceptions and preferences first form? A cognitive developmental investigation', *Journal of Consumer Research* 13 (December 1986): 382–93.

80. Deborah L. Roedder, 'Age differences in children's responses to television advertising: An information processing approach', *Journal of Consumer Research* 8 (September 1981): 1, 44–53; see also Deborah Roedder John and Ramnath Lakshmi-Ratan, 'Age differences in children's choice behavior: The impact of available alternatives', *Journal of Marketing Research* (29 May 1992): 216–26; Jennifer Gregan-Paxton and Deborah Roedder John, 'Are young children adaptive decision makers? A study of age differences in information search behavior', *Journal of Consumer Research* (1995).

81. http://www.bbc.co.uk/news/topics/cql0269k80xt/metoo-campaign (accessed 1 August 2018).

82. https://www.telegraph.co.uk/cricket/2018/03/31/australias-three-disgraced-cricketers-expected-launch-legal/ (accessed 1 August 2018).

83. http://socialmarketing.org/archives/generations-xy-z-and-the-others/ (accessed 1 August 2018).

84. Bickley Townsend, 'Où sont les neiges d'antan?' ('Where are the snows of yesteryear?'), *American Demographics* (October 1988): 2.

85. Martin Lindstrom, 'Bottling the past: Using nostalgia to connect with consumers', *Fast Company* (23 August 2011).

86. 'Same kids, more money', *Marketing* (29 June 1995): 37.

87. Birgitte Tufte and Jeanetter Rasmussen, 'Children on the Net: State of the Art and Future Perspectives Regarding Danish Children's Use of the Internet', in Darach Turley and Stephen Brown (eds), *European Advances in Consumer Research: All Changed, Changed Utterly?* 6 (Valdosta, GA: Association for Consumer Research, 2003): 142–6; Anthony Patterson, Kim Cassidy and Steve Baron, 'Communication and Marketing in a Mobilized World: Diary Research on "Generation Txt"', in Turley and Brown (eds), *European Advances in Consumer Research*: 147–52; Natalie Hanman, 'The kids are all writing', *The Guardian* (9 June 2005).

88. 'Same kids, more money', op. cit.; Scott McCartney, 'Society's subcultures meet by modem', *Wall Street Journal* (8 December 1994): B1 (2).

89. Junu Bryan Kim, 'For savvy teens: Real life, real solutions', *Advertising Age* (23 August 1993): Special Report 1.

90. 'Hopes and fears: Young European opinion leaders', GfK, adapted from *Marketing Week* (25 June 1998) – a study of 500 opinion leaders aged 14–20 from 16 western and eastern European countries.

91. 'Generation next', *Marketing* (16 January 1997): 25.

92. 'Trends in households in the European Union: 1995–2025', op. cit.: 38.

93. Eurostat: Statistics Explained (May 2014): 7; see also 'Europe in Figures', *Eurostat Yearbook,* 2008, Figure SP.9: 29.

94. Hope Schau, Mary C. Gilly and Mary Wolfinbarger (2009), 'Consumer identity renaissance: The resurgence of identity-inspired consumption in retirement', *Journal of Consumer Research* 36, August, in press.

95. Fahmida Rahman and Daniel Tomlinson, 'Cross countries: International comparisons of intergenerational trends', Resolution Foundation (February 2018), http://www.resolutionfoundation.org/app/uploads/2018/02/IC-international.pdf (accessed 1 August 2018).

96. Patrick Collinson, 'UK millennials second worst-hit financially in developed world, says study', *The Guardian* (19 Feb 2018), https://www.theguardian.com/money/2018/feb/19/uk-millennials-second-worst-hit-financially-in-developed-world-says-study (accessed 1 August 2018).

97. Sally Weale, 'Boomerang offspring damage parents' wellbeing, study finds', *The Guardian* (7 March 2018), https://www.theguardian.com/society/2018/mar/07/boomerang-offspring-damage-parents-wellbeing-study-finds (accessed 1 August 2018); see also Marco Tosi, 'Parents' lives made more miserable by boomerang generation', (3 March 2018) http://www.lse.ac.uk/News/Latest-news-from-LSE/2018/03-March-2018/Boomerang-generation (accessed 1 August 2018); also Marco Tosi and Emily Grundy, 'Returns home by children and changes in parents' well-being in Europe', *Social Science and Medicine* 200 (2018): 99–106, https://ac.els-cdn.com/S0277953618300169/1-s2.0-S0277953618300169-main.pdf?_tid=6654de52-f182-49f9-af97-ee476fe980d4&acdnat=1522756067_806a4966745a73964dbcb2f49b1383ba (accessed 1 August 2018).

98. Marco Tosi and Emily Grundy, op cit.; they cite G.H. Elder Jr., M.K. Johnson and R. Crosnoe, 'The Emergence and Development of Life Course Theory', in *Handbook of the Life Course* (New York: Springer, 2003): 3–19.

99. Sally Weale, 'Boomerang children can be good for family relationships – study', *The Guardian* (29 June 2018), https://www.theguardian.com/education/2018/jun/29/boomerang-children-can-be-good-for-family-relationships-study (accessed 1 August 2018).

100. Sally Weale, op cit.

101. 'Living conditions in Europe: statistical handbook', https://ec.europa.eu/eurostat/web/products-statistical-books/-/KS-DZ-18-001 (accessed 12 December 2018).

102. 'Trends in households in the European Union: 1995–2025', op. cit.: 93.

103. David B. Wolfe, 'Targeting the mature mind', *American Demographics* (March 1994): 32–6.

104. 'Shades of grey', op. cit.

105. Allyson Steward-Allen, 'Marketing in Europe to the consumer over age fifty', *Marketing News* 31(16) (4 August 1997): 18.

106. Gabriele Morello, 'Old is Gold, But What is Old?', ESOMAR seminar on 'The Untapped Gold Mine: The Growing Importance of the Over-50s' (Amsterdam: ESOMAR, 1989); Gabriele Morello, 'Sicilian time', in *Time and Society* (London: SAGE, 1997): 6(1): 55–69; see also 'Living conditions in Europe: statistical handbook', op. cit.: 9–21.

107. Benny Barak and Leon G. Schiffman, 'Cognitive Age: A Nonchronological Age Variable', in Kent B. Monroe (ed.),

Advances in Consumer Research 8 (Provo, UT: Association for Consumer Research, 1981): 602–6.

108. David B. Wolfe, 'An ageless market', *American Demographics* (July 1987): 27–55.

109. Hope Jensen Schau, Mary C. Gilly, and Mary Wolfinbarger, 'Consumer identity renaissance: The resurgence of identity-inspired consumption in retirement', *Journal of Consumer Research* 36 (August 2009): 255–76; cf. also Michelle Barnhart and Lisa Peñaloza, 'Who are you calling old? Negotiating old age identity in the elderly consumption ensemble', *Journal of Consumer Research* 39(6) (April 2013): 1,133–53.

110. 'Baby boom generatie moet oud-zijn modieus maken', op. cit.

111. 'Demographic statistics 1997', *Eurostat* (Luxembourg: Office for Official Publications of the European Communities, 1997); see also https://europa.eu (accessed 1 August 2018); Lenore Skenazy, 'These days, it's hip to be old', *Advertising Age* (15 February 1988).

112. This segmentation approach is based on the US population and follows William Lazer and Eric H. Shaw, 'How older Americans spend their money', *American Demographics* (September 1987): 36; see also 'Living conditions in Europe: statistical handbook', op. cit.: 9–21.

113. Ellen Day, Brian Davis, Rhonda Dove and Warren A. French, 'Reaching the senior citizen market(s)', *Journal of Advertising Research* (December/January 1987/88): 23–30; Warren A. French and Richard Fox, 'Segmenting the senior citizen market', *Journal of Consumer Marketing* 2 (1985): 61–74; Jeffrey G. Towle and Claude R. Martin Jr, 'The Elderly Consumer: One Segment or Many?', in Beverlee B. Anderson (ed.), *Advances in Consumer Research* 3 (Provo, UT: Association for Consumer Research, 1976): 463.

114. Catherine A. Cole and Nadine N. Castellano, 'Consumer behavior', *Encyclopedia of Gerontology* 1 (1996): 329–39.

115. Senior Citizens' Marketing, AdAge (15 September 2003) https://adage.com/article/adage-encyclopedia/senior-citizens-market/98875/ accessed 6 November 2018)

Chapter 11
Income and social class

Chapter objectives

When you finish reading this chapter you will understand why:

11.1 Both personal and social conditions influence how we spend our money.

11.2 We group consumers into social classes based on factors such as income, occupation and education.

11.3 Social class has a fundamental impact on our consumer tastes.

11.4 Social stratification creates a status hierarchy, where some goods come to signify the social status of their owners.

11.5 Our lifestyles are shaped not only by economic but also by cultural capital, and are expressed in the form of daily consumer practices.

FINALLY, the big day has come! David is going home with Julia to meet her parents. David had been doing some contracting work at the publishing company where Julia works, and it was love at first sight. Even though David had attended the 'School of Hard Knocks' on the streets of Liverpool, while Julia studied Classics at Trinity College, Oxford, somehow they knew they could work things out despite their vastly different social backgrounds. Julia's been hinting that the Caldwells have money from *several* generations back, but David doesn't feel intimidated. After all, he knows plenty of guys from both Liverpool and London who have wheeled-and-dealed their way into six figures; he thinks he can handle one more big shot in a silk suit, flashing a roll of bills and showing off his expensive modern furniture with mirrors and gadgets everywhere you look.

When they arrive at the family estate 90 minutes outside London, David looks for a Rolls-Royce parked at the end of the long, tree-lined driveway, but he sees only a Jeep Cherokee – which, he decides, must belong to one of the servants. Once inside, David is surprised by how simply the house is decorated and by how understated everything seems.

The hall floor is covered with a faded Oriental rug, and all the furniture looks really old – in fact, there doesn't seem to be a stick of new furniture anywhere, just a lot of antiques.

David is even more surprised when he meets Mr Caldwell. He had half-expected Julia's father to be wearing a tuxedo and holding a large glass of cognac like the people he saw in the movie *Gosford Park.* In fact, David had put on his best Italian silk suit in anticipation and was wearing his large cubic zirconium ring so Mr Caldwell would know that he had money too. When Julia's father emerges from his study wearing an old rumpled cardigan and plim-solls, David realises he's definitely not in the same world. . .

Gary Bamossy

Introduction

Both personal and social conditions influence how we spend our money.

As David's eye-opening experience at the Caldwells' suggests, there are many ways to spend money, and a wide gulf exists between those who have it and those who don't. Perhaps an equally wide one exists between those who have had it for a long time and those who made it more recently. This chapter begins by considering briefly how general economic conditions affect the way consumers allocate their money. Then, reflecting the adage, 'The rich are different', it will explore how people who occupy different positions in society consume in very different ways. Whether a person is a skilled worker like David or a child of privilege like Julia, their **social class** has a profound impact on what they do with their money and on how consumption choices reflect the person's 'place' in society.

As this chapter illustrates, these choices serve another purpose as well. The specific products and services we buy are often intended to make sure *other* people know what our social standing is – or what we would like it to be. Products are frequently bought and displayed as markers of social class: they are valued as **status symbols**. Indeed, it is quite common for a product to be positioned on the basis of its (presumed) place in the **social hierarchy**. The chapter continues with an assessment of the evolving nature of such status symbols, and it considers some reasons why status-driven products are not always accurate indicators of a consumer's true social standing.

The way income and social class influences consumer behaviour can be approached from an individual or a more social perspective. The field of **behavioural economics**, or economic psychology, is concerned with the 'individual' and 'psychological' side of economic decisions. Beginning with the pioneering work of the psychologist George Katona, this discipline studies how consumers' motives and their expectations about the future affect their current spending, and how these individual decisions add up to affect a society's economic welfare.[1]

The chapter concludes with a section reflecting on the relation between social class and lifestyle, based on the work of French sociologist Pierre Bourdieu.[2] Bourdieu has also been very influential in formulating a theory of practices, describing how culture is learned not so much by personal choices, nor by subjecting ourselves to explicit values and norms, but by adopting routinised types of behaviour that, for us, represent the 'ways things are done'. This approach is decisive in arguing why social inequalities have a tendency to reproduce themselves in society.

Consumer spending and economic behaviour

Income patterns

In Europe, we have been used to many years of relatively steady growth in income, so the average European's standard of living has continued to improve. Gross Domestic Product more than doubled, and in some EU countries quadrupled, between 1980 and 1995. Although there were a few conjuncture-based fluctuations and although this boom was by no means shared equally among all consumer groups,[3] optimism generally endured until 2008. Individual income shifts were linked to two key factors: a shift in women's roles and increases in educational attainment.[4] But the financial crisis turned into an economic crisis and into a crisis of public debt. In the subsequent years (i.e., since 2008) we have witnessed first a growing pessimism and an economic recession that has had a serious impact on people's income and livelihoods, and from about 2013 onwards a renewed confidence in a better future. Unemployment rates soared across Europe and are still high in several countries, mainly Spain and Greece[5] – especially in terms of young people, where countries such as Spain (38.6 per cent), Italy (34.7 per cent) and Greece (43.6 per cent) are experiencing youth unemployment rates above a third of the youth population. If it is any consolation, Spain and Greece were hovering above 50 per cent in the years 2012 to 2014.[6] It is obvious that such unemployment rates severely influence income and consumption patterns. For example, many more young people stay with their parents for a longer period. Research has demonstrated how, in some Greek families, solidarity may grow as an outcome of the crisis but also how such disruptive changes in lifestyle and economic situation may lead to more social reclusiveness, since keeping up with the peers in terms of consumer spending is no longer possible.[7]

Furthermore, Europe may be experiencing a new phenomenon – the 'working poor': people who are employed but making less than necessary to make ends meet. This struggling population, known from American society, is increasingly found not just in Spain and Greece but also in France[8] and Germany. Usual welfare systems are ill-suited to cater for such people, who are employed and therefore technically self-sustained.[9]

Woman's work

One reason for the increase in income in European households up until the recent recession is that there has also been a larger proportion of people of working age participating in the labour force. While men are more likely to have paid employment than women, the greatest increases in paid employment in EU countries over the past decades have been among women. This steady increase in the numbers of working women is a primary cause of the pre-recession steady increase in household incomes. However, even now, in the post-recession period, women seem more vulnerable on the job market when it comes to full-time jobs disappearing.[10]

Furthermore, throughout the EU, women's average full-time earnings are less than men's, and over 30 per cent of women in employment are working part-time, against only about 10 per cent of men. Female part-time work is particularly prevalent in the Netherlands, where it accounts for more than 58 per cent of female employment, and in Switzerland (44 per cent). In the UK, Austria, Germany, Italy and Ireland female part-time employment rates are above 30 per cent.[11] As can be seen in Figure 11.1, in 2016 the European average gross hourly wage of women working on a full-time basis was approximately 16 per cent lower than the earnings of their male equivalents. The explanations for this are related to the kinds of jobs typically held by women, the consequences of breaks in careers for child-bearing and a number of other factors. Men are not only more concentrated in higher-paid sectors and occupations, but within these sectors and occupations they are also more likely than women to hold supervisory responsibilities and if they do so their earnings tend to be relatively higher.[12] That women are more likely to be in part-time work reflects the fact that they take on the more traditional activities of caring for the household and for children living at home – activities that are still seen as primarily a woman's responsibility. As discussed in the previous chapter, the family situation, number and age of children living at home and the educational level of women all heavily influence their employment activities.

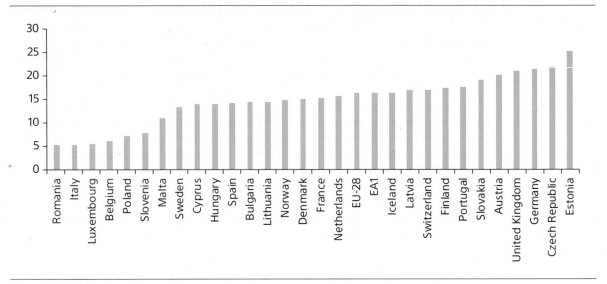

Figure 11.1 The unadjusted gender pay gap, 2016 – the difference between average gross hourly earnings of male and female employees as percentage of male gross earnings

http://ec.europa.eu/eurostat/tgm/table.do?tab=table&plugin=1&language=en&pcode=tesem180 [0]

Yes, it pays to go to school!

Another factor that determines who gets a bigger slice of the pie is education. Although the expense of going to college often entails great sacrifice, it still pays in the long run. University and higher professional-study graduates earn about 50 per cent more than those who have only gone through secondary school during the course of their lives. Close to half of the increase in consumer spending power during the past decade came from these more highly educated groups. Full-time employees with a tertiary education qualification earn, on average, considerably more than those who have completed upper secondary school (defined as A-levels, *Baccalauréat*, Abitur, HBO or equivalent). In general, the trend is that the younger generation of Europeans is better qualified than older generations. In 2013, 88 per cent of the younger generation aged 20–24 had completed at least upper secondary education. This figure has been rising steadily over the years – a development driven by the increase in the outsourcing of jobs requiring lower skills and thus the smaller number of job opportunities for the less skilled. Still, more than 5 million youngsters in Europe are without any form of secondary training, and their chances of getting a job will only fall in the coming years.[13]

To spend or not to spend, that is the question

A basic assumption of economic psychology is that consumer demand for goods and services depends on both our ability *and* willingness to buy. While demand for necessities tends to be stable over time, other expenditures can be postponed or eliminated if people do not feel that now is a good time to spend.[14] For example, a person may decide to 'make do' with their current car for another year rather than buy a new car now.

Discretionary spending

Discretionary income is the money available to a household over and above that required for a comfortable standard of living. European consumers are estimated to have discretionary spending power in billions of euros per year, and it is consumers aged 35–55 (whose incomes are at a peak) who account for the greatest amounts. As might be expected, discretionary income increases as overall income goes up – and it goes down for many people during recessionary times, such as the current one.

While some populations are struggling, the crisis obviously did not hit everyone equally hard. All countries have felt a degree of recession, but the burdens are far from equally distributed. Income inequality is on the rise and is a potential source for unrest in much of the Western world.[15] In some parts of the world, such as Indonesia and Russia, the rise in income inequality is due to the growth of an upper and upper-middle class (and in Russia also a class of super rich), whereas in the developed economies the rise may well be due to the fact that not all parts of the population carry the same burden of economic recession. And even if there are large differences among the developed countries (ranging from the US, with the highest income inequality, to Norway with the lowest), the inequality is growing pretty much everywhere.[16] This is seen in Figure 11.2, which shows the *Gini index,* a measure of social inequality, for selected countries between 2006 and 2011. The Gini coefficient continues to rise in almost all countries, indicating growing national inequality. According to OECD, the average for its countries grew from 0,315 in 2010 to 0,318 in 2014. The UK, for example, is above average with 0.36.[17]

Within Europe, the top (richest) 20 per cent of the population received five times as much of the total income as the bottom (poorest) 20 per cent. For EU countries in 2016, this gap between the most and least well-off persons (known as the *share ratio S80/S20*) is smallest in the Czech Republic (3.5), Finland, Slovakia, Slovenia (3.6) and Norway (3.7). It is generally widest in the Balkans – Bulgaria (7,7) and Romania (7.1) – but also high in other parts of Southern Europe (Spain and Greece 6.6) and in the Baltic states of Lithuania (7.1) and Latvia (6.2).[18] While discretionary income is a powerful tool for predicting certain types of consumer behaviour, it is not always a measure from which straightforward comparisons between countries can be easily made. Factors such as different levels of sales tax (VAT) or varying levels of direct family benefits for children under 19 years of age living at home in various EU countries account for differences in what constitutes true discretionary income. Price levels also vary, in spite of the homogenising effect of the European free market. Buying power is, therefore, often a better measurement of wealth, at least in relation to the daily costs of living. Figure 11.3 gives a graphic overview of regional buying power for Europe in 2017.

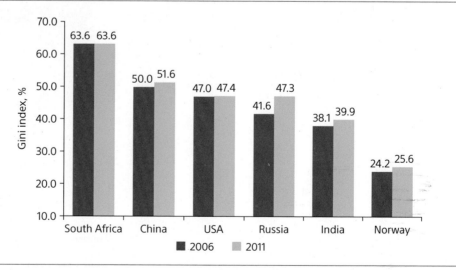

Figure 11.2 Gini index of selected countries, 2006–2011 Note: A society that scores 0 per cent on the Gini index has perfect equality, where every inhabitant has the same income. The higher the number over 0 per cent, the higher the inequality, and a score of 100 per cent indicates total inequality, where only one person receives all the income.

Source: Euromonitor International from national statistics.

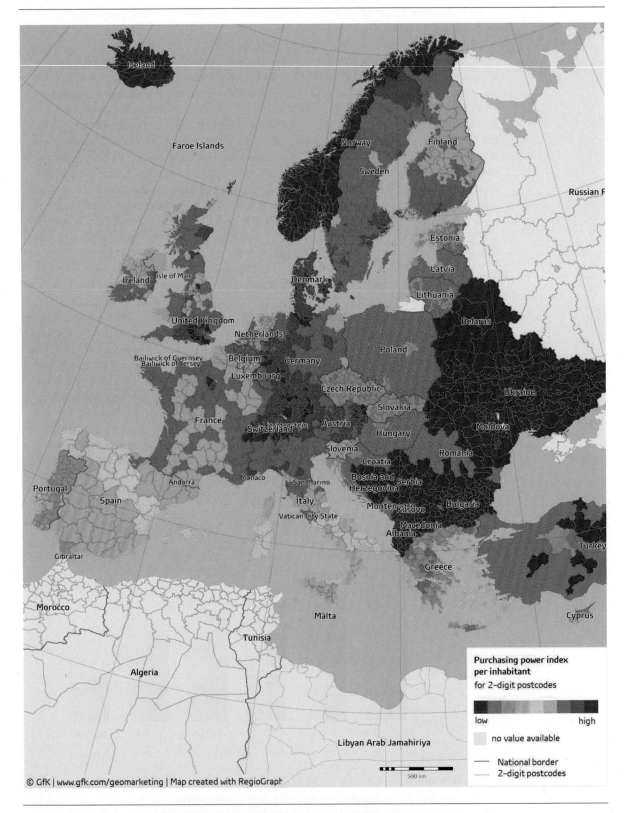

Figure 11.3 Buying power per capita across Europe, by region, 2017

Source: http://www.gfk.com/insights/news/map-of-the-month-gfk-purchasing-power-europe-2017/

Individual attitudes towards money

Many consumers are entertaining doubts about their individual and collective futures, and are anxious about holding on to what they have. A consumer's anxieties about money are not necessarily related to how much they actually have: acquiring and managing money is sometimes more a state of mind than of wallet. Researchers have, for example, investigated what they call 'personal saving orientation' – a propensity to build economic prudence and sustainable savings into one's lifestyle.[19] Times of crisis, impact a lot of people directly on their income, as we have seen. But even those that are not directly touched by the recession tend to be more prudent with their money and their spending, both out of precaution for an uncertain future but also because crisis can be 'talked up'. This psychological mechanism has been demonstrated for financial markets[20] but it also works for ordinary people, for example when they are experiencing talk of crisis in all media. Based on this particular 'crisis mood', they may alter their spending patterns without it really being a measure of caution or some other rational decision. The change may, however, go in two directions, since instead of being more cautious, young people especially might decide that since the future is not to be relied upon, they might as well have the fun they can right away.

Money can have a variety of complex psychological meanings: it can be equated with success or failure, social acceptability, security, love, freedom and . . . sex appeal.[21] Some clinical psychologists even specialise in treating money-related disorders, and report that people feel guilty about their success and deliberately make bad investments to ease this feeling! Other clinical conditions include atephobia (fear of being ruined), harpaxophobia (fear of becoming a victim of robbers), peniaphobia (fear of poverty) and aurophobia (fear of gold).[22] A study that approached money as a social resource explored some interesting links between our need for acceptance and our feelings about cash. In one case, participants were led to believe that a group either had rejected them or had accepted them. They then completed a number of measures that reflected their desire for money. Those whom the group had 'rejected' expressed a greater desire for money. At another stage, subjects counted either real money or pieces of paper and then experienced physical pain. Those who counted the real money reported feeling less pain than those who just counted paper![23]

Consumer confidence

A consumer's beliefs about what the future holds is an indicator of **consumer confidence**, which reflects the extent to which people are optimistic or pessimistic about the future health of the economy and how they will fare in the future. These beliefs influence how much money a consumer will pump into the economy when making discretionary purchases.

Hence it is no surprise that many businesses take forecasts about anticipated spending very seriously, and periodic surveys attempt to 'take the pulse' of the European consumer. The Henley Centre conducts a survey of consumer confidence, as does Eurostat and the *EuroMonitor*. The following are the types of attitudinal statements presented to consumers in these surveys:[24]

> *'My standard of living will change for the better over the next year.'*
>
> *'My quality of life will improve over the next year.'*
>
> *'I will have a lack of money when I retire.'*
>
> *'I spend too much of my income, and intend to spend less next year.'*
>
> *'I am concerned about the amount of free time I have.'*

When people are pessimistic about their prospects and about the state of the economy, they tend to cut-back their spending and take on less debt. On the other hand, when they are optimistic about the future, they tend to reduce the amount they save, take on more debt and buy discretionary items. Thus, the overall **savings rate** is influenced by individual consumers' pessimism or optimism about their personal circumstances (e.g. the fear of being laid off *vs* a steady increase in personal wealth due to rising real estate prices or a sudden increase in personal wealth due to an inheritance), as well as by world events (e.g. the election of a new government or an international crisis such as the collapse of Lehman Brothers in September 2008; or the current EU financial-sector crisis – think of Italy, Spain and Greece, and the current tensions of the euro).[25]

The financial crisis that started in the autumn of 2008 and was marked by the collapse of Lehman Brothers is a good example of how mass psychology is linked to the economy. When financial markets go up, the rise is based on expectations (and a lot of what is bought and sold in the financial markets are expectations, and even expectations of expectations). Likewise, when the market goes down. When everybody expects greater risks of losses (rather than gains) due to bankruptcies, failing demand, unemployment, etc., investors, buyers *and* consumers become more prudent, which slows down the turnover in the marketplace and aggravates the symptoms of crisis. This is why indexes of consumer confidence are received and read with great interest, and sometimes anxiety, these days.

Seeking value *vs* quality

In an era of diminished resources, Europeans are redefining traditional relationships among price, value and quality. In the past (most notably in the 1980s), people seemed to be willing to pay almost anything for products and services. Consumers still claim to want quality – but at the right price. In surveys, most people report that they regret the conspicuous consumption of the 1980s and feel the need to live with less. The attitude of the 1990s was more practical and reflected a 'back to basics' orientation. People today want more hard news instead of 'hype' from advertising, and they appreciate ads that feature problem-solving tips or that save money or time – or both. This is at the roots of the access-based economy (discussed in Chapter 1). Online and app-based services offering consumer-to-consumer buying and selling opportunities are proliferating, car-sharing programmes are popping up in many places[26] and the 'sharing economy' in general is becoming the new buzzword in marketing and consumer research.[27]

Nonetheless, the general quality of life and life satisfaction of European consumers is high, with some important distinctions: there are big differences between the EU15 countries and the new member states with respect to perceived quality of life and life satisfaction. A higher degree of materialism is often found in relatively poorer countries that have a direct way of comparing themselves to richer 'relatives', such as the Central and East European countries still undergoing a marketising process.[28] Also, levels of satisfaction are more heterogeneous among citizens of the new member states and in the EU15.

Marketing opportunity
(Virtual) Second-hand stores – the new in-place for consumers?

With the financial crisis turning into an economic crisis, new market opportunities replace the ones that went away with the carefree years that opened the twenty-first century. Second-hand shops are experiencing a boom in many European countries, indeed all over the world,[29] not only for reasons of frugality but also because many consumers consider this type of recycling a more ethical approach to consumption than the use-and-throw-away logic of former days. In Denmark, second-hand shopping has also soared, and growth rates in some online second-hand services have exceeded 40 per cent over the last few years. This can hardly be explained by the crisis alone – it probably also reflects a changed attitude towards second-hand consumption. 'Old stuff' makes it easier to feel unique through one's finds (there may be more stories attached to the old things), and in a contemporary consumer society of relative affluence, it might no longer be seen as socially down-grading to shop for recycled things, since it might be a sign of smartness and ability to locate 'good stuff', rather than a lack of means. In particular, the Web 2.0 has made it possible for consumers to reach other consumers very easily. The result: a booming online second-hand market. In the UK, the online market for second-hand furniture as well as for second-hand clothing continues to grow. So-called 'mumpreneurs' make extra money selling second-hand children's clothing.[30] One company, World of Books, has made a fortune buying and selling unwanted second-hand books – 80 per cent goes to recycling and 20 per cent to readers. With an app developed since 2014, it is easy for people to get a quick offer for their unwanted, old, dust-collecting paperbacks.[31] If you can contribute to prolonged life cycles of goods, there are good business opportunities!

Social class

11.2

We group consumers into social classes based on factors such as income, occupation and education.

All societies can be roughly divided into the haves and the have-nots (though sometimes 'having' is a question of degree). While social equality is a widely held value throughout Europe, the fact remains that some people seem to be more equal than others. As David's encounter with the Caldwells suggests, a consumer's standing in society, or social class, is determined by a complex set of variables including income, family background and occupation.

The place one occupies in the social structure is not just an important determinant of how *much* money is spent. It also influences *how* it is spent. David was surprised that the Caldwells, who clearly had a lot of money, did not seem to flaunt it. This understated way of living is oftentimes a hallmark of so-called 'old money'. People who have had it for a long time do not need to prove they have it. In contrast, consumers who are relative newcomers to affluence might allocate the same amount of money very differently.

Striving for access to resources

In many animal species, a social organisation develops whereby the most assertive or aggressive animals exert control over the others and have the first pick of food, living space and even mating partners. Chickens, for example, develop a clearly defined dominance–submission hierarchy. Within this hierarchy, each hen has a position in which she is submissive to all of the hens above her and dominates all of the ones below her (hence the origin of the term *pecking order*).[32]

People are not much different. We also develop a pecking order that ranks us in terms of our relative standing in society. This ranking, to a large degree, determines our access to such resources as education, housing and consumer goods. Unlike chicken, though, we can change this politically. And people try to improve their ranking by moving up the social order whenever possible. This desire to improve one's lot, and often to let others know that one has done so, is at the core of many marketing strategies.

Just as marketers try to carve society into groups for segmentation purposes, sociologists have developed ways to describe meaningful divisions of society in terms of people's relative social and economic resources. Some of these divisions involve political power, while others revolve around purely economic distinctions. Karl Marx argued that position in a society was determined by one's relationship to the *means of production.* Some people (the haves) control resources, and they use the labour of others to preserve their privileged positions. The have-nots lack control and depend on their own labour for survival, so these people have the most to gain by changing the system. Distinctions among people that entitle some to more than others are perpetuated by those who will benefit from doing so.[33] The German sociologist Max Weber showed that the rankings people develop are not one-dimensional. Some involve prestige or 'social honour' (he called these *status groups*), some rankings focus on power (or *party*) and some revolve around wealth and property (*class*).[34]

The term 'social class' is now used more generally to describe the overall rank of people in a society. People who are grouped within the same social class are approximately equal in terms of their social standing in the community. They work in roughly similar occupations, and they tend to have similar lifestyles by virtue of their income levels and common tastes. These people tend to socialise with one another and share many ideas and values regarding the way life should be lived.[35] Indeed, 'birds of a feather do flock together'. We tend to marry people in a similar social class to ours – a tendency sociologists call **homogamy**, or 'assortative mating'.

Social class is as much a state of being as it is of having: as David saw, class is also a question of what one *does* with one's money and how one defines one's role in society. Although people may not like the idea that some members of society are better-off or 'different' from others, most consumers do acknowledge the existence of different classes and the effect of class membership on consumption. It is not uncommon to divide social classes into five categories, A to E from top to bottom, where class A is defined as having an income of +200 per cent of average gross income, B between 150 and 200 per cent, C 100–150 per cent, D 50–100 per cent and E less than 50 per cent of average gross income. Generally speaking, in most countries, classes A and B have between 5 and 10 per cent of the population each, class C between 10 and 20 per cent and classes D and E between 30 and 40 per cent each. These figures point to a fairly uneven distribution of income; as we shall see a little later, the distribution of wealth is even more unequal.

Marketing pitfall

What do the super-rich do with their gold? Well, some decide to eat it! Since 2004, one New York-based restaurant has experimented with gold as an ingredient in its dishes – one of its 'popular' menu items is the 'Burger Extravagant' with a gold-coated bun ($295). If there is more appetite (and money left), you can top the burger off with a sundae called 'Frr-rozen Haute Chocolate' for the not insignificant sum of $25,000![36] In 2018, a video from a publicist and self-proclaimed fancy-food influencer, who renamed himself 'Foodgōd', went viral. Together with another US-based restaurant, he was promoting golden hotwings on Instagram – and proposing the modest price of $45 for 10. The video was immensely popular – so why isn't this a marketing opportunity? Well, because such extravagance, while fascinating, is also often looked down upon as unnecessary bragging and idiotic conspicuous consumption (see later in the chapter). As one British commenter noted: 'Gold needs to be in its purest 24k form to be safe to eat. The problem is, it tastes of nothing. Your body can't digest it and it has no nutritional value. You might as well be lighting a fag with a burning tenner – the joy, it seems, is in destroying it.'[37]

Social stratification

In virtually every context, some people seem to be ranked higher than others. Patterns of social arrangements evolve whereby some members get more resources than others by virtue of their relative standing, power and/or control in the group.[38] The phenomenon of **social stratification** refers to this creation of such culturally instituted divisions in a society: 'those processes in a social system by which scarce and valuable resources are distributed unequally to status positions that become more-or-less permanently ranked in terms of the share of valuable resources each receives'.[39] We see these distinctions both offline and online as the reputation economy takes shape; recall that this term refers to the 'currency' people earn when they post online and others recommend their comments.[40] Retailers may 'sort' clientele in terms of their ability to afford the retailers' products or services (e.g. some investment firms only accept clients with a certain net worth). Since 2013, Facebook engaged with some powerful data mining companies in order to give particular brands access to the Facebook traffic and liking data. Paired with other information about purchasing behaviour and demographic data, the insights from our online behaviour provide a powerful marketing segmentation tool. As we all know now, this is a practice that has backfired and generated a renewed and far more critical view of such commercial use of our private data. Facebook lost more than $ 134 billion in stock value after the Cambridge Analytica scandal – but at the time of writing all that value has been regained.[41] We still love Facebook, scandals or not. . .

Achieved *vs* ascribed status

If you recall groups you've belonged to, both large and small, you will probably agree that in many instances some members seemed to get more than their fair share while others were not so lucky. Some of these resources may have gone to people who earned them through hard work or diligence. This allocation is due to **achieved status**. Other rewards may have been obtained because the person was lucky enough to be born into wealthy circles. Such good fortune reflects **ascribed status**. The most obvious contemporary example of ascribed status is the existence of royal families in a number of European countries. But, possibly in particular in the UK, the imagery of the aristocratic 'landed class' also continues to be an important reference of ascribed social status, although the dominance of inherited wealth appears to be fading in Britain's traditionally aristocratic society. According to a survey, 86 of the 200 wealthiest people in England made their money the old-fashioned way: they earned it. Even the sanctity of the Royal Family, which epitomises the aristocracy, has been diluted because of tabloid exposure and the antics of younger family members, who have been transformed into celebrities more like rock stars than royalty.[42] However, according to some researchers, the royal families in most countries still have a degree of magic surrounding them and they remain a source of inspiration for aspirational and conspicuous consumption.[43]

Although we tend to believe that in modern democratic societies there should be few inherited privileges, experience shows that ascribed status is more difficult to overcome than we would (like to) think. We already saw how wealth was a better source of accumulation than salary, and we will return to this issue in our discussion about social mobility below, but one reason for this might be how we raise our children. A research report looked at the way different social classes spend their money on activities and products oriented towards children's learning and development. In the early 1970s, the gap between the top and bottom fifth of the population in the US meant that the former spent about four times as much on their children's learning and development as the bottom fifth. By 2006 the gap had widened to approximately seven times as much.[44]

Whether rewards go to the 'best and the brightest' or to someone who happens to be related to the boss, allocations are rarely equal within a social group. Most groups exhibit a structure, or status hierarchy, in which some members are somehow better off than others. They may have more authority or power, or they are simply more liked or respected. It is important to note that in contemporary societies, status hierarchies may be of different types and they are not necessarily congruent. In other words, it is possible to have high status in some hierarchies but lower in others (see the discussion of status crystallisation, below).

Components of social class

When we think about a person's social class, there are a number of pieces of information we can consider. Two major ones are occupation and income. A third important factor is educational attainment, which is strongly related to income and occupation.

Occupational prestige

In a system where (like it or not) a consumer is defined to a great extent by what they do for a living, *occupational prestige* is one way to evaluate the 'worth' of people. Hierarchies of occupational prestige tend to be quite stable over time, and they also tend to be similar in different societies. Similarities in occupational prestige have been found in countries as diverse as Brazil, Ghana, Guam, Japan and Turkey.[45]

A typical ranking includes a variety of professional and business occupations at the top (e.g. director of a large corporation, doctor or university professor), while those jobs hovering near the bottom include shoe-shiner, unskilled labourer and dustman. Because a person's occupation tends to be strongly linked to their use of leisure time, allocation of family resources, political orientation and so on, this variable is often considered to be the single best indicator of social class.

Wealth

The distribution of wealth is of great interest to social scientists and to marketers, since it determines which groups have the greatest buying power and market potential. Wealth is by no means distributed evenly across the classes. While there is a more equitable distribution of wealth across European countries relative to Latin America, Asia and America – the top fifth of the population in the US controls about 85 per cent of all assets (and what is worse, the top 0.1 per cent equals the bottom 90 per cent in terms of control over value assets)[46] – there is still a disproportionate share of wealth controlled by a small segment of the European population. In Figure 11.4, you can compare the US with various European countries. In OECD countries, the top 10 per cent dispose of 50 per cent of the wealth, and countries such as Austria, the Netherlands and Germany are well above average.[47] One economist made the headlines when he pointed out that in order to understand contemporary inequality, it would be much better to look at the distribution of wealth than of income, and that it was easier to increase one's wealth through investment of existing funds than through salaried work.[48]

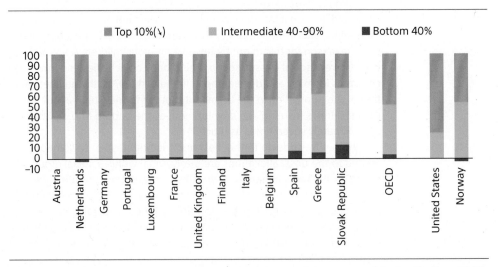

Figure 11.4 Wealth shares of top, middle and bottom of the net wealth distribution, 2010 or latest year

Source: Calculations from OECD Wealth Distribution Database, https://www.oecd.org/els/soc/cope-divide-europe-2017-background-report.pdf [0](accessed 29 August 2018)

The relationship between income and social class

Although consumers tend to equate money with class, the precise relationship between other aspects of social class and income is not clear and has been the subject of debate among social scientists.[49] The two are by no means synonymous, which is why many people with a lot of money try to use it to improve their social class.

The UK, in many ways, still seems very much a class-conscious country and, at least until recently, consumption patterns were pre-ordained in terms of one's inherited position and family background. Members of the upper class were educated at public schools such as Eton and Harrow and had a distinctive accent. Remnants of this rigid class structure can still be found. 'Hooray Henrys' (wealthy young men) play polo at Windsor and, at the time of writing, hereditary peers can still take their seat in the House of Lords. The UK, closely followed by Poland and the Baltic states, is the country in northern Europe with the highest inequality in income distribution.[50]

That said, a straightforward relationship between income and social class is not so easily established. One problem is that even if a family increases its household income by adding wage earners, each additional job is likely to be of lower status. For example, a housewife who gets a part-time job is not as likely to get one that is of equal or greater status than the primary wage earner's. In addition, the extra money earned may not be pooled for the common good of the family. Instead it may be used by the individual for their own personal spending. More money does not then result in increased status or changes in consumption patterns, since it tends to be devoted to buying more of the same, rather than upgrading to higher-status products.[51]

The following general conclusions can be made regarding the relative value of social class (i.e. place of residence, occupation, cultural interests, etc.) *vs* income in predicting consumer behaviour:

- Social class appears to be a better predictor of purchases that have symbolic aspects but low-to-moderate prices (e.g. cosmetics, alcohol).

- Income is a better predictor of major expenditures that do not have status or symbolic aspects (e.g. major appliances).

- Social class and income data together are better predictors of purchases of expensive, symbolic products (e.g. cars, homes, luxury goods).[52]

Social mobility

To what degree do people tend to change their social class? In some traditional societies, social class is very difficult to change, but in Europe, any man or woman can become prime minister. **Social mobility** refers to the 'passage of individuals from one social class to another'.[53] Internationally speaking, social mobility is lower in countries such as the US, the UK and France, while mobility is highest in Nordic countries such as Denmark.[54]

This mobility can be upward, downward or even horizontal. *Horizontal mobility* refers to movement from one position to another roughly equivalent in social status, such as becoming a nurse instead of a junior school teacher. *Downward mobility* is, of course, not very desirable, but this pattern is unfortunately quite evident in recent years as redundant workers have been forced to join the unemployment queue or have joined the ranks of the homeless.[55] Even temporary downward mobility may be experienced as an embarrassment that requires various coping strategies, such as, for example, being downgraded in airplane seating.[56]

Despite the discouraging trends generated by the crisis, hitting harder in countries such as Spain and Greece but nevertheless felt all over Europe, demographics decree that there must be *upward mobility* in European society. The middle and upper classes reproduce less than the lower classes (an effect known as *differential fertility*), and they tend to restrict family size below replacement level. Therefore, so the reasoning goes, positions of higher status over time must be filled by those of lower status.[57] Overall, though, the offspring of blue-collar consumers tend also to be blue-collar, while the offspring of white-collar consumers tend also to be white-collar.[58] People tend to improve their positions over time, but these increases are not usually dramatic enough to catapult them from one social class to another.

Measurement of social class

Because social class is a complex concept that depends on a number of factors, it has not surprisingly proved difficult to measure. Early measures included the Index of Status Characteristics developed in the 1940s and the Index of Social Position developed by Hollingshead in the 1950s.[59] These indices used various combinations of individual characteristics (such as income and type of housing) to arrive at a label of class standing. The accuracy of these composites is still a subject of debate among researchers; one study claimed that, for segmentation purposes, raw education and income measures work as well as composite status measures.[60] A more recent study suggested an easy-to-apply 34-item instrument for indicating social class. By answering yes or no to 34 questions, the respondent can be placed in one of six categories of social class.[61] Easy as that – or what do you think?

Social class is a tricky thing to measure. Blue-collar workers with relatively high-income jobs still tend to view themselves as working class, even though their income levels may be equivalent to those of many white-collar workers.[62] This fact reinforces the idea that the labels 'working class' or 'middle class' are very subjective. Their meanings say at least as much about self-identity as they do about economic well-being.

Problems with measures of social class

Market researchers were among the first to propose that people from different social classes can be distinguished from each other in important ways. While some of these dimensions still exist, others have changed.[63] Unfortunately, many of these measures are badly dated and are not as valid today for a variety of reasons, some of which are discussed here.[64]

Most measures of social class were designed to accommodate the traditional nuclear family, with a male wage earner in the middle of his career and a female full-time home-maker. Such measures have trouble accounting for the two-income families, young singles living alone or households headed by women that are so much more prevalent in today's society (see Chapter 10).

Another problem with assigning people to a social class is that they may not be equal in their standing on all of the relevant dimensions. A person might come from a low-status background but have a high-status job, for example, while another may live in a fashionable part of town but have not completed secondary school. The concept of **status crystallisation** was developed to assess the impact of inconsistency on the self and social behaviour.[65] A particular type of such inconsistency is often felt by middle-class black Americans, who are stigmatised due to their skin colour but in all other aspects of life strive to be 'respected' as ordinary citizens with 'respectable consumption patterns'.[66] A related problem occurs when a person's social-class standing creates expectations that are not met. Some people find themselves in the not unhappy position of making more money than is expected of those in their social class. This situation is known as an *overprivileged condition* and is usually defined as an income that is at least 25–30 per cent over the median for one's class.[67] In contrast, *underprivileged* consumers, who earn at least 15 per cent less than the median, must often devote their consumption priorities to sacrificing in order to maintain the appearance of living up to class expectations.

Lottery winners are examples of consumers who become overprivileged overnight. As attractive as winning is to many people, it has its problems. Consumers with a certain standard of living and level of expectations may have trouble adapting to sudden affluence and may engage in flamboyant and irresponsible displays of wealth. Ironically, it is not unusual for lottery winners to report feelings of depression in the months after the win. They may have trouble adjusting to an unfamiliar world, and they frequently experience pressure from friends, relatives and business people to 'share the wealth'.

One cross-cultural study investigated incongruent relationships between status and identity due to transitions of one or both, and found a significant difference between vertically based transitions (changes in status) and horizontally based transitions, or in other words changes in status that lead to changes in identity versus changes in identity that lead to changes in status. Consumption, it was found, played a far more significant role for the former than the latter, indicating that status-driven life changes are more significant for consumption patterns than identity-driven life changes. One outcome of this is that forced status changes, for example for single women following a divorce, can be a very traumatic experience.[68]

The traditional assumption was that husbands define a family's social class, while wives must live it. Women borrowed their social status from their husbands.[69] Indeed, the evidence indicates that physically attractive women tend to 'marry up' to a greater extent than attractive men. Women trade the resource of sexual appeal, which historically has been one of the few assets they were allowed to possess, for the economic resources of men.[70] The accuracy of this assumption in today's world must be questioned. Many women now contribute equally to the family's well-being and work in positions of comparable or even greater status than their spouses. This process can be found on a global scale.[71] *Cosmopolitan* magazine offered this revelation: 'Women who've become liberated enough to marry any man they please, regardless of his social position, report how much more fun and spontaneous their relationships with men have become now that they no longer view men only in terms of their power symbols'.[72]

Problems with social class segmentation: a summary

Social class remains an important way to categorise consumers. Many marketing strategies do target different social classes. However, marketers have failed to use social class information as effectively as they could for the following reasons:

- they have ignored status inconsistency
- they have ignored intergenerational mobility
- they have ignored subjective social class (i.e. the class a consumer identifies with rather than the one they objectively belong to)
- they have ignored consumers' aspirations to change their class standing
- they have ignored the social status of working wives.

Multicultural dimensions

Elite consumer segments are becoming increasingly significant in a number of emerging markets. These elite segments share some similarities with social elites elsewhere in the world, but they also have their own particular characteristics – for example, in terms of their preferences for the country of origin of their luxury goods. One study demonstrated how the Pakistani elite tends to value luxury items originating in either the US or Japan. A luxury giant such as France is only preferred when it comes to perfumes.[73]

Class structure around the world

Every society has some type of hierarchical class structure, where people's access to products and services is determined by their resources and social standing. Of course, the specific 'markers' of success depend on what is valued in each culture. We may consider these class structures 'exotic', since we are used to considering that consumer societies are located in Western or 'Westernised' contexts. But consider the prediction of OECD for 2050 (see Figure 11.5) in terms of the size of the consuming middle classes – Westerners will increasingly be the 'oddity', while the majority of the consuming middle classes will be Asian.

Profound changes in global income distribution drive this shift. Traditionally, it was common to find a huge gulf between the rich and the poor countries: you were either one or the other. Today, rising incomes in many rapidly developing countries, such as South Korea and China, coupled with decreasing prices for quality consumer goods and services has somewhat levelled the playing field. More and more consumers around the globe participate in the global economy. The biggest emerging markets go by the acronym BRIC: Brazil, Russia, India and China. These four countries today account for 15 per cent of the $60 trillion global economy, but analysts project they will overtake the European and American economies by 2030.[74] (As an aside, sometimes they are referred to as BRICS, throwing South Africa in there for good measure.) And now there is also talk around the town about the MINT countries, Mexico, Indonesia, Nigeria and Turkey, all with huge populations and growing middle classes (but also haunted by internal strife and big income gaps), as new markets of huge interest.[75]

This change fuels demand for mass-consumed products that still offer some degree of panache. Companies such as H&M, Zara, EasyJet and L'Oréal provide creature comforts to a consumer segment that analysts label 'mass class'. This refers to the hundreds of millions of global consumers who now enjoy a level of purchasing power that's sufficient to let them afford high-quality products.

China

In China, an economic boom has created a middle class of more than 430 million people that analysts project to grow to more than 780 million by the mid-2020s.[76] During the Cultural Revolution, Mao's Red Guards seized on even the smallest possessions – a pocket watch or silk scarf – as evidence of 'bourgeois consciousness'. Change came rapidly in the early 1990s,

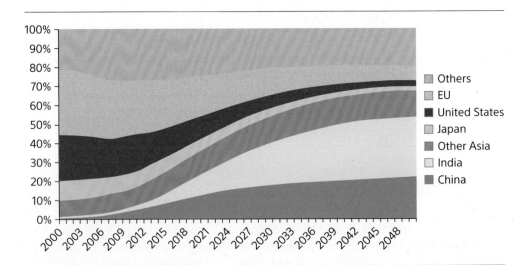

Figure 11.5 Shares of global middle class consumption 2000–2050

Source: Homi Kharas, 'The Emerging Middle Class in Developing Countries', OECD Development Centre, Working Paper no. 285 (OECD 2010). © OECD 2010.

after Mao's successor Deng Xiaoping uttered the phrase that quickly became the credo of the new China: 'To get rich is glorious'. Because costs are low, a family with an annual income of €10–12,000 can enjoy middle-class comforts, including stylish clothes, Chinese-made colour televisions, DVD players and mobile phones. Wealthier Chinese entrepreneurs can indulge in Cuban Cohiba cigars that sell for €20 each – a quarter of the average Chinese labourer's monthly wage. In bustling Shanghai, newly minted 'yuppies' drop their kids off for golf lessons, visit Maserati and Ferrari showrooms, buy some luxury items from Louis Vuitton, Hugo Boss or Prada and then pick up some Häagen-Dazs ice cream before heading to an Evian spa to unwind. One cultural difference that may help to account for this love of branded goods is that Asians tend to be highly sensitive to cues that communicate social standing, and well-known brand names help to manage this impression. Indeed, even in the US, researchers report that Asian immigrants and Asian Americans have a higher preference for branded goods over generic products compared to other Americans.[77]

However, China is one of the countries with the highest Gini coefficient. The class differences in China are very much a question of rural and urban populations. This high and still-increasing inequality is causing concern for the stability of Chinese society.[78] Furthermore, the changes in Chinese consumption standards and the nation's role as the world's consumer goods workshop (which has enabled the wealth accumulation) have come at the price of a tremendous pollution problem. The air quality in many of China's metropolitan areas, particularly Beijing, now frequently reaches 'hazardous' levels and is destructive for the tourism industry, which is why the Chinese government is adopting policies to make Chinese consumers scrap their old, highly polluting cars,[79] and why local government restricts the issue of new licence plates.

India

As with China, India's economy has undergone a big booming period, and many higher-end global brands are catching on. India's economy is among the fastest-growing in the world, and brands such as Gucci, Hermès and others are scrambling to open stores. One of Bollywood's biggest stars, Shahrukh Khan, was 'brand ambassador' for Tag Heuer watches, which cost thousands of dollars. He gave them away on the Indian version of *Who Wants to Be a Millionaire?*. India's ascendancy is fairly recent; for decades after the country became independent from Britain, its economy was a relatively closed one. Today, a lot of young consumers watch satellite TV, surf the internet, read international fashion magazines and are embracing the power of plastic; credit-card spending in India rose by 275 per cent a year from 2012 to 2017.[80] Indian consumers have even (re-)discovered yoga! As a recent study points out, Indians are increasingly consuming yoga in a variety of fitness and wellness centres, both as a modern relaxation and wellness technique but also as a sign of traditional cultural identity. As such, it has become a new middle-class marker in India.[81]

Not everybody is invited to the party, though. Inequality in India as well as China is out of proportion compared to what we know in the Western world, and economic development often happens at the expense of the poor population of so-called subaltern consumers – typically farmers, fishermen, unskilled workers and people of other traditional occupations.[82]

Marketing pitfall

One marketing incident illustrates the divide in Indian society. *Vogue India* ran a 16-page spread of poor people surrounded by luxury goods: a toothless old woman holds a child who wears a Fendi bib; a woman and two other people ride on a motorbike as she sports a Hermès bag that sells for more than $10,000; a street beggar grips a Burberry umbrella. A columnist denounced the spread as 'not just tacky but downright distasteful'. The magazine's editor commented that the shoot's message is simply that 'fashion is no longer a rich man's privilege. Anyone can carry it off and make it look beautiful'.[83] While that is a gross overstatement, the Indian middle class is indeed growing a lot. However, they are not free from suffering from the downsides of consumerism. As of 2017, it was reported that demands for 'keeping up with the Joneses' in India (see later in the chapter under 'Status symbols') has led to an unhealthy consumption pattern where much too many purchases are loan- and credit-financed. The consequences: eternal financial worries, even among many relatively well-off middle-class consumers.[84]

Japan

Japan is a highly status-conscious society, where upmarket, designer labels are popular and new forms of status are always being sought. In spite of this modernisation of the Japanese consumer society, spiritual dimensions remain very important for the meanings Japanese attach to a variety of consumption rituals.[85]

Although the devastation wrought by the 2011 earthquake and tsunami reduced demand for luxury goods among many Japanese, their love affair with top brands started in the 1970s when the local economy was booming and many Japanese could buy Western luxury accessories for the first time. Some analysts say Japan's long slump since that time may have fostered a psychological need to splurge on small luxuries to give people the illusion of wealth and to forget their anxieties about the future. Single, working women are largely responsible for fuelling Japan's luxury-goods spending; about three-quarters of Japanese women aged 25 to 29 work outside the home. These 'office ladies' (as we saw in Chapter 10) save money by living with their parents, so this leaves them with cash in hand to spend on clothes, accessories and holidays.

Middle East

In contrast to the Japanese, few Arab women work, so searching for the latest in Western luxury brands is a major leisure activity. Dressing rooms are large, with antechambers to accommodate friends and family members who often come along on shopping sprees. A major expansion of Western luxury brands is under way across the Middle East, home to some of the fashion industry's best customers. High-end retailers such as Saks Fifth Avenue and Giorgio Armani operate opulent stores to cater to this growing market. However, fashion retailers must take cultural and religious considerations into account. Missoni makes sure that collections include longer trousers and skirts, and evening gowns with light shawls to cover heads or bare shoulders. And advertising and display options are more limited: erotic images don't work. In the strict religious culture of Saudi Arabia, mannequins cannot reveal a gender or human shape. At Saks' Riyadh store, models are headless and do not have fingers. Half of the two-level store is off-limits to men.[86] This division of gendered spaces for consumption is not only established in public but also in private homes.[87]

Among the extremely wealthy locals in the Gulf states of Qatar and the United Arab Emirates, balancing modesty and vanity has led to a particular status game. The local dresses, the *abaya,* supposedly covering the body and preventing desire, have become another status and fashion item – both separating the (often extremely wealthy) locals from the (often poorer) expatriate workers, and providing tailors and fashion designers and brands with a new playground for innovativeness.[88]

Africa

The consumer market in a variety of African countries is booming, beyond the already mentioned countries of South Africa and Nigeria. The International Monetary Fund estimated that six of the ten fastest-growing economies in the world in 2018 will be in Africa.[89] Economic growth has reached an impressive 7–8 per cent in countries such as Ghana, Ethiopia, Ivory Coast, Djibouti, Senegal and Tanzania,[90] while the oil economy of Nigeria is of an impressive size, even if growth is slower. New consumer middle classes in Kenya, for example, enjoy standards of consumption of many services and goods that do not trail behind many European countries. However, it is also obvious that such estimates depend very much on how you define 'middle classes' – ranging from people being able to spend $2 per day to the afore-mentioned benefiters of Kenyan urban life.[91]

Marketing opportunity

In Kenya, one of the hot status symbols in 2018 is the door! Rather than mere separators between the inside and the outside or between various rooms, doors have become stylised expressions of taste and class. 'When viewing a house, it is one of the first things buyers or renters see when they enter', says one housing market agent. A plethora of styles are available, and the choices between, say, vintage-looking or Arab-style décor is carefully made.[92]

How social class affects purchase decisions

Social class has a fundamental impact on our consumer tastes.

Different products and stores are often, and possibly rightly so, perceived by consumers to be appropriate for certain social classes.[93] And income inequalities are growing in many societies in the West, notably in the US but also elsewhere – a fact that contributed to the 'Occupy Wall Street' and 'We are the 99 per cent' protest movements. However, due to other changes in market society, it has become tougher for the casual observer to accurately place a consumer in a certain class by looking at the products he buys. That's because a lot of 'affordable luxuries' are now within reach of many consumers who could not have acquired them in the past. In addition, the widespread use of credit – one of the core constituents of consumer culture[94] – has blurred the direct class-signalling effect of many consumer goods. This being said, social differences persist in forming different consumer cultures in different layers of the population.

Class differences in worldview

A major social-class difference involves the *worldview* of consumers. The world of the working class (including the lower-middle class) is more intimate and constricted. For example, working-class men are more likely to name local sports figures as heroes and are less likely to take long holidays in out-of-the-way places.[95] Immediate needs, such as a new refrigerator or TV, tend to dictate buying behaviour for these consumers, while the higher classes tend to focus on more long-term goals, such as saving for college fees or retirement.[96]

Working-class consumers depend heavily on relatives for emotional support and tend to orient themselves in terms of the community rather than the world at large. They are more likely to be conservative and family oriented. Maintaining the appearance of one's home and property is a priority, regardless of the size of the house. One recent study that looked at social class and how it relates to consumers' feelings of *empowerment* reported that lower-class men are not as likely to feel they have the power to affect their outcomes. Respondents varied from those who were what the researcher calls *potent actors* (those who believe they have the ability to take actions that affect their world) to *impotent reactors* (those who feel they are at the mercy of their economic situations). This orientation influenced consumption behaviour: for example, the professionals in the study, who were likely to be the potent actors, set themselves up for financial opportunity and growth by taking very broad perspectives on investing and planning their budgets strategically.[97]

While good things appear to go hand in hand with higher status and wealth, the picture is not that clear. The social scientist Emile Durkheim observed that suicide rates are far higher among the wealthy. He wrote in 1897, 'the possessors of most comfort suffer most'.[98] The quest for riches has the potential to result in depression, deviant behaviour and ruin. In fact, a survey

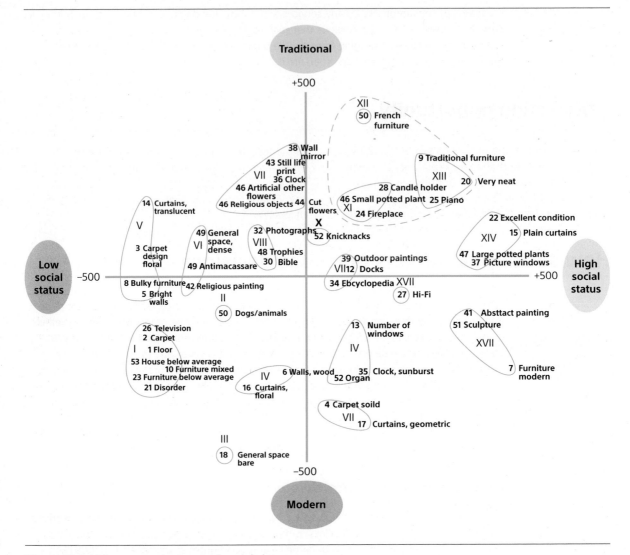

Figure 11.6 Living room clusters and social class

Source: Edward O. Laumann and James S. House, 'Living room styles and social attributes: The patterning of material artifacts in a modern urban community', Sociology and Social Research 54 (April 1970): 321–42.

of affluent American consumers supports this notion. Although these people are in the top 2.5 per cent income bracket in the US, only 14 per cent said they felt very well off.[99]

The concept of a **taste culture**, which differentiates people in terms of their aesthetic and intellectual preferences, is helpful in understanding the important yet subtle distinctions in consumption choices among the social classes. Taste cultures largely reflect education (and are also income-related).[100] A distinction is often made between low cultural-capital and high cultural-capital groups (this is discussed in more detail towards the end of this chapter), which reflects shared tastes in literature, art, home decoration and so on. In one classic study of social differences in taste, researchers catalogued home-owners' possessions while asking more typical questions about income and occupation. Clusters of furnishings and decorative items that seemed to appear together with some regularity were identified, and different clusters were found depending on the consumer's social status. For example, religious objects, artificial flowers and still-life portraits tended to be found together in relatively lower-status living rooms, while a cluster containing abstract paintings, sculptures and modern furniture was more likely to appear in a higher-status home (see Figure 11.6).[101]

Another study investigating the highly popular blog and indoor decoration site 'Apartment Therapy' applied the notion of 'taste regimes' rather than taste culture in order to underline how such tastes are also forming our practices, how we live and act in daily life. One example discusses the notion of making a 'landing strip' in one's home, allowing people to have places for keys, coats, etc., a mirror for last-minute correction of hair and other aspects of 'look', a space for dropping off one's bag, etc. In other words, the taste for a 'landing strip' engendered a certain way of 'coming home' and 'going out'. A taste culture is therefore not just something one 'has' but something one 'gets' through social mediations.[102] Likewise, an orchestra hall made strategic use of its lobby space as one such social mediator and thereby succeeded in influencing consumer tastes in classical music.[103]

We all carry stereotypical imagery of taste cultures in our heads. If you are told about one person that they like to visit museums and attend live theatre and about another that they like camping and fishing and like to attend a boxing match, which one would you place in the highest social-class segment? You were probably right.[104]

Another approach to social class focuses on differences in the types of *codes* (the ways meanings are expressed and interpreted by consumers) used within different social strata. Discovery of these codes is valuable to marketers, since this knowledge allows them to communicate to markets using concepts and terms most likely to be understood and appreciated by specific consumers. The nature of these codes varies among social classes. **Restricted codes** are dominant among the working classes, while elaborated codes tend to be used by the middle and upper classes. Restricted codes focus on the content of objects, not on relationships among objects. **Elaborated codes**, in contrast, are more complex and depend upon a more sophisticated worldview. Some differences between these two general types of codes are provided in Table 11.1. As this table indicates, these code differences extend to the way consumers approach such basic concepts as time, social relationships and objects. The brand as a code in itself constitutes an interesting issue: a study of the importance of brands in a choice of lunch boxes among British school children confirmed the importance of the brand code among those children, recruited from the lower class.[105] A study of high-end consumers in Scandinavia reached the exact opposite conclusion – that brands were something to be highly sceptical about.[106] We might conclude that, according to an elaborated code, brands are not as trustworthy.

Marketing appeals that are constructed with these differences in mind will result in quite different messages. For example, a life insurance ad targeted at a lower-class person might depict in simple, straightforward terms a hard-working family man who feels good immediately after purchasing a policy. An upmarket appeal might depict a more affluent older couple surrounded by photos of their children and grandchildren and contain extensive copy emphasising the satisfaction that comes from planning for the future and highlighting the benefits of a whole-life insurance policy.

Targeting the poor

While poor people obviously have less to spend than rich ones, they have the same basic needs as everyone else. Low-income families purchase such staples as milk, bread and tea at the same rates as average-income families. And minimum-wage-level households spend a greater than average share on over-the-counter medicine, rent and food consumed at home. Equality among the poor raises overall satisfaction levels, but paradoxically also generates a tendency to destroy this equality (as it increases the propensity to spend a little extra since it can improve one's relative position).[107] The risk of poverty is a good measure of economic crisis. In 2016, the percentage of people at risk of poverty in the EU was just over 17 per cent,[108] almost the same as in 2008, whereas it was 23 per cent in 2010.[109] This average figure, however, covers big differences in the different EU countries. Certain household types are typically more likely to be at risk of poverty: single parents with dependent children (these single parents are overwhelmingly female parents), old people living alone, single females and two-adult households with three or more dependent children.

Table 11.1 Effects of restricted versus elaborated codes

	Restricted codes	Elaborated codes
General characteristics	Emphasise description and contents of objects	Emphasise analysis and interrelationships between objects, i.e. hierarchical organisation and instrumental connections
	Have implicit meanings (context dependent)	Have explicit meanings
Language	Use few qualifiers, i.e. few adjectives or adverbs	Have language rich in personal, individual qualifiers
	Use concrete, descriptive, tangible symbolism	Use large vocabulary, complex conceptual hierarchy
Social relationships	Stress attributes of individuals over formal roles	Stress formal role structure, instrumental relationships
Time	Focus on present; have only general notion of future	Focus on instrumental relationship between present activities and future rewards
Physical space	Locate rooms and spaces in context of other rooms and places: e.g. 'front room', 'corner shop'	Identify rooms and spaces in terms of usage; formal ordering of spaces: e.g. 'dining room', 'financial district'
Implications for marketers	Stress inherent product quality, contents (or trustworthiness, goodness of 'real-type'), spokesperson	Stress differences, advantages vis-à-vis other products in terms of some autonomous evaluation criteria
	Stress implicit fit of product with total lifestyle	Stress product's instrumental ties to distant benefits
	Use simple adjectives, descriptors	Use complex adjectives, descriptors

Source: Adapted from Jeffrey F. Durgee, 'How Consumer Sub-Cultures Code Reality: A Look at Some Code Types', in Richard J. Lutz (ed.), Advances in Consumer Research 13 (Provo, UT: Association for Consumer Research, 1986): 332.

The unemployed do feel alienated in a consumer society, since they are unable to obtain many of the items that our culture tells us we 'need' to be successful. However, idealised advertising portrayals do not seem to appeal to low-end consumers who have been interviewed by researchers. Apparently, one way to preserve self-esteem is by placing oneself outside the culture of consumption and emphasising the value of a simple way of life with less emphasis on materialism. If you remain in the consumer culture, however, your relative feeling of powerlessness might induce you to choose larger portion sizes, as one American study concluded, adding worse to bad in terms of the health and obesity problems often associated with lower social classes.[110]

In some cases, lower-income consumers enjoy advertising as entertainment without actually yearning for the products. A comment by one 32-year-old British woman is typical: 'They're not aimed at me, definitely not. It's fine to look at them, but they're not aimed at me so in the main I just pass over them'.[111] A more recent study identified other coping strategies among poorer people when confronted with the consumption consequences of their own poverty. Such coping strategies could be rooted in the fulfilling of role expectations – for example, through the feeling of being a good mother in spite of not being able to give the children a lot in material terms, in the feeling of independence coming from not being dependent on others in spite of a low income, or in the consolation that others are worse off.[112] Furthermore, a variety of strategies for avoiding conflict are applied in order to avoid poverty-generated conflict in the family – for example, by being open about the economic troubles of the household.[113]

The headline of this section is treacherous, since it suggests that the poor are a homogeneous group. In fact, although they share a lack of economic resources, their lifestyles and value profiles may be highly diverging, as testified by one study of the population of an American trailer-park neighbourhood. Just in this micro-community, the study identified five different 'lifestyles', including 'nesters', 'community builders' and 'outcast'.[114] Consumer researchers, usually belonging to a quite different social status group, should therefore be cautious to draw too many rapid and stereotypical conclusions about 'how the poor live'.

Consumer behaviour as I see it . . .

Coping with poverty

Kathy Hamilton, University of Strathclyde

Within our consumer culture, people use consumption to send identity messages to others. However, building consumer identity requires access to financial resources. What happens when you can't afford to buy the latest on-trend trainers for your children? What happens when you can't afford to participate in social activities and go on regular holidays? It was questions of this kind that guided my research with low-income families.

My qualitative research with low-income families considered the coping strategies that are employed by those who are restricted in their opportunities for consumption. Findings revealed that consumers on low incomes can become skilled at managing the family budget. Coping strategies include price comparisons, turning to the second-hand market, shopping in discount stores, searching for bargains and selling possessions.

However, as well as dealing with material hardships, consumers on low incomes have to cope with negative attitudes and reactions from others. They are subject to marketplace stigma, meaning that they encounter labelling, stereotyping, and devaluation for going against perceived norms of consumer culture. Stigmatization can have a negative impact on well-being. As a result, the coping strategies employed by low-income families are often aimed at disguising poverty and portraying a socially acceptable image.

Disguising poverty appears to be especially important for young people who do not want to appear different from their peers. Within consumer culture there is a large emphasis on designer brand names that have high brand-awareness among children, even those younger than school age. By displaying brand-name or 'on-trend' products that are regarded as socially acceptable among peer groups, low-income consumers distance themselves from the stigma of poverty.

Parents often make sacrifices and place the desires of their children before their own, ensuring that the family budget in managed in such a way that children have the material resources necessary to 'fit in' with their peers. The result is that low-income families may prioritise the consumption of visible goods, such as brand-name clothing, over invisible, private goods, such as food and other goods consumed in the home. Thus, current categories of 'discretionary' and 'non-discretionary' spending need to be revisited when considering the behaviour of those experiencing poverty, as do hierarchy-of-needs frameworks that suggest consumers meet basic needs for food and shelter before buying the more discretionary 'social' goods, such as branded trainers.

Questions

Is coping through consumption an effective response to poverty?

What is the relationship between stigma and the marketplace? What role do marketers play in fuelling both stigmatisation and destigmatisation?

Kathy Hamilton

Still, a lot of companies are taking a second look at marketing to the poor because of their large numbers. The economist C.K. Prahalad added fuel to this fire with his book *The Fortune at the Bottom of the Pyramid,* which argued that big companies could profit and help the world's four billion poor or low-income people by finding innovative ways to sell them soap and refrigerators.[115] And maybe he was not all wrong in pointing out this potential. A recent report by the market research agency Nielsen concluded that much of the impressive Brazilian retail growth of 5.5 per cent in value in 2010 was driven by low-income groups.[116]

Some companies are getting into these vast markets by revamping their distribution systems or making their products simpler and less expensive. When Nestlé Brazil shrank the package size of its Bono cookies (no relation to the U2 singer) from 200 grams to 140 grams and dropped the price, sales jumped 40 per cent. In Uganda, very small packages of tea are marketed as 'economy packs' (quite the contrary of what we usually understand by that concept). And in Mexico, the cement company Cemex improved housing in poor areas after it introduced a pay-as-you-go system for buying building supplies.[117]

Muhammad Yunus, a Bangladeshi economist, won the 2006 Nobel Prize in Economics for pioneering the concept of **microfinance**. His Grameen Bank loans small sums – typically less than $100 – to entrepreneurs in developing countries. Today, there are a number of such microfinancial institutions, and in many circles they have gained a reputation as a highly ethical business practice. However, in recent years growing critique has been raised against the microfinance-business, indicating not only that they are exporting a particular Western model of market and consumer,[118] but also that their lending techniques are exploitative, the interest rates too high and that, at the end of the day, they do not contribute much to alleviate poverty.[119]

Targeting the rich

We live in an age where elite department stores sell Donna Karan and Calvin Klein Barbies, and Mattel's Pink Splendor Barbie comes complete with crystal jewellery and a bouffant gown sewn with 24-carat threads.[120] To dress the 'living doll', Victoria's Secret offers its Million Dollar Fantasy Bra, with over 100 carats of real diamonds.[121] *Somebody* must be buying this stuff. . .

Many marketers try to target affluent markets. This practice often makes sense, since these consumers obviously have the resources to expend on costly products (often with higher profit margins). *The Robb Report,* a magazine targeted at the very affluent, has traditionally focused on the American market, but today also publishes reports on countries such as China, Russia, Brazil and Turkey. In these times of crisis, they have had to defend themselves against attacks from journalists and citizens who are bringing these super-rich lifestyles into discredit.[122]

However, it is a mistake to assume that everyone with a high income should be placed in the same market segment. As noted earlier, social class involves more than absolute income: it is also a way of life, and affluent consumers' interests and spending priorities are significantly affected by such factors as where they got their money, how they got it and how long they have had it.[123] For example, the marginally rich tend to prefer sporting events to cultural activities, and are only half as likely as the super rich to frequent art galleries or the opera.[124]

Multicultural dimensions

In a nation where one-child families are the rule, Chinese parents spare few expenses when bringing up baby. But the relatively uncontrolled Chinese market generates new class differences in Chinese parenting. Food scandals in China are not only routine, but difficult to control and contain; years after the 2008 melamine-tainted infant formula scandal sickened nearly 300,000 Chinese babies, the chemical continued to make scattered appearances across the country. How do Chinese consumers cope with the constant danger that what they buy for themselves or their families may have fatal consequences? When buying products with a potential for bodily harm, particularly those for children or infants, educated consumers (those with cultural capital – see the final section of this chapter) focus on channel of purchase rather than brand. Concerned that the government cannot be trusted to ensure goods on the Chinese market, some consumers seek out goods originally designated for markets with strong legal and regulatory systems, producer accountability and activist consumers. This has led to a thriving market in informally imported infant formula and other goods for babies. Online marketplaces such as *Taobao* boast hundreds of stores selling infant formula purchased in Australia, the US, the UK and many European nations and sold directly to Chinese consumers at as much as 400 per cent of the original price. Although many of the brands sold through these channels are available in China, the products available domestically are perceived as inferior to the nearly identical products sold abroad.[125]

Old money

When people have enough money for all intents and purposes, to buy just about anything they want, social distinctions ironically no longer revolve around the amount of money they have. Instead, it appears to be important to consider *where* the money came from and *how* it is spent. The 'top out-of-sight class' (such as Julia's parents) live primarily on inherited money. People who have made vast amounts of money from their own labour do not tend to be included in this select group, though their flamboyant consumption patterns may represent an attempt to prove their wealth.[126] The mere presence of wealth is thus not sufficient to achieve social prominence. It must be accompanied by a family history of public service and philanthropy, which is often manifested in tangible markers that enable these donors to achieve a kind of immortality (e.g. Rockefeller University or the Whitney Museum).[127] 'Old money' consumers tend to make distinctions among themselves in terms of ancestry and lineage rather than wealth.[128] Old money people (like the Caldwells) are secure in their status. In a sense, they have been trained their whole lives to be rich and hence feel less urgency to demonstrate their wealth at any given opportunity. As the saying goes, discretion is a matter of honour.

The nouveaux riches

Other wealthy people do not know how to be rich. The Horatio Alger myth, the dream of going from 'rags to riches' through hard work and a bit of luck, is still a powerful force in Western society and, more recently, in Asian societies as well. Although many people do in fact become 'self-made millionaires', they often encounter a problem (although not the worst problem one could think of!) after they have become wealthy and have changed their social status: consumers who have achieved extreme wealth and have relatively recently become members of upper social classes are known as the *nouveaux riches,* a term that is sometimes used in a derogatory manner to describe newcomers to the world of wealth.

The *nouveau riche* phenomenon is also widespread in Russia and other Eastern European countries, where the transition to capitalism has paved the way for a new class of wealthy consumers who are spending lavishly on luxury items. One study of wealthy Russians identified a group of 'super-spenders', who spend as much on discretionary items as they do on rent. They would like to spend more money, but are frustrated by the lack of quality products and services available to them.[129]

Alas, many *nouveaux riches* are plagued by *status anxiety.* They monitor the cultural environment to ensure that they are doing the 'right' thing, wearing the 'right' clothes, being seen in the 'right' places, using the 'right' caterer and so on.[130] Flamboyant consumption can thus be viewed as a form of symbolic self-completion, where the excessive display of symbols thought to denote 'class' is used to make up for an internal lack of assurance about the 'correct' way to behave.[131]

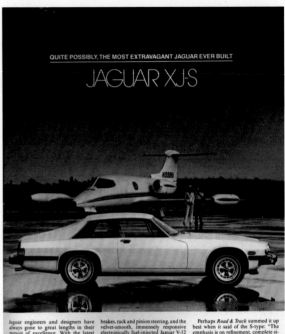

"If you can afford this car, you probably also have a private jet" – high social status at display...

Magic Car Pics/Shutterstock

Status symbols

Social stratification creates a status hierarchy, where some goods come to signify the social status of their owners.

People have a deep-seated tendency to evaluate themselves, their professional accomplishments, their material well-being and so on, in relation to others. The popular phrase 'keeping up with the Joneses' (in Japan, 'keeping up with the Satos', in Uganda, 'keeping up with the Mukasas') and the popular reality TV programme *Keeping Up with the Kardashians*, refer to the comparison between one's standard of living and that of one's neighbours. This is true even in the details of life. One study demonstrated how we assign value to loyalty programmes (e.g. when airlines award you special status based on the number of miles you fly) at least in part based on our level in the hierarchy relative to other members. Subjects were assigned to 'gold status' in a programme where they were in the only tier, or a programme where there was also a silver tier. Although both groups were 'gold', those in the programme that also offered a lower level felt better about it.[132]

Satisfaction is a relative concept, however. We hold ourselves to a standard defined by others that is constantly changing. Unfortunately, a major motivation for the purchase and display of products is not to enjoy them, but rather to let others know that we can afford them. In other words, these products function as status symbols. The desire to accumulate these 'badges of achievement' is summarised by the slogan 'He who dies with the most toys, wins'. Status-seeking is a significant source of motivation to procure appropriate products and services that the user hopes will let others know that they have 'made it'. The popular movie *The Joneses* from 2009 illustrates the consequences of this logic – but also that the chase of 'the most toys' may end up taking your life.

Conspicuous consumption

The motivation to consume for the sake of consuming was first discussed by the social analyst Thorstein Veblen at the turn of the last century. Veblen felt that a major role of products was for invidious distinction – they are used to inspire envy in others through display of wealth or power. Veblen coined the term **conspicuous consumption** to refer to people's desire to provide prominent visible evidence of their ability to afford luxury goods. Veblen's work was motivated by the excesses of his time. He wrote in the era of the robber barons, where the likes of J.P. Morgan, Henry Clay Frick, William Vanderbilt and others were building massive financial empires and flaunting their wealth by throwing lavish parties. Some of these events of excess became legendary, as described in this account:

> there were tales, repeated in the newspapers, of dinners on horseback; of banquets for pet dogs; of hundred-dollar bills folded into guests' dinner napkins; of a hostess who attracted attention by seating a chimpanzee at her table; of centerpieces in which lightly clad living maidens swam in glass tanks, or emerged from huge pies; of parties at which cigars were ceremoniously lighted with flaming banknotes of large denominations.[133]

Marketing opportunity

In this age of fitness and active lifestyles, cycling has been taken up by many as a new way of getting exercise, getting around in the cities without getting stuck in the traffic and even getting out into nature and the countryside (provided you don't live in the centre of a metropolitan area!). As a reference to some of the world's 'bicycling capitals', terms such as 'Copenhagenising' or 'Amsterdamising' are now being used to describe other cities' attempts to make life easier for cyclists through the introduction of bike paths and separate traffic, etc.

With the increased focus on bicycling comes also an increased consciousness of its status value, and the inconspicuous bicycle is rapidly becoming, for some, a new way of showing off in many countries in Europe, such as Germany.[134] Even in China, where consumers have rushed from bicycle to car transportation, a few up-market consumers are following the biking trend.[135]

For the really wealthy among you, what about a Damien Hirst-designed Butterfly Trek Madone Bike auctioned at 500,000 USD? But that is of course one of a kind – in terms of (small) serial products, what about a 24-carat gold-coated Montante bike with python leather finish and 11,000 Swarovski crystals for adornment – only 46,000 USD? No? Well then check out some of the other possibilities for really showing off on your bike.[136]

The modern potlatch

Veblen was inspired by anthropological studies of the Kwakiutl Indians, who lived in the American Pacific Northwest. These Indians had a ceremony called a **potlatch** – a feast where the host showed off his wealth and gave extravagant presents to the guests. The more one gave away, the better one looked to the others. Sometimes the host would use an even more radical strategy to flaunt his wealth. He would publicly destroy some of his property to demonstrate how much he had.

This ritual was also used as a social weapon: since guests were expected to reciprocate, a poorer rival could be humiliated by being invited to a lavish potlatch. The need to give away as much as the host, even though he could not afford it, would essentially force the hapless guest into bankruptcy. If this practice sounds 'primitive', think for a moment about many modern weddings. Parents commonly invest huge sums of money to throw a lavish party and compete with others for the distinction of giving their daughter the 'best' or most extravagant wedding, even if they have to save for 20 years to do so. However, even though many buy into the lavish spending logic for the wedding, not everybody engages in the 'wedding potlatch' the exact same way. Young females engage in profound reflections on 'how to waste the best way'.[137]

The leisure class

This process of conspicuous consumption was, for Veblen, most evident among what he termed the *leisure class,* people for whom productive work is taboo. In Marxist terms, this reflects a desire to link oneself to ownership or control of the means of production, rather than to the production itself. Any evidence that one actually has to work for a living is to be shunned, as suggested by the term the 'idle rich'.

There seems to be a modern paradox about the contemporary 'leisure class': the people who can afford the most to not work are also those who work the most.[138] Conspicuous busyness, rather than leisure time, has become a status symbol for many, both in the US and in Europe, although more in the former than the latter.[139] However, social psychological research consistently underlines that we gain more happiness from extra time than from extra money.[140] And many people *talk* about the possibility of getting off the rat race, but quite few realise this dream.

Like the potlatch ritual, the desire to convince others that one has a surplus of resources creates the need for evidence of this abundance. Accordingly, priority is given to consumption activities that use up as many resources as possible in non-constructive pursuits. This *conspicuous waste* in turn shows others that one has the assets to spare. Veblen noted that 'we are told of certain Polynesian chiefs, who, under the stress of good form, preferred to starve rather than carry their food to their mouths with their own hands'.[141]

Multicultiral dimensions
Passports as new luxury

The luxury goods sector has seen some strange phenomena. One of the stranger ones is the current rise in passports as a commodity, and this time not in the black market. Twenty or so countries (in Europe, Cyprus, Portugal, Malta and Moldova) offer national passports in exchange for investments. This makes it possible for businessmen (both the honest and the not-so-honest ones), notably from China or Russia, to 'buy' passports, thus securing them visa-free entry to a much larger number of countries than their Chinese or Russian passports. One of the most attractive (but also expensive) citizenships is for Cyprus – a €2 million investment in either real estate or in Cypriot national bonds will secure you the craved-for document. Also, Canada, the US and the UK offer similar opportunities, but the path to citizenship is somewhat more difficult here than in the most 'open' countries.[142]

The death – and rebirth – of status symbols

While ostentatious products fell out of favour in the 1970s as a result of the rebellious previous decade, the 1990s and the early part of the twenty-first century (at least until the crisis set in in 2008) saw a resurgence of interest in luxury goods. European companies such as Hermès International, Moët Hennessy Louis Vuitton (LVMH) and Baccarat enjoyed sales gains of between 13 and 16 per cent, as affluent consumers once again indulged their desires for the finer things in life. One market researcher termed this trend 'the pleasure revenge' – people were tired of buying moderately, eating low-fat foods and so on, and, as a result, sales boomed for self-indulgent products from fur coats to premium ice creams and caviar. As the Chairman of LVMH put it: 'The appetite for luxury is as strong as ever. The only difference is that in the 1980s, people would put a luxury trademark on anything. Today only the best sells'.[143] Think of the earlier quote concerning the conspicuous consumption around the end of the nineteenth and early twentieth century – which examples of similarly spectacular (and excessive?) conspicuous consumption can you find dating from the more recent turn of the century?

Inconspicuous consumption

As the competition to accumulate status symbols escalates, sometimes the best tactic is to switch gears and go into reverse. One way to do this is to deliberately *avoid* status symbols. One of the most proliferated consumer concepts of 2014 was the 'normcore' phenomenon. After its introduction by a group of New York-based artists, who wanted to ironise over consumer society and its eternal fashion and status games, it immediately spread through social media and generated a new 'style' of 'not being styled'. The ironic statement hit a note among consumers who might have suffered from 'hipster-style fatigue' and were seeking not to have to communicate through anything they wore.[144] Well, 'normcore' may be a short-lived fad, only time will tell. But the spreading of luxury consumption to more and more parts of the world and larger and larger segments (allegedly 94 per cent of Tokyo women in their twenties own a Louis Vuitton item, while 92 per cent own a Gucci), the fact that lower-status groups may be more inclined to engage in luxury brand consumption since it is one way of standing out and 'borrowing' some of the status of higher social classes, and a general growing discontent with the ostentatious display of luxury brands, also in countries such as China,[145] has made inconspicuous and discrete luxury brands a growing market globally. This combination of subtlety and snobbery allows for a more complex way of thinking about the relationships between consumption and social status.[146]

Capital and practices: class-based lifestyles

11.5

Our lifestyles are shaped not only by economic but also by cultural capital, and are expressed in the form of daily consumer practices.

We can now try to summarise the relationship between social class and consumption, by integrating a lot of what we have described in the preceding pages into one conceptual framework. The French sociologist Pierre Bourdieu described society in terms of a competition for different types of **capital**.[147] Capital, for Bourdieu, is resources that are acknowledged and can be used as assets in various contexts. He distinguished primarily between economic (money, as well as access to money, i.e. financing possibilities), cultural (education, cultural knowledge) and social (networks, social connections) capital. Cultural capital, however, is not exclusively a matter of formal education but also, more generally speaking, a matter of 'manners'. Take the example of dining out. This is one domain (or 'field' as Bourdieu would call it), where there can be a lot at stake. Remember that scene from *Pretty Woman,* where Julia Roberts is trying to learn which fork is used for what in a highly formal dinner setting? This is an example of trying to pick up cultural capital. But it does not have to be as high-brow as that. Just knowing a little about what to expect from an Indian versus a Thai or a Chinese restaurant, how to compose a meal from a menu, what to drink with which course – all these little 'knowledges' also constitute cultural capital. And that capital must be mobilised whenever we are eating out, whereby we reveal something about how much of it we have, and which kinds of class and other distinctions are brought into play, when we sit down at the table.[148]

For Bourdieu, social life can be seen as a number of games, which people constantly win or lose to varying degrees. Social domination, then, is an outcome of how these resources or types of capital are distributed and brought to use strategically in the social games. Business, of course, is one such game. But family (how to make a good one) is also considered a game. As such, the games are played in different fields, such as the already mentioned business and family, but also politics, sports, news, education, entertainment, science, art and so on. Hence, it is obvious that the same types of capital do not apply in all fields – it is difficult to qualify as a sports hero based on a doctoral dissertation. But not all great sports people become sports heroes – only certain of them seem have this extra 'star quality', which may be rooted in their abilities to play the games well and exploit their capital to the maximum. And speaking of sports: the notion of cultural capital was used to analyse the distinction between the inner circle of hardcore football fans and the larger circle of the wider fan community in the football clubs Liverpool FC (England) and Cork City (Ireland). It was found that part of the build-up of cultural capital for the die-hard fans was through the sacrifices made for the club and for attending the matches. Thus, having sacrificed a lot of time, money, effort and even family events for the club provided a particular status for the football consumers.[149] Indeed, as some researchers have suggested based on a recent study, 'fandom' may be one of the domains where consumers without so many assets at their disposal can act out their status aspirations and acquire cultural capital.[150]

The position of each individual in these status games and their resources constitutes the basis for a person's **habitus** – a structuring set of classifications and tastes that permeates our lives and determines our ways of behaviour, as well as our judgement of different social phenomena – in short, our lifestyles. This kind of tacit status display permeates our lives and choices and has been shown to be relevant even for understanding choices of private schools in the UK.[151] Differences in habitus also permits the lower-class people to not necessarily be envious of the rich, since apart from the lack of economic worries (which, as we have seen, the lower-class people also attribute to the higher-class people), there is not much to be envious about. Much of the high-cultural and economic-capital leisurely activities appear to be outright boring to the lower class, just as there is a tendency to consider high-class social gatherings as less warm and heartfelt compared to lower-class social gatherings. Hence, the driver of this whole system, according to Bourdieu, is the process of **distinction**. This process works in terms of the social differences that exist in society, the aspirations to overcome them through social mobility or the aspirations to keep them (from above as well as from below) in order to reconfirm one's own social universe.

Figure 11.7 presents a simplified lifestyle mapping based on Bourdieu's work. Bourdieu distinguishes between the general level of capital (since there is a high correlation between cultural and economic capital in society – remember, going to school pays off) and the relative weight of cultural versus economic capital. We can see the clear positioning and correlation between reading *Le Monde* (an intellectual daily newspaper), going to the opera and being a university professor, being a manager in the private sector, playing golf and reading the more conservative and business-friendly *Le Figaro,* being a worker, reading *L'Humanité* (traditionalist communist newspaper) and engaging in car repair and finally being a craftsman, reading the popular newspaper *France-Soir* and engaging in betting on horses in one's spare time. This approach has been applied within American consumer research to distinguish between consumer tastes among various social groupings.[152]

Practice theory and consumer behaviour

When Bourdieu was doing fieldwork in Algeria, he noticed the following things about the relation between what people *actually* did and what they *said* they did (remember the attitude–behaviour gap from Chapter 7). First of all, as we have already discussed, there was

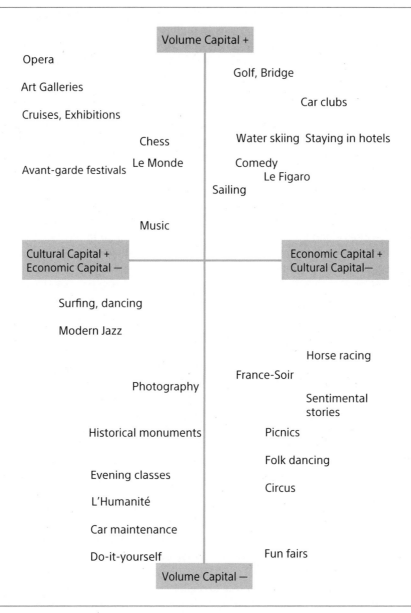

Figure 11.7 Bourdieu's lifestyle map with examples of leisure consumption

Source: Adapted from B. Moingeon, 'La sociologie de P. Bourdieu et son apport au marketing', Recherches et Applications en Marketing 8(2) (1993): 123.

not a very good correspondence between people's actions and their own accounts of these actions. In other words, people are not very accurate in accounting for their own behaviour. But what was more revealing was that the way people acted was not really in accordance with their own explicit values and norms either.[153] In other words, it was as if people often behaved in ways that were difficult to explain based on their own individual accounts. In order to find a word that would take into consideration this distance between our reflections and our behaviour, Bourdieu came up with a theory of 'practice'.

Remember Bourdieu's fondness for considering social life as constituted of competitive games? **Practice theory** is normally described in terms of the sportsperson's 'feel' for their game.[154] It is very difficult for, say, a footballer to explain how to play football. It is also impossible for the same footballer to go through a lot of conscious decision processes when deciding how to move on the field, what to do with the ball, etc. There is simply no time for evaluating alternatives. Instead they act spontaneously based on experiences with how the game may unfold. That is not to say that their behaviour is determined, but it does follow certain logics or templates that the footballer can master to a greater or lesser degree.

A practice then, is, a routinised type of behaviour that involves both bodily and mental activities (the footballer moves and 'thinks', even if they do not engage in rational decision-making as we have described it earlier), it involves things and their use (a football field of a certain size and design), a ball (rather important) and possibly appropriate clothes (in specific colours, goals with posts, net, etc.) and some background knowledge (knowing what all this is used for, what the different lines mean, etc.).[155]

Now, the trick is to consider not just playing a football match but applying all our daily activities along those lines. How do we know how to go to the movies? To ride a bike? To shop in the supermarket? Or, as one study from Finland asked: 'How do we know whether our ordinary daily meal has been "a proper one", particularly in relation to child-rearing and family care?'[156] And so on and so forth. According to practice theory, all these things are embedded in certain routines (that is, we do not make decisions in the classical sense while doing them). The fact that practices are routinised explains why they are discussed in this chapter on social class – quite simply because, as we have already seen, there is strong sociological evidence that our routines, as well as our ways of combining our own personal sources and the marketplace resources at our disposal,[157] are highly dependent on our upbringing and the capitals we have acquired. This is also what was concluded by the Finnish study of daily meals.[158] Many other studies have confirmed how class background forms our consumer practices. In the UK, consumption among children aged 8–13 years old was shown to be deeply embedded in daily routines and practices and inextricably linked to social background.[159] In the US, it was demonstrated how, for late teens/emerging adults, working-class youth differs from middle-class youth in longing for stability and seeking the familiar for the former, and a far more exploratory consumer behaviour for the latter.[160]

The routines are also embedded in the things and their design. We grab a cup by its handle, because it is there – and we are made aware of this when, for instance, offered tea in glasses in Turkey or elsewhere in the Middle East. This is why practice theory is especially interested in how the presence and design of the things around us influence the way we act.[161] In fact, not even digital consumption is without materiality – there are iPods, hard drives and other devices that are crucial to digital consumption. Certain types of materiality may lose importance, but others seem to replace them.[162] One very obvious type of object that directs and orients our practices is the self-tracking instrument that allows us to personally monitor the level of our physical activity, so we can adjust our behaviour accordingly. It is, thus, to a large extent, the consumer object that decides how we are supposed to behave (walk more, run faster, get our pulse higher . . .).[163] From these examples, ranging from the family meal to self-tracking devices, it is also obvious how practices form our experience of time. It has been argued that part of what makes certain consumption activities more (or less) attractive is a congruent relationship between the practices involved and their time flow. Whether it is the calm of the build-up to a family dinner or the hectic pace of a dance party, or the oscillation between waiting and adrenalin-pumping action in leisure activities such as free-skiing and paintball, the practices we engage in form our experience of time.[164] To give a brief example: waiting is completely OK if we consider it a normal part of the practices that form a particular activity (think of the difference between going to a fast-food restaurant and a normal restaurant).

Just as practice theory considers whether the design of things determines their use (rather than the other way round), so it also suggests that activities generate wants (remember the discussion of effect hierarchies). In other words, it is because we engage in certain activities that we generate personal wants and desires, not our wants and desires that make us participate in certain activities. This might not sound very revolutionary, but a lot of consumer research actually assumes that wants (motivations, that is) come first and lead us to engage in certain types of consumption. Practice theorists say that practices in many cases are more likely to come first, and then generate wants.[165] For example, if we have established certain types of cooking routines (or cooking practices) in our family (for example, cooking from scratch and not relying on ready-to-eat meals), these practices generate the wants for fresh produce.

Practice theory does not turn us into robots of our own social background, because the schemes of social practice are hardly ever very precise about what exactly to do. Consider how to eat 'properly'. How do we know when that practice is 'obeyed'? Not because of a very precise manual. In fact, our children can point out our practice when they act how to 'perform' it: cutting the meat with excessively pointy little fingers; lifting the fork with great care to the mouth slowly and without smearing anything on the side of the mouth; putting the bite in; then chewing it carefully with an exaggerated expression of satisfaction and happiness on their faces. In other words, if practices are performed consciously, they often stop being 'normal social practices' and become overdramatised performances instead. A good actor is someone who knows about this and can perform the practices of a persona in such a way that the audience cannot see that the actor is just performing a newly learned script. Another reason why practices do not make us robots is that, in our lives, we are constantly subjects to larger or smaller disruptions. When such disruptions are considerable, for example following natural disasters or extreme conditions, or moving in with a vegan (no direct comparison intended), we do not change practices altogether but usually engage in an adaptation process called *practice alignment.* This alignment may institute a 'new normal' set of practices.[166]

Why is practice theory important to consumer research? Well, for one thing it reminds us how much of our consumption is carried out without our being really conscious about it, since it is neither part of a calculation of benefits nor is it part of our explicit identity projects, and we do not consider it a symbolic expression of anything in particular (others might still interpret it that way, but that is a different story!).[167] Secondly, it might contribute to our understanding of why it is so difficult to alter people's consumption behaviour to more sustainable types and possibly help to solve that problem, since a lot of our daily unsustainable consumption seems to be embedded in practices rather than deliberate choices. We all know we ought to recycle, right? Why don't we then just do it (as the Nike slogan goes)? Well, maybe it is because changing practices is not so easy. One study looked at the effects of a behaviour change initiative in a corporate setting – so-called 'Environment Champions' – and how the material environment and employee practices created obstacles or opportunities, and in particular obstacles, for implementing a recycling policy.[168]

Sustainability, then, seems largely practice-driven.[169] Likewise, other things we do often without even thinking about them may be absolutely crucial to the degree to which we live sustainable lives. Mundane activities such as energy consumption in the household (switching lights on and off, putting electronic equipment on stand-by) have attracted the attention of practice theorists.[170] Or consider the consumption of water! How many of you shower more or less 'on autopilot' in the morning, or maybe several times during the day? Do you 'choose' to shower? Well, not really, right? You just do it (here is that Nike logic again). Not so many decades ago, showering was not a daily routine for most people; the most critical places were washed in front of the washbowl, and the weekly-or-so bath took care of the thorough cleaning. How did showering become such a 'normal routine' in a few decades that we hardly think about it anymore?[171] Well, this is a good example of how practices work.

Since practices are embedded in our social background, with its resources of capital, they can also profoundly alter the way we look at decision-making and the way our social-class background influences it. You would believe that the choice of where to study is an extremely rational one, since it basically influences your career opportunities and thereby to a large extent determines a lot of your social and economic possibilities for the rest of your life. One study examined the choice of college from a practice perspective and concluded that, especially for people of a working-class background, the fit of the school with previous life experiences was the deciding factor for choice. So, students from this background tended to choose based on how much they felt 'at home' during the college visit rather than based on 'abstract information' such as academic reputation and the academic quality of the curricula.[172] Hence, it was the practical experience of the school 'fitting like a glove' to oneself that proved decisive. Again, this helps explain why social inequalities and class backgrounds tend to reproduce themselves from generation to generation.

Chapter summary

Now that you have finished reading this chapter you should understand why:

11.1 **Both personal and social conditions influence how we spend our money.** The field of behavioural economics considers how consumers decide what to do with their money. In particular, *discretionary expenditures* are made only when people are able and willing to spend money on items above and beyond their basic needs. *Consumer confidence* – the state of mind consumers have about their own personal situation, as well as their feelings about their overall economic prospects – helps to determine whether they will purchase goods and services, take on debt or save their money.

11.2 **We group consumers into social classes based on factors such as income, occupation and education.** A consumer's *social class* refers to their standing in society. It is determined by a number of factors, including education, occupation and income. However, research has demonstrated that social class today is a fairly complex concept and is not so easy to use as a straight means of market segmentation.

11.3 **Social class has a fundamental impact on our consumer tastes.** Virtually all groups make distinctions among members in terms of relative superiority, power and access to valued resources. This *social stratification* creates a status hierarchy, where some goods are preferred over others and are used to categorise their owners' social class. While income is an important indicator of social class, the relationship is far from perfect since social class is also determined by such factors as place of residence, cultural interests and worldview.

11.4 **Social stratification creates a status hierarchy, where some goods come to signify the social status of their owners.** Purchase decisions are sometimes influenced by the desire to 'buy up' to a higher social class or to engage in the process of *conspicuous consumption,* where one's status is flaunted by the deliberate and non-constructive use of valuable resources. This spending pattern is characteristic of the *nouveaux riches,* whose relatively recent acquisition of income, rather than ancestry or breeding, is responsible for their increased *social mobility.*

11.5 **Our lifestyles are shaped not only by economic but also by cultural capital, and are expressed in the form of daily consumer practices.** Theories of capital explain how resources come in different types and for different uses in various social settings.

Most important are cultural capital (education, knowledge, manners) and economic capital (wealth or access to financing), but social capital (the networks you can draw from) is also important. Different types of capital distinguish different social classes. Theories of practice explain our behaviour, rooted in routinised patterns that we have learned, most significantly from our class background. Practice thus offers a different perspective on consumer behaviour that is less dependent on conscious decision-making.

Key terms

Achieved status (p. 437)
Ascribed status (p. 437)
Behavioural economics (p. 428)
Capital (p. 455)
Conspicuous consumption (p. 453)
Consumer confidence (p. 433)
Discretionary income (p. 430)
Distinction (p. 456)
Elaborated codes (p. 447)
Habitus (p. 456)
Homogamy (p. 436)
Microfinance (p. 450)

Potlatch (p. 453)
Practice theory (p. 457)
Restricted codes (p. 447)
Savings rate (p. 433)
Social class (p. 428)
Social hierarchy (p. 428)
Social mobility (p. 439)
Social stratification (p. 436)
Status crystallisation (p. 440)
Status symbols (p. 428)
Taste culture (p. 446)

Consumer behaviour challenge

1 How important is social class in your society? Can you think of societies where social class matters more? Or less?

2 What are some of the obstacles to measuring social class in European societies? Discuss some ways to get around these obstacles.

3 What consumption differences, if any, might you expect to observe between a family characterised as underprivileged *vs* one whose income is average for its social class?

4 When is social class likely to be a better predictor of consumer behaviour than mere knowledge of a person's income?

5 How do you assign people to social classes, or do you at all? What consumption cues do you use (e.g. clothing, speech, cars, etc.) to determine social standing?

6 Thorstein Veblen argued that women were often used as a vehicle to display their husbands' wealth. Is this argument still valid today?

7 What are some contemporary examples of potlatch and waste? Can you identify either in your everyday consumption?

8 Some people argue that status symbols are dead. Do you agree?

9 What role do counterfeit brands play in contemporary conspicuous consumption?

10 The chapter observes that some marketers are finding 'greener pastures' by targeting low-income people. How ethical is it to single out consumers who cannot afford to waste their precious resources on discretionary items? Under what circumstances should this segmentation strategy be encouraged or discouraged?

→

For additional material see the companion website at **www.pearsoned.co.uk/solomon**

See Case studies D.1, D.2, and D.3 at the end of Part D:

Case study D.1: 'Influencer marketing: monetising online audiences through customer reviews,' Ben Koeck and David Marshall (University of Edinburgh Business School, UK)

Case study D.2: 'What is generational marketing ? And how does consumption contribute to strengthen links between generations?', Elodie Gentina (IESEG, Paris, France)

Case study D.3: 'Consumption ambivalence in family sharing: the case of intergenerational support in economically challenging times, Katerina Karanika (Exeter University, UK)

Notes

1. Fred van Raaij, 'Economic psychology', *Journal of Economic Psychology* 1 (1981): 1–24.
2. Pierre Bourdieu, *Distinction: A Social Critique of the Judgment of Taste* (Cambridge, MA: Harvard University Press, 1984).
3. Peter S.H. Leeflang and W. Fred van Raaij, 'The changing consumer in the European Union: A meta-analysis', *International Journal of Research in Marketing* 12 (1995): 373–87.
4. Data in this section are adapted from Fabian Linden, *Consumer Affluence: The Next Wave* (New York: The Conference Board, Inc., 1994); 'Trends in households in the European Union: 1995–2025', *Eurostat, Statistics in Focus,* Theme 3–24/2003 (Luxembourg: Office for Official Publications of the European Communities, 2004).
5. http://ec.europa.eu/eurostat/tgm/table.do?tab=table&init=1&plugin=1&pcode=tipsun20&language=en (accessed 29 August 2018).
6. http://ec.europa.eu/eurostat/tgm/table.do?tab=table&init=1&plugin=1&pcode=tipslm80&language=en (accessed 29 August 2018).
7. Vissiliki Grougiou and George Moschis, 'Antecedents of young adults' materialistic values', *Journal of Consumer Behaviour* 14 (2015): 115–26.
8. See, for example, Hélène Gorge and Nil Özçaglar-Toulouse, 'Expériences de consommation des individus pauvres en France: apports du Bas de la Pyramide et de la Transformative Consumer Research', *Décisions Marketing* 72 (2013): 139–56.
9. https://www.eurofound.europa.eu/topic/working-poor (accessed 30 August 2018).
10. https://www.theguardian.com/commentisfree/2017/feb/21/latest-job-stats-full-time-work-is-disappearing-for-women-but-not-for-men (accessed 29 August 2018).
11. https://data.oecd.org/emp/part-time-employment-rate.htm (accessed 29 August 2018).
12. http://www.pewresearch.org/fact-tank/2015/04/14/on-equal-pay-day-everything-you-need-to-know-about-the-gender-pay-gap/ (14 April 2015) (accessed 29 August 2018).
13. European Centre for the Development of Vocational Training, http://www.cedefop.europa.eu/en/publications-and-resources/statistics-and-indicators/statistics-and-graphs/keeping-young-people (accessed 29 August 2018).
14. Christopher D. Carroll, 'How does future income affect current consumption?', *Quarterly Journal of Economics* 109(1) (February 1994): 111–47.
15. *Information* (1 May 2012).
16. http://blog.euromonitor.com/2012/03/special-report-income-inequality-rising-across-the-globe.html (accessed 29 August 2018).
17. http://www.oecd.org/social/income-distribution-database.htm (accessed 29 August 2018).
18. http://appsso.eurostat.ec.europa.eu/nui/show.do?dataset=ilc_di11&lang=en (accessed 29 August 2018).
19. U. Dholakia, L. Tam, S. Yoon and N. Wong, 'The Ant and the Grasshopper: Understanding personal saving orientation of consumers', *Journal of Consumer Research* 43(1) (2016): 134–55.
20. Oliver Fischer and Lorenz Fischer, 'The financial crisis: An economic psychological analysis', *Wirtschaftspsychologie,* 13 (2011): 5–23.
21. Jose J.F. Medina, Joel Saegert and Alicia Gresham, 'Comparison of Mexican-American and Anglo-American attitudes toward money', *Journal of Consumer Affairs* 30(1) (1996): 124–45.
22. Kirk Johnson, 'Sit down. Breathe deeply. This is *really* scary stuff', *New York Times* (16 April 1995): F5. For a scale that measures consumer frugality, see John L. Lastovicka, Lance A. Bettencourt, Renee Shaw Hughner and Ronald J. Kuntze, 'Lifestyle of the tight and frugal: Theory and measurement', *Journal of Consumer Research* 26 (June 1999): 85–98.
23. Xinyue Zhou, Kathleen D. Vohs and Roy F. Baumeister, 'The symbolic power of money: Reminders of money alter social distress and physical pain', *Psychological Science* 20(6) (2009): 700–6.
24. 'Frontiers: Planning or consumer change in Europe 96/97', 2 (London: The Henley Centre, 1996).
25. George Katona, 'Consumer saving patterns', *Journal of Consumer Research* 1 (June 1974): 1–12.
26. Fleura Bardhi and Giana Eckhardt, 'Access-based consumption', *Journal of Consumer Research* 39(4) (2012): 881–98.
27. Russell W. Belk, 'Sharing', *Journal of Consumer Research* 36 (February 2010): 715–34; Russell W. Belk and Rosa Llamas, 'The nature and effect of sharing in consumer behavior', in D.G. Mick, S. Pettigrew, C. Pechmann and J.L. Ozanne (eds),

Transformative Consumer Research for Personal and Collective Well-being (London: Routledge, 2011): 625–46.

28. Güliz Ger and Russell Belk, 'Cross cultural differences in materialism', *Journal of Economic Psychology* 17(1) (1996): 55–77; Güliz Ger and Russell Belk, 'Accounting for materialism in four cultures', *Journal of Material Culture* 4(2) (1999): 183–204.

29. Euromonitor International, Daphne Kasriel-Alexander, 'The "Thrill of Thrift": From Circular Economics to Online Bargain Hunting in the Americas (10 May 2015), http://blog.euromonitor.com/2015/05/the-thrill-of-thrift-from-circular-economics-to-online-bargain-hunting-in-the-americas.html (accessed 29 August 2018).

30. https://www.telegraph.co.uk/family/parenting/meet-mums-making-mint-selling-second-hand-baby-clothes/ (accessed 29 August 2018).

31. Jonathan Margolis, 'How unwanted second-hand books became big business', *Financial Times* (21 August 2016).

32. Floyd L. Ruch and Philip G. Zimbardo, *Psychology and Life,* 8th edn (Glenview, IL: Scott, Foresman, 1971).

33. Jonathan H. Turner, *Sociology: Studying the Human System,* 2nd edn (Santa Monica, CA: Goodyear, 1981).

34. Ibid.

35. Richard P. Coleman, 'The continuing significance of social-class to marketing', *Journal of Consumer Research* 10 (December 1983): 265–80; Turner, *Sociology,* op. cit.

36. https://www.cnbc.com/2016/12/27/heavenly-taste-the-obsession-with-edible-gold.html (accessed 29 August 2018).

37. https://www.theguardian.com/lifeandstyle/2018/may/30/golden-chicken-you-might-as-well-be-lighting-a-fag-with-a-burning-tenner (accessed 29 August 2018).

38. Turner, *Sociology,* op. cit.

39. Ibid.

40. Anya Kamenetz, 'The perils and promise of the reputation economy', *Fast Company* (25 November 2008), www.fastcompany.com/magazine/131/on-the-internet-everyone-knows-youre-a-dog.html (accessed 29 August 2018).

41. https://www.cbsnews.com/news/facebook-stock-price-recovers-all-134-billion-lost-in-after-cambridge-analytica-datascandal/ (accessed 29 August 2018).

42. Robin Knight, 'Just you move over, 'Enry 'Iggins: A new regard for profits and talent cracks Britain's old class system', *U.S. News & World Report* 106 (24 April 1989): 40.

43. C.C. Otnes and P. MacLaran. 'Royalty: Marketplace icons', *Consumption Markets & Culture* 21(1) (2018): 65–75.

44. Greg Duncan and Richard Murnane (eds), *Whither Opportunity? Rising Inequality, Schools and Children's Life Chances* (New York: Russell Sage Foundation, 2011).

45. Richard Coleman, Lee Rainwater and Kent McLelland, *Social Standing in America: New Dimensions of Class* (New York: Basic Books, 1978): 220.

46. http://www.theguardian.com/business/2014/nov/13/us-wealth-inequality-top-01-worth-as-much-as-the-bottom-90 (accessed 29 August 2018).

47. https://www.oecd.org/els/soc/cope-divide-europe-2017-background-report.pdf (accessed 29 August 2018).

48. Thomas Piketty, *Capital in the Twenty-First Century* (Cambridge, MA: Harvard University Press, 2014).

49. See Coleman, 'The continuing significance of social class to marketing', op. cit.; Charles M. Schaninger, 'Social class versus income revisited: An empirical investigation', *Journal of Marketing Research* 18 (May 1981): 192–208.

50. https://ec.europa.eu/eurostat/web/products-datasets/product?code=ILC_PNS4 and https://www.equalitytrust.org.uk/scale-economic-inequality-uk (both accessed 30 August 2018).

51. Coleman, 'The continuing significance of social class to marketing', op. cit.

52. Bernard Dubois and Gilles Laurent, 'Is There a Euro-consumer for Luxury Goods?' in W. Fred Van Raaij and Gary J. Bamossy (eds), *European Advances in Consumer Research* 1 (Provo, UT: Association for Consumer Research, 1993): 59–69; Bernard Dubois and Gilles Laurent, 'Luxury Possessions and Practices: An Empirical Scale', in F. Hansen (ed.), *European Advances in Consumer Research* 2 (Provo, UT: Association for Consumer Research, 1995): 69–77; Bernard Dubois and Patrick Duquesne, 'The market for luxury goods: Income versus culture', *European Journal of Marketing* 27(1) (1993): 35–44.

53. Turner, *Sociology,* op. cit.: 260.

54. https://www.theguardian.com/society/2018/jun/15/social-mobility-in-richest-countries-has-stalled-since-1990s (accessed 30 August 2018).

55. See Sofia Ulver-Sneistrup and Jacob Östberg, 'The nouveaux pauvres of liquid modernity', *Research in Consumer Behavior* 13 (2011): 217–32.

56. Iain R. Black, 'Sorry not today: Self and temporary consumption denial', *Journal of Consumer Behaviour* 10 (2011): 267–78.

57. Joseph Kahl, *The American Class Structure* (New York: Holt, Rinehart & Winston, 1961).

58. Leonard Beeghley, *The Structure of Social Stratification in The United States,* 3rd edn (Boston, MA: Allyn and Bacon, 2000).

59. August B. Hollingshead and Fredrick C. Redlich, *Social Class and Mental Illness: A Community Study* (New York: John Wiley, 1958).

60. John Mager and Lynn R. Kahle, 'Is the whole more than the sum of the parts? Re-evaluating social status in marketing', *Journal of Business Psychology* 10(1) (1995): 3–18.

61. John Rossiter, 'A new measure of social class', *Journal of Consumer Behaviour* 11 (2012): 89–93.

62. R. Vanneman and F.C. Pampel, 'The American perception of class and status', *American Sociological Review* 42 (June 1977): 422–37.

63. Donald W. Hendon, Emelda L. Williams and Douglas E. Huffman, 'Social class system revisited', *Journal of Business Research* 17 (November 1988): 259.

64. Coleman, 'The continuing significance of social class to marketing', op. cit.

65. Gerhard E. Lenski, 'Status crystallization: A non-vertical dimension of social status', *American Sociological Review* 19 (August 1954): 405–12.

66. D. Crockett, 'Paths to respectability: Consumption and stigma management in the contemporary black middle class', *Journal of Consumer Research* 44(3) (2017): 554–81.

67. Richard P. Coleman, 'The Significance of Social Stratification in Selling', in Martin L. Bell (ed.), *Marketing: A Maturing Discipline, Proceedings of the American Marketing Association 43rd National Conference* (Chicago: American Marketing Association, 1960): 171–84.

68. Sofia Ulver and Jacob Östberg, 'Moving up, down or sideways? Exploring consumer experience of identity and status incongruence', *European Journal of Marketing* 48(5/6) (2014): 833–53.

69. N.J. Paris and R.V. Robinson (1988), 'Class Identification of Men and Women in the 1970s and 1980s', *American Sociological Review*: 103–12.

70. R.F. Baumeister and K.D. Vohs (2004), 'Sexual economics: Sex as a female resource for social exchange in heterosexual

interactions', *Personality and Social Psycology Review* 8(4): 339–63.

71. World Bank, 'The effect of womens' economic power in Latin America and the Caribbean' (August 2012), http://www.bancomundial.org/content/dam/Worldbank/document/PLBSummer12latest.pdf (accessed 29 August 2018).

72. Ibid.

73. Hina Khan, David Bamber and Ali Quazi, 'Relevant or redundant: Elite consumers' perception of foreign made products in an emerging market', *Journal of Marketing Management* 28(9/10) (2012): 1,190–216.

74. Gleb Bryanski and Guy Faulconbridge, 'BRIC Demands More Clout, Steers Clear of Dollar Talk', Reuters (16 June 2009), www.reuters.com/article/ousiv/idUSTRE55F47D20090616 (accessed 29 August 2018); Guy Faulconbridge, 'BRIC Seeks Global Voice at First Summit', Reuters (14 June 2009).

75. http://www.forbes.com/sites/chriswright/2014/01/06/after-the-brics-the-mints-catchy-acronym-but-can-you-make-any-money-from-it/ (accessed 29 August 2018).

76. https://foreignpolicy.com/2018/02/01/chinas-middle-class-is-pulling-up-the-ladder-behind-itself/ (accessed 30 August 2018).

77. Heejung S. Kim and Aimee Drolet, 'Cultural differences in preferences for brand name versus generic products', *Personality & Social Psychology* 35(12) (December 2009): 1,555–66.

78. Issaku Harada and Tetsushi Takahashi, 'Rising inequality imperils China's push for "quality" growth, *Nikkei Asian Review* (14 February 2018), https://asia.nikkei.com/Economy/Rising-inequality-imperils-China-s-push-for-quality-growth (accessed 30 August 2018).

79. Jennifer Duggan, 'China to scrap millions of cars to ease pollution', *The Guardian* (27 May 2014), http://www.theguardian.com/environment/chinas-choice/2014/may/27/china-scrap-millions-cars-reduce-air-pollution (accessed 29 August 2018).

80. https://qz.com/india/998098/after-years-of-diffidence-among-users-credit-cards-hit-a-record-high-in-india/ (accessed 30 August 2018).

81. Søren Askegaard and Giana Echardt, 'Glocal yoga: Re-appropriation in the Indian consumptionscape, *Marketing Theory* 12(1) (2012): 45–60.

82. Rohit Varman and Ram Manohar Vikas, 'Freedom and consumption: Towards conceptualizing systemic constraints for subaltern consumers in a capitalist society', *Consumption, Markets and Culture* 10(2) (2007): 117–31.

83. Heather Timmons, 'Vogue's fashion photos spark debate in India', *New York Times* (31 August 2008), www.nytimes.com/2008/09/01/business/worldbusiness/01vogue.html?_r1&refbusi (accessed 29 August 2018).

84. https://economictimes.indiatimes.com/small-biz/policy-trends/the-problem-of-being-caught-in-the-circle-of-conspicuous-consumption/articleshow/59191638.cms (accessed 29 August 2018).

85. Yuko Minowa, 'Practicing *Qi* and consuming *Ki:* Folk epistemology and consumption rituals in Japan', *Marketing Theory* 12(1) (2012): 27–44.

86. Cecilie Rohwedder, 'Design houses build stores, pamper demanding shoppers in fashion-industry hot spot', *Wall Street Journal on the Web* (23 January 2004).

87. Rana Sobh and Russell W. Belk, 'Privacy and gendered spaces in Arab Gulf homes', *Home Cultures* 8 (3 November 2011): 317–40.

88. Rana Sobh, Russell Belk and Justin Gressel, 'Modest seductiveness: Reconciling modesty and vanity by reverse assimilation and double resistance', *Journal of Consumer Behaviour* 11 (2012): 357–67.

89. http://www.imf.org/external/pubs/ft/weo/2012/02/index.htm (accessed 29 August 2018).

90. https://qz.com/africa/1179387/africas-economic-outlook-is-promising-for-2018-but-there-clouds-on-the-horizon/ (accessed 30 August 2018).

91. Katrina Mansson, 'Africa: Aspiration drives consumption boom', *Financial Times* (1 March 2013).

92. https://www.businessdailyafrica.com/lifestyle/design/Doors-new-status-symbol-Kenyan-homes/4258320-4305908-I5mfix/index.html (accessed 29 August 2018).

93. J. Michael Munson and W. Austin Spivey, 'Product and brand-user stereotypes among social classes: Implications for advertising strategy', *Journal of Advertising Research* 21 (August 1981): 37–45.

94. Jean Baudrillard, *The Consumer Society* (London: SAGE, 1998).

95. Coleman, 'The continuing significance of social class to marketing', op. cit.

96. Jeffrey F. Durgee, 'How Consumer Sub-Cultures Code Reality: A Look at Some Code Types', in Richard J. Lutz (ed.), *Advances in Consumer Research* 13 (Provo, UT: Association for Consumer Research, 1986): 332–7.

97. Paul C. Henry, 'Social class, market situation, and consumers' metaphors of (dis)empowerment', *Journal of Consumer Research* 31 (March 2005): 766–78.

98. Durkheim (1958), quoted in Roger Brown, *Social Psychology* (New York: The Free Press, 1965).

99. Lenore Skenazy, 'Affluent, like masses, are flush with worries', *Advertising Age* (10 July 1989): 55.

100. Herbert J. Gans, 'Popular Culture in America: Social Problem in a Mass Society or Social Asset in a Pluralist Society?' in Howard S. Becker (ed.), *Social Problems: A Modern Approach* (New York: Wiley, 1966); Helga Dittmar, 'Material possessions as stereotypes: Material images of different socio-economic groups', *Journal of Economic Psychology* 15 (1994): 561–85; Helga Dittmar and Lucy Pepper, 'To have is to be: Materialism and person perception in working class and middle class British adolescents', *Journal of Economic Psychology* 15 (1994): 233–5.

101. Edward O. Laumann and James S. House, 'Living room styles and social attributes: The patterning of material artifacts in a modern urban community', *Sociology and Social Research* 54 (April 1970): 321–42; see also Stephen S. Bell, Morris B. Holbrook and Michael R. Solomon, 'Combining esthetic and social value to explain preferences for product styles with the incorporation of personality and ensemble effects', *Journal of Social Behavior and Personality* 6 (1991): 243–74.

102. Zeynep Arsel and Jonathan Bean, 'Taste regimes and market-mediated practices', *Journal of Consumer Research* 39(5) (2013): 899–917.

103. A. Skandalis, E. Banister and J. Byrom, 'Marketplace orchestration of taste: Insights from the Bridgewater Hall', *Journal of Marketing Management* 32(9/10) (2016): 926–43.

104. Eugene Sivadas, George Mathew and David J. Curry, 'A preliminary examination of the continuing significance of social class to marketing: A geodemographic replication', *Journal of Consumer Marketing* 41(6) (1997): 463–79; see also Morris B. Holbrook, Michael J. Weiss and John Habich,

'Class-related distinctions in American cultural tastes', *Empirical Studies of the Arts* 22(1) (2004): 91–115.

105. Stuart Roper and Caroline La Niece, 'The importance of brands in the lunch-box choices of low income British school children', *Journal of Consumer Behaviour* 8 (2009): 84–99.

106. Sofia Ulver-Sneistrup, Søren Askegaard and Dorthe Brogård Kristensen, 'The new work ethics of consumption and the paradox of mundane brand resistance', *Journal of Consumer Culture* 11(2) (2011): 215–38.

107. Nadaliya Ordabayeva and Pierre Chandon, 'Getting ahead of the Joneses: When equality increases conospicuous consumption among bottom-tier consumers', *Journal of Consumer Research* 38 (June 2011): 27–41.

108. https://ec.europa.eu/eurostat/statistics-explained/index.php/People_at_risk_of_poverty_or_social_exclusion (accessed 30 August 2018).

109. http://epp.eurostat.ec.europa.eu/cache/ITY_PUBLIC/3-08022012-AP/EN/3-08022012-AP-EN.PDF and http://epp.eurostat.ec.europa.eu/cache/ITY_PUBLIC/3-18012010-AP/EN/3-18012010-AP-EN.PDF (both accessed ???).

110. David Dubois, Derek Rucker and Adam Galisnky, 'Super size me: Product size as signal of status', *Journal of Consumer Research* 38 (April 2012): 1,047–62.

111. Quoted in Richard Elliott, 'How do the unemployed maintain their identity in a culture of consumption?' in Hansen (ed.), *European Advances in Consumer Research* 2: 1–4, at 3.

112. Kathy Hamilton and Miriam Catterell, 'I Can Do It! Consumer Coping and Poverty', in A.Y. Lee and D. Soman (eds), *Advances in Consumer Research* 35 (2008): 551–6.

113. Kathy Hamilton, 'Consumer decision making in low-income families: The case of conflict avoidance', *Journal of Consumer Behavior* 8 (2009): 252–67.

114. Bige Saatciglu and Julie Ozanne, 'Moral habitus and status negotiation in a marginalized working-class neighrborhood', *Journal of Consumer Research* 40(4) (2013): 692–710.

115. C.K. Pralahad, *The Fortune at the Bottom of the Pyramid: Eradicating Poverty Through Profits* (Philadelphia: Wharton School Publishing, 2004).

116. http://blog.nielsen.com/nielsenwire/consumer/lower-income-groups-drive-brazilian-retail-growth-in-2010/ (accessed 29 August 2018).

117. Antonio Regalado, 'Marketers Pursue the Shallow-Pocketed', *Wall Street Journal* (26 January 2007): B3.

118. Samuel Bonsu and Pia Polsa. 'Governmentality at the Base-of-the-Pyramid', *Journal of Macromarketing* 31(3) (2011): 236–44.

119. Marek Hudon and Joakim Sandberg, 'The ethical crisis in microfinance: Issues, findings and implications', *Business Ethics Quarterly* 23(4) (2013): 561–89.

120. Cyndee Miller, 'New Line of Barbie dolls targets big, rich kids', *Marketing News* (17 June 1996): 6.

121. Cyndee Miller, 'Baubles are back', *Marketing News* (14 April 1997): 1(2).

122. The Robb Report, 'Putting luxury into perspective', editorial (1 June 2009).

123. 'Reading the Buyer's Mind', *U.S. News & World Report* (16 March 1987): 59.

124. Rebecca Piirto Heath, 'Life on easy street', *American Demographics* (April 1997): 33–8.

125. Erika Kuever, 'Mapping the Real and the False: Globalization and the Brand in Contemporary China', *Research in Consumer Behavior* 14 (London: Emerald Publishing, 2014): 173–89.

126. Paul Fussell, *Class: A Guide Through the American Status System* (New York: Summit Books, 1983): 29.

127. Elizabeth C. Hirschman, 'Secular immortality and the American ideology of affluence', *Journal of Consumer Research* 17 (June 1990): 31–42.

128. Coleman, Rainwater and McLelland, *Social Standing in America,* op. cit.: 150.

129. M.H. Moore, 'Homing in on Russian "Super Spenders"', *Adweek* (28 February 1994): 14–16; see also Carol Vogel, 'Fabergé collection bought by Russian for a return home', *The New York Times* (5 February 2004), http://www.nytimes.com/2004/02/05/arts/design/05FABE.html?th=&pagewanted=print&position (accessed 29 August 2018).

130. Jason DeParle, 'Spy anxiety: The smart magazine that makes smart people nervous about their standing', *Washingtonian Monthly* (February 1989): 10.

131. For an examination of retailing issues related to the need for status, see Jacqueline Kilsheimer Eastman, Leisa Reinecke Flynn and Ronald E. Goldsmith, 'Shopping for status: The retail managerial implications', *Association of Marketing Theory and Practice* (Spring 1994): 125–30.

132. Xavier Drèze and Joseph C. Nunes, 'Feeling superior: The impact of loyalty program structure on consumers perceptions of status', *Journal of Consumer Research* 35 (April 2009): 890–905.

133. John Brooks, *Showing off in America* (Boston: Little, Brown, 1981): 13.

134. https://www.deutschland.de/en/topic/life/sports-leisure/the-bicycle-becomes-a-status-symbol (accessed 30 August 2018).

135. https://www.cnbc.com/id/100338066 (accessed 30 August 2018).

136. https://www.bicycling.com/bikes-gear/g20028599/luxury-bikes/ (accessed 30 August 2018).

137. Kira Strandby and Søren Askegaard, 'Weddings as waste', *Research in Consumer Behavior* 15 (2013): 145–65.

138. https://www.forbes.com/sites/modeledbehavior/2018/02/19/free-time/#50c49ff79e00 (accessed 29 August 2018).

139. S. Bellezza, N. Paharia and A. Keinan, 'Conspicuous consumption of time: When busyness and lack of leisure time become a status symbol', *Journal of Consumer Research* 44(1) (2017): 118–38.

140. H.E. Hershfield, C. Mogilner and U. Barnea, 'People who choose time over money are happier', *Social Psychological and Personality Science* 7(7) (2016): 697–706.

141. Thorstein Veblen, *The Theory of the Leisure Class* (1899; reprint, New York: New American Library, 1953): 45.

142. https://www.telegraph.co.uk/business/2017/10/24/forget-fast-cars-yachts-passports-new-status-symbol-ultra-rich/ (accessed 29 August 2018).

143. Quoted in Miller, 'Baubles are back', op. cit.; Elaine Underwood, 'Luxury's tide turns', *Brandweek* (7 March 1994): 18–22; see also Ball, 'Italy's Finpart to acquire Cerruti', op. cit.

144. http://politiken.dk/kultur/mode/ECE2495700/normcore-er-aarets-modeord/ (accessed 29 August 2018).

145. Z.Y. Wu, J.F. Luo, J.E. Schroeder and J.L. Borgerson, 'Forms of inconspicuous consumption: What drives inconspicuous luxury consumption in China?', *Marketing Theory* 17(4) (2017): 491–516.

146. Giana Eckhardt, Russell Belk and Jonathan Wilson, 'The rise of inconspicuous consumption', *Journal of Marketing Management* 31(7/8) (2015): 807–26.

147. Pierre Bourdieu, *La Distinction: Critique Social du Jugement* (Paris: Editions de Minuit, 1979; Eng. trans. 1984).

148. Alan Warde, Lydia Martens and Wendy Olsen, 'Consumption and the problem of variety: Cultural omnivorousness, social distinction, and dining out', *Sociology* 33(1) (1999): 105–27.

149. Brendan Richardson and Darach Turley, 'It's Far More Important Than That: Football Fandom and Cultural Capital', in S. Borghini, M.A. McGrath and C. Otnes (eds), *European Advances in Consumer Research* (Duluth, MN: Association for Consumer Research, 2008): 33–8.

150. A. Seregina and J.W. Schouten, 'Resolving identity ambiguity through transcending fandom', *Consumption Markets & Culture* 20(2) (2017): 107–30.

151. B. Hill and A.L. Lai, 'Class talk: Habitus and class in parental narratives of school choice', *Journal of Marketing Management* 32(13/14) (2016): 1,284–307.

152. Douglas B. Holt, 'Does cultural capital structure American consumption?', *Journal of Consumer Research* 25 (June 1998): 1–25.

153. Giana Eckhardt, Russell W. Belk and Timothy M. Devinney, 'Why don't consumers consume ethically?', *Journal of Consumer Behavior* 9 (2010): 426–36.

154. Pierre Bourdieu, *The Logic of Practice* (Stanford, CA: Stanford University Press, 1990).

155. Andreas Reckwitz, 'Toward a theory of social practices: A development in culturalist theorizing', *European Journal of Social Theory* 5(2) (2002): 243–63.

156. Heli Holttinen, 'How practices inform the materialization of cultural ideals in mundane consumption', *Consumption, Markets and Culture* 17(6) (2014): 573–94.

157. Richard Elliott, 'Making Up People: Consumption as a Symbolic Vocabulary for the Construction of Identity', in K. Ekström and H. Brembeck (eds) *Elusive Consumption* (Oxford: Berg, 2004): 129–43.

158. Holttinen, op. cit.

159. A. Nairn and F. Spotswood, 'Obviously in the cool group they wear designer things: A social practice theory perspective on children's consumption', *European Journal of Marketing* 49(9/10) (2015): 1,460–83.

160. M.F. Weinberger, J.R. Zavisca and J.M. Silva, 'Consuming for an imagined future: Middle-class consumer lifestyle and exploratory experiences in the transition to adulthood', *Journal of Consumer Research* 44(2) (2017): 332–60.

161. Elizabeth Shove, Matthew Watson, Martin Hand and Jack Ingram, *The Design of Everyday Life* (Oxford: Berg, 2007).

162. Paolo Magaudda, 'When materiality "bites back": Digital music consumption practices in the age of dematerialization', *Journal of Consumer Culture* 11(1) (2011): 15–36.

163. Mika Pantzar and Minna Ruckenstein, 'The heart of everyday analytics: Emotional, material and practical extensions in the self-tracking market', *Consumption, Markets and Culture* 18(1) (2015): 92–109.

164. Niklas Woermann and Joonas Rokka, 'Timeflow: How consumption practices shape consumers' temporal experiences', *Journal of Consumer Research* 41(6): 1,486–508.

165. Alan Warde, 'Consumption and theories of practice', *Journal of Consumer Culture* 5(2) (2005): 131–53.

166. M. Phipps and J.L. Ozanne, 'Routines disrupted: Reestablishing security through practice alignment', *Journal of Consumer Research* 44(2) (2017): 361–80.

167. Søren Askegaard and Jeppe Trolle Linnet, 'Towards an epistemology of consumer culture theory: Phenomenology and the context of context', *Marketing Theory* 11(4) (2011): 381–404.

168. Tom Hargreaves, 'Practicing behavior change: Applying social practice theory to pro-environmental behavior change', *Journal of Consumer Culture* 11(1) (2011): 77–99.

169. Iain Black and Helene Cherrier, 'Anti-consumption as part of daily living a sustainable lifestyle: Daily practices, contextual motivations and subjective values', *Journal of Consumer Behaviour* 9 (2010): 437–53.

170. Kirsten Gram-Hanssen, 'Understanding change and continuity in residential energy consumption', *Journal of Consumer Culture* 11(1) (2011): 61–78.

171. Elisabeth Shove, 'Users, technologies and experiences of comfort, cleanliness and convenience', *Innovation: The European Journal of Social Science Research* 16(2) (2003): 193–206.

172. Douglas E. Allen, 'Toward a theory of consumer choice as sociohistorically shaped practical experience: The fits-like-a-glove (FLAG) framework', *Journal of Consumer Research* 28 (March 2002): 515–32.

Case study D.1

Influencer marketing: monetising online audiences through customer reviews

Benjamin Koeck and **David Marshall**, University of Edinburgh Business School, UK

Introduction

Word of mouth is growing in computer-mediated environments. The shift of marketing communications to digital platforms such as blogs or social networking sites provides new outlets for information distribution, particularly with respect to products and services. Blogs provide a particularly critical channel for disseminating information. There are currently more than 200 million blogs online and 100,000 are being added every day. A majority of internet users read more than one blog per day. These consist of dated entries displayed in chronological order.[1] Although bloggers use similar technologies, their communicative practices can vary widely. The blog format is predominantly textual, although an increasing percentage of bloggers include rich media such as videos, audio, music and photos. Some of these blogs are for personal display, whereas others offer information to a wider audience.

Content posted on these blogs is considered powerful because it is long-lasting, far-reaching and has been shown to influence readers' choices.[2] Compared to websites, blogs are more influential thanks to their interactive characteristics as bloggers maintain an online dialogue. Regular readers of a particular blog represent a potentially large and loyal community. Thus, blogs allow ordinary consumers and individuals (endogenous) and companies (exogenous) to access a mass audience – the 'megaphone effect'.[3]

A 'new generation' of bloggers is emerging that has the ability to attract a potentially large audience, or 'followership', with activities such as product tests. Acting as intermediaries between companies and consumers, the bloggers build an online reputation by reviewing products as part of their blogging activities and add further value by drawing on their own personal experiences with the product. Building on the communication concepts of key individuals (opinion leader, market maven, etc.) in traditional word of mouth, this case study examines how these 'tech bloggers' utilise their audience to generate income, and considers the implications for marketing.

Brandon's blog

Brandon is a final-year medical student and the sole author of his blog 'AllAboutTech', on which he publishes around three articles a day. His blog is one of the fastest-growing and most successful blogs in the area of consumer electronics. Most of his content is devoted to product news about smartphones or tablets, and features a series of product reviews where he evaluates new devices. Since Brandon started his blog in 2011, his audience has grown continuously and in 2015 attracted around 400,000 blog visitors every month. In addition, he has more than 6,000 followers on Twitter and over 11,000 user 'likes' on his Facebook page. According to Brandon, part of the success of his blog is simply based on his passion for consumer electronics. His writing style is distinct from that of traditional product reviews, and rather than reviewing devices in a lab, he tests them in real-life situations. Typically, he will use a device as his primary technology for a couple of weeks and then share his experiences on his blog. These reviews have evolved over the past few years from written reviews to multimedia reviews that include pictures and videos. The latter is particularly important to Brandon. He argues that producing videos allows him to present and review devices in a more flexible and authentic fashion and to actually show the device in use.

This shift towards visual reviews has attracted more readers to his blog, but has required additional economic resources to purchase the necessary camera equipment and increased the time he takes to produce the review. For each review, he needs to write the text, produce and edit the video and shoot additional pictures. In order to maintain the high quality of his reviews and further develop his blog he has had to find ways to generate income. First, he began to incorporate banner advertising on his blog in order to cover the costs of his webserver. He also incorporated affiliate links at the end of his reviews, which allowed readers to purchase products directly. In addition, every purchase through his site gives him 5 per cent commission on the purchase price, which adds up to a small four-figure monthly income. Although still driven by his passion for consumer electronics, Brandon is becoming more business-oriented by including advertising and collaborating with marketers, particularly where the latter have become increasingly interested in his blog and his audience of dedicated followers.

The value of influencer marketing

Influencer marketing is a relatively new form of marketing that involves companies building links and establishing long-term relationships with bloggers like Brandon. Rather than addressing the whole population through mass online marketing, the focus is on targeting specific individuals with a large social network. A variety of marketing activities are aimed at these individuals. In contrast to traditional mass audience marketing activities, collaboration with these 'influencers' is seen as an efficient and cost-effective form of communication. Unlike traditional marketing campaigns, influencer marketing is not restricted to a certain period of time.

For manufacturers, retailers and marketers of consumer electronics, Brandon is seen as one of those targeted individuals. His blog is a successful one, with his reviews read by a large audience. Even more importantly, his audience is very concentrated as it mainly consists of technology enthusiasts, the majority of whom, he claims, visit his blog on a weekly basis. Cooperation with Brandon allows marketers to exploit a new target audience for certain products, an audience that they would not be able to reach otherwise. With highly opinionated and unique product reviews, his articles not only serve as a multiplier, but may also persuade people to buy a certain product. From Brandon's perspective, collaboration with marketers adds further value to his blog. This support takes the form of product seeding, giving him access to information about products and providing funding.

Product seeding

A critical part of influencer marketing is to provide products, normally free of charge. This is known as product seeding. Normally, Brandon purchases devices for the sole purpose of reviewing them and sells them at a later stage at a significant loss. Product seeding allows him to review more products in a given time without additional costs. In most cases, marketers provide devices before they are on general sale to the public, which gives him a critical time advantage and makes his review more appealing to potential readers. These types of collaboration have become more formalised in that devices are lent out for two weeks for Brandon to review in advance of the official launch. Normally these products have to be returned to the company, but occasionally Brandon is allowed to keep them. For example, he held a raffle for his blog anniversary where his readership could win a Samsung Galaxy phone provided by a retailer. According to him, it was a good opportunity to increase site traffic and gave the new Samsung phone increased visibility.

Access to information

As well as supporting Brandon with access to new devices, marketers are able to provide further information about their products. This includes both direct online communication, for example via email, and face-to-face interaction including invitations to events such as product introductions or conferences. These events are essential to Brandon as they provide a unique opportunity to get hands-on experience of unreleased devices and to speak directly to representatives of device manufacturers.

Further funding

These factors underline the importance of Brandon being part of such events. Nevertheless, travel and accommodation are costly. In some cases, marketers fund him to participate in events and reimburse him for travel and accommodation. However, Brandon has found that marketers are very selective in terms of the funding they are willing to give. Providing access to, or lending, devices can be much more expensive for marketers.

Conclusion

Although the relationship between Brandon and marketers can be beneficial for both, it can also be controversial. In contrast to banner advertising, influencer marketing is less formalised, largely due to its novelty. While there is a clear benefit for Brandon in this relationship, less is known about the return on investment from the marketer's perspective.

Questions

1 How do 'tech bloggers' differ from traditional opinion leaders or market mavens?

2 To what extent do you think that cooperating with companies in these ways – product seeding, access

to information and funding – compromises Brandon's review? What might be the consequence of a negative review for both parties?

3 Do you think that marketers prefer bloggers who provide a positive or an authentic evaluation of their products? How would it be perceived by the audience if marketers were to pay bloggers for product reviews?

4 What can Brandon do to sustain relationships with both the marketers and his readership?

Sources

[1]R. Blood, 'How blogging software reshapes the online community', *Communications of the ACM* 47(12) (2004): 53; E. Vaast, E.J. Davidson and T. Mattson, 'Talking about technology: the emergence of a new actor category through new media', *MIS Quarterly* 37(4) (2013): 1,069–92.

[2]J. Graham and W. Havlena, 'Finding the "missing link": Advertising's impact on word-of-mouth, web searches, and site visits', *Journal of Advertising Research* 47(4) (2007): 427–35.

[3]E. McQuarrie, J. Miller and B. Phillips, 'The megaphone effect: Taste and audience in fashion blogging', *Journal of Consumer Research* 40(1) (2013): 136–58.

Further reading

D. Godes and D. Mayzlin. (2009), 'Firm-created word-of-mouth communication: evidence from a field test', *Marketing Science*, 28(4), 721–39.

R. Kozinets, K. de Valck, A. Wojnicki and S. Wilner. (2010), 'Networked narratives: Understanding word-of-mouth marketing in online communities', *Journal of Marketing*, 74(2), 71–89.

Case study D.2

What is generational marketing? And how does consumption contribute to strengthen links between generations?

Elodie Gentina, IESEG School of Management, Paris and Lille, France

We know that teenage daughters influence their mothers' clothing consumption behaviour, telling them which fashionable clothes to buy, for example – that is not new. But teenage girls don't just socialise their mothers, they also affect the fashion products mothers consume for themselves, which in turn affects their own identity.[1]

As evidenced by this, companies are increasingly recognising the need to focus not just on individual products, but also on products that facilitate the creation and strengthening of social bonds between individuals within the same family unit. That is, retailers are positioning products from the transgenerational standpoint by targeting two members of the same family at the same time (for instance, a mother and daughter).[2] For example, by aiming its communications at the mother–teenage daughter relationship, Comptoir des Cotonniers (Fast Retailing Co.), which has risen to success in Europe and is expanding in the United States, has succeeded in becoming a key shopping destination for mothers and teenage daughters. Despite the promise of this generational approach, however, when examining the practitioner and academic literature, we find that most of the retailers tend to look at their products and brands from an individual perspective rather than from a relational perspective. Consistent with recent research,[3] firms must take into account not only the individual dimensions but also the relational dimensions of consumption.

Mothers and their teenage daughters are the targets for a vast body of information about the nature of their relationship and associated consumption activities. The press, books[4] and even movies depict the specificities of mother–teenage daughter relationships. The film *LOL* (2012) sparked popular interest in the mother–teenage daughter relationship and explored the shared day-to-day characteristics of the lives of mothers and teenage daughters: similar temperaments, common tastes and values and shared consumption activities. Specifically, some retailers observed that many ordinary mothers are following their teenage daughters' clothing style and often share clothing co-consumption practices with them (for example, shopping for clothes together, joint ownership of purchases and swapping clothes).[5] Thus, retailers recognise the benefits of targeting these teenage girls' mothers. On average, US women aged between 35 and 60 spent $800 per year on clothing in 2009.[6] Why do mothers engage in these clothing co-consumption practices with their teenage daughters and why are they willing to change their clothing purchase habits in relation to fashion brands, stores and styles according to their daughters' influence? What processes underlie mothers' adoption of such clothing co-consumption practices with their teenage daughters? Insights into the motives that drive mothers to adopt these practices can provide retailers with a set of cues they might use to appeal to this attractive segment more effectively.

Marketers argue that intergenerational mother–daughter relationships are universal and their co-consumption behaviours are 'global' consumption practices. An important and under-researched question is this: is the mother–teenage daughter relationship universal, which would explain universal clothing co-consumption practices? Hofstede's cultural dimensions theory examines the effects of a society's culture on the values of its members, and how these values might relate to behaviours.[7] There have been many lively debates about how Hofstede's research might be applied outside its original organisational context, and marketers' often unquestioning approach in adopting Hofstede's research for their own purposes has attracted particular criticism. However, while recognising the importance of this criticism, we will put aside these issues for a moment and think about how Hofstede's insights might offer a starting point for us here. Hofstede's line of research holds that Japan is a highly collectivistic national culture, with high power distance, a strongly masculine culture and low uncertainty avoidance. In contrast, Hofstede sees France as an individualistic culture, with a more feminine culture and lower uncertainty avoidance. In this case study I take the opportunity to focus first on understanding the role of national culture (however it might be characterised) in co-consumption practices between mothers and teenage daughters; second, on how mothers' attitudes and purchase habits change in relation to fashion brands, stores and styles; and third, on how the daughters' influential role differs across cultures.[8]

In the following stories, we will spend an afternoon with each mother–teenage daughter dyad: Isabelle, 50, and Inès, 17, from France; and Tomoko, 47, and Naho, 16, from Japan, and will take a look at their approach to clothing co-consumption practices.

Daughter leads, mum follows

Isabelle works full time as a management assistant for a medium-sized firm outside town. She works 35 hours per week. She likes her job since it allows her to spend time with her teenage daughter, Inès. They regularly go shopping together in the nearby mall and always know the different clothing stores that they want to visit. This Saturday afternoon, Isabelle and Inès spent four hours in the shops looking for new jeans. Isabelle felt unsure about her outfit and needed her daughter's advice to be sure she was making 'appropriate' clothing purchases. They went to the first clothing store, Zara, where they browsed the various sections of the store, shared the same changing room and chatted. Both mother and daughter find shopping a bonding experience and an opportunity to have intimate conversations like friends. Isabelle found it reassuring to be with her daughter because Inès has an up-to-date and youthful view of fashion trends and gave her advice on the most fashionable new jeans to purchase. Isabelle ended up buying jeans in a new clothing store that her daughter knows well, but that she rarely visits herself. Thanks to her daughter, Isabelle adopted a new look that her daughter found both fashionable and age-appropriate. Once home, Isabelle hurried to look in her daughter's wardrobe so that she could perhaps borrow a sweater or a shirt. This was not unusual; Isabelle often borrows clothes from her daughter, and views her as the 'depository' of all things feminine. Thus, borrowing clothes from her teenage daughter enables Isabelle to renew and rediscover her own femininity. At the same time, Inès is very happy to lend her mother clothes because it shows that their fashion styles are converging and that her mother is aiming for a more youthful and feminine look. Inès also used to borrow everything from shorts to underwear from her mother. She did not seek any prior permission and nor was she obliged to return the item within a precise time period. Looking at these experiences, it can be seen that age and size are not major determinants in whether mothers and daughters can share clothing. Understanding the motives underlying sharing practices between mothers and teenage daughters is more subtle. Sharing clothing items with family members removes interpersonal distance, creates bonds and increases feelings of unity. Sharing implies, in France at least, that mothers and daughters have a 'body in common', which helps to eliminate differences.

Mother leads, daughter follows

Tomoko is a former flight attendant. Last Saturday, Tomoko and Naho went to the Aeron mall, which is one of the biggest shopping malls in western Japan. They spent three hours there so that Tomoko could purchase new jeans. They visited several clothing stores together, including Global Work, Coen, SpRay, Ciqueto Vence Exchange and Melrose Claire. Naho was always chasing after her mother, saying 'Mummy, mummy'. Her mother would like her daughter to be more mature and more independent from her. Thus, when both of them visited the last clothing store, Chikyuoto, Tomoko encouraged her daughter to go to different sections and browse by herself. Tomoko went to the women's section while Naho browsed the teenage section. Afterwards, Tomoko and Naho met up to discuss what they had found. Naho did not buy anything because she found it very difficult to choose any item and make decisions on her own. Tomoko, on the other hand, ended up finding and purchasing new jeans, without asking her daughter's opinion. Tomoko, in general, was not subject to any form of influence from her teenage daughter. Although mother and daughter get along very well, Tomoko is a pretty directive mother who prefers to maintain her authoritative position in relation to her daughter, even during shopping trips. For Tomoko, it is essential to retain her status within the family and clearly distinguish the generations that structure a family. She considers that clothing is a social indicator of the position occupied by mothers, both within the family and within society. Once home, Tomoko put the new jeans away in her wardrobe and Naho knew that she would not be allowed to borrow them.

Questions

1 Do these examples of shared clothing practices between mothers and daughters illustrate an 'epiphenomenon' – a trend that characterises our society today that is focused on the cult of youth? Or, on the contrary, do you think that these practices reveal a real change that refers to a cultural and social phenomenon transmitted across generations?

2 How would you explain clothing co-consumption practices as a generational marketing approach? That is, how are they used and what role do sharing practices play?

3 Are these shared clothing consumption practices universal? What is the impact of national culture on co-consumption practices? How would you explain the fact that co-consumption practices differ according to different cultures?

4 When you were a child, did you have an influence on your parents' consumption behaviour? Are there any products or services in which you have a strong influence on your parents? What factors might impact children's influence on their parents' consumption behaviours?

5 What are the potential risks for marketers in depicting 'the same and undifferentiated' mothers and teenage daughters in their communication campaigns? What is the ethical role of the marketer in these circumstances?

6 For which kinds of companies would the idea of targeting mothers and teenage daughters through a generational marketing approach *not* work well? And, in contrast, for which kinds of companies would this generational marketing strategy work especially well? Why?

Sources

[1] A. Considine, 'Daughter leads, mom follows in fashion sync', *New York Times* (5 August 2011).

[2] E. Gentina, M. Sakashita, J.Y. Kimura and I. Decoopman, 'How national culture affects clothing sharing practices: French versus Japanese daughters and mothers', in A. Valenzuela, E. Reutskaja and G. Cornelissen (eds), *Advances in Consumer Research* 10 (Provo, UT: Association for Consumer Research, 2013): 1–4; A. Ruvio, Y. Gavish and A. Shoham, 'Consumer doppelganger: A role model perspective on intentional consumer mimicry', *Journal of Consumer Behaviour* 12(1) (2011): 60–9.

[3] A. Epp and L.L. Price, 'Designing solutions around customer network identity goals', *Journal of Marketing* 75(2) (2011): 36–54.

[4] The concept of mother-and-daughter clothes sharing is examined in S. Mathieson (2009), *Steal This Style: Moms and Daughters Swap Wardrobe Secrets.* New York: Clarkson Potter.

[5] A. Considine, 'Daughter leads, mom follows in fashion sync', *New York Times* (5 August 2011).

[6] 'Prêt-à-porter féminin: signes de reprise' ('Women's ready-to-wear: signs of recovery'), *Le Figaro* (25 February 2011): 4.

[7] G. Hofstede, *Culture's Consequences: Comparing Values, Behaviors, Institutions, and Organizations across Nations* (Thousand Oaks, CA: SAGE, 2001).

[8] E., Gentina, I. Decoopman and A. Ruvio, 'Social comparison motivation of mothers with their adolescent daughters and its effects on the mother's consumption behaviour', *Journal of Retailing and Consumer Services* 20(1) (2012): 94–101.

Case study D.3

Consumption ambivalence in family sharing: the case of intergenerational support in economically challenging times

Katerina Karanika, Exeter University, UK

Outline summary

Consumer research tends to present a positive view of the family, highlighting the concepts of love, conflict avoidance and conflict resolution within the family,[1] including for low-income consumers.[2] However, Epp and Price discuss how each family accommodates interacting bundles of identities that may not be consistent with one another under some circumstances (thus suggesting a less harmonious view of family life).[3] These include the family's collective identity, relational identities (e.g., parent–child dyads) and individual family members' identities. Consumer research on families neglected that sharing can be difficult[4] and overlooked ambivalence (mixed, both positive and negative feelings)[5] in family sharing that may reflect inconsistent family identity bundles. Moreover, consumer research has tended to concentrate on the nuclear family (a couple with their underage children), rather than on intergenerational relationships of adult family members, and has overlooked the experience of adult intergenerational support and sharing that is widespread. In order to address these gaps, a study with downwardly mobile Greek consumers involved in familial intergenerational support and sharing captured the voices of adult recipients and providers of resources.[6] Three types of consumer ambivalence were identified that reflected different types of conflicts between consumption choices and different levels of family identity (collective, relational and individual). This case study problematises previously positive views of the family in consumer research and highlights family sharing as a major antecedent of consumer ambivalence.

Context

Adult intergenerational support is widespread. Globally, a significant number of adult children remain in their parental homes, or move back into their parental homes (boomerang children), or receive parental financial support; grandparents support financially and/or practically their grandchildren; and adults live with or provide financial or practical aid to ageing parents.[7] Adult intergenerational sharing may be experienced differently from (and with more ambivalence compared to) the taken-for-granted, obligatory sharing within families with underage children, where sharing takes place as a matter of entitlement[8] and on which consumer research has largely concentrated. Intergenerational support and intergenerational sharing can be breeding grounds for ambivalence in family relationships and in consumption. This is because intergenerational support and sharing can be associated not only with affection, compassion for others and mutual aid, but also with failed expectations and ideals for adult children achieving financial independence, the sacrifice of autonomy, conformity pressures and the desire to dominate and exercise control.[9]

A qualitative study was conducted with Greek downwardly mobile consumers who were coping with financial difficulties and consumption restrictions and were involved in familial intergenerational support and sharing.[10] Intergenerational ambivalence (i.e., mixed feelings – both positive and negative feelings in family relationships)[11] accompanied intergenerational support and was the lens through which these downwardly mobile consumers experienced consumption. The findings reveal the following three types of consumer ambivalence[12] in family sharing (see also Figure 1):

1 **Guilt-evoking and shame-evoking consumption of goods experienced as 'reflectors of egoism':** The first type of consumption ambivalence was experienced for goods that prioritised individual over relational and collective identity.[13] For example, Vivian (a retired woman aged 67) felt guilty for buying a dress instead of spending the money on her two unemployed daughters (aged 35 and 39). The dress objectified guilt for favouring personal identity over relational and collective identity. At the same time, the fact that Vivian had not bought any clothes for two years as 'the expenses are so many due to the daughters' unemployment', and her daughters' insistence on her dress purchase, contributed to Vivian also having positive feelings about the dress. Reflecting intergenerational ambivalence, Vivian expressed mixed feelings toward certain consumption activities and objects, such as her new dress. She said: 'Our daughters are both unemployed and

we are supporting them. [. . .] All these [bills] are depriving us of a lot of things [. . .] I was submissive to my parents, my parents-in-law, my husband, my children. . . What about me? I won't get to live? [. . .] but it's impossible for my daughters to find a job due to unemployment [. . .] I felt guilty for buying the dress. I could buy something for my daughters instead.'

Moreover, many informants (often unemployed, low-paid employees or students) who were supported by their families had mixed feelings about their possessions and the goods and activities they were consuming as these often represented others' sacrifice and their own guilt and shame for favouring personal rather than relational or collective identity. An example is Mark (aged 37) who is unemployed, has moved back to his parents' house and feels guilt and shame for receiving parental support. This means that he experiences many of the products and services he consumes with ambivalence. He said: 'I'm ashamed I live in my parents' house. When I was self-sufficient I was paying for my health insurance but since I became unemployed my father does. I didn't want him to; it's a dignity issue but if something bad happens we wouldn't be able to deal with it.'

This type of consumer ambivalence for goods experienced as 'reflectors of egoism' was accompanied by doubts about the purchase and the continuation of the consumption that were often addressed by reducing the use of or sharing the possession in an effort to pursue voluntary simplicity. Participants tried to avoid the market for 'reflector of egoism' goods in order to avoid 'temptations', but they also often engaged in extensive market search regarding these goods.

2 **Regretful consumption of goods experienced as 'burdens':** The second type of consumer ambivalence was experienced for goods that partly supported but mainly burdened individual, relational and collective identity.[14] For example, Vivian (aged 67), who, as discussed above, supported financially her adult daughters, experienced her car as a burden and said: 'we don't know how to pay the instalments. . . It has got us to a dead end. . . You try to support your family, your children who live in a different house; it's very hard.'

Even though Vivian felt that the car offered her and her husband short escapes to the countryside, supporting individual and relational identity, she also experienced the car as a 'burden' to her individual and collective (family) identity. Participants

also expressed feelings of guilt for receiving financial intergenerational support in order to pay for expenses related to possessions, such as cars, experienced as 'burdens'. Some participants also saw their houses (first houses and especially second houses that they used to let for additional income) as 'burdens' due to the increased taxation, the pain of mortgage payments, the houses' reduced sale value and reduced saleability, as well as the increased need to provide or receive intergenerational support.

This type of consumer ambivalence was accompanied by remorse for the purchase, which was often addressed by reducing the use of the product, or sharing the possession, or by researching the market and trying to sell the possession in an effort to pursue voluntary simplicity.

3 **Involuntary simplicity, goods experienced as compromises and lost self-extension goods:** The third type of ambivalence was experienced for consumption that prioritised relational or collective over individual identity.[15] Here, participants engaged in involuntary simplicity by firstly accepting 'compromises' and secondly giving up possessions that represented 'self-extensions'.[16]

Compromises represented lowering living standards and included lower-quantity and -quality products that participants such as Vivian had started buying in order to provide intergenerational support. Although the low quality of such products was not particularly appreciated, informants felt positive about the fact that buying cheaper products (e.g., cheaper cosmetics) allowed them to provide more support for their families. Moreover, some participants like Mark had to make lifestyle and consumption compromises in order to reduce their expenses and to release their relatives from the anxiety of providing financial support. Similarly, participants who continued or started living together with relatives experienced co-habitation and their homes as compromises imposed by economic conditions. Feelings of gratitude but also a sense of personal failure accompanied informants remaining with or moving in with relatives. For example, Beatrice (aged 55), who is an architect and single, recently moved in with her mother due to recession-related difficulties and said: 'I have less work due to the crisis. I get by on my savings. I feel I didn't make it in my life [. . .] I'd like to have a house of my own that would suit my needs. I now share a very small house with my mother. It's really difficult. There's always the other person's presence and her needs; it's a big compromise.'

Participants also expressed ambivalence at being forced to abandon favourite activities or sell beloved possessions that were part of their extended selves to raise resources for themselves and their families, and often in order to favour relational and collective identity by abandoning a personal identity.[17] For example, George (aged 69) expressed his disappointment at being forced to abandon favourite activities (e.g., trips, cinema) in order to support his adult children. He said: 'I'm now forced to help my children (aged 35, 33 and 26). . . They are grown up. They should be self-sufficient. . . They haven't cut their umbilical cords yet [. . .] they have jobs but due to the financial crisis they aren't fully self-sufficient.'

This type of consumer ambivalence was not accompanied by doubts about the continuation of the behaviour and the consumption, but rather it was accompanied by efforts to accept consumption simplicity. To this end, participants avoided the market for 'lost self-extension' goods and engaged in extensive market search to find the best 'compromise' goods possible. An internal locus of control facilitated the acceptance of both 'compromises' and losses.

These three types of consumer ambivalence reflected different types of conflicts between consumption choices and different levels of family identity (collective, relational and individual).[18] The study problematises previously positive views of the family in consumer research.[19] The findings highlight family sharing – and particularly adult intergenerational support in situations of economic adversity – as a major antecedent of consumer ambivalence. Table 1 summarises the ways consumers coped with these three types of ambivalence. Even though some of the strategies participants followed to cope with ambivalence were the same for all three types of consumer ambivalence identified, the consequences of consumer ambivalence and some of the coping strategies were specific to each type of consumer ambivalence.

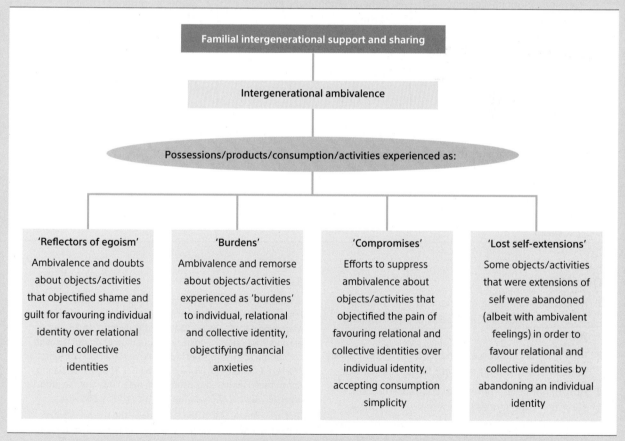

Figure 1 Consumption experiences coloured by familial intergenerational support and sharing within a context of increased economic difficulty

K. Karanika and M.K. Hogg, 'Consumption through the ambivalent prism of intergenerational support', *European Journal of Marketing* 50(3/4) (2016): 575–601.

Table 1 Coping with ambivalence

Reflectors of egoism: guilt-evoking and shame-evoking consumption	Burdens: regretful consumption	Compromises and lost self-extensions: involuntary simplicity
Consequences of consumer ambivalence: • Doubts about the purchase and the continuation of the consumption • Considerations of disposing of or selling the goods	Consequences of consumer ambivalence: • Remorse for the purchase	Consequences of consumer ambivalence: • No doubts about continuing the consumption and the behaviour
Practical coping: • Reduced use of and sharing the possession • Both avoiding the market and extensive market search	Practical coping: • Reduced use of and sharing the possession • Researching the market and trying to sell the possession	Practical coping: • Avoiding the market of 'lost self-extension' goods • Extensive market search to find the best 'compromise' good possible
Emotional coping: • General emotional coping strategies	Emotional coping: • General emotional coping strategies	Emotional coping: • General emotional coping strategies • Internal locus of control facilitates acceptance of 'compromises' and acceptance of losses
General emotional coping strategies: • External locus of control (e.g. attributing constraints to the economy and the weak welfare state) • Social emotional support and self-consolation • Escapism		

Questions

1 How is family sharing experienced in your family? What are instances of ambivalence when sharing within your family?

2 How is family sharing experienced in different family structures and during different family transitions?

3 How might intergenerational support affect consumption experiences in societies with stronger welfare states and societies less affected by austerity measures that nevertheless experience a significant rise in intergenerational support?[21]

4 What might be the implications of this study for marketing managers?

Sources

[1]E. Gótze, C. Prange and I. Uhrovska, 'Children's impact on innovation decision making: a diary study', *European Journal of Marketing* 43(1/2) (2009): 264–95; M.K. Hogg, C. Folkman Curasi and P. Maclaran, 'The (re-)configuration of production and consumption in empty nest households/families', *Consumption Markets & Culture* 7(3) (2004): 239–59; C.J. Thompson, 'Caring consumers: gendered consumption meanings and the juggling lifestyle', *Journal of Consumer Research* (1996): 388–407.

[2]B. Cappellini, A. Marilli and E. Parsons, 'The hidden work of coping: gender and the micro-politics of household consumption in times of austerity, *Journal of Marketing Management* 30(15/16) (2014): 1,597–624; K. Hamilton and M. Catterall, 'Consuming love in poor families: children's influence on consumption decisions', *Journal of Marketing Management* 22(9/10)

(2006): 1,031–52; T. Kochuyt, 'Giving away one's poverty: On the consumption of scarce resources within the family', *The Sociological Review* 52(2) (2004): 139–61.

[3] A.M. Epp and L.L. Price, 'Family identity: a framework of identity interplay in consumption practices', *Journal of Consumer Research* 35(1) (2008): 50–70.

[4] R. Belk, 'Sharing', *Journal of Consumer Research* 36(5) (2010): 715–34; R. Belk and R. Llamas, 'The nature and effects of sharing in consumer behavior', in D.G Mick, S. Pettigrew, C.C. Pechmann and J.L. Ozanne (eds), *Transformative Consumer Research for Personal and Collective Well-Being* (London: Routledge, 2012): 625–64.

[5] C. Otnes, T.M. Lowrey and L.J. Shrum, 'Toward an understanding of consumer ambivalence', *Journal of Consumer Research* 24(1) (1997): 80–93.

[6] K. Karanika and M.K. Hogg, 'Consumption through the ambivalent prism of intergenerational support', *European Journal of Marketing* 50(3/4) (2016): 575–601.

[7] V.L. Bengtson, 'Beyond the nuclear family: The increasing importance of multigenerational bonds', *Journal of Marriage and Family* 63(1) (2001): 1–16; M. Choroszewicz and P. Wolff, '51 million young EU adults lived with their parent(s) in 2008', *Eurostat Statistics in Focus* (2010); ONS Office for National Statistics (UK), 'Large increase in 20 to 34-year-olds living with parents since 1996', (2014), http://www.ons.gov.uk/ons/rel/family-demography/young-adults-living-with-parents/2013/sty-young-adults.html (accessed 3 September 2018).

[8] R. Belk, 'Sharing', *Journal of Consumer Research* 36(5) (2010): 715–34; R. Belk and R. Llamas, 'The nature and effects of sharing in consumer behavior', in D.G Mick, S. Pettigrew, C.C. Pechmann and J.L. Ozanne (eds), *Transformative Consumer Research for Personal and Collective Well-Being* (London: Routledge, 2012): 625–64.

[9] K. Lüscher, 'Ambivalence: A "sensitizing construct" for the study and practice of intergenerational relationships', *Journal of Intergenerational Relationships* 9(2) (2011): 191–206; K. Lüscher and K. Pillemer, 'Intergenerational ambivalence: A new approach to the study of parent–child relations in later life', *Journal of Marriage and the Family* (1998): 413–25; A.E. Willson, K.M. Shuey and G.H. Elder, 'Ambivalence in the Relationship of Adult Children to Aging Parents and In-Laws', *Journal of Marriage and Family* 65(4) (2003): 1,055–72.

[10] K. Karanika and M.K. Hogg, 'Consumption through the ambivalent prism of intergenerational support', *European Journal of Marketing* 50(3/4) (2016): 575–601.

[11] K. Lüscher and K. Pillemer, 'Intergenerational ambivalence: A new approach to the study of parent–child relations in later life', *Journal of Marriage and the Family* (1998): 413–25.

[12] C. Otnes, T.M. Lowrey and L.J. Shrum, 'Toward an understanding of consumer ambivalence', *Journal of Consumer Research* 24(1) (1997): 80–93.

[13] A.M. Epp and L.L. Price, 'Family identity: a framework of identity interplay in consumption practices', *Journal of Consumer Research* 35(1) (2008): 50–70.

[14] Ibid.

[15] Ibid.

[17] R.W. Belk, 'Possessions and the Extended Self', *Journal of Consumer Research* 15 (1988): 139–67.

[18] Ibid.

[19] A.M. Epp and L.L. Price, 'Family identity: a framework of identity interplay in consumption practices', *Journal of Consumer Research* 35(1) (2008): 50–70.

[20] B. Cappellini, A. Marilli and E. Parsons, 'The hidden work of coping: gender and the micro-politics of household consumption in times of austerity, *Journal of Marketing Management* 30(15/16) (2014): 1,597–624; E. Gótze, C. Prange and I. Uhrovska, 'Children's impact on innovation decision making: a diary study', *European Journal of Marketing* 43(1/2) (2009): 264–95; K. Hamilton and M. Catterall, 'Consuming love in poor families: children's influence on consumption decisions', *Journal of Marketing Management* 22(9/10) (2006): 1,031–52; M.K. Hogg, C. Folkman Curasi and P. Maclaran, 'The (re-)configuration of production and consumption in empty nest households/families', *Consumption Markets & Culture* 7(3) (2004): 239–59; T. Kochuyt, 'Giving away one's poverty: On the consumption of scarce resources within the family', *The Sociological Review* 52(2) (2004): 139–61; C.J. Thompson, 'Caring consumers: gendered consumption meanings and the juggling lifestyle', *Journal of Consumer Research* (1996): 388–407.

[21] M. Choroszewicz and P. Wolff, '51 million young EU adults lived with their parent(s) in 2008', *Eurostat Statistics in Focus* (2010).

Further reading

P. Bourdieu, *Distinction: A Social Critique of The Judgement of Taste* (London: Routledge, 1984).

K. Karanika and M.K. Hogg, 'Trajectories across the lifespan of possession-self relationships', *Journal of Business Research* 66(7) (2013): 910–16.

S. Ulver and J. Óstberg, 'Moving up, down or sideways? Exploring consumer experience of identity and status incongruence', *European Journal of Marketing* 48(5/6) (2014): 833–53.

Part E
Culture and European consumers

The final part of the text considers consumers as members of a broad cultural system. Chapter 12 starts this part by examining some of the basic building blocks of culture and consumption, and shows how consumer behaviours and culture are constantly interacting with each other. Chapter 13 then looks at the perpetual production of culture, and how the 'gatekeepers' of culture help shape our sense of fashion and consumer culture. In other words, we focus on processes of cultural change.

Chapter 12
Culture and consumer behaviour

Chapter objectives

When you finish reading this chapter you will understand why:

12.1 Culture is the accumulation of shared meanings, practices and traditions that permeates everything we do.

12.2 Myths are stories that express the shared ideals of a culture, and modern myths are transmitted through the media.

12.3 We perform rituals every day, in gift-giving as well as many other routines, but also on big occasions such as graduations, weddings and funerals – modern rites of passage that require consumption of ritual artefacts.

12.4 Consumer activities can be divided into sacred and profane domains.

12.5 Religion can be an influential factor on consumption.

I T'S THURSDAY NIGHT, 7.30. Sean puts down the phone after speaking with Colum, his study partner in his consumer behaviour class. The weekly night out for the Irish marketing students has begun! Sean has just spent the summer months travelling in Europe. He was always amazed, and delighted, to find a place claiming to be an Irish pub. Regardless of how unauthentic the place was, an Irish pub always sold Guinness – a true symbol of Ireland, he reflected. Sean had begun to drink when he started university. Initially, bottled beers straight from the fridge had been his preference. However, now that he was in his third year and a more sophisticated, travelled and rounded person, he feels that those beers were just a little too – well, fashionable. He has thus recently begun to drink Guinness. His dad, uncle and grandad, in fact most of the older men he knows, drink Guinness. That day in consumer behaviour the lecturer had discussed the 'Guinness Time' TV commercial. It featured a young

Consider a ritual that many beer drinkers in the UK and Ireland hold near and dear to their hearts: the spectacle of a pub bartender 'pulling' the perfect pint.
Oli Scarff/Getty Images

man doing a crazy dance around a settling pint of Guinness. The young man saved his most crazed expression for the point when he took his first sip. The lecturer had pointed out that the objectives of the ad were to associate Guinness with fun – an important reason why young people drink alcohol – and to encourage them to be patient with the stout, as a good pint takes a number of minutes to settle.[1]

Sean has arranged to meet his friends in the local pub at 8.30. They will order 'three pints of the finest black stuff' and then have their own Guinness ritual. To begin, they watch it being poured and then look for the rising rings of the head – the best indication of a good pint. Once settled, a small top-up, and then ready for action. But they always wait and study their glasses before taking the first mouthful together – what a thing of beauty!

Damien McLoughlin, University College, Dublin, Ireland

Introduction

As we have already seen in the earlier parts of this text, consumption choices cannot be understood without considering the cultural context in which they are made: culture is the 'prism' through which people view products and try to make sense of their own and other people's consumer behaviour.

Sean's beer-drinking reflects his desire to associate with and dissociate from (with help from the media and marketers) a certain style, attitude and trendiness. Being an Irishman, his attachment to Guinness has a very different meaning in his world than it would have in, for example, trendy circles in continental cities, where Guinness may be associated with the very fashionability that Sean is trying to avoid.

Indeed, it is quite common for cultures to modify symbols identified with other cultures and present these to a new audience. As this occurs, these cultural products undergo a process of **co-optation**, where their original meanings are transformed and often trivialised by outsiders. In this case, the Irish beer has been, to a large extent, divorced from its original connection with the Irish traditional working class or rurality and is now used as a trendy way of consuming 'Irishness' abroad (but without the rural or lower-class aspect).[2]

We have seen (in Chapter 1) how contemporary society can be regarded as a consumer society or a consumer culture – a culture in which consumption has become a central vehicle for organising social meanings. This chapter considers culture from a somewhat broader perspective. We will take a look at how some of the characteristics not only of contemporary consumer culture but of all cultures contribute to the shaping of consumer behaviour. Myths, rituals and the sacred are not just features of so-called 'primitive' societies but are basic elements in all cultures. We will take a look at how myths and rituals of the culture in which we live create the meaning of everyday products and how these meanings move through a society to consumers.

This chapter deals mainly with the way in which very basic cultural values and symbols are expressed in goods and how consumers appropriate these symbols through consumption rituals. The next chapter will then take a closer look at fashion and other change processes in consumer culture. The first part of this chapter reviews what is meant by culture and how cultural priorities are identified and expressed. These social guidelines often take the form of *values,* which have already been discussed (see Chapter 5). The second part considers the role of myths and rituals in shaping the cultural meaning of consumer products and consumption activities. The chapter concludes by exploring the concepts of the sacred and the profane and their relevance for consumer behaviour.

Culture and consumption

12.1

Culture is the accumulation of shared meanings, practices and traditions that permeates everything we do.

Culture, a concept crucial to the understanding of consumer behaviour, may be thought of as the collective memory of a society. Culture is the accumulation of shared meanings, rituals, norms and traditions among the members of an organisation or society. It is what defines a human community, its individuals, its social organisations, as well as its economic and political systems. It includes both abstract ideas, such as values and ethics, and the material objects and services, such as cars, clothing, food, art and sports, that are produced or valued by a group of people. Thus, individual consumers and groups of consumers are but part of culture, and culture is the overall system within which other systems are organised.

Some of the pioneers in exploring the relationship between consumption and culture were an anthropologist, Mary Douglas, and an economist, Baron Isherwood.[3] They underlined how goods are always used as social markers, not only in the traditional sense of displaying social status (although that is an important feature) but more generally by underlining how uses of goods express particular social relationships (such as friendship), particular times (for example, 'a party'), particular moods (such as relaxation) and so on. Most importantly, these marking functions are performed through a variety of daily and not-so-daily consumption rituals. We will take a closer look at consumption rituals later in this chapter. The basic learning from this and other works on consumption and culture is that any consumption activity must be understood in the cultural context in which it is taking place.

Ironically, the effects of culture on consumer behaviour are so powerful and far-reaching that this importance is sometimes difficult to grasp or appreciate.[4] We are surrounded by a lot of practices, from seemingly insignificant behaviours such as pressing the start button of our iPod to larger movements such as flying to an exotic honeymoon in Tanzania. What is important is that these practices have meaning for us – that we know how to interpret them. Culture is basically this interpretation system, which we use to understand all those daily or extraordinary **signifying practices**[5] around us. Culture as a concept is like a fish immersed in water – we do not always appreciate this power until we encounter a different environment, where suddenly many of the assumptions we had taken for granted about the clothes we wear, the food we eat, the way we address others and so on no longer seem to apply. The effect of encountering such differences can be so great that the term 'culture shock' is not an exaggeration. However, this might be changing, since with increased globalisation we encounter other cultures all the time, in the real or the virtual world. And this, in turn, might make us more reflexive about who we are and what we represent ourselves. Such reflexive culture may challenge the 'water fish swim in' metaphor and make culture just as much an outcome as an antecedent to our consumption.[6] We learn to 'design' our culture through consumption choices.

This does not alter the fact that the strength of culture often comes as a surprise to marketers (although that might, in itself, be a little surprising!). But the importance of cultural expectations is often only discovered when they are violated, as some Danish companies learned the hard way through market shares lost in the Middle East following the so-called cartoon crisis.[7] Research has shown that it is not the evaluation of the product quality that has changed as much as the evaluation of the brand. In other words, the negativity of the brand in this case is more significant than the positivity about the product quality.[8] This case illustrates that sensitivity to cultural issues, whether by journalists or by brand managers, can come only by understanding these underlying dimensions – and that is the goal of this chapter.

A consumer's culture determines the overall priorities they attach to different activities and products. It also determines the success or failure of specific products and services. A product that provides benefits consistent with those desired by members of a culture at a particular time has a much better chance of attaining acceptance in the marketplace. It may be difficult to guess the success or failure of certain products. Some years ago, the business magazine *Financial Times* analysed the downfall of the Danish toy manufacturing company LEGO, and presented it as an excellent case of how good companies go bad.[9] Today, a good decade later, LEGO is hailed as an absolute leader in the toy market and a great example of very good product innovation, not least through its understanding of cultural processes – including the rise of programmable toys and the role of Hollywood blockbusters in cultural mythologies.[10]

The relationship between consumer behaviour and culture is a two-way street. On the one hand, products and services that resonate with the priorities of a culture at any given time have a much better chance of being accepted by consumers. On the other hand, the study of new products and innovations in product design successfully produced by a culture at any point in time provides a window on the dominant cultural ideals of that period. Consider, for example, some products that reflect underlying cultural processes at the time they were introduced:

- convenience foods and ready-to-eat meals, hinting at changes in family structure and the decline of the full-time housewife;
- cosmetics such as those of The Body Shop, made of natural materials and not tested on animals, which reflected consumers' apprehensions about pollution, waste and animal rights;
- unisex fragrances, indicating new views on sex roles and a blurring of gender boundaries, as exemplified by Calvin Klein.

Cultural systems

Cultures are organised as open systems of interrelated elements. What this means is that culture is not static. It is continually evolving, synthesising old ideas with new ones. A cultural system can be said to consist of three interrelated functional areas:[11]

1 *Ecology*: the way in which a system is adapted to its habitat. This area is shaped by the technology used to obtain and distribute resources (for example, industrialised societies *vs* less-affluent countries). One example is the Japanese interest in space-saving devices, since living space is often very sparse in Japanese cities.

2 *Social structure*: the way in which orderly social life is maintained. This area covers the domestic and political groups that are dominant within the culture, including, for example, the importance of the nuclear family *vs* the extended family, different gender roles and degrees of male and female dominance in different areas of life.

3 *Ideology*: the mental characteristics of a people and the way in which they relate to their environment and social groups. This area revolves around the belief that members of a society possess a common **worldview** – that is, they share certain ideas about principles of order and fairness. They also share an **ethos**, or a set of moral and aesthetic principles. In Europe, contemporary Turkey is a good example of a clash of ethos within a culture, where rapid modernisation and the construction of a consumer society is enchanting a lot of people but also challenging traditional pious values and thereby provoking people with a different ethos to seek alternative solutions. One consequence is that many Turkish women are confronted with dilemmas concerning respecting a certain piety by wearing a headscarf (a practice that has gone from stigmatised to more legitimate, based on cultural reflexivity on Turkey's 'Islamic heritage'), and appearing modern, fashionable and seductive at the same time. Fashion veiling is born! Hence, the consumption of the headscarf becomes inscribed right in the middle of contemporary Turkish cultural politics.[12]

How cultures vary

Although every culture is different, a lot of research has been aimed at reducing the cultural variation to simpler principles. We have already made reference to the specificity of the Japanese relationship with living space. People's culturally formed relationship to space, also called **proxemics**, is one of the fundamental distinctions between different cultures.[13] This is valid both in terms of the public space and the intimate private space immediately surrounding them. Another fundamental distinction between cultures is the relationship with time. It has been suggested that there are **monochronic** (stressing 'one thing at a time and according to schedule' principles) and **polychronic** (stressing 'several things at a time and completion of task') cultural time systems.[14] Which cultural time system do you think you belong to? Notice that when assessing such differences in cultural styles, there may not only be national cultural differences at stake here, but also other kinds of cultural distinction such as urban versus rural cultures. This is one of the problems with such grand reductions of cultural differences to a simple scheme. The problem is not that proxemics or time styles are irrelevant, but that they may not be very good descriptors of what distinguishes a particular nation. It should be remembered that everyone is a member of several cultures. You are not only British, or Swedish or. . . , but also a student (which constitutes a particular culture sub-divided into subcultures), with perhaps an upper middle-class background, coming from a relatively small town, etc. As one final example, cultures also differ in their emphasis on individualism *vs* collectivism. In **collectivist cultures**, people subordinate their personal goals to those of a stable in-group. By contrast, consumers in **individualist cultures** attach more importance to personal goals, and people are more likely to change memberships when the demands of the group (e.g. workplace, church, etc.) become too costly. A Dutch researcher on culture, Geert Hofstede, has proposed this and three other dimensions – the relation to differences in social power, handling of uncertainty and risk and the degree of masculine and feminine values – to account for much of this variability.[15] However, Hofstede's and similar approaches have been much criticised.[16] The four dimensions do not account for the differences in the meaning and the role of the concepts in each culture. That each culture has to cope with problems of power, risk and uncertainty, gender roles and the relationship between the individual and society is obvious. But that the solutions to these problems are reducible to different levels on one-and-the-same scale is dubious, to say the least.

Although we must be able to compare behaviour across cultures by using general concepts, we must do so by initially understanding and analysing every culture (and hence every consumer culture) on the basis of its own premises – an approach known as ethnoconsumerism.[17] In Figure 12.1, the principles of an ethnoconsumerist methodology are depicted. Note how central the notions of cultural categories and cultural practices (introduced in Chapters 1 and Chapter 11) are to this approach to studying consumption. To illustrate the contribution of such an approach to the study of consumer behaviour, consider a study of foreign tourist behaviour in Britain that concluded that a sheer indication of nationality in and by itself was a bad predictor of how tourists coped with their confrontation with the (strange) British culture, whereas an ethnoconsumerist study permitted the researchers to isolate a number of cultural factors and types of behaviour that generated a much richer portrayal of touristic coping behaviour.[18] The point is, that whatever consumers do, if we want to understand it fully we will have to be aware of the cultural background to the activity. Even a simple thing such as drinking a cup of coffee has a different meaning in different cultures.[19]

Rules for behaviour

Values (as we saw in Chapter 5) are very general principles for judging between good and bad goals, etc. They form the core principles of every culture. From these flow norms, or rules, dictating what is right or wrong, acceptable or unacceptable. Some norms, called *enacted norms,* are explicitly decided upon, such as the rule that a green traffic light means 'go' and

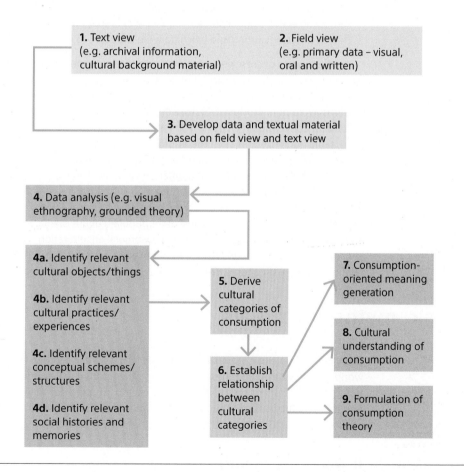

Figure 12.1 Principles for an ethnoconsumerist approach to studying consumption

Source: Laurie Meamber and Alladi Venkatesh, 'Ethnoconsumerist Methodology for Cultural and Cross-Cultural Consumer Research', in R. Elliott and S. Beckmann (eds), *Interpretive Consumer Research* (Copenhagen: Copenhagen Business School Press, 2000): 87–108.

a red one means 'stop'. Many norms, however, are far more subtle. These *crescive norms* are embedded in a culture and are only discovered through interaction with other members of that culture. Crescive norms include the following:[20]

- A **custom** is a norm handed down from the past that controls basic behaviours, such as division of labour in a household or the practice of particular ceremonies. Offering visitors a small thing to eat or drink, such as a cup of coffee or a cup of tea, is in many cultures part of custom, whether the visit is a professional or a private one.

- **Mores** are customs with a strong moral overtone. Mores often involve a taboo, or forbidden behaviour, such as incest or cannibalism. Violation of mores often meets with strong censure from other members of a society. As we saw above, the rise of a highly fashion-conscious and modern Islamic consumer in Turkey (and elsewhere in the Middle East) has led to the construction of a parallel fashion scene, where the mores of displaying the female body parts are not violated.[21]

- **Conventions** are norms regarding the conduct of everyday life. These rules deal with the subtleties of consumer behaviour, including the 'correct' way to furnish one's house, wear one's clothes, host a dinner party and so on. Consider that the classical races at Royal Ascot recently felt compelled to introduce a stricter dress code, since the hats and clothes on display had become a little too fanciful for the organisers' taste – according to a spokesperson, it was important to obey the formality of the occasion and not dress as on a visit to a nightclub.[22] Sometimes conventions cause cross-cultural problems. For example, the Chinese were grappling with a cultural problem as they prepared for the 2008 Olympics in Beijing: local habits of public spitting and belching were expected to offend many a foreign visitor.[23]

All three types of crescive norms may operate to define a culturally appropriate behaviour. For example, mores may tell us what kind of food it is permissible to eat. Note that mores vary across cultures, so eating a dog may be taboo in Europe, while Hindus would shun beef and Muslims avoid pork products. Custom dictates the appropriate hour at which the meal should be served. Conventions tell us how to eat the meal, including such details as the utensils to be used, table etiquette and even the appropriate apparel to be worn at dinner time.

We often take these conventions for granted, assuming that they are the 'right' things to do (again, until we are exposed to a different culture!). And it is good to remember that much of what we know about these norms is learned *vicariously* (see Chapter 6), as we observe the behaviours of others in our peer groups but also actors and actresses in films and TV series, television commercials, print ads and other popular culture media. In the long run, marketers have a great deal to do with influencing consumers' enculturation, which is the process whereby you learn your own society's values, as opposed to acculturation, which refers to processes of relating to different cultures. We shall take a look at acculturation processes in the next chapter.

Magic, myths and rituals

Myths are stories that express the shared ideals of a culture, and modern myths are transmitted through the media.

Every culture develops stories and practices that help its members to make sense of the world. When we examine these activities in other cultures, they often seem strange or even unfathomable. Yet our *own* cultural practices appear quite normal – even though a visitor may find them equally bizarre. The following section will discuss magic, myths and rituals – three aspects of culture common to all societies, from the ancient to the modern world.

It works like magic!

To appreciate how so-called 'primitive' belief systems, which some may consider irrational or superstitious, continue to influence our supposedly 'modern', rational society, consider the avid interest of many Western consumers in magic. Marketers of health foods, anti-ageing cosmetics, exercise programmes and gambling casinos often imply that their offerings have 'magical' properties that will ward off sickness, old age, poverty or just plain bad luck. People by the millions carry lucky charms to ward off 'the evil eye', or have 'lucky' clothing or other products that they believe will bring them good fortune. Many of us have a lucky number that we use on various occasions, such as in sports games (whether we are playing ourselves, betting, or just watching), and lotteries. Beliefs in magic structure major consumer events in the West as well as the East. When the calendar hit 7 July 2007 – 7/7/07 – many people in the US scrambled to take advantage of its link to lucky 777. Western culture associates the number 7 with good fortune (for example, the seven sacraments in Roman Catholicism), and US marketers from Wal-Mart to Las Vegas casinos jumped on the bandwagon.[24] Keep in mind that these beliefs are culture-centric, so they take on different forms around the world. For example, in China the number 8 is the luckiest number. The Chinese word for 8 is *ba,* which rhymes with *fa,* the Chinese character for wealth. It was no coincidence that the Summer Olympics in Beijing opened on 8/8/08 at 8.08 pm.

But the magic most prevalent in consumer culture is the magic that pertains to the transformations of our bodies. The health, wellness and beauty industries are replete with suggestions of magical transformations of our bodies, which will help us cleanse our bodily organs, shed excess weight, restore youthful looks and create a new and more harmonious and balanced self. Research has demonstrated the role of magical thinking in the way consumers relate to weight-loss programmes,[25] and how such weight-loss programmes as Weight Watchers, for example, constitute spiritual and therapeutic ways of coping with what is perceived as effects of overconsumption.[26] Note the magic of consumer society – that you can consume (e.g., a therapeutic programme) in order to cope with the effects of overconsumption!

Such hopes for a magic transformation lie behind a lot of contemporary consumption pertaining to the self, from the very manifest consumption of cosmetic surgery[27] to the more spiritual consumption of self-enhancement programmes.[28] Often, advertisers and consumers construct marketplace mythologies to serve multiple and sometimes competing ideological agendas – this is particularly true in the product categories that consumers use to deal with issues of health, healing and well-being.[29]

An interest in the occult tends to be popular, perhaps even more so when members of a society feel overwhelmed or powerless – magical remedies simplify our lives by giving us 'easy' answers. Marketing efforts are replete with more-or-less open references to magical practices.[30] And it is not just a matter of fooling consumers: magic is also an active part of our modern lives. Customers on river-rafting trips in the US speak about the magical capacities of the river to transform their lives, heal psychological wounds and bring out the best in people.[31] Even a computer was once regarded with awe by many consumers as a sort of 'electronic magician', with the ability to solve our problems (or in other cases to make data magically disappear!).[32] However, some scholars argue that the use of the magic metaphor oversimplifies the way persuasion works in marketing and contributes to a demonisation.[33] In this text, magic should not be understood as a demonisation of persuasive techniques, but as a fundamental anthropological phenomenon.

Marketing opportunity

Magic has been the order of the beginning of the twenty-first century. As some researchers have suggested, we live in a period characterised by stories of magic and the magic of stories.[34] Never before (or at least since the Middle Ages) has the market been so populated with magicians, sorcerers, witches, spirits, druids and other beings of the magical universe. Possibly the single most influential factor here is the marketing genius of – or rather behind – *Harry Potter.* The completely engineered world of Harry Potter, with the cathedral of magic at Hogwarts, the variety of shops in Diagon Alley, the experience economy of Quidditch and the plethora of sweets at Honeydukes sweetshop, is all based on a very enriching encounter between a society hungry for sorcery and the magic of marketing, if you are to believe one

→

marketing wizard writing under the name of Stephen Brown. The success of the Harry Potter brand is immersed in a contemporary (postmodern?) demand for magic fairy tales and a skilful construction of a complete universe reflecting all of contemporary consumer society's wonderful and not-so-wonderful consequences of marketplace practices. Can we finally learn the trick? Magic matters! It is marketing for Muggles![35] Is magic a has-been? Consider the success of Kevin the carrot – Aldi's commercial Christmas mascot in the UK since 2016.[36] And fantasy literature is still a big genre for youngsters, so the question might very well be: where might the next marketing magic be coming from?

Myths

Every society possesses a set of myths that define that culture. A **myth** is a story containing symbolic elements, which expresses the shared emotions and ideals of a culture. The story may feature some kind of conflict between two opposing forces, and its outcome serves as a moral guide. In this way, a myth reduces anxiety because it provides consumers with guidelines about their world. For example, a couple of researchers used the concept of myth to analyse how media resolved anxieties among mainstream consumers (not everyone had their anxieties resolved!) concerning major environmental disasters such as the oil spills of Exxon Valdez (1989) and the BP Deepwater Horizon Spill in the Mexican Gulf (2010).[37] For a mythological resolution to a daily life problem, consider, for example, the significance of the relationship between order and disorder in many of the ways in which we relate to our possessions and how deeply-rooted ideas of what is orderly and disorderly orient us in our daily lives.[38]

An understanding of cultural myths is important to marketers, who in some cases (most likely unconsciously) pattern their strategy along a mythic structure.[39] Consider, for example, the way that a company such as McDonald's takes on 'mythical' qualities.[40] The golden arches are a universally recognised symbol, one that is virtually synonymous with American culture. Not only do they signify the possibility for the whole world symbolically to consume a bite of Americana and modernity, but they also offer sanctuary to Americans around the world, who know exactly what to expect once they enter. Basic struggles involving good *vs* evil are played out in the fantasy world created by McDonald's advertising, as when Ronald McDonald confounds the Hamburglar. McDonald's even has a 'seminary' (Hamburger University) where inductees go to learn appropriate behaviours and be initiated into the culture. In short, McDonald's is a kind of mythical utopia representing modernity, leisurely eating and lifestyle, and the American dream – a mythical utopia it shares with other brands such as Disneyland or Disney World.[41]

Corporations often have myths and legends in their history, and some make a deliberate effort to be sure newcomers to the organisation learn these. Nike (a name drawn from Greek mythology) designates senior executives as 'corporate storytellers', who explain the company's heritage to the hourly workers at Nike stores.[42] The strongest brands often base their strength on how well they resonate with current mythologies.[43] One example provided is the whisky producer Jack Daniels, which has skilfully used and contributed to the American 'gunfighter myth'.[44] What is this myth about? Consider detective stories in TV and on the big screen – often the hero does not just have to fight the villains, but also his superordinate boss, as a representative of the 'system'. This 'man versus system' is what the gunfighter myth is all about. How many other brands and types of consumption depend on such mythology? A similar mythological narrative of 'the morally good real American' versus 'the morally corrupt and un-American environmentalists', was evoked by consumers of the Hummer brand in order to defend their car choice.[45] Sometimes consumers react against what they see as industry-created myths. In Denmark, a country known for its dairy industry, one set of consumers started to react very strongly against what they saw as a 'corporate-generated myth' that dairy products are healthy. The conflict escalated to the point where the Danish health authorities, for the first time ever, issued a public warning against following the dietary recommendations of this consumer movement, especially for small children.[46] Myths are a battleground!

Of course, one of the most fundamental myths of the Western world is the myth of the 'exotic Other', which is basically different from ourselves, as expressed by Kipling in his lines, 'East is East and West is West, and never the twain shall meet'. This myth is reflected in a lot of consumer behaviour, such as in the experiences promised by the tourist industry, where myths about destinations are sometimes supported by similar mythologies inherent in music, or imagined lifestyles. For example, Hawaii[47] (and surf culture[48] in particular) has been studied as such a mythological universe. We also find this myth, however, in more home-based activities such as in the attraction to and collection of exotic goods such as Oriental carpets.[49] One version of this myth is the myth of the primitive, the unspoiled natural and immaculate, which may be seen to be at the roots of the allure of surfer culture.[50]

The functions and structure of myths

Myths serve four interrelated functions in a culture:[51]

1 *metaphysical*: they help to explain the origins of existence;

2 *cosmological*: they emphasise that all components of the universe are part of a single picture;

3 *sociological*: they maintain social order by authorising a social code to be followed by members of a culture;

4 *psychological*: they provide models for personal conduct.

Myths can be analysed by examining their underlying structures – a technique pioneered by the anthropologist Claude Lévi-Strauss. Lévi-Strauss noted that many stories involve *binary opposition,* where two opposing ends of some dimension are represented (good *vs* evil, nature *vs* technology). Characters and products often appear in advertisements to be defined by what they are *not,* rather than by what they *are* (for example, this is *not* a product for those who feel old, *not* an experience for the frightened, *not* music for the meek, etc.). Such structures have been used to analyse food categories, dividing food into hot *vs* cold, for children, for adults and for old people, for men and for women, etc.[52] Myths are often the fundamental element in folk tales, where they represent eternal conflicts between good and evil, innocence and guilt, male and female, civility and bestiality. It has been argued that the success of *The Twilight Saga,* one of the biggest franchises in the history of popular culture, is not least due to its skillful application of fundamental mythical structures that can be played out in its occult universe of vampires, love, attraction and repulsion.[53]

According to Freudian theory, the ego functions as a kind of 'referee' between the opposing needs of the id and the superego. In a similar fashion, the conflict between mythical opposing forces is sometimes resolved by a *mediating figure,* who can link the opposites by sharing characteristics of each. For example, many myths contain animals that have human abilities (e.g. a talking snake) to bridge the gap between humanity and nature, just as cars (technology) are often given animal names such as Jaguar or Mustang.

Myths are found everywhere in modern popular culture. While we generally equate myths with the ancient Greeks or Romans, modern myths are embodied in many aspects of popular culture, including comic books, films, holidays and even commercials. Sports consumption is replete with myths – for instance, myths about 'super-athletes' or 'the eternal no. 2', or the favourites who always fail, such as the Spanish football team until their victory in the 2008 European Championship. Music is also full of myths – myths about the garage band who makes it big, or the myth of the self-destructive artist maintained by many a dead music star.[54]

Comic book superheroes demonstrate how myths can be communicated to consumers of all ages. Indeed, some of these fictional figures represent a **monomyth** – a myth that is common to many cultures.[55] The most prevalent monomyth involves a hero who emerges from the everyday world with supernatural powers and wins a decisive victory over evil forces. He then returns with the power to bestow good things on his fellow men. This basic theme can be found in such classic heroes as Lancelot, Hercules and Ulysses. The success of the Disney movie *Hercules* reminds us that these stories are timeless and appeal to people through the ages. Comic book heroes are familiar to most consumers, and they are viewed as more credible and effective than celebrity endorsers. Film spin-offs and licensing deals aside, comic books are a multi-million-dollar industry. The American version of the monomyth is best-epitomised by Superman – an almost Christ-like figure who renounces worldly temptations and restores harmony to his community. But there are many other, less obvious, mythological figures surrounding us. For example, the role of Albert Einstein as a mythological figure – one that is used for giving meaning to and promoting certain consumable objects in films or posters, or in advertisements as a sort of indirect endorsement, and which has been studied by consumer researchers.[56]

Many blockbuster films and hit TV programmes draw directly on mythic themes. *Spiderman* draws both on the myth of the superhero as well as the myth of one's eternal fight with one's own negative sides (especially in *Spiderman 3*).[57] So, while dramatic special effects or attractive stars certainly do not hurt, a number of these films perhaps owe their success to their presentation of characters and plot structures that follow mythic patterns. Consider, for example, the two film classics *E.T.* and *Jaws*:[58]

- *E.T.: The Extraterrestrial.* E.T. represents a familiar myth involving Messianic visitation. The gentle creature from another world visits Earth and performs miracles (e.g. reviving a dying flower). His 'disciples' are local children, who help him combat the forces of modern technology and an unbelieving secular society. The metaphysical function of myth is served by teaching that the humans chosen by God are pure and unselfish. In an inverse format, a similar story is told in the more recent blockbuster *Avatar*.

- *Jaws.* This and films constructed around similar themes draw on myths of the beast, representing the wild, dangerous, untamed nature that is culture's (human beings') enemy. Such myths are known from Christianity and other religious mythologies, such as Norse mythology (the Midgaard Snake, the Fenris Wolf), and have played a central role in the way the Western world has regarded nature over the centuries.

- But also the more contemporary movie *Titanic* plays on and strengthens a mythology about human hubris – a human tendency to overestimate one's own powers and control over things – and its adjacent mythology about some of the negative sides of modernity and technology. A mythology that was not least strengthened (and consumed!) during the marking of the 100 years of the world's most-famous shipwreck.[59]

Commercials and products as myths

More mundane consumer objects can be the subject of mythological narratives. Even such an organisation as the UK's Post Office has been considered an institution connected to national mythologies.[60] The Danish and Swedish postal systems merged in 2009 and in 2016 it was decided to make the uniforms of the newly-formed 'PostNord' organisation the colour blue in both countries. The disappearance of the red postman, an iconic figure in Danish popular culture, was called a 'symbolic castration' of a national icon.[61] Can you think of other such controversial remakings of iconic products or figures in your own country?

Even when objects stay more or less the same, they change over place and time since they are culturally constructed. Consider, for example, a classic study of the meanings and roles of the Italian scooter in the Italian and British market contexts. Whereas in Italy the scooter was mainly positioned as a symbol of the new, modern and liberated Italian woman, epitomised in the Italian superstar actresses of the 1950s, the scooter in Britain became caught in a cultural clash between the more 'masculine' heavy industry and the blue-collar jobs expressed in subcultural terms among the 'rockers' and their motorcycles, and the more white-collar youth subculture of the 'mods', heavily engaged in conspicuous consumption activities. The latter adopted the scooter as their prime symbol and dominant mode of transport.[62] Today, the scooter (revived by consumer nostalgia and retro-marketing)[63] has become a modern myth object referring to the happy and innocent youth culture of 40 to 50 years ago, as depicted by this bag for sale at London's Portobello Road market.

Commercials can be analysed in terms of the underlying cultural themes they represent. Myths of particular places (for example, of the lost paradise of Shangri-La – lost but never found, somewhere in Tibet) have inspired Westerners captured by Eastern mythology for years. However, the search could be over, since the Chinese Government has now founded an official Shangri-La – a Disneyfied tourist destination based on spiritual and sacred themes.[64] But it's not just particular places that are mythical, it's also particular times. For example, commercials for various food products ask consumers to 'remember' the mythical 'good old days', when products were wholesome and natural. The mythical theme of the underdog prevailing over the stronger foe (David and Goliath) has been used by the car rental firm Avis in a now-classic campaign where they stated, 'when you're no. 2, you try harder'. Other figures from mythical narratives have been used by advertisers, such as the villain (a brand teasing its competitors), the hero (the brand in control) or the helper (the brand that helps you accomplish something).[65]

The interest in such mythological foundations has soared since the turn of the millennium, not least through the influential work of one brand analyst introducing the notion of *iconic brands.*[66] Since then, a whole series of products has been suggested as being of a particular status in the contemporary marketplace, ranging from the vinyl record[67] and the electric guitar[68] to champagne.[69] Even celebrities have been suggested to be such iconic brands[70] – we will talk more about the role of celebrities as cultural icons when we discuss sacred people below.

A bag depicting a modern myth object – the scooter

Photo courtesy of Caroline Penhoat

Rituals

12.3

We perform rituals every day, in gift-giving as well as many other routines, but also on big occasions such as graduations, weddings and funerals – modern rites of passage that require consumption of ritual artefacts.

A **ritual** is a set of multiple, symbolic behaviours that occur in a fixed sequence and that tend to be repeated periodically.[71] Although bizarre tribal ceremonies, perhaps involving animal or virgin sacrifice, may come to mind when people think of rituals, in reality, many contemporary consumer activities are ritualistic. Rituals are traditionally thought of as patterns of behaviour that serve to uphold the social order, but drinking rituals such as Sean's can also be thought of as transgressive and transformative, especially among younger consumers. Hence, drinking as a ritual constitutes a time and space to enter another state of being, of being intoxicated! This relationship to drinking rituals is probably more characteristic of northern European consumers compared to southern Europeans.[72]

Multicultural dimensions

What kind of extras do you think of, when you consider buying a car? You may think of upgraded sound systems, GPS and other digital equipment that makes driving easier and safer, plus all kinds of chromium additions. But maybe there is one thing that did not occur to you: a blessing. Some car dealers in countries such as India and Malaysia delight their customers with a free blessing, a *puja,* as a service either performed on the spot at the dealers or at a nearby temple.[73] Blessing things before their usage is a common ritual among Hindu communities. It is a way of seeking the gods' good will and of protecting the object from bad influences. How to do it? There is an online guide, obviously.[74]

A study conducted by the advertising agency BBDO Worldwide illustrates just how crucial rituals are to many brands.[75] It labels brands that we closely link to our rituals as **fortress brands**, because once they become embedded in our rituals – whether that be brushing our teeth, drinking a beer, or shaving – we are unlikely to replace them. The study ran in 26 countries, and the researchers found that, overall, people worldwide practice roughly the same consumer rituals. The study claims that 89 per cent of people repeatedly use the same brand for these sequenced rituals, and three out of four are disappointed or irritated when something disrupts their ritual, or their brand of choice is not available. For example, the report identifies one common ritual category it calls *preparing for battle.* For most of us this means getting ready for work. Relevant rituals include brushing teeth, taking a shower or bath, having something to eat or drink, talking to a family member or partner, checking email, shaving, putting on makeup, watching TV or listening to the radio and reading a newspaper.

Rituals can occur at a variety of levels, as noted in Table 12.1. Some of the rituals described are specifically American, but the US Super Bowl may be compared to the English FA Cup Final or the traditional ski-jump competition in Germany on the first day of the new year. Some rituals affirm broad cultural or religious values, like the differences in the ritual of tea drinking in the UK and France. Whereas tea seems a sensuous and mystical drink to the French, the drinking of coffee is regarded as having a more functional purpose. For the British, tea is a daily drink and coffee is seen more as a drink to express oneself.[76]

The ritual of going to a café offering a selection of coffee opportunities was unknown outside most of the metropolitan areas of the US until recent times. No longer. The Starbucks Corporation has experienced phenomenal success by turning the coffee break into a cultural event that, for many, has assumed almost cult-like status. The average Starbucks customer visits 18 times a month, and 10 per cent of the clientele stops by twice a day.[77] Starbucks has opened shops in many countries in Europe, re-exporting a new kind of coffee-shop culture to places with long traditions for café culture, such as France. Thus, several types of places for different 'coffee rituals' may co-exist. One study suggested at least three kinds of coffee shops in the Scandinavian context: the traditional 'Viennese' style, where a lot of focus is on the baked goods; the 'starbuckified' modern coffee shop (such as Starbucks but also Baresso,

Table 12.1 Types of ritual experience

Primary behaviour source	Ritual type	Examples
Cosmology	Religious	Baptism, meditation, Mass
Cultural values	Rites of passage	Graduation, marriage
	Cultural	Festivals, holidays (Valentine's Day), Super Bowl
Group learning	Civic	Parades, elections, trials
	Group	Business negotiations, office luncheons
	Family	Mealtimes, bedtimes, birthdays, Mother's Day, Christmas
Individual aims and emotions	Personal	Grooming, household rituals

Source: Dennis W. Rook, 'The ritual dimension of consumer behavior', *Journal of Consumer Research* 1985 12(3): 251–64, *The Journal of Consumer Research* Copyright © 1985, Oxford University Press by permission of Oxford University Press.

etc.); and the 'local' coffee shop, with a less streamlined interior decoration than the modernist ones, and often a devoted clientele of 'alternative-minded' people.[78] Rituals also travel over borders – as witnessed by the celebration of Halloween (see section on Holiday Rituals below). More American rituals are finding their way to Europe – researchers underlined the importance of processes of inclusion and exclusion in the introduction of the American high-school prom in a British context.[79]

Ritual artefacts

Many businesses owe their livelihoods to their ability to supply **ritual artefacts**, or items used in the performance of rituals, to consumers. Birthday candles, diplomas, specialised foods and beverages (e.g. wedding cakes, ceremonial wine, or even sausages at the stadium), trophies and plaques, band costumes, greetings cards and retirement watches are all used in consumer rituals. In addition, consumers often employ a ritual script, which identifies the artefacts, the sequence in which they are used and who uses them. The proliferation of 'manners and style' books in recent years bears witness to the renewed interest in rituals after the belief of the beat generation that they could abolish ritual behaviour and just act 'normal' and be 'natural'. Of course, such behaviour required a whole new set of rituals. . .

But rituals are not restricted to the special occasions described above. Daily life is full of ritualised behaviour. Wearing a tie on certain occasions can be seen as a ritual, for example. The daily meal is a ritual, albeit one that some see as being under threat, for example by the inclusion of media in the ritual. The question is, however, whether watching TV abolishes or just changes the ritual of the daily meal.[80] The significance attached to rituals will vary across cultures (Valentine's Day is slowly gaining popularity in several European countries and in the Middle East),[81] and will often be a mixture of private and public (generally shared) symbolism.[82]

In the model of movement of meaning in the world of goods (see Chapter 1) it is suggested that there are four types of rituals that are central for consumption: possession rituals, exchange rituals, grooming rituals and divestment rituals.[83] Let us begin with considering the first and the last together, since they are logically intertwined: one consumer's divestment can often be linked to another consumer's acquisition of a possession.

Possession and divestment rituals

Whether it is in the form of putting magnets on the refrigerator door, objects hanging from the mirror in the car or stickers and badges put on jackets and bags, consumers often perform various rituals that provide a certain degree of alteration to a newly purchased object. The

Weddings are important rites of passage that often include lavish spending and a number of additional rituals such as cutting the cake – an important ritual artefact.

RubberBall/Alamy Stock Photo

object is thereby transformed from a mass-produced good to a personalised possession. Possession rituals mark that the object is no longer just any object, it is *my* object. The blank and boring computer screen is personalised through the installation of our background for the desktop, our own set of preferred photos as screensavers and in a multitude of other ways. We personalise the screen and the ringtone of our cellphone. Through these ritualistic inclusions of the mass-produced goods in our own little sphere of being, we are transforming them into objects that are visibly or audibly one's own and also expressions of identity (as we discussed in Chapter 4).

Since we invest personal meanings in our things, we also, often, invest some effort in removing the elements of identity when we are getting rid of the things. We call these efforts rituals of disposition. When you move out of your flat, you make sure to clean it of everything that belongs to you, not only because the contract says so, but also because you do not want to allow other people a look into your private life through the personal items or traces left. You may clean it thoroughly, but possibly the new tenant will perform yet another cleaning (another divestment ritual – making sure the flat is divested of its former owne) and a possession ritual of repainting in order to make sure the flat is now truly theirs. Divestment rituals also occur when cherished possessions are ritualistically transferred from

Marketing pitfall

Product launches in the cultural industry have always been surrounded with important rituals, such as pre-screenings of (what is expected to be) new blockbuster movies with invited guests (celebrities, by and large) and a red carpet, etc., the premiere of a theatre play or the long-awaited new book from a celebrity author, complete with signature tours and public readings. In the later years, the tech giants have jumped on this bandwagon and also surrounded their product launchings with ritualistic elements, which the consumers usually happily play along with – queuing overnight to get the phone first, and being part of the festive balloons, confetti and free morning coffee get-together. Usually. . . When Apple's iPhone8 was launched in 2017, it produced little of former times' excitement. It was arguably overshadowed by the expected launching of the iPhone X in 2018.[84] Maybe these launchings have outlived themselves, since the tech companies, eager to always be at the pinnacle of progress, launch multiple versions and improvements of their models so that the 'big makeover' has been replaced by several small, and less-ritualised makeovers.

one generation to the next. Such rituals of handing over things to a younger generation can contribute to lower the anxieties that the new generations will cherish and protect the family heirloom as well as former generations.

Consequently, rituals of disposition are not only performed in order to remove personalisation from consumer objects but, in a way, also to keep it since it confirms if not the individual then the family identity. They can also be performed in order to maintain a moral identity. Consider the great efforts some consumers go to in terms of sorting their garbage for maximal recycling. We can consider this sorting behaviour an expression of environmental values, but it is also a ritual that is performed in order to divest the objects 'properly' – that is, in the morally and socially (and environmentally) correct way. The concept of 'freecycling' also illustrates such a moral approach to divestment;[85] increasingly, consumers are willing to share what they no longer need and are turning trash for themselves into treasures for other people (see also the discussion in Chapter 5).[86] Indeed, consumers can experience the yearning to get rid of some of their possessions as some kind of sacrifice ritual in order to obtain a purer, almost sacred kind of consumer life.[87] We will return to the sacred shortly, but let us add that this idea of divestment as a sacrifice does not only pertain to voluntary simplists and downshifters. A story of ordinary British families found the same kind of sacrifice ritual in the way people related to their left-over food.[88] And what initially seems an abnormal practice undergoes a slow normalisation process until it becomes an increasingly socially acceptable ritual.[89]

Grooming rituals

Whether brushing one's hair 100 strokes a day or talking to oneself in the mirror, virtually all consumers undergo private grooming rituals. These are sequences of behaviours that aid in the transition from the private self to the public self, or back again. These rituals serve various purposes, ranging from inspiring confidence before confronting the world to cleansing the body of dirt and other profane materials. Traditionally a female market, the grooming sector for men is now also a booming business. For example, at the turn of the millennium Unilever opened a new chain of barber shops in the UK that also offer facial treatments and manicures on top of the shaves and beard trims. The adaptation to the male market is almost perfect: the waiting rooms feature PlayStations instead of glossy magazines.[90]

When consumers talk about their grooming rituals, some of the dominant themes that emerge from these stories reflect the almost mystical qualities attributed to grooming products and behaviours. Many people emphasise a before-and-after phenomenon, where the person feels magically transformed after using certain products (similar to the *Cinderella* myth).[91]

Two sets of binary oppositions that are expressed in personal rituals are *private/public* and *work/leisure.* Many beauty rituals, for instance, reflect a transformation from a natural state to the social world (as when a woman 'puts on her face') or vice versa. In these daily rituals, women reaffirm the value placed by their culture on personal beauty and the quest for eternal youth.[92] This focus is obvious in ads for Oil of Olay beauty cleanser, which proclaim: 'And so your day begins. The Ritual of Oil of Olay'. Similarly, the bath is viewed as a sacred, cleansing time – a way to wash away the sins of the profane world.[93]

Exchange rituals

It would be fair to say that the whole marketplace of exchanging goods, services and information through sharing, buying and selling is one big set of exchange rituals. But sometimes the social context of the exchange proves that it is important that the exchange is *not* commercialised.[94] Think about the party where everyone is supposed to bring a contribution to the buffet – and imagine someone starts comparing expenses and asks for compensation if it turns out they spent more on ingredients than others! Indeed, the form of exchange rituals that most ordinary consumers would think of first and foremost is probably giving and receiving gifts, which is *not* seen as a commercial exchange. Nevertheless, the promotion of appropriate gifts for every conceivable holiday and occasion provides an excellent example of the influence consumer rituals can exert on marketing phenomena and vice versa. In the **gift-giving ritual**, consumers procure the perfect object (artefact), meticulously remove the price tag (symbolically changing the item from a commodity to a unique good), carefully wrap it and deliver it to the recipient.[95]

Gift-giving used to be viewed by researchers primarily as a form of economic exchange, where the giver transfers an item of value to a recipient, who in turn is somehow obliged to reciprocate. However, gift-giving is interpreted increasingly as a symbolic exchange, where the giver is motivated by acknowledging the social bonds between people.[96] These might then be seen as more economic and reciprocal, but may also be guided by unselfish factors such as love or admiration, without expectation of anything in return. Some research indicates that gift-giving evolves as a form of social expression: it is more exchange-oriented (instrumental) in the early stages of a relationship, but becomes more altruistic as the relationship develops.[97] One set of researchers identified multiple ways in which giving a gift can affect a relationship.[98] These are listed in Table 12.2.

Every culture prescribes certain occasions and ceremonies for giving gifts, whether for personal or professional reasons. The giving of birthday presents alone is a major undertaking. Things we receive as gifts immediately take on a different meaning compared to if we had just bought it ourselves, because they come to represent a social relationship. Likewise, research has demonstrated how experiential gifts might be more effective in fostering strong relationships than material gifts.[99] Today, it may also be much nicer to receive a home-made gift rather than something bought in a shop. But it was of course not always like that. Historically, the gift that was bought rather than made emerged in the last half of the 19th century, indicating the rise of contemporary market-based consumer culture.[100]

The gift-giving ritual can be broken down into three distinct stages.[105] During *gestation,* the giver is motivated by an event to procure a gift. This event may be either *structural* (i.e. prescribed by the culture, as when people buy Christmas presents), or *emergent* (i.e. the decision is more personal and idiosyncratic). The second stage is *presentation,* or the process of gift exchange. The recipient responds to the gift (either appropriately or not), and the donor evaluates this response.

Table 12.2 Effects of gift-giving on social relationships

Relational effect	Description	Example
Strengthening	Gift-giving improves the quality of a relationship	An unexpected gift such as one given in a romantic situation
Affirmation	Gift-giving validates the positive quality of a relationship	Usually occurs on ritualised occasions such as birthdays
Negligible effect	Gift-giving has a minimal effect on perceptions of relationship quality	Non-formal gift occasions and those where the gift may be perceived as charity or too good for the current state of the relationship
Negative confirmation	Gift-giving validates a negative quality of a relationship between the gift-giver and the receiver	The selection of gift is inappropriate, indicating a lack of knowledge of the receiver. Alternatively, the gift is viewed as a method of controlling the receiver
Weakening	Gift-giving harms the quality of the relationship between giver and receiver	When there are 'strings attached' or gift is perceived as a bribe, a sign of disrespect or offensive
Severing	Gift-giving harms the relationship between the giver and the receiver to the extent that the relationship is dissolved	When the gift forms part of a larger problem, such as a threatening relationship, or when a relationship is severed through the receipt of a 'parting' gift

Source: Adapted from Julie A. Ruth, Cele C. Otnes and Frederic F. Brunel, 'Gift receipt and the reformulation of interpersonal relationships', *Journal of Consumer Research* 1999 25(4): 385–402, Table 1: 389. Copyright © 1999, Oxford University Press by permission of Oxford University Press.

Multicultural dimensions

The importance of gift-giving rituals is underscored by considering Japanese customs, where the wrapping of a gift is as important (if not more so) as the gift itself. The economic value of a gift is secondary to its symbolic meaning.[101] To the Japanese, gifts are viewed as an important aspect of one's duty to others in one's social group. Giving is a moral imperative (known as *giri*).

Highly ritualised gift-giving occurs during the giving of both household/personal gifts and company/professional gifts. Each Japanese person has a well-defined set of relatives and friends with whom they share reciprocal gift-giving obligations (*kosai*).[102] In keeping with the Japanese emphasis on saving face, presents are not opened in front of the giver, so that it will not be necessary to hide one's possible disappointment with the present.

Personal gifts are given on social occasions, such as at funerals, to people who are hospitalised, to mark movements from one stage of life to another (such as weddings, birthdays) and as greetings (when one is meeting a visitor). Company gifts are given to commemorate the anniversary of a corporation's founding or the opening of a new building, as well as being a routine part of doing business, as when rewards are given at trade meetings to announce new products.

Some of the items most desired by Japanese consumers to receive as gifts include gift coupons, beer and soap.[103] Consider this in relation to another country, Turkey, where the highly important tradition of giving gold objects as gifts has a meaning that goes way beyond the mere economic value of the gold. The importance of gold as a gift, it has been argued, is exactly its capacity of maintaining high economic *and* symbolic value without reducing one to the other.[104]

Gift-giving has long been a cultural trait among the Japanese. In recent years, it has become popular within the context of a westernised Christmas season in Japan.

Gen Nishino/Taxi/Getty Images

In the third stage, known as *reformulation,* the bonds between the giver and receiver are adjusted (either looser or tighter) to reflect the new relationship that emerges after the exchange is complete. (One study of such a reformulation process underlined the role of gift-giving rituals for community building, and thereby the success of a larger consumption ritual, the New Orleans *Mardi Gras* festival.[106]) Negativity can arise if the recipient feels the gift is inappropriate or of inferior quality. Both participants may feel resentful for being 'forced' to participate in the ritual.[107] Indeed, since people may feel fear of becoming either subject to or the cause of a feeling of indebtedness by engaging in gift-giving, some may even 'escape' to the market and sell some of their stuff rather than giving it away, not so much to make money but rather to avoid creating a relationship of indebtedness.[108]

People commonly find (or devise) reasons to give themselves something; they 'treat' themselves. Consumers purchase **self-gifts** as a way to regulate their behaviour. This ritual provides a socially acceptable way of either rewarding oneself (and sometimes others in a shared format) for good deeds, celebrating (or motivating) some accomplishment, remembering or bonding, marking a departure or to compensate and feel consolation.[109] It is useful to analyse the reasons people view as legitimate for rewarding themselves with self-gifts. For example, one theme might emerge that, for example, the purchaser has had a particularly gruelling

Consumer behaviour as I see it . . .

The dark side of the gift

Stephen Brown, University of Ulster

Russ Belk, an eminent consumer researcher, once observed that 'you can learn more. . . from a reasonably good novel than from a "solid" piece of social science research'. Much the same sentiments have been expressed by leading thinkers and creative writers, from Walter Benjamin to Bob Dylan. It is often said that *Debt of Honor,* a bestselling blockbuster novel by Tom Clancy, not only anticipated but inspired the terrorist attacks of 9/11. Science-fiction writer J.G. Ballard has been credited with many prescient predictions about contemporary consumer society, including social media and reality television. The best description of consumer 'scavenging' is not found in the pages of an academic journal but in an essay of that name by renowned American novelist Jonathan Franzen.

In this regard, consider the 'dark side of the gift'. That is, a situation where we give or are given an embarrassingly inappropriate present. We've all done it. We've all had it done to us. I know I have. A few years ago, for example, I gave my wife what I thought was the prefect Christmas gift. Taking into account that she has a natural flair for – and gets great satisfaction from – home decoration, do-it-yourself and domestic construction projects of all kinds, I decided to buy her a stepladder. Yes, a stepladder. For Christmas.

This was no ordinary stepladder, let it be said. This was the Lotus Elan of stepladders, the Louis Vuitton of stepladders, the Louboutin stilettos of stepladders. It was made of adonised aluminium. It came with non-slip steps. It had all sorts of special features. I wrapped it up in beautiful marbled Christmas paper, moreover, and placed it tenderly beneath our bauble-bedecked, tinsel-swaddled, star-surmounted Christmas tree. Where, I have to admit, it looked a little bit like an ancient Egyptian mummy in its alabaster sarcophagus.

Well, on Christmas Day, we did our traditional ritual thing. All our extended family of aunts, uncles, nieces, nephews etc, gather round the tree and we open the presents in turn, oohing and aaahing and clapping as each perfectly-chosen gift is unwrapped.

When my wife unwrapped her stepladder, there was total silence, dead silence, sepulchral silence. A howling wind picked up from nowhere. A bell tolled mournfully in the distance. As I recall, a ball of tumbleweed rolled across the floor in front of me.

It took me months, months of flowers, chocolates, cards and the like to repair the damage. To this very day, whenever we do the Christmas ritual thing, someone will always say 'Do you remember the year with the stepladder?'. And everybody laughs at sad old Stephen's gift-giving mortification.

Question

What is the worst present you've ever received? Or given? Or heard about? While you're ruminating, read *The Gift,* by David Flusfeder. This brilliant novel is a sublime account of how innocent gift-giving can get completely out of hand and how the principle of reciprocity – where the value of gifts given and received are roughly equivalent – can lead to ruinous consequences.

No, don't thank me. It's my little gift to you, dear reader. If you feel moved to buy my books in return, you'll have fallen for the oldest trick in the marketers' book.

Stephen Brown

It is useful to analyse the reasons people view as legitimate for rewarding themselves with self-gifts

Drazen/E+/Gettty Images

day at work and needed a pick-me-up in the form of a new fragrance. This theme could then be incorporated into a promotional campaign for a perfume. With the growing evidence of hedonic motives for consumption in recent decades, self-gifts may represent an increasingly importance part of the overall consumption pattern.

One final gift-giving ritual that is worth mentioning – since the rise of the internet and its digitalised world has made it far easier and present in our lives – is the idea of sharing and of giving away (in a digital form) what one already possesses, but without losing it oneself. In what may well be the largest gift-giving system in history, the now bygone Napster music sharing community, and its successors such as Limewire and Piratebay, have opened a whole new world of consumer exchange rituals with its own specific set of norms for reciprocity and contribution within the online community. For example, people who download files without leaving their files available to others are labelled as 'leeches'.[110] As we all know, this form of gift-giving has not been embraced by all. Copyright holders in the form of music publishers (and musicians) are generally less than amused, so since then we have witnessed what might best be described as a drama between producers protecting their intellectual property rights and consumers underlining their rights to do what they want with their possessions (including online sharing and community building), as long as it remains a non-commercial activity.[111] These and other moral arguments such as 'fair use' and the fact that buying copies might help other people than the copyright holders make a living are also evoked in order to justify ethical issues in music access.[112] A British study suggests that there are four types of 'pirates': (1) the serious ones actively and quite often seeking out occasions to pirate (known as 'Devils'); (2) the opportunistic ones that will occasionally take a chance on pirating but not very frequently ('Chancers'); (3) pirates who are not actively pirating but accept receiving pirated material ('Receivers'); and (4) the 'Angels', who refrain from any sort of pirating.[113] Which type are you?

Holiday rituals

Holidays are important rituals in both senses of the word. Going on holiday was one of the most widespread rituals and tourism one of the biggest industries of the late twentieth century, and the trend looks set to continue.[114] On holiday, consumers step back from their everyday lives and perform ritualistic behaviours unique to those times.[115] For example, going to Disneyland in Paris may mean a ritualised return to the memories of our own dreams of a totally free (of obligations, duties and responsibilities) fantasy land of play.[116] Holiday occasions are filled with ritual artefacts and scripts and are increasingly cast as a time for giving gifts by enterprising marketers. Holidays mean big business to hotels, restaurants, travel agents and so on. They are even related to particular sacred beliefs (more on those later). In a modern society, everybody wants to go on holiday. Thus, the Turkish tourist industry has provided a fancy new hotel industry for faithful Muslims, with separate male and female pool and beach areas and entertainment facilities.[117]

Holidays also exist in terms of special celebratory occasions. For many businesses, Christmas is the single most important season. Concerning the holidays of celebrations, most such holidays are based on a myth, and often a real (Guy Fawkes) or imaginary (Cupid on Valentine's Day) character is at the centre of the story. These holidays persist because their basic elements appeal to deep-seated patterns in the functioning of culture.[118]

The Christmas holiday is bursting with myths and rituals, from adventures at the North Pole to those that occur under the mistletoe. One of the most important holiday rituals involves Santa Claus, or an equivalent mythical figure, eagerly awaited by children the world over. Unlike Christ, this person is a champion of materialism. Perhaps it is no coincidence, then, that he appears in stores and shopping centres – secular temples of consumption. In an American context, Christmas is such an important ritual that it has been found that even people who do not celebrate Christmas, for example subcultures of other religious observance, construct a separate set of rituals in order to maintain some kind of symbolic linkage with the celebrating majority.[119] Obviously, certain consumers resist the materialism and marketisation of Christmas. These 'anti-Christmas' groups may draw upon a counter-mythological figure, such as the cynical Christmas-hater Ebenezer Scrooge from Dickens' *A Christmas Carol*, as a symbol to flock around online in order to share and reinforce their anti-consumerism Christmas ideals.[120]

Whatever the origins of Santa Claus, the myth surrounding him serves the purpose of socialising children by teaching them to expect a reward when they are good and that members of society get what they deserve. Needless to say, Christmas, Santa Claus and other associated rituals and figures change when they enter into other cultural settings. In the Netherlands he has to compete with his doppelgänger Sint Niklaas, who even has his own day of celebration on 6 December. In Denmark, Norway and Sweden, Santa Claus competes or is confused with Julenissen (in Sweden, Jultomten), who is a kind of amalgamation between gnomes from ancient pagan beliefs and a contemporary Santa Claus figure. Some of the transformations of Santa Claus in a Japanese context include a figure called 'Uncle Chimney', Santa Claus as a stand-in for the newborn Christ, and Santa Claus crucified at the entrance of one department store with the words 'Happy Shopping' written above his head.[121] What does this tell us about the globalisation process?

On Valentine's Day, standards regarding sex and love are relaxed or altered as people express feelings that may be hidden during the rest of the year. In addition to cards, a variety of gifts are exchanged, many of which are touted by marketers to represent aphrodisiacs or other sexually related symbols. It seems as if many people in consumer societies are always on the lookout for new rituals to fill their lives. This ritual was once virtually unknown in Scandinavia but is slowly becoming part of their consumption environment.[122] Also, the American ritual of celebrating Halloween has now become more fashionable in Europe. In

Christmas marks the biggest consumption ritual in today's world, in Uganda also.

Photo: Kira Strandby

Denmark, Halloween has become a significant consumer ritual. Between 2005 and 2008 the sales of 'scary stuff' from toy stores had gone up 10–20 per cent each year, and the sale of pumpkins (which Danes generally do not eat) multiplied by 30 between 1999 and 2008. In 2016, it was reported that the Halloween turnover in Denmark was about three times as big as during the traditional occasion for children's disguises and costumes – *Fastelavn*.[123] As for many modern rituals, supermarket chains and other commercial agents have played a significant role in spreading these occasions for having a good time but also for boosting sales across borders.

Rites of passage

What does a dance for recently divorced people have in common with 'college initiation cere-monies'? Both are examples of modern **rites of passage**, or special times marked by a change in social status. Every society, both primitive and modern, sets aside times where such changes occur. Some of these changes may occur as a natural part of consumers' lifecycles (puberty or death), while others are more individual in nature (divorce and re-entering the dating market). For example, one particular rite that marks the entrance to youth and puberty for young girls is typically starting to wear make-up. As such, this grooming ritual also becomes a rite of passage for adolescent girls.[124] As we saw with some of the other rituals, there seems to be a

The myth of Santa Claus permeates our culture and have done so for quite some years
Heritage Images/ Hulton Archive/Getty Imahes

renewed interest in transition rites. They are increasingly becoming consumption objects in themselves, as well as occasions for consumption. In order to satisfy the 'need' for rituals, not only do we import new ones from abroad, as we have seen, but in times of globalisation many cultures also experience a renewed interest in the old rituals that have traditionally framed the cultural identity.[125]

Some marketers attempt to reach consumers on occasions in which their products can enhance a transition from one stage of life to another.[126] A series of Volkswagen ads, for example, underlined the role of the car in the freedom of women who were leaving their husbands or boyfriends.

Stages of role transition

Much like the metamorphosis of a caterpillar into a butterfly, consumers' rites of passage consist of three phases.[127] The first stage, *separation,* occurs when the individual is detached from their original group or status (for example, the first-year university student leaves home). *Liminality* is the middle stage, where the person is literally in between statuses (the new arrival on campus tries to work out what is happening during orientation week). The last stage, *aggregation,* takes place when the person re-enters society after the rite of passage is complete (the student returns home for the Christmas holiday as a 'real university student'). Rites of passage mark many consumer activities, as exemplified by confirmation or other rites of going from the world of the child to the world of the adult. A similar transitional state can be observed when people are prepared for certain occupational roles. For example, athletes and fashion models typically undergo a 'seasoning' process. They are removed from their normal surroundings (athletes are taken to training camps, while young models are often moved to Paris or Milan), indoctrinated into a new subculture and then returned to the real world in their new roles.

The final passage: marketing death

The marketplace is full of references to death! From death metal[128] to crime fiction,[129] death themes are replete in marketing.[130] Consumer researchers are also increasingly interested in the role of the 'real' death as a 'consumption object', since it represents one of the most significant elements in human life.[131] The rites of passage associated with death support an entire industry. Death is a complex symbolic phenomenon for humans and should be studied with methods that respect this symbolic complexity.[132] Survivors must make expensive purchase decisions, often at short notice and driven by emotional and superstitious concerns. Funeral ceremonies help the living to organise their relationships with the deceased,[133] and action tends to be tightly scripted down to the costumes (the ritual black attire, black ribbons for mourners, the body in its best suit) and specific behaviours (sending condolence cards or holding a wake). However, more and more seem to emphasise a certain personal touch to commemorate the individuality of the deceased. Mourners 'pay their last respects', and seating during the ceremony is usually dictated by mourners' closeness to the individual. Even the cortège is accorded special status by other motorists, who recognise its separate, sacred nature by not overtaking as it proceeds to the cemetery.[134] Even after the funeral service, the consumption involved in maintaining and embellishing the grave can be considered the final gift we give to the deceased.[135]

Funeral practices vary across cultures, but they are always rich in symbolism. For example, a study of funeral rituals in Ghana found that the community there determines a person's social value after he has died; this status depends on the type of funeral his family gives him. One of the main purposes of death rituals is to negotiate the social identities of deceased persons. This occurs as mourners treat the corpse with a level of respect that indicates what they think of him. The Asante people, who were the subjects of a study, do not view death as something to fear but rather as a part of a broader, ongoing process of identity negotiation.[136]

Sacred and profane consumption

12.4

Consumer activities can be divided into sacred and profane domains.

As we saw when considering the structure of myths, many types of consumer activity involve the demarcation, or binary opposition, of boundaries, such as good *vs* bad, male *vs* female – or even 'regular' *vs* 'low-fat'. One of the most important of these sets of boundaries is the distinction between the sacred and the profane. **Sacred consumption** involves objects and events that are 'set apart' from normal activities, and are treated with some degree of respect or awe. They may or may not be associated with religion, but most religious items and events tend to be regarded as sacred. **Profane consumption** involves consumer objects and events

Funeral ceremonies are a rite of passage that include scripted symbolism, including a cortège.
Stephen Barnes/Northern Ireland News/Alamy Stock Photo

that are ordinary, everyday objects and events that do not share the 'specialness' of sacred ones. (Note that profane does not mean vulgar or obscene in this context.)

Religion, as we know, plays a role in establishing rules about what is proper and improper to consume. Varying rules about pork, alcohol, beef and meat in general, but also about caffeine and other stimulants, shape particular religious consumption universes. However, the significance of religion may go beyond such rules. 'Infidels! Infidels!', one child of a pious Muslim family in Turkey shouted, when confronted with the Nestlé brand during a research project in Turkey. For reasons of religious opposition, such pious Turkish consumers may consider certain Western brands such as Nestlé but also McDonalds and Coca-Cola 'haram' (forbidden according to religious law) because they are seen as co-responsible for Israëli–American repression of Palestinians.[137] We shall return to religion at the end of the chapter, but let us first consider some less obvious (but not less common!) forms of the sacred.

Domains of sacred consumption

Sacred consumption events permeate many aspects of consumers' experiences, not just the ones that are 'officially' religious. We find ways to 'set apart' a variety of places, people and events. In this section, we will consider some examples of ways that 'ordinary' consumption is sometimes not so ordinary after all.

Sacred places

Sacred places have been 'set apart' by a society because they have religious or mystical significance (e.g. Bethlehem, Mecca, Stonehenge) or because they commemorate some aspect of a country's heritage (e.g. the Kremlin, Versailles, the Colosseum in Rome). Other places are created from the profane world and imbued with sacred qualities. When Ajax, the local football team of Amsterdam, moved from their old stadium (De Meern) to a larger, more modern stadium (De Arena), the turf from the old stadium was carefully lifted from the ground and sold to a local churchyard. The churchyard offers the turf to fans willing to pay a premium price to be buried under authentic Ajax turf!

Even the modern shopping centre can be regarded as a secular 'cathedral of consumption', a special place where community members come to practise shopping rituals.[138] Theme parks are a form of mass-produced fantasy that takes on aspects of sacredness. In particular, the various Disneylands are destinations for pilgrimages from consumers around the globe. Disneyland displays many characteristics of more traditional sacred places, especially for Americans, but Europeans too may consider these parks the quintessence of America. It is even regarded by some as the epitome of child(ish) happiness.[139] A trip to a theme park is the most common 'last wish' for terminally ill children.[140]

In many cultures, the home is a particularly sacred place. It represents a crucial distinction between the harsh, external world and consumers' 'inner space'. In northern and western Europe the home is a place where you entertain guests (in southern Europe it is more common to go out), and fortunes are spent each year on interior decorators and home furnishings; the home is thus a central part of consumers' identities.[141] But even here there are vast differences between, for example, the dominant traditionalist style of British homes and the modernist style of Danish homes.[142] Consumers all over the world go to great lengths to create a special environment that allows them to create the quality of homeliness. This effect is created by personalising the home as much as possible, using such devices as door wreaths, mantel arrangements and a 'memory wall' for family photos.[143] Even public places, such as various types of cafés and bars, strive for a home-like atmosphere that shelters customers from the harshness of the outside world.

Sacred people

People themselves can be sacred, when they are idolised and set apart from the masses. Souvenirs, memorabilia and even mundane items touched or used by 'sacred' people take on special meanings and acquire value in their own right. Indeed, many businesses thrive on consumers' desire for products associated with famous people. This is true not least among young consumers, for whom identification with star celebrities plays a particular role.[144] Obviously, charities also may use celebrities in promoting their good causes.[145] There is a thriving market for celebrity autographs, and objects once owned by celebrities, whether Princess Diana's gowns or John Lennon's guitars, are often sold at auction for astronomical prices. For example, in early 2015, one website that specialises in selling authenticated celebrity possessions offered earrings worn by Lisa Kudrow, a bag that used to belong to Melanie Griffith and various clothes worn by Jim Carrey in the movie *Fun with Dick and Jane,* among other necessities![146]

Sacred events

Many consumers' activities have taken on a special status. Public events, in particular, resemble sacred, religious ceremonies – as exemplified by the playing of the national anthems before a sporting game or the reverential lighting of matches and lighters at the end of a rock concert.[147]

For many people, the world of sport is sacred and almost assumes the status of a religion. The roots of modern sports events can be found in ancient religious rites, such as fertility festivals (e.g. the original Olympics).[148] Indeed, it is not uncommon for teams to join in prayer prior to a game. The sports pages are like the Scriptures (and we describe ardent fans as reading them 'religiously'), the stadium is a house of worship and the fans are members of the congregation. After the first Scottish victory in many years in a football match against England at Wembley Stadium, Scottish fans tore down the goals to bring pieces back home as sacred relics. Indeed, grass from stadiums after important matches, such as World Cup finals, has been sold in small portions at large prices (cf. the Ajax story mentioned above).

Devotees engage in group activities, such as tailgate parties (eating and drinking in bars or even the car park prior to the event) and the 'Mexican Wave', where (resembling a revival meeting) participants on cue join the wave-like motion as it makes its way around the stadium.

The athletes that fans come to see are god-like; they are reputed to have almost superhuman powers (especially football stars in southern Europe and Latin America). Athletes are central figures in a common cultural myth – the hero tale. As exemplified by mythologies of the barefoot Olympic marathon winner (Abebe Bikila from Ethiopia, 1960), or of boxing heroes (legally) fighting their way out of poverty and misery, often the heroes must prove themselves under strenuous circumstances. Victory is achieved only through sheer force of will. Of course, sports heroes are popular endorsers in commercials, but only a few of these sports personalities 'travel' very well, since sports heroes tend to be, first and foremost, national heroes. However, a few people are known worldwide, at least within the key target market for the ads, so that they can be used in international campaigns.

If sport is one domain that is becoming increasingly sacred (see the section on sacralisation below), then the traditionally sacred realm of fine arts is considered by some in danger of desacralisation. In a sale of a publishing company of classical music, various representatives voiced the fear that a takeover by one of the giants such as Sony, Polygram or EMI would mean the introduction of a market logic that would destroy its opportunities to continue to sponsor unknown artists and make long-term investments in them. It is argued that classical music is not a product that can be handled by any marketer, but requires special attention and a willingness to accept financial losses in order to secure artistic openness and creativity.[149] Such reactions (as justified as they may be) indicate that artists and managers conceive of themselves as dealing with sacred objects that cannot be subjugated to what is conceived as the profane legitimacy of the market.[150] Indeed, art and marketing is the subject of study for more and more marketing and consumer researchers, for example in considering art as a kind of service.[151] Famous film directors make commercial campaigns and music videos (and music video-makers turn into great film directors), while commercial film-makers celebrate each other with their own sets of prizes for creativity. The great documentary *Exit Through the Gift Shop,* by the famous British street artist Banksy, about the unfolding of the global street art scene, provides a wonderful example of the intricate relationship between art and marketing in a consumer society.[152] Art and marketing, in short, are becoming increasingly blurred (see the section 'Desacralisation' below).[153]

Tourism is another example of a sacred, non-ordinary experience of extreme importance to marketers. When people travel on holiday, they occupy sacred time and space. The tourist is continually in search of 'authentic' experiences that differ from their normal world.[154] This travelling experience involves binary oppositions between work and leisure and being 'at home' *vs* 'away'. Norms regarding appropriate behaviour are modified as tourists scramble for illicit experiences they would not dream of engaging in at home. The desire of travellers to capture these sacred experiences in objects forms the bedrock of the souvenir industry, which may be said to be in the business of selling sacred memories. Whether a personalised matchbook from a wedding or a little piece of the Berlin Wall, souvenirs represent a tangible piece of the consumer's sacred experience.[155]

In addition to personal mementoes, such as ticket stubs saved from a favourite concert, the following are other types of sacred souvenir icons:[156]

- local products (such as goose liver from Périgord or Scotch whisky);
- pictorial images (postcards);
- 'piece of the rock' (seashells, pine cones), although sometimes this can be problematic. For example, it is forbidden to bring home corals and seashells from a lot of diving places around the world, in order to prevent tourists from 'tearing down' the coral reef. But temptations are great. Even at Nobel Prize dinners, approximately 100 of the noble guests each year cannot resist bringing home something, typically a coffee spoon, as a souvenir;[157]
- symbolic shorthand in the form of literal representations of the site (a miniature London double-decker bus, a Little Mermaid or an Eiffel Tower);
- markers (Hard Rock Café T-shirts).

Increasingly, we see peculiar blends of the sacred and the secular in tourism and in sacred places promoting themselves. One such case is the town of Glastonbury, England. Being an ancient site for pagan as well as Christian worship, it today profiles itself on an amalgamation of 'serious' New Age beliefs and tongue-in-cheek promotion of experience economy witchcraft à la Harry Potter.[158]

From sacred to profane, and back again

Just to make life interesting, in recent times many consumer activities have moved from one sphere to the other. Some things that were formerly regarded as sacred have moved into the realm of the profane, while other, everyday phenomena are now regarded as sacred.[159] Both these processes are relevant to our understanding of contemporary consumer behaviour. A recent study of tea preparation in Turkey illustrates this movement. Although we are more likely to think of thick Turkish coffee, in reality Turks consume more tea per capita than any other country. In this culture, people drink tea continuously, like (or instead of) water. Tea is an integral part of daily life; many households and offices boil water for tea in the traditional *çaydanlik* (double teapot) first thing in the morning, and keep it steaming all day so that the beverage is ready at any time. The tea-drinking process links to many symbolic meanings – including the traditional glasses, clear to appreciate the tea's colour, and hourglass-shaped like a woman's body – and rituals, such as blending one's own tea, knowing how finely to grind the tea leaves, and how long to steep the tea for optimal flavour. When Lipton introduced the modern tea bag in 1984, Turkey was intent on modernisation and soon consumers were buying electric *çaydanlik,* and mugs instead of small, shapely tea glasses. Tea became a symbol of the quick and convenient and the drinking act became more of a fashion statement – it was desacralised. Now, the authors report, many Turkish consumers opt to return to the sacred, traditional rituals as a way to preserve authenticity in the face of rapid societal changes.[160]

Desacralisation

Desacralisation occurs when a sacred item or symbol is removed from its special place or is duplicated in mass quantities, becoming profane as a result. For example, souvenir reproductions of sacred monuments such as the Leaning Tower of Pisa or the Eiffel Tower, 'pop' artworks of the *Mona Lisa* or adaptations of important symbols such as the Union Jack flag by clothing designers, tend to eliminate their special aspects by turning them into inauthentic commodities, produced mechanically and representing relatively little value.[161]

Religion itself has, to some extent, been desacralised. Religious symbols, such as stylised crosses or New Age crystals, have moved into the mainstream of fashion jewellery.[162] What used to be deeply religious expressions thus become fashion. In fact, religion itself becomes fashion. We are witnessing an interesting period, where a lot of religions are competing with each other for the consumers' interest and are marketed as identity construction projects.[163] Indeed, religious consumption for many these days takes the form of consuming spirituality in a variety of ways, sometimes sampled by consumers themselves from various sources as a kind of tailor-made belief system where consumers actually like being uncertain and 'shopping around' in the spiritual market.[164] Not all of these are New Age creations based on some sympathetic Asian philosophy. In Iceland and Norway, the ancient Norse Viking religion worshipping Thor and Odin is a recognised religious community, and it has asked for recognition in Denmark as well. Even in deeply Catholic Italy, there is a revival of a pagan community of believers in ancient magic and mystery.[165]

Religious holidays, particularly Christmas, are regarded by many (and criticised by some) as having been transformed into secular, materialistic occasions devoid of their original sacred significance. Benetton, the Italian clothing manufacturer, has been at the forefront in creating vivid (and often controversial) messages that expose us to our cultural categories and prejudices, but at times they have touched upon the issue of desacralisation.[166]

Multicultural dimensions

The American 'market for religious belief', with its televangelists and its heavy promotion of various churches and sects, is a very exotic experience for many Europeans. The ad below for a church to help recruit worshippers is typical of the American trend towards secular practices being observed by many organised religions.

Even the clergy are increasingly adopting secular marketing techniques. Especially in the US, televangelists rely upon the power of television, a secular medium, to convey their messages. The Catholic Church generated a major controversy after it hired a prominent public relations firm to promote its anti-abortion campaign.[167] Nonetheless, many religious groups have taken the secular route, and are now using marketing techniques to increase the number of believers. The question is whether the use of marketing changes the 'product' or 'service' of the churches.[168]

The ad for church, discussed in the multicultural dimensions boxed feature
Church Ad Project, 1021 Diffley, Eagen, MN 55123.
ullstein bild/Contributor/Getty Images

Sacralisation

Sacralisation occurs when objects, events and even people take on sacred meaning to a culture or to specific groups within a culture. For example, events such as the Cannes Film Festival or Wimbledon and people such as Elvis Presley or Princess Diana have become sacralised to some consumers. But the process of sacralisation can be used to understand more mundane phenomena than such super-events or popular culture heroes. An interesting study of devoted fans of the Apple corporation and its Macintosh computers concluded that the devotion of the Apple fans was comparable to a religious feeling, portraying the late Steve Jobs, co-founder and later re-installed CEO of Apple, as a kind of prophet with a message of salvation for the 'chosen few' in a PC-dominated world.[169]

Objectification occurs when sacred qualities are attributed to mundane items. One way that this process can occur is through *contamination,* where objects associated with sacred events or people become sacred in their own right. This explains the desire by many fans for items belonging to, or even touched by, famous people. One standard procedure through which objects become sacralised occurs when they become included in the collection of a museum. Visiting museums and, in particular, seeing and sometimes feeling the objects belonging to a particularly significant historical period allows consumers to maintain and renew narratives of the importance of cultural heritage, as exemplified by one study of the consumption of a museum of the Byzantine Empire in Greece.[170]

In addition to museum exhibits displaying rare objects, even mundane, inexpensive things may be set apart in private *collections,* where they are transformed from profane items to sacred ones. An item is sacralised as soon as it enters a collection, and it takes on a special significance to the collector that, in some cases, may be hard to comprehend by the outsider. **Collecting** refers to the systematic acquisition of a particular object or set of objects, and this widespread activity can be distinguished from hoarding, which is merely unsystematic collecting.[171] Collecting typically involves both rational and emotional components, since collectors are fixed by their objects, but they also carefully organise and exhibit them.[172]

Name an item, and the odds are that a group of collectors is lusting after it. The contents of collections range from various popular culture memorabilia, rare books and autographs, to Barbie dolls, tea bags, lawnmowers and even junk mail.[173] Consumers are often ferociously attached to their collections; this passion is exemplified by the comment made in one study by a woman who collects teddy bears: 'If my house ever burns down, I won't cry over my furniture, I'll cry over the bears'.[174]

Some consumer researchers have the idea that that collectors are motivated to acquire their 'prizes' in order to gratify a high level of materialism in a socially acceptable manner. By systematically amassing a collection, the collector is allowed to 'worship' material objects without feeling guilty or petty. Another perspective is that collecting is an aesthetic experience: for many collectors the pleasure emanates from being involved in creating the collection, rather than from passively admiring the items one has scavenged or bought. A third perspective that one can apply to collections is that they are an expression of nostalgia, of times gone by.[175] Whatever the motivation, hard-core collectors often devote a great deal of time and energy to maintaining and expanding their collections, so for many this activity becomes a central component of their extended selves (see Chapter 4).[176]

Marketing opportunity

Make your brand a collectable, and enhance your exposure and your brand loyalty. Certain products and brands become cult objects for devoted collectors. In the early 1990s, 'Swatch fever' infected many people. The company made more than 500 different models, some of which were special editions designed by artists. Collectors' interest made a formerly mundane product into a rare piece of art (e.g. a 'Jelly Fish' that originally sold for $30 was sold at auction for $17,000). Although thousands of people still collect the watches, the frenzy began to fade by around 1993.[177] Some collectors' items are more stable. One of the corporations exploiting this opportunity to its fullest is the Coca-Cola Company. With the plethora of Coca-Cola collectables, a lot of devoted and often highly specialised collectors have been created all over the world. They appear as 'spokespersons' for the brand when they account for their sometimes-fabulous collections in the media, and they create a lot of extra and extremely positive exposure for the brand. As one researcher noted: 'These are brand owners. Coca-Cola is theirs'.[178] A recent fad is to collect Adidas sneakers.[179] In Denmark, the company has backed up this tendency by creating an online community for the collectors.[180]

The impact of religion on consumption

12.5

Religion can be an influential factor on consumption.

Religion *per se* has not been studied extensively in marketing, possibly because it is seen as a taboo subject. The very low-key or non-existent approach by large multinational or pan-European companies reflects the same sort of caution that these companies have in targeting ethnic groups – companies are having to decide whether religiously or ethnically tailored programmes foster greater brand loyalty or whether any advantage is outweighed by the risks of misreading the target market and causing offence. Without question, the most successful companies targeting and serving both ethnic and religious segments are small businesses, whose managers and owners are often members of the target group.[181] However, the little evidence that has been accumulated indicates that religious affiliation has the *potential* to be a valuable predictor of consumer behaviour.[182] Religious subcultures have been shown to exert an impact on such consumer variables as personality, attitudes towards sexuality, birth rates and household formation, income and political attitudes.

Christianity has dominated the history and cultural development of Europe and has played an important role in the shaping of the European continent. While the many denominations of Christians make it the largest religious grouping in Europe (roughly 600 million), active membership is on the decline, with fewer and fewer adults attending services on any given Sunday.[183] In response to this trend, the Vatican has been involved in a variety of events aimed at developing closer and more active relationships with Europe's youth.[184] Divided roughly into the more Protestant north and the predominantly Catholic south, Christianity still makes up the majority religion in Europe in terms of claimed membership. Its major holidays of Easter and Christmas and celebrations such as 'Carnival' (*Faschung* in Germany) are celebrated or observed to such an extent that large industries such as travel and retailing rely on these seasons as the times of the year when they earn the most revenues. However, the pious believers often have a problem with consumer culture, which is much too preoccupied with the hedonic pleasures and material rewards of this life. As a protest against such shallow entertainment, evangelical Christians in the US made their own theme park – the 'Holy Land'![185]

Marketing opportunity
Christianity as default is gone: the rise of a non-Christian Europe

Europe's march towards a post-Christian society has been starkly illustrated by research showing a majority of young people in a dozen countries do not follow a religion.

The survey of 16- to 29-year-olds found the Czech Republic is the least religious country in Europe,[186] with 91% of that age group saying they have no religious affiliation. Between 70 and 80 per cent of young adults in Estonia, Sweden and the Netherlands also categorise themselves as non-religious. The most religious country is Poland, where 17% of young adults define themselves as non-religious, followed by Lithuania with 25%. In the UK, only 7% of young adults identify as Anglican, fewer than the 10% who categorise themselves as Catholic. Young Muslims, at 6%, are on the brink of overtaking those who consider themselves part of the country's established church.[187]

The figures are published in a report, 'Europe's Young Adults and Religion',[188] by Stephen Bullivant, a professor of theology and the sociology of religion at St Mary's University in London. They are based on data from the European Social Survey 2014–16:

"And we know the Muslim birthrate is higher than the general population, and they have much higher [religious] retention rates."

In Ireland, there has been a significant decline in religiosity over the past 30 years, "but compared to anywhere else in western Europe, it still looks pretty religious", Bullivant said.

"The new default setting is 'no religion', and the few who are religious see themselves as swimming against the tide", he said.

"In 20 or 30 years' time, mainstream churches will be smaller, but the few people left will be highly committed."'[189]

Islamic marketing

Muslims will be more than one-quarter of the Earth's population by 2030, and during that same time-period analysts expect the number of US Muslims to more than double. In several European countries, if immigration patterns and Muslims' comparatively higher birth rates continue, experts predict that Muslim populations will exceed 10 per cent of the total.[190] That's a consumer market to take seriously.

Nike committed a legendary error when it released a pair of athletic shoes in 1996 with a logo on the sole that some Muslims believed resembled the Arabic lettering for Allah. Muslims consider the feet unclean, and the company had to recall 800,000 pairs of the shoes globally. Today, some companies listen more closely to the needs of this religious subculture. For example, a Malaysian commercial for Sunsilk's Lively Clean & Fresh Shampoo depicts a young, smiling woman – but there is not a strand of hair in sight. Her head is completely covered by a *tudung,* the head scarf worn by many Muslim women in that country. Sunsilk's pitch is that it helps remove excess oil from the scalp and hair, a common problem among wearers of *tudungs*.

Mindful of the success of kosher certification, some Muslims recognise that halal foods (permissible under the laws of Islam) also may appeal to mainstream consumers. The Islamic Food and Nutrition Council of America certifies halal products with a 'crescent M', much like the circled 'O' of the Orthodox Union, the largest kosher certifier. Both kosher and halal followers are forbidden to eat pork, and both require similar rituals for butchering meat. Religious Jews don't mix milk and meat, nor do they eat shellfish, whereas religious Muslims don't drink alcohol. Neither group eats birds of prey or blood.[191]

Halal as a descriptor is being used for more and more commodities, services and activities, including milk, water, non-prescription medicine, holidays,[192] washing powder, tissues, cosmetics, websites and music. Many major companies are taking steps to reassure consumers that all of their products – not just food – are *halal* by having them officially certified. Colgate-Palmolive claims to be the first international company to have obtained *halal* certification in Malaysia for toothpaste and mouthwash products. Some mouthwashes may contain alcohol, which would be forbidden under *halal* guidelines. Colgate's products now bear the *halal* logo, which also is featured in the company's television commercials. Nokia introduced a phone for the Middle East and North Africa markets that came loaded with an 'Islamic Organiser', with alarms for the five daily prayers, two Islamic e-books and an e-card application that lets people send SMS greeting cards for Ramadan. Ogilvy & Mather established a new arm, Ogilvy Noor (Noor means 'light' in Arabic), which the company describes as 'the world's first bespoke Islamic branding practice'. Ogilvy also introduced the Noor index, which rates the appeal of brands to

Muslim consumers. The index was formulated on the basis of how consumers ranked more than 30 well-known brands for compliance with *Shariah,* or Islamic law. Lipton tea, owned by Unilever, topped the list, followed by Nestlé. Ogilvy's research shows that young Muslim consumers are different from their Western counterparts; they believe that by staying true to the core values of their religion, they are more likely to achieve success in the modern world.[193] Other research suggests that 'rather than. . . Muslims becoming "Westernised". . . Muslim youth is in fact entering a new age of becoming. . . [and] evidence for [this]. . . perspective lies in the increase in visible practice of Islam by Muslim youth – most notably in their dress and the conversations on the internet. . . Muslim youth are consuming commodities that were thought of not to necessarily have any Islamic reference or relevance and they are Islamifying them'.[194] The view of the increasing Islamification of brands is illustrated in Figure 12.2.

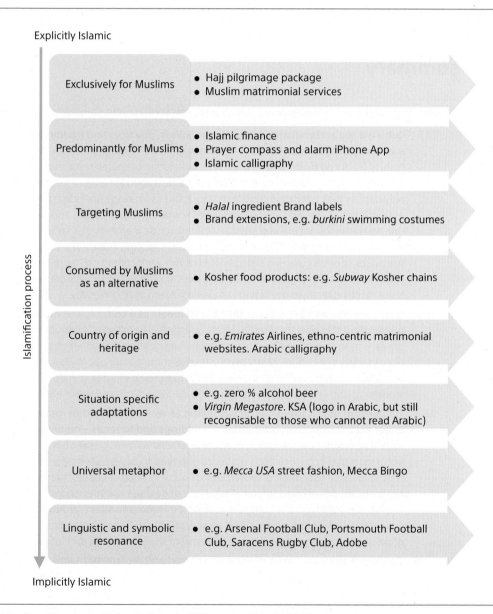

Figure 12.2 Classification of Islamic brands (Wilson and Liu 2011: 4)

Source: Jonathan Bilal, A.J. Wilson and J. Liu, 'The Challenges of Islamic Branding: Navigating Emotions and Halal', Figure 4: Classification of Islamic Brands (p. 34), *Journal of Islamic Marketing* 2(1): 28–42.

Marketing opportunity
Islamic economy

'Consider the following information:

- The halal and lifestyle industry was estimated to be worth $1.8tn in 2014 and is forecast to grow to $2.6tn in 2020.
- By 2030 Muslims will make up 26.5 % of the global population.

- Muslim populations are young and growing. In 2010 they had the youngest median age of any religious group – 23.
- The Muslim middle class is expected to triple from an estimated 300 million in 2015 to 900 million in 2030.'

Source: Shelina Janmohamed, *Generation M: Young Muslims Changing the World* (London: I.B. Tauris, 2016).[195]

Chapter summary

Now that you have finished reading this chapter you should understand why:

12.1 Culture is the accumulation of shared meanings, practices and traditions that permeates everything we do. A society's culture includes its values, ethics and the material objects produced by its people. It is the accumulation of shared meanings and traditions among members of a society. A culture can be described in terms of ecology (the way people adapt to their habitat), its social structure and its ideology (including people's moral and aesthetic principles). This chapter describes some aspects of culture and focuses on how cultural meanings are created and transmitted across members of a society. Members of a culture share a system of beliefs and practices, including values. The process of learning the values of one's culture is called enculturation. Each culture can be described by a set of core values. Values can be identified by several methods, though it is often difficult to apply these results directly to marketing campaigns due to their generality.

12.2 Myths are stories that express the shared ideals of a culture, and modern myths are transmitted through the media. Myths are stories containing symbolic elements that are central to understanding basic tensions and conflicts (good and bad, useful and useless, etc.) in a culture. Many myths involve some binary opposition, where values are defined in terms of what they are and what they are not (e.g. nature *vs* technology). Modern myths are transmitted through advertising, films and other media.

12.3 We perform rituals every day, in gift-giving as well as many other routines, but also on major occasions such as graduations, weddings and funerals – modern rites of passage that require consumption of ritual artefacts. A ritual is a set of multiple, symbolic behaviours that occur in a fixed sequence and tend to be repeated periodically. Rituals are related to many consumption activities that occur in popular culture; these include holiday observances, gift-giving and grooming. A rite of passage is a special kind of ritual that involves the transition from one role to another. These passages typically entail the need to acquire products and services, called ritual artefacts, to facilitate the transition. Modern rites of passage include graduations, initiation ceremonies, weddings and funerals.

12.4 Consumer activities can be divided into sacred and profane domains. Sacralisation is the process whereby ordinary, profane objects obtain a particular 'sacred' status, for instance by being included in a museum or in a private collection. Desacralisation occurs when formerly sacred objects or activities become part of the every day. This can, for example, be when objects that used to be 'one-of-a-kind' works of art are reproduced in large quantities – particularly when the reproduction happens through non-authentic media. For many, there's a difference between a reproduction of Van Gogh on the wall and one on a t-shirt.

12.5 **Religion can be an influential factor on consumption.** While various consumption activities have replaced religion as the most important factor in giving meaning and structure to daily lives, religious belief still deeply influences consumption for a significant part of the population.

Key terms

Collecting (p. 510)	Mores (p. 486)
Collectivist cultures (p. 484)	Myth (p. 488)
Conventions (p. 486)	Polychronic (p. 484)
Co-optation (p. 481)	Profane consumption (p. 504)
Culture (p. 482)	Proxemics (p. 484)
Custom (p. 486)	Rites of passage (p. 502)
Desacralisation (p. 508)	Ritual (p. 492)
Ethnoconsumerism (p. 485)	Ritual artefacts (p. 493)
Ethos (p. 484)	Sacralisation (p. 510)
Fortress brands (p. 492)	Sacred consumption (p. 504)
Gift-giving ritual (p. 496)	Self-gifts (p. 498)
Individualist cultures (p. 484)	Signifying practices (p. 482)
Monochronic (p. 484)	Worldview (p. 484)
Monomyth (p. 490)	

Consumer behaviour challenge

1 Culture can be thought of as a society's personality. If your culture were a person, could you describe its personality traits?

2 What is the difference between an enacted norm and a crescive norm? Identify the set of crescive norms operating when a man and woman in your culture go out for dinner on a first date. What products and services are affected by these norms?

3 How do the consumer decisions involved in gift-giving differ from other purchase decisions?

4 The chapter argues that not all gift-giving is positive. In what ways can this ritual be unpleasant or negative?

5 Construct a ritual script for a wedding in your culture. How many artefacts can you list that are contained in this script?

6 What are some of the major motivations for the purchase of self-gifts? Discuss some marketing implications of these.

7 Describe the three stages of the rite of passage associated with graduating from university.

8 Identify the ritualised aspects of various kinds of sports that are employed in advertising.

9 Which sacred objects do you own, and how did they become sacred to you?

10 Interview two or three of your fellow students about collecting – talking about either their own collections or a collection of somebody they know. Use concepts about the sacred to analyse the responses.

11 Religious symbolism is being used increasingly in advertising, even though some people object to this practice. For example, the French fashion house Marithe and François Girbaud used a poster of well-dressed women posed in a version of Leonardo da Vinci's *The Last Supper*. The poster was banned in Milan.[196] In another example, a French Volkswagen ad for the relaunch of the Golf model of car showed a modern version of *The Last Supper* with the tag line, 'Let us rejoice, my friends, for a new Golf has been born'.[197] A group of clergy in France sued the company and the ad had to be removed from 10,000 hoardings. One of

the bishops involved in the suit said, 'Advertising experts have told us that ads aim for the sacred in order to shock, because using sex does not work anymore'. Do you agree? Should religion be used to market products? Do you find this strategy effective or offensive? When and where is this appropriate, if at all?

For additional material see the companion website at **www.pearsoned.co.uk/solomon**

Notes

1. See Dennis W. Rook, 'The ritual dimension of consumer behavior', *Journal of Consumer Research* 12 (December 1985): 251–64; Mary A. Stansfield Tetreault and Robert E. Kleine III, 'Ritual, Ritualized Behavior, and Habit: Refinements and Extensions of the Consumption Ritual Construct', in Marvin Goldberg, Gerald Gorn, and Richard W. Pollay (eds), *Advances in Consumer Research* 17 (Provo, UT: Association for Consumer Research, 1990): 31–8.

2. See for example, A. Fuat Firat, 'Consumer Culture or Culture Consumed', in Janeen A. Costa and G. Bamossy (eds), *Marketing in a Multicultural World: Ethnicity, Nationalism, and Cultural Identity* (Thousand Oaks, CA: SAGE, 1995): 105–25.

3. Mary Douglas and Baron Isherwood, *The World of Goods,* 2nd edn (London: Routledge, 1996).

4. A classic work on this is, for example, Edward T. Hall, *The Silent Language* (New York: Doubleday, 1959).

5. Paul du Gay, Stuart Hall, Linda Janes, Hugh MacKay and Keith Negus, *Doing Cultural Studies: The Story of the Sony Walkman* (London: SAGE, 1997).

6. Søren Askegaard, Dannie Kjeldgaard and Eric J. Arnould, 'Reflexive culture's consequences', in C. Nakata (ed.), *Beyond Hofstede: Culture Frameworks for Global Marketing and Management* (Chicago: Palgrave Macmillan, 2009): 101–24.

7. See Hans Rask Jensen, 'The Mohammed cartoons controversy and the boycott of Danish products in the Middle East', *European Business Review* 20(3) (2008): 275–89.

8. Ibrahim Abosag and Maya Farah, 'The influence of religiously motivated consumer boycotts on brand image, loyalty and product judgment', *European Journal of Marketing* 48(11/12) (2014): 2,262–83.

9. Donald N. Sull, 'Why good companies go bad,' *Financial Times* 3 (2005).

10. David Robertson and Bill Breen, *Brick by Brick: How LEGO Rewrote the Rules of Innovation and Conquered the Global Toy Industry* (London: Random House Business, 2014).

11. Clifford Geertz, *The Interpretation of Cultures* (New York: Basic Books, 1973); Marvin Harris, *Culture, People and Nature* (New York: Crowell, 1971); John F. Sherry Jr, 'The Cultural Perspective in Consumer Research', in Richard J. Lutz (ed.), *Advances in Consumer Research* 13 (Provo, UT: Association for Consumer Research, 1986): 573–5.

12. Özlem Sandikci and Güliz Ger, 'Veiling in style: How does a stigmatized practice become fashionable?', *Journal of Consumer Research* 37 (June 2010): 15–36.

13. Edward T. Hall, *The Hidden Dimension* (New York: Doubleday, 1966).

14. Edward T. Hall, *The Dance of Life: The Other Dimension of Time* (New York: Doubleday, 1983).

15. Geert Hofstede, *Culture's Consequences* (Beverly Hills, CA: SAGE, 1980); see also Laura M. Milner, Dale Fodness and Mark W. Speece, 'Hofstede's Research on Cross-Cultural Work-Related Values: Implications for Consumer Behavior', in W.F. van Raaij and G. Bamossy (eds), *European Advances in Consumer Research* 1 (Provo, UT: Association for Consumer Research, 1993): 70–6.

16. See for example Brendan McSweeney, 'Hofstede's model of national cultural differences and their consequences: A triumph of faith – a failure of analysis', *Human Relations* 55(1) (2002): 89–118.

17. Alladi Venkatesh, 'Ethnoconsumerism: A Proposal for a New Paradigm to Study Cross Cultural Consumer Behavior', in Costa and Bamossy (eds), *Marketing in a Multicultural World:* 26–67.

18. Andrea Davies and James Fitchett, 'Crossing culture: A multi-method enquiry into consumer behaviour and the experience of cultural transition', *Journal of Consumer Behaviour* 3(4) (2006): 315–30.

19. Brad Weiss, 'Coffee Breaks and Coffee Connections: The Lived Experience of a Commodity in Tanzanian and European Worlds', in D. Howes (ed.), *Cross-Cultural Consumption* (London: Routledge, 1996): 93–105.

20. George J. McCall and J.L. Simmons, *Social Psychology: A Sociological Approach* (New York: The Free Press, 1982).

21. Özlem Sandikci and Güliz Ger, 'Constructing and representing the Islamic consumer in Turkey', *Fashion Theory* 11(2/3) (2007): 189–210.

22. http://www.guardian.co.uk/sport/2012/jan/18/royal-ascot-fascinators-hats-dresscode (accessed 4 September 2018).

23. Jim Yardley, 'No spitting on the road to Olympic glory, Beijing says', *New York Times Online* (17 April 2007).

24. Laura Petrecca, 'Ad Track: Marketers Bet on lucky 777; That's July 7, 2007', *USA Today Online* (29 May 2007).

25. Yannik St. James, Jay M. Handelman and Shirley F. Taylor, 'Magical thinking and consumer coping', *Journal of Consumer Research* 38 (December 2011): 632–49.

26. Risto Moisio and Mariam Beruchashvili, 'Questing for well-being at Weight Watchers: The role of the spiritual-therapeutic model in a support group', *Journal of Consumer Research* 36 (February 2010): 857–75.

27. Søren Askegaard, Martine Cardel Gertsen and Roy Langer, 'The body consumed: Reflexivity and cosmetic surgery', *Psychology & Marketing* 19(10) (2002): 793–812.

28. Jennifer Rindfleisch, 'Consuming the self: New age spirituality as "social product" in consumer society', *Consumption Markets & Culture* 8(4) (2005): 343–60.

29. Craig J. Thompson, 'Marketplace mythology and discourses of power', *Journal of Consumer Research* 31 (June 2004):

162–80. The author formulates the construct of marketplace mythology to explore how cultural myths are used to create marketplace mythologies that serve multiple and often competing ideological agendas. He develops his arguments within the context of the natural health market. While this market is positioned as alternative to mainstream scientific medicine, both practitioners' and consumers' quest for scientific support to validate their holistic healing treatments generate a fundamental paradox. This paper examines the mythic constructions of nature, technology and science and their relations to both natural health's marketplace mythology of holistic well-being and key competitive forces.

30. Eric Arnould, Cele Otnes and Linda Price, 'Magic in the Marketing Age', in S. Brown, A.M. Doherty and B. Clarke (eds), *Proceedings of the Marketing Illuminations Spectacular* (Belfast: University of Ulster, 1997). 167–78.

31. Eric Arnould and Linda Price, 'River magic: Extraordinary experience and the extended service encounter', *Journal of Consumer Research* 20 (June 1993): 24–45.

32. Molly O'Neill, 'As life gets more complex, magic casts a wider spell', *New York Times* (13 June 1994): A1(2).

33. Chris Miles, 'Persuasion, marketing communication, and the metaphor of magic', *European Journal of Marketing* 47(11/12) (2013): 2,002–19.

34. T. Heath and M. Heath, 'Once upon a time there was a consumer: Stories of magic and the magic of stories', *Journal of Marketing Management* 32 (9/10) (2016): 811–26.

35. Stephen Brown, *Wizard: Harry Potter's Brand Magic* (London: Cyan Books, 2005).

36. https://www.liverpoolecho.co.uk/whats-on/whats-on-news/aldi-2017-christmas-advert-sees-13868556 and https://www.walesonline.co.uk/lifestyle/tv/aldi-releases-second-christmas-advert-14008304 (both accessed 4 September 2018).

37. Ashlee Humphreys and Craig Thompson, 'Branding disaster: Reestablishing trust through the ideological containment of systemic risk anxieties', *Journal of Consumer Research* 41(4) (2013): 877–910.

38. Janice Denegri-Knott and Elizabeth Parsons, 'Disordering things', *Journal of Consumer Behaviour* 13 (2014): 89–98; Delphine Dion, Ouidade Sabri and Valérie Guillard, 'Home sweet messy home: Managing Symbolic Pollution, *Journal of Consumer Research* 41(3) (2014): 565–89.

39. Douglas B. Holt and Craig J. Thompson, 'Man-of-Action heroes: The pursuit of heroic masculinity in everyday consumption', *Journal of Consumer Research* 31 (September 2004): 425–40.

40. Conrad Phillip Kottak, 'Anthropological Analysis of Mass Enculturation', in Conrad P. Kottak (ed.), *Researching American Culture* (Ann Arbor, MI: University of Michigan Press, 1982): 40–74.

41. Benoît Heilbrunn, 'Brave New Brands: Cultural Branding between Utopia and A-topia', in J. Schroeder and M-Salzer-Mörling (eds), *Brand Culture* (London: Routledge, 2006): 103–17.

42. Eric Ransdell, 'The Nike story? Just tell it!', *Fast Company* (January–February 2000): 44. For example, they recount tales about the coach of the Oregon track team who poured rubber into his family waffle iron to make better shoes for his team – the origin of the Nike waffle sole. The stories emphasise the dedication of runners and coaches to reinforce the importance of teamwork. Rookies even visit the track where the coach worked to be sure they grasp the importance of the Nike legends. And rumour has it that senior Nike executives (including the CEO) have a 'swoosh' tattoo on their backsides.

43. Douglas B. Holt and Douglas Cameron, *Cultural Strategy: Using Innovative Ideologies to Build BreakThrough Brands* (Oxford, UK: Oxford University Press, 2010).

44. Douglas B. Holt, 'Jack Daniels' America: Iconic brands as parasites and proselytizers', *Journal of Consumer Culture* 6(3) (2006): 355–77.

45. Marius K. Luedicke, Craig J. Thompson and Markus Giesler, 'Consumer identity work as moral protagonism: How myth and ideology animate a brand-mediated moral conflict', *Journal of Consumer Research* 36 (April 2010): 1,016–32.

46. Dorthe Brogård Kristensen, Heidi Boye and Søren Askegaard, 'Leaving the Milky Way! The formation of a consumer counter mythology', *Journal of Consumer Culture* 11(2) (2011): 195–214.

47. Jonathan E. Schroeder and Janet L. Borgerson, 'Packaging Paradise: Consuming Hawaiian Music', in Eric Arnould and Linda Scott (eds), *Advances in Consumer Research* 26 (Provo, UT: Association for Consumer Research, 1999): 46–50.

48. Robin Canniford and Avi Shankar, 'Marketing the Savage: Appropriating Tribal Tropes', in B. Cova, R. Kozinets and A. Shankar (eds), *Consumer Tribes* (London: Butterworth Heinemann, 2007): 35–48.

49. Güliz Ger and Fabian Csaba, 'Flying Carpets: The Production and Consumption of Tradition and Mystique', in S. Hoch and R. Meyer (eds), *Advances in Consumer Research* 27 (Provo, UT: Association for Consumer Research, 2000): 132–7.

50. Robin Canniford and Eminegül Karababa, 'Partly primitive: Discursive constructions of the domestic surfer', *Consumption Markets & Culture* 16(2) (2013): 119–44.

51. Joseph Campbell, *Myths, Dreams, and Religion* (New York: E.P. Dutton, 1970).

52. Sidney J. Levy, 'Interpreting consumer mythology: A structural approach to consumer behavior', *Journal of Marketing* 45 (Summer 1981): 49–61.

53. Carol Donelan, 'Vampires suck, Twihards rule!!! Myth and meaning in the Twilight Saga franchise', *Quarterly Review of Film and Video* 32(3) (2015): 240–50.

54. Alan Bradshaw and Morris Holbrook, 'Remembering Chet: Theorizing the mythology of the self-destructive bohemian artist as self-producer and self-consumer in the market for romanticism', *Marketing Theory* 7(2) (2007): 115–36.

55. Jeffrey S. Lang and Patrick Trimble, 'Whatever happened to the man of tomorrow? An examination of the American monomyth and the comic book superhero', *Journal of Popular Culture* 22 (Winter 1988): 157.

56. James Fitchett, Douglas Brownlie and Michael Saren, 'On the Cultural Location of Consumption: The Case of Einstein as a Commodity', in J. Berács, A. Bauer and J. Simon (eds), *Marketing for an Expanding Europe,* Proceedings of the 25th EMAC Conference (Budapest: Budapest University of Economic Sciences, 1996): 435–53; James Fitchett and Michael Saren, 'Consuming Einstein: The Nine Billion Names of the Commodity', in Brown, Doherty and Clarke (eds), *Proceedings of the Marketing Illuminations Spectacular*: 252–63.

57. See Russell Belk, Güliz Ger and Søren Askegaard, 'The fire of desire: A multisited inquiry into consumer passion', *Journal of Consumer Research* 30(3) (2003): 326–51.

58. Elizabeth C. Hirschman, 'Movies as Myths: An Interpretation of Motion Picture Mythology', in Jean Umiker-Sebeok (ed.), *Marketing and Semiotics: New Directions in the Study of Signs for Sale* (Berlin: Mouton de Guyter, 1987): 335–74.

59. Stephen Brown, Pierre McDonagh and Clifford Shultz II, 'Titanic: Consuming the myths and meanings of an ambiguous brand', *Journal of Consumer Research* 40(4) (2013): 595–614; see also Stephen Brown, 'I'm buying, Jack! Fooling around an ambiguous brand', *Journal of Consumer Behavior* 13 (2014): 108–21.

60. M. Heller, '"Outposts of Britain", the General Post Office and the birth of a corporate iconic brand, 1930–1939', *European Journal of Marketing* 50 (3/4) (2016): 358–76.

61. https://www.dr.dk/nyheder/indland/nu-forsvinder-den-roede-farve-postbude-faar-blaa-uniform (accessed 7 September 2018).

62. Dick Hebdige, 'Object as Image: The Italian Scooter Cycle', in J.B. Schor and D.B. Holt (eds), *The Consumer Society Reader* (New York: The New Press, 2000): 117–54.

63. Stephen Brown, 'Retro-marketing: Yesterday's tomorrows, today', *Marketing Intelligence and Planning* 17(7) (1999): 363–76.

64. Russell W. Belk and Rosa Llamas, 'Paradise lost: The making of Shangri-La', videography presented at the Association for Consumer Research European Conference, London: Royal Holloway (30 June, 3 July 2010).

65. Benoît Heilbrunn, 'My Brand the Hero? A Semiotic Analysis of the Consumer–Brand Relationship', in M. Lambkin et al. (eds), *European Perspectives on Consumer Behaviour* (London: Prentice-Hall, 1998): 370–401.

66. D.B. Holt, 'What becomes an icon most?', *Harvard Business Review* 81(3) (2003): 43–9.

67. D. Bartmanski and I. Woodward, 'Vinyl record: A cultural icon', *Consumption Markets & Culture* 21(2) (2018): 171–7.

68. J. Östberg and B.J. Hartmann, 'The electric guitar – marketplace icon', *Consumption Markets & Culture* 18(5) (2015): 402–10.

69. J. Rokka, 'Champagne: Marketplace icon', *Consumption Markets & Culture* 20(3) (2017): 275–83.

70. C. Hackley and R.A. Hackley, 'The iconicity of celebrity and the spiritual impulse', *Consumption Markets & Culture* 19(3) (2016): 269–74.

71. See Rook, 'The ritual dimension of consumer behavior', op. cit.; Tetreault and Kleine, 'Ritual, ritualized behavior, and habit', op. cit.

72. Kieran Tucker, 'The Value of Ritual Theory for Understanding Alcohol Consumption Behaviours', in K. Ekström and H. Brembeck (eds), *European Advances in Consumer Research* 7 (Duluth, MN: Association for Consumer Research, 2006): 635–40; Emma Banister and Maria Piacenitini, 'Drunk and (Dis)Orderly: The Role of Alcohol in Supporting Liminality' in A.Y. Lee and D. Soman (eds), *Advances in Consumer Research* 35 (Duluth, MN: Association for Consumer Research, 2008): 311–18.

73. https://timesofindia.indiatimes.com/india/Buy-a-car-and-get-its-puja-done-for-free/articleshow/2721588.cms and https://www.thestar.com.my/news/nation/2017/12/13/a-prayer-for-the-new-car-and-peace-of-mind/ (both accessed 5 September 2018).

74. https://www.thoughtco.com/car-puja-guide-1770548 (accessed 5 September 2018).

75. Karl Greenberg, 'BBDO: Successful brands become hard habit for consumers to break', *Marketing Daily* (14 May 2007), http://www.mediapost.com/publications/article/60233/bbdo-successful-brands-become-hard-habit-for-cons.html (accessed 5 September 2018).

76. 'The skill of the chase', *Marketing Week* (30 April 1993): 38–40.

77. Bill McDowell, 'Starbucks is ground zero in today's coffee culture', *Advertising Age* (9 December 1996): 1 (2 pp.). For a discussion of the act of coffee drinking as ritual, see Susan Fournier and Julie L. Yao, 'Reviving Brand Loyalty: A Reconceptualization within the Framework of Consumer–Brand Relationships', working paper 96–039, Harvard Business School, 1996.

78. Dannie Kjeldgaard and Jacob Östberg, 'Coffee grounds and the global cup: Glocal consumer culture in Scandinavia', *Consumption Culture & Markets* 10(2) (2007): 175–88; see also Craig Thompson and Zeynep Arsel, 'The Starbucks brandscape and consumers' (anti-corporate) experiences of glocalization', *Journal of Consumer Research* 31 (December 2004): 631–42.

79. J. Tinson, M. Piacentini, P. Nuttall and H. Cocker, 'Social belonging and the social collective: Understanding how processes shape youth markets', *Marketing Theory* 17(2) (2017): 201–17.

80. Pepukayi Chitakunye and Pauline Maclaran, 'Materiality and family consumption: The role of the television in changing mealtime rituals', *Consumption Markets & Culture* 17(1) (2014): 50–70.

81. Farnaz Fassisi, 'As authorities frown, Valentine's Day finds place in Iran's heart', *The Wall Street Journal* (12 February 2004).

82. Robert Grafton Small, 'Consumption and significance: Everyday life in a brand-new second-hand bow tie', *European Journal of Marketing* 27(8) (1993): 38–45.

83. Grant McCracken, *Culture and Consumption* (Bloomington, IN: Indiana University Press, 1988).

84. https://www.theguardian.com/technology/2017/sep/22/iphone-8-small-queues-muted-reaction-questions-demand-iphone-x (accessed 5 September 2018).

85. Michelle R. Nelson, Mark A. Rademacher and Hye-Jin Park, 'Downshifting consumer = upshifting citizen? An examination of a local freecycle community', *ANNALS of the American Academy of Political and Social Science* 611 (2007): 141–56.

86. Pia A. Albinsson and B. Yasanthi Perera, 'From trash to treasure and beyond: The meaning of voluntary disposition', *Journal of Consumer Behaviour* 8 (2009): 340–53.

87. Helene Cherrier, 'Disposal and simple living: Exploring the circulation of goods and the development of sacred consumption', *Journal of Consumer Behaviour* 8 (2009): 327–39.

88. Benedetta Cappellini, 'The sacrifice of re-use: The travels of leftovers and family relations', *Journal of Consumer Behaviour* 8 (2009): 365–75.

89. J.F. Gollnhofer, 'Normalising alternative practices: The recovery, distribution and consumption of food waste', *Journal of Marketing Management* 33 (7/8) (2017): 624–43.

90. 'Lynx to create chain of male grooming stores', *Marketing* (24 August 2000): 5.

91. Dennis W. Rook and Sidney J. Levy, 'Psychosocial Themes in Consumer Grooming Rituals', in Richard P. Bagozzi and Alice M. Tybout (eds), *Advances in Consumer Research* 10 (Provo, UT: Association for Consumer Research, 1983): 329–33.

92. Diane Barthel, *Putting on Appearances: Gender and Attractiveness* (Philadelphia: Temple University Press, 1988).

93. Quoted in ibid.

94. T.W. Bradford and J.F. Sherry, 'Domesticating public space through ritual: Tailgating as vestaval', *Journal of Consumer Research* 42(1) (2015): 130–51.

95. Russell W. Belk, Melanie Wallendorf and John Sherry Jr, 'The sacred and the profane in consumer behavior: Theodicy on the odyssey', *Journal of Consumer Research* 16 (June 1989): 1–38.

96. Tina M. Lowrey, Cele C. Otnes and Julie A. Ruth, 'Social influences on dyadic giving over time: A taxonomy from the giver's perspective', *Journal of Consumer Research* 30 (March 2004): 547–58.

97. Russell W. Belk and Gregory S. Coon, 'Gift giving as agapic love: An alternative to the exchange paradigm based on dating experiences', *Journal of Consumer Research* 20(3) (December 1993): 393–417.

98. Julie A. Ruth, Cele C. Otnes and Frederic F. Brunel, 'Gift receipt and the reformulation of interpersonal relationships', *Journal of Consumer Research* 25 (March 1999): 385–402.

99. C. Chan and C. Mogilner, 'Experiential gifts foster stronger social relationships than material gifts', *Journal of Consumer Research* 43(6) (2017): 913–31.

100. M.F. Weinberger, 'Gifts: Intertwining market and moral economies and the rise of store-bought gifts', *Consumption Markets & Culture* 20(3) (2017): 245–57.

101. Colin Camerer, 'Gifts as economic signals and social symbols', *American Journal of Sociology* 94 (Supplement 1988): 5,180–214.

102. Robert T. Green and Dana L. Alden, 'Functional equivalence in cross-cultural consumer behavior: Gift-giving in Japan and the United States', *Psychology and Marketing* 5 (Summer 1988): 155–68.

103. Hiroshi Tanaka and Miki Iwamura, 'Gift Selection Strategy of Japanese Seasonal Gift Purchasers: An Explorative Study', paper presented at the Association for Consumer Research, Boston, October 1994.

104. Burçak Ertimur and Özlem Sandikci, 'Alienable gifts: Uses and meanings of gold in Turkey', *Journal of Consumer Behaviour* 13 (2014): 204–11.

105. John F. Sherry Jr, 'Gift-giving in anthropological perspective', *Journal of Consumer Research* 10 (September 1983): 157–68.

106. Michelle Weinberger and Melanie Wallendorf, 'Intracommunity gifting at the intersection of contemporary moral and market economies', *Journal of Consumer Research* 39(1) (2012): 74–92.

107. John F. Sherry Jr, Mary Ann McGrath and Sidney J. Levy, 'The dark side of the gift', *Journal of Business Research* 28(3) (1993): 225–45.

108. Jean-Sebastien Marcoux, 'Escaping the gift economy', *Journal of Consumer Research* 36 (December 2009): 671–85.

109. T.P. Heath, C. Tynan and C. Ennew, 'Accounts of self-gift giving: nature, context and emotions', *European Journal of Marketing* 49(7/8) (2015): 1,067–86.

110. Markus Giesler, 'Consumer gift systems', *Journal of Consumer Research* 33 (September 2006): 283–90.

111. Markus Giesler, 'Conflict and compromise: Drama in marketplace evolution', *Journal of Consumer Research* 34 (April 2008): 739–53.

112. Ercilia Garcia-Alvarez, Jordi Lopez-Sintas and Konstantina Zerva, 'A contextual theory of accessing music: Consumer behavior and ethical arguments', *Consumption Markets & Culture* 12 (3 September 2009): 243–64.

113. Antje Cockrill and Mark M.H. Goode, 'DVD pirating intentions: Angels, devils, chancers and receivers', *Journal of Consumer Behaviour* 11 (2012): 1–10.

114. On tourism as a central part of modern life, see John Urry, *The Tourist Gaze: Leisure and Travel in Contemporary Societies* (London: SAGE, 1990) and John Urry, *Consuming Places* (London: Routledge, 1995). Scandinavians (or those who read Swedish) may also consult Tom Odell (ed.), *Nonstop! Turist i upplevelsesindustrialismen* (Lund: Historiska Media, 1999).

115. See, for example, Russell W. Belk, 'Halloween: An Evolving American Consumption Ritual', in Pollay, Gorn and Goldberg (eds), *Advances in Consumer Research* 17: 508–17; Melanie Wallendorf and Eric J. Arnould, 'We gather together: The consumption rituals of Thanksgiving Day', *Journal of Consumer Research* 18 (June 1991): 13–31.

116. Marc Augé, 'Un ethnologue à Euro Disneyland', *Le Monde Diplomatique* (September 1994).

117. Güliz Ger and Özlem Sandikci, 'In-Between Modernities and Postmodernities: Theorizing Turkish Consumption-scape', in S. Broniarczyk and K. Nakamoto (eds), *Advances in Consumer Research* 29 (Valdosta, GA: Association for Consumer Research, 2002): 465–70.

118. Bruno Bettelheim, *The Uses of Enchantment: The Meaning and Importance of Fairy Tales* (New York: Alfred A. Knopf, 1976).

119. M.F. Weinberger, 'Dominant consumption rituals and intra-group boundary work: How non-celebrants manage conflicting relational and identity goals', *Journal of Consumer Research* 42(3) (2015): 378–400.

120. Ilona Mikkonen, Johanna Moisander and A. Fuat Firat, 'Cynical identity projects as consumer resistance – the Scrooge as a social critic?', *Consumption Markets &Culture* 14 (March 2011): 99–116.

121. Brian Moeran and Lise Skov, 'Cinderella Christmas: Kitsch, Consumerism and Youth in Japan', in D. Miller (ed.), *Unwrapping Christmas* (Oxford: Oxford University Press, 1993). 105–33.

122. *Markedsføring* 1 (1999): 4.

123. http://nyheder.tv2.dk/erhverv/2016-10-29-fastelavn slaaet-omkuld-halloween-er-tre-gange-stoerre (accessed 7 September 2018).

124. Elodie Gentina, Kay Plan and Marie Helène Fosse-Gomez, 'The practice of using make-up: A consumption ritual of adolescent girls', *Journal of Consumer Behaviour* 11 (2012): 115–23.

125. Tuba Ustuner, Güliz Ger and Douglas B. Holt, 'Consuming Ritual: Reframing the Turkish Henna-Night Ceremony', in Hoch and Meyer (eds), *Advances in Consumer Research* 27: 209–14.

126. Michael R. Solomon and Punam Anand, 'Ritual Costumes and Status Transition: The Female Business Suit as Totemic Emblem', in Elizabeth C. Hirschman and Morris Holbrook (eds), *Advances in Consumer Research* 12 (Washington, DC: Association for Consumer Research, 1985): 315–18.

127. Arnold Van Gennep, *The Rites of Passage,* trans. Maika B. Vizedom and Gabrielle L. Caffee (London: Routledge & Kegan Paul, 1960; orig. published 1908); Solomon and Anand, 'Ritual costumes and status transition', op. cit.

128. J.S. Podoshen, S.A. Andrzejewski, J. Wallin and V. Venkatesh, 'Consuming abjection: An examination of death and disgust in the black metal scene', *Consumption Markets & Culture* 21(2) (2018): 107–28.

129. See K.T. Hansen and A.M. Waade, *Locating Nordic Noir* (London: Palgrave Macmillan, 2017).

130. Stephanie O'Donohoe and Darach Turley, 'Dealing with Death: Art, Mortality and the Marketplace', in S. Brown and A. Patterson (eds), *Imagining Marketing, Art, Aesthetics, and the Avant-Garde* (London: Routledge, 2001): 86–106.

131. S. Dobscha and J.S. Podoshen, 'Death consumes us – dispatches from the "death professors" introduction the special issue', *Consumption Markets & Culture* 20(5) (2017): 383–6.

132. Sidney J. Levy, 'Olio and intègraphy as method and the consumption of death', *Consumption Markets & Culture* 18(2) (2015): 133–54; see also Susan Dobscha (ed.), *Death in Consumer Culture* (London: Routledge, 2015).

133. C. Nations, S.M. Baker and E. Krszjzaniek, 'Trying to keep you: How grief, abjection, and ritual transform the social meanings of a human body', *Consumption Markets & Culture* 20(5) (2017): 403–22.

134. Walter W. Whitaker III, 'The Contemporary American Funeral Ritual', in Ray B. Browne (ed.), *Rites and Ceremonies in Popular Culture* (Bowling Green, OH: Bowling Green University Popular Press, 1980): 316–25.

135. J. Drenten, K. McManus and L.I. Labrecque, 'Graves, gifts, and the bereaved consumer: A restorative perspective of gift exchange', *Consumption Markets & Culture* 20(5) (2017): 423–55.

136. Samuel K. Bonsu and Russell W. Belk, 'Do not go cheaply into that good night: Death-ritual consumption in Asante, Ghana', *Journal of Consumer Research* 30 (June 2003): 41–55; see also Stephanie O'Donohoe and Darach Turley, 'Till death do us part? Consumption and the negotiation of relationships following a bereavement', *Advances in Consumer Research* 32(1) (2005): 625–6.

137. Elif Izberk-Bilgin, 'Infidel brands: Unveiling alternative meanings of global brands at the nexus of globalization, consumer culture, and Islamism', *Journal of Consumer Research* 39(4) (2012): 663–87.

138. Robert V. Kozinets, John F. Sherry Jr, Diana Storm, Adam Duhachek, Krittinee Nuttavuthisit and Benet DeBerry-Spence, 'Ludic agency and retail spectacle', *Journal of Consumer Research* 31 (December 2004): 658–72.

139. Simone Pettigrew, 'Hearts and minds: Children's experiences of Disney World', *Consumption Markets & Culture* 14 (June 2011): 145–61; see also Shona Bettany and Russell W. Belk, 'Disney discourses of self and Other: Animality, primitivity, modernity and postmodernity', *Consumption Markets & Culture* 14 (June 2011): 163–76.

140. Kottak, 'Anthropological analysis of mass enculturation', op. cit.: 40–74.

141. Gerry Pratt, 'The House as an Expression of Social Worlds', in James S. Duncan (ed.), *Housing and Identity: Cross-Cultural Perspectives* (London: Croom Helm, 1981): 135–79; Michael R. Solomon, 'The role of the surrogate consumer in service delivery', *Service Industries Journal* 7 (July 1987): 292–307.

142. Malene Djursaa and Simon Ulrik Kragh, 'Syntax and Creolization in Cross-Cultural Readings of Rooms', in B. Dubois, T. Lowrey, L.J. Shrum and M. Vanhuele (eds), *European Advances in Consumer Research* 4 (Provo, UT: Association for Consumer Research, 1999): 293–303.

143. Grant McCracken, "'Homeyness": A Cultural Account of One Constellation of Goods and Meanings', in Elizabeth C. Hirschman (ed.), *Interpretive Consumer Research* (Provo, UT: Association for Consumer Research, 1989): 168–84.

144. H.L. Cocker, E.N. Banister and M.G. Piacentini, 'Producing and consuming celebrity identity myths: Unpacking the classed identities of Cheryl Cole and Katie Price', *Journal of Marketing Management* 31(5/6) (2015): 502–24.

145. G.C. Hopkinson and J. Cronin, "'When people take action...": Mainstreaming malcontent and the role of the celebrity institutional entrepreneur', *Journal of Marketing Management* 31(13/14) (2015): 1,383–402.

146. http://www.heavenandearthandyou.com (accessed 5 September 2018).

147. Emile Durkheim, *The Elementary Forms of the Religious Life* (New York: Free Press, 1915).

148. Susan Birrell, 'Sports as ritual: Interpretations from Durkheim to Goffman', *Social Forces* 60(2) (1981): 354–76; Daniel Q. Voigt, 'American Sporting Rituals', in Browne (ed.), *Rites and Ceremonies in Popular Culture,* op.cit.: 125–40.

149. 'Sale of UK publisher of classical music strikes a sour note', *Wall Street Journal Europe* (9 September 1997): 1, 4.

150. Søren Askegaard, 'Marketing, the performing arts, and social change: Beyond the legitimacy crisis', *Consumption Markets & Culture* 3(1) (1999): 1–25.

151. Simona Botti, 'What Role for Marketing in the Arts? An Analysis of Art Consumption and Artistic Value', in Y. Evrard, W. Hoyer and A. Strazzieri (eds), *Proceedings of the Third International Research Seminar on Marketing Communications and Consumer Behavior* (Aix-en-Provence: IAE, 1999).

152. See also Luca M. Visconti, John F. Sherry Jr, Stefania Borghini and Laurie Anderson, 'Street art, sweet art? Reclaiming the "public" in public space', *Journal of Consumer Research* 37 (October 2010): 511–29.

153. Brown and Patterson (eds), *Imagining Marketing, Art, Aesthetics, and the Avant-Garde* (London: Routledge, 2000).

154. Urry, *The Tourist Gaze,* op. cit.

155. Belk et al., 'The sacred and the profane in consumer behavior', op. cit.

156. Beverly Gordon, 'The souvenir: Messenger of the extraordinary', *Journal of Popular Culture* 20(3) (1986): 135–46.

157. 'Even at the dinner for the Nobel prizes, they steal the spoons', *Wall Street Journal* (7 December 2000): A1, A16.

158. Pauline Maclaran and Linda Scott, 'Spiritual Tourism: Mystical Merchandise and Sacred Shopping in Glastonbury', paper presented at the Association for Consumer Research conference, San Francisco (October 2008).

159. Belk et al., 'The sacred and the profane in consumer behavior', op. cit.

160. Güliz Ger and Olga Kravets, 'Rediscovering Sacred Times in the Mundane: Tea Drinking in Turkey', Consuming Routines: Rhythms, Ruptures, and the Temporalities of Consumption, International Workshop, European University Institute, Florence, Italy (3–5 May 2007); see also Güliz Ger 'Religion and consumption: The profane sacred', *Advances in Consumer Research* 32(1) (2005): 79–81.

161. Belk et al., 'The sacred and the profane in consumer behavior', op. cit.

162. Deborah Hofmann, 'In jewelry, choices sacred and profane, ancient and new', *New York Times* (7 May 1989).

163. James McAlexander, Beth Dufault, Diane Martin and John Schouten, 'The marketization of religion: Field, capital, and consumer identity', *Journal of Consumer Research* 41(3) (2014): 858–75.

164. Deirdre Shaw and Jennifer Thomson, 'Consuming spirituality: the pleasure of uncertainty', *European Journal of Marketing* 47(3/4) (2013): 557–73.

165. Diego Rinallo, 'Living a Magical Life: Sacred Consumption and Spiritual Experience in the Italian Neo-Pagan Community', paper presented at the Association for Consumer Research conference, San Francisco (October 2008).

166. Roberto Grandi, 'Benetton's Advertising: A Case History of Postmodern Communication', unpublished manuscript, Center for Modern Culture and Media, University of Bologna, 1994; Shawn Tully, 'Teens: The most global market of all', *Fortune* (16 May 1994): 90–7.

167. Quoted in 'Public relations firm to present anti-abortion effort to bishops', *New York Times* (14 August 1990): A12.

168. Per Østergaard, 'The Broadened Concept of Marketing as a Manifestation of the Postmodern Condition', in R. Varandarajan and B. Jaworski (eds), *Marketing Theory and Applications,* Proceedings of the AMA Winter Educators Conference 4 (Chicago: American Marketing Association, 1993): 234–9.

169. Russell W. Belk and Gülnur Tumbat, 'The cult of Macintosh', *Consumption Markets & Culture* 8(3) (2005): 205–17.

170. Atyhinodoros Chronis, 'Substantiatin Byzantium: The role of artifacts in the co-construction of narratives', *Journal of Consumer Behaviour* 14 (2015): 180–92.

171. Dan L. Sherrell, Alvin C. Burns and Melodie R. Phillips, 'Fixed Consumption Behavior: The Case of Enduring Acquisition in a Product Category', in Robert L. King (ed.), *Developments in Marketing Science* 14 (1991): 36–40.

172. Russell W. Belk, 'Acquiring, Possessing, and Collecting: Fundamental Processes in Consumer Behavior', in Ronald F. Bushard and Shelby D. Hunt (eds), *Marketing Theory: Philosophy of Science Perspectives* (Chicago: AMA, 1982): 185–90.

173. For an extensive bibliography on collecting, see Russell W. Belk, *Collecting in a Consumer Culture* (London: Routledge, 1995), or Russell W. Belk, Melanie Wallendorf, John F. Sherry Jr and Morris B. Holbrook, 'Collecting in a Consumer Culture', in Russell W. Belk (ed.), *Highways and Buyways* (Provo, UT: Association for Consumer Research, 1991): 178–215. See also Janine Romina Lovatt, 'The People's Show Festival 1994: A Survey', in S. Pearce (ed.), *Experiencing Material Culture in the Western World* (London: Leicester University Press, 1997): 196–254; Werner Muensterberg, *Collecting: An Unruly Passion* (Princeton, NJ: Princeton University Press, 1994); Melanie Wallendorf and Eric J. Arnould, '"My favorite things": A cross-cultural inquiry into object attachment, possessiveness, and social linkage', *Journal of Consumer Research* 14 (March 1988): 531–47. See also Nia Hughes 'Consumption and Collections: the impact of collecting on the construction of identity', unpublished doctoral thesis Lancaster University (July 2008); N Hughes and M.K. Hogg, 'Conceptualizing and exploring couple dyads in the world of collecting', in C. Pechman and L. Price Duluth (eds), *Advances in Consumer Research* 33 (MN: Association for Consumer Research, 2006): 124–30; N. Hughes and M.K. Hogg, 'Problematizing gendered interpretations of collecting behaviour', in Lorna Stevens and Janet Borgerson (eds), *Gender, Marketing and Consumer Behavior, Eighth Conference* (Edinburgh: Association for Consumer Research, June 2006).

174. Quoted in Ruth Ann Smith, 'Collecting as Consumption: A Grounded Theory of Collecting Behavior', unpublished manuscript, Virginia Polytechnic Institute and State University, 1994: 14.

175. G. Cross, 'Nostalgic collections', *Consumption Markets & Culture* 20(2) (2017): 101–6.

176. See Belk, *Collecting in a Consumer Culture,* op. cit.

177. 'A feeding frenzy for Swatches', *New York Times* (29 August 1991): C3; Patricia Leigh Brown, 'Fueling a frenzy: Swatch', *New York Times* (10 May 1992): 1, 9; Mary M. Long and Leon G. Schiffman, 'Swatch fever: An allegory for understanding the paradox of collecting', *Psychology and Marketing* 14(5) (August 1997): 495–509.

178. Jan Slater, 'Collecting the Real Thing: A Case Study Exploration of Brand Loyalty Enhancement Among Coca-Cola Brand Collectors', in Hoch and Meyer (eds), *Advances in Consumer Research* 27: 202–8.

179. https://www.highsnobiety.com/2017/07/03/dasslers-finest-adidas-sneaker-collector-interview/ (accessed 5 September 2018).

180. https://www.adidas.dk/collect (accessed 5 September 2018).

181. Elizabeth C. Hirschman, 'Religious Affiliation and Consumption Processes: An Initial Paradigm', in *Research in Marketing* (Greenwich, CT: JAI Press, 1983): 131–70.

182. See, for example, Nejet Delener, 'The effects of religious factors on perceived risk in durable goods purchase decisions', *Journal of Consumer Marketing* 7 (Summer 1990): 27–38.

183. Madeline Bunting, 'Churchgoing bottoms out', *The Guardian* (10 August 1996): 2; 'Catholic Church loses mass appeal', *The Guardian* (30 January 1996): 4; 'België is nietlangerkatholiek (Belgium is no longer Catholic)', *Trouw* (19 September 1996); Madeline Bunting, 'Revolving door throws doubt on evangelical churches' revival', *The Guardian* (28 August 1996); for a comprehensive website on the world's religions and their populations, see http://www.religious tolerance.org/worldrel.htm (accessed 7 September 2018).

184. Amy Barrett, 'John Paul II to share stage with marketers', *Wall Street Journal Europe* (19 August 1997): 4.

185. D. Crockett and L. Davis, 'Commercial mythmaking at the Holy Land Experience', *Consumption Markets & Culture* 19(2) (2016): 206–27.

186. https://www.theguardian.com/world/europe-news (accessed 4 September 2018).

187. https://www.theguardian.com/world/2017/may/13/uk-losing-faith-religion-young-reject-parents- beliefs (accessed 5 December 2018).

188. https://www.theguardian.com/world/religion (accessed 5 December 2018).

189. Harriet Sherwood, '"Christianity as default is gone": The rise of a non-Christian Europe', *The Guardian* (21 March 2018), https://www.theguardian.com/world/2018/mar/21/christianity-non-christian-europe-young-people-survey-religion (accessed 5 September 2018).

190. Cathy Lynn Grossman, 'Number of U.S. Muslims to double', *USA Today* (27 January 2011), http://www.usatoday.com/news/religion/2011-01-27-1Amuslim27_ST_N.htm (accessed 5 September 2018). For a theoretical account, see E. Izberk-Bilgin, 'Infidel brands: Unveiling alternative meanings of global brands at the nexus of globalization, consumer culture, and Islamism', *Journal of Consumer Research* 39(4) (2012): 663–87.

191. Barry Newman, 'Halal meets Kosher in health-food aisle', *Wall Street Journal* (5 May 2006): B1; Louise Story, 'Rewriting the ad for Muslim-Americans', *New York Times Online* (28 April 2007).

192. Mourad Touzani and Elizabeth Hirshman, 'The celebration of Ramadan in France among North African émigrés . . . [exploring particularly] . . . how they transfer their religious rituals during Ramadan to this cultural setting'; Mourad Touzani and Elizabeth Hirschman, 'Minority Religious Rituals in the Past Colonial World: Ramadan in France', in Alan Bradshaw, Chris Hackley and Pauline Maclaran (eds), *European Association for Consumer Research Conference* (RHUL, 2010): 9.

193. Liz Gooch, 'Advertisers seek to speak to Muslim consumers', *New York Times* (11 August 2010).

194. Jonathan Bilal and A.J. Wilson, 'Muslim youth culture: A new wave of hip-hop grunge', *The Halal Journal,* World Halal Forum 2012 Special Edition 32–38: 34, www.halaljour nal.com (accessed 5 September 2018); see also Jonathan Bilal, A.J. Wilson and J. Liu, 'The challenges of Islamic branding: Navigating emotions and Halal', *Journal of Islamic Marketing* 2(1): 28–42.

195. Harriet Sherwood, 'How Britain's young Muslims are tapping into a £2 trillion market', *The Guardian* (15 October 2016), https://www.theguardian.com/lifeandstyle/2016/oct/15/muslim-consumers-entrepreneurs-economy (accessed 5 September 2018). See also Harriet Sherwood, 'Meet Generation M: the young, affluent Muslims changing the world', *The Guardian* (3 September 2016), https://www.theguardian.com/world/2016/sep/03/meet-generation-m-the-young-affluent-muslims-changing-the-world (accessed 5 September 2018).

196. Sophie Arie, 'Supper is off: Milan bans Da Vinci parody', *The Guardian* (4 February 2005): 15.

197. Claudia Penteado, 'Brazilian ad irks Church', *Advertising Age* (23 March 2000): 11.

Chapter 13
Cultural change processes

Chapter objectives

When you finish reading this chapter you will understand why:

13.1 Cultural change can be seen as an outcome of a production system including many agents.

13.2 New products, services and ideas spread through a population, and different types of people are more or less likely to adopt them.

13.3 Fashion is organised as a cyclical cultural system that communicates symbolic meanings of imitation and differentiation to consumers.

13.4 Acculturation is the process whereby consumers adapt to living in a new cultural setting. This process not only influences those consumers migrating, but also the consumers already living in the host culture.

JOOST AND LIEKE have just arrived in Chicago from Amsterdam, and they are checking-in to a new hotel, Eden, not too far from the Chicago downtown area. Joost is tired after the flight and looks forward to throwing himself on the bed and maybe grabbing a small bottle of something from the minibar, just to wind down. When they arrive in the room, the first thing that catches Joost's attention is a funny kind of thin mattress rolled up in the closet. 'I hope this is not the bed' he thinks to himself, and quickly reassures himself that there are indeed nice big and comfortable beds. He searches – in vain – for the minibar, and finally asks Lieke if she has any idea whether there is one in the room. 'I suppose not', she answers. 'The Eden hotels are oriented towards wellness, fitness, relaxation for mind and body and healthy eating, so I guess a minibar does not really fit into that concept.' Joost looks very puzzled. 'Did you not see the yoga mattress when we entered the room?', Lieke asks. Joost's reply is prompt – 'Why on earth did you book a hotel room in a fitness centre?', he almost shouts. 'Well, I saw this on the internet – it is a kind of new concept and I felt that it might be good to not have to give up my yoga and exercise programmes just because we are away from home – and you know how the food can be so greasy in the United States. I am sure it will do us both good to spend the next week in a healthy environment.' Joost sits down on the bed with a big sigh – 'A "luxury hotel" without a minibar but with yoga mattress and health food – what is the world coming to?', he thinks to himself. Not exactly the kind of arrival he had had in mind. . . [1]

Gary Bamossy

Introduction

Fashion tattoos. Vuitton handbags. Free-range eggs. Lady Gaga. High-tech furniture. Flash mobs. Postmodern architecture. *Angry Birds.* Personal coaching. Tablets. Hybrid cars. Costa Rican ecotours. Gladiator sandals. We inhabit a world that brims with different styles and possibilities. The food we eat, the cars we drive, the clothes we wear, the places we live and work, the music we listen to – the ebb and flow of popular culture and fashion influences all of them. This ebb and flow, obviously, is also what is behind a certain process of regret ('Oh, can you believe how we were into that thing. . . ') and sometimes generating a feeling of such, as in regretting having had a particular tattoo.[2]

Consumers may, at times, feel overwhelmed by the sheer choice in the marketplace. A person trying to decide on something as routine as what to have for lunch has many hundreds of alternatives from which to choose. Despite this seeming abundance, however, the options available to consumers at any point in time actually represent only a *small fraction* of the total set of possibilities. In this chapter, we shall follow marketers' and cultural gatekeepers' attempts to set their marks on which possibilities get the most attention and which trends and tendencies become victorious in the battle for a place in our minds as consumers. Some styles become so prevalent that they almost become part of national identity and image-building, as has arguably been the case for Britpop and British society.[3] We will take a closer look at the processes of change driving the ever-changing styles of consumption we are presented with. Already (back in Chapter 1), we have seen how culture and consumption are related through a meaning system, linking culture with consumption through systems of fashion and advertising and through a variety of consumer rituals. In Chapter 12, we took a closer look at the rituals and at some of the cultural mythologies of the advertising system. In this final chapter, we will look at how fashions and consumption styles spread within and among societies.

Modes of cultural production

13.1

Cultural change can be seen as an outcome of a production system including many agents.

Even though most of the consumers we have been dealing with in this text may live in Western middle-class areas, each with their national and local characteristics, they are often able to 'connect' symbolically with millions of other young consumers by relating to styles that originated far away – even though the original meanings of those styles may have little relevance to them. The spread of fashions in consumption is just one example of what happens when the meanings created by some members of a culture are interpreted and produced for mass consumption.

Take the example of rap music. Baggy jeans and outfits featuring gold vinyl skirts, huge gold chains and bejeweled baseball caps, which used to be seen only on the streets of impoverished urban areas, are being adapted by *haute couture* fashion designers for the catwalks of Manhattan and Paris. In addition, a high proportion of people who buy recordings of rap music are white. How did rap music and fashions, which began as forms of expression in the black urban subculture, make it to mainstream America and the rest of the world? A brief chronology is given in Table 13.1.

It's common for mainstream culture to modify symbols from 'cutting-edge' subcultures for a larger audience to consume. As this occurs, these cultural products undergo a process of **co-optation**, where outsiders transform their original meanings. This happened to rap music, which is divorced to a large extent from its original connection with the struggles of young

Table 13.1 The mainstreaming of popular music and fashion

Date	Event
1968	Bronx DJ Kool Herc invents hip-hop.
1973–8	Urban block parties feature break-dancing and graffiti.
1979	A small record company named Sugar Hill becomes the first rap label.
1980	Manhattan art galleries feature graffiti artists.
1981	Blondie's song 'Rapture' hits number one in the US charts.
1985	Columbia Records buys the Def Jam label.
1988	MTV begins *Yo! MTV Raps,* featuring Fab 5 Freddy.
1990	Hollywood gets into the act with the hip-hop film *House Party;* Ice-T's rap album is a big hit on college radio stations; amid controversy, white rapper Vanilla Ice hits the big time; NBC launches a new sitcom, *Fresh Prince of Bel Air.*
1991	Mattel introduces its Hammer doll (a likeness of the rap star Hammer, formerly known as M.C. Hammer); designer Karl Lagerfeld shows shiny vinyl raincoats and chain belts in his Chanel collection; designer Charlotte Neuville sells gold vinyl suits with matching baseball caps for $800; Isaac Mizrahi features wide-brimmed caps and take-offs of African medallions; Bloomingdale's launches Anne Klein's rap-inspired clothing line by featuring a rap performance in its Manhattan store.
1992	Rappers start to abandon this look, turning to low-fitting baggy jeans, sometimes worn backwards; white rapper Marky Mark appears in a national campaign wearing Calvin Klein underwear, exposed above his hip-hugging trousers; composer Quincy Jones launches *Vibe* magazine and it wins over many white readers.[4]
1993	Hip-hop fashions and slang continue to cross over into mainstream consumer culture. An outdoor ad for Coca-Cola proclaims, 'Get Yours 24–7'. The company is confident that many viewers in its target market will know that the phrase is urban slang for 'always' (24 hours a day, 7 days a week).[5]
1994	The (late) Italian designer Versace pushes oversized overalls favoured by urban youngsters. In one ad, he asks, 'Overalls with an oversize look, something like what rappers and homeboys wear. Why not a sophisticated version?'.[6]
1996	Tommy Hilfiger, a designer who was the darling of the preppie set, turns hip-hop. He gives free wardrobes to rap artists such as Grand Puba and Chef Raekwon, and in return finds his name mentioned in rap songs – the ultimate endorsement. The September 1996 issue of *Rolling Stone* magazine features the Fugees; several band members prominently display the Hilfiger logo. In the same year the designer uses rap stars Method Man and Treach of Naughty by Nature as runway models. Hilfiger's new Tommy Girl perfume plays on his name but also is a reference to the New York hip-hop record label Tommy Boy.[7]
1997	Coca-Cola features rapper L.L. Cool J. in a commercial that debuts in the middle of the sitcom *In the House,* a TV show starring the singer.[8]
1998	In their battle with Dockers for an increased share of the khaki market, Gap launches its first global advertising campaign. One of the commercials, 'Khakis Groove', includes a hip-hop dance performance set to music by Bill Mason.[9]
1999	Rapper-turned-entrepreneur Sean (Puffy) Combs introduces an upscale line of menswear he calls 'urban high fashion'. New companies FUBU, Mecca and Enyce attain financial success in the multibillion-dollar industry.[10] Lauryn Hill and the Fugees sing at a party sponsored by upscale Italian clothier Emporio Armani and she proclaims, 'We just wanna thank Armani for giving a few kids from the ghetto some great suits'.[11]
2000	360hip-hop.com, a Web-based community dedicated to the hip-hop culture, is launched. In addition to promoting the hip-hop lifestyle, the site allows consumers to purchase clothing and music online while watching video interviews with such artists as Will Smith and Busta Rymes.[12]
2001	Hip-hop dancing becomes the rage among China's youth, who refer to it as *jiew,* or street dancing.[13]

Table 13.1 The mainstreaming of popular music and fashion (*continued*)

Date	Event
2003	Hip-hop finds its way into toy stores. Toy manufacturers start mimicking the hip-hop practice of using the letter 'Z' instead of the letter 'S' in names. This trend started with the 1991 film *Boyz N The Hood* (a title that was itself borrowed from a 1989 song by the rap group N.W.A.).[14]
2005	The fusion of hip-hop and brand culture becomes ever more prevalent. The global fast-food chain McDonald's offers to pay rappers €4.15 every time a song is played that drops the name of the 'Big-Mac'. Artists who have 'referenced' well-known products include Jay-Z, 50 Cent and Snoop Dogg. Among the happy beneficiaries have been brands such as Courvoisier, Gucci, Dom Perignon, Bentley and Porsche.[15]
2008	Glocal hip-hop: hip-hop increasingly disengages from its American roots as artists around the world develop their own localised interpretations, for example aboriginal Australian hip-hop,[16] a Portuguese thriving hip-hop scene based on immigrant populations[17] and an Islamic hip-hop and rap with lyrics promoting moralities very different from the original 'booze and girls'.[18]
2012	The 'domestication' of hip-hop: some of the outrageousness seems to have gone from the scene. Jay-Z and Beyoncé have become parents, and companies such as Rocawear offer hip-hop outfits for kids.
2015	Rap is now big business. Jay-Z is now worth in excess of $500 million, with much of the value coming from business outside the music industry.[19] Kanye West was 2015's number 37 on *Time* magazine's list of the most influential persons in the world. As a musical trendspotter, activist, clothing designer and provocateur, he seems almost omni-present. All is not well in Kanye-land, though. When he was announced as the 2015 headline act at the Glastonbury music festival, more than 130,000 protesters objected to this 'insult to music'. Kanye West remained the headline act. . . [20]
2017	LL Cool J becomes the first rapper to be awarded the Kennedy Center Honor – the highest award for performing arts in the USA.[21]
2018	Kendrick Lamar becomes the first non-jazz or non-classical musician to win the Pulitzer Prize for music.[22]

African Americans and is now a mainstream entertainment format.[23] One writer sees the white part of the 'hip-hop nation' as a series of concentric rings. In the centre are those who actually know African Americans and understand their culture. The next ring consists of those who have indirect knowledge of this subculture via friends or relatives but who do not actually rap, spray-paint or break-dance. Then, there are those a bit further out who simply play hip-hop between other types of music. Finally, come the more suburban 'wiggers', who simply try to catch on to the next popular craze.[24] As was mentioned in Table 13.1, these cultural expressions also change when they move from one cultural context to another. Although, on the surface of it, Afro-American and French Arab and African urban and suburban street cultures may look alike, both in terms of musical styles and an affectionate relationship with sneakers, the consumption of the sneaker (which in the American context is included in the countercultural statement) is more a fashion statement in the French context.[25] The spread of hip-hop fashions and music is only one example of what happens when the marketing system takes a set of subcultural meanings, reinterprets them and produces them for mass consumption.[26]

Cultural selection

The selection of certain alternatives over others – whether cars, dresses, computers, recording artists, political candidates, religions or even scientific methodologies – is the culmination of a complex filtration process resembling a funnel, as depicted in Figure 13.1. Many possibilities initially compete for adoption, and these are steadily narrowed down as they make their way along the path from conception to consumption in a process of **cultural selection** – a process in which, not least, the advertising and communication agencies play a central role.[27]

The internet has made the spotting and selection of the various trends and changes in society – the symbol pool – easier. New trend-watching services can be paid for scouring the world for new possibilities in colours, fabrics, designs or combinations. They can access pictures from runways of great fashion shows, look at store decorations from H&M or Zara, or look at photos of cool London/Paris/Amsterdam/Berlin youngsters sporting the latest rebellious twist to the clothing companies' standard offerings. Even though the subscription to these services is costly, many companies think they are well worth their price, because they save in business trips and other types of costly trend-spotting fieldwork.[28]

The development of the internet has made the communication system for the trends and fashion even more complex, but also more democratic. With the rise of fashion blogs, 'everyone' can become a gatekeeper (see section on cultural gatekeepers below) and promoter for trends and fashions, provided you are capable of building the necessary trust in your site. This is what some researchers have called the 'megaphone effect'.[29] Some of these blogs can be very good income sources. For example, Forbes offers an overview over the bloggers with the highest earnings in 2017 – blogs whose topics typically revolve around lifestyle or technology trends.[30] Consumers (would like to believe that consumers) have the power. . .

Social media is not just a playground for consumers but something that is strategically used by major brands – for example, when making the best possible presence on Instagram.[31] Our tastes and product preferences, then, are obviously not formed in a vacuum.

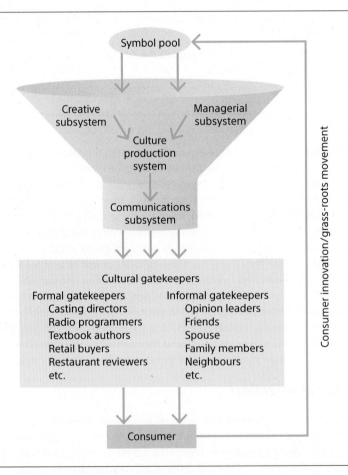

Figure 13.1 The cultural production process

Source: Adapted from Michael R. Solomon, 'Building Up and Breaking Down: The Impact of Cultural Sorting on Symbolic Consumption', in J. Sheth and E.C. Hirschman (eds), *Research in Consumer Behavior* (Greenwich, CT: JAI Press, 1988): 325–51.

Choices are driven by the images presented to us in mass media, our observations of those around us and even by our desires to live in the fantasy worlds created by marketers. These options are constantly evolving and changing. A clothing style or type of cuisine that is 'hot' one year may be 'out' the next. Some general characteristics of the evolution of styles and fashions include:

- Styles are a reflection of more fundamental societal trends (e.g. politics and social conditions).
- A style begins as a risky or unique statement by a relatively small group of people and then spreads as others increasingly become aware of the style and feel confident about trying it.
- Styles usually originate as an interplay between the deliberate inventions of designers and businesspeople and spontaneous actions by ordinary consumers who modify styles to suit their own needs. Designers, manufacturers and merchandisers who can anticipate what consumers want will succeed in the marketplace. In the process, they help to fuel the fire when they encourage distribution of the item.
- These cultural products travel widely, often across countries and even continents.
- Influential people in the media play a significant role in deciding which will succeed.
- Most styles eventually wear out as people continually search for new ways to express themselves and marketers scramble to keep up with these desires.

Culture production systems

No single designer, company or advertising agency is solely responsible for creating popular culture. Every product, whether a hit record, a car or a new fashion, requires the input of many different participants. The set of individuals and organisations responsible for creating and marketing a cultural product is a **cultural production system (CPS)**.[32] The nature of these systems helps to determine the types of product that eventually emerge from them. Factors such as the number and diversity of competing systems and the amount of innovation versus conformity that is encouraged are important.

The different members of a cultural production system may not necessarily be aware of or appreciate the roles played by other members, yet many diverse agents work together to create popular culture.[33] Each member does their best to anticipate which particular images will be most attractive to a consumer market. Of course, those who are able to forecast consumers' tastes consistently will be successful over time.

With the increasing power of bloggers, the boundaries between formal and informal gatekeepers are blurring. It seems as if everyone with an internet connection can assume a self-announced position as gatekeeper, passing judgement on topics as diverse as fashion, music and food to a potentially global audience. And consumers seeking information online seem more than willing to absorb the opinions of 'real' people – peers who seemingly have no financial interest in the products they endorse. As a consequence of this 'democratisation' of the cultural production process, formal gatekeepers are losing power and can merely watch as the Justin Biebers and One Directions of tomorrow flood the gates, building audiences autonomously and earning fame through YouTube videos, not record companies. Just as everyone with an internet connection can be aspire to be a gatekeeper, so everyone with a video camera has the potential to be a star.

Components of a CPS

A cultural production system has three major subsystems: (1) a *creative subsystem* responsible for generating new symbols and/or products; (2) a *managerial subsystem* responsible for selecting, making tangible, mass-producing and managing the distribution of new symbols and/or products; and (3) a *communications subsystem* responsible for giving meaning to the new product and providing it with a symbolic set of attributes that is communicated to consumers.

A classic example of the three components of a cultural production system for a music record would be: (1) a singer (e.g. Madonna, a creative subsystem); (2) a company (e.g. Atlantic Records, which manufactures and distributes Madonna's records – a managerial subsystem); and (3) the advertising and publicity agencies hired to promote the albums (a communications subsystem). Of course, all artistic domains experience conflicts between the market-driven forces and the artistic ambitions, which may not always draw in the same direction. This is notably true for those genres characteristically driven by 'authentic artistic aspirations' rather than marketplace success, such as jazz.[34] Table 13.2 illustrates some of the many *cultural specialists,* operating in different subsystems, who are required to create a hit CD.

But again, in a YouTube age, there are if not easier then at least more easily accessible ways to stardom. The music industry is under increasing pressure from the digital world. With some decent computer equipment, it is possible to create a home studio and nice-sounding recordings (provided you can play and sing . . . usually!) that you can upload to YouTube yourself – and the rest may be history. Or so at least was the history of Justin Bieber! Spotify and similar organisations increasingly take the place of the shop owners (how many music shops are left in your area?), and sites such as Cloudmusic or Sellaband provide facilities for hopeful artists to make a splash. One study investigated the role of consumer co-creation in the music industry and found five different

Table 13.2 Cultural specialists in the music industry

Specialist	Functions
Songwriters	Compose music and lyrics; must reconcile artistic preferences with estimates of what will succeed in the marketplace
Performers	Interpret music and lyrics; may be formed spontaneously, or may be packaged by an agent to appeal to a predetermined market (e.g. Elton John or *Green Day*)
Teachers and coaches	Develop and refine performers' talents
Agents	Represent performers to record companies
A&R (artist & repertoire) executives	Acquire artists for the record label
Publicists, image consultants	Create an image for the artist or group that is transmitted to the buying public, designers, stylists
Recording technicians, producers	Create a recording to be sold
Marketing executives	Make strategic decisions regarding performer's appearances, ticket pricing, promotional strategies and so on
Video directors	Interpret the song visually to create a music video that will help to promote the record
Music reviewers	Evaluate the merits of a recording for listeners
Disc jockeys, radio programme directors	Decide which records will be given airplay and/or placed in the radio stations' regular rotations. A recent article discussed the relatively high power of programme directors over the single DJs and radio hosts[35]
Record-shop owners and digital platforms	Decide which of the many records produced will be stocked and/or promoted heavily in the retail environment

ways in which consumers participate in the making and marketing processes in the music industry, ranging from being participants in viral marketing processes to being actual 'prosumers' of music – we will return to the prosumer in a short while.[36]

Cultural gatekeepers

Many judges, or 'tastemakers', influence the products that are eventually offered to consumers. These judges, or **cultural gatekeepers**, are responsible for filtering the overload of information and materials intended for consumers. Gatekeepers include film, restaurant and car reviewers, interior designers, disc jockeys, retail buyers and magazine editors. Collectively, this set of agents has been known as the *throughput sector*.[37] Increasingly, however, these 'occupations responsible for the production and legitimation of various images, experiences, identities and lifestyles'[38] are known as **cultural intermediaries**.[39] Advertising agencies, in spite of possibly losing some of their significance as advertising makers but then shifting their business to being general and social media communication consultants, remain very significant cultural intermediaries,[40] not least in emerging economies where other parts of civil society may have less striking power.[41] Such cultural intermediaries can also promote anti-fashion fashion – that is, tips about how to dress fashionably without following fashion, as is the case with either the normcore style or what, in Finnish contexts, is called the 'Wardrobe Self-Help' movement.[42]

Speaking the language of beauty

One study of cultural gatekeepers in the fashion and beauty industry illustrates how some cultural 'products' (in this case, fashion models) are selected and championed over other stylistic possibilities.[43]

In this study, decision-makers at a group of influential magazines identified a small set of 'looks' that characterise many of the diverse fashion models they evaluate on a daily basis – what is more, though each editor was studied independently, overall respondents exhibited a very high level of agreement among themselves regarding what the 'looks' are, what they are called, which are more or less desirable *and* which they expect to be paired with specific

The recent 'Normcore' style reflects the fashion of not being in fashion.
Eugenio Marongiu/Shutterstock

product advertisements. This research suggests that cultural gatekeepers tend to rely on the same underlying cultural ideals and priorities when making the selections that in turn get passed down the channel of distribution for consideration by consumers.

Editors at such women's magazines as *Cosmopolitan, Vogue, Marie Claire, Depêche Mode* and *Elle* thus play an important role in selecting the specific variations of beauty that will appear in the pages of these 'bibles of fashion'. If you're interested in the role of editors, you might want to check the influence of someone such as Anna Wintour, currently the chief editor at *Vogue*. She has put a big mark on fashion through many years. The images promoted by such editors, in turn, will be relied on by millions of readers to decide what 'look' they would like to adopt – and, of course, which particular products and services (such as hairstyles, cosmetics, clothing styles, exercise regimes) they will need to attain these images.

We have already encountered numerous examples of the mini revolution we call consumer-generated content; companies today pay attention to everyday people's opinions when they design new products, create advertising messages or improve upon shopping experiences. The rise of social networking changes the basic process of innovation, as the consumer feedback loop in Figure 13.1 grows stronger and stronger. This shift from a top-down to a bottom-up process is a symptom of the transition from *marketerspace,* where companies exert total control over the market, to *consumerspace.*

Consumerspace is where customers act as partners with companies to decide what the marketplace will offer.[44] One study underlined how consumer discourses – that is, how consumers speak about something – are important building blocks for the making of luxury brand meaning, thereby slightly challenging McCracken's movement of meaning model (which we saw in Chapter 3).[45] Others underline how even new markets are increasingly designed by participant consumers.[46] This process is becoming more and more common – in terms of your car, your cell phone and a lot of other technology products, basically in a lot of contemporary purchase processes, the consumer contributes to the end-design of the product, thereby taking on the role of the **prosumer**. The process of engaging consumers as prosumers is nowadays often called **crowdsourcing**.[47] This process can be used for a number of innovation processes for various goods and services. The value of crowdsourcing has been demonstrated for sectors as different as fashion in Bangkok[48] and map-making.[49]

Even the foods you eat can be prosumed. In one study, researchers investigated the so-called community-supported agriculture, where farmers and consumers operate on shared rewards and risks. This system, the researchers underlined, is in a way countercultural to even the organic producers, who have in many cases become too large to be seen as being close to the interests of local consumers. The basic idea is that the consumer can rear their own beef, make sure that animals are living a good life, as well as support local business of high-quality and high-morality food products.[50] It should be added that some consumer researchers prefer to use the term 'working consumer' instead, in order to underline that just because the consumer gets a role in the production process, it does not mean that the interests of producers and consumer are necessarily harmonious.[51]

High culture and popular culture

Do Beethoven and Beyoncé have anything in common? While both the famous composer and the American singer are associated with music, many would argue that the similarity stops here. We think it doesn't. Cultural production systems create many diverse kinds of products, but in terms of how they relate to consumer culture, they might be quite similar. For example, it is not only the followers of Beyoncé and other pop music stars who can be considered from a fan culture perspective and be divided according to their degree of investment and commitment in a particular type of music.[52] The audiences of classical music also share some of these traits.[53] Some basic distinctions can be offered regarding the characteristics of most cultural products.

Arts and crafts

One distinction can be made between arts and crafts.[54] An **art product** is viewed primarily as an object of aesthetic contemplation without any functional value. A **craft product**, in contrast, is admired because of the beauty with which it performs some function (e.g. a ceramic bowl or hand-carved fishing lures). A piece of art is original, subtle and valuable, and is associated with the elite of society. A craft tends to follow a formula that permits rapid production. According to this framework, elite culture is produced in a purely aesthetic context and is judged by reference to recognised classics. It is high culture – 'serious art'.[55] However, many businesses and consumption practices operate in some grey area in between the two. Consider the tattoo business. Whereas tattooists are basically subject to providing the tattoos the consumers order them to produce, many do consider themselves as artists and only unwillingly accept to do such things as brand logo tattoos because they consider it a sell-out to commercial forces where the consumer could have had an artistic expression.[56]

High art *vs* low art

It is not just that these grey areas exist. The whole distinction between high and low culture is not as clear as it may first appear. In addition to the possible class bias that drives such a distinction (i.e. we assume that the rich have culture while the poor do not), high and low culture are blending together in interesting ways. Popular culture reflects the world around us; these phenomena touch rich and poor. In many places in Europe, advertising is widely appreciated as an art form and the TV/cinema commercials have their own Cannes Festival. In France and the UK, certain advertising executives are public figures in their respective countries.

The arts are big business. All cultural products that are transmitted by mass media become a part of popular culture.[57] Classical recordings are marketed in much the same way as Top-40 albums,[58] and museums use mass-marketing techniques to sell their wares. A multinational team of consumer researchers extended the study of high and low art to the realm of *street art,* where artists create paintings, murals and other pieces in public places. They identified numerous sites where the art became an instrument that was used

This advertisement demonstrates the adaptation of famous paintings ('high art') to sell products ('low art').

Alfredo Dagli Orti/Shutterstock

531

for 'transactions' between the artists and the people who lived in the area. Although not all reactions were positive, it was common to observe that people's experiences of public spaces were enhanced because the street art created a feeling of empowerment and ownership in formerly barren places.[59]

Marketers often incorporate high art imagery in their promotion of products, trying to find a style that is believed to fit with the brand image.[60] They may sponsor artistic events to build public goodwill or feature works of art on shopping bags.[61] When observers from Toyota watched customers in luxury car showrooms, the company found that these consumers tended to view a car as an art object.

However, we also find movement of value in the opposite direction. Value is not just taken from the artworld and given to commercial objects. The market value of the artwork or exhibition event is also generated in a co-creation process by the consumers.[62] Indeed, in the contemporary world, the creative art scene, marketing techniques and consumer involvement are highly intertwined, and may be mobilised for political protest.[63] Creativity is in the streets! Certain companies have taken to the use of crowdsourced snapshots or videos in order to generate a maximum sense of authenticity in their visual communication. Indeed, 'authenticity' is the 'holy grail' of much cultural marketing.[64] But whether companies are using high art, street art or snapshot aesthetics, everything happens in order to create a visual gimmick that is powerful enough to break through the clutter of our contemporary, overcommunicating marketplace. One final twist to the relation between art and marketing: if brands are good at applying (indeed parodying) artistic expression format, one artist found it appropriate to inverse the process and parody the branding techniques. In a satire on how a tool company anaesthetised the axe, he made a spoof of the campaign, putting a toilet plunger at the centre of attention instead. The art project was supposed to draw attention to the question: 'What happens when we transform a useful object to an aesthetic symbol?', How do working-class elements such as tools contribute to form middle-class fantasies (of authenticity, masculinity, etc.)?[65]

Cultural formulae

Mass culture, in contrast, churns out products specifically for a mass market. These products aim to please the average taste of an undifferentiated audience and are predictable because they follow certain patterns. As illustrated in Table 13.3, many popular art forms, such as detective stories or science fiction, generally follow a **cultural formula**, where certain roles and props often occur consistently.[66] Computer programs even allow users to 'write' their own romances by systematically varying certain set elements of the story. Romance novels are an extreme case of a cultural formula. The romance novel and other formulae reflect the consumer society by the way consumption events and different brands play a role in the story and in the construction of the different atmospheres described.[67] **Subcultures** often draw heavily on particular cultural formulae – for example, the 'Goth' subculture uses references to the vampire universe to challenge norms about gender identity and sexuality.[68]

Reliance on these formulae also leads to a postmodern *recycling* of images, as members of the creative subsystem reach back through time for inspiration. Thus, young people in Britain watch retro channels such as Granada Plus and UK Gold that broadcast classic decades-old soaps, and old themes are recycled for new soap series. Who, for example, would have believed that the 'dead and gone' vinyl record that all but disappeared from the market some 25 years ago has made a remarkable resurrection and is becoming the major physical medium for selling commercial music?[69] Designers modify styles from Victorian England or colonial Africa, DJs sample sound bites from old songs and combine them in new ways, and Gap runs ads featuring now-dead celebrities including Humphrey

Table 13.3 Cultural formulae in public art forms

Art form/genre	Classic Western	Science fiction	Hard-boiled detective	Family sitcom
Time	1800s	Future	Present	Any time
Location	Edge of civilisation	Space	City	Suburbs
Protagonist	Cowboy (lone individual)	Astronaut	Detective	Father (figure)
Heroine	Schoolmistress	Spacegirl	Damsel in distress	Mother (figure)
Villain	Outlaws, bandits	Aliens	Killer	Boss, neighbour
Secondary characters	Townsfolk, Native Indians	Technicians in spacecraft	Police, underworld	Children, dogs
Plot	Restore law and order	Repel aliens	Find killer	Solve problem
Theme	Justice	Triumph of humanity	Pursuit and discovery	Chaos and confusion
Costume	Cowboy hat, boots, etc.	High-tech uniforms	Raincoat	Normal clothes
Locomotion	Horse	Spaceship	Beat-up car	Family estate car
Weaponry	Six-gun, rifle	Raygun	Pistol, fists	Insults

Source: Arthur A. Berger, *Signs in Contemporary Culture: An Introduction to Semiotics* (New York: Longman, 1984): 86. Copyright © 1984. Reissued 1989 by Sheffield Publishing Company, Salem, WI. Reprinted with permission of the publisher.

Bogart, Gene Kelly and Pablo Picasso dressed in khaki trousers.[70] With easy access to photoshopping and all other kinds of digital software, virtually anyone can 'remix' the past.[71]

Artists and companies in the popular music or film industry may be more guided by ideas of what could make a 'hit' than by any wish for artistic expression. And creators of aesthetic products are increasingly adapting conventional marketing methods to fine-tune their mass-market offerings, which is why it is not completely beside the point to talk about the 'film brandscape', as two British researchers suggest.[72] In the US, market research is used, for example, to test audience reactions to film concepts. Although testing cannot account for such intangibles as acting quality or cinematography, it can determine if the basic themes of the film strike a responsive chord in the target audience. This type of research is most appropriate for blockbuster films, which usually follow one of the formulae described earlier. In some cases, research is combined with publicity, as when the producers of the film *Men in Black,* featuring Will Smith, showed the first 12 minutes of the film to an advance audience and then let them meet the stars to create a pre-release buzz.[73]

Even the content of films is sometimes influenced by this consumer research. Typically, free invitations to pre-screenings are handed out in shopping centres and cinemas. Attendees are asked a few questions about the film, then some are selected to participate in focus groups. Although groups' reactions usually result in only minor editing changes, occasionally more drastic effects result. When initial reaction to the ending of the film *Fatal Attraction* was negative, Paramount Pictures spent an additional $1.3 million to shoot a new one.[74] Of course, this feedback is not always accurate – before the mega-hit *E.T.: The Extra-Terrestrial* was released, consumer research indicated that no one over the age of four would go to see the film![75]

Reality engineering

The mythical and much-beloved Simpsons family debuted in real life as 7-Eleven transformed many of its stores into Kwik-E-Marts to promote the cartoon series' movie. During the promotion, customers snapped up Krusty O's cereal, Buzz Cola and Ice Squishees, all products from the show.[76] The Simpsons were also used as an exemplar of particular tribal consumption patterns in one European study.[77] With the increasing importance of such media becoming reality, and reality televisions' reality in the media, no wonder consumer researchers increasingly look for clues concerning contemporary consumption patterns in the media in addition to looking at consumers.

Like the Simpsons universe, many of the environments in which we find ourselves, whether shopping centres, sports stadiums or theme parks, are composed at least partly of images and characters drawn from products, marketing campaigns or the mass media. Reality engineering occurs as elements of popular culture are appropriated by marketers and converted to vehicles for promotional strategies.[78] These elements include sensory and spatial aspects of everyday existence, whether in the form of products appearing in films, scents pumped into offices and shops, advertising hoardings, theme parks or video monitors attached to shopping trolleys and so on.

The people of Disney Corporation are probably the best worldwide-known reality engineers, through their theme parks in California and Florida and their newer parks in Japan and Europe. Disneyland-Paris got off to a problematic start when it opened in 1991. Fewer-than-expected

The Food Hotel in Germany is completely done in a food theme, from can-shaped furniture to barstools made of beer crates. Each guest room is sponsored by a food brand, like the Prinzen biscuits seen in the right-hand picture. A room by the chocolate manufacturer Ferrero recreates the scene of a TV commercial for its Rafaello coconut candies set on a desert island, with palm trees, shells, summer hats, photos of sandy beaches and books about beach holidays. Another room by potato crisp brand, Chio, features a rotating mirrored disco ball and flashing bathroom lights with an integrated sound system.

Thomas Frey/EPA/Shutterstock

visitors, and especially too few clients for the hotel and conference facilities, created economic problems. But the conceptualisation of the park was changed, made less American and more European, and now the park is drawing huge crowds. Consequently, some of the most notable providers of consumable experiences are theme parks and amusement parks emulating the Disneylands, such as the Legolands, Parc Asterix or other thematised spaces of leisurely consumption. But experience economy has also found its way to more mundane consumption activities, such as going to a café.

One final recent example of reality engineering is that, in homage to the famous movie *Casablanca,* a former US diplomat opened a Rick's Café in the Moroccan city that gave the film its name. The new 'Rick's' has the same warm atmosphere as the film original (which was created on a sound stage in Hollywood). Waiters in traditional fez caps and wide-legged pants serve customers at candle-lit tables. The owner commented, 'Because there has never been a Rick's Café here, I could be reasonably assured that it would succeed. It was already an institution, and it never even existed. It's not often you get a chance to turn myth into reality'.[79]

Experience economy

These examples resonate with the argument from some marketers who have suggested that the contemporary economy can be characterised as an experience economy.[80] They argue that the competition among different market offers has driven producers to distinguish otherwise almost-identical products – initially through the services attached to acquiring the product but now increasingly through differentiating the experience that comes with consuming the product. This historical shift, it is argued, can be exemplified through the consumption of a birthday cake. Historically, the standard way of creating a birthday party for one's child has gone from buying the ingredients for making a cake, to buying a cake at the baker's/confectioner's shop, to buying the cake as well as a number of other objects supposedly providing a thematised birthday (a Spiderman birthday, a ghost birthday, a Barbie birthday), to buying the whole birthday party at the local McDonald's, the local toy store, the local zoo or any other provider of a 'complete birthday experience'. Although it has been argued that we should probably look for the origins of the experience economy somewhat earlier, for example in the rise of hedonic consumer culture in post-war Californian myths of 'fun in the sun',[81] it is obvious that contemporary corporations are doing their utmost to play the game. To the extent that consumers demand and companies provide more and more 'total experiences', we live in an experience economy.

Consumer behaviour as I see it . . .
Cultural change as glocalisation

Professor Dannie Kjeldgaard University of Southern Denmark

My view on consumer behaviour started with the observation in the late 1990s that marketers and social commentators claimed that young consumers increasingly shared styles, tastes and values globally, to the extent that they would have more in common with each other than with other age groups in their native countries. Young consumers were, in other words, a global consumer segment. This lead me to ask two questions: how did this segment come about? And while the marketing and consumer behaviour theories were quick to buy into this myth of a uniform group of consumers, what differences might there be globally?

→

The segment is an outcome of broader societal developments in the industrialized world accelerating after WWII: a growing middle class and prolonged education for younger people. Youth culture, as a life stage with a specific cultural meaning, emerged as a cultural category. A key element in youth culture is the notion of style: that each new generation assemble specific styles (clothing, music taste, grooming, transportation and communication technologies) that distinguish them from the contemporary adult culture. Youth culture in that sense is also often hailed as a site of cultural innovation, and therefore intrinsically interesting for marketers. A third characteristic of youth culture is that it is often associated with non-conformity and cultural and stylistic innovation that speaks against mainstream market expressions, or even rests on anti-market and anti-capitalist sentiments as has been seen in many subcultures. However, marketing was implicated in the very constitution of youth culture. The word 'teenager', for example, gained more widespread use after the publication of a market research report in 1956 in the UK labelled 'The Teenage Consumer'. This mutuality of (rebellious) youth culture, broader societal developments, and marketing's perpetual search for new innovations hence lead to the emergence of the youth segment as a cultural category. A cultural category that was mediated through popular culture such as movies and music and ultimately spread globally.

So, does this mean that a common stylistic expression among consumers in different contexts means the same thing? Obviously not. My research demonstrated that the meaning of a symbol of global youth culture such as tattooing had very different meanings for a young consumer on the West Coast of Greenland than to a young consumer in central Copenhagen. For the Greenlandic consumer the tattoo was a matter of signalling a belonging to global youth culture and thereby signifying a modern and global Greenland distinct from an identity based on the mythology of Inuit hunter-gatherer culture, whereas for the consumers in Copenhagen it was a symbol of individual distinction from other young consumers locally. This is why we can speak of a glocal (global and local at the same time) phenomenon.

Consumer behaviour, as I see it, always means taking as a starting point that marketers, consumers and other cultural intermediaries can be seen as 'reality engineers' and therefore a site of cultural innovation and market-change processes.

Question

Try to find various examples of glocal consumption styles in your own surroundings – global styles or tendencies that are altered or given a local format.

Dannie Kjeldgaard

Product placement

Reality engineering is accelerating due to the current popularity of product placements by marketers. It is quite common to see real brands prominently displayed or to hear them discussed in films and on television. In many cases, these 'plugs' are no accident. **Product placement** refers to the insertion of specific products and/or the use of brand names in film and TV scripts. Today most major releases are brimming with real products. Directors like to incorporate branded props because they contribute to the film's realism. 2014's top scorer in terms of product placement was (no surprise, we guess) Apple.[82]

Some researchers claim that product placement can aid in consumer decision-making because the familiarity of these props creates a sense of cultural belonging while generating feelings of emotional security.[83] Another study found that placements consistent with a show's plot do enhance brand attitudes, but incongruent placements that are not consistent with the plot affect brand attitudes *negatively* because they seem out of place.[84] On the other hand, a study of children concluded that product placement of snack products increased the snacking but did not alter brand attitude.[85] There may, however, be a growing discontent with product placement, as witnessed by the success of film-maker Morgan Spurlock and his film *The Greatest Movie Ever Sold*.[86] In all cases, product placement should be used with care. Based on experiments, researchers have argued that it does not take that much product placement to harm the host brand, even if the host brand is James Bond[87] (see Marketing pitfall below).

Other researchers found, however, that a small amount of product placement renders movies more popular, whereas beyond a certain limit it subtracts from the popularity. Consumers of mainstream films are also far more tolerant of product placement than consumers of independent movies.[88]

Marketing opportunity

Product placement may no longer be enough – now companies want to integrate the brands in the plot and dialogue. The year 2018 saw a 'groundbreaking attempt to blend advertising and editorial in an episode of the hit US sitcom *Black-ish,* which involved consumer goods firm Procter & Gamble paying for a plotline'.[89]

The problem may, of course, be that consumers of the series and movies start to consider the product an advertisement in itself, and hence maybe less worth watching. If the filmmakers have to twist the storylines in odd ways to make the brand fit in, then it may backfire. When Heineken attempted to interfere with a very established cultural formula, by making James Bond a beer drinker rather than staying a fan of the 'shaken-not-stirred' Dry-Martini (in *Skyfall*), it was actually not very well received by many fans but it also did not backfire to a largescale on the company. In the following movie *Spectre*, Mr Bond was back to a more classic vodka martini, since a sponsoring deal had been made between Sony and Belvedere Vodka.[90]

Marketing pitfall

Product placement can be so heavy that it almost takes attention away from the cultural product, the movie, itself. For example, product placement was already very visible in the first *Jurassic Park* movie back in 1993. But in the most recent sequel, *Jurassic World,* it has gone to unprecedented heights. As one source noted, 'kids ignore their parents while immersed in Beats by Dre headphones, parkgoers can be seen swilling Starbucks and the velociraptor trainer (played by Chris Pratt) takes a big, refreshing gulp of Coca-Cola. A Jurassic World visitor's pamphlet used as a movie prop is loaded with logos for FedEx Office, Coke, Starbucks and Samsung – the latter of which has its logo on every phone, tablet and TV, as well as the park's 'Samsung Innovation Center'. The dinosaur park's main shopping center includes a Pandora, the charm-jewellery store, and Jimmy Buffett's Margaritaville, the parrothead-themed restaurant.'[91] Maybe most featured of all is German car maker Mercedes-Benz, whose vehicles play central roles in several of the movie's most action-filled scenes.

As one film critic noted in her *New York Times* review, 'There are so many plugs for Mercedes that you may wonder if the targeted viewers are studio executives'.[92]

Here are a few further examples to illustrate the power of product placement:

- The Chinese talent programme *Lycra My Show* is partly funded by Invista, the maker of Lycra fabric, so contestants sing while wearing stretchy Lycra-based clothing. Also in China, Ford produced a *Survivor* clone called *Ford Maverick Beyond Infinity,* where 12 contestants on a tropical island hunt for treasure in a Ford Maverick sport utility vehicle, leap onto rafts while wearing Nike clothing and cool off with Nestlé drinks. Ford's marketing director in China noted, 'We really built the show around the product'.[93]
- Lady Gaga prominently showed off a Virgin Mobile phone, Miracle Whip dressing and several other brands in her hit video 'Telephone'.[94]

One of the newer types is product placement in blogs by highly influential young fashion and style bloggers. Certain fashion and cosmetics companies will send products to influential bloggers for 'testing' in the hope that this will lead to a promotion through the blog. Of course, this practice is risky business, since bloggers exist based on their being credible and savvy. Any suspicion that the blog is just another series of ads will be devastating. Still many bloggers do make a living out of this.

Marketing pitfall

Product placement can also be non-intended from the corporate perspective, and detrimental too. One little sentence in the blockbuster *Sideways* from 2004 virtually destroyed the American market for Merlot wines, 'If anybody's drinking Merlot, I'm outta here. I am not drinking any f . . . Merlot', exclaimed the self-designated wine connoisseur Miles in one scene in the movie. This led to a veritable flight from Merlot wines by American consumers and a lot of producers instead tried to sell their Merlot wines overseas – some even removed Merlot from their fields and started to plant other types of grapes.[95] This is a good example that marketers do not own their product or brand – that they are out there as signs in consumer culture, and culture producers (consumers or film-makers or others) can do with them what they want within the laws of copyright infringement.

As gaming goes mass market, marketers turn to **advergaming**, where online games merge with interactive advertisements that let companies target specific types of consumers. Clearly, computer gaming is not what it used to be. Not long ago, the typical players were scruffy teenage boys shooting at TV screens in their basements. But with the online gaming explosion of recent years, gamers have become a more sophisticated lot and are now more representative of the general population.

The mushrooming popularity of user-generated videos on YouTube and other sites creates a growing market to link ads to these sources as well. This strategy is growing so rapidly that there's even a new (trade-marked) term for it. Plinking™ is the act of embedding a product or service link in a video. Why is this medium one of the hottest things in the last decade?[96] Here's a few reasons:

- Compared to a 30-second TV spot, advertisers can get viewers' attention for a much longer time. Players spend an average of 5–7 minutes on an advergame site.

- Physiological measures confirm that players are highly focused and stimulated when they play a game.

- Marketers can tailor the nature of the game and the products in it to the profiles of different users. They can direct strategy games to upscale, educated users, while they gear action games to younger users.

Although it sounds like play, it is far from innocent. The advergaming practice has been accused of having very negative consequences – for instance, in terms of altering child gamers' eating habits to the worse due to product placement of fatty and salty products.[97] Studies of the **cultivation hypothesis**, which relates to media's ability to shape consumers' perceptions of reality, have shown that heavy television viewers tend to overestimate the degree of affluence in the country, and these effects also extend to such areas as perceptions of the amount of violence in one's culture.[98] Others have underlined the role of media and celebrity spokespersons – in this particular case David Beckham – in shaping children's moral attitudes.[99] Also, the depiction of consumer environments in programmes and advertisements may lead to further marginalisation of, for example, unemployed people, who cannot afford to buy into the depicted lifestyle,[100] or may lead to outright addicted consumers, who cannot refrain from constantly buying various goods even though they may not use them at all. However, as other researchers have shown, you can counter that by training children to be better at spotting product placement.[101]

The diffusion of innovations

13.2

New products, services and ideas spread through a population, and different types of people are more or less likely to adopt them.

New products and styles termed 'innovations' constantly enter the market. An **innovation** is any product or service that is perceived to be new by consumers. These new products or services occur in both consumer and industrial settings. Innovations may take the form of a clothing or fashion accessory style (such as Panda's eco-friendly bamboo watch[102]), a new manufacturing technique or a novel way to deliver a service.

If an innovation is successful (most are not), it spreads through the population. First it is bought and/or used by only a few people, and then more and more consumers decide to adopt it until, in some cases, it seems that almost everyone has bought or tried the innovation. Diffusion of innovations refers to the process whereby a new product, service or idea spreads through a population. There is a tendency for technical goods, especially, to diffuse more rapidly these days. The cell phone, PC and internet all spread far more rapidly than, for example, TV and radio, and far more rapidly than the use of, for example, aeroplanes and cars.[103] Furthermore, it has been argued that emotionally laden innovations (in this particular research, the products investigated related to funeral services) require lengthier adoption processes.[104]

Marketing opportunity

As the new millennium is maturing, the long-predicted tipping point where more consumers' access of the internet is done through mobile devices than through desktop computers has been reached – in late 2013 according to one source.[105] So, how do consumers search for product information?

Well, 48 per cent (still) start on search engines, but 33 per cent start on branded websites and 26 per cent directly on branded apps. The conclusion: branded apps are becoming increasingly important as informational devices for consumers.

Adopting innovations

A consumer's adoption of an innovation may resemble the decision-making sequence discussed earlier (see Chapter 8). The person moves through the stages of awareness, information search, evaluation, trial and adoption, although the relative importance of each stage may differ depending on how much is already known about a product,[106] as well as on cultural factors that may affect people's willingness to try new things.[107] A study of 11 European countries found that consumers in individualistic cultures are more innovative than consumers in collective cultures.[108]

One of the more curious large-scale product adoptions in recent history is the victorious introduction of bottled water in modern consumer markets, based on a variety of mythological beliefs about nature, purity, cleansing and health, as well as the increased demand for portable drinks in our highly mobile and efficient society. Notice, too, how we have also adopted the American habit of 'coffee-to-go' in Europe. In spite of the fact that numerous studies have demonstrated that in a lot of places there is no particular reason why we should drink bottled water rather than tap water, bottled water has become a symbol of the modern, healthy lifestyle. As the advertisement depicted below demonstrates, it has also become associated with particular cultural ways of life – in this case living the Italian way. In fact, as Table 13.4 demonstrates, the Mexicans were the world's leading consumers of bottled water in 2013, but a market such as Thailand has shown immense growth in the per capita consumption of bottled water, as have other emerging markets. This trend is obviously not just for consumers' good in terms of immediate access to clean water, since it is putting a lot of strain on a number of resources and creating a huge waste problem.[109]

Table 13.4 Global bottled water market: per capita consumption by leading countries 2008–13(P)

Rank	Countries	Gallons per capita	
		2008	**2013**
1	Mexico	56.6	67.3
2	Thailand	25.8	59.5
3	Italy	51.8	51.9
4	Belgium-Luxembourg	36.9	39.1
5	Germany	34.6	38.0
6	United Arab Emirates	27.0	37.3
7	France	34.5	36.5
8	United States	28.5	32.0
9	Spain	27.8	31.9
10	Hong Kong	21.3	31.2
11	Lebanon	28.7	29.8
12	Croatia	25.4	28.5
13	Slovenia	25.9	28.5
14	Hungary	28.2	28.4
15	Saudi Arabia	26.6	28.2
16	Switzerland	26.0	27.7
17	Austria	23.1	24.6
18	Poland	19.4	24.4
19	Brazil	19.7	23.9
20	Romania	18.7	22.6
	Global Average	7.8	9.9

Source: Beverage Marketing Corporation. http://www.bottledwater.org/public/2011%20BMC%20Bottled%20Water%20Stats_2.pdf\#overlay-context=economics/industry-statistics (accessed 5 September 2018).

However, even within the same culture, not all people adopt an innovation at the same rate. Some do so quite rapidly, and others never do at all. Consumers can be placed into approximate categories based upon the likelihood of adopting an innovation. The categories of adopters, shown in Figure 13.2, can be related to phases of the product life cycle concept used widely by marketing strategists.

As can be seen in Figure 13.2, roughly one-sixth of the population (innovators and early adopters) is very quick to adopt new products, and one-sixth of the people (laggards) is very slow. The other two-thirds are somewhere in the middle, and these majority adopters represent the mainstream public. In some cases people deliberately wait before adopting an innovation because they assume that its technological qualities will be improved, or that its price will fall after it has been on the market a while.[110] Keep in mind that the proportion of consumers falling into each category is an estimate; the actual size of each depends upon such factors as the complexity of the product, its cost and other product-related factors, and possibly also varies from country to country.

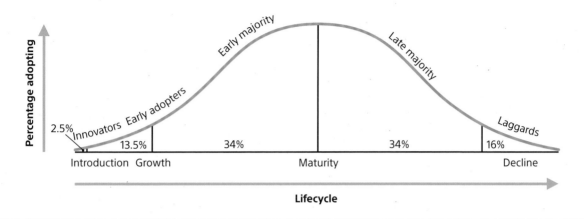

Figure 13.2 Types of adopters

Even though innovators represent only 2.5 per cent of the population, marketers are always interested in identifying them. According to standard theory, these are the brave souls who are always on the lookout for novel developments and will be the first to try a new offering. Just as generalised opinion leaders do not appear to exist, innovators tend to be category-specific. A person who is an innovator in one area may even be a laggard in another (cf. also the associated discussion about opinion leaders in Chapter 9). For example, someone who prides themselves on being at the cutting edge of fashion may have no conception of new developments in recording technology and stereo equipment.

Despite this qualification, some generalisations can be offered regarding the profile of innovators.[111] Not surprisingly they tend to have more favourable attitudes towards taking risks. They are also, at least in an American context, likely to have higher educational and income levels and to be socially active. However, in a European study of the fashion and clothing market, the same correlation between socio-demographic variables and innovative or early adopting behaviour could not be found.[112] On the other hand, a Spanish study, perhaps not surprisingly, concluded that innovators tend to be younger and, more interestingly, that publicity and advertisement would have the biggest influence on product adoption in the early years of commercialisation of a product, whereas word of mouth and other non-producer-controlled information becomes more important thereafter.[113]

How do we locate innovators? Ad agencies and market research companies are always on the prowl for people who are on top of developing trends. The internet bloggers, already mentioned quite a few times, YouTube, Facebook and other social media are of course an invaluable source. The agency DDB runs a service it calls SignBank, which collects thousands of snippets of information from its 13,000 employees around the world about cultural change in order to advise its clients on what it all means for them.[114]

Early adopters share many of the same characteristics as innovators, but an important difference is their degree of concern for social acceptance, especially with regard to expressive products such as clothing, cosmetics and so on. Generally speaking, an early adopter is receptive to new styles because they are involved in the product category and also place high value on being 'in fashion'. The universality of the dichotomy of innovators and adopters has been challenged by research pertaining to health foods, suggesting that (1) three groups can be distinguished (namely, innovators, more-involved adopters and less-involved adopters), and (2) there is not a big difference between the purchase rate of new products between innovators and adopters – rather, the difference lies in the kind of innovations tried and the approach to trying new products.[115] Table 13.5 gives a brief description of the different types of consumers and their approach to new product trials.

Table 13.5 Decision styles of market segments based on adoption, innovation and personal involvement

Adoption-decision process stage	Less-involved adopters	Innovators	More-involved adopters
Problem recognition	Passive, reactive	Active	Proactive
Search	Minimal, confined to resolution of minor anomalies caused by current consumption patterns	Superficial but extensively based within and across product-class boundaries	Extensive within relevant product category; assiduous exploration of all possible solutions within that framework
Evaluation	Meticulous, rational, slow and cautious; objective appraisal using tried-and-tested criteria	Quick, impulsive, based on currently accepted criteria; personal and subjective	Careful, confined to considerations raised by the relevant product category: but executed confidently and (for the adopter) briskly within that frame of reference
Decision	Conservative selection within known range of products, continuous innovations preferred	Radical: easily attracted to discontinuously new product class and able to choose quickly within it; frequent trial, followed by abandonment	Careful selection within a product field that has become familiar through deliberation, vicarious trial and sound and prudent pre-purchase comparative evaluation
Post-purchase evaluation	Meticulous, tendency to brand loyalty if item performs well	Less loyal; constantly seeking novel experiences through purchase and consumption innovations	Loyal if satisfied, but willing to try innovations within the prescribed frame of reference; perhaps tends towards dynamically continuous

Source: Gordon R. Foxall and Seema Bhate, 'Cognitive style and personal involvement as explicators of innovative purchasing of health food brands', *European Journal of Marketing* 27(2) (1993): 5–16. Used with permission.

Innovative companies understand the value of involving their most forward-thinking customers in business decisions before they introduce the final product. More than 650,000 customers tested a beta version of Microsoft Windows 2000. Many were even prepared to pay Microsoft a fee to do this because working with the program would help them understand how it could create value for their own businesses. The value of the research and development investment by customers to Microsoft was more than $500 million.

This approach is more prevalent in high-tech industries that consult their **lead users** about ideas; these are very experienced and knowledgeable customers. Indeed, it is common for these people to propose product improvements – because they have to live with the consequences. According to one estimate, users rather than manufacturers developed 70 per cent of the innovations in the chemical industry![116]

Types of innovations

Innovations can contain a technological level and involve some functional change (for example, car air bags), or be of a more intangible kind, communicating a new social meaning (such as a new hairstyle). However, contrary to what much literature states,[117] both are symbolic in the sense that one refers to symbols of technical performance and safety and the other to less tangible symbols, such as courage and individuality. Both types refer to symbols of progress.[118] New products, services and ideas have characteristics that determine the degree to which they will probably diffuse. Innovations that are more novel may be less likely to diffuse, since they require bigger changes in people's lifestyles and thus more effort. On the other hand, most innovations are close to being of the 'me too' kind, and thus do not necessarily possess qualities that would persuade the consumer to shift from existing product types. In any case, it should be noted that in spite of all the good intentions of the marketing concept to ensure that there is a market before the product is developed, the failure rate of new products is as high as ever, if not higher.[119]

Behavioural demands of innovations

Innovations can be categorised in terms of the degree to which they demand changes in behaviour from adopters. Three major types of innovation have been identified, though these three categories are not absolutes. They refer, in a relative sense, to the amount of disruption or change they bring to people's lives.

A **continuous innovation** refers to a modification of an existing product, as when a breakfast cereal is introduced in a sugar-coated version, or Levi's promoted 'shrink-to-fit' jeans. This type of change may be used to set one brand apart from its competitors. The launch of Coke Zero was one such continuous innovation, where the idea was to produce a sugar-free cola targeted to men, as opposed to the Diet Coke that was mainly popular among the female segment. This was the idea; however, in many countries, including Denmark, Coke Zero has gained as much popularity among women as the men.[120] Most product innovations are evolutionary rather than revolutionary. Small changes are made to position the product, add line extensions or merely to alleviate consumer boredom.

Consumers may be lured to the new product, but adoption represents only minor changes in consumption habits, since innovation perhaps adds to the product's convenience or to the range of choices available. A typewriter company, for example, many years ago modified the shape of its product to make it more user friendly. One simple change was the curving of the tops of the keys, a convention that was carried over on today's computer keyboards. One of the reasons for the change was that secretaries with long fingernails had complained about the difficulty of typing on flat surfaces.

A **dynamically continuous innovation** is a more pronounced change in an existing product, as represented by self-focusing cameras or touch-tone telephones. These innovations have a modest impact on the way people do things, creating some behavioural changes, although the touch-tone telephone is an expression of a larger innovation involving many discontinuous renewals of daily life: the digitalisation of communication. When introduced, the IBM electric typewriter, which used a 'golf ball' rather than individual keys, enabled typists to change the typeface of manuscripts simply by replacing one ball with another.

A **discontinuous innovation** creates major changes in the way we live. Major inventions, such as the aeroplane, the car, the computer and television have radically changed modern lifestyles, although, as can be seen from these examples, major changes normally take some time from the point of introduction. For people in the richer parts of the world, the personal computer has supplanted the typewriter, and it has created the phenomenon of 'telecommuters' by allowing many people to work from their homes. Of course, the cycle continues, as new innovations such as new versions of software are constantly being made; dynamically continuous innovations such as the 'mouse' and trackballs compete for adoption, and discontinuous innovations such as streaming video transmitted on cell phones start to appear in stores.

Marketing opportunity

There are mega trends pointing in the right direction in terms of alleviation of the climate crisis: the introduction of lab-grown meat and plant-based alternatives for meat and dairy products; the rise of renewable energy sources; the upsurge of electric cars and improved batteries for them; improved energy efficiency; and (more potential than real) reforestation. Tendencies worth keeping an eye on.[121] But a lot of efforts are put into technological solutions for more sustainable lifestyles that are a bit more into the future. Five technologies to watch out for seem to be: (1) transparent solar cells in the form of a thin film that can be put on glass; (2) bio-degradable batteries; (3) induction-charging cars that will 'charge as you go', solving the problem of reaching a charging station within the range of how far you can go on a full battery; (4) hydrogen-fuel cells that may make us skip the bio-fuel age rapidly before we even get to Doc Brown's compost-fuelled DeLorean; and (5) microgeneration boilers that simultaneously generate electricity and heat the house in a sustainable manner.[122] Of these projects, the biodegradable battery is probably the closest one to realisation here in 2018.

Prerequisites for successful adoption

Regardless of how much behavioural change is demanded by an innovation, several factors are desirable for a new product to succeed:[123]

- *Compatibility.* The innovation should be compatible with consumers' lifestyles. As an illustration, a manufacturer of personal care products tried unsuccessfully several years ago to introduce a hair-removal cream for men as a substitute for razors and shaving cream. This formulation was similar to that used widely by women to remove hair from their legs. Although the product was simple and convenient to use, it failed because men were not interested in a product they perceived to be too feminine and thus threatening to their masculine self-concepts.

- *Trialability.* Since an unknown is accompanied by high perceived risk, people are more likely to adopt an innovation if they can experiment with it prior to making a commitment. To reduce this risk, companies often choose the expensive strategies of distributing free 'trial-size' samples of new products. But trialability can also be a steady state of affairs. Apple stores are famous for the freedom they offer to walk in from the street and try their products, even without having to interact with staff members.

- *Complexity.* The product should be low in complexity. A product that is easier to understand and use will often be preferred to a competitor's. This strategy requires less effort from the consumer, and it also lowers perceived risk. Manufacturers of various apps, for example, have put a lot of effort into simplifying usage to encourage adoption.

- *Observability.* An innovation that is easily observable is more likely to spread, since this quality makes it more likely that other potential adopters will become aware of its existence. The rapid proliferation of coffee-on-the-go may be due to such observability factors – it was easy for others to see the convenience offered. The 'iconic whiteness' of the Apple iPod earplugs may also have played such a role.[124]

- *Relative advantage.* Most importantly, the product should offer relative advantage over alternatives. The consumer must believe that its use will provide a benefit that other products cannot offer. For example, the success of many environmentally friendly product alternatives may be due to the fact that, once consumers have been convinced about the environmental advantages of the product, it is a clear and easily understandable advantage compared to competing products.

Today, with new objects often coming with increased capacities in terms of being digitally interconnected with other objects – the so-called 'smart objects' and *Internet of Things* – new factors in terms of consumer resistance towards new stuff must also be considered. One recent study found that the most salient factors determining whether an innovation would be positively received or not was perceived uselessness (no real improvement), perceived price, intrusiveness (violating my privacy), perceived novelty (very different) and self-efficacy (degree to which it enables me to do things I couldn't do before).[125]

The social context of innovations

One critical but relatively little-researched aspect is the importance of the social context of product adoption behaviour.[126] This is linked to the importance of visibility of the product innovation as well as the influence of the reference group that is seen as related to the new product. As some researchers have suggested, the success of new products depends very much on their ability to being 'told' by marketers and consumers alike.[127] How well do they lend themselves to a good story? For example, Western products are admired in many contexts in Asia and Africa, or the marketising economies of Eastern Europe, for the sole reason of being linked to the status of the Western world, which is seen as 'better', more 'developed' and generally of a higher status.[128] Likewise, in Europe the association of new products with the American way of life will have a significant impact on the adopting behaviour of various groups in society, but will differ in different European countries. As a consequence, it is important to note that what is 'new' is not just an objective fact about a thing or a service but that 'newness' can change as it travels across users and contexts.[129]

Do you ever find that new products are being introduced at an ever-increasing speed? Well, you're not wrong, as historical analyses of technological innovations have shown.[130] A backside to the temporal dimension of innovation is the pitfall of being caught up in too many continuous innovations due to an ever-finer market segmentation and customisation approach. This may take resources away from more strategic considerations of changing 'the way things are done'.[131]

The fashion system

13.3

Fashion is organised as a cyclical cultural system that communicates symbolic meanings of imitation and differentiation to consumers.

The **fashion system**[132] consists of all those people and organisations involved in creating symbolic meanings and transferring these meanings to cultural goods. Although people tend to equate fashion with clothing, be it *haute couture* or street wear, it is important to keep in mind that fashion processes affect *all* types of cultural phenomena from the more mundane (what do you think of high-fashion nappy bags in unisex style?)[133] to high art, including music, art, architecture and even science (i.e. certain research topics and scientists are 'hot' at any point in time). Even business practices are subject to the fashion process; they evolve and change depending on which management techniques are in vogue, such as total quality management or 'the learning organisation'.

Fashion can be thought of as a *code,* or language, that helps us to decipher these meanings.[134] However, fashion seems to be *context-dependent* to a larger extent than language. That is, the same item can be interpreted differently by different consumers and in different situations.[135] In semiotic terms (see Chapter 3) the meaning of many products is *undercoded* – that is, there is no one precise meaning, but rather plenty of room for interpretation among perceivers. This said, remember the concept of iconic products from Chapter 12? Some products indeed have many potential meanings in different contexts, but there still seem to be a quite fundamental meaning that follows this product around and allows for a general analysis of this fashion object as a cultural item. This is true of, for example, the tissue of denim,[136] but maybe even more so for the global symbol of feminine elegance that high heels seem to constitute.[137]

At the outset, it may be helpful to distinguish between some confusing terms. **Fashion** is the process of social diffusion by which a new style is adopted by some group(s) of consumers. In contrast, *a fashion* (or style) refers to a particular combination of attributes. And, to be *in* *fashion* means that this combination is currently positively evaluated by some reference group. Thus, the term *Danish Modern* refers to particular characteristics of furniture design (i.e. a fashion in interior design); it does not necessarily imply that Danish Modern is a fashion that is currently desired by consumers.[138]

Collective selection

Fashions tend to sweep through countries; it seems that all of a sudden 'everyone' is doing the same thing or wearing the same styles. Some sociologists view fashion as a form of *collective behaviour,* or a wave of social conformity. How do so many people get tuned in to the same phenomenon at once, as happened with hip-hop styles? However, it has also been shown how fashion magazines were helpful in teaching women around the late nineteenth and early twentieth century to conceive of themselves as free and self-determining individuals.[139] We see here, again, how fashion is a process that links the macro-level cultural changes with micro-level individual behaviour.

Remember that creative subsystems within a cultural production system attempt to anticipate the tastes of the buying public. Despite their unique talents, members of this subsystem are also members of mass culture. Like the fashion magazine editors discussed earlier, cultural gatekeepers are drawing from a common set of ideas and symbols, and are influenced by the same cultural phenomena as the eventual consumers of their products.

The process by which certain symbolic alternatives are chosen over others has been termed **collective selection**.[140] As with the creative subsystem, members of the managerial and communications subsystems also seem to develop a common frame of mind. Although products within each category must compete for acceptance in the marketplace, they can usually be characterised by their adherence to a dominant theme or motif – be it the goth look, sixties nostalgia, the urban skater scene or New Nordic Cuisine.

Behavioural science perspectives on fashion

Fashion is a very complex process that operates on many levels. At one extreme, it is a macro, societal phenomenon affecting many people simultaneously. At the other, it exerts a very personal effect on individual behaviour. A consumer's purchase decisions are often motivated by their desire to be in fashion. Fashion products are aesthetic objects, and their origins are rooted in art and history. For this reason, there are many perspectives on the origin and diffusion of fashion. Although these cannot be described in detail here, some major approaches can be briefly summarised.[141]

Psychological models of fashion

Many psychological factors help to explain why people are motivated to be in fashion. These include conformity, variety-seeking, personal creativity and sexual attraction. For example, many consumers seem to have a 'need for uniqueness': they want to be different, but not too different.[142] For this reason, people often conform to the basic outlines of a fashion, but try to improvise and make a personal statement within these guidelines.

One of the earliest theories of fashion proposed that 'shifting **erogenous zones**' accounted for fashion changes. Different parts of the female body are the focus of sexual interest, and clothing styles change to highlight or hide these parts. For example, people in the Victorian era found shoulders exciting, a 'well-turned ankle' was important at the beginning of the twentieth century, while the back was the centre of attention in the 1930s.

While these shifts may be due to boredom, some have speculated that there are deeper reasons for changes in focus; body areas symbolically reflect social values. In medieval times, for example, a rounded belly was desirable. This preference was most likely a reflection of

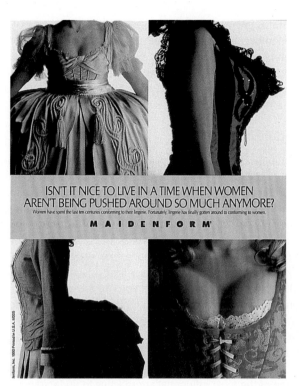

ISN'T IT NICE TO LIVE IN A TIME WHEN WOMEN AREN'T BEING PUSHED AROUND SO MUCH ANYMORE?

Women have spent the last ten centuries conforming to their lingerie. Fortunately, lingerie has finally gotten around to conforming to women.

M A I D E N F O R M

This ad for Maidenform illustrates that fashions have accentuated different parts of the female anatomy throughout history. The underlying premise is that today (thanks to Maidenform!) we can look 'natural'. What do you think about this underlying premise – aren't women's bodies pushed around anymore?

the fact that multiple pregnancies were necessary to maintain population growth in an age when infant mortality was high. Interest in the female leg in the 1920s and 1930s coincided with women's new mobility and independence, while the exposure of breasts in the 1970s signalled a renewed interest in breastfeeding.[143] Breasts were de-emphasised in the 1980s as women concentrated on careers, but some analysts have theorised that a larger bust size is now more popular as women try to combine professional activity with child-rearing. Now, some suggest that the current prevalence of the exposed midriff reflects the premium our society places on fitness.[144] It is important to note that until very recently, the study of fashion focused almost exclusively on its impact on women. More recently, consumer researchers have started to focus also on fashion consumers among other groups. First and foremost, men are not exempt from being 'fashion victims', and the rise of the 'metrosexual man'[145] has underlined, for marketers as well as for researchers, the importance of gaining insight into male fashion consumption.

Psychological research suggests that it is possible to distinguish between two different personality types, respectively more- or less-sensitive to the opinion of their social surroundings (also called high and low self-monitors). The high self-monitors have been demonstrated to stress the brand of a consumer good (specifically clothing) more than low self-monitors, who are, on the other hand, more positive to functional product attributes.[146]

Economic models of fashion

Economists approach fashion in terms of the model of supply and demand. Items that are in limited supply have high value, while those readily available are less desirable. Rare items command respect and prestige.

Veblen's notion of conspicuous consumption (see Chapter 11) proposed that the wealthy consume in order to display their prosperity – for example, by wearing expensive (and at times impractical) clothing. The functioning of conspicuous consumption seems more complex in today's society, since wealthy consumers often engage in *parody display,* where they deliberately adopt formerly low-status or inexpensive products, such as jeeps or jeans. On the other hand, new hierarchies develop between generic jeans, signalling a traditional, work-oriented, classless or lower-class environment, and designer jeans expressing an urban, upmarket, class-distinctive and more contemporary lifestyle.[147] Other factors also influence the demand curve for fashion-related products. These include a *prestige-exclusivity effect,* where high prices still create high demand, and a *snob effect,* where lower prices actually reduce demand.[148]

Sociological models of fashion

The collective selection model discussed previously is an example of a sociological approach to fashion. This perspective focuses on a subculture's adoption of a fashion (idea, style, etc.) and its subsequent diffusion into society as a whole. This process often begins with youth subcultures, such as the hip-hop segment. Another current example is the integration of Goth culture into the mainstream. This fashion started as an expression of rebellion by young outcasts who admired nineteenth-century romantics and who defied conventional styles with their black clothing (often including over-the-top fashion statements such as Count Dracula capes, fishnet stockings, studded collars and black lipstick) and punk music from bands such as Siouxsie & the Banshees and Bauhaus. Today, you can buy vampire-girl lunchboxes, and mall outlets sell tons of clunky cross jewellery and black lace, and the success of the *Twilight* series has all but mainstreamed this counter-culture. Hard-core Goths are not amused, but hey, that's fashion for you.[149]

In addition, much attention has been focused on the relationship between product adoption and class structure. The **trickle-down theory**, first proposed in 1904 by Georg Simmel, has been one of the most influential approaches to understanding fashion. It states that there are two conflicting forces that drive fashion change. First, subordinate groups try to adopt the status symbols of the groups above them as they attempt to climb up the ladder of social mobility. Dominant styles thus originate with the upper classes and *trickle down* to those below. However, this is where the second force comes into play: those people in the super-ordinate groups are constantly looking below them on the ladder to ensure that they are not imitated. They respond to the attempts of lower classes to 'impersonate' them by adopting even *newer* fashions. These two processes create a self-perpetuating cycle of change – the engine that drives fashion.[150]

The trickle-down theory was quite useful for understanding the process of fashion changes when applied to a society with a stable class structure, which permitted the easy identification of lower- versus upper-class consumers. This task is not so easy in modern times. In contemporary Western society, this approach must be modified to account for new developments in mass culture:[151]

- A perspective based on class structure cannot account for the wide range of styles that are simultaneously made available in our society. Modern consumers have a far greater degree of individualised choice than in the past because of advances in technology and distribution. Just as an adolescent is almost instantly aware of the latest style trends by watching reality shows on TV, elite fashion has been largely replaced by mass fashion, since media exposure permits many groups to become aware of a style at the same time. Stores such as Zara and H&M can replenish their inventories in weeks rather than months, and the 'fast-fashion' market has become the fastest growing within the clothing sector.[152]

- Consumers tend to be more influenced by opinion leaders who are similar to them. As a result, each social group has its own fashion innovators who determine fashion trends. It is often more accurate to speak of a trickle-across effect, where fashions diffuse horizontally among members of the same social group.[153]

- In times of individualism, standing out is just as important as fitting in. Style reflexivity and confirmation of one's individuality have become crucial parts of the contemporary fashion scene, in particular among youngsters.[154] We try to resolve this paradox, that you have to confirm your individuality at the same time as you want to avoid being an outcast, by making stories for ourselves that we wear – 'what we like to wear' and what 'expresses who we are', rather than what is dictated by fashion.[155] Essentially, as another study demonstrated, fashion consumers are able to follow the Dr Martens slogan: 'We make the shoes, you make the story'.[156]

- Anybody who has been on a skiing holiday will have noticed the subcultural fashions demonstrated among the skiers. In fact, more and more consumption-based subcultures, sailing enthusiasts for instance, adopt their own fashions in order to reinforce their community feeling and distinguish themselves from outsiders.[157]

- Subcultural fashions are also expressed through the variation in ethnic populations. This is not only true in terms of migrants from the Middle East, Asia or Africa, but also among different but neighbouring ethnic populations, for example, Russians and Estonians in Estonia, where ethnic and subcultural identity can be expressed through fashion.[158]

- Finally, current fashions often originate with the lower classes and trickle up. Grassroots innovators are typically people who lack prestige in the dominant culture (such as urban youth). Since they are less concerned with maintaining the status quo, they are more free to innovate and take risks.[159] Whatever the direction of the trickling, one thing is sure: fashion is always a complex process of variation, of imitation and differentiation, of adoptions and rejections in relation to one's social surroundings.[160]

This blurring of the origins of fashion has been attributed to the condition of postmodernity when there is no fashion, only fashions, and no rules, only choices,[161] and where the norms and rules can no longer be dictated solely by the *haute couture* or other cultural gatekeepers but where the individual allows themselves more freedom in creating a personal look by mixing elements from different styles.[162] This obviously has the consequence that the relatively linear models of fashion cycles discussed below become less able to predict actual fashion developments.[163]

A French researcher followed the development in the editorial content of a French fashion magazine since 1945. It turned out that the content became more global and less 'French' over the years, but also that the magazine gradually shifted away from dictating one certain fashion style at each point in time, to an approach in the 1990s where several styles were promoted in each issue and consumers were invited to mix and match and create their own personal style independently of high fashion.[164] Swedish retailer H&M has been pioneering the blurring of high and low fashion through their collections in collaboration with, for example, Jimmi Choo and Karl Lagerfeld. A similar blurring of high and low fashion was demonstrated by a prize-winning campaign, where a charity organisation used former international top model Renee Toft Simonsen for promoting clothes from their second-hand shops.[165] Neither she nor the agency received any payment for their participation. Some British fashion-hungry women go to *swishing parties* – a kind of clothes-swapping meeting, where the participants can nibble a little something to eat and sip a glass of wine while checking out the garments brought by other participants. The VISA corporation has stepped in with an organising principle, securing points given for what you hand in, and those can then be used for taking away clothes. This ensures that the swapping does not end up in chaos and free-riding behaviour, but becomes a true fashion event. Hence, your access is dependent on bringing a clean, good-quality garment, or shoes, that has just spent a little too much time in the wardrobe. This is both economical and environmental, underline the patrons. A total of 900,000 tons of clothing and shoes are thrown away each year in the UK. A swishing party allows people to recycle and embellish themselves at the same time – and it is a cosy event where they meet new friends who are also into fashion.[166]

Swishing parties are popular among female British fashion consumers.

keith morris/Alamy Stock Photo

Multicultural dimensions

What do you think of invisible fashion? The particular use of fashion in the Middle East is a phenomenon that has evoked increasing interest among consumer researchers. The simultaneous demands of fashionable conspicuousness and religious piety and modesty lead female fashion consumers to negotiate a particular type of 'layering' through which the fashionable and 'sexy' clothes are hidden behind what is morally deemed appropriate public attire. But, as indicated, this does not prevent women in the Gulf States from wearing a lot of highly expensive fashion clothing in private contexts and underneath their *abayas.* By exercising modesty and vanity at the same time, these women can 'have their cake and eat it'[167] – or what do you think? Such dressing may be one way of compensating for the lack of access to overt expression of female sexuality and dating rituals – they simply manifest and exert their femininity and seductiveness through a different practice.[168]

The fashion system, then, is becoming increasingly complex. Brands may be very significant to consumers and they may be less ashamed to admit that than previously, but they are less committed to any one brand over a longer period. The fashion industry is trying to compensate for this by overexposing their brands, putting the brand name very conspicuously all over clothing, bags, accessories, etc. in order to get a maximum exposure out of the 'catch'.[169] The fashion industry is also exploring the individual styles for new market opportunities and new meanings of fashion goods for wider distribution.[170] Even those trying to rebel against fashion dictates by turning to ugliness as a motif for their choice of 'look' cannot escape. Ugliness in a variety of forms is becoming increasingly fashionable; as one consumer said: 'These shoes were so ugly I just had to have them'.[171]

An institutional model of fashion

Recently, it has become increasingly common to consider fashion from an institutional angle. This means that fashion is not considered a simple innovation process and subsequent distribution, but a more complex set of organisations that work together to solve a set of issues or problems that are deemed important for social and/or individual well-being. Fashion as an institution is obviously tightly interwoven with the marketing institution.[172] Key issues in such an institutional perspective are:[173]

- *Legitimacy*: which kinds of acts and actors are deemed appropriate within a field, such as fashion?
- *Institutional logics*: these define the content and meaning of institutions. Usually, it is assumed that the key logics in fashion are the institutional logics of art and commerce.[174]
- *Institutional work*: this is indicative of how processes unfold in the institution. For example, in the fashion scene, who does what, how and when?
- *Institutional boundaries*: these help to define what is inside an institution and what is outside – or, in this case, what is included and not included in fashion processes.

Such an approach has been used to demonstrate how some consumers can feel excluded from the institution and thus the market, almost as if it was a result of a classical apartheid system. One study studied fat or overweight women and their frustrations with the offerings of the fashion producers and their brand and product policies, not allowing these larger-sized consumers a place in the market. As a consequence, these women feel that they cannot be part of the fashion institution, something which is deemed important for your social- and self-esteem in a current consumer culture.[175] What this study also showed, was that consumers are increasingly playing (or trying to play) a role in the formation of fashion, similar to what we discussed under the term 'megaphone effect' earlier. The inclusion of such 'connected consumers' in the market formation processes may alter fundamentally the way the fashion market functions as an institution.[176]

Marketing opportunity

A *knock-off* is a style that has been deliberately copied and modified, often with the intent to sell to a larger or different market. *Haute couture* clothing styles presented by top designers in Paris and elsewhere are commonly 'knocked off' by other designers and sold to the mass market. The Web is making it easier than ever for firms to copy these designs – in some cases so quickly that their pirated styles appear in stores at the same time as the originals. Design company Balenchiaga is making a point out of blending well-known brand designs with a slight twist into, for example, their t-shirts. Brands are becoming such a strong cultural marker, that anything vaguely familiar is useful, even for other strong brands.[177] Isn't imitation the sincerest form of flattery? But it doesn't end there. . . if you can't beat them join them. A pop-up fashion store opened in New York in early 2018 replete with Deisel wear. Alright, the order of the e and the I was inverse, but otherwise the models of all kinds of garments were awfully close to the original. . . and the price was about a third of the regular Diesel brand. Did Diesel come after these knock-off villains? Nope. . . it was all created by Diesel. If we are to be knocked off, we might as well do it ourselves. . .[178]

Cycles of fashion adoption

In 1997, a little digital animal swept across the planet. After enjoying considerable success in Japan in 1996 with about three million units sold, it spread throughout the world during 1997 where its population by the summer had increased to a total of seven million (with approximately twice that number in back orders). The *Tamagochi,* as it was known, was an electronic pet that must be nurtured, played with and taken care of, just like a living being. Failure to do so meant that it would weaken and show signs of maltreatment until it eventually died. That is, in the Japanese version it died. This unhappy ending did not appeal to Americans, who therefore created their own version where it flies off to another planet if not treated well. Needless to say, the Japanese 'authentic' versions quickly became collectors' items (see the discussion of collections in the previous chapter). Today, many consumers might not know what a Tamagochi is, but anybody with children will know what a Pokémon is. Even the Pokémon were disappearing, when the little creatures went through a great revival thanks to the Pokémon Go app.[179]

The stories of the Tamagochi or the Pokémon or the Pokémon Go – or indeed many other brands – show how quickly a consumer craze can catch on globally. Although the longevity of a particular style can range from a month to a century, fashions tend to flow in a predictable sequence. The **fashion life cycle** is quite similar to the more familiar product lifecycle. An item or idea progresses through basic stages from birth to death, as shown in Figure 13.3.

Variations in fashion life cycles

The diffusion process discussed earlier in this chapter is intimately related to the popularity of fashion-related items. To illustrate how this process works, consider how the **fashion acceptance cycle** works in the popular music business. In the *introduction stage,* a song is listened to by a small number of music innovators. It may be played in clubs or on 'cutting-edge' radio stations, which is exactly how 'grunge rock' groups such as Nirvana got their start. During the *acceptance stage,* the song enjoys increased social visibility and acceptance by large segments of the population. A record

The revived coolness of the vinyl record is used by a vodka producer to make a local statement about the coolness of a particular neighborhood in Berlin (and of course the coolness of the Absolut brand). A particular local use of this long-lasting and highly popular campaign, using the shape of the Absolut bottle in all kinds of contexts.

Agencja Fotograficzna Caro/Alamy Stock Photo

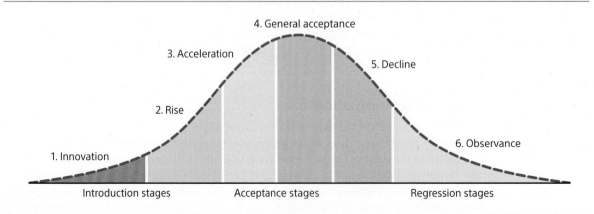

Figure 13.3 A normal fashion cycle

Source: Susan Kaiser, *The Social Psychology of Clothing* (New York: Macmillan, 1985).

may get wide airplay on 'Top-40' stations, steadily rising up the charts 'like a bullet'. This process may, of course, be supported or even generated by marketing efforts from the record company.

In the *regression stage,* the item reaches a state of social saturation as it becomes overused, and eventually it sinks into decline and obsolescence as new songs rise to take its place. A hit record may be played once an hour on a Top-40 station for several weeks. At some point, though, people tend to get sick of it and focus their attention on newer releases. The former hit record stagnates in terms of the downloads and the number of plays on Spotify. A neat division into such stages, however, is challenged by the internet, where the development may be so rapid that the stages are hardly distinguishable anymore (think of Justin Bieber's road to fame). Likewise, retro-marketing and retro-styles ensure that not all 'old stuff' disappears into oblivion.

Not everybody shares the same musical tastes. Nor, as we discussed above, is everybody necessarily influenced by the same fashion in clothing anymore. As society may become more characterised by lifestyles than by generalisable consumption patterns spreading through social classes, as in the class-based fashion models, the social groups in question may consist more of a particular lifestyle than actual social classes. For example, one may distinguish generally between the more risk-prone and the more prudent fashion consumers, and each of these two groups have their own independent fashion cycles that do not necessarily influence the other groups.[180]

Figure 13.4 illustrates that fashions are characterised by slow acceptance at the beginning, which (if the fashion is to 'make it') rapidly accelerate and then taper off. Different classes of fashion can be identified by considering the relative length of the fashion acceptance cycle. While many fashions exhibit a moderate cycle, taking several years to work their way through the stages of acceptance and decline, others are extremely long lived or short lived.

A **classic** is a fashion with an extremely long acceptance cycle. It is in a sense 'anti-fashion', since it guarantees stability and low risk to the purchaser for a long period of time. One anthropologist reflected on the continued success of 'the little black dress' (introduced by Coco Chanel in the early twentieth century) and concluded that this type of dress was a classic exactly because there were so many contemporary possibilities of dressing up – including a number of ways that would be inappropriate – that in a lot of situations it remains nice for the women to have something tried and tested – a classic – to fall back upon.[181]

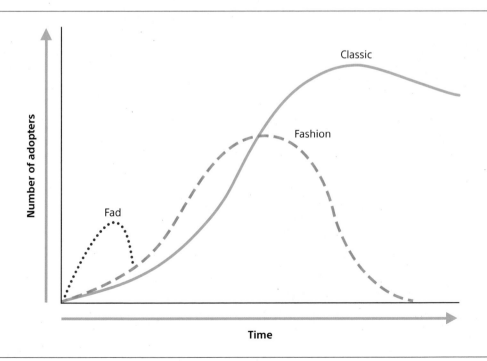

Figure 13.4 Comparison of the acceptance cycle of fads, fashions and classics

A **fad** is a very short-lived fashion. Fads are usually adopted by relatively few people. Adopters may all belong to a common subculture, and the fad 'trickles across' members but rarely breaks out of that specific group.[182] Indeed, others are likely to ridicule the fad (which may add fuel to the fire). For example, a pair of researchers recently studied adults who resisted the Harry Potter craze. They found some of these consumers avoid the Hogwarts world because they pride themselves on 'not being taken in'. These adults react negatively to the 'evangelical' enthusiasts who try to convert them to fandom. They recount the resentment of one newlywed on her honeymoon (as related in an essay by her new husband): 'My new page-turning obsession did not go down too well with my new life partner. When on our first night in the Maldives and expecting some form of conjugal rites [she found] herself in second place to a fictional 11-year-old trainee wizard and something called the Sorting Hat'.[183]

Fads are not 'one size fits all' in terms of spread and impact. Figure 13.5 illustrates different types of fads. However, whatever the fad cycle, some key characteristics of fads include:

- the fad is non-utilitarian – that is, it does not perform any explicit purpose function;
- the fad is often adopted on impulse; people do not undergo stages of rational decision-making before joining in;
- the fad diffuses rapidly, gains quick acceptance and is short lived.

How do you tell whether a fad is 'true', 'cyclical' or one of the other types? For example, experts are discussing whether the current interest in Scandinavian food in the UK is a short-lived fad (since it does not come with the same imagery of a lifestyle to support it as, for example, Mediterraenean food) or whether it will last longer, based on the new Scandinavian cuisine's striving for what is natural and seasonal.[184] The interest in Scandinavian food has been sparked by the celebration of Scandinavian chefs and restaurants at world competitions, but possibly also due to the media exposure of Scandinavian culture through a set of highly popular TV series, including *The Killing,*

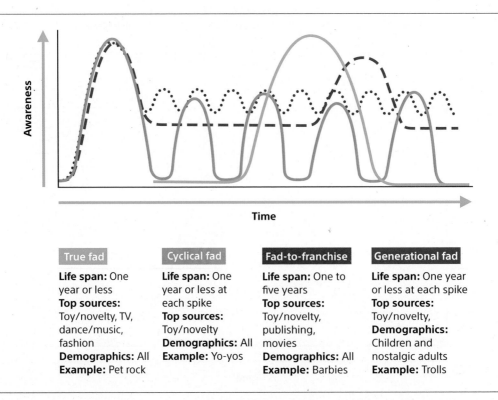

Figure 13.5 The behaviour of fads

The Bridge and *Borgen*. Distinguishing between fads or more lasting tendencies of change is not easy, and many consulting agencies make a living out of being trend-spotters. However, here are a few points that may be helpful in distinguishing short-lived fads from longer-lasting innovations:[185]

- *Does it fit with basic lifestyle changes*? If a new hairstyle is hard to care for, this innovation will not be consistent with women's increasing time demands. On the other hand, the movement to shorter-term holidays is more likely to last because this innovation makes trip planning easier for harried consumers.

- *What are the benefits*? The switch to leaner meats and cuts came about because these meats are perceived as healthier, so a real benefit is evident.

- *Can it be personalised*? Enduring trends tend to accommodate a desire for individuality, whereas styles such as mohawk haircuts or the grunge look are inflexible and do not allow people to express themselves.

- *Is it a trend or a side effect*? An increased interest in exercise is part of a basic trend towards health consciousness, although the specific form of exercise that is 'in' at any given time will vary (e.g. low-impact aerobics *vs* inline skating).

- *What other changes have occurred in the market*? Sometimes the popularity of products is influenced by carry-over effects. The miniskirt fad in the 1960s brought about a major change in the hosiery market, as sales of tights grew from 10 per cent of this product category to more than 80 per cent in two years. Now, sales of these items are declining due to the casual emphasis in dressing.

- *Who has adopted the change*? If the innovation is not adopted by working mothers, baby boomers or some other important market segment, it is not likely to become a trend.

Acculturation processes

Acculturation is the process whereby consumers adapt to living in a new cultural setting. This process not only influences those consumers migrating, but also the consumers already living in the host culture.

We will address one final important process of social change that is relevant for many marketers and consumers in this age of global movement. We term the process of learning the values, beliefs and behaviours endorsed by one's own culture **enculturation**.[186] In contrast, we call the process of learning the value system and behaviours of another culture (often a priority for those who wish to understand consumers and markets in foreign countries) **acculturation**.[187] Acculturation is the process of movement and adaptation to one country's cultural environment by a person from another country.[188] This is a very important issue for marketers because of our increasingly global society. In 2017, the total population within EU28 alone was estimated at nearly 512 million.[189] In 2015, nearly five million people immigrated to the EU.[190]

As people move from place to place, they may quickly assimilate to their new homes, or they may resist this blending process and choose to insulate themselves from the mainstream culture. One important way to distinguish between members of a subculture is to consider the extent to which they retain a sense of identification with their country of origin *vs* their host country.

As Figure 13.6 shows, many factors affect the nature of this transition process. Individual differences, such as whether the person speaks the host-country language, influence how difficult the adjustment will be. The person's contacts with **acculturation agents** – people and institutions that teach the ways of a culture – are also crucial. Some of these agents are aligned with the *culture of origin*. These include family, friends, religious institutions, local businesses and heritage language media that keep the consumer in touch with their country of origin. Other agents are associated with the *culture of immigration* (e.g. one of the EU28 countries), and help the consumer to learn how to navigate in the new environment, including such institutions as schools and the media, in the host culture's language. Media is an important socialisation agent. We learn a lot about a culture's priorities by looking at the values communicated by advertising.

As immigrants adapt to their new surroundings, several processes come into play. *Movement* refers to the factors motivating people to uproot themselves physically from one location and go to another. On arrival, immigrants encounter a need for *translation.* This means attempting to master a set of rules for operating in the new environment, whether learning how to decipher a different currency or understanding the social meanings of unfamiliar clothing styles. This cultural learning leads to a process of *adaptation,* where new consumption patterns are formed. A study of Romanian women in Italy, and their food consumption practices, for instance, identified the different strategies that they employed 'to negotiate the traditional gender script based on the dominant discourses in their home culture, and the modern woman myth featured in the marketplace representations in the host culture'.[191]

As consumers experience acculturation, several things happen. Many immigrants undergo (at least to some extent) *assimilation,* where they adopt products, habits and values that are identified with the mainstream culture. At the same time, there is an attempt at *maintenance* of practices associated with the culture of origin. Immigrants stay in touch with people in their country, and many continue to eat ethnic foods and read ethnic newspapers. Their continued identification with their home culture may cause *resistance,* as they resent the pressure to submerge their identities and take on new roles. Finally, immigrants (voluntarily or not) tend to exhibit *segregation;* they are likely to live and shop in places physically separated from the host community. Figure 13.6 provides an overview of the processes involved in consumer acculturation. Research evidence argues against the notion that assimilation necessarily involves losing identification with the person's original group. The best indicator of assimilation, these researchers argue, is the extent to which members of a minority group have social interactions with members of other ethnic groups in comparison with their own.[192]

The progressive learning model helps us to understand the acculturation process. This perspective assumes that people gradually learn a new culture as they increasingly come into contact with it. Thus, we expect that when people acculturate they will mix the practices of

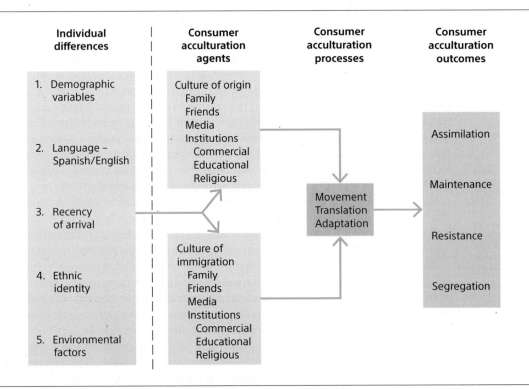

Figure 13.6 A model of consumer acculturation

Source: Adapted from Lisa Peñaloza, '*Atravesando fronteras*/border crossings: A critical ethnographic exploration of the consumer acculturation of Mexican immigrants', *Journal of Consumer Research* 21(1) (1994): 32–54. Copyright © 1994, Oxford University Press by permission of Oxford University Press.

their original culture with those of their new or **host culture**.[193] Research that examines such factors as shopping orientation, the importance people place on various product attributes, media preference and brand loyalty generally supports this pattern.[194] When researchers take into account the intensity of ethnic identification, they find that consumers who retain a strong ethnic identification differ from their more assimilated counterparts in these ways:[195]

- they have a more negative attitude towards business in general (probably caused by frustration as a result of relatively low income levels);
- they are higher users of media that is in their native language;
- they are more brand loyal;
- they are more likely to prefer brands with prestige labels;
- they are more likely to buy brands that specifically advertise to their ethnic group.

There is also evidence that for second-generation citizens, their 'ethic identification tends to decrease even as their cultural affiliation continues to inform their consumption'.[196,197] The acculturation process thus embraces all kinds of moves, including those that involve relocating from one place to another within the same country. If you have ever moved (and it is likely you have), you no doubt remember how difficult it was to give up old habits and friends and adapt to what people in your new location do. A recent study of Turkish people who move from the countryside to an urban environment illustrates how people cope with change and unfamiliar circumstances. The authors describe a process of *warming,* which involves transforming objects and places into those that feel cosy, hospitable and authentic. The study's informants described what happened when they tried to turn a cold and unfamiliar house into a home as *güzel* ('beautiful and good', 'modern and warm'). In this context, that means incorporating symbols of village life into their new homes by blanketing them with the embroidered, crocheted and lace textiles that people traditionally make by hand for brides' dowries in the villages. The researchers reported that migrants' homes contained far more of these pieces than they would have in their village homes because they used them to adorn the modern appliances they acquired. These dowry textiles symbolise traditional norms and social networks composed of friends and family in the villages, so they link the 'cold' modern objects with the owner's past. Thus, the unfamiliar becomes familiar.[198]

Of course, it's not unusual for consumers who don't belong to a subculture to use products they associate with that group. De-ethnicisation occurs when a product we link to a specific ethnic group detaches itself from its roots and appeals to other groups as well. Think about the popularity of croissants across Western Europe; and different types of Italian coffee across all of Europe.

Another group of researchers examined the plight of people who were forced to leave their homes and settle in a foreign country with little planning and few possessions.[199] As 'strangers in a strange land', they must essentially start all over again and completely re-socialise. The authors did an in-depth study of refugees from a number of countries who lived in an Austrian refugee shelter. They found that teenagers are traumatised by their experience and turn to adaptive consumption strategies to cope. For example, the adolescents (including the boys) all had stuffed animals they used to comfort themselves. And all of the teenage boys wore earrings as a way to create their own community.

An ethnographic study of Turkish women squatters has proposed a new model, dominated consumer acculturation (see Figure 13.7), in contrast to the model of postmodern consumer acculturation covered by earlier research. The goal of these authors was to identify the role played by particular sociocultural structures in acculturation by examining Turkish women peasants who were part of the widespread global phenomenon of mass migration of the rural poor into urban areas. In contrast to earlier studies, this research allowed for a more contextual model of acculturation, which took account of the variety of acculturation outcomes. This model proposed 'three modes of acculturation structured by this context: migrants reconstitute their village culture in the city, shutting out the dominant ideology; or

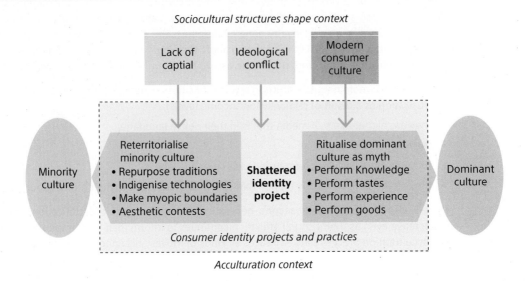

Figure 13.7 Dominated consumer acculturation

Source: Tuba Ustuner and Douglas B. Holt, 'Dominated consumer acculturation: The Social Construction of Migrant Women's Consumer Identity Projects in a Turkish Squatter', *Journal of Consumer Research* 34 (June 2007) Figure 2.53. *The Journal of Consumer Research* by American Association for Public Opinion Research. Reproduced with permission of University of Chicago Press.

they collectively pursue the dominant ideology as a myth through ritualised consumption; or they give up on both pursuits, resulting in a shattered identity project'.[200]

More recently, research has synthesised a series of studies of the intricate processes involved in migrants' 'sociocultural adaptation to unfamiliar economic (income, status), biological (food, health), physical (urbanization), social (family, friendships, discrimination), and cultural (clothing, religion, language) conditions'.[201] This offers an alternative modelling of consumer acculturation processes (see Figure 13.8), which captures 'the sociocultural discourses, consumption practices, and resources that affect how locals and migrants construct their identities in a circle of mutual observation, translation, and recreation of discourses and practices [symbolised by the outer arrows]. Rather than adopting an individualist or in-group-centric perspective, this model focuses on co-constitutive social relations mediated by consumption and communication. . . For example, most industrialized societies have cemented discourses of multiculturalism and integration into their constitutions, political programmes, moral norms, and brands. But they also produce more local and ephemeral, but nonetheless influential discourses of xenophobia, segregation, and discrimination[202] that affect the cultural adaptation system (see upper boxes [in Figure 13. 8]). . . The model equally highlights the importance of studying consumption behaviours of migrants and locals that translate these discourses into practices (lower boxes [in Figure 13.8]). . . This alternative conceptualization no longer models acculturation as a progressive, directed process of culture learning but as a circular system of mutual observation and adaptation, [so that] cultural adaptation is no longer a question of voluntary decision-making but is rather an inescapable fact for all parties. The globalizing consumer cultures thrive on constant change, innovation, fashion, and variation[203] and migrants and locals become co-producers of meanings and practices that affect brand meanings, and the social desirability of goods.'[204]

In the most recent model of acculturation, we move beyond the perspective of the immigrant to incorporate the perspective of the local community into our understanding of acculturation. From this perspective, consumer acculturation is redefined as 'a relational, interactive adaptation process that involves not only immigrant consumption practices but also indigenes who interpret and adjust to these practices, thereby shaping the paths of possibility for mutual adaptation'.[205]

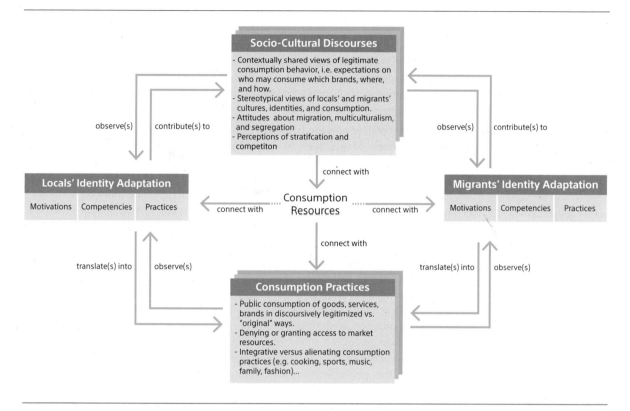

Figure 13.8 A model of recursive consumer cultural adaptation to migration

Source: Marius K. Luedicke, 'Consumer acculturation theory: (crossing) conceptual boundaries', *Consumption Markets & Culture* 14(3) (2011): 239, Figure 2.

Acculturation now becomes about the adjustments that both communities (immigrant and host) make, involving 'those phenomena that occur when consumers (immigrants or indigenes) adjust their established consumption practices, brand relationships, territorial claims, status hierarchies, and (collective) identities to their evolving relationships to consumers from unfamiliar national, social, or cultural backgrounds'.[206] We are all influenced by migration in our consumption practices and in the way goods and practices become meaningful to us (discourses), whether we stay put and acculturate or go away and acculturate.

Chapter summary

Now that you have finished reading this chapter you should understand why:

13.1 Cultural change can be seen as an outcome of a production system including many agents. The styles prevalent in a culture at any point in time often reflect underlying political and social conditions. The set of agents responsible for creating stylistic alternatives is termed a cultural production system. Factors such as the types of people involved in this system and the amount of competition from alternative product forms influence the choices that eventually make their way to the marketplace for consideration by end consumers. Culture is often described in terms of high (or elite) forms and low (or popular) forms. Products of popular culture tend to follow a cultural formula and contain predictable components. On the other hand, these distinctions are blurring in modern society as imagery from 'high art' is increasingly being incorporated into marketing efforts, and marketed products (or even marketing products such as advertisements) are treated and evaluated as high art. Many modern marketers are reality engineers. Reality engineering occurs when marketers appropriate elements of popular culture to use in their promotional strategies. These elements include sensory and spatial aspects of everyday existence, whether in the form of products that appear in movies, scents pumped into offices and stores, billboards, theme parks, or video monitors attached to shopping carts.

13.2 **New products, services and ideas spread through a population, and different types of people are more- or less-likely to adopt them.** A consumer's decision to adopt a new item depends on their personal characteristics (if they are inclined to try new things) and on the characteristics of the item. Products sometimes stand a better chance of being adopted if they demand relatively little change in behaviour from consumers and are compatible with current practices. They are also more likely to diffuse if they can be tested prior to purchase, if they are not complex, if their use is visible to others and, most importantly, if they provide a relative advantage vis-à-vis existing products.

13.3 **Fashion is organised as a cyclical cultural system that communicates symbolic meanings of imitation and differentiation to consumers.** The fashion system includes everyone involved in the creation and transference of symbolic meanings. Meanings that express common cultural categories (for instance, gender distinctions) are conveyed by many different products. New styles tend to be adopted by many people simultaneously in a process known as collective selection. Perspectives on motivations for adopting new styles include psychological, economic and sociological models of fashion. Fashions tend to follow cycles that resemble the product life cycle. The two extremes of fashion adoption, classics and fads, can be distinguished in terms of the length of this cycle. Fashion is increasingly considered a market institution, where different organisations and other types of agents co-create the change processes. The internet in general, and social media in particular, change the ways in which fashions are created and disseminated in contemporary consumer culture. Bloggers experience an increasing amount of market power as cultural gatekeepers, democratising the cultural production system along the way.

13.4 **Acculturation is the process whereby consumers adapt to living in a new cultural setting. This process not only influences those consumers migrating, but also the consumers already living in the host culture.** Consumers' degree of acculturation into mainstream society varies; and there are important cultural differences among subgroups that marketers need to recognise, while also acknowledging the views of the host community. Recently, several minority groups have caught the attention of marketers as their economic power has grown. Segmenting consumers by their ethnicity can be effective, but care must be taken not to rely on inaccurate (and sometimes offensive) ethnic stereotypes.

Key terms

Acculturation (p. 555)
Acculturation agents (p. 555)
Advergaming (p. 538)
Art product (p. 531)
Classic (p. 553)
Collective selection (p. 546)
Continuous innovation (p. 543)
Co-optation (p. 523)

Craft product (p. 531)
Crowdsourcing (p. 530)
Cultivation hypothesis (p. 538)
Cultural formula (p. 532)
Cultural gatekeepers (p. 529)
Cultural intermediaries (p. 529)
Cultural production system (CPS) (p. 527)
Cultural selection (p. 525)

Discontinuous innovation (p. 543)
Dynamically continuous innovation (p. 543)
Early adopters (p. 541)
Enculturation (p. 555)
Erogenous zones (p. 546)
Fad (p. 554)
Fashion (p. 545)
Fashion acceptance cycle (p. 552)
Fashion life cycle (p. 552)

Fashion system (p. 545)
Host culture (p. 557)
Innovation (p. 539)
Lead users (p. 542)
Product placement (p. 536)
Prosumer (p. 530)
Reality engineering (p. 534)
Subculture (p. 532)
Trickle-down theory (p. 548)

Consumer behaviour challenge

1 Think of the last piece of clothing you bought. Trace the origins of this piece of clothing through the cultural production system. How did it end up at the store?

2 Some consumers complain that they are 'at the mercy' of designers: they are forced to buy whatever styles are in fashion because nothing else is available. Do you agree that there is such a thing as a 'designer conspiracy'?

3 How has the internet contributed in democratising the cultural production process?

4 What is the difference between an art and a craft? Where would you characterise advertising within this framework?

5 Think about some innovative products that you can remember, but which disappeared. Try to reflect on the reasons why these innovations ultimately failed.

6 Now try to remember some successful innovations. What characteristics made them successful? Do the successes and failures fit with the criteria mentioned in this chapter?

7 The marketing opportunity of introducing product placements in, for example, news programmes may have some problematic ethical and political side-effects. Would you be comfortable with product placement in the news? Why, or why not?

8 The chapter mentions some instances where market research findings influenced artistic decisions, as when a film ending was reshot to accommodate consumers' preferences. Many people would oppose this use of consumer research, claiming that books, films, records or other artistic endeavours should not be designed merely to conform to what people want to read, see or hear. What do you think?

9 Many are claiming there is now a more individualistic style of fashion. Discuss whether individualism in style and fashion has actually increased, or whether we are being conformist in new ways.

10 What does it mean to have an 'institutional view' on fashion?

11 Locate one or more consumers (perhaps family members) who have immigrated from another country. Interview them about how they adapted to their host culture. In particular, what changes did they make in their consumption practices over time?

For additional material see the companion website at **www.pearsoned.co.uk/solomon**

See Case studies E.1, E.2 & E.3 at the end of Part E:

Case study E.1: 'Keep the faith: mediating Catholicism and consumption', Leighanne Higgins (Lancaster University, UK)

Case study E.2: '"Miss u loads": online consumer memorialisation practices', Darach Turley (Dublin City University, Ireland) and Stephanie O'donohoe (University of Edinburgh, UK)

Case study E.3: 'Routes to heritage: acculturation among second-generation British Indian women', Anuja Pradhan and Hayley Cocker' (Lancaster University, UK)

Notes

1. See https://healinghotelsoftheworld.com/ (accessed 20 December 2018).

2. Deniz Atik and Cansu Yildirim, 'Motivations behind acquiring tattoos and feelings of regret: Highlights from an Eastern Mediterranean context', *Journal of Consumer Behaviour* 13 (2014): 212–23.

3. B. Navarro, 'Creative industries and Britpop: The marketisation of culture, politics and national identity', *Consumption Markets & Culture* 19(2) (2016): 228–43.

4. Nina Darnton, 'Where the homegirls are', *Newsweek* (17 June 1991): 60; 'The idea chain', *Newsweek* (5 October 1992): 32.

5. Cyndee Miller, 'X marks the lucrative spot, but some advertisers can't hit target', *Marketing News* (2 August 1993): 1.

6. Ad appeared in *Elle* (September 1994).

7. Marc Spiegler, 'Marketing street culture: Bringing hip-hop style to the mainstream', *American Demographics* (November 1996): 23–7; Joshua Levine, 'Badass sells', *Forbes* (21 April 1997): 142–8.

8. Jeff Jensen, 'Hip, wholesome image makes a marketing star of rap's LL Cool J', *Advertising Age* (25 August 1997): 1.

9. Alice Z. Cuneo, 'Gap's 1st global ads confront dockers on a khaki battlefield', *Advertising Age* (20 April 1998): 3–5.

10. Jancee Dunn, 'How hip-hop style bum-rushed the mall', *Rolling Stone* (18 March 1999): 54–9.

11. Quoted in Teri Agins, 'The rare art of "gilt by association": How Armani got stars to be billboards', *The Wall Street Journal Interactive Edition* (14 September 1999).

12. Eryn Brown, 'From rap to retail: Wiring the hip-hop nation', *Fortune* (17 April 2000): 530.

13. Martin Fackler, 'Hip hop invading China', *The Birmingham News* (15 February 2002): D1.

14. Maureen Tkacik, '"Z" zips into the zeitgeist, subbing for "S" in hot slang', *The Wall Street Journal Interactive Edition* (4 January 2003); Maureen Tkacik, 'Slang from the 'hood now sells toyz in target', *The Wall Street Journal Interactive Edition* (30 December 2002).

15. 'Return of the Mac – coming soon' (29 March 2005), http://news.bbc.co.uk/2/hi/business/4389751.stm (accessed 6 September 2018).

16. Damien Arthur, 'Authenticity and consumption in the Australian hip hop culture', *Qualitative Market Research* 9(2) (2005): 140.

17. http://www.icce.rug.nl/~soundscapes/DATABASES/MIE/Part2_chapter08.shtml (accessed 6 September 2018).

18. Danmarks Radio, P1 (5 November 2008).

19. http://www.forbes.com/sites/zackomalleygreenburg/2015/05/07/jay-zs-net-worth-in-2015-550-million/ (accessed 6 September 2018).

20. Simon Lund, 'Kanye', *Politiken,* Kultur (20 June 2015): 10–15.

21. https://www.billboard.com/articles/columns/hip-hop/8085226/ll-cool-j-kennedy-center-honors-tribute-performance (accessed 6 September 2018).

22. https://www.theguardian.com/culture/2018/apr/16/kendrick-lamar-pulitzer-prize-weinstein-new-york-times (accessed 6 September 2018).

23. Elizabeth M. Blair, 'Commercialization of the rap music youth subculture', *Journal of Popular Culture* 27 (Winter 1993): 21–34; Basil G. Englis, Michael R. Solomon and Anna Olofsson, 'Consumption imagery in music television: A bi-cultural perspective', *Journal of Advertising* 22 (December 1993): 21–34.

24. Marc Spiegler, 'Marketing street culture: Bringing hip-hop style to the mainstream', *American Demographics* (November 1996): 29–34.

25. Janice Brace-Govan and Hélène de Burgh-Woodman, 'Sneakers and street culture: A postcolonial analysis of marginalized cultural consumption', *Consumption Markets & Culture* 11(2) (2008): 93–112.

26. See, for example, Thomas Frank, *The Conquest of Cool* (Chicago: University of Chicago Press, 1997).

27. G. Eckhardt and A. Arvidsson, 'Ad agencies', *Consumption Markets & Culture* 19(2) (2016): 167–71.

28. Teri Agins, 'To track fickle fashion, apparel firms go online', *The Wall Street Journal* (11 May 2000): B1.

29. Edward McQuarrie, Jessica Miller and Barbara Phillips, 'The megaphone effect: Taste and audience in fashion blogging', *Journal of Consumer Research* 40(1) (2013): 136–58.

30. https://www.forbes.com/sites/robertadams/2017/03/02/top-income-earning-blogs/#3d68c1da2377 (accessed 6 September 2018).

31. https://blog.hubspot.com/marketing/best-brands-on-instagram (accessed 7 September 2018).

32. Richard A. Peterson, 'The Production of Culture: A Prolegomenon', in Richard A. Peterson (ed.), *The Production of Culture,* Sage Contemporary Social Science Issues (Beverly Hills, CA: SAGE, 1976) 33: 7–22.

33. Elizabeth C. Hirschman, 'Resource exchange in the production and distribution of a motion picture', *Empirical Studies of the Arts* 8(1) (1990): 31–51; Michael R. Solomon, 'Building Up and Breaking Down: The Impact of Cultural Sorting on Symbolic Consumption', in J. Sheth and E.C. Hirschman (eds), *Research in Consumer Behavior* (Greenwich, CT: JAI Press, 1988): 325–51.

34. T. Mordue and N. Dennis, 'Performing jazz and the jazz constellation: Movements, moments and connections', *Marketing Theory* 17(2) (2017): 241–57.

35. Iben Foss, 'Lytternes ekkorum', *Weekendavisen,* Kultur (8 May 2015): 8–9.

36. Jordan Gamble and Audrey Gilmore, 'A new era of consumer marketing? An application of co-creational marketing in the music industry', *European Journal of Marketing* 47(11/12) (2013): 1,859–88.

37. See Paul M. Hirsch, 'Processing fads and fashions: An organizational set analysis of cultural industry systems', *American Journal of Sociology* 77(4) (1972): 639–59; Russell Lynes, *The Tastemakers* (New York: Harper & Brothers, 1954); Michael R. Solomon, 'The missing link: Surrogate consumers in the marketing chain', *Journal of Marketing* 50 (October 1986): 208–19.

38. Jennifer Smith Maguire, 'Provenance and the liminality of production and consumption: The case of wine promoters', *Marketing Theory* 10(3) (2010): 269–82.

39. A concept originally introduced by Pierre Bourdieu. See, for example, Paul du Gay, 'Devices and Dispositions: Promoting consumption', *Consumption Markets & Culture* 7 (June 2004): 99–105; and Anne M. Cronin, 'Regimes of mediation: Advertising practitioners as cultural intermediaries, *Consumption Market & Culture* 7 (December 2004): 349–69.

40. K. Kobayashi, S.J. Jackson and M.P. Sam, 'Multiple dimensions of mediation within transnational advertising production: Cultural intermediaries as shapers of emerging cultural capital', *Consumption Markets & Culture* 21(2) (2018): 129–46.

41. M.E. Drumwright and S. Kamal, 'Habitus, doxa, and ethics: Insights from advertising in emerging markets in the Middle East and North Africa', *Consumption Markets & Culture* 19(2) (2016): 172–205.

42. Ilona Mikkonen, Handan Vicdan and Annu Markkula, 'What not to wear? Oppositional ideology, fashion and governmentality in wardrobe self-help', *Consumption Markets & Culture* 17(3) (2014): 254–73.

43. Michael R. Solomon, Richard Ashmore and Laura Longo, 'The beauty match-up hypothesis: Congruence between types of beauty and product images in advertising', *Journal of Advertising* 21 (December 1992): 23–34.

44. Michael R. Solomon, *Conquering Consumerspace: Marketing Strategies for a Branded World* (New York: AMACOM, 2003).

45. Stuart Roper, Robert Caruana, Dominic Medway and Phil Murphy, 'Constructing luxury brands: Exploring the role of consumer discourse', *European Journal of Marketing* 47(3/4) (2013): 375–400.

46. Diane Martin and John Schouten. 'Consumption-driven market emergence', *Journal of Consumer Research* 40(5) (2014): 855–70.

47. R.L. Gruner and D. Power, 'What's in a crowd? Exploring crowdsourced versus traditional customer participation in the innovation process', *Journal of Marketing Management* 33(13/14) (2017): 1,060–92.

48. A. Arvidsson and B. Niessen, 'Creative mass: Consumption, creativity and innovation on Bangkok's fashion markets', *Consumption Markets & Culture* 18(2) (2015): 111–32.

49. A. Darmody, M. Yuksel and M. Venkatraman, 'The work of mapping and the mapping of work: Prosumer roles in crowdsourced maps', *Journal of Marketing Management* 33(13/14) (2017): 1,093–119.

50. Craig J. Thompson and Gökcen Coskuner-Balli, 'Countervailing market responses to corporate co-optation and the ideological recruitment of consumption communities', *Journal of Consumer Research* 34(2) (August 2007): 135–52.

51. Bernard Cova and Daniele Dalli, 'Working consumers: The next step in marketing theory?', *Marketing Theory* 9(3) (2009): 315–39. See also Detlev Zwick, Sammy Bonsu and Aron Darmody, 'Putting consumers to work: "Co-creation" and the new marketing govern-mentality', *Journal of Consumer Culture* 8(2) (2008): 163–96.

52. Peter Nuttall, 'Insiders, regulars and tourists: Exploring selves and music consumption in adolescence', *Journal of Consumer Behaviour* 8 (2009): 211–24.

53. Terry O'Sullivan, 'All together now: A symphony orchestra audience as a consuming community', *Consumption Markets & Culture* 12 (September 2009): 209–23.

54. Howard S. Becker, 'Arts and crafts', *American Journal of Sociology* 83 (January 1987): 862–89.

55. Herbert J. Gans, 'Popular Culture in America: Social Problem in a Mass Society or Social Asset in a Pluralist Society?', in Howard S. Becker (ed.), *Social Problems: A Modern Approach* (New York: Wiley, 1966).

56. Anders Bengtsson, Jacob Östberg and Dannie Kjeldgaard, 'Prisoners in paradise: Subcultural resistance to the marketization of tattooing', *Consumption Markets & Culture* 8(3) (2005): 261–74.

57. Michael R. Real, *Mass-Mediated Culture* (Englewood Cliffs, NJ: Prentice-Hall, 1977).

58. For websites that show 'Top-40' music sales in the US and UK, see http://top40-charts.com/chart.php?cid=27 (accessed 6 September 2018) and http://www.bbc.co.uk/radio1/chart/singles.shtml (accessed 6 September 2018).

59. Luca M. Visconti, John F. Sherry Jr., Stefania Borghini and Laurel Anderson, 'Street Art, Sweet Art? Reclaiming the "Public" in Public Place', *Journal of Consumer Research* 37(3) (October 2010): 511–29.

60. A.M. Peluso, G. Pino, C. Amatulli and G. Guido, 'Luxury advertising and recognizable artworks: New insights on the "art infusion" effect', *European Journal of Marketing* 51(11/12) (2017): 2,192–206.

61. Annetta Miller, 'Shopping bags imitate art: Seen the sacks? Now visit the museum exhibit', *Newsweek* (23 January 1989): 44.

62. C. Preece, F. Kerrigan and D. O'Reilly, 'Framing the work: The composition of value in the visual arts', *European Journal of Marketing* 50(7/8) (2016): 1,377–98.

63. G. Patsiaouras, A. Veneti and W. Green, 'Marketing, art and voices of dissent: Promotional methods of protest art by the 2014 Hong Kong's Umbrella Movement', *Marketing Theory* 18(1) (2018): 75–100.

64. P. Freathy and I. Thomas, 'Marketplace metaphors: Communicating authenticity through visual imagery', *Consumption Markets & Culture* 18(2) (2015): 178–94.

65. R. Modrak, 'Learning to talk like an urban woodsman: An artistic intervention', *Consumption Markets & Culture* 18(6) (2015): 539–58.

66. Arthur A. Berger, *Signs in Contemporary Culture: An Introduction to Semiotics* (New York: Longman, 1984).

67. Stephen Brown, 'Psycho Shopper: A Comparative Literary Analysis of "The Dark Side"', in Flemming Hansen (ed.), *European Advances in Consumer Research* 2 (Provo, UT: Association for Consumer Research, 1995): 96–103; Stephen Brown, 'Consumption Behaviour in the Sex'n'Shopping Novels of Judith Krantz: A Post-structuralist Perspective', in J. Lynch and K. Corfman (eds), *Advances in Consumer Research* 23 (Provo, UT: Association for Consumer Research, 1996): 96–103.

68. Christina Goulding and Michael Saren, 'Performing identity: An analysis of gender expression at the Whitby goth festival', *Consumption Markets & Culture* 12 (March 2009): 27–46.

69. Dominik Bartmanski and Ian Woodward, 'The vinyl: The analogue medium in the age of digital representation', *Journal of Consumer Culture* 15(1) (2015): 3–27.

70. Jonathan Guthrie, 'Why using a dead celebrity sells', *Financial Times* (26 April 2005).

71. Michiko Kakutani, 'Art is easier the 2nd time around', *New York Times* (30 October 1994): E4. See also Stephen Brown, *Retro-Marketing* (London: Routledge, 2001).

72. Daragh O'Reilly and Finola Kerrigan, 'A view to a brand: Introducing the film brandscape', *European Journal of Marketing* 47(5/6) (2013): 769–89.

73. Nigel Andrews, 'Filming a blockbuster is one thing; striking gold is another', *Financial Times,* accessed via Simon & Schuster College Newslink (20 January 1998).

74. Helene Diamond, 'Lights, camera. . . research!', *Marketing News* (11 September 1989): 10.

75. Andrews, 'Filming a blockbuster is one thing; striking gold is another', op. cit.

76. Nina M. Lentini, 'Doh! Looks like 7-Eleven stores may get Homered', *Marketing Daily* (30 March 2007).

77. Steve Cooper, Damien McLoughlin and Andrew Keating, 'Individual and neo-tribal consumption: Tales from the Simpsons of Springfield', *Journal of Consumer Behaviour* 4(5) (2005): 330–44.

78. Michael R. Solomon and Basil G. Englis, 'Reality engineering: Blurring the boundaries between marketing and popular culture', *Journal of Current Issues and Research in Advertising* 16(2) (Fall 1994): 1–17.

79. Nicolas Marmie, 'Casablanca Gets a Rick's', *Montgomery Advertiser* (9 May 2004): 3AA.

80. B. Joseph Pine and James Gilmore, 'Welcome to the experience economy', *Harvard Business Review* (July/August 1998): 97–105.

81. Søren Askegaard, 'Experience economy in the making: Hedonism, play and coolhunting in automotive song lyrics', *Consumption Markets & Culture* 13(4) (2010): 351–71.

82. http://www.theverge.com/2015/3/4/8147063/apple-transformers-age-of-extinction-product-placement (accessed 6 September 2018).

83. Denise E. DeLorme and Leonard N. Reid, 'Moviegoers' experiences and interpretations of brands in films revisited', *Journal of Advertising* 28(2) (1999): 71–90.

84. Cristel Antonia Russell, 'Investigating the effectiveness of product placement in television shows: The role of modality and plot connection congruence on brand memory and attitude', *Journal of Consumer Research* 29 (December 2002): 306–18.

85. Jörg Matthes and Brigitte Naderer, 'Children's consumption behavior in response to food product placements in movies', *Journal of Consumer Behaviour* 14 (2015): 127–36.

86. See also Spurlock's TED talk on https://www.youtube.com/watch?v=Y2jyjfcp1as (accessed 6 September 2018).

87. A. Marchand, T. Hennig-Thurau and S. Best, 'When James Bond shows off his Omega: does product placement affect its media host?', *European Journal of Marketing* 49(9/10) (2015): 1,666–85.

88. J. Meyer, R. Song and K. Ha, 'The effect of product placements on the evaluation of movies', *European Journal of Marketing* 50(3/4) (2016): 530–49.

89. https://www.theguardian.com/media/2018/jan/20/forget-product-placement-advertisers-buy-storylines-tv-blackish (accessed 6 September 2018).

90. http://www.telegraph.co.uk/news/celebritynews/11294887/James-Bond-to-drink-sponsored-vodka-martinis-in-Spectre.html (accessed 6 September 2018).

91. https://www.washingtonpost.com/news/wonk/wp/2015/06/12/jurassic-world-shows-just-how-weird-product-placement-has-become/?noredirect=on&utm_term=.3dbe4a6fbe99 (accessed 6 September 2018).

92. Ibid.

93. Geoffrey A. Fowler, 'New star on Chinese TV: Product placements', *Wall Street Journal Online Edition* (2 June 2004): B1.

94. Joseph Plambeck, 'Product Placement Grows in Music Videos', *New York Times* (5 July 2010), http://www.nytimes.com/2010/07/06/business/media/06adco.html?_r=1&emc=eta1 (accessed 6 September 2018).

95. 'Filmreplik ødelagde Merlot i USA', *Berlingske Kultur* (15 April 2008): 3.

96. Nick Wingfield, 'Sony's PS3 to get in-game ads', *Wall Street Journal* (4 June 2008): B7; Jeffrey Bardzell, Shaowen Bardzell and Tyler Pace, 'Player Engagement and In-Game Advertising' (23 November 2008).

97. Agnes Nairn and Haiming Hang, 'Advergames: It is not an advert – it says play. A review of research', research report (University of Bath: Family and Parenting Institute, December 2012).

98. Stephen Fox and William Philber, 'Television viewing and the perception of affluence', *Sociological Quarterly* 19 (1978): 103–12; W. James Potter, 'Three strategies for elaborating the cultivation hypothesis', *Journalism Quarterly* 65 (Winter 1988): 930–9; Gabriel Weimann, 'Images of life in America: The impact of American T.V. in Israel', *International Journal of Intercultural Relations* 8 (1984): 185–97.

99. Patricia Gaya Wicks, Agnes Nairn and Christine Griffin, 'The role of commodified celebrities in children's moral development: The case of David Beckham', *Consumption Markets & Culture* 10(4) (2007): 401–24.

100. Stephanie O'Donohue, 'On the Outside Looking In: Advertising Experiences Among Young Unemployed Adults', in Flemming Hansen (ed.), *European Advances in Consumer Research* 2 (Provo, UT: Association for Consumer Research): 264–72; Richard Elliott, 'How Do the Unemployed Maintain Their Identity in a Culture of Consumption?', in Hansen (ed.), *European Advances in Consumer Research* 2: 273–6.

101. S. De Jans, L. Hudders and V. Cauberghe, 'Advertising literacy training: The immediate versus delayed effects on children's responses to product placement', *European Journal of Marketing* 51(11/12) (2017): 2,156–74.

102. See http://inhabitat.com/accessories-and-fashion/ (accessed 6 September 2018) for this and many more innovations of this type.

103. Adam Therer, 'On measuring technology diffusion rates', techliberation.com/2009/05/28/on-measuring-technology-diffusion-rates (accessed 6 September 2018).

104. L. Hurmerinta and B. Sandberg, 'Sadness bright as glass: The acceptance of emotionally sensitive radical innovation', *Journal of Marketing Management* 31(9/10) (2015): 918–39.

105. http://www.smartinsights.com/mobile-marketing/mobile-marketing-analytics/mobile-marketing-statistics/ (accessed 6 September 2018).

106. Susan B. Kaiser, *The Social Psychology of Clothing* (New York: Macmillan, 1985); Thomas S. Robertson, *Innovative Behavior and Communication* (New York: Holt, Rhinehart & Winston, 1971).

107. Eric J. Arnould, 'Toward a broadened theory of preference formation and the diffusion of innovations: Cases from Zinder Province, Niger Republic', *Journal of Consumer Research* 16 (September 1989): 239–67.

108. Jan-Benedict E.M. Steenkamp, Frenkel ter Hofstede and Michel Wedel, 'A cross-national investigation into the individual and national cultural antecedents of consumer innovativeness', *Journal of Marketing* 63(2) (1999): 55–69.

109. Richard Wilk, 'Bottled water: The pure commodity in the age of branding', *Journal of Consumer Culture* 6(3) (2006): 303–25.

110. Susan L. Holak, Donald R. Lehmann and Farena Sultan, 'The role of expectations in the adoption of innovative consumer durables: Some preliminary evidence', *Journal of Retailing* 63 (Fall 1987): 243–59.

111. Hubert Gatignon and Thomas S. Robertson, 'A propositional inventory for new diffusion research', *Journal of Consumer Research* 11 (March 1985): 849–67.

112. Frank Huber, 'Ein konzept zur ermittlung und bearbeitung des frühkäufersegments im bekleidungsmarkt', *Marketing ZFP* 2 (2nd Quarter 1995): 110–21.

113. Eva Martinez, Yolanda Polo and Carlos Flavián, 'The acceptance and diffusion of new consumer durables: Differences between first and last adopters', *Journal of Consumer Marketing* 15(4) (1998): 323–42.

114. Sofie Møller Bjerrisgaard and Dannie Kjeldgaard. 'How market research shapes market spatiality a global governmentality perspective', *Journal of Macromarketing* 33(1) (2013): 29–40. See also John A. McCarthy, Martin I. Horn, Mary Kate Szenasy and Jocelyn Feintuch, 'An exploratory study of consumer style: Country differences and international segments', *Journal of Consumer Behaviour* 6(1) (January–February 2007): 48–59.

115. Gordon R. Foxall and Seema Bhate. 'Cognitive style and personal involvement as explicators of innovative purchasing of health food brands', *European Journal of Marketing* 27(2) (1993): 5–16.

116. Adage.com/article/news/ad-age-agency-year-consumer/114132/ (accessed 6 September 2018).

117. Elizabeth C. Hirschman, 'Symbolism and Technology as Sources of the Generation of Innovations', in Andrew Mitchell (ed.), *Advances in Consumer Research* 9 (Provo, UT: Association for Consumer Research, 1982): 537–41.

118. Søren Askegaard and A. Fuat Firat, 'Towards a Critique of Material Culture, Consumption and Markets', in Susan M. Pearce (ed.), *Experiencing Material Culture in the Western World* (London: Leicester University Press, 1997): 114–39.

119. Stephen Brown, *Postmodern Marketing* (London: Routledge, 1995).

120. 'Mange kvinder er begyndt at drikke mandecola', *Berlingske Tidende* (19 August 2008), Business: 11.

121. https://www.theguardian.com/environment/2017/nov/08/seven-megatrends-that-could-beat-global-warming-climate-change (accessed 6 September 2018).

122. http://www.theguardian.com/sustainable-business/2015/jun/22/five-clean-technologies-to-watch-solar-cells-biodegradable-batteries (accessed 6 September 2018).

123. Everett M. Rogers, *Diffusion of Innovations,* 3rd edn (New York: Free Press, 1983).

124. http://brandgenetics.com/why-observable-innovation-is-key-to-success/ (accessed 6 September 2018).

125. Z. Mani and I. Chouk, 'Drivers of consumers' resistance to smart products', *Journal of Marketing Management* 33(1/2) (2017): 76–97.

126. Robert J. Fisher and Linda L. Price, 'An investigation into the social context of early adoption behavior', *Journal of Consumer Research* 19 (December 1992): 477–86.

127. S. Geiger and J. Finch, 'Promissories and pharmaceutical patents: Agencing markets through public narratives', *Consumption Markets & Culture* 19(1) (2016): 71–91.

128. Güliz Ger and Russell W. Belk, 'I'd like to buy the world a Coke: Consumptionscapes of the "less affluent world"', *Journal of Consumer Policy* 19 (1996): 271–304; Robin A. Coulter, Linda L. Price and Lawrence Feick, 'Rethinking the origins of involvement and brand commitment: Insights from postsocialist Central Europe', *Journal of Consumer Research* 30 (September 2003): 151–69.

129. Gökcen Coskuner-Balli and Özlem Sandikci, 'The aura of new goods: How consumers mediate newness', *Journal of Consumer Behaviour* 13 (2014): 122–30.

130. N. Dholakia, I. Reyes and J. Bonoff, 'Mobile media: From legato to staccato, isochronal consumptionscapes', *Consumption Markets & Culture* 18(1) (2015): 10–24.

131. W. Chan Kim and Renée Mauborgne, 'Value innovation: The strategic logic of high growth', *Harvard Business Review* (January–February 1997): 103–12.

132. Roland Barthes, *Système de la mode* (Paris: Seuil, 1967); English translation: Roland Barthes, *The Language of Fashion* (Oxford: Berg Publishers, 2006).

133. 'Diaper bag double take', *Discount Merchandiser* (March 2000).

134. Umberto Eco, *A Theory of Semiotics* (Bloomington, IN: Indiana University Press, 1979).

135. Fred Davis, 'Clothing and Fashion as Communication', in Michael R. Solomon (ed.), *The Psychology of Fashion* (Lexington, MA: Lexington Books, 1985): 15–28.

136. D. Miller, 'Denim', *Consumption Markets & Culture* 18(4) (2015): 298–300.

137. M.A. Parmentier, 'High heels', *Consumption Markets & Culture* 19(6) (2016): 511–19.

138. Melanie Wallendorf, 'The Formation of Aesthetic Criteria Through Social Structures and Social Institutions', in Jerry C. Olson (ed.), *Advances in Consumer Research* 7 (Ann Arbor, MI: Association for Consumer Research, 1980): 3–6.

139. Christine Delhaye, 'The development of consumption culture and the individualization of female identity', *Journal of Consumer Culture* 6(1) (2006): 87–115.

140. Herbert Blumer, *Symbolic Interactionism: Perspective and Method* (Englewood Cliffs, NJ: Prentice-Hall, 1969); Howard S. Becker, 'Art as collective action', *American Sociological Review* 39 (December 1973); Richard A. Peterson, 'Revitalizing the culture concept', *Annual Review of Sociology* 5 (1979): 137–66.

141. For more details, see Kaiser, *The Social Psychology of Clothing,* op. cit.; George B. Sproles, 'Behavioral Science Theories of Fashion', in Solomon (ed.), *The Psychology of Fashion,* op. cit.: 55–70.

142. C.R. Snyder and Howard L. Fromkin, *Uniqueness: The Human Pursuit of Difference* (New York: Plenum Press, 1980).

143. Alison Lurie, *The Language of Clothes* (New York: Random House, 1981).

144. Linda Dyett, 'Desperately seeking skin', *Psychology Today* (May/June 1996): 14.

145. Diego Rinallo, 'Producing and Consuming the Metro-sexual', in S. Borghini, M.A. McGrath and C. Otnes (eds), *European Advances in Consumer Research* (Duluth, MN: Association for Consumer Research, 2008): 306–8.

146. Susan Auty and Richard Elliott, 'Social Identity and the Meaning of Fashion Brands', in B. Englis and A. Olofsson (eds), *European Advances in Consumer Research* 3 (Provo, UT: Association for Consumer Research, 1998): 1–10.

147. John Fiske, *Understanding Popular Culture* (Boston: Unwin Hyman, 1989): especially 1–21.

148. Harvey Leibenstein, *Beyond Economic Man: A New Foundation for Microeconomics* (Cambridge, MA: Harvard University Press, 1976).

149. Nara Schoenberg, 'Goth culture moves into mainstream', *Montgomery Advertiser* (9 January 2003): 1G.

150. Georg Simmel, 'Fashion', *International Quarterly* 10 (1904): 130–55.

151. Grant D. McCracken, 'The Trickle-Down Theory Rehabilitated', in Solomon (ed.), *The Psychology of Fashion,* op. cit.: 39–54.

152. 'Fast Fashion in 11 per cent Sales Surge', *Marketing* (20 April 2005): 14.

153. Charles W. King, 'Fashion Adoption: A Rebuttal to the "Trickle-Down" Theory', in Stephen A. Greyser (ed.), *Toward Scientific Marketing* (Chicago: American Marketing Association, 1963): 108–25.

154. Dannie Kjeldgaard, 'The meaning of style? Style reflexivity among Danish high school youths', *Journal of Consumer Behavior* 8 (2009): 71–83.

155. Terry Newholm and Gillian C. Hopkinson, 'I just tend to wear what I like: Contemporary consumption and the paradoxical construction of individuality', *Marketing Theory* 9 (2009): 439–62.

156. Gilles Marion and Agnes Nairn, '"We make the shoes, you make the story": Teenage girls' experiences of fashion: Bricolage, tactics and narrative identity', *Consumption Markets & Culture* 14 (March 2011): 29–56.

157. Gillian Hogg, Suzanne Horne and David Carmichael, 'Fun, Fashion, or Just Plain Sailing? The Consumption of Clothing in the Sailing Community', in B. Dubois, T. Lowrey, L.J. Shrum and M. Vanhuele (eds), *European Advances in Consumer Research* 4 (Provo, UT: Association for Consumer Research, 1999): 336–40.

158. Triin Vihalemm and Margit Keller, 'Looking Russian or Estonian: Young consumers constructing the ethnic "self" and "other"', *Consumption, Markets & Culture* 14 (September 2011): 293–309.

159. Alf H. Walle, 'Grassroots innovation', *Marketing Insights* (Summer 1990): 44–51.

160. Patrick Hetzel, 'The Role of Fashion and Design in a Postmodern Society: What Challenges for Firms?', in M.J. Baker (ed.), *Perspectives on Marketing Management* 4 (London: John Wiley & Sons, 1994): 97–118.

161. Stuart and Elizabeth Ewen, cited in Mike Featherstone, *Consumer Culture and Postmodernism* (London: SAGE, 1993): 83.

162. Hetzel, 'The Role of Fashion and Design in a Postmodern Society: what challenges for firms?', op. cit.

163. Anne F. Jensen, 'Acknowledging and Consuming Fashion in the Era after "Good Taste" – From the Beautiful to the Hideous', Doctoral Dissertations from the Faculty of Social Science, no. 40 (Odense: University of Southern Denmark, 1999).

164. Patrick Hetzel, 'A Socio-Semiotic Analysis of the Media/ Consumer Relationships in the Production of Fashion Systems: The Case of the "Elle-France" Magazine', in Englis and Olofsson (eds), *European Advances in Consumer Research* 3: 104–7.

165. 'Topmodel i genbrugstøj', *Fyens Stiftstidende, Erhverv* (1 November 2000): 1.

166. http://news.bbc.co.uk/2/hi/uk_news/magazine/7563318. stm and http://www.guardian.co.uk/lifeandstyle/2007/ may/18/fashion.ethicalliving (both accessed 6 September 2018).

167. Rana Sobh, Russell Belk and Justin Gressel, 'Mimicry and modernity in the Middle East: Fashion invisibility and young women in the Arabian Gulf', *Consumption Markets & Culture* 17(4) (2014): 392–412.

168. Fajer Saleh al-Mutawa, Richard Elliott and Peter Nuttall, 'Foreign brands in local cultures: A socio-cultural perspective of postmodern brandscapes', *Journal of Consumer Behaviour* 14 (2015): 137–44.

169. 'Panik i mode-fabrikken', Intervju med Alladi Venkatesh, *Dagens Nyheter* (27 June 2000): B1.

170. Don Slater, *Consumer Culture and Modernity* (Cambridge: Polity Press, 1997).

171. Anne F. Jensen and Søren Askegaard, 'In Pursuit of Ugliness: Searching for a Fashion Concept in the Era After Good Taste', Working Paper in Marketing, no. 17 (Odense: Odense University, 1998).

172. Heltnormalt.dk/truthfacts/2012/01/10 (accessed 28 April 2012).

173. Pierre-Yann Dolbec and Eileen Fischer, 'Re-fashioning a field? Connected consumers and institutional dynamics in the markets', *Journal of Consumer Research* 41(6) (2015); 1,447–68.

174. Pierre Bourdieu and Yvette Delsaut, 'Le couturier et sa griffe. Contribution a une théorie de la magie', *Actes de la Recherche en Sciences Sociales* 1(1) (1975): 7–36.

175. Daiane Scaraboto and Eileen Fischer. 'Frustrated fatshionistas: An institutional theory perspective on consumer quests for greater choice in mainstream markets', *Journal of Consumer Research* 39(6) (2013): 1,234–57.

176. Dolbec and Fischer, op. cit.

177. https://www.theguardian.com/fashion/2017/dec/30/ bootleg-logos-designers-copyright-fashion (accessed 6 September 2018).

178. https://www.nytimes.com/2018/02/11/fashion/diesel-deisel-new-york-fashion-week-pop-up.html (accessed 6 September 2018).

179. A.K. Tang, 'Key factors in the triumph of Pokémon GO', *Business Horizons* 60(5) (2017): 725–8.

180. Anne F. Jensen and Per Østergaard, 'Dressing for Security or Risk? An Exploratory Study of Two Different Ways of Consuming Fashion', in Englis and Olofsson (eds), *European Advances in Consumer Research* 3: 98–103.

181. Daniel Miller, 'The little black dress is the solution, but what was the problem?', K. Ekström and H. Brembeck, (eds), *Elusive Consumption* (Oxford: Berg, 2004): 113–27.

182. B.E. Aguirre, E.L. Quarantelli and Jorge L. Mendoza, 'The collective behavior of fads: The characteristics, effects, and career of streaking', *American Sociological Review* (August 1989): 569.

183. Quoted in Stephen Brown and Anthony Patterson, '"You're a Wizard, Harry!" Consumer responses to the Harry Potter phenomenon', *Advances in Consumer Research* 33 (2006): 155–60.

184. Maddy Savage, 'Scandinavian food: Why is it becoming popular in the UK?', *BBC News Magazine* (25 February 2012).

185. Martin G. Letscher, 'How to tell fads from trends', *American Demographics* (December 1994): 38–45.

186. See Chapter 5 for a discussion of core values and how underlying values potentially influence individuals' motivations to consume (or not to consume).

187. See, for instance, the discussion of acculturation issues and British South East Asian women in A.M. Lindridge, M.K. Hogg and M. Shah, 'Imagined multiple worlds: How South Asian women in Britain use family and friends to navigate the "border crossings" between household and societal contexts', *Consumption Markets & Culture* 7(3) (September 2004): 211–38.

188. See Lisa Peñaloza, 'Atravesando Fronteras/Border Crossings: A critical ethnographic exploration of the consumer acculturation of Mexican immigrants', *Journal of Consumer Research* 21 (June 1994): 32–54; Lisa Peñaloza and Mary C. Gilly, 'Marketer acculturation: The Changer and the Changed', *Journal of Marketing* 63 (July 1999): 84–104;

Carol Kaufman-Scarborough, 'Eat bitter food and give birth to a girl; Eat sweet things and give birth to a cavalryman: Multicultural health care issues for consumer behaviour', *Advances in Consumer Research* 32(1) (2005): 226–69; Søren Askegaard, Eric J. Arnould and Dannie Kjeldgaard, 'Post-assimilationist ethnic consumer research: Qualifications and extensions', *Journal of Consumer Research* 32(1) (2005): 160.

189. http://ec.europa.eu/eurostat/tgm/table.do?tab=table&init=1&language=en&pcode=tps00001&plugin=1 (accessed 13 February 2018)

190. http://ec.europa.eu/eurostat/statistics-explained/index.php/Migration_and_migrant_population_statistics, (accessed ??).

191. Sante J. Achille, 'Italians dislike online publicity', http://www.multilingual-search.com/italians-dislike-online-publicity/22/07/2008 (accessed 13 February 2018).

192. A. Fuat Firat, 'Consumer Culture or Culture Consumed?', in Costa and Bamossy (eds), *Marketing in a Multicultural World*: 105–25; Michael Laroche, Chankon Kim, Michael K. Hui and Annamma Joy, 'An empirical study of multidimensional ethnic change: The case of the French Canadians in Quebec', *Journal of Cross-Cultural Psychology* 27(1) (January 1996): 114–31.

193. Melanie Wallendorf and Michael Reilly, 'Ethnic migration, assimilation, and consumption', *Journal of Consumer Research* 10 (December 1983): 292–302.

194. Ronald J. Faber, Thomas C. O'Guinn and John A. McCarty, 'Ethnicity, acculturation and the importance of product attributes', *Psychology & Marketing* 4 (Summer 1987): 121–34; Humberto Valencia, 'Developing an Index to Measure Hispanicness', in Elizabeth C. Hirschman and Morris B. Holbrook (eds), *Advances in Consumer Research* 12 (Provo, Utah: Association for Consumer Research, 1985): 118–21.

195. Rohit Deshpande, Wayne D. Hoyer and Naveen Donthu, 'The intensity of ethnic affiliation: A study of the sociology of hispanic consumption', *Journal of Consumer Research* 13 (September 1986): 214–20.

196. Lisa Penaloza, 'Ethnic marketing practice and research at the intersection of market and social development: A macro study of the past and present, with a look to the future', *Journal of Business Research* 82 (2018): 273–80; see also L. Visconti, A. Jafari, W. Batat, A. Broeckerhoff, Ö. Dedeoglu, C. Demangeot and M. Weinberger, 'Consumer

ethnicity three decades after: A TCR agenda', *Journal of Marketing Management* 30(17/18) (2014): 1,882–922; Z. Yang, 'Ethnic youth: Parental style and consumer socialization', in A. Jamal, L. Peñaloza and M. Laroche (eds), *The Routledge Companion to Ethnic Marketing* (London: Routledge, 2015): 36–50.

197. See Case study 13 by Pradhan and Cocker 'Routes to heritage: acculturation among second-generation British Indian women' in this text.

198. Guliz Ger, 'Warming: Making the new familiar and moral', in Richard Wilk and Orvar Lofgren (eds), *Journal of European Ethnology* (special issue of the journal *Ethnologia Europea*) 35(1/2) (2005): 19–22.

199. Elisabeth Kriechbaum-Vitellozzi and Robert Kreuzbauer, 'Poverty consumption: Consumer behaviour of refugees in industrialized countries', *Advances in Consumer Research* 33(1) (2006); see also L. Wamwara-Mbugua, T. Wakiuru, Bettina Cornwell and Gregory Boller, 'Triple acculturation: The role of African Americans in the consumer acculturation of Kenyan immigrants', *Advances in Consumer Research* 33(1) (2006).

200. Tuba Ustuner and Douglas B. Holt, 'Dominated consumer acculturation: The social construction of poor migrant women's consumer identity projects in a Turkish squatter', *Journal of Consumer Research* 34 (June 2007): 41.

201. Marius K. Luedicke, 'Consumer acculturation theory: (crossing) conceptual boundaries', *Consumption Markets & Culture* 14(3) (2011): 223.

202. A. Marsh and M. Sahin-Dikmen, 'Discrimination in Europe', *Policy Studies Institute* (London 2002).

203. Z. Bauman, *Liquid Modernity* (Cambridge: Polity Press, 2000); A. Marsh and M. Sahin-Dikmen, *Discrimination in Europe (Report B)* (London: Policy Studies Institute, 2002); O. Sandikct and G. Ger., 'Veiling in style: How does a stigmatized practice become fashionable?', *Journal of Consumer Research* 37 (June 2010): 15–36. All cited in Luedicke 2011, op. cit.

204. Marius K. Luedicke (2011) op. cit.: 239–40.

205. Marius K. Luedicke, 'Indigenes' responses to immigrants' consumer acculturation: A relational configuration analysis', *Journal of Consumer Research* 42(1) (June 2015): 109–29.

206. Ibid.

Case study E.1

Keep the faith: mediating Catholicism and consumption

Leighanne Higgins, Lancaster University, UK

We are said today to be living in an historical moment governed by the ideology of consumerism,[1] an ideology that many scholars believe is at times replacing traditional institutional pillars such as religion, family and education.[2] Yet we continue to live in a world where approximately 6.5 billion people out of the total population of 7.4 billion continue to belong to a religious institution, with approximately 2.4 billion Christians (approximately 1.2 billion of whom are Roman Catholic), 1.7 billion Muslims and 2.3 billion followers of the Hindu, Buddhist, Sikh, Jewish and Folk religions.[3] How, then, in a world of consumerism do the faithful remain so? We will see through the following narratives how three modern-day Scottish Catholic consumers, Kevin and married couple Sally and Ryan, manage to mediate and balance their religious faith with consumer culture; in short, how they manage to 'keep the faith'.

The deaconate route: Kevin's story

Kevin admits to often falling prey to 'those pesky marketing trappings', finding consumerism very difficult both as an individual and as a family man, because not only do his kids want the latest Xbox or smartphone, but he, too, desires the myriad of electronic gadgets offered to him. He tells himself and others that he needs these gadgets for work, but admits: 'If I am being really honest that's a load of crap, I don't need these things, I want them', going on to say that marketing is like sugar, 'deeply enticing' and 'drawing you in'. At times, he feels 'torn' between his faith and the market, as his faith positions itself doctrinally as contrary to marketplace and consumerist ideologies. He claims, however, that this 'torn-ness' is not necessarily a bad feeling. For Kevin it is a false belief that life is about finding peace and satisfaction with absolutely everything. Rather, he believes that 'it's good to have a bit of tension', that such tension between religious faith and consumerist ideologies is 'healthy' and that people should aim to be more aware of and live better with that tension.

A few years ago, Kevin had a serious and defining decision to make when he received two great job opportunities within a week of one another. One job would take him down the business management, personal development route, leading to greater opportunities for promotion, more money, a different lifestyle, power and all the associated material things that people often find attractive. The alternative was to go down the spiritual route and train to become an ordained deacon (a level below a Catholic priest). He spoke about his dilemma, considering what his wife and children would think and how they would cope. Would the money and material route be more helpful with the kids fast becoming teenagers? He thought, too, about how his employers would they react if he left his job or became a deacon. Perhaps leaving would be easier than explaining his faith-based decision. Would his friends judge him? Would they wonder how Kevin, the life and soul of the party, the guy who literally dances on tables at parties, could become a deacon? He asked this same question of himself many a time before realising that the money, the house and the material goods would all be helpful, but they would not bring him what he really wanted in life: time with family, time with friends and, most importantly, more time with God. He admitted that at times he sees things advertised and thinks that it would be nice to have them, but the 'wallet-strings won't allow it' and, regardless of how attractive the new electronic gadget is, for Kevin it will 'lose its shine, become chipped, fall in a puddle and eventually break, but the time with my family, my parish, my friends and Him [God], that continues to grow brighter, lighter, stronger, making me happier every day'.

Keeping the Christ in Christian life: Ryan and Sally's story

Sally and Ryan were in their late thirties when they met, fell in love and married. Prior to meeting Sally, Ryan, like many students, worked part-time as a means of putting himself through university. His part-time work often meant he had to work on Sundays and could not keep the Sabbath. Although the Sabbath is not often observed by Christians today, working on Sundays irritated Ryan because when he was growing up Sunday was always the day spent with family and with God. Consequently, when he graduated he strove to build a career for himself that would allow him to keep Sundays free. Thus, he became a college lecturer and, even today, to the best of his ability he refrains from working and shopping on a Sunday. Instead, Ryan tries to ensure Sunday is 'a different kind of day'.

Being older, Sally and Ryan never in a million years believed they would have a family, but 'God gave us a miracle in Aaron'. Their son is so much of a miracle to them that just before they took him home for the first time, they popped into church to say thanks to God. A few years ago, Aaron started school. Sally spoke of how a family tradition was born following the end of Aaron's first school year, when the three of them journeyed to Loch Lomond in Scotland for a picnic. She went on to mention that, as she is not currently working, money is tight and their family laptop is fast approaching the end of its life. She spoke extensively about the dilemma of whether they should buy a new laptop or not. She and Ryan made a decision as a family to wait a while, for, as Sally explained, 'taking Aaron away for our family day is more important to us; it means that we have a family day out, which means God comes too, which means we have a great time, and that kind of makes you think "well if we can get by, we will make do with out it"'.

Consequently, Ryan and Sally often discussed the idea of their 'strategically complying' with consumerist society, meaning that they follow the consumerist rules up to a point that they feel comfortable with, but at the same time they actually 'play the consumption game we want to play'. They believe their relationship with consumerism is such that they comply as long as they feel it is not impinging on their religious beliefs and lifestyle, and if it does begin to encroach on the religious aspect of their lives, they 'opt out'. This, for Sally and Ryan, is 'how we ensure we keep Christ in our Christian lives'.

Consumer researchers are becoming increasingly aware of the important role religion can play in influencing consumer behaviour, with recent research documenting different consumer-balancing strategies that aid in the mediation between religion and consumption.[4] The above narratives are illustrative of such strategies. Catholic consumers acknowledge the ubiquitous and 'enticing' nature of consumer culture and often suffer feelings of guilt and tension when partaking in consumer cultural norms. Yet these feelings of 'tension' and 'guilt' with regard to consuming are not necessarily viewed negatively, but rather are perceived as a 'healthy tension', enabling them to become more mindful of their actions as consumers and to strike a balance between religion and consumption.

Questions

1 What do you think about the statistics offered in this case – does it surprise you that so many people remain affiliated with and practise religion today? Would you say we live in a secular age? If so, why? Provide examples to support your views.

2 Do you have any friends like Kevin, Sally or Ryan whose consumption habits and behaviours are affected by religious, political or cultural influences? If so, what are some of these influences?

3 Think about your own life experiences. Can you see how religious beliefs, cultural learnings and/or family influences have all played a part in shaping you as a consumer today? What are some of these personal influences and can you trace where they have stemmed from?

4 Palmer and Gallagher[5] and McAlexander et al.[6] both found that lapsed Catholics and ex-Mormons, years after leaving their religious faiths, remained influenced by the religious dogmas of the Catholic and Mormon faith respectively. The faith rulings were embedded within the consumers to such a degree that they had become 'habits of the heart'. Can you think of any such 'habits of the heart' that you or a fellow family member have?

5 Do you think consumer research is correct in its claim that a 'detraditionalisation' of institutional pillars such as family, education and religion is occurring? Is consumer culture the new ideology and religion of the 21st century?

Sources

[1]E.J. Arnould, 'Should consumer citizens escape the market?', *The Annals of the American Academy of Political and Social Science* 611 (2007): 96–111.

[2]R.W. Belk, M. Wallendorf and J.F. Sherry Jr, 'The sacred and the profane in consumer behaviour: Theodicy on the Odyssey', *Journal of Consumer Research* 16(1) (1989): 1–38; J.H. McAlexander, B. Leavenworth Dufault, D.M. Martin and J.W. Schouten, 'The marketization of religion: Field, capital, and consumer identity', *Journal of Consumer Research* 41(3) (2014): 858–75.

[3]S. Ross, 'The Harvest Fields Statistics 2018', http://www.wholesomewords.org/missions/greatc.html (accessed 3 September 2018).

[4]M. Touzani and E.C. Hirschman, 'Cultural syncretism and Ramadan observance: Consumer research visits Islam', *Advances in Consumer Research* 35 (2009): 374–80; O. Sandikci and G. Ger, 'Veiling in style: How does a stigmatized practice become fashionable?', *Journal of Consumer Research* 37(1) (2010): 15–36; E.C. Hirschman, A.A. Ruvio and M. Touzani, 'Breaking bread with Abraham's children: Christians, Jews and Muslims' holiday consumption in dominant, minority and diasporic communities', *Journal of the Academy of Marketing Science* 39 (2011): 429–48; D. Rinallo, S. Borghini, G. Bamossy and R.V. Kozinets, 'When sacred objects go brand: Fashion rosaries and the contemporary linkage of religion and commerciality', in D. Rinallo, L. Scott, and P. Maclaren (eds), *Consumption and Spirituality* (London: Routledge, 2013): 29–40.

[5]A. Palmer and D. Gallagher, 'Religiosity, relationships and consumption: A study of church-going in Ireland', *Consumption Markets & Culture* 10(1) (2007): 31–49.

[6]J.H. McAlexander, B. Leavenworth Dufault, D.M. Martin and J.W. Schouten, 'The marketization of religion: Field, capital, and consumer identity', *Journal of Consumer Research* 41(3) (2014): 858–75.

Case study E.2

'Miss u loads': online consumer memorialisation practices

Darach Turley, Dublin City University, Ireland, and

Stephanie O'donohoe, University of Edinburgh, UK

People can live, work and play alongside spouses, siblings and friends for years without ever having to ask themselves 'who exactly is this person and what do they mean to me?'. For many, this question only arises after a death. Indeed, answering this question is now widely seen as an integral part of the grieving process and may explain why one of the most instinctive reactions on the part of bereaved family and friends is to begin telling stories about the deceased person. It is more than just a matter of filling in the uncomfortable silences that can linger in a household when someone dies; stories are a vital part of regaining a sense of order and control following a major loss.

In many countries, this process of creating a biography or narrative of the dead person begins with relatives and friends exchanging stories and memories with immediate family members, often during visits to the bereaved family home. In this sense, family members typically act as custodians and censors of the loved one's biography, exercising a certain control over what should or should not be included in it. This biographical pride of place in finalising the dead person's identity mirrors the way in which immediate family members were also first to be informed of the death, first to issue funeral details, appeared at the top of the death notice, occupied the front seats during the funeral service and stood closest to the grave at the moment of burial.

Chapter 4 of this text reviews the self-concept of the consumer, its elements and its influence on purchasing. It makes the point that consumers' virtual selves are an increasingly important element of this self-concept. This virtual self can include our identities on gaming sites and our avatars in cyber worlds such as *Second Life,* together with the identities we create on our social media profiles. Social media profiles such as those on Facebook are instances of anonymous identities that are 'anchored', at least to a degree, in our offline identities; this need not be the case for our gaming avatars, where we can be anyone we want.

Although many other social networking sites such as Instagram and Snapchat exist, Facebook is the colossus of cyberspace, with, as of January 2018, a global reach of over 2.2 billion people.[1] Given its dominance, it is hardly surprising that death and mourning make their presence felt on this platform. This sometimes takes the form of dedicated memorial sites set up by family or friends of the deceased. More commonly, however, memorialisation is practised in spaces effectively co-created by the living and the dead. Personal Facebook sites have often been crafted interactively by their owners over years, and are replete with photos, video clips, links, lists of friends, comments and conversation. Employers will often check a Facebook site to gain a fuller picture of a prospective employee's offline identity.

When a Facebook user dies, their profile remains 'live' and friends can continue to post comments as before. The site they post on is the same site they have always posted on and, because Facebook is asynchronous, replies are not necessarily expected, so in one sense it appears to be business as usual. Obviously the content and emotional tone of postings will alter dramatically, and the deceased owner is no longer active, but the online process of identity creation continues nonetheless. By addressing the dead person, by expressing one's sense of loss, by sharing reminiscences, regrets and sometimes revelations, the identity creation process of the dead person continues unabated. This virtual identity of a deceased consumer may no longer be anchored in a physical body, but it can still evolve and endure. In this sense, social media such as Facebook look set to change the complexion and ground rules of mourning in the years ahead.

The post-mortem identity-making and narrative creation evidenced on Facebook raise a number of interesting issues both for bereaved people and for those who manage such networks. At a general level, some media commentators feel that having survivors speak openly about death, grief and their relationship with the deceased person will help normalise death. In many cultures death is seen as a taboo topic, something not to be spoken about in public; having ordinary posters weave their sense of loss and longing into their daily online exchanges may change this significantly. In a similar vein, friends who post on a deceased friend's profile continue to use the same informal, conversational language and, in so doing, may serve to mainstream mourning and demystify dying and death. For example, Kasket reports comments such as 'I know u can read this, it just sux that u can't talk back . . . '.[2] In this way, Facebook users continue to weave dead 'friends' into the social fabric of their everyday lives, both proclaiming and enacting continuing bonds between the living and the dead.

Many personal profiles contain a rich variety of audio and visual resources and can therefore tell the story of the deceased person in much greater detail and to a much broader audience. Some bereaved family members may welcome the opportunity to discover aspects of the life, loves and leisure pursuits of their loved one for the first time, to get to know hitherto unknown friends, work colleagues and team-mates, to read how they were valued and how deeply they are now missed. For example, a *Time* magazine article[3] reports that when 21-year-old UCLA student Amy Weiss died suddenly, her mother Pam found some solace in the traces she left on Facebook, logging in to her daughter's Facebook account, Pam found many photographs of Amy that she would never have seen otherwise, and posts she had written offering fresh insights into her life and aspirations. Pam even began communicating with her daughter's friends on Facebook, sharing memories and learning more about what she had meant to them.

While Amy's mother found consolation in accessing her profile, interactions between family members, online 'friends' and content can also cause tension and distress. Immediate family members logging in and using the dead person's password may be upset by some of what they find on Facebook – parents may find photos of their deceased children doing things they disapprove of, for example, or posting about family issues that they had not expected to be shared online. They may feel uncomfortable about how online friends talk about – or to – the person who died. They may also take umbrage at being given unsolicited advice on grieving from Facebook friends of their loved one who are total strangers to them.

Friends and family members may find that their grief is exacerbated by actions and policies of Facebook itself. Many report being upset by automated messages encouraging them to get back in touch with people who have died, or even to send them 'happy birthday' wishes. This has led to the introduction of a memorialisation option: on receiving proof of a death, an account will be frozen and no one can log in or post from it. To protect it from voyeurs, trolls or 'grief tourists', only those who were already Facebook friends can find it or interact with the profile. In most cases, the majority of these 'friends' are non-family members, offline pals and work colleagues, people who would formerly have been on the sidelines of the story-telling exercise. The

traditional 'hierarchy of intimacy' among mourners would have left these occupiers of non-kinship roles somewhat marginalised. We may now see this asymmetry reversed, with the mourners who really mattered to the deceased profile owner becoming enfranchised and having their say. In this sense, the migration of mourning to digital platforms such as Facebook looks set to change and challenge traditional custom and practice, particularly with reference to the long-established pecking order of family ownership and control over the dead person's biography.

It is Facebook policy not to allow family members to access a dead person's account if they don't know the password, and they cannot even interact with the profile if they were not already friends on Facebook. The distress this can cause is highlighted by the case of John Berlin, who uploaded a YouTube video pleading with Facebook to allow him to see the automatically generated one-minute 'Look Back' video featuring the 'highlights' of his dead 22-year-old son Jesse's posts, even though he did not have his son's password.[4] In other cases, even parents who knew their child's password have found themselves suddenly locked out of the account because someone else notified Facebook about the death, leading the account to be memorialised.

Facebook does, however, allow family members, regardless of their 'friend' status, to delete a dead person's account. This can have major repercussions for online friends who found comfort and community in continuing to interact online; indeed, some people have described the sudden disappearance of their friend's Facebook profile as a second bereavement. Furthermore, since online social networks are, by definition, co-created, Facebook's privileging of family over 'friends' in this way raises important questions over ownership as well as privacy. Concerns such as these regarding post-mortem privacy and ownership have led to a recent change in Facebook policy – users can now appoint a 'legacy contact' to manage their account when they die.[5]

Questions

1 To what extent do digital and social media technologies change the rituals surrounding death and remembrance?

2 Recent theories of bereavement emphasise that death changes but does not sever the bonds between the living and the dead. Discuss the role of consumption, online and offline, in continuing bonds.

3 Users may now nominate someone to manage their 'digital legacy' on Facebook. What else might be part of a consumer's digital legacy, and what concerns might there be about how this is managed?

Sources

[1]https://en.wikipedia.org/wiki/Facebook (accessed 5 December 2018).

[2]E. Kasket, 'Continuing bonds in the age of social networking: Facebook as a modern-day medium', *Bereavement Care* 31(2) (2012): 62–9.

[3]G. Faure, 'Managing your online afterlife', *Time* 174(10) (2009): 51.

[4]D. Lee, 'Facebook reviews family memorials after dad's plea', BBC News (6 February 2014), http://www.bbc.co.uk/news/technology-26066688 (accessed 3 September 2018).

[5]V. Callison-Burch, J. Probst and M. Govea, 'Adding a legacy contact', Facebook newsroom (2015), http://newsroom.fb.com/news/2015/02/adding-a-legacy-contact/ (accessed 3 September 2018).

Case study E.3

Routes to heritage: acculturation among second-generation British Indian women

Anuja Pradhan and **Hayley Cocker**, Lancaster University, UK

Introduction

Acculturation theories conceptualise what happens when people from one culture live in a different cultural context, i.e., how migrant consumers experience a new 'host' culture. Post-assimilationist acculturation studies such as that by Peñaloza[1] explain that not all migrants choose to assimilate into the host culture (assimilation). Instead, they may physically separate themselves from the host culture (segregation), completely resist the host culture (resistance), or maintain aspects of both cultures (maintenance).

In this case, we show how current acculturation models do not completely account for the unique lived experiences of second-generation ethnic consumers. In contrast to previous acculturation studies that have focused on the shattered identities[2] and ethnic group conflicts,[3] we bring to the fore the uplifting stories of acculturation that develop in part due to higher social class positions, historical ties between host and home cultures and a multicultural setting (e.g. the UK). We emphasise the important role social class plays in the lived experiences of second-generation ethnic consumers. Unlike previous studies that make distinctions between home and host, we articulate the prevalence of creole symbols of culture – for example, British Indian films and 'curry' – that are interwoven in second-generation consumers' lived experiences.

Our case is about ethnic consumers born in the 'host' country to parents who have migrated from the 'home' country. We understand the lives of second-generation British Indian women (hereafter known as G2) through Geetha's story (see below). G2s are different from their parents' generation (hereafter known as G1) since they acquire dominant cultural practices through the public spheres of education, media and government *inter alia*, while learning 'home' (i.e. heritage cultural practices) from family, friends and community. British Indians make the case even more complex because they are a group of heterogeneous communities originating from different states of India (e.g. Punjab, Gujarat, Tamil Nadu, etc). Each community speaks a different language, may practice a different religion and has different cultural practices, customs and traditions. G2s, through G1s, learn and identify with these differences in Britain much like they identify with being English, Scottish, Welsh or Irish. Owing to India's and Britain's colonial history, British society has a familiarity with Indian culture, and has integrated some Indian practices, traditions and customs in a way that they are now a part of British culture, the best example being curry. In the next section, we use the example of Geetha to show that present acculturation theories need to be revised to include the complexities of G2 experiences.

Geetha – a second-generation British Indian woman

Geetha is a 21-year-old middle-class British Indian woman studying for an undergraduate degree in biology at a university close to London. She chose this university because it's close to home, meaning she can bring dirty laundry back at weekends for her mum to do. Geetha's mum is a psychologist and her dad a general physician. Both her parents were born in small towns in the state of Tamil Nadu in India and migrated to Britain in 1989 for better work opportunities. Born and raised in Britain, Geetha grew up in a home dominated by Indian cultural practices. Her mum ensured, as good Hindus, that Geetha and her sister, Lila, prayed every morning, and her dad played Tamil music CDs enough times for the kids to know the lyrics without understanding the words. Her parents enrolled their daughters in dance and music lessons to learn Bharatnatyam (a traditional south Indian dance) and Carnatic singing (traditional south Indian music). They enjoyed these weekly lessons for seven years. It was a place for them to engage in their heritage with other G2s.

At home, every evening meal is Indian food lovingly prepared by her mum using ingredients bought during their trips to India. Geetha says her mum tried to teach Lila and her some Indian cooking before they went off to university, but it was too complicated. She much prefers getting chicken tikka masala from the local takeaway on weekends with her flat mates, though it never compares to her mum's chicken curry and homemade naan. Geetha has, however, taken her mum's practice of having a leisurely afternoon Yorkshire tea with scones to university with her.

At university Geetha has white British friends, Kenyan friends and North Indian friends, but primarily identifies with her Sri Lankan friends whom she feels are most like her. She feels different from North Indians based on language, skin colour and attitudes. 'They're two shades lighter than me, I look nothing like them. They're all in the Indian society and speak in Hindi to each other so I have no idea what they're saying. Also, they're so loud it's annoying', Geetha complains.

Geetha visits India almost every year with her parents and sister. She loves visiting India for the food, shopping and, most importantly, spending time with her grandparents. As Geetha's grandparents do not speak English, visiting them for three weeks in the summer gives her the opportunity to practise speaking Tamil – the language spoken by her parents and grandparents. She discovers the latest fashion trends from her Indian cousins and then shows these off back home in Britain. She likes cycling around her palatial ancestral home in the village, being chased by stray dogs. Every Sunday her family visits the temples her ancestors built, giving Geetha and Lila a sense of finding a spiritual home. These visits help Geetha learn about her heritage, and act as an important route to Indian culture, in addition to her parents' stories.

Back in the UK, Geetha and her Sri Lankan friends religiously go to the local cinema each time a new Bollywood film is released. She loves the clothes and the dancing but has to watch the movies with subtitles. While Geetha understands and is able to speak some Tamil, she does not understand Hindi, the language used in most Bollywood productions. 'I prefer Bollywood to British Indian cinema. It's so much more colourful and fun! Though my friends and I love *Bend It Like Beckham* (a British Indian film) because it's so relatable. We all have that one 'aunty' who's into everybody's business!' Bollywood becomes another route for Geetha to understand her heritage culture, while British Indian movies help her identify more locally.

Acculturation among the second generation

Like Geetha, many ethnic consumers in multicultural societies find routes to reclaim cultural heritage through trips to their homeland, media and food. Most importantly, G1 consumers play a key role in socialising G2s in the culture of heritage from an early age through religion, celebrations and food. They also educate G2s about intercommunity differences within their culture (e.g. the difference between those from Punjab and those from Tamil Nadu). G2s find liberation in belonging to more than one culture,

and enjoy sharing this with others. This is especially possible in urban cities, where multiple resources for exploring cultural heritage exist – in Geetha's case this means access to Bollywood movies at the cinema, easy trips to India, Indian food and dance and music lessons.

Geetha does not feel the need to be completely Indian – she does not speak her language of heritage or wear traditional Indian clothes or cook Indian food. However, it is important for her to do what she can, while also being British. We often see competition among ethnic consumers about who is more attuned to their heritage – it's a mark of superiority and pride to successfully identify diversely.

Contribution to acculturation theory

- *Uplifting lived experiences*: we highlight how it is possible for second-generation ethnic consumers to have uplifting lived experiences. We show how a combination of factors, including acculturating to home culture, higher social class, historical ties between host and home cultures and a multicultural society, contribute towards G2 consumers experiencing an integrative environment for cultural performance.

- *Home and host*: in the case of second-generation ethnic consumers, concepts of home and host do not fit quite neatly. Aspects of the dominant culture – British culture in Geetha's case – form their 'home' culture, while aspects of the minority culture – Indian culture for Geetha – are dominant in their actual home and community setting. For G2 ethnic consumers, cultures are creolised, mythologised and fluid.

- *Assimilation, maintenance, segregation and resistance*: G2s have a different set of strategies for identification compared to G1s. Their identification is greatly influenced by their parents' strategies of socialising them into their culture of heritage. Their identification also depends on the society they live in and how accepting it is of their heritage. In Geetha's case, she lives in an urban, multicultural city where she can freely express herself. Her sister, Lila, works in a small town in the south of England where she believes people might not be as accepting and so saves her cultural performances for when she's home in London.

- *Access to resources*: Geetha is lucky to have grown up in a city where she has multiple routes to access her heritage culture – she can watch Bollywood movies, learn South Indian dance and eat authentic Indian food. Some of her North Indian friends had very different experiences growing up in small towns – they travelled to far off cities to watch Bollywood cinema (and not very often), and as Buddhists they didn't find any temples close to home. Thinking about the progressive learning model (see Chapter 13), we see the difficulties G2 ethnic consumers face if they don't have contact with, and access to, the culture they want to perform/ identify with.

- *Mythologised cultures*: G2s' understanding and performance of cultures is often mythologised. They are socialised into the dominant and minority cultures by their parents and other G1s – experiencing stories of these cultures and seeing them through a first-generation lens. In Geetha's case she is able to experience India through regular trips, but her friend Priya has never had the chance to visit. Priya's version of Indian culture is informed by her parents' stories, Bollywood movies and BBC documentaries.

Questions

1 How do the experiences of second-generation ethnic consumers such as Geetha differ from those of first-generation consumers typically discussed in acculturation studies, and how does this change our understanding of acculturation?

2 What acculturation agents influence the process of acculturating to heritage culture?

3 Why is it important to understand positive and uplifting migrant stories?

Sources

[1]Lisa Peñaloza, '*Atravesando Fronteras*/Border Crossings: A Critical Ethnographic Exploration of the Consumer Acculturation of Mexican Immigrants', *Journal of Consumer Research* 21 (June 1994): 32–54.

[2]T. Üstüner and D. Holt, 'Dominated consumer acculturation: The social construction of poor migrant women's consumer identity projects in a Turkish squatter', *Journal of Consumer Research* 34(1) (2007): 41–56.

[3]M.K. Luedicke, 'Indigenes' responses to immigrants' consumer acculturation: A relational configuration analysis', *Journal of Consumer Research* 42(1) (2015): 109–29.

Further reading

S. Askegaard, E. Arnould and D. Kjeldgaard, 'Postassimilationist ethnic consumer research: Qualifications and extensions. *Journal of Consumer Research* 32(1) (2005): 160–70.

D. Crockett, 'Paths to Respectability: Consumption and Stigma Management in the Contemporary Black Middle Class', *Journal of Consumer Research* 44(3) (2017): 554–81.

C. Demangeot, A. Broeckerhoff, E. Kipnis, C. Pullig and L. Visconti, 'Consumer mobility and well-being among changing places and shifting ethnicities', *Marketing Theory* 15(2) (2014): 271–8.

D. Kjeldgaard and S. Askegaard, 'The Glocalization of Youth Culture: The Global Youth Segment as Structures of Common Difference', *Journal Of Consumer Research* 33(2) (2006): 231–47.

A. Takhar, P. Maclaran and L. Stevens, 'Bollywood Cinema's Global Reach: Consuming the "Diasporic Consciousness"', *Journal of Macromarketing* 32(3) (2012): 266–79.

E. Veresiu and M. Giesler, 'Beyond Acculturation: Multiculturalism and the Institutional Shaping of an Ethnic Consumer Subject', *Journal Of Consumer Research* (2018).

Glossary

80/20 rule The rule of thumb (or heuristic) whereby only 20 per cent of a product's users accounts for 80 per cent of the volume of that product that a company sells (p. 183)

Abandoned products Grocery items that shoppers buy but never use (p. 62)

ABC model of attitudes A multidimensional perspective, stating that attitudes are jointly defined by affect, behaviour and cognition (p. 254)

Absolute threshold The minimum amount of stimulation that can be detected by a sensory channel (p. 94)

Access-based consumption Transactions that can be market mediated but where no transfer of ownership takes place (see also 'Sharing economy') (p. 26)

Accommodative purchase decision The process to achieve agreement among a group whose members have different preferences or priorities (p. 401)

Acculturation The process of learning the beliefs and behaviours endorsed by another culture (pp. 188, 555)

Acculturation agents Friends, family, local businesses and other reference groups that facilitate the learning of cultural norms (p. 555)

Achieved status A status that is based on merit. In other words, a status that reflects one's skills, which has been obtained through one's activities and accomplishments, and as such the status is earned and chosen. To be a top athlete or a professor is an achieved status (p. 436)

Activation models of memory Approaches to memory stressing different levels of processing that occur and activate some aspects of memory rather than others, depending on the nature of the processing task (p. 233)

Activity stores A retailing concept that lets consumers participate in the production of the products or services being sold in the store (p. 57)

Actual self A person's realistic appraisal of his or her qualities (p. 120)

Adaptation The process that occurs when a sensation becomes so familiar that it is no longer the focus of attention (p. 98)

Advergaming Online games merged with interactive advertisements that let companies target specific types of consumers (p. 538)

Affect The way a consumer feels about an attitude object (p. 254, 324)

Age cohort A group of consumers of the same approximate age who have undergone similar experiences (p. 409)

Agentic goals Goals that stress self-assertion and mastery and are associated with males (p. 132)

AIOs (activities, interests and opinions) The psychographic variables used by researchers in grouping consumers (p. 182)

Alternate reality games (ARGs) Games that take place in an interactive networked narrative that uses the real world as a platform and media across multiple platforms to deliver a story that can be altered by players' actions (p. 176)

Anchoring A concept in behavioural economics that refers to a piece of information (such as price, or a feature of a consumer good or service) that people use as a standard for future judgements (p. 319)

Androgyny The possession of both masculine and feminine traits (p. 134)

Anti-brand communities Groups of consumers who share a common disdain for a celebrity, store or brand (p. 375)

Anti-conformity This is about defiance and, in the context of consumption, is where people go out of their way *not* to buy whatever happens to be in fashion or on trend (p. 359)

Anti-consumption The actions taken by consumers involving the deliberate defacement or mutilation of products (p. 20)

Appeal The basis of the persuasive message in an advertisement, which can be linked to a range of emotions (e.g. fear or surprise) and message types (e.g. humour) (p. 276)

Approach–approach conflict A person must choose between two desirable alternatives (p. 166)

Approach–avoidance conflict A person desires a goal but wishes to avoid it at the same time (p. 167)

Art product A creation viewed primarily as an object of aesthetic contemplation without any functional value (p. 531)

Ascribed status Status that one has inherited through birth or which is assigned to one later in life. It is not chosen but given to you. To be a prince or to be born into a wealthy family is an ascribed status. Also, such phenomena as gender prejudice are based on ascribed status, where certain characteristics of 'being a woman' can be ascribed to you (p. 436)

Atmospherics The use of space and physical features in store design to evoke certain effects in buyers (p. 57)

Attention The assignment of cognitive capacity to selected stimuli (p. 85)

Attitude A lasting, general evaluation of people (including oneself), objects or issues (p. 251)

Attitude object (A_o) Anything towards which one has an attitude (p. 251)

Attitude towards the act of buying (A_{act}) The perceived consequences of a purchase (p. 271)

Attitude towards the advertisement (A_{ad}) A predisposition to respond favourably to a particular advertising stimulus during an exposure situation (p. 260)

Augmented reality (AR) This term refers to media that combine a physical layer with a digital layer to create a combined experience. If you've ever watched a 3D movie with those clunky glasses, you've experienced one form of augmented reality (pp. 58, 96)

Autocratic decisions Purchase decisions that are made exclusively by one spouse (p. 402)

Avoidance–avoidance conflict Occurs when we face a choice between two undesirable alternatives (p. 168)

Balance theory Considers relations among elements a person might perceive as belonging together and people's tendency to change relations among elements in order to make them consistent or balanced (p. 264)

Behavioural economics The study of the behavioural determinants of economic decisions (pp. 318, 428)

Behavioural learning theories The perspectives on learning that assume that learning takes place as the result of responses to external events (p. 215)

Behavioural targeting Refers to presenting people with specific advertisements based on their use of the internet and social media (p. 184)

Being space A retail environment that resembles a residential living room where customers are encouraged to congregate (p. 56)

Belief systems The set of a person's underlying beliefs, i.e. what they believe at heart; the extent to which people share a belief system is a function of individual,

social and cultural forces. Believers tend to be exposed to information that supports what they believe (p.186)

Bitcoin A form of digital currency that is created and held electronically (p. 51)

Body cathexis A person's feelings about aspects of his or her body (p. 140)

Body image A consumer's subjective evaluation of his or her physical appearance (p. 140)

Boomerang generation Children or dependents who find themselves needing to return to their parents/guardians' home, primarily for financial reasons (p. 413)

Bounded rationality A concept in behavioural economics that states that since we rarely have the resources (especially the time) to weigh every possible factor into a decision, we settle for a solution that is just 'good enough' (p. 319)

Brand The name associated by a manufacturer with their product in order to distinguish their product from similar products in the marketplace; it can often also be a trademark (p. 104)

Brand addiction A psychological state involving both mental and behavioural near-obsession with a particular brand, seen in the drive to possess the brand's products. This behaviour involves positive affectivity and gratification (pp. 173, 324)

Brand advocates Consumers who supply product reviews online (pp. 303, 377)

Brand communities A group of consumers who share a set of social relationships based on usage or interest in a product (p. 359)

Brand equity A brand that has strong positive associations and consequently commands a lot of loyalty (p. 223)

Brand-fests Usually organised by companies to promote and celebrate their brands and often used to encourage the development of brand communities in order to build brand loyalty and reinforce group membership (p. 360)

Brand loyalty A pattern of repeat product purchases accompanied by an underlying positive attitude towards the brand (pp. 175, 317)

Brand personality A set of traits people attribute to a product as if it were a person (p. 14)

Buzz Word of mouth that is viewed as authentic and generated by customers (p. 363)

Capital Following Bourdieu, capital involves a variety of resources (e.g. economic, cultural and social) that can be used as assets in various contexts (p. 455)

Carbon footprint The impact human activities have on the environment in terms of the amount of greenhouse gases they produce; measured in units of carbon dioxide (p. 197)

Category exemplars Brands that are particularly relevant examples of a broader classification (p. 309)

Classic A fashion with an extremely long acceptance cycle (p. 553)

Classical conditioning The learning that occurs when a stimulus eliciting a response is paired with another stimulus that initially does not elicit a response on its own, but will cause a similar response over time because of its association with the first stimulus (p. 217)

Co-branding strategies Strategies that employ a marketing partnership between two or more different brands to jointly promote a product or service (p. 181)

Co-consumers Other patrons in a consumer setting (p. 43)

Coercive power Influencing a person by social or physical intimidation (p. 349)

Cognition The beliefs a consumer has about an attitude object (p. 254)

Cognitive development The ability to comprehend concepts of increasing complexity as a person ages (p. 408)

Cognitive learning The learning that occurs as a result of internal mental processes (p. 221)

Cognitive processing style A predisposition to process information. Some of us tend to have a *rational system of cognition* that processes information analytically and sequentially using roles of logic, while others rely on an *experiential system of cognition* that processes information more holistically and in parallel (p. 293)

Cohesiveness The degree to which members of a group are attracted to each other and how much each values their membership in this group (p. 353)

Collecting The accumulation of rare or mundane and inexpensive objects, which transforms profane items into sacred ones (p. 510)

Collective interest Denotes the commonalities of bonds that link groups either offline (such as family or social activities) or online (such as white-wine enthusiasts) (p. 377)

Collective selection The process whereby certain symbolic alternatives tend to be chosen jointly in preference to others by members of a group (p. 546)

Collective value creation The process whereby brand community members work together to develop better ways to use and customise products (p. 360)

Collectivist culture A cultural orientation that encourages people to subordinate their personal goals to those of a stable in-group (p. 484)

Communal goals Goals that stress affiliation and the fostering of harmonious relations and are associated with females (p. 132)

Communities of practice Groups of people engaged in some mutual endeavour or activity (p. 362)

Community In a digital context, a group of people who engage in supportive and sociable relationships with others who share one or more common interests (p. 373)

Compensatory decision rules Allow information about attributes of competing products to be averaged; poor standing on one attribute may be offset by good standing on another (p. 312)

Conformity A change in beliefs or actions as a reaction to real or perceived group pressure (p. 355)

Conjunctive rule A type of consumer decision rule that entails processing by brand. Having established cut-offs for each attribute, the decision-maker chooses a brand if it meets all of the cut-offs, while failure to meet any one cut-off means they will reject it. If none of the brands meets all of the cut-offs, they may delay the choice, change the decision rule, or modify the cut-offs they choose to apply. See also **Non-compensatory decision rules** (p. 312)

Conscientious consumerism A new value that combines a focus on personal health with a concern for global health (p. 196)

Consensual purchase decision A decision in which the group agrees on the desired purchase and differs only in terms of how it will be achieved (p. 401)

Consideration set The products a consumer actually deliberates about choosing (p. 307)

Conspicuous consumption The purchase and prominent display of luxury goods as evidence of the consumer's ability to afford them (p. 453)

Constructive processing The term for a thought process in which the effort needed to make a particular choice is evaluated, and the amount of 'cognitive effort' expended to get the job done is then tailored (p. 293)

Consumer behaviour The processes involved when individuals or groups select, purchase, use or dispose of products, services, ideas or experiences to satisfy needs or desires (p. 3)

Consumer confidence The state of mind of consumers relative to their optimism or pessimism about economic decisions; people tend to make more discretionary purchases when their confidence in the economy is high (p. 433)

Consumer culture The relationship between market forces, consumption processes and the key characteristics of what is normally understood to be 'a culture' (p. 13)

Consumer culture theory (CCT) An interdisciplinary field of research oriented towards a better understanding of consumers and their behaviour from what could broadly be termed a 'cultural perspective', and why consumer culture unfolds as it does – see http://cctweb.org/ (p. 13)

Consumer-generated content (CGC) A hallmark of Web 2.0; everyday people voice their opinions about products, brands and companies on blogs, podcasts and social networking sites and film their own commercials, which they post on websites (p. 177)

Consumer hyperchoice A condition where the large number of available options forces us to make repeated choices that drain psychological energy and diminish our ability to make smart decisions (p. 292)

Consumer identity renaissance The redefinition process people undergo when they retire (p. 418)

Consumer policy Concern of public bodies (including many national and international agencies) to oversee consumer-related activities for the welfare of consumers, e.g. health-and-safety issues around the consumption of legal and illegal substances such as alcohol, cigarettes and drugs, or sustainability issues and the environment (p. 19)

Consumer satisfaction/dissatisfaction (CS/D) The overall attitude a person has about a product after it has been purchased (p. 315)

Consumer socialisation The process by which young people acquire skills that enable them to function in the marketplace (p. 404)

Consumer society A society where social life is organised less around our identities as producers or workers in the production system, and more according to our roles as consumers in the consumption system (p. 13)

Consumer tribe Group of people who share a lifestyle and who can identify with each other because of a shared allegiance to an activity or a product (p. 361)

Consumption communities Consumption communities are groups of people who share the consumption of a particular brand or product (p. 4)

Consumption constellations Clusters of complementary products, specific brands and/or consumption activities used by consumers to define, communicate and enact social roles (p. 181)

Consumption situation The setting or context in which a product or service is consumed (p. 37)

Continuous innovation A product change or new product that requires relatively little adaptation in the consumer's behaviour (p. 543)

Conventions Norms regarding the conduct of everyday life (pp. 189, 486)

Conversations Communications or exchanges between two or more people, either offline (usually in real time) or online (synchronous or asynchronous), based on talking or writing, or sometimes a hybrid of the two. If you communicate with a friend via Facebook chat, for instance, you may feel that you actually 'talked' to her, even if the timing was asynchronous (i.e. the exchange of views was not at the same time) (p. 377)

Co-optation A cultural process where the original meaning of a product or other symbol associated with a subculture is modified by members of mainstream culture (pp. 481, 523)

Core values Common general values held by a culture (p. 186)

Counteractive construal An exaggeration of the negative aspects of behaviours that will interfere with an ultimate goal (p. 294)

Country of origin Original country in which a product is produced; can be an important piece of information in the decision-making process (p. 321)

Co-variation The associations made between events that may or may not actually influence each other (p. 320)

Craft product A creation valued because of the beauty with which it performs some function; this type of product tends to follow a formula that permits rapid production; it is easier to understand than an art product (p. 531)

Crescive norms Unspoken rules that govern social behaviour (p. 189)

Crowdsourcing A term coined in the early 21st century to describe the strategic use of the general public (consumers, audiences) as a source of ideas or other forms of input for some kind of corporate use such as campaigns or product or service development (p. 530)

Cryptocurrency A digital or virtual currency in which encryption techniques are used to regulate the generation of units of currency and verify the transfer of funds (p. 51)

Cultivation hypothesis A perspective emphasising media's ability to distort consumers' perceptions of reality (p. 538)

Cult products Products with a committed customer base (p. 173)

Cultural categories The grouping of ideas and values that reflect the basic ways members of society characterise the world (p. 103)

Cultural formula Where certain roles and props often occur consistently in many popular art forms, such as detective stories or science fiction (p. 532)

Cultural gatekeepers Individuals who are responsible for determining the types of message and symbolism to which members of mass culture are exposed (p. 529)

Cultural intermediaries Cultural agents who mediate information between high culture and popular mass culture (p. 529)

Cultural production system (CPS) The set of individuals or organisations responsible for creating and marketing a cultural product (p. 527)

Cultural selection The process where some alternatives are selected in preference to those selected by cultural gatekeepers (p. 525)

Culture The values, ethics, rituals, traditions, material objects and services produced or valued by members of society (p. 482)

Custom A norm that is derived from a traditional way of doing something (pp. 189, 486)

Cybercrime Illegal activities undertaken on the internet that can result in identity theft and data loss for consumers (p. 186)

Cybermediary Intermediary that helps to filter and organise online market information so that consumers can identify and evaluate alternatives more efficiently (p. 300)

Cyberplace An online social community (p. 373)

Cyberspace Refers to the virtual world created by the internet, where individuals can engage in a variety of activities including the buying and selling of goods and services, and also games playing (p. 46)

Decision polarisation The process whereby individuals' choices tend to become more extreme (polarised), in either a conservative or risky direction, following group discussion of alternatives (p. 355)

Default bias A tendency in decision-making that makes it more likely for people to comply with a requirement than to make an effort not to comply (p. 319)

De-individuation The process whereby individual identities are submerged within a group, reducing inhibitions against socially inappropriate behaviour (p. 353)

Democracy In a social media context, a term that refers to rule by the people; community leaders are appointed or elected based on their demonstrated ability to add value to the group (p. 377)

Demographics The observable measurements of a population's characteristics, such as birth rates, age distribution or income (p. 4, 182)

Desacralisation The process that occurs when a sacred item or symbol is removed or is duplicated in mass quantities, and as a result becomes profane (p. 508)

Determinant attributes The attributes actually used to differentiate among choices (p. 310)

Differential threshold The ability of a sensory system to detect changes or differences among stimuli (p. 94)

Digital detoxing Refers to periods of time when consumers choose to go offline from their various digital gadgets (e.g. smartphones, iPads, laptops) and disconnect from social media activities *inter alia* (p. 379)

Digital self The mask people put on to engage the technological world (p. 129)

Digital virtual consumption Purchases of virtual goods for use in online games and social communities (p. 382)

Digital wallets Electronic devices that allow an individual to make electronic commerce transactions (p. 51)

Discontinuous innovation A product change or new product that requires a significant amount of adaptation of behaviour by the adopter (p. 543)

Discretionary income The money available to an individual or household over and above that required for maintaining a comfortable standard of living (p. 430)

Dissociative groups Dissociative groups These are sets of people with whom one would prefer not to be associated with or linked to (e.g. via the symbolic meaning(s) of brand associations) (p. 348)

Dispreferred Marker Effect The tendency to couch negative product reviews in softer terms to avoid looking harsh or judgemental (p. 396)

Distinction A term used by French sociologist Pierre Bourdieu for establishing a class system based on consumer tastes (p. 456)

Divestment rituals The steps people take to gradually distance themselves from things they treasure so that they can sell them or give them away (p. 67)

Drive theory Focuses on the desire to satisfy a biological need in order to reduce physiological arousal (p. 163)

Dynamically continuous innovation A product change or new product that requires a moderate amount of adaptation of behaviour by the adopter (p. 543)

Early adopters People receptive to new styles because they are involved in the product category and place high value on being fashionable (p. 541)

Economics of information A branch of microeconomic theory that studies how information affects an *economy* and economic decisions. Information has special characteristics. It is easy to create but hard to trust. It is easy to spread but hard to control. It influences many decisions (p. 297)

Elaborated codes Ways of expressing and interpreting meanings that are complex and depend on a sophisticated worldview; tend to be used by the middle and upper classes (p. 447)

Elaboration likelihood model (ELM) The approach that one of two routes to persuasion (central *vs* peripheral) will be followed, depending on the personal relevance of a message; the route taken determines the relative importance of message contents *vs* other characteristics, such as source attractiveness (p. 281)

Electronic recommendation agent A software tool that tries to understand a human decision-maker's multi-attribute preferences for a product category by asking the user to communicate his or her preferences. Based on these data, the software then recommends a list of alternatives sorted by the degree that they fit with the person's preferences (p. 302)

E-sports A multi-player video game played competitively for spectators, typically by professional gamers (p. 178)

Elimination-by-aspects rule A consumer rule by which the buyer evaluates brands on their most important attributes but imposes specific cut-offs (p. 312)

Embodied cognition The concept that mental activity is linked to how we perceive the physical world around us. In marketing it refers to the way that changes in self-concept can arise from usage of brands that convey different meanings (p. 129)

Emotions Intense feelings that often relate to a specific triggering event (p. 261)

Enclothed cognition A term coined by researchers to express how the symbolic meaning of clothing changes the way that people behave (p. 129)

Encoding The process in which information from short-term memory is entered into long-term memory in recognisable form (p. 229)

Enculturation The process of learning the beliefs and behaviours endorsed by one's own culture (pp. 188, 555)

Endowed progress effect A term used to describe anything whereby people are allowed to achieve small goals in pursuit of a bigger goal (p. 227)

Erogenous zones Areas of the body considered by members of a culture to be foci of sexual attractiveness (p. 546)

Ethical consumer A consumer often taking ethical, environmental, social and/or political issues into consideration when making purchase and consumption decisions (p. 21)

Ethnocentrism The belief in the superiority of one's own country's practices and products (p. 321)

Ethnoconsumerism The understanding and analysis of each culture, including consumer culture, on the basis of its own premises (p. 485)

Ethos A set of moral, aesthetic and evaluative principles (p. 484)

Evaluative criteria The dimensions used by consumers to compare competing product alternatives (p. 310)

Evoked set Those products already in memory, plus those prominent in the retail environment, that are actively considered during a consumer's choice process (p. 234, 307)

Exchange The process whereby two or more organisations or people give and receive something of value (p. 6)

Exchange theory The perspective that every interaction involves an exchange of value (p. 59)

Executive control centre A term used by scientists for the part of the brain used for important decision-making (p. 294)

Expectancy disconfirmation model The perspective that consumers form beliefs about product performance based on prior experience with the product and/or communications about the product that imply a certain level of quality; their actual satisfaction depends on the degree to which performance is consistent with these expectations (p. 315)

Expectancy theory The perspective that behaviour is largely 'pulled' by expectations of achieving desirable 'outcomes' or positive incentives, rather than 'pushed' from within (p. 164)

Expert power Authority derived from possessing a specific knowledge or skill (p. 349)

Exposure An initial stage of perception, where some sensations come within range of consumers' sensory receptors (p. 85)

Extended family Traditional family structure where several generations and/or relatives, such as aunts, uncles and cousins, live together (p. 396)

Extended problem-solving An elaborate decision-making process often initiated by a motive that's fairly central to the self-concept and accompanied by perceived risk; the consumer tries to collect as much information as possible and carefully weighs product alternatives (p. 295)

Extended self The definition of self, created by the external objects with which one surrounds oneself (p. 128)

Extinction The process whereby learned connections between a stimulus and response are eroded so that the response is no longer reinforced (p. 217)

Fad A short-lived fashion (p. 554)

Family financial officer (FFO) The family member who is in charge of making financial decisions (p. 402)

Family household A household unit containing at least two people who are often, but not necessarily, related by blood or marriage (p. 397)

Family life cycle (FLC) A classification scheme that segments consumers in terms of changes in income and family composition and the changes in demands placed on this income (p. 400)

Fashion The process of social diffusion by which a new style is adopted by a group or groups of consumers (p. 545)

Fashion acceptance cycle The diffusion process of a style through three stages: introduction, acceptance and regression (p. 552)

Fashion life cycle The 'career' or stages in the life of a fashion as it progresses from launch to obsolescence (p. 552)

Fashion system Those people or organisations involved in creating symbolic meanings and transferring these meanings to cultural goods (p. 545)

Fatshionistas Consumer activists representing overweight or fat women fighting against the fashion industry's neglect of larger-size women. They try to make the fashion brands offer a better plus-size selection and/or strive to build a parallel market that better caters to large-size women (p. 144)

Fear of Missing Out (FOMO) The compulsion to constantly check social networks in the desire to stay on top of the activities of online friends (p. 372)

Feature bloat Another term for feature creep, denoting the increasing complexity of products and the associated difficulties of comprehension for consumers in learning how to use the products (p. 314)

Feature creep Trend towards an increasing number of options a product offers, which makes it more difficult for consumers to decide among competitors (p. 314)

Feature fatigue Another term for feature creep, denoting the increasing complexity of products and the associated difficulties of comprehension for consumers in learning how to use the products (p. 314)

Feedback loop A channel or pathway formed by an 'effect' returning to its cause (p. 294)

Fertility rate A rate determined by the number of births per year per 1,000 women of child-bearing age (p. 397)

Flaming A violation of digital etiquette when a post is written in all capital letters (p. 375)

Flow state Situation in which consumers are truly involved with a product, an ad or a website (p. 174)

Folksonomy An online posting system where users categorise entries themselves rather than relying upon a pre-established set of labels (p. 373)

Foot-in-the-door technique Based on the observation that a consumer is more likely to comply with a request if he or she has first agreed to comply with a smaller request (p. 266)

Fortress brands Brands that consumers closely link to rituals; this makes it unlikely they will be replaced (p. 492)

Framing A concept in behavioural economics that suggests the way a problem is posed to consumers (especially in terms of gains or losses) influences the decision they make (p. 317)

Freecycling The practice of giving away useful but unwanted goods to keep them out of landfills (p. 66)

Freegans A play on *vegans,* who shun all animal products, freegans are anti-consumerists who live off discards as a political statement against corporations and materialism (p. 66)

Frequency marketing A marketing technique that reinforces regular purchasers by giving them prizes with values that increase along with the amount purchased (p. 226)

Functional theory of attitudes A pragmatic approach that focuses on how attitudes facilitate social behaviour; attitudes exist because they serve some function for the person (p. 252)

Generation X (Gen-Xers or baby busters) The cohort of consumers born between 1966 and 1976, who were profoundly affected by the economic recession of the early 1990s (p. 411)

Gestalt psychology A school of thought that maintains that people derive meaning from the totality of a set of stimuli rather than from an individual stimulus (p. 100)

Gift-giving ritual The events involved in the selection, presentation, acceptance and interpretation of a gift (p. 496)

Global consumer culture A culture in which people around the world are united through their common devotion to brand-name consumer goods, movie stars, celebrities and leisure activities (p. 14)

Globalisation The process whereby geographical distance is decreasing in importance for the constitution of the social world. Instead, the social world is structured by how groups and societies are positioned in relation to global flows of people, money, technology, mediated information and ideas (p. 14)

Glocalisation The basic principle that the flows that constitute globalisation (see above) are always adopted into local cultures (p. 19)

Goal A consumer's desired end-state (p. 162)

Greenwashing Inflated claims about a product's environmental benefits. A play on the word 'whitewash', but employed here to describe activities of firms that seek to create the perception that they are conscientious about the potential environmental impact of their activities and thus that they are environmentally friendly, although it is unclear how far the espoused environmental values feed through into actual company policy (p. 198)

Grey market Term used to describe the phenomenon of a fast-growing segment of consumers aged 62 or older (p. 415)

Guerrilla marketing Promotional strategies that use unconventional locations and intensive word-of-mouth campaigns (p. 364)

Habitual decision-making The consumption choices that are made out of habit, without additional information search or deliberation among products (p. 316)

Habitus Systems of classification of phenomena adopted from our socialisation processes (p. 456)

Halal Food and other products whose usage is permissible according to the laws of Islam (p. 531)

Haul videos Video recordings posted to the internet that display recently purchased items (p. 378)

Hedonic consumption The multisensory, fantasy and emotional aspects of consumers' interactions with products (p. 88)

Heuristics The mental rules of thumb that lead to a speedy decision (p. 319)

Hierarchy of effects A fixed sequence of steps that occurs during attitude formation; this sequence varies depending on such factors as the consumer's level of involvement with the attitude object (p. 254)

Hierarchy of needs Psychologist Abraham Maslow developed a system whereby needs were ranked in ascending order of importance, starting with the lower-order needs (physiological, i.e. requirements for water, sleep and food), through safety, belongingness and ego needs and culminating in individuals' desire for self-actualisation (p. 170)

Highlighting effect The order in which consumers learn about brands determines the strength of association between these brands and their attributes (p. 237)

Homeostasis The state of being where the body is in physiological balance; goal-oriented behaviour attempts to reduce or eliminate an unpleasant motivational state and return to a balanced one (p. 163)

Home shopping party A selling format where a company representative makes a sales presentation to a group of people who gather at the home of a friend or acquaintance (p. 355)

Homogamy The tendency for individuals to marry others similar to themselves in social class and background (p. 435)

Homophily The degree to which a pair of individuals is similar in terms of education, social status and beliefs (p. 366)

Hook An element in a title that increases the likelihood people will click on it (p. 302)

Host culture A new culture to which a person must acculturate (p. 557)

Hybrid products Products that feature characteristics from two distinct domains (p. 308)

Hype Corporate propaganda planted by companies to create product sensation – often dismissed as inauthentic by customers (p. 363)

Hyperreality A phenomenon associated with modern advertising in which what is initially stimulation or hype becomes real (p. 111)

Ideal self One's personality is composed of the *real self* and the *ideal self*. Your real self is who you actually are, while your ideal self is the person you want to be. The ideal self is an idealised version of yourself created out of what you have learned from your life experiences, the demands of society and what you admire in your role models (p. 120)

Identificational membership reference group A group that has a significant effect on an individual's aspirations such that the individual forms an attitude towards the group and seeks to conform to the group's expectations and to join it (p. 352)

Implementation intentions A self-regulatory strategy in the form of an 'if-then plan' that can lead to better goal attainment (p. 294)

Impression management The process by which consumers work hard to 'manage' what others think of them by strategically choosing clothing and other cues that will put them in a good light (p. 121)

Impulse buying A process that occurs when the consumer experiences a sudden urge to purchase an item that he or she cannot resist (p. 58)

Incidental brand exposure Where consumers are influenced by brand stimuli they don't realise they have experienced, such as unplanned exposure to brand logos (p. 162)

Incidental similarity Points of commonality between a buyer and a seller, such as a shared birthday (p. 60)

Individualism Personal value orientation that encourages people to attach more importance to personal goals than to group goals; values such as personal enjoyment and freedom are stressed (p. 194)

Individualist culture A cultural orientation that encourages people to attach more importance to personal goals than to group goals; values such as personal enjoyment and freedom are stressed (p. 484)

Inertia The process whereby purchase decisions are made out of habit because the consumer lacks the motivation to consider alternatives (pp. 173, 317)

Influence impressions Brand-specific mentions on social media posts (p. 380)

Influence network A two-way dialogue between participants in a social network and opinion leaders (p. 366)

Information cascades An online communication process where one piece of information triggers a sequence of interactions (p. 366)

Information power Power gained simply because one knows something others would like to know (p. 348)

Information-processing perspective Traditionally a classic cognitive or rational approach to understanding consumer decision-making: people carefully integrate and evaluate as much information as they can collect about a product or service before making a consumer choice (p. 296)

Information search The process whereby a consumer searches for appropriate information to make a reasonable decision (p. 297)

Informational social influence The conformity that occurs because the group's behaviour is taken as evidence about reality (p. 355)

Innovation A product or style that is perceived as new by consumers (p. 539)

Innovative communicators Opinion leaders who are also early purchasers (p. 368)

Instrumental values Those goals that are endorsed because they are needed to achieve desired end-states or terminal values (p. 192)

Intelligent agents Software programs that learn from past user behaviour in order to recommend new purchases (p. 301)

Interactions In a social media context, behaviour-based ties between participants such as talking with each other, attending an event together, or working together (p. 366)

Interactive mobile marketing Real-time promotional campaigns targeted to consumers' mobile phones (p. 177)

Interference A process whereby additional learned information displaces earlier information, resulting in memory loss for the item learned previously (p. 238)

Interpretant The meaning derived from a symbol (p. 105)

Interpretation The process whereby meanings are assigned to stimuli (p. 85)

Interpretivism A research perspective that produces a 'thick' description of a consumer's subjective experiences and stresses the importance of the individual's social construction of reality (p. 12)

Involvement The motivation to process product-related information (p. 172)

JND (just-noticeable difference) The minimum change in a stimulus that can be detected by a perceiver (p. 95)

Kin network system The rituals intended to maintain ties among family members, both immediate and extended (p. 402)

Knowledge structures Organised systems of concepts relating to brands, stores and other concepts (pp. 233, 308)

Laddering A technique for uncovering consumers' associations between specific attributes and general consequences (p. 194)

Lateral cycling A process where already purchased objects are sold to others or exchanged for other items (p. 64)

Latitudes of acceptance and rejection Formed around an attitude standard, ideas that fall within a latitude will be favourably received, while those falling outside this zone will not (p. 267)

Lead users Involved, experienced customers (usually corporate customers) who are very knowledgeable about their field (p. 542)

Learning A relatively permanent change in a behaviour as a result of experience (p. 215)

Legitimate power Influence over others due to a position conferred by a society or organisation (p. 349)

Lexicographic rule A consumer decision rule whereby consumers select the brand that is the best on the most important attribute selected. If they feel two or more brands are equally good on that attribute, the consumer then compares them on the second most-important attribute. This selection process goes on until the tie is broken (p. 311). See also **Non-compensatory decision rules**

Lifestyle A set of shared values or tastes exhibited by a group of consumers, especially as these are reflected in consumption patterns (p. 178)

Lifestyle marketing perspective A perspective that recognises that people are increasingly conscious that we sort ourselves and each other into groups on the basis of the things we/they like to do and how we/they spend our/their disposable income (p. 180)

Limited problem-solving A problem-solving process in which consumers are not motivated to search for information or evaluate rigorously each alternative; instead, they use simple decision rules to arrive at a purchase decision (p. 295)

Lifestyle segmentation typologies The classifications of the category divisions of a potential market, based on what people spend their money on (p. 184)

List of Values (LOV) A scale developed to isolate values with more direct marketing applications. Identifies consumer segments based on the values members endorse and relates each value to differences in consumption behaviours (p. 193)

LOHAS An acronym for 'lifestyles of health and sustainability'; a consumer segment that worries about the environment, wants products to be produced in a sustainable way and who spend money to advance what they see as their personal development and potential (p. 196)

Long-term memory The system that allows us to retain information for a long period (p. 233)

Long tail Rather than the conventional approach of many companies to marketing, which is to sell a lot of one product to most customers, here the notion is that companies should pursue 'the long tail', i.e. a strategy of selling a large variety of products to a smaller number of customers to achieve the same level of business, so that there is a shift from mass markets to many, many niche markets (p. 302)

Looking-glass self The process of imagining the reaction of others towards oneself (p. 122)

Lurkers Passive members of an online community who do not contribute to interactions (p. 375)

Market beliefs Common assumptions about relationships between product quality and other factors such as price (p. 320)

Market maven A person who often serves as a source of information about marketplace activities (p. 368)

Market segmentation Strategies targeting a brand only to specific groups rather than to everybody (p. 8)

Masculinism Study devoted to the male image and the cultural meanings of masculinity (p. 137)

Mass customisation The personalisation of products and services for individual customers at a mass-production price (p. 174)

Mass connectors Highly influential members of social media networks (p. 380)

Materialism The importance consumers attach to worldly possessions (p. 258)

Maximising A decision strategy that seeks to deliver the best possible result (p. 319)

Meaning The fundamental of unit of human society. All cultures are systems of meaning. As sociologists Nisbet and Perrin (1970) formulated it: The symbol is to the social world what the atom is to the physical world and the cell is to the biological world (The Social Bond, 1970) (p. 38)

Means–end chain model Assumes that people link very specific product attributes (indirectly) to terminal values such as freedom or safety (p. 194)

Media multiplexity In a social media context, when flows of communication go in many directions at any point in time and often on multiple platforms (p. 375)

Megaphone Effect The term used to describe the fact that the Web makes a huge audience potentially available to the ordinary consumer (p. 378)

Membership reference group Ordinary people whose consumption activities provide informational social influence (p. 355)

Memory A process of acquiring information and storing it over time (p. 228)

Mental accounting Principle that states that decisions are influenced by the way a problem is posed (p. 318)

Mental budgets Consumers' pre-set expectations of how much they intend to spend on a shopping trip (p. 57)

Mere exposure phenomenon The tendency to like persons or things if we see them more often (p. 352)

Metrosexual A straight, urban male who exhibits strong interests and knowledge regarding product categories such as fashion, home design, gourmet cooking and personal care, which runs counter to the traditional male sex role (p. 137)

Microfinance A source of financial services for entrepreneurs and small businesses that lack access to banks (p. 450)

Millennials Generally viewed as people born between 1986 and 2002, also known as 'Gen Y'; note that different year spans can be employed in different research studies (p. 431)

Minimal group paradigm A methodology from Social Psychology which is employed to investigate the minimal (lowest number of) conditions under which discrimination might occur (p. 348)

MMOGS (massively multi-player online games) Social games where large numbers of people in different physical locations participate (p. 382)

Mobile shopping apps Smartphone applications that retailers provide to guide shoppers in stores and malls (p. 58)

Monochronic A cultural relation to time that stresses its linearity and attaches importance to engaging in one task at a time; time is conceived mechanically, as in a clockwork (p. 484)

Monomyth A myth with basic characteristics that are found in many cultures (p. 490)

Moods Temporary positive or negative affective states accompanied by moderate levels of arousal (p. 261)

Mores Norms with strong moral overtones (p. 486)

Morning Morality Effect The term used to describe the finding that people are more likely to lie, cheat or commit other minor misdemeanours in the afternoon than in the morning (p. 294)

Motivation An internal state that activates goal-oriented behaviour (p. 162)

Motivational research A qualitative research approach based on psychoanalytical (Freudian) interpretations, with a heavy emphasis on unconscious motives for consumption (p. 181)

Multi-attribute attitude models Those models that assume that a consumer's attitude (evaluation) of an attitude object depends on the beliefs he or she has about several or many attributes of the object; the use of a multi-attribute model implies that an attitude towards a product or brand can be predicted by identifying these specific beliefs and combining them to derive a measure of the consumer's overall attitude (p. 268)

Multitasking The best performance by an individual of appearing to handle more than one task at the same time. The term is derived from computer multitasking. An example of multitasking is taking a phone call while typing an email. Some believe that multitasking can result in time wasted due to human context switching and apparently causing more errors due to insufficient attention (p. 97)

Myth A story containing symbolic elements, which expresses the shared emotions and ideals of a culture (p. 488)

Narrative transportation The result of a highly involving message where people become immersed in the storyline (p. 176)

Near Field Communications (NFC) Technology that allows devices near to one another (such as a smartphone and a NFC terminal in a store) to establish radio communication (p. 56)

Need A basic biological motive (p. 162)

Negative reinforcement The process whereby a negative reward weakens responses to stimuli so that inappropriate behaviour is avoided in the future (p. 219)

Negative word of mouth The passing on of negative experiences involved with products or services by consumers to other potential customers to influence others' choices (p. 364)

Neuromarketing A new technique that uses a brain-scanning device called functional magnetic resonance imaging (fMRI), which tracks blood flow as people perform mental tasks. Scientists know that specific regions of the brain light up in these scans to show increased blood flow when a person recognises a face, hears a song, makes a decision, senses deception and so on. Now they are trying to harness this technology to measure consumers' reactions to movie trailers, choices about automobiles, the appeal of a pretty face and loyalty to specific brands (p. 313)

Neuroscience Study of the brain via experimental methods to assess the different types and levels of reactions to various forms of marketing stimuli (e.g. advertisements) (p. 313)

Nodes Members of a social network connected to others via one or more shared relationships (p. 373)

Non-compensatory decision rules A set of simple rules used to evaluate competing alternatives; a brand with a low standing on one relevant attribute is eliminated from the consumer's choice set (p. 311)

Normative influence The process by which a reference group helps to set and enforce basic standards of conduct (p. 351)

Normative social influence The conformity that occurs when a person alters his or her behaviour to meet the expectations of a person or group (p. 356)

Norms The informal rules that govern what is right and wrong (p. 355)

Nostalgia A bittersweet emotion when the past is viewed with sadness and longing; many 'classic' products appeal to consumers' memories of their younger days (p. 239)

Nuclear family A contemporary living arrangement composed of a married couple and their child(ren) (p. 396)

Nudge A subtle change in a person's environment that results in a change in their behaviour (p. 318)

Object A semiotic term – the product that is the focus of the message (p. 105)

Object sociality The extent to which an object (text, image, video) is shared among members of online social networks (p. 376)

Observational learning The process in which people learn by watching the actions of others and noting the reinforcements they receive for their behaviours (p. 221)

Open rates The percentage of people who open an email message from a marketer (p. 39)

Operant conditioning The process by which the individual learns to perform behaviours that produce positive outcomes and to avoid those that yield negative outcomes (p. 218)

Opinion leaders Those people who are knowledgeable about products and who are frequently able to influence others' attitudes or behaviours with regard to a product category (p. 365)

Opinion seekers Usually opinion leaders who are also involved in a product category and actively search for information (p. 368)

Paradigm A widely accepted view or model of phenomena being studied. The perspective that regards people as rational information processors is currently the dominant paradigm, though this approach is now being challenged by a new wave of research that emphasises the frequently subjective nature of consumer decision-making (p. 12)

Parental yielding The process that occurs when a parental decision-maker is influenced by a child's product request (p. 403)

Pastiche The playful and ironic mixing of existing categories and styles (p. 110)

Peak experiences Term coined by the American psychologist Abraham Maslow to describe moments of elation (p. 170)

Perceived age How old a person *feels*, rather than his or her chronological age (p. 417)

Perceived risk The belief that use of a product has potentially negative consequences, either physical or social (p. 303)

Perception The process by which stimuli are selected, organised or interpreted (p. 86)

Perceptual defence People see what they want to see – and don't see what they don't want to see. If a stimulus is threatening to us we may not process it – or we may distort its meaning so that it is more acceptable. For example, a heavy smoker may block out images of cancer-scarred lungs because these vivid reminders hit too close to home (p. 98)

Perceptual map A research tool used to understand how a brand is positioned in consumers' minds relative to competitors' brands (p. 87)

Perceptual selection The process in which people attend to only a small portion of the stimuli to which they are exposed (p. 98)

Perceptual vigilance Stimuli that consumers attend to because it relates to their current needs (p. 98)

Personality A person's unique psychological makeup, which consistently influences the way the person responds to his or her environment (p. 4)

Personality traits Identifiable characteristics that define a person (p. 200)

Persuasion An active attempt to change attitudes (p. 274)

Phablets A combination of the features of a mobile phone and a tablet (p. 46)

Point-of-purchase stimuli (POP) The promotional materials that are deployed in shops or other outlets to influence consumers' decisions at the time products are purchased (p. 59)

Polychronic A cultural relation to time that stresses its circularity and allows for engaging in multiple tasks at a time; time is conceived organically, as in natural cycles (life, seasons. . .) (p. 484)

Popular culture The music, films, sports, books, celebrities and other forms of entertainment consumed by the mass market (p. 14)

Pop-up stores Temporary locations that allow a company to test new brands without a huge financial commitment (p. 56)

Positive reinforcement The process whereby rewards provided by the environment strengthen responses to stimuli (p. 218)

Positivism A research perspective that relies on the principles of the 'scientific method' and assumes that a single reality exists, events in the world can be objectively measured and the causes of behaviour can be identified, manipulated and predicted (p. 12)

Postmodernism A theory that questions the search for universal truths and values and the existence of objective knowledge (p. 108)

Post-purchase evaluation Post-purchase evaluation occurs when we experience a product or service and decide whether it meets our expectations (p. 314)

Potlatch A Kwakiutl Indian feast at which the host displays his wealth and gives extravagant gifts (p. 453)

Power posing The term used to describe the adoption of stances associated with confidence, power and achievement (p. 129)

Power users Opinion leaders in online networks (p. 372)

Practice theory A theoretical framework that stresses how much of human behaviour is inscribed in routines that we have picked up over time through our socialisation. As such, it is heavily based on our social backgrounds and our learned skills and tastes (see Distinction) (p. 457)

Presence The effect that people experience when they interact with a computer-mediated environment (p. 377)

Pretailer An e-commerce site that provides exclusive styles by prodding manufacturers to produce catwalk pieces they wouldn't otherwise make to sell in stores (p. 50)

Priming The process in which certain properties of a stimulus are more likely to evoke a schema than others (p. 318)

Principle of closure Implies that consumers tend to perceive an incomplete picture as complete (p. 100)

Principle of cognitive consistency The belief that consumers value harmony among their thoughts, feelings and behaviours and that they are motivated to maintain uniformity among these elements (p. 263)

Principle of least interest The person who is least committed to staying in a relationship has the most power (p. 357)

Principle of similarity The gestalt principle that describes how consumers tend to group objects that share similar physical characteristics (p. 100)

Problem recognition The process that occurs whenever the consumer sees a significant difference between his or her current state and some desired or ideal state; this recognition initiates the decision-making process (p. 297)

Product complementarity Term used to describe the situation where symbolic meanings of different products relate to one another (p. 181)

Product disposal The choices people make regarding how to get rid of items once they are no longer of value to them (p. 60)

Product involvement The level of a consumer's interest in purchasing a certain product type (p. 174)

Product placement The process of obtaining exposure for a product by arranging for it to be inserted into a film, television programme or some other medium (p. 536)

Product signal Communicates an underlying quality of a product through the use of aspects that are visible (p. 320)

Productivity orientation A continual striving to use time constructively (p. 165)

Profane consumption The process of consuming objects and events that are ordinary or of the everyday world (p. 504)

Propinquity As physical distance between people decreases and opportunities for interaction increase, they are more likely to form relationships (p. 352)

Prospect theory A descriptive model of how people make choices (p. 318)

Prosumer A consumer who reflects the tendency to blur production and consumption processes, as in tailor-made solutions, consumer involvement in production and assembling processes, etc. (p. 530)

Proxemics The study of the social construction of personalised space. How close or distant can you stand, sit, etc. to family, friends, strangers. Proxemics often cause cross-cultural discomfort as 'comfortable distance' from strangers is not defined in the same way across cultures (p. 484)

Psychographics The use of psychological, sociological and anthropological factors to construct market segments (pp. 4, 178, 181)

Psychology of loss aversion (PLA) A concept from economics that argues that, when making decisions, individuals tend to have a stronger preference to avoid losses rather than to acquire gains (p. 318)

Psychophysics The science that focuses on how the physical environment is integrated into the consumer's subjective experience (p. 94)

Punishment The process or outcome that occurs when a response is followed by unpleasant events (p. 219)

Purchase momentum Initial impulses to buy in order to satisfy our needs increase the likelihood that we will buy even more (p. 292)

Queuing theory The mathematical study of waiting lines (p. 40)

Rational perspective A view of the consumer as a careful, analytical decision-maker who tries to maximise utility in purchase decisions (p. 296)

Reactance A boomerang effect that may occur when consumers are threatened with a loss of freedom of choice; they respond by doing the opposite of the behaviour advocated in a persuasive message (p. 359)

Reader-response theory A theory that stresses the role of an interpreting reader in the constitution of human communication. It is thus critical of the idea that the sender's intended meaning can be used to define what a communication is (or should be) about (p. 274)

Reality engineering The process whereby elements of popular culture are appropriated by marketers and become integrated into marketing strategies (e.g. product placement) (p. 534)

Reclaimers Businesses that seek to rescue and recycle items of potential historical interest or collectable value, e.g. architectural features of houses undergoing demolition such as fireplaces, doors, windows (p. 64)

Recommerce The recovery of products over electronic systems, such as the internet, or through physical distribution channels (p. 64)

Red Sneakers Effect The concept that someone who makes unconventional choices is more powerful and competent (p. 356)

Reference group An actual or imaginary individual or group that has a significant effect on an individual's evaluations, aspirations or behaviour (p. 349)

Referent power The power of prominent people to affect others' consumption behaviours by virtue of product endorsements, distinctive fashion statements or championing causes (p. 348)

Reputation economy A reward system based on recognition of one's expertise by others who read online product reviews (p. 302)

Response bias A form of contamination in survey research where some factor, such as the desire to make a good impression on the experimenter, leads respondents to modify their true answers (p. 243)

Restricted codes Ways of expressing and interpreting meanings that focus on the content of objects; tend to be used by the working classes (p. 447)

Retail theming Strategy where stores create imaginative environments that transport shoppers to fantasy worlds or provide other kinds of stimulation (p. 53)

Retail therapy Shopping as a means of making oneself feel happier (p. 164)

Retrieval The process whereby desired information is accessed from long-term memory (p. 229)

Reward power A person or group with the means to provide positive reinforcement (p. 349)

Risk society A term coined by a German sociologist to describe a situation where modernity and scientific progress are no longer perceived to increasingly reduce risk but, on the contrary, are perceived to increasingly produce risks (global warming, nuclear waste) (p. 21)

Risky shift effect Group members show a greater willingness to consider riskier alternatives following group discussions than they would if each member made his or her own decision without prior discussion (pp. 354)

Rites of passage Special occasions marked by a change in social status (p. 502)

Ritual A set of multiple, symbolic behaviours that occur in fixed sequence and that tend to be repeated periodically (p. 492)

Ritual artefacts Items or consumer goods used in the performance of rituals (p. 493)

Role theory The perspective that much of consumer behaviour resembles action in a play (p. 6)

Sacralisation A process that occurs when ordinary objects, events or people take on sacred meaning to a culture or to specific groups within a culture (p. 510)

Sacred consumption The process of consuming objects and events that are set apart from normal life and treated with some degree of respect or awe (p. 504)

Satisficing A decision strategy that aims to yield an adequate solution rather than the best solution, in order to reduce the costs of the decision-making process (p. 319)

Savings rate The amount of money saved for later use, influenced by consumers' pessimism or optimism about their personal circumstances and perceptions of the economy (p. 433)

Schema An organised collection of beliefs and feelings represented in a cognitive category (pp. 86, 235)

Search engine optimisation (SEO) Procedures used by companies to design the content of websites and posts to maximise the likelihood that their content will show up when someone searches for a relevant term (p. 301)

Search engines Software (such as Google) that helps consumers access information based upon their specific requests (p. 301)

Self-concept The attitude a person holds towards him- or herself (p. 119)

Self-gifts The products or services bought by consumers for their own use, as a reward or consolation (p. 498)

Selfies Pictures a smartphone user takes of himself or herself (p. 380)

Self-image congruence models The approach based on the prediction that products will be chosen when their attributes match some aspect of the self (p. 127)

Self-perception theory An alternative explanation of dissonance effects; it assumes that people use observations of their own behaviour to infer their attitudes towards an object (p. 266)

Self-regulation A person's deliberate efforts to change or maintain his/her actions over time (p. 294)

Semiotics A field of study that examines the correspondence between a sign and the meaning(s) it conveys (p. 105)

Sensation The immediate response of sensory receptors to such basic stimuli as light, colour and sound (p. 86)

Sensory marketing This occurs where companies pay extra attention to the impact of sensations on our product experiences (p. 88)

Sensory memory The temporary storage of information received from the senses (p. 233)

Sensory overload Sensory overload occurs when consumers are exposed to far more information than they can process (p. 97)

Sentiment analysis A process (sometimes also called *opinion mining*) that scours the social media universe to collect and analyse the words people use when they describe a specific product or company (p. 261)

Serial reproduction A technique to study how information changes as people transmit it to another person, where each person has to repeat the stimulus for the next person (p. 380)

Sex-typed traits Characteristics that are stereotypically associated with one sex or the other (p. 133)

Sharing economy A notion referring to the increasing tendency to give other people access to the resources that one has at one's disposal, or to team with fellow consumers for joint consumption of equipment, etc. Since things are rarely actually 'shared' (for free), better terms for this may be 'access-based consumption' or 'mutuality-based consumption' (p. 25)

Sharing sites E-commerce sites that allow users to share, exchange and rent goods in a local setting (p. 64)

Shopping orientation A consumer's general attitudes and motivations regarding the act of shopping (p. 42)

Short-term memory (STM) The system that allows us to retain information for a short period (p. 233)

Sign The sensory imagery that represents the intended meanings of the object (p. 105)

Signifying practices Practices that have meaning to individuals, who know how to interpret them thanks to the understanding of culture as the interpreting system (p. 482)

Situational involvement Differences that may occur when buying the same object for different contexts (p. 177)

Social class The overall rank of people in society; people who are grouped within the same social class are approximately equal in terms of their social standing, occupations and lifestyles (p. 428)

Social comparison theory The perspective that people compare their outcomes with others' as a way to increase the stability of their own self-evaluation, especially when physical evidence is unavailable (p. 357)

Social game A multi-player, competitive, goal-oriented activity with defined rules of engagement and online connectivity among a community of players (p. 177)

Social graphs Social networks; relationships among members of online communities (p. 374)

Social hierarchy A ranking of social desirability in terms of consumers' access to such resources as money, education and luxury goods (p. 428)

Social identity theory A theory that argues that each of us has several 'selves' that relate to groups. These linkages are so important that we think of ourselves not just as 'I', but also as 'we' (p. 348)

Social judgement theory The perspective that people assimilate new information about attitude objects in the light of what they already know or feel; the initial attitude acts as a frame of reference, and the new information is categorised in terms of this standard (p. 267)

Social loafing The tendency for people not to devote as much to a task when their contribution is part of a larger group effort (p. 354)

Social media Social media are the online means of communication, conveyance, collaboration, and cultivation among interconnected and interdependent networks of people, communities and organisations, enhanced by technological capabilities and mobility (p. 18)

Social mobility The movement of individuals from one social class to another (p. 439)

Social network A group of people who connect with one another online due to some shared interest or affiliation (p. 373)

Social networking A growing practice whereby websites let members post information about themselves and make contact with others who share similar interests and opinions or who want to make business contacts (p. 376)

Social power The capacity of one person to alter the actions or outcome of another (p. 348)

Social recycling Consumers dispose of used (or pre-loved) goods by allowing other consumers to acquire them – for instance, via charity shops or even at no cost at all (p. 63)

Social stratification The process in a social system by which scarce and valuable resources are distributed unequally to status positions, which become more-or-less permanently ranked in terms of the share of valuable resources each receives (p. 436)

Sociometric methods The techniques for measuring group dynamics that involve tracing of communication patterns in and among groups (p. 371)

Source attractiveness The dimensions of a communicator that increase his or her persuasiveness; these include expertise and physical attractiveness (p. 276)

Source credibility A communication source's perceived expertise, objectivity or trustworthiness (p. 275)

Spacing effect The tendency to recall printed material to a greater extent when the advertiser repeats the target item periodically, rather than presenting it over and over in a short period of time (p. 236)

Spectacles A marketing message that takes the form of a public performance (p. 177)

Stage of cognitive development Segmentation of children by age in terms of their ability to comprehend concepts of increasing complexity (p. 408)

Status crystallisation The extent to which different indicators of a person's status are consistent with one another (p. 440)

Status symbols Products that are purchased and displayed to signal membership of a desirable social class (p. 428)

Stereotype An example regarded as typical of a particular group of people or products (p. 321)

Stimulus discrimination The process that occurs when behaviour caused by two stimuli is different, as when consumers learn to differentiate a brand from its competitors (p. 218)

Stimulus generalisation The process that occurs when the behaviour caused by a reaction to one stimulus occurs in the presence of other, similar stimuli (p. 217)

Storage The process that occurs when knowledge entered in long-term memory is integrated with what is already in memory and 'warehoused' until needed (p. 229)

Store gestalt Consumers' global evaluation of a store (p. 56)

Store image The 'personality' of a shop, composed of attributes such as location, merchandise suitability and the knowledge and congeniality of the sales staff (p. 56)

Subculture A group whose members share beliefs and common experiences that set them apart from the members of the main culture (p. 532)

Sunk-cost fallacy The belief that if we pay more for something we should not waste it (p. 318)

Surrogate consumer A professional who is retained to evaluate and/or make purchases on behalf of a consumer (p. 369)

Swishing A movement where people organise parties to exchange clothing or other personal possessions with others (p. 64)

Symbol A sign that is related to a product through either conventional or agreed-upon associations (p. 105)

Symbolic interactionism A sociological approach, stressing that relationships with people play a large part in forming the self; people live in a symbolic environment and the meaning attached to any situation or object is determined by a person's interpretation of those symbols (p. 122)

Symbolic self-completion theory The perspective that people who have an incomplete self-definition in some context will compensate by acquiring symbols associated with a desired social identity (p. 125)

Syncratic decisions Purchase decisions that are made jointly by spouses (p. 402)

Taste culture A group of consumers who share aesthetic and intellectual preferences (p. 446)

Terminal values End-states desired by members of a culture (p. 192)

Theory of cognitive dissonance Theory based on the premise that people have a need for order and consistency in their lives and that a state of tension is created when beliefs or behaviours conflict with one another (p. 166)

Theory of reasoned action A version of the Fishbein multi-attitude theory that considers such factors as social pressure and the attitude towards the act of buying a product rather than attitudes towards just the product itself (p. 270)

Tie strength The nature and potency of the bond between members of a social network (p. 371)

Time poverty A feeling of having less time available than is required to meet the demands of everyday living (p. 39)

Time style Determined by an individual's priorities, it incorporates such dimensions as economic time, past or future orientation, time submissiveness and time anxiety (p. 39)

Torn self Where individuals struggle between retaining their original authentic culture while enjoying the cultural freedoms offered by the Western society in which they live (p. 122)

Transactional advertising An advertising message in a social game that rewards players if they respond to a request (p. 177)

Transformative consumer research (TCR) A movement that seeks to study and rectify social problems in the marketplace (p. 24)

Transitional economies Countries that are in the process of transforming their economic system from a controlled, centralised system to a free market one (p. 18)

Tribal marketing Linking a product's identity to an activity-based 'tribe', such as basketball players (p. 361)

Trickle-down theory The perspective that fashions spread as a result of status symbols associated with the upper classes trickling down to the other social classes as these consumers try to emulate those with higher status (p. 548)

Two-step flow model of influence Proposes that a small group of *influencers* disseminate information since they can modify the opinions of a large number of other people (p. 366)

Unboxing videos Videos that illustrate how to remove electronics products from their boxes and assemble them for use (p. 378)

Underground economy Secondary markets (such as flea markets) where transactions are not officially recorded (p. 64)

Unplanned buying When a shopper buys merchandise they did not intend to purchase, often because they recognise a new need while in the store (p. 58)

Valuable virality Companies create online content that they hope consumers will view and share with their friends and family to spread the message about their product or service via social media (p. 378)

Value A belief that some condition is preferable to its opposite (p. 186)

Value system A culture's ranking of the relative importance of values (p. 187)

Values and Lifestyles System (VALS2™) A psychographic segmentation system used to categorise consumers into clusters (p. 184)

Variety-seeking The desire to choose new alternatives over more familiar ones (p. 176)

Virtual makeovers Platforms that allow the shopper to superimpose images on their faces or bodies so that they can quickly and easily see how a product looks – without taking the risk of actually buying the item first (p. 121)

Viral marketing The strategy of getting customers to sell a product on behalf of the company that creates it (p. 378)

Virtual goods Digital items that people buy and sell online (p. 382)

Virtual reality (VR) A computer-simulated interface that creates the impression that the user is physically present (p. 58)

Virtual water footprint Represents how much total water is required to produce a product, taking account of the use of water resources throughout the production process (p. 197)

Virtual worlds Immersive, 3D, virtual (online and Web-based) environments such as *Second Life* (p. 382)

Visual search A software app that allows consumers to upload a picture (often taken from a magazine or social media website) of the product they are looking for onto a retailer's website as they search for a similar outfit or product (p. 50)

Vlogger A video blogger (p. 378)

Want The particular form of consumption chosen to satisfy a need (p. 163)

Wearable computing Computer-powered devices or equipment (e.g. watches, glasses) that can be worn by a user (p. 130)

Web Internet exchange system that has evolved from its original roots as a form of one-way transmission from producers to consumers to a social, interactive medium (Web 2.0) (p. 171)

Weber's Law The principle that the stronger the initial stimulus, the greater its change must be for it to be noticed (p. 95)

Word-of-mouth communication (WOM) The information transmitted by individual consumers on an informal basis (p. 362)

Worldview The ideas shared by members of a culture about principles of order and fairness (p. 484)

Zipf's Law Pattern that describes the tendency for the most robust effect to be far more powerful than others in its class; applies to consumer behaviour in terms of buyers' overwhelming preferences for the market leader in a product category (p. 322)

Indexes

Index of personal names

Index of Companies and Products

Subject Index

Note: Page numbers in **bold** refer to terms in the Glossary